A SHAKESPEARE GLOSSARY

PLAYWRIGHTS

HORIZONS

THEATRE

SCHOOL

C. T. ONIONS

A SHAKESPEARE
GLOSSARY

Enlarged and revised throughout by
ROBERT D. EAGLESON

OXFORD
AT THE CLARENDON PRESS
1986

Oxford University Press, Walton Street, Oxford OX2 6DP

Oxford New York Toronto
Delhi Bombay Calcutta Madras Karachi
Kuala Lumpur Singapore Hong Kong Tokyo
Nairobi Dar es Salaam Cape Town
Melbourne Auckland

and associated companies in
Beirut Berlin Ibadan Nicosia

Oxford is a trade mark of Oxford University Press

Published in the United States
by Oxford University Press, New York

British Library Cataloguing in Publication Data

Onions, Charles Talbut
A Shakespeare glossary.—[3rd ed].,
rev. and enl.
1. Shakespeare, William—Dictionaries,
indexes, etc.
I. Title II. Eagleson, Robert D.
822.3'3 PR2892
ISBN 0-19-811199-1
ISBN 0-19-812521-6 Pbk

Library of Congress Cataloging in Publication Data

Onions, C. T. (Charles Talbut), 1873-1965.
A Shakespeare glossary.
Bibliography: p.
1. Shakespeare, William, 1564-1616—Language—Glossaries, etc.
I. Eagleson, Robert D. II. Title.
PR2892.0'6 1985 822.3'3 84-7912
ISBN 0-19-811199-1
ISBN 0-19-812521-6 (pbk.)

Printed in Great Britain
at the University Printing House, Oxford
by David Stanford,
Printer to the University

PREFACE

SHAKESPEARE justly retains our high esteem and praise as a supreme master of English Literature, a never-ending source of pleasure and illumination. As the years separate us from Elizabethan times, however, changes arise in the English language which become obstacles to our enjoyment and appreciation of the riches in his works. Very obvious are the words which have disappeared from common use, such as *acture, eke, gest*, and *whiffler*. But in some ways even more critical to our full understanding because their continuing currency can mislead us into accepting them with today's values are the many words and phrases which have undergone important shifts in meaning since Shakespeare wrote: *bandy, humour, politician, silly, vicious, wake*—indeed the majority of items in this *Glossary*. Then there are the familiar words, such as *gallow, line, nameless*, and *try*, which function in the plays with regional dialect meanings alongside the standard ones known to us.

A Shakespeare Glossary has been designed to offer readers immediate and practical assistance at these crucial points where they are likely to be led astray or mystified. Rather than providing an exhaustive account of Shakespeare's vocabulary, it concentrates, in the words of its original editor, 'in supplying definitions and illustrations of words or senses of words which are now obsolete or which survive only in archaic or provincial use'. It thus contributes to the elucidation and appreciation of the plays and poems by directing attention to the features of words which are potential causes of difficulty and confusion. The first and second editions of this *Glossary* were compiled by C. T. Onions, a noted editor of the *Oxford English Dictionary*. In fact, the first edition of the *Glossary* was prompted by the progress with the *Dictionary*, though Dr Onions sensitively modified the material he had at his disposal, perceptively applying it in the context of Shakespeare and making an individual and important contribution from his own resources. This third edition is based solidly on the earlier editions, and much that Dr Onions originally prepared remains. But in the intervening years scholarly study in Shakespeare's text and language and in Elizabethan English generally has contributed towards resolving previous difficulties and clarifying past obscurities. In addition, the publication of two computer-generated concordances, one based on the Folio and Quarto texts and the other on a modern edition, has provided a valuable support to the close reading and related investigations undertaken in preparing this edition by making readily available for comparison all the occurrences and variants of a particular word. The cumulative result has been a significant expansion of the material in the earlier editions in the form of completely new entries or additions to the original entries. It has also been possible to make amendments and corrections to a number of other entries.

Other purely editorial modifications have been made in the process of revising and enlarging the *Glossary*. At least one citation from the text of a play or poem now accompanies every definition. The treatment of different parts of speech has been arranged under the one headword to emphasize the connection of the various senses and uses of the words. Foreign words and phrases have been included in the appropriate alphabetical position in the *Glossary* proper rather than located in a separate section at the end. The use of special symbols has been regularized and reduced. All these and other changes have been introduced to make the reader's task easier, but the original conception of the *Glossary* has been assiduously preserved.

The preparation of this third edition has been supported by generous awards from the Australian Research Grants Committee which enabled the engagement as Research Assistants of Miss L. Auld and the late J. Britton, and as computer-terminal operator of Mrs E. Massie. The University of Sydney through a University research grant made all the computing facilities available to compile the material by computer. Mr Gary Newell of the University Computing Centre gave invaluable advice in the development and operation of the necessary computer programs. All four displayed a high sense of commitment to and personal involvement in the project. The debt to past and present scholars is extensive. The bibliography can serve only as a partial acknowledgement.

R. D. E.

CONTENTS

ARRANGEMENT OF THE ENTRIES

WHEREVER possible three references to the Shakespearean text are given to illustrate every definition. Because it is not practicable to cite every instance of a word in a given sense, and because the many editions of Shakespeare's works vary in text and especially in the numeration of act, scene, and line, an adequate quotation from the Shakespearean text generally follows the first cited reference. In this way we plan to provide the reader with sufficient material for comparison should he be investigating the use of a word in a play not specifically cited in the entry, and to reduce confusion caused by the fluctuations in numeration. The entries in the *Glossary* should be accessible to readers, no matter what particular edition of Shakespeare's works they are using.

Because the Spevack Concordance was used in the preparation of this third edition, for convenience the text used in the illustrative quotations and act-scene-line numeration used in all references are those of the Riverside edition, on which the Concordance was based. On occasions, however, the text has been set aside for some special reason, and from time to time the spelling of items has been modified where Riverside has preserved an older form. The illustrative quotations are printed in italic type.

The spelling of headwords is normally the preferred form in *OED*. Important variants are listed with a cross-reference to the appropriate headword.

Definitions which are uncertain or disputed are preceded by the symbol (?). Alternative explanations, where available, are arranged under numerals (1), (2), etc., e.g. PAJOCK.

Ancillary material which may be important for the understanding of the use of a word is given immediately after the entry in a special note, e.g. ACROSS.

Paraphrases of obscure passages are introduced by 'i.e.' and are given between round brackets, e.g. ALMS-BASKET.

Etymological statements are placed within square brackets and usually follow the indication of word-class.

Variant readings are given in round brackets immediately after the citation if they are drawn only from the Folio and Quarto editions. The procedure is illustrated by the following example:

find *vb.*[3] . . . H5 1.2.72 *To fine his title with some show of truth* (Qq1-3; F1 *find*)—means the First, Second, and Third Quartos read *fine*, while the First Folio reads *find*.

If a variant reading derives from an emendation or conjecture, its source is indicated in a special note, e.g. ABSTRACT *n.* sense 5.

Foreign words and phrases have been incorporated into the general alphabetical listing on the basis of the spelling of the first item.

Small capitals indicate a cross-reference to another entry.

ABBREVIATIONS OF TITLES
OF PLAYS AND POEMS

ADO	*Much Ado about Nothing*	LUC	*The Rape of Lucrece*
AWW	*All's Well that Ends Well*	MAC	*Macbeth*
ANT	*Antony and Cleopatra*	MM	*Measure for Measure*
AYL	*As You Like It*	MND	*A Midsummer Night's*
LC	*A Lover's Complaint*		*Dream*
COR	*Coriolanus*	MV	*The Merchant of Venice*
CYM	*Cymbeline*	OTH	*Othello, the Moor of Venice*
ERR	*The Comedy of Errors*	PER	*Pericles, Prince of Tyre*
HAM	*Hamlet*	PHT	*The Phoenix and the Turtle*
1H4	*The First Part of King*	PP	*The Passionate Pilgrim*
	Henry IV	R2	*The Tragedy of King*
2H4	*The Second Part of King*		*Richard II*
	Henry IV	R3	*The Tragedy of King*
H5	*The Life of King Henry V*		*Richard III*
1H6	*The First Part of King*	ROM	*Romeo and Juliet*
	Henry VI	SHR	*The Taming of the Shrew*
2H6	*The Second Part of King*	SON	*Sonnets*
	Henry VI	TGV	*The Two Gentlemen of*
3H6	*The Third Part of King*		*Verona*
	Henry VI	TIM	*Timon of Athens*
H8	*The Famous History of the*	TIT	*Titus Andronicus*
	Life of King Henry VIII	TMP	*The Tempest*
JC	*Julius Caesar*	TN	*Twelfth Night*
JN	*The Life and Death of King*	TRO	*Troilus and Cressida*
	John	VEN	*Venus and Adonis*
LLL	*Love's Labours Lost*	WIV	*The Merry Wives of Windsor*
LR	*King Lear*	WT	*The Winter's Tale*

ABBREVIATIONS OF TECHNICAL TERMS

absol.	absolute(ly), i.e. without some usual construction (e.g. a verb without an object)
adj.	adjective
adv.	adverb
app.	apparently
arch.	archaic
Arg.	Argument
attrib.	attributive
C	century
cf.	compare
Ch.	Chorus
conj.	conjunction
const.	construction
co-ord.	co-ordinate
corr.	corruption
Ded.	Dedication
det.	determiner
dial.	dialect
e.g.	for example
edd.	editions
Eliz.	Elizabethan
ellipt.	elliptical(ly)
Epil.	Epilogue
esp.	especially
F1	First Folio (1623)
F2	Second Folio (1632)
F3	Third Folio (1663)
F4	Fourth Folio (1685)
Ff	Folios
fig.	figuratively
Fr.	French
freq.	frequent(ly)
gen.	general(ly)
Gk.	Greek
i.e.	that is
imper.	imperative
Ind.	Induction
infin.	infinitive
interj.	interjection
interr.	interrogative
intr.	intransitive
It.	Italian
L.	Latin
lit.	literal(ly)
midl.	Midland
mod.	modern
mod. edd.	modern editions (from Rowe, 1709 onwards)
n.	noun
O	Octavo
O1	Octavo 1, etc.
occas.	occasionally
O. Fr.	Old French
orig.	original(ly)
pa. pple.	past participle
pa. t.	past tense
pass.	passive voice
perh.	perhaps
phr.	phrase
pl.	plural
ppl. adj.	participial adjective
pple.	participle
prep.	preposition
prob.	probably
Prol.	Prologue
pron.	pronoun
Q1, etc.	Quarto 1, etc.
Qq	Quartos
q.v.	quod vide ('which see')
ref.	reference
refl.	reflexive
rel.	relative
SD.	stage direction
Sp.	Spanish
spec.	specifically
sing.	singular
sub.	subordinate
trans.	transitive
transf.	in a transferred sense
usu.	usually
var.	variant
vb.	verb

BIBLIOGRAPHY

This is a composite bibliography, covering the first, second, and third editions.

1. Editions of Shakespeare

ALEXANDER, P., *Complete Works* (1951; 1960).

BARNET, S. (Gen. Ed.), *The Complete Signet Classic Shakespeare* (1972).

BOSWELL, J., *Plays and Poems* (1821).

BROOKS, H. F.: see ELLIS-FERMOR, U.

CAMPBELL, T., *Works* (1838).

CAPELL, E. C., *Comedies, Histories and Tragedies* (1767-8).

CASE, R. H.: see CRAIG, W. J.

CHALMERS, A., *The Plays* (1805).

CLARK, W. G., GLOVER, J., and WRIGHT, W. A., *The Cambridge Shakespeare* (1863-5; reissued 1891-3).

CLARK, W. G., and WRIGHT, W. A., *The Globe Edition* (1866).

—— and —— *Clarendon Press Series* (1868 etc.).

COLLIER, J. P., *Works* (1842-4).

COWDEN CLARKE, C. and M., *Cassell's Illustrated Shakespeare* (1864-8).

CRAIG, H., *Works* (1951; revised by Bevington, D. 1973).

CRAIG, W. J., *The Oxford Shakespeare* (1892; 1911-12).

——and CASE, R H. (Gen. Eds.), *The Arden Shakespeare* (1891, etc.; see also ELLIS-FERMOR, U.).

DELIUS, N., *The Leopold Shakespeare* (1877).

DYCE, A., *Works* (1857; 1864-7).

ELLIS-FERMOR, U., BROOKS, H. F., JENKINS, H., and MORRIS, B. (Gen. Eds.), *The Arden Shakespeare* (new edn., 1951 etc.; see also CRAIG, W. J.).

EVANS, G. BLAKEMORE (Gen. Ed.), *The Riverside Shakespeare* (1974).

FARJEON, H., *The Nonesuch Edition* (1929).

FURNESS, H. H., *The New Variorum Edition* (1879 etc.; reprint 1963-5).

HARBAGE, A. (Gen. Ed.), *The Complete Pelican Shakespeare* (1969).

HALLIWELL, J. O., *Works* (1851-3).

HANMER, T., *Works* (1743-4).

HARNESS, W., *Works* (1825).

HEATH, B., *A Revisal of Shakespear's Text* (1765).

HUDSON, H. N., *The Harvard Edition* (1851-6).

INGRAM, W. G., and REDPATH, T., *Shakespeare's Sonnets* (1964).

JENKINS, H.: see ELLIS-FERMOR, U.

JOHNSON, S., *Plays* (1765).

KEIGHTLEY, T., *Plays* (1865).

KNIGHT, C., *Pictorial Edition* (1838-43).

KOKERITZ, H., and PROUTY, C. T., *The Yale Shakespeare* (1954-9).

MALONE, E., *Plays and Poems* (1790).

MORRIS, B.: see ELLIS-FERMOR, U.

MUNRO, J., *The London Shakespeare* (1958).

POPE, A., *Works* (1723–5; 1728).

PROUTY, C. T.: see KOKERITZ, H.

QUILLER-COUCH, A., and DOVER WILSON, J. (Gen. Eds.), *New Cambridge Shakespeare* (1921–66).

RANN, J., *Dramatic Works* (1786–94).

REED, I., *Plays* (1785; first variorum edn., 1803; second variorum edn. with notes by Malone, 1813).

ROLFE, W. J., *The Friendly Edition* (1871–96).

ROWE, N., *Works* (1709; 1714).

SEYMOUR-SMITH, M. *Shakespeare's Sonnets* (1963).

SINGER, S. W., *Dramatic Works* (1826).

SISSON, C. J. *Complete Works* (1954).

SPENCER, J. T. B. (Gen. Ed.), *The New Penguin Shakespeare* (1967 etc.).

STAUNTON, H., *Plays* (1858–60).

STEEVENS, G. (with JOHNSON, S.) *Plays* (1773).

THEOBALD, L., *Works* (1733).

WARBURTON, W., *Works* (1747).

WELLS, S. (Gen. Ed.), *The Oxford Shakespeare* (1982 (H5, SHR, TRO)).

WHITE, R. G., *Works* (1857–9; 1883).

WILSON, J. DOVER: see QUILLER-COUCH, A.

WRIGHT, W. A.: see CLARK, W. G.

WYNDHAM, G., *Poems* (1898).

2. Concordances

HOWARD-HILL, T., *Oxford Shakespeare Concordances* (1969–72).

SPEVACK, M., *Complete and Systematic Concordance to the Works of Shakespeare* (1968–70).

3. Other Works

This is only a select list. It has not been feasible to acknowledge the large number of articles which have appeared, for example, in journals.

ABBOTT, E. A., *A Shakespearian Grammar* (3rd edn., 1870).

ASCHAM, R., *Toxophilus* (1545; treatise on archery).

BAILEY, N., *An Universal Etymological English Dictionary* (1721).

BAILEY, R. W., *et al.*, *Michigan Early Modern English Materials* (1975).

BALDWIN, T. W., *William Shakespere's 'Small Latine and Lesse Greeke'* (1944).

BARET, J., *An Alvearie or triple Dictionarie in Englishe, Latin, and French* (1573).

—— *An Alvearie or quadruple dictionarie, containing foure sundrie tongues, English, Latine, Greeke, and French* (1580).

BLOUNT, T., *Glossographia* (1656, 1661, 1674).

—— *A Law-Dictionary* (1670, 1691).

BLUNDEVILLE, T., *The Art of Writing [with] The Order of Curing Horses diseases* (1580).

BORDE, A., *A compendyous Regyment or Dyetary of Helth* (1542).

BOTONER OF WORCESTER, W., *Itinerarium* (14—).

BOURNE, W., *A Regiment for the Sea: conteyning most profitable rules . . . of navigation* (1574).

BROOK, G. L., *The Language of Shakespeare* (1976).

CAWDREY, R., *A Table Alphabeticall of Hard Usual English Words* (1604).

COKE, E., *The First Part of the Institvtes of the Lawes of England* (1628).

COLMAN, E. A. M., *The Dramatic Use of Bawdy in Shakespeare* (1974).

Constitutions and Canons Ecclesiasticall (1604).

COOPER, T., *Thesaurus Linguae Romanae and Britannicae* (1578).

COTGRAVE, R., *A Dictionarie of the French and English Tongues* (1611; another edition by Sherwood, 1632).

COWELL, J., *The Interpreter; or Booke containing the signification of Words . . . mentioned in the Lawe-writers or Statutes* (1607).

CUNNINGTON, C. W. and P., and BEARD, C., *A Dictionary of English Costume* (1960).

DENT, A., *World of Shakespeare: Plants* (1971).

—— *World of Shakespeare: Animals and Monsters* (1972).

DENT, R. W. *Shakespeare's Proverbial Language* (1981).

DYER, T. F. THISELTON, *Folk-lore of Shakespeare* (c.1883).

DYMMOK, J., *A Treatice of Ireland* (c.1600).

B. E. GENT., *A New Dictionary of the Terms Ancient and Modern of the Canting Crew* (c.1700).

ELYOT, SIR THOMAS, *The Dictionary of syr Thomas Eliot knyght* (1538).

EVANS, A. B. and S., *Leicestershire Words, Phrases and Proverbs* (1881).

FALCONER, A. F., *A Glossary of Shakespeare's Sea and Naval Terms including Gunnery* (1965).

FARMER, R., *An Essay on the Learning of Shakespeare* (1767).

FARMER, J. S., and HENLEY, W. E., *Slang and Its Analogues Past and Present* (1890–1904).

FLORIO, J., *A Worlde of Words, or most copious and exact Dictionarie in Italian and English* (1598; enlarged edn. 1611).

FOXE, J., *Actes and Monuments of these latter and perillous dayes* (1563, 1570, etc.; known as 'The Book of Martyrs').

FULLER, T., *The Church-History of Britain* (1655).

GASCOIGNE, G., *A Hundred Sundry Flowers* (1575).

GERARDE, G., *The Herball, or generall historie of plantes* (1597).

GOLDING, A., *The xv. Bookes of P. Ovidius Naso entytuled Metamorphosis, translated oute of Latin into English meeter* (1567).

GREENE, R., *The Scottish Historie of James the fourth* (15—).

GUILLIM, J., *A Display of Heraldrie* (1610).

HALL, E., *The Union of the two noble and illustre famelies of Lancastre and Yorke* (1550; 'Hall's Chronicle').

HALL, J., *Virgidemiarum, sixe bookes of . . . satyrs* (1597).

HARSNET, S., *A Declaration of egregious Popish Impostures . . . vnder the pretence of casting out diuels* (1603).

HARTING, J. E., *The Ornithology of Shakespeare* (1864; 1978).

HENN, T. R., *The Living Image* (1972).

HESLOP, O., *Northumberland Words* (1892-4).

HEYWORD, J., *A Dialogue, conteyninge the number in effecte of all the Proverbes in the Englishe tunge* (1561).

HOLINSHED, R., *The Chronicles of Englande, Scotlande, and Irelande* (1577).

HOLLAND, P., *The Historie of the World, commonly called the Naturall Historie of C. Plinius Secundus* (1601).

—— *The Philosophie, commonly called the Morals, written by . . . Plutarch of Chaeronea* (1603).

HOLME, R., *The Academy of Armory, or a storehouse of armory and blazon* (1688).

HULME, H. M., *Explorations in Shakespeare's Language* (1962; 1977).

JOHNSON, S., *A Dictionary of the English Language* (1755).

JORGENSEN, P. A., *Shakespeare's Military World* (1956).

KEETON, G. W., *Shakespeare's Legal and Political Background* (1967).

KINNEAR, B. G., *Cruces Shakespearianae* (1883).

KURATH, E., *Middle English Dictionary* A-P3 (1963-82).

LATHAM, S., *Lathams Falconry, or the Faulcons Lure and Cure* (1615-18).

LELAND, J., *Itinerarium* (1534-43).

LILY, W., *Brevissima Institutio* (1522; Latin grammar).

LINTHICUM, M. C., *Costume in the Drama of Shakespeare and his Contemporaries* (1936).

MADDEN, D. H., *The Diary of Master William Silence: A Study of Shakespeare and of Elizabethan Sport* (1897).

MAHOOD, M. M., *Shakespeare's Word-play* (1957).

MANWAYRING, H., *The Seaman's Dictionary* (1644).

MILWARD, P., *Shakespeare's Religious Background* (1973).

MINSHEU, J., *Ductor in Linguas, The Gvide into Tongves* (1617).

NARES, R., *A Glossary . . . of English Authors, particularly Shakespeare* (1822).

NAYLOR, E. W., *Shakespeare and Music* (1935).

NOBLE, R. *Shakespeare's Biblical Knowledge and Use of the Book of Common Prayer* (1935).

NORTH, T., *The Lives of the noble Grecians and Romanes, compared together by Plutarch of Chaeronea; translated out of Greeke into French by J. Amyot . . . and out of French into Englishe by T. North* (1579).

ORTON, H., and DEITH, E., *Survey of English Dialects* (1962-71).

Oxford English Dictionary (1884-1928); *Supplements* (1933; 1972-82).

PALSGRAVE, J., *Lesclarcissement de la Langue Francoyse* (1530; French grammar and vocabulary).

PARTRIDGE, E., *A Dictionary of Catch Phrases* (1977).

PARTRIDGE, E., *A Dictionary of Slang and Unconventional English* (7th edn., 1970).

—— *Shakespeare's Bawdy* (rev. 1968).

PHILLIPS, O. HOOD, *Shakespeare and the Lawyers* (1972).

RAY, J., *A Collection of English Words not generally used . . . in two Alphabetical Catalogues. The one of such as are Proper to the Northern, the other to the Southern Counties* (1674).

RIDER, J., *Bibliotheca Scholastica, a double Dictionarie* (1589).

ROWSE, A. L., *Shakespeare's Sonnets: The Problems Solved* (2nd edn., 1973).

RUSHTON, W., *Shakespeare a Lawyer* (1858).

—— *Shakespeare's Testamentary Language* (1869).

SCHMIDT, A. *A Shakespeare-Lexicon* (1874-5; revised by Sarrazin, G., 6th edn. 1971).

SCOTT-GILES, C. W., *Shakespeare's Heraldry* (1971).

Shakespeare Survey (passim).

SHERWOOD: see COTGRAVE.

SISSON, C. J., *New Readings in Shakespeare* (1956).

SKINNER, S., *Etymologicon Linguae Anglicanae* (1671).

SMITH, T., *The Common Welth of England* (1583).

SMYTH, J., *Certain Discourses . . . concerning the formes and effects of diuers sorts of Weapons, and other verie important matters Militarie* (1590).

SPURGEON, C., *Shakespeare's Imagery and What It Tells Us* (1935).

STERNHOLD, T., and HOPKINS, J., *The whole booke of Psalmes collected into Englyshe Meter* (1564).

STEWART, C. D., *Some Textual Difficulties in Shakespeare* (1914).

STOW, J., *A breviat Chronicle contaynynge all the Kynges* (1561).

STUBBES, P., *The Anatomie of Abuses* (1583).

SUGDEN, E. H., *A Topographical Dictionary to the Works of Shakespeare and his Fellow Dramatists* (1925).

TILLEY, M. P., *A Dictionary of Proverbs in England in the Sixteenth and Seventeenth Centuries* (1950).

TORRIANO, G., *Vocabolario Italiano et Inglese, a Dictionary of Italian and English* (1659).

TURBERVILE, G., *The Noble Arte of Venerie or Hunting* (1575).

TYRWHITT, T., *Observations and Conjectures upon Some Passages of Shakespeare* (1766).

WALKER, A., *Textual Problems of the First Folio* (1953).

WALKER, W. S., *A Critical Examination of the Text of Shakespeare* (1860).

—— *Shakespeare's Versification* (1854).

WATERS, D. W., *The Art of Navigation in England in Elizabethan and Early Stuart Times* (1958).

WHITING, B. J., *Proverbs, Sentences, and Proverbial Phrases from English Writings Mainly before 1500* (1968).

WILSON, F. P. (ed.), *Oxford Dictionary of English Proverbs* (1970).

WITHALS, J., *A Dictionarie in English and Latine* (1616).

WRIGHT, J., *English Dialect Dictionary* (1896-1905).

WRIGHT, T., *Dictionary of obsolete and provincial English* (1857).

A

a *vb.* (contraction for) HA (=HAVE) LLL 5.2.17 *She might 'a' been grandam ere she died,* HAM 4.5.65.

a *pron.* (contraction for) HA (=HE) SHR 5.2.60 *a has a little gall'd me, I confess.*

a *interj.* (variant of) Ah 2H4 2.1.50 *A, thou honey-suckle villain!*

a *prep.* (reduced form of OE, 'of' and 'on')
1 Of R2 1.3.76 *John a' Gaunt,* ERR 2.1.11 *out a'door.*
2 On 2H4 2.4.313 *a' mine honour.*
3 In R2 2.1.251 *a' God's name.*
4 To MND 2.2.7 *Seeing me now a sleepe.*
5 By COR 1.3.58 *A' my troth.*
▷ Similarly, *a* before a gerund is a reduced form of 'on' SHR 3.1.34 *Lucentio that comes a wooing* (F. Mod. edd. often hyphenate, e.g. *a-wooing.*)

a *det.* One AWW 1.3.238 *He and his physicians Are of a mind,* HAM 5.2.265 *These foils have all a length?* (i.e. one and the same length).
▷ S. freq. inserted *a* before a numeral when the objects enumerated were regarded as a unit, e.g., JN 4.2.199 *a many thousand warlike French.*

a *prefix.* (in Ff and Qq freq. separated from the stem) LLL 4.3.157 *a shamed* (Q).

-a an extra syllable often added in songs for the sake of rhythm WT 4.4.317 *My dainty duck, my dear-a,* HAM 4.5.172.

abandon *vb.*
1 Banish, keep away SHR Ind.2.115 *Being all this time abandon'd from your bed.*
2 Give up absolutely OTH 3.3.369 *Never pray more; abandon all remorse.*

abandoned *ppl. adj.* Surrendered unreservedly TN 1.4.19 *If she be so abandon'd to her sorrow.*

abase *vb.* Lower R3 1.2.246 *And will she yet abase her eyes on me,* 2H6 1.2.15.

abashed *ppl. adj.* Showing shame, error or guilt TRO 1.3.18 *Do you with cheeks abash'd behold our works.*

abate *vb.*
1 Lessen, shorten MND 3.2.432 *Abate thy hours.*
2 Curtail, deprive of LR 2.4.159 *She hath abated me of half my train.*
3 Depreciate (a person) CYM 1.4.68 *I would abate her nothing.*
4 Blunt R3 5.5.35 *Abate the edge of traitors,* 2H4 1.1.117.
5 Bar, except LLL 5.2.544 *Abate throw at novum, and the whole world again Cannot pick out five such.*

abated *ppl. adj.* Humiliated COR 3.3.132 *as most Abated captives to some nation.*

abatement *n.*
1 Reduction, diminution LR 1.4.60 *There's a great abatement of kindness appears,* HAM 4.7.120, CYM 5.4.21.
2 Depreciation of character TN 1.1.13 *But falls into abatement and low price.*

abhominable, abhomination See ABOMINATION *note.*

abhor *vb.*
1 Horrify, disgust OTH 4.2.162 *It does abhor me now I speak the word,* HAM 5.1.187.
2 (term of canon law) Protest against H8 2.4.81 *I utterly abhor, yea, from my soul Refuse you for my judge.*

abhorred *ppl. adj.* Abominable MAC 5.7.10 *Thou liest, abhorred tyrant,* JN 4.2.224.

abhorring *n.*
1 Abhorrence, loathing COR 1.1.168 *He...will flatter Beneath abhorring.*
2 Object of disgust ANT 5.2.60 *and let the water-flies Blow me into abhorring!*

abide *vb.*
1 Stay briefly WT 4.3.93 *yet it will no more but abide.*
2 Face in fight MND 3.2.422 *Abide me, if thou dar'st,* 2H4 2.3.36, CYM 3.4.183.
3 Pay the penalty for, atone for, take the consequences of (perhaps from confusion with 'aby') JC 3.1.94 *let no man abide this deed, But we the doers;* (esp. with *dear*) JC 3.2.114 *If it be found so, some will dear abide it,* MND 3.2.175 (F1).

abiliments *n. (pl.)* Habiliments, attire ANT 3.6.17 *In th' abiliments of the goddess Isis.*

ability *n.*
1 Wealth, means TN 3.4.344 *Out of my lean and low ability I'll lend you something,* 2H4 1.3.45.
2 Strength WT 2.3.164 *Any thing, my lord, That my ability may undergo And nobleness impose;* (hence) strength in means of defence OTH 1.3.25 *But altogether lacks th' abilities That Rhodes is dress'd in.*

abject *n.* Contemptible thing; (hence) most servile subject R3 1.1.106 *We are the Queen's abjects, and must obey.*
~ *adj.* Contemptible, despicable, degraded 1H6 5.5.49 *That he should be so abject, base, and poor.*

abjectly *adv.* Basely TIT 2.3.4 *Let him that thinks of me so abjectly.*

able *vb.* Vouch for LR 4.6.168 *None does offend none, I say none, I'll able 'em.*
~ *adj. able for* Sufficient for, equal to, competent to deal with AWW 1.1.65 *Be able for thine enemy Rather in power than use.*

abode *n.*
1 Delay MV 2.6.21 *Sweet friends, your patience for my long abode.*
2 Remaining, stay ANT 1.2.175 *especially that of Cleopatra's, which wholly depends on your abode.*
3 Residence TGV 4.3.23 *To Mantua, where I hear he makes abode,* SHR 4.5.38.

abode *vb.* Foretell, forbode H8 1.1.93 *this tempest ...aboded The sudden breach on't,* 3H6 5.6.45.

abodement *n.* Foreboding, omen 3H6 4.7.13 *Tush, man, abodements must not now affright us.*

abomination *n.*
1 Hateful act ANT 3.6.94 *Only th' adulterous Antony, most large In his abominations.*
2 State of being greatly hated or loathed, abominableness LUC 704 *Ere he can see his own abomination.*
▷ From 14 to 17C, and in S., *abominable* and *abomination* were commonly spelt 'abhom-', as if from 'ab' and 'homin-' (i.e. away from man, inhuman).

abortive *n.* Untimely or monstrous birth JN 3.4.158 *Abortives, presages, and tongues of heaven.*
~ *adj.* Born prematurely; (hence) untimely, un-natural, monstrous (lit. and fig.) 2H6 4.1.60 *and allay this thy abortive pride,* R3 1.2.21, LLL 1.1.104.

abound *vb.* Be wealthy H8 1.1.83 *They shall abound as formerly.*

about *adv.* (only in imperative; perhaps remnant of a larger construction) (Be) on the move, afoot, astir JC 3.2.204 *Revenge! About! Seek! Burn! Fire*, HAM 2.2.588, WIV 5.5.55.

above *adv.* Upstairs ERR 2.2.207 *Husband, I'll dine above with you to-day*, WIV 4.2.76.

Abraham Cupid See ADAM *n.* sense 3.

abram *adj.* (corr. of 'abron', 'abrun') Auburn Cor 2.3.19 *our heads are some brown, some black, some abram, some bald.*

abridge *vb.*
1 Deprive, debar MV 1.1.126 *Nor do I now make moan to be abridg'd.*
2 Reduce JC 3.1.104 *So are we Caesar's friends, that have abridg'd His time of fearing death*, TGV 3.1.247.

abridgement *n.*
1 Means of shortening time, pastime, (perh.) shortened play for an evening's entertainment MND 5.1.39 *what abridgement have you for this evening?*, Ham 2.2.420.
2 Reduction (of time, of an account) H5 5.Ch.44 *Then brook abridgement, and your eyes advance.*

abroach *vb. set abroach* Set on foot, start flowing ROM 1.1.104 *Who set this ancient quarrel new abroach?*, 2H4 4.2.14, R3 1.3.324.

abroad *adv.*
1 Away or apart from one's own body or person CYM 1.2.4 *there's none abroad so wholesome as that you vent*, LC 137, LC 183.
2 *abroad displayed* Outstretched (with allusion to 'sails abroad', i.e. sails set or spread) 2H6 3.2.172 *His hands abroad display'd, as one that grasp'd.*

abrogate *vb.* Abstain from LLL 4.2.54 *good Master Holofernes, perge, so it shall please you to abrogate squirility.*

abrook *vb.* Brook, endure 2H6 2.4.10 *Sweet Nell, ill can thy noble mind abrook The abject people gazing on thy face.*

abruption *n.* Breaking off TRO 3.2.65 *What makes this pretty abruption?*

absent *adj.* Of absence R2 2.3.79 *To take advantage of the absent time.*

Absey book *n.* ABC-book, primer, hornbook JN 1.1.196 *And then comes answer like an Absey book.*

absolute *adj.*
1 Free from imperfection, complete H5 3.7.25 *Indeed, my lord, it is a most absolute and excellent horse*, MM 5.1.54, HAM 5.2.107.
2 Unrestricted, unconditional 1H4 4.3.50 *And pardon absolute for yourself*, COR 3.1.116.
3 Positive, perfectly certain, decided MAC 3.6.40 *And with an absolute 'Sir, not I', The cloudy messenger turns me his back*, MM 3.1.5.

absque hoc nihil est See OBSQUE.

abstenious *adj.* Abstemious, abstinent TMP 4.1.53 *Be more abstenious, Or else good night your vow.*

abstract *n.*
1 Epitome, symbol ANT 1.4.9 *A man who is th' abstract of all faults.*
2 Summary account R3 4.4.28 *Brief abstract and record of tedious days.*
3 Short catalogue or inventory WIV 4.2.62 *an abstract for the remembrance of such places.*
4 Summary proceeding AWW 4.3.86 *an abstract of success.*
5 Abridgement, short cut ANT 3.6.61 *an abstract 'tween his lust and him.*
◇ F1; Theobald's emendation *obstruct* 'impediment'.

absurd *adj.* Tasteless, incongruous HAM 3.2.60 *let the candied tongue lick absurd pomp.*
◇ Hulme observes that 'ab' is etymologically an intensive and 'surdus' is defined as 'that which hath no sauour' in Cooper's 'Thesaurus' (1578).

abuse *n.*
1 Ill-usage, injury, wrong, offence 3H6 3.3.188 *th' abuse done to my niece*, WIV 5.3.7; (fig.) H5 2.Ch.32 *We'll digest Th' abuse of distance.*
2 Imposture, deception, delusion HAM 4.7.50 *Or is it some abuse, and no such thing?*
3 Corrupt practice MM 2.1.43 *If these be good people in a commonweal that do nothing but use their abuses in common houses, I know no law*, JC 2.1.115, VEN 792.
~ *vb.* 1 Do violence to, ill-use R3 1.3.52 *But thus his simple truth must be abus'd*, WIV 1.1.3, SHR 5.1.108.
2 Impose upon, cheat, deceive ADO 5.2.98 *the Prince and Claudio mightily abus'd*, HAM 2.2.603, CYM 1.4.114.
3 Insult, malign ANT 5.2.43 *Do not abuse my master's bounty*, CYM 2.3.149.
4 Disgrace, dishonour WIV 2.2.292 *My bed shall be abus'd*, 1H6 4.5.41.

abuser *n.* Corrupter OTH 1.2.78 *For an abuser of the world.*

abusing *ppl. adj.* Harmful, injurious, bringing evil R3 3.7.199 *From the corruption of abusing times.*

aby *vb.* Pay the penalty for, atone for MND 3.2.175 *Lest, to thy peril, thou aby it dear.*

academe *n.* Academy, philosophical school LLL 1.1.13 *Our court shall be a little academe.*

accent *n.*
1 Word, speech, language JN 5.6.14 *any accent breaking from thy tongue*, ROM 2.4.29, 1H4 1.1.3.
2 *second accent* Echo H5 2.4.126 *That cares... shall...return your mock In second accent of his ordinance.*

accept *ppl. adj.* Decisive H5 5.2.82 *Pass our accept and peremptory answer.*

accepted *ppl. adj.* Acceptable TRO 3.3.30 *Shall quite strike off all service I have done, In most accepted pain.*

accidence *n.* Rudiments of grammar WIV 4.1.16 *ask him some questions in his accidence.*

accident *n.* Occurrence, incident, event MND 4.1.68 *And think no more of this night's accidents*, ADO 2.1.181, TMP 5.1.306.

accite *vb.*
1 Summon, cite 2H4 5.2.141 *we will accite... all our state.*
2 (prob. confusion for) Excite 2H4 2.2.60 *And what accites your most worshipful thought to think so?* (Ff3–4 *excites*).

accommodate *vb.*
1 Furnish, equip LR 4.6.81 *The safer sense will ne'er accommodate His master thus*, 2H4 3.2.66.
◇ Hulme proposes that *safer sense*, i.e. saner sense, refers not to Lear but to Gloucester, and that S. here used *accommodate* in the sense, also current at the time, of 'adapt itself to', i.e. 'maintain itself when confronted by'.
2 Favour CYM 5.3.32 *Accommodated by the place.*

accommodation *n.*
1 Provision, entertainment OTH 1.3.238 *With such accommodation and besort As levels with her breeding.*
2 (pl.) Conveniences, comforts MM 3.1.14 *For all th' accommodations that thou bear'st.*

accommodo [L.] (First person singular present indicative form of 'accommodare') Accommodate 2H4 3.2.72 *Accommodated! it comes of 'accommodo'.*

accomplice *n.* Comrade in arms, ally 1H6 5.2.9 *And happiness to his accomplices!*

accomplish *vb.*
1 Equip perfectly H5 4.Ch.12 *The armourers, accomplishing the knights*, MV 3.4.61, R2 2.1.178.

2 Gain, obtain 3H6 3.2.152 *Than to accomplish twenty golden crowns.*

accompt *n.* Reckoning LLL 5.2.200 *That we may do it still without accompt.*

accord *n.*
1 Harmony, concord, agreement H5 5.2.353 *Plant neighbourhood and Christian-like accord,* AYL 1.1.64; (of sounds) SHR 3.1.73 *the ground of all accord.*
2 Assent, consent TRO 1.3.238 *Good arms, strong joints, true swords, and, great Jove's accord* (i.e.with Jove on their side), HAM 1.2.123, ERR 2.1.25.
~ *vb.* Agree, assent, consent H5 2.2.86 *You know how apt our love was to accord,* AYL 5.4.133.

accordant *adj.* Agreeing, consenting ADO 1.2.14 *and if he found her accordant.*

according *ppl. adj.* Agreeing, assenting ROM 1.2.19 *And she agreed, within her scope of choice Lies my consent and fair according voice.*

accost *vb.* (nautical) Go alongside of, hail; (hence) approach, make up to, address TN 1.3.49 *Accost, Sir Andrew, accost.*

accountant *adj.* Accountable, liable to give an account MM 2.4.86 *And his offence is so, as it appears, Accountant to the law upon that pain,* OTH 2.1.293.

accoustrements *n.* (spelling based on OFr. original) Accoutrements AYL 3.2.383 *you are rather point-device in your accoustrements.*

accusativo [L.] In the accusative case WIV 4.1.45.

accuse *n.* Accusation 2H6 3.1.160 *By false accuse doth level at my life.*

acerb *adj.* Sour and bitter OTH 1.3.349 *The food... shall be to him shortly as acerb as the coloquintida.*

ache *n.* Continuous pain or pain of some duration TMP 1.2.370 *Fill all thy bones with aches.*
▷ Pronounced [eɪtʃ], hence pl. 'aches' is dissyllabic; when used as verb, pronounced [eik], and spelt 'ake' in orig. edd.

achieve *vb.*
1 Gain, succeed in obtaining AWW 1.1.45 *she derives her honesty, and achieves her goodness,* COR 1.9.33, SON 67.3.
2 Make an end of, finish H5 4.3.91 *Bid them achieve me, and then sell my bones.*
3 Accomplish one's purpose COR 4.7.23 *and does achieve as soon As draw his sword.*

achievement *n.*
1 Something accomplished or acquired 2H4 4.5.189 *For all the soil of the achievement goes With me into the earth,* TRO 1.2.293.
2 Heraldic device to commemorate a feat of arms H5 3.5.60 *And for achievement offer us his ransom.*

achiever *n.* One who accomplishes, winner, victor ADO 1.1.8 *A victory is twice itself when the achiever brings home full numbers.*

Achilles' spear *n.* A spear, the rust from which is capable of curing a wound inflicted by it 2H6 5.1.100 *like to Achilles' spear Is able with the change to kill and cure.*
▷ An allusion to the incident of Telephus in classical mythology.

acknow *vb.* be acknown confess knowledge of OTH 3.3.319 *Be not acknown on't.*

a-cold *adj.* Cold, chilled LR 3.4.58 *Tom's a-cold.*

aconitum *n.* Poisonous extract of wolf's-bane or monk's-hood 2H4 4.4.48 *As aconitum or rash gunpowder.*

acquit *vb.*
1 Atone for LUC 1071 *Till life to death acquit my forc'd offence.*
2 Pay back, requite H5 2.2.144 *And God acquit them of their practices,* MV 5.1.138.

3 (refl.) Perform one's part, discharge the duties of one's position, prove oneself AYL 1.1.128 *He that escapes me without some broken limb shall acquit him well.*
~ *ppl. adj.* Free, rid of WIV 1.3.24 *I am glad I am so acquit of this tinderbox.*

acquittance *n.*
1 Writing in evidence of a discharge LLL 2.1.160 *you can produce acquittances For such a sum.*
2 Acquittal HAM 4.7.1 *Now must your conscience my acquittance seal.*
~ *vb.* Acquit, clear, discharge R3 3.7.233 *Your mere enforcement shall acquittance me.*

across *adv.*
1 Crossed, folded JC 2.1.240 *Musing and sighing, with your arms across,* LUC 1662.
2 Not straight, obliquely; (hence) clumsily, amiss AWW 2.1.67 *Good faith, across!*
▷ In tilting the blow was delivered with the point; it would be an unskilled tilter who broke his lance 'across' instead of head-on.

act *n.*
1 Performance, action, operation MV 1.3.83 *Between these woolly breeders in the act,* AWW 1.2.30, JN 3.1.274.
2 Event OTH 5.2.371 *This heavy act with heavy heart relate.*
~ *vb.* Carry out, put into action ANT 5.2.45 *let the world see His nobleness well acted,* ROM 3.2.16, 2H6 5.1.103.

action *n.* Gesture, gesticulation JC 3.2.222 *nor words, nor worth, Action, nor utterance, nor the power of speech,* HAM 3.2.17; movement, demeanour SHR Ind.1.110 *bear himself with honourable action.*

action-taking *adj.* Litigious, seeking redress at law rather than by his own hand LR 2.2.18 *a lily-liver'd, action-taking...rogue.*

actor *n.* Doer MM 2.2.37 *Condemn the fault, and not the actor of it?,* AWW 2.3.24, LUC 608.

actual *adj.* Active, consisting in action MAC 5.1.12 *besides her walking and other actual performances* (i.e. physical acts), OTH 4.2.153.

acture *n.* Action, performance LC 185 *Love made them not, with acture they may be.*

Adam *n.*
1 Natural depravity, human frailty (ref. to the sinfulness inherited by mankind as Adam's descendants) H5 1.1.29 *And whipt th' offending Adam out of him.*
2 (jocular) Bailiff's officer (the buff or leather jerkin of the officer suggesting Adam who, after the fall, wore skins) ERR 4.3.13 *What, have you got the picture of old Adam new apparell'd?*
3 Adam Bell, a famous archer ADO 1.1.259 *he that hits me, let him be clapp'd on the shoulder, and call'd Adam.*
▷ Hence proposed emendation of *Abraham Cupid* (F1 and Qq) to *Adam Cupid* in mod. edd. in ROM 2.1.13 *Young Abraham Cupid, he that shot so trim* (i.e. Cupid the Archer).

adamant *n.*
1 Imaginary stone or mineral of impenetrable hardness 1H6 1.4.52 *And spurn in pieces posts of adamant.*
2 Lodestone, magnet MND 2.1.195 *You draw me, you hard-hearted adamant,* TRO 3.2.179.

ad Apollinem [L.] To Apollo TIT 4.3.54.

addiction *n.* Natural inclination, bent H5 1.1.54 *Since his addiction was to courses vain,* OTH 2.2.6.

addition *n.* Mark of distinction, something added to a man's name or coat of arms to denote his rank, title MAC 1.3.106 *In which addition, hail, most worthy thane.*

addle *adj.* Addled, rotten ROM 3.1.24 *yet thy head hath been beaten as addle as an egg for quarrelling.*

address *vb.*
1 Direct MND 2.2.143 *and, all my powers, address your love and might To honour Helen,* TN 1.4.15, LLL 5.2.92.
2 Prepare, make ready WT 4.4.53 *Address yourself to entertain them sprightly,* MND 5.1.106, H5 3.3.58.

adhere *vb.* Hang together, agree WIV 2.1.62 *They do no more adhere...than the hundred Psalms to the tune of 'Greensleeves',* MAC 1.7.52.

ad Jovem [L.] To Jupiter TIT 4.3.54.

adjunct *n.*
1 Something annexed LLL 4.3.310 *Learning is but an adjunct to ourself.*
2 Aid, assistant SON 122.13 *To keep an adjunct to remember thee Were to import forgetfulness in me* (i.e. an added help to memory).
~ *adj.* Connected, annexed JN 3.3.57 *Though that my death were adjunct to my act,* SON 91.5.

ad manes fratrum [L.] To the departed spirits of our brothers TIT 1.1.98.

ad Martem [L.] To Mars TIT 4.3.55.

admirable *adj.* Wonderful, to be wondered at MND 5.1.27 *But howsoever, strange and admirable.*

admiral *n.* Flagship ANT 3.10.2 *Th' 'Antoniad', the Egyptian admiral, With all their sixty, fly.*
▷ Eliz. practice was to call the flagship the 'Admiral' or 'Vice-Admiral' depending on the rank of the commanding officer.

admiration *n.*
1 Quality of exciting wonder or approbation TMP 3.1.38 *Admir'd Miranda, Indeed the top of admiration.*
2 Object of wonder, marvel AWW 2.1.88 *Bring in the admiration, that we with thee May spend our wonder too.*
3 Wonderment, astonishment LR 1.4.237 *This admiration, sir, is much o' th' savour Of other your new pranks.*
4 *note of admiration* The exclamation mark (!) WT 5.2.11 *the changes...were very notes of admiration.*

admire *vb.* Wonder TMP 5.1.154 *At this encounter do so much admire That they devour their reason.*

admired *ppl. adj.*
1 Admirable ANT 2.2.119 *Admir'd Octavia,* TMP 3.1.37.
2 Amazing MAC 3.4.109 *You have...broke the good meeting, With most admir'd disorder.*
3 Wondering TIM 5.1.51 *'Tis thou that rig'st the bark and plough'st the foam, Settlest admired reverence in a slave.*

admittance *n.*
1 Acceptance, sanction; (hence) vogue, fashion WIV 3.3.58 *the ship-tire, the tire-valiant, or any tire of Venetian admittance,* WIV 2.2.226.
2 Reception LLL 2.1.80 *Now, what admittance, lord?*

admonish *vb.* Warn (no suggestion of moral exhortation) 1H6 5.3.3. *And ye choice spirits that admonish me And give me signs of future accidents.*

a'door, adoor See A (*prep.*).

adoptedly *adv.* By adoption MM 1.4.47 *adoptedly, as school-maids change their names.*

adoptious *adj.* Adopted AWW 1.1.174 *with a world Of pretty fond adoptious christendoms.*

adorning *n.* That which is beautiful in itself or which adds to the grace and beauty of another ANT 2.2.208 *And made their bends adornings.*

adsum [L.] I am here 2H6 1.4.23.

adulterate *vb.* Commit adultery JN 3.1.56 *Sh' adulterates hourly with thine uncle John.*
~ *adj.* Adulterous SON 121.5 *false adulterate eyes.*

advance *vb.* Raise, lift up TMP 1.2.409 *The fringed curtains of thine eye advance,* R3 1.2.40, H5 5.Ch.44.

advantage *n.*
1 Favourable opportunity, chance TMP 3.3.13 *The next advantage Will we take throughly,* OTH 1.3.297, VEN 129.
2 Pecuniary profit, interest on money MV 1.3.70 *you neither lend nor borrow Upon advantage;* (fig.) JN 3.3.22 *with advantage means to pay thy love.*
3 Embellishments H5 4.3.50 *But he'll remember with advantages.*
~ *vb.*
1 Be of benefit TMP 1.1.32 *for our own doth little advantage.*
2 Benefit from, derive advantage from H5 4.1.284 *Whose hours the peasant best advantages.*
3 Augment R3 4.4.323 *Advantaging their love with interest.*

advantageable *adj.* Profitable, advantageous H5 5.2.88 *as your wisdoms best Shall see advantageable for our dignity.*

adventerous *adj.* Adventurous, i.e. wandering in search of adventure HAM 2.2.320 *the adventerous knight shall use his foil and target.*

adventure *n.* Hazard, chance WT 5.1.156 *Th' adventure of her person; at all adventures* at all hazards, whatever happens ERR 2.2.216 *And in this mist at all adventures go?,* H5 4.1.116.
~ *vb.* Run risks ROM 2.2.84 *I should adventure for such merchandise,* WT 1.2.38, R3 1.3.115.

adversity *n.* Quibbler TRO 5.1.12 *Well said, adversity!*

advertise *vb.* Inform, instruct 3H6 5.3.18 *We are advertis'd by our loving friends.*

advertisement *n.*
1 Information 1H4 3.2.172 *For this advertisement is five days old.*
2 Advice, counsel 1H4 4.1.36 *Yet doth he give us bold advertisement,* AWW 4.3.213, ADO 5.1.32.

advertising *adj.* Attentive MM 5.1.383 *Advertising and holy to your business.*

advice *n.*
1 Consideration, deliberation MV 4.2.6 *My Lord Bassanio upon more advice Hath sent you here this ring,* H5 2.2.43, MV 4.2.6.
2 Discretion, forethought AWW 3.4.19 *Rinaldo, you did never lack advice so much As letting her pass so.*

advise *vb.*
1 Consider, bethink oneself of TN 4.2.94 *Advise you what you say,* ROM 3.5.190, LR 2.1.27.
2 Inform, apprise TGV 3.1.122 *Advise me where I may have such a ladder,* H8 1.2.107, AWW 3.5.25.

advised *ppl. adj.* Considerate, deliberate, cautious JN 4.2.214 *More upon humour than advis'd respect,* MV 1.1.142, R2 1.3.188.
▷ See also WELL-ADVISED.

advocation *n.* Pleading of an advocate OTH 3.4.123 *My advocation is not now in tune.*

aedile *n.* Roman official whose duties included responsibility for public buildings and public order COR 3.1.182 *Seize him, aediles!*

aerial *adj.* Of the atmosphere OTH 2.1.39 *Even till we make the main and th' aerial blue An indistinct regard.*

aerie, aery *n.* Nest, or brood of a bird of prey, particularly of an eagle JN 5.2.149 *And like an eagle o'er his aerie tow'rs;* HAM 2.2.339 *But there is, sir, an aery of children, little eyases, that cry out on the top of question* (a reference to the young choristers of the Chapel Royal and St. Paul's, who acted plays).

afar off *adv.* Remotely, indirectly WIV 1.1.208 *there is as 'twere a tender, a kind of tender, made afar off by Sir Hugh here,* WT 2.1.104.

affect *n.*
1 Kind feeling, affection R2 1.4.30 *As 'twere to banish their affects with him.*
2 Disposition, inclination, passions LLL 1.1.151 *For every man with his affects is born,* OTH 1.3.263.
~ *vb.*
1 Be fond of, like, love TN 2.5.24 *Maria once told me she did affect me,* LR 1.1.1, 2H6 4.7.98.
2 Desire, be inclined ANT 1.3.71 *Thy soldier, servant, making peace or war As thou affects.*
3 Aim at, aspire to COR 3.3.1 *In this point charge him home, that he affects Tyrannical power,* WT 4.4.420.
4 Imitate, resemble JN 1.1.86 *The accent of his tongue affecteth him.*

affected *ppl. adj.*
1 In love LLL 2.1.232 *With that which we lovers entitle 'affected',* VEN 157.
2 Disposed, inclined TGV 1.3.60 *And how stand you affected to his wish?,* LR 2.1.98.

affectedly *adv.* Lovingly LC 48 *With sleided silk feat and affectedly Enswath'd.*

affecting *ppl. adj.* Using affectation, affected WIV 2.1.141 *I never heard such a drawling, affecting rogue.*

affection *n.*
1 Emotion, passion JC 2.1.20 *When his affections sway'd More than his reason,* LLL 1.1.9.
2 Thoughts and feelings, natural disposition MV 1.1.16 *The better part of my affections would Be with my hopes abroad,* MAC 4.3.77.
3 Inclination, bent TMP 1.2.482 *My affections Are then most humble,* ADO 2.2.6, COR 1.1.104.
4 Affectation LLL 5.1.4 *witty without affection, audacious without impudency,* LLL 5.2.407.
~ *vb.* Have affection for WIV 1.1.227 *But can you affection the oman?*

affectioned *ppl. adj.* Full of affectation, affected TN 2.3.148 *an affection'd ass.*

affeer *vb.* Confirm, settle authoritatively MAC 4.3.34 *The title is affeer'd!*

affiance *n.* Trust, confidence H5 2.2.127 *O, how hast thou with jealousy infected The sweetness of affiance!*

affined *ppl. adj.*
1 Closely related TRO 1.3.25 *The hard and soft, seem all affin'd and kin.*
2 Bound, obliged OTH 1.1.39 *Whether I in any just term am affin'd To love the Moor.*

affinity *n.* Family connections OTH 3.1.46 *That he you hurt is of great fame in Cyprus, And great affinity.*

affirm *vb.* Confirm, maintain (a statement) H5 5.2.114 *I said so...and I must not blush to affirm it.*

affirmation *n.* Confirmation Cym 1.4.59 *upon warrant of bloody affirmation* (i.e. pledge to confirm his assertion by shedding blood).

affray *vb.* Frighten ROM 3.5.33 *Since arm from arm that voice doth us affray.*

affront *n.* Stand CYM 5.3.87 *There was a fourth man, in a silly habit, That gave th' affront with them* (i.e. made the stand).
~ *vb.*
1 Meet, accost HAM 3.1.31 *That he, as 'twere by accident, may here Affront Ophelia.*
2 Face, encounter CYM 4.3.29 *Your preparation can affront no less,* WT 5.1.75.
3 Confront, equal, balance TRO 3.2.166 *Might be affronted with the match and weight Of such a winnowed purity in love!*

affy *vb.*
1 Trust TIT 1.1.47 *so do I affy In thy uprightness and integrity.*
2 Betroth 2H6 4.1.80 *daring to affy a mighty lord Unto the daughter of a worthless king.*

afoot *adv.* Up and about TIT 4.2.29 *But were our witty Empress well afoot, She would applaud Andronicus' conceit.*

afore *conj.* Before, sooner than 2H4 2.4.205 *I'll forswear keeping house afore I'll be in these tirrits.*
~ *prep.*
1 (of place) Before, in front of H5 3.6.31 *with a muffler afore his eyes* (i.e. over his eyes), 1H4 2.4.138, PER 4.6.136.
2 (esp. in oaths) In the presence of R2 2.1.200 *afore God,* TMP 4.1.7, ROM 2.4.161.
3 (of time) Before, previously to TMP 2.2.75 *if he have never drunk wine afore,* WIV 1.2.205, LR 1.5.5.

a(-)front *adv.* Abreast 1H4 2.4.200 *These four came all afront.*

after *adj.* (nautical) Rear OTH 1.3.35 *Have there injointed them with an after fleet* (i.e. a rear squadron of a fleet).

after *prep.*
1 According to TMP 2.2.73 *He's in his fit now, and does not talk after the wisest* (i.e. in the wisest fashion).
2 At the rate of MM 2.1.241 *I'll rent the fairest house in it after threepence a bay.*
~ in combination with n.

after-debt Debt to be paid at a later time AWW 4.3.226 *He ne'er pays after-debts.* **after-dinner** Time following dinner, afternoon MM 3.1.33 *But as it were an after-dinner's sleep.* **after-hours** Later times R3 4.4.293 *Which after-hours gives leisure to repent.* **after-inquiry** Subsequent investigation CYM 5.4.182 *or jump the after-inquiry on your own peril.* **after-loss** Later or second loss, future grief SON 90.4 *And do not drop in for an after-loss.* **after-love** Future love TGV 3.1.95 *For scorn at first makes after-love the more.* **after-meeting** Later or second meeting COR 2.2.39 *As the main point of this our after-meeting.* **after-nourishment** Later sustenance PER 1.2.13 *Have after-nourishment and life by care.* **after-supper** Late supper MND 5.1.34 *three hours Between our after-supper and bed-time?* **after-times** Future 2H4 4.2.51 *much too shallow, To sound the bottom of the after-times.*
~ in combination with vb.
after-eye Gaze after CYM 1.3.16 *ere left To after-eye him.*

again *adv.* Back, in return AYL 3.5.132 *I marvel why I answer'd not again,* SHR 2.1.218, SON 79.8.

against *conj.* In expectation of the time when, by the time that MND 3.2.99 *I'll charm his eyes against she do appear,* SHR 4.4.103.
~ *prep.* In expectation of, just before, in time for HAM 2.2.483 *But as we often see, against some storm, A silence in the heavens,* ROM 4.2.46, TRO 1.2.176.
⇨ See also the aphetic form 'GAINST.

agate *n.* (fig.) Very diminutive person 2H4 1.2.16 *I was never mann'd with an agate till now* (F1 *agot*).
⇨ An allusion to small figures cut in agates for seals.

agaz'd *ppl. adj.* Astounded, amazed 1H6 1.1.126 *All the whole army stood agaz'd on him.*

age *n.* Lifetime 1H6 4.5.46 *My age was never tainted with such shame.*

agent *n.* Organ (of body) VEN 400 *But when his glutton eye so full hath fed, His other agents aim at like delight?*

aggravate *vb.* Increase, add to WIV 2.2.284 *I will aggravate his style.*
⇨ In MND 1.2.81 *I will aggravate my voice so that I will roar you as gently as any sucking dove,* and in 2H4 2.4.162 *aggravate your choler, aggravate* is a comic malapropism for 'moderate'.

aglet-baby n. Small metal female figure serving as the tag, or figure carved on the tag of a lacing cord SHR 1.2.79 *marry him to a puppet or an aglet-baby.*

agnize vb. Acknowledge, confess OTH 1.3.231 *I do agnize A natural and prompt alacrity.*

agone ppl. adj. Ago TGV 3.1.85 *long agone*, TN 5.1.198.

agood adv. In earnest, plentifully TGV 4.4.165 *I made her weep agood.*

agot See AGATE.

ague n. Malarial fever or the shivering caused by such a fever JC 2.2.113 *As that same ague which hath made you lean,* MV 1.1.23.

agued adj. Trembling, shivering (as if with malarial fever) COR 1.4.38 *and faces pale With flight and agued fear!*

a-height adv. On high LR 4.6.58 *Look up a-height.*

a-high adv. Aloft R3 4.4.86 *One heav'd a-high to be hurl'd down below.*

a-hold adv. Close to the wind (in order to hold or keep to it) TMP 1.1.49 *Lay her a-hold, a-hold! Set her two courses off to sea again.*

aid n. *pray in aid* (legal) Claim assistance in defending an action from one who has a joint interest in the defence ANT 5.2.27 *A conqueror that will pray in aid for kindness.*

aidance n. Assistance, aid 2H6 3.2.165 *for aidance 'gainst the enemy,* VEN 330.

aidant adj. Helpful LR 4.4.17 *aidant...In the good man's distress.*

aim n.

1 Mark, object, butt R3 4.4.89 *To be the aim of every dangerous shot,* MM 1.3.5, TGV 5.4.101.

2 Conjecture, guess JC 1.2.163 *What you would work me to, I have some aim.*

3 (fig.) Help, encouragement TIT 5.3.149 *But, gentle people, give me aim a while.*

4 (exclamation) 'Good shot!' WIV 3.2.44 *and to these violent proceedings all my neighbours shall cry aim.*

~ vb.

1 Guess, conjecture 2H6 2.4.58 *Ah, Nell, forbear! thou aimest all awry,* HAM 4.5.9.

2 Aim at, mean, intend ERR 3.2.66 *Call thyself sister, sweet, for I aim thee* (Ff *am*).

Aio (te), Aeacida, Romanos vincere posse [L.] (ambiguous answer given by the Delphic oracle to Pyrrhus) I say that thou, Aeacides, canst conquer the Romans, or, that the Romans can conquer thee Aeacides 2H6 1.4.62.

air n.

1 Breath WT 5.3.78 *There is an air comes from her,* 2H6 3.2.371.

2 *take air* Get abroad TN 3.4.132 *lest the device take air, and taint.*

3 Manner, style WT 4.4.731 *Seest thou not the air of the court in these enfoldings?,* TIM 5.1.22.

4 Mien, demeanour WT 5.1.128 *Your father's image is so hit in you (His very air) that I should call you brother.*

5 Tune MND 1.1.183 *and your tongue's sweet air More tuneable than lark to shepherd's ear.*

~ vb.

1 Wear openly, expose to public view CYM 2.4.96 *I beg but leave to air this jewel.*

2 *air'd abroad* Exposed to the airs of foreign lands, lived abroad WT 4.2.5 *though I have for the most part been air'd abroad.*

airy adj. (fig.) Lofty, elevated, or widely talked of TRO 1.3.144 *Having his ear full of his airy fame.*

a-land adv.

1 On land, ashore PER 2.1.28 *Why, as men do a-land; the great ones eat up the little ones.*

2 To the land or shore, ashore (implying motion) PER 3.2.69 *If e'er this coffin drives a-land.*

alarm, alarum n. (differentiated spellings of the same word, used indiscriminately in old edd., but in mod. edd. *alarum* is usu. appropriated to senses 1 and 2, and *alarm* to 3,4, and 5. Often in aphetic forms *'larm, 'larum*).

1 Cry or signal 'allarme' (to arms) 2H6 5.2.3 *Now when the angry trumpet sounds alarum,* R3 4.4.149.

2 Call to arms R3 1.1.7 *Our stern alarums chang'd to merry meetings*; (fig.) OTH 2.3.26.

3 Loud noise, disturbance SHR 1.1.127 *though it pass your patience and mine to endure her loud alarums,* R2 1.1.205.

4 Attack, battle MAC 5.2.4 *Would to the bleeding and the grim alarm Excite the mortified man,* VEN 424.

5 State of surprise or excitement HAM 2.2.509 *A blanket, in the alarm of fear caught up.*

~ vb. Call to arms, rouse to action; (fig.) MAC 2.1.53 *Alarum'd by his sentinel, the wolf,* LR 2.1.53.

alarum-bell n. Bell rung as a signal of danger MAC 2.3.74 *Ring the alarum-bell! Murder and treason!*, 2H6 3.1.17.

alderliefest adj. Dearest of all 2H6 1.1.28 *With you, mine alderliefest sovereign.*

ale n.

1 *in his ales* Under the influence of ale H5 4.7.38 *being a little intoxicates in his prains, did, in his ales and his angers.*

2 Church-ale, a festivity at which ale was sold to raise funds for the church TGV 2.5.58 *Because thou hast not so much charity in thee as to go to the ale with a Christian.*

alien n. Stranger 1H4 3.2.34 *And art almost an alien to the hearts Of all the court.*

~ adj. Belonging to others SON 78.3 *As every alien pen hath got my use.*

a-life adv. On my life, dearly WT 4.4.261 *I love a ballet in print, a-life.*

all adj. Any MAC 3.2.11 *Things without all remedy.*

~ adv.

1 Entirely TIM 1.1.139 *I will choose Mine heir from forth the beggars of the world, And dispossess her all*; (hence) exclusively LR 1.1.104 *Sure, I shall never marry like my sisters, To love my father all.*

2 (intensifier) Quite SHR 3.2.102 *all so long.*

~ conj. Although R3 4.4.226 *Thy head (all indirectly) gave direction.*

~ in combination

1 (n. (genitive) with n.) Of all: **all-seer** R3 5.1.20 *That high All-Seer which I dallied with.* **all-our** JN 4.2.102 *This will break out To all our sorrows* (i.e. to the sorrows of us all).

2 (n. (objective) with vb. (pres. pple.)) All: **all-cheering** Cheering all ROM 1.1.134 *the all-cheering sun.* **all-hating** Hating all, (hence) full of hate R2 5.5.66 *this all-hating world.*

3 (adj. with n.) Every: **all-thing** MAC 3.1.13 *And all-thing unbecoming* (i.e. in every way, wholly).

4 (adv. with adj. and pple.) Wholly, completely, infinitely: **all-worthy** CYM 3.5.94 *All-worthy villain.* **all-oblivious** SON 55.9 *all-oblivious enmity*; (with pple. freq. agentive or instrumental) By all: **all-abhorred** 1H4 5.1.16 *This churlish knot of all-abhorred war.* **all-obeying** ANT 3.13.77 *his all-obeying breath.* **all-amort** (Fr. 'à la mort' to death) Sick to death, dispirited, dejected SHR 4.3.36 *How fares my Kate? What, sweeting, all amort?*

Alla nostra casa ben venuto, molto honorato signor mio Petrucio [It.] Welcome to our house, my much honoured Signor Petruchio! SHR 1.2.25.

alla stoccato [It.] At the thrust ROM 3.1.74.

allay n. Means of abatement WT 4.2.8 *to whose feeling sorrows I might be some allay.*
~ vb. Weaken, qualify, dilute ANT 2.5.50 *I do not like 'but yet', it does allay The good precedence.*

allaying adj. Diluting COR 2.1.49 *a cup of hot wine with not a drop of allaying Tiber in't.*

allayment n.
1 Antidote CYM 1.5.22 *and apply Allayments to their act, and by them gather Their several virtues and effects.*
2 Dilution TRO 4.4.8 *Or brew it to a weak and colder palate, The like allayment could I give my grief.*

allegiant adj. Giving allegiance, loyal H8 3.2.176 *Can nothing render but allegiant thanks.*

all-hallond eve n. Eve of All Saint's Day (1 Nov.) MM 2.1.126 *Was't not at Hallowmas, Master Froth?—All-hallond eve.*

All-hallown summer n. Spell of fine weather in the late autumn, Indian summer; (fig.) vigour lasting into later life 1H4 1.2.158 *Farewell, the latter spring! Farewell, All-hallown summer!*

all hid phr. Children's cry at the game of hide-and-seek or blindman's buff LLL 4.3.76 *'All hid, all hid', an old infant play.*

alliance n. Marriage ADO 2.1.318 *Good Lord, for alliance! Thus goes every one to the world but I,* ROM 2.3.91.

allied ppl. adj. Related, connected TGV 4.1.47 *An heir and near allied unto the Duke,* MM 3.2.102.

allons [Fr.] Let us go! LLL 5.1.152.

allot vb. Appoint, destine 1H6 5.3.55 *Thou art allotted to be ta'en by me.*

allottery n. Share, portion AYL 1.1.73 *the poor allottery my father left me by testament.*

allow vb.
1 Grant, admit, concede 2H4 1.3.5 *I well allow the occasion of our arms,* LUC 1845, TN 4.2.59.
2 Assign as one's due MV 4.1.303 *The law allows it, and the court awards it.*
3 Approve, sanction LR 2.4.191 *if your sweet sway Allow obedience,* TN 1.2.59, TIM 5.1.162.
4 (refl.) Permit (itself) to LR 3.7.105 *his roguish madness Allows itself to any thing.*

allowance n.
1 Admission or acknowledgement of a claim TRO 1.3.376 *Give him allowance for the better man,* HAM 3.2.27, OTH 2.1.49.
2 Assent, permission, authorization H8 3.2.322 *to conclude, Without the King's will or the state's allowance, A league.*

allowed ppl. adj. Approved, licensed TN 1.5.94 *There is no slander in an allow'd fool.*

allusion n. Riddle LLL 4.2.41 *Th' allusion holds in the exchange.*

ally n. Kinsman, relative ROM 3.1.109 *This gentleman, the Prince's near ally.*

allycholly n. Melancholy TGV 4.2.27 *Now, my young guest, methinks you're allycholly.*
▷ Corr. of *malycoly,* old form of *melancholy.*

Almain n. German OTH 2.3.83 *He sweats not to overthrow your Almain.*

almanac n. Calendar ANT 1.2.149 *they are greater storms and tempests than almanacs can report.*
▷ Such compilations also carried predictions of various sorts.

almost adv. (used to intensify a rhetorical question) Even JN 4.3.43 *Or do you almost think, although you see, That you do see?*

alms-basket n. Basket containing alms to be distributed LLL 5.1.38 *They have liv'd long on the alms-basket of words* (i.e. lived on charity).

alms-deed n. Act of charity 3H6 5.5.79 *Murder is thy alms-deed.*

alms-drink n. Drink given in charity, remains of liquor usually saved for alms-folk ANT 2.7.5 *They have made him drink alms-drink.*

almsman n. Man supported by alms, beadsman R2 3.3.149 *thy gay apparel for an almsman's gown.*

aloft prep. Above the surface of JN 4.2.139 *but now I breathe again Aloft the flood.*

alone adj. Having no equal, unique TGV 2.4.167 *She is alone,* ANT 4.6.29.

along adv. At full length, stretched out AYL 2.1.30 *as he lay along.*
~ prep. Throughout the length of AYL 2.1.32 *Upon the brook that brawls along this wood.*

alter vb. Exchange TN 2.5.158 *She that would alter services with thee.*

amain adv. Suddenly, at once, with all speed LLL 5.2.546 *The ship is under sail, and here she comes amain,* TMP 4.1.74.

amaze n. Extreme astonishment LLL 2.1.246 *His face's own margent did cote such amazes.*
~ vb. Bewilder, perplex JN 4.3.140 *I am amaz'd, methinks, and lose my way,* VEN 684.

amazement n. Bewilderment, perplexity, distraction TRO 5.3.85 *Behold, distraction, frenzy, and amazement,* HAM 3.4.112, JN 5.1.35.

Amazonian adj. Resembling an Amazon (fabled race of female warriors) 3H6 1.4.114 *To triumph like an Amazonian trull,* COR 2.2.91.

ambassy Var. of EMBASSY.

ambling adj. Walking with affected gait R3 1.1.17 *To strut before a wanton ambling nymph.*

ambuscado n. Ambush ROM 1.4.84 *Of breaches, ambuscadoes, Spanish blades.*

amend vb. (cf. MEND).
1 Correct, reform, improve LLL 4.3.74 *God amend us,* 1H4 3.1.178, 2H4 1.2.123.
2 Become better, recover TMP 5.1.115 *Th' affliction of my mind amends,* TN 1.5.49.

amends n. Improvement in health SHR Ind.2.97 *Now Lord be thanked for my good amends.*

amerce vb. Punish ROM 3.1.190 *But I'll amerce you with so strong a fine.*

ames-ace n. Two aces, the lowest possible throw at dice AWW 2.3.79 *I had rather be in this choice than throw ames-ace for my life.*

amiable adj.
1 Of love WIV 2.2.234 *to lay an amiable siege to the honesty of this Ford's wife,* ADO 3.3.151.
2 Lovable, lovely MND 4.1.2 *While I thy amiable cheeks do coy,* OTH 3.4.59, ADO 5.4.48.

amiss n.
1 Misbehaviour, misdeed, fault SON 35.7 *Myself corrupting, salving thy amiss,* SON 151.3.
2 Calamity HAM 4.5.18 *prologue to some great amiss.*

among adv. ever among All the while 2H4 5.3.22 *And ever among so merrily.*

amorous adj. Pertaining to or expressing love AWW 5.3.68 *Send forth your amorous token for fair Maudlin,* ADO 1.1.325.

amort See ALL-AMORT.

ample adv. Fully, completely TIM 1.2.130 *how ample y'are belov'd.*

an, an' sub. conj. (a clipped form of) AND.

an prep.
1 On WT 4.3.7 *Doth set my pugging tooth an edge,* 2H6 3.2.318.
2 still an end Continually TGV 4.4.62 *A slave, that still an end turns me to shame.*

anatomize, annothanize vb.
1 Dissect LR 3.6.76 *Then let them anatomize Regan.*
2 Analyse, lay bare AWW 4.3.32 *I would gladly have him see his company anatomiz'd;* (hence) explain, interpret LLL 4.1.68 *which to annothanize in the vulgar.*

anatomy *n.*
1 Skeleton ERR 5.1.239 *A mere anatomy, a mountebank,* JN 3.4.40 *that fell anatomy* (i.e. Death).
2 The body (in a depreciative sense) ROM 3.3.106 *In what vile part of this anatomy.*

anchor *n.* Anchorite, hermit HAM 3.2.219 *An anchor's cheer in prison be my scope.*

anchor *vb.* Fix firmly R3 4.4.232 *Till that my nails were anchor'd in thine eyes;* (fig.) MM 2.4.4 *Whilst my invention, hearing not my tongue, Anchors on Isabel.*

anchorage *n.* Ship's set of anchors TIT 1.1.73 *From whence at first she weigh'd her anchorage.*

anchoring *ppl. adj.*
1 Riding at anchor LR 4.6.18 *And yond tall anchoring bark.*
2 Securing, holding firm TGV 3.1.118 *with a pair of anchoring hooks.*

ancient *n.* (corr. of 'ensign' by association of such forms as 'ensyne' and 'ancien')
1 Ensign, standard 1H4 4.2.31 *ten times more dishonourable ragged than an old feaz'd ancient.*
2 Standard-bearer, ensign 1H4 4.2.24 *my whole charge consists of ancients, corporals...,* OTH 1.1.33, 2H4 2.4.69.

ancientry *n.*
1 Old-fashioned, traditional style ADO 2.1.77 *A measure, full of state and ancientry.*
2 Old people WT 3.3.62 *wronging the ancientry.*

and, an, an' *co-ord. conj.*
1 (Used to join two nouns to form the figure hendiadys) R2 2.3.12 *The tediousness and process of my travel* (i.e. tedious process), LUC 335, HAM 1.1.87.
2 (Used to join two adjectives with the first in adverbial relationship to the second) H5 2.4.13 *the fatal and neglected English* (i.e. fatally neglected), TN 1.2.51.
3 (Used to introduce a phrase, consisting of n. or pron. with pple. or adj., equivalent to absol. const.) HAM 1.3.62 *Those friends thou hast, and their adoption tried, Grapple them unto thy soul.*
~ *sub. conj.*
1 If; even if, though 1H4 2.4.283 *Ah, no more of that, Hal, and thou lovest me,* MV 1.2.89, OTH 1.1.159.
⇨ Sometimes duplication found TMP 2.2.116 *These be fine things and if they be not sprites.*
2 As if H5 2.3.11 *'A made a finer end, and went away and it had been any christom child.*
3 Whether MND 5.1.193 *To spy and I can hear my Thisby's face.*

andirons *n.* Fire-dogs CYM 2.4.88 *Her andirons ...were two winking Cupids.*

angel *n.*
1 Evil genius, demon MAC 5.8.14 *the angel whom thou still hast serv'd.*
2 Good genius, darling (i.e. someone considered incapable of evil) JC 3.2.181 *For Brutus, as you know, was Caesar's angel.*
3 Gold coin, having as its device the archangel Michael, with a value from a third to half a pound according to the period JN 2.1.590 *When his fair angels would salute my palm?;* (hence, fig.) *ancient angel* a fellow of the good old stamp SHR 4.2.61 *An ancient angel coming down the hill.*

angerly *adv.* Angrily TGV 1.2.62 *How angerly I taught my brow to frown,* MAC 3.5.1.

angle *n.¹* Fishing-hook or line ANT 2.5.10 *Give me mine angle, we'll to the river;* (hence fig.) WT 4.2.46 *the angle that plucks our son thither,* HAM 5.2.66.

angle *n.²* Corner TMP 1.2.223 *In an odd angle of the isle.*

an-heires See MYNHEERS.

an-hungry *adj.* Hungry COR 1.1.205 *They said they were an-hungry.*

a-night *adv.* At night AYL 2.4.48 *coming a-night to Jane Smile.*

annexion *n.* Addition, adjunct LC 208 *With th' annexions of fair gems enrich'd.*

annexment *n.* Adjunct, appendage HAM 3.3.21 *Each small annexment, petty consequence.*

annothanize *vb.* (old form of) ANATOMIZE.

annoy *n.*
1 Pain, suffering, grief VEN 497 *life was death's annoy.*
2 Injury, harm R3 5.3.151 *guard thee from the boar's annoy.*
~ *vb.* Harm, injure JC 1.3.22 *and went surly by, Without annoying me.*

annoyance *n.*
1 Injury, harm MAC 5.1.76 *Remove from her the means of all annoyance.*
2 That which hurts or harms JN 5.2.150 *To souse annoyance that comes near his nest.*

anon *adv.*
1 Soon, shortly, presently TN 3.4.320 *I'll be with you anon,* 1H4 2.1.4 (equivalent to mod. 'coming').
2 *now...anon* At one moment...at the next LLL 4.2.6 *now hangeth like a jewel...and anon falleth like a crab.*
3 *ever and anon* Every now and then LLL 5.2.101 *And ever and anon they made a doubt.*
4 *till anon* For a moment ANT 2.7.39 *Forbear me till anon.*

answer *n.*
1 Reply made to a charge, defence, account 2H6 2.1.199 *And call these foul offenders to their answers,* JC 1.3.114, COR 3.1.176.
2 Punishment, retaliation, anything done in return H5 2.2.143 *Arrest them to the answer of the law,* H5 4.7.136, CYM 5.3.79; (in fencing) the return hit TN 3.4.277 *on the answer, he pays you,* HAM 5.2.269.
~ *vb.*
1 Return, requite WIV 4.6.10 *Who mutually hath answer'd my affection.*
2 Atone for, pay for JC 3.2.80 *And grievously hath Caesar answer'd it.*
3 Be responsible for 1H4 4.2.8 *I'll answer the coinage.*
4 Defend, satisfactorily account for HAM 4.1.16 *Alas, how shall this bloody deed be answer'd?,* CYM 3.5.42.
5 Act in conformity with, obey TMP 1.2.190 *I come To answer thy best pleasure.*

answerable *adj.*
1 Accountable 1H4 2.4.522 *If he have robb'd these men, He shall be answerable.*
2 Corresponding, suitable SHR 2.1.359 *all things answerable to this portion,* OTH 1.3.345.

anthem *n.* Song of grief or mourning TGV 3.1.242 *As ending anthem of my endless dolour,* VEN 839, PHT 21.

Anthropophaginian *n.* One of the Anthropophagi or cannibals WIV 4.5.9 *he'll speak like an Anthropophaginian.*

antic *n.*
1 Grotesque entertainment, or with characters in grotesque or fantastic costumes LLL 5.1.112 *or pageant, or antic, or firework.*
2 Buffoon, burlesque performer, jester TRO 5.3.86 *Like wretches antics, one another meet,* R2 3.2.162, ADO 3.1.63.
~ *vb.* Make buffoons of ANT 2.7.125 *the wild disguise hath almost Antick'd us all.*
~ *adj.* Fantastic, grotesque, ludicrous ROM 1.5.56

cover'd with an antic face (i.e. grotesque mask), HAM 1.5.172, SON 19.10.
▷ In Ff and Qq *antick* or *antique*.

anticly *adv.* Fantastically (dressed) ADO 5.1.96 *Go anticly, and show outward hideousness.*

antiquary *adj.* Ancient TRO 2.3.251 *Instructed by the antiquary times.*

antique *adj.* Old-fashioned, out of date COR 2.3.119 *The dust on antique time would lie unswept* (i.e. on old-fashioned institutions and customs).
▷ See also ANTIC NOTE.

antiquity *n.* Old age 2H4 1.2.184 *and every part about you blasted with antiquity,* SON 62.10.

antre *n.* Cavern OTH 1.3.140 *Wherein of antres vast and deserts idle.*

apaid *ppl. adj.* Contented, satisfied LUC 914 *He gratis comes, and thou art well apaid.*

ape *n.*
1 Imitator CYM 2.2.31 *O sleep, thou ape of death, lie dull upon her,* WT 5.2.100.
2 Fool (or similar term of reproach) CYM 4.2.194 *Triumphs for nothing, and lamenting toys, Is jollity for apes, and grief for boys.*
3 term of endearment 2H4 2.4.217 *Alas, poor ape, how thou sweat'st!*
▷ *lead apes in hell* a fate proverbially assigned to old maids: SHR 2.1.34 *for your love to her lead apes in hell.*

ape-bearer *n.* One who carries or leads a monkey for exhibition WT 4.3.95 *he hath been since an ape-bearer.*

a-pieces *adv.* In or to pieces H8 5.3.76 *Not being torn a-pieces.*

apology *n.* Explanatory statement, justification LLL 5.1.135 *I will have an apology for that purpose.*

apoplexed *ppl. adj.* Paralysed HAM 3.4.73 *that sense Is apoplex'd.*

aporn *n.* Apron 2H6 2.3.75 *I give thee my aporn.*

apostrophas *n.* Apostrophe LLL 4.2.119 *You find not the apostrophas, and so miss the accent* (i.e. disregard the marks indicating contractions).
▷ *Apostrophus* was the usu. 16C form. Some edd. suggest that Holofernes might have been using a pedantic word for caesura (a turning-point of the line since *apostrophus* lit. = a turning away).

apparent *adj.* (fig. use from 'heir apparent') Closest WT 1.2.177 *Next to thyself...he's Apparent to my heart.*

apparently *adv.* Openly ERR 4.1.78 *If he should scorn me so apparently.*

apparition *n.* Strange look or expression ADO 4.1.159 *I have mark'd A thousand blushing apparitions To start into her face.*

appeach *vb.* Inform against, impeach R2 5.2.102 *were he twenty times my son, I would appeach him.*

appeal *n.* Accusation, impeachment ANT 3.5.11 *upon his own appeal, seizes him,* R2 1.1.4.
~ *vb.* Accuse, impeach R2 1.1.9 *If he appeal the Duke on ancient malice.*

appearance *n.* Semblance 2H4 1.1.128 *whose well-labouring sword Had three times slain th' appearance of the King.*

appeared *ppl. adj.* Made evident or manifest COR 4.3.9 *Your favour is well appear'd by your tongue.*

appearer *n.* One who appears to have a certain quality or status PER 5.3.18 *Reverent appearer, no, I threw her overboard.*

appellant *n.* One who 'appeals' or accuses another of treason, R2 1.1.34 *Come I appellant to this princely presence*; (hence) one who challenges another to single combat to prove the treason or felony of which he 'appealed' him, challenger R2 1.3.4 *the summons of the appellant's trumpet,* 2H6 2.3.49.

appendix *n.* (said of a bride) Addition, adjunct SHR 4.4.104 *You come with your appendix.*

apperil *n.* Peril, risk TIM 1.2.33 *Let me stay at thine apperil, Timon.*

appertaining *n.* Belonging, appurtenance LC 115 *His real habitude gave life and grace To appertainings and to ornament.*
~ *adj.* Appropriate to ROM 3.1.63 *the reason...Doth much excuse the appertaining rage To such a greeting.*

appertainment *n.* That which belongs (because of rank), prerogative, right TRO 2.3.80 *we lay by Our appertainments* (F1).

appertinent *n.* (usu. pl.) Thing pertaining to a person, appurtenance H5 2.2.87 *To furnish him with all appertinents.*
~ *adj.* Belonging, appropriate *to* 2H4 1.2.171 *All the other gifts appertinent to man,* LLL 1.2.16.

apple-john *n.* Kind of apple which ripened about St. John's Day (midsummer) and was said to keep two years and to be in perfect condition when shrivelled and withered 2H4 2.4.5 *The Prince once set a dish of apple-johns before him.*

apple of the eye *n. phr.* Pupil of the eye, so called because it was supposed to be a globular solid body; (sometimes, perhaps by error) eyeball MND 3.2.104 *Sink in apple of his eye.*
▷ LLL 5.2.475 *And laugh upon the apple of her eye* various interpretations: (1) laugh, looking closely into her eyes; (2) laugh upon her in a very affectionate manner.

appliance *n.* (the medicinal sense colours most uses)
1 Service, skill in administering AWW 2.1.113 *I come to tender...my appliance, With all bound humbleness.*
2 Remedy, cure, medicament H8 1.1.124 *temp'rance, that's th' appliance only Which your disease requires*; (fig.) MM 3.1.88 *Thou art too noble to conserve a life In base appliances.*
3 Device, apparatus 2H4 3.1.29 *With all appliances and means to boot.*

application *n.* Administration of a medicament, medicinal treatment AWW 1.2.74 *The rest have worn me out With several applications.*

apply *vb.*
1 Attend assiduously *to* MAC 3.2.30 *Let your remembrance apply to Banquo.*
2 Be suitable *to* WIV 2.2.238 *Would it apply well to the vehemency of your affection.*
3 *apply for* Interpret as, explain as JC 2.2.80 *these does she apply for warnings.*

appoint *vb.*
1 Equip, furnish WT 4.4.592 *my care To have you royally appointed,* TIT 4.2.16.
2 Assign, grant, allot JC 4.1.30 *I do appoint him store of provender.*
3 Arrange (e.g. a meeting), make an appointment for TIT 4.4.102 *appoint the meeting,* WIV 2.1.94.
4 Direct, order WIV 4.2.94 *I'll appoint my men to carry the basket,* SHR 4.4.102.

appointment *n.*
1 Equipment, accoutrement R2 3.3.53 *Our fair appointments may be well perus'd,* ANT 4.10.8.
2 Direction, instruction H8 2.2.133 *That good fellow... follows my appointment.*

apprehend *vb.* Imagine, conceive MND 5.1.5 *Such shaping fantasies, that apprehend More than cool reason ever comprehends,* 1H4 1.3.209.

apprehension *n.*
1 Sensory perception MND 3.2.178 *The ear more quick of apprehension makes,* COR 2.3.224.
2 Mental perception, understanding, common

sense H5 3.7.135 *If the English had any apprehension, they would run away*, Tro 2.3.115, Ado 3.4.68.
3 Conception, imagination MM 3.1.77 *The sense of death is most in apprehension*, R2 1.3.300, Cym 4.2.110.

apprehensive *adj.* Possessed of intelligence or understanding, quick to perceive AWW 1.2.60 *younger spirits, whose apprehensive senses*, JC 3.1.67.

apprenticehood *n.* Apprenticeship R2 1.3.271 *serve a long apprenticehood To foreign passages.*

approach *n.* Hostile advance, attack Tim 5.1.164 *we shall drive back Of Alcibiades th' approaches wild*, Jn 5.2.131, H5 2.4.9.

approbation *n.*
1 Confirmation, attestation, proof WT 2.1.177 *nought for approbation But only seeing*, Cym 1.4.124, H5 1.2.19.
2 Sanction, approval H8 1.2.71 *By learned approbation of the judges.*
3 Probation, novitiate MM 1.2.178 *my sister should the cloister enter, And there receive her approbation.*

approof *n.*
1 Proof, trial AWW 2.5.3 *of very valiant approof* (i.e. of proved valour), Ant 3.2.27.
2 Approval MM 2.4.174 *Either of condemnation or approof.*

appropriation *n.* Special attribute or excellence MV 1.2.41 *he makes it a great appropriation to his own good parts.*

approve *vb.*
1 Prove, confirm, demonstrate to be true MV 3.2.79 *approve it with a text*, AWW 3.7.13, Mac 1.6.4.
2 Convict, find guilty Oth 2.3.211 *he that is approv'd in this offence.*
3 Put to the proof, test, try MND 2.2.68 *I might approve This flower's force in stirring love*, 1H4 4.1.9, Shr 1.1.7.
4 Commend Ham 5.2.135 *it would not much approve me*, Per 2.1.51.

approved *ppl. adj.*
1 Proven Ado 4.1.44 *an approved wanton.*
2 Tested, tried 1H4 1.1.54 *valiant and approved Scot*, R2 2.3.44.

approver *n.* Tester, one who makes a trial Cym 2.4.25 *make known To their approvers they are people such That mend upon the world.*

appurtenance *n.* That which belongs to something Ham 2.2.371 *th' appurtenance of welcome is fashion and ceremony.*

apricock *n.* Apricot MND 3.1.166 *Feed him with apricocks and dewberries*, R2.3.4.29.

apron-man *n.* Mechanic, artisan Cor 4.6.96 *You have made good work, You and your apron-men.*

apt *adj.*
1 Ready, prepared, willing H5 2.2.86 *You know how apt our love was to accord*, Ado 1.1.292, JC 3.1.160.
2 Easily impressed, impressionable JC 5.3.68 *Why dost thou show to the apt thoughts of men The things that are not?*, Ven 354.
3 Natural, likely Oth 2.1.287 *That she loves him, 'tis apt and of great credit*, Cym 5.5.444.

Arabian bird *n.* Phoenix; (fig.) unique specimen Cym 1.6.17 *If she be furnish'd with a mind so rare She is alone th' Arabian bird.*

araise *vb.* Raise from the dead AWW 2.1.76 *whose simple touch Is powerful to araise King Pippen.*

arbitrement *n.*
1 Settlement, decision H5 4.1.160 *if it come to the arbitrement of swords*, TN 3.4.261.
2 Judicial inquiry, inspection, evaluation 1H4 4.1.70 *we of the off'ring side Must keep aloof from strict arbitrement.*

arch *n.*[1] *vaulted arch* Sky,heaven Cym 1.6.33; *watery arch* rainbow Tmp 4.1.71.

arch *n.*[2] Chief, master Lr 2.1.59 *The noble Duke my master, My worthy arch and patron.*
~ *adj.* Chief, pre-eminent, principal R3 4.3.2 *The most arch deed of piteous massacre* (i.e. heinous deed), 3H6 2.2.2, Oth 4.1.70.

argal, argo *adv.* (corr. of 'ergo') Therefore Ham 5.1.19 *he drowns not himself; argal, he that is not guilty of his own death shortens not his own life*, 2H6 4.2.29.

argosy *n.* Merchant vessel of the largest size and burden MV 3.1.100 *Hath an argosy cast away*, Shr 2.1.376.

argue *vb.* Prove, evince, show, betoken Rom 2.3.33 *it argues a distempered head*, Ham 5.1.11, Luc 65.

argument *n.*
1 Proof, evidence Ado 2.3.234 *no great argument of her folly*, TN 3.2.11.
2 Subject of contention H5 3.1.21 *sheath'd their swords for lack of argument*, Tro 1.1.92, Mac 2.3.120.
⇨ In Ham 2.2.355 *There was for a while no money bid for argument, unless the poet and the players went to cuffs in the question*, a quibble on two senses: (1) cause of contention, and (2) plot of a play.

arithmetic *n.* Computation, number Cor 3.1.244 *But now 'tis odds beyond arithmetic*, Ham 5.2.114 *though I know to divide him inventorially would dozy th' arithmetic of memory* (i.e. mental arithmetic).

arm *vb.* Take in one's arms, lift up Cym 4.2.400 *Come, arm him.*

armado *n.* Fleet of warships or of armed merchant vessels Err 3.2.137 *Spain, who sent whole armadoes of carrects to be ballast at her nose*, Jn 3.4.2.

armed and reverted *adj. phr.* In arms and in revolt Err 3.2.123 *In her forehead, arm'd and reverted, making war against her heir.*
⇨ Perh. also 'scarred by venereal disease' (*armed* = with eruptions, and *reverted* = receding (alluding to the loss of hair from this disease)).

arm-gaunt *adj.* In good condition, in fine fettle, excellent Ant 1.5.48 *And soberly did mount an arm-gaunt steed.*

armigero *n.* One entitled to bear heraldic arms, esquire Wiv 1.1.10 *who writes himself 'Armigero', in any bill, warrant, quittance or obligation.*

armipotent *adj.* Powerful in arms LLL 5.2.651 *The armipotent Mars, of lances the almighty*, AWW 4.3.236.

aroint *vb.* or *interj. aroint thee* Avaunt, begone Mac 1.3.6 *'Aroint thee witch!' the rump-fed ronyon cries*, Lr 3.4.124.

a-row *adv.* In a row, one after another Err 5.1.170 *Beaten the maids a-row.*

arrant *n.* (abbreviation of 'arrant thief') Thief, robber Err 2.1.72 *So that my arrant, due unto my tongue.*
⇨ Generally agreed that Dromio uses *arrant* for 'errand' here.
~ *adj.* (from **errant**, orig. applied to a thief) Notorious, downright, out and out, thoroughgoing Tim 4.3.437 *the moon's an arrant thief*, H5 3.6.61.

arras *n.* Hanging screen of tapestry placed round the walls of rooms, often at such a distance from them that people could be concealed in the intervening space Ham 2.2.163 *Be you and I behind an arras then*, Wiv 3.3.90.

arrearages *n.* (pl.) Arrears, back payment of tribute Cym 2.4.13 *He'll grant the tribute, send th' arrearages.*

arrest *n.* Order, decree binding a person to be re-

sponsible to the law HAM 2.2.67 *sends out arrests On Fortinbras.* ~ *vb.*
1 Seize (property) by legal warrant WIV 5.5.115 *His horses are arrested for it.*
2 (fig.) Take as security MM 2.4.134 *I do arrest your words* (i.e. take you at or hold you to your word), LLL 2.1.159.

arrivance *n.* Arrivals, company coming OTH 2.1.42 *For every minute is expectancy Of more arrivance.*

arrive *vb.*
1 Land at or on 3H6 5.3.8 *those powers...have arriv'd our coast,* JC 1.2.110.
2 Reach COR 2.3.181 *arriving A place of potency,* LUC 781.
3 *arrive at* Attain to TIM 4.3.505 *For many so arrive at second masters.*

art *n.*
1 Learning, science WIV 3.1.107 *Boys of art, I have deceiv'd you both*; (pl., with allusion to the 'liberal arts' studied in the Middle Ages) PER 2.3.82 *My education been in arts and arms,* LLL 2.1.45, SHR 1.1.2.
2 Magic TMP 1.2.1 *If by your art, my dearest father, you have Put the wild waters in this roar,* 1H6 2.1.15.

artere *n.* (var. spelling of 'artery') Ligament, sinew HAM 1.4.82 *makes each petty artere in this body As hardy as the Nemean lion's nerve.*

Arthur *n.*
1 *Arthur's show* Annual exhibition at Mile-end Green by a company of London archers, each of whom took the name of one of King Arthur's knights 2H4 3.2.280 *I was then Sir Dagonet in Arthur's show.*
2 *Arthur's bosom* (malapropism for) Abraham's bosom H5 2.3.9 *He's in Arthur's bosom.*

article *n.*
1 Particular piece of business, matter, concern HAM 5.2.117 *I take him to be a soul of great article* (i.e. of great moment, of importance).
2 Character WIV 2.1.53 *thou shouldst not alter the article of thy gentry.*
3 Term, provision ANT 2.2.82 *You have broken The article of your oath.*
4 Regulation COR 2.3.196 *his surly nature, Which easily endures not article.*

articulate *vb.*
1 Arrange terms, enter into negotiations COR 1.9.77 *Send us to Rome The best, with whom we may articulate.*
2 State in articles, specify 1H4 5.1.72 *These things indeed you have articulate.*

artificial *adj.*
1 Skilled in art, able to create MND 3.2.203 *We, Hermia, like two artificial gods.*
2 Skilful PER 5.1.72 *If that thy prosperous and artificial feat Can draw him but to answer thee in aught.*
3 Produced by art, artful, cunning MAC 3.5.27 *Shall raise such artificial sprites* (i.e. spirits produced by magic arts), ROM 1.1.140.
4 *artificial strife* The striving of art (to outdo nature) TIM 1.1.37 *Artificial strife Lives in these touches, livelier than life.*

artist *n.*
1 Scholar TRO 1.3.24 *the artist and unread,* POR 2.3.15.
2 Medical practitioner AWW 2.3.10 *To be relinquish'd of the artists.*

artless *adj.* Unskilful, crude HAM 4.5.19 *So full of artless jealousy is guilt* (i.e. uncontrolled suspicion).

arts-man *n.* Learned man, scholar LLL 5.1.81 *Arts-*

man, *preambulate, we will be singuled from the barbarous.*

as *rel.* That R3 1.4.279 *Go, coward, as thou art,* ROM 2.1.36.
~ *conj.*
1 (after *so* and *such*) That LUC 1372 *such signs of rage they bear as it seem'd,* 3H6 1.1.234.
2 So that SHR Ind.1.70 *As he shall think by our true diligence He is no less...,* SON 62.8.
3 If SHR Ind.1.109 *Tell him from me, as he will win my love.*
4 As if TMP 2.1.122 *As stooping to relieve him,* H5 2.4.20, HAM 4.7.87.
5 *as...as* Though, however ADO 1.1.115 *As like him as she she is* (i.e. whatever like him she may be).
⇨ When used as correlatives, the first *as* is sometimes omitted COR 4.5.20 *A strange one as ever I looked on.*
6 Inasmuch as TN 2.2.38 *As I am woman (now alas the day!),* 1H4 3.3.145.
7 As for example, to wit LLL 1.1.37 *But there are other strict observances: As not to see a woman in that term,* SON 46.13.
⇨ Redundant in *as how* AYL 4.3.141 *As how I came into that desert place*; and in phrases expressing time JC 5.1.71 *This is my birthday; as this very day Was Cassius born.* Some edd. consider that it has an intensifying force before time phrases ROM 5.3.247 *That he should hither come as this dire night* (i.e. this very night); others regard its use here as prepositional (i.e. on this night).

ash *n.* Wood of the ash-tree from which spears were made; (by metonymy) the spear itself COR 4.5.108 *My grained ash an hundred times hath broke.*

asinico, assinego *n.* [Sp.] (lit. 'little ass') Blockhead TRO 2.1.44 *Thou hast no more brain than I have in mine elbows, an asinico may tutor thee.*

askance, askaunce *vb.* Turn aside LUC 637 *That from their own misdeeds askaunce their eyes!*

askaunt *prep.* Aslant, across in a slanting direction HAM 4.7.166 *There is a willow grows askaunt the brook* (Q2; Ff *aslant*).

aspect *n.*
1 Look, glance ERR 2.2.111 *Some other mistress hath thy sweet aspects,* ANT 1.5.33.
2 Position and influence of a heavenly body WT 2.1.107 *There's some ill planet reigns; I must be patient, till the heavens look With an aspect more favourable,* TRO 1.3.92, SON 26.10.
3 Sight R2 1.3.127 *our eyes do hate the dire aspect Of civil wounds,* LLL 4.3.256.

aspersion *n.* Sprinkling (of dew or rain) TMP 4.1.18 *No sweet aspersion shall the heavens let fall.*

aspic *n.* Asp, venomous serpent ANT 5.2.351 *This is an aspic's trail,* OTH 3.3.450.

aspire *vb.*
1 Be ambitious TGV 3.1.154 *Wilt thou aspire to guide the heavenly car,* R2 5.2.9.
2 Rise, mount up WIV 5.5.97 *Fed in heart, whose flames aspire,* LUC 5.
3 Mount up to ROM 3.1.117 *That gallant spirit hath aspir'd the clouds.*

aspray See OSPREY.

ass *n.* (often a term of reproach) Dolt COR 2.1.58 *I find the ass in compound with the major part of your syllables* (i.e. a mixture of stupidity in all you say; a play on the suffix 'as' which was often compounded with other words, like 'whereas', so freq. over-used in legal documents), TN 2.3.18.
⇨ A related quibble in HAM 5.2.43 *many such-like as's,* where *as's* refers both to the plural of 'as' used as a noun and to 'ass'.

assail *vb.* Address with offers of love, woo, attempt

to seduce SON 41.6 *Beauteous thou art, therefore to be assailed*, ROM 1.1.213, TN 1.3.57.

assault *n*. Proposal of love, wooing MM 3.1.184 *The assault that Angelo hath made to you*, ADO 2.3.115.

assay *n*.
1 Trial, test OTH 1.3.18 *This cannot be By no assay of reason*, MM 3.1.162, HAM 2.1.62.
2 Effort, endeavour MAC 4.3.143 *Their malady convinces The great assay of art* (i.e. efforts of medical science).
3 Attack, assault H5 1.2.151 *Galling the gleaned land with hot assays*, HAM 2.2.71.
~ *vb*.
1 Try, attempt MM 1.4.76 *Assay the, ɔw'r you have*, OTH 2.3.207, HAM 4.7.152.
2 Learn by experience, make trial of LC 156 *The destin'd ill she must herself assay.*
3 Assail with words, accost, address with proposals of love WIV 2.1.25 *that he dares in this manner assay me?*, MM 1.2.181.
4 Challenge to a trial of strength or skill 1H4 5.4.34 *I will assay thee, and defend thyself*, HAM 3.1.14.

assemblance *n*. Semblance, appearance 2H4 3.2.259 *Care I for the limb, the thews, the stature, bulk, and big assemblance of a man?*

ass-head *n*. Dolt, blockhead TN 5.1.206 *an ass-head and a coxcomb and a knave*, MND 3.1.116.

assign *n*. Appurtenance, accessory HAM 5.2.150 *and poniards, with their assigns, as girdle, hangers, and so on.*

assinego See ASINICO.

assist *vb*. Attend, accompany, join TMP 1.1.54 *The King and Prince at prayers, let's assist them*, WT 5.1.113, COR 5.6.154.

assistance *n*. Body of associates COR 4.6.33 *And affecting one sole throne, Without assistance.*

assistant *adj*. In attendance HAM 1.3.3 *And convey is assistant* (i.e. conveyance is available).

associate *vb*. Accompany, escort, attend ROM 5.2.6 *One of our order, to associate me*, COR 4.6.76.

assubjugate *vb*. Debase TRO 2.3.192 *assubjugate his merit.*

assume *vb*.
1 (a technical term from demonology for a devil's disguising himself in the form of a dead person) Put or take on a garb, aspect or character HAM 1.2.243 *If it assume my noble father's person.*
2 Claim, lay claim to MV 2.9.51 *I will assume desert*, PER 1.1.61.

assurance *n*.
1 Pledge, guarantee 3H6 4.1.141 *Give me assurance with some friendly vow*, TN 1.5.180, TN 4.3.26.
2 Legal guarantee of settlement of property Shr 2.1.387 *let your father make her the assurance.*
3 Certainty, security ADO 2.2.49 *such seeming truth of Hero's disloyalty, that jealousy shall be call'd assurance*, MAC 4.1.83, MND 3.1.21.

assure *vb*.
1 Convey (property) to a person SHR 2.1.343 *and he of both That can assure my daughter greatest dower.*
2 Promise in marriage, betroth ERR 3.2.141 *swore I was assur'd to her*, JN 2.1.535.

astonish *vb*. Stun, dismay JC 1.3.56 *Such dreadful heralds to astonish us*, H5 5.1.39, LUC 1730.

astringer *n*. Falconer who trains goshawks AWW 5.1.SD *Enter a [Gentleman, an] astringer.*

astronomer *n*. Astrologer, one who predicts future events by the situation of the stars CYM 3.2.27 *O, learn'd indeed were that astronomer That knew the stars as I his characters*, TRO 5.1.92.

astronomical *adj*. Pertaining to astrology LR 1.2.150 *How long have you been a sectary astronomical?* (i.e. believer in astrology).

astronomy *n*. Astrology SON 14.2 *And yet methinks I have astronomy* (i.e. understand astrology).

at *prep*. (reduced form of ME. 'atte') At the MV 2.5.40 *Mistress, look out at window for all this.*

Ate *n*. Goddess of mischief; (hence, in pl.) incitements to mischief, provocation LLL 5.2.688 *Pompey is mov'd. More Ates, more Ates! stir them on, stir them on!*

athwart *adv*. Perversely, topsy-turvy, from an unexpected quarter MM 1.3.30 *The baby beats the nurse, and quite athwart Goes all decorum*, 1H4 1.1.36.

a-tilt *adv*. In a joust or tourney 2H6 1.3.51 *Thou ran'st a-tilt in honour of my love.*

atomy *n*.
1 Atom, mote, minute speck AYL 3.2.232 *It is as easy to count atomies as to resolve the propositions of a lover.*
2 Tiny being, mite ROM 1.4.57 *Drawn with a team of little atomy.*
▷ The use of *atomy* in the sense of 'living skeleton' is a malapropism resulting from confusion of 'anatomy' and 'atom' in 2H4 5.4.29 *Thou atomy, thou!*

atone *vb*.
1 Reconcile, set at one R2 1.1.202 *Since we cannot atone you, we shall see Justice design the victor's chivalry*, OTH 4.1.233.
2 Appease, set at peace TIM 5.4.58 *to atone your fears With my more noble meaning.*
3 Agree, be in concord AYL 5.4.110 *When earthly things made even Atone together*, COR 4.6.73.

atonement *n*. Reconciliation 2H4 4.1.219 *If we do now make hour our atonement well*, R3 1.3.36.

attach *vb*.
1 Arrest or seize, as by authority of a writ 2H4 4.2.109 *Of capital treason I attach you both*, ERR 4.1.73; (fig.) seize on, affect 2H4 2.2.3 *I had thought weariness durst not have attach'd one of so high blood*, TMP 3.3.5, TRO 5.2.161.
2 Seize with the hands LLL 4.3.372 *Then homeward every man attach the hand Of his fair mistress.*

attachment *n*. Arrest, imprisonment TRO 4.2.5 *And give as soft attachment to thy senses As infants empty of all thought.*

attainder *n*.
1 Condemnation LLL 1.1.157 *Stands in attainder of eternal shame*; dishonouring accusation R2 4.1.24 *the attainder of his slanderous lips.*
2 Stain of dishonour R3 3.5.32 *He liv'd from all attainder of suspects* (i.e. free from all taint of suspicion), H8 2.1.41 (F1 *attendure*).

attaint *n*.
1 Impeachment LR 5.3.83 *I arrest thee On capital treason, and in thy attaint, This gilded serpent.*
2 Infection, impairment, exhaustion H5 4.Ch.39 *overbears attaint With cheerful semblance and sweet majesty*, VEN 741.
3 Stain on honour, disgrace ERR 3.2.16 *What simple thief brags of his own attaint?*, TRO 1.2.25, LUC 825.
~ *vb*.
1 Convict, condemn (one convicted of treason or felony) 1H6 2.4.96 *My father was attached, not attainted*, 2H6 2.4.59.
2 Sully, disgrace 1H6 2.4.92 *And by his treason, stand'st not thou attainted*, SON 88.7.
▷ See TAINT.
~ *ppl. adj.*
1 Infected 1H6 5.5.81 *My tender youth was never yet attaint With any passion.*
2 Sullied, dishonoured LLL 5.2.819 *You are attaint with faults and perjury.*

attainture *n*. (1) Conviction; (2) disgrace 2H6 1.2.106

And her attainture will be Humphrey's fall (perh. with play on both senses).

attask, attax *vb.* Take to task, blame, censure LR 1.4.343 *You are much more attax'd for want of wisdom.*

attempt *n.* Warlike enterprise, attack JN 5.2.111 *Till my attempt so much be glorified*, MAC 3.6.39; (fig.) CYM 3.4.182.

~ *vb.*

1 Try to win, obtain, or subdue WIV 4.2.212 *he will never, I think, in the way of waste, attempt us again*, LR 2.2.122, TIM 1.1.126.

2 Try to move or influence, urge MV 4.1.421 *Dear sir, of force I must attempt you further.*

attemptable *adj.* Open to attempts (at seduction) CYM 1.4.60 *less attemptable than any the rarest of our ladies in France.*

attend *vb.*

1 Listen to TMP 1.2.78 *Dost thou attend me?*, CYM 1.6.142, LUC 818.

2 Apply oneself to AWW 1.1.4 *I must attend his Majesty's command*, ANT 2.2.60, 1H6 1.1.173.

3 Tend, watch, guard CYM 1.6.197 *They are in a trunk, Attended by my men*, TGV 5.1.10.

4 Wait for, await MAC 3.1.44 *Attend those men Our pleasure?*, WIV 1.1.269, SHR 2.1.168.

5 Expect TIM 3.5.101 *Attend our weightier judgment.*

6 Be present CYM 3.3.77 *and we will fear no poison, which attends In place of greater state.*

attendure See ATTAINDER.

attent *adj.* Attentive, heedful HAM 1.2.193 *Season your admiration for a while With an attent ear*, PER 3. GOWER 11.

attest *n.* Evidence, testimony TRO 5.2.122 *That doth invert th' attest of eyes and ears.*

~ *vb.*

1 Certify, vouch for, represent H5 Prol.16 *O, pardon! since a crooked figure may Attest in little place a million*, TN 5.1.158.

2 Call to witness TRO 2.2.132 *But I attest the gods.*

attired *adj.* Enwrapped ADO 4.1.144 *For my part I am so attir'd in wonder*, LUC 1601.

attorney *n.*[1]

1 Agent, deputy ERR 5.1.100 *And will have no attorney but myself.*

2 Advocate, pleader R3 4.4.413 *Be the attorney of my love to her*, AWW 2.2.21, VEN 335.

3 *attorney-general* Deputy appointed to represent his principal in all legal matters R2 2.1.203 *By his attorneys-general to sue.*

attorney *n.*[2] Appointment of a legal representative or deputy; (hence) *by attorney* by proxy AYL 4.1.94 *No, faith, die by attorney*, R3 5.3.83.

~ *vb.*

1 Perform by proxy WT 1.1.27 *their encounters (though not personal) hath been royally attorney'd with interchange of gifts.*

2 Employ as an attorney MM 5.1.385 *I am still attorneyed at your service.*

attorneyship *n.* Proxy 1H6 5.5.56 *Than to be dealt in by attorneyship.*

attribute *n.* Reputation, credit HAM 1.4.22 *The pith and marrow of our attribute*, PER 4.3.18, TRO 2.3.116.

attribution *n.* Praise, recognition 1H4 4.1.3 *Such attribution should the Douglas have.*

attributive *adj.* Ascribing excellent qualities TRO 2.2.58 *the will dotes that is attributive To what infectiously itself affects.*

audible *adj.* Quick of hearing COR 4.5.223 *it's sprightly, waking, audible, and full of vent.*

~ *adv.* Audibly MM 5.1.408 *The very mercy of the law cries out Most audible.*

audience *n.* Hearing, attention to what is said COR 3.3.40 *List to your tribunes. Audience! peace, I say*, HAM 1.3.93; *give, lend, vouchsafe audience* listen JC 3.2.2 *follow me, and give me audience*, LC 278, LLL 5.2.313.

audit *n.* (chiefly fig.) Statement of account HAM 3.3.82 *how his audit stands who knows save heaven*, H8 3.2.141, SON 4.12.

▷ Commonly used in a theological sense of a solemn rendering of account to God.

augur *n.* Prophet, prognosticator SON 107.6 *the sad augurs mock their own presage*, PHT 7.

▷ In the technical sense S. uses AUGURER.

augure *n.* Augury, the practice of divination MAC 3.4.123 *Augures and understood relations have By maggot-pies and choughs and rooks brought forth The secret'st man of blood.*

augurer *n.* Augur, sooth-sayer, religious official among the Romans who professed to foretell events from omens, derived chiefly from birds and inspection of entrails JC 2.2.37 *What say the augurers?*, COR 2.1.1.

auguring *ppl. adj.* Prophesying ANT 2.1.10 *My powers are crescent, and my auguring hope Says it will come to th' full.*

augury *n.* Art and practice of the augur (augurer), divination by omens HAM 5.2.219 *Not a whit, we defy augury*; prophetic skill TGV 4.4.68 *if my augury deceive me not.*

aunt *n.*

1 Old woman, gossip MND 2.1.51 *The wisest aunt, telling the saddest tale.*

2 Woman of loose morals WT 4.3.11 *Are summer songs for me and my aunts, While we lie tumbling in the hay.*

auricular *adj.* Perceived by the ear LR 1.2.92 *and by an auricular assurance have your satisfaction.*

auspicious *adj.* Cheerful HAM 1.2.11 *With an auspicious, and a dropping eye.*

austerely *adv.* Plainly ERR 4.2.2 *Might'st thou perceive austerely in his eye.*

authentic *adj.* Authoritative, duly qualified WIV 2.2.226 *authentic in your place and person*, AWW 2.3.12.

authority *n.* Those in office or of rank COR 1.1.16 *What authority surfeits on would relieve us.*

authorize *vb.*

1 Sanction, justify SON 35.6 *Authorizing thy trespass with compare.*

2 Vouch for MAC 3.4.65 *A woman's story at a winter's fire, Authoriz'd by her grandam.*

avail *n.* Benefit, profit AWW 3.1.22 *When better fall, for your avails they fell.*

~ *vb.*

1 Be of use to 1H6 3.1.178 *Now will it best avail your Majesty*, LUC 1273.

2 Benefit, profit MM 3.1.234 *But how out of this can she avail?*

avaunt *n.* Order to be off H8 2.3.10 *To give her the avaunt, it is a pity.*

~ *interj.* Begone! away! WIV 1.3.81 *Rogues, hence, avaunt, vanish like hailstones; go!*

ave *n.* Shout of welcome, acclamation MM 1.1.70 *Their loud applause and aves vehement.*

Ave-Mary *n.* A specific set of prayers 3H6 2.1.162 *Numb'ring our Ave-Maries with our beads* (i.e. say the rosary).

aver *vb.* Assert the existence of, cite CYM 5.5.203 *averring notes Of chamber-hanging.*

avert *vb.* Turn away LR 1.1.211 *T'avert your liking a more worthier way.*

avise (var. of) ADVISE.

avoid *vb.*

1 Get rid of TRO 2.2.65 *how may I avoid...The wife I chose?*, AYL 1.1.25, WIV 3.5.149.

2 Withdraw, depart, retire TMP 4.1.142 *Well done, avoid; no more*, WT 1.2.462, COR 4.5.30.

3 Quit, depart from COR 4.5.23 *Pray you avoid the house*, H8 5.1.86.

4 (legal term) Make void, refute MM 3.1.196 *he will avoid your accusation*, AYL 5.4.98.

avoirdupois See HABERDEPOIS.

avouch *n.* Guarantee, assurance HAM 1.1.57 *Without the sensible and true avouch Of mine own eyes.*

avouchment *vb.* (used by Welshman Fluellen for) Avouch H5 4.8.36 *and will avouchment, that this is the glove of Alanson.*

await *vb.*

1 Look out *for* 1H6 1.1.48 *Posterity, await for wretched years.*

2 Be in store for 2H6 1.4.64 *what fate awaits the Duke of Suffolk?*

award *vb.* Adjudge, decree R3 2.1.14 *Lest He...award Either of you to be the other's end*, MV 4.1.300.

away *adv.*

1 (with a verb in ellipsis) Tolerate, get on with 2H4 3.2.201 *She never could away with me.*

2 (with *bring, come*) Along, here MM 2.1.41 *bring them away*, TN 2.4.51 *come away, death.*

⇨ Joined to some verbs, *away* carries the idea of spending or destroying by the action LLL 5.2.324 *That kiss'd his hand away in courtesy.*

aweless *adj.*

1 Fearless JN 1.1.266 *The aweless lion could not wage the fight.*

2 Inspiring no awe R3 2.4.52 *Insulting tyranny begins to jut Upon the innocent and aweless throne.*

awful *adj.*

1 Commanding fear or respect, inspiring awe SHR 5.2.109 *An awful rule and right supremacy*, 2H6 5.1.98.

2 Full of awe, respectful, reverential R2 3.3.76 *To pay their awful duty to our presence*, PER 2.Gower.4.

awkward *adj.*

1 Perverse, indirect H5 2.4.85 *no sinister nor no awkward claim.*

2 Adverse, contrary, unfavourable 2H6 3.2.83 *by awkward wind from England's bank*, PER 5.1.93.

axle-tree *n.*

1 Piece of timber on which the wheel turns 1H4 3.1.130 *a dry wheel grate on the axle-tree.*

2 axis of revolution of the heavens TRO 1.3.66 *Should with a bond of air strong as the axle-tree On which heaven rides.*

ay *adv.*

1 Yes TMP 1.2.268 *Ay, sir;* (but sometimes used to introduce a more forcible statement than the preceding one) WT 2.1.138 *For every inch of woman in the world, Ay, every dram of woman's flesh is false.*

2 (used to introduce a question) Come! Why! SHR 5.2.42 *Ay, mistress bride, hath that awakened you?*, ANT 3.10.28.

ay *interj.* Ah! alas! JN 3.1.305 *O husband hear me! ay, alack*, HAM 3.4.51.

ayword *n.* Byword, proverb TN 2.3.135 *gull him into an ayword.*

⇨ See also NAYWORD.

B

babe of clouts *n. phr.* Rag doll JN 3.4.58 *Or madly think a babe of clouts were he.*

baby *n. baby of a girl* (term of contempt) Weak, cowardly person MAC 3.4.104 *If trembling I inhabit them, protest me the baby of a girl* (perh. with play on sense of 'doll' for *baby*).

bacare, baccare (var. of) BACKARE.

Bacchanal *n.*

1 Priest, priestess, or devotee of Bacchus, god of wine MND 5.1.48 *The riot of the tipsy Bacchanals.*

2 Dance in honour of Bacchus ANT 2.7.104 *Shall we dance now the Egyptian bacchanals And celebrate our drink?*

back *n.*

1 Rear (of an armed force) 2H4 1.3.79 *To French and Welsh he leaves his back unarm'd*, 3H6 5.1.61.

2 Support, backing HAM 4.7.153 *this project Should have a back or second* (i.e. a second plot in reserve).

3 *to the back* All through (said orig. of a sword which is all steel from edge to back) TIT 4.3.48 *But metal, Marcus, steel to the very back.*

~ *vb.*

1 Mount 1H4 2.3.71 *That roan shall be my throne. Well, I will back him straight*, CYM 5.5.427, VEN 419.

2 *be backed with* Have (something) at the back of it MM 4.1.29 *Whose western side is with a vineyard back'd.*

backare *vb.* [pseudo-L.] Stand back SHR 2.1.73 *Backare! you are marvellous forward* (F1 *Bacare*).

back-friend *n.* Pretended friend ERR 4.2.37 *A back-friend, a shoulder-clapper.*

⇨ With a quibble on an officer's clapping a man on the back or shoulder to signify arrest.

backside *n. th' backside the town* The back streets of the town CYM 1.2.13 *His steel was in debt, it went o' th' backside the town.*

backsword man *n.* Fencer at single stick 2H4 3.2.64 *I knew him a good backsword man.*

back-trick *n.* Step taken backwards in the galliard TN 1.3.123 *I have the back-trick simply as strong as any man in Illyria.*

backward *n.* What lies behind, the past TMP 1.2.50 *What seest thou else In the dark backward and abysm of time?*

backwardly *adv.* Perversely, unfavourably TIM 3.3.18 *And does he think so backwardly of me now.*

back-wounding *adj.* Backbiting MM 3.2.186 *back-wounding calumny The whitest virtue strikes.*

bacon *n.* 'Chaw-bacon', rustic 1H4 2.2.90 *No, ye fat chuffs, I would your store were here! On, bacons, on!* (with play on senses of 'pig's flesh' and 'fattened pig').

badge *vb.* Mark as with a badge MAC 2.3.102 *Their hands and faces were all badg'd with blood.*

baffle *vb.* Subject (a perjured knight) to public disgrace by exhibiting a painting of him hanging by the heels 1H4 1.2.101 *An I do not, call me villain and baffle me*; (hence) disgrace, treat with contumely TN 2.5.162 *I will baffle Sir Toby*, R2 1.1.170.

bag and baggage *phr.* All the property of an army AYL 3.2.161 *Come, shepherd, let us make an honourable retreat, though not with bag and baggage, yet with scrip and scrippage*, WT 1.2.206.

⇨ To march out with bag and baggage, i.e. with nothing surrendered, was an honourable retreat.

bail *vb.* Confine, enclose Son 133.10 *But then my friend's heart let my poor heart bail.*
▷ Connected with *bail*, the external wall of a feudal castle.

bailiff *n.* Officer of justice under a sheriff who executes writs, distrains, and arrests WT 4.3.96 *he hath been...a process-server, a bailiff.*

baillez [Fr.] Give, fetch Wiv 1.4.87 *Rugby, baillez me some paper* (Ff, Q3 *ballow*).

bait *n.* Food, refreshment, (esp.) light snack Tro 5.8.20 *My half-supp'd sword that frankly would have fed, Pleas'd with this dainty bait, thus goes to bed.*
~ *vb.*
1 take refreshment, drink H8 5.3.81 *here ye lie baiting of bombards, when Ye should do service.*
2 Entice or catch with bait MV 3.1.53 *To bait fish withal;* (fig.) Err 2.1.94 *Do their gay vestments his affections bait?*
3 Set dogs upon, attack with dogs (e.g. a bear, bull) 2H6 5.1.148 *We'll bait thy bears to death;* (hence) harass Mac 5.8.29 *to be baited with the rabble's curse*, R2 4.1.238.

baiting-place *n.* Bear-pit 2H6 5.1.150 *bring them to the baiting-place.*

bake *vb.* Cake together Rom 1.4.90 *and bakes the elflocks in foul sluttish hairs.*

baked meats *n.* (pl.) Food in pastry Rom 4.4.5 *Look to the baked meats, good Angelica.*
▷ Possibly a type of mince pie, see Rom 4.4.2 *They call for dates and quinces in the pastry.*

baker's daughter *n.* Allusion to the Gloucestershire legend of the daughter who offered a miserably small piece of bread to Christ and was turned into an owl for her meanness Ham 4.5.43 *They say the owl was a baker's daughter.*
▷ To the Elizabethans *baker's daughter* denoted a prostitute; the expression is associated with sensuality and harlotry.

balance *n.*
1 (uninflected pl.) Scales for weighing MV 4.1.255 *Are there balance here to weigh The flesh?*
2 (fig.) Scale-pan of a balance R2 3.4.87 *in the balance of great Bullingbrook, Besides himself, are all the English peers.*
3 (fig.) An equal weight AWW 2.3.176 *if not to thy estate A balance more replete.*
~ *vb.* Give due weight to 2H6 5.1.9 *I cannot give due action to my words, Except a sword or sceptre balance it.*

bald *adj.*
1 Bare-headed, with no covering on head Cor 4.5.194 *they stand bald before him.*
2 Trivial, paltry, stupid Err 2.2.108 *'twould be a bald conclusion* (with quibble in the normal sense 'without hair'), 1H4 1.3.65.

bale *n.* Harm, injury, disaster Cor 1.1.163 *Rome and her rats are at the point of battle, The one side must have bale.*

balk *vb.*
1 Heap up in balks or mounds 1H4 1.1.69 *Ten thousand bold Scots, two and twenty knights, Balk'd in their own blood.*
2 Neglect, let slip TN 3.2.24 *This was look'd for at your hand, and this was balk'd*, Luc 696.
3 *balk logic* Bandy arguments, quibble Shr 1.1.34 *Balk logic with acquaintance.*

ball *n.*
1 Golden orb (a symbol of sovereignty) H5 4.1.260 *'Tis not the balm, the sceptre, and the ball*, Mac 4.1.121.
2 Hand-ball or tennis-ball AWW 2.3.297 *Why, these balls bound, there's noise in it*, H5 1.2.261.

3 Any round object H5 5.2.17 *The fatal balls of murdering basilisks.*
▷ Since 'basilisks' could refer to the fabulous creatures whose glance caused death or to large cannon, *balls* here provides word-play on two senses, (1) eyeballs and (2) cannon-balls.

ballad *vb.* Make ballads on, make (one) the subject of a popular song Ant 5.2.216 *scald rhymers Ballad's out a' tune.*

ballast *vb.* Load with ballast or cargo Err 3.2.137 *who sent whole armadoes of carrects to be ballast at her nose.*
▷ In Cym 3.6.77 *then had my prize Been less, and so more equal ballasting To thee, Posthumus*, possible confusion with *balance*.

ballow *n.* [North-Midland] Cudgel Lr 4.6.241 *whither your costard or my ballow be the harder.*
▷ For Wiv 1.4.87 *ballow* (Ff, Q3) see BAILLEZ.

balm *vb.*
1 Anoint with fragrant oil or liquid Shr Ind.1.48 *Balm his foul head in warm distilled waters*, Per 3.2.65.
2 Soothe, heal Lr 3.6.98 *This rest might yet have balm'd thy broken sinews.*

balmy *adj.*
1 Deliciously fragrant Oth 5.2.16 *balmy breath.*
2 Soothing, of healing virtue Son 107.9 *with the drops of this most balmy time My love looks fresh*, Oth 2.3.258.

balsamum, balsom *n.* Balm, balsam Err 4.1.89 *The oil, the balsamum, and aqua-vitae.*

Banbury cheese *n.* Cheese which, when pared, was very thin Wiv 1.1.128 *You Banbury cheese!* (a reference to Slender's physique).

band *n.*
1 (pl.) Fetters, bonds 3H6 1.1.186 *And die in bands for this unmanly deed*, Tmp Epil.9.
2 Obligation, bond, tie Ado 3.1.114 *my kindness shall incite thee To bind our loves up in a holy band*, Ham 3.2.160.
3 Agreement, promise R2 1.1.2 *according to thy oath and band*, Err 4.2.49.
4 Deed, legal document by which a person binds himself 1H4 3.2.157 *the end of life cancels all bands.*

bandetto, banditto *n.* Outlaw, brigand; (attrib.) 2H6 4.1.135 *A Roman sworder and bandetto slave Murder'd sweet Tully.*

ban-dog *n.* Ferocious dog kept tied or chained up 2H6 1.4.18 *The time when screech-owls cry and ban-dogs howl.*

bandy *vb.*
1 Strike or throw a ball to and fro as in games of tennis and bandy; (mostly fig.) give and take (blows, words, looks etc.) LLL 5.2.29 *Well bandied both, a set of wit well played*, Lr 1.4.84, Rom 2.5.14.
2 Contend, strive, fight AYL 5.1.55 *I will bandy with thee in faction*, Tit 1.1.312.

bandying *n.* Contention, quarrelling 1H6 4.1.190 *This factious bandying of their favourites*, Rom 3.1.89.

bane *n.*
1 Cause of death 2H6 5.1.120 *The sons of York...Shall be their father's bail, and bane to those That for my surety will refuse the boys!*, Tit 5.3.73.
2 Poison (cf. RATSBANE) MM 1.2.129 *Like rats that ravin down their proper bane.*
3 Murder, destruction Mac 5.3.59 *I will not be afraid of death and bane*, Ven 372.
~ *vb.* Poison MV 4.1.46 *to give ten thousand ducats To have it ban'd.*

banished *ppl. adj.*
1 Outlawed TGV 5.4.152 *These banish'd men...Are men endu'd with worthy qualities.*
2 *banished years* Years of banishment R2 1.3.210.

bank *n.*
1 Sea coast or shore 1H4 3.1.44 *the sea That chides the banks of England*, Son 56.11.
2 Shelving elevation in the sea or bed of a river, shelf, sand bank Tmp 1.2.390 *Sitting on a bank...This music crept by me upon the waters*, Mac 1.7.6.
~ *vb.* Skirt, sail by Jn 5.2.104 *Have I not heard these islanders shout out 'Vive le roi!' as I have bank'd their towns* (probable quibble here on *bank* as a card-playing term, meaning 'win').

banket See BANQUET.

bankrout *n., vb., adj.* (var. of) Bankrupt; (*n.*) Rom 3.2.57 *O, break, my heart, poor bankrout, break at once!* (with play on *break* 'go bankrupt'); (*vb.*) LLL 1.1.27 *but bankrout quite the wits*; (*adj.*) MND 3.2.85 *bankrout sleep.*

banner *n.* Little fringed flag on a trumpet H5 4.2.61 *I will the banner from a trumpet take.*

banneret *n.* Small banner, pennant, streamer AWW 2.3.204 *yet the scarfs and the bannerets about thee did manifoldly dissuade me from believing thee a vessel of too great a burden.*

banquet *n.*
1 *running banquet* Slight repast between meals, hurried repast (with a bawdy overtone) H8 1.4.12 *some of these Should find a running banquet, ere they rested* (F1 *banket*); (fig.) H8 5.3.65 *the running banquet of two beadles* (i.e. public whipping).
2 Dessert, course or slight repast of fruit and sweetmeats Shr 5.2.9 *My banquet is to close our stomachs After our great good cheer* (F1 *banket*), Rom 1.5.122.

bar *n.*
1 Plea or objection strong enough to halt a lawsuit or claim Shr 1.1.135 *this bar in law makes us friends*, Wiv 3.4.7, H5 1.2.35.
2 Obstruction, obstacle, barrier Ado 2.2.4 *Any bar, any cross, any impediment will be med'cinable to me*, JC 1.3.96, MV 2.7.45.
3 Tribunal, court H5.5.2.27 *To bring your most imperial Majesties Unto this bar and royal interview*, R3 5.3.199.

barbarism *n.* Ignorance, lack of culture LLL 1.1.112 *though I have for barbarism spoke more Than for that angel knowledge.*

Barbary *n.*
1 (short for) Barbary horse R2 5.5.78 *When Bullingbrook rode on roan Barbary* (here the name of the horse as well as its breed).
⇨ Cf. Ham 5.2.147 *six Barbary horses.*
2 *Barbary hen* Guinea hen (whose feathers are already ruffled); (euphemism for) prostitute 2H4 2.4.99 *He'll not swagger with a Barbary hen, if her feathers turn back in any show of resistance.*
3 *Barbary cock-pigeon* Pigeon orig. from the Barbary coast; (also widely applied to) Eastern non-Christians who vigilantly secluded their wives from other men AYL 4.1.150 *I will be more jealous of thee than a Barbary cock-pigeon over his hen.*

barbed *ppl. adj.* Having breast and flanks protected by armour R2 3.3.117 *His glittering arms he will commend to rust, His barbed steeds to stables*, R3 1.1.10.

barber-monger *n.* Constant frequenter of the barber's shop; (hence) conceited, effeminate person Lr 2.2.33 *you whoreson cullionly barber-monger, draw!*

bare *n.* Bareness, naked skin LC 95 *Whose bare outbragg'd the web it seem'd to wear.*
~ *vb.* Shave MM 4.2.176 *Shave the head, and tie the beard, and say it was the desire of the penitent to be so bar'd before his death.*

~ *adj.*
1 Threadbare, napless TGV 2.4.45 *for it appears by their bare liveries that they live by your bare words*; (fig.) AWW 4.5.98 *his right cheek is worn bare.*
2 Lean, poor, needy Rom 5.1.68 *Art thou so bare and full of wretchedness*, 1H4 4.2.74.

bare-bone *n.* Lean, skinny person 1H4 2.4.326 *Here comes lean Jack, here comes bare-bone.*

bare-boned *adj.* Consisting only of bones, skeletal Luc 1761 *a bare-bon'd death.*

bare-gnawn *ppl. adj.* Worn away by continued biting Lr 5.3.122 *my name is lost, By treason's tooth bare-gnawn and canker-bit.*

barely *adv.* In an exposed, naked state AWW 4.2.19 *but when you have our roses, You barely leave our thorns to prick ourselves.*

bareness *n.* Leanness 1H4 4.2.71 *and for their bareness, I am sure they never learn'd that of me.*

barful *adj.* Difficult, full of impediments TN 1.4.41 *a barful strife!*

bargain *n. sell a bargain* Ridicule LLL 3.1.101 *The boy hath sold him a bargain, a goose, that's flat.*

barge *n.* Boat of any kind; (freq.) vessel propelled by oars and used on state occasions, normally ornamented and elegantly furnished H8 2.1.98 *See the barge be ready; And fit it with such furniture as suits The greatness of his person*, Ant 2.2.191.

baring *n.* Shaving off AWW 4.1.49 *the baring of my beard.*

bark *vb.*
1 Kill by stripping off the bark; (fig.) Ant 4.12.23 *and this pine is bark'd, That overtopp'd them all.*
2 *bark about* Cover as with bark, encrust Ham 1.5.71 *a most instant tetter bark'd about Most lazar-like, with vile and loathsome crust All my smooth body.*

barky *adj.* Covered with bark MND 4.1.44 *female ivy so Enrings the barky fingers of the elm.*

barley-broth *n.* Ale H5 3.5.19 *Can sodden water,... their barley-broth, Decoct their cold blood to such valiant heat?*

barm *n.* Yeast, froth MND 2.1.38 *make the drink to bear no barm.*

barn, barne *n.* Child, bairn AWW 1.3.25 *I shall never have the blessing of God till I have issue a' my body; for they say barnes are blessings*, Ado 3.4.49.

barn *vb.* Store as in a barn Luc 859 *barns the harvest of his wits.*

barnacle *n.* Kind of goose formerly supposed to develop from the fruit of a tree or from the shellfish so named Tmp 4.1.248 *all be turn'd to barnacles, or to apes.*

barren *adj.* Lacking in mental power or energy, dull TN 1.5.84 *I marvel your ladyship takes delight in such a barren rascal*; unresponsive Ham 3.2.41 *barren spectators.*

barrenness *n.* Patch of hard skin (callous) on the palm of a kitchen drudge, or dryness of the hand Err 3.2.120 *Where Scotland?—I found it by the barrenness, hard in the palm of the hand.*
⇨ A moist hand was considered a sign of fruitfulness; see OILY. Perh. a pun on 'barren ness' (Scotch for promontory).

Bartholomew boar-pig *n.* Pig sold at the Bartholomew Fair held annually at West Smithfield 2H4 2.4.231 *Thou whoreson little tidy Bartholomew boar-pig.*
⇨ Roast pig was a chief attraction at the fair.

Bartholomew tide *n.* Feast of St. Bartholomew, 24th August H5 5.2.308 *like flies at Bartholomew tide.*

Basan *n.* Land noted for its cattle ('bulls of Basan') and its hills (Psalm 22.12) Ant 3.13.127 *O that I* *were Upon the hill of Basan, to outroar The horned herd.*

base *n.*¹ Foundation TN 5.1.75 *Though I confess, on base and ground enough, Orsino's enemy* (i.e. reason).

base *n.*² Prisoner's base (a children's chasing game) CYM 5.3.20 *lads more like to run The country base*; *bid the base* challenge to a test of speed TGV 1.2.94 *Indeed I bid the base for Proteus*, VEN 303.

base, bass *vb.* Utter in a deep voice, sound with a deep note TMP 3.3.99 *it did base my trespass* (F1).

base *adj.*
1 Low, low-lying R2 2.4.20 *I see thy glory like a shooting star Fall to the base earth from the firmament*, LUC 664.
2 Base-born, illegitimate LR 1.2.10 *Why brand they us with base? with baseness? bastardy?*

base-court *n.* [Fr. 'basse-cour'] Lower or outward court of a mansion R2 3.3.176 *My lord, in the base court he doth attend.*

bases *n.* (pl.) Skirt-like garment of cloth, velvet or rich brocade worn by a mounted knight PER 2.1.161 *Only, my friend, I yet am unprovided Of a pair of bases.*

base-string *n.* String of the lowest pitch in a musical instrument; (fig.) 1H4 2.4.6 *the very base-string of humility.*

base-viol *n.* Form of viol, for producing the lowest sounds ERR 4.3.24 *he that went like a base-viol in a case of leather.*

Basilisco-like *adj.* Resembling Basilisco, a braggart knight in Kyd's 'Soliman and Perseda' JN 1.1.244 *Knight, knight, good mother, Basilisco-like.*

basilisk *n.*
1 Fabulous reptile, also called 'cockatrice', alleged to be hatched by a serpent from a cock's egg and said to kill by its breath and look WT 1.3.388 *Make me not sighted like the basilisk*, CYM 2.4.107.
2 Large cannon, generally made of brass 1H4 2.3.53 *Of basilisks, of cannon*, H5 5.2.17 (with pun on sense 1; see BALL).

Basimecu *n.* (contemptuous term for a) Frenchman 2H6 4.7.28 *What canst thou answer to my Majesty for giving up of Normandy unto Monsieur Basimecu, the Dauphin of France?*
▷ Prob. pseudo-French pun on 'baise mon cul' (kiss my backside).

basis *n.*
1 Base, foot, foundation TMP 2.1.121 *To th' shore, that o'er his wave-worn basis bowed*, TN 3.2.34.
2 Pedestal JC 3.1.115 *That now on Pompey's basis lies along.*

basket-hilt *n.* (short for) Basket-hilt sword, a sword with a curved hand guard shaped like a basket 2H4 2.4.131 *you basket-hilt stale juggler you!*
▷ Prob. used here as a term of contempt, suggesting a swordsman whose sword and hence style were old-fashioned.

bass See BASE *vb.*

basta *adv.* [It.] Enough SHR 1.1.198 *Basta, content thee; for I have it full.*

bastard *n.*
1 Sweet Spanish wine, resembling muscadel MM 3.2.3 *we shall have all the world drink brown and white bastard*, 1H4 2.4.27.
2 *Nature's bastard* Product of artificial crossing, not a natural breed WT 4.4.83 *the fairest flow'rs o' th' season Are our carnations and streak'd gillyvors (Which some call Nature's bastards).*
~ *adj.* Counterfeit, spurious MV 3.5.13 *a kind of bastard hope indeed*, SON 68.3.

baste *vb.* Sew loosely ADO 1.1.287 *the guards are but slightly basted on.*

bastinado *n.* Beating with a stick or cudgel AYL

5.1.54 *I will deal in poison with thee, or in bastinado, or in steel*; (fig.) JN 2.1.463 *He gives the bastinado with his tongue; Our ears are cudgell'd.*

bat *n.* Stick, club COR 1.1.161 *make you ready your stiff bats and clubs*, LR 4.6.241 (Qq).

batch *n.* Quantity of bread produced at one baking; (fig.) TRO 5.1.5 *Thou crusty batch of nature.*

bate *n.* Strife, discord 2H4 2.4.250 *and breeds no bate with telling of discreet stories.*

bate *vb.*¹ (a term from falconry when a hawk attempts to escape from a falconer's wrist) Beat the wings 1H4 4.1.99 *All plum'd like estridges, that with the wind Bated like eagles having lately bath'd*, SHR 4.1.196; (fig.) ROM 3.2.14 *Hood my unmann'd blood, bating in my cheeks, With thy black mantle*, H5 3.7.112 (with quibble on *bate* vb.² sense 2).
▷The falconer controlled the hawk by putting a hood over its head; hence, the fig. use of both *bate* and *hood.*

bate *vb.*²
1 Blunt, dull LLL 1.1.6 *That honour which shall bate his scythe's keen edge.*
2 Reduce, diminish, weaken TIM 3.3.26 *Who bates mine honour shall know my coin*, MV 3.3.32, MV 4.1.72; decrease, fall off 1H4 3.3.2 *do I not bate? do I not dwindle?*, H5 3.7.112 (with quibble on *bate* vb.¹).
3 Deduct, remit TMP 1.2.250 *Thou did promise To bate me a full year*, HAM 5.2.23, 2H4 Epil.14; (absol.) CYM 3.2.54 *O let me bate!*
4 Except, omit MND 1.1.190 *Were the world mine, Demetrius being bated.*

bate-breeding *adj.* Strife-creating VEN 655 *this bate-breeding spy.*
▷ See BREED-BATE.

bateless *adj.* Keen, not to be blunted LUC 9 *This bateless edge on his keen appetite.*

bat-fowling *n.* Catching of birds at night by dazing them with lights and knocking them down with poles or netting them TMP 2.1.185 *and then go a-batfowling.*

batler See BATLET.

batlet *n.* Wooden bat, paddle (used in washing clothes) AYL 2.4.49 *I remember the kissing of her batlet* [Ff2-4; F1 *batler*].

battalia *n.* Forces, army R3 5.3.11 *Why our battalia trebles that account* [F1; Qq *battalion*), HAM 4.5.79 (F1).

batten *vb.* Grow fat on COR 4.5.32 *batten on cold bits*, HAM 3.4.67.

battery *n.*
1 Beating, assailing with blows JN 2.1.446 *This union shall do more than battery can To our fast-closed gates*; (fig.) CYM 1.4.22 *to fortify her judgment, which else an easy battery might lay flat*; (in law) unlawful attack on another by beating or wounding TN 4.1.34 *I'll have an action of battery against him*, HAM 5.1.103.
2 Breach in a fortification; (fig.) VEN 426 *For where a heart is hard they make no batt'ry.*
3 Wound 3H6 3.1.37 *Her sighs will make a batt'ry in his breast.*

battle *n.*
1 Single combat R2 1.1.92 *Besides I say, and will in battle prove.*
2 Body or line of troops in battle array, battalion 1H4 4.1.129 *What may the King's whole battle reach unto?*; (fig.) VEN 619 *a battle...of bristly pikes.*
3 Main body of an armed force MAC 5.6.4 *You, worthy uncle, Shall...Lead first battle*, R3 5.3.299.

batty *adj.* Bat-like MND 3.2.365 *With leaden legs and batty wings.*

bauble *n.*
1 Showy trinket of little worth SHR 4.3.82 *it is a paltry cap,...a bauble.*

2 Mere toy CYM 3.1.27 *his shipping (Poor ignorant baubles!) on our terrible seas.*
3 Stick carried by a court fool TIT 5.1.79 *An idiot holds his bauble for a god,* AWW 4.5.30.
4 Foolish, childish person, trifler CYM 3.2.20 *Senseless bauble, Art thou a feodary for this act?,* OTH 4.1.135.
~ *attrib.* bauble boats Toy boats TRO 1.3.35.

baubling, bawbling *adj.* Trifling, paltry, of no account TN 5.1.54 *A baubling vessel was he captain of, For shallow draught and bulk unprizable.*

bavin *n.* Brushwood, faggots 1H4 3.2.61 *With shallow jesters, and rash bavin wits, Soon kindled and soon burnt.*

bawcock *n.* [Fr. 'beau coq'] Fine fellow H5 3.2.25 *Good bawcock, bate thy rage.*

bawd *n.*[1] [dial.] Hare ROM 2.4.130 *A bawd, a bawd, a bawd! So ho!*
▷ Sustained punning here, first on *bawd* and then on *hare,* slang word for prostitute.

bawd *n.*[2] Procurer H5 3.6.62 *I remember him now; a bawd, a cutpurse.*

bay *n.*[1] Section of a house lying under one gable or between two party-walls MM 2.1.242 *I'll rent the fairest house in it after threepence a bay.*

bay *n.*[2]
1 Deep prolonged barking TIT 2.2.3 *let us make a bay, And wake the emperor.*
2 State of a chase when the hunted animal is obliged to turn and defend itself 1H6 4.2.52 *desperate stags, Turn on the bloody hounds...And make the cowards stand aloof at bay,* VEN 877; (fig.) TIT 4.2.42 *I would we had a thousand Roman dames At such a bay, by turn to serve our lust,* PP 11.13.
~ *vb.*
1 Bark at JC 4.3.27 *bay the moon,* CYM 5.5.223.
2 Pursue or drive to bay, with barking 2H4 1.3.80 *Baying him at the heels,* MND 4.1.113.
3 Bring to bay, hold at bay; (fig.) JC 4.1.49 *bay'd about with many enemies.*

be *vb.*
1 *be off* See OFF.
2 *be with* See WITH.

bead *n.*
1 (pl.) Drops (of liquid), tears JN 1.171 *Ay, with these crystal beads heaven shall be brib'd To do him justice,* JC 3.1.284.
2 Any very small thing MND 3.2.330 *Get you gone, you dwarf,... You bead, you acorn,* WIV 5.5.49 (Ff Bede).
3 (pl.) Rosary ERR 2.2.188 *O for my beads!,* R2 3.3.147.

beaded *ppl. adj.* In the form of beads LC 37 *Of amber, crystal, and of beaded jet.*

beadle *n.* Officer of a parish with power to punish petty offences LR 4.6.160 *Thou rascal beadle...Why dost thou lash that whore?,* 2H6 2.1.134, H8 5.3.66; (fig.) H5 4.1.169 *War is his beadle, war is his vengeance,* LLL 3.1.175.

beadsman *n.* One paid or endowed to pray for others, pensioner bound to pray for the souls of his benefactors R2 3.2.116 *Thy very beadsmen learn to bend their bows...against thy state,* TGV 1.1.18.

beagle *n.* Small dog, used for hunting hares; (fig., used for a woman, sometimes contemptuously) TIM 4.3.175 *Get thee away, and take Thy beagles with thee;* (sometimes respectfully) TN 2.3.179 *She's a beagle true-bred.*

beak *n.* Pointed and ornamented projection at the prow of ancient vessels TMP 1.2.196 *I boarded the King's ship; now on the beak.*

beam *n.*
1 Wooden roller in a loom on which the warp is wound WIV 5.1.22 *I fear not Goliath with a weaver's beam.*
▷ Allusion to 1 Samuel 17.7 'the staff of [Goliath's] spear was like a weaver's beam'.
2 Lance TRO 5.5.9 *And stands Colossus-wise, waving his beam, Upon the pashed corses of the kings.*
3 (fig.) Something large LLL 4.3.160 *You found his mote, the King your mote did see; But I a beam do find in each of three.*
▷ Allusion to Matthew 7.3: 'why beholdest thou the mote that is in thy brother's eye, but considerest not the beam that is in thine own eye'.
4 *beam of sight* Range of vision COR 3.2.5 *That the precipitation might down stretch Below the beam of sight.*

bear *vb.*
1 Contain (a meaning or the like) 1H4 4.1.20 *His letters bears his mind, not I, my lord,* LC 19, AYL 3.2.166.
2 Carry with it or as a consequence TIM 1.1.131 *His honesty rewards him in itself, It must not bear my daughter.*
3 Sustain, keep going WT 4.4.295 *I can bear my part, you must know 'tis my occupation,* TMP 1.2.426, LUC 1132.
4 Carry on, conduct, manage MAC 3.6.3 *Things have been strangely borne,* JN 3.4.149, ADO 2.3.221.
5 Carry, win, conquer OTH 1.3.23 *So may he with more facile question bear it, For that it stands not in such warlike brace; bear it* carry the day 2H4 4.1.133 *He ne'er had borne it out of Coventry,* TRO 2.3.217.
6 (refl. and intr.) Behave, comport oneself MM 1.3.47 *How I may formally in person bear Like a true friar,* H8 2.1.30.
~ in combination
bear away Sail away ERR 4.1.87 *That stays but till her owner comes aboard, And then, sir, she bears away.* **bear back** Move or go back JC 3.2.168 *Stand back; room, bear back!,* LUC 1417. **bear down** Overwhelm, overthrow MV 4.1.214 *If this will not suffice, it must appear That malice bears down truth,* 2H4 1.1.11, TIT 2.1.30. **bear hard** Bear ill will to JC 1.2.313 *Caesar doth bear me hard.* **bear in hand** Pretend CYM 5.5.43 *Whom she bore in hand to love with such integrity;* delude, deceive ADO 4.1.303 *What bear her in hand until they come to take hands;* abuse, take advantage of HAM 2.2.67 *whereat griev'd, That so his sickness, age, and impotence was falsely borne in hand.* **bear off** Keep off, ward off TMP 2.2.18 *Here's neither bush nor shrub to bear off any weather at all.* **bear out** 1 Support, back up JN 4.1.6 *I hope your warrant will bear out the deed,* 2H4 5.1.48. 2 (with *it*) Have the upper hand, carry the day SON 116.12 *Love...bears it out even to the edge of doom,* TN 1.5.20, OTH 2.1.19. **bear up** Put the helm up in order to put the vessel before the wind; (fig.) TMP 3.2.2 *therefore bear up and board 'em.*

beard *vb.* Face defiantly, oppose resolutely HAM 2.2.424 *thy face is valanc'd since I saw thee last; com'st thou to beard me in Denmark?* (with pun on 'beard' on chin).

bearer *n.* Possessor, holder 2H4 4.5.29 *O majesty! When thou dost pinch thy bearer,* TRO 3.3.104, H8 2.3.15.

bear-herd, beaard, berard, berrord, bearward *n.* Keeper of a tame bear SHR Ind.2.20 *by education a card-maker, by transmutation a bear-herd, and now by present profession a tinker,* ADO 2.1.40, 2H4 1.2.169.

bearing *n.*
1 Behaviour, demeanour, carriage, deportment COR 2.3.249 *but you have found, Scaling his present*

bearing with his past, That he's your fixed enemy, H5 4.7.177, Ado 2.1.160.

2 Endurance (of suffering) LR 3.6.107 *But then the mind much sufferance doth o'erskip, When grief hath mates, and bearing fellowship.*

bearing-cloth *n.* Child's christening robe WT 3.3.115 *look thee, a bearing-cloth for a squire's child!*, 1H6 1.3.42.

beastly *adv.* Like a beast, in a beastly manner, lewdly SHR 4.2.34 *Fie on her, see how beastly she doth court him!*, ANT 1.5.50, CYM 5.3.27.

beat *vb.*
1 Flap the wings with force SHR 4.1.196 *these kites That bate and beat.*
2 Think or ponder laboriously HAM 3.1.174 *Whereon his brains still beating puts him thus From fashion of himself*, 2H6 2.1.20; (hence) engross the mind LR 3.4.14 *this tempest in my mind Doth from my senses take all feeling else, Save what beats there*, TMP 1.2.176.

beated *pa. pple.* Beaten, battered SON 62.10 *Beated and chop'd with tann'd antiquity.*

beauty *vb.* Embellish, adorn, beautify HAM 3.1.50 *The harlot's cheek, beautied with plast'ring art.*

beaver *n.* Visor, face-guard of a helmet HAM 1.2.230 *Then saw you not his face.—O yes, my lord, he wore—his beaver up*, 2H4 4.1.118, H5 4.2.44; (sometimes) the whole helmet R3 5.3.50 *What? is my beaver easier than it was?*

because *conj.* In order that, so that SHR 1.1.184 *closely mew'd her up, Because she will not be annoy'd with suitors.*

beck *n.*
1 Summoning gesture HAM 3.1.124 *with more offences at my beck than I have thoughts to put them in*, 3H6 1.1.68, SON 58.5.
2 Bow TIM 1.2.231 *What a coil's here! Serving of becks and jutting-out of bums.*
~ *vb.* Beckon, command, call by a nod JN 3.3.13 *When gold and silver becks me to come on*, ANT 4.12.26.

become *vb.*
1 Agree with, befit MV 5.1.57 *Soft stillness and the night Become the touches of sweet harmony*; be fitting, suitable TIT 1.1.347 *But let us give him burial as becomes*, 1H6 5.3.170.
2 Adorn, grace CYM 5.5.406 *He would have well becom'd this place, and grac'd The thankings of a king*, CYM 2.1.258, TMP 3.2.104.
3 Come, arrive 3H6 2.1.10 *Where our right valiant father is become* (i.e. what has happened to him).

becomed *ppl. adj.* Befitting, proper ROM 4.2.26 *And gave him what becomed love I might, Not stepping o'er the bounds of modesty.*

becoming *n.* Grace ANT 1.3.96 *Since my becomings kill me when they do not Eye well to you*, SON 150.5.

bed *n.*
1 *bed of Ware* Enormous bed, approx. 3.5 metre square TN 3.2.47 *although the sheet were big enough for the bed of Ware in England.*
2 (fig.) Marriage AYL 5.4.190 *You to a long and well-deserved bed.*
3 (fig.) Grave TMP 2.1.284 *lay to bed forever*, CYM 4.4.52.
4 (pl.) 'Bed-time' or close of life, old age TN 5.1.401 *But when I came unto my beds.*

bedded *ppl. adj.* Laid flat HAM 3.4.121 *Your bedded hair, like life in excrements, Start up and stand on end.*

Bedlam, Bedlem *n.*
1 Hospital of St.Mary of Bethlehem in London, used for an asylum for the mentally deranged 2H6 5.1.131 *To Bedlam with him! is the man grown mad?*, LR 1.2.136.

2 Lunatic, madman JN 2.1.183 *Bedlam, have done*, LR 3.7.103.
~ *adj.* Mad 2H6 3.1.51 *Did instigate the bedlam brain-sick Duchess*, 2H6 5.1.132, H5 5.1.19.

bed-presser *n.* Lazy fellow 1H4 2.4.242 *this bed-presser, this horse-back-breaker, this huge hill of flesh.*

bedred, bed-rid *ppl. adj.* Bed-ridden LLL 1.1.138 *To her decrepit, sick, and bedred father* (Q1; F1 *bed-rid*), LUC 975, HAM 1.2.29.

bed-right *n.* Conjugal due(s) TMP 4.1.96 *Whose vows are, that no bed-right shall be paid.*

bed-swerver *n.* Adulterer WT 2.1.93 *that she's A bed-swerver, even as bad as those That vulgars give bold'st titles.*

bed-vow *n.* Marriage vow SON 152.3 *In act thy bed-vow broke.*

bed-work *n.* Easy work such as could be done in bed TRO 1.3.205 *They call this bed-work, mapp'ry, closet-war.*

beef *n.* Ox, or any animal of the ox kind MV 1.3.167 *flesh of muttons, beefs, or goats.*

beef-witted *adj.* Brainless as an ox, thick-headed TRO 2.1.13 *thou mongrel beef-witted lord!*

beesom See BISSON.

beetle *n.* three-man beetle Implement with a heavy head, requiring three men to lift it, used in ramming paving stones 2H4 1.2.228 *If I do, fillip me with a three-man beetle.*

beetle *vb.* Project like beetle brows, overhang threateningly HAM 1.4.71 *the dreadful summit of the cliff That beetles o'er his base into the sea.*
~ *adj.* Prominent ROM 1.4.32 *beetle brows.*

beetle-headed *adj.* Wooden headed, stupid SHR 4.1.157 *A whoreson, beetle-headed, flap-ear'd knave!*

befall *vb.* Become of ERR 1.1.123 *What hath befall'n of them.*

before *adv.*
1 In front MAC 5.9.12 *Had he his hurts before?*, SHR 3.2.56.
2 Forward! On! 2H4 4.1.226 *Before, and greet his Grace.—My Lord, we come.*
3 God before With God as our leader, with God's help H5 1.2.307 *for, God before, We'll chide this Dauphin at his father's door.*
4 the better foot before Best foot forward JN 4.2.170 *Nay, but make haste; the better foot before*, TIT 2.3.192.
~ *conj.* Rather than (that) MM 2.4.182 *he'll yield them up, Before his sister should her body stoop To such abhorr'd pollution*, MV 3.2.301, R3 3.2.44.
~ *prep. before me!* On my soul! TN 2.3.178 *Before me, she's a good wench*, OTH 4.1.145.

before-breach *n.* Earlier violation H5 4.1.170 *here men are punish'd for before-breach of the King's laws in now the King's quarrel.*

beforehand *adv.* been beforehand with Forestalled, anticipated JN 5.7.111 *let us pay the time but needful woe, Since it hath been beforehand with our griefs.*
▷ Derives from commercial metaphor, to have money in hand, to draw money in advance.

beg *vb.* Petition the Court of Wards for the custody of (a minor, an heiress or an idiot) LLL 5.2.490 *You cannot beg us, sir,... we know what we know* (i.e. prove us fools).

beget *vb.*
1 Obtain HAM 3.2.7 *you must acquire and beget a temperance.*
2 Produce LLL 2.1.69 *His eye begets occasion for his wit*, SHR 1.1.45.

beggar *n.* One who begs a favour, suppliant AWW 1.3.20 *Wilt thou needs be a beggar?*

~ vb.
1 Reduce to beggary R3 1.4.141 *It beggars any man that keeps it*, MV 2.6.19.
2 Make valueless, esteem as worthless TRO 2.2.91 *Beggar the estimation which you priz'd Richer than sea and land?*
3 Exhaust the resources of ANT 2.2.198 *For her own person, It beggar'd all description.*
4 beggared *of* Made destitute of HAM 4.5.92 *Wherein necessity, of matter beggar'd*, SON 67.10.

beggary *n.* Contemptible meanness CYM 1.6.115 *Not I Inclin'd to this intelligence pronounce The beggary of his change.*

begnaw *vb.* Gnaw, corrode R3 1.3.221 *The worm of conscience still begnaw thy soul*, SHR 3.2.54.

beguild See BEGUILE sense 3.

beguile *vb.*
1 Deprive, rob *of* LLL 1.1.77 *Light, seeking light, doth light of light beguile*, OTH 1.3.156.
2 Cheat, disappoint (hopes) TGV 5.4.64 *treacherous man, Thou hast beguil'd my hopes!*
3 Deceive LUC 1544 *Tarquin armed to beguild With outward honesty.*
◇ *Beguild* is taken by some as a var. of *beguile* for the sake of rhyme. A common emendation is *armed, so beguil'd With outward honesty* (i.e. so disguised).

behalf *n.*
1 in (the) behalf of, on behalf of In the interest of, in favour of, for the benefit of AYL Epil.9 *nor cannot insinuate with you in the behalf of a good play*, JN 1.1.7, AWW 4.3.320; on the part of, in the name of 1H4 1.3.48 *amongst the rest demanded My prisoners in your Majesty's behalf*, R3 3.4.19, TIM 3.1.17.
2 in that behalf In respect of that LLL 2.1.27 *and in that behalf, Bold of your worthiness, we single you As our best-moving fair solicitor*, JN 2.1.264.

behave *vb.*
1 as he is behav'd According to his behaviour HAM 3.1.34 *And gather by him, as he is behav'd, If 't be th'affliction of his love or no.*
2 Control, regulate TIM 3.5.22 *He did behave his anger, ere 'twas spent* (F1 *behoove*).

behaviour *n.*
1 Words and deeds, 'person' JN 1.1.3 *Thus, after greeting, speaks the King of France In my behaviour to the majesty* (i.e. through me).
2 (pl. = sing.) Conduct JC 1.2.42 *Which give some soil, perhaps, to my behaviours.*

behind-hand *adj.* Backward, tardy WT 5.1.151 *my behind-hand slackness.*

beholding *n.*
1 Sight LR 3.7.9 *the revenges we are bound to take upon your traitorous father are not fit for your beholding*, COR 1.3.9.
2 Looks, aspect PER 5.1.222 *I am wild in my beholding.*
~ *ppl. adj.* Indebted, beholden, under obligation WIV 1.1.273 *A Justice of Peace sometime may be beholding to his friend for a man.*

behoof, behove *n.* Benefit, advantage 2H6 4.7.78 *This tongue hath parley'd unto foreign kings For your behoof*, HAM 5.1.63, LC 165.

behoofeful, behoveful *adj.* Advantageous, expedient ROM 4.3.8 *such necessaries As are behoofeful for our state* (Q1; F1 *behoouefull*).

behoove See BEHAVE.

behowl *vb.* Bay MND 5.1.372 *And the wolf behowls the moon* (F *beholds*).

being *n.*
1 Life, existence HAM 2.1.93 *As it did seem to shatter all his bulk And end his being*, SHR 1.1.11, OTH 1.2.21.
2 Stay, abode, dwelling CYM 1.5.54 *To shift his be-

ing Is to exchange one misery with another, ANT 2.2.35.
~ *conj.* Seeing that, since 2H4 2.1.186 *You loiter here too long, being you are to take soldiers up in counties as you go*; (with *that*) ADO 4.1.249 *Being that I flow in grief, The smallest twine may lead me.*

belching *ppl. adj.* Spouting TRO 5.5.23 *And there they fly or die, like scaling sculls Before the belching whale.*

beldam, beldame *n.*
1 Grandmother LUC 953 *To show the beldame daughters of her daughter*, 1H4 3.1.31.
2 Loathsome old woman, hag MAC 3.5.2. *Have I not reason, beldams as you are?*, JN 4.2.185.

belee *vb.* Place a ship in such a position that the wind is cut off and it becomes stationary; (fig.) OTH 1.1.30 *And I...must be belee'd and calm'd By debitor and creditor.*

belie *vb.*
1 Tell lies about, calumniate, misrepresent 2H4 1.1.98 *And he doth sin that doth belie the dead*, ADO 4.1.146, OTH 4.1.36.
2 Fill with lies CYM 3.4.35 *whose breath Rides on the posting winds and doth belie All corners of the world*, LUC 1533.

bell *n.*
1 Little bell attached to a falcon's leg 3H6 1.1.47 *Dares stir a wing if Warwick shake his bells.*
2 Word used in the ritual of excommunication which closed with 'Do to the book, quench the candle, ring the bell' JN 3.3.12 *Bell, book, and candle shall not drive me back.*

bellman *n.* Crier who, as night-watchman calling the hours, rang a bell at midnight outside the cell of a prisoner destined for execution in the morning MAC 2.2.3 *It was the owl that shriek'd, the fatal bellman, Which gives the stern'st good-night.*

bell-wether *n.*
1 Leading sheep of a flock, on whose neck a bell is hung AYL 3.2.80 *to be bawd to a bell-wether.*
2 (term of contempt) Clamorous person WIV 3.5.114 *a jealous rotten bell-wether.*

belly-doublet See GREAT-BELLY, THIN-BELLY.

belonging *n.*
1 Equipment COR 1.9.62 *My noble steed...With all his trim belonging.*
2 (pl.) Qualities, endowments MM 1.1.29 *Thyself and thy belongings Are not thine even so proper as to waste Thyself upon thy virtues.*

beloving *ppl. adj.* Loving ANT 1.2.23 *You shall be more beloving than beloved.*

below *adv.*
1 Downstairs WIV 2.2.144 *Sir John, there's one Master Brook below would fain speak with you.*
◇ Ado 5.2.10 *below stairs* downstairs, i.e. in the servants' quarters.
2 In Hell (as opposed to earth) TMP 4.1.31 *Or Night kept chain'd below.*

bemadding *ppl. adj.* Maddening LR 3.1.38 *unnatural and bemadding sorrow.*

bemete, be-mete *vb.* Measure SHR 4.3.112 *I shall so bemete thee with thy yard As thou shalt think on prating whilst thou liv'st* (i.e. measure, thrash).

bemoil *vb.* Befoul with mire, cover with mud SHR 4.1.75 *Thou shouldst have heard in how miry a place, how she was bemoil'd.*

bemonster *vb.* Make monstrous LR 4.2.63 *Bemonster not thy feature.*

bench *n.* Court, deliberative body COR 3.1.106 *who puts his 'shall', His popular 'shall', against a graver bench*, COR 3.1.166 *th' greater bench* (i.e. the Senate).

~ vb.

1 Raise to authority, give official status WT 1.2.314 *whom I from meaner form Have bench'd and rear'd to worship.*

2 Sit on the bench, as a judge LR 3.6.38 *And thou, his yoke-fellow of equity, Bench by his side.*

bencher *n.* Member of a court or deliberative body COR 2.1.82 *you are well understood to be a perfecter giber for the table than a necessary bencher in the Capitol* (i.e. a senator).

bench-hole *n.* Hole in a latrine ANT 4.7.9 *We'll beat 'em into bench-holes.*

bend *n.* Glance, look JC 1.2.123 *that same eye whose bend doth awe the world Did lose his lustre,* ANT 2.2.208.

~ vb.

1 Level, aim, direct LR 2.1.46 *'Gainst parricides did all the thunder bend,* JN 2.1.379, R3 1.2.95.

2 (intr. and refl.) Direct oneself, turn, proceed AWW 3.2.55 *Thither we bend again,* WT 5.1.165, 1H4 5.5.36.

3 *bend up* Strain, nerve H5 3.1.16 *Hold hard the breath, and bend up every spirit To his full height,* MAC 1.7.79.

4 *bend the brows, one wrinkle* Knit the brow, frown, scowl JN 4.2.90 *Why do you bend such solemn brows on me?,* R2 2.1.170 *bend one wrinkle on my sovereign's face,* PP 18.25.

bending *ppl. adj.* Courteous, respectful R3 4.4.95 *the bending peers that flattered thee,* TRO 1.3.236.

⮡ H5 Epil.2 *Our bending author* prob. play on two meanings: (1) bowing to the audience, respectful, and (2) stooped with the labour of composition.

beneath *adv.* (used attrib.) Underneath TIM 1.1.44 *I have, in this rough work, shap'd out a man Whom this beneath world doth embrace and hug.*

benedicite [L.] (salutation used by friars) Bless you! MM 2.3.39 *Grace go with you, Benedicite!*

benediction *n.* Blessing LR 2.2.161 *Thou out of heaven's benediction com'st To the warm sun.*

⮡ Usu. form of the proverb is 'out of God's blessing into the warm sun'.

beneficial *adj.*

1 Beneficent H8 1.1.56 *Take up the rays o' th' beneficial sun,* ERR 1.1.151.

2 Advantageous, profitable OTH 2.2.6 *beneficial news.*

benefit *n.*

1 Bestowal of property rights, benefaction 1H6 5.4.152 *Either accept the title thou usurp'st, Of benefit proceeding from our king,* R3 3.7.196.

2 Natural gift or advantage H8 1.2.115 *When these so noble benefits shall prove Not well dispos'd,* AYL 4.1.34.

benet *vb.* Ensnare HAM 5.2.29 *Being thus benetted round with villainies.*

benevolence *n.* Forced loan or aid levied with legal authority of the king R2 2.1.250 *And daily new exactions are devis'd, As blanks, benevolences, and I wot not what.*

⮡ An anachronism here, since benevolences were first raised by Edward IV in 1473.

benison *n.* Blessing MAC 2.4.40 *God's benison go with you,* LR 1.1.265.

bent *n.*

1 Extent to which a bow may be bent, degree of tension; (hence, when applied to mental state) degree of intensity, of endurance, capacity Ado 2.3.223 *It seems her affections have their full bent* (i.e. are at full stretch), HAM 3.2.384, TN 2.4.37.

2 Mental inclination, tendency, bias ADO 4.1.186 *the very bent of honour* (i.e. perfect inclination toward), JC 2.1.210.

3 Cast or inclination (of the eye) CYM 1.1.13

Although they wear their faces to the bent Of the King's look, H5 5.2.16.

4 Arch (of eyebrows) ANT 1.3.36 *Eternity was in our lips and eyes, Bliss in our brows' bent.*

~ ppl. adj. Inclined (to), intent (upon), determined MND 3.2.145 *you all are bent To set against me for your merriment,* 2H6 2.1.163, VEN 618.

ben venuto, bien venuto *n.* [It. salutation] Welcome SHR 1.2.280 *Petruchio, I shall be your 'ben venuto'* (i.e. host).

berattle *vb.* Rattle away at, rail at; (hence) cry down, satirize HAM 2.2.342 *These are now the fashion, and so berattle the common stages.*

beray *vb.* Defile, make filthy TIT 2.3.222 *Lord Bassanius lies beray'd in blood.*

bereave *vb.*

1 Take away (a thing) from (a person) 2H6 3.1.85 *That all your interest in those territories Is utterly bereft you,* OTH 1.3.257.

2 Rob of strength or beauty; (hence) impair, spoil ERR 2.1.40 *to see like right bereft,* VEN 797.

bereaved *ppl. adj.* Impaired LR 4.4.9 *his bereaved sense.*

Bergomask dance *n.* Dance after the manner of the people of Bergamo (a province in the state of Venice) who were noted for the rusticity of their manners and speech MND 5.1.353 *hear a Bergomask dance between two of our company.*

berhyme, be-rime *vb.* Celebrate in rhyme, make rhymes upon ROM 2.4.41 *she had a better love to berhyme her,* AYL 3.2.176.

berlady, berlakin (var. of) BY'R LADY.

bescreen *vb.* Conceal ROM 2.2.52 *What man art thou that thus bescreen'd in night So stumblest on my counsel?*

beseech *n.* Beseeching, entreaty TRO 1.2.293 *Achievement is command; ungain'd, beseech.*

beseek *vb.* (old Northern and North-Midland form of) Beseech 2H4 2.4.162 *I beseek you now.*

beseeming *n.* Appearance CYM 5.5.409 *The soldier that did company these three In poor beseeming.*

~ ppl. adj. Appropriate ROM 1.1.93 *their grave beseeming ornaments.*

beside *adv.* By, past VEN 981 *Yet sometimes falls an orient drop beside.* **~ prep.** Out of ADO 5.1.128 *Never any did so, though very many have been beside their wit,* JC 3.1.180.

besides *prep.* Out of, beyond CYM 2.4.149 *Quite besides The government of patience!,* ERR 3.2.78, SON 23.2.

beslubber *vb.* Daub, smear 1H4 2.4.310 *then to beslubber our garments with it and swear it was the blood of true men.*

besonian, Bezonian *n.* [from It. 'bisogno' need] Beggar, scoundrel 2H4 5.3.113 *Under which king, besonian? Speak, or die,* 2H6 4.1.134.

besort *vb.* Suitable company OTH 1.3.238 *With such accommodation and besort As levels with her breeding.*

~ vb. Befit LR 1.4.251 *To be such men as may besort your age.*

bespeak *vb.* Speak to, address TN 5.1.189 *But I bespake you fair,* HAM 2.2.140, R2 5.2.20.

bespice *vb.* Season with spice WT 1.2.316 *mightst bespice a cup, To give mine enemy a lasting wink* (i.e. add poison to).

best *adj.* (absol.)

1 *have the best* Have the advantage 3H6 5.3.20 *having now the best at Barnet field.*

2 *at the best* In the best possible way OTH 1.3.173 *Take up this mangled matter at the best,* 3H6 3.1.8; in the best condition ROM 1.5.119 *the sport is at the best,* TIM 1.2.152.

3 *in the best* At best HAM 1.5.27 *Murder most foul, as in the best it is.*

best-conditioned *adj.* Best-natured, of the best disposition MV 3.2.293 *the kindest man, The best-condition'd and unwearied spirit In doing courtesies.*

bestead, bested *adj.* In a (worse) plight, in (worse) circumstances 2H6 2.3.56 *I never saw a fellow worse bested* (F1 *bestead*).

best-moving *adj.* Most persuasive, eloquent LLL 2.1.28 *we single you As our best-moving fair solicitor.*

bestow *vb.*
1 Give in marriage AYL 5.4.7 *You will bestow her on Orlando here?*
2 (refl.) Behave, conduct (oneself) TGV 3.1.87 *How and which way I may bestow myself*, JN 3.1.225, 2H4 2.2.169.
3 Apply, employ, devote; (hence) spend (time) JC 5.5.61 *bestow thy time with me*; lay out (money) 2H4 5.5.12 *I would have bestow'd the thousand pound I borrow'd.*
4 Lodge, put up MAC 3.1.29 *our bloody cousins are bestow'd In England.*
5 Stow away, place, dispose of TMP 5.1.299 *bestow your luggage where you found it*, ERR 1.2.78.

bestowing *n.* Proper use, functions TRO 3.2.37 *And all my powers do their bestowing lose.*

bestraught *adj.* Distracted, mad SHR Ind.2.25 *What! I am not bestraught.*

bestride *vb.* Stand over (a fallen man) to protect him ERR 5.1.192 *When I bestrid thee in the wars, and took Deep scars to save thy life*, MAC 4.3.4, 2H4 1.1.207.

best-tempered *adj.* Tempered like fine steel, of the truest 'metal' 2H4 1.1.115 *took fire and heat away From the best-temper'd courage in his troops, For from his metal was his party steeled.*

beteem *vb.*
1 Grant, afford MND 1.1.131 *Belike for want of rain; which I could well Beteem them from the tempest of my eyes.*
◇ Perhaps with secondary reference to 'teem' = pour.
2 Allow HAM 1.2.141 *he might not beteem the winds of heaven Visit her face too roughly.*

bethink *vb.*
1 Think of, devise 3H6 3.3.39 *calm the storm, While we bethink a means to break it off*, HAM 1.3.90.
2 (pass.) Have in mind, intend LR 2.3.6 *and am bethought To take the basest and most poorest shape.*

betime *adv.*
1 In good time JN 4.3.98 *Put up thy sword betime.*
2 Early ANT 4.4.20 *To business that we love we rise betime.*

betray *vb.*
1 Give over or expose to punishment, or some evil WIV 3.3.195 *to betray him to another punishment?*, H8 3.1.56, AYL 4.1.6.
2 Lead astray, mislead, deceive MAC 1.3.125 *The instruments of darkness tell us truths...to betray 's In deepest consequence*, WIV 5.3.22, OTH 5.2.6; (absol.) TIM 4.3.147 *betray with them.*
3 Cheat, disappoint TIT 5.2.147 *a complot to betray thy foes.*

better *vb. I were better* It would be better for me AYL 3.3.91 *I were better to be married of him than of another*; (with *thou*) OTH 3.3.362 *Thou hadst been better.*
~ *adv.* Rather H8 3.2.253 *Within these forty hours Surrey durst better Have burnt that tongue than said so*, AWW 3.6.88.

bettering *n.* Improvement SON 32.5 *the bett'ring of the time.*

betumbled *ppl. adj.* Disordered LUC 1037 *This said, from her betumbled couch she starteth.*

between *n.* Interval (of time) WT 3.3.61 *for there is nothing in the between but getting wenches with child.*

bevel *adj.* Slanting; (hence) crooked, deviating from uprightness SON 121.11 *I may be straight though they themselves be bevel.*

bevy *n.* Company (properly, of ladies) H8 1.4.4. *None here, he hopes, In all this noble bevy, has brought with her One care abroad*, HAM 5.2.189 (Qq *breed*).

beware *vb.* Take care of 1H6 1.3.47 *beware your beard.*

beweep *vb.*
1 Weep over, deplore SON 29.2 *I all alone beweep my outcast state*, R3 1.3.327.
2 Wet with tears HAM 4.5.39 *sweet flowers, Which bewept to the ground did not go With true-love showers.*

bewet *vb.* Wet TIT 3.1.146 *His napkin, with his true tears all bewet.*

bewray *vb.* Reveal COR 5.3.95 *our raiment And state of bodies would bewray what life We have led*, 3H6 1.1.211, TIT 2.4.3.

Bezonian See BESONIAN.

bias *n. assays of bias* Indirect attempts HAM 2.1.62 *with assays of bias, By indirections find directions out.*
~ *adj.* Swollen as the bowl on the biased side TRO 4.5.8 *till thy sphered bias cheek Outswell the colic of puff'd Aquilon.*
~ *adv.* Awry, out of a straight line TRO 1.3.15 *trial did draw Bias and thwart, not answering the aim.*
◇ All uses of *bias* in S. have allusion to the game of bowls.

bias-drawing *n.* Divergence from the straight line, deviation (from the truth) TRO 4.5.169 *faith and troth, Strain'd purely from all hollow bias-drawing.*

biddy *n.* Fowl, chicken TN 3.4.115 *Ay, biddy, come with me.*

bide *vb.*
1 Endure, bear SON 58.7 *And patience, tame to sufferance, bide each cheek*, R3 4.4.304.
2 Dwell or insist *upon* WT 1.2.242 *To bide upon't.*

biding *n.* Abode, refuge, resting-place LR 4.6.224 *I'll lead you to some biding.*

bifold *adj.* Double, twofold TRO 5.2.144 *Bi-fold authority.*

big *adj.*
1 Strong, stout, mighty H5 4.2.43 *Big Mars seems bankrupt in their beggar'd host*, OTH 3.3.349.
2 Pregnant CYM 1.1.39 *and his gentle lady, Big of this gentleman*, WT 2.1.61.
3 Full to overflowing JC 3.1.282 *Thy heart is big; get thee apart and weep.*
4 Haughty, inflated H8 1.1.119 *Buckingham Shall lessen this big look*, AWW 1.3.95.

bigamy *n.* Marriage with a widow (formerly an ecclesiastical offence) R3 3.7.189 *loath'd bigamy.*

biggen *n.* Hood for the head, nightcap 2H4 4.5.27 *As he whose brow with homely biggen bound Snores out the watch of night.*

bilberry *n.* [Midland dial.] Vaccinium myrtillus, whortleberry, blueberry (U.S.) WIV 5.5.45 *There pinch the maids as blue as bilberry.*

bilbo *n.* Well-tempered sword (orig. of Bilbao) WIV 3.5.111 *next, to be compass'd like a good bilbo, in the circumference of a peck, hilt to point.*
◇ A test to establish the quality of a blade was to see if it could be bent from hilt to point.

bilboes *n.* Shackles or fetters sliding on an iron bar

which is locked to the floor, used for mutinous sailors HAM 5.2.6 *Worse than the mutines in the bilboes.*

bile, byle *n.* (earlier forms of) Boil COR 1.4.31 *Biles and plagues Plaster you o'er*, LR 2.4.223.

bill *n.*[1] Weapon varying in form from a concave blade with a long wooden handle to a kind of concave axe with a spike at the back and its shaft ending in a spearhead, carried by soldiers and watchmen ADO 3.3.178 *We are likely to prove a goodly commodity, being taken up of these men's bills* (with play on BILL *n.*[2]), R2 3.2.118, 2H6 4.7.127.
▷ In 16C and 17C bills were often painted or varnished in different colours, hence 2H6 4.10.12 *brown bill*, LR 4.6.91.

bill *n.*[2]
1 Note, written order, memorandum SHR 4.3.145 *Error i' th' bill, sir, error i' th' bill!*, JC 5.2.1.
2 List, catalogue, inventory MAC 3.1.99 *Particular addition, from the bill That writes them all alike*, MND 1.2.105.
3 Label AYL 1.2.123 *With bills on their necks, 'Be it known unto all men by these presents'.*
4 Public notice, placard ADO 1.1.39 *He set up his bills here in Messina, and challeng'd Cupid at the flight*, JC 4.3.173.

billet *n.* Thick stick used as a weapon, club MM 4.3.55 *they shall beat out my brains with billets.*

billet *vb.* Enrol COR 4.3.44 *the centurions and their charges, distinctly billeted* (i.e. separately enrolled).

bird *n.*
1 The young of birds, nestling 1H4 5.1.60 *the cuckoo's bird*, TIT 2.3.154, 3H6 2.1.91.
2 Game-bird; (fig.) prey, object of attack SHR 5.2.46 *Am I your bird?*
3 Term of familiar endearment HAM 1.5.116 *come, bird, come*, TMP 4.1.184.

bird-bolt, burbolt *n.* Blunt-headed arrow for shooting birds at short distances TN 1.5.93 *To be generous, guiltless, and of free disposition, is to take those things for bird-bolts that you deem cannon-bullets*, ADO 1.1.42.

birding *n.* Hawking with a sparrow-hawk at small birds which were thus driven out of bushes and shot WIV 3.3.230 *we'll a-birding together. I have a fine hawk for the bush.*

birding-piece *n.* Fowling-piece WIV 4.2.58 *discharge their birding-pieces.*

birladie, birlady (var. of) BY'R LADY.

birth *n.*
1 That which is born, offspring 2H4 4.4.122 *Unfather'd heirs and loathly births of nature.*
2 Parentage, descent; (esp.) noble lineage ADO 2.1.165 *she is no equal for his birth*, JN 2.1.430.
3 Nature, innate goodness ROM 2.3.20 *Revolts from true birth.*
4 Nativity, horoscope 2H6 4.1.34 *calculate my birth.*

birth-child *n.* Person born in a particular place PER 4.4.41 *Thetis' birth-child* (i.e. born in the sea).

birthdom *n.* Inheritance, birthright MAC 4.3.4 *Bestride our downfall birthdom.*

bis coctus [L.] Twice cooked LLL 4.2.22 *Twice sod simplicity, bis coctus!*

bisson *adj.*
1 Partially blind COR 2.1.64 *What harm can your bisson conspectuities glean out of this character?* (Ff *beesom*).
2 Blinding HAM 2.2.506 *threat'ning the flames With bisson rheum.*

bite *vb.*
1 Inveigh, rail TRO 2.2.33 *you bite so sharp at reasons.*

2 *bite by the ear* Show affection ROM 2.4.77 *I will bite thee by the ear for that jest.*
3 *bite by the nose* Treat with contempt MM 3.1.108 *bite the law by th' nose.*
4 *bite one's tongue* Be silent or speechless 2H6 1.1.230 *So York must sit, and fret, and bite his tongue.*
5 *bite the thumb at* Insult, defy 'by putting the thumbe naile into the mouth, and with a ierke from the upper teeth make it knack' (Cotgrave) ROM 1.1.42 *I will bite my thumb at them.*

bitumed *adj.* Made watertight with bitumen PER 3.1.71 *a chest beneath the hatches, caulk'd and bitum'd ready*, PER 3.2.56 (Q *bottomed*).

Black Monday *n.* Easter Monday MV 2.5.25 *my nose fell a' bleeding on Black Monday last.*

blackness *n.* Wickedness PER 1.2.89 *How many worthy princes' bloods were shed To keep his bed of blackness unlaid ope.*

bladder *n.* Boil, pustule TRO 5.1.21 *bladders full of imposthume.*

bladed *adj.* In the blade (i.e. not yet in the ear) MAC 4.1.55 *Though bladed corn be lodg'd*, MND 1.1.211.

blain *n.* Blister, sore TIM 4.1.28 *Itches, blains.*

blame *vb. to blame* To be blamed, deserving blame, at fault MV 5.1.166 *You were to blame*, H8 4.2.101 (F1 *too*), ROM 3.5.169; (ellipted construction) ERR 4.1.47 *And I, to blame, have...* (i.e. who am to blame; F1 *too*).
▷ In Ff freq. *too*, so that *blame* is misinterpreted by some as an adj.

blank *n.*
1 White spot in the centre of a target, bull's-eye HAM 4.1.42 *As level as the cannon to his blank;* (fig.) *anything aimed at, range of such aim* LR 1.1.159 *let me still remain The true blank of thine eye*, OTH 3.4.128, WT 2.3.5.
2 Lottery ticket which does not win a prize COR 5.2.10 *it is lots to blanks My name hath touch'd your ears* (see LOT).
3 Open charter (document given to the agents of the crown in Richard II's reign to fill up as they pleased) R2 2.1.250 *new exactions are devis'd, As blanks, benevolences.*

blank *vb.* Blanch, make pale (a symptom of grief) HAM 3.2.220 *Each opposite that blanks the face of joy.*

blast *vb.*
1 Split (the ears) with a din ANT 4.8.36 *Trumpeters, With brazen din blast you the city's ear.*
2 Wither, fall under a blight TGV 1.1.48 *by love the young and tender wit Is turn'd to folly, blasting in the bud*, LUC 49.
3 (from gunnery) Blow up, fail, burst HAM 4.7.154 *therefore this project Should have a back or second, that might hold If this did blast in proof.*

blastment *n.* Withering blight HAM 1.3.42 *And in the morn and liquid dew of youth Contagious blastments are most imminent.*

blazon *n.*
1 (heraldry) Armorial bearings, coat of arms, banner bearing the arms WIV 5.5.64 *With loyal blazon;* (fig.) TN 1.5.293 *Thy tongue...thy actions, and spirit Do give thee fivefold blazon.*
2 Description of armorial bearings according to rules of heraldry; (hence) description, ADO 2.1.296 *I think your blazon to be true.*
3 Proclamation, publication HAM 1.5.21 *this eternal blazon*, SON 106.5.
~ *vb.*
1 Describe fitly, set forth honourably in words LC 217 *With wit well blazon'd*, ROM 2.6.26.
2 Proclaim, make public TIT 4.4.18 *blazoning our injustice everywhere*, CYM 4.2.170.

blazoning *ppl. adj.* Eulogistic, laudatory OTH 2.1.63 *One that excels the quirks of blazoning pens.*

bleak *adj.* Pale, wan AWW 1.1.104 *Looks bleak i' th' cold wind.*

blear *vb. blear the eyes* Hoodwink, deceive (one) SHR 5.1.117 *While counterfeit supposes blear'd thine eyne.*

bleeding *adj.*
1 Running or suffused with blood, bloody JN 2.1.304 *Whose sons lie scattered on the bleeding ground*, MAC 3.1.168.
2 (fig.) Unstaunched, unhealed COR 2.1.77 *dismiss the controversy bleeding* (i.e. not adjudicated).
3 Attended by loss of blood LC 275 *Now all these hearts that on mine depend, Feeling it break, with bleeding groans they pine.*
◇ Allusion to the belief that every sigh lessened life by drawing a drop of blood from the heart.

blench *n.* Turning aside, swerving away, inconstancy SON 110.7 *These blenches gave my heart another youth.*
~ *vb.* Start aside, swerve away, flinch MM 4.5.5. *Though sometimes you do blench from this to that*, HAM 2.2.597, TRO 1.1.28.

blend *ppl. adj.* Blended LC 215 *The heaven-hu'd sapphire and the opal blend With objects manifold.*

blent *ppl. adj.* Blended MV 3.2.181 *Where every something, being blent together, Turns to a wild of nothing*, TN 1.5.239.

bless *vb.*
1 Guard, keep *from* R3 3.3.5 *God bless the Prince from all the pack of you!*
2 Make happy (with some gift) TMP 2.1.125 *would not bless our Europe with your daughter*, H8 2.4.36; (used ironically) ERR 2.1.79 *he will bless that cross with other beating.*
3 (refl.) Count oneself supremely happy 2H4 2.4.95 *You would bless you to hear what he said*, WT 3.3.113.

blest *ppl. adj.* Endowed with healing virtues PER 3.2.35 *the blest infusions That dwells in vegetives, in metals, stones.*

blind *adj.*
1 Heedless, regardless, reckless, indiscriminate H5 3.3.34 *The blind and bloody soldier*, TN 5.1.229, R3 1.4.252.
2 Dark, obscure R3 5.3.62 *the blind cave of eternal night*, LUC 675, R3 3.7.129 (F1 *dark*).

blindfold *adj.*
1 Without sight R2 1.3.224 *blindfold Death not let me see my son.*
2 Reckless VEN 554 *With blindfold fury she begins to forage.*

blindness *n.* Concealment ERR 3.2.8 *Muffle your false love with some show of blindness.*

blistered *ppl. adj.* Puffed out H8 1.3.31 *tall stockings, Short blist'red breeches.*

bloat *adj.* Soft-bodied, puffed, bloated HAM 3.4.182 *Let the bloat king tempt you again to bed.*
◇ Warburton's emendation. Ff *blunt*; Qq *blowt*. 'Blowty' in the same sense is used in Lincolnshire.

block *n.* Wooden mould for a hat; (hence) shape or fashion (of hat) ADO 1.1.77 *He wears his faith as the fashion of his hat: it ever changes with the next block*, LR 4.6.183.

blood *n.*
1 Vital fluid; (hence) life ROM 3.1.183 *the price of his dear blood.*
2 Supposed seat of emotion; (hence) passion ADO 2.1.180 *Against whose charms faith melteth into passion*; temper, mood, disposition ADO 1.3.28 *it better fits my blood*, 2H4 4.4.38, HAM 3.2.69; (emphatically) high temper, mettle, anger LR 4.2.64

Were't my fitness To let these hands obey my blood, MV 1.2.18.
3 Supposed seat of animal appetite; (hence) fleshly nature of man, carnal tendency TMP 4.1.53 *th' fire i' th' blood*, LC 162, OTH 1.3.328.
4 *in blood* Full of life, in excellent physical condition COR 4.5.211 *when they shall see, sir, his crest up again and the man in blood*, LLL 4.2.4, 1H6 4.2.48.
5 Blood-relationship; (hence) parentage, descent, stock, kindred MAC 2.3.140 *the near in blood, The nearer bloody*, MND 1.1.135, JN 4.2.99.
6 Good parentage or stock TGV 3.1.121 *a gentleman of blood*, TRO 3.3.26.
7 Man of mettle, fire or spirit JC 1.2.151 *the breed of noble bloods*, ADO 3.3.132, LLL 5.2.708.

blood-boltered *adj.* Having the hair matted with blood MAC 4.1.123 *the blood-bolter'd Banquo.*

blood-drinking *adj. blood-drinking sighs* Sighs drawing blood 2H6 3.2.63.
◇ See BLEEDING sense 3 and note.

blood-sucker *n.* One who takes or sheds the blood of another; (hence) murderer 2H6 3.2.225 *Pernicious blood-sucker of sleeping men*, R3 3.3.6.

bloody *adj.*
1 Consisting of or containing blood JN 4.2.210 *the bloody house of life* (i.e. the body), AYL 3.5.7.
2 Portending bloodshed JC 5.1.14 *Their bloody sign of battle*, H5 1.2.101.
3 Intent on bloodshed, cruel, bloodthirsty TN 3.4.223 *thy intercepter, full of despite, bloody as the hunter*, MV 3.3.34, MAC 4.1.79.

blossom *n.*
1 One that is full of youth and promise TIT 4.2.72 *Sweet blowse, you are a beauteous blossom sure*, WT 3.3.46.
2 *in the blossoms* In the prime, in full flourish WT 5.2.125 *already appearing in the blossoms of their fortune*, HAM 1.5.76.

blot *vb.*
1 Tarnish, stain, sully SHR 5.2.139 *It blots thy beauty*, LLL 4.3.237.
2 Slander, calumniate JN 2.1.132 *There's a good mother, boy, that blots thy father.*
3 Obscure VEN 184 *Like misty vapours when they blot the sky.*

blow *n.* Blasting noise SHR 1.2.208 *gives not half so great a blow to hear.*
~ *vb.*[1]
1 Inflate, swell, puff up TN 2.5.43 *Look how imagination blows him*, ANT 4.6.33.
2 (of flies) Deposit eggs; (hence) defile TMP 3.1.63 *to suffer The flesh-fly blow my mouth.*

blow *vb.*[2] Blossom, bloom MND 2.1.249 *I know a bank where the wild thyme blows*, TGV 1.1.46; (fig.) TRO 1.3.317 *the seeded pride That hath to this maturity blown up In rank Achilles.*

blown *ppl. adj.*[1] Swollen, inflated PER 5.1.255 *Toward Ephesus Turn our blown sails*, COR 5.4.47, 1H4 4.2.49; (fig.) LR 4.4.27 *blown ambition.*
◇ OTH 3.3.182 *Exchange me for a goat, When I shall turn the business of my soul To such exsufflicate and blown surmises* (Ff *blowed*) could involve a mixture of the senses (1) inflated and (2) fly-blown, tainted.

blown *ppl. adj.*[2] Blossomed; (hence) past its prime ANT 3.13.39 *Against the blown rose may they stop their nose That kneel'd unto the buds.*

blowse *n.* (term of endearment) Ruddy, fat-faced girl TIT 4.2.72 *Sweet blowse, you are a beauteous blossom sure.*

blowt See BLOAT.

blubbered *pa. pple.* Swollen and disfigured with weeping 2H4 2.4.390 *She comes blubber'd.*

blue *adj.*
1 Usual colour of servants' clothing, not dark but resembling the sky-blue of a clear Spring day SHR 4.1.91 *let their heads be slickly comb'd, their blue coats brush'd*, 1H6 1.3.47.
2 Leaden-coloured, livid WIV 5.5.45 *pinch the maids as blue as bilberry*, WIV 4.5.112.
3 With bluish-black circles (caused by weeping and lack of sleep) AYL 3.2.373 *a blue eye and sunken*, LUC 1587.

blue-bottle *n.* (used attrib.) Beadle 2H4 5.4.19 *you blue-bottle rogue, you filthy famished correctioner*.
▷ Nickname based on the blue coat worn by a beadle. Ff *blew bottl'd*.

blue-cap *n.* (term of contempt) Scot 1H4 2.4.357 *one Mordake, and a thousand blue-caps more*.
▷ A broad round flat cap of blue woollen material was formerly common in Scotland. *Blue-cap* was, therefore, a contemptuous term for Scots since servants wore blue caps in England.

blue-eyed *adj.* (See BLUE sense 3) With dark circles around the eyes TMP 1.2.269 *This blue-ey'd hag was hither brought with child*.

blunt *adj.*
1 Stupid, dull-witted TGV 2.6.41 *I'll quickly cross By some sly trick blunt Thurio's dull proceeding*, 2H4 Ind.18.
2 Rude, unpolished 3H6 4.8.2 *hasty Germans and blunt Hollanders*, LUC 1300; (hence) harsh, unfeeling 3H6 5.1.86 *Clarence is so harsh, so blunt, unnatural*, R3 1.3.103, VEN 884.

blurt *vb.* Pooh-pooh *at*, make light *of* PER 4.3.34 *ours was blurted at and held a mawkin*.

board *vb.*
1 Make advances to, address, accost WIV 2.1.88 *he would never have boarded me in this fury*, SHR 1.2.95, AWW 5.3.211.
2 *bear up and board 'em* Attack the bottle again TMP 3.2.3.
▷ Both senses are a fig. use of the naval term, meaning to come alongside or aboard a ship, usually in order to attack.

boar-pig *n.* Young male pig 2H4 2.4.231 *Thou whoreson little tidy Bartholomew boar-pig*.

boast *n.* Display TIT 2.3.11 *When every thing doth make a gleeful boast?*
~ *vb.*
1 Display proudly LUC 55 *When beauty boasted blushes*.
2 *boast off* Praise highly TMP 4.1.9 *Do not smile at me that I boast her off*.

bob *n.* Jibe, taunt, quip AYL 2.7.55 *senseless of the bob.*
~ *vb.*[1]
1 Cheat *out of* TRO 3.1.68 *You shall not bob us out of our melody.*
2 Filch, swindle OTH 5.1.16 *Of gold and jewels that I bobb'd from him.*

bob *vb.*[2] Bang, thump TRO 2.1.69 *I have bobb'd his brain more than he has beat my bones*, R3 5.3.334.

bodement *n.* Omen, augury, prophecy MAC 4.1.96 *Sweet bodements!*, TRO 5.3.80.

bodge *vb.* (var. of) Budge, flinch, give way 3H6 1.4.19 *We bodg'd again.*

bodkin *n.*[1]
1 Dagger HAM 3.1.75 *When he himself might his quietus make With a bare bodkin.*
2 Small pointed instrument for piercing holes in cloth, etc. WT 3.3.86 *betwixt the firmament and it you cannot thrust a bodkin's point.*
3 Long pin or pin-shaped ornament for the hair LLL 5.2.611 *The head of a bodkin.*

bodkin *n.*[2] Little body HAM 2.2.529 *God's bodkin.*
▷ Ff *bodykins*. Cf. BODYKINS.

body *vb. body forth* Give mental shape to MND 5.1.14 *imagination bodies forth The forms of things unknown.*

bodykins *interj.* By God's little body WIV 2.3.44 *Bodykins, Master Page.*
▷ A diminutive formation on 'body' used in oaths, referring orig. to the consecrated wafer in the Mass.

boggler *n.* Waverer, shifty, capricious person ANT 3.13.110 *You have been a boggler ever.*

boil See BILE.

boiled *ppl. adj.* Sweated (i.e. treated for venereal disease by being sweated in a tub) CYM 1.6.125 *such boil'd stuff As well might poison poison.*

boiled-brains *n.* Senseless, hot-headed creatures WT 3.3.64 *Would any but these boil'd-brains of nineteen and two-and-twenty hunt this weather?*
▷ Cf. TMP 5.1.59 and MND 5.1.4. *Lovers and madmen have such seething brains.*

boisterous *adj.* Painful, painfully rough JN 4.1.94 *Then feeling what small things are boisterous there*, ROM 1.4.26.

bold *vb.* Embolden, encourage LR 5.1.26 *This business...Not bolds the king.*
~ *adj.* Confident *of*, trusting *in* CYM 2.4.2 *as I am bold her honour Will remain hers*, LLL 2.1.28, OTH 2.1.51.

bold-beating *adj.* Bold-faced and brow-beating WIV 2.2.28 *your bold-beating oaths.*
▷ Possible confusion of 'bold-faced' and 'brow-beating'. Other edd. suggest a misprint for 'bowl-beating' (i.e. pot-thumping), or for 'bull-baiting'.

boldness *n.* Confidence MM 4.2.155 *but in the boldness of my cunning, I will lay myself in hazard.*

bolin *n.* (early form of) Bowline PER 3.1.43 *Slack the bolins there!*

bollen *adj.* Swollen, puffed (with anger) LUC 1417 *Here one being throng'd bears back, and boll'n and red.*

bolster *vb.* Lie on a bolster OTH 3.3.399 *If ever mortal eyes do see them bolster More than their own* (i.e. go to bed together).

bolt *n.*
1 Arrow, esp. the stouter and shorter kind with blunt or thickened head MND 2.1.165 *Yet mark'd I where the bolt of Cupid fell*, CYM 4.2.300, H5 3.7.122; (hence) *make a shaft or a bolt* (lit.) use a slender, sharp arrow or a thick blunt one; (fig.) take a risk one way or another WIV 3.4.24 *I'll make a shaft or a bolt on't.*
2 Fetter MM 5.1.346 *Away with him to prison! Lay bolts enough upon him*, CYM 5.4.10.
~ *vb.*[1] (fig.) Fetter ANT 5.2.6 *Which shackles accidents and bolts up change.*

bolt *vb.*[2] (lit and fig.) Sift WT 4.4.364 *or the fann'd snow that's bolted By th' northern blasts twice o'er.*

bolted *ppl. adj.* Sifted; (hence fig.) refined COR 3.1.320 *ill school'd In bolted language.*

bolter *n.* Piece of cloth used for sifting 1H4 3.3.70 *they have made bolters of them.*

bolting *n.* Sifting TRO 1.1.17 *Ay, the grinding; but you must tarry the bolting.*

bolting-hutch *n.* Bin used in sifting flour from bran; (fig.) 1H4 2.4.450 *Why dost thou converse with that trunk of humours, that bolting-hutch of beastliness.*

bombard, bumbard *n.* Leather jug for liquor (prob. resembling the cannons formerly so called) TMP 2.2.21 *Yond same black cloud, yond huge one, looks like a foul bumbard that would shed his liquor*, 1H4 2.4.451, H8 5.3.81.

bombast, bumbast *n.* Cotton wool used for padding or stuffing 1H4 2.4.327 *How now, my sweet creature of bumbast, how long is't ago, Jack, since* *thou sawest thine own knee?*; (fig.) LLL 5.2.781 *As bombast and as lining to the time.*

bona-roba *n.* [It. 'buona roba' = good material] High-class courtesan 2H4 3.2.23 *we knew where the bona-robas were.*

bona terra, mala gens [L.] A good land, a bad people 2H6 4.7.56.

bone *n.*
1 *young bones* Unborn child or children LR 2.4.163 *Strike her young bones.*
2 *ten bones* Fingers 2H6 1.3.190 *By these ten bones.*
3 (pl.) Simple, unsophisticated musical instrument of bone clappers held between the fingers MND 4.1.29 *Let's have the tongs and the bones.*
4 Bobbin, made of trotter bones, for weaving bone lace TN 2.4.45 *And the free maids that weave their thread with bones.*

bonnet *vb.* Take off the bonnet (in token of respect or in flattery) COR 2.2.27 *who, having been supple and courteous to the people, bonneted.*

bonny *adj.*
1 Stout, stalwart, strapping AYL 2.3.8 *to overcome The bonny priser.*
2 Gladsome ADO 2.3.67 *be you blithe and bonny.*

bonos dies [L.] (wrong form for 'bonus dies') Good day TN 4.2.12.

book *n.*
1 Document 1H4 3.1.221 *By that time will our book, I think, be drawn.*
2 *book of words* Screed, rigmarole ADO 1.1.307 *tire the hearer with a book of words.*
3 Erudition, book-learning, study H8 1.1.122 *A beggar's book Outworths a noble's blood,* TMP 3.1.94.
4 *by the book* According to prescription, with due formality ROM 1.5.110 *You kiss by th' book,* AYL 5.4.90.
5 *without book* From memory, by rote TRO 2.1.20 *learn a prayer without book,* TN 1.3.27.
6 Bible LLL 4.3.246 *O, who can give an oath? Where is a book?,* WIV 1.4.146.
7 Account book LR 3.4.97 *keep...thy pen from tenders' books,* CYM 3.3.26; memorandum-book, note-book or book of records, (often fig.) 1H6 2.4.101 *I'll note you in my book of memory,* COR 5.2.15, HAM 1.5.100.
~ *vb.* Record, list H5 4.7.73 *To book our dead, and then to bury them.*

book-man *n.* Scholar, student LLL 2.1.227 *This civil war of wits were much better used On Navarre and his book-men.*

book-mate *n.* Fellow student LLL 4.1.100 *one that makes sport To the Prince and his book-mates.*

book-oath *n.* Oath taken on the Bible 2H4 2.1.103 *I put thee now to thy book-oath.*

boor *n.* Peasant WT 5.2.160 *Let boors and franklins say it.*

boorish *n.* Illiterate speech AYL 5.1.48 *the society— which in the boorish is company.*

boot *n.*[1]
1 Something given in addition WT 4.4.637 *Though the pennyworth on his side be the worst, yet hold thee, there's some boot,* R3 4.4.65, TRO 5.4.40; (freq. in phr.) *to boot* into the bargain MAC 4.3.37 *And the rich East to boot,* SON 135.2.
2 Advantage, profit ANT 4.1.9 *Make boot of his distraction; it is no boot* it is of no avail or use SHR 5.2.176; *to boot* to our help WT 1.2.80 *Grace to boot!,* R3 5.3.301.
3 Booty, plunder 1H4 2.1.82 *they ride up and down on her, and make her their boots,* H5 1.2.194, 2H6 4.1.13.
~ *vb.*
1 Avail, profit: (intr.) R2 3.4.18 *And what I want it*

boots not to complain; (trans.) TGV 1.1.28 *No, I will not; for it boots thee not.*
2 Enrich with an additional gift, compensate ANT 2.5.71 *And I will boot thee with what gift beside Thy modesty can beg.*

boot *n.*[2] *give (a person) the boots* Fool, make fun of (a person) TGV 1.1.27 *Nay, give me not the boots.*
~ *vb.* Put on one's boots 2H4 5.3.134 *Boot, boot, Master Shallow!*

boot-hose *n.* Over-stocking which covers the leg like a jack-boot SHR 3.2.67 *with a linen stock on one leg, and a kersey boot-hose on the other.*

bootless *adj.* Unavailing, unprofitable, useless VEN 422 *this idle theme, this bootless chat,* OTH 1.3.209, MV 3.3.20.
~ *adv.* Without profit, unavailingly MND 2.1.37 *And bootless make the breathless housewife churn,* TIT 3.1.36.

border *vb.* Keep within bounds LR 4.2.32 *That nature which contemns it origin Cannot be bordered certain in itself.*

bore *n.*
1 Small hole COR 4.6.87 *confin'd Into an auger's bore*; (fig.) CYM 3.2.57 *Love's counsellor should fill the bores of hearing* (i.e. the ears).
2 (fig.) Calibre, importance HAM 4.6.26 *yet are they much too light for the bore of the matter.*
~ *vb.*
1 Perforate, pierce MND 3.2.53 *This whole earth may be bor'd* (i.e. have a hole bored through it), R2 3.2.170.
2 Cheat H8 1.1.128 *He bores me with some trick.*

boresprit See BOWSPRIT.

borrow *n.* BORROWING, LOAN WT 1.2.39 *I'll adventure The borrow of a week.*
~ *vb.*
1 Derive, receive TRO 4.5.133 *any drop thou borrow'dst from thy mother,* SON 153.5.
2 Assume, put on LR 1.4.1 *If but as well I other accents borrow.*

borrowed *ppl. adj.* Not one's own, assumed H5 2.4.79 *The borrowed glories*; (hence) counterfeit, false LUC 1549 *these borrowed tears,* ROM 4.1.104.

bosky *adj.* Shrubby or wooded TMP 4.1.81 *My bosky acres and my unshrubb'd down.*

bosom *n.*
1 *Abraham's bosom* (Luke 26.22) Paradise R3 4.3.38 *The sons of Edward sleep in Abraham's bosom.*
2 Seat of affection, thoughts, feelings ROM 5.1.3 *My bosom's lord sits lightly in his throne* (i.e. love); (hence) repository of secrets LR 4.5.26 *I know you are of her bosom* (i.e. in her confidence), JC 5.1.7, MM 5.1.10; intimate thoughts OTH 3.1.55 *where you shall have time To speak your bosom freely,* MM 4.3.134.
3 Pocket in front part of a bodice, used for the safe keeping of love-letters and love-tokens TGV 1.2.111 *Poor wounded name: my bosom as a bed Shall lodge thee till thy wound be throughly heal'd,* HAM 2.2.113.
4 (of things) Surface JN 4.1.3 *When I strike my foot Upon the bosom of the ground,* ROM 2.2.32; depths, inmost recesses JN 2.1.410 *send destruction Into this city's bosom,* R3 1.1.4, LLL 4.3.30.
~ *vb.*
1 Take to the bosom, embrace; (hence) admit to close companionship LR 5.1.13 *I am doubtful that you have been conjunct And bosom'd with her.*
2 *bosom up* Hide in the bosom, take to heart H8 1.1.112 *Bosom up my counsel, You'll find it wholesome.*

botch *n.* Flaw resulting from unskilful workmanship MAC 3.1.133 *To leave no rubs nor botches in the work.*

~ *vb.* (with *up*) Patch together in a clumsy way HAM 4.5.10 *botch the words up to fit their own thoughts*, TN 4.1.56, H5 2.2.115.

botcher *n.* Mender of old clothes COR 2.1.88 *and your beards deserve not so honourable a grave as to stuff a botcher's cushion*, AWW 4.3.185.

botchy core *n. phr.* Hard mass of tissue at the centre or core of a boil or tumour TRO 2.1.6 *And those biles did run—say so—did not the general run then? Were not that a botchy core?*

both-sides *adj.* Two-faced AWW 4.3.222 *Damnable both-sides rogue!*

bots *n.* Disease of horses caused by the presence of botfly larvae in the stomach SHR 3.2.55 *begnawn with the bots*, 1H4 2.1.10; (in oaths) PER 2.1.118 *bots on't* (cf. 'a plague on it').

bottle *n.* Bundle, truss (of hay) MND 4.1.33 *a bottle of hay*.

bottle-ale *adj.* (pejorative term) Not respectable, low-class TN 2.3.28 *My lady has a white hand, and the Mermidons are no bottle-ale houses* (i.e. low inns); low, dissolute 2H4 2.4.131 *Away, you bottle-ale rascal!*

bottled *ppl. adj.* Shaped like a bottle, swollen, big-bellied R3 1.3.241 *Why strew'st thou sugar on that bottled spider Whose deadly web ensnareth thee about?*, R3 4.4.81.

bottom *n.*
1 Low-lying land, valley AYL 4.3.78 *down in the neighbour bottom*, 1H4 3.1.104; (attrib.) growing in a bottom VEN 236 *Sweet bottom grass and high delightful plain*.
2 Keel or hull; (hence) ship, vessel MV 1.1.42 *My ventures are not in one bottom trusted*, TN 5.1.57, JN 2.1.73.
3 Ball of thread (properly, the core of the skein upon which the weaver wound his wool) SHR 4.3.137 *beat me to death with a bottom of brown thread*.
~ *vb.* Wind (as a skein of thread) TGV 3.2.53 *as you unwind her love from him,...You must provide to bottom it on me.*

bounce *n.* Explosive noise, bang, boom JN 2.1.462 *He speaks plain cannon-fire, and smoke, and bounce*; (used as interj.) 2H4 3.2.284 *'bounce', would 'a say.*

bound *n.*
1 Boundary, limit, barrier (lit. and fig.) TMP 1.2.97 *A confidence sans bound*, JN 3.1.23, HAM 4.7.128.
2 (pl.) Territory, district, precinct, areas ERR 1.1.133 *Roaming clean through the bounds of Asia*, TIM 5.4.61; (occas. sing.) area TMP 2.1.153 *contract, succession, Bourn, bound of land, tilth, vineyard, none*, 1H4 5.4.90.
~ *vb.*[1] Enclose, confine, restrict JN 2.1.431 *Whose veins bound richer blood than Lady Blanch?*, TRO 4.5.129, HAM 2.2.254.

bound *vb.*[2]
1 Recoil, rebound, leap AWW 2.3.297 *Why, these balls bound*, R2 1.2.58.
2 Cause to leap H5 5.2.140 *if I might buffet for my love, or bound my horse for her favours.*

bound *ppl. adj.*[1]
1 Ready, prepared HAM 1.5.6 *Speak, I am bound to hear*, LR 3.7.10, 3H6 2.4.3.
2 Destined, intending to go ERR 4.1.3 *I am bound To Persia*, SON 86.2, HAM 4.6.11.

bound *ppl. adj.*[2]
1 Obliged, under obligation 1H6 2.1.37 *How much in duty I am bound to both.*
2 *dare be bound* Be certain CYM 4.3.18 *I dare be bound he's true.*

bounded *ppl. adj.* Enclosed, confined TRO 1.3.111 *the bounded waters.*

bounden *adj.* Obliged, indebted AYL 1.2.286 *I rest much bounden to you*, JN 3.3.29.

bounding *ppl. adj.* Enclosing, confining LUC 1119 *like a gentle flood, Who being stopp'd, the bounding banks o'erflows.*

bounteous *adj.* Liberal, generous HAM 1.3.93 *you yourself Have of your audience been most free and bounteous*, MM 5.1.443, OTH 1.3.265.

bounteously *adv.* Liberally TN 1.2.52 *I'll pay thee bounteously.*

bountiful *adj.*
1 Liberal, generous PP 20.38 *If that one be prodigal, Bountiful they will him call*, AYL 1.2.35.
2 Ample, of rich contents AWW 2.2.15 *Marry, that's a bountiful answer that fits all questions.*
~ *adv.* In full measure COR 2.3.102 *I will counterfeit the bewitchment of some popular man, and give it bountiful to the desirers.*

bountifully *adv.* Plenteously, abundantly TIM 3.2.52 *Commend me bountifully to his good Lordship.*

bounty *n.*
1 Liberality, munificence ROM 2.2.133 *my bounty is as boundless as the sea*, TGV 1.1.144.
2 An act of generosity, a gift TIM 1.2.123 *to all That of his bounties taste*, ANT 4.6.21.
3 Active benevolence, disposition to do good AWW 4.3.10 *the King, who had even tun'd his bounty to sing happiness to him*, MV 3.4.9.

bourn *n.*[1] Brook, small stream LR 3.6.25 *Come o'er the bourn, Bessy, to me.*

bourn *n.*[2] Boundary, limit WT 1.2.134 *one that fixes No bourn 'twixt his and mine*, ANT 1.1.16, LR 4.6.57.

bout *n.* Turn, round (in fencing) TN 3.4.306 *the gentleman will for his honour's sake have one bout with you*, HAM 4.7.158; (transf. to dancing) ROM 1.5.17 *Ladies that have their toes Unplagu'd with corns will walk a bout with you* (i.e. dance a turn) (Q1 *have about*; Qq, Ff *walke about*).

bow *n.* Yoke for oxen AYL 3.3.79 *As the ox hath his bow.*
~ *vb.* Cause to bend, make crooked SHR 2.1.150 *bow'd her hand to teach her fingering*, H8 2.3.36, PER 4.2.88; (fig.) H5 1.2.14 *wrest, or bow your reading*, COR 5.6.24.

bow-back *n.* Curved or arched back VEN 619 *On his bow-back he hath a battle set.*

bow-boy *n.* Cupid (boy with the bow) ROM 2.4.16 *the very pin of his heart cleft with the blind bow-boy's butt-shaft.*

bow-case *n.* Case in which a bow is kept; (fig.) lean starveling 1H4 2.4.247 *you tailor's yard, you sheath, you bow-case.*

bowels *n.* Offspring MM 3.1.29 *For thine own bowels, which do call thee sire.*

bower *vb.* Embower, enclose ROM 3.2.81 *When thou didst bower the spirit of a fiend In mortal paradise Of such sweet flesh?*

bowget See BUDGET.

bow-hand *n.* Hand in which an archer held the bow (i.e. the left hand) LLL 4.1.133 *Wide a' the bow-hand!* (i.e. too far to the left.)

bowl *vb.*
1 Play at bowls LLL 4.1.138 *challenge her to bowl.*
2 Pelt (with rolling missiles) WIV 3.4.87 *And bowl'd to death with turnips!*

bowsprit *n.* Spar running out from the bows of a vessel to support sails and stays TMP 1.2.200 *on the topmast, The yards and bowsprit* (Ff *boresprit*).

boy *vb.* Play a woman's part as a boy would ANT 5.2.220 *Some squeaking Cleopatra boy my greatness* (i.e. reduce my greatness to the crude imitation of a boy player).

▷ Allusion to the playing of female parts by boys on the stage in Shakespeare's time.

boy-queller *n.* Boy-killer TRO 5.5.45 *Come, come, thou boy-queller, show thy face.*

brabble *n.* Quarrel, brawl TN 5.1.65 *In private brabble did we apprehend him,* TIT 2.1.62.

brabbler *n.* Quarreller, brawler JN 5.2.162 *We hold our time too precious to be spent With such a brabbler.*

brace *n.*
1 Mailed arm-piece PER 2.1.127 *'Keep it, my Pericles, it hath been a shield 'Twixt me and death'— and pointed to this brace.*
2 State of defence, readiness OTH 1.3.24 *stands not in such warlike brace.*
3 Pair 3H6 2.5.129 *Edward and Richard, like a brace of greyhounds,* TMP 5.1.126, ROM 5.3.295.
~ *vb.* Make tense, tighten (the skin of a drum) JN 5.2.169 *a drum is ready brac'd That shall reverberate all as loud as thine.*

brach *n.* Dog (esp. a bitch) that hunts by scent LR 3.6.69 *Hound or spaniel, brach or lym,* 1H4 3.1.235, SHR Ind.1.17.

brag *vb.*
1 Boast of CYM 5.3.93 *He brags his service.*
2 Speak with proper pride of ROM 1.5.67 *Verona brags of him To be a virtuous and well-govern'd youth.*

braggartism *n.* Excessive praise, bragging speech TGV 2.4.164 *Why, Valentine, what braggartism is this?* (F1 *braggadism*).

bragged *ppl. adj.* Boasted COR 1.8.12 *your bragg'd progeny.*

bragless *adj.* Without vain boasting TRO 5.9.5 *bragless let it be, Great Hector was as good a man as he.*

braid *vb.* Upbraid PER 1.1.93 *'Twould braid yourself too near for me to tell it.*

braid *adj.* (?) Deceitful AWW 4.2.73 *Since Frenchmen are so braid, Marry that will, I live and die a maid.*
▷ Pa. pple. of 'braid' (vb.) twist in and out; but could be from Scots 'braid' broad, i.e. loose, licentious.

brain *n.*
1 *bear a brain* Have a good mind or memory ROM 1.3.29 *Nay, I do bear a brain.*
2 *beat with brains* Satirize, mock ADO 5.4.103 *if a man will be beaten with brains, 'a shall wear nothing handsome about him.*
~ *vb.*
1 Bring to an end by dashing out the brains, defeat MM 5.1.396 *That brain'd my purpose.*
2 Understand, grasp with the mind CYM 5.4.146 *or else such stuff as madmen Tongue and brain not* (i.e. utter without understanding).

brained *ppl. adj.* Endowed with brains TMP 3.2.6 *if th' other two be brain'd like us.*

brainish *adj.* Headstrong, passionate HAM 4.1.11 *And in this brainish apprehension kills The unseen good old man.*

brake *n.* Thicket VEN 876 *her fawn hid in some brake;* H8 1.2.75 *the rough brake That virtue must go through.*

branch *n.*
1 (pl.) Hands TIT 2.4.18 *lopp'd and hew'd, and made thy body bare Of her two branches?*
2 Division, section, part ERR 5.1.106 *a branch and parcel of mine oath,* CYM 5.5.383, MV 2.2.63.

branched *adj.* Adorned with a figured pattern suggesting branches or flowers TN 2.5.47 *Calling my officers about me, in my branch'd velvet gown.*

branchless *adj.* (fig.) Destitute ANT 3.4.24 *Better I were not yours Than yours so branchless.*

brand *n.* Cupid's torch SON 153.1 *Cupid laid by his brand,* SON 154.2.

brass *n.* Symbol of hardness, imperishableness MM 5.1.11 *When it deserves, with characters of brass, A forted residence,* H5 4.3.97; insensibility SON 120.4 *Unless my nerves were brass or hammered steel* (i.e. utterly unfeeling); obduracy LLL 5.2.395 *Can any face of brass hold longer out?*

brassed, brazed *adj.* Hardened (as if plated with brass) HAM 3.4.37 *If damned custom have not brass'd it so* (Qq2–5 *brasd*; Ff, Q1 *braz'd*), LR 1.1.11 (F1 *brazed*).

brassy *adj.* Hard as brass MV 4.1.31 *brassy bosoms and rough hearts of flint.*

brave *n.* Bravado, defiant threat or behaviour SHR 3.1.15 *Sirrah, I will not bear these braves of thine,* JN 5.2.159, TIT 2.1.30.
~ *vb.*
1 Challenge, defy (lit. and fig.) JN 4.3.87 *Out, dunghill! dar'st thou brave a nobleman?,* R3 4.3.57, SHR 4.3.110 (with quibble on sense 3).
2 *brave it* Play the brave, show oneself defiantly TIT 4.1.121 *Lucius and I'll go brave it at the court.*
3 Make splendid, adorn R3 5.3.279 *He should have brav'd the east an hour ago,* SHR 4.3.125.
~ *adj.*
1 Finely arrayed; (hence) showy, splendid SHR Ind.1.40 *And brave attendants near him when he wakes,* SON 15.8, PP 12.4.
2 Excellent, capital, fine (general epithet of praise of persons and things) ADO 5.4.128 *I'll devise thee brave punishments for him,* AYL 3.4.41, 1H4 4.1.7.
3 Defiant, insolent COR 4.5.17 *Are you so brave? I'll have you talk'd with anon.*

bravely *adv.*
1 Valiantly, fearlessly MND 5.1.147 *He bravely broach'd his boiling bloody breast,* AWW 3.5.52, H5 3.6.73.
2 Excellently, worthily, finely TMP 3.3.83 *Bravely the figure of this harpy hast thou Perform'd, my Ariel,* SHR 4.3.54.
▷ The various meanings are often blended, e.g. MAC 5.7.26 *The noble thanes do bravely in the war.*

bravery *n.*
1 Defiance, bravado CYM 3.1.18 *The natural bravery of your isle,* CYM 3.1.18.
2 Splendour, finery, fine clothes SHR 4.3.57 *With scarfs and fans, and double change of brav'ry,* MM 1.3.10, AYL 2.7.80.
3 Ostentatious display HAM 5.2.79 *But sure the bravery of his grief did put me Into a tow'ring passion.*

braving *adj.* Defiant, menacing R2 2.3.112 *In braving arms against thy sovereign,* AWW 1.2.3.

brawl *n.*1 French figure dance resembling a cotillon LLL 3.1.9 *Master, will you win your love with a French brawl?*

brawl *n.*2 Quarrel, squabble TIT 4.3.93 *a matter of a brawl betwixt my uncle and one of the Emperal's men.*
~ *vb.*
1 Quarrel, contend; (hence) be noisy or discordant, make a disturbance SHR 4.1.206 *I'll rail and brawl, And with the clamour keep her still awake,* 2H4 1.3.70.
2 (of a stream) Course noisily AYL 2.1.32 *Upon the brook that brawls along this wood.*
3 *brawl down* Beat down with clamour JN 2.1.383 *Till their soul-fearing clamours have brawl'd down The flinty ribs of this contemptuous city.*

brawling *ppl. adj.* Discordant, clamorous MM 4.1.9 *my brawling discontent,* ROM 1.1.176.

brawn *n.*
1 Fleshy part of the body, (esp.) the arm, calf of the

leg or buttock Cym 4.2.311 *The brawns of Hercules*, Tro 1.3.297. ~ *attrib.* Fleshy AWW 2.2.18 *the brawn-buttock*.
2 Boar fattened for the table; (fig.) 2H4 1.1.19 *Harry Monmouth's brawn, the hulk Sir John.*

brazed See BRASSED.

brazen *adj.* Extremely strong, as if made of brass 2H6 3.2.89 *And he that loos'd them forth their brazen caves*, 3H6 2.4.4.

brazier *n.* Worker in brass H8 5.3.41 *he should be a brazier by his face.*

breach *n.*
1 Fissure or gap caused by breaking VEN 1175 *She crops the stalk, and in the breach appears Green-dropping sap*, Jn 4.2.32; (hence) wound Tro 4.5.245 *the very breach whereout Hector's great spirit flew*, VEN 1066.
2 *breach of the sea* Breaking of sea waves on a shore or rock, breakers or surf TN 2.1.22 *you took me from the breach of the sea.*

bread *n.*
1 *God's bread* (used in oaths) Sacramental bread ROM 3.5.176 *God's bread, it makes me mad!*
2 *bread and cheese* Simple fare Wiv 2.1.136 *I love not the humour of bread and cheese.*

bread-chipper *n.* One who cuts the crust off the bread 2H4 2.4.315 *Not to dispraise me, and call me pantler and bread-chipper.*

break *vb.*
1 Cut open (esp. a person's head) Wiv 1.1.122 *Slender, I broke your head*, ERR 1.2.79, ROM 1.3.38.
2 Crack (a joke) SHR 4.5.72 *Like pleasant travellers, to break a jest Upon the company you overtake?*, ADO 2.3.236, Tro 1.3.148.
3 Reveal, disclose MAC 1.7.48 *What beast was't then That made you break this enterprise to me?*, H5 5.2.245; (hence intr. constr. *with* or *to*) make a revelation or disclosure TGV 3.1.59 *I am to break with thee of some affairs*, ADO 1.1.309, H8 5.1.47.
4 Interrupt Wiv 3.4.22 *Break their talk, Mistress Quickly*, ANT 4.14.31, 2H4 4.5.68.
5 Train, make docile *to* SHR 2.1.147 *break her to the lute*, ERR 3.1.77.
6 (intr.) Disband, disperse AWW 4.4.11 *The army breaking, My husband hies him home.*
7 Become bankrupt, fail MV 3.1.115 *Antonio's creditors... swear he cannot choose but break*, ROM 3.2.57.
8 (of darkness) Be dispersed by light R3 5.3.86 *And flaky darkness breaks within the east.*
9 Fall out or quarrel (*with*) TGV 2.5.18 *What, are they broken?*, COR 4.6.49.
10 *break up* Tear open (seals) WT 3.2.131 *Break up the seals, and read*, MV 2.4.10.
~ in phrases
break a comparison Indulge in word play ADO 2.1.146 *he'll but break a comparison...on me* (see next item). **break a lance** Have a tilting match 1H6 3.2.50 *Break a lance, And run a-tilt at Death.* **break parle** Open negotiations TIT 5.3.19 *Rome's emperor, and nephew, break the parle* (sense 4 above is perhaps also possible to give a reading 'interrupt or stop the dispute'). **break (one's) wind** Become broken-winded 1H4 2.2.13 *If I travel but four foot by the squier further afoot, I shall break my wind.* **break a word** Exchange words ERR 3.1.75 *A man may break a word with you, sir.*

break-neck *n.* Ruinous course WT 1.2.363 *To do't, or no, is certain To me a break-neck.*

break-promise *n.* Breaker of promises AYL 4.1.192 *I will think you the most pathetical break-promise.*

break-vow *n.* Breaker of vows Jn 2.1.569 *That daily break-vow, he that wins of all.*

breast *n.* Pair of lungs, voice TN 2.3.20 *the fool has an excellent breast.*

breath *n.*
1 Power of breathing HAM 5.2.271 *The King shall drink to Hamlet's better breath*, ERR 4.1.57.
2 Breathing-space, short interval TRO 2.3.112 *But for your health and your digestion sake, An after-dinner's breath*, R3 4.2.24, Jn 3.4.134.
3 Speech, language MND 3.2.44 *Lay breath so bitter on your bitter foe*, ADO 5.1.263, LR 1.1.60.

breathe *vb.*
1 Speak HAM 2.1.44 *The youth you breathe of*, WIV 4.5.2; (trans.) voice, give utterance to TIM 5.4.7 *and breath'd Our sufferance vainly*, Jn 4.2.36.
2 Exercise briskly AWW 2.3.256 *thou wast created for men to breathe themselves upon thee.*

breathed *ppl. adj.* Exercised, trained LLL 5.2.653 *A man so breathed, that certain he would fight, yea, From morn till night*, AYL 1.2.218, SHR Ind.2.48; (hence) inured TIM 1.1.10 *A most incomparable man, breath'd, as it were, To an untirable and continuate goodness.*

breather *n.*
1 One who breathes, living creature SON 81.12 *When all the breathers of this world are dead*, AYL 3.2.280.
2 Speaker MM 4.4.28 *But it confounds the breather.*

breathing *n.*
1 Utterance ANT 1.3.14 *I am sorry to give breathing to my purpose.*
2 Pause, interval, delay ADO 2.1.363 *Come, you shake the head at so long a breathing*, LUC 1720.
3 Exercise PER 2.3.100 *Come, sir, here's a lady that wants breathing too*, AWW 1.2.17; (attrib.) *breathing time* time for exercise HAM 5.2.174 *it is the breathing time of day with me.*
4 *breathing while* Length of a breath, short time R3 1.3.60 *Cannot be quiet scarce a breathing while.*
~ *ppl. adj.* *breathing lives* Living beings Jn 2.1.419 *Rescue those breathing lives to die in bed.*

breech *n.* Symbol for authority of the husband 3H6 5.5.24 *stol'n the breech from Lancaster*, 2H6 1.3.146.

breeched *adj.* Covered (as with breeches) MAC 2.3.116 *their daggers Unmannerly breech'd with gore.*

breeching scholar *n.* Young scholar or schoolboy still liable to be whipped SHR 3.1.18 *I am no breeching scholar in the schools.*

breed *n.*
1 Race, strain R2 2.1.45 *This happy breed of men*, Cym 4.2.25; family MAC 4.3.108 *and does blaspheme his breed*; kind, species LLL 5.2.266 *Are these the breed of wits so wondered at?*, HAM 3.2.315.
2 Offspring, descendants SON 12.14 *And nothing 'gainst Time's scythe can make defence Save breed*; (fig.) MV 1.3.134 *A breed for barren metal.*
~ *vb.*
1 *bred out* Exhausted, degenerated H5 3.5.29 *Our mettle is bred out*, TIM 1.1.250.
2 Bring up, keep, support LR 4.2.73 *A servant that he bred*, Cym 2.3.114, WT 3.3.48; cherish, nurture SON 112.13 *You are so strongly in my purpose bred.*

breed-bate *n.* Mischief-maker Wiv 1.4.12 *and I warrant you, no tell-tale nor no breed-bate.*
⇨ See BATE *n.*

breeding *n.*
1 Parentage, descent WT 4.4.719 *your names? your ages? of what having? breeding?*, 2H4 5.3.107.
2 Upbringing H8 4.2.134 *Beseeching him to give her virtuous breeding.*

breeze, breese *n.* Gadfly TRO 1.3.48 *The herd hath more annoyance by the breeze Than by the tiger*, ANT 3.10.14.

brewage *n*. Brewed drink Wɪᴠ 3.5.32 *I'll no pullet-sperm in my brewage.*

bribed *ppl. adj*. Stolen, purloined Wɪᴠ 5.5.24 *Divide me like a brib'd buck, each a haunch.*
⇨ Poachers would quickly cut up a deer after stealing it.

briber *n*. Something which wins indulgence Tɪᴍ 3.5.61 *a sufficient briber for his life.*

bride *n*. Bridegroom Rᴏᴍ 3.5.144 *we have wrought So worthy a gentleman to be her bride* (Q2; F1 *Bridegroome*).
~ *vb*. bride it Play the bride Sʜʀ 3.2.251 *Shall sweet Bianca practise how to bride it?*

brief *n*.
1 Letter, dispatch 1H4 4.4.1 *Hie, good Sir Michael, bear this sealed brief.*
2 Short account, summary, abstract MND 5.1.42 *There is a brief how many sports are ripe,* AWW 5.3.137, Aɴᴛ 5.2.138; (fig.) Jɴ 2.1.103 *draw this brief into as huge a volume.*
⇨ Occurs in variants of 'the short and the long' AWW 2.3.29 *that is the brief and the tedious of it.*

briefly *adv*. In a short time, soon, quickly Aɴᴛ 4.4.10 *Go put on thy defences.—Briefly, sir,* Cʏᴍ 5.5.106, Pᴇʀ 3.1.53; a short time ago Cᴏʀ 1.6.16 *'Tis not a mile; briefly we heard their drums.*

briefness *n*. Quickness, expedition Lʀ 2.1.18 *Briefness and fortune, work!,* Pᴇʀ 5.2.15.

brim fulness *n. phr*. Condition of being full to the brim H5 1.2.150 *With ample and brim fulness of his force.*

brinded *adj*. Brindled, marked with streaks of a different hue from the body colour Mᴀᴄ 4.1.1 *Thrice the brinded cat hath mew'd.*

brine *n*. Salt water; (hence) tears Rᴏᴍ 2.3.69 *what a deal of brine Hath wash'd thy sallow cheeks for Rosaline!,* Lᴜᴄ 796.

bring *vb*.
1 Escort or accompany (a person) on his way TGV 1.1.55 *And thither will I bring thee,* H5 2.3.1, JC 3.2.52.
2 Report, inform Aɴᴛ 4.13.10 *And bring me how he takes my death,* Hᴀᴍ 5.2.196.
3 Derive 1H6 2.5.77 *whereas he From John of Gaunt doth bring his pedigree.*
4 Bring forth, bring into the world, give birth to WT 2.1.148 *fourteen they shall not see To bring false generations,* Sᴏɴ 32.11.
5 (with *be with*) Gain the upper hand Tʀᴏ 1.2.279 *I will be with you, niece, by and by—To bring, uncle?* (with quibble).
~ in combination
bring about Cause to make a complete revolution, complete (a cycle of time) R2 1.3.220 *For ere the six years that he hath to spend Can change their moons and bring their times about,* 3H6 2.5.27.
bring forth 1 Express, put forth Tʀᴏ 1.3.242 *If that the prais'd himself bring the praise forth.* 2 Set in public view Aɴᴛ 5.2.219 *Antony Shall be brought drunken forth,* AWW 5.3.151. **bring in** Place or establish in one's position Oᴛʜ 3.1.50 *And needs no other suitor but his likings...To bring you in again.* **bring off** Deliver, rescue, acquit Tʀᴏ 5.6.25 *I'll be ta'en too, Or bring him off,* H8 3.2.220. **bring on** Induce Hᴀᴍ 3.1.9 *When we would bring him on to some confession Of his true state,* Aɴᴛ 3.2.44. **bring out** Produce Tɪᴍ 4.3.188 *Let it no more bring out ingrateful man!* WT 4.3.121. **bring up** Move, dispose, raise to the pitch of WT 4.4.533 *And bring him up to liking.*

bringings-forth *n*. (*pl*.) Achievements MM 3.2.145 *Let him be but testimonied in his own bringings-forth.*

brinish *adj*. Having the taste of salt Lᴜᴄ 1213 *And wip'd the brinish pearl from her bright eyes* (i.e. salt tear).

brisk *adj*.
1 Quick and active Rᴏᴍ 1.5.15 *Cheerly, boys, be brisk a while*; (of the times) fast TN 2.4.6 *These most brisk and giddy-paced times.*
2 Smartly dressed, spruce 1H4 1.3.54 *for he made me mad To see him shine so brisk and smell so sweet.*
3 Agreeably acid 2H4 5.3.46 *A cup of wine that's brisk and fine.*

brisky *adj*. Brisk, lively MND 3.1.95 *Most brisky juvenal, and eke most lovely Jew.*

broach *vb*.
1 Pierce, impale, stick (something) on a spit or pointed weapon H5 5.Ch.32 *Bringing rebellion broached on his sword,* Tɪᴛ 4.2.85.
2 Tap (a cask); (fig.) MND 5.1.147 *he bravely broach'd his boiling bloody breast,* Tɪᴍ 2.2.177, 1H6 3.4.40.
3 Begin, introduce in conversation or discussion Sʜʀ 1.2.84 *I will continue that I broach'd in jest,* H8 2.4.150, Aɴᴛ 1.2.173.

broad *adj*.
1 Free, unrestrained Hᴀᴍ 3.4.2 *his pranks have been too broad to bear with,* Mᴀᴄ 3.6.21.
2 Widely diffused, spread abroad Mᴀᴄ 3.4.22 *As broad and general as the casing air.*
3 Arrogant, contemptuous Tʀᴏ 1.3.190 *in full as proud a place As broad Achilles.*
4 Obvious, plain, clear Rᴏᴍ 2.4.87 *which, added to the goose, proves thee far and wide a broad goose* (perh. with a pun on the sense 'indecent').
~ *adv*. Freely, unrestrainedly Tɪᴍ 3.4.63 *Who can speak broader than he*; broad awake wide awake Tɪᴛ 2.2.17 *I have been broad awake two hours and more*; broad blown in full bloom Hᴀᴍ 3.3.81 *With all his crimes broad blown, as flush as May*; broad-spreading wide-spreading R2 3.4.50 *The weeds which his broad-spreading leaves did shelter.*

broad-fronted *adj*. With broad forehead Aɴᴛ 1.5.29 *Broad-fronted Caesar.*

brock *n*. (lit.) Badger; (term of contempt applied to persons) stinking fellow, skunk TN 2.5.103 *Marry, hang thee, brock!*

brogue *n*. Roughly made shoe, ankle-high, of untanned hide, worn by poor persons in Ireland and Scotland and by soldiers Cʏᴍ 4.2.214 *put My clouted brogues from off my feet.*

broil *n*. Confused tumult, battle Mᴀᴄ 1.2.6 *Say to the King the knowledge of the broil As thou didst leave it.*
~ *vb*. Suffer great heat H8 4.1.56 *Where have you been broiling?*; become heated with excitement Tʀᴏ 1.3.378 *the great Myrmidon, Who broils in loud applause.*

broke *vb*. Bargain, traffic, trade as a procurer AWW 3.5.71 *And brokes with all that can in such a suit Corrupt the tender honour of a maid.*

broken *ppl. adj*.
1 Fragmentary, incomplete H5 5.2.246 *Katherine, break thy mind to me in broken English,* AWW 2.3.60; broken meats remains of food, as eaten by servants Lʀ 2.2.15 *A knave, a rascal, an eater of broken meats.*
2 Interrupted H8 1.4.61 *You have now a broken banquet,* WT 5.2.9.
3 *broken music* Music arranged for instruments of more than one kind, 'part' music AYL 1.2.141 *to see this broken music in his sides?* (with a pun on the sense of the noisy breaking of ribs), H5 5.2.243, Tʀᴏ 3.1.49.
4 Ruined, bankrupt Cʏᴍ 5.4.19 *Who of their broken*

debtors take a third, A sixt, a tenth, AYL 2.1.57, R2 2.1.257.

5 *broken bosoms* Broken hearts LC 254.

broker *n.* Agent or intermediary (freq. with implied censure), (esp.) go-between in love affairs JN 2.1.568 *that sly devil, That broker that still breaks the pate of faith,* 3H6 4.1.63; (fig.) HAM 1.3.127 *Do not believe his vows, for they are brokers,* LC 173.

broker-between *n.* Go-between TRO 3.2.203 *Let all constant men be Troiluses, all false women Cressids, and all brokers-between Pandars!*

broking *adj.* Belonging to the trade of broking or lending R2 2.1.293 *Redeem from broking pawn the blemish'd crown.*

brooch *n.* Any jewel ornament, (esp.) one worn round the neck, or in the hat; (fig.) HAM 4.7.93 *He is the brooch indeed And gem of all the nation,* R2 5.5.66.

~ *vb.* Adorn (as with a jewel) ANT 4.15.25 *Not th' imperious show Of the full-fortun'd Caesar ever shall Be brooch'd with me.*

brood *n. sits on brood* Sits brooding like a hen HAM 3.1.165 *There's something in his soul O'er which his melancholy sits on brood.*

brooded *adj.* Having a brood to watch over, brooding JN 3.3.52 *Then, in despite of brooded watchful day, I would into thy bosom pour my thoughts.*

▷ Many edd. support Pope's emendation 'broadeyed', i.e. all-seeing.

brook *n. flying at the brook* Hawking with a goshawk at the river for waterfowl 2H6 2.1.1 *Believe me, lords, for flying at the brook, I saw not better sport these seven years' day.*

brook *vb.* Tolerate, endure H5 5.Ch.44 *Then brook abridgement.*

▷ A pun; Brooke's 'Abridgement' was the most famous of legal text books before the days of Coke.

broom-grove *n.* Wooded area containing broom, a shrub bearing yellow flowers TMP 4.1.66 *and thy broom-groves, Whose shadow the dismissed bachelor loves.*

broom-staff *n.* Broom-handle H8 5.3.54 *at length they came to th' broomstaff to me* (i.e. to close quarters).

brother *n.*

1 Brother-in-law ERR 2.2.152 *Fie, brother, how the world is chang'd with you.*

2 Step-brother R3 5.3.95 *thy brother, tender George.*

brother-love *n.* Brotherly affection H8 5.2.206 *With a true heart And brother-love I do it.*

brow *n.*

1 (fig.) Aspect, appearance 1H4 4.3.83 *by this face, This seeming brow of justice,* MAC 4.3.23, HAM 1.2.4.

2 (ellipsis for) Brow-antler LLL 4.1.117 *You still wrangle with her, Boyet, and she strikes at the brow* (i.e. takes good aim, the brow-antler being the correct aim for an archer).

Brownist *n.* Adherent of the Congregationalist scheme of Church government, founded in Elizabeth's reign by the Puritan Robert Browne and adopted in a modified form by the Independents TN 3.2.31 *I had as lief be a Brownist as a politician.*

bruise *vb.* Crush or mangle with a heavy blow MM 2.1.6 *fall, and bruise to death.*

bruit *n.* Rumour, report 3H6 4.7.64 *The bruit thereof will bring you many friends,* TIM 5.1.193.

~ *vb.*

1 Noise abroad, report, rumour 1H6 2.3.68 *I find thou art no less than fame hath bruited.*

2 Announce, herald with noise MAC 5.7.22 *By this great clatter, one of greatest note Seems bruited.*

3 *bruit again* Echo HAM 1.2.127 *the King's rouse the heaven shall bruit again.*

brush *n.* Hostile encounter TRO 5.3.34 *And tempt not*

yet the brushes of the war; (fig.) TIM 4.3.264 *have with one winter's brush Fell from their boughs.*

bubble *n.* (fig.) Empty, unsubstantial thing AYL 2.7.152 *Seeking the bubble reputation Even in the cannon's mouth,* AWW 3.6.5.

bubukle, bubuncle *n.* (confusion by Fluellen of 'bubo', inflamed swelling, and carbuncle) A type of skin eruption H5 3.6.102 *His face is all bubukles, and whelks, and knobs.*

buck *n.* Lye or suds in which clothes are soaked when being washed; (hence) pile of soiled clothes 2H6 4.2.48 *she washes bucks here at home.*

buck-basket *n.* Basket for dirty clothes WIV 3.5.143 *This 'tis to be married! This 'tis to have linen and buck-baskets!*

bucking *n.* Washing WIV 3.3.131 *and throw foul linen upon him, as if it were going to bucking.*

bucket *n.* Beam of a brewer's crane used in hoisting 2H4 3.2.264 *come off and on swifter than he that gibbets on a brewer's bucket.*

buckle *vb.*

1 *buckle in* Enclose, encompass AYL 3.2.132 *That the stretching of a span Buckles in his sum of age.*

2 Contend, join in close combat *with* 1H6 4.4.5 *In single combat thou shalt buckle with me,* 1H6 4.4.5.

3 Bend (under pressure) 2H4 1.1.141 *whose fever-weak'ned joints, Like strengthless hinges, buckle under life.*

buckler *n.* Shield ADO 5.2.17 *I give thee the bucklers* (i.e. I acknowledge that you are the better man or the victor).

~ *vb.*

1 Shield, defend SHR 3.2.239 *I'll buckler thee against a million,* 2H6 3.2.216, 3H6 3.3.99.

2 Catch or ward off (blows) 3H6 1.4.50 *buckler with thee blows, twice two for one.*

Bucklersbury *n.* Street of London off Cheapside where apothecaries sold herbs WIV 3.3.72 *smell like Bucklersbury in simple time.*

buckram, buckrom *n.* Strong, coarse linen cloth, stiffened with gum or paste 1H4 2.4.212 *These nine in buckrom that I told thee of.*

~ *attrib.* (fig.) Stiff, stuck-up 2H6 4.7.25 *thou buckram lord!*

buck-washing *n.* Process of washing dirty linen by boiling it in an alkaline lye (see BUCK) and afterwards beating and rinsing it in clear water WIV 3.3.155 *You were best meddle with buck-washing.*

bud *n.* Shoot of a plant used for ingrafting under the bark of a different stock WT 4.4.95 *And make conceive a bark of baser kind By bud of nobler race;* (fig.) JN 3.4.82 *now will canker-sorrow eat my bud* (i.e. Arthur).

~ *vb.* (fig.) Develop H8 1.1.94 *The sudden breach ...is budded out.*

budding *ppl. adj.* (fig.) Developing SHR 4.5.37 *Young, budding virgin.*

budge *vb.* Flinch, retreat COR 1.6.44 *The mouse ne'er shunn'd the cat as they did budge From rascals,* 1H4 2.4.354, JC 4.3.44.

▷ Various spellings in F: *boudge, bouge, budge.*

budger *n.* One who flinches COR 1.8.5 *Let the first budger die the other's slave.*

budget *n.* Wallet or bag WT 4.3.20 *And bear the sow-skin budget* (F1 *bowget*).

buff *n.* Stout leather made of ox-hide dressed with oil, used for the attire of soldiers, and (in S.) sergeants and bum-bailiffs ERR 4.2.36 *A wolf, nay worse, a fellow all in buff;* (attrib.) 1H4 1.2.42 *is not a buff jerkin a most sweet robe of durance?*

buffet *vb.* (intr.) Fight, contend H5 5.2.140 *if I might buffet for my love.*

bug, bugbear *n.* Hobgoblin, bogey, imaginary object of terror SHR 1.2.210 *Tush, tush, fear boys with* *bugs* (i.e. frighten children with bogeymen), HAM 5.2.22; TRO 4.2.33 *A bugbear take him!*; (fig.) 3H6 5.2.2 *Warwick was a bug that fear'd us all*, CYM 5.3.51.

bugle *n*. (attrib.) Tube-shaped glass bead, commonly black, used to decorate wearing apparel; WT 4.4.222 *Bugle-bracelet, necklace amber, Perfume for a lady's chamber*, AYL 3.5.47.

building *n*.
1 Fixed place PER 2.1.156 *This jewel holds his building on my arm* (i.e.keeps its place).
2 (fig.) Edifice, structure TRO 4.2.103 *the strong base and building of my love*, COR 2.1.200.
3 Build, construction (of a ship) SON 80.12 *I am a worthless boat, He of tall building*.

bulk *n*.¹
1 Trunk, body (of a person) R3 1.4.40 *But smother'd it within my panting bulk*, HAM 2.1.92, LUC 467.
2 Body of great proportions, huge frame TRO 4.4.128 *Though the great bulk Achilles be thy guard*.
3 Hull of a ship TN 5.1.55 *A baubling vessel was he captain of, For shallow draught and bulk unprizable*, TRO 1.3.37.

bulk *n*.² Framework projecting from the front of a shop, forming a shop-stall OTH 5.1.1 *Here, stand behind this bulk, straight will he come*, COR 2.1.210.

Bull *n*. Taurus, one of the signs of the zodiac TIT 4.3.72 *The Bull, being gall'd, gave Aries such a knock*.

bull-beef *n*. Flesh of bulls 1H6 1.2.9 *They want their porridge and their fat bull-beeves*.

bully *n*. (term of endearment and familiarity) Fine fellow, good friend H5 4.1.48 *I love the lovely bully*, WIV 2.1.217; (often prefixed as a sort of title to a proper name or designation) gallant MND 4.2.19 *O sweet bully Bottom*, WIV 2.3.18, TMP 5.1.258.

bully-rook *n*. (See BULLY) Fine fellow, boon companion WIV 1.3.2 *What says my bully-rook?*

bully-stale See STALE n².

bum-baily *n*. Sheriff's officer who made arrests for debt TN 3.4.177 *scout me for him at the corner of the orchard like a bum-baily*.
◇ Some mod. edd. have 'bum-bailiff', but *bum-baily* is the regular form found in Midland dialects.

bumbard See BOMBARD.

bumbast See BOMBAST.

bunch-backed *adj*. Hump-backed R3 1.3.245 *help thee curse this poisonous bunch-back'd toad*, R3 4.4.81 (later Qq *hunch-back'd*).

bung *n*. Pickpocket 2H4 2.4.128 *Away, you cutpurse rascal! you filthy bung, away!*

buoy *vb*. Rise *up* LR 3.7.60 *The sea...would have buoy'd up*.

burbolt See BIRDBOLT.

burden, burthen *n*.
1 Freight, cargo, carrying capacity of a ship AWW 2.3.205 *a vessel of too great a burden*, TRO 1.3.71.
2 Birth ERR 5.1.344 *That bore thee at a burden two fair sons* (i.e. at one birth), WT 4.4.264, JN 3.1.90.
3 Bass, undersong AYL 3.2.247 *I would sing my song without a burden*; (fig.) SHR 1.2.68 *As wealth is burden of my wooing dance*; refrain TMP 1.2.380 *And, sweet sprites, the burden bear*, WT 4.4.194.
◇ Sometimes, a play between the sense of 'load' and sense 2 or 3, e.g. TGV 1.2.82 *It is too heavy for so light a tune.—Heavy? belike it hath some burden then?*, R3 4.4.168.
4 *burdens of the dead* False hair, wigs made from the hair of the dead TIM 4.3.146 *thatch your poor thin roofs With burdens of the dead*.
◇ *burthen* the more common spelling in Ff and Qq.

burdened, burthened *adj*. Burdensome R3 4.4.111 *thy proud neck bears half my burden'd yoke*.

burdenous, burthenous *adj*. Oppressive R2 2.1.260 *His burdenous taxations*.

burden-wise, burthen-wise *adv*. As a burden or undersong LUC 1133 *For burden-wise I'll hum on Tarquin still*.

burgomaster *n*. Magistrate corresponding to an alderman 1H4 2.1.76 *burgomasters and great oney'rs*.

burgonet *n*. Helmet with a vizor so fitted to the gorget or neck-piece that the head could be turned without exposing the neck 2H6 5.1.200 *I'll write upon thy burgonet*; (fig.) ANT 1.5.24 *The demi-Atlas of this earth, the arm and burgonet of men* (F1 *burganet*).

burial *n*. Burying-place, grave MV 1.1.29 *Vailing her high top lower than her ribs To kiss her burial*.

burly-boned *adj*. Bulky 2H6 4.10.57 *the burly-bon'd clown*.

burn *vb*.
1 *burn daylight* Burn candles in daytime; (hence) waste daylight or time WIV 2.1.54 *We burn daylight*, ROM 1.4.43; (similarly) ANT 4.2.41 *burn this night with torches*.
2 Make (drink) hot TN 2.3.190 *burn some sack*.
3 (intr. and refl.) Be on fire, wax hot, glow, consume oneself with love, etc. TGV 2.5.53 *though he burn himself in love*, JN 4.2.103, LR 4.6.40.

burning zone See ZONE.

burnt *ppl. adj*. Heated, warmed WIV 2.1.215 *burnt sack*.

burthen See BURDEN.

bury *vb*. (fig.) Consign to oblivion, put out of sight, conceal JC 4.3.159 *In this [bowl of wine] I bury all unkindness*, 3H6 4.1.55.

bush *n*. Bush of ivy formerly hung out as a vintner's sign AYL Epil.4 *good wine needs no bush*.

busil'est *adv*. Most busily TMP 3.1.15 *these sweet thoughts do even refresh my labours, Most busil'est when I do it*.
◇ Kermode; F *busie lest*; Singer *busiest*; Theobald *busyless*.

buskined *ppl. adj*. Wearing buskins or half-boots MND 2.1.71 *Your buskin'd mistress*.

busky *adj*. Bosky, bushy 1H4 5.1.2 *yon busky hill*.

buss *n*. Kiss 2H4 2.4.268 *Thou dost give me flattering busses*.
~ *vb*. Kiss JN 3.4.35 *buss thee as thy wife*; (fig.) TRO 4.5.220 *Yon towers, whose wanton tops do buss the clouds*, COR 3.2.75.

busyless See BUSIL'EST.

but *adv*.
1 Only ERR 4.1.33 *For he is bound to sea, and stays but for it*, OTH 4.1.87, TMP 1.2.169; (strengthened by *only*) 2H4 1.1.192, MAC 5.9.6, 3H6 4.2.25.
2 *but now* Just now, only this moment MV 3.2.169 *and even now, but now, now*, VEN 497.
~ *conj*.
1 (after negative sentences containing a comparison) Than MND 1.2.81 *they would have no more discretion but to hang us*, TN 1.4.13.
2 If...not, unless, except CYM 5.5.41 *And but she spoke it dying, I would not Believe her lips in opening it*, MND 3.2.150, TGV 1.1.85.
3 (esp. after verbs of thinking, doubting, etc.) That...not 1H4 4.3.38 *And God defend but still I should stand so*, TMP 3.1.44, OTH 3.3.225.
4 Anything else than, otherwise than TMP 1.2.119 *I should sin To think but nobly of my grandmother*, MND 3.2.56.
5 (after negatived vb. of denying) That ADO 1.3.32 *it must not be denied but I am a plain-dealing villain*, AWW 5.3.167.

6 If, provided that PER 3.1.45 *But sea-room, and the brine and cloudy billow kiss the moon, I care not.*
7 Only with the result that, if only that, so that SHR 2.1.15 *I'll plead for you myself, but you shall have him,* CYM 3.6.69.
8 (used as a negative rel.) Who, which, or that...not 1H6 1.2.5 *What towns of any moment but we have?*, R3 1.3.185.

butcher sire *n.* Murderous father VEN 766 *Or butcher sire that reaves his son of life.*

butcherly *adj.* Murderous 3H6 2.5.89 *What stratagems! how fell! how butcherly!*

butt *n.*¹ Large cask for wine or ale (567 litres of wine or 486 litres of ale) TMP 2.2.121 I escap'd upon a butt of sack; (fig.) TRO 5.1.28 *you ruinous butt.*
▷ In TMP 1.2.146 *A rotten carcass of a butt, not rigg'd, Nor tackle, sail, nor mast* the meaning is doubtful but prob. a contemptuous term with sense of 'a tub'.

butt *n.*² Target, mark for archery practice; (properly) the mound on which the target was placed 3H6 1.4.29 *I am your butt, and I abide your shot,* H5 1.2.186; (hence) goal, object OTH 5.2.267 *Here is my journey's end, here is my butt.*

butt *n.*³ Butting of a horned animal SHR 5.2.41 *an hasty-witted body Would say your head and butt were head and horn.*
▷ Here prob. refers to the part of the head which gives the butt.

butt-end *n.* Thick and heavy end, remnant; (fig.) the concluding part R3 2.2.110 *the butt-end of a mother's blessing.*

butterfly *n.* Vain person in gaudy attire (e.g. one who flutters about a court) LR 5.3.13 *and laugh At gilded butterflies.*

butter-woman *n.* Dairy-woman AYL 3.2.98 *It is the right butter-women's rank to market,* AWW 4.1.41.

buttery *n.* Store-room (orig.) for liquor (kept in butts); (later) for provisions generally SHR Ind.1.102 *Go, sirrah, take them to the buttery, And give them friendly welcome every one.*

buttery-bar *n.* Ledge on the top of the buttery hatch or half-door, to rest tankards on TN 1.3.70 *bring your hand to th' butt'ry-bar.*

button *n.*
1 *'tis in his buttons* He is sure to succeed, he has it in him WIV 3.2.70 *he will carry't—'tis in his buttons*; *butcher of a silk button.* Expert fencer who could strike any designated button on his opponent's attire ROM 2.4.23 *the very butcher of a silk button, a duellist.*
2 Knob on the top of a cap HAM 2.2.229 *on Fortune's cap we are not the very button.*
3 Bud HAM 1.3.40 *The canker galls the infants of the spring Too oft before their buttons be disclos'd.*

button-hole *n.* *take (a person) a button-hole lower* Humiliate, take down a peg LLL 5.2.700 *Master, let me take you a button-hole lower.*

butt-shaft *n.* Unbarbed arrow used in shooting at the butts LLL 1.2.176 *Cupid's butt-shaft is too hard for Hercules' club* (i.e. Cupid's dart), ROM 2.4.16.

buxom *adj.* Brisk, lively H5 3.6.26 *a soldier firm and sound of heart, And of buxom valour,* PER 1.Gower.23.

buy *vb.*
1 *buy and sell* Barter, traffic in or with (in a bad

sense) H8 1.1.192 *the Cardinal Does buy and sell his honour as he pleases*; (hence) *bought and sold* betrayed ERR 3.1.72 *It would make a man mad as a buck to be so bought and sold,* R3 5.3.305, JN 5.4.10.
2 Pay for, atone for 3H6 5.1.68 *Thou and thy brother both shall buy this treason.*
3 *buy out* Ransom, redeem ERR 1.2.5 *And not being able to buy out his life*; remove, get rid of by a money payment 1H4 4.2.33 *to fill up the rooms of them as have bought out their services* (i.e. paid money to be released from military service), JN 3.1.164, HAM 3.3.60.

buzz *n.* Baseless rumour LR 1.4.325 *Each buzz, each fancy, each complaint, dislike, He may enguard his dotage with their pow'rs.*
~ *vb.* Spread a rumour, whisper, suggest mischief 3H6 5.6.86 *I will buzz abroad such prophecies.*
~ *interj.* Exclamation of impatience or contempt when a person states news already known HAM 2.2.393 *The actors are come hither, my lord.—Buzz, buzz!*

buzzard *n.*¹ Inferior kind of hawk, useless for falconry R3 1.1.133 *kites and buzzards prey at liberty.*
▷ In SHR 2.1.207 *O slow-wing'd turtle, shall a buzzard take thee?* a fig. extension (=fool) of this sense prob. applies, with a switch to buzzard *n.*² in SHR 2.1.208.

buzzard *n.*² Buzzing insect SHR 2.1.208 *Ay, for a turtle, as he takes a buzzard.*

buzzer *n.* Whispering informer HAM 4.5.90 *wants not buzzers to infect his ear With pestilent speeches of his father's death.*

buzzing *n.* Rumour H8 2.1.148 *buzzing of a separation.*

by *adv.* Aside, out of the way JN 4.3.94 *Stand by, or I shall gall you, Faulconbridge.*
~ *prep.*
1 About, concerning ADO 5.1.303 *virtuous In any thing that I do know by her,* 2H6 2.1.16, OTH 1.3.17.
2 By reason of 3H6 4.4.12 *Fell Warwick's brother, and by that our foe.*
3 According to, in the opinion of ANT 3.3.40 *Why, methinks, by him, This creature's no such thing.*
~ in combination
by-dependance Additional, dependent, secondary circumstances CYM 5.5.390 *And all the other by-dependances, From chance to chance.* **by-drinking** Drinking at odd times 1H4 3.3.73 *You owe money here besides, Sir John, for your diet and by-drinkings.* **bi-fold, by-fold** Double, ambiguous TRO 5.2.144 *Bi-fold authority, where reason can revolt Without perdition.* **by-gone day** Yesterday WT 1.2.32 *this satisfaction The by-gone day proclaim'd.* **by-peeping** Looking aside, peeping sidelong CYM 1.6.108 *then by-peeping in an eye Base and illustrious as the smoky light.* **by-room** Side or private room 1H4 2.4.29 *do thou stand in some by-room, while I question my puny drawer.* **by-word** Object of derision 3H6 1.1.42 *whose cowardice Hath made us by-words to our enemies.*

by'r lady *interj.* By our Lady H8 1.3.46 *and, by'r lady, Held current music too,* ADO 3.3.77, ROM 1.5.33.
▷ Other variants: *berlady, ber Lady, birdladie, byrlady, by'r Lady.*

C

cabbage *n.* Cabbage-head, fool WIV 1.1.121 *Good worts? good cabbage.*
cabilero See CAVALEIRO.

cabin *n.*
1 Hut, temporary shelter TN 1.5.268 *Make me a willow cabin at your gate,* PP 14.3.

2 Den of a wild beast VEN 637 *the boar...his loath-some cabin*; cave, (hence) eye-socket VEN 1038 *eyes are fled Into the deep-dark cabins of her head.*

~ *vb.*

1 Lodge TIT 4.2.179 *suck the goat, And cabin in a cave.*

2 Shut up within narrow bounds MAC 3.4.23 *I am cabin'd, cribb'd, confin'd.*

cabinet *n.*

1 Tent, hut, small place of habitation LUC 442 *They must'ring to the quiet cabinet Where their dear governess and lady lies* (i.e. rallying to the heart).

2 Bird's nest VEN 854 *the gentle lark, weary of rest, From his moist cabinet mounts up on high.*

cable *n.* Scope OTH 1.2.17 *The law...Will give him cable.*

cacodemon *n.* Evil spirit R3 1.3.143 *Thou caco-demon, there thy kingdom is.*

caddis *n.* (short for) Caddis ribbon, worsted tape or binding used for garters by poor people WT 4.4.207 *inkles, caddises, cambrics, lawns.*

caddis-garter *n.* Garter made of caddis ribbon 1H4 2.4.70 *Wilt thou rob this leathern-jerkin...puke-stocking, caddis-garter.*

⇨ Nares: 'Garters were then worn in sight, and therefore to wear a coarse, cheap sort, was reproachful'.

cade *n.* Barrel of 500 herrings 2H6 4.2.34 *stealing a cade of herrings.*

cadent *adj.* Falling LR 1.4.285 *With cadent tears fret channels in her cheeks.*

caduceus *n.* Wand having two serpents twined round it, which was carried by Hermes (Mercury), the messenger of the gods TRO 2.3.12 *lose all the serpentine craft of thy caduceus.*

Caesar *n.* Absolute ruler, emperor 3H6 3.1.18 *No bending knee will call thee Caesar now.*

cage *n.* Prison for petty criminals, lock-up 2H6 4.2.52 *for his father had never a house but the cage.*

caged *ppl. adj.* Closed like a cage LC 249 *she would the caged cloister fly.*

cagion, 'casion *n.* (aphetic form of) Occasion LR 4.6.235 *Chill not let go, zir, without vurther cagion.*

Cain-coloured *adj.* Reddish-yellow, the traditional colour of Cain's beard in tapestries WIV 1.4.23 *with a little yellow beard, a Cain-colour'd beard.*

⇨ Ff, Q3; Qq1-2 *kane*; some mod. edd. *cane-coloured.*

caitiff *n.*

1 (expressing pity) Wretched, miserable person, one in a piteous case OTH 4.1.108 *Alas, poor caitiff*, R3 4.4.101.

2 (expressing contempt) Base, mean, despicable wretch MM 2.1.174 *O thou caitiff! O thou varlet!*, LR 3.2.55, TIM 4.3.235.

~ *adj.* Vile, base, despicable R2.1.2.53 *A caitiff recreant to my cousin* (F1 *caitive*), MM 5.1.88.

cake *n.*

1 *my cake is dough* My project has failed SHR 5.1.140.

2 *cake of roses* See ROSE.

calculate *vb.* Ascertain beforehand the time of an event by astrology, forecast 2H6 4.1.34 *A cunning man did calculate my birth.*

calendar *n.*

1 Guide, directory HAM 5.2.109 *he is the card or calendar of gentry.*

2 Record AWW 1.3.4 *the calendar of my past endeavours.*

calf *n.*

1 Stupid fellow, dolt HAM 3.2.106 *It was a brute part of him to kill so capital a calf there.*

2 (term of endearment) WT 1.2.127 *Art thou my calf?*

caliver *n.* Light kind of musket introduced during 16C, which seems to have been fired without a rest 1H4 4.2.19 *such as fear the report of a caliver worse than a struck fowl*, 2H4 3.2.270.

call *n.* Decoy, decoy-bird JN 3.4.174 *a dozen French... would be as a call To train ten thousand English to their side.*

~ *vb.* Visit (a person) at his house, call upon MM 4.4.16 *I'll call you at your house*, TN 3.2.52.

~ in combination

call back

1 Summon to return TGV 1.2.51 *to call her back again.* 2 Revoke H8 2.4.235 *to call back her appeal.* 3 Recall to memory SON 3.10 *and she in thee Calls back the lovely April of her prime.* **call in** With-draw from action 2H4 4.3.25 *Call in the powers.* **call on, upon** 1 Make claim for payment TIM 2.2.22 *My master is awak'd by great occasion To call upon his own*, 1H4 5.1.129. 2 Call (somebody) to account ANT 1.4.28 *Full surfeits and the dryness of his bones Call on him for't.* **call up** Rouse in any way COR 2.3.194 *As cause had call'd you up.*

callat, callet, callot *n.* Whore, trull OTH 4.2.121 *A beggar in his drink Could not have laid such terms upon his callet*, 2H6 1.3.83, 3H6 2.2.145.

calling *n.* Name, appellation AYL 1.2.233 *I am more proud to be Sir Rowland's son...and would not change that calling.*

calm *n.* (confused with 'qualm') Sensation of nausea 2H4 2.4.37 *and they be once in a calm, they are sick.*

~ *vb.* Becalm (a ship) 2H6 4.9.33 *Like to a ship that, having scap'd a tempest, Is straightway calm'd*, OTH 1.1.30.

calves-guts *n.* Fiddle-strings CYM 2.3.29 *which horsehairs and calves'-guts,...can never amend.*

Cambyses *n. in King Cambyses' vein* In a style of ludicrous and old-fashioned ranting, like that of Thomas Preston's 'Cambyses', an early Eliz. tra-gedy 1H4 2.4.387 *for I must speak in passion, and I will do it in King Cambyses' vein.*

camel *n.* Awkward, hulking fellow TRO 1.2.249 *Achilles! a drayman, a porter, a very camel.*

camlet *n.* Rough cloth, in 16 and 17C made of the hair of the Angora goat H8 5.3.89 *You i' th' camlet* (F1 *chamblet*).

camp *vb.* Provide lodging for ANT 4.8.33 *Had our great palace the capacity To camp this host.*

can *vb.[1]*

1 (trans.) Know, have skill in PHT 14 *Let the priest in surplice white, That defunctive music can*, TMP 4.1.27, CYM 4.2.392.

2 (intr.) Be skilled HAM 4.7.84 *they can well on horseback.*

can *vb.[2]* (altered form of 'gan', past tense of 'gin', used for 'did') Began to LLL 4.3.104 *the wind, All unseen, can passage find*, PER 3.Gower.36.

canakin, cannakin *n.* Small can or drinking-vessel OTH 2.3.69 *And let me the canakin clink, clink.*

canary *n.*

1 Light, sweet wine from Canary Islands WIV 3.2.88 *drink canary with him*, TN 1.3.80, 2H4 2.4.26.

2 Lively, energetic, Spanish dance AWW 2.1.74 *and make you dance canary With spritely fire and motion.*

~ *vb.* Dance a canary LLL 3.1.12 *canary to it with your feet.*

cancel *vb. cancel off* Strike off, annul PER 1.1.113 *We might proceed to cancel off your days* (Ff; Qq *counsel of*).

Cancer *n.* Sign of the zodiac, associated with heat, which the sun (Hyperion) enters at the summer solstice, June 21 TRO 2.3.196 *And add more coals* *to Cancer when he burns With entertaining great Hyperion.*

candidatus *n.* [L.] (lit.) One clothed in white; (transf.) candidate for office in Rome, who would wear a white toga TIT 1.1.185 *Be candidatus then and put it on, And help to set a head on headless Rome.*

candied *ppl. adj.*
1 Covered with anything crystalline or glistening (e.g. frost) TIM 4.3.226 *Will the cold brook, Candied with ice, caudle thy morning taste...?*; (hence) congealed TMP 2.1.279 *Twenty consciences...candied they be.*
2 Sugared, honeyed HAM 3.2.60 *let the candied tongue lick absurd pomp* (i.e. flattering tongue).

candle *n.* (fig.)
1 Star ROM 3.5.9 *Night's candles are burnt out,* MAC 2.1.5.
2 'Light' of life 3H6 2.6.1 *Here burns my candle out; ay, here it dies,* MAC 5.5.23.

candle-case *n.* Case to keep candles in SHR 3.2.45 *a pair of boots that have been candle-cases, one buckled, another lac'd.*

candle-holder *n.* Attendant who provides light for others; (hence) mere onlooker ROM 1.4.38 *I'll be a candle-holder and look on.*

candle-mine *n.* Store of tallow 2H4 2.4.300 *You whoreson candle-mine.*

candle-waster *n.* Student who sits late over his books, book-worm ADO 5.1.18 *make misfortune drunk With candle-wasters.*

candy *n.* (attrib.) Sugared 1H4 1.3.251 *what a candy deal of courtesy This fawning greyhound then did proffer me!* (Ff1-2 *caudie*).

cane-coloured See CAIN-COLOURED.

canganet See CANZONET.

canker *n.*
1 (usu. fig.) Spreading, persistent ulcer JN 5.2.14 *heal the inveterate canker of one wound,* 2H6 1.2.18, TIM 4.3.50.
2 (freq. fig.) Worm that destroys buds and leaves TGV 1.1.43 *as in the sweetest bud The eating canker dwells,* MND 2.2.3, ROM 2.3.30.
3 Wild rose, dog-rose 1H4 1.3.27 *I had rather be a canker in a hedge than a rose in his grace,* 1H4 1.3.176.

canker-bit *adj.* Worm-eaten LR 5.3.122 *Know, my name is lost, By treason's tooth bare-gnawn and canker-bit.*

canker-bloom *n.* Wild rose SON 54.5 *The canker-blooms have full as deep a dye As the perfumed tincture of the roses.*

canker-blossom *n.* Worm that cankers or destroys the blossom (of love) MND 3.2.282 *O me, you juggler, you canker-blossom, You thief of love!*

cankered *ppl. adj.*
1 Rusted, tarnished, corroded 2H4 4.5.71 *The cank'red heaps of strange-achieved gold.*
2 Infected with evil, corrupt COR 4.5.91 *for I will fight Against my cank'red country.*
3 Malignant 1H4 1.3.137 *this ingrate and cank'red Bullingbrook,* ROM 1.1.95, JN 2.1.194.

canker-sorrow *n.* Sorrow that destroys like a canker JN 3.4.82 *But now will canker-sorrow eat my bud.*

canon *n.* (properly) Law or decree of the Church; *the canon canon law* AWW 1.1.145 *self-love, which is the most inhibited sin in the canon;* (hence) law or rule in general LLL 1.1.260 *contrary to thy established proclaimed edict and continent canon,* HAM 1.2.132.

canonize *vb.* (fig.) Enrol among famous persons TRO 2.2.202 *And fame in time to come canonize us.*

canonized *ppl. adj.* Buried with the prescribed rites of the Church HAM 1.4.47 *Why thy canoniz'd bones, hearsed in death Have burst their cerements.*

canopy *n.* Sky COR 4.5.38 *Where dwell'st thou?— Under the canopy,* HAM 2.2.300.
~ *vb.* Provide a shelter or covering SON 12.6 *When lofty trees I see barren of leaves, Which erst from heat did canopy the herd,* TN 1.1.40, CYM 2.2.21.

canstick *n.* Candlestick 1H4 3.1.129 *I had rather hear a brazen canstick turn'd.*

cantherizing *n.* Cauterizing TIM 5.1.133 *For each true word, a blister, and each false Be as a cantherizing to the root o' th' tongue.*
⋄ Ff1 *canth-*; Ff2-4 *cath-*. Some edd. substitute *cauterizing* but S. might well have been thinking of the action of the dried powder of cantharides (Spanish flies or blister flies), used by doctors in cauterizing by caustics. Support for the portmanteau word, *cantherizing,* is given by use of *blister* in the preceding line.

cantle *n.* (lit.) Corner-piece; (hence) part, segment ANT 3.10.6 *The greater cantle of the world.*
⋄ 1H4 3.1.99 *A huge half-moon, a monstrous cantle out:* Ff1 *cantle*; Q1 *scantle*.

canton *n.* Canto, song TN 1.5.270 *Write loyal cantons of contemned love, And sing them loud.*

canvas-climber Sailor, (espec.) an upper-yardman who goes aloft to trim sails PER 4.1.61 *And from the ladder-tackle washes off A canvas-climber.*

canus *n.* (incorrect form of L. 'canis') Dog LLL 5.2.589 *Whose club kill'd Cerberus, that three-headed canus.*

canvass *vb.* Toss in a canvas sheet as a sport or punishment; (hence) belabour, deal with severely 1H6 1.3.36 *I'll canvass thee in thy broad cardinal's hat,* 2H4 2.4.225.

canzonet *n.* Short song LLL 4.2.120 *Let me supervise the canzonet* (Ff1 *canganet*).

cap *n.*
1 Cardinal's biretta 1H6 5.1.33 *If once he come to be a cardinal, He'll make his cap co-equal with the crown,* H8 3.2.282.
2 Chief, head TIM 4.3.358 *Thou art the cap of all the fools alive.*
3 *throw their caps at* Give up for lost (from throwing one's cap after a rival in a foot race as a concession of defeat) TIM 3.4.101 *our masters may throw their caps at their money.*
4 *gain the cap of* Win the approval of CYM 3.3.25 *Such gain the cap of him that makes him fine.*
⋄ Throwing the cap in the air as a mark of joy occurs in several phrases, e.g. R3 3.7.35 *some followers of mine own, At lower end of the hall, hurl'd up their caps,* HAM 4.5.108.

capable *adj.*
1 Capacious, comprehensive OTH 3.3.459 *a capable and wide revenge.*
2 Sensitive, receptive HAM 3.4.127 *His form and cause conjoin'd, preaching to stones, Would make them capable,* AYL 3.5.23.
3 Intelligent, gifted TRO 3.3.307 *Let me bear another to his horse, for that's the more capable creature,* R3 3.1.155.
4 Legally able to inherit, qualified to possess LR 2.1.85 *I'll work the means To make thee capable.*
5 *capable of* Open to, susceptible to, apt to be affected by TMP 1.2.353 *Abhorred slave...Being capable of all ill!,* AWW 1.1.95, WT 4.4.764.

capacity *n.*
1 Power of receiving or containing TN 1.1.10 *That notwithstanding thy capacity Receiveth as the sea,* H8 2.3.31, ANT 4.8.32.
2 Intelligence, understanding TN 2.5.117 *Why, this is evident to any formal capacity;* (hence) *to my capacity* as far as I am able to understand, in my

opinion MND 5.1.105 *Love, therefore, and tongue-tied simplicity In least speak most, to my capacity.*

cap-and-knee *adj.* Obsequiously deferential because always raising their hats and bowing TIM 3.6.97 *Cap-and-knee slaves, vapours, and minute-jacks!*

cap-a-pe *adv.* [from OFr. 'cap-à-pie'] From head to foot HAM 1.2.200 *Armed at point exactly, cap-a-pe,* WT 4.4.736.

caparison *n.*
1 Cloth or covering spread over the saddle or harness of a horse, often gaily ornamented; trappings VEN 286 *rich caparisons, or trappings gay,* COR 1.9.12.
2 (transf.) Dress and ornaments of persons WT 4.3.27 *With die and drab I purchas'd this caparison.*
~ *vb.* Cover with a caparison, put trappings on R3 5.3.289 *Caparison my horse.*

caparisoned *ppl. adj.* Decked out, dressed AYL 3.2.195 *though I am caparison'd like a man,* SHR 3.2.65.

capital *adj.*
1 Principal, pre-eminent H5 5.2.96 *She is our capital demand,* 1H4 3.2.110.
2 Deadly, fatal COR 5.3.104 *to poor we Thine enmity's most capital.*

capitulate *vb.* Draw up articles of agreement, combine 1H4 3.2.120 *The Archbishop's grace of York, Douglas, Mortimer, Capitulate against us,* COR 5.3.82.

capocchia *n.* [fem. of It. 'capocchio'] Simpleton, innocent TRO 4.2.31 *Ha, ha! Alas, poor wretch! A poor capocchia!*

capon *n.*
1 Love-letter LLL 4.1.56 *Boyet, you can carve, Break up this capon.*
◇ A play on Fr. 'poulet' in the same sense.
2 Dullard (with overtone of being a cuckold) ERR 3.1.32 *Mome, malt-horse, capon, coxcomb, idiot, patch!*
◇ Corrupt justices were called 'capon justices', hence the ref. in AYL 2.7.154 *And then the justice, In fair round belly with good capon lin'd* (because bribed by gifts of capons).

capriccio [It.] Caprice AWW 2.3.293 *Will this capriccio hold in thee, art sure?*

capricious *adj.* Characterised by play of wit or fancy, ingenious, fantastic AYL 3.3.8 *I am here with thee and thy goats as the most capricious poet, honest Ovid, was among the Goths.*
◇ Punning allusion to L. 'caper', (goat), whence ultimately *capricious*. *Goths* was also pronounced in the same way as 'goats' in Eliz. English.

captain *n.*
1 (fig. from military sense) Chief, head OTH 2.1.74 *She that I spake of, our great captain's captain,* R2 4.1.99, ROM 2.4.20.
2 Subordinate officer R2 4.1.126 *the figure of God's majesty, His captain, steward, deputy, elect,* R3 5.3.108.
3 Familiar term of address without implying any rank TIM 2.2.73 *Why, how now, captain? what do you in this wise company?,* WT 1.2.123.
~ *adj.* Chief, principal SON 52.8 *Or captain jewels in the carcanet.*

captain-general *n.* Chief general, commander-in-chief TRO 3.3.277 *captain-general of the army, Agamemnon.*

captious *adj.* Capacious AWW 1.3.202 *Yet in this captious and intenible sieve.*

captivate *vb.* Take prisoner, make captive LLL 3.1.125 *thou wert immured, restrained, captivated, bound*; (fig.) subjugate, subdue 3H6 1.4.115 *Upon their woes whom fortune captivates!*; fascinate, charm VEN 281 *And this I do to captivate the eye Of the fair breeder.*
~ *pa. pple.* Captured, taken prisoner 1H6 2.3.42 *And sent our sons and husbands captive.*

captive *n.* Person vanquished or subdued LLL 4.1.75 *The captive is enrich'd,* COR 3.3.132.
~ *vb.* Take captive H5 2.4.55 *And all our princes captiv'd by the hand Of that black name.*
~ *adj.* Vanquished LUC 730 *a captive victor that hath lost in gain,* TRO 5.3.40, ANT 2.5.44.

captived *pa. pple.* Taken captive H5 2.4.55 *And all on princes captiv'd by the hand Of that black name.*

car *n.* Chariot of the sun-god TGV 3.1.154 *Wilt thou aspire to guide the heavenly car?,* MND 1.2.35, ANT 4.8.29.

carack See CARRACK.

caract *n.*[1] Mark, sign; symbol of office MM 5.1.56 *Even so may Angelo, In all his dressings, caracts, titles, forms, Be an arch-villain* (Ff *charact*).

caract *n.*[2] See CARRACK.

caraway *n.* Caraway seeds (which were often eaten with apples), or sweetmeat containing caraway seeds 2H4 5.3.3 *we will eat a last year's pippin of mine own graffing, with a dish of caraways.*

carbonado, carbinado *n.* Meat scored across and broiled COR 4.5.187 *he scotch'd him and notch'd him like a carbonado.*
~ *vb.* Make a carbonado of WT 4.3.267 *toads carbonadoed*; (hence) cut, slash, hack LR 2.2.38 *I'll so carbonado your shanks.*

carbonadoed *ppl. adj.* Cut, slashed AWW 4.5.101 *your carbonado'd face* (F1 *carbinado'd*).

carbuncle *n.* Precious stone of a red or fiery colour CYM 5.5.189 *a carbuncle Of Phoebus' wheel,* ERR 3.2.135.

carbuncled *adj.* Adorned with carbuncles ANT 4.8.28 *He has deserv'd it, were it carbuncled Like holy Phoebus' car.*

carcanet *n.* Ornamental collar or necklace, usu. of gold or set with jewels ERR 3.1.4 *To see the making of her carcanet,* SON 52.8.

card *n.*
1 Compass-card, on which the 32 points of the compass are marked MAC 1.3.17 *th' shipman's card*; (fig.) guide, directory HAM 5.2.109 *he is the card or calendar of gentry*; speak by the card be exact to a point, express oneself with nicety HAM 5.1.138.
2 Playing card; (hence) *fac'd it with a card of ten* put on a bold front SHR 2.1.405 *Yet I have fac'd it with a card of ten* (i.e. bluffed it with only a ten); *cooling card* (term of an unknown card-game, used fig.) something that cools one's ardour, check, deterrent 1H6 5.3.84 *there lies a cooling card*; *pack cards with* Make a fraudulent arrangement with ANT 4.14.19 *she, Eros, has Pack'd cards with Caesar's* (i.e. stacked the cards in Caesar's favour).

card *vb.* (a term from cloth-making but also used for mixing different kinds of drink) Mix 1H4 3.2.62 *carded his state, Mingled his royalty with cap'ring fools.*

cardecu, cardecue *n.* [Fr. 'quart d'ecu' quarter of a crown] Old French silver coin AWW 4.3.278 *Sir, for a cardecue he will sell the fee-simple of his salvation.*

carder *n.* One who cards wool (i.e. combs out its impurities) H8 1.2.33 *spinsters, carders, fullers, weavers.*

cardinally *adv.* (malapropism for) Carnally MM 2.1.80 *a woman cardinally given.*

card-maker *n.* Maker of cards for combing wool

Shr Ind.2.19 *by birth a pedlar, by education a card-maker.*

carduus benedictus *n.* Blessed Thistle, noted for its medicinal properties Ado 3.4.73 *Get you some of this distill'd carduus benedictus.*

care *n.*
1 *have (a) care* Be attentive, pay attention, take care Tmp 1.1.9 *Good boatswain, have care,* Ado 3.3.41 *have a care that your bills be not stol'n,* Wiv 4.5.75.
2 *keep, make a care of* Care for Tmp 2.1.303 *If of life you keep a care,* WT 4.4.355 *if you make a care Of happy holding her.*
~ *vb.* Take care 2H6 3.1.173 *those that care to keep your royal person From treason's secret knife.*

career, careire, carier *n.*
1 (a jousting term) Short gallop at full speed Ado 5.1.135 *Sir, I shall meet your wit in the career* (i.e. at full speed).
2 Quick movements this way and that of a nimble horse; (hence) caper, frolic H5 2.1.126 *he passes some humours and careers.*
3 Running, course; (esp. fig.) rapid and continuous course of action WT 1.2.286 *stopping the career Of laughter with a sigh,* LLL 5.2.482, R2 1.2.49.

careful *adj.* Full of care or anxiety, uneasy R3 1.3.82 *By Him that rais'd me to this careful height,* R2 2.2.75, H5 4.1.231.

careless *adj.*
1 Free from care or anxiety Wiv 5.5.52 *careless infancy,* Ham 4.7.79, Tro 5.5.40.
2 Uncared-for Mac 1.4.11 *To throw away the dearest thing he ow'd, As 'twere a careless trifle,* AWW 2.3.163.

carelessly *adv.*
1 Without care or anxiety AYL 1.1.118 *fleet the time carelessly.*
2 With indifference, heedlessly Rom 3.4.25 *It may be thought we held him carelessly* (i.e. did not value him highly), JC 1.2.118.

caret *vb.* [L.] (It) is wanting or lacking LLL 4.2.123 *but for the elegancy, facility, and golden cadence of poesy, caret.*

care-tuned *adj.* Tuned to the key or sounds or sorrow R2 3.2.92 *my care-tun'd tongue.*

carl, carle *n.* Countryman, churl, peasant Cym 5.2.4 *this carl, A very drudge of nature's.*

carlot *n.* Peasant AYL 3.5.108 *the bounds That the old carlot was master of.*

carman *n.* Wagoner, carter, carrier 2H4 3.2.317 *he heard the carmen whistle.*

carnal *adj.* Carnivorous R3 4.4.56 *this carnal cur Preys on the issue of his mother's body.*

carnation *n.* Flesh-colour H5 2.3.33 *'A could never abide carnation—'twas a colour he never lik'd*; (used attrib.) LLL 3.1.145 *how much carnation ribbon may a man buy for a remuneration?*

carol *n.*
1 (orig.) A ring-dance with a song; (hence) any kind of song sung at times of festival AYL 5.3.26 *This carol they began that hour.*
2 Song of religious joy MND 2.1.102 *with hymn or carol blest.*

carouse *n.* Cup filled to the brim and drunk right out, esp. for drinking toasts Shr 1.2.275 *And quaff carouses to our mistress' health.*

carpet *n. on carpet consideration* Because of exploits on 'the carpet' (i.e. carpeted chambers, drawing rooms or the court), not in the field TN 3.4.236 *He is knight, dubb'd with unhatch'd rapier, and on carpet consideration.*

carpet-monger *n.* Carpet-knight, one who frequents ladies' boudoirs or carpeted chambers

rather than fields of battle Ado 5.2.32 *a whole bookful of these quondam carpet-mongers.*

carrack *n.* Large trading vessel, also fitted for warfare, galleon Err 3.2.137 *whole armadoes of carracks* (F1 *Carrects*); (fig.) Oth 1.2.50 *he tonight hath boarded a land carrack* (Ff2–4; F1 *carract*).
▷ In Oth 1.2.50 prob. also a ref. to 'prostitute', for which 'land-frigate' was freq. used.

carrect See CARRACK.

carriage *n.*
1 Act of carrying, conveyance removal Cym 3.4.187 *I be suspected of Your carriage from the court.*
2 Power of, or capacity for, carrying Rom 1.4.94 *Making them women of good carriage,* LLL 1.2.71 (with play on sense 5 or 6).
3 Conduct, handling, execution WT 3.1.17 *The violent carriage of it Will clear or end the business,* Tro 2.3.131.
4 Manner of carrying one's body, deportment 1H4 2.4.424 *a cheerful look...a most noble carriage.*
5 Demeanour, behaviour, Err 3.2.14, *Teach sin the carriage of a holy saint,* LLL 5.2.306.
6 Moral conduct Tim 3.2.81 *his right noble mind, illustrious virtue, And honourable carriage,* LLL 1.2.69 (see sense 2).
7 Burden, load Wiv 2.2.173 *take all, or half, for easing me of the carriage,* Tmp 5.1.3.
8 Import, significance Ham 1.1.94 *as by the same comart And carriage of the article design'd.*
9 Hanger of a sword (based on an original sense 'gun-carriage') Ham 5.2.151 *Three of the carriages, in faith, are very dear to fancy, very responsive to the hilts.*

carrier *n.* Messenger, deliverer of letters Tit 4.3.87 *Why, villain, art not thou the carrier?,* Wiv 2.2.135.

carrion *n.*
1 Dead putrefying flesh Ham 2.2.182 *if the sun breed maggots in a dead dog, being a good kissing carrion.*
2 Term of contempt for a living person (as being no better than carrion) H5 4.2.39 *Yond island carrions, desperate of their bones, Ill-favouredly become the morning field,* Rom 3.5.156, Wiv 3.3.193; the living human body, the flesh MV 3.1.35 *Out upon it, old carrion, rebels it at these years?*
~ *attrib.*
1 Dead, putrefying JC 3.1.275 *carrion men.*
2 Belonging to the body MV 4.1.41 *I rather choose to have a weight of carrion flesh.*
3 Feeding on carrion Rom 3.3.35 *carrion flies,* 2H6 5.2.11.
4 Carrion-lean, skeleton-like MV 2.7.63 *carrion Death.*

carry *vb.*
1 Win, obtain, achieve Cor 2.1.238 *rather Than carry it but by the suit of the gentry; carry it* win the day Wiv 3.2.69 *he will carry't,* AWW 4.1.27, Oth 1.1.67.
2 Take by assault, conquer Cor 4.7.27 *think you he'll carry Rome?,* AWW 3.7.19.
3 Conduct, manage Lr 5.3.36 *carry it so As I have set it down,* MM 3.1.256, Ado 4.1.210; (refl.) behave or conduct oneself H8 2.4.144 *And like her true nobility she has Carried herself towards me,* AWW 4.3.104; (hence) *carry it* conduct matters, behave, act TN 3.4.137 *We may carry it thus, for our pleasure.*
4 Endure, put up with Lr 3.2.48 *Man's nature cannot carry Th' affliction nor the fear,* Ham 4.5.118; (hence) *carry coals* tolerate affronts, submit to insults H5 3.2.46 *I knew by that piece of service the men would carry coals.*
5 *carry it away* (from a hawking term = fly away

with the game) Carry or win the day ROM 3.1.74 *'Alla stoccato' carries it away.*

6 *carry out my side* Win my game LR 5.1.61.

7 *carry through itself* Be successful LR 1.4.3 *My good intent May carry through itself to that full issue.*

carry-tale *n.* Tale-bearer LLL 5.2.463 *Some carry-tale, some please-man,* VEN 657.

cart *n.*

1 Hangman's cart 1H4 2.4.496 *If I become not a cart as well as another man.*

2 Chariot of the sun-god HAM 3.2.155 *Phoebus' cart.*

~ *vb.* Drive around in an open cart (a punishment esp. for prostitutes and disorderly women) SHR 1.1.55 *To cart her rather; she's too rough for me.*

carve *vb.*

1 Plan, consider, form ADO 2.3.17 *carving the fashion of a new doublet,* SHR 4.3.89.

2 *carve for* Indulge HAM 1.3.20 *He may not, as un-valued persons do, Carve for himself,* OTH 2.3.173.

3 Show courtesy and affability, make affected gestures with the hand WIV 1.3.45 *She discourses, she carves, she gives the leer of invitation,* LLL 5.2.323.

carver *n.* be his own carver Be a law unto himself, take or choose at his own discretion R2 2.3.144 *in braving arms, Be his own carver.*

case *n.*¹

1 Condition, circumstances TMP 3.2.26 *I am in case to justle a constable* (i.e. in fit condition); *in good case* prosperous, well-off 2H4 2.1.106 *She hath been in good case.*

2 State of facts legally considered, cause or suit LR 3.2.87 *When every case in law is right,* 1H6 5.3.166; (hence) question CYM 1.6.42 *in this case of favour* (i.e. in this question of beauty).

3 Form of legal procedure (more fully called 'action upon the case') ERR 4.2.42 *I do not know the matter, he is 'rested on the case.*

4 *if case* In case, if perchance 3H6 5.4.34 *If case some of you would fly from us.*

case *n.*²

1 Container, covering; (applied to) a mask LLL 5.2.387 *There then, that vizard, that superfluous case,* ROM 1.4.29; the body (often as enclosing the soul) ANT 4.15.89 *This case of that huge spirit now is cold,* TN 5.1.165; eye-sockets LR 4.6.144 *What, with the case of eyes?,* WT 5.2.12; the skin (technical term for skin of the fox or other vermin) WT 4.4.814 *but though my case be a pitiful one, I hope I shall not be flay'd out of it* (with reference to both skin and plight); clothes 1H4 1.2.179 *I have cases of buckrom,* MM 2.4.13.

2 Set H5 3.2.4 *I have not a case of lives.*

~ *vb.*

1 Encase, cover ERR 2.1.85 *If I last in this service you must case me in leather,* 1H4 2.2.53, CYM 5.3.22.

2 Enclose, shut up, surround TRO 3.3.187 *And case thy reputation in thy tent,* JN 3.1.259.

3 Skin, strip AWW 3.6.103 *We'll make you some sport with the fox ere we case him.*

cased *ppl. adj.* Caged JN 3.1.259 *A cased lion.*

casing *ppl. adj.* Enveloping MAC 3.4.22 *the casing air.*

'casion See CAGION.

cask *n.* Casket 2H6 3.2.409 *A jewel, lock'd into the woefull'st cask.*

casque, caske *n.* Headpiece or helmet H5 Prol.13 *the very casques That did affright the air at Agincourt;* (used as a symbol of military life or authority) COR 4.7.43 *not moving From th' casque to th' cushion.*

cassock *n.* Loose, wide-sleeved cloak worn by soldi-

ers in 16–17C AWW 4.3.169 *shake the snow from off their cassocks.*

cast *n.*

1 Throw of the dice 1H4 4.1.47 *Were it good To set the exact wealth of all our states All at one cast?,* R3 5.4.9.

2 Casting or founding (of cannon) HAM 1.1.73 *And why such daily cast of brazen cannon.*

3 Dash or shade of colour, tinge HAM 3.1.84 *the native hue of resolution Is sicklied o'er with the pale cast of thought.*

~ *vb.*

1 Throw in wrestling MAC 2.3.41 *though he took up my legs sometime, yet I made a shift to cast him.*

2 Drive away 1H6 5.4.146 *Be cast from possibility of all,* CYM 5.4.60.

3 Throw up, vomit MM 3.1.92 *His filth within being cast;* (esp. with *up*) H5 3.2.53 *Their villainy goes against my weak stomach, and therefore I must cast it up,* PER 2.1.42; *cast the gorge* vomit violently TIM 4.3.41 *She, whom the spittle-house and ulcerous sores Would cast the gorge at.*

4 Throw off, get rid of, dismiss OTH 1.1.149 *the state... Cannot with safety cast him.*

5 Reckon, calculate 2H4 1.1.166 *You cast th' event of war...And summ'd the accompt of chance,* 2H6 4.2.86; (hence) *cast beyond ourselves* be over-calculating, go too far HAM 2.1.112 *it is as proper to our age To cast beyond ourselves in our opinions,* ANT 3.2.17.

6 *cast the water* Analyse or inspect urine (as a means of diagnosing disease) MAC 5.3.50 *If thou couldst, doctor, cast The water of my land, find her disease.*

~ *in combination*

cast away Wreck (a ship) MV 3.1.100 *Hath an argosy cast away,* JN 5.5.13. **cast by** Throw aside ROM 1.1.93 *citizens Cast by their grave beseeming ornaments.*

cast, casted *ppl. adj.* Disused, abandoned, forsaken AYL 3.4.15 *a pair of cast lips of Diana,* H5 4.1.23 *With casted slough.*

castigate *vb.* Chasten, mortify TIM 4.3.240 *If thou didst put this sour cold habit on To castigate thy pride.*

castigation *n.* Chastisement, corrective discipline or punishment OTH 3.4.41 *fasting and prayer, Much castigation, exercise devout.*

Castiliano vulgo [pseudo-Sp.] (?) Polite or decent language TN 1.3.42 *What, wench! Castiliano vulgo! for here comes Sir Andrew Agueface.*

▷ Some edd. emend to *Castiliano volto* (i.e. put on your Castilian (i.e. solemn) face) with ref. to the proverbial gravity and decorum of the Castilians.

castle *n.*

1 *old lad of the castle* (cant phrase for) Roisterer, swaggering, noisy reveller 1H4 1.2.42 *As the honey of Hybla, my old lad of the castle.*

▷ Perh. allusion to Sir John Oldcastle, the name S. originally intended for Falstaff.

2 (fig.) Stronghold, strong protection TRO 5.2.187 *Stand fast, and wear a castle on thy head!,* TIT 3.1.169.

casual *adj.*

1 Happening by chance, accidental HAM 5.2.382 *accidental judgements, casual slaughters.*

2 Subject to chance or accident, precarious CYM 1.4.91 *so your brace of unprizable estimations, the one is but frail and the other casual.*

casually *adv.* Accidentally CYM 2.3.141 *Search for a jewel that too casually Hath left mine arm.*

casualty *n.* Chance, risk PER 5.1.93 *awkward casualties,* MV 2.9.30, LR 4.3.44.

cat *n.*

1 Civet-cat or musk-cat Lʀ 3.4.105 *Thou ow'st...the cat no perfume,* AYL 3.2.68.

2 (term of contempt for a human being) Object of aversion, AWW 4.3.237 *I could endure any thing before but a cat, and now he's a cat to me,* Cor 4.2.34.

3 *tear a cat* Rant violently MND 1.2.30 *I could play...a part to tear a cat in.*

4 *give language to a cat* Allusion to proverb 'Good liquor will make a cat speak' Tᴍᴘ 2.2.83 *Open your mouth; here is that which will give language to you, cat* (i.e. help you to talk).

Cataian *n.* (lit.) Person from Cathay, i.e. China; (hence) scoundrel, one whose word cannot be trusted Wɪᴠ 2.1.144 *I will not believe such a Cataian, though the priest o' th' town commended him for a true man.*

cataplasm *n.* Poultice, plaster Hᴀᴍ 4.7.143 *no cataplasm so rare...can save the thing from death.*

catastrophe *n.*

1 Denouement, that which produces the conclusion or final event of a dramatic piece LLL 4.1.77 *The catastrophe is a nuptial,* Lʀ 1.2.134.

2 Conclusion, end AWW 1.2.57 *This his good melancholy oft began, On the catastrophe and heel of pastime;* (hence jocularly) posterior 2H4 2.1.60 *Away, you scullion!...I'll tickle your catastrophe.*

catch *n.*

1 That which is caught or is worth catching Sʜʀ 2.1.331 *No doubt but he hath got a quiet catch,* Tʀᴏ 2.1.100.

2 Short, part-time musical composition sung by three or more voices, each taking up the melody in succession, the second singer beginning the first line, as the first goes on to the second line, and so on TN 2.3.93 *We did keep time, sir, in our catches,* Tᴍᴘ 3.2.126.

~ *vb.*

1 Attain, get possession of, obtain 3H6 3.2.179 *to catch the English crown,* Mᴀᴄ 1.7.3; (absol.) Jɴ 1.1.173 *have is have, however men do catch.*

2 (fig. from contracting a disease) Become infected with, acquire by sympathy MND 1.1.189 *My tongue should catch your tongue's sweet melody.*

3 *catch the air* Gasp for breath 2H6 3.2.371 *That makes him gasp...and catch the air.*

4 Make a sudden snatch (as a hound when it reaches its quarry) Aᴅᴏ 5.2.12 *Thy wit is as quick as the greyhound's mouth, it catches.*

5 *catch cold* Become chilled by exposure to cold Lʀ 1.4.101 *and thou canst not smile as the wind sits, Thou'lt catch cold shortly.*

cate-log *n.* (Launce's pronunciation) Catalogue TGV 3.1.274 *Here is the cate-log of her condition.*

cater-cousins *n.* Good friends MV 2.2.131 *His master and he (saving your worship's reverence) are scarce cater-cousins.*

caterpillar *n.* (fig.) Rapacious person R2 2.3.166 *The caterpillars of the commonwealth.*

cates *n.* (pl.) Delicacies 1H4 3.1.161 *feed on cates,* Eʀʀ 3.1.28.

⟡ Sʜʀ 2.1.189 *For dainties are all Kates* (with play on name).

catling *n.* String made of catgut, for a violin, lute or similar musical instrument Tʀᴏ 3.3.304 *unless the fiddler Apollo get his sinews to make catlings on.*

cat-o'-mountain *n.* Wild cat, leopard, panther Tᴍᴘ 4.1.261 *pard or cat-o'-mountain;* (attrib.) Wɪᴠ 2.2.26 *your cat-o'- mountain looks.*

caudie See CANDY.

caudle *n.*

1 Warm drink given to the sick, made of thin gruel mixed with wine or ale, sweetened and spiced LLL 4.3.172 *Where lies thy pain?...A caudle ho!*

2 *hempen caudle* Halter 2H6 4.7.90 *Ye shall have a hempen caudle then, and the help of hatchet* (i.e. a hanging).

~ *vb.* Give a warm, soothing drink to Tɪᴍ 4.3.226 *Will the cold brook, Candied with ice, caudle thy morning taste.*

cause *n.*

1 Matter in dispute 2H6 3.1.289 *What counsel give you in this weighty cause?,* Sʜʀ 4.4.26.

2 Offence, charge, accusation Lʀ 4.6.109 *What was thy cause? Adultery?*

3 Affair, business, matter of concern Lᴜᴄ 1295 *The cause craves haste,* LLL 5.2.792, H5 1.1.45.

4 Disease AWW 2.1.111 *touch'd with that malignant cause,* Cor 3.1.234.

5 (term from duelling) One of the situations or grounds set out in the code of honour which justified a duel LLL 1.2.178 *The first and second cause will not serve my turn.*

ˈ**cause** *conj.* (aphetic form of) Because Tɪᴛ 5.2.63 *called so 'Cause they take vengeance,* Mᴀᴄ 3.6.21.

causeless *adj.* Inexplicable in terms of natural law, not to be explained by any natural cause AWW 2.3.3 *things supernatural and causeless.*

cautel *n.* Deceit, trickery, legal wile Hᴀᴍ 1.3.15 *no soil nor cautel doth besmirch The virtue of his will,* LC 303.

cautelous *adj.* Crafty, deceitful Cor 4.1.33 *caught With cautelous baits and practice,* JC 2.1.129.

cauterizing See CANTHERIZING.

caution *n.* Precaution, taking heed Mᴀᴄ 3.6.44 *And that well might Advise him to a caution.*

cavaleiro *n.* Cavalier, gentleman trained in arms; (hence) gallant 2H4 5.3.59 *all the cabileros about London* (Q; Ff *cavaleros*); (used as a title) Wɪᴠ 2.3.74 *Master Page, and eke Cavaleiro Slender,* MND 4.1.23 (F1 *Cauallery*).

cavalery (var. of) CAVALEIRO.

cavalleria *n.* [It.] Cavaliers, body of gentlemen Pᴇʀ 4.6.12 *or she'll disfurnish us of all our cavalleria* (Q *Caualereea*).

cave *vb.* Live in a cave Cʏᴍ 4.2.138 *such as we Cave here.*

cave-keeper *n.* Cave-dweller, one who lives in a cave Cʏᴍ 4.2.298 *I thought I was a cave-keeper.*

cave-keeping *adj.* (fig.) Concealed (like beasts keeping to their lairs), secret Lᴜᴄ 1250 *Cave-keeping evils.*

Caveto [L.] Beware, take care H5 2.3.53 *Therefore Caveto be thy counsellor.*

caviary, caviare *n.* Roe of the sturgeon pressed and salted Hᴀᴍ 2.2.437 *the play...pleas'd not the million, 'twas caviary to the general* (i.e. unpalatable to those who had not acquired a taste for it).

cease *n.* See CESS.

cease *vb.*

1 Halt, end, arrest Cʏᴍ 5.5.255 *A certain stuff, which, being ta'en, would cease The present pow'r of life.*

2 *be not ceas'd* Do not allow yourself to be silenced Tɪᴍ 2.1.16 *be not ceas'd With slight denial.*

ceinture See CENTER.

celestial *n.* (jocular) One concerned with heavenly or spiritual matters Wɪᴠ 3.1.106 *Give me thy hand, celestial* (i.e. the parson).

censer *n.* Perfuming-pan with a perforated lid, generally ornamented Sʜʀ 4.3.91 *Here's a snip and nip and cut and slish and slash, Like to a censer in a barber's shop,* 2H4 5.4.18.

censor *n.* One of the two magistrates in ancient Rome who drew up the census and had general supervision of public morals COR 2.3.244 *Censorinus...And nobly nam'd so, twice being censor.*

censure *n.*
1 Judicial sentence, esp. a condemnatory one COR 5.6.141 *Your heaviest censure*, OTH 5.2.368.
2 Opinion, judgement HAM 1.3.69 *Take each man's censure, but reserve thy judgement*, AYL 4.1.7, R3 2.2.144.
3 Adverse judgement, unfavourable opinion, blame H8 3.1.64 *your late censure Both of his truth and him*, MM 3.2.186, LR 1.4.210.
~ *vb.*
1 Pass sentence upon MM 2.1.29 *When I, that censure him, do so offend*, LR 5.3.3.
2 (trans.) Form or give an opinion of, estimate JN 2.1.328 *both your armies, whose equality By our best eyes cannot be censured*, COR 2.1.22, JC 3.2.16.
3 (intr.) Give an opinion (on) TGV 1.2.19 *That I... Should censure thus on lovely gentlemen*, HAM 3.2.87.

center *n.* [Fr. ceinture] Cincture, girdle, belt JN 4.3.155 *Now happy he whose cloak and center can Hold out this tempest.*
▷ Ff *center*; some mod. edd *cincture, ceinture.*

centre *n.*
1 Middle point of the earth HAM 2.2.159 *I will find Where truth is hid, though it were hid indeed Within the centre*, MND 3.2.54.
2 Earth (in the Ptolemaic system the centre of the universe) TRO 1.3.85 *The heavens themselves, the planets, and this centre Observe degree, priority and place.*
3 Heart or soul, taken as the centre of the body WT 1.2.138 *Affection! thy intention stabs the centre*, ROM 2.1.2, SON 146.1.

century *n.*
1 Division of the Roman army, prob. consisting orig. of 100 men COR 1.7.3 *dispatch Those centuries to our aid.*
2 Hundred CYM 4.2.391 *a century of prayers.*

cerecloth *n.* Winding sheet, shroud, properly one impregnated with wax MV 2.7.51 *To rib her cerecloth in the obscure grave* (F1 *searecloath*).

cerements *n.* (pl.) Waxed wrappings for the dead; (hence) graveclothes HAM 1.4.48 *thy canoniz'd bones, hearsed in death, Have burst their cerements* (F1, Qq *cerments*, Ff2–4 *cearments*).

ceremony *n.*
1 External accessory or symbol of state H5 4.1.104 *the King...His ceremonies laid by*, MM2.2.59; (applied to) festal ornaments JC 1.1.65 *Disrobe the images, If you do find them deck'd with ceremonies.*
2 Portent, omen JC 2.1.197 *dreams, and ceremonies.*

'cern *vb.* (aphetic form of) Concern SHR 5.1.75 *what 'cerns it you if I wear pearl.*

certainly *adv.* Steadfastly, fixedly 1H6 5.1.37 *and therefore are we certainly resolv'd.*

certes *adv.* Certainly LLL 4.2.163 *And certes the text most infallibly concludes it*, TMP 3.3.30, OTH 1.1.16.

certificate *n.* Licence or patent, certifying the status, or acquirements, etc. of the bearer 2H4 2.2.121 *Why, this is a certificate* (i.e. written in legal style).

certify *vb.* Assure, inform with certainty MV 2.8.10 *Antonio certified the Duke They were not with Bassanio in his ship*, 1H6 2.3.32, R3 1.4.96.

cess, cease *n.*[1] (partly an aphetic form of 'decease') Cessation, death HAM 3.3.15 *The cess of majesty Dies not alone*, LR 5.3.265 (Ff *cease*; Qq *cesse*).

cess *n.*[2] (aphetic form of 'assess') Assessment 1H4 2.1.7 *Poor jade is wrung in the withers, out of all cess* (i.e. beyond all calculation).

cesse *vb.* (var. spelling of) Cease AWW 5.3.72 *Or, ere they meet, in me, O nature, cesse!*

cestern, cesterne *n.* Cistern, receptacle for storing liquid OTH 4.2.61 *Or keep it as a cestern for foul toads.*

chace (var. of) CHASE (see esp. n. sense 4).

chafe *n.* Rage, passion, angry demeanour ANT 1.3.85 *How this Herculean Roman does become The carriage of his chafe.*
~ *vb.*
1 Vex, irritate, enrage SHR 2.1.241 *I chafe you if I tarry.*
2 (of the sea or a river against its banks) Rage, fret JC 1.2.101 *The troubled Tiber chafing with her shores*, LR 4.6.21, WT 3.3.88.

chafed *ppl. adj.* Angry, enraged 3H6 2.5.126 *And Warwick rages like a chafed bull*, TRO Prol.2.

chaffless *adj.* Without chaff; (hence) with nothing worthless in his character CYM 1.6.178 *but the gods made you (Unlike all others) chaffless.*

chain *vb.* Surround as with a chain, embrace ANT 4.8.14 *O thou day o' th' world, Chain my arm'd neck.*

chair *n.*
1 Seat of authority (e.g. a throne, a judgement seat) WIV 5.5.61 *The several chairs of order look you scour*, 3H6 1.4.97, JC 3.2.63.
2 Sedan chair OTH 5.1.82 *O for a chair To bear him easily hence!*
3 Invalid's chair (used as a symbol of old age) 1H6 4.5.5 *When sapless age and weak unable limbs Should bring thy father to his drooping chair.*

chair-days *n.* Days of rest (i.e. old age) 2H6 5.2.48 *And in thy reverence, and thy chair-days, thus To die in ruffian battle?*

chaliced *adj.* Having a cup-like blossom CYM 2.3.23 *chalic'd flowers.*

challenge *n.*
1 Claim 1H6 5.4.153 *And not of any challenge of desert.*
2 (legal) Formal objection, exception taken against either persons or things H8 2.4.77 *and make my challenge You shall not be my judge.*
3 Summons to single combat or duel ROM 2.4.8 *A challenge, on my life*, ADO 1.1.41.
~ *vb.*
1 Accuse, bring a charge against TIT 1.1.340 *Dishonoured thus and challenged of wrongs?*, MAC 3.4.41.
2 Lay claim to, demand or urge as a right R2 2.3.134 *I am a subject, And I challenge law*, LLL 5.2.805, OTH 2.1.211.
3 Summon to fight or (freq.) single combat ADO 1.1.42 *challeng'd him at the burbolt*, H8 1.1.34, TN 2.3.127.

challenger *n.* Claimant H5 2.4.95 *Your crown and kingdom, indirectly held From him, the native and true challenger*, HAM 4.7.28.

chamber *n.*
1 *of (a person's) chamber* One of his attendants, chamberlain to him MAC 1.7.76 *When we have mark'd with blood those sleepy two Of his own chamber*, AYL 2.2.5, PER 1.1.151.
2 Metropolis, capital R3 3.1.1. *Welcome, sweet Prince, to London, to your chamber.*
▷ London was known as 'the King's Chamber' or 'the Chamber of the Kings of England'.
3 Small piece of ordnance (16 and 17C) 2H4 2.4.52 *to venture upon the charg'd chambers bravely* (i.e. the loaded cannon, but with a bawdy second sense), H5 3.Ch.SD.

chamber-councils *n.* Private affairs WT 1.2.237 *I have trusted thee, Camillo, With all the nearest things to my heart, as well My chamber-councils* (F *Chamber-Councels*).

chambered *ppl. adj.* Lodged R2 1.1.149 *the best blood chamber'd in his bosom.*

chamberer *n.* Frequenter of ladies' chambers; (hence) gallant OTH 3.3.265 *those soft parts of conversation That chamberers have.*

chamberlain *n.*
1 One who waits on a king or lord in his bedchamber; (fig.) Tim 4.3.222 *think'st That the bleak air, thy boisterous chamberlain, Will put thy shirt on warm?*
2 Officer having charge of the king's private apartments and household R3 1.1.123 *As much unto my good Lord Chamberlain.*
3 Attendant in an inn in charge of the bedrooms 1H4 2.1.47 *What ho! chamberlain!*

chamber-lye *n.* Urine 1H4 2.1.20 *and your chamber-lye breeds fleas like a loach.*

chambermaid *n.* Lady's maid TN 1.3.51 *My niece's chambermaid.*

chamblet See CAMLET.

chameleon *n.* Lizard-like creature having the power of changing colour and formerly supposed to live on air HAM 3.2.93 *Excellent, i' faith, of the chameleon's dish: I eat the air, promise-cramm'd,* 3H6 3.2.191; (attrib.) TGV 2.1.172 *though the chameleon Love can feed on the air.*

champaign *n.* Flat open country LR 1.1.64 *With shadowy forests and with champaigns rich'd,* TN 2.5.160; (attrib.) LUC 1247 *a goodly champaign plain* (Ff1–2 *champian,* Ff3–4 *champion*).

champion *n.*
1 Fighting man, man of valour 1H6 3.4.19 *A stouter champion never handled sword,* TIT 1.1.65.
2 One who does battle in his own cause or for another in single combat R2 1.3.5 *Why then the champions are prepar'd,* PER 1.1.61, VEN 596.
~ *vb.* Challenge, oppose, fight against MAC 3.1.71 *come fate into the list, And champion me to th' utterance.*

chance *n.*
1 Event, occurrence (esp. an unfortunate one) 2H4 4.2.81 *Against ill chances men are ever merry,* HAM 5.2.334, MAC 2.3.91.
2 *main chance* Chief or paramount issue, most important eventuality 2H4 3.1.83 *a man may prophesy...of the main chance of things.*
~ *vb.*
1 *may chance* (with infinitive) May possibly TRO 1.1.26 *ye may chance burn your lips,* ADO 2.3.235, 2H4 2.1.11.
2 *how chance* How does it come about that?, How is it that? LR 2.4.63 *How chance the King comes with so small a number?,* WIV 5.5.217, 2H4 4.4.20.

chancellor *n.* Secretary H8 2.1.20 *Sir Gilbert Peck his chancellor;* (spec.) 'The King's Chancellor', the Lord High Chancellor, the keeper of the Great Seal and highest judicial authority in England H8 3.2.394 *Sir Thomas More is chosen Lord Chancellor in your place,* 3H6 1.1.238.

change *n.*
1 Exchange ADO 4.1.183 *or that I yesternight Maintain'd the change of words with any creature,* H5 4.8.29, TRO 3.3.27.
2 Changefulness, caprice LR 1.1.288 *You see how full of changes his age is,* CYM 1.6.115, SON 20.4.
3 Variation or modulation (in music) TGV 4.2.68 *Hark, what fine change is in the music;* (in verse) SON 76.2 *Why is my verse...So far from variation or quick change.*
4 Round or figure in dancing LLL 5.2.209 *Then in our measure do but vouchsafe one change.*
~ *vb.*
1 Exchange AYL 1.3.91 *Wilt thou change fathers?,* LLL 5.2.134; (hence) *change eyes* fall in love TMP

1.2.442 *At the first sight They have chang'd eyes;* (intr. with *for* before the thing taken in exchange) OTH 1.3.349 *She must change for youth,* PER 4.6.164.
2 Change colour, alter expression, (sometimes) turn pale, blush CYM 1.6.11 *Change you, madam: The worthy Leonatus is in safety,* ADO 5.1.140, H5 2.2.73.

changeable *adj.* Varying in colour in different lights or with movement, shot TN 2.4.74 *the tailor make thy doublet of changeable taffeta, for thy mind is a very opal.*

changeful *adj.* Inconstant TRO 4.4.97 *When we will tempt the frailty of our powers, Presuming on their changeful potency.*

changeling *n.*
1 Fickle or inconstant person COR 4.7.11 *yet his nature In that's no changeling,* 1H4 5.1.76.
2 Child left by the fairies in exchange for one stolen MND 2.1.23 *She never had so sweet a changeling;* (attrib.) MND 2.1.120 *I do but beg a little changeling boy;* (fig.) a letter substituted for another HAM 5.2.53 *Folded the writ up in the form of th' other,...The changeling never known.*

channel *n.* Street gutter 2H4 2.1.48 *Throw me in the channel?,* 3H6 2.2.141.
~ *vb.* Furrow 1H4 1.1.7 *No more shall trenching war channel her fields.*

chanson *n.* Song HAM 2.2.419 *the first row of the pious chanson.*

chantry *n.* Small, privately endowed chapel where mass was sung daily for the souls of the founders or others TN 4.3.24 *go with me, and with this holy man, Into the chantry by.*

chaos *n.*
1 Gaping void, abyss of infinite darkness LUC 767 *Vast sin-concealing chaos, nurse of blame!,* VEN 1020.
2 State resembling that of the formless void of primordial matter, utter confusion TRO 1.3.125 *This chaos, when degree is suffocate,* OTH 3.3.92 (prob. also sense 1).
3 Confused mass or mixture, conglomeration of parts or elements without order or correction ROM 1.1.179 *O heavy lightness, serious vanity, Misshapen chaos of well-seeming forms.*
4 (transf.) Amorphous mass, shapeless lump 3H6 3.2.161 *To disproportion me in every part, Like to a chaos, or an unlick'd bear-whelp.*

chap *n.*[1] Crack in the skin TIT 5.3.77 *chaps of age.*

chap *n.*[2] (pl.) Jaws as unitedly forming the mouth TMP 2.2.86 *Open your chaps again,* 2H4 2.4.130, ANT 3.5.13.

chape *n.* Metal plate or mounting of a scabbard, esp. that which covers the point AWW 4.3.143 *the chape of his dagger.*

chapeless *adj.* Without a CHAPE SHR 3.2.48 *an old rusty sword...with a broken hilt, and chapeless.*

chapless *adj.* Lacking the lower jaw ROM 4.1.83 *With reeky shanks and yellow chapless skulls* (F1, Qq2–3 *cha(p)els*), HAM 5.1.89.

chapman *n.*
1 Merchant, trader LLL 2.1.16 *Not utt'red by base sale of chapmen's tongues.*
2 Buyer, customer, haggler TRO 4.1.76 *Fair Diomed, you do as chapmen do, Dispraise the thing that they desire to buy.*

charact See CARACT.

character *n.*
1 (in collective sing.) Writing, printing TIM 5.3.6 *What's on this tomb I cannot read; the character I'll take with wax* (i.e. wax impression of the engraved letters), SON 59.8; (in pl.) letters CYM 4.2.49 *he cut our roots in characters.*

2 Handwriting HAM 4.7.51 *Know you the hand?–
'Tis Hamlet's character*, MM 4.2.193, TN 5.1.346.
3 Cipher for secret correspondence, secret handwriting; (fig.) MM 1.1.27 *There is a kind of character in thy life.*
4 Appearance, demeanour, face or features as be-
tokening moral qualities TN 1.2.51 *thou hast a
mind that suits With this thy fair and outward
character*, COR 2.1.65.
~ *vb.* Write, inscribe, engrave; (fig.) HAM 1.3.59
*And these few precepts in thy memory Look thou
character*, TGV 2.7.4, 2H6 3.1.300.
characterless *adj.* Leaving no written record or
mark behind them TRO 3.2.188 *And mighty states
characterless are grated To dusty nothing.*
charactery *n.* Writing WIV 5.5.73 *Fairies use flow'rs
for their charactery*; (fig.) JC 2.1.308 *I will construe
to thee, All the charactery of my sad brows.*
Charbon *n.* Name prob. derived from Fr. 'chair
bonne' (good flesh); (hence) flesh-eater, one who
rejected the ordinance of fasting, as opposed to
Poysam (from 'poisson') who obeyed it AWW
1.3.52 *for young Charbon the puritan and old Poysam the papist.*
chare *n.* Chore, job (esp. of household work) ANT
4.15.75 *as the maid that milks And does the meanest
chares.*
charge *n.*
1 Load, burden WIV 1.4.98 *'Tis a great charge to
come under one body's hand*, ADO 1.1.103, WT
1.2.26.
2 Luggage, baggage 1H4 2.1.46 *They will along with
company, for they have great charge.*
3 Importance, weight WT 4.4.258 *many parcels of
charge* (i.e. valuable articles), ROM 5.2.18.
4 Expense, cost; (hence) *on your charge* at your
expense MV 4.1.257 *Have by some surgeon, Shylock, on your charge To stop his wounds*, 2H6 1.1.61;
be at charges buy spend something R3 1.2.255 *I'll
be at charges for a looking-glass.*
5 Order; (hence) *on charge* at command TRO
4.4.133 *I'll nothing do on charge*; *give in charge*
command TMP 5.1.8 *Confin'd together In the same
fashion as you gave in charge*, 2H6 2.4.80, R3 1.1.85;
have in charge have an order or commission 2H6
1.1.2 *As by your high imperial Majesty I had in
charge at my depart for France* (i.e. I was commanded).
6 Military post or command; (also) the troops
under an officer's command 1H4 2.4.546 *I'll procure this fat rogue a charge of foot*, JC 4.2.48, COR
4.3.44; (hence) *limits of the charge* distribution of
commands in an army 1H4 1.1.35 *And many limits
of the charge set down But yesternight.*
7 (of a weapon) Position for attack 2H4 4.1.118
Their armed staves in charge.
~ *vb.*
1 Load, burden; (fig.) MAC 5.1.54 *The heart is sorely
charg'd*, WIV 2.2.165, H5 1.2.15.
2 Lay a command upon, command, order JN
3.1.151 *Thou canst not, Cardinal, devise a name So
slight...To charge me to an answer, as the Pope* (i.e.
order me to give an answer), MV 5.1.298.
3 Direct, level (e.g. a weapon) ADO 5.1.136 *I shall
meet your wit in the career, and you charge it
against me*, LLL 5.2.88.
chargeful *adj.* Costly ERR 4.1.29 *The fineness of the
gold, and chargeful fashion* (i.e. expensive design
or workmanship).
charge-house *n.* House in which youth are taken
charge of, boarding-school LLL 5.1.83 *Do you not
educate youth at the charge-house on the top of the
mountain?*
chariness *n.* Scrupulous integrity WIV 2.1.99 *I will*

*consent to any villainy against him, that may not
sully the chariness of our honesty.*
charitable *adj.* Loving TIM 1.2.91 *Why have you that
charitable title from thousands, did not you chiefly
belong to my heart?*
Charles' wain *n.* Charlemagne's wagon, i.e. the
constellation of the Great Bear 1H4 2.1.2 *Charles'
wain is over the new chimney.*
charm *n.*
1 Person or thing that charms ANT 4.12.16 *For
when I am reveng'd upon my charm, I have done
all*, OTH 5.1.35.
2 Magic spell, enchantment TMP 5.1.54 *To work
mine end upon their senses that This airy charm is
for*; (fig.) ROM 2.Prol.6 *bewitched by the charm of
looks*, LR 5.3.48.
~ *vb.*
1 Entreat or conjure (usu.) by some potent invocation JC 2.1.271 *I charm you, by my once commended beauty.*
2 *charm the tongue* Keep the tongue silent OTH
5.2.184 *I will not charm my tongue; I am bound to
speak*, SHR 4.2.58, 2H6 4.1.64.
charmed *ppl. adj.*
1 Endowed with magic or occult power MAC 4.1.9
Boil thou first i' th' charmed pot, LC 146.
2 Fortified by a spell MAC 5.8.12 *a charmed life.*
charmer *n.* One who has magic powers or uses
spells OTH 3.4.57 *She was a charmer, and could
almost read The thoughts of people.*
charming *ppl. adj.* Having the power of a magic
charm CYM 1.3.35 *two charming words.*
charneco *n.* Sweet Portuguese wine 2H6 2.3.63 *a cup
of charneco.*
charter *n.* Acknowledged right, privilege, im-
munity AYL 2.7.48 *as large a charter as the wind,
To blow on whom I please*, OTH 1.3.245, R3 3.1.54.
chartered *adj.* Privileged, licensed H5 1.1.48 *The
air, a charter'd libertine, is still.*
chary *adj.* Careful, shy, particular HAM 1.3.36 *The
chariest maid.*
~ *adv.* Carefully SON 22.11 *thy heart, which I will
keep so chary As tender nurse her babe.*
chase *n.*
1 Pursuit MND 2.2.88 *I am out of breath in this
fond chase*; *race* JC 1.2.8 *in this holy chase*; *in chase*
(used both of the chaser and the chased) in pursuit
TGV 5.4.15 *Have some unhappy passenger in chase,*
JN 1.1.223, SON 143.5; *by this kind of chase* by pursuing this course of argument AYL 1.3.32 *By this
kind of chase, I should hate him.*
2 *the chase* The sport of hunting OTH 2.3.363 *I do
follow here in the chase*, VEN 3.
3 Hunting-ground TIT 2.3.255 *Upon the northside
of this pleasant chase.*
4 Hunted animal WT 3.3.57 *This is the chase.*
5 (term of tennis) Second impact on the floor (or
in a gallery) of a ball which the opponent has
failed or declined to return; (used loosely in pl.)
tennis play H5 1.2.266 *That all the courts of France
will be disturb'd With chases* (with pun on sense
1; F1 *Chaces*).
~ *vb.*
1 Harass, persecute WT 5.1.217 *Though Fortune,
visible an enemy, Should chase us with my father.*
2 *chas'd your blood Out of appearance* Driven the
colour out of your face H5 2.2.75.
chaste *adj.*
1 Celibate, unmarried ROM 1.1.217 *she will still live
chaste?*, MV 1.2.107.
2 Stainless OTH 5.2.2 *you chaste stars.*
chat *vb.* Chatter or gossip about COR 2.1.208 *she
chats him.*

chawdron, chaudron *n.* Entrails MAC 4.1.33 *Add thereto a tiger's chawdron.*

che *pron.* (form of South-Western dial. 'ch' used before consonants) I LR 4.6.240 *keep out, che vor' ye* (i.e. I warrant you).

cheapen *vb.* Bargain or bid for ADO 2.3.31 *I'll never cheapen her,* PER 4.6.10.

cheat *n.* Swindle, fraud WT 4.3.28 *my revenue is the silly cheat.*

cheater *n.*
1 Escheator, officer appointed to look after the king's escheats (i.e. property forfeited to the king); (fig.) WIV 1.3.70 *I will be cheaters to them both, and they shall be exchequers to me,* TIT 5.1.111, Son 151.3.
▷ With a play in all three on the sense of 'one who deals fraudently, swindler'.
2 *tame cheater* Decoy duck or other tame animal used as a decoy in hunting 2H4 2.4.97 *He's no swagg'rer, hostess, a tame cheater, i' faith, you may stroke him as gently as a greyhound puppy.*
▷ With play on sense of 'swindler'. At 2H4 2.4.102 the hostess plays on sense 1 'escheator'.

check *n.* Reproof, censure WIV 3.4.80 *against all checks, rebukes, and manners,* OTH 3.3.67, ANT 4.4.31.
~ *vb.*
1 Rebuke, reprove JC 4.3.97 *Check'd like a bond-man, all his faults observ'd,* AWW 1.1.67, LR 2.2.142.
2 Curb, control JN 2.1.123 *thou mayst be a queen, and check the world!,* 3H6 3.2.166; (hence) rein in (a horse) 3H6 2.6.12 *check thy fiery steeds.*
3 (of a hawk) Stop pursuing its proper quarry and fly at a chance and inferior prey that crosses its path TN 3.1.64 *like the haggard, check at every feather That comes before his eye,* TN 2.5.113.
4 Stop short at HAM 4.7.62 *If he be now returned As checking at his voyage.*

cheek-roses *n.* Rosy cheeks MM 1.4.16 *Hail, virgin, if you be, as those cheek-roses Proclaim you are no less!*

cheer *n.*
1 Face, complexion MND 3.2.96 *All fancy-sick she is and pale of cheer.*
2 Countenance, aspect MV 3.2.312 *show a merry cheer,* TIT 1.1.264.
3 Disposition, mood AWW 3.2.64 *I prithee, lady, have a better cheer,* TIT 2.3.188, SON 97.13; (hence) *what cheer?* how goes it with you? TMP 1.1.2 *Here, master; what cheer?; good cheer* good heart, courage MV 3.5.5, R3 4.1.37.
4 Cheerfulness, mirth ADO 1.3.71 *their cheer is the greater that I am subdu'd,* HAM 1.2.116, HAM 3.2.164.
5 Kindly welcome, hospitable entertainment LUC 89 *So guiltless she securely gives good cheer And reverend welcome to her princely guest,* ERR 3.1.66. ~ *vb.*
1 *how cheer'st thou?* What cheer?, How is it with you? MV 3.5.70 *How cheer'st thou, Jessica?*
2 Encourage, incite 3H6 2.4.9 *And cheers these hands that slew thy sire and brother To execute the like upon thyself,* TIM 1.2.42; (fig.) SON 15.6 *Cheered and check'd even by the self-same sky.*
3 Salute with joyful sounds MND 4.1.125 *A cry more tuneable Was never hollow'd to, nor cheer'd with horn.*

cheerly *adv.* Blithely, cheerily R3 5.2.14 *In God's name cheerly on, courageous friends,* H5 2.2.192; (as a cry of encouragement among sailors) heartily TMP 1.1.5 *Heigh, my hearts! cheerly, cheerly, my hearts!,* R3 5.2.14.

chequin *n.* Sequin, gold coin of Italy and Turkey

PER 4.2.26 *Three or four thousand chequins were as pretty a proportion to live quietly.*

cherish *vb.*
1 Foster 3H6 2.6.21 *For what doth cherish weeds but gentle air?,* LUC 950.
2 Entertain (a guest) with kindness 1H4 3.3.172 *love thy husband, look to thy servants, cherish thy guests.*

cherry-pit *n.* Children's game in which cherry stones are thrown into a hole TN 3.4.116 *'tis not for gravity to play at cherry-pit with Satan.*

cherubin *n.* (transf. applied to a woman) Person with angelic qualities OTH 4.2.63 *Patience, thou young and rose-lipp'd cherubin,* TMP 1.2.152.
~ *attrib.* Angelic TIM 4.3.64 *For all her cherubin look.*

chest *n.* Breast LUC 761 *Some purer chest to close so pure a mind.*

chevalry (var. of) CHIVALRY.

cheverel, cheveril *n.* (short for) Cheverel-leather, kid-leather ROM 2.4.83 *here's a wit of cheverel, that stretches from an inch narrow to an ell broad.*
~ *attrib.* Of the nature of cheverel-leather; (fig.) stretching, flexible, pliant H8 2.3.32 *which gifts ...the capacity Of your soft cheveril conscience would receive If you might please to stretch it,* TN 3.1.12.
▷ Cheverel-leather was noted for its pliancy and capability of being stretched.

chew *vb.* Keep mumbling over MM 2.4.5 *As if I did but only chew his name.*

chewet *n.* Chough, jackdaw; (fig.) chatterer 1H4 5.1.29 *Peace, chewet, peace!*

chick *n.* (used as term of endearment) Dear one TMP 5.1.317 *My Ariel, chick.*

chicken *n.*
1 (fig.) Child MAC 4.3.218 *all my pretty chickens, and their dam, At one fell swoop.*
2 (fig.) One who is as timorous or defenceless as a chicken CYM 5.3.42 *Forthwith they fly Chickens, the way which they stoop'd eagles.*

chide *vb.*
1 (intr.) Scold, quarrel, speak loudly SHR 1.2.95 *though she chide as loud As thunder,* LLL 4.3.130, SON 111.1.
2 (trans.) Drive away with scolding MND 3.2.312 *he hath chid me hence,* TGV 4.2.103.
3 Strike against with angry noise (e.g. the sounds of crashing waves) 1H4 3.1.44 *the sea That chides the banks of England, Scotland, Wales.*
4 Proclaim with noise H5 2.4.125 *caves and womby vaultages of France Shall chide your trespass and return your mock.*

chiding *n.* Brawling or angry noise MND 4.1.115 *Never did I hear Such gallant chiding,* AYL 2.1.7.
~ *ppl. adj.* Brawling, noisy H8 3.2.197 *As doth a rock against the chiding flood,* TRO 1.3.54, PER 3.1.32.

chidden *ppl. adj.* Struck with angry blasts (of the wind) OTH 2.1.12 *The chidden billow seems to pelt the clouds* (i.e. storm-tossed).

chief *n. in chief* Mainly, principally MM 5.1.220 *but in chief For that her reputation was disvalued,* 2H4 4.1.31.

child *n.*
1 Female infant, daughter WT 3.3.70 *A boy, or a child, I wonder?*
▷ *my child* is always used by S. of a daughter e.g. TMP 5.1.198, ADO 4.1.76, LR 4.7.69.
2 (used in ballads as a kind of title) Youth of noble birth LR 3.4.182 *Child Rowland to the dark tower came.*

child-changed *adj.* Changed by the conduct of his

children LR 4.7.16 *Th' untun'd and jarring senses, O, wind up Of this child-changed father!* ⇨ Perh. also with the sense of 'changed into a child'.

childed *ppl. adj.* Provided with children LR 3.6.110 *He childed as I fathered.*

childhood *n.* Filial relation LR 2.4.178 *The offices of nature, bond of childhood.*

childing *ppl. adj.* Fertile, fruitful MND 2.1.112 *The childing autumn.*

childishness *n.* second childishness Second childhood AYL 2.7.165 *second childishness, and mere oblivion. Sans teeth, sans eyes, sans taste, sans every thing.*

chill *vb.* [dial., cf. CHE] I will LR 4.6.242 *Chill be plain with you.*

chimney *n.* Fireplace 1H4 2.1.20 *And then we leak in your chimney,* WIV 5.5.43, CYM 2.4.81.

chimney-piece *n.* Piece of sculpture or carving placed as an ornament over a fireplace CYM 2.4.81 *The chimney Is south the chamber, and the chimney-piece Chaste Dian bathing.*

chinks *n.* Money ROM 1.5.117 *I tell you, he that can lay hold of her Shall have the chinks.*

chip *n.* Key of a spinet or harpsichord Son 128.10 *those dancing chips O'er whom thy fingers walk with gentle gait.*

chip *vb.* Pare by cutting away the crusts 2H4 2.4.238 *'a would 'a' chipp'd bread well.*

chipped *ppl. adj.* Cut in many places, hacked Tro 5.5.34 *his mangled Myrmidons, that noseless, handless, hack'd and chipp'd.*

chirrah *vb.* (prob. corruption of Gk. 'chaere') Hail! LLL 5.1.32 *Chirrah!—Quare chirrah, not sirrah?*

chirurgeonly *adv.* Like a skilled surgeon TMP 2.1.141 *And most chirurgeonly.*

chivalry *n.*
1 (Eliz. name for) Men-at-arms, the mounted and fully armed fighting men of the Middle Ages H5 1.2.157 *When all her chivalry hath been in France,* 2H4 2.3.20.
2 Knighthood, knightly qualities 1H4 5.1.94 *I have a truant been to chivalry,* TRO 1.2.229.
3 Bravery or prowess in war LUC 109 *Made glorious by his manly chivalry, With bruised arms and wreaths of victory,* R2 1.1.203, 3H6 2.1.71.
4 *wreath of chivalry* Heraldic representation of a twisted band (or two bands of different colours twisted together), encircling a helmet and supporting a crest PER 2.2.29 *his device, a wreath of chivalry.*

choice *n.*
1 Abundant and well selected supply 1H6 5.5.17 *So full replete with choice of all delights.*
2 Picked or select company JN 2.1.72 *a braver choice of dauntless spirits...Did never float upon the swelling tide.*
3 Special value, estimation AWW 3.7.26 *This ring he holds In most rich choice.*
~ *adj.* Excellent 1H6 5.3.3 *ye chcice spirits that admonish me,* JC 3.1.163.

choice-drawn *adj.* Chosen with special care H5 3.Ch.24 *These cull'd and choice-drawn cavaliers.*

choicely *adv.* With discrimination 2H6 3.1.313 *a band of men, Collected choicely.*

choke *vb.*
1 Obstruct, prevent the free play of MAC 1.2.9 *As two spent swimmers that do cling together And choke their art.*
2 Silence SHR 2.1.376 *What, have I chok'd you with an argosy?*
3 *choke up* Smother R2 3.4.44 *her fairest flowers chok'd up.*

choler *n.*
1 (orig.) Bile, one of the 'humours'; (hence) bilious disorder R2 1.1.153 *Let's purge this choler without letting blood,* HAM 3.2.303 (in both passages with quibble on sense 2).
2 Anger ROM 1.1.3 *and we be in choler, we'll draw,* 1H4 2.4.324, JC 4.3.39; (pl.) H5 4.7.35 *his wraths and his cholers.*

choleric *adj.*
1 Causing bile SHR 4.3.19 *I fear it is too choleric a meat.*
2 Inclined to wrath, irascible LR 1.1.299 *in firm and choleric years,* ERR 2.2.62.
3 Angry, enraged, wrathful MM 2.2.130 *a choleric word,* JC 4.3.43, 2H6 1.2.51.

choose *vb.*
1 Do as one likes, take one's own course MV 1.2.47 *And you will not have me, choose;* (hence) be allowed to proceed SHR 5.1.47 *I hope I may choose, sir* (i.e. allow me, sir!).
2 *cannot choose* Have no alternative TMP 1.2.186 *I know thou canst not choose,* COR 4.3.37; (followed by but) MV 3.1.114 *he cannot choose but break,* 2H4 3.2.207, VEN 79.
3 *to choose* To select, to prefer one way to another, to determine WT 4.4.175 *I think there is not half a kiss to choose Who loves another best* (i.e. there is no ground of preference or difference).

chop *n.*[1] Chap, crack in the skin LUC 1452 *Her cheeks with chops and wrinkles were disguis'd.*

chop *n.*[2] (usu. pl.)
1 Jaw MAC 1.2.22 *unseam'd him from the nave to th' chops.*
2 (transf.) Person with fat or bloated cheeks 1H4 1.2.136 *You will, chops?,* 2H4 2.4.218.

chop-fallen *adj.* With the lower jaw fallen; (fig.) dejected, downcast, crest-fallen HAM 5.1.192 *Not one now to mock your own grinning - quite chop-fall'n.*

chopine *n.* Kind of shoe raised on a thick sole, prob. of cork, worn in Spain and Italy HAM 2.2.427 *Your ladyship is nearer to heaven than when I saw you last, by the altitude of a chopine.*

chopless *adj.* Lacking the lower jaw HAM 5.1.89 *my Lady Worm's, Chopless.*

chop-logic *n.* Contentious, sophistical arguer ROM 3.5.149 *How how, how how, chop logic!* ⇨ Q1; Ff, Qq2-3 *chopp'd logic* i.e. sophistical or contentious argument.

chopped *adj.* Chapped, chafed AYL 2.4.50 *the cow's dugs that her pretty chopp'd hands had milk'd.*

chopping *ppl. adj.* Making frequent changes, switching from one sense to another, changing the meaning of words R2 5.3.124 *The chopping French we do not understand.*

choppy *adj.* Chapped, chafed MAC 1.3.44 *By each at once her choppy finger laying Upon her skinny lips.*

chorl (var. of) CHURL.

chorus *n.* (orig.) Organised band of singers and dancers in the religious festivals and dramatic performances of ancient Greece; in English drama reduced by S. and others to a single personage who spoke the prologue and commented upon the course of events H5 Prol.32 *for the which supply, Admit me Chorus to this history,* HAM 3.2.245, WT 4.1.SD.

chorus-like *adv.* Like a chorus, serving as a commentator VEN 360 *And all this dumb play had his acts made plain With tears which chorus-like her eyes did rain.*

chosen *adj.* Choice PER 5.1.46 *with her sweet harmony, And other chosen attractions.*

chough *n.* Bird of the crow family, esp. the jackdaw MND 3.2.21 *Or russet-pated choughs, many in sort*

(*Rising and cawing at the gun's report*), Mac 3.4.124, WT 4.4.617.

▷ In some instances reference is intended to the traditional belief that choughs were capable of learning to speak, e.g. AWW 4.1.19 *choughs' language, gabble enough, and good enough*, TMP 2.1.266.

christen *adj.* Christian 1H4 2.1.17 *ne'er a king christen* (Ff in *Christendom*).

christendom *n.*
1 Christianity, Christian faith JN 4.1.16 *By my christendom, So I were out of prison...I should be as merry*, H8 1.3.15.
2 Christian name AWW 1.1.174 *a world Of pretty, fond, adoptious christendoms.*

christom-child *n.* A child in its chrisom-cloth or christening robe; (hence) innocent babe H5 2.3.12 *and it had been any christom child.*

▷ A corruption by association with 'christen' of 'chrisom'.

chrysolite *n.* Gem of green colour, formerly one of such types as zircon, tourmaline, topaz and apatite OTH 5.2.145 *such another world Of one entire and perfect chrysolite.*

chuck *n.* (term of endearment) Chick LLL 5.1.111 *the Princess* (*sweet chuck*), MAC 3.2.45, ANT 4.4.2.

chuff *n.* Miser, avaricious person, one who does not know how to put his wealth to good use 1H4 2.2.89 *No, ye fat chuffs, I would your store were here!*

church *n.*
1 *I am of the church* I am a 'churchman', i.e. a clergyman WIV 1.1.32.
2 *fetch, go, hie to church* Be married ADO 2.1.356 *County Claudio, when mean you to go to church?*, ROM 2.5.72, ADO 3.4.97.
3 *like a church* With little haste 2H4 2.4.230 *thou follow'dst him like a church.*
4 *old church* Unregenerate or corrupt community or group 2H4 2.2.150 *Ephesians, my lord, of the old church.*

church-like *adj.* Befitting connection with a church 2H6 1.1.247 *Whose church-like humours.*

churchman *n.* Ecclesiastic, clergyman H8 1.3.55 *That churchman bears a bounteous mind indeed*, TN 3.1.4, R3 3.7.48.

churl *n.*
1 Countryman, peasant, rustic ERR 3.1.24 *Good meat, sir, is common; that every churl affords*; (hence) rude, low-bred fellow ROM 5.3.163 *O churl, drunk all, and left no friendly drop To help me after*, TIM 1.2.26.
2 Miser, niggard SON 1.12 *And, tender churl, mak'st waste in niggarding*; (fig.) SON 69.11 *Then, churls, their thoughts...To thy fair flower add the rank smell of weeds.*

churlish *adj.*
1 Rude, rough, brutal HAM 5.1.240 *I tell thee, churlish priest, A minist'ring angel shall my sister be*, AYL 5.4.77, VEN 134.
2 (of beasts, natural objects and agencies) Rough, rude, violent AYL 2.1.7 *And churlish chiding of the winter's wind*, H5 4.1.15, TRO 1.2.21.
3 Niggardly, miserly AYL 2.4.80 *My master is of churlish disposition*, JN 2.1.519 *churlish thoughts* (i.e. grudging, niggardly in praise).
4 Stiff, hard 1H4 5.1.16 *unknit This churlish knot of all-abhorred war?*

cicatrice *n.* Scar COR 2.1.148 *There will be large cicatrices to show the people*, HAM 4.3.60; (loosely) mark, impression AYL 3.5.23 *lean upon a rush, The cicatrice and capable impressure Thy palm some moment keeps.*

'cide *vb.* (aphetic form of 'decide') Award, assign to a side or party SON 46.9 *To 'cide this title.*

▷ Sewell's conjecture, adopted by most mod. edd. Q *side.*

cincture See CENTER.

cinder *n.*
1 (pl.: loosely used for) Ashes TIT 2.4.37 *burn the heart to cinders*, OTH 4.2.75, PHT 55.
2 *cinders of the element* Stars 2H4 4.3.52 *as much as the full moon doth overshine the cinders of the element.*

cinquepace *n.* Lively dance, the steps of which were prob. based on the number five ADO 2.1.74 *wooing, wedding, and repenting, is as a Scotch jig, a measure, and a cinquepace*, TN 1.3.130 (F1 *Sinke-a-pace*).

cinque-spotted *adj.* Having five spots CYM 2.2.38 *On her left breast A mole cinque-spotted.*

cipher *n.* Zero; (usu. fig.) nonentity, a mere nothing, a person or thing of no importance or worth AYL 3.2.290 *Which I take to be either a fool or a cipher*, MM 2.2.39, LLL 1.2.56; (with ref. to a zero increasing the value of figures preceding it) H5 Prol.17 *And let us, ciphers to this great accompt, On your imaginary forces work* (with quibble), WT 1.2.6.
~ *vb.*
1 Express, show forth, make manifest LUC 207 *To cipher me how fondly I did dote*, LUC 1396.
2 Decipher LUC 811 *To cipher what is writ in learned books.*

circle *n.*
1 Ring used in magic or necromancy within which a magician was supposed to be safe during his dealing with spirits AYL 2.5.60 *'Tis a Greek invocation, to call fools into a circle*; (transf.) ROM 2.1.24 *to raise a spirit in his mistress' circle*, H5 5.2.293.
▷ In ROM 2.1.24 and H5 5.2.293 with play on sense of 'vulva'.
2 Crown, diadem H5 1.2 *yielded up into your hand The circle of my glory*, ANT 3.12.18.
3 Circuit, compass JN 5.2.136 *From out the circle of his territories*, AYL 5.4.34.
4 *come full circle* Turn quite round LR 5.3.175 *The wheel is come full circle.*

circled *ppl. adj.* Rounded, circular ROM 2.2.110 *th' inconstant moon, That monthly changes in her circled orb*, LUC 1229.

circuit *n.* Circlet, diadem 2H6 3.1.352 *the golden circuit on my head*, 3H6 1.2.30.

circummured *adj.* Walled around MM 4.1.28 *He hath a garden circummur'd with brick.*

circumstance *n.*
1 Adjunct of an action, condition (time, place, etc.) in which an action takes place MM 4.2.105 *neither in time, matter, or other circumstance*, TN 3.4.80, HAM 3.2.76; (pl.) R3 3.7.176, *All circumstances well considered*, LUC 1262.
2 Adjuncts of a fact which provide evidence one way or another OTH 3.3.406 *strong circumstances Which lead directly to the door of truth*, WT 5.2.31, HAM 2.2.157; (hence) circumstantial evidence R3 1.2.77 *Of these supposed crimes, to give me leave By circumstance but to acquit myself.*
3 Detailed and circuitous narration or discourse; (hence, collective sing. and pl.) details, particulars TGV 3.2.36 *it must with circumstance be spoken By one whom she esteemeth as his friend*, ERR 5.1.16, ROM 5.3.181; detailed proof or inference TGV 1.1.36 *So, by your circumstance, you call me fool.*
4 Condition, state of affairs HAM 1.3.102 *You speak like a green girl, Unsifted in such perilous circumstance*, TGV 1.1.36 (with quibble).
5 Ceremony, trappings, formality WT 5.1.90 *His*

approach, *So out of circumstance and sudden* (i.e. so unceremonious), SHR 5.1.27, HAM 1.5.127.
6 Mere contingency, accident OTH 3.3.16 *Or breed itself so out of circumstance,* WT 3.2.18, 2H6 5.2.39.

circumstanced *ppl. adj.* Subject to, or governed by, circumstances OTH 3.4.201 *I must be circumstanc'd.*

circumstantial *adj.*
1 Indirect AYL 5.4.85 *the Lie Circumstantial.*
2 Detailed CYM 5.5.383 *This fierce abridgement Hath to it circumstantial branches.*

circumvention *n.* Means or power of circumventing COR 1.2.6 *That could be brought to bodily act ere Rome Had circumvention.*

cital *n.* (law) Citation, summons; (hence) 'impeachment' (Johnson) 1H4 5.2.61 *He made a blushing cital of himself.*

cite *vb.*
1 Summon to appear in court H8 4.1.29 *to which She was often cited by them, but appear'd not.*
2 Call, urge, incite 2H6 3.2.281 *And had I not been cited so by them, Yet did I purpose as they do entreat,* TGV 2.4.85, 3H6 2.1.34.
3 Call to mind, make mention of H5 5.2.70 *Whose want gives growth to th' imperfections Which you have cited,* TGV 4.1.51, TIT 5.3.117; (with *up*) LUC 524 *have thy trespass cited up in rhymes,* R3 1.4.14.
4 Testify to, be evidence of AWW 1.3.210 *Whose aged honour cites a virtuous youth.*

citizen *adj.* City bred CYM 4.2.8 *But not so citizen a wanton as To seem to die ere sick.*

cittern *n.* Cithern, wire-stringed instrument whose head was often grotesquely carved, a kind of guitar; (attrib.) LLL 5.2.610 *A cittern-head.*

city *n.*
1 *the City* London 3H6 1.1.67 *Ah, know you not the city favours them?*
2 Self-governing city or state COR 3.1.199 *The people are the city.*
3 (fig.) Maiden innocence LC 176 *long upon these terms I held my city, Till thus he gan besiege me,* LUC 469, AWW 1.1.126.
~ *attrib. city feast* Official, formal banquet (with seating strictly by rank) TIM 3.6.67 *Make not a city feast of it, to let the meat cool ere we can agree upon the first place.*

city-woman *n.* Citizen's wife AYL 2.7.75 *the citywoman bears The cost of princes on unworthy shoulders?*

civet *n.* Perfume derived from the civet cat AYL 3.2.67 *civet...the very uncleanly flux of a cat,* LR 4.6.130.

civil *adj.*
1 Of or belonging to citizens ROM Prol.4 *Where civil blood makes civil hands unclean.*
2 Well governed, orderly ANT 5.1.16 *civil streets,* TGV 5.4.156, H5 1.2.199.
3 Responsible, showing restraint, civilized CYM 3.6.23 *who's here? If any thing that's civil, speak; if savage, Take or lend.*
4 Of civil law MV 5.1.210 *No woman had it, but a civil doctor.*
5 Associated with civil war ANT 1.3.45 *Our Italy Shines o'er with civil swords,* R2 3.3.102.

civility *n.* Civilised behaviour, culture, civilisation MV 2.2.195 *all the observance of civility,* WIV 4.2.27, OTH 1.1.131.

clack-dish *n.* Beggar's bowl with wooden cover that could be clacked to attract attention MM 3.2.126 *Yes, your beggar of fifty; and his use was to put a ducat in her clack-dish.*

claim *vb.* Demand the fulfilment of (a promise) TGV 4.4.87 *I claim the promise for her heavenly picture,* R3 3.1.197.

clamo(u)r *vb.* (in bell-ringing) Repeat the strokes more quickly, when they are at the height, in order to cease them; (hence) silence WT 4.4.247 *Clamor your tongues, and not a word more* (F1).

clap *n. at a clap* At one stroke LR 1.4.294 *What, fifty of my followers at a clap?*
~ *vb.*
1 Strike (hands) reciprocally in token of a bargain H5 5.2.129 *Give me your answer, i' faith, do, and so clap hands and a bargain,* WT 1.2.104; (hence) *clap up* settle (a bargain) SHR 2.1.325 *was ever match clapp'd up so suddenly?,* JN 3.1.235.
2 *clap to* Shut smartly 1H4 2.4.276 *Hostess, clap to the doors!,* COR 1.4.51.
3 *clap up* Put in prison 2H6 1.4.50 *Away with them, let them be clapp'd up close;* (fig.) ANT 4.2.17 *all of you clapp'd up together in An Antony.*
4 Impose (fines) H8 5.3.80 *on your heads Clap round fines for neglect.*
5 Put or set smartly and vigorously WIV 2.2.136 *Clap on more sails, pursue,* R2 3.2.114, ROM 3.1.6; (absol.) 2H4 3.2.46 *'a would have clapp'd i' th' clout at twelve-score.*
6 *clap into* Begin speedily, strike *into* (a song) MM 4.3.41 *I would desire you to clap into your prayers,* AYL 5.3.11.

clapper-claw *vb.* Exchange blows, thrash, maul WIV 2.3.68 *he shall clapper-de-claw em;* (fig.) TRO 5.4.1 *they are clapper-clawing one another.*

claret wine *n.* Light-red wine 2H6 4.6.4 *the pissing-conduit run nothing but claret wine this first year of our reign.*
▷ The name 'claret' was orig. opposed to 'white' and to 'red' wine.

clatpole (var. of) CLOTPOLE.

claw *vb.*
1 Seize, grip HAM 5.1.72 *But age with his stealing steps Hath clawed me in his clutch.*
2 Scratch gently or soothingly 2H4 2.4.259 *the wither'd elder hath not his pole claw'd like a parrot.*
3 Flatter, cajole ADO 1.3.17 *laugh when I am merry, and claw no man in his humour.*

clay-brained *adj.* Stupid 1H4 2.4.227 *thou clay-brain'd guts.*

cleanly *adj.* Adroit, deft, dextrous, 1H4 2.4.456 *wherein neat and cleanly, but to carve a capon and eat it?*
~ *adv.*
1 Cleverly, adroitly, deftly, artfully TIT 2.1.94 *often struck a doe, And borne her cleanly by the keeper's nose,* LUC 1073.
2 Completely, quite VEN 694 *till they have singled With much ado the cold fault cleanly out.*

clean-timbered *adj.* Clean-limbed, well built LLL 5.2.638 *Hector was not so clean-timber'd.*

cleap See CLIP *vb.*²

clear *vb.*
1 Get (one) clear of a place WT 1.2.439 *will by twos and threes at several posterns Clear them o' th' city.*
2 Settle (affairs) AYL 1.1.172 *this wrastler shall clear all,* WT 3.1.18.
3 Get rid of, cancel (debts) MV 3.2.319 *all debts are clear'd between you and I,* WT 1.2.74; set (a person) free from debt TIM 2.2.226 *I clear'd him with five talents.*
~ *adj.*
1 Bright, fully light MM 4.2.210 *it is almost clear dawn,* H8 1.1.226.
2 (of looks) Serene, cheerful WT 1.2.343 *with a countenance as clear As friendship wears at feasts,* MND 3.2.60, SHR 2.1.172.
3 Glorious, illustrious LR 4.6.73 *the clearest gods,* MV 2.9.42, LUC 11.

4 Unspotted, blameless, innocent MAC 1.7.18 *this Duncan... hath been So clear in his great office*, TMP 3.3.82, ANT 5.2.122.

5 Free of debt or other encumbrances TIM 3.4.76 *he should the sooner pay his debts, And make a clear way to the gods*.

~ *adv.* Serenely, cheerfully MAC 1.5.72 *look up clear*.

clearness *n.* Freedom from suspicion MAC 3.1.132 *I require a clearness*.

clearstories See CLERESTORY.

cleave *vb.* cleave the pin (archery) Hit the pin or peg in the centre of the target ROM 2.4.16 *the very pin of his heart cleft with the blind bow-boy's butt-shaft*.

clef *n.* Key in music SHR 3.1.77 *'D sol re, one clef, two notes have I'*; (fig.) TRO 5.2.11 *any man can sing her, if he can take her cleff; she's noted.* (prob. with play on 'cleft' (= pudenda)).
◇ Ff and Q *cliff*, except in TRO where Ff have *find her...take her life.*

cleft *ppl. adj.* Divided, twofold LC 293 *O cleft effect!*

clepe *vb.* Call LLL 5.1.22 *he clepeth a calf, 'cauf'*, MAC 3.1.93, HAM 1.4.19.

clerestory, clear store, clearstory *n.* Upper part of the nave, choir or transept of a large church, containing windows to admit light; also applied to similar features in other buildings TN 4.2.37 *and the clerestories toward the south north are as lustrous as ebony* (F1 *cleere stores*; Ff2-4 *clear(e) stones*).

clerk *n.*
1 Man of learning, scholar MND 5.1.93 *great clerks have purposed To greet me with premeditated welcomes*, H8 2.2.91, PER 5.Gower.5.
2 Saint Nicholas' clerks See NICHOLAS.

clerk-like *adv.* In a scholarly way WT 1.2.392 *a gentleman, thereto Clerk-like experienc'd*.

clerkly *adj.* Scholarly, book-learned WIV 4.5.57 *thou art clerkly, Sir John*.
~ *adv.* In a scholarly manner TGV 2.1.108 *I thank you, gentle servant—'tis very clerkly done*, 2H6 3.1.179.

clew *n.* Ball of thread AWW 1.3.182 *you have wound a goodly clew*.

cliff See CLEF.

climate *n.* Region, country, clime (without ref. to climatic conditions) R2 4.1.130 *That in a Christian climate souls refin'd Should show so heinous...a deed*, JC 1.3.32; region or part of the sky, heavens JN 2.1.344 *That sways the earth this climate overlooks*.
~ *vb.* Reside WT 5.1.170 *whilest you Do climate here!*

climature *n.* Region HAM 1.1.125 *Have heaven and earth together demonstrated Unto our climatures and countrymen*.

climb *vb.* Reach by climbing TGV 2.4.181 *how I must climb her window*, ROM 2.5.74; (fig.) TIM 1.1.76 *Bowing his head against the steepy mount To climb his happiness*.

cling *vb.* Cause (the body, etc.) to shrink, shrivel MAC 5.5.39 *Upon the next tree shall thou hang alive, Till famine cling thee*.

clinquant *adj.* Glittering H8 1.1.19 *the French, All clinquant, all in gold*.

clip *vb.*[1]
1 Cut PER 5.3.74 *This ornament...will I clip to form*.
2 Curtail, abbreviate LLL 5.2.599 *Judas Machabeus clipt is plain Judas*, LR 4.7.6.

clip *vb.*[2] Embrace, surround JN 5.2.34 *That Neptune's arms, who clippeth thee about*, 1H4 3.1.43, 2H6 4.1.6 (Ff *cleap(e)*).

clip *vb.*[3] See CLEPE.

clipper *n.* One who (fraudulently) 'clips' or cuts off

the edges of coins H5 4.1.229 *it is no English treason to cut French crowns, and to-morrow the King himself will be a clipper* (with play on 'cutting of heads').

clip-winged *adj.* Having the wings clipped 1H4 3.1.150 *A clip-wing'd griffin*.

cloak-bag *n.* Portmanteau CYM 3.4.169 *'Tis in my cloak-bag*; (fig.) 1H4 2.4.452 *that stuff'd cloak-bag of guts*.

clock *n.* 'twixt clock and clock Between the striking of one hour and the next, hour by hour CYM 3.4.42 *To weep 'twixt clock and clock?*; tell the clock count the strokes of the clock R3 5.3.276 *Tell the clock there*, TMP 2.1.289.

clock-setter *n.* One who attends to and regulates clocks JN 3.1.324 *Old Time the clock-setter*.

clodpole *n.* Blockhead TN 3.4.190 *it comes from a clodpole*.

clog *n.* (fig.) Encumbrance, impediment, burden R2 5.6.20 *clog of conscience*.

cloistered *adj.* (fig.) Restricted, confined as in a cloister MAC 3.2.41 *ere the bat hath flown His cloister'd flight*.

cloistress *n.* Nun TN 1.1.27 *like a cloistress she will veiled walk*.

close *n.*[1] Enclosure TIM 5.1.205 *a tree, which grows here in my close*.

close *n.*[2]
1 Conclusion of a piece of music, cadence H5 1.2.182 *Congreeing in a full and natural close, Like music*, R2 2.1.12.
2 Union TGV 5.4.117 *come, a hand from either. Let me be blest to make this happy close*, TN 5.1.158.
3 Struggle, encounter, grapple 1H4 1.1.13 *Did lately meet in the intestine shock And furious close of civil butchery*.
~ *vb.*
1 Enclose MAC 3.1.98 *According to the gift which bounteous nature Hath in him clos'd* (prob. with extended sense, 'set, like a jewel'), LUC 761.
2 Join, clasp (hands) JN 2.1.533 *close your hands*, ROM 2.6.6.
3 Meet, be united H5 1.2.210 *As many lines close in the dial's centre*, MAC 3.2.14.
4 Grapple 2H4 2.1.18 *If I can close with him, I care not for his thrust*.
5 Come to terms, agree HAM 2.1.45 *He closes with you in this consequence*, JC 3.1.202, TGV 2.5.12.
~ *adj.*
1 Enclosed, shut in, shut up, confined TGV 3.1.237 *close prison*, OTH 5.2.335, MND 3.2.7.
2 Concealed, secret 2H6 2.4.73 *This is close dealing*, R3 1.1.158, TIM 4.3.143.
3 Practising secrecy, not open, uncommunicative MM 4.3.118 *Show your wisdom, daughter, in your close patience*, MAC 3.5.7, 1H4 2.3.110.
~ *adv.* Secretly SHR Ind.1.127 *in a napkin (being close convey'd)*.

closely *adv.*
1 In close confinement SHR 1.1.183 *And therefore has he closely mew'd her up*, R3 1.1.38.
2 Secretly, covertly, privately HAM 3.1.29 *we have closely sent for Hamlet hither*, LLL 4.3.135, ROM 5.3.255.

closeness *n.* Retirement, seclusion TMP 1.2.90 *dedicated To closeness and the bettering of my mind*.

close-stool *n.* Piece of furniture in the form of a stool or chair enclosing a chamber pot, commode AWW 5.2.17 *Fortune's close-stool*.

closet *n.*
1 Study, private room JN 4.2.267 *to my closet bring The angry lords*, H5 5.2.198, JC 2.1.35.
2 Private repository or cabinet for papers MAC

5.1.6 *unlock her closet, take forth paper,* LR 3.3.11, JC 3.2.129.

close-tongued *adj.* Uncommunicative LUC 770 *whisp'ring conspirator With close-tongu'd treason and the ravisher!*

closet-war *n.* War conducted in the closet or study TRO 1.3.205 *They call this bed-work, mapp'ry, closet-war.*

closure *n.*
1 Enclosure, bound, limit R3 3.3.11 *Within the guilty closure of thy walls,* VEN 782, SON 48.11.
2 Conclusion, end TIT 5.3.134 *make a mutual closure of our house.*

cloth *n.*
1 Handkerchief, napkin 3H6 1.4.157 *This cloth thou dipp'dst in blood of my sweet boy,* PER 3.2.87, CYM 5.1.1.
2 Dress, livery CYM 2.3.123 *A hilding for a livery, a squire's cloth.*
3 *painted cloth* Wall-hanging painted with scenes and mottoes, tapestry TRO 5.10.46 *Good traders in the flesh, set this in your painted cloths,* LLL 5.2.576, LUC 245.
4 *cloth of gold* Fabric woven at least partly of gold thread ANT 2.2.199 *she did lie In her pavilion— cloth of gold, of tissue.*
▷ See TISSUE.

clothier's yard See YARD.

clotpole *n.*
1 Thick or 'wooden' head CYM 4.2.184 *I have sent Cloten's clotpole down the stream In embassy to his mother.*
2 Blockhead, clodpole LR 4.1.56 *Call the clotpole back,* TRO 2.1.117.
▷ Q; 'clat' (clod of earth) is a widespread dial. form alongside 'clot' and 'clod'.

cloud *n.*
1 Dark spot, esp. on the face of a horse ANT 3.2.51 *He has a cloud in's face.*
▷ The cloud was considered a blemish.
2 (fig.) Anything that obscures or conceals (e.g. a mask) LLL 5.2.204 *blessed are clouds, to do as such clouds do.*
~ *vb.*
1 Overspread with gloom, cast a shadow over 3H6 4.1.74 *your dislikes...Doth cloud my joys.*
2 Defame, sully WT 1.2.280 *My sovereign mistress clouded so.*
3 (fig.) Become gloomy LLL 5.2.721 *the scene begins to cloud.*

cloudy *adj.* Gloomy, sullen MAC 3.6.41 *The cloudy messenger turns me his back.*

clout *n.*
1 Piece of cloth, rag; (hence) handkerchief R3 1.3.176 *a clout Steep'd in the faultless blood of pretty Rutland,* ROM 2.4.206, HAM 2.2.506.
▷ See also BABE OF CLOUTS.
2 Square piece of canvas in the centre of the archery target LLL 4.1.134 *Indeed 'a must shoot nearer, or he'll ne'er hit the clout,* 2H4 3.2.46, LR 4.6.92.

clouted *adj.* Hobnailed CYM 4.2.214 *My clouted brogues... whose rudeness Answer'd my steps too loud.*
▷ In 2H6 4.2.185 *such as go in clouted shoon...are thrifty honest men* the meaning may be either 'hobnailed' or 'patched'.

cloy *vb.* Claw CYM 5.4.118 *His royal bird...cloys his beak.*

cloyless *adj.* That does not cloy or satiate ANT 2.1.25 *epicurean cooks Sharpen with cloyless sauce his appetite.*

cloyment *n.* Satiety TN 2.4.99 *That suffer surfeit, cloyment, and revolt.*

club *n.* Weapon used by apprentices 1H6 1.3.84 *I'll*

call for clubs, *if you will not away* (i.e. I'll summon assistance), H8 5.3.51, ROM 1.1.73.
▷ 'Prentices and clubs' was the rallying cry of the London apprentices.

cluster *n.* Crowd, mob COR 4.6.122 *cowardly nobles gave way unto your clusters.*

clustering *ppl. adj.* Thronging, closely-knit 1H6 4.7.13 *Into the clust'ring battle of the French* (i.e. into the closely grouped forces of the French).

clutch *vb.* Clench, close up (in refusal) JN 2.1.589 *Not that I have the power to clutch my hand,* MM 3.2.47.

clyster-pipe *n.* Tube or pipe for administering an injection or enema OTH 2.1.177 *Would they were clyster-pipes for your sake* (F1 cluster-pipes).

coach-fellow *n.* Horse teamed with another in drawing a coach; (fig.) companion, close associate WIV 2.2.8 *three reprieves for you and your coach-fellow Nym.*

co-act *vb.* Act together TRO 5.2.118 *how these two did co-act.*

co-active *adj.* Acting in concert with WT 1.2.141 *With what's unreal thou co-active art.*

coal *n.*
1 *dead coal(s)* Cinder(s), charred fuel WT 5.1.68 *Stars, stars, And all eyes else dead coals*; (fig.) JN 5.2.83 *Your breath first kindled the dead coal of wars*; (hence, sing.) ashes COR 4.6.137 *If he could burn us all into one coal.*
2 *carry coals* See CARRY *vb.* sense 4.

coarse *adj.* Inferior H8 3.2.239 *Of what coarse metal ye are moulded.*

coarsely *adv.* Slightingly, harshly AWW 3.5.57 *a gentleman... Reports but coarsely of her.*

coast *n.* Quarter, direction, region 2H6 1.2.93 *Yet have I gold flies from another coast.*
~ *vb.*
1 Go a roundabout way, travel circuitously (as if following a coastline) H8 3.2.38 *how he coasts And hedges his own way.*
2 Make one's way *to* VEN 870 *And all in haste she coasteth to the cry.*
3 Approach (esp. with hostility), attack, assail, accost 3H6 1.1.268 *Whose haughty spirit...Will coast my crown* (F cost).

coasting *adj.* Accosting; (hence) friendly, ready TRO 4.5.59 *O, these encounterers, so glib of tongue, That give a coasting welcome ere it comes.*

coat *n.*
1 Coat of arms or coat-armour WIV 1.1.17 *the dozen white luces in their coat,* MND 3.2.213, R2 3.1.24.
2 Coat of mail R2 1.3.75 *steel my lance's point, That it may enter Mowbray's waxen coat,* 1H4 4.1.100.

cobloaf *n.* 'little loafe made with a round head' (Minsheu 1617) TRO 2.1.38 *Thou shouldst strike him—Cobloaf!*

cock *n.*[1]
1 Weather-cock LR 3.2.3 *Till you have drench'd our steeples, drown'd the cocks!*
2 Spout or pipe to let out liquor, tap TIM 2.2.162 *I have retir'd me to a wasteful cock, And set mine eyes at flow.*

cock *n.*[2] Small ship's boat, cockboat LR 4.6.19 *yond tall anchoring bark, Diminish'd to her cock.*

cock *n.*[3] (in oaths, var. of) God SHR 4.1.118 *Cock's passion, silence!,* HAM 4.5.61, WIV 1.1.303.

cock-a-hoop *n.phr. set cock-a-hoop* Cast off all restraint, set loose disorder ROM 1.5.81 *You will set cock-a-hoop! you'll be the man!*

cockatrice *n.* BASILISK *n.* sense 1 ROM 3.2.47 *the death-darting eye of cockatrice,* TN 3.4.196.

cockered *adj.* Indulged, pampered JN 5.1.70 *A cock'red silken wanton.*

cockle *n.*[1] Weed (prob. darnel) LLL 4.3.380 *Sow'd*

cockle reap'd no corn; (fig.) Cor 3.1.70 *The cockle of rebellion, insolence, sedition.*

cockle *n.*²
1 Scallop or any other bivalve, or the shell of a cockle Shr 4.3.66 *a cockle or a walnut-shell.*
2 Small shallow boat resembling a cockle shell Per 4.4.2 *Sail seas in cockles* (could perh. be simply cockle-shells—see sense 1).
3 *cockle hat* Hat with a cockle-shell stuck in it, worn by pilgrims as a sign of their having been to the shrine of St. James of Compostela in Spain Ham 4.5.25 *By his cockle hat and staff.*

cockled *adj.* Furnished with a shell LLL 4.3.335 *Love's feeling is more soft and sensible Than are the tender horns of cockled snails.*

cockney *n.*
1 Effeminate or foppish fellow TN 4.1.15 *this great lubber, the world, will prove a cockney.*
2 Squeamish woman Lr 2.4.122 *Cry to it, nuncle, as the cockney did to the eels when she put 'em i' th' paste alive.*

cockpit *n.* (orig.) Enclosed place for fighting cocks; (transf.) circular theatre H5 Prol.11 *Can this cock-pit hold The vasty fields of France?*

cock-shut *adj.* Sunset or twilight R3 5.3.70 *Much about cock-shut time.*

cock-sure *adv.* With perfect security 1H4 2.1.86 *We steal, as in a castle, cock-sure.*

coctus See BIS COCTUS.

codding *adj.* Lustful, lecherous Tit 5.1.99 *That codding spirit had they from their mother.*

codling *n.* Immature or half-grown apple TN 1.5.158 *a codling when 'tis almost an apple.*

codpiece *n.* Baggy appendage at the front of breeches, indelicately conspicuous (esp. with clowns) in S.'s time; (fig.) penis MM 3.2.115 *for the rebellion of a codpiece to take away the life of a man!*

coffin *n.* Pie-crust Tit 5.2.188 *of the paste a coffin I will rear, And make two pasties of your shameful heads.*
⬦ Cf. CUSTARD-COFFIN.

cog *vb.*
1 Employ fraud or deceit, cheat Ado 5.1.95 *fashion-monging boys, That lie and cog and flout, deprave and slander,* LLL 5.2.235, Tim 5.1.95.
2 Flatter, fawn Wiv 3.3.70 *I cannot cog and say thou art this and that.*
3 Beguile, wheedle (something from someone) Cor 3.2.133 *I'll mountebank their loves, Cog their hearts from them.*

cogging *ppl. adj.* Deceiving, cheating Oth 4.2.132 *Some cogging, cozening slave.*

cognition *n.* Knowledge, consciousness, rational apprehension Tro 5.2.63 *nor have cognition Of what I feel.*

cognizance *n.* (in heraldry) Device or emblem worn by retainers JC 2.2.89 *that great men shall press For tinctures, stains, relics, and cognizance;* (hence) mark, badge or token by which a thing is known 1H6 2.4.108 *this pale and angry rose, As cognizance of my blood-drinking hate,* Cym 2.4.127.

cohere *vb.* Agree with MM 2.1.11 *time coher'd with place, or place with wishing,* TN 5.1.252.

coherence *n.* Agreement 2H4 5.1.65 *the semblable coherence of his men's spirits and his.*

coherent *adj.* Suitable, in accord AWW 3.7.39 *That time and place with this deceit so lawful May prove coherent.*

cohort *n.* Band or troop of soldiers Lr 1.2.148 *banishment of friends, dissipation of cohorts, nuptial breaches.*

coif See QUOIF.

coign *n.* Corner-stone Cor 5.4.1 *See you yond coign a' th' Capitol, yond cornerstone?,* Per 3.Gower.17; *coign of vantage* corner or position convenient for observation or action Mac 1.6.7 *no jutty, frieze, Buttress, nor coign of vantage, but this bird Hath made his pendant bed.*

coil *n.*
1 Noisy disturbance, tumult Err 3.1.48 *What a coil is there, Dromio?*
2 Fuss, ado Ado 5.2.96 *yonder's old coil at home,* Jn 2.1.165; *mortal coil* turmoil of this mortal life Ham 3.1.66 *When we have shuffled off this mortal coil.*

coining *n.* Making of money, minting Lr 4.6.82 *They cannot touch me for coining, I am the King himself* (F *crying;* Q *coyning*).

coistrel *n.* Knave, base fellow TN 1.3.40 *He's a coward and a coistrel* (F1 *coystrill*), Per 4.6.166 (Qq *custerell*).

cold *n.* Coldness H8 4.2.98 *How pale she looks, And of an earthy cold!*
~ *adj.*
1 Deliberate, cool Cym 2.3.2 *the most patient man in loss, The most coldest that ever turn'd up ace,* 2H4 3.2.123.
2 Devoid of sensual heat, chaste Cym 5.5.181 *He spake of her, as Dian had hot dreams, And she alone were cold,* Tmp 4.1.66, MND 1.1.73.
3 Gloomy, dispirited, hopeless 3H6 3.2.133 *A cold premeditation for my purpose!,* AWW 2.1.144, 1H4 2.3.30.
4 Chilling, damping 2H6 3.1.86 *Cold news, Lord Somerset; but God's will be done!,* R3 4.4.534.
5 Without power to move or influence, having lost the power of exciting the emotions TGV 4.4.181 *I hope my master's suit will be but cold.*
⬦ Perh. also MV 2.7.73 *Fare you well, your suit is cold.*
6 (of scent) Faint, not strong TN 2.5.121 *He is now at a cold scent,* Ven 694.
⬦ *catch cold* See CATCH.

coldly *adv.*
1 Calmly, coolly, rationally Err 5.1.273 *If he were mad, he would not plead so coldly,* Ado 3.2.129, Jn 2.1.53.
2 Lightly, with indifference Ham 4.3.62 *thou mayst not coldly set Our sovereign process.*

cold-moving *adj.* Frigid, distant Tim 2.2.212 *With certain half-caps and cold-moving nods, They froze me into silence.*

co-leagued, colleagued *adj.* Allied, joined Ham 1.2.21 *Co-leagued with this dream of his advantage.*

collar *n.*
1 Hangman's halter 2H4 5.5.87 *A collar that I fear you will die in, Sir John* (punning; Q *collor;* F *colour.* See COLOUR *n.* sense 4).
2 *Collars of Esses* Ornamental gold chains, part of the insignia of knighthood, fashioned of S-shaped links H8 4.1.SD.

collateral *adj.* Shining from a different sphere, indirect, subordinate AWW 1.1.88 *In his bright radiance and collateral light Must I be comforted,* Ham 4.5.207.
⬦ In Ptolemaic astronomy the spheres moved 'collaterally', i.e. in parallel motion.

collect *vb.* Gather, deduce, infer 2H6 3.1.35 *The reverent care I bear unto my lord Made me collect these dangers in the Duke,* H8 1.2.130.

collection *n.* Inference, deduction, attempt to gather the meaning Ham 4.5.9 *Her speech is nothing, Yet the unshaped use of it doth move The hearers to collection,* Cym 5.5.432.

collied *adj.* Dark, blackened (as if by coal) MND 1.1.145 *the collied night,* Oth 2.3.206.

collop *n.* Piece of flesh; (hence) part of a man,

offspring 1H6 5.4.18 *God knows thou art a collop of my flesh*, WT 1.2.137.

coloquintida *n*. Colocynth or bitter apple, used as a purgative OTH 1.3.349 *The food...shall be to him shortly as acerb as the coloquintida.*

colour *n*.

1 (pl.) Military ensigns; (hence) *fear no colours* fear no enemy, have no fear TN 1.5.6 *He that is well hang'd in this world needs to fear no colours*; *under her colours* in her party, led by her CYM 1.4.20 *those that weep this lamentable divorce under her colours.*

2 Appearance, semblance 1H6 2.4.34 *without all colour Of base insinuating flattery*, HAM 3.4.130.

3· Tone, character, kind LR 2.2.138 *a fellow of the self-same colour*, AYL 1.2.101.

4 Pretext, pretence TGV 4.2.3 *Under the colour of commending him*, 2H4 5.5.86 (see also COLLAR *n.* sense 1), ANT 1.3.32.

5 Allegeable ground or reason, excuse CYM 3.1.50 *Against all colour here Did put the yoke upon 's* (i.e. in opposition to all reason), 2H4 1.2.246.

~ *vb*.

1 Dye SHR 4.1.134 *There was no link to colour Peter's hat*, CYM 5.1.2.

2 Gloss, disguise, give a specious appearance to HAM 3.1.44 *That show of such an exercise may colour Your loneliness*, MM 2.1.220, 1H4 1.3.109.

colourable *adj*. Specious, plausible LLL 4.2.149 *I do fear colourable colours.*

coloured *ppl. adj*. Depicted in colour, painted LUC 1497 *pencill'd pensiveness and colour'd sorrow.*

colt *n*.

1 (fig.) Young, inexperienced fellow MV 1.2.40 *Ay, that's a colt indeed, for he doth nothing but talk of his horse.*

2 (fig.) Lascivious fellow, wanton LLL 3.1.31 *No, master, the hobby-horse is but a colt, and your love perhaps a hackney.*

3 *colt's tooth* Youthful desires, wanton inclinations and impulses H8 1.3.48 *Well said, Lord Sands, Your colt's tooth is not cast yet.*

~ *vb*.

1 Befool, trick 1H4 2.2.37 *What a plague mean ye to colt me thus?*

2 Have sexual intercourse with, possess sexually CYM 2.4.133 *She hath been colted by him* (with possible play on sense 1).

co-mart, comart *n*. Agreement, bargain HAM 1.1.93 *as by the same comart And carriage of the article design'd*, *His fell to Hamlet* (Ff *Cou'nant* 'covenant').

combat *n*. Fight between two, duel 2H6 1.3.219 *the day of the combat*, TRO 1.3.335, HAM 1.1.84.

combinate-husband *n*. Man bound by oath to be one's husband, betrothed MM 3.1.222 *her combinate-husband, this well-seeming Angelo.*

combination *n*. Agreement, treaty, alliance H8 1.1.169 *The articles o' th' combination*, HAM 3.4.60; (hence) marriage TN 5.1.383 *A solemn combination shall be made Of our dear souls.*

combine *vb*. Tie, bind MM 4.3.144 *For my poor self, I am combined by a sacred vow*, AYL 5.4.150.

combustion *n*. Tumult, civil disorder MAC 2.3.58 *And prophesying, with accents terrible, Of dire combustion and confus'd events.*

combustious *adj*. Combustible VEN 1162 *Subject and servile to all discontents, As dry combustious matter is to fire.*

come *vb*.

1 Become HAM 5.1.156 *How came he mad?*, MND 2.2.92.

2 Come around, relent MM 2.2.125 *he will relent. He's coming; I perceive't.*

~ in phrases

come from thy ward Leave thy posture of defence TMP 1.2.472 *Come, from thy ward, For I can here disarm thee with this stick*. **come home** Come away from its hold so as to drag WT 1.2.214 *You had much ado to make his anchor hold, When you cast out it, still came home.* **come short, come slack** Fall short *of* MM 5.1.220 *her promised proportions Came short of composition*, LR 1.3.9 *If you come slack of former services.* **come to it** Reach the age of puberty or of manhood TRO 1.2.84 *Th' other's not come to 't.* **come to oneself** Recover consciousness JC 1.2.269 *When he came to himself again.*

~ in combination

come about 1 Veer round MV 2.6.64 *the wind is come about.* 2 Turn out to be true ROM 1.3.45 *To see now how a jest shall come about!* **come away** Come along 1H4 2.1.22 *What, ostler! come away and be hang'd!* **come behind** Approach from the rear (in order to attack) 2H6 4.7.84 *O monstrous coward! What, to come behind folks?* **come by** Get hold of, become possessed of TMP 2.1.292 *I'll come by Naples*. **come in** 1 Make a pass or a home-thrust, get within the opponent's guard 2H4 3.2.283 *'a would about and about, and come you in.* 2 Give in, yield, relent JN 5.2.70 *King John hath reconcil'd Himself to Rome, his spirit is come in.* **come near** See NEAR. **come off** 1 Escape, retire from combat JN 5.5.4 *O, bravely came we off* 2 Turn out TIM 1.1.29 *This comes off well and excellent.* 3 Pay up, disburse WIV 4.3.11 *I'll make them pay...they must come off.* **come over** 1 Surpass ADO 5.2.7 *no man living shall come over it.* 2 Take possession of; (fig.) OTH 4.1.20 *it comes o'er my memory.* 3 Light upon TIM 3.2.78 *Nor came any of his bounties over me.* 4 Taunt, twit H5 1.2.267 *How he comes o'er us with our wilder days.* **come up** 1 Come into fashion 2H6 4.2.9 *it was never merry world in England since gentlemen came up.* 2 Rise *to* WT 2.1.193 *Whose ignorant credulity will not Come up to th' truth.* **come upon** 1 Approach TRO 4.3.3 *the hour prefix'd...Come fast upon.* 2 Attack, riposte against LLL 4.1.119 *Shall I come upon thee with an old saying?*

comeddle *vb*. Mix, blend HAM 3.2.69 *Whose blood and judgement are so well co-meddled* (Ff *co-mingled*; Qq *com(m)edled*).

comedian *n*. Actor, stage-player TN 1.5.182 *Are you a comedian?*

comely *adv*. Fittingly LC 65 *And comely distant sits he by her side* (i.e. at a decorous distance).

comfit-maker *n*. Confectioner 1H4 3.1.248 *Heart, you swear like a comfit-maker's wife.*

comfort *n*.

1 Pleasure, gladness, delight CYM 5.5.403 *Let them be joyful too, For they shall taste our comfort.*

2 Succour, support, assistance LR 4.1.16 *Thy comforts can do me no good at all*, MM 3.2.41.

~ *vb*.

1 Relieve, minister relief to TIT 2.3.209 *Why dost not comfort me and help me out From this unhallow'd and blood-stained hole?*, LLL 4.2.44, WT 2.3.56.

2 Take comfort, be consoled AYL 2.6.5 *Live a little, comfort a little, cheer thyself a little.*

~ *interj*. Cheer up, take heart WT 4.4.818 *Comfort, good comfort! We must to the King, and show our strange sights*, R3 2.2.89; *what comfort* what cheer MM 3.1.54, R2 2.1.72; *have comfort, be of (good) comfort* be of good cheer TMP 1.2.496, TN 3.4.338, JN 5.3.9.

comfortable *adj*.

1 Affording comfort or consolation, helpful AWW

1.1.76 *Be comfortable to my mother, your mistress*, ROM 5.3.148, LR 1.4.306.
2 Cheerful AYL 2.6.9 *For my sake be comfortable*, COR 1.3.2, TIM 3.4.71.

comfortless *adj.*
1 Unconsoled, inconsolable H8 2.3.105 *The Queen is comfortless*, ERR 5.1.80.
2 Giving no comfort TIT 3.1.250 *that kiss is comfortless As frozen water to a starved snake*, LR 3.7.85, JN 5.6.20.

coming(s)-in *n.* Income H5 4.1.243 *What are thy rents? What are thy comings-in?*, MV 2.2.163.

co-mingle See CO-MEDDLE.

coming-on *adj.* Complaisant, agreeable AYL 4.1.112 *now I will be your Rosalind in a more coming-on disposition.*

comma *n.*
1 Small part of a sentence, detail TIM 1.1.48 *no levell'd malice Infects one comma in the course I hold.*
2 Break in continuity, pause, interval HAM 5.2.42 *peace should...stand a comma 'tween their amities* (spoken ironically).

command *n.* *upon command* At a given order R3 1.4.193 *What we will do, we do upon command*; at pleasure AYL 2.7.125 *take upon command what help we have.*
~ *vb.*
1 Demand with authority CYM 1.5.8 *wherefore you have Commanded of me these most poisonous compounds*, 2H6 5.1.49.
2 Lay commands *upon* MAC 3.1.16 *Let your Highness Command upon me.*
3 Force, compel 3H6 2.6.36 *As doth a sail, fill'd with a fretting gust, Command an argosy to stem the waves*, VEN 584.
4 Commend, entrust CYM 3.7.9 *and to you the tribunes, For this immediate levy, he commands His absolute commission.*
5 (pass.) Be entrusted with a command COR 1.1.262 *But I do wonder His insolence can brook to be commanded Under Cominius.*

commanded *ppl. adj.* Forced SHR Ind.1.125 *a shower of commanded tears.*

commandment *n.*
1 *at my, your commandment* At my, your service 2H4 5.3.137 *Let us take any man's horses, the laws of England are at my commandment*, MV 2.2.32; *at commandment* at pleasure 2H4 3.2.24 *we knew where the bona robas were and had the best of them all at commandment.*
2 *ten commandments* The fingers 2H6 1.3.142 *I could set my ten commandments in your face.*
⬦ In Ff and Qq usu. *commandement* or *command'ment* to represent pronunciation.

commeddle See CO-MEDDLE.

commence *vb.* Admit to a university degree; (hence) qualify, make fit or competent (to do something); (fig.) 2H4 4.3.116 *learning a mere hoard of gold kept by a devil, till sack commences it and sets it in act and use.*
⬦ Prob. an allusion to the commencement at Cambridge University.

commend *vb.*
1 Commendation PER 2.2.49 *speak in his just commend.*
2 (pl.) Greetings, remembrances, compliments R2 3.1.38 *Tell her I send to her my kind commends.*
~ *vb.*
1 Deliver, commit, entrust LLL 3.1.168 *And to her white hand see thou do commend This seal'd-up counsel*, MAC 1.7.11, H8 5.1.17.
2 Commit to the care or attention of COR 4.5.144

Let me commend thee first to those that shall Say yea to thy desires, TGV 1.1.17.
4 Present or convey one's greetings and kind remembrances WIV 1.4.157 *If thou seest her before me, commend me*, TGV 1.1.146, MM 1.4.88; (refl.) send one's greetings, ask to be kindly remembered MV 3.2.232 *Signior Antonio Commends him to you*, TRO 3.1.66, HAM 1.5.183.

commendations *n.* (pl.) Greetings, kind remembrances TGV 1.3.53 *a word or two Of commendations sent from Valentine.*

comment *n.* Observation, judgement HAM 3.2.79 *Even with the very comment of thy soul Observe my uncle.*

commenting *n.* Meditating, pondering R3 4.3.51 *fearful commenting Is leaden servitor to dull delay.*

commerce *n.* Intercourse, dealings TN 3.4.174 *he is now in some commerce with my lady*, HAM 3.1.108.

commission *n.*
1 Order, mandate LR 5.3.253 *He hath commission from thy wife and me To hang Cordelia in the prison*, MM 1.1.13.
2 Warrant AWW 2.3.261 *more saucy with lords and honourable personages than the commission of your birth and virtue gives you heraldry*, 1H6 5.4.95, ROM 4.1.64.
3 *in commission* Entrusted with an office MAC 1.4.2 *Are not Those in commission yet return'd?*; *in commission with* serving as a justice of the peace with 2H4 3.2.88 *my cousin Silence, in commission with me.*
4 Body of persons charged with a specific office LR 3.6.38 *You are o' th' commission* (i.e. appointed one of the judges).

commit *vb.* Sin TGV 5.4.77 *I do as truly suffer As e'er I did commit*; (spec.) commit adultery LR 3.4.81 *commit not with man's sworn spouse.*

commixtion *n.* Commingling, mixture, blending together TRO 4.5.124 *Were thy commixtion Greek and Troyan so That thou couldst say...*

commixture *n.*
1 Compound 3H6 2.6.6 *thy tough commixtures melt.*
2 Complexion, bodily constitution LLL 5.2.296 *Dismask'd, their damask sweet commixture shown.*

commodious *adj.* Accommodating TRO 5.2.194 *The parrot will not do more for an almond than he for a commodious drab.*

commodity *n.*
1 Convenience, commercial privileges MV 3.3.27 *the commodity that strangers have With us in Venice*, WT 3.2.93.
2 Expediency JN 2.1.597 *Since kings break faith upon commodity.*
3 Advantage, profit 2H4 1.2.248 *I will turn diseases to commodity*, LR 4.1.21.
4 Quantity of wares, parcel, consignment TN 3.1.44 *Now Jove, in his next commodity of hair, send thee a beard!*, 1H4 1.2.83; (spec.) parcel of goods sold on credit by a usurer to a needy person who then raised cash by re-selling at a lower price, often to the usurer himself MM 4.3.5 *he's in for a commodity of brown paper and old ginger, nine-score and seventeen pounds, of which he made five marks ready money.*

common *n.*
1 Common people, commonalty COR 1.1.151 *the weal a' th' common*; (usu. pl.) R2 1.1.246 *The commons hath he pill'd*, H8 1.2.104.
2 Common land JC 4.1.27 *graze in commons*; (fig. or allusively) ERR 2.2.29 *And make a common of my serious hours* (i.e. a public playground), LLL 2.1.223.
3 *the common* That which is usual or ordinary COR 4.1.32 *your son Will or exceed the common or be*

caught With cautelous baits; the vulgar tongue
AYL 5.1.49 this female—which in the common is
woman.
~ adj.
1 Belonging equally to all MAC 3.1.68 the common
enemy of man (i.e. the devil), 1H4 2.1.95.
2 Public, free to be used by everyone MM 4.2.9 a
common executioner, AYL 2.3.33, ADO 4.1.65.
3 General AWW 2.5.52 common speech Gives him
a worthy pass (i.e. general report), 2H6 1.1.206;
(hence) generally known or spoken of JN 4.2.187
Young Arthur's death is common in their mouths.
4 Usual, prevalent SON 102.12 And sweets grown
common lose their dear delight, TGV 5.4.62.
5 Ordinary, undistinguished TGV 5.4.62 Thou
common friend, that's without faith or love, VEN
293; common sense ordinary or untutored percep-
tions LLL 1.1.57 Things hid and barr'd (you mean)
from common sense.
6 Belonging to the commonalty, of the people or
the multitude COR 1.6.43 The common file (i.e.
plebeian soldiers), ERR 3.1.101, 2H4 1.3.97.
common vb. (var. of) COMMUNE.
commoner n. Prostitute, common harlot AWW
5.3.194 He gave it to a commoner a' th' camp, OTH
4.2.73.
common-hackneyed adj. Cheapened, vulgarized
1H4 3.2.40 So common-hackney'd in the eyes of men.
common-kissing adj. Kissing all alike CYM 3.4.163
to the greedy touch Of common-kissing Titan.
commonty n. (humorous blunder for) Comedy SHR
Ind.2.138 Is not a commonty a Christmas
gambold...? (F1 comonty).
commotion n.
1 Tumult, sedition 2H6 3.1.358 To make commotion, as full well he can, 2H4 2.4.363.
2 Mental perturbation TRO 2.3.175 Kingdom'd
Achilles in commotion rages, H8 3.2.112.
commune vb.
1 Talk, converse MM 4.3.104 For I would commune
with you of such things (F1 commone), WT 2.1.162.
2 Talk over SHR 1.1.101 For I have more to commune with Bianca.
3 Take a part in common, share with HAM 4.5.203
Laertes, I must commune with your grief (F1
common).
community n. Commonness, familiarity 1H4 3.2.77
with such eyes As, sick and blunted with
community, Afford no extraordinary gaze.
commutual, comutual adj. Mutual, reciprocal,
answering to each other as one HAM 3.2.160 Since
love our hearts and Hymen did our hands Unite
commutual in most sacred bands (F1 comutuall).
comonty See COMMONTY.
compact n. Plot, conspiracy ERR 2.2.161 What is the
course and drift of your compact?
~ ppl. adj.¹
Joined in compact, leagued MM 5.1.242 Thou foolish friar, and thou pernicious woman, Compact
with her that's gone, LR 2.2.118.
compact vb.
1 Combine, incorporate LUC 530 The poisonous
simple sometime is compacted In a pure compound.
2 Confirm, strengthen LR 1.4.339 And thereto add
such reasons of your own As may compact it more.
~ ppl. adj.²
1 Knit together LR 1.2.7 When my dimensions are
as well compact.
2 Made up or composed of ERR 3.2.22 make us but
believe (Being compact of credit) that you love us
(i.e. entirely composed of credulity).
3 Solid LUC 1423 much imaginary work was there,
Conceit deceitful, so compact, so kind.
companion n. (term of contempt) Fellow AWW

5.3.250 What an equivocal companion is this!, ERR
4.4.61, 2H4 2.4.123.
~ vb. Make companion ANT 1.2.30 Find me to
marry me with Octavius Caesar, and companion
me with my mistress.
companionship n. all of companionship All in a
body or party TIM 1.1.242 'Tis Alcibiades, and some
twenty horse, All of companionship.
company n.
1 from company Alone, in solitude 1H6 5.5.100 And
so conduct me where, from company, I may revolve
and ruminate my grief; for company by way of
sociableness, for company's sake SHR 4.1.177 And
for this night we'll fast for company.
2 Companion AWW 4.3.32 I would gladly have him
see his company anatomiz'd, MND 1.1.219, H5
1.1.55.
⬦ Perh. pl. of the collective—i.e. various groups
of companions or associates.
3 (pl.) Companionship HAM 2.2.14 by your companies To draw him on to pleasures.
~ vb. Accompany CYM 5.5.408 The soldier that did
company these three.
comparative n. One who devises comparisons
(esp. satirical ones) 1H4 3.2.67 stand the push Of
every beardless vain comparative.
~ adj.
1 Skilful at making (satirical) comparisons 1H4
1.2.80 Thou hast the most unsavoury similes and
art indeed the most comparative, rascalliest, sweet
young prince.
2 made comparative (?) Made (1) to serve as a
means of comparison; or (2) comparable (with)
CYM 2.3.129 Thou wert dignified enough...if 'twere
made Comparative for your virtues, to be styl'd The
under-hangman of his kingdom.
compare n. Comparison TN 2.4.101 Make no compare Between that love, SON 21.5, MND 3.2.290.
~ vb.
1 Draw a comparison R2 2.1.185 Or else he never
would compare between.
2 compare with Bear comparison with, rival, vie
with HAM 5.2.138 lest I should compare with him in
excellence, MND 2.2.99, 2H4 2.4.166.
comparison n.
1 (pl.) Advantages which appear when we are
compared ANT 3.13.26 I dare him therefore To lay
his gay comparisons apart.
2 Satirical or scoffing simile LLL 5.2.844 Full of
comparisons and wounding flouts, ADO 2.1.146.
compass n.
1 Circle, circumference TGV 2.7.51 What compass
will you wear your farthingale?, WIV 5.5.66, 3H6
4.3.47.
2 Circuit, circular course JC 5.3.25 My life is run
his compass, OTH 3.4.71.
3 Bounds, limits, range, reach R2 3.4.40 Why
should we in the compass of a pale Keep law and
form and due proportion, H8 1.1.36, OTH 3.4.21.
~ vb. Obtain, win WT 4.3.96 then he compass'd a
motion of the Prodigal Son, TGV 2.4.214, H5 4.1.294;
achieve, accomplish VEN 567 Things out of hope
are compass'd oft with vent'ring, TN 1.2.44.
compassed, compast ppl. adj. Round, arched, circular SHR 4.3.139 a small compass'd cape;
compass'd window semi-circular bay-window TRO
1.2.111 She came to him th' other day into the compass'd window.
compassion vb. Pity TIT 4.1.124 O heavens, can you
hear a good man groan And not relent, or not compassion him?
compassionate adj. Pitying, self-pitying R2 1.3.174
It boots thee not to be compassionate, After our sentence plaining comes too late.

compeer *n.* Companion, associate SON 86.7 *neither he, nor his compeers by night Giving him aid.* ~ *vb.* Equal, rival LR 5.3.69 *he compeers the best.*

compel *vb.* Take or get by force AWW 4.3.321 *And I were not a very coward, I'd compel it of you,* H5 3.6.109, H8 1.2.57.

compelled *ppl. adj.* Enforced, unsought H8 2.3.87 *fie upon This compell'd fortune!*; involuntary MM 2.4.57 *our compell'd sins Stand more for number than for accompt.*

competence *n.* Adequate supply, modest allowance 2H4 5.5.66 *For competence of life I will allow you.*

competency *n.* Sufficient supply COR 1.1.139 *From me receive that natural competency Whereby they live.*

competent *adj.* Sufficient, adequate TN 3.4.247 *his indignation derives itself out of a very competent injury,* HAM 1.1.90.

competitor *n.* Associate, partner TGV 2.6.35 *Myself in counsel his competitor,* R3 4.4.505, ANT 5.1.42.

compile *vb.* Compose as an original work LLL 4.3.132 *Longaville Did never sonnet for her sake compile,* SON 78.9.

complain *vb.* Bewail, lament R2 3.4.18 *And what I want it boots not to complain,* ROM 2.Prol.7, LUC 1839.

compleat See COMPLETE.

complement *n.*
1 That which 'completes' the character of a gentleman in matters of external appearance or demeanour LLL 1.1.168 *A man of complements, whom right and wrong Have chose as umpeer of their mutiny,* OTH 1.1.63, H5 2.2.134; (hence) actions belonging to or associated with a gentleman LLL 3.1.22 *these are complements, these are humours.*
2 See COMPLIMENT.

complete, compleat *adj.*
1 Fully equipped, perfect, accomplished H8 3.2.49 *She is a gallant creature, and complete In mind and feature,* TRO 3.3.181, TIM 3.1.10.
2 Filled (*with*), full TGV 2.4.73 *He is complete in feature and in mind With all good grace to grace a gentleman,* TIM 4.3.244.

complexion *n.*
1 Bodily habit or constitution, orig. supposed to be composed of the four 'humours' HAM 5.2.99 *very sultry and hot for my complexion.*
2 Constitution or habit of mind, disposition, temperament MV 3.1.29 *and then it is the complexion of them all to leave the dam,* ADO 2.1.295.
3 Natural colour and appearance of the skin, esp. of the face ERR 3.2.101 *What complexion is she of?—Swart, like my shoe,* TMP 1.1.29, OTH 4.2.62.
4 (fig.) Colour 2H4 2.2.5 *though it discolours the complexion of my greatness to acknowledge it,* WT 1.2.381, H5 2.2.73.
5 Visible aspect, appearance (of objects in general) R2 3.2.194 *Men judge by the complexion of the sky The state and inclination of the day.*

complice *n.* Confederate, comrade R2 2.3.165 *Bushy, Bagot, and their complices.*

compliment *n.* Observance of ceremony in social relations, formal civility, politeness, courtesy LLL 4.2.142 *Stay not thy compliment; I forgive thy duty,* ADO 4.1.319, LR 1.1.302.
◊ Ff and Qq *complement*, a form which was gradually replaced in this sense by *compliment* in 17-18C, which is now usu. adopted in mod. edd.

complimental *adj.* Courteous, polite, observing due ceremony TRO 3.1.39 *I will make a complimental assault upon him.*

complot *n.* Plot, conspiracy 2H6 3.1.147 *their complot is to have my life,* R3 3.1.192, TIT 2.3.265.
~ *vb.* Combine in plotting, concert covertly R2 1.3.189 *To plot, contrive, or complot any ill,* R2 1.1.96.

comply *vb.*
1 Fulfil, accomplish OTH 1.3.263 *Nor to comply with heat...and proper satisfaction.*
2 Observe the formalities of courtesy and politeness, 'use complements, or ceremonies, or kind offices' (Florio) HAM 2.2.372 *Let me comply with you in this garb.*

compose *vb.*
1 Make up, construct, produce MAC 1.7.73 *thy undaunted mettle should compose Nothing but males,* MND 1.1.48, TRO 5.2.170.
2 Come to a settlement, agree ANT 2.2.15 *If we compose well here, to Parthia.*

composed *ppl. adj.* Elaborately put together TGV 3.2.69 *composed rhymes.*

composition *n.*
1 Constitution JN 1.1.88 *some tokens of my son In the large composition of this man?,* R2 2.1.73.
2 Compact, agreement ANT 2.6.58 *I crave our composition may be written And seal'd between us,* MM 1.2.2, MAC 1.2.59.
3 Consistency OTH 1.3.1 *There's no composition in these news That gives them credit.*

composture *n.* Manure, compost TIM 4.3.441 *feeds and breeds by a composture stol'n From gen'ral excrement.*

composure *n.*
1 Temperament, disposition TRO 2.3.240 *thou art of sweet composure,* ANT 1.4.22.
2 Combination, alliance TRO 2.3.99 *But it was a strong composure a fool could disunite* (Ff *counsel*).

compound *n.*
1 Compound word SON 76.4 *To new-found methods and to compounds strange?*
2 Mass, lump 2H4 2.4.294 *Thou whoreson mad compound of majesty,* 1H4 2.4.123.
~ *vb.*
1 Construct, form, make up, constitute H5 5.2.207 *Shall not thou and I...compound a boy, half French, half English,* TIM 4.2.35.
2 Settle (a difference) SHR 1.2.27 *we will compound this quarrel,* R3 2.1.75; (also intr.) agree, make terms MM 4.2.24 *If you think it meet, compound with him by the year,* JN 2.1.281, LR 1.2.128.

comprehend *vb.* (malapropism for) Apprehend ADO 3.3.25 *This is your charge: you shall comprehend all vagrom men.*

compromise *n.*
1 Settlement by arbitration WIV 1.1.33 *I am of the church, and will be glad to do my benevolence to make atonements and compromises between you.*
2 Coming to terms by concessions on both sides JN 5.1.67 *Shall we...Send fair-play orders and make compromise, Insinuation, parley, and base truce To arms invasive?,* R2 2.1.253, 1H6 5.4.149.
~ *vb. be compromised* Be agreed as the result of compromise, have come to terms MV 1.3.78 *When Laban and himself were compromis'd That all the eanlings which were streak'd and pied Should fall as Jacob's hire.*

compt *n.* Account, reckoning AWW 5.3.57 *strikes some scores away From the great compt; at compt* at the day of reckoning, the Judgement Day OTH 5.2.273 *when we shall meet at compt, This look of thine will hurl my soul from heaven* (Q1 *count*); *in compt* subject to account MAC 1.6.26 *Your servants ever Have theirs, themselves, and what is theirs, in compt, To make their audit at your Highness' pleasure.*

compter *n.* Counter, metal disc used in calculating WT 4.3.36 *I cannot do't without compters,* TRO 2.2.28 (Q; F1 *Counters*).

comptible *adj.* Liable to answer to; (hence) susceptible, sensitive *to* TN 1.5.175 *I am very comptible, even to the least sinister usage.*

comptless *adj.* Countless, that cannot be counted VEN 84 *And one sweet kiss shall pay this comptless debt.*

comptroller *n.* Officer in a great household whose duties were primarily to check or control expenditure and so to manage in general H8 1.3.67 *For I was spoke to, with Sir Henry Guilford This night to be comptrollers.*

compulsative, compulsatory *adj.* Involving force HAM 1.1.103 *to recover of us, by strong hand And terms compulsatory, those foresaid lands* (Qq; Ff *compulsative*).

compulsion *n.* Compelling circumstances JN 5.2.44 *what a noble combat hast thou fought Between compulsion and a brave respect!*

compulsive *adj.* Exercising compulsion, coercive HAM 3.4.86 *Proclaim no shame When the compulsive ardure gives the charge*; (in physical sense) having the property of driving or forcing onward OTH 3.3.454 *the Pontic Sea Whose icy current and compulsive course Nev'r feels retiring ebb.*

compunctious *adj.* Remorseful MAC 1.5.45 *That no compunctious visitings of nature Shake my fell purpose.*

con *vb.*
1 Learn by heart MND 1.2.100 *and desire you, to con them by tomorrow night,* TRO 2.1.17, JC 4.3.98.
2 *con thanks* Acknowledge one's gratitude, offer thanks AWW 4.3.152 *I con him no thanks for't,* TIM 4.3.425.

con tutto (il) core, ben trovato [It.] With all my heart, well met SHR 1.2.24.

concave *adj.* Hollow AYL 3.4.24 *I do think him as concave as a cover'd goblet,* LC1.

concealed *adj.* Secretly married ROM 3.3.98 *and what says My conceal'd lady to our cancell'd love?*

concealment *n.* Secret, mystery 1H4 3.1.165 *a worthy gentleman,...profited In strange concealments* (i.e. expert in secret arts).

conceit *n.*
1 What is conceived in the mind, conception, idea OTH 3.3.115 *hadst shut up in thy brain Some horrible conceit,* LLL 2.1.72, MV 3.4.2.
2 Faculty of conceiving, apprehension, understanding, mental capacity AYL 5.2.54 *a gentleman of good conceit,* ERR 4.2.65, PER 3.1.16.
3 Personal opinion or estimate TGV 3.2.17 *Proteus, the good conceit I hold of thee,* H8 2.3.74.
4 Imagination, fancy R2 2.2.33 *'Tis nothing but conceit, my gracious lady,* AYL 2.6.8, LR 4.6.42; (hence) fanciful thought or brooding HAM 4.5.45 *Conceit upon her father*; gaiety of imagination, wit 2H4 2.4.241 *There's no more conceit in him than is in a mallet.*
5 Fanciful design, device, invention HAM 5.2.153 *Three of the carriages, in faith, are very dear to fancy...and of very liberal conceit,* TIT 4.2.30, 1H6 4.1.102; fancifully made articles MND 1.1.33 *rings, gawds, conceits.*

~ *vb.*
1 Form a conception or opinion of JC 1.3.162 *Him and his worth, and our great need of him, You have right well conceited.*
2 (intr.) Form a conception, conceive OTH 3.3.149 *One that so imperfectly conceits* (Qq *conjects*).

conceited *ppl. adj.*
1 Full of imagination or fancy, ingenious WIV 1.3.23 *He was gotten in drink. Is not the humour conceited?,* LUC 1371; (hence) *well conceited* aptly put 2H4 5.1.36; *conceited characters* fanciful designs LC 16 *her napkin...had conceited characters.*

2 Possessed of an idea TN 3.4.294 *He is so horribly conceited of him* (i.e. has a terrifying notion of).

conceitless *adj.* Witless TGV 4.2.96 *so shallow, so conceitless, To be seduced by thy flattery.*

conceive *vb.*
1 Take the meaning of (a person), understand WIV 1.1.242 *Nay, conceive me, conceive me, sweet coz,* MM 2.4.141, MND 4.1.213.
2 Have an opinion or estimate of H8 1.2.105 *The grieved commons Hardly conceive of me.*

concent *n.* Harmony, concord H5 1.2.181 *For government...doth keep in one concent, Congreeing in a full and natural close, Like music.*
◇ F1, Qq *consent,* a common 16–17C spelling.

conception *n.*
1 That which is conceived in the mind, idea, notion, plan TRO 1.3.312 *I have a young conception in my brain,* MM 2.4.7, H8 1.2.139.
2 Mere fancy OTH 3.4.156 *Pray heaven it be state matters... And no conception nor no jealous toy Concerning you.*

conceptious *adj.* Fruitful, prolific TIM 4.3.187 *thy fertile and conceptious womb.*

concern *vb.*
1 (trans.) Have reference to, relate to 2H4 4.1.30 *Say on, my Lord of Westmerland, in peace, What doth concern your coming* (i.e. what is the purpose of), TGV 3.1.256.
2 Be of importance to MM 1.1.77 *it concerns me To look into the bottom of my place,* OTH 1.3.22, MND 1.1.126.
3 (intr.) Be of importance LLL 4.2.142 *deliver this paper into the royal hand of the King; it may concern much,* TGV 1.2.73, 1H6 5.3.116.
4 Befit MND 1.1.60 *how it may concern my modesty.*

concernancy *n.* Import, relevance HAM 5.2.122 *The concernancy, sir? Why do we wrap the gentleman in our more rawer breath?*

concerning *n.* Concern, affair MM 1.1.56 *As time and our concernings shall importune,* HAM 3.4.191.

conclude *vb.*
1 *be it concluded* To conclude, in brief WT 1.2.203 *Be it concluded, No barricado for a belly.*
2 Come to a final arrangement or decision R2 1.1.156 *Forget, forgive, conclude and be agreed,* 1H6 5.1.5, HAM 3.4.201.
3 Decide, resolve R3 1.3.15 *It is determin'd, not concluded yet,* JC 2.2.93, MAC 3.1.140.
4 (intr.) Be decisive, settle the matter JN 1.1.127 *This concludes: My mother's son did get your father's heir.*

conclusion *n.*
1 Action of concluding or inferring ANT 4.15.28 *Your wife Octavia, with her modest eyes And still conclusion, shall acquire no honour Demuring upon me.*
2 Problem, riddle PER 1.1.56 *Scorning advice, read the conclusion then.*
3 Experiment ANT 5.2.355 *for her physician tells me She hath pursu'd conclusions infinite Of easy ways to die,* OTH 1.3.329, HAM 3.4.195.

concupiscible *adj.* Desirous, lustful MM 5.1.98 *by gift of my chaste body To his concupiscible intemperate lust.*

concupy *n.* Concubine TRO 5.2.177 *He'll tickle it for his concupy.*
◇ Possibly a var. of 'concuby.'

condemn *vb.* Discredit ANT 5.2.100 *nature's piece 'gainst fancy, Condemning shadows quite,* SON 99.6.

condemned *ppl. adj.* Unfit, useless COR 1.8.15 *you have sham'd me In your condemned seconds.*

condign *adj.* Worthily deserved, merited, fitting LLL 1.2.25 *In thy condign praise,* 2H6 3.1.130.

condition *n.*
1 (used ellipt. for) On condition that TRO 1.2.74 *Condition I had gone barefoot to India.*
2 Covenant, contract MV 1.3.148 *such sum or sums as are Express'd in the condition,* TMP 1.2.117, AWW 4.2.30.
3 Mode or state of being JC 2.1.236 *to commit Your weak condition to the raw cold morning,* AYL 1.2.15, OTH 1.2.26.
4 Social or official position, rank TMP 3.1.59 *I am, in my condition, A prince,* 2H4 4.3.84, H5 4.3.63.
5 Mental disposition, temper, character MV 1.2.129 *If he have the condition of a saint,* LLL 5.2.20, TIM 4.3.140.
6 Property, quality, characteristic, attribute TGV 3.1.274 *Here is the cate-log of her condition,* ADO 3.2.66, SHR 5.2.167.

conditionally *adv.* On condition 3H6 1.1.196 *Conditionally that here thou take an oath.*

conditioned *ppl. adj.* Subjected to conditions, in specified circumstances TIM 4.3.526 *Go, live rich and happy, But thus condition'd.*

condole *vb.*
1 Sorrow greatly, lament MND 1.2.27 *I will condole in some measure.*
2 Grieve with (a sufferer) H5 2.1.127 *Let us condole the knight.*

condolement *n.*
1 Grief, sorrowing HAM 1.2.93 *to persevere In obstinate condolement is a course Of impious stubbornness.*
2 Tangible expression of sympathy PER 2.1.150 *There are certain condolements, certain vails.*

conduce *vb.* Go on, proceed TRO 5.2.147 *Within my soul there doth conduce a fight.*

conduct *n.*
1 Guidance, leading LR 3.6.97 *that will to some provision Give thee quick conduct.*
2 Escort, guard TN 3.4.242 *I will return again into the house, and desire some conduct of the lady,* R3 1.1.45, 1H4 3.1.91.
3 Guide, leader, conductor ROM 5.3.116 *Come, bitter conduct, come, unsavoury guide!;* (fig.) TMP 5.1.244 *there is in this business more than nature Was ever conduct of,* 2H4 5.2.36, LUC 313.
4 Leadership, command AYL 5.4.157 *which were on foot In his own conduct,* TIT 4.4.65.

conductor *n.* Leader, commander-in-chief LR 4.7.87 *Who is conductor of his people?*

confection *n.* Mixture, compound; a medicinal preparation compounded of various drugs CYM 1.5.15 *our great King himself doth woo me oft For my confections;* (spec.) prepared poison CYM 5.5.246 *given his mistress that confection Which I gave him for cordial.*

confectionary *n.* Place where confections or sweetmeats are made or kept TIM 4.3.260 *But myself, Who had the world as my confectionary.*
▷ Some interpret in the sense of 'maker of confections'.

conference *n.*
1 Conversation, talk JC 4.2.17 *Nor with such free and friendly conference As he hath us'd of old,* SHR 2.1.251, ANT 1.1.45.
2 Debate, discussion JC 1.2.188 *Being cross'd in conference by some senators.*

confidence *n.* (prob. malapropism for) Conference WIV 1.4.160 *I will tell your worship more of the wart the next time we have confidence,* ADO 3.5.2, ROM 2.4.127.

confident *adj.*
1 Confiding, trustful TIT 1.1.61 *Rome, be as just... to me As I am confident and kind to thee.*
2 *three thousand confident* Having the confidence of three thousand CYM 5.3.29.

confine *n.*
1 (pl.) Boundaries, bounds ROM 3.1.6 *when he enters the confines of a tavern.*
2 (pl.) Region, territory R3 4.4.3 *Here in these confines slily have I lurk'd,* R2 1.3.137; (sing., fig.) JN 4.2.246 *this confine of blood and breath.*
3 Confinement, limitation OTH 1.2.27 *I would not my unhoused free condition Put into circumscription and confine For the sea's worth,* LC 265.
4 Place of confinement, prison, cell HAM 1.1.155 *Th' extravagant and erring spirit hies To his confine,* TMP 4.1.121, ANT 3.5.12.
~ *vb.* Relegate to certain limits, banish WT 2.1.194 *So have we thought it good From our free person she should be confin'd.*

confineless *adj.* Boundless MAC 4.3.55 *being compar'd With my confineless harms.*

confiner *n.* Inhabitant CYM 4.2.337 *The Senate hath stirr'd up the confiners And gentlemen of Italy.*

confirmed *ppl. adj.* Firm, steady, resolute ADO 2.1.379 *he is of a noble strain, of approv'd valour, and confirm'd honesty,* COR 1.3.59; *Thy age confirm'd thy settled maturity, riper manhood R3 4.4.172.

confiscate *ppl. adj.* Confiscated, appropriated by way of penalty, adjudged forfeited ERR 1.1.20 *His goods confiscate to the Duke's dispose,* MV 4.1.332, CYM 5.5.323.

confix *vb.* Fix firmly, fasten MM 5.1.232 *Or else for ever be confixed here A marble monument.*

conflux *n.* Flowing together, confluence TRO 1.3.7 *As knots, by the conflux of meeting sap, Infects the sound pine.*

conformable *adj.* Compliant, submissive SHR 2.1.278 *from a wild Kate to a Kate Conformable as other household Kates,* H8 2.4.24.

confound *vb.*
1 Destroy ANT 3.2.58 *What willingly he did confound he wail'd,* AWW 2.3.120, H5 4.5.3; (used in curses or imprecations) bring to ruin or perdition TIM 1.1.239 *thy god confound thee,* TRO 2.3.75, ANT 2.5.92.
2 Waste, consume, spend 1H4 1.3.100 *He did confound the best part of an hour,* COR 1.6.17, ANT 1.1.45.
3 Mingle so that the elements become indistinguishable R2 4.1.141 *tumultuous wars Shall kin with kin and kind with kind confound.*

confounded *ppl. adj.* Wasted, worn away H5 3.1.13 *as doth a galled rock O'erhang and jutty his confounded base, Swilled with the wild and wasteful ocean.*

confounding *ppl. adj.* Ruinous TIM 4.3.391 *by thy virtue Set them into confounding odds.*

confusion *n.*
1 Ruin, destruction MAC 3.5.29 *Shall draw him on to his confusion,* ERR 2.2.180; (used as an imprecation) LR 2.4.95 *Vengeance! plague! death! confusion!,* 2H6 5.2.31.
2 Mental agitation HAM 3.1.2 *get from him why he puts on this confusion,* MV 3.2.177.
3 (pl.) Disorders, commotions ROM 4.5.66 *Confusion's cure lives not In these confusions.*

congee, congie *vb.*
1 Take ceremonious leave AWW 4.3.87 *I have congied with the Duke.*
2 Bow in courtesy H8 4.2.SD *They first congee unto her, then dance.*

conger *n.* Large species of eel living in salt water 2H4 2.4.245 *eats conger and fennel;* (used as term of abuse) 2H4 2.4.53 *Hang yourself, you muddy conger* (Q *cunger*).

congest *vb.* Collect, gather together LC 258 *Must for your victory us all congest.*

congratulate *vb.* Salute LLL 5.1.88 *it is the King's most sweet pleasure and affection to congratulate the Princess.*

congree *vb.* Agree, accord H5 1.2.182 *Congreeing in a full and natural close, Like music* (Qq *congrueth with a mutual consent*).

congreet *vb.* Greet mutually, meet amicably H5 5.2.31 *That face to face, and royal eye to eye, You have congreeted.*

congrue *vb.* Agree HAM 4.3.64 *By letters congruing to that effect* (Ff *conjuring*).
▷ H5 1.2.182: see CONGREE.

conject *vb.* Conjecture, guess, surmise OTH 3.3.149 *From one that so imperfectly conjects* (Q1; Ff *conceits*).

conjectural *adj.* Of the nature of conjecture, based on opinion or the reading of omens, not on proof AWW 5.3.114 *And mak'st conjectural fears to come into me* (i.e. dreadful surmises; F2; F1 *connecturall*).

conjecture *n.*
1 Supposition H5 4.Ch.1 *Now entertain conjecture of a time When creeping murmur and the poring dark Fills the wide vessel of the universe.*
2 Evil surmise, suspicion HAM 4.5.15 *dangerous conjectures in ill-breeding minds,* Ado 4.1.106, WT 2.1.176.

conjunct *adj.* Joined together, conjoined, closely connected LR 5.1.12 *conjunct And bosom'd with her,* LR 2.2.118 (Ff *compact*).

conjunction *n.*
1 Apparent proximity of two planets; the position of two planets when they are in the same, or nearly the same direction as viewed from the earth 2H4 2.4.263 *Saturn and Venus this year in conjunction!*
▷ Formerly in astrology two planets were said to be 'in conjunction' when they were in the same sign of the zodiac, or even in adjacent signs.
2 United force 1H4 4.1.37 *That with our small conjunction we should on.*

conjunctive *adj.* Closely joined HAM 4.7.14 *She is so conjunctive to my life and soul,* OTH 1.3.367 (F1; Q1 *communicative;* Q2 *conjective*).

conjuration *n.*
1 Solemn appeal or entreaty, adjuration HAM 5.2.38 *An earnest conjuration from the King,* ROM 5.3.68, H5 1.2.29.
2 Incantation, charm OTH 1.3.92 *what drugs, what charms, What conjuration, and what mighty magic,* 2H6 1.2.99.

conjure *vb.*
1 Call upon solemnly, adjure TGV 2.7.2 *I do conjure thee...To lesson me,* ERR 4.4.57, MAC 4.1.50.
2 Call upon, constrain (a devil or spirit) to appear or to do one's bidding by incantation or the use of some spell, raise or bring into existence as by magic: (intr. or absol.) TRO 5.2.125 *I cannot conjure,* ERR 3.1.34, H5 5.2.288; (trans.) TIM 1.1.7 *all these spirits thy power Have conjur'd to attend,* H5 2.1.54; (fig.) ADO 2.1.257 *I would...some scholar would conjure her;* (with adverb) conjure down ROM 2.1.26 *conjur'd it down;* conjure up JC 2.1.323 *Thou, like an exorcist, has conjur'd up My mortified spirit,* MND 3.2.158; affect or influence by incantation, charm or magic OTH 1.3.105 *with some dram (conjur'd to this effect) He wrought upon her.*

conjurer *n.* One who conjures spirits, magician, wizard ERR 4.4.47 *Good Doctor Pinch, you are a conjurer, Establish him in his true sense again.*
▷ Pinch, as a schoolmaster, would have enough Latin to address the evil spirits in the language

they were supposed to understand and so could exorcise them.

conjuro te [L.] I conjure you 2H6 1.4.SD.

connectural See CONJECTURAL.

conscience *n.*
1 Consciousness, inward knowledge, inmost thought, internal conviction H5 4.1.118 *By my troth, I will speak my conscience of the King,* WT 3.2.46, CYM 1.6.116.
2 Sound judgement, reasonableness TIM 2.2.175 *Canst thou the conscience lack To think I shall lack friends?*
3 Regard for the dictates of conscience, conscientiousness WT 4.4.646 *Indeed I have had earnest, but I cannot with conscience take it,* OTH 3.3.203.
4 Matter about which scruples are or should be felt JN 4.2.229 *And thou...Made it no conscience to destroy a prince.*

conscionable *adj.* Conscientious, bound by the dictates of conscience OTH 2.1.238 *no further conscionable than in putting on the mere form of civil and humane seeming.*

consent *n.*[1] (var. of) CONCENT.

consent *n.*[2]
1 Agreement as to a course of action LLL 5.2.460 *here was a consent...To dash it like a Christmas comedy,* TMP 2.1.203, AYL 2.2.3.
2 Agreement or unity of opinion, unanimity H5 2.2.22 *We carry not a heart with us from hence That grows not in a fair consent with ours,* 2H4 5.1.70; *consent of* agreement about COR 2.3.23 *their consent of one direct way.*
3 Opinion, or the expression of it WT 5.3.136 *O, peace, Paulina! Thou shouldst a husband take by my consent As I by thine a wife,* 1H6 1.2.44, 3H6 4.6.36.
~ *vb.*
1 Agree together in opinion or statement, be of the same mind AYL 5.1.43 *all your writers do consent that 'ipse' is he.*
2 *consent in* Come to an agreement about, agree in planning OTH 5.2.297 *Did you and he consent in Cassio's death?*

consequence *n.* the consequence o' th' crown Royal succession CYM 2.3.121.

consequently *adv.* Subsequently, thereafter TN 3.4.71 *and consequently sets down the manner how,* JN 4.2.240.

conserve *n.* (pl.) *conserves of beef* Preserved or salted beef SHR Ind.2.7 *give me conserves of beef.*
~ *vb.*
1 Preserve MM 3.1.87 *Thou art too noble to conserve a life In base appliances.*
2 Make into a conserve OTH 3.4.75 *And it was dy'd in mummy which the skilful Conserv'd of maidens' hearts.*

consider *vb.* Requite, reward, recompense WT 4.2.17 *which if I have not enough consider'd...to be more thankful to thee shall be my study,* CYM 2.3.28.

considerance *n.* Reflection 2H4 5.2.98 *After this cold considerance, sentence me.*

considerate *adj.* Thoughtful, reflective R3 4.2.30 *None are for me That look into me with considerate eyes,* ANT 2.2.110.

considered *adj.* Suitable for consideration or deliberate thought HAM 2.2.81 *And at our more considered time we'll read.*

consign *vb.* Set one's seal H5 5.2.90 *we'll consign thereto;* (hence) assent 2H4 5.2.143 *God consigning to my good intents;* submit CYM 4.2.275 *all lovers must Consign to thee and come to dust.*

consigned *ppl. adj.* Added by way of ratification TRO 4.4.45 *With distinct breath and consign'd kisses.*

consist *vb.*
1 *consist on, upon* Insist upon 2H4 4.1.185 *As our conditions shall consist upon*, PER 1.4.83.
2 *consist in* Reside or inhere in R3 4.4.406 *In her consists my happiness and thine.*

consistory *n.* Council-chamber; (fig.) R3 2.2.151 *My other self, my counsel's consistory*; college of cardinals presided over by the pope H8 2.4.92 *By a commission from the consistory, Yea, the whole consistory of Rome.*

consonancy *n.* Agreement, accord, correspondence TN 2.5.129 *there is no consonancy in the sequel that suffers under probation*, HAM 2.2.284.

consonant *n.* A sound which, unlike a vowel, cannot form a syllable by itself; (hence) insignificant person, nonentity LLL 5.1.53 *'Quis, quis', thou consonant?*

consort *n.*
1 Fellowship, company TGV 4.1.62 *wilt thou be of our consort?*, LR 2.1.97.
2 Harmonious music TGV 3.2.83 *Visit by night your lady's chamber-window With some sweet consort.*
3 Band of musicians 2H6 3.2.327 *And boding screech-owls make the consort full!*
~ *vb.* Accompany, attend LLL 2.1.177 *Sweet health and fair desires consort your Grace!*, ERR 1.2.28, ROM 3.1.130.

conspectuity *n.* Sight COR 2.1.64 *What harm can your bisson conspectuities glean out of this character?*

conspire *vb.* (said of a single person) Plot secretly, contrive TRO 5.1.63 *to be Menelaus, I would conspire against destiny*, TGV 1.2.43, OTH 3.3.142.

constable *n.* In France and England, a principal officer in the royal household, having jurisdiction in matters of arms and chivalry H5 2.4.41 *Well, 'tis not so, my Lord High Constable*, H8 2.1.1u2.

constancy *n.*
1 Persistence, perseverance H8 3.2.2 *force them with a constancy.*
2 Certainty MND 5.1.26 *grows to something of great constancy.*

constant *adj.*
1 Firm in opinion, certain TN 4.2.48 *make the trial of it in any constant question* (i.e. rational discourse.)
2 Settled, steady TMP 2.2.115 *do not turn me about, my stomach is not constant.*

constantly *adv.*
1 Resolutely, faithfully JC 5.1.91 *resolv'd To meet all perils very constantly*, HAM 1.2.234, CYM 3.5.118.
2 Confidently TRO 4.1.41 *I constantly believe...My brother Troilus lodges there to-night*, MM 4.1.21.
3 Continuously, steadily TN 2.3.148 *or any thing constantly but a time-pleaser.*

constant-qualified *adj.* Endowed with constancy, steadfast, faithful CYM 1.4.60 *to be more fair, virtuous, wise, chaste, constant-qualified* (Ff and many edd. *constant, qualified*).

constellation *n.* Configuration or position of 'stars' or planets in regard to one another, as supposed to influence men and events; (hence) a person's character as determined by his 'stars' TN 1.4.35 *I know thy constellation is right apt For this affair.*

conster (var. of) CONSTRUE.

constitution *n.* Frame (of mind) MV 3.2.246 *Could turn so much the constitution Of any constant man*; (of body) TN 1.3.132 *the excellent constitution of thy leg.*

constrain *vb.*
1 Assume by an effort LR 2.2.97 *some fellow who...constrains the garb Quite from his nature.*

2 Violate TIT 5.2.177 *her spotless chastity...you constrain'd.*

constrained *ppl. adj.* Produced by compulsion, forced ANT 3.13.59 *he Does pity, as constrained blemishes, Not as deserved*, CYM 5.4.15.

constringe *vb.* Compress, constrict TRO 5.2.173 *Constring'd in mass by the almighty sun.*

construe *vb.*
1 Explain TN 3.1.56 *I will construe to them whence you come.*
2 Translate orally SHR 3.1.30 *Construe them*, SHR 3.1.41.
▷ *Conster*, a common var. spelling in 16–18C, occurs in Ff in these quotations.

consul *n.* Senator OTH 1.2.43 *And many of the consuls, rais'd and met, Are at the Duke's already*, CYM 4.2.385.

consummation *n.* Death CYM 4.2.280 *Quiet consummation have, And renowned be thy grave*, LR 4.6.129 (Ff *consumption*).

consumption *n.* Wasting disease TIM 4.3.151 *Consumptions sow In hollow bones of man*, ADO 5.4.96, 2H4 1.2.236.
▷ Not restricted to pulmonary consumption or phthisis.

contagion *n.* Contagious or poisonous influence JC 2.1.265 *To dare the vile contagion of the night*, HAM 3.2.390; poison HAM 4.7.147 *I'll touch my point With this contagion, that if I gall him slightly, It may be death.*

contagious *adj.* Pestilential, noxious MND 2.1.90 *from the sea Contagious fogs*, JN 5.4.33, H5 3.3.31.
▷ TN 2.3.54 *A contagious breath*: quibbling on 'a catchy song' and 'a bad breath'.

contain *vb.* Retain, keep MV 5.1.201 *Or your own honour to contain the ring*, SON 77.9.

containing *n.* Contents, tenor CYM 5.5.430 *This label on my bosom, whose containing Is so from sense in hardness.*

contemn *vb.*
1 Despise, disdain, scorn TGV 2.4.129 *I have done penance for contemning Love*, CYM 1.6.41, ANT 3.6.1.
2 Refuse scornfully VEN 205 *What am I that thou shouldst contemn me this?*

contemned *ppl. adj.* Despised, scorned, treated with contempt TN 1.5.270 *cantons of contemned love*, LR 2.2.143, JN 5.2.13.

contemptible *adj.*
1 Despicable 1H6 1.2.75 *my contemptible estate.*
2 Disdainful, contemptuous ADO 2 3.180 *a contemptible spirit.*

contemptuous *adj.* CONTEMPTIBLE *adj.* sense 1, despicable 2H6 1.3.83 *Contemptuous base-born callot as she is.*

contend *vb.* Strive earnestly MM 3.2.232 *One that, above all other strifes, contended especially to know himself*; strive to go SON 60.4 *In sequent toil the waves all forwards do contend.*

contending *adj.* Making war, warlike SHR 5.2.159 *What is she but a foul contending rebel*, VEN 82.

content *n.* Desire, wish, or fulfilment of one's desire R2 5.2.38 *To whose high will we bound our calm contents*, TRO 1.2.294, 2H6 1.1.35 (with play on other sense of 'capacity').
~ *vb.*
1 Please, gratify TGV 3.1.93 *A woman sometime scorns what best contents her*, SHR 4.3.178, HAM 3.1.24.
2 (refl. and pass. used imper.) *content thee, be contented* Be calm, do not trouble ADO 5.1.87 *Content yourself*, SHR 1.1.80; WIV 3.3.166 *Good Master Ford, be contented*, LR 3.4.110.
3 Remunerate, reward, pay OTH 3.1.1 *Masters,*

play here, I will content your pains, R3 3.2.111, SHR
1.1.163.
4 (intr.) Acquiesce, endure VEN 61 *Forc'd to content, but never to obey.*
~ *adj.*
1 *be content* (used imper.) Be calm, be not uneasy
R2 5.2.82 *Good mother, be content*, JC 4.2.41; (elliptically) LR 1.4.313 *Pray you, content.*
2 (elliptically as an exclamation) Agreed, I am
content 3H6 3.2.183 *And cry 'Content' to that which
grieves my heart*, SHR 5.2.70, ANT 4.3.22.
contented *adj.*
1 *Well contented* Agreed, CONTENT *adj.* sense 2 MAC
2.3.134.
2 Marked by contentment R3 1.3.83 *From that contented hap which I enjoy'd.*
contention *n.* Combat TRO 4.5.205 *I would my arms
could match thee in contention*, 1H4 1.1.60.
contentless *adj.* Discontented TIM 4.3.245 *Best state,
contentless, Hath a distracted and most wretched
being.*
continent *n.*
1 Something that holds or contains: cover, enclosure, receptacle HAM 4.4.64 *Which is not tomb enough and continent To hide the slain*, LR 3.2.58,
ANT 4.14.40; bounding or enclosing land MND
2.1.92 *Hath every pelting river made so proud That
they have overborne their continents*, 1H4 3.1.109.
2 Earth, 'terra firma' 2H4 3.1.47 *and the continent,
Weary of solid firmness, melt itself Into the sea.*
3 *orbed continent* 'Solid globe' or sphere of the sun
TN 5.1.271 *that orbed continent the fire That severs
day from night.*
4 Summary, sum LLL 4.1.109 *my continent of beauty*, MV 3.2.130, HAM 5.2.110.
~ *adj.*
1 Self-restrained, temperate LR 1.2.166 *have a continent for bearance.*
2 Restraining, restrictive MAC 4.3.64 *and my desire
All continent impediments would o'erbear*, LLL
1.1.259.
continuance *n.* Permanence TN 1.4.6 *you call in
question the continuance of his love*, MM 3.1.240,
ROM Prol.10.
continuantly *adv.* (malapropism) Continually 2H4
2.1.26 *'A comes continuantly to Pie-corner.*
continuate *ppl. adj.*
1 Uninterrupted, continuous OTH 3.4.178 *But I
shall in a more continuate time Strike off this core
of absence.*
2 Lasting, habitual TIM 1.1.11 *an untirable and
continuate goodness.*
continue *vb.*
1 Retain H8 2.4.33 *What friend of mine...did I Continue in my liking;* keep, let live, MM 4.3.84 *And
how shall we continue Claudio...?*
2 Come as a sequel TIM 2.2.5 *nor resumes no care
Of what is to continue.*
continuer *n.* One who persists or keeps on, one
with staying power ADO 1.1.142 *I would my horse
had the speed of your tongue, and so good a continuer.*
contract *vb.* Betroth, affiance WT 4.4.390 *But come
on, Contract us 'fore these witnesses*, WIV 5.5.223;
(fig.) SON 1.5 *thou, contracted to thine own bright
eyes.*
~ *pa. pple.* Contracted, espoused, betrothed R3
3.7.179 *For first was he contract to Lady Lucy.*
contracting *n.* Betrothal MM 3.2.282 *And perform
an old contracting.*
contraction *n.* Marriage-contract, betrothal HAM
3.4.46 *As from the body of contraction plucks The
very soul.*

contrarious *adj.* Adverse 1H4 5.1.52 *And the contrarious winds that held the King So long.*
~ *adv.* In the contrary direction, inconsistently,
antagonistically MM 4.1.61 *and most contrarious
quest Upon thy doings.*
contrary *n.*
1 Opposite side WT 1.2.372 *Wafting his eyes to th'
contrary* (i.e. averting his glance), H8 2.1.15.
2 *in the contrary* To the contrary H8 3.2.182 *as i'
th' contrary The foulness is the punishment*, OTH
4.2.174.
3 *by contraries* In a manner opposite to what is
customary TMP 2.1.148 *I' th' commonwealth I
would, by contraries, Execute all things.*
~ *vb.* Oppose, thwart ROM 1.5.85 *You must contrary me!*
~ *adj.* Wrong MV 1.2.96 *I pray thee set a deep glass
of Rhenish wine on the contrary casket*, JN 4.2.198.
~ *adv.* In an opposite direction 1H4 5.5.4 *And
wouldst thou turn our offers contrary?*
contrive *vb.*¹ Devise, plan, (esp.) plot HAM 2.2.212
*and suddenly contrive the means of meeting be-
tween him and my daughter*, R2 1.1.96, MV 4.1.352.
contrive *vb.*² Spend, pass (time) SHR 1.2.274 *Please
ye we may contrive this afternoon.*
contriving *adj.* Conspiring ANT 1.2.182 *our contriving friends in Rome.*
control *vb.*
1 Overpower COR 3.1.161 *th' ill which doth control't*, LUC 678, TMP 1.2.373.
2 Refute, rebuke TMP 1.2.440 *The Duke of Milan
And his more braver daughter could control thee*,
LUC 189, LR 2.4.246.
controller *n.* Censurer, detractor TIT 2.3.60 *Saucy
controller of my private steps*, 2H6 3.2.205.
controlment *n.* Restraint, compulsion JN 1.1.20
*Here have we war for war and blood for blood,
Controlment for controlment*, ADO 1.3.20, TIT 2.1.68.
controversy *n.: hearts of controversy* Hearts that
dispute or contend (with another) with stout courage JC 1.2.109 *And stemming it with hearts of
controversy.*
convenience *n.*
1 Fitness, propriety AWW 3.2.72 *all the honour
That good convenience claims*, MM 3.1.248.
2 (pl.) Comforts, advantages TRO 3.3.7 *expos'd myself From certain and possess'd conveniences To
doubtful fortunes*, OTH 2.1.231.
convenient *adj.* Proper, fitting TIT 5.2.90 *It were
convenient you had such a devil*, MM 4.3.103, MND
3.1.2.
conveniently *adv.* Properly MV 2.8.45 *such fair
ostents of love As shall conveniently become you
there.*
convent *vb.* Summon, convene COR 2.2.54 *We are
convented Upon a pleasing treaty*, MM 5.1.158, H8
5.1.52.
◊ In TN 5.1.382 *When that is known, and golden
time convents* some propose 'be convenient, suit',
rather than 'summon'.
conventicle *n.* Secret meeting 2H6 3.1.166 *Myself
had notice of your conventicles.*
conversation *n.*
1 Intercourse, give-and-take AWW 1.3.234 *the conversation of my thoughts*, HAM 3.2.55, CYM 1.4.103.
2 Behaviour, conduct OTH 3.3.264 *And had not
these soft parts of conversation That chamberers
have*, WIV 2.1.24, ANT 2.6.123; (pl.) manners 2H4
5.5.100 *banish'd till their conversations Appear
more wise and modest to the world.*
converse *n.* Intercourse; (hence) conversation HAM
2.1.42 *Your party in converse, him you would
sound*, OTH 3.1.38, LLL 5.2.735.
~ *vb.* Hold intercourse, associate *with* LLL 5.2.851

You shall...Visit the speechless sick, and still converse With groaning wretches, TGV 1.3.31, AYL 5.2.60.

conversion n. Change to something better or higher AYL 4.3.136 *I do not shame To tell you what I was, since my conversion So sweetly tastes*, JN 1.1.189.

convert vb.
1 (trans.) Turn in another direction AYL 5.4.161 *was converted Both from his enterprise and from the world*, SON 7.11.
2 (intr.) Turn away or aside SON 11.4 *when thou from youth convertest*, SON 14.12.
3 Appropriate MV 3.2.167 *Myself, and what is mine, to you and yours Is now converted* (i.e. made yours).
4 Change *into* something else HAM 5.1.211 *why of that loam whereto he was converted*, ADO 2.3.68; (intr. for pass.) undergo a change MAC 4.3.229 *let grief Convert to anger*, ADO 1.1.122, ROM 1.5.92.

convertite n. Convert, penitent JN 5.1.19 *But since you are a gentle convertite*, AYL 5.4.184, LUC 743.

convey vb.
1 (euphemism for) Steal R2 4.1.317 *O, good! convey! Conveyers are you all, That rise thus nimbly by a true king's fall*, WIV 1.3.29.
2 (refl.) Represent oneself, pass oneself off H5 1.2.74 *Convey'd himself as th' heir to th' Lady Lingare.*
3 Manage with secrecy MAC 4.3.71 *You may Convey your pleasures in a spacious plenty*, LR 1.2.101.

conveyance n.
1 Escort, convoy OTH 1.3.285 *To his conveyance I assign my wife*, HAM 4.4.3.
2 Removal R3 4.4.283 *Mad'st quick conveyance with her good aunt Anne.*
3 Document by which the transference of property is effected HAM 5.1.110 *The very conveyances of his lands.*
4 Cunning management, underhand dealing, trickery 1H6 1.3.2 *Since Henry's death, I fear, there is conveyance*, ADO 2.1.245, 3H6 3.3.160.
5 Channel for conveying liquid COR 5.1.54 *These pipes and these conveyances of our blood.*
6 Means of transport WIV 3.3.127 *bethink you of some conveyance.*

conveyer n. Thief R2 4.1.317 *Conveyers are you all.*

convict pa. pple. Proved guilty R3 1.4.187 *Before I be convict by course of law.*

convicted ppl. adj. Vanquished, defeated JN 3.4.2 *A whole armado of convicted sail Is scattered.*
◇ Hulme [220–2] proposes that *convicted* is a spelling var. of 'convected' from L. 'con' (with, together) and 'vehere' (carry, convey) to give a reading of 'assembled'.

convince vb.
1 Overcome MAC 1.7.64 *his two chamberlains Will I with wine and wassail so convince*, OTH 4.1.28, PER 1.2.123.
2 Convict, prove guilty of TRO 2.2.130 *Else might the world convince of levity As well my undertakings as your counsels.*
3 Give proof of LLL 5.2.746 *The holy suit which fain it would convince.*

convive vb. Feast together TRO 4.5.272 *There in the full convive we.*

convocation n. Assembly HAM 4.3.20 *a certain convocation of politic worms are e'en at him*; gathering of provincial synod of clergy H5 1.1.76 *For I have made an offer to his Majesty, Upon our spiritual convocation* (i.e. on behalf of the assembly of clergy).

convoy n. Means of conveyance or transport H5

4.3.37 *And crowns for convoy put into his purse*, ROM 2.4.191, AWW 4.3.89.

convulsion n. Cramp, painful seizure TMP 4.1.259 *grind their joints With dry convulsions.*

cony n. Adult rabbit AYL 3.2.339 *As the cony that you see dwell where she is kindled*, VEN 687.

cony-catch vb. Cheat SHR 5.1.99 *Take heed Signior Baptista, lest you be cony-catch'd in this business*, WIV 1.3.33.

cony-catching n. Trickery, evasion SHR 4.1.43 *so full of cony-catching.*
~ ppl. adj. Cheating WIV 1.1.124 *I have matter in my head...against your cony-catching rascals.*

coop vb. Enclose for protection or defence JN 2.1.25 *And coops from other lands her islanders*, 3H6 5.1.109.

copatain adj. High-crowned SHR 5.1.67 *a scarlet cloak, and a copatain hat!*

cope n. Firmament, canopy (of the sky) PER 4.6.123 *the cheapest country under the cope.*

cope vb.
1 (intr.) Come into contact *with*, have to do *with* HAM 3.2.55 *Horatio, thou art e'en as just a man As e'er my conversation cop'd withal*, WT 4.4.424, LUC 99.
2 (trans.) Meet, encounter, tackle AYL 2.1.67 *I love to cope him in these sullen fits*, H8 1.2.78, OTH 4.1.86.
3 Match (a thing) *with* (an equivalent) MV 4.1.412 *Three thousand ducats...We freely cope your courteous pains withal.*

copesmate n. Companion LUC 925 *Misshapen Time, copesmate of ugly Night.*

copped adj. Peaked PER 1.1.101 *The blind mole casts Copp'd hills towards heaven.*

copper n. Money made of copper LLL 4.3.383 *our copper buys no better treasure.*
~ attrib.
1 Of copper as a base metal, often with notion of spurious, pretentious, worthless MM 4.4.105 *some with cunning gild their copper crowns*, MM 4.3.13 *Master Copper-spur* (i.e. Master Pretentious).
2 *copper nose* Red nose caused by acne, by intemperance, etc. TRO 1.2.106 *I had as lieve Helen's golden tongue had commended Troilus for a copper nose.*

copulative n. (used humorously) Person about to be married AYL 5.4.56 *the rest of the country copulatives.*

copy n.
1 Copyhold, tenure of land held at the will of the lord of the manor by 'copy' of the manorial court-roll; (fig.) MAC 3.2.38 *But in them nature's copy's not eterne.*
2 Model, example AWW 1.2.46 *Such a man Might be a copy to these younger times*, JN 4.2.113, TIM 3.3.32.
3 Original (writing, text, etc.) SON 11.14 *Thou shouldst print more, not let that copy die.*
4 Minutes or memoranda of a conference; (hence) subject-matter, theme ERR 5.1.62 *It was the copy of our conference.*

coram n. (used erroneously for) Quorum, a title of certain justices whose presence was necessary to constitute a bench WIV 1.1.6 *In the county of Gloucester, Justice of Peace and Coram.*

coranto n. Quick running dance H5 3.5.33 *swift corantos.*

cordial n. Restorative medicine CYM 5.5.247 *that confection Which I gave him for cordial*, ROM 5.1.85, R3 2.1.41.
~ adj. Restorative, comforting WT 1.2.318 *Which draught to me were cordial*, CYM 1.5.64.

core n.
1 Central part of an ulcer TRO 2.1.6 *Were not that*

a botchy core; (fig.) Tro 5.1.4 *How now, thou core of envy?*

2 *heart's core* Heart of my heart Ham 3.2.73 *I will wear him In my heart's core* (perhaps with a play on L. 'cor' = heart).

Corinth *n.* House of ill-fame, brothel district Tim 2.2.70 *Would we could see you at Corinth!*

Corinthian *n.* Spirited fellow 1H4 2.4.12 *I am no proud Jack like Falstaff, but a Corinthian, a lad of mettle.*

co-rivall (mod. var. of) CORRIVAL.

corky *adj.* Withered Lr 3.7.29 *Bind fast his corky arms.*

cormorant *n.* Glutton; (fig.) R2 2.1.38 *Light vanity, insatiate cormorant, Consuming means, soon preys upon itself.*

~ *attrib.* Ravenous, rapacious Tro 2.2.6 *In hot digestion of this cormorant war,* LLL 1.1.4, Cor 1.1.121.

corn *n.* *pipes of corn* Musical instrument made of oat stalks MND 2.1.67 *Playing on pipes of corn.*

corner *n.*

1 (fig.) Place of concealment H8 3.1.31 *There's nothing I have done yet, o' my conscience, Deserves a corner.*

2 *the three corners of the world* Europe, Asia, and Africa Jn 5.7.116 *Come the three corners of the world in arms.*

3 *corner of the moon* Horn of the moon Mac 3.5.23 *Upon the corner of the moon There hangs a vap'rous drop.*

corner-cap *n.* Cap with three (or four) corners worn by divines, by members of the universities and by judges when passing sentence of death; (fig.) LLL 4.3.51 *Thou makest the triumphery, the corner-cap of society, The shape of love's Tyburn.*

⬦ With considerable play on the notion of three, *triumphery* being a var. of 'triumviry' (triumvirate), and the gallows at Tyburn being triangular in shape.

cornet *n.* Company of cavalry, so called from its standard, which was orig. a long horn-shaped pennon 1H6 4.3.25 *Somerset, who in proud heart Doth stop my cornets.*

cornuto *n.* Cuckold Wiv 3.5.70 *the peaking cornuto her husband.*

corollary *n.* Surplus Tmp 4.1.57 *bring a corollary, Rather than want a spirit.*

coronet *n.* Chaplet, garland MND 4.1.52 *For she his hairy temples then had rounded With coronet of fresh and fragrant flowers,* Ham 4.7.172.

corporal *n.* *a corporal of his field* A superior field officer who acted as assistant or aide-de-camp to the sergeant-major; (fig.) LLL 3.1.187 *I to be a corporal of his field.*

corporal *adj.*

1 Bodily Mac 1.7.80 *bend up Each corporal agent to this terrible feat,* MM 3.1.79, JC 4.1.33.

2 Material, physical Mac 1.3.81 *and what seem'd corporal melted, As breath into the wind,* AWW 1.2.24.

correspondent *adj.* Responsive, obedient Tmp 1.2.297 *I will be correspondent to command.*

corresponsive *adj.* Corresponding Tro Prol.18 *with massy staples And corresponsive and fulfilling bolts.*

corrigible *adj.*

1 Submissive Ant 4.14.74 *bending down His corrigible neck.*

2 Correcting, corrective Oth 1.3.325 *the power and corrigible authority of this lies in our wills.*

corrival, co-rival *n.*

1 Rival 1H4 1.3.207 *So he...might wear Without corrival all her dignities.*

2 Partner, associate 1H4 4.4.31 *many moe corrivals and dear men of estimation.*

~ *vb.* Vie with Tro 1.3.44 *Whose weak untimber'd sides but even now Corrivall'd greatness.*

corroborate *adj.* (?) (Misuse by Pistol; lit. 'strengthened') H5 2.1.124 *His heart is fracted and corroborate.*

corrosive *n.* Sharp or caustic remedy 2H6 3.2.403 *though parting be a fretful corrosive, It is applied to a deathful wound.*

~ *adj.* Fretting, wasting 1H6 3.3.3 *care is no cure, but rather corrosive.*

corrupted *ppl. adj.* Prevented from inheriting property and titles by 'corruption of the blood' 1H6 2.4.93 *Corrupted, and exempt from ancient gentry.*

⬦ Under the legal state of 'corruption of the blood', a person's blood was held to have become tainted or 'corrupted' by his crime, so that he and his descendants lost all rights of rank and title.

corruptibly *adv.: touch'd corruptibly* Infected to the point of being corrupt or decomposed Jn 5.7.2 *the life of all his blood Is touch'd corruptibly.*

corse *n.* Corpse R3 1.2.32 *whiles I lament King Henry's corse,* JC 3.1.199, Tim 5.4.70.

cost *n.*

1 Expense, outlay Ado 1.1.98 *The fashion of the world is to avoid cost,* Rom 4.4.6, Ant 3.4.37.

2 Costly thing MM 1.3.10 *Where youth, and cost, witless bravery keeps,* AYL 2.7.76, 2H4 1.3.60.

costard *n.* Large kind of apple; (jocularly) the head R3 1.4.154 *Take him on the costard with the hilts of thy sword,* Wiv 3.1.14, Lr 4.6.241.

costermonger *n.* Seller of fruits (orig. of costard apples) and vegetables; (used contemptuously) 2H4 1.2.169 *Virtue is of so little regard in these costermongers' times* (i.e. commercial times).

costly *adj.* Lavish, rich MV 2.9.94 *To show how costly summer was at hand.*

co-supremes *n.* (pl.) Joint sovereigns PhT 51 *Co-supremes and stars of love.*

cote *n.* Cottage AYL 3.2.427 *come every day to my cote and woo me.*

cote *vb.*[1] (orig. a coursing term) Outstrip Ham 2.2.317 *We coted them on the way.*

cote *vb.*[2] See QUOTE.

cot-quean *n.* Man who busies himself unduly with the housewife's duties Rom 4.4.6 *Go, you cot-quean, go, Get you to bed.*

couch *vb.*

1 Cause to cower or crouch Luc 507 *a falcon tow'ring in the skies, Coucheth the fowl below.*

2 Lower to the position of attack 1H6 3.2.134 *A braver soldier never couched lance.*

3 Lie hidden or in ambush Wiv 5.2.1 *we'll couch i' th' castle-ditch,* Lr 3.1.12, AWW 4.1.21; (fig.) R2 1.3.98 *I espy virtue with valour couched in thine eye,* Tro 1.1.39.

4 Put into words, express (esp. in a veiled way) 2H6 3.1.179 *With ignominious words, though clerkly couch'd.*

couching *n.* Low bowing, grovelling JC 3.1.36 *These couchings and these lowly courtesies.*

~ *adj.* (heraldic term) Couchant 1H4 3.1.151 *A couching lion and a ramping cat.*

Council *n.* (spec.) Body of the king's privy councillors R2 1.3.124 *And list what with our Council we have done,* Wiv 1.1.35, H8 4.1.112.

counsel *n.*

1 Consultation, deliberation, consideration WT 4.4.409 *The father...should hold some counsel In such a business,* Ado 2.3.202, 1H4 4.3.11.

2 Private or secret purpose, secret, inmost thought Cor 1.2.2 *That they of Rome are ent'red in* *our counsels,* ADO 3.3.86, HAM 4.2.11; *in counsel* in private, in secret WIV 1.1.119.

counsel-keeper *n.* One who keeps secrets 2H4 2.4.267 *his note-book, his counsel-keeper.*

counsel-keeping *adj.* Keeping secrets TIT 2.3.24 *And curtain'd with a counsel-keeping cave.*

counsellor *n.*
1 Privy councillor 2H4 4.5.121 *all you sage counsellors hence,* H8 5.2.17 (F1 *Councellor*).
2 Legal advocate MM 1.2.106 *good counsellors lack no clients.*

count *n.*
1 Reckoning, account ROM 1.3.71 *By my count, I was your mother much upon these years,* ANT 2.6.54, SON 2.11; *out of all count* incalculable TGV 2.1.57 *the one is painted, and the other out of all count.*
2 Legal indictment HAM 4.7.17 *to a public count I might not go.*
~ *vb.* Make account *of* TGV 2.1.60 *so painted to make her fair, that no man counts of her beauty.*

Count Comfect *n.* Lord Lollipop ADO 4.1.316 *a goodly count, Count Comfect, a sweet gallant surely!*
▷ Prob. with play on the legal sense of 'count' (charge, indictment) and also on 'conte comfect' (a made-up story).

counted *ppl. adj.* Accounted, esteemed R3 4.1.46 *Nor mother, wife, nor England's counted queen.*

countenance *n.*
1 Bearing, demeanour AYL 2.7.108 *the countenance Of stern command'ment,* SHR 4.2.65, 1H4 5.1.69.
2 Assumed appearance, pretence, hypocritical show MM 5.1.118 *the evil which is here wrapt up In countenance.*
3 Favour, patronage 2H4 4.2.13 *Would he abuse the countenance of the King,* 1H4 1.2.29, HAM 1.3.113.
▷ The precise meaning of many instances is doubtful, and often several meanings can be operating at once.
~ *vb.* Be in keeping with, give a suitable accompaniment to MAC 2.3.80 *walk like sprites, To countenance this horror,* SHR 4.1.103.

counter *n.* Disc or coin used in calculating JC 4.3.80 *To lock such rascal counters from his friends* (i.e. debased coin), TRO 2.2.28 (F1); (hence) object of no value AYL 2.7.63 *What, for a counter, would I do but good?*
▷ See also COMPTER.

counter *adv.* (hunting term) Following the trail in a direction opposite to that which the game has taken, backwards ERR 4.2.39 *A hound that runs counter,* 2H4 1.2.90, HAM 4.5.111.

counter-caster *n.* (lit. one who calculates with metal counters) Contemptuous name for an arithmetician or a reckoner OTH 1.1.31 *this counter-caster, He (in good time!) must his lieutenant be.*

counterchange *n.* Exchange CYM 5.5.396 *The counterchange Is severally in all.*

countercheck *n.* Rebuke in reply to one from another person AYL 5.4.80 *the Countercheck Quarrelsome;* check JN 2.1.224 *Have brought a countercheck before your gates.*

counterfeit *n.* Image, likeness, portrait MV 3.2.115 *Fair Portia's counterfeit!,* TIM 5.1.80, MAC 2.3.76.
~ *vb.* Represent (in an art form) TIM 5.1.82 *Thou counterfeit'st most lively.*
~ *adj.*
1 Portrayed, painted HAM 3.4.54 *The counterfeit presentment of two brothers.*
2 Deceitful, false H5 3.6.61 *an arrant counterfeit rascal,* TIM 4.3.113, SHR 4.4.92.

Counter-gate *n.* Gate of the Counter, a name for debtors' prisons in London, Southwark and elsewhere WIV 3.3.78 *I love to walk by the Counter-gate.*

countermand *vb.*
1 Oppose (the power of) LUC 276 *My heart shall never countermand mine eye.*
2 Prohibit ERR 4.2.37 *one that countermands The passages of alleys.*

counterpart *n.* Copy, reproduction SON 84.11 *And such a counterpart shall fame his wit.*

counterpoint *n.* Counterpane SHR 2.1.351 *In cypress chests my arras counterpoints.*

counterpoise *n.* Compensation, equal amount, equivalent AWW 2.3.175 *A counterpoise—if not to thy estate A balance more replete.*
~ *vb.* Compensate, give an equivalent for TIM 1.1.145 *What you bestow, in him I'll counterpoise,* ADO 4.1.28, COR 2.2.87.

counterseal *vb.* Seal with an additional seal to give further sanction COR 5.3.205 *On like conditions, will have counter-seal'd.*

countervail *vb.* Equal, counterbalance ROM 2.6.4 *It cannot countervail the exchange of joy,* PER 2.3.56.

country *n.*
1 District, region 1H6 5.4.3 *Have I sought every country far and near,* WIV 1.1.219, 3H6 3.1.75.
2 *man of countries* Traveller JN 1.1.193.
~ *attrib.*
1 *country base* Prisoner's base (a boys' game) CYM 5.3.20 *lads more like to run The country base than to commit such slaughter.*
2 *country matters* (oblique, perhaps indecent reference to) The pudendum HAM 3.2.116 *Do you think I meant country matters?*

county *n.* Count ROM 5.3.195 *here lies the County Paris slain,* MV 1.2.45, TN 1.5.301.

couple a gorge (malapropism for) 'Coupe la gorge' [Fr.] (i.e. cut the throat) H5 2.1.71.

couplement *n.*
1 Coupling, union SON 21.5 *Making a couplement of proud compare.*
2 Couple, pair LLL 5.2.532 *most royal couplement.*

couplet *n.* Couple, pair HAM 5.1.287 *the female dove When that her golden couplets are disclosed* (the pigeon lays only two eggs at a time and the newly hatched birds are covered with yellow down), TN 3.4.378.

courage *n.*
1 Spirit, disposition 3H6 2.2.57 *this soft courage makes your followers faint,* COR 3.3.92.
2 Desire, inclination TIM 3.3.24 *courage to do him good;* sexual inclination, lust VEN 276 *his hot courage.*

courageous *adj.* (used blunderingly for) Splendid, brave MND 4.2.27 *O most courageous day!*

courb See CURB.

course *n.*
1 Current (of air) 2H4 4.5.150 *found no course of breath within your Majesty.*
2 Customary procedure, habit HAM 3.3.83 *in our circumstance and course of thought,* MM 3.2.225, TRO 1.3.9; (esp. pl.) habits, way of life, goings-on OTH 4.1.279 *And his own courses will denote him so,* MM 2.1.187, H5 1.1.24.
3 Regular order or process ADO 5.4.6 *the true course of all the question,* JN 1.1.113, LR 3.7.101; *in course* in due course, as a matter of course MM 3.1.249.
4 Line of action, method of procedure LR 1.3.26 *To hold my very course* (i.e. to take the same line of action as I do), TMP 2.1.287.
5 (in bear baiting) One of a succession of attacks MAC 5.7.2 *bear-like I must fight the course,* LR 3.7.54.

6 *two courses* The principal sails of a ship, namely the mainsail and foresail T*MP* 1.1.49 *Set her two courses: off to sea again!*
▷ Some edd. have no punctuation between *courses* and *off*, when the meaning is possibly 'two points of the compass'.

7 *course of the sun* Path followed by the sun in a year; (hence) a year H8 2.3.6 *now after So many courses of the sun enthroned*, S*ON* 59.6; (similarly) *yearly course* J*N* 3.1.81 *The yearly course that brings this day about.*

~ *vb.* Pursue L*R* 3.4.57 *to course his own shadow*, AYL 2.1.39, M*AC* 1.6.21.

courser *n.* Horse, charger H5 3.7.44 *to my courser, for my horse is my mistress*, A*NT* 1.2.193, R2 1.2.51.

coursing *ppl. adj.* Marauding H5 1.2.143 *the coursing snatchers.*

court *n.*
1 *court of guard* Guard room, guard house O*TH* 2.1.218 *The lieutenant to-night watches on the court of guard*, A*NT* 4.9.31, 1H6 2.1.4.
2 (attrib.) *court holy-water* (fig.) Flattery L*R* 3.2.10 *court holy-water in a dry house is better than this rain-water out o'door.*

court-cupboard *n.* Sideboard or cabinet used to display plate, etc. R*OM* 1.5.7 *remove the court-cupboard, look to the plate.*

courteous *adj.* (as a formula of address, orig. to superiors) Gracious T*RO* 5.2.184 *My courteous lord, adieu*, R*OM* 3.2.62.

courtesy *n.*
1 Good manners MND 3.2.147 *If you were civil and knew courtesy*; sense of what good manners require MV 5.1.217 *I was beset with shame and courtesy.*
2 Obeisance, bow JC 3.1.36 *These couchings and these lowly courtesies*, LLL 1.2.63, T*RO* 2.3.105; *make courtesy* bow, make obeisance A*DO* 2.1.55, AYL Epil.23.
3 *courtesy of nations* Usage of civilised peoples AYL 1.1.46 *The courtesy of nations allows you my better, in that you are the first born.*
▷ In Ff and Qq freq. *cursie, curtsie.*

court(-)hand *n.* Style of handwriting in use in English law-courts from 16 to 18C 2H6 4.2.93 *and write court-hand.*

courtier *n.* One who courts, wooer A*NT* 2.6.17 *courtiers of beauteous freedom.*

courtlike *adj.* Befitting the court, elegant, refined W*IV* 2.2.229 *your many war-like, court-like and learned preparations.*

courtly *adj.*
1 Belonging to or connected with the court AWW 3.4.14 *courtly friends*, 2H6 1.1.27.
2 Befitting the court, elegant, refined AYL 3.2.70 *You have too courtly a wit for me*, T*RO* 3.1.28, C*YM* 3.5.71.
3 (in an unfavourable sense) Characteristic of the false manners of courtiers T*IM* 5.1.27 *To promise is most courtly and fashionable.*

courtship *n.*
1 Courtliness of manners, ways of court AYL 3.2.346 *one that knew courtship too well* (with play on sense of 'wooing'), LLL 5.2.363, 2H6 1.3.54.
2 State befitting a court or courtier R*OM* 3.3.34 *more courtship lives In carrion flies than Romeo.*
3 Paying of court (*to* anyone) R2 1.4.24 *Observ'd his courtship to the common people.*

cousin *n.*
1 Collateral relative beyond the immediate family circle: nephew or niece A*DO* 1.2.1, AYL 1.2.155; uncle TN 1.5.123; brother-in-law 1H4 3.1.51.
2 (in earlier legal language) Next of kin, including

direct ancestors and descendants; (applied to) grandchild J*N* 3.3.17, O*TH* 1.1.113, R3 2.2.8.
3 Title used by a sovereign in formally addressing or mentioning another sovereign or a nobleman MM 5.1.165 *Come, cousin Angelo*, R3 3.4.35.

covenants *n.* (pl.) Clauses or articles of a contract; the contracts themselves S*HR* 2.1.127 *That covenants may be kept on either hand*, 1H6 5.4.114, C*YM* 1.4.164.

covent *n.* (earlier form of) Convent MM 4.3.128 *One of our covent, and his confessor*, H8 4.2.19.

cover *vb.*
1 Spread the cloth for a meal; (trans.) MV 3.5.53 *bid them cover the table, serve in the meat*; (intr.) 2H4 2.4.10 *Why then cover and set them down.*
2 Put on one's hat or head covering; (intr.) MV 2.9.44 *How many then should cover that stand bare?*; (pass.) AYL 3.3.77 *pray be cover'd.*

covered *ppl. adj. covered goblet* Empty goblet AYL 3.4.24 *as concave as a cover'd goblet or a worm-eaten nut.*
▷ Goblets were generally fitted with ornamental covers, which were removed when the goblet was in use.

coverture *n.* Covering, cover 3H6 4.2.13 *in night's coverture*, A*DO* 3.1.30.
▷ Steevens' conjecture for C*OR* 1.9.46. See OVER-TURE.

coward *vb.* Make cowardly, render timorous H5 2.2.75 *That have so cowarded and chas'd your blood Out of appearance?*
~ *adj.* Cowardly P*ER* 4.3.25 *how coward a spirit*, AYL 3.5.13, S*ON* 74.11.

cowardship *n.* Cowardice TN 3.4.388 *and for his cowardship.*

cowish *adj.* Cowardly L*R* 4.2.12 *cowish terror.*

cowl-staff *n.* Pole on which a 'cowl' or basket is borne between two persons W*IV* 3.3.147 *Where's the cowl-staff?*

cox *n.* (var. spelling of) Cock's (i.e. God's) AWW 5.2.40 *Cox my passion.*
▷ See C*OCK* *n.³.*

coxcomb *n.*
1 Cap worn by a professional fool, like a cock's comb in shape and colour S*HR* 2.1.225 *What is your crest? a coxcomb?*, W*IV* 5.5.138, 1H4 4.1.104.
2 (jocular) The head TN 5.1.176 *a bloody coxcomb*, H5 5.1.43, W*IV* 3.1.89.

coy *vb.*
1 Disdain C*OR* 5.1.6 *he coy'd To hear Cominius speak.*
2 Caress, stroke lovingly MND 4.1.2 *While I thy amiable cheeks do coy.*
~ *adj.* Distant, disdainful S*HR* 2.1.243 *you were rough and coy and sullen*, TGV 1.1.30, V*EN* 96.

coying *n.* Affectation (of modesty or shyness) R*OM* 2.2.101 *Than those that have [more] coying to be strange.*

coystrill See COISTREL.

coz (abbreviation for) COUSIN (in its various meanings) AYL 1.2.255 *Will you go, coz?*, R*OM* 1.1.183, 1H4 1.1.91.

cozen *vb.* Cheat, dupe WT 4.4.251 *I was cozen'd by the way, and lost all my money*, L*R* 5.3.155, AWW 4.5.27.

cozenage *n.* The practice of cozening, trickery, deception H*AM* 5.2.67 *with such coz'nage*, E*RR* 1.2.97, W*IV* 4.5.63.

cozened *ppl. adj.* Deceived, duped AWW 4.4.23 *cozen'd thoughts.*

cozener *n.* Cheat, imposter L*R* 4.6.163 *The usurer hangs the cozener*, W*IV* 4.5.66, WT 4.4.253.

cozening *ppl. adj.* Cheating, defrauding O*TH* 4.2.132

Some cogging, cozening slave, WIV 4.2.172, R2 2.2.69.

cozier *n.* Cobbler TN 2.3.90 *coziers' catches*.

crack *n.*
1 Charge of explosive put into the breach of cannons, cannon shot MAC 1.2.37 *As cannons overcharg'd with double cracks*.
2 Flaw, defect WT 1.2.322 *I cannot Believe this crack to be in my dread mistress*, LLL 5.2.415; breach OTH 2.3.324 *this crack of your vone*.
3 Lively or pert little boy 2H4 3.2.31 *when 'a was a crack not thus high*, COR 1.3.68.
~ *vb.* Utter (a boast) loudly or smartly CYM 5.5.177 *our brags Were crack'd*; boast, brag LLL 4.3.264 *Ethiops of their sweet complexion crack*.

cracker *n.* Boaster, bragger JN 2.1.147 *What cracker is this same that deafs our ears*.

crack-hemp *n.* Gallows-bird SHR 5.1.46 *Come hither, crackhemp*.

cradle *n.* Place of repose MND 3.1.78 *So near the cradle of the Fairy Queen?*, VEN 1185.
~ *vb.* Lie as in a cradle TMP 1.2.464 *husks Wherein the acorn cradled*.

craft *vb.* Ply one's trade, work at a job, make a (good) job of it COR 4.6.118 *You have crafted fair!* (perh. with pun on sense of 'act craftily').

crafty *adj.*
1 Skilfully wrought ADO 3.1.22 *little Cupid's crafty arrow*.
2 Feigned JN 4.1.53 *you may think my love was crafty love*.

crafty-sick *adj.* Feigning sickness 2H4 Ind.37 *old Northumberland, Lies crafty-sick*.

crammed *ppl. adj.* Filled or stuffed to excess, fed with excess (to fatten for the table) TRO 2.2.49 *would they but fat their thoughts With this cramm'd reason*.

crank *n.* A winding path or course COR 1.1.137 *through the cranks and offices of man*.
~ *vb.* Run in a winding course, zigzag 1H4 3.1.97 *See how this river comes me cranking in*.

crannied *ppl. adj.* Like a cranny MND 5.1.158 *had in it a crannied hole or chink*.

crants *n.* (var. of ?) Garland, wreath (carried before a maiden's bier and hung over her grave) HAM 5.1.232 *here she is allow'd her virgin crants*.

crare *n.* (var. of ?) Crayer, small trading vessel CYM 4.2.205 *thy sluggish crare* (F1 *care*).

crasing See CRAZING.

crave *vb.* Beg to know SHR 2.1.179 *I'll crave the day When I shall ask the banes*.

craven *n.* Cock that is not game SHR 2.1.227 *No cock of mine, you crow too like a craven*; (hence) coward H5 4.7.133 *He is a craven and a villain else*.
~ *vb.* Render cowardly CYM 3.4.78 *a prohibition…That cravens my weak hand*.

craver *n.* Beggar PER 2.1.88 *I'll turn craver too*.

craze *vb.*
1 Break, impair R3 4.4.17 *So many miseries have craz'd my voice*.
2 Impair in intellect, render insane, drive mad, distract LR 3.4.170 *The grief hath craz'd my wits*.

crazed *ppl. adj.* Impaired, unsound MND 1.1.92 *Thy crazed title to my certain right*.

crazing *n.* Shattering H5 4.3.105 *the bullet's crazing*.
◇ F1, Qq *crasing*; F2 *grasing*. See GRAZE *vb.²*

crazy *adj.* Decrepit, broken down 1H6 3.2.89 *crazy age*.

cream *vb.* Form a scum MV 1.1.89 *cream and mantle like a standing pond*.

cream-faced *adj.* Pale MAC 5.3.11 *thou cream-fac'd loon!*

create *pa. pple.* Created H5 2.2.31 *With hearts create of duty and of zeal*, MND 5.1.405, JN 4.1.106.

creature *n.* One who owes his position to another, servant H8 3.2.36 *A creature of the Queen's*; (hence) puppet, instrument TIM 1.1.116 *this thy creature*.

credent *adj.*
1 Believing, trustful HAM 1.3.30 *with too credent ear*, LC 279.
2 Credible MM 4.4.26 *my authority bears of a credent bulk*, WT 1.2.142.

credit *n.*
1 Credibility, trustworthiness OTH 2.1.287 *that she loves him, 'tis apt and of great credit*.
2 Reputation PER 4.2.30 *our credit comes not in like the commodity*, AYL 1.1.127, LLL 4.1.26.
3 Report TN 4.3.6 *I found this credit*.
~ *vb.* Do credit to, honour SHR 4.1.104 *I call them forth to credit her*.

creek *n.*
1 Tidal estuary of a river CYM 4.2.151 *I'll throw't into the creek…and let it to the sea*.
2 Narrow or winding passage ERR 4.2.38 *The passages of alleys, creeks, and narrow lands*.

crescent *adj.* Growing, increasing ANT 2.1.10 *My powers are crescent*, HAM 1.3.11, CYM 1.4.2.

crescive *adj.* Growing H5 1.1.66 *crescive in his faculty*.

cresset *n.* Vessel of iron (etc.) to hold fire used for light or a beacon, fire-basket; (transf.) 1H4 3.1.15 *full of fiery shapes Of burning cressets*.

crest *n.*
1 (only fig.) Comb, tuft of feathers, or the like, on an animal's head 1H4 1.1.99 *bristle up The crest of youth*, TRO 1.3.379, COR 4.5.210.
2 (often fig.) Device placed on a wreath, coronet, etc. and borne above the shield and helmet in a coat of arms WIV 5.5.63 *Each fair instalment, coat, and sev'ral crest*, MND 3.2.214, JN 4.3.46.
3 Helmet (orig. plume of feathers, etc., on a helmet or the conical top of it) MAC 5.8.11 *Let fall thy blade on vulnerable crests*, JN 2.1.317, VEN 104.
4 Ridge of the neck of a horse or dog VEN 272 *his braided hanging mane Upon his compass'd crest*, JC 4.2.26.
◇ Fig. uses of senses 1 and 4 coincide.
~ *vb.* Serve as a crest to, top ANT 5.2.83 *his rear'd arm Crested the world*.
◇ Some heraldic crests were of the form of a raised arm on a wreath.

crestless *adj.* Having no heraldic crest 1H6 2.4.85 *Spring crestless yeomen from so deep a root?*

crest-wounding *adj.* Disgracing the crest or cognizance LUC 828 *crest-wounding private scar!*

crewel *n.* Fine, coloured, worsted yarn used for embroidery and tapestry LR 2.4.7 *he wears crewel garters*.
◇ Ff12 *cruell* Possible play on the sense 'painful'.

cribbed *ppl. adj.* Confined, hampered MAC 3.4.23 *I am cabin'd, cribb'd, confin'd*.

crimeful *adj.* Criminal LUC 970 *this cursed crimeful night*, HAM 4.7.7 (F1; Qq *criminall*).

cringe *vb.* Distort (the face) ANT 3.13.100 *you see him cringe his face*.

cripple *adj.* Lame H5 4.Ch.20 *the cripple tardy-gaited night* (F1 *creeple*).

crisp *adj.* Curled, rippled TMP 4.1.130 *Leave your crisp channels*, 1H4 1.3.106.
◇ TIM 4.3.183 *crisp heaven* either 'curled with clouds' (cf. Schmidt), or 'shining, clear'.

crisped *ppl. adj.* Curled MV 3.2.92 *those crisped snaky golden locks*.

critic *n.* Fault-finder, caviller LLL 3.1.176 *a critic, nay, a night-watch constable*, SON 112.11, TRO 5.2.131.
~ *adj.* Censorious, fault-finding LLL 4.3.168 *critic Timon laugh at idle toys!*

critical *adj.* Censorious, fault-finding MND 5.1.54 *some satire, keen and critical*, OTH 2.1.119.

crone *n.* Withered old woman WT 2.3.77 *give't to thy crone.*

crook-back *n.* Hunchback 3H6 5.5.30 *this scolding crook-back.*
~ *adj.* Hunchbacked 3H6 1.4.75 *that valiant crook-back prodigy.*

crooked *adj.*
1 With bent back, deformed ERR 4.2.19 *He is deformed, crooked, old, and sere.*
2 False H5 1.2.94 *their crooked titles.*
3 Perverse, malignant TGV 4.1.22 *If crooked fortune had not thwarted me*, H8 5.2.79, 2H6 5.1.158.

crooked-pated *adj.* Having a curved head AYL 3.2.82 *betray a she-lamb of a twelve-month to a crooked-pated old cuckoldly ram.*

crop *vb.*
1 Reap, gather, pluck R2 2.1.134 *To crop at once a too long withered flower*, 1H4 5.4.73.
2 Cut off, lop off R3 1.2.247 *That cropp'd the golden prime of this sweet prince*; (fig.) PER 1.1.141 *lest my life be cropp'd.*
3 Bear a crop ANT 2.2.228 *He ploughed her, and she cropp'd* (i.e. had a child).

crop-ear *n.* Crop-eared animal 1H4 2.3.69 *What horse? Roan? a crop-ear, is it not?*

cross *n.* (usu. quibbling) Coin, usu. with the representation of a cross on it AYL 2.4.12 *Yet I should bear no cross if I did bear you, for I think you have no money in your purse*, AYL 2.4.12, 2H4 1.2.226.

cross *vb.*
1 Cross the path of, meet HAM 1.1.127 *I'll cross it* [the Ghost].
2 Thwart, obstruct, go counter to ADO 1.3.67 *If I can cross him any way*, MND 1.1.150, MAC 3.1.80; contradict SHR 2.1.28 *When did she cross thee with a bitter word*, PER 4.3.16, LLL 1.2.34.
3 Debar *from* 3H6 3.2.127 *To cross me from the golden time I look for!*
4 (pass.) Have one's debt crossed off or cancelled TIM 1.2.162 *When all's spent, he'ld be cross'd then.*
~ *adj.*
1 Passing from side to side JC 1.3.50 *the cross blue lightning* (i.e. forked), LR 4.7.34.
2 Perverse ROM 4.3.5 *my state, Which…is cross and full of sin*, H8 3.2.214; inclined to quarrel or disagree SHR 2.1.249 *cross in talk*, R3 3.1.126, TIT 2.3.53.
~ *adv.* Across the course (of something), obliquely crosswise ADO 5.1.139 *give him another staff, this last was broke cross* (i.e. broken across the adversary's body or shield).

cross-gartered *adj.* Wearing the garters crossed on the leg TN 2.5.154 *wish'd to see thee ever cross-garter'd.*

cross-gartering *n.* Wearing the garters crossed on the leg TN 3.4.21 *This does make some obstruction in the blood, this cross-gartering.*

crossing *n.* Contradiction 1H4 3.1.35 *I do not bear these crossings.*

crossly *adv.* Adversely, unfavourably R2 2.4.24 *And crossly to thy good all fortune goes.*

crossness *n.* Contrariness, disposition to contradict, perversity ADO 2.3.177 *rather than she will bate one breath of her accustom'd crossness.*

cross-row *n.* (more fully 'Christ-row' or 'criss-cross-row') The alphabet, so called from the cross formerly prefixed to it in primers R3 1.1.55 *And from the cross-row plucks the letter G.*

crotchet *n.* (used with play on two senses) (1) Whimsical fancy; and (2) musical note ADO 2.3.56 *these are the very crotchets that he speaks*, ROM 4.5.118.

crow *n.* Crowbar ROM 5.2.21 *Get me an iron crow*, ERR 3.1.80.

crowd *vb.* (lit. and fig.) Squeeze, crush JC 2.4.36 *Will crowd a feeble man almost to death*, 2H4 4.2.34.

crow-flower *n.* Buttercup HAM 4.7.169 *Of crow-flowers, nettles, daisies.*
⇨ So in mod. North-Midland use; Gerarde (1597) gives the name to the Ragged Robin.

crow-keeper *n.*
1 One employed to keep rooks away from cornfields LR 4.6.88 *That fellow handles his bow like a crow-keeper.*
2 Scarecrow ROM 1.4.6 *Scaring the ladies like a crow-keeper.*

crown *n.* *triple crown* The papal tiara 2H6 1.3.63.

crowner *n.* (reduced form, with assimilation to 'crown', of) Coroner HAM 5.1.4 *The crowner hath sate on her*, TN 1.5.13+.

crownet *n.* (reduced form, with assimilation to 'crown', of) Coronet ANT 5.2.91 *crowns and crownets*, TRO Prol.6.

crown-imperial *n.* Fritillaria imperialis, a native of the Levant WT 4.4.126 *Bold oxlips, and The crown imperial.*

crudy *adj.* 'Curdy', thick 2H4 4.3.98 *all the foolish and dull and crudy vapours.*

cruel *n.* (pl.) Cruelties, cruel beings LR 3.7.65 *All cruels else subscribe.*
~ *adj.* See CREWEL.

cruelly *adv.* Exceedingly, excessively H5 5.2.203 *I love thee cruelly.*

cruelty *n.* (concrete use) Cruel being TN 1.5.288 *Farewell, fair cruelty.*

crusado, cruzado *n.* Portuguese coin, orig. of gold, bearing the figure of a cross OTH 3.4.26 *Full of crusadoes.*

crush *vb.*
1 Force, put a strained sense upon (words) TN 2.5.140 *to crush this a little.*
2 Drink, quaff ROM 1.2.80 *crush a cup of wine.*

crushed *ppl. adj.* Forced, strained H5 1.2.175 *a crush'd necessity.*

crutch *n.* (fig.) Old age CYM 4.2.200 *turn'd my leaping time into a crutch.*

cry *n.*
1 Public report, rumour OTH 4.1.123 *the cry goes that you marry her*, TRO 3.3.184.
2 Pack (esp. of hounds) OTH 2.3.364 *not like a hound that hunts, but one that fills up the cry*, MND 4.1.124, COR 3.3.120; (transf.) a company (of people) HAM 3.2.278 *a cry of players.*
~ *vb.*
1 Appeal, supplicate 1H6 5.4.53 *cry for vengeance at the gates of heaven*, TIM 2.1.20.
2 Beg for (something) LC 42 *Where want cries some*; *cry mercy* cry pardon R3 5.3.224 *Cry mercy, lords*; call for, demand loudly OTH 1.3.276 *th' affair cries haste.*
3 Extol, praise PER 4.2.93 *hast thou cried her through the market?*, H8 1.1.27.
4 *cry a match* Claim the match, claim the victory ROM 2.4.69.
~ in combination
cry down Put down, overwhelm by vehement action H8 1.1.137 *cry down This Ipswich fellow's insolence.* **cry on** 1 Invoke with outcry TRO 5.5.35 *Crying on Hector.* 2 Proclaim HAM 5.2.364 *This quarry cries on havoc.* 3 cry upon HAM 4.5.110 *How cheerfully on the false trail they cry.* **cry out** 1 Tell plainly ROM 3.3.109 *Thy form cries out thou art.* 2 Be in labour H8 5.1.67 *What, is she crying out?* **cry out of** Complain loudly of H5 2.3.27 *he cried out of sack.* **cry out upon** Denounce, exclaim against 1H4 4.3.81 *Cries out upon abuses.* **cry up** Praise

H8 1.2.84 *what worst...is cried up.* **cry upon** (of hounds) Yelp on the scent of TN 2.5.123 *Sowter will cry upon't.*

crystal *n.* (fig.) Eye H5 2.3.54 *clear thy crystals* (i.e. dry your eyes), VEN 963.

crystal-button *n.* Button worn on the jerkins of wine merchants or innkeepers who sell wine 1H4 2.4.69 *this leathern-jerkin, crystal-button.*

cub-drawn *adj.* Sucked dry by her cubs; (hence) ravenous, fierce LR 3.1.12 *the cub-drawn bear would couch.*

cubiculo *n.* [ablative of L. 'cubiculum'] Small chamber, apartment TN 3.2.52 *We'll call thee at the cubiculo.*

cuckoldly *adj.* Having an unfaithful wife WIV 2.2.270 *poor cuckoldly knave,* AYL 3.2.82.

cuckoo *n.* Fool 1H4 2.4.353 *A' horseback, ye cuckoo.*
▷ Associated with cuckoldry in LLL 5.2.907, MND 3.1.135, AWW 1.3.63 because the cuckoo's call was traditionally considered as proclaiming to married men that they were cuckolds.

cuckoo-bud *n.* A yellow flower LLL 5.2.896 *cuckoo-buds of yellow hue.*

cuckoo-flower *n.* Name of several kinds of flower; (here prob.) lady's smock LR 4.4.4 *hardocks, hemlock, nettles, cuckoo-flow'rs.*

Cucullus non facit monachum [L.] The cowl does not make the monk MM 5.1.262.
▷ Cf. H8 3.1.23 *all hoods make not monks.*

cudgelled *ppl. adj.* Produced by a cudgel H5 5.1.88 *These cudgell'd scars.*

cuisses See CUSHES.

cullion *n.* Base fellow SHR 4.2.20 *such a cullion,* H5 3.2.21.

cullionly *adj.* Base LR 2.2.33 *you whoreson cullionly barber-monger.*

culverin [ultimately from Fr. 'couleuvre', adder] Cannon, very long in proportion to its base 1H4 2.3.53 *Of basilisks, of cannon, culverin.*

cum privilegio [L.] With exclusive right H8 1.3.34.

cum privilegio ad impremendum solum [L.] With exclusive copyright; (fig. with ref. to marriage rights) SHR 4.4.93.

cumber *vb.* Harass, trouble JC 3.1.264 *Shall cumber all the parts of Italy,* TIM 3.6.46.

cunger See CONGER.

cunning *n.*
1 Knowledge OTH 3.3.49 *That errs in ignorance and not in cunning,* TRO 5.5.41, TIM 5.4.28.
2 Skill, ability H5 5.2.144 *I have no cunning in protestation,* ROM 2.2.101, ANT 2.3.35.
3 Profession TIM 4.3.209 *By putting on the cunning of a carper.*
~ *adj.*
1 Knowledgeable, skilful, clever ROM 4.2.2 *cunning cooks,* ADO 2.2.52, HAM 3.4.139.
2 Dexterously wrought or devised, ingenious R2 1.3.163 *a cunning instrument,* OTH 5.2.333, 1H4 2.4.90.
3 Possessing magical knowledge or skill, having the power of fortune-telling 2H6 1.2.75 *the cunning witch;* **cunning man** fortune teller, wizard 2H6 4.1.34 *A cunning man did calculate my birth.*

cup *vb.* Ply with drink, intoxicate ANT 2.7.117 *Cup us till the world go round.*

cupboard *vb.* Hoard COR 1.1.100 *Still cupboarding the viand.*

Cupid's flower *n.* The pansy, (also called) heartease MND 4.1.73 *Dian's bud o'er Cupid's flower.*

cur *n.* (used without depreciation) Dog, freq. of the mastiff or other large kind MAC 3.1.92 *hounds and greyhounds...curs.*

curate *n.* Priest having a cure or charge of souls,

parish priest TN 4.2.2 *Sir Topas the curate,* LLL 5.1.113.

curb *n.* Chain or strap attached to a bit, used for checking an unruly horse AYL 3.3.80 *The horse his curb.*

curb *vb.* Bow, bend HAM 3.4.155 *curb and woo for leave to do him good* (F courb).

curdy *vb.* (fig.) Congeal COR 5.3.66 *the icicle That's curdied by the frost.*
▷ Perh. misprint for 'curdled'.
~ *adj.* See CRUDY.

cure *n.*
1 Remedy 1H6 3.3.3 *Care is no cure,* H8 1.4.33.
2 *stand in bold, hard cure* Be in a healthy, desperate state OTH 2.1.51, LR 3.6.100.
~ *vb.* Get well again, be remedied ROM 1.2.48 *One desperate grief cures with another's languish.*

cureless *adj.* Incurable 3H6 2.6.23 *cureless are my wounds,* MV 4.1.142, LUC 772.

curiosity *n.* Fastidiousness, nicety, delicacy LR 1.1.6 *equalities are so weigh'd, that curiosity in neither can make choice of either's moi'ty,* TIM 4.3.303.

curious *adj.*
1 Made with care, skilfully wrought, dainty, delicate 3H6 2.5.53 *a curious bed,* LR 1.4.33, CYM 5.5.361.
2 Fastidious, particular SHR 4.4.36 *For curious I cannot be with you,* AWW 1.2.20, LC 49; careful in observation ROM 1.4.31 *What curious eye doth quote deformities?*
3 Anxious, concerned CYM 1.6.191 *curious...To have them in safe stowage;* causing or involving care WT 4.4.514 *curious business,* TRO 3.2.65.
~ *adv.* Delicately, nicely LLL 1.1.246 *curious-knotted garden,* LUC 1300.

curiously *adv.* Fastidiously, delicately SHR 4.3.143 *The sleeves curiously cut,* ADO 5.1.156, HAM 5.1.205.

curled *ppl. adj.* Having hair artificially curled; (hence) elegant OTH 1.2.68 *The wealthy curled darlings of our nation.*

currance *n.* Current H5 1.1.34 *With such a heady currance, scouring faults* (Ff2–3 *currant,* F4 *current*).

current *n.* Unimpeded course or progress MV 4.1.64 *The current of thy cruelty,* 1H4 2.3.55.

current *adj.* (often used allusively in ref. to 'current coin')
1 common R2 5.3.123 *Speak 'pardon' as 'tis current in our land.*
2 Sterling, genuine R3 1.2.84 *thou canst make No excuse current;* hold current prove true 1H4 2.1.54 *It holds current that I told you yesternight; current from suspicion* sound; (hence) free from suspicion R3 2.1.95 *go current from suspicion.*

currish *adj.* Displaying characteristics of Cynic philosophy; (hence) cynical, captious, disposed to find fault and sneer at sincerity and goodness 3H6 5.5.26 *Let Aesop fable in a winter's night, His currish riddles sorts not with this place.*
▷ In Greek 'cynic' is derived from a word with the sense of 'dog-like, currish'. Onions tentatively proposed 'involving stories about beasts', i.e. an extension of 'cur' (dog) to animals in general.

curry *vb.* Use flattery to gain advantage 2H4 5.1.73 *I would curry with Master Shallow.*

cursie See COURTESY.

cursitory *adj.* Cursory H5 5.2.77 *I have but with a cursitory eye O'erglanc'd the articles.*
▷ Qq12 *cursenary;* Q3 *cursory;* Ff *curselarie. curslary.* Ff prob. misspelling of *cursitory* or *cursetary.*

cursorary See CURSITORY.

curst *ppl. adj.* (usu. spelling of 'cursed' in the foll. senses)
1 Malignant, perverse, shrewish, cantankerous

SHR 1.1.180 *so curst and shrew'd*, TN 3.2.42, LLL 4.1.36.

2 Savage, vicious ADO 2.1.23 *God sends a curst cow short horns*, WT 3.3.130, VEN 887.

curstness *n.* Malignancy, ill-humour ANT 2.2.25 *Nor curstness grow to th' matter.*

curtal *adj.* Having the tail docked or shortened WIV 2.1.110 *Hope is a curtal dog in some affairs* (i.e. a dog of no value), ERR 3.2.146, PP 17.19.

curtle-axe *n.* (perverted form of 'cutlass', Fr. 'coutelas') Broad cutting sword AYL 1.3.117 *A gallant curtle-axe upon my thigh*, H5 4.2.21.

curtsy See COURTESY.

curvet *n.* In the manege, an intricate leap AWW 2.3.282 *the bound and high curvet of Mars's fiery steed.*

~ *vb.* Execute a curvet; (fig.) leap about, frisk AYL 3.2.244 *Cry 'holla' to thy tongue, I prithee; it curvets unseasonably.*

cushes *n.* (pl.) Armour for the thighs 1H4 4.1.105 *His cushes on his thighs.*

cushion *n.*
1 Seat (of a ruler) COR 3.1.101 *Let them have cushions by you* (i.e. seats in the Senate alongside you).
2 Symbol of peace and ease COR 4.7.43 *From the casque to th' cushion.*
3 Swelling simulating pregnancy 2H4 5.4.14 *you shall have a dozen of cushions.*

custalorum *n.* (corruption of L. 'custos rotulorum') Keeper of the rolls WIV 1.1.7 *cousin Slender, and Custa-lorum.—Ay, and Rato-lorum too.*

custard-coffin *n.* Crust over a custard SHR 4.3.82 *A custard-coffin, a bauble, a silken pie.*

custerell (var. of) COISTRELL.

custom *n.*
1 *of custom* Customary WIV 5.5.75 *Our dance of custom*, MAC 3.4.96, OTH 3.3.122.
2 *with a custom* From habit WT 4.4.12 *Digest't with a custom.*

customer *n.* Prostitute, harlot OTH 4.1.119 *I marry her! What? a customer!*, AWW 5.3.286.

custom-shrunk *adj.* Having fewer customers MM 1.2.84 *I am custom-shrunk.*

cut *n.*
1 Slash in a garment ADO 3.4.19 *cloth a' gold and cuts*, SHR 4.3.90.
2 Common or working horse; (a proper name) 1H4

2.1.5 *beat Cut's saddle*; (term of abuse, cf. HORSE) TN 2.3.187 *call me cut.*

3 *draw cuts* Draw lots ERR 5.1.423.

~ *vb.*
1 Carve, represent in stone MV 1.1.84 *cut in alabaster*, WT 5.3.79.
2 Preclude *from* 1H4 5.2.90 *he cuts me from my tale.*
~ in combination
cut off
1 Make an end of, break off, cancel LR 2.4.174 *cut off my train.* **2** Put to death MM 5.1.35 *Cut off by course of justice*, H5 3.6.107. **cut out** Shape according to a pattern WT 4.4.382 *By th' pattern of mine own thoughts I cut out The purity of his.*
⇨ cut bowstrings See HOLD.

cut and long-tail *n.phr.* (lit.) Horses or dogs with docked and undocked (long) tails (i.e. every kind of horse, etc.); (fig.) all sorts of people WIV 3.4.47 *come cut and long-tail.*

cutpurse *n.* Pickpocket, thief H5 5.1.86 *cutpurse of quick hand*, LR 3.2.90, HAM 3.4.99; (attrib.) 2H4 2.4.128 *you cutpurse rascal.*

cutter *n.* Sculptor CYM 2.4.83 *The cutter Was as another Nature.*

cutter-off *n.* Interrupter, curtailer AYL 1.2.49 *the cutter-off of Nature's wit.*

cuttle *n.* Cutthroat, bully 2H4 2.4.130 *play the saucy cuttle with me.*

cyme *n.* Medicinal drug used as an emetic MAC 5.3.55 *What rhubarb, cyme, or what purgative drug.*
⇨ Some see this as a misspelling of 'cumin', or 'thyme', or of 'cynne' (a var. of 'senna').

cynic *n.* One holding the principles of Cynic philosophy, which despised ease, wealth and enjoyments of life; (hence) surly, currish, rude, sneering fellow JC 4.3.133 *how vilely doth this cynic rhyme!*

cypress *n.*[1] Tree of hard durable wood and dense dark foliage, symbolical of mourning and used at funerals TN 2.4.52 *come away, death, And in sad cypress let me be laid*; (attrib.) SHR 2.1.351 *In cypress chests*, 2H6 3.2.323, COR 1.10.30.

cypress *n.*[2] Light, transparent material of silk and linen, when black often used in mourning WT 4.4.219 *Cypress black as e'er was crow*; kerchief or veil made of this and worn in sign of mourning TN 3.1.121 *a cypress, not a bosom, Hides my heart.*

D

daff *vb.*
1 Put off (clothes, armour) ANT 4.4.13 *till we do please To daff't for our repose*, LC 297.
2 Put, turn, thrust aside ADO 5.1.78 *Canst thou so daff me? Thou hast kill'd my child*, PP 14.3.
3 Put off (with an excuse) OTH 4.2.175 *thou daff'st me with some device* (F1 *dafts*, Qq *dofftst*).

dagger *n.*
1 *rapier* or *sword and dagger* Method of fighting introduced towards the end of the 16C and taking the place of sword-and-buckler fighting WIV 1.1.284 *playing at sword and dagger*, HAM 5.2.145; (attrib.) MM 4.3.14 *the rapier and dagger man.*
2 *dagger of lath* Wooden weapon borne by Vice in the morality plays 1H4 2.4.137 *beat thee...with a dagger of lath*, TN 4.2.126.
⇨ Cf. H5 4.4.72 *pare his nails with a wooden dagger*; 2H4 3.2.319 *Vice's dagger.*

3 *speak daggers* Speak so as to wound HAM 3.2.396 *I will speak daggers to her, but use none.*

dainty *n.*
1 Daintiness, fastidiousness 2H4 4.1.196 *the King is weary Of dainty.*
2 *make dainty* Be chary, act coyly ROM 1.5.19 *She that makes dainty, She I'll swear hath corns.*
~ *adj.* dainty *of* Scrupulous or fastidious about MAC 2.3.144 *let us not be dainty of leave-taking.*

daisied *adj.* Full of daisies CYM 4.2.398 *the prettiest daisied plot.*

dalliance *n.* Idle delay 1H6 5.2.5 *keep not back your powers in dalliance.*

dally *vb.*
1 Talk lightly or idly 1H4 5.3.55 *What, is it a time to jest and dally now?*
2 Trifle SHR 4.4.68 *Dally not with the gods*, TN 2.4.47, LLL 5.1.104.

damask n.
1 Colour of the damask rose: pink or light-red COR 2.1.216 *the war of white and damask*; mixture of red and white AYL 3.5.123 *mingled damask.*
~ adj. Of such colour (in both senses of n.) TN 2.4.112 *her damask cheek*, LLL 5.2.296 *their damask sweet commixture*, PP 7.5.
damasked ppl. adj. Having the hue of a damask rose (see DAMASK) SON 130.5 *I have seen roses damask'd, red and white.*

dame n.
1 Mistress (of a household, etc.) WT 4.4.57 *Both dame and servant*, LUC 1034.
2 Woman of rank, lady MND 5.1.293 *the fairest dame That liv'd*, MAC 4.2.65, LUC 21; (prefixed to a name) 2H6 1.2.39 *Henry and Dame Margaret.*
3 Form of address to a lady ANT 4.4.29 *Fare thee well, dame.*
4 Mother 2H4 3.2.112 *my old dame will be undone now*, LUC 1477.
damnation n. (abusive address) Damned person ROM 3.5.235 *Ancient damnation! O most wicked fiend!*
damp n. Vapour, fog, mist AWW 2.1.163 *twice in murk and occidental damp*, AYL 4.9.13, LUC 778.
dan n. Master, Sir LLL 3.1.180 *Dan Cupid* (Ff, Q2 *don*).
dance vb. dance barefoot (said of an elder sister when a younger one is married before her) Be unaccompanied by a husband, go as an old maid SHR 2.1.33 *I must dance barefoot on her wedding day.*
dancing horse n. A famous performing horse named Morocco, which had been trained to beat out numbers with its hoof LLL 1.2.53 *the dancing horse will tell you.*
dancing-rapier n. Sword worn only for ornament in dancing TIT 2.1.39 *a dancing-rapier by your side.*

danger n.
1 Power to harm; reach or range (e.g. of a weapon) JN 4.3.84 *Nor tempt the danger of my true defence; in, into, out of the danger of* in (etc.) the power or mercy of HAM 1.3.35 *Out of the shot and danger of desire*, TN 5.1.87, MAC 3.2.15.
2 Mischief, harm, damage MV 4.1.38 *let the danger light Upon your charter*, JC 2.1.17.
3 Debt MV 4.1.180 *You stand within his danger* (with play on sense 1 also).
~ vb. Endanger ANT 1.2.192 *whose quality, going on, The sides o' th' world may danger.*
dangerous adj. Threatening 1H4 5.1.69 *dangerous countenance*, ADO 5.1.97.
dankish adj. Dank, humid ERR 5.1.248 *in a dark and dankish vault.*
Dansker n. [Danish form] Dane HAM 2.1.7 *what Danskers are in Paris.*

dare n.
1 Defiance, challenge ANT 1.2.184 *Pompeius Hath given the dare to Caesar.*
2 Boldness, daring 1H4 4.1.78 *It lends...A larger dare to our great enterprise.*
~ vb.¹
1 Have boldness or courage (to do something), be willing *to*, go so far as *to* MV 5.1.251 *I dare be bound*, H8 5.1.17; *dare better* would rather AWW 3.6.88 *and dares better be damn'd than to do't.*
2 Challenge, defy 1H6 1.3.45 *am I dar'd and bearded to my face?*, MND 3.2.413, ROM 2.4.12.
~ vb.² Daze, dazzle (larks) and so entrap them (e.g. by means of a piece of scarlet cloth and a mirror) H8 3.2.282 *And dare us with his cap, like larks*, H5 4.2.36.
dareful adj. Defiant MAC 5.5.6 *We might have met them dareful, beard to beard.*

daring adv. Daringly R2 1.3.43 *no person be so bold Or daring-hardy.*
dark adj. (fig.)
1 Iniquitous, evil R2 1.1.169 *dark dishonour's use.*
2 Gloomy, dismal MV 5.1.87 *his affections dark as Erebus*, ROM 3.5.36, SON 97.3; frowning, clouded VEN 182 *a heavy, dark, disliking eye.*
3 Obscure in meaning LLL 5.2.19 *What's your dark meaning, mouse, of this light word?*; indistinct, indiscernible TMP 1.2.50 *the dark backward and abysm of time*, VEN 760.
4 Concealed, secret LR 1.1.36 *our darker purpose.*
5 *dark house, dark room* Place of confinement for madmen TN 3.4.135 *We'll have him in a dark room and bound*, ERR 4.4.94, AYL 3.2.401; *keep him dark* keep him confined in a dark room AWW 4.1.94.
~ vb. Obscure, eclipse PER 4.Gower.35 *This so darks In Philoten all graceful marks.*
~ adv. Darkling in the dark AYL 3.5.39 *without candle may go dark to bed.*
darken vb. Deprive of lustre or renown, eclipse COR 2.1.259 *their blaze Shall darken him forever*, ANT 3.1.24.
darkening n. Setting, growing dark TRO 5.8.7 *the vail and dark'ning of the sun* (F1 *darking*).
darking See DARKENING.
darkling adv. In the dark, in darkness ANT 4.15.10 *Burn the great sphere thou mov'st in! darkling stand The varying shore o' th' world!*, MND 2.2.86, LR 1.4.217.

darkly adv.
1 Secretly MM 3.2.177 *have dark deeds darkly answer'd*, AWW 4.3.11.
2 Obscurely JN 4.2.232 *When I spake darkly what I purposed*, LLL 5.2.23, R3 1.4.169.
3 Gloomily R3 1.4.169 *How darkly and how deadly dost thou speak!*, TN 2.1.3.
darkness n. Death MM 3.1.83 *I will encounter darkness as a bride.*
darnel n. A grass, Lolium temulentum, a weed injurious to growing corn LR 4.4.5 *Darnel, and all the idle weeds that grow In our sustaining corn*, H5 5.2.45, 1H6 3.2.44.
▷ In 1H6 3.2.44 there is possibly a ref. to the belief that 'darnell hurteth the eies and maketh them dim, if it happen in corne' (Gerarde).
darraign vb. Set in array 3H6 2.2.72 *Darraign your battle, for they are at hand.*
dart vb. Throw, shoot, cast LLL 5.2.396 *lady, dart thy skill at me*, LR 2.4.165, CYM 4.2.314.
darting ppl. adj. Shooting darts ANT 3.1.1 *darting Parthia.*
▷ Ref. to the practice of Parthian horsemen, who retreated shooting flights of arrows backward upon the enemy.

dash n.
1 Stroke of the pen, brush, etc. LUC 206 *Some loathsome dash the herald will contrive.*
2 Trace, touch, stain WT 5.2.113 *the dash of my former life.*
3 *at first dash* From the first 1H6 1.2.71 *She takes upon her bravely at first dash.*
~ vb.
1 Destroy, frustrate 3H6 2.1.118 *To dash our late decree in parliament*, LLL 5.2.462.
2 Daunt, dispirit, abash LLL 5.2.582 *an honest man, look you, and soon dash'd*, OTH 3.3.214.
dastard n. One who meanly shrinks from danger; (esp.) one who does malicious acts in a cowardly way 3H6 2.2.114 *Ay, like a dastard and a treacherous coward*, R2 1.1.190, 2H6 4.8.27.
~ adj. Meanly shrinking from danger, showing base cowardice, dastardly COR 4.5.75 *our dastard nobles*, 1H6 1.1.144.

date n.
1 Duration, term of existence MND 3.2.373 *Whose date till death shall never end*, ERR 1.2.41, JN 4.3.106.
2 Limit or end of a period or term SON 14.14 *Thy end is truth's and beauty's doom and date*.

date-broke adj. Overdue TIM 2.2.37 *demands of date-broke bonds*.
◇ Emendation proposed by Steevens because of the metrical irregularity in F1 *demands of debt, broken Bonds*.

dateless adj. Without term, endless, limitless R2 1.3.151 *The dateless limit of thy dear exile*, ROM 5.3.115, SON 30.6.

daub vb.
1 Cover with a specious exterior, disguise, white-wash R3 3.5.29 *daub'd his vice with show of virtue*.
2 *daub it* Dissemble, pretend LR 4.1.52 *I cannot daub it further* (Qq *dance it*).

daw n. (lit.) Jackdaw; (fig.) fool, simpleton 1H6 2.4.18 *I am no wiser than a daw*, COR 4.5.44.

daubery, daubry n. The practice of daubing, false show WIV 4.2.177 *such daub'ry as this is*.

dawning n. Morning LR 2.2.1 *Good dawning to thee, friend*, MM 4.2.94; *bird of dawning* the cock HAM 1.1.160.

day n.
1 *by days* Daily, day by day, every day in its turn TRO 4.1.10 *how Diomed, a whole week by days, Did haunt you*.
2 *How's the day?* What time is it? TMP 5.1.3; (hence) *by the day* o'clock 1H4 2.1.1 *an' it be not four by the day*.
3 *take no longer days* Be no longer about it TIT 4.2.165.
4 *days of nature* Days of one's life HAM 1.5.12 *Till the foul crimes done in my days of nature*.
5 Space of time, period 2H6 2.1.2 *I saw not better sport these seven years' day*.
6 Day of battle JN 3.4.116 *What have you lost by losing of this day?*, 2H4 1.2.208; (hence) victory JN 2.1.393 *To whom in favour she shall give the day*, 1H4 5.4.159, 2H6 5.2.89.
7 (fig.) Light ANT 4.8.13 *O thou day o' th' world*.
8 *duty of the day* Morning salutation CYM 3.5.32 *Nor to us both tender'd The duty of the day*.

day-bed n. Sofa, couch TN 2.5.48 *having come from a day-bed, where I have left Olivia sleeping*, R3 3.7.72 (Qq; F1 *love-bed*).

day-woman See DEY-WOMAN.

dazzle vb. Lose the faculty of steady vision or the distinctness of vision, esp. from gazing at too bright light 3H6 2.1.25 *Dazzle mine eyes, or do I see three suns?*, TIT 3.2.85, VEN 1064.

dead adj.
1 Deadly, mortal WT 4.4.434 *the dead blow of it*, MND 3.2.57.
2 Of or pertaining to death JN 5.7.65 *You breathe these dead news*.
3 Deathlike, deathly, deadly pale 2H4 1.1.71 *So dull, so dead in look, so woe-begone*, OTH 2.3.177.
4 *is dead* Has died ROM 5.3.210 *my wife is dead to-night*, ADO 5.1.242, LR 5.3.293.
5 *a dead man* A man marked out for death WIV 4.2.43 *You are utterly sham'd, and he's but a dead man*.

dead-killing adj. Mortal R3 4.1.35 *this dead-killing news*, LUC 540.

deadly adj. Deathlike, deathly ERR 4.4.93 *Their pale and deadly looks*, TN 1.5.265, LR 5.3.291.
~ adv.
1 In a manner resembling or suggesting death R3 3.7.26 *look'd deadly pale*.
2 Mortally TRO 5.5.12 *Thoas is deadly hurt*.

3 Implacably, to the death ADO 5.1.177 *hate him deadly*, AWW 5.3.117, 3H6 1.4.84.

deadly-handed adj. Murderous 2H6 5.2.9 *The deadly-handed Clifford slew my steed*.

deadly-standing adj. Fixed with a deathly stare TIT 2.3.32 *What signifies my deadly-standing eye*.

dead men's fingers n. The early purple orchis, Orchis mascula HAM 4.7.171 *our cull-maids do dead men's fingers call them*.

deal n.
1 *no deal* Not at all PP 17.17 *My shepherd's pipe can sound no deal*.
2 *some deal* A little TIT 3.1.244 *To weep with them that weep doth ease some deal*.

deal vb. Act, proceed JN 5.2.22 *We cannot deal but with the very hand Of stern injustice*, WIV 1.3.101, 1H4 2.4.169.
~ in combination
deal in 1 Proceed or act in (a matter) ADO 5.1.101 *Do not you meddle, let me deal in this*. 2 Have to do with TMP 5.1.271 *deal in her command*. **deal on lieutenantry** Act (and hence) fight by proxy ANT 3.11.39 *He alone Dealt on lieutenantry*. **deal upon** Set to work against, proceed against R3 4.2.74 *they that I would have thee deal upon*.

dealer See PLAIN adj. sense 3.

dealing n. *in plain dealing* Putting it plainly MM 2.1.249 *in plain dealing, Pompey, I shall have you whipped*.

dear adj.[1]
1 Precious, valuable, worthy MV 1.1.62 *Your worth is very dear in my regard*, R2 1.3.151, 1H4 4.4.31.
2 Important, significant ROM 5.3.32 *a ring that I must use In dear employment*, LR 3.1.19, 1H4 4.1.34.
3 Affectionate, fond, loving SON 131.3 *my dear doting heart*, TGV 4.3.14, WT 2.3.150.
4 Hearty; (hence) energetic, zealous LLL 2.1.1 *summon up your dearest spirits*, 1H4 5.5.36, TRO 5.3.9.
◇ ROM 3.3.28 *dear mercy* 'rare, unusual' or senses 1 and 3. Q1 *meere* 'mere'.
~ adv.
1 (with *aby, buy, cost*) At a high price, dearly MND 3.2.175 *Lest, to thy peril, thou aby it dear*, ERR 4.1.81, OTH 5.2.255.
2 (with *love*) As one who is held dear, fondly ROM 2.3.66 *thou didst love so dear*, SHR 2.1.337, MV 3.2.313.
3 (with *grieve*) Keenly, sorely JC 3.1.196 *Shall it not grieve thee dearer than thy death*, LR 1.1.56.

dear adj.[2] Hard, grievous, dire HAM 1.2.182 *my dearest foe*, TMP 2.1.136, AWW 4.5.11.

deared ppl. adj. Endeared, held dear ANT 1.4.44 *the ebb'd man...Comes dear'd by being lack'd* (F1 *fear'd*).

dearly adv.
1 Richly, finely CYM 2.2.18 *Rubies unparagon'd, How dearly they do't!*, CYM 2.2.18.
2 Heartily WT 5.1.130 *dearly welcome*.
3 Deeply, keenly HAM 4.3.41 *we dearly grieve*, ERR 2.2.130, AYL 1.3.33.

dearness n. Affection, fondness ADO 3.2.98 *in dearness of heart*.

dearn See DERN.

dearth n. Costliness, high value HAM 5.2.117 *his infusion of such dearth and rareness*.

death n.
1 *the death* The last extremity ERR 1.1.146 *Though thou art adjudged to the death*, MND 1.1.65, R3 1.2.178; *to the death* on pain or peril of death, though it cost me my life R3 3.2.55 *God knows I will not do it, to the death!*, LLL 5.2.146, ADO 1.3.70.

2 Skeleton, or skull Jn 5.2.177 *A bare-ribb'd death*, MV 2.7.63.

deathful *adj.* Deadly, mortal 2H6 3.2.404 *a deathful wound*.

deathlike *adj.* Deadly Per 1.1.29 *death-like dragons*.

death-marked *adj.* Marked out for death Rom Prol.9 *The fearful passage of their death-mark'd love*.

death-practised *adj.* Whose death is plotted Lr 4.6.277 *the death-practis'd Duke*.

deathsman *n.* Executioner 3H6 5.5.67 *As, deathsmen, you have rid this sweet young prince!*, Luc 1001, Lr 4.6.258.

death-token *n.* Plague-spot indicating the approaching death of the patient Tro 2.3.177 *He is so plaguy proud that the death-tokens of it Cry 'No recovery'*.

debase *vb.* Degrade the dignity of R2 3.3.127 *We do debase ourselves*, Cor 3.1.135.

debate *n.* Contention, quarrel MND 2.1.116 *comes From our debate, from our dissension*, Son 89.13, 2H4 4.4.2.
~ *vb.*
1 (intr.) Fight, quarrel Luc 1421 *they would debate with angry swords*.
2 (trans.) Contest, dispute AWW 1.2.75 *Nature and sickness Debate it at their leisure*, Ham 4.4.26.

debatement *n.* Deliberation, consideration Ham 5.2.45 *Without debatement further*, MM 5.1.99.

debater *n.* Disputant Luc 1019 *Where leisure serves with dull debaters*.

debile *adj.* Weak AWW 2.3.34 *In a most weak—And debile minister*, Cor 1.9.48.

debitor and creditor *n. phr.* Statement of account, account book Cym 5.4.168 *You have no true debitor and creditor but it*; (hence) book-keeper Oth 1.1.31 *belee'd and calm'd By debitor and creditor*.

debonair *adj.* Gentle, meek Tro 1.3.235 *Courtiers as free, as debonair, unarm'd*.

debosh *vb.* Vilify AWW 5.3.206 *With all the spots a'th'world tax'd and debosh'd*.

deboshed *ppl. adj.* Corrupted, depraved Lr 1.4.242 *Men so disorder'd, so debosh'd and bold* (Ff; Qq *deboyst*), Tmp 3.2.26, AWW 2.3.138.

deboyst See DEBOSHED.

debted *ppl. adj.* Indebted Err 4.1.31 *I stand debted to this gentleman*.

debuty (var. of) DEPUTY.

decay *n.*
1 Downfall, destruction, ruin Jn 4.3.154 *The imminent decay of wrested pomp*, 2H6 3.1.194, R3 4.4.409; cause of ruin Son 80.14 *my love was my decay*.
2 (fig.) A ruin Lr 5.3.298 *this great decay*.
~ *vb.*
1 Perish, be destroyed Ant 2.1.4 *decays the Thing we sue for*, 1H6 1.1.34, Son 71.12.
2 Destroy Cym 1.5.56 *to decay A day's work*.

decayer *n.* Destroyer Ham 5.1.172 *your water is a sore decayer of your whoreson dead body*.

deceased *ppl. adj.* Bygone 2H4 3.1.81 *times deceas'd*.

deceivable *adj.* Deceitful, deceptive R2 3.84 *Whose duty is deceivable and false*, TN 4.3.21.

deceive *vb.*
1 Be false to, betray 1H4 5.1.11 *You have deceiv'd our trust*.
2 Cheat, defraud of Son 4.10 *Thou of thyself thy sweet self dost deceive*.

deceptious *adj.* Delusive, deceiving Tro 5.2.123 *As if those organs had any deceptious functions*.

decimation *n.* Selection of every tenth man for punishment by death Tim 5.4.31 *By decimation, and a tithed death*.

decipher *vb.*

1 Reveal, detect 1H6 4.1.184 *we should have seen decipher'd there More rancorous spite*, Tit 4.2.8.
2 Make known, indicate Wiv 5.2.9 *The white will decipher her well*, Err 5.1.335.

deck *n.*
1 Pack of cards 3H6 5.1.44 *The king was slyly finger'd from the deck!*
2 *above deck* Above board Wiv 2.1.91 *I'll be sure to keep him above deck*.
~ *vb.* Cover Tmp 1.2.155 *When I have deck'd the sea with drops full salt*.

declension *n.* Falling away from a high standard R3 3.7.189 *base declension*, 2H4 2.2.173; decline, deterioration Ham 2.2.149 *by this declension Into the madness*.

decline *vb.*
1 Incline or lean *to* Err 3.2.44 *to you do I decline*.
2 Fall, sink Cor 1.1.193 *Who thrives, and who declines*, Tro 4.5.189, Ham 2.2.478; (fig.) fall *upon* (an unworthy object) Ham 1.5.50 *to decline Upon a wretch*.
3 Bend (the head, etc.) Lr 4.2.22 *Decline your head*, Err 3.2.135.
4 Inflect a word Wiv 4.1.41 *Articles...be thus declin'd*; (hence) go through (a matter) thoroughly and in order Tro 2.3.52 *I'll decline the whole question*, R3 4.4.97.

declined *ppl. adj.* Fallen, decayed, deteriorated, enfeebled Ant 3.13.27 *And answer me declin'd, sword against sword*, Tro 3.3.76.

declining *ppl. adj.* Failing, decaying, deteriorating, falling off R2 2.1.240 *this declining land*, Lr 1.2.73.

decoct *vb.* Warm up H5 3.5.20 *Decoct their cold blood to such valiant heat?*

decree *vb.* Determine, resolve (to do something) Tit 2.3.274 *Where we decreed to bury Bassianus*, Ado 1.3.34, Rom 3.3.146.

dedicate *ppl. adj.* Dedicated MM 2.2.154 *Whose minds are dedicate To nothing temporal*, 2H6 5.2.37.

dedicated *ppl. adj.* The dedicated words Words of dedication, dedicatory epistle Son 82.3.

deed *n.* Performance (of what is promised) Ham 1.3.27 *May give his saying deed*, AWW 3.6.94, Lr 1.1.71.

deed-achieving *adj.* Achieved by acts of valour Cor 2.1.173 *deed-achieving honour*.

deedless *adj.* Inactive Tro 4.5.98 *deedless in his tongue*.

deem *n.* Thought, surmise Tro 4.4.59 *what wicked deem is this?*

deep *n.* (of night) Depths JC 4.3.226 *The deep of night is crept upon our talk*, JC 4.3.226.
~ *adj.* (fig.)
1 Grave, serious, weighty 1H4 1.3.190 *matter deep and dangerous*, Cym 2.3.91, Mac 1.3.126; grievous, heinous R3 2.2.28 *deep vice*, Tim 3.4.30, Mac 1.7.20.
2 Profound in learning, knowledge or insight R3 3.7.75 *deep divines*, Tmp 2.1.266, 2H4 4.2.17.
3 Profound in craft or subtlety 2H6 3.1.57 *deep deceit*, R3 1.3.223.
~ *in combination*
deep(-) **1** To a depth, deeply, profoundly, intensely AYL 2.7.31 *deep contemplative*; Err 2.2.138 *deep-divorcing*; Tro Prol.12 *deep-drawing* (i.e. of deep draught); Luc 1100 *deep drenched*; LC 213 *deep-green*; 1H6 3.1.1 *deep premeditated*; R3 4.2.42 *deep-revolving*; LLL 1.1.85 *deep search'd*; Ven 432 *deep sore*; Ven 432 *deep-sweet*; Jn 3.1.231 *deep-sworn* (i.e. solemnly); PP 9.10 *deep-wounded*. **2** From the depths 2H6 2.4.33 *my deep-fet groans* (i.e. fetched from the depths).
✧ **deep-brained** Full of profound thoughts LC 209 *deep-brained sonnets*. **deep-mouthed** *adj.* (of

dogs) Having a loud bay or bark SHR Ind.1.18 *the deep-mouthed brach*; (transf.) loud and sonorous H5 5.Ch.11 *deep-mouth'd sea*, JN 5.2.173.

deeply *adv.*
1 Profoundly, thoroughly TN 2.5.42 *now he's deeply in*; with profound craft SHR 4.4.42 *dissemble deeply.*
2 Solemnly HAM 3.2.225 *'Tis deeply sworn.*
3 Intensely WT 2.3.14 *took it deeply*, TIT 4.1.98, 2H4 4.5.26.
4 With deep sound SHR 2.1.193 *thy beauty sounded, Yet not so deeply*, VEN 832.

deer *n.* Beast, animal LR 3.4.138 *mice and rats and such small deer.*

deface *vb.* Efface, obliterate, cancel MV 3.2.299 *deface the bond*, 2H6 1.1.102.

defame *n.* Evil repute, infamy LUC 768 *dark harbour for defame.*

defamed *ppl. adj.* Made of ill-repute 2H6 3.1.123 *England was defam'd by tyranny.*

default *n.*
1 Lack AWW 2.3.229 *I may say in the default* (i.e. at need).
2 Fault 1H6 2.1.60 *this was your default*, ERR 1.2.52.

defeat *n.* Destruction, ruin ADO 4.1.47 *defeat of her virginity*, HAM 2.2.571.
~ *vb.*
1 Destroy, ruin, undo OTH 4.2.160 *his unkindness may defeat my life*, TIM 4.3.163.
2 Disfigure, deface OTH 1.3.340 *defeat thy favour with an usurp'd beard.*
3 Defraud (anyone) *of* SON 20.11 *Nature...by addition me of thee defeated*, MND 4.1.157.

defeated *ppl. adj.* Destroyed, ruined HAM 1.2.10 *a defeated joy.*

defeature *n.* Disfigurement ERR 5.1.300 *strange defeatures in my face*, VEN 736.

defect *n.* Defectiveness, faultiness MAC 2.1.18 *the servant to defect*, SON 149.11.

defence *n.*
1 Capacity of defending (itself) 3H6 5.1.64 *the city being but of small defence.*
2 Art of defending oneself, practice or skill in self-defence HAM 4.7.97 *art and exercise in your defence*, AYL 3.3.62, JC 4.3.202.
3 Arms, armour ANT 4.4.10 *Go, put on thy defences*, ROM 3.3.134, TN 3.4.220.

defend *vb.*
1 Forbid 1H4 4.3.38 *God defend but still I should stand so*, ADO 2.1.94, ANT 3.3.43.
2 (intr.) Make a defence H5 1.2.137 *defend Against the Scot.*

defendant *adj.* Defensive H5 2.4.8 *means defendant.*

defensible *adj.* Able to make a defence H5 3.3.50 *For we no longer are defensible*, 2H4 2.3.38.

defer *vb.* Put off (time), linger 1H6 3.2.33 *Defer no time, delays have dangerous ends.*

defiance *n.*
1 Challenge to fight JC 5.1.64 *Defiance, traitors, hurl we in your teeth*, R2 3.3.130, ROM 1.1.110.
2 Declaration of aversion, rejection MM 3.1.142 *Take my defiance! Die, perish!*

deficient *adj.* Failing, fainting LR 4.6.23 *The deficient sight.*

define *vb.* Describe H5 4.Ch.46 *as may unworthiness define.*

definement *n.* Description HAM 5.2.112 *his definement suffers no perdition in you.*

definite *adj.* Resolute CYM 1.6.43 *idiots...would Be wisely definite.*

definitive *adj.* Resolute MM 5.1.427 *Never crave him, we are definitive.*

defunct *n.* The deceased CYM 4.2.358 *abhor to make his bed With the defunct.*

~ *adj.* Dead, deceased H5 4.1.21 *The organs, though defunct and dead before*, OTH 1.3.264 (F1).

defunction *n.* Decease H5 1.2.58 *After defunction of King Pharamond.*

defunctive *adj.* Pertaining to death or dying, funeral PHT 14 *defunctive music.*

defuse See DIFFUSE.

defy *vb.*
1 Challenge (esp. to a fight) H5 2.1.72 *I thee defy again*, ERR 5.1.32, JN 2.1.406.
2 Reject, despise HAM 5.2.219 *we defy augury*, MV 3.5.70, PER 4.6.26.

degree *n.*
1 (fig.) Step or stage in a process TIM 4.3.253 *The sweet degrees that this brief world affords*, 2H4 1.2.232, TN 1.5.135.
2 A step in direct line of descent R2 1.4.36 *And he our subjects' next degree in hope* (i.e. heir presumptive to the throne).
3 *in any fair degree* To any reasonable extent R2 1.1.80.

deign *vb.* Condescend to take, accept without grudging ANT 1.4.63 *thy palate then did deign The roughest berry*, TGV 1.1.152.

deject *ppl. adj.* Downcast, dejected HAM 3.1.155 *most deject and wretched*, TRO 2.2.50.

dejected *ppl. adj.* Abased, humbled, downcast LR 4.1.3 *The lowest and most dejected thing of Fortune*, PER 2.2.46, WIV 5.5.162.

dejectitude *n.* Lowered or humiliated estate, condition COR 4.5.208 *whilest he's in dejectitude.*
◇ Collier's conjecture, a word coined on 'dejected'; F1 *directitude.*

delated *ppl. adj.* (var. of) DILATED: expanded, detailed HAM 1.2.38 *more than the scope Of these delated articles allow* (Qq; Ff *dilated*; Q1 *related*).

delation *n.* Unfavourable information, accusation OTH 3.3.123 *They're close delations, working from the heart.*
◇ Johnson *delation. Dilation* was a 16-17C variant of *delation.* Ff,Qq2-3 *dilations*; Q1 *denotements.*

delicate *n.* Delicacy 3H6 2.5.51 *a prince's delicates.*
~ *adj.*
1 Delightful, pleasant WT 3.1.1 *The climate's delicate*, MAC 1.6.10, OTH 1.3.353.
2 Graceful, dainty, elegant TMP 1.2.442 *Delicate Ariel*, TIM 4.3.384, OTH 2.3.20.
3 Voluptuous ADO 1.1.303 *soft and delicate desires.*
4 Tender, not robust HAM 4.4.48 *a delicate and tender prince*, LR 3.4.12.
5 Exquisite in nature, beauty, etc. TMP 1.2.272 *a spirit too delicate To act her earthy...commands.*
6 Finely skilful, ingenious LR 4.6.184 *a delicate stratagem*, CYM 5.5.47, OTH 4.1.187; skilfully or finely made HAM 5.2.152 *most delicate carriages*, AWW 4.5.104.

delight *n.* Charm, delightfulness ROM 1.3.82 *And find delight writ there with beauty's pen*, LLL 5.2.897, SON 91.11; *of delight* delightful SON 98.11 *figures of delight.*

delighted *adj.* Endowed with or affording delight, delightful OTH 1.3.289 *delighted beauty*, MM 3.1.120, CYM 5.4.102.

deliver *vb.*
1 (lit. and fig., chiefly pass.) Bring forth (offspring) OTH 1.3.370 *many events in the womb of time which will be deliver'd*, ERR 5.1.403, LLL 4.2.69.
2 Send AWW 1.1.1 *In delivering my son from me.*
3 Present, exhibit TN 1.2.42 *that I...might not be delivered to the world*, COR 5.3.39.
4 Declare, communicate, report, relate, tell WT 5.2.4 *deliver the manner how he found it*, ERR 2.2.164, JC 3.1.181.

5 (intr.) Speak, discourse COR 1.1.95 *and't please you, deliver*, R2 3.3.34.

deliverance *n.*
1 Bringing forth of offspring CYM 5.5.370 *Ne'er mother Rejoic'd deliverance more.*
2 Utterance, enunciation, delivery 3H6 2.1.97 *at each word's deliverance,* AWW 2.1.82.

delivery *n.* Statement, account WT 5.2.9 *I make a broken delivery of the business.*

demean *vb.* (refl.) Behave oneself ERR 5.1.88 *he demean'd himself rough, rude, and wildly,* 2H6 1.1.188, 3H6 1.4.7.

demerit *n.*
1 (pl.) Merits, deserts OTH 1.2.22 *my demerits,* COR 1.1.272.
2 (pl.) Offences, sins MAC 4.3.226 *Not for their own demerits, but for mine.*

demesne *n.*
1 (pl.) Lands, estates ROM 3.5.180 *Of fair demesnes.*
2 (pl.) Regions, domains CYM 3.3.70 *This rock and these demesnes have been my world,* ROM 2.1.20.

demi- *prefix*
1 (often contemptuous) Half, semi, half-sized, curtailed TMP 5.1.272 *demi-devil,* HAM 4.7.87, OTH 5.2.301.
2 *demi-Atlas* One that holds up half the world ANT 1.5.23.
3 *demi-cannon* Gun of about 6½ inches (165 mm) bore SHR 4.3.88 *a sleeve? 'tis like a demi-cannon.*

demise *vb.* Convey, transmit R3 4.4.248 *Canst thou demise to any child of mine?*

demon *n.*
1 Attendant or ministering spirit ANT 2.3.20 *Thy demon...is Noble, courageous.*
2 Evil spirit, devil H5 2.2.121 *that same demon that hath gull'd thee thus.*

demonstrable *adj.* Evident, apparent OTH 3.4.142 *Made demonstrable here in Cyprus to him.*

demonstrate *vb.*
1 Exhibit, manifest, show HAM 1.1.124 *even the like...Have heaven and earth together demonstrated,* AYL 3.2.380, H5 4.2.54.
2 Prove OTH 3.3.431 *other proofs That do demonstrate thinly,* AWW 1.2.47.

demure *adj.* Grave, sober, serious H8 1.2.167 *with demure confidence,* LUC 1219, 2H4 4.3.90.
~ *vb.* Look demurely ANT 4.15.29 *Your wife Octavia, with her modest eyes...shall acquire no honour Demuring upon me.*

demurely *adv.* Gravely MV 2.2.192 *look demurely;* with solemn sound ANT 4.9.30 *the drums Demurely wake the sleepers.*

den See GOOD-DEN.

denay *n.* Denial TN 2.4.124 *bide no denay.*
~ *vb.* (var. of) deny 2H6 1.3.104 *let him be denay'd the regentship.*

denier *n.* Small copper coin, the tenth of an English penny (Cotgrave); (hence) a very small sum R3 1.2.251 *My dukedom to a beggarly denier,* 1H4 3.3.79, SHR Ind.1.9.
◇ Orig. a French coin, the twelfth of a sou.

denotement *n.* Indication, token, sign OTH 2.3.317 *the contemplation, mark and denotement of her parts and graces.*
◇ Q2; Q1,F1 *deuotement:* see DEVOTEMENT. OTH 3.3.123: Q1 *denotements;* other edd. *delations, dilations.*

denounce *vb.* Proclaim, declare ANT 3.7.5 *[war] denounc'd against us,* JN 3.1.319, R3 1.3.179.

denunciation *n.* Formal declaration MM 1.2.148 *we do the denunciation lack.*

deny *n.*
1 Refuse *to* (do something) SHR 2.1.179 *If she deny to wed.*

2 Refuse permission *to,* forbid R2 2.3.129 *I am denied to sue my livery here,* TIT 2.3.174.
3 Refuse to accept R2 2.1.204 *If you...deny his off'red homage.*
4 Refuse admittance to 1H4 2.4.495 *you will deny the sheriff,* H5 5.2.296.
5 Disown ROM 2.2.34 *Deny thy father and refuse thy name.*

depart *n.* Departure TGV 5.4.96 *At my depart,* 2H6 1.1.2, 3H6 4.1.92; (hence) death 3H6 2.1.110 *your loss and his depart.*
~ *vb.*
1 Take leave of one another TIM 1.1.254 *Ere we depart,* CYM 1.1.108.
2 Leave, quit, go away from 3H6 2.2.73 *depart the field,* LR 3.5.1, SON 11.2.
3 *depart with(al)* Part with, give up JN 2.1.563 *Hath willingly departed with a part,* LLL 2.1.146.

departing *n.* Separation 3H6 2.6.43 *like life and death's departing.*
◇ *praise in departing* See PRAISE.

depend *vb.*
1 Lean CYM 2.4.91 *Cupids...Depending on their brands.*
2 Be in a position of dependence LR 1.4.250 *the remainders that shall still depend,* MM 3.2.27, TRO 3.1.4.
3 Impend, be imminent, hang over ROM 3.1.119 *This day's black fate on moe days doth depend,* LUC 1615, TRO 2.3.19 (Ff *dependant*).
4 Remain in suspense CYM 4.3.23 *but our jealousy Does yet depend.*

dependancy, dependency *n.* Dependence MM 5.1.62 *Such a dependancy of thing on thing,* ANT 5.2.26, CYM 2.3.118.

dependant *adj.* Impending TRO 2.3.19 *the curse dependant on those* (Ff; Qq *depending:* see DEPEND *vb.* sense 3).

depender *n.* Dependant CYM 1.5.58 *To be depender on a thing that leans.*

deplore *vb.* Tell with grief TN 3.1.162 *Will I my master's tears to you deplore.*

deploring *ppl. adj.* Tearful, doleful TGV 3.2.84 *a deploring dump.*

depose *vb.*
1 Deprive (a person of something), take away R2 4.1.192 *You may my glories and my state depose.*
2 Testify, give evidence upon an oath MM 5.1.198 *I'll depose I had him in mine arms,* 3H6 1.2.26.
3 Examine on oath R2 1.3.30 *Depose him in the justice of his cause.*

depositary *n.* A person with whom anything is lodged in trust LR 2.4.251 *Made you my guardians, my depositaries.*

depravation *n.* Defamation, detraction TRO 5.2.132 *apt without a theme For depravation.*

deprave *vb.* (trans. and intr.) Vilify, detract TIM 1.2.140 *Who lives that's not depraved or depraves,* ADO 5.1.95.

depress *vb.* Bring down, humble R2 3.4.68 *Depress'd he is already, and deposed.*

deprive *vb.* Take away (a possession) HAM 1.4.73 *deprive your sovereignty of reason,* LUC 1186.

deputation *n.*
1 Appointment to act on behalf of another, office of deputy MM 1.1.20 *And given his deputation all the organs Of our own pow'r.*
2 *by deputation* By means of a deputy 1H4 4.1.32 *his friends by deputation could not So soon be drawn; in deputation* as deputy, vice-regent 1H4 4.3.87 *In deputation left behind him here.*

depute *vb.* Appoint OTH 4.2.221 *to depute Cassio in Othello's place.*

deputed *ppl. adj.* Appointed as an emblem of office

or dignity MM 2.2.60 *the deputed sword* (i.e. the sword of justice).

deputy *n.*
1 Lord Lieutenant H8 2.1.42 *Deputy of Ireland.*
2 *deputy of the ward* Member of the Common Council of London, who acts instead of an alderman in his absence 1H4 3.3.114 *Maid Marian may be the deputy's wife of the ward to thee,* 2H4 2.4.85 (Ff; Q1 *debuty*).

deracinate *vb.* Uproot H5 5.2.47 *That should deracinate such savagery,* TRO 1.3.99.

derive *vb.*
1 (refl.) Pass by descent, be descended or inherited ADO 4.1.135 *This shame derives itself from unknown loins,* 2H4 4.5.43.
2 Inherit AWW 1.1.45 *She derives her honesty,* AYL 1.3.62.
3 Draw upon, direct to (a person) AWW 5.3.265 *would derive me ill will,* H8 2.4.32.
4 (refl.) Originate *out of* TN 3.4.246 *his indignation derives itself out of a very competent injury.*
5 Trace the origin of, show how (it) comes about TRO 2.3.61 *Derive this.*

derived *ppl. adj.* Descended MND 1.1.99 *I am, my lord, as well deriv'd as he,* JC 2.1.322.

dern, dearn *adj.* Dark, drear, dread PER 3.Gower.15 *many a dern and painful perch,* LR 3.7.63 (Qq12).

derogate *vb.* Act in a way derogatory to one's position CYM 2.1.44 *You cannot derogate, my lord;* degenerate CYM 2.1.47 *therefore your issues, being foolish, do not derogate* (with quibble).
~ *ppl. adj.* Debased LR 1.4.280 *her derogate body.*

derogately *adv.* Disparagingly ANT 2.2.34 *name you derogately.*

derogation *n.* Disparagement CYM 2.1.43 *Is there no derogation in't?*

descant *n.* Melody sung extempore upon a plainsong, ground, or bass, to which it forms the air TGV 1.2.91 *And mar the concord with too harsh a descant;* (hence fig.) comment R3 3.7.49 *on that ground I'll make a holy descant.*
~ *vb.* Sing a descant or air; (hence) 'sing with a small, yet pleasant and shrill voice as birds doe' (Minsheu), warble LUC 1134 *While thou on Tereus descants better skill;* (hence fig.) comment R3 1.1.27 *descant on mine own deformity.*

descend *vb.* Come down from 3H6 1.1.74 *descend my throne,* LC 31.

descending *n.* Descent, lineage PER 5.1.128 *that thou cam'st From good descending?* (Qq 1–3 *discending;* Qq 4–6 *discent;* F 3–4 *descent*).

descension *n.* Descent 2H4 2.2.173 *From a God to a bull? a heavy descension!* (Q; Ff *declension*).

descent *n.*
1 That to which one descends, lowest part LR 5.3.138 *To the descent and dust below thy foot.*
2 (legal) The passing of property to the heir(s) without disposition by will, transmission by inheritance R2 2.3.136 *my inheritance of free descent* (i.e. through legitimate succession); step in descent AWW 3.7.24 *From son to son, some four or five descents.*

description *n.* Sort, species, kind, variety MV 3.2.301 *a friend of this description.*

descry *n.* Sight of a distant object LR 4.6.213 *the main descry Stands on the hourly thought* (i.e. sight of the main body of troops).
~ *vb.* Reconnoitre, investigate LR 4.5.13 *to descry The strength o' th' enemy,* R3 5.3.9.

desert *n.*
1 Action meriting reward CYM 1.5.73 *that set thee on to this desert.*
2 *without desert* Undeservedly, without cause R3

2.1.68 *all without desert have frown'd on me,* TGV 2.4.57, ERR 3.1.112.

deserve *vb.*
1 (intr.) Be entitled to reward, be worthy CYM 3.3.54 *many times Doth ill deserve by doing well,* ADO 3.1.115.
2 Requite, pay back OTH 1.1.183 *I will deserve your pains.*

deserved *ppl. adj.* Deserving, meritorious COR 3.1.290 *Rome, whose gratitude Towards her deserved children is enroll'd,* AWW 2.1.189.

deserving *n.*
1 That which one deserves, desert, due reward LR 5.3.305 *The cup of their deservings,* MM 5.1.477, SON 87.6.
2 That for which one deserves well, merit 2H4 4.3.44 *more of his courtesy than your deserving,* AWW 1.3.6, LR 3.3.23.

design *n.* Enterprise, project WT 4.4.502 *not prepar'd For this design,* LLL 4.1.86, MAC 2.1.55.

design *vb.* Indicate, point out R2 1.1.203 *see Justice design the victor's chivalry,* HAM 1.1.94.

designment *n.* Enterprise, undertaking OTH 2.1.22 *their designment halts,* COR 5.6.34.

desire *vb.*
1 Request the boon or favour (*of* something from a person) MV 4.1.402 *desire your Grace of pardon,* AYL 5.4.54.
◇ Ff 1–2 and Qq omit *of* in MND 3.1.195 *I desire you more acquaintance,* but retain it in MND 3.1.182 and MND 3.1.188.
2 Invite H5 4.1.27 *Desire them all to my pavilion,* LLL 5.2.145, TRO 4.5.150.

desired *ppl. adj.* Loved OTH 2.1.204 *you shall be well desir'd in Cyprus.*

despair *vb.* Be without hope of MAC 5.8.13 *Despair thy charm.*

desperate *adj.*
1 Reckless, utterly careless TN 5.1.64 *desperate of shame and state.*
2 (of debts) Without hope (of repayment), irrecoverable, irretrievable TIM 3.4.102 *These debts may well be call'd desperate ones,* R2 5.3.20 (with quibble).

desperately *adv.* In despair, without hope LR 5.3.293 *desperately are dead,* MM 4.2.145.

desperation *n.* Despair leading to recklessness or thoughts of (self-)destruction HAM 1.4.75 *The very place puts toys of desperation...into every brain* (i.e. thoughts or fancies of desperate action), TMP 1.2.210.

despised *ppl. adj.* Despicable, hateful ROM 3.2.77 *Despised substance of divinest show!,* TIM 4.3.459, VEN 135.

despite *n.*
1 Contempt, scorn, disdain ADO 1.1.235 *an obstinate heretic in the despite of beauty,* OTH 4.2.116.
2 Malice, ill-will 1H6 3.2.52 *hag of all despite,* TN 3.4.222; *in despite* out of ill-will, spitefully OTH 4.3.91 *scant our former having in despite,* H5 3.5.17.
3 *in despite* In defiance of another's wish SHR Ind.1.128 *An onion...Shall in despite enforce a watery eye,* MND 5.1.112, ROM 5.3.48; (esp.) *in despite of, in* (*a person's*) *despite* in spite of, notwithstanding the opposition of ERR 3.1.108 *in despite of mirth,* WIV 5.5.125, CYM 4.1.15.
~ *vb.* Vex, torment ADO 2.2.31 *Only to despite them, I will endeavour any thing.*
~ *prep.* In spite of ADO 5.1.75 *Despite his nice fence,* MM 1.2.26.

despiteful *adj.* Malicious, spiteful, cruel AYL 5.2.80 *To seem despiteful and ungentle to you,* AWW 3.4.13; (fig. of things) SHR 4.2.14 *despiteful love,* R3 4.1.36, TIT 4.4.50.

destitute *adj.* Deserted, forsaken Luc 441 *Left their round turrets destitute and pale.*

detain *vb.* Withhold Lr 1.2.41 *I shall offend either to detain or give it,* Err 2.1.107, R2 1.1.90.

detect *vb.* Expose, lay bare (esp. in wrong-doing) Tit 2.4.27 *lest thou shouldst detect him, cut thy tongue,* Wiv 2.2.310, MM 3.2.121.

detection *n.* Exposure, accusation Wiv 2.2.246 *could I come to her with any detection.*

detector *n.* One who detects, exposes, uncovers Lr 3.5.13 *O heavens! that this treason were not; or not I the detector!*

detention *n.* Withholding Tim 2.2.38 *the detention of...debts.*

determinate *vb.* Determine, fix R2 1.3.150 *shall not determinate the dateless limit of thy dear exile.*
~ *ppl. adj.*
1 (legal metaphor) Ended, expired Son 87.4 *My bonds in thee are all determinate.*
2 Decisive H8 2.4.177 *a determinate resolution,* Oth 4.2.227.
3 Intended TN 2.1.11 *my determinate voyage.*

determination *n.*
1 (legal metaphor) Cessation, end Son 13.6 *So should that beauty which you hold in lease Find no determination.*
2 Decision, sentence MM 3.2.244 *the determination of justice,* Tro 2.2.170.
3 Resolution, intention, mind Ham 3.1.168 *I have in quick determination Thus set it down,* Wiv 3.5.68, MV 1.2.102.

determine *vb.*
1 End, put an end to 2H4 4.5.81 *Till his friend sickness have determin'd me?,* 1H6 4.6.9.
2 Come to an end Ant 4.3.2 *It will determine one way,* Cor 3.3.43, Cor 5.3.120.

determined *ppl. adj.* Limited, restricted 1H6 4.6.9 *my determin'd time,* MM 3.1.69.

detested *ppl. adj.* Detestable, odious Lr 1.2.76 *Abhorred villain! unnatural, detested, brutish,* TN 5.1.139, R2 2.3.109; held in abhorrence TN 5.1.139 *Ay me, detested! how am I beguil'd!*

detract *vb.* Subtract, take away 1H6 5.4.142 *Shall I...Detract so much from that prerogative.*

deuce-ace *n.* Low throw at dice, a two and a one LLL 1.2.46 *you know how much the gross sum of deuce-ace amounts to.*

devest (var. of) DIVEST.

device *n.*
1 'Manner of thinking, cast of mind' (Schmidt) AYL 1.1.167 *full of noble device,* Ven 789.
2 Design (of an object), shape, cut Cym 1.6.189 *plate of rare device,* Jn 1.1.210.
3 Emblematic figure borne as a heraldic charge or cognizance Per 2.2.15 *The labour of each knight in his device.*
4 Something devised for dramatic representation Tim 1.2.150 *And entertain'd me with mine own device,* LLL 5.2.663, MND 5.1.50.
5 Clever or skilful piece of work LC 232 *this device was sent me from a nun.*

devil-porter *n.* play the devil-porter Act the porter of hell Mac 2.3.17.

devise *vb.*
1 Think Cor 1.1.102 *see and hear, devise, instruct, walk, feel.*
2 Decide, resolve 1H6 1.2.124 *What devise you on?*
3 Conceive, imagine Rom 3.1.69 *I...love thee better than thou canst devise.*
4 Invent Ant 2.2.189 *There she appear'd indeed; or my reporter devis'd well for her,* LLL 1.2.184.
5 Enlighten, instruct Ham 4.7.53 *Can you devise me?* (i.e. explain it to me).

devote *ppl. adj.* Devoted, dedicated, addicted Shr 1.1.32 *Or so devote to Aristotle's checks,* Oth 2.3.316.

devoted *ppl. adj.* Consecrated, holy R3 1.2.35 *devoted charitable deeds,* TGV 2.7.9.

devotement *n.* Devotion, worship Oth 2.3.317 *contemplation, mark and devotement of her parts and graces.*
◇ F1,Q1 *deuotement,* Ff 2–4, Q3 *devotement;* Q2 *denotement.* See DENOTEMENT.

devotion *n.*
1 Devout purpose or object R3 4.1.9 *Upon the like devotion as yourselves.*
2 Earnest application, zeal Oth 5.1.8 *I have no great devotion to the deed.*

devour *vb.* (fig.) *devour the way* Cover it with great rapidity 2H4 1.1.47 *He seem'd in running to devour the way.*

devoured *ppl. adj.* Swallowed up, absorbed Per 4.4.25 *in sorrow all devour'd.*

devout *adj.* Zealous, earnest LLL 5.2.782 *more devout than this in our respects.*

devoutly *adv.* Earnestly, sincerely Ham 3.1.63 *Devoutly to be wish'd.*

dew *n.* (fig. uses)
1 Tears R2 5.1.9 *That you in pity may dissolve to dew,* LLL 4.3.28, Luc 1829.
2 Something likened to dew, as coming with refreshing power or with gentle fall R3 4.1.83 *the golden dew of sleep,* Cor 5.6.22.
~ *vb.* Wet as with dew, moisten Rom 5.3.14 *Which with sweet water nightly I will dew,* MND 2.1.9, Mac 5.2.30.

dewberry *n.* A species of blackberry or brambleberry; (? in S.) gooseberry MND 3.1.166 *Feed him with apricocks and dewberries.*

dewlap, dewlop *n.* Fold of loose skin hanging from the throat or neck MND 2.1.50 *her withered dewlap* (Qq, F *dewlop*).

dewlapped *adj.* Having a DEWLAP Tmp 3.3.45 *Dewlapp'd, like bulls,* MND 4.1.122.

dexter *adj.* Right Tro 4.5.128 *the dexter cheek.*

dexteriously *adv.* (17C var. of) Dexterously TN 1.5.60 *Can you do it?—dexteriously.*

dexterity *n.* Agility, nimbleness Ham 1.2.157 *to post With such dexterity to incestuous sheets.*

dey-woman *n.* Dairy-woman LLL 1.2.131 *she is allow'd for the dey-woman* (F1 *Day-woman*).

Di faciant laudis summa sit ista tuae [L. Ovid, *Heroides* 2.66] The gods grant that this may be the summit of thy glory 3H6 1.3.43.

diable [Fr.] Devil Wiv 3.1.91.

diablo [Sp.] Devil Oth 2.3.161.

dial *n.* Clock, watch, pocket sun-dial AYL 2.7.20 *he drew a dial from his poke,* R2 5.5.53; *dial's point* minute hand R2 5.5.53 *like a dial's point,* Luc 327.

dial(-)hand *n.* Hand of a watch or dial Son 104.9 *yet doth beauty, like a dial-hand, Steal from his figure.*

dialogue *vb.*
1 Hold a conversation Tim 2.2.51 *Dost dialogue with thy shadow?*
2 Express in dialogue form LC 132 *And dialogue'd for him what he would say.*

diameter *n.* Extent from side to side Ham 4.1.41 *O'er the world's diameter.*

Dian's bud *n.* (?) (1) The plant Artemisia (i.e. the herb of Artemis or Diana, the moon goddess); or (2) the Agnus castus (the Chaste Tree), to which very similar powers to preserve chastity were ascribed by ancient herbalists MND 4.1.73 *Dian's bud o'er Cupid's flower Hath such force.*

diapason *n.* A bass accompaniment in exact concord, i.e. in octaves with the air Luc 1132 *And with deep groans the diapason bear.*

diaper *n.* Towel, napkin SHR Ind.1.57 *Another bear the ewer, the third a diaper.*

dibble *n.* Instrument for making holes in the ground for seeds or young plants WT 4.4.100 *I'll not put The dibble in earth.*

dich *vb.* [Warwickshire dial.] Adhere to, stick to TIM 1.2.72 *Much good dich thy good heart.*

dick *n.* Fellow, lad LLL 5.2.464 *some Dick, That smiles his cheek in years,* TN 5.1.197, COR 2.3.116.

dictator *n.* Chief magistrate with absolute power, elected in Ancient Rome in times of emergency COR 2.2.89 *Our then dictator.*

diction *n.* Expression or description in words HAM 5.2.118 *to make true diction of him.*

die *n.* (orig. sing. of) Dice R3 5.4.10 *The hazard of the die,* MND 5.1.307, WT 4.3.26.

die *vb.*
1 *die the death* Be put to death, suffer the penalty of capital punishment MND 1.1.65 *Either to die the death, or to abjure For ever the society of men,* CYM 4.2.96.
2 *die and live* Pass one's whole life, exist AYL 3.5.7 *he that dies and lives by bloody drops* (i.e. by shedding blood).

diet *n.*
1 Course of life R3 1.1.139 *an evil diet.*
2 Prescribed course of food, regimen TIM 4.3.88 *The tub fast and the diet,* TGV 2.1.24, MM 2.1.112.
3 Food, fare, victuals, board OTH 3.3.15 *feed upon such nice and waterish diet,* TN 3.3.40, 1H4 3.3.73.
~ *vb.*
1 Feed 1H6 1.2.10 *dieted like mules;* (fig.) OTH 2.1.294 *to diet my revenge.*
2 Prescribe a diet for (as a regimen of health) ERR 5.1.99 *be his nurse, Diet his sickness;* (fig.) 2H4 4.1.64 *To diet rank minds sick of happiness,* LC 261; (hence) cause to conform, restrict, be tied *to* COR 5.1.57 *dieted to my request,* AWW 4.3.29.

dieter *n.* Regulator of diet CYM 4.2.51 *And he had been her dieter.*

Dieu de batailles [Fr.] God of battles H5 3.5.15.

Dieu vous garde, monsieur.—Et vous aussi, votre serviteur [Fr.] God keep you, sir.—And you too, your servant TN 3.1.71.

difference *n.*
1 Diversity, variety PER 4.2.80 *you shall have the difference of all complexions.*
2 Diversity of opinion, disagreement, dispute MV 4.1.171 *Are you acquainted with the difference,* JC 1.2.40; *at difference* at variance, in disagreement COR 5.3.201 *thou hast set thy mercy and thy honour At difference in thee.*
3 Characteristic or distinguishing feature HAM 5.2.107 *full of most excellent differences;* distinction (of rank or quality) H8 1.1.139 *or proclaim there's difference in no persons.*
4 (heraldic term) Alteration in or addition to a coat of arms to distinguish a younger or lateral branch of a family from the chief line; (fig.) ADO 1.1.69 *let him bear it for a difference between himself and his horse,* HAM 4.5.183.
5 *make difference* Discriminate WIV 2.1.57 *as long as I have an eye to make difference of men's liking.*

differency *n.* Difference COR 5.4.11 *There is differency between a grub and a butterfly.*

difficult *adj.* difficult weight Not easy to be estimated OTH 3.3.82 *full of poise and difficult weight.*

diffidence *n.* Distrust, suspicion JN 1.1.65 *And wound her honour with this diffidence,* 1H6 3.3.10, LR 1.2.147.

diffuse *vb.*
1 Pour, shed TMP 4.1.79 *Diffusest honey-drops, refreshing show'rs.*
2 Confuse, render indistinguishable LR 1.4.2 *If...I*

other accents borrow, That can my speech diffuse (Ff, Qq *defuse*).

diffused *ppl. adj.* Disordered, confused, disorderly WIV 4.4.55 *some diffused song,* R3 1.2.78, H5 5.2.61 (F3; F1 *defus'd*).

digest *vb.*
1 Arrange R3 3.1.200 *digest our complots in some form,* HAM 2.2.439, ANT 2.2.176.
2 Put up with, swallow, stomach, bear without resistance LLL 5.2.289 *digest this harsh indignity,* MV 3.5.90.
3 Assimilate, amalgamate LR 1.1.128 *With my two daughters' dow'rs digest the third,* AWW 5.3.74.
4 Dispose of, get rid of H5 2.Ch.31 *we'll digest Th' abuse of distance;* disperse, dissipate 1H6 4.1.167 *digest Your angry choler on your enemies.*
5 Comprehend, understand COR 1.1.150 *digest things rightly Touching the weal a' th' common.*
◇ In F1, etc., often spelt *digest,* which is retained in places in some mod. edd.

dignity *n.* Dignitary 1H6 1.3.50 *In spite of Pope or dignities of church.*

digress *vb.*
1 Depart, deviate ROM 3.3.127 *Digressing from the valour of a man,* SHR 3.2.107.
2 Transgress, offend TIT 5.3.116 *I do digress too much, Citing my worthless praise,* R2 5.3.66.

digressing *ppl. adj.* Transgressing R2 5.3.66 *This deadly blot in thy digressing son.*

digression *n.* Transgression, moral going astray LLL 1.2.116 *my digression by some mighty precedent,* LUC 202.

dig-you-den See GOD AND GOOD EVEN.

dilate *vb.* Relate at length OTH 1.3.153 *all my pilgrimage dilate,* ERR 1.1.122.

dilated *ppl. adj.*
1 Spread far and wide TRO 2.3.250 *Which like...a shore confines Thy spacious and dilated parts.*
2 Extended, expressed at length AWW 2.1.57 *take a more dilated farewell,* HAM 1.2.38.

dilation *n.* (?) (1) Delay, postponement; or (2) (var. of) DELATION OTH 3.3.123 *They're close dilations, working from the heart* (Ff, Qq 2–3; Q1 *denotements*).

dild See GOD'ILD.

dildo *n.* (lit.) Male sex organ, phallus WT 4.4.195 *and with such delicate burthens of dildos and fadings.*
◇ The word is used in refrains of ballads; its use by the Clown in WT is contradictory.

diligence *n.*
1 Assiduity (esp. in service) HAM 5.2.91 *all diligence of spirit,* 1H6 5.3.9, CYM 4.3.20; (quasi-personified) one in whom the quality is personified, a diligent person TMP 5.1.241 *Bravely, my diligence.*
2 Speed, dispatch LR 1.5.4 *If your diligence be not speedy,* TMP 1.2.304.

diligent *adj.*
1 Assiduous (esp. in service) LR 5.1.53 *diligent discovery,* SHR 4.3.39, LR 5.1.53.
2 Attentive, heedful TMP 3.1.42 *diligent ear.*

diluculo surgere [L.] To rise early TN 2.3.2.
◇ Abbreviation of 'diluculo surgere saluberrimum est' (to rise early is most wholesome).

dim *adj.* Not bright, dull, lustreless WT 4.4.120 *violets, dim,* JN 3.4.85, LUC 403.

dimension *n.* Bodily frame TN 1.5.261 *in dimension, and the shape of nature;* (pl.) bodily parts or proportions LR 1.2.7 *my dimensions are as well compact,* MV 3.1.60, TN 1.5.261.

diminish *vb.* Impair TMP 3.3.64 *as diminish One dowle that's in my plume,* VEN 417.

diminutive *n.* Very small thing or being TRO 5.1.34 *diminutives of nature,* ANT 4.12.37.

dint *n.* Force JC 3.2.194 *you feel The dint of pity.*

direct *vb.* Address (words) 1H6 5.3.179 *Words sweetly plac'd and modestly directed.*

direction *n.* Capacity for directing R3 5.3.16 *men of sound direction.*

directitude (humorous blundered form) (?) Cast down, overthrown, discredited COR 4.5.208 *whilest he's in directitude.*
▷ See *dejectitude.*

directive *adj.* Subject to direction TRO 1.3.356 *...than are swords and bows Directive by the limbs.*

directly *adv.*
1 Straight OTH 3.3.407 *lead directly to the door of truth,* JN 3.4.129, JC 4.1.32.
2 Immediately, at once HAM 3.2.209 *Directly seasons him his enemy,* MV 4.1.359, OTH 2.3.350.
3 Straightforwardly OTH 4.2.208 *I have dealt most directly in thy affair,* CYM 3.5.113.
4 Plainly, pointedly, without ambiguity OTH 2.1.219 *directly in love with him,* 1H4 2.3.86, COR 4.5.185.
5 Exactly, precisely, just HAM 3.4.210 *When in one line two crafts directly meet,* TN 3.4.66, JC 1.2.3.

direness *n.* Horror MAC 5.5.14 *Direness, familiar to my slaughterous thoughts.*

dirge *n.* Funeral song, song of mourning ROM 4.5.88 *Our solemn hymns to sullen dirges change,* HAM 1.2.12, LUC 1612.

dirty *adj.* (used as epithet of disgust or aversion) Foul, repulsive CYM 3.6.55 *those Who worship dirty gods.*

disable *vb.* Depreciate, disparage, belittle AYL 4.1.34 *disable all the benefits of your own country,* 1H6 5.3.67.

disabling *n.* Disparagement MV 2.7.30 *a weak disabling of myself.*

disallow *vb.* Disapprove *of* JN 1.1.16 *What follows if we disallow of this?*

disanimate *vb.* Discourage 1H6 3.1.182 *it disanimates his enemies.*

disappointed *ppl. adj.* Unprepared HAM 1.5.77 *Unhous'led, disappointed, unanel'd.*

disaster *n.* Unfavourable aspect of a star HAM 1.1.118 *Disasters in the sun;* (hence) ill-luck MAC 3.1.111 *So weary with disasters, tugg'd with fortune.*
~ *vb.* Ruin ANT 2.7.16 *the holes where eyes should be, which pitifully disaster the cheeks.*

disbench *vb.* Cause (a person) to leave his seat, displace COR 2.2.71 *I hope My words disbench'd you not?*

disbranch *vb.* (fig.) Sever LR 4.2.34 *She that herself will sliver and disbranch From her material sap.*

discandy *vb.* Dissolve or melt out of a solid condition ANT 4.12.22 *The hearts...do discandy, melt their sweets On blossoming Caesar.*

discard *vb.* Dismiss, discharge TN 3.4.89 *Go off, I discard you.*

discase *vb.* Undress TMP 5.1.85 *I will discase me,* WT 4.4.633.

discerner *n.* Person of judgement, critic H8 1.1.32 *no discerner Durst wag his tongue in censure.*

discernings *n.* Intellectual faculties LR 1.4.228 *his discernings Are lethargied.*

discharge *n.* (theatrical term) Performance TMP 2.1.254 *What's past is prologue, what to come In yours and my discharge.*
~ *vb.*
1 Unburden, disburden, deliver, free ROM 5.1.63 *that the trunk may be discharg'd of breath,* ADO 5.1.319, 2H4 2.4.137.
2 (fig. from letting off cannon) Let fly, fire off, give vent to H8 1.2.206 *He did discharge a horrible oath,* LUC 1605.

3 Pay, settle with (a creditor) MV 3.2.273 *to discharge the Jew,* ERR 4.1.32, TIM 2.2.12.
4 Perform MND 4.2.8 *not a man in all Athens able to discharge Pyramus but he,* COR 3.2.106.

disciple *vb.* Teach, train AWW 1.2.28 *He...was Discipled of the bravest.*

discipline *n.*
1 Instruction, teaching SHR 1.1.30 *this moral discipline,* TGV 3.2.87, TRO 2.3.30.
2 Training in military affairs, military experience JN 2.1.39 *our chiefest men of discipline,* H5 3.2.72, R3 3.7.16.
~ *n.*
1 Instruct, train, teach TRO 2.3.244 *he that disciplin'd thine arms to fight,* LC 261.
2 Chastise, punish COR 2.1.126 *Has he disciplin'd Aufidius soundly?*

disclaim *vb.*
1 Renounce, disavow all share LR 2.2.54 *Nature disclaims in thee.*
2 Repudiate connection with, disown R2 1.1.70 *Disclaiming here the kindred of the King,* JN 1.1.247, LR 1.1.113.

disclaiming *n.* Disavowal HAM 5.2.241 *my disclaiming from a purpos'd evil.*

disclose *n.* (fig.) Incubation; (hence) the action of bringing forth to view HAM 3.1.166 *the hatch and the disclose Will be some danger.*
~ *vb.*
1 Unfold HAM 1.3.40 *before their buttons be disclos'd,* SON 54.8.
2 (pass.) Be hatched HAM 5.1.287 *When that her golden couplets are disclosed.*

discolour *vb.* Cause to blush, bring a blush to 2H4 2.2.4 *it discolours the complexion of my greatness to acknowledge it.*

discoloured *ppl. adj.* Pale LUC 708 *lean discolour'd cheek.*

discomfit *n.* Complete disconcertment, defeat 2H6 5.2.86 *uncurable discomfit Reigns in the hearts.*
~ *vb.* Defeat, rout 1H4 3.2.114 *This infant warrior, in his enterprises Discomfited great Douglas,* 2H6 5.1.63.

discomfited *ppl. adj.* Disconcerted, discouraged SHR 2.1.163 *be not so discomfited.*

discomfiture *n.* Defeat, rout 1H6 1.1.59 *Of loss, of slaughter, and discomfiture.*

discomfort *n.*
1 Discouragement MAC 1.2.28 *Discomfort swells,* R2 3.2.65.
2 Sorrow ANT 4.2.34 *What mean you, sir, To give them this discomfort?,* 2H4 1.2.104, MAC 4.2.29.
~ *vb.*
1 Discourage TRO 5.10.10 *My lord, you do discomfort all the host,* JC 5.3.106.
2 Grieve HAM 3.2.166 *Discomfort you, my lord, it nothing must.*

discomfortable *adj.* Causing discouragement, destroying comfort or happiness R2 3.2.36 *Discomfortable cousin.*

discommend *vb.* Express disapprobation of, not commend LR 2.2.109 *My dialect, which you discommend.*

discontent *n.* Malcontent 1H4 5.1.76 *fickle changelings and poor discontents,* ANT 1.4.39.

discontented *ppl. adj.* Full of discontent OTH 5.2.314 *another discontented paper.*

discontenting *ppl. adj.* Dissatisfied WT 4.4.532 *Your discontenting father.*

discontinue *vb.* Cease to frequent, give up ADO 5.1.189 *I must discontinue your company,* MV 3.4.75.

discordant *adj.* Disagreeing 2H4 Ind.19 *The still-discordant wav'ring multitude.*

discourse n.

1 Reasoning, thought, reflection HAM 4.4.36 *with such large discourse, Looking before and after,* MM 1.2.185; *discourse of reason,* thought process or faculty of reasoning or thought HAM 1.2.150 *discourse of reason,* OTH 4.2.153 *discourse of thought.*

2 Talk, conversation R3 5.3.99 *ample interchange of sweet discourse,* TGV 2.4.109, H5 1.1.43.

3 Faculty of conversing, conversational power ERR 3.1.109 *a wench of excellent discourse,* TRO 1.2.253.

4 Familiar intercourse HAM 3.1.107 *your honesty should admit no discourse to your beauty.*

~ vb.

1 Hold discourse, talk, converse JC 3.1.295 *discourse...of the state of things,* MND 5.1.151.

2 Pass (the time) in talk CYM 3.3.38 *shall we discourse The freezing hours away?*

3 Tell, narrate TIT 5.3.81 *he did discourse...The story,* ERR 5.1.396; (absol.) 1H6 1.4.26.

4 Utter, say OTH 2.3.280 *and discourse fustian with one's own shadow?*

5 Give forth (musical sound) HAM 3.2.359 *it will discourse most eloquent music.*

discourser n. Narrator H8 1.1.41 *a good discourser.*

discover vb.

1 Uncover, expose to view MV 2.7.1 *discover The several caskets,* TN 2.5.160, R3 4.4.241.

2 Divulge, reveal, disclose (a thing), make known TGV 2.1.167 *that might her mind discover,* WIV 2.2.183, ADO 5.1.233; (hence) show, exhibit JC 1.2.69 *Will modestly discover to yourself,* TGV 3.2.76, WT 3.1.20.

3 Spy out, reconnoitre ANT 4.10.8 *Where their appointment we may best discover,* ERR 1.1.91, R2 2.3.33.

4 Reveal the identity of, betray (a person) LR 2.1.66 *I threaten'd to discover him.*

5 Distinguish, discern JC 2.1.75 *discover them By any mark of favour,* MM 4.2.172, COR 2.1.43.

discoverer n. Scout, spy, explorer 2H4 4.1.3 *Here stand, my lords, and send discoverers forth.*

discovery n.

1 Revelation, disclosure (of a secret) H5 2.2.162 *the discovery of...treason,* WT 1.2.441, HAM 2.2.294.

2 Exploration, reconnoitring AYL 3.2.197 *a South-Sea of discovery,* TMP 2.1.243, MAC 5.4.6.

3 Bringing to view, showing TIM 5.1.36 *a discovery of the infinite flatteries.*

4 Discoverer, revealer VEN 828 *the fair discovery of her way.*

discretion n. do, use your discretion Act as you think fit OTH 3.3.34 *Well, do your discretion,* AYL 1.1.146 *therefore use thy discretion.*

discuss vb. Declare, tell, make known H5 4.4.29 *Discuss the same in French unto him,* WIV 1.3.95.

disdain n. Indignation, vexation TRO 1.2.34 *the disdain and shame whereof.*

disdained ppl. adj. Disdainful 1H4 1.3.183 *Revenge the jeering and disdain'd contempt.*

disease n. Absence of ease, trouble, grievance, vexation 1H6 2.5.44 *And in that ease, I'll tell thee my disease,* AYL 5.4.65, LR 1.1.164.

~ vb. Trouble, disturb COR 1.3.105 *she will but disease our better mirth.*

▷ MAC 5.3.21 *This push will cheer me ever, or disease me now:* Ff 234; F1 *dis-eate,* perh. in this sense, but see also DISSEAT, DISSEISE.

disedge vb. Satisfy the appetite of CYM 3.4.93 *thou shalt be disedg'd by her.*

disfurnish vb. Deprive TGV 4.1.14 *if you should here disfurnish me,* TIM 3.2.44, PER 4.6.11.

disgest, disgestion (var. of) DIGEST, DIGESTION.

disgrace n.

1 Misfortune, adverse fortune COR 1.1.94 *to fob off our disgrace with a tale.*

2 Disfigurement LLL 1.1.3 *in the disgrace of death,* SON 33.8.

disgraced ppl. adj. Disgraceful WT 1.2.188 *so disgrac'd a part.*

disgraceful adj. Devoid of grace, unbecoming 1H6 1.1.86 *these disgraceful wailing robes.*

disgracious adj. Out of favour, disliked R3 4.4.178 *If I be so disgracious in your eye.*

disguise n. Drunkenness, intoxication ANT 2.7.124 *the wild disguise hath almost Antick'd us all.*

dishabit vb. Dislodge JN 2.1.220 *stones...Had been dishabited.*

dishclout n. Dishcloth ROM 3.5.219 *Romeo's a dishclout to him,* LLL 5.2.714.

dishonest adj. Unchaste, immodest AYL 5.3.4 *I hope it is no dishonest desire to desire to be a woman of the world,* WIV 3.3.185, TN 1.5.45.

dishonesty n. Lewdness, unchaste behaviour WIV 4.2.134 *if you suspect me in any dishonesty.*

dishonourable adv. Dishonourably 1H4 4.2.31 *ten times more dishonourable ragged.*

dishonoured ppl. adj. Dishonourable LR 1.1.228 *No...dishonoured step,* COR 3.1.60.

disjoin vb. (intr.) Sever oneself VEN 541 *Till breathless he disjoin'd.*

disjoint vb. Fall to pieces MAC 3.2.16 *let the frame of things disjoint.*

~ ppl. adj. Out of joint, distracted HAM 1.2.20 *thinking...Our state to be disjoint and out of frame.*

dislike n. Disagreement, discord LR 1.4.325 *Each buzz, each fancy, each complaint, dislike,* 1H4 5.1.26, TRO 2.3.225.

~ vb.

1 Displease ROM 2.2.61 *if either thee dislike* (Q1 *displease*), OTH 2.3.47.

2 (intr.) Disapprove of AWW 2.3.123 *thou dislik'st Of virtue for the name.*

disliken vb. Disguise WT 4.4.652 *disliken The truth of your own seeming.*

dislimn vb. Obliterate the outlines of, blot out, efface ANT 4.14.10 *the rack dislimns, and makes it indistinct* (Ff *dislimes*).

dismal adj.

1 Ill-boding, sinister 3H6 2.6.58 *Now death shall stop his dismal threat'ning sound,* VEN 889, AWW 5.3.128.

2 Disastrous, calamitous ROM 4.3.19 *My dismal scene I needs must act alone.*

dismal-dreaming adj. Full of ill-boding dreams PP 14.20 *dismal-dreaming night.*

dismantle vb.

1 Divest of a mantle or cloak or clothing in general WT 4.4.652 *Dismantle you;* (fig.) remove (a covering) LR 1.1.217 *dismantle So many folds of favour.*

2 Deprive, strip (of covering, fortifications, etc.) HAM 3.2.282 *This realm dismantled was Of Jove himself.*

dismask vb. Unmask LLL 5.2.296 *Dismask'd, their damask sweet commixture shown.*

dismay vb. Be discouraged 1H6 3.3.1 *Dismay not, princes.*

disme n. Tenth man sacrificed TRO 2.2.19 *Every tithe soul, 'mongst many thousand dismes.*

dismissed ppl. adj.

1 Discarded, rejected TMP 4.1.67 *the dismissed bachelor.*

2 Forgiven, remitted MM 2.2.102 *a dismiss'd offence.*

dismission n.

1 Discharge from service or office ANT 1.1.26 *your dismission Is come from Caesar.*

2 Rejection CYM 2.3.52 *When command to your dismission tends.*

dismount *vb.*
1 (fig.) Unseat, unhorse H5 3.7.77 *your horse ...would trot as well, were some of your brags dismounted.*
2 Lower LC 281 *his...eyes he did dismount.*
3 dismount *thy tuck* Draw thy rapier out of its sheath TN 3.4.224.

disnatured *adj.* Unnatural LR 1.4.283 *a thwart disnatur'd torment.*

disorbed *ppl. adj.* Removed from its natural sphere TRO 2.2.46 *like a star disorb'd?* (i.e. a shooting star).

disorder *n.*
1 Disorderly act or practice, misdemeanour LR 1.2.113 *Machinations, hollowness, treachery, and all ruinous disorders,* TN 2.3.97.
2 Disturbance of mind, discomposure JN 3.4.102 *such disorder in my wit,* VEN 742.

disordered *ppl. adj.* Disorderly, unruly LR 1.4.242 *Men so disorder'd, so debosh'd and bold.*

dispark *vb.* Throw open (park land) for common use R2 3.1.23 *Dispark'd my parks.*

dispatch *n.*
1 Dismissal, leave to go COR 5.3.180 *give us our dispatch,* LLL 4.1.5, LR 2.1.125.
2 Execution, settlement MM 4.4.12 *a dispatch of complaints,* AWW 3.2.54; *quick dispatch* prompt execution LLL 2.1.31; (hence) speed, expedition OTH 1.3.46 *post-post-haste. Dispatch!,* H5 2.4.6, SON 143.3.
3 Conduct, management MAC 1.5.68 *into my dispatch.*
4 Act of putting away hastily LR 1.2.32 *What needed then that terrible dispatch of it.*
~ *vb.*
1 Make away with, kill R2 3.1.35 *see them dispatch'd*; (absol.) JN 4.1.27 *I will be sudden, and dispatch,* R3 1.2.181, LR 2.1.58.
2 Deprive HAM 1.5.75 *Of life, of crown, of queen, at once dispatch'd.*
3 Settle, conclude (a business), execute promptly AWW 4.3.85 *I have to-night dispatch'd sixteen businesses*; (absol.) WIV 5.5.179 *have you dispatched,* ANT 5.2.230; settle or have done *with* MM 3.1.266 *dispatch with Angelo,* ANT 3.2.2.

dispensation *n.*
1 Licence granted by ecclesiastical authority to do what is forbidden or omit what is enjoined by ecclesiastical law or by any solemn obligation LLL 2.1.87 *seek a dispensation for his oath,* 1H6 5.3.86.
2 *make dispensation with* Set aside LUC 248 *with good thoughts makes dispensation.*

dispense *vb.* (always in the constr. *dispense with*)
1 Make an arrangement with (for an offence, etc.) 2H6 5.1.181 *Canst thou dispense with heaven for such an oath?*
2 Give exemption or relief from LLL 1.1.147 *dispense with this decree,* 1H6 5.5.28.
3 Set aside, disregard WIV 2.1.47 *Dispense with trifles.*
4 Forgo, do without MM 3.1.153 *dispense with your leisure,* TIM 3.2.86.
5 Condone by dispensation, pardon MM 3.1.134 *Nature dispenses with the deed,* ERR 2.1.103, LUC 1070.

dispiteous *adj.* Pitiless JN 4.1.34 *dispiteous torture* (Ff *dispitious*).

displace *vb.* Remove, banish MAC 3.4.108 *You have displac'd the mirth,* LUC 887.

displant *vb.* (fig.) Uproot ROM 3.3.59 *Displant a town.*

displanting *n.* Deposition from office OTH 2.1.276 *the displanting of Cassio.*

display *vb.* Behave ostentatiously LR 2.4.41 *the very fellow which...Display'd so saucily against your Highness.*

displeasure *n.*
1 Offence, wrong ERR 4.4.116 *Do outrage and displeasure to himself,* ERR 5.1.142.
2 *your displeasure* The unpopularity you are in H8 3.2.392, *your displeasure with the King,* OTH 3.1.42.
3 *take a displeasure* Take offence TMP 4.1.202 *If I should Take a displeasure against you.*

disponge See DISPUNGE.

disport *n.* Pastime OTH 1.3.271 *that my disports corrupt...my business,* LUC Arg.19.
~ *vb.* (refl.) Amuse oneself 3H6 4.5.8 *Comes hunting this way to disport himself,* TIM 1.2.136.

dispose *n.*
1 Disposal TGV 2.7.86 *All that is mine I leave at thy dispose,* ERR 1.1.20, JN 1.1.263.
2 Bent of mind, temperament TRO 2.3.164 *carries on the stream of his dispose.*
3 External manner OTH 1.3.397 *a smooth dispose.*
~ *vb.*
1 Place, distribute, bestow TRO 4.5.116 *His blows are well dispos'd,* H5 4.Ch.51, H8 1.2.116.
2 Put away, stow away, deposit ERR 1.2.73 *how thou hast dispos'd thy charge,* TIT 4.2.173, TMP 1.2.225.
3 Regulate, order, direct H5 4.3.133 *how thou pleasest, God, dispose the day!*; (refl.) direct one's action PER 1.2.117 *by whose letters I'll dispose myself,* WT 1.2.179.
4 Settle matters, come to terms ANT 4.14.123 *you did suspect She had dispos'd with Caesar.*

disposed *ppl. adj.* Inclined to merriment, in a merry mood LLL 2.1.250 *Come to our pavilion—Boyet is dispos'd,* LLL 5.2.466, TN 2.3.81.

disposer *n.* One who arranges or manages, one who does what one will (with someone or something) TRO 3.1.87 *my disposer Cressida,* TRO 3.1.89.

disposing *n.* Direction, arrangement JN 5.7.92 *put his cause and quarrel To the disposing of the Cardinal,* H8 1.1.43, VEN 1040.

disposition *n.*
1 Arrangement OTH 1.3.236 *fit disposition for my wife.*
2 Inclination, humour, mood AYL 4.1.113 *a more coming-on disposition,* COR 1.6.74, ROM 1.3.65.
3 Natural constitution, temperament WIV 4.5.109 *the villainous inconstancy of man's disposition,* ROM 3.3.115, HAM 1.2.169.

disprise, disprize *vb.* Hold in contempt TRO 4.5.74 *great deal disprising The knight oppos'd* (F1; Q *misprising*).

disprized *ppl. adj.* Held in contempt HAM 3.1.71 *pangs of dispriz'd love* (F1; Qq *despiz'd*).

disproperty *vb.* Alienate (a possession) COR 2.1.248 *would Have...Dispropertied their freedoms.*

disproportion *n.* Want of fitness OTH 3.3.233 *Foul disproportions, thoughts unnatural* (Ff *disproportions,* Qq *disproportion*).
~ *vb.* Make out of proportion 3H6 3.2.160 *To disproportion me in every part.*

disproportioned *ppl. adj.*
1 Out of proportion TMP 5.1.291 *as disproportion'd in his manners As in his shape.*
2 Inconsistent OTH 1.3.2 *they are disproportioned.*

dispunge, disponge *vb.* Pour down as from a squeezed sponge ANT 4.9.13 *The poisonous damp of night dispunge upon me.*

dispurse *vb.* Disburse 2H6 3.1.117 *many a pound of mine own...store...Have I dispursed to the garrisons.*

disputable *adj.* Inclined to dispute AYL 2.5.35 *He is too disputable for my company.*

disputation *n.* Conversation 1H4 3.1.203 *a feeling disputation* (i.e. a conversation by exchange of feelings not words), H5 3.2.95.

dispute *vb.*
1 Discuss WT 4.4.400 *dispute his own estate*, ROM 3.3.63.
2 Strive against, resist MAC 4.3.220 *Dispute it like a man.*

disquantity *vb.* Diminish LR 1.4.249 *to disquantity your train.*

disquietly *adv.* In a disturbing manner LR 1.2.114 *disorders follow us disquietly to our graves.*

disseat *vb.* Unseat MAC 5.3.21 *This push Will cheer me ever, or disseat me now.*
◇ F1 *dis-eate*; Ff 2–4 *disease*. See DISEASE, DISSEISE.

disseise *vb.* Dispossess MAC 5.3.21 *This push Will cheer me ever, or disseise me now.*
◇ Ff 2–4 *disease.* 'Disseise' and 'dysseise' are 16C forms of *disseise.* See DISEASE, DISSEAT.

dissemble *vb.* Disguise TN 4.2.4 *I will dissemble myself in't.*

dissembling *n.* Falseness, hypocrisy 3H6 3.3.119 *all dissembling set aside, Tell me for truth...*, ANT 1.3.79.
~ *ppl. adj.* False, hypocritical ERR 4.4.100 *Dissembling villain, thou speak'st false*, TRO 5.4.2; (fig.) MND 2.2.98 *dissembling glass.*

dissembly *n.* (Dogberry's malapropism) Assembly ADO 4.2.1 *Is our whole dissembly appear'd'?*

dissipation *n.* Dispersal, breaking-up LR 1.2.148 *dissipation of cohorts.*

dissolution *n.*
1 Liquefaction WIV 3.5.116 *continual dissolution and thaw*, LUC 355.
2 Destruction, ruin R2 2.1.258 *Reproach and dissolution*, MM 3.2.223, LR 1.2.145.

dissolve *vb.*
1 Loosen, undo R2 2.2.71 *dissolve the bands of life*, TRO 5.2.156.
2 Part, separate AWW 1.2.66 *I...were dissolved from my hive*, WIV 5.5.224, COR 1.1.204.
3 (trans.) Destroy, put to an end LR 4.4.19 *Lest his ungovern'd rage dissolve the life*; (intr.) come to an end TMP 5.1.64 *The charm dissolves apace*, TMP 4.1.154.
4 Melt R2 3.2.108 *As if the world were all dissolv'd to tears*; (intr.) TGV 3.2.8 *ice, which...Dissolves to water*, LR 5.3.204, MND 1.1.245.

dissuade *vb.* Discourage AWW 3.5.23 *dissuade succession* (i.e. discourage others from following the same course).

distaff *n.* Cleft stick on which wool or flax was formerly wound; (used as the type for woman's work) wifely duties LR 4.2.17 *give the distaff Into my husband's hands*, CYM 5.3.34.

distaff-woman *n.* Spinning woman R2 3.2.118 *distaff-women manage rusty bills Against thy seat.*

distain *vb.* Defile, sully, dishonour LUC 786 *The silver-shining queen he would distain*, R3 5.3.322, PER 4.3.31 (Q1 *disdaine*).

distance *n.*
1 Disagreement MAC 3.1.115 *such bloody distance.*
2 (in fencing) Definite interval of space to be kept between the combatants WIV 2.3.27 *thy reverse, thy distance, thy montant*, WIV 2.1.225, ROM 2.4.21.
3 Remoteness in intercourse, the reverse of intimacy or familiarity LC 151 *With safest distance I mine honour shielded*, OTH 2.3.56, OTH 3.3.13.

distaste *vb.*
1 Have no taste for, dislike TRO 2.2.66 *Although my will distaste what it elected*, LR 1.3.14 (Qq 1-2 *dislike*).

2 Offend the taste, cause disgust OTH 3.3.327 *poisons, Which at the first are scarce found to distaste.*
3 Render distasteful TRO 2.2.123 *Her brain-sick raptures Cannot distaste the goodness of a quarrel.*
◇ TRO 4.4.48: F1 *Distasting with the salt of broken tears* (i.e. sense 2); Qq *Distasted...*(i.e. sense 3).

distasteful *adj.* Expressing dislike or aversion TIM 2.2.211 *distasteful looks.*

distemper *n.*
1 Ill humour, bad temper WIV 3.5.76 *instigated by his distemper*, WT 1.2.385, HAM 3.2.337.
2 Deranged condition of body or mind, illness, disease HAM 2.2.55 *your son's distemper*, CYM 3.4.191.
3 Intoxication H5 2.2.54 *little faults, proceeding on distemper.*
~ *vb.* Disturb, disorder TN 2.1.5 *The malignancy of my fate might perhaps distemper yours*, VEN 653.

distemperance *n.* DISTEMPERATURE *n.* sense 2 PER 5.1.27 *Upon what ground is his distemperance?* (Qq 1-2 *distemperature*).

distemperature *n.*
1 Physical disorder or derangement, illness ERR 5.1.82 *pale distemperatures*, 1H4 3.1.33.
◇ Sometimes the word also includes, along with sense 1, the old sense 'inclemency of weather', e.g. MND 2.1.106 *thorough this distemperature we see The seasons alter*, 1H4 5.1.3.
2 Disturbance of mind ROM 2.3.40 *up-rous'd with some distemp'rature*, PER 5.1.27.

distempered *ppl. adj.*
1 Inclement JN 3.4.154 *no distemper'd day*; (transf.) AWW 1.3.151 *this distempered messenger of wet* (i.e. the rainbow).
2 Out of humour or temper TMP 4.1.145 *Never...Saw I him touch'd with anger, so distemper'd*, JN 4.3.21, HAM 3.2.301.
3 Physically disordered, diseased TN 1.5.91 *a distemper'd appetite*, 2H4 3.1.41, TRO 2.2.169.
4 Mentally or morally deranged ROM 2.3.33 *a distempered head*, MAC 5.2.15.

distempering *ppl. adj.* Intoxicating, disturbing OTH 1.1.99 *distemp'ring draughts.*

distil *vb.*
1 Fall in minute drops TIT 3.1.17 *rain, That shall distil from these two ancient urns* (i.e. his eyes).
2 Let fall in minute drops TIT 2.3.201 *dew distill'd on flowers*, ROM 5.3.15.
3 Melt HAM 1.2.204 *distill'd Almost to jelly with the act of fear.*

distillation *n.* Product of distilling WIV 3.5.113 *like a strong distillation*, SON 5.9.

distilment *n.* Distillation, product of distilling HAM 1.5.64 *The leprous distilment.*

distinct *n.* Separate thing PHT 27 *Two distincts.*

distinction *n.* Discrimination TRO 3.2.27 *lose distinction in my joys*, TRO 1.3.27.

distinctively *adv.* Distinctly OTH 1.3.155 *by parcels she had something heard, But not distinctively* (Ff 2-4 *distinctiuely*; F1 *instinctiuely*; Qq *intentively*).

distinctly *adv.* Separately, individually TMP 1.2.200 *on the topmast, The yards and boresprit, would I flame distinctly, Then meet*, OTH 2.3.289, COR 3.1.205.

distinguishment *n.* Distinction WT 2.1.86 *mannerly distinguishment leave out Betwixt the prince and beggar.*

distract *vb.*
1 Separate, divide, scatter ANT 3.7.43 *Distract your army*, OTH 1.3.323.
2 Perplex, confuse, bewilder, agitate WIV 2.2.134 *This news distracts me!*, OTH 2.3.256.
3 Make mad 2H4 2.1.107 *poverty hath distracted her.*

~ *ppl. adj.*
1 Separated, divided LC 231 *Their distract parcels.*
2 Perplexed, confused ERR 4.3.42 *The fellow is distract and so am I,* JC 4.3.155.
3 Deranged in mind, crazy, mad, insane LR 4.6.281 *Better I were distract, So should my thoughts be sever'd from my griefs,* HAM 4.5.2, TN 5.1.280.
distracted *ppl. adj.* Perplexed, confused, bewildered, agitated HAM 1.5.97 *this distracted globe,* TIM 3.4.113, AWW 5.3.35.
distractedly *adv.* Disjointedly TN 2.2.21 *speak in starts distractedly,* LC 28.
distraction *n.*
1 Division, detachment ANT 3.7.76 *His power went out in such distractions as Beguil'd all spies.*
2 Frenzy, madness, mental derangement SON 119.8 *the distraction of this madding fever.*
distrain vb. Levy a distress upon, seize (property, etc.) by way of distress R2 2.3.131 *My father's goods are all distrain'd and sold;* (hence) confiscate 1H6 1.3.61 *Hath here distrain'd the Tower to his use.*
distraught *adj.* Mentally deranged, driven to madness R3 3.5.4 *distraught and mad with terror,* ROM 4.3.49.
distressful *adj.* Hard-earned, gained by hard toil H5 4.1.270 *distressful bread.*
distribute vb. Administer (justice) COR 3.3.99 *the ministers That doth distribute it.*
distrustful *adj.* Diffident 1H6 1.2.126 *Distrustful recreants, Fight till the last gasp.*
disturb *n.* Disturbance R3 4.2.73 *my sweet sleep's disturbs* (Ff *disturbers;* Qq 1-6 *disturbs*).
disvalue vb. Disparage MM 5.1.221 *her reputation was disvalued In levity.*
disvouch vb. Contradict MM 4.4.1 *Every letter he hath writ hath disvouch'd other.*
dive-dapper *n.* Dabchick, little grebe VEN 86 *a dive-dapper peering through a wave.*
divers *adj.*
1 Different in kind AYL 3.2.308 *Time travels in divers paces with divers persons,* 2H4 3.1.53, H5 1.2.184.
▷ In H8 5.2.53 *new opinions, Divers and dangerous* the old meaning 'wrong, perverse' may also be involved.
2 Various, sundry, several WIV 1.1.229 *divers philosophers hold that...,* JC 4.1.20, H5 1.2.184; (absol.) MV 3.1.113 *divers of Antonio's creditors.*
divest vb. (refl.)
1 Undress OTH 2.3.186 *Divesting them for bed* (Qq; Ff *Devesting*).
2 Strip or dispossess oneself (*of*) H5 2.4.78 *That you divest yourself* (Ff *devest*), LR 1.1.49.
dividable *adj.* Having the function of dividing, that divides TRO 1.3.105 *dividable shores.*
dividant *adj.* Divided, separate TIM 4.3.5 *Twinn'd brothers...Whose procreation...and birth Scarce is dividant.*
divided *ppl. adj.*
1 Incomplete, imperfect JN 2.1.439 *she a fair divided excellence, Whose fulness of perfection lies in him.*
2 Distributed or parted among a number of things or persons TIM 1.2.48 *divided draught.*
divine *n.* Priest WT 3.1.19 *Apollo's great divine.*
~ *adj.* Immortal, blessed R2 1.1.38 *my divine soul.*
divinely *adv.* Piously, religiously JN 2.1.237 *most divinely vow'd,* R3 3.7.62.
divineness *n.* Superhuman excellence CYM 3.6.43 *divineness No elder than a boy.*
diviner *n.* Soothsayer, seer ERR 3.2.140 *this...diviner...told me what privy marks I had about me.*
division *n.*
1 (in music) The execution of a rapid melodic pass-

age, orig. conceived as the dividing of each of a succession of long notes into several short ones; such a passage itself, a florid piece of melody, a run ROM 3.5.29 *the lark makes sweet division,* 1H4 3.1.208; (hence, fig.) variation, modulation MAC 4.3.96 *abound In the division of each several crime, Acting it many ways.*
2 Definite portion of a battalion or squadron 2H4 1.3.70 *his divisions...Are in three heads;* (hence) orderly arrangement OTH 1.1.23 *the division of a battle.*
divorce *n.* That which causes separation H8 2.1.76 *as the long divorce of steel falls on me* (i.e. executioner's axe), TIM 4.3.381, VEN 932.
divulge vb. Proclaim (a person) to be so-and-so WIV 3.2.42 *divulge Page himself for a secure and wilful Actaeon,* TN 1.5.260.
divulging *n.* Becoming known, being revealed HAM 4.1.22 *To keep it from divulging.*
dizzy vb. Make 'dizzy', confuse TRO 5.2.174 *dizzy with more clamour Neptune's ear,* HAM 5.2.114 (Q2(u) *dosie;* Q2(c) *dazzie;* Qq4-6 *dizzie*).
dizzy-eyed *adj.* Giddy, whirling 1H6 4.7.11 *Dizzy-ey'd fury.*
do vb.
1 *do to death, do dead* Put to death 2H6 3.2.179 *who should do the Duke to death?,* ADO 5.3.3; 3H6 1.4.108 *do him dead.*
2 Play the part of, enact MND 1.2.68 *You may do it extempore,* MND 1.2.26, ADO 2.1.117.
3 (imperative) 'Go on!' TRO 2.1.42 *Do! do!,* TMP 4.1.239.
4 'Do with' LUC 1092 *day hath nought to do what's done by night.*
5 (euphemism) Have sexual intercourse with TIT 4.2.76 *I have done thy mother.*
6 Be sufficient 1H4 2.4.170 *all would not do.*
7 *to do* To be done MM 1.2.112 *What's to do here...?,* AYL 1.2.115.
~ in combination
do good Succeed WT 2.2.52 *I shall do good.* **do withal** Do otherwise, help it MV 3.4.72 *I could not do withal.*
docked *ppl. adj.* Put in dock MV 1.1.27 *dock'd in sand.*
▷ Rowe's emendation; F1, Qq *docks.*
doctrine *n.*
1 Instruction, lesson ANT 5.2.31 *A doctrine of obedience,* LLL 4.3.298, ROM 1.1.238.
2 Learning AWW 1.3.241 *the schools, Embowell'd of their doctrine.*
document *n.* Instruction, lesson HAM 4.5.178 *A document in madness.*
do de *interj.* Used to represent shivering or the chattering of the teeth from cold LR 3.4.58 *Tom's a-cold—O do de, do de, do de.*
dodge vb. Be shifty ANT 3.11.62 *dodge And palter in the shifts of lowness.*
doff See DAFF.
dog *n.*
1 *dog at* Adept at TGV 4.4.13 *a dog at all things,* TN 2.3.60.
2 *the dog's name* The letter R (because its sound was thought to resemble a dog's growl) ROM 2.4.209 *R—...that's the dog's name.*
dog-ape *n.* Dog-faced baboon, cynocephalus AYL 2.5.27 *th' encounter of two dog-apes.*
dog-days *n.* (*pl.*) The days about the time of the heliacal rising of the Dog-star, the hottest and most unwholesome period of the year in the northern hemisphere, about July 3 to August 15 H8 5.3.42 *twenty of the dog-days now reign in's nose.*
dogfish *n.* Name of a kind of small shark; (applied

opprobriously to a person) 1H6 1.4.107 *Pucelle or puzzel, Dolphin or dogfish.*

dog-fox *n.* Male fox; (fig.) a man likened for craftiness to a fox Tro 5.4.11 *the policy of those crafty...rascals...that...dog-fox, Ulysses...*

dogged *adj.* Like a dog Jn 4.3.149 *Now for the bare-pick'd bone of majesty Doth dogged war bristle his angry crest*; (hence) cruel, malicious Jn 4.1.128 *these dogged spies*, 2H6 3.1.158.

dog-hearted *adj.* Cruel Lr 4.3.45 *his dog-hearted daughters.*

dog-hole *n.* Filthy or disorderly place unfit for human habitation AWW 2.3.274 *France is a dog-hole.*

dog's-leather *n.* Leather made of dogskin 2H6 4.2.24 *He shall have the skins of our enemies, to make dog's-leather of.*

dog-weary *adj.* Tired out Shr 4.2.60 *I have watch'd so long That I am dog-weary.*

doing *n.*
1 Deed, action, performance H8 1.2.74 *ignorant tongues, which...yet will be The chronicles of my doing*, R3 2.2.90, Cor 1.9.40; (also pl.) Cor 1.9.23 *hide your doings.*
2 (euphemism) Sexual intercourse H5 3.7.99 *Doing is activity, and he will still be doing*, AWW 2.3.233.

doit *n.* Former Dutch coin, equivalent to half a farthing, used as a type of a small sum Per 4.2.51 *I cannot be bated one doit of a thousand pieces*, Tmp 2.2.32, Cor 4.4.17.

dole *n.*[1]
1 Share, portion AWW 2.3.169 *what dole of honour Flies where you bid it.*
2 Portion or lot in life, destiny 1H4 2.2.76 *happy man be his dole!* (i.e. may his lot be to be called 'Happy man!'), Wiv 3.4.65, Shr 1.1.140.

dole *n.*[2] Grief, sorrow Ham 1.2.13 *weighing delight and dole*; lamentation, mourning AYL 1.2.130 *making such pitiful dole*; sorrowful, piteous object MND 5.1.278 *What dreadful dole is here!*

dollar *n.* (in S.'s time, English name for) German thaler and Spanish piece of eight (eight reals) Mac 1.2.62 *Till he disbursed...Ten thousand dollars*, Tmp 2.1.18.

Dolphin *n.* (var. in Ff and Qq of) Dauphin 1H6 5.3.37 *Charles the Dolphin*, Jn 5.1.32, H5 1.2.288.

domination *n.* Dominion Jn 2.1.176 *The dominations, royalties, and rights Of this...boy.*

dominator *n.* Ruler, lord LLL 1.1.220 *sole dominator of Navarre*, Tit 2.3.31.

domineer *vb.* Feast riotously Shr 3.2.224 *revel and domineer.*

dominical *n.* (short for) 'Dominical letter', the letter, marked in red on old almanacs, used to denote the Sundays in a particular year LLL 5.2.44 *My red dominical, my golden letter.*
▷ The seven letters A, B, C, D, E, F, G are used in succession to denote the first seven days of the year (January 1–7), and then in rotation the next seven days, so that, e.g. if January 3 is a Sunday the dominical letter for the year is C, and it would be printed in red for that year.

don *n.* Master Ado 5.2.84 *Don Worm, his conscience.*
▷ See also DAN.

done *pa. pple.*
1 Agreed! Shr 5.2.74 *A match!* '*tis done*, Tmp 2.1.32, Cor 1.4.2.
2 Ruined, lost, 'done for' AWW 4.2.65 *though there my hope be done*, R2 1.1.183, Ham 3.2.162.

doom *n.*
1 Judgement, sentence R2 1.3.148 *for thee remains a heavier doom*, Tit 5.3.182.
2 Last or great judgement at the end of the world, day of the last judgement Rom 3.2.67 *dreadful trumpet, sound the general doom*, Mac 4.1.117.

3 Final fate, death, destruction R3 4.4.12 *If yet your gentle souls...be not fix'd in doom perpetual*, Son 14.14, Wiv 5.5.58.
4 *day of doom* Last day of one's life R2 3.2.189 *To change blows with thee for our day of doom*, Tit 2.3.42.
▷ In S. not 'day of last judgement'.
~ *vb.*
1 Judge Cor 1.8.6 *the gods doom him after!*
2 Condemn R3 3.4.65 *To doom th'offenders...*; they have deserved death, Jn 4.3.39, Tit 3.1.47.
3 Decree R3 2.1.103 *to doom my brother's death*, Tit 4.2.114.
4 Decide Cym 5.5.420 *Nobly doom'd!*

doomsday *n.* A day of judgement, day one faces judgement, last day of one's life 1H4 4.1.134 *Doomsday is near, die all, die merrily*, Rom 5.3.234, R3 5.1.12.

door *n.*
1 Quarter 1H4 3.3.88 *is the wind in that door...?* (i.e. is that the tendency of affairs?).
▷ A popular tag; Tilley W 419.
2 *Speak within door* Lower your tone, do not talk so loud Oth 4.2.144 (Qq *dores*).
3 *out of door* External, visible Cym 1.6.15 *All of her that is out of door most rich!*

door-keeper *n.* Pander, procurer Per 4.6.118 *thou damned door-keeper!*, Per 4.6.165.

door particulars *n.* Home or private affairs Lr 5.1.30 *these domestic door particulars* (Qq 1–2; Ff *these domestic and particular broils*).

dormouse *n.* (attrib.) Sleepy, dormant TN 3.2.19 *your dormouse valour.*

dotage *n.*
1 Feebleness of mind Lr 1.4.326 *He may enguard his dotage with their powers.*
2 Excessive fondness Oth 4.1.27 *by their...voluntary dotage of some mistress.*

dotant *n.* Dotard, one whose intellect is impaired by age, one who is in his dotage Cor 5.2.44 *a decay'd dotant.*

dote *vb.*
1 Act or talk foolishly Ven 1059 *franticly she doteth.*
2 Be excessively fond or in love TGV 4.4.82 *You dote on her that cares not for your love*, Ham 5.2.189, Ven 837.

doter *n.* Fond lover LLL 4.3.256 *It mourns that painting...Should ravish doters with a false aspect.*

doting *ppl. adj.*
1 Fond R3 4.4.300 *the doting title of a mother*, Luc 1064.
2 Foolish Err 4.4.58 *Peace, doting wizard, peace!*

double *n.* Sharp turn Ven 682 *He cranks and crosses with a thousand doubles.*
~ *vb.*
1 Be twice as much as Lr 2.4.259 *Thy fifty yet doth double five and twenty*; (fig.) Cym 3.4.177 *honourable, And doubling that, most holy.*
2 Speak with repetition of sounds, stutter (under the influence of drink) 2H6 2.3.91 *This knave's tongue begins to double.*
~ *adj.*
1 (of the tongue) Forked MND 2.2.9 *snakes with double tongue*; (fig.) deceitful LLL 5.2.245 *You have a double tongue within your mask* (also with allusion to the leather tongue on the inside of a mask, held in the mouth to keep the mask in place).
2 Signed by two people Ham 5.1.105 *his double vouchers.*
3 *as double as* Having twice the power or influence of Oth 1.2.14 *a voice potential As double as the Duke's.*

4 *double beer* Strong beer 2H6 2.3.64.

5 *double man* Spectre, wraith 1H4 5.4.138.

~ *adv.*

1 Doubly, twice MAC 4.1.83 *make assurance double sure*, AWW 2.3.239, WT 5.3.107.

2 Deceitfully ROM 2.4.168 *if you should deal double with her.*

3 *double-fatal* Lethal in two ways R2 3.2.117 *to bend their bows of double-fatal yew.*

▷ The yew has poisonous leaves, and its wood was used for instruments of death.

double-henned *adj.* Having two hens TRO 5.7.11 *my double-henned sparrow* (i.e. with two wives, alluding to Paris, husband of Œnone and Helen).

▷ The sparrow was often described as lecherous in M.E. and Eliz. literature (Hulme). Q *double hen'd spartan*; Kellner conjecture *double-horned Spartan.*

doublet *n.* Close-fitting body-garment, with or without sleeves, worn by men from 14C to 18C TMP 2.1.103 *Is not...my doublet as fresh as the first day I wore it?*, SHR Ind.2.9, 1H4 2.4.74; *doublet and hose* typical male attire AYL 2.4.6 *as doublet and hose ought to show itself courageous to petticoat;* (also) a kind of undress, or dress for active pursuits, implying absence of the warm cloak, or the dignified gown or long coat WIV 3.1.46 *in your doublet and hose, this raw rheumatic day?*, 2H6 4.7.51.

double-vantage *vb.* Benefit doubly SON 88.12 *Doing thee vantage, double-vantage me.*

doubt *n.*

1 Suspicion, conjecture OTH 3.3.429 *'Tis a shrewd doubt*, OTH 3.3.188.

2 Fear 3H6 4.8.37 *The doubt is that he will seduce the rest*, CYM 4.4.14.

3 *in doubt* Ambiguous HAM 4.5.6 *speaks things in doubt That carry but half sense.*

~ *vb.*

1 Suspect HAM 1.2.255 *I doubt some foul play.*

2 Fear COR 3.1.152 *You...That love the fundamental part of state More than you doubt the change on't*, OTH 3.3.19.

3 (refl.) Fear TIM 1.2.154 *I doubt me.*

doubtful *adj.*

1 Inclined to suspect, suspicious LR 5.1.12 *I am doubtful that you have been...bosom'd with her*, TN 4.3.27; apprehensive MAC 3.2.7 *dwell in doubtful joy*, JN 5.1.36.

2 Causing dread, awful, to be feared 1H6 4.1.151 *this doubtful strife*, ERR 1.1.68.

doubtfully *adv.*

1 Undecidedly TGV 2.1.111 *being ignorant to whom it goes, I write at random, very doubtfully.*

2 Ambiguously, in ambiguous language TIM 4.3.122 *the oracle Hath doubtfully pronounc'd...* (i.e. with ambiguity typical of an oracle), ERR 2.1.50.

3 Dreadfully ERR 2.1.53 *he struck...so doubtfully, that I could scarce understand them.*

doubtless *adj.* and *adv.* Without fear or suspicion 1H4 3.2.20 *I am doubtless I can purge Myself*; JN 4.1.129 *pretty child, sleep doubtless.*

dout *vb.* Put out, extinguish; (fig.) H5 4.2.11 *dout them with superfluous courage*, HAM 4.7.191.

▷ F1 *doubts*; in HAM 4.7.191 Qq, Ff 2–4 *drown(e)s.*

dove *n.* Common type of gentleness and harmlessness; (hence) simpleton, innocent SHR 3.2.157 *she's a lamb, a dove, a fool to him!*

dower *n.*

1 Portion of his estate that a husband settles on his wife in his will SHR 2.1.343 *he...That can assure my daughter greatest dower.*

2 Dowry, portion, property given with the wife AWW 4.4.19 *Hath brought me up to be your daughter's dower.*

dowered *ppl. adj.* Endowed LR 1.1.204 *Dow'r'd with our curse.*

dowlas *n.* Coarse kind of linen 1H4 3.3.69 *Dowlas, filthy dowlas.*

dowl(e) *n.* Soft fine feather TMP 3.3.65 *One dowle that's in my plume.*

down *interj.* Used in ballad refrains without appreciable meaning WIV 1.4.43 *And down, down, adown-a*, HAM 4.5.171.

down-gyved *adj.* Hanging down like gyves or fetters HAM 2.1.77 *his stockings...down-gyved to his ankle.*

downright *adj.*

1 Directed straight downwards, vertical 2H6 2.3.90 *a downright blow*, 3H6 1.1.12.

2 Direct, straightforward, plain, definite MM 3.2.105 *this downright way of creation*, H5 5.2.144, OTH 1.3.249.

~ *adv.*

1 Straightway, forthwith VEN 645 *and fell I not downright?*

▷ Other sense of 'straight down' could also apply here.

2 Positively, absolutely, out and out LLL 5.2.389 *they'll mock us now downright*, ROM 3.5.128.

3 Plainly, definitely AYL 3.4.29 *You have heard him swear downright he was.*

down-roping See ROPING.

down sleeves *n.* Long, close-fitting sleeves padded with down ADO 3.4.20 *lac'd with silver, set with pearls, down sleeves, side sleeves.*

doxy *n.* (vagabonds' cant) Beggar's mistress WT 4.3.2 *With heigh, the doxy over the dale!*

drab *n.* Harlot TRO 5.1.96 *he keeps a Troyan drab*, 2H6 2.1.153.

drabbing *n.* Associating with drabs or harlots HAM 2.1.26 *quarrelling, Drabbing—you may go so far.*

draff *n.* Pig-wash, hog's-wash 1H4 4.2.35 *prodigals lately come from swine-keeping, from eating draff and husks*, WIV 4.2.107 (Ff, Q3 *draugh*).

dragon's tail *n.* The descending node of the moon's orbit with the ecliptic LR 1.2.129 *under the Dragon's tail.*

drain *vb.* Let fall in drops 2H6 3.2.142 *to drain Upon his face an ocean of salt tears.*

dram *n.*

1 One-eighth of an ounce apothecaries' weight, one-sixteenth of an ounce avoirdupois weight; (hence) very small quantity WT 2.1.138 *every dram of woman's flesh is false*, TIM 5.1.151, AWW 2.3.221.

2 One-eighth of a fluid ounce; (hence) dose, small draught ROM 5.1.60 *let me have A dram of poison*, WT 1.2.320.

draught *n.* Cesspool, privy, sewer TRO 5.1.75 *Sweet draught!...sweet sewer*, TIM 5.1.102.

draw *vb.*

1 (intr.) Pull a vehicle; (fig.) act in concert OTH 4.1.67 *Think every bearded fellow that's but yok'd May draw with you*, TRO 5.5.44.

2 Bend (a bow), pull back (an arrow) on the string SHR 5.2.47 *as you draw your bow*, R3 5.3.339 *draw your arrows to the head!*; (absol.) TIT 4.3.3 *Look ye draw home enough*, TIT 4.3.64.

3 (intr.) Draw the bow across a fiddle ADO 5.1.128 *I will bid thee draw, as we do the minstrels, draw to pleasure us.*

4 (of a ship) Displace so much water; (absol.) TRO 2.3.266 *greater hulks draw deep.*

5 Gather, collect, assemble JN 4.2.118 *That such an army could be drawn in France*, 1H4 3.1.88, COR 2.3.253.

6 Withdraw 2H4 2.1.149 *Go wash thy face, and draw the action*, 3H6 5.1.25.

7 (intr.) Draw liquor, obtain (drink) from a cask, etc.; exercise the trade of a drawer WIV 1.3.10 *he shall draw, he shall tap.*

8 (trans.) Empty, drain dry MM 2.1.205 *...tapsters; they will draw you* (with quibble on sense 11).

9 Receive (money), win (a stake) WT 1.2.248 *seest...the rich stake drawn*, MV 4.1.87, LR 1.1.85; (fig.) HAM 4.5.143 *That, swoopstake, you will draw both friend and foe.*

10 Bring (something into a person's hands) LR 3.3.23 *must draw me That which my father loses*, CYM 3.3.18.

11 Disembowel (usu. with quibble) JN 2.1.504 *Drawn in the flattering table of her eye! Hang'd...And quarter'd...*, ADO 3.2.22.

12 Write out, frame, compose MND 1.2.105 *I will draw a bill of properties*, MV 4.1.394, SHR 3.1.70.

~ in combination
draw on 1 Involve as a consequence 3H6 3.3.75 *that...Thou draw not on thy danger.* **2** Entice, lead on MAC 3.5.29 *draw him on to his confusion.* **3** (intr.) Approach WIV 5.3.23 *The hour draws on*, WIV 5.5.2, MND 1.1.2. **draw out** Extend, lengthen R3 5.3.293 *My foreward shall be drawn out all in length*, JC 3.1.100. **draw up 1** Set in array LR 5.1.51 *draw up your powers.* **2** Inhale VEN 929 *draws up her breath.*

drawer *n.* Tapster ROM 3.1.9 *draws him on the drawer*, WIV 2.2.159.

drawn *ppl. adj.*
1 Having one's sword drawn MND 3.2.402 *Here, villain, drawn and ready*, TMP 2.1.308, ROM 1.1.70.
2 *drawn fox* Fox driven from cover (and therefore wily in his attempts to get back again) 1H4 3.3.113 *no more truth in thee than in a drawn fox.*
3 *drawn of* Emptied of CYM 5.4.165 *the purse too light, being drawn of heaviness.*

dread *n.* One deeply revered VEN 635 *wondrous dread!*
~ *vb.* Be anxious about PP 7.10 *Dreading my love, the loss whereof still fearing!*
~ *adj.*
1 Dreadful, terrible TMP 1.2.206 *his dread trident.*
2 Held in awe, revered 2H6 5.1.17 *our dread liege*, HAM 3.4.108.

dread-bolted *adj.* Accompanied by terrible lightning or thunderbolts LR 4.7.32 *the deep dread-bolted thunder.*

dreadful *adj.* Full of dread HAM 1.2.207 *In dreadful secrecy*, R3 1.1.8, OTH 2.3.175.

dreadfully *adv.*
1 With dread MM 4.2.143 *apprehends death no more dreadfully but as a drunken sleep.*
2 Appallingly HAM 2.2.269 *I am most dreadfully attended.*

dreg *n.* (usu. pl.; always fig.)
1 Worthless part of something, impurity, corrupt matter TRO 3.2.65 *What too curious dreg espies my sweet lady in the fountain of our love?*, TIM 1.2.233, SON 74.9.
2 Residue, last remains TMP 2.2.40 *till the dregs of the storm be past*, R3 1.4.121, COR 5.2.77.

dress *vb.*
1 Cultivate (a plot of ground) R2 3.4.73 *set to dress this garden*, R2 3.4.56.
2 Train, break (a horse) R2 5.5.80 *That horse that I so carefully have dress'd.*

dressing *n.*
1 Refashioning SON 123.4 *They are but dressings of a former sight.*
2 Ornament of office MM 5.1.56 *In all his dressings.*

dribbling *ppl. adj.* (of an arrow) Falling short or wide of the mark MM 1.3.2 *the dribbling dart of love.*

drift *n.*
1 Shower (of bullets) JN 2.1.412 *Our thunder...Shall rain their drift of bullets on this town.*
2 What one is driving at, aim, tenor, tendency TMP 5.1.29 *The sole drift of my purpose*, HAM 4.7.151, ROM 2.3.55.
3 Scheme, plot, design TGV 2.6.43 *wit to plot this drift*, 3H6 1.2.46, ROM 4.1.114.

drink *n.* Drinking-bout(s), carousal TIM 3.5.73 *His days are foul and his drink dangerous*, ANT 2.7.105.
~ *vb.*
1 Inhale ANT 5.2.213 *forc'd to drink their vapour.*
2 Toast, drink in honour of, drink the health of TIM 1.2.137 *spend our flatteries to drink those men.*
3 *drink (a person) dead drunk, dead to bed* Out-drink (someone), drink (a person) under the table OTH 2.3.82, *he drinks you, with facility, your Dane dead drunk*, ANT 2.5.21.

drive *vb.*
1 Rush *at* or *upon* TIT 2.3.64 *the hounds Should drive upon thy...limbs*, HAM 2.2.472 *Pyrrhus at Priam drives.*
2 *let drive* Aim blows, strike 1H4 2.4.196 *Four rogues...let drive at me*, 1H4 2.4.223.
3 *drive away* Cause (the time) to pass 1H4 2.4.28 *to drive away the time till Falstaff come.*
◇ Past tense sometimes *drave*, e.g. TRO 3.3.190 *drave great Mars to faction*; pa. pple. *droven*, e.g. ANT 4.7.5 *Had we done so...,we had droven them home.*

driven *ppl. adj.*
1 (of snow) Drifted WT 4.4.218 *as white as driven snow.*
2 (of down) Separated from the heavier down by a current of air OTH 1.3.231 *My thrice-driven bed of down.*

drollery *n.* Puppet-show TMP 3.3.21 *A living drollery*; comic picture 2H4 2.1.144 *for thy walls, a pretty slight drollery.*

drone *n.* Bass pipe of a bagpipe, which emits one continuous note 1H4 1.2.76 *the drone of a Lincolnshire bagpipe.*

drooping chair *n.* Chair of old age 1H6 4.5.5. *When...age...Should bring thy father to his drooping chair.*

drop *n.*
1 Spot of colour CYM 2.2.38 *like the crimson drops I' th' bottom of a cowslip.*
2 (short for) Tear-drop TMP 1.2.155 *drops full salt*, VEN 981, LUC 1228.
3 (short for) Drop of blood COR 5.1.10 *the drops That we have bled together*, H5 3.5.25, TRO 4.5.133.
4 (fig.) Small quantity OTH 4.2.53 *A drop of patience*, MV 2.2.186, CYM 4.2.304.
~ *vb.* Move or come casually or in an apparently undesigned manner TIM 1.2.SD *Then comes, dropping after all, Apemantus.*
~ in combination
drop forth Bring forth, produce AYL 4.3.34 *drop forth such...invention*, AYL 3.2.237. **drop in for** Come in for SON 90.4 *do not drop in for an after-loss.*

dropping *ppl. adj.*
1 Dripping wet PER 4.1.62 *with a dropping industry they skip From stem to stern.*
2 Tearful HAM 1.2.11 *a dropping eye.*

dropsied *adj.* Inflated AWW 2.3.128 *a dropsied honour.*

drossy *adj.* Frivolous HAM 5.2.189 *the drossy age.*

drouth *n.* Lack of moisture, thirst PER 3.Gower.8 *crickets...Are the blither for their drouth*, VEN 544.

drovier *n.* Cattle-dealer ADO 2.1.194 *that's spoken like an honest drovier.*

drown *vb.* Make completely drunk TN 1.5.133 *a third [draught] drowns him.*

drowsy *adj.* Inducing sleep OTH 3.3.331 *drowsy syrups*, ROM 4.1.96.

drug *n.* (spec.) Poisonous or injurious concoction OTH 1.2.74 *Abus'd her delicate youth with drugs or minerals That weakens motion*, HAM 3.2.255, TIT 1.1.154.

drug-damned *adj.* 'Damnable for its use of poison' (New Cambridge, 1968) CYM 3.4.15 *That drugdamn'd Italy hath outcraftied him.*

drum *n.* 'Rallying-point' (Arden, 1961) 1H4 3.3.206 *I could wish this tavern were my drum!*

drumble *vb.* Be sluggish, move sluggishly WIV 3.3.147 *Look how you drumble!*

dry *vb.* Cause (the brain) to lose its substance WIV 5.5.135 *Have I laid my brain in the sun and dried it, that it wants matter...*, HAM 4.5.155.

~ *adj.*
1 (properly) That does not draw blood; severe, hard ERR 2.2.63 *dry basting.*
2 (of jests, etc.) Dull, stupid LLL 5.2.373 *This jest is dry to me*, TN 1.5.41, AYL 2.7.39.
3 Thirsty; (hence) eager TMP 1.2.112 *So dry he was for sway.*
4 Sterile, barren TRO 2.3.224 *his ambition is dry* (with quibble on sense 'thirsty').
◇ *a dry hand* was associated with age and impotence 2H4 1.2.181 *Have you not...a dry hand, a yellow cheek, a white beard*, TN 1.3.73.

dry-beat *vb.* Beat soundly LLL 5.2.263 *all dry-beaten with pure scoff!* ROM 3.1.79, ROM 4.5.123.

dry-foot *adv. draw dry-foot* Track game by the scent of the foot ERR 4.2.39 *A hound that runs counter, and yet draws dry-foot well.*

dub *vb.* Confer the rank of knighthood 2H4 5.3.74 *dub me knight*, TN 3.4.235, H5 4.8.86; (with simple object) 3H6 2.2.59 *dub him presently*; (hence) invest with a dignity R3 1.1.82 *dubb'd them gentlewomen*; invest with an opprobrious name H5 2.2.120 *dub thee with the name of traitor.*

ducat *n.* Gold coin of varying value, formerly in use in most European countries HAM 3.4.24 *Dead, for a ducat, dead!*, MM 3.2.126; silver coin of Italy MV 2.8.18 *two sealed bags of ducats*, TN 1.3.22, TGV 1.1.137.

ducdame *interj.* (?) (a corr. of Romany 'dukra me') 'I foretell, I tell fortunes' (New Cambridge, 1926) AYL 2.5.54 *Ducdame, ducdame, ducdame!*

dudgeon *n.* Hilt of a dagger of wood of the same name MAC 2.1.46 *on thy blade and dudgeon gouts of blood.*

due *n.*
1 Debt MV 4.1.37 *the due and forfeit of my bond*, TIM 2.2.16.
2 Justice H8 5.1.131 *due o' th' verdict* (i.e. just verdict).
3 Right MAC 3.6.25 *the due of birth* (i.e. birthright), TRO 1.3.106.

~ *adj.*
1 (nautical use) Straight, direct H5 3.Ch.17 *Holding due course to Harflew*, OTH 1.3.34.
2 Applicable WT 3.2.58 *'tis a saying, sir, not due to me.*

~ *adv.* Duly 2H4 3.2.307 *duer paid to the hearer than the Turk's tribute.*

due *vb.* Endue, invest 1H6 4.2.34 *I thy enemy due thee withal.*

duello *n.* Established code of duellists LLL 1.2.179 *the duello he regards not*, TN 3.4.307.

duke *vb. duke it* Play the duke MM 3.2.94 *Lord Angelo dukes it well in his absence.*

dull *adj.*
1 Wanting acuteness in the bodily senses WT 1.2.421 *A savour that may strike the dullest nostril*, ERR 5.1.317; (fig.) TIT 2.1.128 *The woods are...deaf, and dull.*
2 Indistinctly sensed SHR Ind.1.24 *the dullest scent.*
3 Slow, inert, inactive HAM 4.4.33 *spur my dull revenge*, 1H4 4.2.80, R3 2.2.92; heavy, drowsy MV 2.7.8 *dull lead*, HAM 3.2.226.
4 Soft, soothing 2H4 4.5.2 *some dull and favourable hand.*
5 Gloomy, melancholy ADO 2.3.71 *dumps so dull and heavy*, ROM 1.4.21, SON 97.13.
6 Not sharp, blunt R3 4.4.227 *the...knife was dull and blunt.*
7 Not bright, obscure, dim, gloomy, overcast H5 3.5.16 *Is not their climate foggy, raw, and dull*, 2H4 4.3.98, CYM 2.4.41.

dull-eyed *adj.*
1 Wanting in perception MV 3.3.14 *a...dull-ey'd fool.*
2 Having the eyes dimmed PER 1.2.2 *dull-ey'd melancholy.*

dumb *vb.* Put to silence PER 5.Gower. 5 *Deep clerks she dumbs*, ANT 1.5.50 (F1 *dumbe*; Theobald *dumb'd*).

dumb-discoursive *adj.* That entices or allures without speech, 'silently persuasive' (Muir) TRO 4.4.90 *a still and dumb-discoursive devil.*

dumbly *adv.* Without speech MND 5.1.98 *dumbly have broke off*, R2 5.1.95, VEN 1059.

dump *n.* (properly) Mournful melody or song TGV 3.2.84 *to their instruments Tune a deploring dump*, ADO 2.3.71; (hence) tune in general ROM 4.5.107 *play me some merry dump.*

dun *adj.* Of dull greyish-brown colour SON 130.3 *If snow be white,...her breasts are dun*, MAC 1.5.51.
◇ ROM 1.4.40 *dun's the mouse...If thou art Dun, we'll draw thee from the mire:* quibble on the word 'done' (Nares) and also ref. to an old Christmas game, called 'Dun is in the mire', in which a heavy log representing a horse was lifted and carried off by players.

dung *n.* Vile or contemptible matter ANT 5.2.7 *never palates more the dung.*

dungy *adj.* (fig.) Vile, contemptible WT 2.1.157 *the whole dungy earth*, ANT 1.1.35.

dup *vb.* (contraction of 'do up') Open HAM 4.5.53 *dupp'd the chamber-door.*

durance *n.*
1 Confinement, imprisonment 2H4 5.5.34 *in base durance and contagious prison*, LLL 3.1.128, TN 5.1.276.
2 Lasting quality, durability 1H4 1.2.43 *is not a buff jerkin a most sweet robe of durance?* (with quibble on senses 1 and 3).
3 Stout, durable cloth ERR 4.3.27 *suits of durance* (with quibble on senses 1 and 2).

dusky *adj.* Somewhat dark or deficient in light, not bright or luminous, dim, obscure 1H6 2.5.122 *the dusky torch.*

dust *n.* Grain of dust, minute particle of dry matter JN 3.4.128 *each dust, each straw*, AWW 5.3.55, R2 2.3.91.

dusty *adj.* Consisting of dust TRO 3.2.189 *mighty states...are grated To dusty nothing;* (applied to death as the state in which all 'turn to dust' (Eccles.3:20)) MAC 5.5.23 *lighted fools The way to dusty death.*

duteous *adj.* Dutiful, submissive LR 4.6.253 *duteous to the vices of thy mistress*, CYM 5.5.86, LUC 1360.

duty *n.*
1 Reverence, respect AYL 5.2.96 *All adoration, duty, and observance*, MND 5.1.101, TN 3.1.95; act

of reverence, compliment LLL 4.2.143 *Stay not thy compliment; I forgive thy duty*, 1H4 5.2.55, H8 1.2.61. **2** (one's) Due SHR 4.1.37 *have thy duty*.

dwell *vb.*
1 Remain, continue (*in* a state) AWW 4.3.11 *dwell darkly with you* (i.e. be kept secret by you), MV 1.3.155, H8 3.2.133.
2 Lie in, rest with, depend on TRO 3.2.157 *for to be wise and love...dwells with gods above*, TRO 1.3.336, H8 3.2.459.
~ in combination

dwell on, upon 1 Stand on, make much of ROM 2.2.88 *Fain would I dwell on form*, WIV 2.2.242. **2** Continue in R3 5.3.100 *vows...And...interchange of...discourse Which...friends should dwell upon*, R3 5.3.239.

dweller *n.* *dweller on* Stickler for SON 125.5 *dwellers on form and favour*.

dwelling *n.* Dwelling-place, home SHR 4.5.55 *my dwelling Pisa*, 2H4 5.3.5, AYL 3.2.342.

E

eager *adj.*
1 Pungent, acrid SON 118.2 *With eager compounds we our palate urge*; acid HAM 1.5.69 *curd, like eager droppings into milk, The...blood;* (of air and of speech) keen, biting HAM 1.4.2 *It is a nipping and an eager air*, 3H6 2.6.68 *vex him with eager words.*
2 Ardent, impetuous LUC 1298 *Conceit and grief an eager combat fight*, R2 5.3.75, 3H6 1.4.3.

eagle-sighted *adj.* Having sight strong enough to gaze at the sun LLL 4.3.222 *What peremptory eagle-sighted eye Dares look upon the heaven of her brow?*

eagle-winged *adj.* That soars aloft R2 1.3.129 *the eagle-winged pride Of...ambitious thoughts.*

eale *n.* (?) (1) Fermenting agent (symbolizing evil); or (2) (aphetic form of) evil HAM 1.4.36 *the dram of eale.*
⇨ Qq 2–3 *eale*; Qq 4–6 *ease*; passage not in F1 or Q1.

ean *vb.* Bring forth (lambs) 3H6 2.5.36 *ere the poor fools will ean.*

eaning *ppl. adj. eaning time* Lambing time MV 1.3.87 *ewes, Who then conceiving did in eaning time Fall parti-colour'd lambs*, PER 3.4.6.

eanling *n.* Young lamb MV 1.3.79 *the eanlings which were streak'd and pied.*

ear *n.*
1 *about* (one's) *ears* (said of a shower of blows, missiles, etc. in expressions denoting severe treatment, punishment) Completely on or about one's person 3H6 5.1.108 *Or shall we beat the stones about thine ears*, ROM 3.1.81, H5 3.7.84.
2 *by the ears* (orig. of animals) Quarrelling, at variance AWW 1.2.1 *The Florentines and Senoys are by th' ears*, COR 1.1.233.
3 *in ear and ear* In everybody's ears HAM 4.5.94 *arraign In ear and ear.*
4 *in the ear* Within hearing HAM 3.1.184 *I'll be plac'd...in the ear Of all their conference.*
5 *o'er ears* Drowned TMP 4.1.213 *I be o'er ears.*
6 *shake* (one's) *ears* Term of ridicule with allusion to the action of an ass TN 2.3.125 *Go shake your ears.*
⇨ Cf. JC 4.1.26 *turn him off* (*Like to an empty ass*) *to shake his ears And graze in commons.*

ear *vb.* Plough, till R2 3.2.212 *To ear the land.*

ear-bussing *adj.* Whispered (the speaker's lips touching the hearer's ear) LR 2.1.8 *the news...the whisper'd ones, for they are yet but ear-bussing arguments* (Qq; Ff *ear-kissing*).

ear-kissing See EAR-BUSSING.

earl *n.* (used for the foreign title) Count AWW 3.5.12 *this French earl*, H5 4.8.103, 1H6 5.5.34.

earn *vb.* Grieve JC 2.2.129 *The heart of Brutus earns to think upon*, H5 2.3.6 (F1 *erne*).

earnest *n.* Money paid as an instalment to secure a bargain WT 4.4.646 *I have had earnest*, TGV 2.1.157, ERR 2.2.24 (with quibble).

earth *n.*
1 Country, land R2 2.1.41 *This earth of majesty*, JN 2.1.344, H8 3.1.143; estate ROM 1.2.15 *lady of my earth.*
2 A type of dull, dead matter R2 3.4.78 *thou little better thing than earth*, LR 5.3.262.
3 The body SON 146.1 *the centre of my sinful earth.*

earthed *ppl. adj.* Buried TMP 2.1.234 *Who shall be of as little memory When he is earth'd.*

earthly *adv.*
1 Existing in the ground 3H6 1.4.17 *an earthly sepulchre.*
2 See EARTHY sense 2.

earth-vexing *adj.* Troubling man's life CYM 5.4.42 *this earth-vexing smart.*

earthy *adj.*
1 Grossly material TMP 1.2.273 *her earthy...commands*, ERR 3.2.34.
2 Pale or lifeless as earth TIT 2.3.229 *the dead man's earthy cheeks* (Q; F1 *earthly*), 2H6 3.2.147.

ease *n.*
1 *do* (a person) *ease* Give pleasure or assistance to SHR 5.2.179 *may it do him ease*, HAM 1.1.131, 3H6 5.5.72.
2 Facility, easiness OTH 1.3.29 *an attempt of ease and gain; with ease* easily TMP 3.1.30 *I should do it With much more ease; at what ease* how easily H8 5.1.131 *At what ease Might corrupt minds procure knaves.*
3 (pl.) Means of relief OTH 5.10.55 *seek about for eases.*

easeful *adj.* Restful 3H6 5.3.6 *his easeful western bed.*

easily *adv.*
1 Comfortably, at ease OTH 5.1.83 *To bear him easily hence*, AYL 3.2.320.
2 Smoothly, freely ADO 5.1.158 *your wit...goes easily.*

easiness *n.*
1 Indifference HAM 5.1.68 *Custom hath made it in him a property of easiness.*
2 Facility HAM 3.4.166 *that shall lend a kind of easiness To the next abstinence.*
3 Indulgence H8 5.2.60 *Out of our easiness and childish pity.*

easy *adj.*
1 Moved without difficulty to action or belief, yielding, compliant CYM 2.4.47 *Your lady being so easy*, H5 2.2.125, H8 3.2.356; *easy for* open to WT 4.4.505 *I would your spirit were easier for advice.*
2 Of small importance, insignificant, slight TIT 3.1.198 *purchas'd at an easy price*, JN 3.1.207, 2H4 5.2.71.
~ *adv.* Easily AWW 5.3.125 *you shall as easy Prove that I husbanded her*, MAC 2.3.137, SON 109.3.

easy-held *adj.* Not oppressive or severe, with little restraint 1H6 5.3.139 *her easy-held imprisonment.*

eat *vb.*
1 *eat the air* Be 'fed' on nothing but words, hopes

or promises HAM 3.2.94 *I eat the air, promise-cramm'd*, 2H4 1.3.28.

2 *eat iron, eat (a) sword(s)* Be stabbed TRO 2.3.217 *'A should not bear it so, 'a should eat swords first*, ADO 4.1.275, 2H6 4.10.28.

ebb *n.*
1 *at ebb* (of the eyes) Dry TMP 1.2.436 *with mine eyes* (*never since at ebb*).
2 *his ebbs, his flows* His capriciousness TRO 2.3.130.
~ *vb.* (fig.) Decline, decay TMP 2.1.222 *To ebb Hereditary sloth instructs me*, AYL 2.7.73, OTH 3.3.458.

ebbed *ppl. adj.* Decayed, declined in power ANT 1.4.43 *the ebb'd man*.

ebon *adj.* Black (like ebony) 2H4 5.5.37 *Rouse up revenge from ebon den*, LLL 1.1.243, VEN 948.

Ebrew *adj.* Hebrew iH4 2.4.179 *an Ebrew Jew*.
▷ Common spelling from 14 to 17C.

ecce signum [L.] Behold the token 1H4 2.4.169.

eche *vb.* Eke out MV 3.2.23 *To eche it, and to draw it out in length* (Ff 1–3 *ich*, Q1 *eck*, Q2 *ech*, Qq 3–4 *eech*, F4 *itch*; some mod. edd. *eke* q.v.), PER 3. Gower.13 (Q1 *each*).

ecstasy *n.*
1 State of being beside oneself, in a frenzy or stupor; excitement, bewilderment, (sometimes) madness HAM 3.4.74 *Nor sense to ecstasy was ne'er so thrall'd*, TMP 3.3.108, TIT 4.1.125.
2 Trance, swoon OTH 4.1.79 *laid good 'scuses upon your ecstasy*.
3 Rapture, delight MV 3.2.111 *O love be moderate, allay thy ecstasy*.

edge *n.*
1 Cutting weapon, sword COR 5.6.112 *Stain all your edges on me*, 2H4 3.2.267, H5 2.1.22.
2 Keenness of appetite or desire SHR 1.2.73 *Affection's edge*, R2 1.3.296, MM 1.4.60.
3 *give (a person) an edge* Stimulate, incite (a person) HAM 3.1.26 *give him a further edge*.
4 Perilous path on a narrow ridge 2H4 1.1.170 *he walk'd...on an edge, More likely to fall in than to get o'er*.
5 Utmost point or limit TRO 4.5.68 *the edge of all extremity*.

edged *ppl. adj.* Sharpened, sharp H5 3.5.38 *with spirit of honour edged More sharper than your swords*, 1H6 3.3.52.

edify *vb.* Instruct, inform HAM 5.2.155 *I knew you must be edified by the margent* (i.e. a marginal note), OTH 3.4.14.

Edward shovel-board *n.* Old broad shilling of Edward VI, worn smooth by age and use, and therefore convenient for the game of shovel-board or shovel-groat WIV 1.1.156 *two Edward shovel-boards, that cost me two shilling and two pence apiece*.

eel-skin See ELF-SKIN.

e'er *adv.* (common contraction of) Ever (in all uses) TMP 1.2.446 *the third man that e'er I saw*, TRO 1.1.27, TN 1.1.22.
▷ In Ff and Qq often *ere*. See also OR.

effect *n.*
1 Contemplated result, purpose, end TGV 2.7.73 *Base men, that use them to so base effect*, 1H6 5.4.102, Oth 1.3.105; *to effect* to the purpose TiT 4.3.60 *I have written to effect*; (hence) in importance LR 3.1.52 *to effect, more than all*.
2 Drift, tenor, meaning HAM 1.3.45 *the effect of this good lesson*, AYL 4.3.35, JN 4.1.38.
3 Outward sign, manifestation, appearance ADO 2.3.107 *what effects of passion shows she?*, MM 3.1.24, LC 202; outward behaviour, external acts, action MAC 5.1.10 *do the effects of watching*; *large effects* pomp and circumstance LR 1.1.131.

4 Something acquired by an action HAM 3.3.54 *those effects for which I did the murder*.
5 Execution, accomplishment, fulfilment, realization MM 2.1.13 *attain'd of th' effect of your own purpose*, TGV 1.1.50, MAC 1.5.47.
6 Reality, fact LR 4.2.15 *Our wishes...May prove effects*, TRO 5.3.109.
~ *vb.*
1 Produce (a state) SHR 1.1.86 *our good will effects Bianca's grief*, 1H6 5.1.15.
2 Give effect to TRO 5.10.6 *effect your rage with speed!*

effectless *adj.* Fruitless TIT 3.1.76 *to effectless use*, PER 5.1.53.

effectual *adj.*
1 Having due effect TGV 3.1.225 *stands in effectual force* (i.e. must take effect).
2 To the point, pertinent, conclusive 2H6 3.1.41 *Or else conclude my words effectual*, TIT 5.3.43.

effectually *adv.*
1 With the due or intended result TIT 4.4.107 *Your bidding shall I do effectually*.
2 In effect, in reality SON 113.4 *mine eye...Seems seeing, but effectually is out*.

effeminate *adj.*
1 Unmanly, feeble, self-indulgent R2 5.3.10 *young wanton and effeminate boy*, 1H6 1.1.35, TRO 3.3.218; (of things) characterized by, or proceeding from, unmanly weakness or softness 1H6 5.4.107 *Shall we last conclude effeminate peace?*
2 Tender, gentle R3 3.7.211 *gentle, kind, effeminate remorse*.

effigies *n.* Likeness AYL 2.7.193 *as mine eye doth his effigies witness...in your face*.

effuse *n.* Pouring out, effusion 3H6 2.6.28 *much effuse of blood*.

effusion *n.*
1 Shedding (of blood, of tears) H5 3.6.130 *th' effusion of our blood*, JN 5.2.49, 1H6 5.1.9.
2 (concrete) That which is poured out MM 3.1.30 *The mere effusion of thy proper loins* (i.e. your very children).

eftest *adj.* (Dogberry's blunder for a word with some such sense as) Easiest, most convenient ADO 4.2.36 *the eftest way*.

eftsoons *adv.* Shortly, soon PER 5.1.255 *eftsoons I'll tell thee*.

egal, egall *adj.* Equal MV 3.4.13 *an egall yoke*, TIT 4.4.4.

egally *adv.* Equally R3 3.7.213 *egally...to all estates*.

egg *n.* Type of a worthless or inferior object AWW 4.3.250 *steal...an egg out of a cloister*, WT 1.2.161; (hence, a term or contempt for a person) MAC 4.2.83 *What, you egg! Young fry of treachery!*

egg-shell *n.* Worthless object HAM 4.4.53 *Even for an egg-shell*.
▷ See EGG.

eglantine *n.* Sweet-briar MND 2.1.252 *With sweet musk-roses and with eglantine*, CYM 4.2.223.

egma *n.* (rustic's blunder for) Enigma LLL 3.1.71 *No Egma, no riddle*.

Ego et Rex meus [L.] I and my King H8 3.2.314.

egress and regress (legal phrase) Right or liberty of going in and out WIV 2.1.217 *thou shalt have egress and regress*.

Egyptian *n.*
1 (?) Gipsy OTH 3.4.56 *That handkerchief Did an Egyptian to my mother give*.
2 *Egyptian thief* Robber in the Greek romance of 'Theagenes and Chariclea', who attempted to kill Chariclea, whom he loved TN 5.1.118 *Why should I not..., Like to th' Egyptian thief at point of death, Kill what I love?*

eight *adj.* *in eight and six* In alternate verses of

eight and six syllables each, the common ballad metre MND 3.1.24.

eight-penny adj. Of little value, trifling 1H4 3.3.104 A trifle, some eight-penny matter.

eisel n. Vinegar HAM 5.1.276 Woo't drink up eisel...?, Son 111.10 (F1 Esile; Q1 vessels; Qq 2-4 Esill).

either pron. Each other TMP 1.2.451 They are both in either's pow'rs, H5 2.2.106, Rom 2.6.29.
~ det. either which Either one or the other HAM 4.7.13 My virtue or my plague, be it either which.

eke vb.
1 Increase, add to MV 3.2.23 To eke it.
⇨ See ECHE.
2 eke out Supplement AWW 2.5.74 to eke out that, AYL 1.2.196.

eke vb. Also WIV 1.3.96 I...shall eke unfold, MND 3.1.100.

elbow n. rub the elbow Show oneself pleased 1H4 5.1.77 discontents, Which...rub the elbow at the news Of...innovation, LLL 5.2.109.
~ vb. Jostle, jog LR 4.3.42 shame so elbows him.

eld n.
1 Old age MM 3.1.36 palsied eld; people of advanced age TRO 2.2.104 Virgins and boys, mid-age and wrinkled eld.
2 People of olden times WIV 4.4.36 The superstitious idle-headed eld.

elder n.[1] heart of elder (jocular alteration of 'heart of oak') Faint heart WIV 2.3.29.

elder n.[2]
1 Aged person 2H4 2.4.258 the wither'd elder, JC 1.2.7.
2 Senator COR 2.2.42 Most reverend...elders.
~ adj.
1 Older CYM 3.6.44 No elder than a boy, MV 4.1.251.
2 Belonging to a later period, more advanced R2 2.3.43 elder days, H5 5.1.14.

elder-gun n. Popgun made of a hollowed shoot of elder (i.e. a harmless weapon) H5 4.1.198 That's a...shot out of an elder-gun.

eldest adj. Oldest, earliest TMP 5.1.186 Your eld'st acquaintance cannot be three hours, HAM 3.3.37, ERR 1.1.124.

elect vb. Pick out, select 1H6 4.1.4 elect no other king but him, MM 1.1.18.

element n.
1 (general name for) Earth, water, air, and fire, which were held in ancient and medieval philosophy to be the simple substances of which all material bodies are compounded TN 2.3.10 Does not our lives consist of the four elements?, JC 5.5.73; (hence) a constituent part of a whole, material or immaterial ADO 2.1.342 There's little of the melancholy element in her, H8 1.1.48; (pl.) materials ANT 2.7.45 the elements once out of it (i.e. at its dissolution), TMP 3.3.61.
2 The air, atmosphere, or sky JC 1.3.128 the complexion of the element, TN 1.1.25, LR 3.1.4.
3 (pl.) Atmospheric agencies or powers, (sometimes) heavens TMP 1.1.21 command these elements to silence, COR 1.10.10, ANT 3.2.40.
4 That one of the 'four elements' which is the natural abode of a being; (hence) appropriate or natural surroundings or sphere ANT 5.2.90 above The element they liv'd in, WIV 4.2.178, TN 3.4.124.

eleven and twenty long adj. phr. Exactly suitable, fitting SHR 4.2.57 That teacheth tricks eleven and twenty long.
⇨ An allusion to the card game 'one-and-thirty'.

elf vb. Twist, tangle LR 2.3.10 elf all my hair in knots.

elf-locks n. (pl.) Tangled mass of hair supposed to be due to the agency of elves ROM 1.4.90 the elf-locks in foul sluttish hairs (Q1 Elfelocks; Qq 2-3, F1 Elklocks).

elf-skin adj. (used contemptuously) A thin person 1H4 2.4.244 you starveling, you elf-skin.
⇨ F elke-skin; Qq 1-2 elsskin; Qq 3-5 elfskin; Hanmer eel-skin.

eliad see OEILLADE.

ell n. Measure of length, about 30cm. ROM 2.4.84 an ell broad!, ERR 3.2.110.

else adv. (sometimes used elliptically)
1 Anything besides, such like JN 2.1.276 Bastards, and else.
2 Elsewhere, in another place or direction TGV 4.2.124 since the substance of your perfect self Is else devoted, ERR 5.1.50.
3 In addition HAM 1.4.33 His virtues else.
4 'If you don't believe it', 'if it is not believed' JN 4.1.107 the fire is dead with grief...See else yourself.
5 nor else Nor MND 5.1.224 A lion fell, nor else no lion's dam; or else or SHR 4.1.159 Will you give thanks, sweet Kate, or else shall I?, R3 3.1.72

elvish-marked adj. Marked at birth by malignant fairies R3 1.3.227 Thou elvish-mark'd, abortive ...hog!

emballing n. Investiture with the ball or orb as the emblem or royalty H8 2.3.47 for little England you'ld venture an emballing.
⇨ Prob. used in indelicate sense.

embarquement n. Laying under embargo; (hence) hindrance, impediment COR 1.10.22 Embarquements all of fury.

embassade n. Mission as an ambassador 3H6 4.3.32 When you disgrac'd me in my embassade.

embassador n. (frequent form in Eliz. English of) Ambassador MC 2.9.92 an embassador of love, 2H6 3.2.276, HAM 4.6.10.

embassage n.
1 Errand ADO 2.1.269 do you any embassage to the Pigmies.
2 Message R3 2.1.3 expect an embassage, LLL 5.2.98, SON 26.3.

embassy n.
1 Mission of an ambassador LLL 1.1.134 comes in embassy, JN 1.1.99, TRO 4.5.216.
2 Ambassador's commission or message JN 1.1.6 hear the embassy, LLL 2.1.3, H5 1.1.95.
3 Message (esp. of love) WT 1.1.28 loving embassies, WIV 3.5.129 (F1 ambassie), TN 1.5.166.

embattle vb.
1 Draw up in battle array WIV 2.2.251 her defences, which now are...embattled against me, JN 4.2.200, H5 4.2.14.
2 (intr.) Be drawn up ANT 4.9.3 we shall embattle By th' second hour.

embayed ppl. adj. Locked in a bay OTH 2.1.18 If that the Turkish fleet Be not...embay'd.

ember-eve n. The vigil of an Ember day PER 1.Gower.6 On ember-eves and holy-ales.

emblaze vb. Set forth, as with a heraldic device 2H6 4.10.71 emblaze the honour.

embodied ppl. adj. Unite to another as if in one body AWW 5.3.173 I by vow am so embodied yours.

emboss vb. Drive (a hunted animal) to extremity, close around, corner; (fig.) AWW 3.6.99 we have almost emboss'd him.

embossed ppl. adj.[1] Driven to extremity, foaming at the mouth from exhaustion SHR Ind. 1.17 the poor cur, is emboss'd, ANT 4.13.3.

embossed ppl. adj.[2] Swollen, tumid AYL 2.7.67 embossed sores, 1H4 3.3.157, LR 2.4.224.

embound vb. Confine JN 4.3.137 Which was embounded in this beauteous clay.

embowel vb. Disembowel 1H4 5.4.109 Embowell'd will I see thee by and by, R3 5.2.10; (fig.) empty AWW 1.3.241 Embowell'd of their doctrine.

embrace *vb.*
1 Welcome back as a friend, companion, or the like COR 4.7.10 *I did embrace him*, TIM 1.1.44, CYM 3.4.176; welcome or receive (a thing) joyfully ADO 1.1.103 *You do embrace your charge too willingly*, TN 2.5.147, R2 1.3.89; (hence) submit to with resignation WIV 5.5.237 *What cannot be eschew'd must be embrac'd*, MAC 3.1.136.
2 Cherish, devot oneself to, cling to AYL 1.2.179 *embrace your own safety*, R2 1.3.184, ANT 3.13.56.
3 Encircle, surround COR 5.2.7. *You'll see your Rome embrac'd with fire*; (fig.) TMP 5.1.214 *Let grief and sorrow still embrace his heart*, TRO 3.2.35.
embraced *ppl. adj.* Cherished MV 2.8.52 *quicken his embraced heaviness.*
embrasure *n.* Embrace TRO 4.4.37 *Our lock'd embrasures.*
embrue (var. of) IMBRUE.
eminence *n.*
1 Advantage TRO 2.3.255 *You should not have the eminence of him.*
2 Acknowledgement of superiority, homage MAC 3.2.31 *Present him eminence both with eye and tongue.*
emmew See ENEW.
empale (var. of) IMPALE.
emperal *n.* Emperor TIT 4.3.94 *one of the Emperal's men.*
emperial *adj.* (var. of) Imperial TIT 4.4.40 *and your mistriship be emperial.*
empery *n.*
1 Status or position of emperor TIT 1.1.201 *thou shalt obtain and ask the empery.*
2 Absolute dominion H5 1.2.226 *Ruling in...empery O'er France*, TIT 1.1.19.
3 Territory of an emperor or absolute ruler, empire R3 3.7.136 *Your right of birth, your empery*, CYM 1.6.120.
emphasis *n.*
1 Intensity of feeling HAM 5.1.255 *whose grief Bears such an emphasis.*
2 Emphatic expression ANT 1.5.68 *Be chok'd with such another emphasis!*
empire *n.* Position, or status of an emperor TIT 1.1.183 *name thee in election for the empire.*
empiric *n.* An ancient sect of physicians who drew their rules of practice entirely from experience; (hence) quack AWW 2.1.122 *To prostitute our pastcure malady To empirics.*
empiricutic *adj.* Empirical, quackish COR 2.1.117 *The most sovereign prescription in Galen is but empiricutic.*
◇ Coined word put in the mouth of Menenius. Ff 1–2 *Emperickqutique*, Ff 3–4 *Empericktique*, whence some mod. edd. *empirictic.*
empleached (var. of) IMPLEACHED.
employ *vb.* Send (a person) with a commission somewhere ANT 5.2.70 *employ me to him*, CYM 2.3.63.
employment *n.*
1 Service JN 1.1.198 At your employment.
2 Purpose, use R2 1.1.90 *for lewd employments.*
empoison *vb.* Embitter, destroy ADO 3.1.86 *How much an ill word may empoison liking*, COR 5.6.10.
empty-hearted *adj.* Unfeeling LR 1.1.153 *Nor are those empty-hearted whose low sounds Reverb no hollowness.*
emulate *adj.* ambitious HAM 1.1.83 *a most emulate pride.*
emulation *n.*
1 Ambitious or jealous rivalry, contention between rivals or factions TRO 2.2.212 *emulation in the army crept*, JC 2.3.14, 1H6 4.1.113.
2 Grudge against the superiority of others, dislike

of those who are superior TRO 1.3.134 *an envious fear Of pale and bloodless emulation.*
emulator *n.* Disparager AYL 1.1.143 *an envious emulator of every man's good parts.*
emulous *adj.* (in a good sense) Ambitious TRO 4.1.29 *mine emulous honour*; (in a bad sense) envious TRO 2.3.773 *emulous factions.*
emure (var. of) IMMURE.
enact *n.* Purpose, resolution TIT 4.2.118 *The close enacts and counsels of thy heart.*
~ *vb.*
1 Ordain, decree MV 4.1.348 *It is enacted in the laws*, 1H6 5.4.123, LUC 529.
2 Act or play the part of (a character in a drama), represent dramatically HAM 3.2.103 *I did enact Julius Caesar*, TMP 4.1.121.
3 Accomplish, perform 1H6 1.1.122 *enacted wonders with his sword and lance*, R3 5.4.2.
enacture *n.* Performance, fulfilment, act HAM 3.2.197 *The violence of either grief or joy Their own enactures with themselves destroy* (Qq; Ff *en(n)actors*).
enamelled *ppl. adj.* Having naturally a hard, shiny surface MND 2.1.255 *the snake throws her enamell'd skin*, TGV 2.7.28, ERR 2.1.109.
enchafed *ppl. adj.* Excited, irritated CYM 4.2.174 *Their royal blood enchaf'd*; furious, stormy OTH 2.1.17 *the enchafed flood.*
enchant *vb.* (fig.) Influence as if by a charm, hold spellbound, attract as if by magic LC 89 *Each eye that saw him did enchant the mind*, 1H6 3.3.40, OTH 1.2.63.
enchanted *ppl. adj.* Invested with magical powers or properties TMP 5.1.112 *some enchanted trifle to abuse me*, MV 5.1.13.
enchantingly *adv.* 'As if under the influence of a charm' (Wright) AYL 1.1.168 *of all sorts enchantingly belov'd.*
enchantment *n.* (applied to a person) Enchantress WT 4.4.434 *And you, enchantment.*
enchased *ppl. adj.* Adorned as with gems 2H6 1.2.8 *Enchas'd with all the honours of the world*?
enclog *vb.* Hinder, encumber OTH 2.1.70 *enclog the guiltless keel.*
encompass *vb.* Outwit, take advantage of WIV 2.2.153 *have I encompass'd you*?
encompassment *n.* Circumvention, 'talking round' a subject HAM 2.1.10 *this encompassment and drift of question.*
encounter *n.*
1 Amatory meeting ADO 3.3.151 *this amiable encounter*, WIV 3.5.73, MM 3.1.251.
2 Accosting, address TGV 2.7.41 *The loose encounters of lascivious men.*
3 Style or manner of address, behaviour HAM 2.2.164 *Mark the encounter*, SHR 4.5.54, WT 3.2.49.
~ *vb.*
1 Go to meet ADO 1.1.98 *The fashion of the world is to avoid cost, and you encounter it*; (used bombastically) go towards TN 3.1.74 *Will you encounter the house*?
2 Light upon upon, befall WT 2.1.20 *Good time encounter her!*, CYM 1.6.112.
encounterer *n.* One who encounters; (hence) 'forward', presumptuous person TRO 4.5.58 *these encounterers, so glib of tongue.*
encrimsoned *ppl. adj.* Red like crimson LC 201 *the encrimson'd mood.*
encumbered *ppl. adj.* Folded HAM 1.5.174 *With arms encumb'red.*
end *n.*
1 Extremity AYL 2.6.10 *at the arm's end* (i.e. at arm's lenght), TN 5.1.285.

2 Fragment, tag, quotation R3 1.3.336 *odd old ends stol'n forth of holy writ*, ADO 1.1.288.

3 Conclusion, close; *an end* no more AWW 2.2.63, COR 5.3.171; (elliptically) *and there an end* this shall be the end, that's all there is about it TGV 1.3.65, MAC 3.4.79; *have (an) end* be finished, completed, concluded SON 2.9.6, LR 5.1.45, ANT 1.2.91; *for an end* to cut the matter short, to conclude COR 2.1.244.

4 Death, destruction R3 2.1.15 *Either of you to be the other's end*, 2H4 4.4.130; *take his end* meet his death 2H6 1.4.33.

5 Purpose H8 1.1.171 *to as much end As give a crutch to th' dead*, MM 1.3.5, ANT 3.2.37.

6 Ultimate cause H8 2.1.40 *The Cardinal is the end of this*.

7 *still an end* Continually TGV 4.4.62 *A slave, that still an end turns me to shame*.

end *vb.* Gather in, harvest, garner (a crop); (fig.) COR 5.6.36 *holp to reap the fame Which he did end all his* (i.e. garner as all his own).

end-all *n.* That which ends all MAC 1.7.5 *this blow Might be the be-all and the end-all here*.
⇨ In Yorks. dial. in the sense of 'finishing stroke'.

endart *vb.* Shoot as a dart ROM 1.3.98 *no more deep will I endart mine eye*.

endeared *ppl. adj.*
1 Enhanced in value, made more precious SON 31.1 *Thy bosom is endeared with all hearts*.
2 Bound by obligation TIM 3.2.31 *so much endear'd to that lord*, 2H4 2.3.11.

ender *n.* Conclusion, ending; (hence) death LC 222 *you, my origin and ender* (i.e. source of my life and death).

ending *n.* Death H5 4.1.156 *the particular endings of his soldiers*, JN 5.7.5, LUC 1612.
~ *ppl. adj.* Dying 2H4 4.5.79 *the ending father*, TGV 3.1.242 *ending anthem* (i.e. requiem).

endue See INDUE.

endurance *n.*
1 Patience ADO 2.1.239 *past the endurance of a block*.
2 Imprisonment, durance H8 5.1.121 *to have heard you Without endurance further* (F1 *indurance*).
3 Hardship PER 5.1.136 *the thousand part Of my endurance* (i.e. what I have endured).

endure *vb.*
1 Continue, last TN 2.3.52 *Youth's a stuff will not endure*, SON 153.6.
2 Remain COR 1.6.58 *To endure friends*, LUC 1659.

enemy *n.* The devil MM 2.2.179 *O cunning enemy, that...With saints dost bait thy hook!*, TN 2.2.28.
~ *adj.* Hostile LR 5.3.221 *his enemy king*, MV 4.1.447, COR 4.4.24.

enew *vb.* (term of falconry) Drive (prey) into the water MM 3.1.90 *Whose...visage and deliberate word..follies doth enew As falcon doth the fowl* (F1 *emmew*).

enfeoff *vb.* Hand over as a fief; (hence, fig.) surrender 1H4 3.2.69 *Enfeoff'd himself to popularity*.

enfoldings *n.* (pl.) Clothes WT 4.4.731 *the air of the court in these enfoldings*.

enforce *vb.*
1 Drive by force H5 4.7.62 *as swift as stones Enforced from the old Assyrian slings*, 2H4 4.1.71.
2 Obtain or produce by physical or moral force AYL 2.3.32 *enforce A thievish living*, LLL 3.1.75, TIM 5.4.45.
3 Use force upon JC 4.3.112 *flint...much enforced, shows a hasty spark;* (hence) press upon, urge, charge (a person) COR 3.3.3 *Enforce him with his envy to the people*.
4 Urge the performance of R2 4.1.90 *we will enforce his trial*, COR 3.3.21, LR 2.3.20.

5 Put forward strongly, lay stress upon JC 3.2.40 *his glory not extenuated...; nor his offences enforc'd*, MM 5.1.266, COR 2.3.219.
6 Obtrude (a thing) AWW 2.1.126 *enforce mine office*.

enforced *ppl. adj.*
1 Ravished, violated CYM 4.1.17 *thy mistress enforc'd*, MND 3.1.200, LUC 668.
2 Compelled: (involuntary) MV 5.1.240 *this enforced wrong*, JN 5.2.30, LR 1.2.124; (constrained, forced) R3 3.5.9 *enforced smiles*, JC 4.2.21.

enforcedly *adv.* Under compulsion TIM 4.3.241 *thou Dost it enforcedly*.

enforcement *n.*
1 Compulsion, constraint R3 3.7.233 *Your mere enforcement shall acquittance me*, 2H4 1.1.120, AWW 5.3.107.
2 Violation R3 3.7.8 *his enforcement of the city wives*.

enfranched *ppl. adj.* Enfranchised, freed ANT 3.13.149 *my enfranched bondman*.

enfranchise *vb.*
1 Set free from political subjection ANT 1.1.23 *Take in that kingdom, and enfranchise that*.
2 Release from confinement TIT 4.2.125 *from...where you imprisoned were He is enfranchised*, ADO 1.3.33, TIM 1.1.106.

enfreed *ppl. adj.* Set free, freed, released TRO 4.1.39 *the enfreed Antenor*.

enfreedom *vb.* Set free, release LLL 3.1.124 *enfreedoming thy person*.

engage *vb.*
1 Pledge, pawn, mortgage TIM 2.2.146 *Let all my land be sold.—'Tis all engag'd*; keep as a hostage 1H4 4.3.95 *to be engag'd in Wales, There without ransom to lie forfeited*.
2 Pledge (one's word, honour, etc.) 1H4 2.4.514 *I will engage my word to thee*, ERR 5.1.162, AYL 5.4.166.
3 Bind by a promise or undertaking R2 1.3.17 *engaged by my oath*, ADO 4.1.331, LLL 4.3.176.
4 Entangle, involve HAM 3.3.69 *O limed soul, that struggling to be free Art more engag'd!*, 2H4 1.1.180.
5 Enlist TRO 2.2.124 *a quarrel Which hath our several honours all engag'd*; (refl.) embark on an enterprise ANT 4.7.1 *Retire, we have engag'd ourselves too far*, TRO 5.5.39.

engagement *n.* What one is pledged to do JC 2.1.307 *All my engagements I will construe to thee*.

engaol *vb.* Imprison R2 1.3.166 *you have engaol'd my tongue*.

engild *vb.* Brighten with golden light MND 3.2.187 *engilds the night*.

engine *n.*
1 Artifice, contrivance, device, plot AWW 3.5.19 *their promises, enticements...and all these engines of lust*, OTH 4.2.216, TIT 2.1.123.
2 Mechanical contrivance, machine, implement TGV 3.1.138 *And here an engine fit for my proceeding* (i.e. a rope ladder); (fig.) VEN 367 *the engine of her thoughts* (i.e. her tongue); instrument of warfare OTH 3.3.355 *mortal engines* (i.e. cannon), TMP 2.1.162, TRO 2.3.134; instrument of torture LR 1.4.268 *Which, like an engine, wrench'd my frame of nature*.

engineer, enginer *n.*
1 Inventor OTH 2.1.65 *in th' essential vesture of creation Does tire the engineer* (F1 *Ingeniuer*).
2 Maker of military engines or works HAM 3.4.206 *have the engineer Hoist with his own petar* (Q2 *enginer*), TRO 2.3.8.

engirt *vb.* Surround, encircle 2H6 5.1.99 *engirt these brows*, VEN 364.

~ *ppl. adj.* Surrounded, beset LUC 1173 *corrupted,...engirt with...infamy*, 2H6 3.1.200.

English *vb.* Put into plain English, describe in plain terms WIV 1.3.48 *to be English'd rightly.*

englut *vb.* Swallow up TIM 2.2.166 *How many prodigal bits have slaves...englutted!*, H5 4.3.83, OTH 1.3.57.

engraffed, ingraffed *ppl. adj.*
1 Implanted, firmly fixed OTH 2.3.140 *one of an engraffed infirmity* (Q1 *ingraft*), LR 1.1.301 (Ff 1-2 *ingraffed*; Qq 1-2 *ingraffed*).
2 Closely attached 2H4 2.2.63 *you have been...so much engraff'd to Falstaff.*

engrafted, ingrafted *ppl. adj.* Implanted, firmly fixed or rooted JC 2.1.184 *the ingrafted love he bears to Caesar*, SON 37.8.

engross, ingross *vb.*
1 Write out in a legal or fair hand R3 3.6.2 *in a set hand fairly is engross'd.*
2 Get together, collect ANT 3.7.36 *people Ingross'd by swift impress*, 1H4 3.2.148, 2H4 4.5.70.
3 Gain exclusive possession of, monopolize WIV 2.2.196 *engross'd opportunities to meet her*, AWW 3.2.65, SON 133.6.
4 Fatten R3 3.7.76 *to engross his idle body.*

engrossing *ppl. adj.* Monopolizing ROM 5.3.115 *A dateless bargain to engrossing death.*

engrossment *n.* Quantity collected, accumulation 2H4 4.5.79 *This bitter taste Yields his engrossments to the ending father.*

enjoin *vb.* Bind (a person) as by an oath or obligation (to do something) ADO 5.1.278 *any heavy weight That he'll enjoin me to*, MV 2.9.9, WT 3.3.53.

enjoined *ppl. adj.* Bound by oath AWW 3.5.94 *enjoin'd penitents.*

enjoy *vb.* Have the possession or use of JN 2.1.240 *king o'er him and all that he enjoys*, ANT 2.6.78, SON 29.8; (absol.) R2 2.4.14 *to enjoy by rage and war.*

enjoyer *n.* Possessor SON 75.5 *proud as an enjoyer.*

enkindle *vb.* (fig.) Incite MAC 1.3.121 *enkindle you unto the crown.*

enlard *vb.* Fatten TRO 2.3.195 *enlard his fat-already pride.*

enlarge *vb.*
1 Widen the limits or scope of, give free scope to, extend WIV 2.2.222 *she enlargeth her mirth*, AYL 3.2.143, HAM 5.1.226; give vent to, give free expression to JC 4.2.46 *enlarge your griefs.*
2 Set at liberty, free H5 2.2.40 *Enlarge the man committed yesterday*, TN 5.1.278.

enlargement *n.*
1 Release from confinement LLL 3.1.5 *take this key, give enlargement to the swain*, 1H4 3.1.30, 1H6 2.5.30.
2 Freedom of action CYM 2.3.120 *curb'd from that enlargement.*

enlighten *vb.* Shed lustre upon SON 152.11 *to enlighten thee gave eyes to blindness.*

enlink *vb.* Connect H5 3.3.18 *Enlink'd to waste and desolation.*

enmesh *vb.* Entangle OTH 2.3.362 *the net That shall enmesh them all.*

enmew See ENEW.

enormity *n.* Irregularity, monstrous wickedness COR 2.1.16 *In what enormity is Martius poor in...?*

enormous *adj.* Disordered, irregular LR 2.2.169 *this enormous state.*

enow *adj.* (pl. form of) Enough ANT 1.4.11 *evils enow*, MV 3.5.22, MAC 4.2.57.

enpatron *vb.* Have under one's patronage LC 224 *Since I their altar, you enpatron me.*

enpierced *ppl. adj.* Pierced ROM 1.4.19 *I am too sore*

enpierced *with his shaft* (F1, Qq *enpearced*, Ff 2-3 *impearced*, F4 *impierced*).

enraged *ppl. adj.*
1 Maddened with love or desire, ardent ADO 2.3.100 *she loves him with an enrag'd affection*, VEN 29.
2 Fevered, heated 2H4 1.1.144 *my limbs,...being now enrag'd with grief.*

enrank *vb.* Draw up in battle array 1H6 1.1.115 *enrank his men.*

enrapt *ppl. adj.* (fig.) Carried away TRO 5.3.65 *like a prophet suddenly enrapt.*

enridged *ppl. adj.* Thrown into ridges LR 4.6.71 *waved like the enridged sea* (Qq 1-2; F1 *enraged*).

enring *vb.* Encircle as with rings MND 4.1.44 *Enrings the barky fingers of the elm.*

enrol *vb.* Write on a roll or parchment LLL 1.1.38 *Which I hope well is not enrolled there*, MM 1.2.166, JC 3.2.38.

enrooted *ppl. adj.* Entangled root with root 2H4 4.1.205 *His foes are so enrooted with his friends.*

enround *vb.* Surround H5 4.Ch.36 *How dread an army hath enrounded him.*

enscheduled *ppl. adj.* Written down H5 5.2.73 *Whose tenures...you have enschedul'd briefly in your hands.*

ensconce, insconce *vb.*
1 Shelter behind or within a 'sconce', earthwork, or fortification; (fig.) WIV 2.2.26 *you...will ensconce your rags...under the shelter of your honour!*, ERR 2.2.38, LUC 1515.
2 (refl.) Place oneself in a position of concealment or security WIV 3.3.89 *I will ensconce me behind the arras.*

enseamed *ppl. adj.* Loaded with grease, greased; (fig.) HAM 3.4.92 *an enseamed bed.*

ensear *vb.* Dry up TIM 4.3.187 *Ensear thy fertile and conceptious womb.*

enshield *ppl. adj.* Shielded MM 2.4.80 *an enshield beauty.*

ensinewed, insinewed *ppl. adj.* Joined as by strong sinews 2H4 4.1.170 *ensinewed to this action.*

enskied *ppl. adj.* Placed in heaven MM 1.4.34 *a thing enskied, and sainted.*

enstate, instate *vb.* Endow, invest MM 5.1.424 *We do enstate and widow you with all.*

ensteeped *ppl. adj.* Immersed, lying under water OTH 2.1.70 *Traitors ensteep'd to enclog the guiltless keel.*

ensue *vb.*
1 Follow upon, succeed LUC 502 *repentant tears ensue the deed*, R2 2.1.197.
2 Follow as a logical conclusion AYL 1.3.31 *Doth it therefore ensue that you should love his son dearly?*
3 *what of her ensues* What becomes of her WT 4.1.25.

entail *n.* Succession of estate AWW 4.3.279 *cut th' entail from all remainders.*
~ *vb.*
1 Bestow as an inalienable possession 3H6 1.1.194 *I here entail The crown to thee and thine heirs.*
2 Appoint as heir 3H6 1.1.235 *To entail him and his heirs unto the crown.*

entame *vb.* Subdue AYL 3.5.48 *can entame my spirits to your worship.*

enter *n.* Entrance on the stage LLL 5.1.134 *his enter and exit.*
~ *vb.*
1 (intr.) Bind oneself by a bond, etc. ERR 4.4.125 *I am here ent'red in bond for you*, R2 5.2.65; engage in OTH 3.3.411 *I am ent'red in this cause*, ADO 2.3.194.
2 Engage in (conversation) 1H6 3.1.63 *Must your bold verdict enter talk with lords?*

3 Introduce, admit (to) ANT 4.14.113 *This sword...Shall enter me with him.*

4 Instruct, initiate COR 1.2.2 *they...are ent'red in our counsels.*

⟡ AWW 2.1.6 *well-ent'red soldiers* (i.e. properly initiated soldiers): see MAN-ENT'RED.

5 Bring (an action before the court in due form) 2H4 2.1.1 *Have you ent'red the action?*

enterlude See INTERLUDE.

entertain *n.* Reception PER 1.1.119 *your entertain shall be As doth befit our honour.*

~ *vb.*

1 Keep up, maintain (a state of things) MM 3.1.74 *Lest thou a feverous life shouldst entertain,* MV 1.1.90, LUC 1514.

2 Take into one's service ADO 1.3.58 *Being entertain'd for a perfumer,* TGV 2.4.104, JC 5.5.60.

3 Treat LR 1.4.58 *your Highness is not entertain'd...as you were wont,* WIV 2.1.86, SHR 2.1.250.

4 Engage (a person's attention or thoughts) WIV 2.1.67 *entertain him with hope,* WT 4.4.53.

5 Occupy, while away (time) LUC 1361 *The weary time she cannot entertain.*

6 Engage (an enemy) H5 1.2.111 *could entertain With half their forces the full pride of France.*

7 Receive, accept ERR 3.1.120 *Since mine own doors refuse to entertain me,* AYL 3.2.416, R3 1.4.132.

entertainer *n.* One who harbours or cherishes (sentiments, feelings etc.) TMP 2.1.17 *to th' entertainer...Dolour comes.*

entertainment *n.*

1 Maintenance of a person in one's service or employ AWW 4.1.15 *strangers i' th' adversary's entertainment,* COR 4.3.44, ANT 4.6.16.

2 Way of spending (time) LLL 5.1.118 *some entertainment of time.*

3 Reception (of persons), manner of reception COR 4.5.9 *I have deserv'd no better entertainment,* SHR 2.1.54; (hence) treatment MM 3.2.321 *the entertainment of death,* TMP 1.2.462, COR 4.5.9; *John Drum's entertainment* (i.e. 'to hale a man in by the heade, and thrust him out by both the shoulders' (Holinshed)), AWW 3.6.38.

4 Accommodation for guests, (esp.) provision for the table AYL 2.4.72 *if...gold Can...buy entertainment,* WT 1.1.8, LR 2.4.206; meal, repast TIM 1.2.147 *Set a fair fashion on our entertainment.*

entire *adj.*

1 Unmixed, pure 2H4 2.4.325 *pure fear and entire cowardice,* LR 1.1.240.

2 Unfeigned, sincere SHR 4.2.23 *heard Of your entire affection.*

entirely *adv.*

1 Without intermission MM 4.2.150 *many days entirely drunk.*

2 Heartily, sincerely ADO 3.1.37 *loves Beatrice so entirely,* MV 3.2.225, AWW 1.3.100.

entitled *ppl. adj. entitled in* Having a claim to or upon LLL 5.2.812 *Neither entitled in the other's heart* (F *intitled*), SON 37.7.

entituled See INTITULED.

entrails *n.* (pl.) (fig.) Interior TIT 2.3.230 *the ragged entrails of this pit.*

entrance *n.*

1 (fig.) Mouth 1H4 1.1.5 *the thirsty entrance of this soil* (i.e. parched surface).

2 Entrance fee SHR 2.1.54 *for an entrance to my entertainment.*

entranced *ppl. adj.* Unconscious, in a swoon PER 3.2.94 *She hath not been Entranc'd above five hours.*

entreasured *ppl. adj.* Stored up 2H4 3.1.85 *in their seeds...lie entreasured* (Q *intreasured*), PER 3.2.65.

entreat *n.* Entreaty TIT 1.1.449 *Yield at entreats* (F1 *intreats*), R3 3.7.225 (F1 *entreaties*).

~ *vb.*

1 Treat R2 3.1.37 *fairly let her be entreated,* 2H6 2.4.81, 3H6 1.1.271.

2 Beguile, pass (the time) ROM 4.1.40 *we must entreat the time alone.*

3 Enter into negotiations 2H6 4.4.9 *I'll send some holy bishop to entreat;* (hence) intercede LR 3.3.5 *entreat for him,* AYL 4.3.72.

entreatment *n.* Negotiation after a truce; (hence) conversation, interview HAM 1.3.122 *Set your entreatments at a higher rate Than a command to parle.*

entrench *vb.* Cut AWW 2.1.44 *this very sword entrench'd it.*

enurned See INURNED.

envenom *vb.* Poison JN 3.1.63 *Envenom him with words,* AYL 2.3.15.

envious *adj.* Malicious, spiteful LLL 1.1.100 *an envious sneaping frost,* R2 2.1.62, 2H6 3.1.157.

enviously *adv.* Maliciously HAM 4.5.6 *Spurns enviously at straws.*

envy *n.* Ill-will, malice MV 4.1.10 *Out of his envy's reach,* TMP 1.2.258, TN 2.1.29.

~ *vb.* Show malice towards COR 3.3.57 *Rather than envy you.*

enwheel *vb.* Encircle OTH 2.1.87 *the grace of heaven...Enwheel thee round!*

enwombed *ppl. adj.* Born of (my) womb AWW 1.3.144 *those That were enwombed mine.*

Ephesian *n.* Boon companion WIV 4.5.18 *thine Ephesian calls,* 2H4 2.2.150.

epicure *n.* One who gives himself to sensual pleasures and luxury; sybarite, glutton MAC 5.3.8 *mingle with the English epicures,* ANT 2.7.52.

Epicurean *adj.*

1 Sensual WIV 2.2.287 *Epicurean rascal.*

2 Suited to the taste of an epicure ANT 2.1.24 *epicurean cooks.*

Epicurism *n.* Sensuality, pursuit of pleasure and luxurious living LR 1.4.244 *Epicurism and lust Makes it more like a tavern or a brothel.*

epigram *n.* Short poem ending with a witty or ingenious turn of thought ADO 5.4.102 *Dost thou think I care for a satire or an epigram?*

epileptic *adj.* Affected by epilepsy; (hence) grimacing, grinning LR 2.2.81 *A plague upon your epileptic visage! Smile you my speeches...?*

epithet *n.* Term, phrase, expression ADO 5.2.66 *Suffer love! A good epithet!* (F1 *epithite*), LLL 4.2.8, OTH 1.1.14.

epitheton *n.* (earlier form of 'epithet') Adjective, indicating some characteristic quality or attribute LLL 1.2.14 *a congruent epitheton appertaining to thy young days.*

epitome *n.* Summary, abstract; (hence) representation in miniature COR 5.3.68 *This is a poor epitome of yours.*

equal *adj.*

1 Forming a perfect balance or counterpoise MM 2.4.68 *equal poise* (i.e. equipoise), MV 1.3.149 *an equal pound* (i.e. an exact pound), 2H4 4.1.67; (fig.) equally balanced AYL 1.2.178 *a more equal enterprise,* LUC 1791.

2 Fair, just, impartial H8 2.4.18 *equal friendship and proceeding,* LLL 4.3.381.

~ *vb.* Cope 2H4 1.3.67 *to equal with the king.*

equinoctial *n.* Equator TN 2.3.24 *passing the equinoctial of Queubus.*

equinox *n.* Equal length of days and nights; (fig.) exact counterpart OTH 2.3.124 *his vice, 'Tis to his virtue a just equinox.*

equipage *n.*

1 The state of being equipped, equipment SON 32.12 *of better equipage.*

equivalent 91 estridge

2 (orig. military; transf.) Things in general, goods Wiv 2.2.1 *I will retort the sum in equipage.*

equivalent *adj.* Equal in power Per 5.1.91 *ancestors Who stood equivalent with mighty kings.*

equivocal *adj.* Expressing himself in ambiguous terms AWW 5.3.250 *an equivocal companion.*

erection *n.* (blunder for) Direction Wiv 3.5.40 *they mistook their erection.*

erewhile *adv.* A short while ago AYL 2.4.89 *that you saw here but erewhile*, LLL 4.1.97, MND 3.2.274.

ergo [L.] Therefore Err 4.3.56 *ergo, light wenches will burn*, MV 2.2.57, AWW 1.3.49.

eringo *n.* Candied root of sea-holly, Eryngium maritimum, formerly used as a sweetmeat and regarded as an aphrodisiac Wiv 5.5.20 *let it...hail kissing-comfits, and snow eringoes.*

ermite See HERMIT.

ern See EARN.

errant *adj.*
1 Wandering Tro 1.3.9 *errant from his course of growth.*
▷ See ARRANT.

erring *ppl. adj.* Wandering AYL 3.2.130 *his erring pilgrimage*, Oth 1.3.355, Ham 1.1.154.

erroneous *adj.* Deviating from the path of right; (hence) criminal 3H6 2.5.90 *Erroneous, mutinous, and unnatural*; misguided R3 1.4.195 *Erroneous vassals.*

error *n.*
1 Transgression, wrongdoing Son 117.9 *Book both my wilfulness and errors down*, TGV 5.4.111, LLL 5.2.771.
2 Wandering, specifically of planetary motion Oth 5.2.109 *the...error of the moon.*
3 Lie, deception Tro 5.3.111 *My love with words and errors still she feeds.*

erst *adv.* Once upon a time, formerly H5 5.2.48 *The ...mead, that erst brought...forth the...cowslip*, Per 1.1.49, AYL 3.5.95.

escape *n.*
1 Sally (of wit) MM 4.1.62 *thousand escapes of wit.*
2 Outrageous transgression Tit 4.2.113 *this foul escape*, Oth 1.3.197.

escapen, escapend *pres. pple.* ne aught escapend Nothing escaping Per 2.Gower.36.

eschew *vb.* Keep clear of, escape Wiv 5.5.237 *What cannot be eschew'd must be embrac'd.*

escot *vb.* Pay a reckoning for, maintain Ham 2.2.346 *Who maintains 'em? How are they escoted?*

esile See EISEL.

esperance *n.* Hope Tro 5.2.121 *An esperance so...strong*, Lr 4.1.4.
▷ At 1H4 5.2.96 *Now Esperance! Percy!* and set on, the motto of the Percy family used as a battle cry.

espial *n.* Spy 1H6 1.4.8 *The Prince's espials have informed me*, Ham 3.1.32.

espouse *vb.* Unite in marriage 2H6 1.1.9 *I...was espous'd*; (fig.) H5 4.6.26 *espoused to death*, Luc 20.

espy *vb.* Watch Tit 2.3.48 *we are espied.*

esquire *n.* Man belonging to the higher order of English gentry, ranking immediately below a knight H5 1.1.14 *Six thousand and two hundred good esquires*, 2H4 3.2.57, 2H6 4.10.43.

essay *n.* Trial, proof Lr 1.2.45 *an essay or taste of my virtue*, Son 110.8

essence *n.*
1 Life, existence PhT 26 *So they loved as love in twain Had the essence but in one.*
2 Entity Oth 4.1.16 *Her honour is an essence that's not seen.*
3 Nature MM 2.2.120 *[man's] glassy essence.*
4 (One's) very being TGV 3.1.182 *She is my essence.*

essential *adj.* Real Oth 2.1.64 *in th' essential vesture of creation Does tire the engineer.*

essentially *adv.*
1 In one's essential nature, fundamentally 2H6 5.2.39 *nor he that loves himself Hath not essentially but by circumstance The name of valour*; in fact, really Ham 3.4.187 *I essentially am not in madness, But mad in craft.*
2 *essentially made* Endowed with the intrinsic genuine 'essential' qualities 1H4 2.4.492 *Thou art essentially made, without seeming so.*
▷ Disputed text; some edd. read *essentially mad*, in which case *essentially* operates in sense 1 'in fact, really'.

establish *vb.*
1 Settle (property) upon Mac 1.4.37 *We will establish our estate upon Our eldest.*
2 Determine, settle, enact, ordain 2H6 3.1.317 *our authority is his consent, And what we do establish he confirms*, MV 4.1.219, H5 1.2.50.

estate *n.*
1 State or condition Lr 5.3.210 *seen me in my worst estate*, MV 3.2.316, Cor 2.1.114; good or settled condition Mac 5.5.49 *wish th' estate o' th' world were now undone.*
2 Status, rank, dignity, (esp.) high rank MV 2.9.41 *O that estates, degrees, and offices Were not deriv'd corruptly!*, Mac 1.4.37, Ham 3.2.261.
3 Class or rank of persons R3 3.7.213 *egally indeed to all estates*, LLL 5.2.845.
4 Property, possessions, fortune H8 1.1.82 *sicken'd their estates*, MV 1.1.43, 2H4 1.3.53.
5 Administration of government H8 2.2.69 *business of estate*, WT 4.4.400, Jn 4.2.128.
~ *vb.* Settle or bestow MND 1.1.98 *all my right of her I do estate unto Demetrius*, Tmp 4.1.85, MND 1.1.98.

esteem *n.*
1 Supposed or estimated value AWW 5.3.1 *We lost a jewel of her, and our esteem Was made much poorer by it.*
2 Account, worth 1H6 3.4.8 *prisoners of esteem*, Cym 5.5.253.
3 Opinion, judgement LLL 2.1.4 *precious in the world's esteem*, MND 3.2.294, Mac 1.7.43.
4 Favourable opinion H8 4.1.109 *in much esteem with th' King*, 2H6 5.2.22.
~ *vb.* Estimate the value of, value Cym 1.4.78 *What do you esteem it at?*, Shr 1.1.119.

esteeming *n.* Value, worth Son 102.3 *That love is merchandiz'd whose rich esteeming The owner's tongue doth publish everywhere.*

estimable *adj.*
1 Valuable MV 1.3.166 *A pound of men's flesh...Is not so estimable...As flesh of muttons.*
2 *estimable wonder* Admiring judgement TN 2.1.26 *I could not with such estimable wonder overfar believe that.*

estimate *n.*
1 Valuation, value AWW 2.1.180 *all that life can rate Worth name of life in thee hath estimate* (i.e. has a claim to be considered in appraising thee), Tro 2.2.54, Tim 1.1.14.
2 Repute, reputation R2 2.3.56 *None else of name and noble estimate*, Cor 3.3.114.

estimation *n.*
1 Value, worth AWW 5.3.4 *lack'd the sense to know Her estimation*, Ado 2.2.24, MV 2.7.26.
2 Thing of value Cym 1.4.91 *your brace of unprizable estimations*, Tro 2.2.91.
3 Repute, reputation TGV 2.4.56 *of worth and worthy estimation*, H5 3.6.14, Ham 2.2.334.
4 Conjecture 1H4 1.3.272 *I speak not this in estimation, As what I think might be.*

estridge *n.* Goshawk Ant 3.13.196 *The dove will peck the estridge*, 1H4 4.1.98.

Et bonum quo antiquius eo melius [L.] And a good thing is the better for being older PER 1. Gower.10.

Et tu, Brute? [L.] You too, Brutus? JC 3.1.77.

eternal *adj.*
1 *Would be eternal in our triumph* Would be recorded eternally ANT 5.1.66.
2 *eternal blazon* Revelation of eternity HAM 1.5.21.
~ *adv.* Eternally, forever WT 1.2.65 *to be boy eternal.*

eterne *adj.* Eternal MAC 3.2.38 *nature's copy's not eterne*, HAM 2.2.490.

Ethiop *n.* Ethiopian; (hence) black person TGV 2.6.26 *a swarthy Ethiop*, ADO 5.4.38.
~ *adj.* Black AYL 4.3.35 *Ethiop words.*

eunuch *n.* Eunuch flute, a type of mirliton, in playing which the performer hums through a hole in the side COR 3.2.114 *a pipe Small as an eunuch.*

even *n. the even of it* The plain truth, the long and the short of it H5 2.1.122.
~ *vb.*
1 (pass.) Be even or quits OTH 2.1.299 *Till I am even'd with him.*
2 Act up to, keep pace with, be equal to CYM 3.4.181 *we'll even All that good time will give us*, AWW 1.3.3.
3 *even o'er* Fill in LR 4.7.79 *make him even o'er the time he has lost.*
~ *adj.*
1 Uniform R2 3.4.36 *All must be even in our government.*
2 Direct, straightforward HAM 2.2.287 *be even and direct with me*, H5 4.8.109.
3 Exact, precise AWW 5.3.326 *the even truth.*
4 Equable, unruffled H8 3.1.166 *A soul as even as a calm*, 1H4 1.3.285, H5 2.2.3; steadfast JC 2.1.133 *The even virtue of our enterprise.*
5 Equally balanced MAC 3.4.10 *Both sides are even*, COR 4.7.37; (hence) impartial MV 2.7.25 *weigh thy value with an even hand.*
6 *make even* Get straight, straighten out AYL 5.4.18 *I have promis'd to make all this matter even.*
7 *make it even* Carry it out, accomplish it, fulfil it AWW 2.1.191 *Make thy demand.—But will you make it even?*
~ *adv.*
1 In exact agreement CYM 1.4.44 *to go even with what I heard*, TN 5.1.239.
2 Equally WIV 4.6.27 *even strong against that match And firm for Doctor Caius.*
3 Exactly, precisely, just VEN 59 *Even so*, MV 1.3.49, AYL 1.1.85.
4 (of time) At the same moment, at the same time, just SON 71.12 *let your love even with my life decay*, JC 1.3.27, TMP 2.1.311.
5 Quite, fully COR 1.4.57 *Thou wast a soldier Even to Cato's wish*, WIV 4.6.12.
6 Used to emphasize the identity of a person, thing or circumstance MV 5.1.242 *I swear to thee, even by thine own fair eyes*, TMP 3.1.14, TGV 2.1.44.

even(-)Christen, even(-)Christian *n.* Fellow-Christian(s) HAM 5.1.28 *more than their even-Christian* (F1; Q2 *even Christen*).

even-handed *adj.* Impartial MAC 1.7.10 *even-handed justice.*

evening mass *n.* (prob.) Mass said in the afternoon ROM 4.1.38 *shall I come to you at evening mass?*

evenly *adv.*
1 In a straight line, directly 1H4 3.1.102 *run In a new channel fair and evenly*, H5 2.4.91.
2 In an even direction or position ADO 2.2.7 *ranges evenly with mine.*

even-plashed See EVEN-PLEACHED.

even-pleached *adj.* Evenly interwoven H5 5.2.42 *her hedges even-pleach'd.*

event *n.*
1 Outcome, issue, consequence MM 3.2.238 *leave we him to his events* (i.e. the issue of his affairs), TMP 1.2.117, SHR 3.2.127.
2 Fate in store for a person 2H6 3.1.326 *you and I must talk of that event.*

ever, e'er *adv.*
1 Throughout all time, eternally TMP 4.1.122 *Let me live here ever*, MAC 5.3.21.
2 (with *how* and *what* forming indefinite relatives) *how dearly ever parted* However richly endowed TRO 3.3.96; *what bloody business ever* whatever the bloodthirsty task be OTH 3.3.469.

ever-during *adj.* Everlasting LUC 224 *an ever-during blame.*

ever-fired *adj.* Always burning OTH 2.1.15 *quench the guards of th' ever-fired Pole* (Qq; Ff *ever-fixed*).

everlasting *n.*
1 *the Everlasting* God HAM 1.2.131 *that the Everlasting had not fix'd His canon 'gainst self-slaughter!*
2 Material used in 16C and 17C for the dress of sergeants and catchpoles, app. identical with DURANCE; (attrib.) ERR 4.2.33 *an everlasting garment* (i.e. a garment of everlasting or durance).

evermore *adv.* (with neg.) At any future time SON 36.9 *not evermore*, H8 2.4.132.

every *n.* Every one ANT 1.2.38 *every of your wishes*, AYL 5.4.172.
~ *adj.*
1 Either, each H8 2.4.52 *a wise council to them Of every realm.*
2 (with pl. n.) All severally TMP 5.1.249 *every These happen'd accidents.*

evidence *n.* Witness or witnesses 2H6 3.2.21 *true evidence of good esteem*, ADO 4.1.37, LR 3.6.35; (treated as pl.) R3 1.4.192 *Where are the evidence?*; *came evidence* came as a witness LUC 1650.

evident *adj.* Indubitable, certain, conclusive COR 5.3.112 *We must find An evident calamity*, CYM 2.4.120.

evil *n.[1]* Offensive building or structure; (hence) brothel MM 2.2.171 *Shall we desire to raze the sanctuary And pitch our evils there?*

evil *n.[2]*
1 Sin, crime LUC 972 *his committed evil*, MM 2.2.91, R3 1.2.79.
2 Misfortune, calamity TN 2.1.6 *I may bear my evils alone*, H8 2.1.141, JC 2.2.81.
3 Disease COR 1.1.179 *A sick man's appetite, who desires most that Which would increase his evil*, WT 2.3.56, JN 3.4.114; sore AYL 2.7.67 *all th' embossed sores, and headed evils*; *the evil* the King's evil, scrofula MAC 4.3.146.
~ *adj.*
1 Ill-boding TRO 1.3.92 *the ill aspects of planets evil* (F1; Q *influence of evill Planets*).
2 Unwholesome R3 1.1.139 *an evil diet.*
~ *adv.* Evilly, in an evil manner, wrongly H8 1.2.207 *were he evil used*, LR 1.1.166, 3H6 4.7.84.

evil-eyed *adj.* Maliciously disposed CYM 1.1.72 *you shall not find me...Evil-ey'd unto you.*

evilly *adv.*
1 With difficulty, reluctantly, impatiently JN 3.4.149 *This act so evilly borne.*
2 Inappropriately TIM 4.3.461 *good deeds evilly bestow'd!*

evitate *vb.* Avoid WIV 5.5.228 *she doth evitate and shun A thousand...hours.*

exact *adj. the exact* The actual AWW 3.6.61 *seldom attributed to the true and exact performer.*

exacting *n.* Exaction MM 3.2.281 *So disguise shall...Pay with falsehood false exacting.*

exactly *adv.*
1 Perfectly, completely HAM 1.2.200 *Armed at point exactly.*
2 In express terms R2 1.1.140 *exactly begg'd Your Grace's pardon.*

exalt *vb.* (refl.) Be elated with pride LR 5.3.67 *In his own grace he doth exalt himself.*

exalted *ppl. adj.* Raised, high JC 1.1.60 *till the lowest stream Do kiss the most exalted shores of all.*

examination *n.* Deposition, or the paper on which it is written H8 1.1.116 *Where's his examination?*

example *n.* Parallel case in the past, precedent JN 3.4.13 *Such temperate order in so fierce a cause, Doth want example.*
~ *vb.*
1 Give an example of LLL 3.1.83 *I will example it,* SON 84.4.
2 Furnish a precedent for LLL 4.3.122 *Ill, to example ill, Would from my forehead wipe a perjur'd note,* JN 4.3.56, TRO 1.3.132.
3 Furnish (one) with instances TIM 4.3.435 *I'll example you with thievery.*

exceed *vb.* (intr.) Be greater or better (than something else), be superior or pre-eminent LUC 229 *The guilt being great, the fear doth still exceed,* ADO 3.4.17, PER 2.3.16.

excellent *adj.* Surpassing, exceptionally great, notable, exceeding; (used in a bad sense) R3 4.4.52 *That excellent grand tyrant,* TIT 2.3.7, LR 1.2.118.
~ *adv.* Eminently, exceedingly ADO 3.1.98 *an excellent good name,* HAM 2.2.174.

excellently *adv.* Exceedingly ADO 3.4.13 *I like the new tire within excellently,* TRO 4.1.25.

except *vb.*
1 (intr.) Make objection TN 1.3.7 *let her except before excepted,* TGV 1.3.83.
▷ In TN, a legal phrase 'exceptis excipiendis' is perverted.
2 (trans.) Object to, take exception to R2 1.1.72 *royalty, Which fear...makes thee to except,* JC 2.1.281, SON 147.8.

exception *n.*
1 Objection (to a person's status or fitness) H5 4.2.25 *'Tis positive against all exceptions...That our superfluous lackeys...were enow.*
2 Disapproval, dislike, dissatisfaction AWW 1.2.40 *Exception bid him speak,* H5 2.4.34, HAM 5.2.231; *take exceptions at,* to disapprove, find fault with TGV 5.2.3 *she takes exceptions at your person,* TN 1.3.6, 1H6 4.1.105.

exceptless *adj.* Making no exception TIM 4.3.495 *Forgive my general and exceptless rashness.*

excess *n.* Interest MV 1.3.62 *neither lend nor borrow By taking nor by giving of excess.*

exchange *n.*
1 Reciprocal giving and receiving ROM 2.2.127 *Th' exchange of thy love's faithful vow for mine; in right great exchange in exchange for persons of great importance* TRO 3.3.21; (in fencing) pass HAM 5.2.269 *in answer of the third exchange.*
2 Money transaction by means of bills SHR 4.2.89 *I have bills for money by exchange.*
3 Change; substitution of one word for another LLL 4.2.41 *Th' allusion holds in the exchange* (i.e. the substitution of Adam's name for Cain's); transmutation, alteration MV 2.6.35 *I am much asham'd of my exchange.*
4 Thing offered or given in exchange LR 5.3.97 *There's my exchange,* ROM 2.6.4.
~ *vb.*
1 Obtain in exchange LLL 4.1.82 *What shalt thou exchange for rags?*

2 Change SON 109.7 *not with the time exchang'd.*

excitement *n.* Incentive, encouragement TRO 1.3.182 *Excitements to the field,* HAM 4.4.58.

exclaim *n.* Outcry TRO 5.3.91 *You are amaz'd...at her exclaim, R2 1.2.2.*
~ *vb.*
1 *exclaim against* Protest against, rail at OTH 2.3.310 *exclaim no more against it,* HAM 2.2.351, LUC 757.
2 *exclaim on* Accuse loudly, blame R3 3.3.16 *she exclaim'd on Hastings,* MV 3.2.174, VEN 930.

exclamation *n.* Complaint, reproach H8 1.2.52 *you suffer Too hard an exclamation,* JN 2.1.558, R3 4.4.154.

excrement *n.* Outgrowth (of hair) LLL 5.1.104 *with my excrement, with my mustachio,* ERR 2.2.78, HAM 3.4.121; *valour's excrement* a brave man's beard MV 3.2.87.

excursion *n.* (stage direction) Rush, sally 1H6 3.2.SD Enter Talbot in an excursion, H5 4.4.SD.

excuse *n.* Indulgence, pardon COR 1.3.102 *Give me excuse, good madam,* LUC 235, SHR Ind.2.124.
~ *vb.*
1 Seek to extenuate (a fault); (absol.) MND 5.1.356 *Never excuse;* (with clause) ERR 3.1.92 *she will well excuse Why at this time the doors are made against you.*
2 Maintain the innocence of; (refl.) clear oneself R3 1.2.82 *leisure to excuse myself,* 2H6 1.3.178.
3 Decline with apologies, beg off from TGV 1.3.71 *be in readiness to go—Excuse it not.*

execute *vb.*
1 Carry into effect; (hence) give practical effect to (a passion, etc.), allow to operate R3 1.4.71 *execute thy wrath,* TMP 1.2.104, LLL 5.2.845; bring (a weapon) into play, wield TRO 5.7.6 *In fellest manner execute your arms.*
2 Inflict capital punishment on; (hence) kill, put to death 1H6 1.4.36 *Whom with my bare fists I would execute,* R2 4.1.82.

execution *n.*
1 The giving of practical effect to a passion, etc.; exercise (of powers) 3H6 2.2.111 *The execution of my...heart Upon that Clifford,* OTH 3.3.466, LR 1.1.137.
2 Slaughter, destruction TRO 5.5.38 *hath done today Mad and fantastic execution,* MAC 1.2.18, TIT 2.3.36.

executioner *n.* Murderer R3 1.2.185 *though I wish thy death, I will not be thy executioner,* 2H6 3.1.276.

executor *n.*
1 Performer, agent TMP 3.1.13 *such baseness Had never like executor.*
2 Executioner H5 1.2.203 *The sad-ey'd justice...Delivering o'er to executors pale The...drone.*

exempt *ppl. adj.* Cut off, debarred, excluded ERR 2.2.171 *you are from me exempt,* AYL 2.1.15, TIM 4.2.31; *exempt from envy* immune from the attacks of slander 3H6 3.3.127.

exempted *pa. pple. Exempted be from me* Far be it from me AWW 2.1.195.

exequies *n.* (pl.) Funeral rites 1H6 3.2.133 *see his exequies fulfill'd in Roan.*

exercise *n.*
1 Habitual practice or employment 3H6 4.6.85 *hunting was his daily exercise,* WT 1.2.166, PER 1.4.38.
2 Acquired skill HAM 4.7.97 *art and exercise in your defence.*
3 Religious devotion or act of worship R3 3.7.64 *his holy exercise,* WT 3.2.341, OTH 3.4.41.
4 Preaching, discourse R3 3.2.110 *I am in your debt for your last exercise.*

94

extent

exhalation n. Meteor H8 3.2.226 *fall Like a bright exhalation in the evening*, Jn 3.4.153, JC 2.1.44.

exhale vb.[1] (in the language of Pistol) Draw (your sword) H5 2.1.62 *death is near, Therefore exhale.*

exhale vb.[2] Draw forth R3 1.2.58 *thy presence that exhales this blood From...empty veins;* (esp. of the sun drawing up vapours and thereby producing meteors) Rom 3.5.13 *some meteor that the sun exhal'd;* (fig.) LLL 4.3.68 *fair sun...Exhal'st this vapour-vow.*

exhaled ppl. adj. Drawn forth by the sun 1H4 5.1.19 *an exhal'd meteor.*
▷ See EXHALE vb.[2]

exhaust vb. Draw forth Tim 4.3.120 *the babe, Whose dimpled smiles from fools exhaust their mercy.*

exhibit vb. (technical term) Submit (a petition, bill) for inspection or consideration Wiv 2.1.28 *exhibit a bill in the parliament*, MM 4.4.10, 1H6 3.1.150.
▷ MV 2.3.10 *tears exhibit my tongue*: (blunder for) inhibit.

exhibiter, exhibitor n. Presenter of a bill H5 1.1.74 *cherishing th' exhibiters against us.*

exhibition n.
1 Allowance of money for a person's support TGV 1.3.69 *What maintenance he...receives, Like exhibition thou shalt have from me*, Lr 1.2.25, Oth 1.3.237.
2 Gift, present Oth 4.3.74 *I would not do such a thing for...any petty exhibition.*

exigent n. State of pressing need, emergency, strait JC 5.1.19 *Why do you cross me in this exigent?*, Ant 4.14.63; (hence) last pinch, end 1H6 2.5.9 *These eyes...Wax dim, as drawing to their exigent.*

exion n. (blunder for) Action 2H4 2.1.30 *since my exion is ent'red.*

exorcizer n. One who calls up spirits Cym 4.2.276 *No exorciser harm thee* (F1 *Exorcisor*).

exorcism n. The calling forth (of a spirit), conjuration 2H6 1.4.4 *behold and hear our exorcisms.*

exorcist n. One who calls up spirits JC 2.1.323 *Thou, like an exorcist, hast conjur'd up My mortified spirit*, AWW 5.3.304.

expect n. Expectation Tro 1.3.70 *be't of less expect.*
~ vb. Wait for, await 1H6 5.3.145 *here I will expect thy coming*, TGV 1.1.54, MV 5.1.49.

expectance n. State of waiting to know (something) Tro 4.5.146 *expectance...What further you will do.*

expectancy n.
1 Expectation Oth 2.1.41 *every minute is expectancy Of more arrivance.*
2 Source of hope Ham 3.1.152 *Th' expectancy and rose of the fair state* (F1; Qq *expectation*).

expectation n.
1 Waiting JC 1.1.41 *with patient expectation*, 2H4 5.2.31, Lr 4.4.23.
2 *full of expectation* Full of promise, hopeful, promising 1H4 2.3.19 *a good plot...and full of expectation.*
3 *note of expectation* List of expected guests Mac 3.3.10.

expecter n. One who waits Tro 4.5.156 *the expecters of our Troyan part.*

expedience n.
1 Speed, dispatch R2 2.1.287 *making hither with all due expedience*, H5 4.3.70.
2 Enterprise, expedition Ant 1.2.178 *our expedience to the Queen*, 1H4 1.1.33.

expedient adj. Speedy, expeditious Jn 4.2.268 *with all expedient haste*, R2 1.4.39, 2H6 3.1.288.

expediently adv. Expeditiously AYL 3.1.18 *Do this expediently, and turn him going.*

expedition n. March, progress R3 4.4.136 *Who intercepts me in my expedition?*; (abstract) motion, progress H5 2.2.191 *Putting it straight in expedition.*

▷ H5 3.2.77 *of great expedition and knowledge in th' aunchiant wars*: blunder on the part of Fluellen.

expense n.
1 Spending, (esp.) extravagant expenditure, squandering Son 94.6 *husband nature's riches from expense*, Wiv 2.2.141, Lr 2.1.100.
2 Expenditure (of breath) LLL 5.2.522 *expense of thy royal sweet breath.*
3 Loss (of a possession) Son 30.8 *th' expense of many a vanish'd sight.*

experimental adj. Pertaining to experience Ado 4.1.166 *experimental seal* (i.e. the stamp of experience).

expert adj. Tried, proved by experience Oth 2.1.49 *his pilot* [is] *Of very expert and approv'd allowance.*

expiate vb. (said of death) End Son 22.4 *Then look I death my days should expiate.*
~ ppl. adj. (of an appointed time) Ended; (hence) fully come R3 3.3.24 *Make haste, the hour of death is expiate.*

expire vb. Bring to an end, conclude Rom 1.4.109 *Shall...expire the term Of a despised life.*

explication n. Explanation LLL 4.2.14 *in way, of explication.*

exploit n. Military enterprise AWW 1.2.17 *sick For breathing and exploit*; *in exploit* in action AWW 4.1.38.

expostulate vb. Set forth one's views, discourse, discuss Ham 2.2.86 *to expostulate What majesty should be*, TGV 3.1.253, Oth 4.1.205.

expostulation n. Discourse, speech, talk Tro 4.4.60 *we must use expostulation kindly.*

exposture n. Exposure Cor 4.1.36 *a wild exposture to each chance...before thee.*

express vb. Manifest, reveal Ham 1.3.71 *Costly thy habit...But not express'd in fancy*, Shr 2.1.77, 2H6 1.1.18.

express adj. Exact, fitted to its purpose, consummate Ham 2.2.305 *in form and moving how express and admirable.*

expressive adj. Open and emphatic in expressing sentiments AWW 2.1.52 *Use a more spacious ceremony...Be more expressive to them.*

expressure n.
1 Expression TN 2.3.157 *the expressure of his eye*, Tro 3.3.204.
2 Imprint, image Wiv 5.5.67 *Th' expressure that it bears, green let it be.*

expulse vb. Expel, banish 1H6 3.3.25 *For ever should they be expuls'd from France.*

exsufflicate ppl. adj. Inflated Oth 3.3.182 *exsufflicate and blown surmises* (F1, Q1 *exufflicate*).

extant adj. (of time) Present Tro 4.5.168 *this extant moment.*

extemporal adj. Impromptu, extempore 1H6 3.1.6 *extemporal speech*, LLL 1.2.183.

extemporally adv. Impromptu, extempore Ven 836 *sings extemporally*, Ant 5.2.217.

extend vb.
1 Prolong in duration Mac 3.4.56 *You shall offend him and extend his passion.*
2 Magnify in presentation, exaggerate Cym 1.4.21 *wonderfully to extend him; extend him within himself* enlarge on him only within the bounds of his merits Cym 1.1.25.
3 Seize upon, take possession of Ant 1.2.101 *hath with his Parthian force Extended Asia.*

extent n.
1 Seizure of lands in execution of a writ AYL 3.1.17 *Make an extent upon his house and lands.*
2 Attack, assault TN 4.1.53 *this uncivil and unjust extent.*

3 Exercise, performance (of justice, kindness) Tit 4.4.3 *for the extent Of egall justice,* Ham 2.2.373.

extenuate *vb.*
1 Mitigate (a law) MND 1.1.120 *the law…(Which by no means we may extenuate).*
2 Depreciate, disparage JC 3.2.39 *his glory not extenuated.*

extenuation *n.* Mitigation 1H4 3.2.22 *such extenuation let me beg.*

extermine *vb.* Put an end to, destroy AYL 3.5.89 *your sorrow and my grief Were both extermin'd.*

extern *n.* Outward appearance, exterior Son 125.2 *With my extern the outward honouring.*
~ *adj.* External, outward Oth 1.1.63 *my outward action doth demonstrate The native act…of my heart In complement extern.*

extinct *pa. pple.* Extinguished, quenched R2 1.3.222 *My…light Shall be extinct with age and endless night,* Ham 1.3.118.

extincted *ppl. adj.* Extinguished, quenched Oth 2.1.81 *Give renew'd fire to our extincted spirits.*

extincture *n.* Extinction LC 294 *cold modesty, hot wrath, Both fire from hence and chill extincture hath.*

extirp *vb.* Root out, extirpate MM 3.2.102 *it is impossible to extirp it quite,* 1H6 3.3.24.

extirpate *vb.* Drive completely *out of* Tmp 1.2.125 *extirpate me and mine Out of the dukedom.*

extort *vb.* Torture, wring MND 3.2.160 *extort A poor soul's patience.*

extracting *ppl. adj.* That draws out or takes away TN 5.1.281 *A most extracting frenzy of mine own From my remembrance clearly banish'd his* (i.e. took remembrance of his frenzy out of my mind).
▷ Perh. error for 'distracting' (Onions).

extraught *pa. pple.* 'Extracted', descended 3H6 2.2.142 *knowing whence thou art extraught.*

extravagancy *n.* Vagrancy TN 2.1.12 *my determinate voyage is mere extravagancy.*

extravagant *adj.* Straying, roaming, vagrant Ham 1.1.154 *Th' extravagant and erring spirit,* LLL 4.2.66, Oth 1.1.136.

extremity *n.*
1 Extreme or utmost degree LR 5.3.208 *would…top extremity,* Err 1.1.141, Luc 969.
2 Extreme severity or rigour Err 5.1.308 *O time's extremity,* WT 5.2.119, JC 2.1.31.
3 Extravagance Wiv 4.2.73 *devise something; any extremity.*

exufflicate See EXSUFFLICATE.

eyas *n.* Young hawk taken from the nest for the purpose of training, or one whose training is in-complete; (fig.) Ham 2.2.339 *an aery of children, little eyases* (F1 *Yases*).

eyas-musket *n.* Young male sparrow-hawk; (fig., used jocularly of a sprightly child) Wiv 3.3.22 *How now, my eyas-musket.*

eye *n.* (pl. *eyne* and *eyes*)
1 *put the finger in the eye and weep* (fig.) Play the child Err 2.2.204.
2 (fig. attributed to heavenly bodies) *eyes of light* Stars MND 3.2.188; *the eye of heaven* the sun Son 18.5.
3 Sight, view Tmp 2.1.127 *banish'd from your eye,* H8 1.1.30, Mac 3.1.124; *tended her i' th' eyes* waited in her sight Ant 2.2.207; *within the eye of honour* within the scope of honour's vision, within the limits of the honourable MV 1.1.137.
4 Look, glance 1H4 1.3.143 *on my face he turn'd an eye of death; have an eye of* watch Ham 2.2.290; *throw out our eyes for* look out for Oth 2.1.38; *change, mingle eyes* exchange (amorous) glances Tmp 1.2.442, Ant 3.13.156.
5 Slight shade, tinge Tmp 2.1.56 *tawny—With an eye of green in't,* Ham 1.3.128.
6 The hole in the bowl in which the lead for the bias was inserted Jn 2.1.583 *this same bias …Clapp'd on the outward eye of fickle France* (with quibble on the sense 'organ of sight': *outward eye* the physical eye as distinct from the inward eye of conscience).
~ *vb.* Appear to the eye Ant 1.3.97 *they do not Eye well to you.*

eye-beam *n.* Glance LLL 4.3.27 *thy eye-beams, when their fresh rays have smote The night of dew.*

eye-drop *n.* Tear 2H4 4.5.87 *tyranny…Would, by beholding him, have wash'd his knife With gentle eye-drops.*

eye-glass *n.* Crystalline lens of the eye WT 1.2.268 *your eye-glass Is thicker than a cuckold's horn.*

eye-offending *adj.*
1 Hurting the eye TN 1.1.29 *eye-offending brine.*
2 Unsightly Jn 3.1.47 *foul moles and eye-offending marks.*

eyestrings *n.* (pl.) Muscles, nerves, or tendons of the eye, supposed to crack at death or loss of sight Cym 1.3.17 *I would have broke mine eye-strings, crack'd them.*

eye-wink *n.* Look, glance Wiv 2.2.71 *they could never get an eye-wink of her.*

eyliad See OEILLADE.

eyrie (var. of) AERIE.

eysell See EISEL.

F

fa *n.* The fourth note of the scale LLL 4.2.100 *Ut, re, sol, la, mi, fa.*
~ *vb.* (jocularly) Rom 4.5.119 *I'll re you, I'll fa you. Do you note me?,* Shr 1.2.17.

fable *n.* Falsehood Err 4.4.73 *Sans fable.*

fabric *n.* Building Cor 3.1.246 *manhood is call'd foolery when it stands Against a falling fabric.*

face *n.*
1 (fig., of immaterial things) Appearance Jn 5.2.88 *to know the face of right,* JC 5.1.10, LR 3.1.20.
2 *full of face* Beautiful Per 1.Gower.23 *buxom, blithe, and full of face.*
3 *turn thy face* Depart Jn 5.2.159.
4 *from face to foot* From head to foot Cor 2.2.108.

~ *vb.*
1 Show a false face, maintain a false appearance 1H6 5.3.142 *Suffolk doth not flatter, face, or feign.*
2 Brave, bully Shr 4.3.124 *Face me out* brazen out H5 3.2.33 *'a faces it out, but fights not,* Tro 2.1.289; *face down* brazenly insist or maintain to a person's face (that…) Err 3.1.6 *here's a villain that would face me down He met me on the mart; face out of* exclude impudently from TN 4.2.93 *to face me out of my wits* (i.e. brazenly deny that I am sane), H5 3.7.82.
3 Give countenance to R2 4.1.285 *the face which fac'd so many follies* (perh. with quibble on sense 2 'brazen out' and sense 4).

4 Trim, put a facing or trimming on SHR 4.3.122 *Thou hast fac'd many things*; (fig.) 1H4 5.1.74 *To face the garment of rebellion With some fine colour.*
faced *ppl. adj.* Patched 1H4 4.2.31 *an old faced ancient* (F1; see FEAZED).
face(-)royal *n.* Face stamped on the coin called a 'royal' 2H4 1.2.24 *He may keep it still at a face royal, for a barber shall never earn sixpence out of it* (i.e. he may keep it at the full value of a royal; with quibble on 'kingly face').
facinerious *adj.* Infamous, vile AWW 2.3.29 *of a most facinerious spirit.*
facing *n.* Trimming MM 3.2.10 *furr'd with fox and lambskins too, to signify that craft, being richer than innocency, stands for the facing.*
fact *n.*
1 Deed, esp. evil deed, crime 1H6 4.1.30 *this fact was infamous*, MAC 3.6.10, MM 4.2.136.
2 *in the fact* In the very act 2H6 2.1.169 *apprehended in the fact.*
faction *n.*
1 Class, set (of persons) TRO 2.1.119 *the faction of fools*, TGV 4.1.37.
2 Self-interested or turbulent party strife, factious spirit, dissension 1H4 4.1.67 *turn the tide of fearful faction*, AYL 5.1.55, ANT 1.3.48; factious quarrel or intrigue TIM 3.5.72 *commit outrages And cherish factions.*
factionary *adj.* Active as a partisan COR 5.2.29 *always factionary on the party of your general.*
factious *adj.* Rebellious, seditious, given to factions 3H6 1.1.74 *Thou factious Duke of York*, 1H6 4.1.113, TRO 1.3.191.
factor *n.* Agent ANT 2.6.10 *factors for the gods.*
faculty *n.*
1 Personal quality, disposition H8 1.2.73 *which neither know My faculties nor person.*
2 Active quality or virtue, essential or peculiar nature (of a thing) JC 1.3.67 *all these things change from their...preformed faculties, To monstrous quality*, AWW 1.3.226.
3 (pl.) Powers, abilities HAM 2.2.304 *What a piece of work is man,...how infinite in faculties*, MAC 1.7.17, 2H4 2.4.251.
fadge *vb.* Fit, be suitable; (hence) succeed, come off TN 2.2.33 *How will this fadge?*, LLL 5.1.147.
fading *n.* Refrain WT 4.4.195 *such delicate burthens of dildos and fadings.*
▷ 'With a fading' was the refrain of an indelicate song.
fadom (var. of) FATHOM.
fail *n.*
1 Failure, omission WT 2.3.170 *the fail Of any point*, H8 2.4.199.
2 Failure of issue H8 1.2.145 *How grounded he his title to the crown Upon our fail?*
3 Fault, offence CYM 3.4.64 *Goodly and gallant shall be false and perjur'd From thy great fail*, TIM 5.1.148 (F1 *fall*).
~ *vb.*
1 Die H8 1.2.184 *the King in his last sickness fail'd.*
2 Be at fault, err AWW 3.1.15 *to fail As often as I guess'd*, MM 3.2.257, MND 3.2.93.
3 Leave undone, omit CYM 3.4.178 *I will never fail Beginning nor supplyment*, MAC 3.6.21, LR 2.4.142.
fain *adj.* Glad, pleased 2H6 2.1.8 *man and birds are fain of climbing high*, 1H6 3.2.114; glad under the circumstances TGV 1.1.120 *I perceive I must be fain to bear with you*, 2H4 2.1.153; (hence) obliged, forced LR 4.7.37 *wast thou fain...To hovel thee with swine...?*
~ *adv.* (always with would) Gladly, willingly TGV 2.1.174 *I...would fain have meat*, TMP 1.1.67, AYL 1.2.160.

faining See FEIGNING.
faint *vb.*
1 Lose heart VEN 569 *faints not like a pale-fac'd coward*, JN 5.7.78, R5 5.3.172; (impersonal) *it faints me* I am depressed H8 2.3.103.
2 Become feeble MND 2.2.35 *you faint with wand'ring*, AYL 2.4.75, LUC 1543.
~ *adj.*
1 Inactive, inert, timid TIM 3.1.54 *such a faint and milky heart*, LR 1.4.68, CYM 3.2.55.
2 Spiritless, weak-spirited VEN 401 *Who is so faint that dares not...?*, 3H6 5.4.51, LUC 1209.
3 Weak, feeble MV 1.1.125 *my faint means*, H5 1.1.16, ROM 4.3.15.
fainting *ppl. adj.* That faints, becomes feeble 1H6 2.5.95 *my fainting words*, 1H6 2.5.40.
faintly *adv.*
1 Like a coward, timidly LUC 740 *He faintly flies.*
2 Weakly, feebly ROM 1.4.7 *faintly spoke After the prompter*, VEN 482, R2 1.3.281; (hence) mildly LR 1.2.174 *I have told you...but faintly.*
3 Half-heartedly, without conviction OTH 4.1.112 *he denies it faintly*, R2 5.3.103, COR 5.1.66.
fair *n.*
1 That which is fair, beautiful thing ROM 1.1.231 *they hide the fair*, CYM 1.6.38, LUC 780.
2 A woman, esp. a beloved woman H5 5.2.167 *speak, my fair*, LLL 5.2.37; (applied to a man) VEN 208 *Speak, fair,...or else be mute.*
3 Beauty ERR 2.1.98 *My decayed fair*, LLL 4.1.17, SON 18.7.
~ *vb.* Beautify SON 127.6 *Fairing the foul.*
~ *adj.*
1 Virtuous, pure ROM 1.1.221 *She is too fair...To merit bliss by making me despair*, TGV 4.2.5, LUC 346.
2 (as a form of courteous address) LLL 5.2.310 *Fair sir, God save you!*, 3H6 2.1.95.
3 Plainly to be seen, distinct ROM 1.1.207 *A right fair mark...is soonest hit.*
4 *Fair daylight* Broad daylight LR 4.7.51.
~ *adv.*
1 Courteously, kindly R3 4.4.152 *entreat me fair*, ERR 3.2.181, MV 4.1.275; on good terms 2H4 2.1.193 *tap for tap, and so part fair.*
2 Equitably, honestly 1H4 5.1.114 *We offer fair, take it advisedly*, MM 3.1.140.
3 Becomingly, fittingly COR 4.6.118 *You have crafted fair!*, SHR 2.1.17.
4 Auspiciously, favourably, fortunately ERR 4.1.91 *the merry wind Blows fair from land*, MV 2.1.20, R2 2.2.123; *Fair be to you* Prosperity attend you TRO 3.1.43.
5 Softly, gently 1H4 3.1.102 *fair and evenly*, ADO 5.4.72; *stand fair* Stand still TRO 4.5.235.
fairest-boding *adj.* Of happiest omen R3 5.3.227 *sweetest sleep and fairest-boding dreams.*
fair-faced *adj.* Of fair complexion ADO 3.1.61 *If fair-fac'd...; If black...;* fair in appearance JN 2.1.417 *peace and fair-fac'd league.*
fairing *n.* Complimentary gift LLL 5.2.2 *we shall be rich...If fairings come thus plentifully in.*
fairly *adv.*
1 Beautifully, handsomely SHR 1.2.145 *I'll have them very fairly bound*, TRO 1.3.84, ROM 3.2.84; in beauty SON 5.4 *which fairly doth excel*; in a neat or elegant hand R3 3.6.2 *Which in a set hand fairly is engross'd*, R3 3.6.2.
2 Courteously, respectfully PER 5.1.10 *greet him fairly*, ERR 5.1.233, TIM 1.2.184.
3 Becomingly, properly, honourably MV 1.1.128 *to come fairly off from the great debts*, COR 4.7.21, H8 1.4.31.

4 Auspiciously, favourably H5 5.2.10 *fairly met,* 1H4 5.3.29, MND 1.1.101.
5 Completely, fully, quite ROM 2.4.45 *you gave us the counterfeit fairly last night,* SHR 1.1.108.
fairness *n.* To *the fairness of my power* As fairly as I can COR 1.9.73.
fair play, fair-play *n.* Equitable conditions of intercourse or action, upright conduct JN 5.2.118 *According to the fair play of the world;* (attrib.) JN 5.1.67 *Send fair-play orders.*
fair-spoken *adj.* Of courteous or pleasant speech H8 4.2.52 *Exceeding wise, fair-spoken, and persuading.*
fairy *n.* Enchantress, charmer ANT 4.8.12 *this great fairy.*
fairy gold *n.* Money given by fairies, supposed to crumble away rapidly WT 3.3.123 *This is fairy gold, boy, and 'twill prove so.*
fairy time *n.* The period between midnight and the rising of the morning star MND 5.1.364 *Lovers, to bed, 'tis almost fairy time.*
faith *n.* Loyalty, fidelity MND 3.2.127 *Bearing the badge of faith to prove them true,* TGV 4.3.26, JC 3.1.137; (esp.) faithfulness in love, true love OTH 1.3.294 *My life upon her faith,* TGV 4.2.11, SON 152.3.
faithed *ppl. adj.* Believed in, credited LR 2.1.70 *Make thy words faith'd.*
faithful *adj.*
1 Believing (in religion) R3 1.4.4 *as I am a Christian faithful man,* H5 1.2.13.
2 True MM 4.3.126 *a faithful verity.*
3 Conscientious, thorough in the fulfilment of one's duty HAM 2.2.115 *I will be faithful.*
~ *adv.* Loyally PER 1.2.110 *Day serves not light more faithful than I'll be.*
faithfully *adv.*
1 Confidently TIM 3.2.41 *urge it half so faithfully,* JN 1.1.252.
2 Assuringly, convincingly AYL 2.7.192 *whisper'd faithfully,* ROM 2.2.94.
3 Truthfully, accurately, exactly MV 5.1.299 *answer all things faithfully* (a formula used in the Court of King's Bench), AWW 4.3.58, H5 1.2.43.
faithless *adj.*
1 Unbelieving MV 2.4.37 *a faithless Jew.*
2 Disloyal H8 2.1.123 *A...faithless service,* JN 2.1.230.
3 Not to be trusted MM 3.1.136 *O faithless coward!*
faitor *n.* Imposter, cheat 2H4 2.4.159 *down, dogs! down, faitors!* (Ff *Fates*; Q *faters*).
falchion *n.* Sword more or less curved with the edge on the convex side R3 1.2.94 *thy murd'rous falchion,* LUC 176, LR 5.3.277.
falcon *n.* Female hawk trained for the sport of hawking MAC 2.4.12 *A falcon, tow'ring in her pride of place,* VEN 1027, MM 3.1.91.
fall *n.*
1 Shedding (of blood) H5 1.2.25 *Without much fall of blood.*
2 Downward stroke (of a sword) R3 5.3.111 *crush down with a heavy fall The...helmets,* OTH 2.3.234.
3 Ebb of the tide; *at fall* at a low ebb; (fig.) TIM 2.2.205 *they are at fall, want treasure.*
4 Musical cadence TN 1.1.4 *a dying fall.*
5 Bout at wrestling AYL 1.2.204 *You shall try but one fall.*
~ *vb.*
1 (of a river) Discharge itself; (fig.) LUC 653 *Thou art...a sea,...And lo there falls into thy...flood ...dishonour.*
2 Shrink, become lean H5 5.2.159 *a good leg will fall.*
3 Become, come to be H8 2.1.35 *fell to himself* (i.e. regained self-control), JC 4.3.155, MV 4.1.266.

4 Let fall, drop TMP 2.1.296 *to fall it on Gonzalo,* AYL 3.5.5, R3 5.3.135; give birth to MV 1.3.88 *Who...did...Fall parti-colour'd lambs.*
5 Happen, come to pass JC 3.1.243 *I know not what may fall,* MM 4.2.178; turn out (in a particular way) MND 5.1.187 *it will fall pat as I told you,* HAM 4.7.70.
6 Happen to, befall ANT 3.7.39 *No disgrace Shall fall you,* LLL 2.1.124, VEN 472.
~ in combination
fall away FALL *vb.* sense 2 1H4 3.3.1 *am I not fall'n away vilely since this last action?,* 1H6 3.1.192. **fall down** Come to grief 2H4 4.2.44 *though we here fall down, We have supplies.* **fall from 1** Forsake the allegiance of, revolt from JN 3.1.320 *England, I will fall from thee,* ADO 1.1.255. **2** (pass.) Have forfeited, have lost AWW 5.1.12 *that you are not fall'n From the report,* H8 3.1.20, HAM 2.2.165. **fall in** Make up a quarrel TRO 3.1.103 *Falling in, after falling out, may make them three.* **fall into** Come within H8 3.2.340 *Fall into th' compass of a praemunire.* **fall off** Withdraw from allegiance, revolt 1H4 1.3.94 *He never did fall off.* **fall over** Desert JN 3.1.127 *And dost thou now fall over to my foes?* **fall to** Apply oneself to, set to (csp. eating or fighting) 1H6 3.1.89 *if we be forbidden stones, we'll fall to it with our teeth,* TMP 1.1.3, AYL 2.7.171. **fall upon** Burst in on ANT 2.2.75 *He fell upon me, ere admitted.*
fallacy *n.* Delusive notion, error ERR 2.2.186 *I'll entertain the offer'd fallacy.*
fallen-off *ppl. adj.* Revolted CYM 3.7.6 *The fall'n-off Britains.*
falliable See FALLIBLE.
fallible *adj.*
1 Liable to be erroneous MM 3.1.169 *hopes that are fallible.*
2 (blunder for) Infallible ANT 5.2.257 *this is most fallible, the worm's an odd worm* (Ff *falliable*).
falling-from *n.* Defection TIM 4.3.400 *the falling-from of his friends.*
falling sickness *n.* Epilepsy JC 1.2.254 *he hath the falling sickness.*
fallow *n.*
1 Arable land H5 5.2.54 *vineyards, fallows, meads.*
2 Ground ploughed and harrowed but left uncropped for a time MM 1.4.42 *That from the seedness the bare fallow brings to teeming foison.*
~ *adj.*[1] Uncultivated H5 5.2.44 *her fallow leas The darnel, hemlock...Doth root upon.*
fallow *adj.*[2] Of pale brownish or reddish yellow colour WIV 1.1.89 *your fallow greyhound.*
false *vb.* Betray their trust, become corrupt CYM 2.3.69 *makes Diana's rangers false themselves, yield up Their deer.*
~ *adj.*
1 Badly woven, hence producing an untrue tone JC 4.3.291 *The strings...are false.*
2 *false fire* A blank discharge of fire-arms; a fire made to deceive an enemy HAM 3.2.266 *What, frighted with false fire?* (F1; Q1 *fires*).
3 *false gallop* Canter; (fig.) ADO 3.4.94 *What pace is this that thy tongue keeps?—Not a false gallop?,* AYL 3.2.113 (perh. quibble on 'riding rhyme', the contemporary name for the Chaucerian heroic couplet).
4 *false generations* Illegitimate offspring WT 2.1.148 *I'll geld 'em all; fourteen they shall not see To bring false generations.*
~ *adv.* Falsely LR 1.4.233 *I should be false persuaded I had daughters,* PER 1.1.124, ADO 4.1.237; perfidiously CYM 3.4.114 *false struck,* ERR 2.2.142, MAC 1.5.21.
falsehood *n.*
1 Falseness, faithlessness, perfidy TGV 4.2.8 *my falsehood to my friend,* TMP 1.2.95, WT 3.2.141.

2 Deception, imposture MM 3.2.281 *Pay with false-hood false exacting*, ANT 1.1.40, SON 137.7.
3 Dishonesty TIM 2.2.157 *If you suspect my hus-bandry or falsehood*, SON 48.4.

falsely *adv.*
1 Wrongly, mistakenly JN 4.2.198 *slippers..falsely thrust on contrary feet*, OTH 5.2.117, SON 148.4.
2 Improperly R3 5.3.251 *England's chair, where he is falsely set.*
3 Perfidiously, treacherously MM 2.4.47 *Falsely to take away a life*, TMP 2.1.68, COR 3.1.60.

falsify *vb.* Prove to be ill-founded 1H4 1.2.211 *falsify men's hopes.*

falsing *ppl. adj.* Deceptive ERR 2.2.94 *not sure, in a thing falsing.*

fame *n.* Common talk or report, rumour 1H6 2.3.68 *thou art no less than fame hath bruited*, H8 1.4.66, ANT 2.2.163; (personified) ADO 2.1.214 *the part of Lady Fame; fame and envy* (hendiadys) *detested reputation* COR 1.8.4.
~ *vb.*
1 *fame for* Report, repute as 3H6 4.6.26 *Your Grace hath still been fam'd for virtuous.*
2 Make renowned or famous SON 84.11 *such a counterpart shall fame his wit*, TRO 2.3.243, JC 1.2.153.

familiar *n.*
1 Intimate friend LLL 5.1.96 *the King is a noble gentleman, and my familiar*, TIM 4.2.10, 2H4 2.2.133.
2 Familiar or attendant spirit (see *adj.* sense 4) 2H6 4.7.108 *he has a familiar under his tongue, he speaks not a' God's name*, LLL 1.2.172, 1H6 3.2.122.
~ *adj.*
1 Belonging to the household or family, service-able OTH 2.3.309 *good wine is a good familiar crea-ture*, WIV 1.1.20; pertaining to home, such as to make one feel at home H5 2.4.52 *haunted us in our familiar paths.*
2 Current, habitual, ordinary MM 1.4.31 *'tis my familiar sin With maids to seem the lapwing*, H5 4.3.52, WIV 1.3.46; (hence) trivial ADO 5.4.70 *let won-der seem familiar*, AWW 2.3.2.
3 Easily understood LLL 1.2.9 *a familiar demon-stration of the working*, TRO 3.3.113.
4 *familiar spirit* Demon supposed to be in associ-ation with or under the power of a man, and to attend at his call 1H6 5.3.10 *ye familiar spirits...Help me*, SON 86.9.

famine *n.* Hunger, starvation MAC 5.5.39 *Upon the next tree shall thou hang alive, Till famine cling thee*, CYM 3.6.19, 2H6 4.10.64.

famous *adj.* Notorious ANT 1.4.48 *famous pirates*, SHR 1.2.252, WT 3.3.12.

famoused *ppl. adj.* Renowned SON 25.9 *famoused for fight.*

famously *adv.*
1 With renown R3 2.3.19 *this land was famously enrich'd.*
2 Gloriously, splendidly COR 1.1.36 *what he hath done famously, he did it to that end.*

fan *n.* Motion of the air such as is made by a fan TRO 5.3.41 *the fan and wind of your fair sword.*
~ *vb.* Winnow; (fig.) test, try CYM 1.6.177 *The love I bear him Made me to fan you thus.*

fanatical *adj.* Extravagant LLL 5.1.18 *I abhor such fanatical phantasimes* (i.e. individuals with crazy but fixed notions).

fancy *n.*
1 Fancifulness, fantasticalness HAM 1.3.71 *Costly thy habit...But not express'd in fancy*, LLL 1.1.170.
2 Amorous inclination, love MV 3.2.63 *Tell me where is fancy bred*, AYL 3.5.29, TN 2.4.33; one in love LC 61 *this afflicted fancy.*

3 Musical composition in an impromptu style 2H4 3.2.318 *sung those tunes...and sware they were his fancies*, SHR 3.2.69.
~ *vb.* Take a fancy to, like, love, fall in love with 2H6 1.3.94 *we fancy not the Cardinal*, SHR 2.1.12, TGV 3.1.67; (with a thing as object) SHR 2.1.16; (intr.) fall in love TN 2.5.25 *should she fancy, it should be one of my complexion*, TRO 5.2.165.

fancy-free *adj.* Free from the power of love MND 2.1.164 *In maiden meditation, fancy-free.*

fancy-monger *n.* One who deals in love AYL 3.2.364 *If I could meet that fancy-monger.*

fancy-sick *adj.* Love-sick MND 3.2.96 *All fancy-sick she is and pale of cheer.*

fane *n.* Temple COR 1.10.20 *nor fane nor Capitol ...shall lift up Their rotten privilege*, CYM 4.2.242.

fang *n.* Canine tooth; tusk; (fig.) AYL 2.1.6 *the icy fang...of the winter's wind*, TN 1.5.184.
~ *vb.* Seize TIM 4.3.23 *Destruction fang mankind!*

fanged *ppl. adj.* Having fangs HAM 3.4.203 *Whom I will trust as I will adders fang'd.*

fangled *ppl. adj.* Fond of finery or foppery CYM 5.4.134 *our fangled world.*

fantasied *ppl. adj.* Full of fancies JN 4.2.144 *I find the people strangely fantasied.*

fantastic *adj.*
1 Imaginary R2 1.3.299 *fantastic summer's heat.*
2 Fanciful, capricious VEN 850 *the humour of fan-tastic wits*, TGV 2.7.47; (said of things) extrava-gant, grotesque TRO 5.5.38 *Mad and fantastic execution*, MM 2.2.121, HAM 4.7.168.

fantastical *adj.*
1 FANTASTIC sense 1 MAC 1.3.53 *Are ye fantastical, or that indeed Which outwardly ye show?*
2 Imaginative TN 1.1.15 *So full of shapes is fancy That it alone is high fantastical.*
3 FANTASTIC sense 2 OTH 2.1.223 *telling her fantast-ical lies*, MM 3.2.92, ADO 2.1.76.

fantastically *adv.* Oddly, strangely 2H4 3.2.311 *a head fantastically carv'd*, H5 2.4.27.

fantastico *n.* Absurd, irrational person ROM 2.4.29 *such antic, lisping, affecting fantasticoes* (Q1; F1, Qq 2-4 *phantacies*).

fantasy *n.*
1 Delusion, hallucination HAM 1.1.54 *Is not this something more than fantasy?*, 1H4 5.4.135.
2 Imagination JC 3.3.2 *And things unluckily charge my fantasy*, WIV 5.5.51, ROM 1.4.98.
3 Product or figment of the imagination, fanciful image, fancy JN 5.7.18 *legions of strange fantasies*, MND 2.1.258, JC 2.1.231.
4 Caprice, whim OTH 3.3.299 *to please his fantasy*, ROM 2.4.29, HAM 4.4.61.

fap *adj.* Drunk WIV 1.1.178 *And being fap, sir, was...cashier'd.*

far See FARRE.

farborough See THARBOROUGH.

farced *ppl. adj.* Stuffed; (fig.) padded out with pomp-ous phrases H5 4.1.263 *The farced title running 'fore the king.*

fardel, farthel *n.* Bundle, pack WT 4.4.754 *What's i' th' fardel?*, HAM 3.1.75.

fardingale See FARTHINGALE.

fare *n.* State of things 3H6 2.1.95 *What fare? What news abroad?* (i.e. How is the state of things?), JN 5.7.35.

far-fet *adj.* (lit. 'far-fetched') Deeply laid, cunningly devised 2H6 3.1.293 *his far-fet policy.*

farm *n. in farm* On a lease (esp. one which lets out taxes for a fixed payment) R2 2.1.256 *the Earl of Wiltshire hath the realm in farm.*
~ *vb.*
1 Rent (land), take a lease on HAM 4.4.20 *To pay five ducats, five, I would not farm it.*

2 Let or lease (land); lease the right of taxing to the highest bidder in consideration of a fixed cash payment R2 1.4.45 *We are enforc'd to farm our royal realm.*

farre *adv.* (compar. of 'far') Farther WT 4.4.431 *Farre than Deucalion off* (F1).

farrow *n.* Litter of pigs; (hence used in singular with numeral to indicate the number of young in the litter) MAC 4.1.65 *Her nine farrow.*

farthel See FARDEL.

farthest *adj.* (absol.) Latest MV 2.2.115 *ready at the farthest by five of the clock.*

farthingale, fardingale *n.* Hooped petticoat SHR 4.3.56 *With ruffs and cuffs, and farthingales,* WIV 3.3.64, TGV 2.7.51.

fashion *n.*[1]

1 Kind, sort TGV 5.4.61 *Thou friend of an ill fashion!,* WT 3.2.104, PER 4.2.79; *in the fashion* to of a kind to MV 1.2.22 *in the fashion to choose me a husband.*
2 Mere form, pretence MV 4.1.18 *leadest this fashion of thy malice To the last hour of act.*
3 *out of fashion* Out of vogue or customary use; (hence) eccentric H5 4.1.83 *Though it appear a little out of fashion, There is...valour in this Welshman;* incoherently OTH 2.1.206 *I prattle out of fashion.*

~ *vb.*

1 Contrive, manage OTH 4.2.236 *which I will fashion to fall out between twelve and one,* MND 3.2.194, 1H4 1.3.297.
2 Make (something) of a specified shape or form JC 2.1.30 *Fashion it thus,* ADO 3.3.133, LR 1.2.184; (fig.) mould to one's own purpose JC 2.1.220 *I'll fashion him.*
3 Counterfeit, pervert H5 1.2.14 *That you should fashion, wrest, or bow your reading,* ADO 1.3.29.
4 Adapt, accommodate to TGV 3.1.135 *How shall I fashion me to wear a cloak?,* ADO 5.4.88, ERR 2.2.33.
5 *fashion in* Introduce, work in, prepare the way for TRO 4.4.65 *'be thou true' say I to fashion in My sequent protestation.*

fashion *n.*[2] (corr. of 'farcin') Disease of horses closely allied to GLANDERS SHR 3.2.52 *infected with the fashions.*

fashion-monger *n.* One who studies and follows the fashion ROM 2.4.33 *these strange flies, these fashion-mongers.*

fashion-monging *adj.* Foppish ADO 5.1.94 *fashion-monging boys.*

fast *n.* Fasting, abstinence MM 1.2.126 *surfeit is the father of much fast.*

~ *vb.* (pa.t.) Fasted CYM 4.2.347 *I fast and pray'd for their intelligence.*

fast *adj.*

1 (of sleep) Deep, sound MAC 5.1.8 *in a most fast sleep;* fast asleep ROM 4.5.1 *Fast, I warrant her...fie, you slug-a-bed!*
2 Firmly adhering *to* OTH 1.3.362 *Wilt thou be fast to my hopes?,* CYM 1.6.138.
3 Shut close H8 5.2.3 *All fast? What means this?*

~ *adv.*

1 Close (by) WT 4.4.501 *A vessel rides fast by,* 2H6 3.2.189.
2 Immovably, unchangeably MM 1.2.147 *she is fast my wife, Save that we do the denunciation lack Of outward order,* OTH 1.2.11.

◇ Perh. with allusion to 'handfast' (i.e. betrothed by joining of hands).

fast and loose *n. phr.* A cheating game played by gipsies ANT 4.12.28 *this grave charm,...Like a right gipsy, hath at fast and loose Beguil'd me.*

fasten *vb. fasten upon* Induce to accept OTH 2.3.48 *fasten but one cup upon him.*

fastened *ppl. adj.* Confirmed, inveterate LR 2.1.77 *strange and fast'ned villain!*

fast-lost *adj.* Lost through a fast TIM 2.2.171 *Feast-won, fast-lost.*

fastly *adv.* Rapidly LC 61 *Towards this afflicted fancy fastly drew.*

fat *n.* (var. of) Vat ANT 2.7.115 *In thy fats our cares be drown'd.*

fat *vb.* Nourish; (hence) delight TIT 3.1.203 *this villainy Doth fat me.*

~ *adj.*

1 Close, stuffy 1H4 2.4.1 *that fat room.*
2 Slow-witted, dull, gross HAM 1.5.32 *duller...than the fat weed...on Lethe wharf,* LLL 3.1.109, TN 5.1.109.

◇ See FAT-BRAINED.

fatal *adj.*

1 Concerned with or fraught with destiny 3H6 4.2.21 *the Thracian fatal steeds* (the instruments of fate), H5 5.1.20.
2 Foreboding mischief, ominous 1H6 3.1.194 *that fatal prophecy,* JC 5.1.87, MAC 1.5.39.

fatal-plotted *adj.* Devised to produce ruin or death TIT 2.3.47 *this fatal-plotted scroll.*

fat-brained *adj.* Heavy-witted, dull-witted H5 3.7.133 *his fat-brain'd followers.*

fate *n.*

1 What one is destined to achieve; good fortune ordained by destiny H5 2.4.64 *let us fear The native mightiness and fate of him,* ANT 3.13.169.
2 *Fate* Goddess of destiny TMP 1.1.30 *Stand fast, good Fate, to my hanging;* (pl.) JC 3.1.98 *Fates, we will know your pleasures.*

~ *vb.* Destine AWW 4.4.20 *heaven...hath fated her to be my...helper.*

fated *ppl. adj.*

1 Destined TMP 1.2.129 *one midnight Fated to th' purpose,* LR 3.4.68, OTH 3.3.276.
2 Invested with the power of destiny AWW 1.1.217 *The fated sky Gives us free scope.*

father *n.* The friend or relative that 'gives away' a bride at the altar ADO 5.4.15 *You must be father to your brother's daughter.*

~ *vb. fathers herself* Shows who her father is ADO 1.1.111.

fathered *ppl. adj.* Provided with a father LR 3.6.110 *He childed as I father'd.*

father-in-law *n.* Stepfather R3 5.3.81 *Be to thy person, noble father-in-law!*

fatherly *adv.* As a father CYM 2.3.35 *He cannot choose but take this service I have done fatherly.*

fathom, fadom *n.* (orig. 'the embracing arms')

1 Measure of approx. 2 metres, used esp. to measure depth; (hence, pl.) depths WT 4.4.491 *In unknown fathoms.*
2 (fig.) Grasp of intellect OTH 1.1.152 *Another of his fathom they have none.*

fathomless *adj.* That cannot be embraced by the arms TRO 2.2.30 *a waist most fathomless.*

fathom-line *n.* Sounding-line 1H4 1.3.204 *Where fathom-line could never touch the ground.*

fatigate *ppl. adj.* Fatigued COR 2.2.117 *Requick'ned what in flesh was fatigate.*

fat-kidneyed *adj.* Gross 1H4 2.2.5 *Peace, ye fat-kidney'd rascal!*

fatness *n.* Grossness HAM 3.4.153 *in the fatness of these pursy times.*

fatting *n.* Growing fat, fattening R3 1.3.313 *He is frank'd up to fatting.*

fat-witted *adj.* Dull-witted 1H4 1.2.2 *Thou art so fat-witted with drinking.*

faucet-seller *n.* Seller of taps for broaching barrels

Cor 2.1.171 *a cause between an orange-wife and a faucet-seller* (F4; Ff 1–3 *Forset-seller*).

fault *n.*
1 Lack, want Wiv 1.4.17 *for fault of a better*, Rom 2.4.122, 2H4 2.2.41.
2 Something wrongly done; a single wrong act Wiv 5.5.8 *A fault done first in the form of a beast*; *make a fault* commit an offence Son 35.5 *All men make faults*, WT 3.2.218, R2 1.2.5.
3 (in hunting) Break in the line of scent, loss of scent TN 2.5.128 *The cur is excellent at faults*; *cold fault* cold or lost scent Ven 694 *hounds...have singled...the cold fault cleanly out*, Shr Ind.1.20.
4 Misfortune Per 4.2.74 *The more my fault To scape his hands where I was to die*, Wiv 1.1.94.

faultful *adj.* Culpable Luc 715 *this faultful lord of Rome*.

faulty *adj.* Guilty 2H6 3.2.202 *I am faulty in Duke Humphrey's death*, 1H4 3.2.27, H8 5.2.110.

fauset See FAUCET-SELLER.

Fauste, precor gelida quando pecus omne sub umbra Ruminat [L.] Prithee, Faustus, while all our cattle chew the cud in the cool shade LLL 4.2.93.
▷ First line of first Eclogue of Joannes Baptista Mantuanus.

favour *n.*
1 Leave, permission, pardon Jn 2.1.422 *Speak on with favour*, LLL 3.1.67, H8 1.1.168.
2 Lenity, leniency 2H6 4.7.67 *Justice with favour have I always done*, MV 4.1.386, Ant 3.13.133.
3 Attraction, charm Ham 4.5.189 *She turns to favour and to prettiness*, 2H6 1.2.4, Oth 4.3.21.
4 Appearance, aspect, look Jn 5.4.50 *the favour and the form Of this most fair occasion*, H5 5.2.63, JC 1.3.129.
5 Countenance, face Tro 1.2.93 *a brown favour*, MM 4.2.33, Ham 5.1.194; (pl.) features 1H4 3.2.136 *stain my favours in a bloody mask*.
6 Something given or worn as a mark of affection or goodwill, colours given to a knight by his lady and worn in the helmet 1H4 5.4.96 *But let my favours hide thy mangled face*, LLL 5.2.30, H5 4.7.153.

favourable *adj.* Gracious, kindly 2H4 4.5.2 *some dull and favourable hand*, R3 3.7.101.

favouring *ppl. adj.* Kindly Ant 4.8.23 *thy favouring hand*.
▷ Theobald's emendation; F1 *sauouring*.

fawn *n.*[1] Young fallow deer AYL 2.7.128 *Whiles, like a doe, I go to find my fawn*.

fawn *n.*[2] Servile cringe Cor 3.2.67 *spend a fawn upon 'em*.
~ *vb.* (of an animal) Swish or wag the tail with delight or fondness, show delight Luc 421 *As the grim lion fawneth o'er his prey*, R3 1.3.289, JC 5.1.41; (fig.) wheedle, cringe LLL 5.2.62 *How I would make him fawn, and beg, and seek*, JC 3.1.45.

fawning *ppl. adj.* Wheedling, cringeing, ingratiating MV 1.3.41 *a fawning publican*, TGV 3.1.158, 1H4 1.3.252.

fay *n.* Faith Shr Ind.2.81 *by my fay*, Rom 1.5.128, Ham 2.2.265.

fazed See FEAZED.

fealty *n.* Obligation of fidelity on the part of a feudal tenant or vassal to his lord R2 5.2.45 *lasting fealty to the new-made king*, 2H6 5.1.50; (hence, gen.) fidelity, loyalty TGV 2.4.91 *she hath enfranchis'd them Upon some other pawn for fealty* (i.e. for some other lover's vow of faithful service), Tit 1.1.257, Cym 5.4.73.

fear *n.*
1 Dread, alarm, apprehension; *give, put fear to* make timid, intimidate MM 1.4.62 *to give fear to*

use and liberty, Ven 1158 *Put fear to valour*; *for fear of trust* fearing to trust (oneself) Son 23.5; *Upon the foot of fear* in flight 1H4 5.5.20; *out of fear* (1) for fear 1H4 4.3.7 *You speak it out of fear and cold heart*; (2) without fear 1H4 4.1.135 *I am out of fear Of death*.
2 Dreadfulness AYL 1.2.177 *the fear of your adventure*, Cym 3.4.9, JC 2.1.190.
3 Object of dread, something to be feared 1H4 1.3.87 *Shall we buy treason? and indent with fears, When they have lost...themselves?*, MND 5.1.21, Ham 3.3.25.
~ *vb.*
1 Frighten, scare MM 2.1.2 *a scarecrow...to fear the birds of prey*, Shr 1.2.210, Lr 3.5.3.
2 Be apprehensive or concerned about Ham 4.5.123 *Let him go,...do not fear our person*; (hence) mistrust, doubt Err 4.4.1 *Fear me not, man, I will not break away*, Wiv 4.4.78, Ado 3.1.31.
3 *fear of* Be afraid *of* Son 115.9 *fearing of Time's tyranny*.
4 *I fear me* I am afraid MM 5.1.33 *her wits, I fear me, are not firm*, Tmp 5.1.283, Ant 2.7.32.

fearful *adj.*
1 Dreadful, terrible R2 2.1.263 *this fearful tempest*, Tmp 5.1.106, Luc 1741.
2 Timorous, apprehensive Err 1.1.67 *our fearful minds*, MM 3.1.208, AYL 3.3.48; *fearful of* concerned about 3H6 5.6.87 *fearful of his life*.

fearfully *adv.* Frighteningly, menacingly, terribly Lr 4.1.74 *a cliff, whose...bending head Looks fearfully in the confined deep*, Rom 5.3.133, H5 3.1.12.

feast *vb.* Keep holiday, enjoy oneself 2H4 3.1.59 *Since Richard and Northumberland...Did feast together*, Per 1.4.107, WT 4.4.347.

feast-finding *adj.* Looking for banquets (at which to perform) Luc 817 *Feast-finding minstrels*.

feast-won *adj.* Won by entertainment Tim 2.2.171 *Feast-won, fast-lost*.

feat *vb.* (?) Constrain to propriety or fitting deeds Cym 1.1.49 *A glass that feated them*.
~ *adj.*
1 Adroit, dexterous Cym 5.5.88 *A page...So feat, so nurse-like*.
2 Neat, trim Tmp 2.1.273 *look how well my garments sit upon me, Much feater than before*.
~ *adv.* Neatly LC 48 *With sleided silk feat and affectedly Enswath'd*.

feather *n.*
1 Kind of plumage 3H6 3.3.161 *birds of self-same feather*; (fig.) Tim 1.1.100 *I am not of that feather*.
2 (pl.) Wings Jn 4.2.174 *set feathers to thy heels*, Rom 1.4.20, Luc 1216.
3 (used with ref. to the wearing of plumes in hats) H8 1.3.25 *those remnants Of fool and feather*, Shr 3.2.69, Ham 3.2.275; *plume of feathers* trifling person, coxcomb LLL 4.1.94.

feathered *ppl. adj.* Winged 1H4 4.1.106 *feathered Mercury*, Oth 1.3.269, Per 5.2.15.

featly *adv.* With graceful agility, nimbly WT 4.4.176 *She dances featly*, Tmp 1.2.379.

feature *n.* Shape or form of body TGV 2.4.73 *complete in feature and in mind*, Tmp 3.1.52, Ham 3.1.159 (F1); shapeliness, comeliness R3 1.1.19 *Cheated of feature by dissembling nature*.

featured *ppl. adj.* Shaped Ado 3.1.60 *How wise,...how rarely featur'd*, Son 29.6.

featureless *adj.* Without shape, ugly Son 11.10 *Harsh, featureless, and rude*.

feazed *ppl. adj.* Frayed, worn thin 1H4 4.2.31 *ten times more dishonourable ragged than an old feaz'd ancient*.
▷ F1, Q6 *old-fac'd*; Qq 1–4 *olde fazd*; Q5 *old faczde*; Vaughan's conjecture *old feaz'd*.

fecks *interj.* (distortion of) Faith WT 1.2.120 *I ' fecks! Why, that's my bawcock.*

fedary *n.* Confederate, accomplice MM 2.4.122 *Else let my brother die, If not a fedary,* CYM 3.2.21, WT 2.1.90 (F1 *Federarie*).

federary See FEDARY.

fee *n.*
1 Estate in land held on condition of homage and service to a superior lord; (fig.) one who owes homage and service TIM 3.6.79 *The rest of your fees, O gods—the senators of Athens…*
2 *in fee* (short for) In fee-simple, in absolute possession HAM 4.4.22 *should it be sold in fee* (i.e. sold without restrictions or outright so that the property passes into full possession of the buyer); *at a pin's fee* at a pin's value HAM 1.4.65.
3 Sum which a public officer is authorized to demand as payment for the exercise of his functions; (fig.) 2H6 3.2.217 *I should rob the deathsman of his fee.*
4 Remuneration paid to any professional man VEN 609 *Her pleading hath deserv'd a greater fee,* MV 4.1.423, LR 1.1.163.
5 Perquisite allowed to a servant 3H6 3.1.22 *a deer whose skin's a keeper's fee.*
6 Payment, recompense ADO 2.2.53 *Be cunning in the working this, and thy fee is a thousand ducats,* R3 1.2.169, HAM 2.2.73.
7 Bribe JN 2.1.170 *[tears] Which heaven shall take in nature of a fee.*
8 Tribute or offering to a superior TRO 3.3.49 *supple knees Feed arrogance and are the proud man's fees.*
~ *vb.* Employ, make use of (an opportunity) as one would a servant WIV 2.2.197 *fee'd every slight occasion that could…give me sight of her,* MV 3.1.126, MAC 3.4.131.

feeble *vb.* Make feeble, weaken JN 5.2.146 *Shall that victorious hand be feebled here,* COR 1.1.195.

feed *n.*
1 Feeding-ground, pasture-land AYL 2.4.83 *bounds of feed.*
2 Fodder TIT 4.4.93 *sheep…rotted with delicious feed* (Q3; F1 *foode*; Qq 1–2 *seede*).

fee'd *ppl. adj.* Hired TN 1.5.284 *I am no fee'd post.*

feeder *n.* One dependent on another for food; (hence) servant AYL 2.4.99 *I will your very faithful feeder be,* TIM 2.2.159, ANT 3.13.109.

feeding *n.*
1 Food 2H4 1.1.10 *a horse Full of high feeding,* COR 5.1.55, SON 118.6.
2 Pasture, pasture land WT 4.4.169 *boasts himself To have a worthy feeding.*

fee-farm *n.* Kind of tenure by which land is held in fee-simple subject to a perpetual fixed rent; (fig.) TRO 3.2.50 *a kiss in fee-farm* (i.e. a long kiss).

fee-grief *n.* Grief that has a particular owner, private grief MAC 4.3.196 *is it a fee-grief Due to some single breast?*

feel *vb.* Test, sound H5 4.1.126 *to feel other men's minds,* LR 1.2.86.

feeling *n.*
1 Experience MM 3.2.119 *He had some feeling of the sport,* LLL 3.1.114.
2 What is felt to belong to a thing, impression produced by it R2 1.3.301 *the apprehension of the good Gives but the greater feeling to the worse.*

feeling *ppl. adj.* Deeply felt, heartfelt LR 4.6.222 *known and feeling sorrows,* WT 4.1.8, ROM 3.5.75; *feeling-painful* acutely painful, wringing the heart LUC 1679 *My woe too sensible thy passion maketh More feeling-painful.*

feelingly *adv.*
1 With just perception, understandingly; (hence)

appropriately, to the purpose, exactly TN 2.3.159 *he shall find himself most feelingly personated,* MM 1.2.34, HAM 5.2.109.
2 With feeling or emotion LUC 1492 *Here feelingly she weeps.*
3 In such a manner as to be felt or to leave an impression AYL 2.1.11 *counsellors That feelingly persuade me what I am,* LR 4.6.149.

fee-simple *n.* Estate belonging to the owner and his heirs for ever 2H6 4.10.25 *the lord of the soil come to seize me for a stray, for entering his fee-simple without leave*; (fig.) absolute possession AWW 4.3.278 *sell the fee-simple of his salvation,* WIV 4.2.210, ROM 3.1.32.

feeze *vb.* Drive or frighten away; (hence) do for, settle the business of SHR Ind.1.1 *I 'll feeze you, in faith* (Q1 *pheeze*), TRO 2.3.205.

feign *vb.* Relate in fiction 3H6 1.2.31 *all that poets feign of bliss and joy,* MV 5.1.80.

feigning *ppl. adj.*
1 Inventive, imaginative AYL 3.3.20 *the truest poetry is the most feigning.*
2 Deceitful MND 1.1.31 *feigning love* (F1, Q1 *faining*).
3 Singing softly MND 1.1.31 *feigning voice* (perh. with play on sense 2. F1, Q1 *faining*).

felicitate *ppl. adj.* Made happy LR 1.1.75 *I am alone felicitate In your dear Highness' love.*

fell *n.* Skin LR 5.3.24 *devour them, flesh and fell* (i.e. altogether); covering of hair or wool, fleece MAC 5.5.11 *my fell of hair,* AYL 3.2.54.

fell *adj.*
1 Fierce, cruel TN 1.1.21 *fell and cruel hounds,* TRO 4.5.269, OTH 5.2.362.
2 Hot, angry MND 2.1.20 *Oberon is passing fell and wrath.*
3 Deadly JN 5.7.9 *that fell poison.*

felloe See FELLY.

fellow *n.*
1 Companion, associate SHR 1.1.223 *my fellow Tranio* (i.e. fellow-servant), TMP 3.3.60, HAM 1.2.177.
2 Partaker, sharer WT 3.2.38 *A fellow of the royal bed.*
3 Consort, spouse TMP 3.1.84 *To be your fellow You may deny me.*
4 Equal, match MAC 2.3.63 *remembrance cannot parallel A fellow to it,* JC 5.3.101, MND 4.1.34.
5 Customary title of address to a servant LLL 4.1.100 *Thou fellow, a word,* R3 3.2.106, ROM 1.2.56.
6 Keeper, forester WIV 5.5.26 *I will keep…my shoulders for the fellow of this walk.*
~ *vb.* Associate oneself with, be a 'fellow' to WT 1.2.142 *fellow'st nothing.*

fellowly *adv.* Sympathetic TMP 5.1.64 *Mine eyes …Fall fellowly drops.*

fellowship *n.*
1 Partnership, membership HAM 3.2.277 *Would not this…get me a fellowship in a cry of players?,* MND 1.1.85.
2 Participation, sharing (in an action, etc.) TIM 5.2.12 *His fellowship i' th' cause against your city.*
3 Companionship, company LLL 4.3.47 *sweet fellowship in shame,* JN 3.4.3, OTH 2.1.93.
4 Intercourse, communion H8 3.1.121 *all the fellowship I hold now with him Is only my obedience,* HAM 2.2.384.

felly *n.* Rim of a wheel; (pl.) the curved pieces of wood which, joined together, form the circular rim of a wheel HAM 2.2.495 *Break all the spokes and fellies from her wheel* (F4; F1 *Fallies*; Q4 *fellowes*).

felonious *adj.* Wicked, criminal 2H6 3.1.129 *foul felonious thief.*

female *adj.* Womanish, effeminate, weak R2 3.2.114

boys...clap their female joints In...arms against thy crown.

femetary (var. of) FUMITORY.

femiter (var. of) FUMITER.

fence *n.*
1 The art of fencing JN 2.1.290 *Teach us some fence!*, WIV 1.1.284, ADO 5.1.75.
2 Defence 3H6 4.1.44 *for fence impregnable.*
~ *vb.* Defend, shield, protect 3H6 3.3.98 *that did ever fence the right*, TIM 4.1.3, LUC 63.

fennel *n.* Fragrant yellow-flowered perennial, Faeniculum vulgare, used in fish-sauces, and regarded as an emblem of flattery 2H4 2.4.245 *eats cunger and fennel*, HAM 4.5.180.

fenny *adj.* Inhabiting marshland MAC 4.1.12 *a fenny snake.*

fen-sucked *adj.* Drawn up from marshes LR 2.4.167 *fen-suck'd fogs.*

feodary See FEDARY.

fere *n.* Spouse TIT 4.1.89 *the woeful fere...of that ...dame*, PER 1.Gower.21 (Qq *Peere*, Ff 3–4 *Peer*).

fern-seed *n.* 'Seed' of the fern, once popularly supposed to be an invisible seed and to be capable of imparting its invisibility to any person who possessed it 1H4 2.1.87 *we have the receipt of fern-seed, we walk invisible.*

ferret *vb.* Worry H5 4.4.29 *I'll...ferret him.*

fertile *adj.*
1 Abundant TN 1.5.255 *fertile tears.*
2 Promoting fertility; (fig.) 2H4 4.3.121 *fertile sherris.*

fertile-fresh *adj.* With luxuriant foliage WIV 5.5.68 *green let it be, More fertile-fresh than all the field.*

fervency *n.* Eagerness ANT 2.5.18 *his hook, which he With fervency drew up.*

festinate *adj.* Hasty LR 3.7.10 *most festinate preparation* (F2; F1 *festiuate*; Qq 1–2 *festuant*).

festinately *adv.* Hastily LLL 3.1.6 *bring him festinately hither.*

festival *adj.* Joyful ADO 5.2.41 *woo in festival terms.*
~ *adv.* Like a feast-day JN 3.1.76 *this blessed day Ever...shall be kept festival.*

fet *pa. pple.* Fetched R3 2.2.121 *Forthwith...the young Prince be fet*, H5 3.1.18.

fetch *n.*¹ (var. of) Vetch TMP 4.1.61 *rye, barley, fetches, oats.*

fetch *n.*² Dodge, stratagem, trick HAM 2.1.38 *a fetch of wit*, LR 2.4.89.
~ *vb.*
1 Draw, derive, borrow from a source MM 3.1.81 *Think you I can a resolution fetch From flow'ry tenderness?*, H5 2.2.116, OTH 1.2.21.
2 Deal a blow at PER 2.1.17 *I'll fetch th' with a wanion.*
3 Perform (a movement) MV 5.1.73 *Fetching mad bounds*, CYM 1.1.81.
4 *fetch and carry* (orig. of dogs, hence fig.) Run backwards and forwards with news, tales, etc. TGV 3.1.275 *She can fetch and carry.*
~ *in combination*
fetch about (nautical) Take a roundabout course JN 4.2.24 *It makes the course of thoughts to fetch about.* **fetch in 1** Close in upon, surround, capture CYM 4.2.141 *swear He'ld fetch us in*, ANT 4.1.14. **2** Take in, cheat ADO 1.1.223 *You speak this to fetch me in, my lord.* **fetch off** Make an end of, get the better of WT 1.2.334 *I...will fetch off Bohemia*, 2H4 3.2.301.

fettle *vb.* Make ready, prepare ROM 3.5.153 *fettle your fine joints 'gainst Thursday next.*

fever *vb.* Throw into a fever ANT 3.13.138 *The white hand of a lady fever thee.*

feverous *adj.* Feverish MM 3.1.74 *a feverous life*, TRO 3.2.36, MAC 2.3.61.

few *adj. in* (*a*) *few* In a few words, in short TMP 1.2.144 *In few, they hurried us aboard a bark*, MM 3.1.227, HAM 1.3.126.

fewness *n. fewness and truth* In few words and truly MM 1.4.39 *Fewness and truth, 'tis thus.*

fico *n.* [It.] fig WIV 1.3.30 *a fico for the phrase.*

fiddlestick *n. the devil rides upon a fiddlestick* Here's a fine commotion! 1H4 2.4.487.

fidelity *n. by my fidelity* Upon my word WIV 4.2.153.

fidiused *ppl. adj.* (jocular formation on the name Aufidius) Thrashed COR 2.1.131 *I would not have been so fidius'd for all the chests in Corioles.*

field *n.*
1 Open country VEN 8 *The field's chief flower*, MND 2.1.96.
2 Country as opposed to town MND 3.2.398 *I am fear'd in field and town*, COR 2.2.121.
3 Land as opposed to water OTH 1.3.135 *by flood and field*, VEN 454.
4 Battle-ground, scene of war; (fig.) VEN 108 *Making my arms his field.*
5 Battle MV 2.1.26 *won three fields*, 1H4 5.5.16, 1H6 5.3.12; army in the field of battle JC 5.5.80 *call the field to rest.*
6 Expanse (of sky) PER 1.1.37 *yon field of stars.*
7 Surface of escutcheon on which the charge is displayed LUC 58 *But beauty, in that white intituled From Venus' doves, doth challenge that fair field.*
8 *green field* (?) (1) Green cloth of a counting-house; or (2) green cloth on a writing table H5 2.3.17 *his nose was as sharp as a pen and a table of green fields.*
◇ F1; Theobald's emendation *a' babbl'd o' green fields* generally accepted.

field-bed *n.* Bed in the open field ROM 2.1.40 *This field-bed is too cold for me to sleep.*

fielded *ppl. adj.* Engaged in (a field of) battle COR 1.4.12 *our fielded friends.*

fierce *adj.*
1 Proud, haughty 2H6 4.9.45 *he is fierce and cannot brook hard language.*
2 Wild, extravagant, excessive MND 4.1.69 *the fierce vexation of a dream*, CYM 5.5.382, TIM 4.2.30.

fife *n.* A small variety of the flute; one who plays a fife MV 2.5.30 *the vile squealing of the wry-neck'd fife.*
◇ Either sense of instrument or player is possible here.

fift *adj.* (old form of) Fifth 1H6 1.1.6 *King Henry the Fift.*

fifteen *n.* Fifteenth; a tax of one-fifteenth formerly imposed on personal property 2H6 4.7.22 *made us pay one and twenty fifteens.*

fig *n.*
1 Type of anything valueless or contemptible 2H6 2.3.67 *a fig for Peter!*, OTH 1.3.319.
2 *fig of Spain* Contemptuous gesture consisting in thrusting the thumb between two of the closed fingers or into the mouth H5 3.6.59.
3 *fig's end* Term used scornfully as a substitute for some word just mentioned OTH 2.1.252 *she's full of most bless'd condition.—Bless'd fig's-end!*
~ *vb.* Insult (a person) by making the 'fig of Spain' 2H4 5.3.118 *fig me like The bragging Spaniard.*

fight *n.*
1 *fights and fireworks* Mock battles and pyrotechnic displays (staged on the Thames as part of wedding celebrations) H8 1.3.27 *all their honourable points of ignorance...,as fights and fireworks.*
2 Kind of screen used during a naval engagement to conceal and protect the crew of the vessel WIV 2.2.136 *up with your fights.*

~ *vb. fight o'er* Fight one after the other TMP 3.3.103 *I'll fight their legions o'er.*

figo *n.* [Sp.] Fig H5 3.6.57 *figo for thy friendship!*

fig's end See FIG sense 3.

figure *n.*
1 Distinctive shape or appearance ADO 1.1.14 *doing in the figure of a lamb the feats of a lion.*
2 Imaginary form, phantasm JC 2.1.231 *no figures nor no fantasies*, WIV 4.2.216.
3 Effigy, sometimes made of a person for the purpose of enchantment; or method of fortune-telling based on interpreting shapes ('figures') formed by casting molten lead into cold water WIV 4.2.177 *She works by...spells, by th' figure.*
4 Represented character, part TMP 3.3.83 *Bravely the figure of this harpy hast thou Perform'd.*
5 Written character, letter TIM 5.1.154 *shall...write in thee the figures of their love*, OTH 1.1.62.
6 Emblems, analogies, any of the various rhetorical forms of expression, which are adopted in order to give beauty, variety, or force LLL 1.2.55 *A most fine figure!*, TGV 2.1.148, HAM 2.2.98.
~ *vb.*
1 Imagine, picture in the mind MM 1.2.53 *Thou art always figuring diseases in me*, SON 108.2, LC 199.
2 Portray, represent R3 1.2.193 *I would I knew thy heart.—'Tis figur'd in my tongue.*
3 Prefigure, foreshow 3H6 2.1.32 *the heaven figures some event.*
4 Be a symbol of, represent typically MND 1.1.237 *Wings, and no eyes, figure unheedy haste*, 2H4 4.1.45.

file *n.*
1 List, roll H8 1.1.75 *the file Of all the gentry*, AWW 4.3.166, MAC 3.1.94.
2 The number of men constituting the depth from front to rear of a formation in line AWW 4.3.270 *the doubling of files* (i.e. putting two files into one and so making the ranks smaller); (often used loosely for) ranks, numbers, army TIM 5.2.1 *are his files As full as thy report?*, ANT 1.1.3, COR 5.5.33.
3 Body (of persons) COR 2.1.23 *us a' th' right-hand file* (i.e. the patricians), H8 1.2.42, CYM 5.3.30; *the great file* the majority MM 3.2.136; *the common file* the common people COR 1.6.43.
~ *vb.*[1] March in line, keep pace H8 3.2.171 *My endeavours Have ever come too short of my desires, Yet fil'd with my abilities* (F1 *fill'd*).

file *vb.*[2] Rub smooth with a file WT 4.4.611 *I would have fil'd keys off*, TN 3.3.5; (hence) polish, refine SON 85.4 *precious phrase by all the Muses fil'd*, LLL 5.1.10; sharpen TIT 2.1.123 *she shall file our engines with advice.*

file *vb.*[3] Defile MAC 3.1.64 *For Banquo's issue have I fil'd my mind.*

fill *n.* (pl.) (var. of) Thills, shafts of a cart TRO 3.2.46 *and you draw backward, we'll put you i' th' fills* (Q, F).

fill *vb.*
1 Satiate, satisfy TIM 1.1.261 *see meat fill knaves*, H5 4.1.269, SON 56.5.
2 Be satiated VEN 548 *glutton-like she feeds, yet never filleth.*
~ *in combination*
fill up 1 Come to the measure of, equal LLL 5.2.193 *How many inches doth fill up one mile.* 2 Fulfil MV 4.1.160 *comes...to fill up your Grace's request in my stead.*

fill-horse *n.* Shaft-horse MV 2.2.95 *Dobbin my fill-horse.*
◇ F1, Q1 *philhorse*; Q2 *pilhorse*. See FILL.

film *n.* Fine thread, as of gossamer ROM 1.4.66 *Her whip of cricket's bone, the lash of film.* (F1, Qq *Philome*).

~ *vb.* Cover with a film HAM 3.4.147 *It will but skin and film the ulcerous place.*

filth *n.* (of persons) Vile creature; slut, prostitute TIM 4.1.6 *To general filths Convert...green virginity.*

filthy *adj.*
1 Murky, thick MAC 1.1.12 *the fog and filthy air*, H5 3.3.31.
2 Disgraceful, contemptible LR 3.7.32 *O filthy traitor!*, SHR 4.3.65, OTH 5.2.149.

finch egg *n.* Term of contempt TRO 5.1.36 *Out, gall!—Finch egg!*

find *vb.*
1 Experience, feel MM 3.1.79 *finds a pang*, COR 5.3.111.
2 Discover the true character of, (esp.) discover the weakness of 1H4 1.3.3 *My blood hath been too cold...And you have found me*, AWW 2.4.34, OTH 2.1.248.
3 Provide, furnish H5 1.2.72 *To find his title with some shows of truth* (F1; Qq1-3 *fine*).
4 *find forth* Find out ERR 1.2.37 *to find his fellow forth*, MV 1.1.143.

find-fault *n.* Fault-finder H5 5.2.272 *stops the mouth of all find-faults.*

finding *n.* Thing found WT 3.3.128 *Go you the next way with your findings.*

fine *n.*
1 End ADO 1.1.245 *the fine is...I will live a bachelor*, AWW 4.4.35, HAM 5.1.106; *in fine* in the end, finally HAM 2.2.69, *and, in fine, Makes vow before his uncle...*, AWW 3.7.19, 1H6 1.4.34.
2 (legal) Final agreement, amicable agreement of a fictitious or collusive suit for the possession of lands, formerly in use as a mode of conveyance where the ordinary modes were not available or equally efficacious HAM 5.1.106 *Is this the fine of his fines, and the recovery of his recoveries...?; fine and recovery* means by which an estate tail was converted into a fee-simple; (hence) absolute ownership WIV 4.2.211 *If the devil have him not in fee-simple, with fine and recovery*, ERR 2.2.74 (with quibble).
~ *vb.*[1]
1 Pay as a fine or penalty H5 4.7.69 *I have fin'd these bones of mine for ransom.*
2 Punish MM 2.2.40 *To fine the faults*, R2 2.1.247.

fine *vb.*[2] Bring to an end LUC 936 *Time's office is to fine the hate of foes.*

fine *vb.*[3] Make fine H5 1.2.72 *To fine his title with some shows of truth* (Qq1-3; F1 *find*).
~ *adj.*
1 (of gold) Containing a certain proportion of pure metal, specified in carats 2H4 4.5.161 *Other, less fine in carat.*
2 (of wine) Clear 2H4 5.3.46 *wine that's brisk and fine.*
3 Consummate, egregious OTH 4.1.150 *a fine fool*, WIV 5.1.18.
4 Highly accomplished or skilful JC 1.1.10 *a fine workman*, SHR 1.2.173, ANT 2.6.63.
5 Exquisitely fashioned, precisely beautiful ROM 2.1.19 *her fine foot*, TMP 1.2.317, HAM 2.2.445.
6 Refined, delicate, subtle AWW 5.3.268 *thou art too fine in thy evidence*, ADO 3.4.22, 1H4 4.1.2.
~ *adv.* Delicately, subtly CYM 1.1.84 *How fine this tyrant Can tickle where she wounds!*; mincingly LLL 5.1.20 *to speak 'dout', fine, when he should say 'doubt'.*

fine-baited *adj.* Subtly alluring WIV 2.1.95 *lead him on with a fine-baited delay.*

fineless *adj.* Infinite OTH 3.3.173 *riches fineless is as poor as winter To him that ever fears he shall be poor.*

fineness n. Subtlety Tro 1.3.209 *those that with the fineness of their souls By reason guide his execution.*

finger n. The measure of the breadth of a finger 1H4 4.2.74 *unless you call three fingers in the ribs bare* (i.e. about 6 cms of fat).

~ vb. Pilfer, filch Ham 5.2.15 *Finger'd their packet,* 3H6 5.1.44.

finical adj. Excessively particular in dress Lr 2.2.19 *glass-gazing...finical rogue* (Qq *superfinicall*).

finish vb. Die Cym 5.5.36 *who...Were present when she finish'd,* Ant 5.2.193.

firago n. (var. of) Virago Tn 3.4.274 *I have not seen such a firago.*

fire n.
1 *give fire* Discharge a volley Wiv 2.2.137 *pursue; up with your fights; Give fire!*
2 *give the fire* Give the order to discharge a volley; (fig.) Tgv 2.4.37 *A fine volley of words...you gave the fire.*
3 *put (one's) finger in the fire* Meddle with dangerous matter Wiv 1.4.86 *I'll ne'er put my finger in the fire, and need not.*
4 *fires of heaven* Sun, moon and stars Cor 1.4.39 *by the fires of heaven, I'll leave the foe.*
~ vb. Drive out by applying fire, smoke out Lr 5.3.23 *fire us hence like foxes;* (fig.) Son 144.14 *Till my bad angel fire my good one out.*

fire-drake n. Fiery dragon, or fiery meteor; (hence) a man with a red nose H8 5.3.44 *that fire-drake did I hit three times.*

fire-eyed adj. Having eyes glowing as with fire, with blazing, glowing eyes 1H4 4.1.114 *the fire-ey'd maid of smoky war.*

fire-new adj. Brand-new Tn 3.2.22 *excellent jests, fire-new from the mint,* Lr 5.3.133, R3 1.3.255.

firework n. Pyrotechnic display H8 1.3.27 *fights and fireworks,* Lll 5.1.112.
⇨ See FIGHT.

firk vb. Beat, trounce H5 4.4.28 *I'll fer him, and firk him, and ferret him.*

firm adj. Well-ascertained, certain Mv 4.1.53 *there is no firm reason.*

first n.
1 *the first* (heraldry) The colour first mentioned in blazoning a coat of arms; (fig.) Mnd 3.2.213 *Two of the first, like coats in heraldry.*
2 The beginning or outset (of one's period of life, action, etc.) Mac 5.2.11 *their first of manhood,* Tim 1.1.118, Ham 2.2.61.
3 *at first* At the beginning, before others Cor 1.1.131 *I receive the general food at first.*
4 *at first and last* From beginning to end 1H6 5.5.102, Mac 3.4.1.
5 *since at first* Ever since, from the time when Err 2.2.5 *I could not speak with Dromio since at first I sent him from the mart!*

first-conceived adj. First heard 2H6 3.2.44 *the first-conceived sound.*

firstlings n. (pl.) First-fruits Mac 4.1.147 *The very firstlings of my heart,* Tro Prol. 27.

firze See FURZE.

fisnamy, fisnomy n. (old form of) physiognomy, Face Aww 4.5.40 *his fisnomy is more hotter in France than here.*

fist vb.
1 Strike with the fist, punch 2H4 2.1.21 *And I but fist him once.*
2 Grasp or seize with the fist Cor 4.5.125 *fisting each other's throat.*

fisting n. Beating Per 4.6.167 *To the choleric fisting of every rogue Thy ear is liable.*

fit n.[1] Paroxysm of lunacy, formerly regarded as a periodic disease Err 4.3.90 *Antipholus is mad...Be-like his wife, acquainted with his fits,...shut the doors,* Tit 4.1.17, Ham 4.1.8; *fit of the face* grimace H8 1.3.7; (fig., applied to critical times) Cor 3.2.33 *The violent fit a' th' time,* Mac 4.2.17.

fit n.[2] Strain of music Tro 3.1.57 *you say so in fits* (with quibble).

fit vb.
1 Be fitting or suitable Rom 1.5.75 *It fits when such a villain is a guest,* Aww 2.1.144.
2 Agree or harmonize *with* Tit 3.1.265 *It fits not with this hour,* Lr 3.2.76; (with *to*) Jn 5.6.19 *news fitting to the night.*
3 Be suitable for, answer the requirements of Wiv 2.1.161 *She'll fit it,* Shr 4.3.69.
4 Furnish Tgv 2.7.42 *fit me with such weeds,* Ado 1.1.319, Aww 2.1.90.
~ adj.
1 Of the right measure or size, well-fitting Lll 4.1.50 *One a' these maids' girdles for your waist should be fit,* Tgv 4.4.162; (fig.) Aww 2.2.20 *Will your answer serve fit to all questions?*
2 Prepared, ready Mv 5.1.85 *fit for treasons,* Mm 3.1.256, Oth 3.4.166.
~ adv. Fitly, properly, appropriately Tgv 4.4.162 *Julia's gown, Which served me as fit...As if the garment had been made for me,* Lr 1.2.184.

fitchew, fitchook n. Polecat Lr 4.6.122 *The fitchew nor the soiled horse,* Tro 5.1.67 (Q *Fichooke*); (fig., as a term of contempt) Oth 4.1.146 *'Tis such another fitchew.*

fitful adj. Marked by fits or paroxysms Mac 3.2.23 *life's fitful fever.*

fitly adv. At a fitting time Lr 1.2.169 *I will fitly bring you to hear my lord speak,* Tim 3.4.110.

fitment n.
1 Preparation, fitting arrangement Cym 5.5.409 *'twas a fitment for The purpose I then follow'd.*
2 Duty, that which is fitting or proper Per 4.6.6 *do for clients her fitment.*

fitness n.
1 Readiness, inclination Ham 5.2.201 *If his fitness speaks, mine is ready.*
2 *my fitness* Proper for me Lr 4.2.63 *Were't my fitness To let these hands obey my blood.*

fitted ppl. adj. Driven, forced as by fits or paroxysms Son 119.7 *How have mine eyes out of their spheres been fitted.*

five-finger-tied adj. Sealed or pledged with the whole hand; (hence) tied very securely, pledged wholeheartedly Tro 5.2.157 *another knot, five-finger-tied* (F1 *five finger tied;* Q *finde finger tied*).
⇨ Perh. also with allusion to the five fingers of the devil. Cf. Chaucer 'The Parson's Tale'.

fives n. (pl.) (var. of) Vives, a disease of the parotid gland in young horses Shr 3.2.54 *past cure of the fives.*

fixed ppl. adj. (of teeth) Clenched 2H6 3.2.313 *Deliver'd strongly through my fixed teeth.*

fixture n.
1 Fixing, setting Wiv 3.3.63 *the firm fixture of thy foot would give an excellent motion to thy gait in a semicircled farthingale.*
2 Fixedness, stability Tro 1.3.101 *rend...The unity and...calm of states Quite from their fixture* (Ff 3-4; F1, Q1 *fixure*).

fixure n. Fixedness, stability Wt 5.3.67 *The fixure of her eye has motion in't,* Tro 1.3.101 (Ff 3-4 *fixture*).

flake n. Lock of hair Lr 4.7.29 *these white flakes.*

flaky adj. Broken into 'flakes' or streaks R3 5.3.86 *And flaky darkness breaks within the east.*

flamen n. Priest in ancient Rome devoted to the service of a particular deity Cor 2.1.213 *Seldshown flamens Do press among the popular throngs,* Tim 4.3.155.

flaming *ppl. adj.* Highly coloured, high-flown Tro 1.2.104 *too flaming a praise for a good complexion.*

flannel *n.* [corr. of Welsh 'gwlanen'] (jocularly or contemptuously) A Welshman Wiv 5.5.163 *I am not able to answer the Welsh flannel.*

flap-dragon *n.* Flaming raisin, put afloat in a glass of liquor, to be snapped up with the mouth (in the game of snap-dragon) LLL 5.1.42 *thou art easier swallow'd than a flap-dragon.*
~ *vb.* Swallow as one would a 'flap-dragon' WT 3.3.98 *how the sea flap-dragon'd it.*

flap-jack *n.* Pancake Per 2.1.82 *puddings and flap-jacks.*

flap-mouthed *adj.* Having broad hanging lips Ven 920 *flap-mouth'd mourner.*

flare *vb.* Stream in the wind Wiv 4.6.42 *ribands pendant, flaring 'bout her head.*

flask *n.* Powder-horn Rom 3.3.132 *powder in a skilless soldier's flask,* LLL 5.2.619.

flat *n.*
1 Level ground, plain Ham 5.1.252 *Till of this flat a mountain you have made,* Cym 3.3.11.
2 Tract of low-lying marshy land, swamp Tmp 2.2.2 *bogs, fens, flats.*
3 Nearly level tract over which the tide flows, shoal MV 1.1.26 *think of shallows and of flats,* Jn 5.6.40.
~ *adj.*
1 Absolute, downright MM 2.2.131 *flat blasphemy,* Ado 2.1.222, Jn 3.1.298; *that's flat* that's the absolute, undeniable truth LLL 3.1.101 *The boy hath sold him a bargain, a goose, that's flat,* 1H4 1.3.218.
2 Stupid, dull H5 Prol.9 *flat unraised spirits,* Tro 4.1.63, Ham 4.7.31.

flat-long *adv.* With the flat side downward Tmp 2.1.181 *And it had not fall'n flat-long.*

flatness *n.* Absoluteness WT 3.2.122 *The flatness of my misery.*

flatter *vb.*¹ (sometimes followed by *with*)
1 Encourage with hopeful or pleasing representations Ven 989 *hope...doth flatter thee in thoughts unlikely,* 2H4 1.3.29, TN 1.5.303; please with the belief or suggestion that Ven 978 *flatters her it is Adonis' voice.*
2 *flatter up* Pamper, coddle LLL 5.2.814 *To flatter up these powers of mine with rest.*

flatter *vb.*² Flutter, throw into confusion; (fig.) Cor 5.6.115 *like an eagle in a dove-cote, I Flatter'd your Volscians in Corioles* (F1; Ff 3-4 *Flutter'd*).

flattering *ppl. adj.* Suggesting pleasurable (usu. delusive) anticipations Shr Ind.1.44 *a flattering dream.*
~ *adv.* Flatteringly Rom 2.2.141 *all this is...Too flattering sweet to be substantial.*
▷ F1, Q2 *flattering sweet;* Theobald *flattering-sweet.*

flattery *n.* Gratifying deception, delusion Oth 4.1.129 *She is persuaded I will marry her, out of her own love and flattery,* Son 42.14, Tim 5.1.36.

flaunts *n.* (pl.) Finery WT 4.4.23 *in these my borrowed flaunts.*

flaw *n.*¹
1 Sudden burst or squall of wind 2H6 3.1.354 *the fury of this mad-bred flaw,* Cor 5.3.74, Ham 5.1.216.
2 Outburst of feeling or passion Mac 3.4.62 *these flaws and starts,* MM 2.3.11.

flaw *n.*²
1 Detached piece of something; flake of snow 2H4 4.4.35 *as sudden As flaws congealed in the spring of day;* spark of fire MM 2.3.11 *Who, falling in the flaws of her own youth, Hath blister'd her report.*
2 Fragment Lr 2.4.285 *this heart Shall break into a hundred thousand flaws.*

~ *vb.* Make a flaw in, damage, mar H8 1.1.95 *France hath flaw'd the league.*

flax *n.* (fig.) Wick 2H6 5.2.55 *beauty...Shall to my flaming wrath be oil and flax.*
▷ Wicks were often made from flax.

flax-wench *n.* Female flax-worker WT 1.2.277 *a name As rank as any flax-wench.*

flay *vb.* Skin; (hence, jocularly) strip (a person of his clothes) WT 4.4.815 *but though my case be a pitiful one, I hope I shall not be flay'd out of it.*

fleckled *ppl. adj.* Dappled Rom 2.3.3 *fleckled darkness* (F1; Qq2-4 *fleckeld;* Q1 *flecked*).

fledge, flidge *vb.*
1 Bring up (a young bird) until its feathers are grown and it can fly MV 3.1.29 *knew the bird was fledg'd* (F1, Q2; Q1 *flidge*).
2 Cover with down 2H4 1.2.20 *the juvenal...whose chin is not yet fledg'd* (F1; Q *fledge*).

flee *vb.* Fly 2H4 1.1.123 *arrows fled not swifter,* LLL 3.1.65, Ven 947.

fleece *n.* (transf.) Head or mass of hair Tit 2.3.34 *My fleece of woolly hair.*

fleer *n.* Sneer Oth 4.1.82 *mark the fleers, the gibes, and notable scorns.*
~ *vb.* Smile or grin contemptuously, gibe, sneer Ado 5.1.58 *never fleer and jest at me,* LLL 5.2.109, Rom 1.5.57.

fleering *ppl. adj.* Sneering, gibing JC 1.3.117 *no fleering tell-tale.*

fleet *vb.*
1 Fade, vanish, die out MV 3.2.108 *How all the other passions fleet to air.*
2 Flit, fly, slip away Son 19.5 *Make glad and sorry seasons as thou fleet'st,* 2H6 2.4.4; pass away from the body Jn 2.1.285 *those souls That to their everlasting residence...shall fleet,* Cym 5.3.25.
3 Be afloat Ant 3.13.171 *our sever'd navy too Have knit again, and fleet.*
4 Pass (time) AYL 1.1.118 *fleet the time carelessly.*

fleeting *ppl. adj.* Inconstant, fickle Ant 5.2.240 *the fleeting moon,* Luc 212, R3 1.4.55.

flesh *n.*
1 Visible surface of the body Ant 1.2.18 *fairer than you are...in flesh.*
2 *piece of flesh* Human being, sample of humanity Ado 4.2.82 *as pretty a piece of flesh,* AYL 3.2.66, TN 1.5.28.
3 Human nature with its limitations and frailties Ham 3.1.62 *the thousand natural shocks That flesh is heir to,* H8 5.2.47, Son 151.8.
4 *in flesh* In good condition Rom 5.1.84 *Buy food, and get thyself in flesh.*
5 *strange flesh* Unusual or loathsome food Ant 1.4.67 *thou didst eat strange flesh, Which some did die to look on.*
6 *flesh and fell* See FELL.
~ *vb.*
1 Initiate in or inure to bloodshed Jn 5.1.71 *flesh his spirit in a warlike soil,* Lr 2.2.46.
2 Inflame the ardour or rage (of a person) by a foretaste of success, etc. 2H4 1.1.149 *princes, flesh'd with conquest,* H5 2.4.50.
3 Plunge (a weapon) into flesh 2H4 4.5.132 *the wild dog Shall flesh his tooth on every innocent,* 1H6 4.7.36; *flesh (one's) maiden sword* use it for the first time in battle 1H4 5.4.130 *bravely hast thou flesh'd Thy maiden sword.*
4 Gratify (lust) AWW 4.3.16 *he fleshes his will in the spoil of her honour.*
▷ Orig., reward a hawk or a hound with a piece of the game killed to excite its eagerness in the chase.

fleshed *ppl. adj.* Inured to bloodshed, hardened H5 3.3.11 *the flesh'd soldier,* R3 4.3.6.

fleshly adj. Consisting of flesh JN 4.2.245 in the body of this fleshly land.

fleshment n. Excitement resulting from a first success LR 2.2.123 in the fleshment of this dread exploit.

flesh-monger n. Fornicator MM 5.1.333 was the Duke a fleshmonger.

flewed ppl. adj. having large chaps MND 4.1.120 My hounds are...So flew'd.

flexure n. Bowing, bending TRO 2.3.106 The elephant hath joints...; his legs are legs for necessity, not for flexure, H5 4.1.255.
▷ It was traditionally believed that elephants had no knee-joints.

Flibbertigibbet n. One of the names of fiends (taken from Harsnet's 'Declaration of egregious Popish Impostures', 1603) LR 3.4.115 the foul fiend Flibbertigibbet.

flickering ppl. adj. Shining with unsteady light LR 2.2.108 the wreath of radiant fire On flick'ring Phoebus' front (F1 flicking; Qq 1-2 flitkering; Q3 fletkering).

flidge (var. of) FLEDGE.

flight n.
1 Flock (of birds) TIT 5.3.68 a flight of fowl; (transf.) company HAM 5.2.360 flights of angels sing thee to thy rest!
2 Power of flight MV 1.1.141 when I had lost one shaft, I shot his fellow of the self-same flight (i.e. of the same size and weight).
3 Long-distance shooting with special arrows called 'flights' or 'flight-arrows' ADO 1.1.40 challeng'd Cupid at the flight.

flighty adj. Swift MAC 4.1.145 The flighty purpose never is o'ertook Unless the deed go with it.

fling vb.
1 Dash, rush TIM 4.2.45 He's flung in rage from this ingrateful seat Of monstrous friends.
2 Kick and plunge violently MAC 2.4.16 Duncan's horses...broke their stalls, flung out.

flirt-gill n. Woman of light or loose behaviour ROM 2.4.153 I am none of his flirt-gills.

float n. Wave, billow; (hence) sea TMP 1.2.234 for the rest o' th' fleet..., they all...are upon the Mediterranean float (F1 Flote).

flock n. Tuft of wool 1H4 2.1.6 beat Cut's saddle, put a few flocks in the point.

flood n.
1 Any large body of water, a river, the sea MV 4.1.72 the main flood, AWW 2.1.139; water as opposed to land MND 2.1.5 Thorough flood, thorough fire; (fig.) stream of tears CYM 1.6.74 with his eyes in flood withal laughter.
2 Flowing in of the tide, the height of a tide JC 4.3.219 a tide...taken at the flood, TGV 2.3.41, JN 5.7.64.

flood-gate n. Sluice; (fig.) 1H4 2.4.394 tears do stop the flood-gates of her eyes, VEN 959.
~ attrib. Torrential OTH 1.3.56 my...grief Is of so flood-gate and o'erbearing nature.

floor n. floor of heaven The sky MV 5.1.58.

flote See FLOAT.

flourish n.
1 Ostentatious embellishment, gloss, varnish LLL 4.3.234 Lend me the flourish of all gentle tongues, R3 1.3.240, HAM 2.2.91.
2 Fanfare (of trumpets, etc.), esp. to announce approach of a distinguished person H8 4.1.SD A lively flourish of trumpets.
~ vb.
1 Embellish MM 4.1.74 the justice of your title to him Doth flourish the deceit.
2 Brandish (a sword) (intr.) TIT 1.1.310 him that flourish'd for her with his sword, JC 3.2.192; (trans.) ROM 1.1.78 flourishes his blade.

3 (of trumpets) Sound a flourish or fanfare TIT 4.2.49 Why do the Emperor's trumpets flourish thus?

flout vb. Quote with sarcastic purpose ADO 1.1.288 Ere you flout old ends any further.

flouting-stock n. Object of mockery WIV 3.1.117 he has made us his flouting-stock; (misused for) flout, gibe WIV 4.5.80 You are...full of gibes and flouting-stocks.
▷ In Evans's speech also in the forms vlouting-stock, vlouting-stog.

flow n.
1 Stream; (fig.) H8 1.1.152 flow of gall, TIM 2.2.3; our brains' flow tears TIM 5.4.76 Scorn'dst our brains' flow; set at flow cause to weep TIM 2.2.163 I have...set mine eyes at flow.
2 Rise of the tide TMP 5.1.270 control the moon, make flows and ebbs; (fig.) TIM 2.2.142 the ebb of your estate And your great flow of debts.
3 Rise of water in general ANT 2.7.17 the flow o' th' Nile, LUC 651.
~ vb.
1 Circulate CYM 3.3.93 The princely blood flows in his cheek, MM 1.3.52.
2 flow over Overflow ANT 5.2.24 so full of grace that it flows over.
3 (fig.) Issue PER 4.3.27 he did not flow From honourable courses.
4 (of the sea, etc.) Rise and advance AYL 2.7.72 Doth it not flow as hugely as the sea, ROM 3.5.133, LUC 1569.
5 Rise and overflow; (fig.) TRO 5.2.41 You flow to great distraction.
6 Fill or overflow with tears COR 5.3.99 Make our eyes flow with joy, SON 30.5, H8 Prol.4.
7 Abound in, overflow with ROM 2.4.39 the numbers that Petrarch flow'd in, WT 5.1.102 your verse Flow'd with her beauty once, ADO 4.1.249.

flower n. Bloom, beauty PER 3.2.95 she gins To blow into life's flower again!, R2 3.3.97.

flower-de-luce n.
1 Iris WT 4.4.127 lilies of all kinds (The flow'r-de-luce being one).
2 The heraldic lily, borne upon the royal arms of France 1H6 1.1.80 Cropp'd are the flower-de-luces in your arms, 2H6 5.1.11; (hence applied to Princess Katherine) H5 5.2.210 What say'st thou, my fair flower-de-luce?

flowered ppl. adj. Pinked, decorated with punched patterns ROM 2.4.60 Why then is my pump well flower'd.

flowering ppl. adj.
1 Blooming; (fig.) H5 3.3.14 your flow'ring infants; flow'ring youth bloom of manhood 1H6 2.5.56.
2 Full of flowers, flowery 2H6 3.1.228 the snake roll'd in a flow'ring bank, ROM 3.2.73.

flowery adj. Full of or expressed in flowers of rhetoric MM 3.1.82 Think you I can a resolution fetch From flow'ry tenderness?

flowing ppl. adj. Abundant, copious H8 2.3.62 honour to you no less flowing Than Marchioness of Pembroke.

fluent adj. Copious H5 3.7.33 it is a theme as fluent as the sea.

flush adj.
1 Full TIM 5.4.8 Now the time is flush.
2 Full of life, lusty, vigorous ANT 1.4.52 flush youth, HAM 3.3.81.

flushing n. Redness HAM 1.2.155 the flushing in her galled eyes.

fluster vb. Excite with drink OTH 2.3.58 Three else...Have I tonight fluster'd with flowing cups.

flux n. Discharge AYL 3.2.68 the very uncleanly flux

of a cat; continuous stream (of people) AYL 2.1.52 *misery doth part The flux of company.*

fluxive *adj.* Flowing (with tears) LC 50 *her fluxive eyes.*

fly *vb.*
1 (of a falconer) Cause a hawk to fly at game HAM 2.2.430 *We'll e'en to 't like French falc'ners—fly at any thing we see*, 2H6 2.1.1.
2 Flee MAC 4.2.1 *make him fly the land*, LLL 5.2.86, SON 143.9.
~ in combination
fly off Desert ANT 2.2.152 *never Fly off our loves again*, LR 2.4.91. **fly out** Rush out, break out COR 1.10.19 *my valour for him Shall fly out of itself*, CYM 3.3.90.

fly-bitten *adj.* Fly-specked 2H4 2.1.146 *fly-bitten tapestries.*

fly-slow *adj.* Slowly passing R2 1.3.150 The fly-slow hours (F2; Ff 1, 3, 4, Q5 *slye slow*, Qq1–4 *slie slow*).

fob, fub *vb.*
1 Cheat, deceive, delude 1H4 1.2.60 *and resolution thus fobb'd as it is with…the law*, OTH 4.2.194 (F1 *fopt*).
⇨ See FOP.
2 *fob, fub off* (1) Put off deceitfully 2H4 2.1.34 *I have borne…and been fobb'd off* (Q *fubb'd*); (2) set aside by a trick COR 1.1.94 *to fob off our disgrace with a tale.*

foil *n.*[1] The setting of a jewel; (hence, fig.) that which sets something off to advantage R3 5.3.250 *A base foul stone, made precious by the foil Of England's chair*, 1H4 1.2.215, HAM 5.2.255.

foil *n.*[2] Light weapon used in fencing, a kind of small sword with edge and point blunted ADO 5.2.13 *as blunt as the fencer's foils*, HAM 2.2.321.

foil *n.*[3]
1 Defeat, repulse, check 1H6 3.3.11 *One sudden foil shall never breed distrust; give the foil, put to the foil* give a check to 1H6 5.3.23, TMP 3.1.46.
⇨ Orig. a term of wrestling = 'the fact of being almost thrown, a throw not resulting in a flat fall'.
2 Dishonourable behaviour, disgraceful action ANT 1.4.24 *yet must Antony No way excuse his foils.*
~ *vb.*
1 Throw (in wrestling) AYL 2.2.14 *did but lately foil the sinowy Charles.*
2 Overcome, defeat SON 25.10 *The painful warrior…After a thousand victories once foil'd*, 3H6 5.4.42, TRO 1.3.371.
3 Frustrate, render nugatory or of no effect CYM 2.3.122 *must not foil The precious note of it with a base slave*, OTH 1.3.269.

foin *n.* A thrust in fencing LR 4.6.245 *no matter vor your foins.*
~ *vb.* Thrust in fencing WIV 2.3.24 *To see thee fight, to see thee foin*, 2H4 2.1.16, ADO 5.1.84.

foison *n.* Plentiful crop or harvest TMP 4.1.110 *Earth's increase, foison plenty, Barns and garners never empty*, MM 1.4.43, ANT 2.7.20; (pl.) resources MAC 4.3.88 *Scotland hath foisons to fill up your will.*

fold *n.* Embrace TRO 3.3.223 *from your neck unloose his amorous fold.*
~ *vb. fold in* Envelop COR 5.6.124 *his fame folds in This orb o' th' earth.*

follow *vb.*
1 Pursue as an enemy COR 4.5.98 *I have ever followed thee with hate*, 2H4 4.3.24, ANT 5.1.36.
2 Prosecute (a thing in hand), carry through 2H4 1.1.21 *such a day! So fought, so followed, and so fairly won*, TN 5.1.365, H5 2.4.68.
3 Imitate, copy AWW 2.1.56 *such are to be follow'd*, MND 2.1.131, WT 5.2.57.
4 Engage in (a pursuit), practise (a calling), apply

oneself to JN 2.1.31 *follow arms*, TN 1.3.94, LR 2.2.150.

follower *n.* Pursuer 3H6 1.4.22 *the fatal followers do pursue*, COR 1.4.44.

following *ppl. adj.* Ensuing LUC 186 *What following sorrow.*

folly *n.* Wantonness TRO 5.2.18 *tempt me no more to folly*, MM 3.1.90, OTH 2.1.137.

folly-fallen *adj.* Lapsed into folly TN 3.1.68 *wise men, folly-fall'n, quite taint their wit.*

fond *vb.* Dote TN 2.2.34 *And I…fond as much on him.*
~ *adj.*
1 Infatuated, foolish, silly ERR 2.1.116 *How many fond fools serve mad jealousy?*, LR 1.2.49, JC 3.1.39.
2 Trifling, trivial HAM 1.5.99 *all trivial fond records*, MM 2.2.149.
3 Eager (for), desirous (of) AYL 2.3.7 *so fond to overcome The bonny priser of the…Duke*; (with *of*) COR 5.3.162 *fond of no second brood*, CYM 1.1.37; (with *with*) LUC 134 *with gain so fond.*
~ *adv.* Foolishly AWW 1.3.72 *Fond done, done fond.*

fondling *n.* One who is fondled or caressed, darling, pet VEN 229 *'Fondling,' she saith, 'since I have hemm'd thee here…'*

fondly *adv.* Foolishly R2 3.3.185 *Makes him speak fondly like a frantic man*, SHR 4.2.31, 3H6 2.2.38.

food *n.* in *food* While eating ERR 5.1.83 *In food, in sport, and life-preserving rest To be disturb'd.*

fool *n.*[1] Kind of custard or dish of whipped cream TRO 5.1.9 *thou full dish of fool* (with quibble).

fool *n.*[2]
1 Term of endearment or pity LR 5.3.306 *my poor fool is hang'd!*, TGV 4.4.93, ROM 1.3.31.
2 (Somebody's) dupe, sport, plaything MM 3.1.11 *thou art death's fool*, TN 3.1.144, MAC 2.1.44.
3 Idiot, feeble-minded person, 'natural fool' AWW 4.3.187 *the shrieve's fool* (i.e. an idiot maintained by the sheriff).
4 Professional jester ADO 2.1.138 *he is the Prince's jester, a very dull fool*, ERR 2.2.27, MND 4.1.210; clown as a character in the old comedy MV 1.1.79 *play the fool.*
⇨ In AYL 5.4.64 *According to the fool's bolt* there is a ref. to the proverb 'a fool's bolt is soon shot'.
~ *vb.* Act as a fool or jester TN 5.1.41 *You can fool no more money out of me at this throw* (i.e. obtain in the role of a professional fool).

fool-begged *adj.* Foolishly urged ERR 2.1.41 *This fool-begg'd patience.*

fool-born *adj.* Proceeding from, devised by a fool 2H4 5.5.55 *a fool-born jest* (F1 *fool-borne*).

fooling *n.* Mood for jesting, condition or humour for fooling TN 1.5.32 *put me into good fooling.*

foolish *adj.* (term of depreciation, esp. in speaking of one's own things) Paltry, insignificant, poor, humble ROM 1.5.122 *We have a trifling foolish banquet*, MV 1.2.118.

foolish-compounded *adj.* Composed of folly 2H4 1.2.7 *this foolish-compounded clay.*

foolish-witty *adj.* Foolish in one's wisdom VEN 838 *How love is wise in folly, foolish-witty.*

foot *n.*
1 Footing, status JN 1.1.182 *A foot of honour better than I was.*
2 *at foot* Close behind HAM 4.3.54 *Follow him at foot*, ANT 1.5.44.
3 *on foot* (1) Standing TRO 1.3.135 *keeps Troy on foot*; (2) moving, astir COR 4.3.45 *to be on foot at an hour's warning*, VEN 679; (3) in active employment or operation LLL 5.2.747 *since love's argument was first on foot.*
4 *foot to foot* With one's foot against one's op-

ponent's, in close combat ANT 3.7.66 *fighting foot to foot.*

5 *foot and hand* Putting the foot forward and dealing a blow at the same time 1H4 2.4.217 *but I follow'd me close, came in, foot and hand.*

6 *set on (one's) foot* Start on one's way JC 2.1.331 *Set on your foot, And…I follow you.*

7 *upon the foot of fear* In flight 1H4 5.5.20 *when he saw…all his men Upon the foot of fear, fled with the rest.*

~ *vb.*

1 (intr.) Go on foot, walk WIV 2.1.122 *thieves do foot by night*; (trans.) tread LR 3.4.120 *Swithold footed thrice the 'old.*

2 Land H5 2.4.143 *he is footed in this land already,* LR 3.3.13.

3 Kick MV 1.3.118 *foot me as you spurn a stranger cur,* CYM 3.5.144.

4 (of birds of prey) Clutch with the talons CYM 5.4.116 *the holy eagle Stoop'd, as to foot us.*

5 *foot it* Dance TMP 1.2.379 *Foot it featly.*

foot-cloth *n.* Large, richly ornamented cloth laid over the back of a horse, etc., and hanging down to the ground on each side 2H6 4.7.46 *Thou dost ride in a foot-cloth, dost thou not?*

~ *attrib.* Wearing richly ornamented trappings (indicating the mount of a dignitary) R3 3.4.84 *my foot-cloth horse,* 2H6 4.1.54.

footing *n.*

1 Step, tread MV 5.1.24 *I hear the footing of a man,* TRO 1.3.156, VEN 722.

2 *set footing* Set foot, enter 2H6 3.2.87 *set no footing on this unkind shore,* H8 3.1.183; gain a footing or firm position R2 2.2.48 *Who strongly hath set footing in this land,* 1H6 3.3.64, TRO 2.2.155.

3 Landing OTH 2.1.76 *Whose footing here anticipates our thoughts.*

4 Dancing TMP 4.1.138 *country footing.*

5 Footprint VEN 148 *Dance on the sands, and yet no footing seen.*

6 Surface for the foot, ground to walk on, foothold, foundation WT 3.3.111 *there your charity would have lack'd footing,* JN 5.1.66, R3 1.4.17.

foot-land-raker *n.* Highwayman who robbed on foot 1H4 2.1.73 *I am join'd with no foot-land-rakers* (F1; Q1 *footlande rakers*).

foot-licker *n.* Obsequious servant TMP 4.1.219 *For aye thy foot-licker.*

footman *n.*

1 Walker, pedestrian WT 4.3.64 *by a horseman, or a footman?*

2 'Running footman', a servant who ran with his master's carriage TIT 5.2.55 *Trot like a servile footman.*

fop *n.* Fool LR 1.2.14 *a whole tribe of fops.*

~ *vb.* Cheat, deceive, delude, fool OTH 4.2.194 *begin to find myself fopp'd in it.*

◇ F1 *fopt*; some mod. edd. *fobb'd.* See FOB.

foppery *n.*

1 Folly MV 2.5.35 *the sound of shallow fopp'ry,* MM 1.2.143.

2 Dupery, deceit WIV 5.5.124 *the grossness of the foppery.*

foppish *adj.* Foolish LR 1.4.167 *For wise men are grown foppish.*

for *conj.*

1 Because TMP 1.2.272 *And for thou wast a spirit too delicate,* OTH 3.4.160, TGV 2.4.175; (with *because*) WT 2.1.7 *Not for because Your brows are blacker,* JN 2.1.588, R2 5.5.3; (with *that*) OTH 2.3.316 *for that he hath…given up himself to the contemplation,* WIV 3.4.78, LR 1.2.5.

2 In order that 3H6 3.1.9 *And for the time shall not seem tedious, I'll tell thee…,* 3H6 3.2.154.

3 *for and* And moreover HAM 5.1.95 *a spade, For and a shrouding sheet.*

~ *prep.*

1 Before AWW 4.4.3 *for whose throne 'tis needful…to kneel* (F1), SHR 1.1.3.

2 *for all* Once for all CYM 2.3.106 *and learn now, for all, That I…care not for you.*

3 In place of HAM 5.1.230 *for charitable prayers, Shards, flints, and pebbles should be thrown on her,* LLL 1.1.281, LUC 1424; *made for* made to represent COR 5.4.22 *He sits in his state, as a thing made for Alexander* (i.e. like an image of Alexander).

4 (part of expressions denoting an amount staked or an object risked) At the price of, in exchange of LLL 5.2.720 *Dead, for my life!,* SHR 1.1.189, HAM 3.4.24.

5 Because of, on account of TGV 4.1.48 *banished …from Mantua, for a gentleman, Who…I stabb'd unto the heart,* MND 5.1.249, SON 27.14.

◇ MM 4.3.19 *for the Lord's sake*: a cry of prisoners beseeching passers-by to place alms or food in the basket which hung outside the prison window.

6 In the character or quality of ERR 2.2.188 *I cross me for a sinner* (i.e. sinner that I am), MM 1.2.34, LR 3.4.57; *What is he for a fool?* What kind of a fool is he? ADO 1.3.47.

7 (in exclamations) R2 3.3.70 *alack for woe.*

8 In spite of, notwithstanding 2H6 1.1.163 *for all this flattering gloss, He will be found a dangerous Protector,* ADO 2.1.54, AYL 5.1.3; (hence in conjunctional phrases) *for all* notwithstanding that, although WIV 5.5.192 *for all he was in woman's apparel,* CYM 5.4.201, VEN 342.

9 As a precaution against, for fear of TGV 1.2.133 *here they shall not lie, for catching cold* (i.e. lest they catch cold), 2H6 4.1.74, PER 1.1.41.

10 *for me* For my part R2 1.4.6 *what store of…tears were shed?—Faith, none for me.*

forage *n.* Raging, ravening LLL 4.1.91 *he from forage will incline to play.*

~ *vb.*

1 Range abroad, seek after, esp. with intent to plunder, ravage JN 5.1.59 *Forage, and run To meet displeasure farther from the doors.*

2 Glut oneself as a wild beast H5 1.2.110 *to behold his lion's whelp Forage in blood of French nobility*; (fig.) VEN 554 *With blindfold fury she begins to forage.*

forbear *vb.* (trans.) Leave alone, withdraw from LR 1.2.160 *forbear his presence until some little time hath qualified the heat of his displeasure,* ANT 1.2.121; (intr.) withdraw, retire 1H6 3.1.105 *Let me persuade you to forbear a while,* WT 5.3.85, ANT 5.2.175.

forbid *pa. pple.* Banned, cursed MAC 1.3.21 *He shall live a man forbid.*

forbiddenly *adv.* Unlawfully WT 1.2.417 *you have touch'd his queen Forbiddenly.*

forbidding *n.* Obstacle LUC 323 *all these poor forbiddings could not stay him.*

force *n.*

1 *of force* Of weight, weighty 1H6 3.1.156 *those occasions…were of force,* 2H6 1.3.163, 3H6 2.2.44; necessarily, inevitably MND 3.2.40 *That when he wak'd, of force she must be ey'd,* LLL 1.1.147, JC 4.3.203.

2 *force perforce* By violent constraint, against one's will JN 3.1.142 *and force perforce Keep Stephen Langton…from that holy see,* 2H4 4.1.114, 2H6 1.1.258; of necessity 2H4 4.4.46 *force perforce, the age will pour it in.*

~ *vb.*[1]

1 Press home, urge H8 3.2.2 *If you will now unite in*

your complaints, And force them with a constancy, MM 3.1.109, COR 3.2.51.

2 Reinforce MAC 5.5.5 *Were they not forc'd with those that should be ours.*

3 Attach importance to, care for LUC 1021 *I force not argument a straw;* (hence) hesitate (to do something) LLL 5.2.440 *Your oath once broke, you force not to forswear.*

force *vb.*² Cram, stuff, farce TRO 2.3.223 *Force him with praises,* TRO 5.1.64, H5 2.Ch.32.

forced *ppl. adj.* Brought about by violent means JN 4.2.98 *His little kingdom of a forced grave.*

forceless *adj.*

1 Devoid of force, effortless TRO 5.5.40 *such a careless force, and forceless care.*

2 Frail, without strength VEN 152 *forceless flowers.*

fordo, foredo *vb.* Kill, put an end to, destroy HAM 5.1.221 *The corse they follow did...Foredo it own life,* LR 5.3.256, OTH 5.1.129.

fordone, foredone *ppl. adj.* Exhausted MND 5.1.374 *All with weary task foredone.*

fore, 'fore *adv.* (aphetic form of) Before (of time) SON 7.11 *The eyes, fore duteous, now converted are.*
~ *conj.* Before JN 5.1.7 *To stop their marches 'fore we are inflam'd,* WT 5.1.226.
~ *prep.*

1 In the presence of, in front of WT 4.4.389 *Contract us 'fore these witnesses,* AWW 4.4.3, H8 2.4.120; (in asseverations) AWW 2.3.45 *Fore God, I think so,* COR 1.1.120.

2 (of time) Before MM 2.2.160 *At any time 'fore noon,* COR 4.7.3.

forecast *n.* Forethought, prudence 3H6 5.1.42 *Alas, that Warwick had no more forecast.*

foredo See FORDO.

foredone See FORDONE.

foredoom Condemn beforehand LR 5.3.292 *Your eldest daughters have foredoom'd themselves* (Q2; Q1 *foredoome;* Ff *foredone).*

fore-end *n.* Early part CYM 3.3.73 *The fore-end of my time.*

foregoer *n.* Predecessor AWW 2.3.137 *Honours thrive, When rather from our acts we them derive Than our foregoers.*

foregone *ppl. adj.* Gone by, past AWW 1.3.134 *remembrances of days foregone,* SON 30.9; *foregone conclusion* act already performed OTH 3.3.428 *this was but his dream.—But this denoted a foregone conclusion.*

forehand, 'forehand *n.*

1 *the forehand* The upper hand or advantage H5 4.1.280 *the forehand and vantage of a king.*

2 Mainstay TRO 1.3.143 *The sinew and the forehand of our host.*
~ *adj.*

1 Done at an earlier time ADO 4.1.50 *extenuate the 'forehand sin.*

2 *forehand shaft* Arrow used for shooting straight ahead (rather than for a curved trajectory) 2H4 3.2.47 *'a would have...carried you a forehand shaft a fourteen.*

forehorse *n.* Foremost horse in a team, leader; (fig.) AWW 2.1.30 *the forehorse to a smock.*

foreign *adj.* Not of one's household or family OTH 4.3.88 *they...pour our treasures into foreign laps,* PER 4.1.33.

fore-past *adj.* Previous AWW 5.3.121 *My fore-past proofs.*

forerun *vb.* Be the precursor of ROM 5.1.53 *thought did but forerun my need,* MM 5.1.8, R2 2.4.15.

foresay *vb.* Decree CYM 4.2.146 *let ord'nance Come as the gods foresay it.*

foresee *vb.* Provide for or against TIM 4.3.159 *him*

that, his particular to foresee, Smells from the general weal, H8 5.1.49.

foreshow *vb.* Show forth, betoken, display PER 4.1.85 *your looks foreshow You have a gentle heart.*

foreslow See FORSLOW.

forespeak See FORSPEAK.

forespent *ppl. adj.*¹ Bestowed previously CYM 2.3.59 *his goodness forespent on us;* (hence) past, former H5 2.4.36 *his vanities forespent.*

forespent *ppl. adj.*² See FORSPENT.

fore-spurrer *n.* Forerunner MV 2.9.95 *this fore-spurrer comes before his lord.*

forestall *vb.*

1 Deprive (a person) *of* something by previous action CYM 3.5.69 *May This night forestall him of the coming day!*

2 Discount or condemn by anticipation TRO 1.3.199 *They...Forestall prescience, and esteem no act But that of hand* (F1; Q *Forstall).*

forestalled *ppl. adj. forestall'd remission* (?) (1) Pardon certain to be prevented in advance; or (2) pardon on conditions which honour would prevent accepting 2H4 5.2.38 *never shall you see that I will beg A ragged and forestall'd remission.*
▷ A. K. McIlwraith (TLS 19.1.1933 p. 40) suggests *forestaled* i.e. 'staled beforehand' (by the ignominy of having to beg for it).

foretell *vb.*

1 Indicate beforehand 3H6 2.1.43 *thou, whose heavy looks foretell Some dreadful story hanging on thy tongue,* WT 2.3.199, JN 5.7.5.

2 Tell beforehand TMP 4.1.149 *These our actors (As I foretold you) were all spirits.*

forethought *ppl. adj.* Predestined JN 3.1.312 *alter not the doom Forethought by heaven!*

foreward *n.* Vanguard R3 5.3.293 *My foreward shall be drawn out all in length.*

forewearied See FORWEARIED.

forfeit *n.*

1 Breach, violation (of an obligation) MV 5.1.252 *I dare be bound again, My soul upon the forfeit, that...,* ROM 1.1.97.

2 Penal fine, penalty for breach of contract or neglect of duty MV 1.3.148 *let the forfeit Be nominated for an equal pound Of your fair flesh,* ROM 1.4.111; (fig.) CYM 5.5.208 *But think her bond of chastity quite crack'd, I having ta'en the forfeit.*

3 Person handed over to the law or death MM 2.2.71 *Your brother is a forfeit of the law,* MM 4.2.158, TRO 4.5.187.

4 *forfeits in a barber's shop* List of penalties for various kinds of misbehaviour, such lists being hung up in barbers' shops MM 5.1.321 *the strong statutes Stand like the forfeits in a barber's shop.*

5 Forfeiture, loss AWW 3.6.32 *the divine forfeit of his soul,* MV 4.1.212, 3H6 2.1.197.
~ *vb.* (intr.) Fail to keep an obligation MV 3.1.51 *if he forfeit thou wilt not take his flesh.*
~ *ppl. adj.*

1 Lost by reason of breach of an obligation or the like, given up as a penalty MV 4.1.365 *thy wealth being forfeit to the state,* LLL 5.2.427, MM 2.2.73.

2 Subject, liable *to* SON 107.4 *forfeit to a confin'd doom,* AWW 4.3.190.

forfeiter *n.* One who fails to keep a bond CYM 3.2.38 *Though forfeiters you cast in prison.*

forfended *ppl. adj.* Forbidden LR 5.1.11 *the forfended place.*

forge *vb.*

1 Shape by heating with forge and hammering HAM 2.2.490 *never did the Cyclops' hammers fall On Mars's armour forg'd for proof eterne.*

2 Frame, fashion AWW 1.1.75 *The best wishes that*

can Be forged in your thoughts, COR 3.1.257, WT 4.4.17.

3 Fabricate, invent (a false story, etc.) TIT 5.2.71 *Whate'er I forge to feed his brain-sick humours*, MAC 4.3.82, R2 4.1.40; (absol.) 1H6 3.1.12 *Think not...That therefore I have forg'd*.

forgery *n.*
1 Invention, fictitious invention HAM 4.7.89 *in forgery of shapes and tricks*.
2 Fraudulent invention, deception, lie HAM 2.1.20 *put on him What forgeries you please*, MND 2.1.81, PP 1.4.

forget *vb.* Drop the practice of (a duty, etc.) ERR 3.2.1 *you have quite forgot A husband's office*, 2H6 2.1.190; (with infin.) forget how to 2H4 5.2.22 *like men that had forgot to speak*, TGV 3.1.85, MM 1.2.39.

forgetfulness *n.* Neglect, ingratitude, inattention TIM 5.1.144 *They confess Toward thee forgetfulness too general*, TGV 2.2.12.

forgetive *adj.* Creative, inventive 2H4 4.3.99 *apprehensive, quick, forgetive*.

forgive *vb.* Remit (a debt), overlook the omission of (a duty, etc.) MV 4.1.26 *Forgive a moi'ty of the principal*, LLL 4.2.143, TN 1.5.192.

fork *n.*
1 The forked tongue (popularly supposed to be the sting) of a snake MAC 4.1.16 *Adder's fork and blind-worm's sting*, MM 3.1.16.
2 Barbed head of an arrow LR 1.1.144 *though the fork invade The region of my heart*.
3 Legs LR 4.6.119 *between her forks*.

forked *ppl. adj.*
1 Cleft at the summit ANT 4.14.5 *A forked mountain*.
2 (of an arrow) Barbed AYL 2.1.24 *with forked heads Have their round haunches gor'd*.
3 Two-legged LR 3.4.107 *a poor, bare, fork'd animal*.
4 'Horned', cuckolded WT 1.2.186 *o'er head and ears a fork'd one!*

forlorn *n.* Forlorn person 3H6 3.3.26 *forc'd to live in Scotland a forlorn.*
~ *pa. pple.* (of 'forlese') Brought to ruin, confounded PP 17.14 *Love hath forlorn me.*
~ *adj.*
1 Lost, destroyed CYM 5.5.405 *The forlorn soldier, that so nobly fought.*
▷ Possibly also with associations with 'forlorn hope' and with the same sense.
2 Abandoned, forsaken, desolate TIT 2.3.153 *ravens foster forlorn children*, LLL 5.2.795, LR 4.7.38; (hence) unhappy, wretched LUC 1500 *who she finds forlorn, she doth lament*, WT 2.2.20, VEN 251.
3 Of wretched appearance, thin, meagre 2H4 3.2.312 *'A was so forlorn, that his dimensions to any thick sight were invisible*, TIT 2.3.94.

form *n.*
1 Image, likeness, portrait JN 5.7.32 *I am a scribbled form, drawn with a pen*, TGV 4.4.198, LLL 2.1.237.
2 Orderly arrangement, good order TRO 1.3.87 *proportion, season, form,...in all line of order*; military formation 2H4 4.1.20 *In goodly form comes on the enemy.*
3 Degree of rank or eminence H5 4.1.246 *place, degree, and form* (with quibble on senses 2 and 5).
4 Ceremony MM 5.1.56 *dressings, caracts, titles, forms*, ADO 4.1.2, ROM 2.2.88.
5 Behaviour, mode of behaving TGV 5.4.56 *change you to a milder form*, JC 1.2.299; (pl.) manners LC 303 *all strange forms...Of burning blushes, or of weeping water*, TN 5.1.350.

formal *adj.*
1 Extremely regular or accurate, stiff, rigid LC 29 *hair...tied in formal plat*, AYL 2.7.155.
2 Conventional, traditional R3 3.1.82 *the formal Vice, Iniquity.*
▷ In 16C morality plays a stock character called Iniquity represented all the vices.
3 Dignified 2H4 5.2.133 *in formal majesty*, JC 2.1.227.
4 Normal or ordinary in intellect, sane ERR 5.1.105 *drugs, and holy prayers, To make of him a formal man again*, TN 2.5.117, ANT 2.5.41.

former *adj.* Front, forward, foremost JC 5.1.79 *on our former ensign Two...eagles fell.*

formerly *adv.* Just now MV 4.1.362 *The danger formerly by me rehears'd.*

forsake *vb.*
1 Decline, refuse 1H6 4.2.14 *If you forsake the offer of their love*, OTH 4.2.125, AWW 2.3.56.
2 Give up, renounce, reject ERR 4.3.21 *forsake your liberty*, LUC 1538.

forset-seller See FAUCET-SELLER.

forslow, foreslow *vb.* Delay 3H6 2.3.56 *Forslow no longer, make we hence amain* (F1 *Foreslow*).

forsooth *adv.* In truth, certainly SHR 4.3.1 *No, no, forsooth I dare not*, ROM 4.2.12, LR 1.4.194.
▷ Sometimes used contemptuously by upper-class persons.

forspeak, forespeak *vb.* Speak against ANT 3.7.3 *Thou hast forspoke my being in these wars* (F1 *forespoke*).

forspent, forespent *ppl. adj.* Worn out, exhausted 3H6 2.3.1 *Forspent with toil* (F1 *forespent*), 2H4 1.1.37.

forswear *vb.*
1 Abandon, renounce on oath TMP 4.1.91 *Her and her blind boy's scandall'd company I have forsworn*; (with infin.) TN 3.4.252 *forswear to wear iron about you*, COR 5.3.80, ROM 1.1.223.
2 Deny or repudiate on oath or with strong words 1H4 5.2.38 *forswearing that he is forsworn*, ERR 5.1.11, SHR 5.1.111.

forted *ppl. adj.* Fortified MM 5.1.12 *A forted residence.*

forth *adv.*
1 Forward (in movement or direction) TIM 1.1.49 *flies an eagle flight, bold, and forth on*, SHR 4.1.146, CYM 4.2.149.
2 Out ERR 4.4.95 *wherefore didst thou lock me forth*, MM 5.1.255, MV 1.1.143; *forth of* out of JC 3.3.3 *forth of doors*, TMP 5.1.160, R2 3.2.204.
3 Abroad, not at home JC 1.2.289 *I am promis'd forth*, WIV 2.2.266, ERR 2.2.210.
4 (of a force) In the field COR 1.3.96 *the Volsces have an army forth*; at sea ANT 4.11.3 *his best force Is forth to man his galleys.*
~ *prep.* Out of MND 1.1.164 *Steal forth thy father's house*, COR 1.4.23, ANT 4.10.7; (with *from*) WIV 4.4.54 *Let them from forth a sawpit rush.*

forthcoming *ppl. adj.* Ready to appear or to be produced when required, e.g. in court SHR 5.1.93 *I charge you to see that he be forthcoming*, 2H6 1.4.53.

forthright *n.* Straight path TMP 3.3.3 *Through forthrights and meanders*, TRO 3.3.158.

fortitude *n.* Physical or structural strength OTH 1.3.222 *the fortitude of the place*, 1H6 2.1.17.

fortressed *ppl. adj.* Protected LUC 28 *weakly fortress'd from a world of harms.*

fortuna de la guerra [Sp.] Fortune of war LLL 5.2.530 (F1, Q1 *Fortuna delaguar*).

fortune *n.*
1 Chance, hap, accident SHR 3.2.23 *Whatever fortune stays him from his word*, MV 1.1.44, OTH 1.3.130; *by fortune* by chance MV 2.1.34 *turn by*

fortune from the weaker hand, AYL 1.2.44, SON 32.3; *at fortune* at random OTH 3.3.263 *To prey at fortune.*

2 (pl. = sing.) A person's possessions, wealth OTH 5.2.366 *seize upon the fortunes of the Moor,* ADO 2.1.303, JN 2.1.69.

~ *vb.*

1 Regulate the fortunes of ANT 1.2.74 *Isis...fortune him accordingly!*

2 Happen TGV 5.4.169 *what hath fortuned.*

forty *adj.*

1 Used indefinitely to express a large number COR 3.1.242 *I could beat forty of them,* ERR 4.3.83, SON 2.1; (so also) *forty thousand* WT 4.4.277 *forty thousand fathom above water,* HAM 5.1.269, OTH 3.3.442.

2 *forty pence* A customary amount for a wager H8 2.3.89 *Is it bitter? Forty pence, no.*

forward *adj.*

1 Situated at the front AWW 5.3.39 *take the instant by the forward top* (i.e. by the forelock), TMP 2.2.90, AWW 3.2.113.

2 Eager, ardent, zealous H8 4.1.9 *they are ever forward In celebration of this,* R2 4.1.317, R3 3.2.46.

3 Early, ripe, premature R3 3.1.94 *Short summers lightly have a forward spring,* SON 99.1, HAM 1.3.8.

forwardness *n.* Eagerness, ardour 1H6 1.1.100 *why doubt'st thou of my forwardness?,* 3H6 4.5.23.

forwearied, forewearied *ppl. adj.* Thoroughly exhausted JN 2.1.233 *Forwearied in this action* (F1 *forewearied*).

fosset-seller See FAUCET-SELLER.

foster *vb.*

1 Feed CYM 2.3.114 *foster'd with cold dishes.*

2 Bring up as a foster-child, be a foster-parent to PER 4.3.15 *Nurses are not the fates To foster it,* JN 5.2.75, TIT 2.3.153.

foul *adj.*

1 Ugly TIM 4.3.29 *make Black white, foul fair,* LLL 4.3.85, OTH 2.1.141.

2 Unattractive, poor in quality TRO 1.3.358 *Let us like merchants first show foul wares.*

3 Stormy TMP 2.1.142 *foul weather,* JN 4.2.108, VEN 456.

4 Grossly abusive MND 3.2.197 *this foul derision.*

5 Harsh, rough VEN 573 *Foul words and frowns must not repel a lover,* H5 2.1.56, TMP 2.2.91.

~ *adv.* FOULLY sense 1 R3 3.2.44 *the crown so foul misplac'd.*

foully *adv.*

1 Shamefully, disgracefully, wickedly MAC 3.1.3 *Thou play'dst most foully for't,* AWW 5.3.154, MM 2.2.173.

2 Insultingly 1H4 1.3.154 *Live scandaliz'd and foully spoken of.*

foulness *n.*

1 Ugliness AYL 3.5.66 *He's fall'n in love with your foulness.*

2 Moral impurity, wickedness LR 1.1.227 *vicious blot, murder, or foulness,* ADO 4.1.153, H8 3.2.183.

foundation *n. God save the foundation!* A phrase used on receiving alms at a house of charity ADO 5.1.318.

founded *ppl. adj.* Solid, steady MAC 3.4.21 *Whole as the marble, founded as the rock.*

founder *vb.* Cause (a horse) to break down or go lame TMP 4.1.30 *Phoebus' steeds are founder'd,* 2H4 4.3.36.

four *adj.* Used for an indefinite number, large or small according to the circumstances TIM 5.1.220 *Lips, let four words go by and language end!,* ANT 2.7.102, 1H4 2.2.12.

⇨ See FORTY.

four-inched *adj.* Four inches wide LR 3.4.57 *over four-inch'd bridges.*

foutra, foutre *n.* Term of contempt 2H4 5.3.99 *A foutre for the world...!*

fox *n.*

1 Symbol or type of ingratitude and sham LR 3.7.28 *Ingrateful fox,* LR 1.4.317, LR 3.6.22.

2 Kind of sword H5 4.4.9 *thou diest on point of fox.*

⇨ The figure of a wolf which was engraved on some makes of sword-blades is supposed to have been mistaken for a fox.

foxship *n.* The character or qualities of a fox; (esp.) ingratitude COR 4.2.18 *Hadst thou foxship To banish that struck more blows for Rome Than thou hast spoken words?*

fracted *ppl. adj.* Broken TIM 2.1.22 *my reliances on his fracted dates,* H5 2.1.124.

fraction *n.*

1 Discord, dissension, rupture TRO 2.3.98 *their fraction is more our wish than their faction.*

2 Fragment TIM 2.2.211 *these hard fractions...froze me into silence* (i.e. fragments of sentences, disjointed utterances), TRO 5.2.158.

fragment *n.* (applied to a person as a term of contempt) Insignificant, incomplete, worthless creature COR 1.1.222 *get you home you, fragments,* TRO 5.1.8.

frame *n.*

1 Contrivance ADO 4.1.189 *toil in frame of villainies.*

2 Structure, form WT 2.3.103 *The very mould and frame of hand, nail, finger*; (hence) constitution, nature TN 1.1.32 *a heart of that fine frame,* MM 5.1.61, AWW 4.2.4.

3 Established order, plan, system MAC 3.2.16 *let the frame of things disjoint,* HAM 4.1.128.

4 Definite form or order LLL 3.1.191 *Still a-repairing, ever out of frame,* HAM 3.2.309.

5 Structure HAM 5.1.43 *that frame outlives a thousand tenants* (F1).

~ *vb.*

1 Shape one's course; (hence) direct one's steps, go PER 1.Gower.32 *many princes thither frame To seek her.*

2 Cause, produce, create, bring to pass 2H6 5.2.32 *Fear frames disorder,* PP 7.15, 2H4 4.1.178.

3 Perform ANT 2.2.211 *hands, That yarely frame the office.*

frampold *adj.* Disagreeable WIV 2.2.90 *She leads a very frampold life with him.*

franchise *n.*

1 Free exercise CYM 3.1.56 *our laws...whose repair and franchise Shall...be our good deed.*

2 (pl.) Liberties, privileges COR 4.6.86 *Your franchises...confin'd Into an auger's bore.*

franchised *ppl. adj.* Free MAC 2.1.28 *keep My bosom franchis'd and allegiance clear.*

Francisco *n.* Frenchman WIV 2.3.28 *Is he dead, my Francisco?*

⇨ Perh. quibble on 'francisc' i.e. battle-axe.

frank *n.* Enclosure for pigs, sty 2H4 2.2.147 *Doth the old boar feed in the old frank?*

frank *adj.*

1 Unrestrained, unrestricted AWW 2.3.55 *Thy frank election.*

2 Liberal, bounteous SON 4.4. *being frank she lends,* AWW 1.2.20, OTH 3.4.44.

3 Open, undisguised TIM 1.3.38 *bearing with frank appearance Their purposes toward Cyprus*; outspoken H5 1.2.244 *with frank...plainness Tell us.*

franked *ppl. adj. franked up* Shut up in a sty R3 1.3.313 *He is frank'd up to fatting.*

franklin *n.* Yeoman WT 5.2.160 *Let boors and franklins say it, I 'll swear it,* 1H4 2.1.55, CYM 3.2.77.

frankly *adv.*

1 Freely, without restraint or constraint, unre-

strictedly HAM 3.1.33 *We may of their encounter frankly judge*, TRO 5.8.19, TIM 2.2.179.
2 Generously, unreservedly TIT 1.1.420 *he frankly gave*, MM 3.1.105, OTH 2.3.298.

fraud *n.* Faithlessness ADO 2.3.72 *The fraud of men was ever so*, TGV 2.7.78, VEN 1141.

fraught *n.* Freight, cargo TIT 1.1.71 *the bark that hath discharg'd his fraught*, TN 5.1.65; (fig.) load, burden OTH 3.3.448 *Swell, bosom, with thy fraught*.
~ *vb.* Load; (fig.) CYM 1.1.126 *If...thou fraught the court With thy unworthiness*.
~ *ppl. adj.* Laden, loaded MV 2.8.30 *A vessel...richly fraught*, TRO Prol.4; (fig.) filled, stored WT 4.4.514 *I am so fraught with curious business*, LR 1.4.220, TGV 3.2.70.

fraughtage *n.* Cargo ERR 4.1.87 *Our fraughtage...I have convey'd aboard*.

fraughted *ppl. adj.* Fraught, loaded PP 17.16 *O cruel speeding, fraughted with gall*.

fraughting *ppl. adj.* Forming the cargo TMP 1.2.13 *The fraughting souls within her*.

frayed *ppl. adj.* Frightened TRO 3.2.32 *as if she were fray'd with a spirit*.

freckled *ppl. adj.* Spotted TMP 1.2.283 *a freckled whelp*, H5 5.2.49.

free *vb.*
1 Secure *from* WT 4.4.433 *full of our displeasure, yet we free thee From the dead blow of it*.
2 Clear from blame or stain, absolve, acquit WT 3.2.111 *mine honour, Which I would free*, H8 2.4.158, HAM 5.2.242.
3 Get rid of, banish MAC 3.6.35 *Free from our feasts...bloody knives*, CYM 3.6.79; obtain remission of (a sin) TMP Epil.18 *frees all faults*.
~ *adj.*
1 Of noble or honourable character, generous, magnanimous OTH 3.3.199 *your free and noble nature*, TN 1.5.260, H8 3.1.60.
2 *free duty* Unqualified expressions of respect OTH 1.3.41 *With his free duty recommends you*.
3 Guiltless, innocent HAM 2.2.564 *Make mad the guilty, and appal the free*, AYL 2.7.85, TN 1.5.92.
4 Not affected with any disease or distress of body or mind MM 1.2.43 *whether thou art tainted or free*; carefree, unconcerned, untroubled OTH 3.3.340 *I slept...well, fed well, was free and merry*, LR 3.4.11, TN 2.4.45.

freedom *n.*
1 Ease H8 5.1.102 *You cannot with such freedom purge yourself*.
2 Privilege, franchise MV 3.2.278 *the freedom of the state*, COR 2.1.248; (fig.) WT 1.1.12 *I speak it in the freedom of my knowledge*, SON 46.4.
3 *at freedom* At liberty, freely TMP 4.1.265 *thou Shalt have the air at freedom*, CYM 3.3.71.

free-hearted *adj.* Liberal TIM 3.1.10 *Complete, free-hearted gentleman*.

freely *adv.* In freedom, with absolute possession of one's privileges MV 3.2.249 *I must freely have the half*, TN 1.4.39.

freeness *n.* Liberality CYM 5.5.421 *Nobly doom'd! We'll learn our freeness of a son-in-law*.

freestone-coloured *adj.* Of the colour of sandstone or limestone AYL 4.3.25 *she has a leathern hand, A freestone-coloured hand*.

French brawl See BRAWL.

French crown *n.*
1 The French coin called 'ecu' 2H4 3.2.221 *four Harry ten shillings in French crowns*, 2H6 4.2.158, H5 4.1.226.
2 Bald head (with reference to the baldness produced by syphilis, 'the French disease') MND 1.2.97 *Some of your French crowns have no hair at all*, MM 1.2.52, LLL 3.1.141.

▷ Quibble on sense 1.
3 *French-crown-colour* Yellowish colour of a gold coin MND 1.2.95 *your French-crown-colour beard*.

French hose *n.* The fashionable Eliz. loose, wide breeches, of 'mid-thigh length, shaped like pumpkins' (Linthicum, 1936) and stuffed with hair, flocks, or bombast H5 3.7.53 *your French hose off, and in your strait strossers*, MAC 2.3.14.

French slop *n.* French hose ROM 2.4.44 *bon jour! there's a French salutation to your French slop*.

French thrift *n.* An economy measure of having one page (often French) and no other servingmen WIV 1.3.84 *French thrift, you rogues—myself and skirted page*.

frequent *vb.* Resort to a place R2 5.3.6 *For there, they say, he daily doth frequent*.
~ *adj.*
1 Addicted *to* WT 4.2.32 *less frequent to his princely exercises than formerly*.
2 Familiar SON 117.5 *I have frequent been with unknown minds*.

fresh *n.* Spring of fresh water TMP 3.2.67 *Where the quick freshes are*.
~ *adj.*
1 Raw, inexperienced JN 3.4.145 *How green you are and fresh in this old world!*
2 Invigorating, refreshing LC 213 *The...em'rald, in whose fresh regard Weak sights their sickly radiance do amend*, OTH 4.3.44, CYM 5.3.71.
3 Refreshing, cool 3H6 2.5.49 *a fresh tree's shade*.
4 Blooming, looking healthy or youthful TMP 4.1.137 *these fresh nymphs*, SHR 4.5.29, OTH 2.3.20.
5 Not exhausted or tired; (hence) still enthusiastic H8 1.1.3 *a fresh admirer Of what I saw*.

fresh(-)fish *n.* Novice H8 2.3.86 *and you...A very fresh fish here...have your mouth fill'd up Before you open it*.

freshly *adv.*
1 Newly TMP 5.1.236 *we, in all our trim, freshly beheld Our...ship*.
2 Anew, afresh CYM 5.4.143 *Be jointed to the old stock, and freshly grow*, MM 1.2.171.
3 With undiminished intensity H5 4.3.55 *freshly rememb'red*, H8 5.2.66.
4 Healthily, bloomingly AYL 3.2.230 *Looks he as freshly as he did the day he wrastled?*, H5 4.Ch.39.

fret *n.* In instruments of the guitar kind, (formerly) a ring of gut (now a bar of wood) placed on the finger-board to regulate the fingering LUC 1140 *as frets upon an instrument*, SHR 2.1.149.
~ *vb.*[1] Furnish (a guitar, etc.) with frets; (quibblingly) HAM 3.2.371 *though you fret me, yet you cannot play upon me*.

fret *vb.*[2]
1 Make or form by wearing away LR 1.4.285 *fret channels in her cheeks*, R2 3.3.167.
2 Become eaten or corroded (through rust, moth, etc.), decay, SHR 2.1.328 *a commodity lay fretting by you*, WIV 3.5.113, 1H4 2.2.2.

fret *vb.*[3] Adorn (a ceiling) with carved or embossed work in decorative patterns CYM 2.4.88 *The roof...With golden cherubins is fretted*; (fig.) HAM 2.2.301 *this majestical roof fretted with golden fire*; chequer JC 2.1.104 *yon grey lines That fret the clouds*.

fretful *adj.*
1 Eating away 2H6 3.2.403 *a fretful corrosive*.
2 Peevish, ill-tempered, impatient 1H4 3.3.11 *you are so fretful you cannot live long*, LR 3.1.4, HAM 1.5.20 (F1).

fretten *ppl. adj.* Chafed, blasted MV 4.1.77 *the mountain pines...When they are fretten with the gusts of heaven*.

fretting *ppl. adj.* (of the wind) Blowing in frets or gusts 3H6 2.6.35 *a sail, fill'd with a fretting gust.*

friar *n.* Member of any one of the four religious mendicant orders SHR 4.1.145 *It was the friar of orders grey* (i.e. a Franciscan); (loosely) any monk or brother H8 1.2.148 *a Chartreux friar.*

friend *n.*
1 Lover, sweetheart MM 1.4.29 *He hath got his friend with child,* ADO 5.2.70, CYM 1.4.69.
2 (usu. pl.) Relatives, kinsfolk TGV 3.1.106 *she...is promis'd by her friends Unto a youthful gentleman,* MM 1.2.151, AYL 1.3.62.
3 *at friend, to friend* As a friend, friendly, on one's side AWW 5.3.182 *you have them ill to friend,* WT 5.1.140, JC 3.1.143.
~ *vb.* Befriend, assist H5 4.5.17 *friend us now!,* MM 4.2.113, H8 1.2.140; (absol.) TRO 1.2.78 *time must friend or end.*

friending *n.* Friendliness HAM 1.5.185 *his love and friending.*

friendship *n.* Friendly act, favour, friendly aid TIM 4.3.71 *What friendship may I do thee?,* MV 1.3.168, LR 3.2.62.

frieze, frize *n.* Kind of coarse woollen cloth with a nap, made in Wales WIV 5.5.138 *Am I ridden with a Welsh goat too? Shall I have a coxcomb of frieze?,* OTH 2.1.126.

frippery *n.* Shop where old clothes are sold TMP 4.1.226 *we know what belongs to a frippery.*

fritters *n.* (pl.) *make fritters of* Make a hash of WIV 5.5.143 *one that makes fritters of English.*

fro *prep.* From CYM 5.5.261 *throw your wedded lady fro you,* ROM 4.1.75.

frolic *adj.* Merry MND 5.1.387 *we fairies...Now are frolic.*
~ *adv.* Merrily SHR 4.3.182 *And therefore frolic, we will hence forthwith, To feast and sport us.*

from *adv.* See FALLING-FROM.
~ *prep.*
1 Among, from among TIM 1.2.91 *Why have you that charitable title from thousands?,* AWW 2.1.127.
2 Away from, apart from, at variance with, not in accordance with, otherwise than JC 2.1.196 *Quite from the main opinion he held once,* TN 5.1.332, JN 4.3.151.
3 *from forth* Out of JN 5.4.45 *From forth the noise and rumour of the field,* WIV 4.4.54.

front *n.*
1 Forehead; (hence) face R3 1.1.9 *smooth'd his wrinkl'd front,* JN 2.1.356, MAC 4.3.232; (hence) forelock (fig.) OTH 3.1.49 *To take the safest occasion by the front.*
2 Foremost line of battle 3H6 1.1.8 *Charg'd our main battle's front,* COR 1.6.8, ANT 5.1.44.
3 First period, beginning WT 4.4.3 *April's front,* SON 102.7.
~ *vb.*
1 Confront, oppose ANT 2.2.61 *those wars Which fronted mine own peace,* 2H4 4.1.25, 1H6 4.2.26.
2 March in the front rank H8 1.2.42 *I.. front but in that file.*

frontier *n.*
1 Outwork in fortification 1H4 2.3.52 *palisadoes, frontiers, parapets;* (fig.) 1H4 1.3.19 *The moody frontier of a servant brow.*
2 Border fortress or town AWW 4.4.16 *Goes it against the main of Poland, sir, Or for some frontier?*

frontlet *n.* Band worn on the forehead; (hence, fig.) a frowning face LR 1.4.189 *what makes that frontlet on?*

frosty *adj.* Characteristic of old age, hoary TIT 5.3.77 *my frosty signs and chaps of age,* 2H6 5.1.167.

froth *vb.* Make drink frothy; (fig.) WIV 1.3.14 *Let me see thee froth.*

froward *adj.* Perverse, refractory, wilful VEN 562 *the froward infant,* TGV 3.1.68, SHR 1.1.69.

frown *n. in frown* Defiantly CYM 5.3.28 *to look back in frown.*

fruit *n.*
1 Dessert HAM 2.2.52 *the fruit to that great feast.*
2 Offspring 3H6 4.4.24 *King Edward's fruit,* H8 5.1.20, SON 97.10.

fruitful *adj.*
1 Abundant, copious MM 4.3.154 *one fruitful meal,* TIM 5.1.150, HAM 1.2.80.
2 Generous, liberal H8 1.3.56 *A hand as fruitful as the land that feeds us,* OTH 2.3.341.

fruitfully *adv.* Copiously, fully AWW 2.2.70 *You understand me?—Most fruitfully,* LR 4.6.265.

fruitfulness *n.* Liberality; (hence) amorousness OTH 3.4.38 *This argues fruitfulness and liberal heart.*

fruitless *adj.* Barren, not producing offspring MND 1.1.73 *the cold fruitless moon,* MAC 3.1.60, VEN 751.

frush *vb.* Smash, batter TRO 5.6.29 *I'll frush it and unlock the rivets.*

frustrate *vb.* Annul 3H6 2.1.175 *To frustrate...his oath.*
~ *ppl. adj.* Frustrated, baffled, defeated ANT 5.1.2 *Being so frustrate,...he mocks The pauses that he makes;* vain TMP 3.3.10 *Our frustrate search.*

frutify *vb.* (comic blunder for) Notify MV 2.2.134 *as my father...shall frutify unto you.*

fry *n. fry of fornication* (term of contempt) Crowd of people, mob H8 5.3.36 *Bless me, what a fry of fornication is at door!*

fub See FOB.

fugitive *n.* Deserter ANT 4.9.22 *let the world rank me...a fugitive,* 1H6 3.3.67.

fulfil *vb.*
1 Fill full, fill up SON 136.5 *fulfil the treasure of thy love,* LLL 4.3.361, LUC 1258.
2 Execute, perform ERR 4.1.113 *servants must their masters' minds fulfil,* 1H6 3.2.133, LUC 1635.

fulfilling *ppl. adj.* Complementary TRO Prol.18 *fulfilling bolts.*

full *n.*
1 *at full* Fully, completely MM 1.1.43 *be thou at full ourself;* at length ERR 1.1.122 *dilate at full,* H5 2.4.140, HAM 4.3.63; at the period or moment of fulness LLL 5.2.214 *took the moon at full,* ANT 3.2.49.
2 *in the full* In full company, all together TRO 4.5.272 *There in the full convive we.*
3 *to the full* Fully 2H6 1.2.84 *effected to the full,* AWW 1.3.199; to its full state TRO 3.3.241 *to my full of view* (i.e. to my eye's complete satisfaction), ANT 2.1.11.
~ *adj. with full voice* Unanimously COR 3.3.59.
~ *adv.*
1 Fully, quite AWW 1.3.61 *full true,* MV 1.3.56, MAC 1.4.54.
2 Very, exceedingly LR 2.1.56 *full suddenly,* VEN 361, OTH 1.2.10.

full-acorned *adj.* Fed full on acorns CYM 2.5.16 *a full-acorn'd boar.*

fullam *n.* Kind of false dice loaded at the corner WIV 1.3.85 *gourd and fullam holds, And high and low beguiles the rich and poor.*

full-charged *adj.* Fully loaded; (fig.) fully prepared H8 1.2.3 *a full-charg'd confederacy.*

fuller *n.* One who cleanses cloth H8 1.2.33 *spinsters, carders, fullers, weavers.*

full-fraught *adj.* Fully laden; (fig.) complete, all-round H5 2.2.139 *thy fall hath left a kind of blot To mark the full-fraught man...With some suspicion.*

full-gorged *adj.* Crammed full with food SHR 4.1.191 *till she stoop, she must not be full-gorg'd.*

fullness *n.* Repletion, satiety SON 56.6 *thou fill Thy hungry eyes even till they wink with fullness*; abundance CYM 3.6.12 *To lapse in fullness* (i.e. to sin in prosperity), MAC 1.4.34.

fully *adv.* To satiety LR 3.5.21 *stuff his suspicion more fully*, COR 1.9.11.

fulsome *adj.*
1 Full with young, pregnant MV 1.3.86 *the fulsome ewes.*
2 Cloying, offensive to good taste TN 5.1.109 *fulsome to mine ear.*
3 Offensive to the senses, physically disgusting R3 5.3.132 *fulsome wine,* JN 3.4.32.
4 Morally foul, filthy OTH 4.1.37 *that's fulsome!*

fumble *vb.* Wrap up clumsily, huddle together TIT 4.2.58 *What dost thou wrap and fumble in thy arms?*; (fig.) TRO 4.4.46 *many farewells...He fumbles up into a loose adieu.*

fume *n.*
1 Exhalation, vapour ROM 1.1.190 *Love is a smoke made with the fume of sighs.*
2 Noxious vapour supposed formerly to rise to the brain from the stomach, chiefly as the result of intoxication; (hence) something which goes to the head and clouds the brain MAC 1.7.66 *his two chamberlains Will I with wine...so convince That memory...Shall be a fume,* TMP 5.1.67, CYM 4.2.301.
3 Rage VEN 316 *bites the poor flies in his fume,* 2H6 1.3.153.
~ *vb.* (fig.) Be clouded with fumes; (hence) be stupefied ANT 2.1.24 *Keep his brain fuming.*

fumiter See FUMITORY.

fumitory, fumiter *n.* Plant of the genus Fumaria, regarded as a weed H5 5.2.45 *rank fumitory* (F1 *Femetary*), LR 4.4.3 *rank fumiter* (Q1 *femiter*).

function *n.*
1 Activity, action (of the faculties) MAC 1.3.140 *function Is smother'd in surmise,* HAM 2.2.556.
2 Particular kind of activity or operation: of a physical organ MND 3.2.177 *Dark night, that from the eye his function takes*; of intellectual or moral powers OTH 2.3.348 *Even as her appetite shall play the god With his weak function.*

funeral *n.*
1 (pl.) Obsequies, funeral rites JC 5.3.105 *His funerals shall not be in our camp,* TIT 1.1.381.
2 Death PER 2.4.32 *cause to mourn his funeral.*

furlong *n.* An area a furlong each way, containing ten acres TMP 1.1.65 *a thousand furlongs of sea,* WT 1.2.95.

furnace *vb.* Exhale as from a furnace CYM 1.6.66 *furnaces The thick sighs.*

furnish *vb.*
1 Supply what is necessary, equip, fit out MV 2.4.9

we have two hours To furnish us, 1H6 4.1.39, ANT 1.4.77.
2 Dress AYL 3.2.245 *He was furnish'd like a hunter,* ADO 3.1.103; decorate, embellish ROM 4.2.35 *ornaments...to furnish me to-morrow.*
~ in combination
furnish forth FURNISH sense 1 2H4 1.2.224 *lend me a thousand pound to furnish me forth,* HAM 1.2.181.
furnish out Provide for TIM 3.4.114 *to furnish out A moderate table.*

furnishings *n.* (pl.) Unimportant appendages, mere externals LR 3.1.29 *or something deeper, Whereof...these are but furnishings.*

furniture *n.*
1 Fitting out, equipping, provision 1H4 3.3.202 *Money and order for their furniture.*
2 Equipment SHR 4.3.180 *this poor furniture and mean array,* 2H6 1.3.169, H8 2.1.99.
3 Trappings, harness AWW 2.3.59 *give bay Curtal and his furniture.*

furrow *n.* Ploughed land, cornfields TMP 4.1.135 *sicklemen,...Come hither from the furrow*; (attrib.) *furrow weeds* Weeds which come up in furrows, esp. in cornfields LR 4.4.3 *rank...furrow weeds.*

furse See FURZE.

further *adj.* More distant or remote H8 2.4.233 *till further day,* LR 5.3.53; (absol.) *no further* no further or additional business, nothing else COR 2.3.173 *I have no further with you,* MM 5.1.481.

fury *n.*
1 Inspired frenzy, poetic rage OTH 3.4.72 *A sibyl ...In her prophetic fury,* LLL 4.3.225, SON 100.3.
2 One of the goddesses sent from Tartarus to avenge wrong and punish crime R3 1.4.57 *Furies, take him unto torment!,* ADO 1.1.191, ANT 2.5.40.

furze *n.* Gorse TMP 4.1.180 *sharp furzes, pricking goss, and thorns* (F1 *firzes*), TMP 1.1.66 (F1 *firrs*).

fust *vb.* Grow mouldy HAM 4.4.39 *[God] gave us not...capability and...reason To fust in us unus'd.*

fustian *n.*
1 Coarse cloth made of cotton and flax SHR 4.1.47 *the serving men in their new fustian.*
2 Gibberish, inflated nonsense OTH 2.3.280 *discourse fustian with one's own shadow.*
~ *adj.* Ridiculously pompous TN 2.5.108 *A fustian riddle!*

fustilarian *n.* (formation on the word fustilugs) Fat, frowzy woman 2H4 2.1.60 *you fustilarian!*

fusty *adj.* Mouldy, stale TRO 1.3.161 *this fusty stuff,* COR 1.9.7.

fut *interj.* God's foot LR 1.2.131 *Fut, I should have that I am...*
⇨ Also perh. var. of 'phut'.

G

gaberdine *n.* Long, loose upper garment MV 1.3.112 *And spit upon my Jewish gaberdine,* TMP 2.2.38.

gad *n.* Sharp spike; (hence) stylus TIT 4.1.103 *I...with a gad of steel will write these words; upon the gad suddenly* LR 1.2.26 *All this done Upon the gad?*

gage *n.*
1 Pawn, pledge, security H5 4.1.208 *Give me any gage of thine, and I will wear it in my bonnet*; lay to gage put in pawn LUC 1351.
2 Pledge (usu. a glove thrown on the ground) of a person's appearance to do battle in support of his assertions, challenge R2 1.1.69 *Pale trembling coward, there I throw my gage,* R2 4.1.34.

~ *vb.*
1 Pledge, stake, risk HAM 1.1.91 *a moi'ty competent Was gaged by our king,* LUC 144.
2 Bind as by oath or promise 1H4 1.3.173 *Did gage them both in an unjust behalf,* TRO 5.1.41.
3 Entangle *in* MV 1.1.130 *the great debts Wherein my time...Hath left me gag'd.*

gain *vb.*
1 Acquire (a language) 2H4 4.4.69 *to gain the language.*
2 Restore CYM 4.2.167 *To gain his colour.*
3 Give victory to CYM 2.4.59 *the foul opinion You had...gains or loses Your sword or mine.*

4 *gain the cap* See CAP.

gain-giving *n.* Misgiving HAM 5.2.216 *such a kind of gain-giving, as would perhaps trouble a woman.*

gainsay *vb.* Forbid TRO 4.5.132 *But the just gods gainsay.*

gainsaying *n.* Refusal WT 1.2.19 *and in that I'll no gainsaying.*

gainst, 'gainst *conj.* By the time that, before HAM 1.1.158 *'gainst that season comes,* TIT 5.2.205.
~ *prep.* In expectation of, in time for, in preparation for SHR 2.1.315 *To buy apparel 'gainst the wedding day,* ROM 3.5.153, R2 5.2.66.
◊ Aphetic form of AGAINST. In mod. edd. usu. *'gainst.*

gait *n.*
1 Walking, going forward WIV 1.4.30 *strut in his gait,* H8 3.2.116; *take his gait* go his way MND 5.1.416 *Every fairy take his gait; address thy gait* go TN 1.4.15 *Therefore, good youth, address thy gait unto her, Be not denied access.*
2 (fig.) Proceeding HAM 1.2.31 *to suppress His further gait herein.*

Galen, Galien *n.* Celebrated physician of the 2C; (hence gen.) a physician WIV 2.3.29 *What says my Aesculapius? my Galen?*

gall *n.* Spirit to resent injury TRO 1.3.237 *But when they would seem soldiers, they have galls, Good arms, strong joints...,* OTH 4.3.92.
~ *vb.*
1 Make sore by chafing or rubbing HAM 5.1.141 *the toe of the peasant comes so near the heel of the courtier, he galls his kibe,* 2H4 1.2.166, PER 4.1.53; irritate 2H4 1.2.147 *I am loath to gall a new-heal'd wound.*
2 Graze with a weapon, wound, hurt SHR 5.2.60 *hath he not hit you here?—'A has a little gall'd me,* HAM 4.7.147, JN 4.3.94.
3 (fig.) Harass, annoy OTH 1.1.148 *this may gall him with some check,* WIV 3.4.5, 1H4 1.3.229.
4 Scoff at H5 5.1.74 *gleeking and galling at this gentleman.*

gallant *n.*
1 Man of fashion and pleasure, fine gentleman AYL 2.2.17 *Send to his brother; fetch that gallant hither,* OTH 2.3.31, ADO 4.1.317.
2 (pl. used as vocative) Gentlemen ADO 3.2.15 *Gallants, I am not as I have been,* 1H4 2.4.277, 1H6 3.2.41.
3 Ladies' man, lover WIV 2.1.22 *to show himself a young gallant!*
~ *adj.* Excellent, splendid, fine AYL 1.2.229 *But fare thee well, thou art a gallant youth,* WT 1.1.38, JC 4.2.24; (of a ship) noble, stately TMP 5.1.237 *Our royal, good, and gallant ship.*

gallantry *n.* Body of gallants TRO 3.1.136 *Deiphobus, Helenus, Antenor, and all the gallantry of Troy.*

gallant-springing *adj.* Full of noble promise, 'growing up in beauty' (Schmidt) R3 1.4.221 *When gallant-springing brave Plantagenet.*

galled *adj.* Full of gall, rancour TRO 1.10.54 *Some galled goose of Winchester would hiss* (with quibble on sense of 'affected with venereal disease').

galled *ppl. adj.* Sore (from chafing) HAM 3.2.242 *Let the gall'd jade winch;* (from crying) R3 4.4.53 *in galled eyes of weeping souls,* HAM 1.2.155; fretted (with salt water) H5 3.1.12 *a galled rock,* LUC 1440.

galley *n.* Low flat-built vessel, propelled by oars but also having masts for sails, formerly in common use in the Mediterranean SHR 2.1.379 *twelve tight galleys,* OTH 1.2.40, TN 3.3.26.

Gallia *n.*
1 Gaul, France H5 5.1.89 *And swear I got them in the Gallia wars,* 1H6 4.7.48, 3H6 5.3.8.

2 Wales WIV 3.1.97 *Gallia and Gaul, French and Welsh.*

Gallian *adj.* French 1H6 5.4.139 *With more than half the Gallian territories,* CYM 1.6.66.

galliard *n.* Quick and lively dance in triple time TN 1.3.120 *What is thy excellence in a galliard, knight?,* H5 1.2.252.

galliass *n.* Heavy low-built vessel, larger than a galley, propelled both by sail and oar, chiefly employed in war SHR 2.1.378 *two galliasses.*

gallimaufrey *n.*
1 Medley, jumble WT 4.4.328 *a gallimaufrey of gambols.*
2 Promiscuous assemblage WIV 2.1.115 *He loves the gallimaufrey.*

gallop *n. false gallop* Canter; (fig.) AYL 3.2.113 *the very false gallop of verses,* ADO 3.4.94.

gallow *vb.* Frighten LR 3.2.44 *Gallow the very wanderers of the dark.*

gallow-glasses *n.* (pl.) Soldiers or retainers formerly maintained by Irish chiefs 2H6 4.9.26 *come from Ireland...with...a mighty power Of gallowglasses,* MAC 1.2.13 (F1 *Gallowgrosses*).

gallows *n.* (short form of) Gallows-bird, one deserving to be hanged LLL 5.2.12 *Ay, and a shrewd unhappy gallows too,* TMP 1.1.30; (with additional pl. suffix) CYM 5.4.205 *desolation of gaolers and gallowses!*

gambol *adj.* Sportive, playful 2H4 2.4.251 *and such other gambol faculties.*

gambold *n.* (var. of) GAMBOL SHR Ind.2.138 *a Christmas gambold, or a tumbling-trick.*

gamboys See VIOL-DE-GAMBOYS.

game *n.*
1 Fun, sport MND 1.1.240 *As waggish boys in game themselves forswear,* LLL 5.2.155.
2 Amorous play OTH 2.3.19 *And I'll warrant her, full of game,* TRO 4.5.63, 3H6 3.2.14 (with quibble on sense 3).
3 Sport derived from the chase LLL 5.2.360 *We have had pastimes here and pleasant game,* 3H6 4.5.11.

gamester *n.*
1 Frolicsome person AYL 1.1.164 *Now will I stir this gamester,* SHR 2.1.400, H8 1.4.45.
2 Lewd person AWW 5.3.188 *And was a common gamester to the camp,* PER 4.6.75.

gamoth, gamouth See GAMUT.

gamut *n.* Musical scale SHR 3.1.72 *Yet read the gamut of Hortensio* (F1 *gamouth*).

gan *vb.* Began COR 2.2.115 *When by and by the din of war gan pierce,* 2H4 1.1.129, CYM 5.5.197.

gap *n.*
1 *gap of breath* Mouth JN 4.4.32 *And stop this gap of breath with fulsome dust.*
2 Point in song where the male singer pauses and interpolates an obscenity or bawdy gesture WT 4.4.197 *and break a foul gap into the matter.*
◊ *Gap* is sometimes emended, esp. to *jest*. See BREAK sense 2.

gape *vb.* Desire eagerly ROM 2.Ch.2 *And young affection gapes to be his heir.*

gaping *n.* Bawling H8 5.3.3 *leave your gaping.*
~ *ppl. adj. gaping pig* Pig's head served on the table, with its mouth wide open MV 4.1.47.

garb *n.* Style, manner, fashion H5 5.1.76 *he could not speak English in the native garb,* LR 2.2.97, HAM 2.2.373.

garboil *n.* Brawl, commotion ANT 1.3.61 *The garboils she awak'd,* ANT 2.2.67.

garden-house *n.* Summer-house MM 5.1.212 *And did supply the at thy garden-house.*

gardon *n.* (blunder for) GUERDON LLL 3.1.170 *Gardon, O sweet gardon! better than remuneration.*

garland n.
1 Royal crown or diadem R3 3.2.40 *Till Richard wear the garland of the realm*, 2H4 5.2.84.
2 Principal ornament or 'glory' COR 1.1.184 *that was your garland*, ANT 4.15.64.

garner n. Storehouse, granary COR 1.1.250 *To gnaw their garners*, TMP 1.1.111.
~ vb. Treasure, store up OTH 4.2.57 *But there, where I have garner'd up my heart*.

garnish n. Outfit, dress MV 2.6.45 *Even in the lovely garnish of a boy*.
~ vb. Fit out, furnish MV 3.5.69 *I do know A many fools, that stand in better place, Garnish'd like him*.

gaskins n. Breeches TN 1.5.25 *if both break, your gaskins fall*.

gasted pa. pple. Terrified LR 2.1.55 *gasted by the noise I made*.

gastness n. Terror OTH 5.1.106 *the gastness of her eye*.

gate n. (short for) Gate-vein, the 'vena porta' HAM 1.5.67 *The natural gates and alleys of the body*.

gaud, gawd n. Plaything, toy, trinket MND 4.1.167 *Seems to me now As the remembrance of an idle gaud*, JN 3.3.36, TRO 3.3.176.

gauded, gawded pple. adj. Adorned COR 2.1.217 *In their nicely gawded cheeks*.
◊ F1; some edd. read *guarded* 'protected'.

gaudy adj. Bright, resplendent, gay LLL 5.2.802 *the gaudy blossoms of your love*, SON 1.10, VEN 1088.

gaudy-night n. Night of rejoicing ANT 3.13.182 *Let's have one other gaudy night*.

gawd See GAUD.

gay adj. (in poetry, esp. ballad) Conventional epithet of praise applied to women PP 15.15 *the lady gay*.

gaze n.
1 That which is gazed at, object of vision MAC 5.8.24 *And live to be the show and gaze o' th' time!*, SON 5.2.
2 at gaze (hunting term) Staring in wonder and bewilderment LUC 1149 *As the poor frighted deer that stands at gaze*.

gear n.
1 Stuff, thing, article MV 2.2.167 *a good wench for this gear*, TRO 3.2.211, ROM 5.1.60.
2 Discourse, talk MV 1.1.110 *I'll grow a talker for this gear*.
3 Matter, affair, business 2H6 1.4.14 *To this gear, the sooner the better*, R3 1.4.153, ROM 2.4.101.

geck n. Fool, dupe TN 5.1.343 *And made the most notorious geck and gull*, CYM 5.4.67.

geld vb. Deprive (of some essential part) R2 2.1.237 *gelded of his patrimony*, LLL 2.1.148, 1H4 3.1.109.

gelidus timor occupat artus See PINE GELIDUS....

gemini [L.] Pair WIV 2.2.9 *a gemini of baboons*.

gender n.
1 Kind, sort, class OTH 1.3.323 *one gender of herbs*; *the general gender* the common sort (of people) HAM 4.7.18.
2 Offspring PHT 18 *That thy sable gender mak'st*.
~ vb. Engender, beget OTH 4.2.62 *To knot and gender in*.

general n.
1 *the general* The whole TRO 1.3.342 *the success ...shall give a scantling Of good or bad unto the general*; *the general sex* all womenkind TRO 5.2.132 *to square the general sex by Cressid's rule*.
2 People in general, the public JC 2.1.12 *I know no personal cause to spurn at him, But for the general*, HAM 2.2.437.
3 That which is common to all TRO 1.3.180 *severals and generals of grace*.
4 *in general* (1) In a body, collectively, without exception 1H4 4.3.26 *So are all the horses of the*

enemy *In general journey-bated*, TRO 4.5.21; (2) in all respects PER 5.1.183 *Most wise in general*; (3) generally JC 2.2.29 *to the world in general as to Caesar*, LUC 1484.
~ adj.
1 All, all collectively, whole 1H4 3.2.178 *Our general forces*, 1H6 4.4.3, LR 1.4.61.
2 Relating to the whole people, common, public JC 3.2.89 *The general coffers*, 2H4 4.1.93, HAM 2.2.563.
~ adv. Generally 1H4 4.1.5 *Should go so general current through the world*.

generally adv.
1 In a body, as a whole AYL 3.2.349 *hath generally tax'd their whole sex withal*, SHR 1.2.88.
2 Universally, without exception R2 2.2.132 *Wherein the King stands generally condemn'd*, AWW 2.3.38, H8 2.1.47.

generation n.
1 Offspring, progeny TRO 3.1.133 *Is love a generation of vipers?*, WT 2.1.148, LR 1.1.117.
2 Breed, race, kind TMP 3.3.33 *Our human generation*, MM 4.3.89, TIM 1.1.201.
3 Procreation, propagation of species PER 3.3.25 *to the end of generation!*, 2H4 4.2.49.
4 Genealogy, pedigree TRO 3.1.131 *Is this the generation of love?*

generative adj. Capable of generation MM 3.2.112 *and he is a motion generative*.

generosity n. Nobility COR 1.1.211 *To break the heart of generosity*.

generous adj. Of noble lineage, high born LLL 5.1.91 *most generous sir*, MM 4.6.13, HAM 1.3.74.

genitivo [L.] In the genitive case WIV 4.1.43 *genitivo, hujus*.

genius n.
1 (in classical pagan belief) Attendant god or spirit supposed to be allotted to every man at birth TN 3.4.129 *His very genius*, TRO 4.4.50, MAC 3.1.55.
2 One of the two mutually opposed (good and evil) spirits supposed to attend every person throughout his life TMP 4.1.27 *Our worser genius*.
3 Embodied type or representation 2H4 3.2.314 *the very genius of famine*.

gennet See JENNET.

gentility n.
1 Good birth, honourable extraction AYL 1.1.21 *mines my gentility with my education*.
2 Politeness LLL 1.1.128 *A dangerous law against gentility*.

gentle n. (pl.) Gentlefolk LLL 4.2.166 *the gentles are at their game*; (chiefly used, sing. and pl., in polite address) WT 4.4.46 *Be merry, gentle*, WIV 3.2.91, H5 Prol.8.
~ vb. Ennoble H5 4.3.63 *gentle his condition*.
~ adj.
1 Well-born WT 1.2.394 *Our parents' noble names, In whose success we are gentle*, 1H6 5.4.8, CYM 4.2.39.
2 Used as a complimentary epithet TGV 1.2.14 *What think'st thou of the gentle Proteus?*, MM 4.2.72; (freq. in polite address) JC 3.2.72 *You gentle Romans*, MM 1.4.7, ERR 3.2.25.
3 Cultivated, domesticated WT 4.4.93 *A gentler scion to the wildest stock*.
◊ COR 4.1.8 *being gentle wounded* i.e. bearing oneself like a gentleman when wounded.

gentleman n.
1 Officer of a company of soldiers H5 4.1.39 *I am a gentleman of a company*, 1H4 4.2.24.
2 Man of 'gentle' (good) birth attached to the household of a person of high rank TN 5.1.180 *The Count's gentleman*, H8 1.2.5, LR 1.3.1; (transf.) 1H4 1.2.29 *Diana's foresters, gentlemen of the shade*.

gentlewoman n. Woman of 'gentle' (good) birth attached to the household of a person of high rank

OTH 3.1.24 *the gentlewoman that attends the general's wife*, ADO 2.3.215, H8 3.2.94.

gently *adv.* Willingly, without resistance TMP 1.2.298 *do my spriting gently*, MAC 5.7.24.

gentry *n.*
1 Rank by birth, quality or rank of a gentleman COR 2.1.238 *by the suit of the gentry to him*, WT 1.2.393, 1H6 2.4.93.
2 Good breeding HAM 5.2.110 *the card or calendar of gentry*; courtesy HAM 2.2.22 *show us so much gentry and good will*.

George *n.* Jewel, on which is a figure of St. George, forming part of the insignia of the Order of the Garter 2H6 4.1.29 *Look on my George*, R3 4.4.366.

germain (var. of) GERMAN and GERMEN.

german, germane *n.* Near relative OTH 1.1.113 *you'll have...jennets for germans* (F1 *Germaines*; Q1 *Iermans*); *cousin-german* first cousin TRO 4.5.121.
~ *adj.*
1 Closely related WT 4.4.773 *those that are germane to him*, TIM 4.3.340.
2 Closely connected, appropriate HAM 5.2.158 *more germane to the matter*.

German clock *n.* Elaborately constructed clock, often containing automatic figures of persons or animals LLL 3.1.190 *that is like a German clock*.

germen *n.* Rudiment of an organism, germ, seed MAC 4.1.59 *the treasure Of nature's germens*, LR 3.2.8 (F1 *germains*).

gest *n.*[1] (pl.) Notable deeds, exploits ANT 4.8.2 *let the Queen know of our gests*.

gest *n.*[2] Time allotted for a halt WT 1.2.41 *behind the gest*.

gesture *n.* Demeanour, bearing AYL 5.2.62 *as your gesture cries it out*, H5 4.Ch.25.

get *vb.*
1 (intr.) Gain 1H6 4.3.32 *they daily get*.
2 Learn, ascertain HAM 3.1.2 *Get from him why he puts on this confusion*, TGV 2.5.39, WT 4.2.50.
3 Beget HAM 2.3.13 *She is with child, And he that got it, sentenc'd*, ADO 2.1.321, MV 3.5.11; (absol.) VEN 168 *to get it is thy duty*; (for pass.) be begotten JN 1.1.259 *were I to get again, Madam, I would not wish a better father*.

getter *n.* Begetter COR 4.5.224 *a getter of more bastard children*.

ghost *n.*
1 Incorporeal being SON 86.9 *that affable familiar ghost Which nightly gulls him with intelligence*.
2 Apparition, spectre VEN 933 *Death—Grim-grinning ghost*.
3 Corpse HAM 1.4.85 *I'll make a ghost of him that lets me*, 2H6 3.2.161.
~ *vb.* Haunt ANT 2.6.13 *Who at Philippi the good Brutus ghosted*.

ghostly *adj.* Spiritual ROM 3.3.49 *a ghostly confessor*, MM 4.3.53, 3H6 3.2.107.

giant-dwarf *n.* Dwarf with a giant's power LLL 3.1.180 *This senior-junior giant-dwarf, Dan Cupid*.

gib(-cat) *n.* Tom-cat 1H4 1.2.74 *I am as melancholy as a gib cat*, HAM 3.4.190.

gibbet *vb.* Hang as on a gibbet 2H4 3.2.264 *swifter than he that gibbets on the brewer's bucket*.

giddily *adv.* Carelessly, lightly TN 2.4.84 *I hold as giddily as fortune*.

giddy *adj.*
1 Whirling round with bewildering rapidity LUC 952 *the giddy round of Fortune's wheel*, H5 3.6.27.
2 Inconstant, fickle H5 1.2.145 *a giddy neighbour to us*, ADO 5.4.108, TN 2.4.33.

gig *n.* Whipping-top LLL 5.1.67 *go whip thy gig*.
~ *vb.* Walk flightily HAM 3.1.144 *You gig and amble* (Q2; F1 *gidge*; Q(1676) *jig*).

giglet, giglot *n.* Lewd, wanton woman MM 5.1.347 *Away with those giglets*; (attrib.) 1H6 4.7.41 *a giglot wench*, CYM 3.1.31.

gild *vb.*
1 Smear with blood JN 2.1.316 *all gilt with Frenchmen's blood*, MAC 2.2.53 (with quibble).
2 Supply with money MV 2.6.49 *I will...gild myself With some moe ducats*.
3 Flash TMP 5.1.280 *liquor that hath gilded 'em*.
4 Give a specious lustre to 1H4 5.4.158 *I'll gild it with the happiest terms*, 2H4 1.2.149, ANT 1.5.37.

gilded *ppl. adj.*
1 Tinged with a golden colour ANT 1.4.62 *the gilded puddle Which beasts would cough at* (i.e. covered with a scum of a golden colour).
2 Supplied with money HAM 3.3.58 *Offence's gilded hand may shove by justice*.

gill, jill *n.* (abbreviation of 'Gillian') Familiar or contemptuous term applied to a woman; lass, wench LLL 5.2.875 *Our wooing doth not end like an old play: Jack hath not Gill*, MND 3.2.461 (F1 *Iill*), SHR 4.1.50 (F1 *Gils*).

gillyvors *n.* Clove-scented pink flower, Dianthus carophyllus WT 4.4.98 *garden rich in gillyvors*.

gilt *n.*
1 Money, gold H5 2.Ch.26 *Have for the gilt of France*.
2 Fine trappings H5 4.3.110 *Our gayness and our gilt are all besmirch'd*, TIM 4.3.302.

gilt *ppl. adj.* Covered with a golden colour; (hence) glazed with the yolk of an egg LLL 5.2.646 *A gilt nutmeg*.
◇ Gilt nutmegs, for spicing ale and wine, were a common lover's gift in S.'s time.

gimmal *n.*
1 (pl.) Joints or connecting parts for transmitting motion in clockwork 1H6 1.2.41 *by some odd gimmals or device, Their arms are set, like clocks* (F1 *gimmors*; Ff 2-3 *Gimmalls*, F4 *Gimmals*).
◇ Also spelt *gimmer*.
2 (attrib.) See GIMMALED.

gimmaled *adj.* Made with joints, consisting of two similar parts hinged together H5 4.2.48 *the gimmal'd bit* (Ff *Iymold*; mod. edd. *gimmal*).

gimmer, gimmor See GIMMAL.

gin *n.* Trap, snare TN 2.5.83 *Now is the woodcock near the gin*, MAC 4.2.35, 3H6 1.4.61.

gin *vb.* Begin MAC 1.2.25 *the sun gins his reflection*; (with infin.) TMP 3.3.106 *their great guilt...Now gins to bite the spirits*, MAC 5.5.49, COR 2.2.115.

ging *n.* Gang WIV 4.2.118 *there's a knot, a ging, a pack, a conspiracy against me* (F1, Q3 *gin*).

gipsy *n.* (allusively identified with) Egyptian ANT 4.12.28 *this grave charm...Like a right gipsy, hath at fast and loose Beguil'd me to the very heart of loss*.
◇ The gipsies in S's. time were believed to have come from Egypt. Cf. ROM 2.4.41 *Cleopatra a gipsy*.

gird *n.* Sharp, biting remark SHR 5.2.58 *I thank thee for that gird*.
~ *vb.* Taunt COR 1.1.256 *he will not spare to gird the gods*; (intr.) 2H4 1.2.6 *take a pride to gird at me*.

girded *ppl. adj.* Encircled; (hence) besieged H5 3.Ch.27 *on girded Harflew*.

girdle *n.*
1 Belt worn round the waist to secure garments; also employed as a means of carrying light articles, esp. a weapon or a purse 2H4 1.2.39 *bunches of keys at their girdles*, LLL 4.1.50, LR 4.6.126; (fig.) 2H4 3.1.50 *The beachy girdle of the ocean*, H5 Prol.19, CYM 3.1.80.
2 *put a girdle round the earth* Make a circuit of the world MND 2.1.175.

give *vb.*
1 'Give away,' hand over the bride at the marriage ceremony AYL 3.3.67 *none here to give the woman?*
2 (of the mind) Suggest, cause to suspect COR 4.5.150 *my mind gave me his clothes made a false report of him*, H8 5.2.144.
3 Display as on armorial bearing WIV 1.1.16 *may give the dozen white luces*, 1H6 1.5.29.
4 Represent, report COR 1.9.55 *us that give you truly*, ANT 1.4.40.
5 Attribute, ascribe, assign MAC 1.3.119 *those that gave the Thane of Cawdor to me*, H8 3.2.262, ROM 4.5.116.
7 Consider, set down WT 3.2.95 *your favour, I do give lost*.
8 Be tearful, exude moisture TIM 4.3.484 *whose eyes do never give*.
▷ In MAC 2.3.35 *giving him the lie* may also contain a quibble on 'lay out flat', as in wrestling.
~ in combination
give away Sacrifice (another's interests) OTH 3.3.28 *thy solicitor shall rather die Than give thy cause away*. **give back** Retreat, fall back TGV 5.4.126 *Thurio, give back, or else embrace thy death*. **give off** **1** Relinquish JN 5.1.27 *My crown I should give off*.
2 Cease ANT 4.3.22 *Let's see how it will give off*. **give over** **1** Abandon, desert TIT 4.2.48 *Pray to the devils, the gods have given us over*, MND 3.2.130, TMP 2.1.11.
2 Pronounce incurable, 'give up' TIM 3.3.12 *His friends, like physicians, Thrice give him over*, 1H4 3.3.36. **3** Yield *to* 2H4 1.1.164 *give o'er To stormy passion*.
4 Cease CYM 2.3.16 *I'll never give o'er*, PER 4.2.28. **give up** **1** Succumb CYM 2.2.46 *Where Philomele gave up*. **2** Deliver, render R3 1.4.184 *have given their verdict up Unto the frowning judge*, HAM 1.3.98.

giving out *n.* Assertion, declaration HAM 1.5.178 *such ambiguous giving out*, MM 1.4.54, OTH 4.1.127.
glad *n.* Gladness PER 2.Gower.38 *to give him glad*.
~ *vb.* Make glad 3H6 4.6.93 *Did glad my heart*, TIT 1.1.166, H8 2.4.197.
glance *n.* (fig.) Satirical hit AYL 2.7.57 *glances of the fool*.
~ *vb.*
1 (of a weapon) Glide off an object struck WIV 5.5.234 *your arrow hath glanc'd*; (fig.) SHR 5.2.61 *the jest did glance away from me*, LR 5.3.149; *glance on* strike obliquely upon and turn aside PER 3.3.7 *Your shakes of fortune…glance full wond'ringly on us*.
2 Dart or spring *aside* SON 76.3 *Why with the time do I not glance aside*.
3 Pass quickly *from* (a subject) MM 5.1.309 *to glance from him To th' Duke himself*.
4 Allude to ERR 5.1.66 *I often glanced it*.
glanders *n.* Contagious disease in horses, causing swellings beneath the jaw SHR 3.2.50 *possess'd with the glanders*.
glass *n.*
1 Sand-glass for the measurement of time; (esp.) hour-glass 1H6 4.2.35 *the glass, that now begins to run*, AWW 2.1.165, WT 1.2.306; (in nautical use) half-hour glass; (hence) half-an-hour TMP 5.1.223 *three glasses since*.
2 Magic mirror or crystal MAC 4.1.119 *who bears a glass Which shows me many more*.
3 Eyeball R2 1.3.208 *the glasses of thine eyes*, COR 3.2.117.
glassed *ppl. adj.* Enclosed or cased in glass LLL 2.1.244 *jewels in crystal…from where they were glass'd*.

glass-eyes *n.* Spectacles LR 4.6.170 *Get thee glass-eyes*.
glass-faced *adj.* Reflecting like a mirror the looks of another TIM 1.1.58 *the glass-fac'd flatterer*.
glass-gazing *adj.* Contemplating oneself in a mirror LR 2.2.18 *whoreson, glass-gazing…rogue*.
glassy *adj.* Frail as glass MM 2.2.120 *His glassy essence*.
glaze *vb.* Stare, glare JC 1.3.21 *Who glaz'd upon me*.
glean *vb.* Collect in one mass HAM 4.2.20 *what you have glean'd*, H8 3.2.284.
gleaned *ppl. adj.* Stripped (of defenders) H5 1.2.151 *Galling the gleaned land with hot assays*.
gleek *n.* Gibe, jest ROM 4.5.114 *No money…but the gleek*, 1H6 3.2.123 (F1 *glikes*).
~ *vb.* Jest MND 3.1.146 *I can gleek upon occasion*, H5 5.1.74.
glib *vb.* Castrate WT 2.1.149 *And I had rather glib myself*.
glimpse *n.* Transient brightness, flash MM 1.2.158 *glimpse of newness*, HAM 1.4.53; (fig.) faint appearance, tinge TRO 1.2.25 *There is no man hath a virtue that he hath not a glimpse of*.
globe *n.* Head or brain HAM 1.5.97 *this distracted globe*.
glooming *adj.* (fig.) Dark ROM 5.3.305 *A glooming peace*.
glorious *adj.* Eager for glory CYM 1.6.7 *the desire that's glorious*, PER 1. Gower.9.
gloss *n.* Speciously fair appearance MAC 1.7.34 *worn now in their newest gloss*; (hence) *set a gloss on* give a speciously fair appearance to TIM 1.2.16, 1H6 4.1.103.
glow *vb.* Make hot ANT 2.2.204 *To glow the delicate cheeks*.
gloze *n.* 'High falutin' talk LLL 4.3.367 *Now to plain-dealing, lay these glozes by*.
~ *vb.*
1 Interpret (a thing) to be (so and so) H5 1.2.40 *the French unjustly gloze*.
2 Comment *on* TRO 2.2.165 *Have gloz'd, but superficially*.
3 Flatter, talk smoothly and speciously R2 2.1.10 *whom youth and ease have taught to gloze*, TIT 4.4.35, PER 1.1.110.
glut *vb.*
1 Swallow greedily, gulp down TMP 1.1.60 *And gape at wid'st to glut him*.
2 Satiate 1H4 3.2.84 *Being with his presence glutted, gorg'd, and full*.
gnarl *vb.* Snarl 2H6 3.1.192 *wolves are gnarling*.
gnarling *ppl. adj.* Snarling R2 1.3.292 *gnarling sorrow hath less power to bite*.
go *vb.*
1 Walk, move on foot at an ordinary pace TGV 4.2.20 *love Will creep in service where it cannot go*, LR 1.4.21, TMP 3.2.72.
2 Go away, depart, leave; (used in imperative as a rebuke) MND 3.2.259 *You are a tame man, go!*, H5 5.1.69, ROM 1.5.86.
3 Be pregnant 2H4 5.4.9 *the child I now go with*, R3 3.5.86, H8 4.1.77; (hence) conceive ANT 1.2.64 *let him marry a woman that cannot go*.
~ in combination
go about Make it one's object *to*, take (it) in hand MND 4.1.207 *if he go about t' expound this dream*, MM 3.2.203, H5 4.1.199. **go along with** Agree with or approve of HAM 1.2.15 *Your better wisdoms, which have freely gone With this affair along*. **go before** Be superior to CYM 1.4.72 *If she went before others I have seen*. **go by** Go unnoticed, pass unheeded SHR 1.2.254 *let her go by*, MM 2.2.41. **go even, hard, near** See EVEN, HARD, NEAR. **go in** Join in ADO 1.1.186 *to go in the song*. **go off** Die

MAC 5.9.2 *Some must go off.* **go through** Do one's utmost MM 2.1.270 *do it for some piece of money, and go through with all,* PER 4.2.43. **go to!** Used to express disapprobation or derisive incredulity MAC 5.1.46 *go to.* **go to it 1** Die, perish HAM 5.2.56 *So Guildenstern and Rosencrantz go to't,* TGV 4.4.4. **2** Copulate LR 4.6.112 *The wren goes to't,* PER 4.6.74. **go up** (of a sword) Be put up in its sheath JC 5.1.52 *When think you that the sword goes up again?*

goal *n.*
1 *get goal for goal of* Be even with ANT 4.8.22.
2 *to the goal* To the point WT 1.2.96 *But to th' goal.*

goatish *adj.* Lascivious, lustful LR 1.2.127 *to lay his goatish disposition.*

gobbet *n.* Piece of raw flesh 2H6 4.1.85 *With gobbets of thy mother's bleeding heart,* 2H6 5.2.58.

god *n.* Deity; (attrib., prefixed, without the article, to the name of a deity, or a person likened to one) ADO 3.3.134 *like god Bel's priests,* TRO 1.3.169.
▷ *God be wi' you*: in Ff and Qq usu. *God buy you* or *ye* (also *bu'y, buy'*), occas. *God be with you, God buy to go. God dig-you-den, God (g)igoden* see GOOD-DEN.
~ *vb.* Deify, idolize COR 5.3.11 *This last old man…godded me indeed.*

god-a-mercy *interj.*
1 God have mercy! SHR 4.3.153 *God-a-mercy, Grumio, then he shall have no odds,* 1H4 3.3.50, HAM 4.5.199 (Ff *Gramercy*).
2 (used in response to a respectful salutation or a wish, usu. expressed by an inferior, for a person's welfare) God reward you, Thank you HAM 2.2.172 *How goes my Lord Hamlet?—Well, God-a-mercy,* JN 1.1.185, TRO 5.4.31.

godfather *n.*
1 Sponsor at baptism; (fig., sometimes with ref. to the godfather's naming the child at baptism) LLL 1.1.88 *These earthly godfathers of heaven's lights, That give a name to every fixed star,* VEN Ded.5.
2 (pl., jocularly) Jurymen whose verdict brings a man to the gallows MV 4.1.398 *In christ'ning shalt thou have two godfathers…To bring thee to the gallows.*

God 'ild, Godild *interj.* (lit. 'God yield', used in returning thanks) Thank you AYL 3.3.74 *God 'ild you for your last company,* MAC 1.6.13, HAM 4.5.42.

godlike *adv.* Divinely, like a god PER 5.1.206 *Thou hast been godlike perfit.*

god's me *interj.* God save me 1H4 2.3.94 *God's me, my horse!*

goer *n.*
1 *goer-back* One who retreats CYM 1.1.169 *that I might prick The goer-back.*
2 *goer-backward* One who deteriorates AWW 1.2.48 *would demonstrate them now But goers-backward.*
3 *goer-between* Go-between TRO 3.2.201 *all pitiful goers-between.*

gog *n.* (corrupt form of) God SHR 3.2.160 *by gogs-wouns.*

gold *n.* Metal used in ornamentation of fabrics, gold thread SHR 2.1.354 *Valens of Venice gold.*

golden *adj.*
1 *golden care* The burden of the crown 2H4 4.5.23; *golden sorrow* sorrow that comes from high rank H8 2.3.22.
2 Rich TIM 4.3.18 *Ducks to the golden fool.*
3 Exceedingly favourable or propitious TN 5.1.382 *golden time convents,* 3H6 3.2.127.

goldenly *adv.* Excellently AYL 1.1.6 *report speaks goldenly of his profit.*

gone *pa. pple.*
1 Dead JN 3.4.163 *If that young Arthur be not gone already.*

2 Far advanced R2 2.1.184 *York is too far gone with grief.*
3 Lost, ruined MM 5.1.300 *Then is your cause gone too,* MV 3.5.18.

good *n.* do good on, upon Prevail upon MM 4.2.68 *Who can do good on him?,* 1H4 3.1.197, ROM 4.2.13.
~ *adj.*
1 Conventional epithet to titles of high rank WT 1.2.220 *At the good Queen's entreaty,* H8 3.1.78; (hence) (*one's*) *good lord* or *lady* patron or patroness, protector AWW 2.3.245 *He is my good lord,* CYM 2.3.153; (hence freq.) an epithet of courteous address or respectful reference TMP 1.1.9 *Good boatswain,* TGV 1.2.115, WT 4.4.200; (absol. used vocatively) good one, dear one TMP 1.1.15 *Nay, good, be patient,* ROM 1.5.7.
2 Comely PER 4.2.47 *She has a good face.*
3 Financially sound; (hence) wealthy, substantial MV 1.3.12 *Antonio is a good man,* MV 1.3.16, COR 1.1.16.
▷ In H8 3.2.356 *good easy man* quasi-adv. use, mildly depreciative intensifying *easy.*
~ in phrases
make good 1 Carry into effect, fulfil, perform TIM 1.2.196 *of no power to make his wishes good,* 2H6 5.1.122, SHR 4.2.115. **2** Prove (a statement, charge) to be true, substantiate R2 1.1.4 *to make good the boist'rous late appeal,* HAM 1.2.210. **3** Show or prove (a person or thing) to be blameless WT 2.3.61 *I…would by combat make her good,* MV 1.3.94. **4** Maintain, hold, defend (a position) COR 1.5.12 *to make good the city,* LR 1.1.172, H8 5.3.54.

good cheap *adj.* Cheap 1H4 3.3.45 *would have bought me lights as good cheap at the dearest chandler's in Europe.*

good conceited *adj.* Well devised CYM 2.3.17 *a very excellent good conceited thing.*

good-deed *n.* In reality, in deed WT 1.2.42 *yet, good-deed, Leontes.*

good-den, good-even *n. phr.* (salutation) Good evening (but used at any time after noon) JN 1.1.185 *Good-den, Sir Richard!,* COR 2.1.93, ROM 2.4.110.
▷ Other spellings, *godden, good(d)en, good e'en.* The full phrase 'God give you good even' is represented in early Ff and Qq as *God gi' god-en* (ROM 1.2.57) and *God dig-you-den* (LLL 4.1.43).

good-faced *adj.* Pretty WT 4.3.115 *No, good-fac'd sir.*

good-jer (var. of) GOOD(-)YEAR.

goodman *n.*
1 Husband SHR Ind.2.105 *I am your goodman.*
2 Title of courtesy prefixed to designations of occupation HAM 5.1.14 *goodman delver*; to names of persons under the rank of gentlemen, esp. yeomen or farmers LLL 4.2.36 *goodman Dull,* 2H4 5.3.89, ADO 3.5.9; (hence, allusively, jocularly or ironically) LR 2.2.45 *goodman boy,* MM 5.1.326, TN 4.2.131.
3 Man of substance, not of noble birth, yeoman LLL 1.1.308 *I'll lay my head to any goodman's hat.*

good morrow *n. phr.* (term of salutation used at meeting in the morning) Good morning MND 4.1.139 *Good morrow, friends,* ANT 4.3.24, 1H4 2.1.32; (hence) salutation, greeting H5 4.1.26 *Do my good morrow to them,* TGV 2.1.96, ROM 2.4.109; (with allusion to the practice of a morning greeting with music under one's window) OTH 3.1.2 *Masters, play here…and bid 'Good morrow, general'.*

goodness *n.* Success, prosperity, good fortune MAC 4.3.136 *the chance of goodness Be like our warranted quarrel!*

good-night *n.* Musical composition sung at night, serenade 2H4 3.2.319 *his fancies or his good-nights.*

good now *interj.* Expression denoting entreaty, ex-

goodwife

postulation, acquiescence HAM 1.1.70 *Good now,*
sit down, and tell me, he that knows, ANT 1.2.26,
ERR 4.4.21.

goodwife *n.* (former title of courtesy prefixed to
surnames) Mrs 2H4 2.1.93 *goodwife Keech, the but-*
cher's wife, WIV 2.2.34.

goodwill *n. by, of (one's) goodwill* Of one's own accord, voluntarily R2 4.1.177 *To do that office of*
thine own goodwill, VEN 479.

good(-)year *n. What the goodyear!* Meaningless ex-
pletive (cf. 'What the deuce!') ADO 1.3.1 *What the*
good-year, my lord, WIV 1.4.122 (F1 good-jer), 2H4
2.4.59; (hence, in imprecatory phrases) malefic
power LR 5.2.34 *The good-years shall devour them,*
flesh and fell.

goose *n.*
1 Tailor's smoothing iron, of which the handle
resembles a goose's neck MAC 2.3.15 *Here you may*
roast your goose.
2 *Winchester goose* Swelling in the groin caused
by venereal disease 3H6 1.3.53 *Winchester goose I*
cry; *goose of Winchester* prostitute TRO 5.10.54
Some galled goose of Winchester.
▷ So-called because the brothels in Southwark
were under the jurisdiction of the bishop of
Winchester.

goose-pen *n.* Quill pen TN 3.2.50 *though thou write*
with a goose-pen.

gorbellied *adj.* Fat-paunched 1H4 2.2.88 *Hang ye,*
gorbellied knaves.

gored *ppl. adj.* (fig.) Wounded deeply LR 5.3.321 *and*
the gor'd state sustain.

gorge *n.* What has been swallowed; (hence) *cast,*
heave the gorge vomit, retch TIM 4.3.41, OTH 2.1.233.

gorget *n.* Piece of armour for the throat TRO 1.3.174
fumbling on his gorget.

gosling *n.* (fig.) Inexperienced, foolish person, one
who is young and green PER 4.2.86 *whip the gos-*
ling, COR 5.3.35.

gospelled *pa. pple.* Imbued with the principles of
the gospel MAC 3.1.87 *Are you so gospell'd To pray*
for this good man.

goss *n.* Gorse, furze, or whin TMP 4.1.180 *pricking*
goss.

gossip *n.*
1 (always in relation to the parents) (One's) child's
godfather or godmother, sponsor H8 5.4.12 *My*
noble gossips, TGV 3.1.270, WT 2.3.41.
2 Friend MV 3.1.7 *my gossip Report,* ROM 2.1.11;
(used as a title prefixed to a woman's surname)
2H4 2.1.94 *call me gossip Quickly,* WIV 4.2.9.
3 Woman's female friend invited to be present at
a birth; (hence) gossiping or tattling woman MND
2.1.47 *sometime lurk I in a gossip's bowl,* MV 3.1.8,
ROM 3.5.174; (fig.) TN 1.5.273 *the babbling gossip of*
the air.
~ *vb.*
1 Be a sponsor to AWW 1.1.175 *pretty, fond,*
adoptious christendoms That blinking Cupid
gossips.
2 Act as a gossip or familiar acquaintance, take
part (in a feast), be a boon companion ERR 5.1.408
I'll gossip at this feast, MND 2.1.125.

gossiping *n.* Merrymaking ERR 5.1.420 *walk in to*
see their gossiping, JN 5.2.59.

gossip-like *adj.* Resembling a gossiping or tattling
woman H5 1.186 *I will leave you now to your*
gossip-like humour.

gourd *n.* Kind of false dice WIV 1.3.85 *for gourd and*
fullam holds.

gout *n.* Drop MAC 2.1.46 *gouts of blood.*

govern *vb.* Direct, regulate, control LR 4.7.18 *Be go-*
vern'd by your knowledge, TGV 2.7.74, WIV
5.1.19.

governess *n.* Ruler, mistress MND 2.1.103 *the*
governess of floods, LUC 443.

government *n.*
1 Control, management CYM 2.4.150 *The go-*
vernment of patience!, MND 5.1.123, ROM 4.1.102.
2 Demeanour, conduct, behaviour, (esp.) becoming conduct, discretion 1H4 3.1.182 *want of govern-*
ment, 3H6 1.4.132, OTH 3.3.256.
3 Command of an army, etc. 1H4 4.1.19 *Under*
whose government, 1H6 2.1.64, OTH 4.1.237.

governor *n.*
1 Military commander OTH 2.1.55 *My hopes do*
shape him for the governor.
2 Tutor 1H6 1.1.171 *ordain'd his special governor.*

gown *n.* Dressing gown, nightgown 2H4 3.2.184 *go*
to the wars in a gown, JC 4.3.231.

grace *n.*
1 *do (a person or thing) grace* Reflect credit on, set
in good light, embellish 1H4 1.2.71 *do the profession*
some grace, HAM 1.1.131, SON 132.11; *in grace of* in
honour of MND 4.1.134 *Came here in grace of our*
solemnity.
2 Ornament H5 2.Ch.28 *this grace of kings.*
3 Favour MAC 1.6.30 *shall continue our graces*
towards him, LLL 5.2.128, H8 3.2.166; good opinion
ADO 2.3.30 *come in my grace*; *do grace* confer a
favour, do a kindness ERR 2.1.87 *His company must*
do his minions grace, SHR 1.2.131, 2H4 5.5.6.
4 Fortune, luck HAM 1.3.53 *A double blessing is a*
double grace, TGV 3.1.146, MM 1.4.69.
5 The source of grace, God ADO 2.1.304 *all grace*
say amen to it, AWW 1.3.220, WT 1.2.80.
6 Beneficent virtue or efficacy R3 2.4.13 *Small*
herbs have grace, ROM 2.3.15.
▷ Cf. HERB-GRACE.
7 Sense of duty or propriety AYL 3.4.2 *have the*
grace to consider, TGV 5.4.165; virtue MAC 4.3.91
The king-becoming graces.
8 Used to form complimentary periphrases; (used
ludicrously) MND 5.1.195 *I am thy lover's grace*
(i.e. thy lover), 1H6 5.3.33.
9 Mercy, pardon LR 3.2.59 *cry These...summoners*
grace, MM 5.1.374, 3H6 2.2.81.
10 One of the sister-goddesses regarded as the be-
stowers of beauty and charm and portrayed as
women of exquisite beauty TRO 1.2.236 *Had I a*
sister were a grace...he should take his choice, LC
316, TGV 5.4.166.
~ *vb.* Gratify, delight R3 4.4.175 *What comfortable*
hour...ever grac'd me in thy company.

graced *ppl. adj.* Endowed with graces, favoured,
adorned with honour MAC 3.4.40 *the grac'd person*
of our Banquo, R2 5.2.24, LR 1.4.246.

graceful *adj.*
1 Full of divine grace WT 5.1.171 *a holy father, A*
graceful gentleman.
2 Favourable ANT 2.2.60 *with graceful eyes.*

gracious *adj.*
1 Finding favour, acceptable 3H6 3.3.117 *gracious*
in the people's eye, AYL 1.2.188, TIT 1.1.11.
2 Attractive, graceful MV 3.2.76 *a gracious voice,*
ADO 4.1.108, JN 3.4.81.
3 (used as a courteous epithet) Kind TMP 5.1.253
my gracious sir, LLL 5.2.729, AWW 2.3.167.
4 Godly, righteous, pious JN 3.4.81 *such a gracious*
creature born, MM 3.2.219, HAM 5.2.84.
5 Happy, fortunate MM 5.1.76 *her gracious fortune,*
WT 3.1.22.

graciously *adv.* Through divine grace, righteously,
virtuously PER 4.6.60 *What he will do graciously,*
MM 2.4.77.

gradation *n.* Process of advancing step by step, course of gradual progress MM 4.3.100 *By cold gra-*
dation and weal-balanc'd form; (hence) rank,

position OTH 1.1.37 *Preferment goes by letter and affection, And not by old gradation.*

graff *n.* Graft, scion PER 5.1.60 *For every graff would send a caterpillar;* (fig.) LUC 1062 *This bastard graff.*

~ *vb.* Insert a graft (in a stock) AYL 3.2.117 *I shall graff it with a medlar,* 2H6 3.2.214, R3 3.7.127.

graffing *n.* The action of inserting a graft, grafting 2H4 5.3.3 *pippin of mine own graffing.*

graft *vb.*

1 (lit. and fig.) Fix, implant, attach as one does a graft or scion WT 1.2.246 *A servant grafted in my serious trust,* AWW 1.2.54, R2 3.4.101.

2 Fix grafts upon (a stock) COR 2.1.189 *some old crab-trees...that will not Be grafted to your relish.*

grafter *n.* Original tree from which a scion has been taken for grafting H5 3.5.9 *And overlook their grafters.*

grain *n.*

1 *in grain* (short for 'dyed in grain') Dyed scarlet or crimson, fast dyed MND 1.2.95 *your purple ingrain beard;* (hence) indelible, ineradicable, ingrained TN 1.5.237 *'Tis in grain, sir, 'twill endure wind and weather,* ERR 3.2.106.

◇ The kermes or scarlet grain was used in making dyes.

2 Arrangement of veins and fibres in wood; (fig.) TRO 1.3.8 *diverts his grain Tortive and errant from his course of growth.*

grained *ppl. adj.*[1] Fast-dyed, ingrained; (fig.) HAM 3.4.90 *such black and grained spots As will not leave their tinct.*

grained *ppl. adj.*[2] Having a grain COR 4.5.108 *My grained ash;* (fig.) furrowed, lined ERR 5.1.312 *this grained face of mine.*

grained *ppl. adj.*[3] Having tines or prongs, pronged, forked LC 64 *his grained bat.*

gramercy *interj.*

1 Thanks, thank you MV 2.2.121 *God bless your worship!—Gramercy,* R3 3.2.106, SHR 1.1.41.

◇ Cf. GOD-A-MERCY sense 2.

2 GOD-A-MERCY sense 1 HAM 4.1.199 *Gramercy on his soul!*

grammar-school *n.* School originally founded for the teaching of Latin 2H6 4.7.33 *in erecting a grammar school.*

grand *adj.*

1 Pre-eminent, chief R2 5.6.19 *The grand conspirator,* TMP 1.2.274, R3 4.4.52; *grand captain* commander ANT 3.1.9.

2 *grand sum* Grand total H8 3.2.293 *the grand sum of his sins.*

3 Main, principal ANT 3.12.10 *his grand sea.*

grandsire *n.* Old man SHR 4.5.50 *Do, good old grandsire.*

~ *attrib.* Ancient ROM 1.4.37 *a grandsire phrase.*

grange *n.* Farmhouse, country house OTH 1.1.106 *My house is not a grange,* WT 4.4.303, MM 3.1.264.

grant *vb.* Assent *to* 3H6 1.1.245 *Before I would have granted to that act.*

grasp *n.* Embrace TRO 4.2.13 *the grasps of love.*

~ *vb.*

1 Clutch 2H6 3.2.172 *grasp'd And tugg'd for life.*

2 Embrace TRO 3.3.168 *Grasps in the comer.*

grass-green *adj.* Green with grass HAM 4.5.31 *At his head a grass-green turf.*

grate *n.* Framework of bars, grating 1H6 1.4.10 *a secret grate of iron bars,* WIV 2.2.9.

grate *vb.*

1 Wear away TRO 3.2.188 *grated To dusty nothing.*

2 Harass, irritate HAM 3.1.3 *Grating so harshly all his days of quiet,* ANT 1.1.18.

3 Oppress or harass with importunities, make exacting demands *upon* or *on* WIV 2.2.7 *I have*

grated upon my good friends for three reprieves for you, 2H4 4.1.90.

gratify *vb.*

1 Reward, requite COR 2.2.40 *To gratify his noble service,* OTH 5.2.213, CYM 2.4.7.

2 Give a gratuity to, remunerate MV 4.1.406 *gratify this gentleman.*

3 Grace, render acceptable or pleasing LLL 4.2.155 *to gratify the table with a grace.*

gratillity *n.* (clown's humorous perversion of) Gratuity TN 2.3.26 *I did impeticos thy gratillity.*

gratulate *vb.* Greet, salute R3 4.1.10 *To gratulate the gentle princes,* TIM 1.2.125; express joy at TIT 1.1.221 *gratulate his safe return.*

~ *adj.* Gratifying, pleasing MM 5.1.529 *There's more behind that is more gratulate.*

grave *vb.*

1 Bury, swallow up as in a grave R2 3.2.140 *grav'd in the hollow ground,* TIM 4.3.166.

2 Cut into VEN 376 *soft sighs can never grave it.*

3 Engrave, record by engraved letters MV 2.7.36 *this saying grav'd in gold,* LC 755, R3 4.4.141 (Ff branded).

gravel *n.* (attrib.; fig.) Hard MM 4.3.64 *O gravel heart!*

gravelled *ppl. adj.* Nonplussed AYL 4.1.74 *were gravell'd for lack of matter.*

gravely *adv.* With dignity 1H4 2.4.435 *If thou dost it half so gravely.*

graves *n.* (var. of) Greaves, leg-armour 2H4 4.1.50 *Turning your books to graves, your ink to blood, Your pens to lances.*

gravy *n.* The fat and juices which exude from flesh during and after the process of cooking; (hence) sweat 2H4 1.2.162 *His effect of gravy.*

graymalkin *n.* (properly) Grey cat; (used as name of a fiend) MAC 1.1.8 *I come, Graymalkin.*

◇ See MALKIN.

graze *vb.*[1] Feed ROM 3.5.188 *Graze where you will.*

graze *vb.*[2] Ricochet H5 4.3.105 *the bullets grazing.*

◇ F2 *grasing;* F1 *crasing.* See CRAZING for alternative interpretation.

grease *vb.* (fig.) Soil, corrupt, make gross or lewd TIM 4.3.195 *greases his pure mind.*

greasily *adv.* Grossly, indecently LLL 4.1.137 *you talk greasily, your lips grow foul.*

greasy *adj.* (fig., term of contempt) Gross, corpulent WIV 2.1.108 *this greasy knight,* AYL 2.1.55.

great *adj.*

1 Pregnant PER 5.1.106 *I am great with woe.*

2 (of the heart) Full of emotion or pride R2 2.1.228 *My heart is great, but it must break with silence,* SHR 5.2.171, 2H4 4.3.111.

3 (of letters) Capital TN 2.5.88 *thus makes she her great P's.*

4 (in titles of office) Grand H5 4.8.95 *Great Master of France, the brave Sir Guichard Dauphin,* 1H6 4.7.70.

5 *great kinsman* Earlier relative, ancestor ROM 4.3.53 *with some great kinsman's bone* (perh. also with sense of 'eminent').

6 *great time* Long while TMP 3.3.105 *to work a great time after; of greater time* older TGV 2.7.48 *a youth Of greater time than I shall show to be.*

7 *great morning* Broad daylight CYM 4.2.61 *It is great morning,* TRO 4.3.1.

~ *adv.* Very 2H6 3.1.379 *'tis great like he will.*

great-bellied *adj.* Advanced in pregnancy MM 2.1.98 *being...with child, and being great-bellied.*

great-belly *n.* (attrib.) *great-belly doublet* Doublet with a thick 'belly' or lower part H5 4.7.48 *the fat knight with the great-belly doublet.*

greatly *adv.* Illustriously H5 Epil.5 *in that small most greatly lived.*

greatness *n.* (used as a title, approximating) Highness, eminence LLL 5.1.107 *it pleaseth his greatness*, TMP 3.2.64, 2H4 2.2.5.

gree *vb.*
1 Agree or determine upon MM 4.1.41 *Are there no other tokens Between you greed concerning her observance.*
2 Come into accord or harmony, come to terms *with* (a person) *on, upon* (a matter) MV 2.2.101 *How gree you now?*, SHR 2.1.297, ANT 2.6.37.
3 Be harmonious or in accord SON 114.11 *What with his gust is greeing.*
◇ Treated as an aphetic form of 'agree' in many mod. edd.

Greek *n. merry Greek* Merry fellow, boon companion TRO 1.2.109 *a merry Greek indeed*, TRO 4.4.56; (hence with ref. to the clown) TN 4.1.18 *foolish Greek.*

green *n.*
1 Verdure SON 12.7 *summer's green all girded up in sheaves*, SON 68.11.
2 Grassy turf or sod PER 4.1.14 *To strow thy green with flowers.*
~ *adj.*
1 (with ref. to colour) Said of the sea, and hence of Neptune ANT 4.14.58 *o'er green Neptune's back*, TMP 5.1.43, WT 4.4.28.
2 Pale, sickly TN 2.4.113 *with a green and yellow melancholy*, ROM 2.2.8, MAC 1.7.37.
3 Young, youthful LLL 1.1.97 *The spring is near when green geese are a-breeding*, TIM 4.1.7, SON 104.8.
4 (of material and immaterial things) Fresh ROM 4.3.42 *green in earth* (i.e. just buried).
5 Raw, inexperienced HAM 1.3.101 *a green girl*, LLL 1.2.89, H5 2.4.136.

green-eyed *adj.* Jealous OTH 3.3.166 *the green-ey'd monster*, MV 3.2.110.

green fields See FIELD sense 8.

greenly *adv.* In an inexperienced manner, like a novice, foolishly, unskilfully HAM 4.5.83 *we have done but greenly In hugger-mugger to inter him*, H5 5.2.143.

green(-)sickness *n.* Kind of anaemia called chlorosis which mostly affects young women and gives a pale or greenish tinge to the complexion PER 4.6.14 *the pox upon her green-sickness*; (transf. of a man) ANT 3.2.6 *Lepidus...is troubled With the green-sickness*, 2H4 4.3.93.

greet *vb.* Gratify PER 5.2.9 *To greet the King.*

grey *n.* Grey or subdued light; (hence) cold sunless light of early morning ADO 5.3.27 *spots of grey*, ROM 3.5.19.
~ *adj.* (fig.) Ancient, hoary 1H4 2.4.453 *that grey Iniquity.*

grief *n.*
1 Hardship, suffering, cause of pain or sorrow ADO 1.1.313 *That know love's grief*, 1H4 5.1.132, 2H4 1.1.144.
2 Grievance 1H4 4.3.42 *The nature of your griefs*, JC 1.3.111, H8 1.2.56.

grief-shot *adj.* Stricken with sorrow COR 5.1.44 *grief-shot With his unkindness.*

grievance *n.*
1 Oppression, annoyance OTH 1.2.15 *Or put upon you what restraint or grievance The law...Will give him cable*, 2H4 4.1.196.
2 Trouble, distress, suffering TGV 4.3.37 *I pity much your grievances*, ROM 1.1.157, SON 30.9.

grieve *vb.*
1 Be a cause of complaint or grievance PER 2.4.19 *no longer grieve without reproof.*
2 Feel grief for, be sorry for, regret R2 2.2.37 *the nothing that I grieve*, 1H4 5.4.29, LR 4.3.53.

grievous *adv.* Very 1H4 4.1.16 *he is grievous sick*, R2 1.4.54 (Ff, Q5 *very*).

grievously *adv.*
1 Dearly, with a heavy penalty JC 3.2.80 *And grievously hath Caesar answer'd it*, WIV 4.4.21.
2 Bitterly, sorrowfully TGV 3.2.14 *My daughter takes his going grievously*, OTH 5.1.53.
3 Strongly, exceedingly JN 4.3.134 *I do suspect thee very grievously.*

griffin *n.* Fabulous animal, half lion, half eagle 1H4 3.1.150 *clip-wing'd griffin*, MND 2.1.232.

grim-looked *adj.* Grim-looking, of a forbidding aspect MND 5.1.170 *O grim-look'd night.*

grind *vb.*
1 Afflict, torment TMP 4.1.258 *they grind their joints.*
2 Whet (the appetite) SON 110.10 *Mine appetite I never more will grind On newer proof.*

gripe *n.*¹ Vulture LUC 543 *the gripe's sharp claws.*

gripe *n.*² Grasp H5 4.6.22 *with a feeble gripe*, H8 5.2.135, MAC 3.1.61.
~ *vb.*
1 Clutch or grasp *at* PER 1.1.49 *Gripe not at earthly joys.*
2 (lit. and fig.) Clutch, seize, grasp WIV 1.3.85 *Let vultures gripe thy guts*, JN 4.2.190, 1H4 5.1.57; (absol.) CYM 3.1.40 *many among us can gripe as hard as Cassibelan.*
3 Grieve, afflict 3H6 1.4.171 *how inly sorrow gripes his soul.*

griping *ppl. adj.* Painful, distressing ROM 4.5.126 *When griping griefs the heart doth wound.*

grise, grize *n.* Step OTH 1.3.200 *as a grise or step*, TN 3.1.124, TIM 4.3.16.

grisled *adj.* Horrible, grisly PER 3.Gower.47 *the grisled north* (Q1; Qq2, 3, 4, 6 *grislee*, Q5 *grieslee*, Ff 3–4 *grisly*).

grizzle *n.* Sprinkling of grey hairs TN 5.1.165 *When time hath sow'd a grizzle on thy case.*

grizzled *ppl. adj.* Grey ANT 3.13.17 *grizzled head*, HAM 1.2.239 (Qq *grissl'd*; Ff *grisly*).

grizzly *adj.* Grey, grizzled HAM 1.2.239 (see GRIZZLED).

groat *n.* Coin, equal to four pence H5 5.1.58 *a groat to heal your pate*, JN 1.1.94; *ten groats* customary fee charged by a lawyer AWW 2.2.21 *as fit as ten groats is for the hand of an attorney.*

groom *n.*
1 Male servant or attendant MAC 2.2.5 *the surfeited grooms Do mock their charge with snores*, 2H6 2.1.181, SHR 4.1.125.
2 Fellow TIT 4.2.164 *you are gallant grooms.*
3 Bridegroom SHR 3.2.152 *a groom indeed*, OTH 2.3.180, CYM 3.6.69.

gross *n.*
1 *by gross, by the gross* In large quantities WT 4.4.207 *though they come to him by th' gross*; wholesale LLL 5.2.319 *we that sell by gross.*
2 *in gross* In a general way, generally, on the whole MV 3.2.158 *which, to term in gross, Is an unlesson'd girl.*
3 (short for) 'Gross sum', sum total, the whole MV 1.3.55 *the gross Of full three thousand ducats*; (fig.) HAM 1.1.68 *the gross and scope of mine opinion.*
~ *adj.*
1 Big, bulky 1H4 2.4.226 *gross as a mountain*, WIV 3.3.41, ADO 5.1.162 (with quibble on sense 5).
2 Corpulent 1H4 2.4.511 *A gross fat man.*
3 Palpable, evident, plain AWW 1.3.172 *to all sense 'tis gross*, WIV 5.5.136, MM 1.2.155.
4 Entire, whole AYL 4.1.195 *the gross band*, LLL 1.2.46, 2H4 2.1.84.
5 Dull, stupid MND 5.1.367 *This palpable-gross play*, ERR 3.2.34, H5 4.1.282.

~ *adv.* Plainly MM 2.4.83 *I'll speak more gross*, LR 1.1.292.

grossly *adv.*
1 Plainly, obviously, palpably AWW 1.3.178 *so grossly shown*, ERR 2.2.169, H5 2.2.107.
2 Excessively, flagrantly 1H4 3.3.132 *slanders thee most grossly*, MM 5.1.472, JN 4.2.94.
3 Materially (opposed to spiritually) TN 5.1.237 *A spirit...grossly clad*, MV 5.1.65.
4 Stupidly OTH 3.3.395 *grossly gape on*, MM 3.1.18, JN 3.1.163.
5 Clumsily WIV 2.2.142 *Let them say 'tis grossly done.*
6 Coarsely, indelicately MV 5.1.266 *Speak not so grossly.*
7 In a state of gross sinfulness HAM 3.3.80 *'A took my father grossly, full of bread* (i.e. without the benefit of absolution or extreme unction).

grossness *n.*
1 Bulkiness TRO 1.3.325 *Whose grossness little characters sum up.*
2 Flagrant character, enormity MV 3.2.80 *Hiding the grossness with fair ornament.*
3 Stupidity TN 3.2.73 *passages of grossness.*

ground *n.*
1 Bottom of sea or other water 1H4 1.3.204 *fathom-line could never touch the ground*; the bottom where the water becomes too shallow for a vessel to float 2H4 4.1.17 *touch ground And dash themselves to pieces*; *on ground* aground 2H4 4.4.40.
2 (in painting or decoration) Main surface or first coating of colour LUC 1074 *My sable ground of sin I will not paint*, 1H4 1.2.212.
3 Bass or plainsong on which a descant is 'raised'; (fig.) R3 3.7.49 *on that ground I'll make a holy descant*, TIT 2.1.70.
4 Space traversed or occupied MV 2.2.104 *have run some ground*; *get ground of* get the better of 2H4 2.3.53 *get ground and vantage of the King*, CYM 1.4.104.
~ *vb.* Fix, establish, found, base AYL 1.2.279 *Grounded upon no other argument*, H8 1.2.144, SON 142.2.

grounded *ppl. adj.* Deeply founded, firmly fixed or established R3 1.3.29 *no grounded malice*, SON 62.4.

groundling *n.* Frequenter of the pit of a theatre HAM 3.2.11 *to split the ears of the groundlings.*

grow *vb.* Accrue, become due ERR 4.1.8 *the sum...Is growing to me*, SON 87.11, ERR 4.4.121.
~ in combination
grow on 1 Advance, proceed PER 4.4.19 *with his steerage shall your thoughts grow on.* 2 Come by degrees MND 1.2.10 *and so grow on to a point* (Ff 1-3; Qq *grow to a point*). **grow on, upon** 1 Increase so as to become troublesome to (a person) LR 5.3.105 *My sickness grows upon me*, H5 3.3.55. 2 Gain ground upon JC 2.1.107 *a great way growing on the south.* 3 Come to take liberties with AYL 1.1.85 *Begin you to grow upon me?* **grow to, unto** 1 Become closely, vitally united to R2 5.3.30 *For ever may my knees grow to the earth*, H8 5.5.49, CYM 1.3.1. 2 Adhere or cling to HAM 4.7.85 *he grew unto his seat*, H8 3.1.89, SON 18.12. 3 Be an integral part of 2H4 1.2.88 *I lay aside that which grows to me.* 4 Advance to, arrive at, come to (a particular stage or state) R3 3.7.20 *grew to an end* (Ff *drew*), 1H6 4.1.36, MV 2.2.18.

growth *n.* Size, stature AYL 1.2.122 *of excellent growth and presence*, WIV 4.4.49, 2H4 1.2.159.

grudge *n.* Murmur, complaint, grumbling TMP 1.2.249 *Without or grudge or grumblings.*
~ *vb. grudge a thought* Think an envious thought 1H6 3.1.175 *That grudge one thought against your Majesty.*

grudging *n.* GRUDGE, murmuring, complaint ADO 3.4.89 *eats his meat without grudging.*
~ *ppl. adj.* Unwilling, reluctant, resentful 1H6 4.1.141 *their grudging stomachs*, R3 2.1.9.

grunt *vb.* Groan HAM 3.1.76 *grunt and sweat under a weary life.*

guard *n.*
1 Custody, keeping, guardianship MV 1.3.175 *in the fearful guard Of an unthrifty knave*, ERR 5.1.149, ANT 5.2.67.
2 (pl.) Caution LC 298 *Shook off my sober guards.*
3 Ornamental border or trimming on a garment ADO 1.1.287 *the guards are but slightly basted on*, MM 3.1.96; (fig.) LLL 4.3.56 *rimes are guards on wanton Cupid's hose.*
4 (pl.) The stars B and Y of the constellation of the Lesser Bear OTH 2.1.15 *the guards of th' ever-fixed Pole.*
5 *at a guard* On his defence MM 1.3.51; *out of guard* unprepared TN 1.5.86.
~ *vb.* Ornament with 'guards', trim MV 2.2.155 *Give him a livery More guarded than his fellows'*, H8 Prol.16; (fig.) ADO 1.1.286 *The body of your discourse is...guarded with fragments*, JN 4.2.10.

guardage *n.* Guardianship OTH 1.2.70 *Run from her guardage.*

guardant *n.* Guardian, protector 1H6 4.7.9 *my angry guardant*, COR 5.2.62.

gudgeon *n.* One who will bite at any bait or swallow anything, credulous or gullible person MV 1.1.102 *For this fool gudgeon.*

guerdon *n.* Reward, recompense ADO 5.3.5 *in guerdon of her wrongs*, LLL 3.1.169.

guerdoned *ppl. adj.* Rewarded 2H6 1.4.46 *See you well guerdon'd for these deserts*, 3H6 3.3.191.

guess *n.* Conjecture H5 1.1.96 *with a ready guess*, TIT 2.3.207, JC 2.1.3.
~ *vb.* Think, judge, suppose COR 1.1.18 *we might guess they reliev'd us humanely*, H8 1.1.47, 1H6 2.1.29.

guessingly *adv.* By conjecture LR 3.7.47 *a letter guessingly set down.*

guide *n.* Conduct, direction TIM 1.1.243 *give them guide to us.*

guidon *n.* Military flag or pennant, broad at the end near the staff, and forked or pointed at the other; or the bearer of it H5 4.2.60 *I stay but for my guidon* (F1 *Guard: on*).

guiled *ppl. adj.* Treacherous MV 3.2.97 *ornament is but the guiled shore.*

guiltless *adj. guiltless blood-shedding* The shedding of innocent blood 2H6 4.7.102.

guilty *adj.*
1 Involving guilt, criminal R3 1.4.273 *guilty murder*, 1H6 2.4.94, ROM 3.2.111.
2 That has incurred guilt, culpable; (transf. to the instrument with which, or the scene where a crime is committed, or the like) ERR 4.4.63 *the guilty doors*, TIT 5.2.183.
3 *guilty to* Guilty of, culpably responsible for (a result) ERR 3.2.163 *guilty to self-wrong*, WT 4.4.538.
4 Prompted by a sense of guilt LUC 1482 *guilty woe.*
5 *guilty instance* Sign of guilt LUC 1511.

guilty-like *adj.* In guilty fashion OTH 3.3.39 *steal away so guilty-like.*

guinea(-)hen *n.* Prostitute OTH 1.3.315 *drown myself for the love of a guinea hen.*

guise *n.* Custom, habit, fashion MAC 5.1.19 *This is her very guise*, 2H6 1.3.42, CYM 5.1.32.

gules *adj.* Heraldic name for 'red' TIM 4.3.60 *paint the ground, gules*, HAM 2.2.457.

gulf *n.* Absorbing eddy, whirlpool H5 2.4.10 *For England his approaches makes as fierce As waters to the sucking of a gulf*, HAM 3.3.16; (fig.) that which devours or swallows up anything R3 3.7.128 *the swallowing gulf Of dark forgetfulness*; (applied to) voracious belly or appetite MAC 4.1.23 *maw and gulf Of the ravin'd salt-sea shark*, LUC 557.

gull n.[1]
1 Unfledged bird 1H4 5.1.60 *that ungentle gull, the cuckoo's bird*, TIM 2.1.31.

gull n.[2]
1 Dupe, fool TN 3.2.69 *Yond gull Malvolio is turn'd heathen*, H5 3.6.67, R3 1.3.327.
2 Trick, deception ADO 2.3.118 *I should think this a gull, but that the white-bearded fellow speaks it.*
~ vb. Dupe, cheat TN 2.3.134 *If I do not gull him into an ayword*, H5 2.2.121, SON 86.10.

gull-catcher n. Trickster, cheat TN 2.5.187 *my noble gull-catcher.*

gum n. Rheum H5 4.2.48 *The gum down-roping from their pale-dead eyes.*

gummed ppl. adj. Stiffened with gum 1H4 2.2.2 *a gumm'd velvet.*

gun-stone n. Stone used for the shot of a gun H5 1.2.282 *turn'd his balls to gun-stones.*

gurnet n. Fish of the genus Triglo; *soused gurnet* a term of approbrium 1H4 4.2.12 *I am a sous'd gurnet.*

gust n. Taste, liking, relish TN 1.3.31 *the gust he hath in quarrelling*, TIM 3.5.54, SON 114.11.
~ vb. (fig.) Taste, relish WT 1.2.219 *When I shall gust it last* (i.e. when I am the last to hear of it).

guts n. Gluttonous or corpulent person 1H4 2.4.227 *thou clay-brain'd guts*; (applied to a dead body) HAM 3.4.212 *I'll lug the guts into the neighbour room.*

guts-griping n. Constricting pains in the 'guts' or bowels TRO 5.1.18 *guts-griping, ruptures.*

Gypsy See GIPSY.

gyve n. Fetter, shackle; (fig.) HAM 4.7.21 *Convert his gyves to graces.*
~ vb. Fetter, shackle OTH 2.1.170 *I will gyve thee in thine own courtship* (Ff 3–4 *give*; Qq *catch*).

H

H n. (quibble on) ACHE ADO 3.4.56 *For the letter that begins them all, H.*

ha vb. (reduced form of) HAVE SHR 5.2.181 *thou shalt ha't.*

ha interj.
1 Exclamation expressing wonder or surprise, eagerness, indignation (often preceded by *ha* or *ah*) TMP 5.1.263 *Ha, ha! What things are these...?*, HAM 1.5.150, MM 2.2.163.
2 (interjectional interr.) 'Eh?' MV 2.5.44 *What says that fool...ha?*, TMP 2.2.59, WIV 2.3.28.

haberdepois n. (Eliz. form of) Avoirdupois 2H4 2.4.254 *between their haberdepois.*

habit n. Dress, garb, bearing TN 5.1.216 *One face, one voice, one habit*, HAM 1.3.70, LR 5.3.189; (fig.) SON 138.11 *love's best habit is in seeming trust.*
~ vb. Dress, attire WT 4.4.546 *She shall be habited*, TIT 2.3.57.

habitude n. Constitution, temperament LC 114 *His real habitude gave life and grace To appertainings.*

hac See HIC.

hack vb. Put to indiscriminate or promiscuous use, make common by such treatment WIV 2.1.52 *These knights will hack, and so thou shouldst not alter the article of thy gentry* (perh. with quibble in the sense of 'make rough cuts, mangle with clumsy cuts').

hackney n. Common woman, prostitute LLL 3.1.32 *your love perhaps a hackney.*

hackneyed See COMMON-HACKNEYED.

hade land See HEADLAND.

haggard n. Wild female hawk caught when in her adult plumage ADO 3.1.36 *wild As haggards of the rock*, SHR 4.1.193, TN 3.1.64; (hence) wild and intractable woman SHR 4.2.39 *I have lov'd this proud disdainful haggard.*
~ adj. Wild, intractable OTH 3.3.260 *If I do prove her haggard.*

haggle vb. Hack, mangle H5 4.6.11 *York, all haggled over.*

hag-seed n. Hag's offspring TMP 1.2.365 *Hag-seed, hence!*

hair n.
1 Type of something small or slight, jot or tittle TMP 1.2.217 *Not a hair perish'd*, 2H4 1.2.24, TRO 3.2.184; *to a hair* to a nicety TRO 3.1.144.

2 Kind, nature, character 1H4 4.1.61 *The quality and hair of our attempt.*
3 *against the hair* Contrary to the natural tendency, against the grain TRO 1.2.27 *and merry against the hair*, WIV 2.3.40, ROM 2.4.96 (with quibble).

halberd n.
1 Military weapon, consisting of a sharp-edged blade ending in a point, and a spearhead mounted on a handle five to seven feet long ERR 5.1.185 *Guard with halberds!*, 3H6 4.3.20, R3 1.2.40.
2 Halberdier, one armed with a halberd R3 1.2.SD. *with halberds to guard it.*

half n. One of two partners LLL 5.2.249 *I'll not be your half*, SHR 5.2.78; (hence) wife JC 2.1.274 *unfold to me, yourself, your half.*
⬦ Cf. ADO 2.3.170 *half myself* (i.e. my wife).

half-blooded adj. Of superior blood by one parent only LR 5.3.80 *Half-blooded fellow.*

half-can n. Drinking vessel larger than a 'pot', which it had put out of fashion among drinkers MM 4.3.17 *and wild Half-can that stabb'd Pots.*

half-cap n. Half-courteous salute TIM 2.2.212 *certain half-caps and cold-moving nods.*

half-checked, half-cheeked adj. *half-check'd bit* Bit in which the bridle is attached half-way up the cheek or side-piece, thus giving insufficient control over the horse's mouth SHR 3.2.57.

half-cheek n. Side-face, face in profile LLL 5.2.616 *Saint George's half-cheek in a brooch.*

half-face n. Thin face JN 1.1.92 *he hath a half-face like my father!*

half-faced adj.
1 With only one half of the face visible 2H6 4.1.98 *our half-fac'd sun*; (orig. of a coin) having a profile stamped upon it like the groats and half-groats first struck in 1503 JN 1.1.94 *A half-fac'd groat* (with quibble on sense 2).
2 Thin-faced, miserable looking 2H4 3.2.264 *this same half-fac'd fellow*; (hence) imperfect, half-and-half 1H4 1.3.208 *this half-fac'd fellowship.*

half-kirtle See KIRTLE.

half part n. Half JN 2.1.437 *He is the half part of a blessed man*, PER 4.1.94.

halfpenny n. (pl.) Small pieces ADO 2.3.140 *she tore the letter into a thousand halfpence.*

~ *attrib.* Minute LLL 5.1.74 *thou halfpenny purse of wit.*
▷ Halfpennies were tiny silver coins in the Eliz. period.

half-supped *adj.* Half-satisfied TRO 5.8.19 *My half-supp'd sword.*

half-sword *n.* at half-sword At close quarters with swords 1H4 2.4.164 *at half-sword with a dozen.*

half-worker *n.* One that performs half of a work; (hence) partner, collaborator CYM 2.5.2 *Is there no way for men to be, but women Must be half-workers.*

half-world *n.* Hemisphere MAC 2.1.49 *o'er the one half-world Nature seems dead.*

halidom *n.* Holy relic; *by my halidom* a weak oath H8 5.1.116 *Now, by my halidom, what manner of man are you* (F1 *holydame*), TGV 4.2.135 (F1 *hallidome*), SHR 5.2.99 (F1 *hollidam*).
▷ Orig. the holy relics upon which oaths were sworn, the ancient formula being 'as help me God and halidome', altered later to 'by my halidome'. The form 'holydame' is due to association with 'dame', the phrase being popularly taken as 'By our Lady.'

hall *n.*
1 Baronial or squire's residence SHR 2.1.188 *Kate of Kate-Hall*, TRO 3.3.134.
2 *the Hall* Westminster Hall, formerly the High Court of Justice H8 2.1.2.
3 *a hall!* Cry to clear the way or make sufficient room ROM 1.5.26 *A hall, a hall! give room!*

hallo, halloo, hallow *vb.* Shout WT 3.3.77 *he hallow'd but even now*; (trans.) TN 1.5.272 *Hallow your name to the reverberate hills.*

balloo (*interj.*) See 'LOO.

Hallowmas *n.* Feast of All Hallows, All Saint's Day, 1st Nov. TGV 2.1.26 *like a beggar at Hallowmas*, MM 2.1.124, R2 5.1.80.

hallowing *n.* Shouting TGV 5.4.13 *What hallowing and what stir is this*, 2H4 1.2.190.

halt *n.* Halt or lame man PP 18.10 *A cripple soon can find a halt.*

halting *adj.* Wavering, shifting JN 5.2.174 *Not trusting to this halting legate.*

hammer *vb.*
1 Devise, plan 2H6 1.2.47 *wilt thou still be hammering treachery; hammer of, upon* deliberate earnestly upon WT 2.2.47 *Who but to-day hammered of this design*, TGV 1.3.18.
2 (of an idea) Be persistently in the mind TIT 2.3.39 *Blood and revenge are hammering in my head.*

hamper *vb.* Obstruct the free movement of by fastening something on (e.g. swaddling-clothes), fetter, bind 2H6 1.3.145 *She'll hamper thee, and dandle thee like a baby.*

hand *n.*
~ in phrases with vb.
bear in hand Delude (a person) with false hopes or pretences, pretend or profess to do something MAC 3.1.80 *How you were borne in hand*, MM 1.4.52, HAM 2.2.67. **give me your hands** Applaud MND 5.1.437 *Give me your hands, if we be friends.* **had ... by the hand** Secured 2H4 1.3.21 *had his assistance by the hand.* **have ... in hand** Have to do with TN 1.3.65 *you have fools in hand.* **holds hands with** Is the equal of JN 2.1.494 *Holds hand with any Princess.* **lay hand on heart** Reflect ROM 3.5.190 *lay hand on heart, advise.* **make a fine hand, fair hands** Succeed, do well H8 5.3.70 *I have made a fine hand*, COR 4.6.117. **will to hand** Call for execution MAC 3.4.138 *Strange things...that will to hand.*
~ in phrases with prep.
at hand 1 At the start JC 4.2.23 *like horses hot at*

hand. **2** By hand JN 5.2.75 *a lion fostered up at hand.* **at, in any hand, of all hands** In any case LLL 4.3.215 *of all hands must we be forsworn*, SHR 1.2.146, AWW 3.6.43. **brief in hand** Shortly to be despatched JN 4.3.158 *A thousand businesses are brief in hand.* **by the hand** At one's side, in hand 2H4 1.3.21 *Till we had his assistance by the hand.* **by my, this hand** By one's own or another's hand (used freq. in oaths) TMP 3.2.49 *by this hand, I will supplant some of your teeth*, AYL 3.2.394, AWW 3.6.72. **for my hand** By my hand SHR 1.1.189. **for, in one's hand** Led or held by one COR 5.3.23 *and in her hand The grandchild*, JN 2.1.236, R3 4.1.2. **in hand with** Occupied or engaged with VEN 912 *In hand with all things.* **of one's hands** In respect of one's actions or valour in fight WT 5.2.166 *thou art no tall fellow of thy hands*, WIV 1.4.26. **on the upper hand** In the place of honour R3 4.4.37 *let my griefs frown on the upper hand.* **out of hand 1** At once 1H6 3.2.102 *gather we our forces out of hand*, 3H6 4.7.63, TIT 5.2.77. **2** Done with 2H4 3.1.107 *were these inward wars once out of hand.* **unto thy hand** Ready for thee ANT 4.14.29 *Is done unto thy hand.*
~ *vb.* Handle TMP 1.1.23 *hand a rope*; deal with WT 2.3.64 *Let him that makes but trifles of his eyes First hand me*, WT 4.4.348.

hand-fast *n.*
1 Firm hold; *in hand-fast* held fast WT 4.4.768 *If that shepherd be not in hand-fast, let him fly.*
2 Marriage contract CYM 1.5.78 *to hold The hand-fast to her lord.*

hand-in-hand *adj. phr.* Well matched CYM 1.4.70 *a kind of hand-in-hand comparison.*

handkercher *n.* Handkerchief AYL 4.3.97 *This handkercher was stain'd*, H5 3.2.48, JN 4.1.42.

handsaw *n.* Saw managed with one hand 1H4 2.4.168 *my sword hack'd like a handsaw.*
▷ In HAM 2.2.379 *I know a hawk from a handsaw* some commentators read 'heronshaw' or 'hernshaw' (i.e. heron). See HAWK.

handsome *adj.* Proper, fitting, becoming ADO 4.2.85 *and everything handsome about him*, HAM 2.2.445.
~ *adv.* Properly, fittingly, in a becoming manner 2H4 2.4.279 *that ever I dress myself handsome.*

handsomely *adv.*
1 Elegantly, neatly TMP 5.1.294 *trim it handsomely*, WT 4.3.779.
2 Conveniently TIT 2.3.268 *if we miss to meet him handsomely.*

handsomeness *n.* Decency, becoming behaviour, courteous conduct TRO 2.1.15 *I will beat thee into handsomeness* (with quibble on sense of 'beauty', 'grace').

handy-dandy *phr.* Choose which you please LR 4.6.153 *and handy-dandy, which is the justice, which is the thief?*
▷ Words used in the children's game, in which a small object is shaken between the hands of one player, and, the hands being suddenly closed, the other player has to guess in which hand the object is.

hang *vb.*
1 *hang off* Leave go MND 3.2.260 *Hang off, thou cat, thou bur.*
2 *hang up* Hang on a gibbet LLL 4.3.52 *love's Tyburn, that hangs up simplicity.*

hanger *n.* Strap on a sword-belt from which the sword hung HAM 5.2.150 *as girdle, hangers, and so.*

hanging *ppl. adj.* Gloomy MM 4.2.33 *a hanging look.*

hangings *n.* (pl.) Fruit on a tree CYM 3.3.63 *my mellow hangings.*

hangman *n.*
1 Executioner MAC 2.2.25 *As they had seen me with these hangman's hands*; (transf. in playful ref. to Cupid as the executioner of human hearts) ADO 3.2.11 *the little hangman dare not shoot.*

hap *n.* Fortune ROM 2.2.189 *and my dear hap to tell* (i.e. good fortune), ERR 1.1.38, ANT 2.3.33; *by haps* by chance ADO 3.1.105 *then loving goes by haps.*

haply *adv.* By hap, by chance, perchance, perhaps TN 1.2.54 *such disguise as haply shall become The form of my intent,* SON 101.5, H5 4.7.173.

happily *adv.* haply, perchance, perhaps SHR 4.4.54 *And happily we might be interrupted,* MM 4.2.95, TN 4.2.52.
⇨ Ff and Qq have *haply* about twice as many times as *happily* in this sense.

happiness *n.* Propriety, appropriateness, felicity HAM 2.2.209 *a happiness that often madness hits on,* ADO 2.3.183.

happy *vb.* Render happy SON 6.6 *usury Which happies those that pay.*
~ *adj.*
1 Propitious, favourable; *in happy time, hour, season* at an appropriate moment, in time JC 2.2.60 *come in very happy time,* AWW 5.1.6, ADO 4.1.283; a propos, to the point ROM 3.5.111 *a sudden day of joy...- Madam, in happy time, what day is that?*
2 Apt, dexterous, skilful TGV 4.1.34 *My youthful travel therein made me happy,* CYM 3.4.174.
3 Appropriate, fitting, felicitous 1H6 3.2.18 *this happy stratagem,* 1H4 5.4.158, TIM 1.1.16.

harbinger *n.* Officer of royal household who went ahead on journeys to procure lodgings MAC 1.4.45 *I'll be myself the harbinger.*

harbour *n.* Shelter, lodging LLL 2.1.174 *denied fair harbour in my house,* MM 1.3.4, TIM 5.4.53.
~ *vb.* Lodge TN 2.3.96 *she harbours you as her kinsman,* ERR 1.1.136, JN 2.1.262; (intr.) TGV 3.1.140 *My thoughts do harbour with my Silvia nightly,* R2 1.1.195, 3H6 4.7.79.

hard *adj.*
1 Hardened, obdurate ANT 3.13.111 *we in our viciousness grow hard,* MAC 3.4.142, TIM 4.3.269.
2 Harsh to the ear ADO 5.2.38 *a hard rhyme.*
3 *too hard for* Too much for, more than one can manage LLL 2.1.258 *You are too hard for me.*
4 *hard consent* Consent difficult to obtain, permission not easily granted HAM 1.2.60 *I seal'd my hard consent.*
~ *adv.*
1 With an uneasy pace AYL 3.2.313 *trots hard.*
2 With difficulty OTH 1.2.10 *I did full hard forbear him,* 3H6 5.1.70; *hard-a-keeping* difficult to keep LLL 1.1.65 *sworn too hard-a-keeping oath*; *hard-rul'd* managed with difficulty H8 3.2.101 *Our hard-rul'd king*; *hard-believing* incredulous VEN 985 *O hard-believing love...!*
3 Close, near HAM 1.2.179 *it followed hard upon,* OTH 2.1.261, WIV 4.2.39.
4 *go hard (with)* Fare ill (with), be hurtful or disadvantageous (to) SHR 4.4.108 *It shall go hard if Cambio go without her,* TGV 4.4.2, MV 3.2.290.
5 *it shall go hard but I will* (introduces a statement of what will happen unless overwhelming difficulties prevent it) I will assuredly TGV 1.1.85 *It shall go hard but I'll prove it by another,* MV 3.1.72, HAM 3.4.207.

hard-favoured *adj.* Unpleasant in countenance, ugly H5 3.1.8 *Disguise fair nature with hard-favour'd rage,* AYL 3.3.29, VEN 133.

hardiment *n.* Boldness, bold exploit 1H4 1.3.101 *changing hardiment with great Glendower,* TRO 4.5.28, CYM 5.4.75.

hardiness *n.* Boldness, daring H5 1.2.220 *the name of hardiness,* CYM 3.6.22.

hardly *adv.*
1 Severely, harshly H8 1.2.105 *Hardly conceive of me,* CYM 3.3.8, R3 2.1.58.
2 With difficulty COR 5.2.72 *I was hardly mov'd,* TGV 1.1.133, MAC 5.3.62.

hardness *n.*
1 Difficulty OTH 3.4.34 *O, hardness to dissemble!,* CYM 5.5.431.
2 Hardship CYM 3.6.21 *hardness ever Of hardness is mother,* OTH 1.3.233.

hardock *n.* Coarse weedy plant, prob. burdock LR 4.4.4 *With hardocks, hemlock, nettles.*
⇨ Ff 1-2 *Hardokes*; Qq *hor-docks*; mod. edd. *hoardocks, harlocks, burdocks.*

hardy *a.* Bold, daring MAC 1.2.4 *a good and hardy soldier,* TN 2.2.10, 3H6 1.4.14.

hare *n.* Prostitute ROM 2.4.132 *No hare, sir, unless a hare, sir, in a lenten pie* (with quibble on the usual animal meaning).

hare-bell *n.* Wild hyacinth CYM 4.2.222 *The azur'd hare-bell.*

hare-finder *n.* (in the sport of coursing) One whose business is to espy a hare in form ADO 1.1.184 *Cupid is a good hare-finder.*

hark *vb.* (imper., used in hunting, etc.) A call to start or urge on dogs in the chase TMP 4.1.257 *there, Tyrant, there! hark, hark!*

harlock See HARDOCK.

harlot *n.* Lewd person (male or female) ERR 5.1.205 *she with harlots feasted,* ROM 2.4.42, COR 3.2.112; (attrib.) WT 2.3.4 *the harlot king,* ERR 2.2.136.

harlotry *n.*
1 Courtesan, harlot OTH 4.2.233 *He sups tonight with a harlotry* (Q1 *harlot*).
2 (term of contempt) Silly wench 1H4 3.1.196 *a peevish self-will'd harlotry,* ROM 4.2.14.
~ *attrib.* Worthless, trashy 1H4 2.4.395 *these harlotry players.*

harmony *n.* Music, tuneful sound TMP 3.3.18 *What harmony is this?,* HAM 3.2.362.

harness *n.* Body-armour MAC 5.5.51 *with harness on our back,* TIM 1.2.52, TRO 5.3.31; (transf.) men in harness, men-at-arms 1H4 3.2.101 *He doth fill fields with harness in the realm.*

harnessed *ppl. adj.* Armed, in armour JN 5.2.132 *This harness'd masque,* TRO 1.2.8.

harp *vb.* Hit upon, guess MAC 4.1.74 *thou hast harp'd my fear.*

harpy *n.* Fabulous monster, rapacious and filthy, having a woman's face and body, and a bird's wings and claws, supposed to be a minister of divine vengeance TMP 3.3.83 *Bravely the figure of this harpy hast thou Perform'd,* ADO 2.1.271, PER 4.3.46.

harrow *vb.* Lacerate or wound (the feelings), vex, distress HAM 1.1.44 *it harrows me with fear,* HAM 1.5.16, COR 5.3.34 (with play on lit. sense).

Harry *n. Harry ten shilling* Ten-shilling piece coined in the reign of Henry V111 2H4 3.2.221 *and here's four Harry ten shillings.*

harsh *adj.*
1 Disagreeably hard and rough to the touch TRO 1.1.58 *The cygnet's down is harsh.*
2 Unpleasantly rough to the taste; (fig.) OTH 5.2.116 *And sweet revenge grows harsh.*
3 Of unpleasant or rough aspect, repulsive SON 11.10 *Harsh, featureless, and rude.*

harvest *n.* Season for reaping and gathering in ripened grain; (fig.) TN 3.1.132 *youth is come to harvest* (i.e. is ripened), ADO 1.3.25, CYM 1.1.46.

harvest-home *n.* (fig.) Occasion of profit WIV 2.2.275 *and there's my harvest-home.*

haste *n.* take haste, put it to the haste Make haste TIM 5.1.210, ANT 5.2.196.

haste-post-haste *n.* Great expedition or speed 3H6 2.1.139 Norfolk, and myself, In haste-post-haste are come to join with you (F1 haste, post-haste).

hasty *adj.*
1 Quick, speedy ROM 5.1.64 as hasty powder fir'd, JC 4.3.112, HAM 2.2.4.
2 In a hurry ADO 5.1.49 Are you so hasty now?, 2H4 4.5.60, R3 4.4.163.

hasty-witted *adj.* Inconsiderate, rash SHR 5.2.40 An hasty-witted body Would say your head and butt were head and horn.

hat *n.* have my hat Doff the hat as a mark of courtesy or civility COR 2.3.99.

hatch *n.*
1 Half-door, gate, or wicket with an open space above ERR 3.1.33 or sit down at the hatch; In at the window, or else o'er the hatch by any way JN 1.1.171 (i.e. born irregularly); take, leap the hatch jump over the hatch JN 5.2.138 and make you take the hatch, LR 3.6.73.
2 (pl.) Movable planks forming a kind of deck in ships TMP 1.2.230 The mariners all under hatches stowed (i.e. below deck), WIV 2.1.92, R3 1.4.13.

hatched *ppl. adj.*[1] Closed with a hatch PER 4.2.33 to keep our door hatch'd.

hatched *ppl. adj.*[2] hatch'd in silver Inlaid with narrow strips of silver; (fig., of hair) streaked with white TRO 1.3.65 venerable Nestor, hatch'd in silver.

hatchment *n.* Square or diamond-shaped tablet displaying the armorial bearings of a deceased person HAM 4.5.215 nor hatchment o'er his bones.

hate *n.* Cause of hatred COR 1.1.183 that was now your hate, JN 3.4.28.

hatefully *adv.* Malignantly VEN 940 But hatefully at random dost thou hit.

haud credo [L.] I do not believe LLL 4.2.20 I said the deer was not a haud credo.

haught *adj.* Haughty, arrogant R2 4.1.254 thou haught insulting man, R3 2.3.28, 2H6 1.3.68 (F1 haughtie).

haughty *adj.* High-spirited, high-minded, exalted 1H6 2.5.79 this haughty great attempt, R3 4.2.37, 1H4 5.2.40.

haul *vb.* Drag 2H4 5.5.35 Hauled thither By most mechanical and dirty hand.
⬦ F1 Hall'd; Q1 halde; some mod. edd. Hal'd.

haunch *n.* (fig.) Latter end 2H4 4.4.92 the haunch of winter.

haunt *n.* Public resort, society of men AYL 2.1.15 our life, exempt from public haunt, ANT 4.14.54; out of haunt secluded HAM 4.1.18 kept...out of haunt This mad young man.
~ *vb.*
1 (trans.) Frequent the company of, accompany, follow persistently MND 2.2.85 do not haunt me thus, ERR 3.2.82, TRO 4.1.11.
2 (intr.) Remain continually, resort habitually OTH 1.1.96 to haunt about my doors, LC 130, MAC 1.6.9.

hautboy *n.* Oboe, wooden double-reed wind instrument of high pitch 2H4 3.2.326 The case of a treble hautboy was a mansion for him (F1 Hoe-boy).

have *vb.*
1 Know, be versed in MV 1.2.71 I have a poor pennyworth in the English, TGV 4.1.33, WT 4.4.607; understand, grasp with the mind HAM 2.1.65 You have me, have you not?
2 (with will) Maintain or assert to be 1H6 3.1.30 As he will have me.
3 (idiomatic uses of the imper.) have after I will follow HAM 11.4.89; have at it I will begin or attempt it WT 4.4.296 Have at it with you, CYM 5.5.315;

have at thee, you (1) I shall come at you, attack you 2H6 2.3.89 have at thee with a downright blow, ROM 4.5.123; (2) I will address you LLL 4.3.286 Have at you then, affection's men-at-arms; have through I will go through 2H6 4.8.61 have through the very middest of you!; have to it I will set about it SHR 1.1.139 then have to't afresh; (similarly) SHR 4.5.78 Have to my widow; have to thee here's to your health SHR 5.2.37 Ha' to thee, lad!; have with thee, you I 'll go along with you WIV 2.1.156, OTH 1.2.53.
4 (idiomatic uses with it) have it (1) Have the victory SHR death blow ROM 3.1.107 I have it, And soundly too; let me have it tell me it WT 1.2.101, H8 2.1.145.

have(-)at(-)him *n.* Stroke, attack H8 2.2.84 I 'll venture one have at him!.
⬦ F1 I 'll venture one; have at him; Ff 2–4 one heave at him. See HAVE *vb.* sense 3 have at.

haver *n.* Possessor COR 2.2.85 dignifies the haver.

having *n.* Possession, property, wealth, estate WIV 3.2.72 The gentleman is of no having, AYL 2.3.62, WT 4.4.719; (pl.) H8 3.2.159 par'd my present havings; allowance OTH 4.3.91 scant our former having; (fig.) endowments, accomplishments LC 235 Whose rarest havings made the blossoms dote, TRO 3.3.97.

haviour *n.* Behaviour, bearing, manner TN 3.4.206 With the same haviour, R2 1.3.77, WIV 1.3.78.

havoc *n.* cry havoc (orig.) Give an army the order 'havoc!' as the signal for pillaging JC 3.1.273 Cry 'Havoc!' and let slip the dogs of war, JN 2.1.357, COR 3.1.273.

hawk *n.* [Northern dial. form] Hack, agricultural tool of the mattock, hoe and pick-axe type HAM 2.2.379 I know a hawk from a handsaw.
⬦ Many commentators interpret hawk here in sense of 'bird of prey': see HANDSAW.

hawk *vb.* Fly at or attack on the wing, as a hawk does MAC 2.4.13 A falcon...Was by a mousing owl hawk'd at.

hawking *adj.* 'Hawk-like', keen' (Schmidt) AWW 1.1.94 his hawking eye.

hay *n.*[1] Country dance having a winding or serpentine movement LLL 5.1.154 let them dance the hay.

hay *n.*[2] (in fencing) Home-thrust ROM 2.4.26 the punto reverso, the hay!

hazard *n.*
1 Game of dice at which the chances are complicated by a number of arbitrary rules; (hence fig.) come, go to hazard run extreme risks MV 2.9.18 That comes to hazard for my worthless self, H5 3.7.85.
2 Chance, venture R3 5.4.10 I have set my life upon a cast, And I will stand the hazard of the die, ANT 3.7.47, MV 2.1.45; (hence) jeopardy, peril, risk JC 3.1.136 Thorough the hazards of this untrod state, HAM 3.3.6, AWW 3.3.6; on (the) hazard at stake TRO Prol.22 Sets all on hazard, JC 5.1.68, 1H4 4.1.48; in hazard in peril MV 4.2.156 I will lay myself in hazard; put in hazard risked COR 2.3.256 This mutiny were better put in hazard.
3 Thing risked or staked MV 1.1.151 Or bring your latter hazard back again.
4 Each of the winning openings in a tennis court H5 1.2.263 Shall strike his father's crown into the hazard.
~ *vb.* Put at risk ANT 3.12.19 hazarded to thy grace (i.e. depending for its fate on thy favour).

he *pron.* he...he One...another MV 4.1.54 Why he cannot abide a gaping pig; Why he, a harmless necessary cat; Why he, a woollen bagpipe, SON 29.6; he as he the one as well as the other TRO 4.1.67.

head *n.*
1 (used for) Ears PER 2.3.97 loud music is too harsh

for ladies' heads, LLL 4.3.333, TRO 4.5.5; mouth CYM 5.5.157 *Our viands...which I heav'd to head*; face MM 4.3.142 *to th' head of Angelo Accuse him home and home*, ADO 5.1.62, MND 1.1.106.

2 Antlers (of a deer, roebuck) 1H6 4.2.51 *Turn on the bloody hounds with heads of steel*; *of the first head* said of a deer at the age when antlers are first developed LLL 4.2.10.

3 Source of a river; (fig.) source, origin AWW 1.3.172 *Your salt tears' head*, HAM 1.1.106, R2 1.1.97.

4 Headland, promontory ANT 3.7.51 *from the head of Actium*.

5 Category, topic TIM 3.5.28 *set quarrelling Upon the head of valour*.

6 Body of people gathered or raised, armed force JN 5.2.113 *this gallant head of war*, 1H4 1.3.284, HAM 4.5.102; *make a head* raise a body of troops 3H6 2.1.141, JC 4.1.42, CYM 4.2.139.

7 *head and front* Height and breadth OTH 1.3.80 *the very head and front of my offending*.

~ *vb.* Behead MM 2.1.238 *If you head and hang all that offend*.

head-borough *n.* Parish officer, having the same functions as a petty constable SHR Ind.1.12 *I must go fetch the Head-borough*.

◇ Mod. edd. *third-borough*.

headed *ppl. adj.* That has come to a head or matured, as a boil AYL 2.7.67 *all th' embossed sores, and headed evils*.

headland *n.* Unploughed strip, used as a boundary and means of access between two portions of a field 2H4 5.1.14 *shall we sow the head land with wheat* (F1; Q1 *hade land*).

headly *adj.* Chief, principal, capital H5 3.3.32 *headly murder* (F1; other Ff *heady*).

headpiece *n.*

1 Helmet H5 3.7.138 *never wear such heavy head-pieces*, LR 3.2.26.

2 Head, brain WT 1.2.227 *Of headpiece extraordinary*.

heady *adj.* Headlong, impetuous, precipitate, violent LR 2.4.110 *my more headier will*, 1H4 2.3.55; (of a stream) H5 1.1.34 *With such a heady currance, scouring faults*.

heady-rash *adj.* Impetuously rash, hasty ERR 5.1.216 *Nor heady-rash, provok'd with raging ire*.

health *n.* Welfare, well being, prosperity 2H4 4.4.81 *Health to my sovereign*, TIM 2.2.197, HAM 1.3.21.

healthful *adj.* Healthy AWW 2.3.48 *with this healthful hand*, H8 1.1.3, JC 2.1.319.

heap *n.*

1 Mass, main body PER 1.1.33 *because thine eye Presumes to reach, all the whole heap must die*.

2 Great company or body R3 2.1.54 *Among this princely heap*; *on heaps, upon a heap* in a body H5 4.5.18 *let us on heaps go offer up our lives*, JC 1.3.23, TRO 3.2.28.

3 *on heaps, on a heap* In a fallen or prostrate mass, in ruins H5 5.2.39 *all her husbandry doth lie on heaps*, TIT 2.3.223, TIM 4.3.102.

heaping *ppl. adj. the heaping friendships* The piling up of friendly relations and services WT 4.2.19.

hear *vb.*

1 Talk together MAC 3.4.31 *We'll hear ourselves again*.

2 Listen, pay attention to JC 1.2.204 *he hears no music*.

3 Hear of, be informed of PER 1.4.54 *hear these tears!*, LUC 263.

hearing *n.* Report, news SHR 5.2.182 *'Tis a good hearing*, CYM 3.1.4.

hearken *vb.*

1 Inquire or seek *after* ADO 5.1.212 *Hearken after their offence*, LLL 1.1.217, R3 1.1.54.

2 Be on the watch, wait *for* SHR 1.2.258 *whom you hearken for*, SHR 4.4.53, 1H4 5.4.52.

hearse *n.* Coffin on a bier JC 3.2.165 *Stand from the hearse*, R3 1.2.2, 2H4 4.5.113.

hearsed *ppl. adj.* Coffined, buried MV 3.1.89 *Would she were hears'd*, HAM 1.4.47; (fig.) LUC 657 *Thy sea within a puddle's womb is hearsed*.

heart *n.*

1 Disposition, temperament ADO 2.1.313 *a merry heart*, MM 5.1.384.

2 Feeling MV 1.2.128 *with so good heart* (i.e. so heartily).

3 Term of endearment, appreciation, commendation and compassion TMP 1.1.6 *cheerly, my hearts!*, LLL 5.1.109, H5 2.1.118.

~ *in phrases*

for his heart To save his life CYM 2.1.55 *Cannot take two from twenty, for his heart*, MV 5.1.165. **in heart** A toast TIM 1.2.53 *My lord, in heart; and let the health go round*. **out of heart** In low spirits, discouraged, disheartened 1H4 3.3.6 *I shall be out of heart shortly*, LLL 3.1.44. **with all my heart** Courteous salutation or response to a greeting OTH 4.1.216 *God save you, worthy general!—With all my heart, sir*, TIM 3.6.25, LR 4.6.32.

heart-blood *n.* Essence TRO 3.1.32 *heart-blood of beauty*.

heart-burn *vb.* Affect with heartburning ADO 2.1.4 *I never can see him but I am heart-burn'd an hour after*, 1H4 3.3.50.

heart-dear *adj.* Beloved 2H4 2.3.12 *my heart-dear Harry* (F1; Q1 *hearts deere Harry*).

hearted *ppl. adj.* Fixed in the heart OTH 1.3.366 *I hate the Moor. My cause is hearted*, OTH 3.3.448.

heartless *adj.*

1 Spiritless, disheartened ROM 1.1.66 *these heartless hinds*, LUC 471, LUC 1392.

2 Sterile, barren PP 17.23 *How sighs resound through heartless ground*.

heartlings *n.* Little heart WIV 3.4.57 *'Od's heartlings*.

heart-offending *adj.* Wounding the heart 2H6 3.2.60 *heart-offending groans*.

heart's ease *n.* Peace of mind, tranquillity H5 4.1.236 *what infinite heart's ease Must kings neglect*.

heart-sore *adj.* Characterized by grief, grieved at heart TGV 1.1.30 *heart-sore sighs*, TGV 2.4.132.

heart-strings *n.* Tendons or nerves supposed, in old anatomy, to brace and sustain the heart TGV 4.2.62 *so false that he grieves my very heart-strings*, R3 4.4.365, OTH 3.3.261; (in sing.) *from heart-string* from my heart H5 4.1.47 *from heart-string I love the lovely bully*.

heart-struck *adj.* Distressing the heart LR 3.1.17 *His heart-struck injuries*.

heart-whole *adj.* Having the affections free, with the heart unengaged AYL 4.1.49 *I'll warrant him heart-whole*.

hearty *adj.* (epithet of compliment) Great-hearted, magnanimous ANT 4.2.38 *my hearty friends!*

heat *n.* Point at which the body becomes warm with moderate drinking TN 1.5.132 *One draught above heat*.

~ *vb.* (?) Run a heat; (hence) race swiftly over WT 1.2.96 *With spur we heat an acre*.

~ *pa. pple.* Heated JN 4.1.61 *The iron of itself, though heat red-hot*.

◇ TN 1.1.25 *The element itself, till seven years' heat*: up to the time in that it has received heat for seven years, i.e. until seven years have passed.

heath See LONG *adj.*[1]

heave n.

1 Deep sigh HAM 4.1.1 *these sighs, these profound heaves.*

2 Thrust H8 2.2.84 *I'll venture one heave at him.*

▷ See HAVE[-]AT[-]HIM.

~ *vb.* Utter (groan or word) AYL 2.1.36 *heav'd forth such groans,* LR 4.3.25.

heaven n.

1 *floor of heaven* Sky MV 5.1.58 *look how the floor of heaven Is thick inlaid.*

2 Each of the 'spheres' or spherical shells, lying above or outside of each other, into which astronomers and cosmographers formerly divided the realms of space around the earth; (fig.) H5 Prol.2 *O for a Muse of fire, that would ascend The brightest heaven of invention!*

heaven-hued adj. Blue LC 215 *heaven-hu'd sapphire.*

heavenly adv. Divinely OTH 5.2.135 *heavenly true.*

heavily adv. Sadly, sorrowfully MAC 4.3.182 *the tidings, Which I have heavily borne,* R3 1.4.1, ADO 5.3.18.

heaviness n.

1 Sadness 2H4 4.2.82 *Against ill chances men are ever merry, But heaviness foreruns the good event,* TMP 5.1.200, ROM 3.4.11.

2 Drowsiness 1H4 3.1.215 *with pleasing heaviness,* TMP 1.2.307.

heaving n. Deep groan or sigh WT 2.3.35 *At each his needless heavings.*

~ *ppl. adj.* Rising TRO 2.2.196 *our heaving spleens.*

heavy adj.

1 Weighty, important, serious LR 5.1.27 *Most just and heavy causes,* AWW 2.5.45, 1H4 2.3.63.

2 Dull, stupid OTH 2.1.143 *O heavy ignorance!,* SON 78.6.

3 Slow, sluggish MND 5.1.368 *The heavy gait of night,* JN 4.1.47, ANT 3.7.38.

4 (of a deed or its agent) Wicked, heinous, grievous HAM 4.1.12 *O heavy deed!,* MM 2.3.28, WT 3.2.208.

heavy-gaited adj. Slow, sluggish R2 3.2.15 *heavy-gaited toads.*

heavy-headed adj. Drowsy, drunken, stupid with drinking HAM 1.4.17 *heavy-headed revel.*

hebenon, hebona n. Substance of uncertain source, having a poisonous juice HAM 1.5.62 *juice of cursed hebenon.*

▷ Ff *hebenon,* Qq *hebona.* Commentators have variously identified the word with 'henbane', 'ebon' (ebony) and German 'eibe' (the yew).

Hecate n. (transf., applied pejoratively to a woman) Hag, witch 1H6 3.2.64 *that railing Hecate.*

hectic n. Hectic or wasting fever HAM 4.3.66 *For like the hectic in my blood he rages.*

Hector n. (transf.) Valiant warrior WIV 1.3.11 *bully Hector,* WIV 2.3.33.

hedge vb.

1 *hedge out* Shut out, debar, exclude TRO 3.1.60 *this shall not hedge us out.*

2 Go *aside from* the straight way TRO 3.3.158 *Or hedge aside from the direct* (Q *turne*); (hence) shift, shuffle, dodge WIV 2.2.25 *to shuffle, to hedge, and to lurch,* H8 3.2.39.

hedge-born adj. Of low or mean birth 1H6 4.1.43 *like a hedge-born swain.*

hedgehog n. (fig.) Person who is regardless of others' feelings R3 1.2.102 *Dost grant me, hedgehog?*

hedge-pig n. Hedgehog MAC 4.1.2 *and once the hedge-pig whin'd.*

hedge-priest n. Illiterate priest of low status LLL 5.2.542 *the braggart, the hedge-priest.*

heed n. That which one heeds or pays attention to LLL 1.1.82 *that eye shall be his heed.*

heel n.

1 (with ref. to punishment) *lay by the heels* Put in irons or the stocks H8 5.3.79 *I'll lay ye all By th' heels*; (similarly) 2H4 1.2.123 *To punish you by the heels*; AWW 4.3.103 *his heels have deserv'd it* (i.e. to be put in the stocks).

2 *out at heels* In unfortunate or decayed circumstances, in distress LR 2.2.157 *A good man's fortune may grow out at heels,* WIV 1.3.31.

~ *vb.* Perform (a dance) TRO 4.4.86 *heel the high lavolt.*

▷ Cf. ADO 3.4.47 *Ye light a' love with your heels!* (i.e. You dance light o' love, with play on 'light' and 'light-heeled', i.e. unchaste).

heft n. Straining, retching WT 2.1.45 *With violent hefts.*

heigh interj. Cry of encouragement TMP 1.1.5 *Heigh, my hearts!,* WT 4.3.2, 1H4 2.4.487.

heigh-ho interj.

1 Exclamation used to summon a person MND 4.1.202 *Heigh-ho! Peter Quince!,* 1H4 2.1.1.

2 Exclamation expressing joy AYL 2.7.182 *heigh-ho, the holly!*

3 Exclamation expressing sadness or dejection ADO 2.1.320 *cry 'Heigh-ho for a husband!',* TRO 3.1.126, AYL 4.3.168.

height n.

1 High rank, degree, or position R2 1.1.189 *with pale beggar-fear impeach my height,* R3 1.3.82, TIT 4.2.34.

2 Highest point, zenith, summit ERR 5.1.200 *the strength and height of injury,* JN 4.3.46, 2H4 2.3.63; *at* (the) *height* at the or its highest point, at its height AYL 5.2.46 *at the height of heart-heaviness,* R3 1.3.41, TIT 3.1.70; *in height of* at the height of R3 5.3.176 *in height of all his pride; in height* at its highest ANT 3.10.20 *Leaving the fight in height; in the height* in the extreme ADO 4.1.301 *in the height a villain,* PER 2.4.6; *on height of* on pain of TIM 3.5.86 *On height of our displeasure; to the height* to the utmost H8 1.2.214 *traitor to th' height,* TRO 5.1.3.

heighten vb. Exalt COR 5.6.21 *who being so heighten'd...watered his new plants with dews of flattery.*

heinously adv. Very badly, shockingly 1H4 3.3.189 *I am heinously unprovided.*

heir n. (transf. uses)

1 Person to whom something is bound to fall due (e.g. sorrow, fate) HAM 3.1.62 *That flesh is heir to,* WIV 5.5.39, R2 2.2.63.

2 Offspring, product 2H4 4.4.122 *Unfather'd heirs,* VEN Ded.5.

heir apparent n. Heir presumptive 2H6 1.1.152 *he is...heir apparent to the English crown* (said of the king's uncle), PER 3.Gower.37.

hell n. Place of confinement for debtors ERR 4.2.40 *carries poor souls to hell.*

hell-hated adj. Hated as hell LR 5.3.148 *With the hell-hated lie.*

hell-hound n. Fiendish person MAC 5.8.3 *Turn, hell-hound,* R3 4.4.48, TIT 5.2.144.

hell-kite n. Person of hellish cruelty MAC 4.3.217 *O hell-kite!*

helm n. Helmet LR 4.2.57 *plumed helm,* ANT 2.1.33, 1H4 3.2.142.

helm vb. (fig.) Steer MM 3.2.143 *the business he hath helm'd.*

help n.

1 *at help* In our favour HAM 4.3.44 *and the wind at help.*

2 Relief, cure, remedy TRO 4.1.48 *There is no help,* ERR 5.1.160, COR 3.1.220.

~ *vb.* Relieve, cure, remedy TMP 2.2.93 *I will help his ague,* TGV 4.2.47, ROM 1.2.47.

▷ Pa.t. and pa. pple. freq. *holp.*

helpless *adj.* Affording no help, unavailing, unprofitable ERR 2.1.39 *urging helpless patience*, R3 1.2.13, LUC 1027.

hem *vb.* Clear *away* with a hem or cough AYL 1.3.18 *Hem them away.*

hemp *n.* Material of the hangman's noose H5 3.6.43 *let not hemp his windpipe suffocate.*

hempen *adj.* (jocular) Made of the hangman's halter 2H6 4.7.90 *Ye shall have a hempen caudle.*

hempseed *n.* Gallows-bird, one deserving to be hanged 2H4 2.1.58 *do, thou hempseed!*

hen *n.* (term of contempt) Chicken-hearted fellow AWW 2.3.213 *Lord have mercy on thee for a hen!*

hence *adv.*
1 In the next world HAM 3.2.222 *Both here and hence*, JN 4.2.89.
2 Henceforward, henceforth OTH 3.3.379 *from hence I 'll love no friend*, LLL 5.2.816, 2H4 5.5.52.

henceforth *adv. for henceforth* For the future ADO 5.1.295 *dispose For henceforth of poor Claudio.*

hence-going *n.* Departure CYM 3.2.63 *from our hence-going.*

henchman *n.* Page of honour MND 2.1.121 *To be my henchman.*

henloft *n.* Hen-house WIV 3.4.41 *stole two geese out of a henloft.*

hent *n.* Clutch, grasp; (hence, fig.) that which is grasped or conceived in the mind, intention HAM 3.3.88 *Up, sword, and know thou a more horrid hent.*
▷ Both the lit. and fig. senses may apply here, but it is possible that *hent* is a var. of HINT.
~ *vb.*
1 Take, seize WT 4.3.124 *And merrily hent the stile-a.*
2 Reach, occupy MM 4.6.14 *Have hent the gates.*

hep See HIP *n.²*

her *poss. det.* (old form of third person pl.) Their 1H6 1.1.83 *her flowing tides*, TRO 1.3.118.

herald *n.*
1 Officer having the duty of (1) making proclamations 2H6 4.2.176 *Herald, away*; (2) bearing messages between princes and hostile forces H5 4.7.66 *Here comes the herald of the French*, JN 2.1.235; (attrib.) TGV 3.1.144 *My herald thoughts*; (3) conveying challenges LR 5.1.48 *let but the herald cry*, H8 1.1.34; (4) arranging public processions, funerals, etc. COR 5.6.143 *the most noble corse that ever herald Did follow*, 1H6 1.1.45; (5) regulating the use of armorial bearings LUC 206 *Some loathsome dash the herald will contrive*, SHR 2.1.224.
2 Messenger, envoy HAM 3.4.58 *the herald Mercury*, R3 1.1.72, LLL 5.2.97.
3 Forerunner, precursor JC 1.3.56 *Such dreadful heralds to astonish us*, ADO 2.1.306, ROM 3.5.6.
~ *vb.* Usher (*into*) MAC 1.3.102 *to herald thee into his sight*, PER 3.1.34.

heraldry *n.*
1 Art or science of a herald, blazoning of armorial bearings MND 3.2.213 *like coats in heraldry*; (fig.) OTH 3.4.47 *our new heraldry is hands.*
2 Heraldic practice or regulation HAM 1.1.87 *Well ratified by law and heraldry* (i.e. heraldic law).
3 Heraldic title or rank AWW 2.3.262 *than the commission of your birth and virtue gives you heraldry.*
4 Heraldic device, armorial bearings; (fig.) HAM 2.2.456 *Hath now this dread and black complexion smear'd* With heraldry more dismal, LUC 64.

herb-grace, herb-of-grace *n.* The plant rue, Ruta graveolens HAM 4.5.182 *we may call it herb-of-grace*, AWW 4.5.17, R2 3.4.105.

herblet *n.* Little herb CYM 4.2.287 *You were as flow'rs, now wither'd; even so These herblets shall.*

here *n.* The present life LR 1.1.261 *Thou losest here, a better where to find.*

hereafter *adj.* Future 1H6 2.2.10 *hereafter ages*, R3 4.4.390.

here-approach *n.* Arrival MAC 4.1.133 *before thy here-approach.*

hereby *adv.* Close by LLL 4.1.9 *Hereby, upon the edge of yonder coppice.*
▷ In LLL 1.2.136 *That's hereby* is app. intended for a derisive comment, but the meaning is uncertain.

here-remain *n.* Stay MAC 4.3.148 *since my here-remain in England.*

hereto *adv.* Hitherto, up to this time COR 2.2.60 *than He hath hereto priz'd them at.*

hermit, ermite *n.*
1 Beadsman MAC 1.6.20 *We rest your hermits* (F1 *Ermites*).
2 *begging hermit* Mendicant friar TIT 3.2.41 *As begging hermits in their holy prayers.*

Herod *n.* Blustering tyrant WIV 2.1.20 *What a Herod of Jewry is this!*, ANT 3.3.3, HAM 3.2.14.
▷ Herod was represented as such a character in the medieval mystery plays. See OUT-HEROD.

hest *n.* Bidding, command TMP 3.1.37 *I have broke your hest*, TMP 4.1.65, 1H4 2.3.62.

hewgh *interj.* Imitation of a whistling sound, 'whew' LR 4.6.92 *i' th' clout—hewgh!*

hey *interj.* Cry expressing surprise, exultation, encouragement, excitement TN 5.1.390 *With hey ho*, AYL 5.3.20, WT 4.3.6; (with *nony, nonino*) ADO 2.3.69, AYL 5.3.17, HAM 4.5.166.
▷ See also HEIGH.

heyday *n.* State of excitement HAM 3.4.69 *The heyday in the blood is tame.*
~ *interj.* Exclamation denoting joy, surprise, wonder, gaiety TMP 2.2.186 *Freedom, hey-day! Hey-day, freedom!*, R3 4.4.459, TIM 1.2.131.
▷ F1 *high-day, hoy-day.*

hey-ho See HEIGH-HO.

hic, hac [L.] This WIV 4.1.66 *teaches him to 'hic' and to 'hac'* (with quibbles on 'hiccup' and 'hack' (i.e. cough)).

hic et ubique [L.] Here and everywhere HAM 1.5.156 *Hic et ubique? Then we'll shift our ground.*

hic ibat Simois, hic est Sigeia tellus; hic steterat Priami . . . regia . . . celsa senis [L.—quotation from Ovid] Here ran the river Simois, here is the Sigeian land; here had stood the lofty palace of old Priam SHR 3.1.28.

hic jacet [L.] Here lies AWW 3.6.62.

hid-fox See KID-FOX.

hide *vb.*
1 Sheath (a sword) AYL 2.7.119 *and hide my sword*, R3 1.2.175.
2 Shield, protect JC 2.1.85 *To hide thee from prevention*, JN 2.1.260, CYM 4.2.388.
3 *hide fox, and all after* Cry formerly uttered in the game of hide and seek, when one player hides and the rest seek him HAM 4.2.30.

hideous *adj.*
1 Detestable, odious LR 1.1.151 *This hideous rashness.*
2 Terrifying, shocking TN 3.4.194 *a most hideous opinion of his rage.*

hie *vb.* (intr. and refl.) Hasten R2 5.1.22 *Hie thee to France*, TGV 4.2.94, MAC 1.5.25.

Hiems *n.* [L.] Winter personified LLL 5.2.891 *This side is Hiems, Winter.*

high *adj.*
1 *higher Italy* The Italian nobility, the higher classes of Italy AWW 2.1.12 *Let higher Italy . . . see.*
2 *at high wish* At the height of one's desires TIM 4.3.245 *The one is filling still, never complete; The other, at high wish.*

3 *the high east* The exact east JC 2.1.110.
~ *adv.*
1 Loudly ANT 1.5.49 *neigh'd so high.*
2 Highly TN 1.1.15 *high fantastical,* LUC 19, VEN 236; deeply, intensely, very AWW 5.3.36 *My high-repented blames,* TIT 4.4.64.
3 Far AWW 4.3.42 *Will he travel higher, or return again...?* (i.e. farther); (fig.) WIV 5.5.105 *hold up the jest no higher,* AWW 2.1.210.
~ in combination
high-battled Having a lofty command ANT 3.13.29 *high-battled Caesar.* **high-blown** Inflated H8 3.2.361 *My high-blown pride.* **high-born** Of high birth JN 5.2.79 *I am too high-born to be propertied.* **high-borne** Exalted, lofty LLL 1.1.172 *high-borne words.* **high-coloured** Flushed ANT 2.7.4 *Lepidus is high-colour'd.* **high cross** Cross set on a pedestal in a market-place or the centre of the town SHR 1.1.132 *whipt at the high cross.* **high-day** 1 Holiday MV 2.9.98 *high-day wit.* **2** See HEYDAY. **high-engendered** Produced in the sky LR 3.2.23 *Your high-engender'd battles.* **high-gravel-blind** (jocular intensive of) Sand-blind MV 2.2.36 *who being more than sand-blind, high-gravel-blind, knows me not.* **high-grown** Overgrown with tall vegetation LR 4.4.7 *in the high-grown field.* **high-judging** Judging from on high; (hence) that is supreme judge LR 2.4.228 *to high-judging Jove.* **high-lone** Quite alone, without support ROM 1.3.36 *stand high-lone.* **high-minded** Arrogant 1H6 1.5.12 *this high-minded strumpet.* **high-pitched** Of lofty character LUC 41 *high-pitch'd thoughts.* **high-proof** In the highest degree ADO 5.1.123 *we are high-proof melancholy.* **high-sighted** Supercilious, arrogant JC 2.1.118 *high-sighted tyranny.* **high-stomached** Haughty R2 1.1.18 *High-stomach'd...and full of ire.* **high-viced** Extremely wicked TIM 4.3.110 *some high-vic'd city.* **high-witted** Cunning TIT 4.4.35 *High-witted Tamora.*

high and low *adj. phr.* (absol., short for) 'High and low men', two kinds of false dice made so as to turn up high and low numbers respectively WIV 1.3.86 *high and low beguiles the rich and poor.*
◇ Perh. a play on this sense also in WT 5.1.207 *The odds for high and low's alike.*

hight *vb.* Is called MND 5.1.139 *which Lion hight by name,* LLL 1.1.170, PER 4.Gower.18.

hild *pa. pple.* (var., used for rhyme's sake, of) Held LUC 1257 *let it not be hild Poor women's fault.*

hilding *n.* Contemptible, worthless person, good-for-nothing AWW 3.6.3 *find him not a hilding,* CYM 2.3.123; (applied to a woman) jade, baggage ROM 3.5.168 *Out on her, hilding!,* SHR 2.1.26.
~ *attrib.* Worthless, mean, good-for-nothing H5 4.2.29 *such a hilding foe,* 2H4 1.1.57.

hilt *n.* Handle of a sword or dagger; (pl. used for sing.) H5 2.1.64 *I'll run him up to the hilts,* JC 5.3.43, R3 1.4.154.

hind *n.*
1 Servant AWW 1.1.19 *lets me feed with his hinds,* WIV 3.1.98, ROM 1.1.66.
2 Rustic, boor 1H4 2.3.15 *cowardly hind,* LLL 1.2.118, ERR 3.1.77.

hinge *n.* (fig.) Pivot OTH 3.3.365 *bear no hinge nor loop.*
~ *vb.* Bend TIM 4.3.211 *hinge thy knee.*

hint *n.* Occasion, opportunity TMP 2.1.3 *Our hint of woe,* COR 3.3.23, ANT 3.4.9.

hip *n.*[1] *on, upon the hip* At a disadvantage MV 4.1.334 *have you on the hip.*

hip *n.*[2] Fruit of the wild rose TIM 4.3.419 *the briers [bear] scarlet hips* (F1 *hep*).

hipped *ppl. adj.* Lamed in the hip SHR 3.2.48 *his horse hipp'd.*

Hiren *n.* (corr. of 'Irene') The name of a female character in Peele's play 'The Turkish Mahamet and Hyrin the fair Greek'; (used allusively by S. and 17C writers) seductive woman, harlot 2H4 2.4.175 *have we not Hiren here?* (perh. with play on 'iron').

his *poss. det.*
1 That one's MAC 4.3.80 *Desire his jewels, and this other's house,* 2H6 2.1.131.
2 Used, after a n., instead of the genitive inflection ('s) TMP 2.1.236 *the King his son's alive* (i.e. the king's), 1H6 4.6.3, TN 3.3.26.
3 Its TMP 1.2.295 *I will rend an oak And peg thee in his knotty entrails,* HAM 3.3.62, SON 9.10.

hist *interj.* Exclamation enjoining silence ROM 2.2.158 *Hist, Romeo, hist.*

history *n.*
1 Narrative, tale, story TN 2.4.109 *And what's her history?,* 3H6 5.6.28, R3 3.5.28.
2 Story represented dramatically, drama; (fig.) AWW 2.7.164 *That ends this strange eventful history;* a drama representing historical events, historical play H5 Prol.32 *Chorus to this history,* HAM 2.2.397, OTH 2.1.258.
~ *vb.* Record, recount 2H4 4.1.201 *and history his loss.*

hit *pron.* (old form of) It AWW 5.3.195 *He blushes, and 'tis hit,* MAC 1.5.47.

hit *vb.*
1 *hit of* Hit upon ERR 3.2.30 *you do hit of mine.*
2 Imitate exactly WT 5.1.127 *Your father's image is so hit in you.*
3 Succeed MV 3.2.267 *What, not one hit?;* be fulfilled AWW 2.1.143 *Oft expectation...hits Where hope is coldest.*
4 (intr.) Fall in suitably or exactly TIM 3.1.6 *this hits right;* (trans.) suit, or fit in with H8 1.2.84 *Hitting a grosser quality,* MAC 3.6.1.
5 Agree LR 1.1.303 *Let us hit together* (Qq *lets hit;* Ff *let vs sit*).

hitherto *adv.*
1 Up to this point, thus far OTH 1.3.185 *I am hitherto your daughter,* HAM 3.2.206.
2 To this place 1H4 3.1.73 *and Severn hitherto.*

hive *n.* Headgear of plaited straw, resembling a hive LC 8 *Upon her head a platted hive of straw.*
~ *vb.* Lodge together MV 2.5.48 *Drones hive not with me.*

hizz *vb.* Hiss LR 3.6.16 *Come hizzing in upon 'em.*

ho *interj.* Expression of derisive laughter, when repeated MND 3.2.421 *Ho, ho, ho!*
◇ See HEIGH-HO, OHO, SOHO, WHAT HO, WHOA HO.

hoar *vb.*
1 Become mouldy ROM 2.4.139 *When it hoars ere it be spent.*
2 (transf.) Smite with 'hoar leprosy' TIM 4.3.155 *hoar the flamen, That scolds...And not believes himself.*
~ *adj.*
1 Greyish-white HAM 4.7.167 *That shows his hoar leaves* (F1; Qq *hoary*).
2 *hoar leprosy* White leprosy, elephantiasis TIM 4.3.36 *Make the hoar leprosy ador'd.*
3 Mouldy ROM 2.4.133 *stale and hoar,* ROM 2.4.134 (with quibble on 'whore').

hoardock See HARDOCK.

hoary See HOAR *adj.* sense 1.

Hob *n.* (by-form of Rob) Familiar rustic variation of the Christian name Robert or Robin; (hence used as a generic name for a rustic) COR 2.3.116 *Hob and Dick.*

hobby-horse n.

1 In the morris dance, figure of a horse made of light material and fastened round the waist of a performer, who went through various antics LLL 3.1.29 *The hobby-horse is forgot*, HAM 3.2.135.

2 (term of contempt) Frivolous fellow, buffoon ADO 3.2.73 *which these hobby-horses must not hear*; loose woman, prostitute WT 1.2.276 *My wife's a hobby-horse* (F1 *holy-Horse*), LLL 3.1.30, OTH 4.1.154.

hob, nob *phr.* (var. of) 'hab, nab' Have, have not TN 3.4.240 *Hob, nob, is his word*.

Hobgoblin See PUCK

hoboy See HAUTBOY.

hodge-pudding n. Pudding made of a medley of ingredients WIV 5.5.151 *What, a hodge-pudding?*

hoeboy See HAUTBOY.

hoise vb.

1 Hoist (sail) R3 4.4.527 *Hois'd sail, and made his course*.

2 Raise aloft, lift up HAM 3.4.207 *have the engineer Hoist with his own petar*, TMP 1.2.148.

3 Lift and move, remove 2H6 1.1.169 *hoise Duke Humphrey from his seat*.

hold n.

1 *in hold(s)* In custody, in prison SHR 1.2.119 *hath the jewel of my life in hold*, MM 4.3.87, R3 4.5.3.

2 Animal's lurking-place CYM 3.6.18 *'tis some savage hold*.

3 Stronghold, fortress 3H6 1.2.52 *And therefore fortify your hold*, JN 5.7.19, 2H4 Ind.35.

~ vb. A. Transitive senses.

1 Endure, bear COR 3.2.80 *that will not hold the handling*, TIM 1.2.154, HAM 5.1.166.

2 Have, keep, retain TMP 2.1.63 *our garments...hold notwithstanding their freshness*, MND 1.1.232, AWW 5.2.3; (refl.) keep or be (so and so) MAC 3.2.54 *hold thee still*, TGV 4.1.32, R3 1.3.156.

3 Keep (one's word) WIV 5.5.244 *you yet shall hold your word*.

4 Restrain, keep back, keep waiting, detain JC 1.2.83 *hold me here so long*, TGV 1.3.2, JN 3.4.18.

5 Entertain (a feeling or thought) HAM 1.2.18 *Holding a weak supposal of our worth*, TGV 3.2.17, JN 3.4.90.

6 Esteem at a certain value, regard in a particular way TN 2.4.84 *I hold as giddily as fortune*, HAM 4.3.58, 3H6 2.2.109.

7 Offer as a wager MV 3.4.62 *I'll hold thee any wager*, SHR 3.2.83.

B. Intransitive senses

8 (imper.) Here, take it JC 1.3.117 *Hold, my hand*, TGV 4.4.127, MAC 2.1.4.

9 Hold one's hand, forbear, cease, stop MAC 5.8.34 *And damn'd be him that first cries, 'Hold, enough!'*, ANT 5.2.39, LR 3.7.75; (hence) refrain AYL 5.1.12 *we cannot hold*, H8 Epil.14.

10 Maintain one's position, 'hold out' ANT 3.13.170 *Our force by land Hath nobly held*.

11 Continue, remain, keep in a state or course, be steadfast, last HAM 5.2.198 *if your pleasure hold to play with Laertes*, ADO 1.1.91, WIV 5.1.1.

12 Be valid or true, 'hold good' LR 4.7.85 *Holds it true, sir*, 1H4 2.1.53, LLL 4.2.42.

13 Take place R2 5.2.52 *Do these justs and triumphs hold?*

~ in combination

hold hand with Be equal with JN 2.1.494 *As she...Holds hand with any princess of the world.*

hold in 1 (intr.) Keep counsel 1H4 2.1.77 *such as can hold in*. **2** (trans.) Keep silent about LR 5.3.203 *If there be more...hold it in*. **hold off** Keep away or at a distance, maintain a reserve HAM 2.2.291 *if you love me, hold not off*, TRO 1.2.286. **hold out 1** Keep out, exclude ROM 2.2.67 *stony limits cannot*

hold love out, 1H4 2.1.84, TIM 1.2.106. **2** Keep up, persist in 3H6 2.6.24 *hold out flight*. **3** Endure to the end JN 4.3.156 *can Hold out this tempest*, 2H4 4.4.117. **4** Remain unsubdued, continue or persist in a course MV 4.1.447 *hold out enemy forever*, TN 4.1.5, MM 5.1.366; (with *it*) WIV 4.2.135 *hold it out.*

hold up Keep going, carry on MND 3.2.239 *hold the sweet jest up*, WIV 5.5.105, ADO 2.3.121. **hold a wing** Keep a course 1H4 3.2.30 *which do hold a wing Quite from the flight of all thy ancestors.*

⟡ MND 1.2.111 *hold, or cut bowstrings* has not been satisfactorily explained. Usu. interpreted as an expression from archery in some such sense as 'keep your word, or give up the enterprise'.

hold-door *adj.* Pandering TRO 5.10.51 *of the hold-door trade*.

hold-fast *adj.*

1 Grasping firmly LUC 555 *in his hold-fast foot*.

2 (used as n.) Name for a dog that holds tenaciously H5 2.3.52 *hold-fast is the only dog*.

holding n.

1 Consistency AWW 4.2.27 *This has no holding*.

2 Refrain of a song ANT 2.7.111 *The holding every man shall bear as loud* (F1 *beat*).

holding-anchor n. Largest of a ship's anchors, sheet-anchor 3H6 5.4.4 *the holding-anchor lost.*

hole n.

1 *find a hole in his coat* Find some fault in him H5 3.6.84.

2 *spit in the hole* Spit in the hollow of the hand in preparation for vigorous action SHR 3.1.40.

holiday n. *speak holiday* Use choice language, different from that of ordinary life WIV 3.2.68 *he writes verses, he speaks holiday*.

~ *attrib.* (of things) Festive, gay, sportive AYL 1.3.14 *holiday foolery*, AYL 4.1.69; choice, dainty 1H4 1.3.46 *holiday and lady terms*; (of persons) idle, trifling TMP 2.2.29 *a holiday fool there*.

holla n. Shout of 'holla' VEN 284 *His flattering 'Holla'.*

~ vb. See HOLLO.

~ interj.

1 Stop!, cease! OTH 1.2.56 *Holla, stand there!*, AYL 3.2.244.

2 Shout to excite attention HAM 1.1.18 *Holla, Barnardo!*, SHR 4.1.11.

3 Shout of exultation or surprise TIT 2.1.25 *Holla, what storm is this?* (F1; Qq *hollo*), LR 5.3.71.

hollo vb.

1 Cry out loud, shout 1H4 1.3.222 *And in his ear I'll hollo 'Mortimer'*, TN 1.5.272, R2 4.1.54.

2 Call to the hounds in hunting MND 4.1.125 *A cry more tuneable Was never hollo'd to.*

3 Call after (in hunting), call or shout to LR 3.1.55 *he that first lights on him, Hollo the other*, COR 1.8.7, VEN 973.

⟡ Spelt variously in Ff and Qq *hallow, holla, hollaw, hollow*.

~ interj. See HOLLA.

hollow (var. of) HOLLO.

hollow *adv.* Hollowly, insincerely TN 3.4.91 *how hollow the fiend speaks*.

holloing n. The action of the vb. HOLLO [esp. sense 1] MV 5.1.43 *Leave holloing, man* [F1 *hollowing*].

holy *adj.* Devoted as a priest *to* MM 5.1.383 *I was...holy to your business.*

holy-ale n. Festive gathering in connection with a church PER 1.Gower.6 *On ember-eves and holy-ales.*

⟡ Emendation adopted in many mod. edd. on analogy with 'church-ale', but there is no evidence for the existence of the word. Q1 *Holydayes*.

holy-horse See HOBBY-HORSE n. sense 2.

holy-rood day *n.* Feast of the Exaltation of the Holy Cross, 14 September 1H4 1.1.52.

holy-thistle *n.* The plant Carduus Benedictus, noted for its medicinal properties ADO 3.4.80 *I meant plain holy-thistle.*

holy(-)water *n.* (fig.) Balm CYM 5.5.269 *My tears that fall Prove holy water on thee*; *court holy-water* gracious but empty promises LR 3.2.10 *court holy-water in a dry house is better than this rain-water out o'door.*

homager *n.* Humble servant ANT 1.1.31 *Caesar's homager.*

home *n.*
1 (fig.) The grave TIT 1.1.83 *These that I bring unto their latest home.*
2 *from home* Abroad JN 4.3.151 *Now powers from home and discontents at home.*
3 *near at home* Near home, near being at home MM 4.3.95 *I am near at home.*
4 *petition us at home* Beg for me to come home ANT 1.2.183.
~ *adj.* Domestic R2 1.1.205 *these home alarms*, TGV 2.4.119.
~ *adv.* To the point aimed at, to the very heart of the matter, so as to reach, touch or affect intimately; (hence in various fig. connections) fully, satisfactorily, thoroughly, plainly (with *speak*, etc.) MM 4.3.143 *Accuse him home*, HAM 3.3.29 *tax him home*, ANT 1.2.105 *Speak to me home*; (with *pay* etc.) LR 3.3.12 *will be reveng'd home*, TMP 5.1.71, WT 5.3.4; (with *know, confirm, satisfy, trust*) MAC 1.3.120 *trusted home*, AWW 5.3.4, CYM 3.5.92; (with *play*) WT 1.2.248 *play'd home* (i.e. played to a finish).

homely *adj.* Plain, uncomely TGV 2.4.98 *Upon a homely object*, ERR 2.1.89, WT 4.4.426.

homespun *n.* Rustic, clown MND 3.1.77 *What hempen homespuns.*

honest *adj.*
1 Holding an honourable position, respectable TMP 3.3.34 *Honest lord*, WIV 2.2.116, H8 4.2.160; (hence a vague epithet of appreciation) COR 1.1.62 *mine honest neighbours*, MND 3.1.184.
2 Decent, seemly, befitting 1H4 3.3.173 *tractable to any honest reason*, WIV 1.1.182, MM 3.2.156.
3 Chaste WIV 4.2.105 *Wives may be merry, and yet honest too*, OTH 3.3.384, HAM 3.1.102; (transf.) ADO 3.1.84 *some honest slanders* (i.e. 'some slanders which do not affect her virtue', Wright).
4 Not seeming other than it is, genuine WIV 4.2.120 *Behold what honest clothes you send forth to bleaching!*

honesty *n.*
1 Honour, honourableness JC 4.3.67 *so strong in honesty*, TGV 2.5.1, ERR 5.1.30.
2 Decency, decorum TN 2.3.87 *no wit, manners, nor honesty*, H8 5.2.28, OTH 4.1.277.
3 Womanly honour, chastity HAM 3.1.109 *Could beauty...have better commerce?*, WIV 1.3.50, LUC 1545.
4 Generosity TIM 3.1.27 *and honesty is his.*
5 *in honesty* In truth CYM 3.6.69 *be your groom in honesty.*

honey *vb.* Talk fondly or sweetly HAM 3.4.93 *Honeying and making love.*

honey-bag *n.* Enlargement of the alimentary canal in which the bee carries its honey MND 3.1.168 *The honey-bags steal from the humble-bees.*

honey-dew *n.* Sweet sticky substance found on the leaves and stems of plants, held to be excreted by aphides, and formerly imagined to be akin to dew in origin TIT 3.1.112 *Tears stood...as doth the honey-dew.*

honeyseed *n.* (Hostess's blunder for) Homicide 2H4 2.1.52 *thou honeyseed rogue!*

honey-stalks *n.* Stalks of clover flowers TIT 4.4.91 *more dangerous, Than...honey-stalks to sheep.*

honeysuckle *adj.* (Hostess's blunder for) Homicidal 2H4 2.1.50 *thou honeysuckle villain!*

Honi soit qui mal y pense [Fr., motto of the Order of the Garter] Evil be to him who evil thinks WIV 5.5.69.

honorificabilitudinitatibus [Medieval L.] Honourableness LLL 5.1.41 *not so long...as honorificabilitudinitatibus.*
▷ Ablative pl. of 'honorificabilitudinatas', a grandiose extension of 'honorificabilitudo'; cited here as a typical long word.

honour *n.* (pl.) Honourable deeds LR 5.3.302 *such addition as your honours Have more than merited.*
~ *vb.* Do honour or homage to, pay worthy respect to 3H6 1.1.198 *To honour me as thy king*, PER 2.3.61, SON 125.2.

honourable *adj.* Respectable, decent, becoming LLL 5.2.327 *In honourable terms*, SHR Ind.1.110.
~ *adv.* Honourably JC 5.1.60 *thou couldst not die more honourable*, 3H6 3.2.123 (F1; Ff 2-4, Qq *honourably*), TRO 2.2.149.

honoured *ppl. adj.* Honourable LR 5.1.9 *honour'd love*, ANT 4.8.11.

honour-flawed *adj.* Of damaged virtue WT 2.1.143 *Be she honourflaw'd.*

honour-owing *adj.* Possessing honour, honourable H5 4.6.9 *honour-owing wounds.*

hood *vb.* Blindfold (a hawk) when it is not pursuing game; (fig.) ROM 3.2.14 *Hood my unmann'd blood.*

hooded *ppl. adj.* Blindfolded; (fig.) *'tis a hooded valour.*

hoodman *n.* Blindfolded player in blind-man's-buff; (allusively) AWW 4.3.118 *Hoodman comes!*

hoodman-blind *n.* Blind-man's-buff HAM 3.4.77 *That thus hath cozen'd you at hoodman-blind.*

hoodwink *vb.* Blindfold AWW 3.6.25 *We will bind and hoodwink him*, ROM 1.4.4, CYM 5.2.16; (fig.) cover up TMP 4.1.206 *Shall hoodwink this mischance.*

hoof *n.* *i', o' the hoof* On foot WIV 1.3.82 *Plod away i' th' hoof!* (F1, Q3 *ith'*; Ff 2-4 *oth'*).

hoop *n.*
1 *tumbler's hoop* Hoop decorated with ribbons of different colours twisted round it LLL 3.1.188 *wear his colours like a tumbler's hoop.*
2 One of the bands placed at equal intervals on a quart pot 2H6 4.2.66 *the three-hoop'd pot shall have ten hoops.*
3 Finger ring MV 5.1.147 *a hoop of gold, a paltry ring.*
~ *vb.*[1] Encircle WT 4.4.439 *hoop his body more with thy embraces.*

hoop *vb.*[2]
1 Shout with astonishment H5 2.2.108 *admiration did not hoop at them.*
2 Drive out with derisive cries COR 4.5.78 *to be Hoop'd out of Rome.*

hop *vb.* *hop without thy head* Be beheaded 2H6 1.3.137 *quickly hop without thy head.*

hope *n.*
1 *out of hope* (1) Without hope TMP 3.3.11 *that he's so out of hope*, SHR 5.1.141; (2) not merely hoping MND 3.2.279 *Therefore be out of hope*; (3) past hope VEN 567 *Things out of hope*; (4) in hopes COR 4.5.79 *not out of hope...to save my life*, H8 Prol.8.
2 Expectation (without implication of desire), prospect OTH 1.3.203 *which late on hopes depended*, 1H4 1.2.211.
~ *vb.* Expect or anticipate (without implication of desire), suppose think ANT 2.1.38 *I cannot hope*

Caesar and Antony shall well greet together, H5 3.7.72.

hopeless *adj*. Of or concerning which there is no hope COR 3.1.16 *pawn his fortunes To hopeless restitution* (i.e. 'in such a way that restitution should be hopeless', Wright).

horn *n*.
1 Attributed to cuckolds, fancifully said to wear horns on the brow ADO 1.1.263 *pluck off the bull's horns, and set them in my forehead*, ANT 1.2.5, LLL 4.1.112.
2 (pl.) Deer LLL 4.1.111 *to kill horns*.
3 *horn of abundance* Cornucopia (symbol of fruitfulness and plenty) 2H4 1.2.46 *for he hath the horn of abundance* (with quibble).
▷ In LR 3.6.75 *thy horn is dry* there is a ref. to the practice of beggars carrying a horn, by blowing which they announced their approach, and in which they received liquor given to them.

horn-beast *n*. Horned animal, deer AYL 3.3.50 *no assembly but horn-beasts*.

horn-book *n*. Leaf of paper containing the alphabet (often with the addition of the ten digits, some elements of spelling, and the Lord's Prayer) protected by a thin plate of translucent horn and mounted on a tablet of wood with a projecting piece for a handle LLL 5.1.46 *he teaches boys the horn-book*.

horning *n*. Cuckolding, cuckoldry TIT 2.3.67 *you have a goodly gift in horning*.

horn-mad *adj*. (orig. of horned beasts) Enraged so as to be ready to horn anybody; (hence, of persons) stark mad, furious WIV 1.4.50 *he would have been horn-mad*; (sometimes, by word-play) mad with rage at being made a cuckold WIV 3.5.152 *I'll be horn-mad*, ERR 2.1.57, ADO 1.1.270.

horn-maker *n*. One who 'horns' or cuckolds AYL 4.1.63 *Virtue is no horn-maker*.

horologe *n*. Clock OTH 2.3.130 *He'll watch the horologe*.

horse *n*.
1 *a horse of that colour* Something of that kind, TN 2.3.167.
2 *I run before my horse to market* I count my gains prematurely R3 1.1.160.
3 Term of contempt applied to a man 1H4 2.4.194 *spit in my face, call me horse*, TRO 3.3.126.
~ *vb*.
1 Set (one thing up *on* another); (hence) engage in amorous play or dalliance WT 1.2.288 *Is whispering nothing?...horsing foot on foot?*
2 Bestride COR 2.1.211 *ridges hors'd With variable complexions*.

horsehair *n*. (transf.) Fiddlestick, fiddle-bow CYM 2.3.29 *a vice in her ears, which horsehairs and calves'-guts...can never amend*.
▷ The fiddlestick is strung with horsehair.

horse-leech *n*. Medicinal leech H5 2.3.55 *like horse-leeches...the very blood to suck!*

horse-way *n*. Road for horse traffic LR 4.1.56 *horse-way and foot-path*.

hose *n*.
1 Long stockings TGV 2.1.78 *cannot see to put on your hose*.
2 Article of clothing, for the legs and loins, close fitting breeches or drawers ADO 5.1.200 *his doublet and hose*, 1H4 2.4.215, WIV 3.1.46; *French hose* large wide breeches MAC 2.3.14 *for stealing out of a French hose*, H5 3.7.53.

host *n*. Inn; *lie at host* be put up at an inn ERR 5.1.411 *Your goods that lay at host*.

host *vb*. Lodge, put up ERR 1.2.9 *the Centaur, where we host*, AWW 3.5.94.

hostage *n*.
1 Security or pledge given to enemies for the fulfilment of an undertaking TIT 4.4.105 *if he stand on hostage*, CYM 4.2.185.
2 (in a general sense) Pledge, security TRO 3.2.107 *You know now your hostages: your uncle's word and my firm faith*.

hot *adj*.
1 Eager, ardent JC 4.2.19 *A hot friend cooling*, TGV 2.5.51, WT 4.4.684.
2 Angry, in a passion ERR 1.2.47 *She is so hot, because the meat is cold*.

hot-house *n*. Brothel MM 2.1.66 *now she professes a hot-house; which, I think, is a very ill house*.

hour *n*. Moment MV 4.1.19 *To the last hour of act*.

hourly *adj*. Marking the hours LUC 327 *hourly dial*.

house *vb. keep (the) house* Stay indoors, remain at home TIM 3.3.41 *Who cannot keep his wealth must keep his house*, MM 3.2.71, CYM 3.3.1.
~ *vb*. Drive or pursue into a house ERR 5.1.188 *Even now we hous'd him in the abbey here*.

household *adj*. Domestic, homely H5 4.3.52 *Familiar in his mouth as household words*, SHR 2.1.278.

housekeeper *n*.
1 Householder TN 4.2.9 *a good housekeeper*.
2 One who keeps at home COR 1.3.51 *You are manifest housekeepers*.
3 Dog kept to guard the house MAC 3.1.96 *The housekeeper, the hunter*.

housekeeping *n*. Hospitality 2H6 1.1.191 *thy plainness, and thy housekeeping*, LLL 2.1.104, SHR 2.1.356.

housewife, huswife *n*.
1 Woman who manages a household MND 2.1.37 *make the breathless housewife churn*, AWW 2.2.60, H8 3.1.24; (applied to Fortune, Nature) AYL 1.2.31 *the good housewife Fortune*, TIM 4.3.420.
2 Woman of low or improper behaviour, hussy OTH 4.1.94 *A housewife that by selling her desires*, 2H4 3.2.317, H5 5.1.80.
▷ *huswife* is the more freq. spelling in Ff and Qq.

housewifery, huswifery *n*. Management of a household, housekeeping OTH 2.1.112 *Players in your housewifery*, H5 2.3.62.

hovel *n*. Shelter as in a hovel LR 4.7.38 *To hovel thee with swine*.

hovering *adj*. Hesitating, wavering WT 1.2.302 *a hovering temporizer*.

how *adv*.
1 How's the day? What hour of the day is it? TMP 5.1.3.
2 *How say you?* What is your opinion? TMP 2.1.254, MM 2.4.58, MAC 3.4.68.
3 *How so?* How is that?, Why? TRO 3.3.246, WIV 3.5.68.
4 (orig. ellipt. for) 'How is that?' or 'How say you?'; (hence) What! MM 2.1.71 *How? thy wife?*, JC 2.1.312, CYM 3.2.1.
5 At what price 2H4 3.2.38 *How a good yoke of bullocks at Stamford fair?*, TRO 4.2.23, PER 4.6.20.

howbeit *adv*. Nevertheless COR 1.9.70 *howbeit, I thank you*, H5 1.2.91.
~ *conj*. Although OTH 2.1.288 *howbeit that I endure him not*.

however, howe'er *adv*.
1 (introducing a clause) However much, notwithstanding that, although JC 1.2.299 *However he puts on this tardy form*, AWW 5.3.88, ADO 5.1.37.
2 In any case, at all events AWW 1.3.183 *howe'er, I charge thee...To tell me*, TGV 1.1.34.

howlet *n*. Owl MAC 4.1.17 *Lizard's leg and howlet's wing*.

howsoever, howsoe'er *adv*.
1 HOWEVER sense 1 COR 5.2.31 *Howsoever you have been his liar*, MM 2.1.220, ADO 2.3.197.

2 HOWEVER sense 2 MND 5.1.27 *But howsoever, strange and admirable*, 1H6 4.1.187, TRO 3.3.296.

howsomever, howsome'er *adv.*
1 (introducing a sub. clause) In whatever manner, to whatever degree HAM 1.5.84 *howsomever thou pursues this act* (Ff *howsoever*).
2 (introducing a sub. clause) HOWEVER sense 1 MV 3.5.89 *howsome'er thou speak'st...I shall disgest it* (Ff 1–2; Q1 *howsoere*), AWW 1.3.52.

hox *vb.* Hamstring WT 1.2.244 *Which hoxes honesty behind.*

hoy *n.* Small coasting vessel ERR 4.3.40 *tarry for the hoy.*

hoy(-)day (var. of) HEYDAY.

huddle *vb.*
1 Pile or heap up ADO 2.1.244 *huddling jest upon jest.*
2 Crowd, throng MV 4.1.28 *That have of late so huddled on his back.*

hugger-mugger *n.* Secrecy HAM 4.5.84 *In hugger-mugger to inter him.*

hulk *n.* Large ship of burden or transport 2H4 2.4.64 *a hulk better stuff'd*, TRO 2.3.266, 1H6 5.5.6; (hence) big unwieldy person 2H4 1.1.19 *the hulk Sir John.*

hull *vb.* Float or drift by the force of the wind or current acting on the hull alone, drift with sails furled TN 1.5.203 *I am to hull here a little longer*, R3 4.4.438; (fig.) H8 2.4.200 *thus hulling in The wild sea of my conscience.*

hum *n.* Utterance of the interj. 'hum' WT 2.1.71 *The shrug, the hum or ha*, WT 2.1.74, COR 5.4.21.

human, humane *adj.*
1 Belonging or pertaining to a man or mankind TMP 1.2.265 *enter human hearing*, ERR 5.1.189, MND 2.1.101.
2 Befitting a man, kindly, courteous, benevolent OTH 2.1.239 *civil and humane seeming*, MND 2.2.57, MV 4.1.25.
▷ The spelling of Ff and Qq is always *humane* for both meanings. Mod. edd. mostly follow modern usage, allotting *human* to sense 1, and *humane* to sense 2.

humanity *n.* Human nature OTH 1.3.316 *change my humanity with a baboon*, TIM 1.1.273, HAM 3.2.35.
2 Mankind LR 4.2.49 *Humanity must perforce prey on itself*, 1H6 2.3.53.

humble-bee *n.* Bumble-bee LLL 3.1.95 *The fox, the ape, and the humble-bee*, MND 3.1.168.

humility *n.* Humanity, kindness, benevolence LLL 4.3.346 *And plant in tyrants mild humility*, R3 2.1.73, MV 3.1.69.

humorous *adj.*
1 Moist, damp ROM 2.1.31 *the humorous night.*
2 Capricious, whimsical, fanciful AYL 1.2.266 *The Duke is humorous*, JN 3.1.119, HAM 2.2.322.
3 Moody, out of humour LLL 3.1.175 *a very beadle to a humorous sigh*, AYL 4.1.19.

humour *n.*
1 Moisture JC 2.1.262 *the humours Of the dank morning.*
2 (in early physiology) Fluid of an animal or vegetable body, either natural or morbid; esp. any of the four chief fluids of the human body (blood, phlegm, choler, melancholy) by the relative proportions of which a person's physical and mental qualities were held to be determined LLL 1.1.233 *the black oppressing humour*, JN 5.1.12, ROM 4.1.96.
3 Mental disposition, temperament JC 4.3.119 *When that rash humour which my mother gave me*, 2H4 2.4.236, R3 4.4.269; (pl.) LLL 2.1.53 *that most his humours know*, 2H6 1.1.247.
4 Temporary state of mind, mood, temper WIV 2.3.77 *See what humour he is in*, OTH 3.4.125, 1H4 3.1.170.

5 Fancy, whim, caprice MV 3.5.63 *let it be as humours...shall govern*, JN 4.2.214, TIT 5.2.140.
6 Inclination or disposition (for something), fancy (to do something) H5 2.1.55 *I have an humour to knock you*, ADO 5.4.101, MND 1.2.28.
~ *vb.*
1 Comply with the humour of, indulge, influence (a person) by observing his inclinations or humours JC 1.2.315 *If I were Brutus...He should not humour me*, ERR 4.4.81, ADO 2.1.380.
2 Comply with the peculiar nature of (something), adapt oneself to LLL 3.1.13 *to jig off a tune at the tongue's end,...humour it with turning up your eyelids.*

Humphrey Hour *n.* Hour at which a meal was provided for the hungry R3 4.4.176 *none, but Humphrey Hour, that call'd your Grace To breakfast once.*
▷ A suggestion here that it would have been an unpalatable meal. The phrase 'dine with Duke Humphrey' meant 'go dinnerless.'

hunch-backed See BUNCH-BACKED.

hundred *n.* and *adj.* (used indefinitely or hyperbolically) A great number TGV 4.4.145 *I have wept a hundred several times*, HAM 1.2.237, 1H6 1.1.123.
▷ ADO 2.1.130 *Hundred Merry Tales*: a popular jest-book published in 1526. WIV 2.1.63 *hundred Psalms*: more likely 'Hundredth Psalm', 'hundred' being a common var. of 'hundredth'.

hundred-pound *n.* (contemptuous epithet) Pretender to the title of gentleman, snob; (attrib.) LR 2.2.16 *a base...hundred-pound, filthy, worsted-stocking knave.*

Hungarian *adj.* Needy, beggarly WIV 1.3.20 *O base Hungarian wight.*
▷ Used, by association, with 'hunger.' A cant term of the Eliz. period.

hungerly *adj.* Starved, famished; (hence) sparse SHR 3.2.175 *his beard grew thin and hungerly.*
~ *adv.* Hungrily TIM 1.1.253 *I feed Most hungerly on your sight*, OTH 3.4.105.

hungry *adj.* Unfertile, barren, sterile COR 5.3.58 *the hungry beach.*
▷ In 1H6 1.2.28 *their hungry prey* = 'prey of their hunger'.

hungry-starved *adj.* Famished with hunger 1H6 1.5.16 *cheer up thy hungry-starved men.*

hunt *n.* Game killed in the hunt, quarry CYM 3.6.89 *we'll go dress our hunt.*

huntsman Manager of a hunt SHR Ind.1.16 *Huntsman, I charge thee, tender well my hounds*, 3H6 4.5.25.

hunt's-up *n.* Orig. 'the hunt is up', the name of an old song sung to awaken huntsmen in the morning; (hence) early morning song ROM 3.5.34 *hunt's-up to the day.*

hurling *adj.* Impetuous, violent HAM 1.5.132 *wild and hurling words.*
▷ F1; Q1 *wherling*; Qq 2–4 *whurling*; Theobald *whirling.*

hurly *n.* Commotion, tumult SHR 4.1.203 *amid this hurly I intend*, JN 3.4.169, 2H4 3.1.25.

hurly-burly *n.* Commotion, tumult MAC 1.1.3 *When the hurly-burly's done.*
~ *adj.* Tumultuous 1H4 5.1.78 *hurly-burly innovation.*

hurricano *n.* Waterspout TRO 5.2.172 *dreadful spout Which shipmen do the hurricano call*, LR 3.2.2.

hurry *n.* Commotion, tumult, disorder COR 4.6.4 *Were in wild hurry.*

hurtle *vb.* (of weapons, battle) Clatter, clash, crash JC 2.2.22 *The noise of battle hurtled in the air*, AYL 4.3.131.

hurtless *adj.* Harmless LR 4.6.166 *the strong lance of justice hurtless breaks.*

husband *n.*

1 One who manages a household, steward 2H4 5.3.11 *your servingman and your husband.*

2 One who manages (well or ill, thriftily or otherwise) H8 3.2.142 *an ill husband* (i.e. a bad economist), MM 3.2.70, SHR 5.1.69.

~ *vb.*

1 Till, farm 2H4 4.3.120 *husbanded, and till'd.*

2 Marry, be a husband to, supply with a husband LR 5.3.70 *if he should husband you,* AWW 5.3.126, JC 2.1.297.

husbandman *n.* One who manages a household, steward 2H4 5.3.11 *he is your servingman and your husbandman* (Ff 3–4; F1 *husband*).

husbandry *n.*

1 Management (of a household) MV 3.4.25 *The husbandry and manage of my house,* COR 4.7.22, H5 4.1.7; good husbandry, economy, thrift TRO 1.2.7 *like as there were husbandry in war,* PER 3.2.20, HAM 1.3.77.

2 Cultivation of the soil, tillage, farming 2H6 3.1.33 *choke the herbs for want of husbandry,* AYL 2.3.65,

2H4 3.2.113; (fig.) MM 1.4.44 *her plenteous womb Expresseth his full tilth and husbandry,* SON 3.6.

hush *adj.* Hushed, silent HAM 2.2.486 *As hush as death.*

husht *interj.* Hush PER 1.3.9 *Husht! here come the lords,* SHR 1.1.68.

husks *n.* (pl., fig.) Refuse H5 4.2.18 *but the shales and husks of men,* TRO 4.5.166.

huswife (var. of) HOUSEWIFE.

huswifery (var. of) HOUSEWIFERY.

Hydra *n.* (attrib.) Difficult to kill like the many-headed snake of Lerna whose heads grew as fast as they were cut off 2H4 4.2.38 *this Hydra son of war.*

Hyems See HIEMS.

hyen *n.* Hyena AYL 4.1.156 *I will laugh like a hyen.*

Hymeneus *n.* The god Hymen; (hence) marriage TIT 1.1.325 *In readiness for Hymeneus stand.*

hyssop *n.* Aromatic herb, Hyssopus officenalis, formerly grown along with thyme OTH 1.3.322 *set hyssop and weed up tine.*

▷ Hyssop was thought by some to be an aphrodisiac, and thyme an anti-aphrodisiac.

hysterica passio [L.] Hysteria LR 2.4.57.

I

I *adv.* (spelling var. in Ff and Qq of) Ay.

Ice (contraction) I shall LR 4.6.241 *keep out...or Ice try whither your costard or my ballow be the harder.*

▷ Ff; Qq 1–2 *ile.* The form '-se', '-s' for 'shall' is mainly northern.

ice-brook *n. the ice-brook's temper* Steel tempered in icy-cold water OTH 5.2.253 *a sword of Spain, the ice-brook's temper.*

▷ Ff *Ice brook(e)s,* Q *Isebrookes.* It was a practice in Spain to harden steel by plunging it red-hot into a river.

Iceland dog *n.* Shaggy sharp-eared white dog formerly in favour as a lap-dog in England; (contemptuously of a person) H5 2.1.42 *Pish for thee, Iceland dog! thou prick-ear'd cur of Iceland!*

idea *n.*

1 Image, likeness R3 3.7.13 *your lineaments, Being the right idea of your father.*

2 Mental image or picture ADO 4.1.224 *Th' idea of her life.*

3 Something merely imagined or fancied LLL 4.2.67 *a...spirit, full of forms,...ideas.*

ides of March *n.* Fifteenth day of March according to the reckoning of the ancient Roman calendar JC 1.2.18 *Beware the ides of March.*

idiot *n.* Professional jester LUC 1812 *esteemed so As seely jeering idiots are with kings,* TRO 2.1.53, TIT 5.1.79.

idle *vb.* Move lazily or uselessly ROM 2.6.19 *the gossamers That idles in the wanton summer air.*

~ *adj.*

1 Ineffective, worthless, vain, trifling TN 3.3.46 *your store...is not for idle markets* (i.e. not for luxuries), LLL 5.2.865, OTH 1.2.95.

2 Foolish, silly MM 4.1.63 *their idle dream,* AWW 2.5.49, LR 1.2.49.

3 Crazy HAM 3.2.90 *I must be idle.*

4 Useless, unprofitable, barren ERR 2.2.178 *idle moss,* R3 3.1.103, OTH 1.3.140.

idle-headed *adj.* Silly, crazy WIV 4.4.36 *superstitious idle-headed eld.*

idlely *adv.* (var. of) IDLY sense 1 JN 5.1.72 *colours idlely spread,* ERR 4.4.129, R2 3.3.171.

idleness *n.*

1 Trifling, frivolous occupation or pastime TGV 1.1.8 *Wear out thy youth with shapeless idleness,* 1H4 1.2.196, ANT 1.3.92.

2 Want of cultivation H5 5.2.51 *The even mead...Conceives by idleness, and nothing teems But hateful docks, rough thistles,* OTH 1.3.324.

idly *adv.*

1 Carelessly, lightly R2 5.2.25 *the eyes of men...Are idly bent on him that enters next,* TIM 1.1.20, H5 1.2.59.

2 By chance JN 4.2.124 *this from rumour's tongue I idly heard.*

i'fecks *interj.* In faith WT 1.2.120 *I 'fecks! Why, that's my bawcock.*

ignis fatuus [L.] Will-o'-the-wisp 1H4 3.3.39.

ignoble *adj.*

1 Of low birth or base descent R3 3.7.127 *Her royal stock graft with ignoble plants,* 1H6 3.1.177, 3H6 4.1.70.

2 Base or dishonourable in character R3 3.5.22 *Here is the head of that ignoble traitor,* TMP 1.2.116, WT 2.3.120.

ignobly *adv.* Basely, dishonourably TIM 2.2.174 *Unwisely, not ignobly, have I given,* 2H6 5.2.23, LR 3.7.35.

ignominy, ignomy *n.* Dishonour, disgrace 1H4 5.4.100 *Thy ignominy sleep with thee in the grave,* MM 2.4.111 (F1 *Ignomie;* Ff 2–4 *Ignominy*), TIT 4.2.115.

ignorance *n.* Stupidity, folly ANT 3.10.7 *The greater cantle of the world is lost With very ignorance.*

ignorant *adj.*

1 Uninformed, unskilled *in* WT 2.3.70 *I am as ignorant in that, as you In so entit'ling me,* CYM 3.2.23.

2 Unconscious *of* MM 2.2.119 *Most ignorant of what he's most assur'd.*

3 Resulting from ignorance OTH 4.2.70 *what ignorant sin have I committed?*

4 That keeps one in ignorance Tмp 5.1.67 *the ignor-ant fumes that mantle Their clearer reason*, WT 1.2.297.

'ild See GODILD.

Ile (spelling var. in Ff and Qq of) I 'll.

iliad See OEILLADE.

ill *n.*
1 Wrong-doing, wickedness, sin Tмp 1.2.353 *cap-able of all ill*, R2 1.1.86, Oтн 4.3.103.
2 Evil inflicted or suffered, mischief, misfortune, disaster Ham 3.1.80 *bear those ills we have*, MV 2.5.17, Son 119.9.
~ *adj.*
1 Morally evil, wicked Per 4.6.109 *with no ill in-tent*, MM 2.1.66, Tмp 1.2.458.
2 Unskilled Rom 4.2.6 *'tis an ill cook that cannot lick his own fingers*, Ham 2.2.120.
~ in combination
1 (n., objective) **ill-breeding** Contriving mischief Ham 4.5.15 *ill-breeding minds*. **ill-dispersing** Scattering misfortune R3 4.1.52 *ill-dispersing wind*. **ill-divining** Misgiving Rom 3.5.54 *an ill-di-vining soul*.
2 (adv., with pres. pple.) **ill-beseeming** Unbecom-ing 2H4 4.1.84 *ill-beseeming arms*, 3H6 1.4.113, Rom 1.5.74. **ill-wresting** That puts a bad construction on everything Son 140.11 *this ill-wresting world*.
3 (adv., with pa. pple.) **ill-annexed** Mischievously joined, unfortunately added Luc 874 *ill-annexed Opportunity*. **ill-composed** Consisting of evil in-gredients Mac 4.3.77 *ill-compos'd affection*. **ill-dis-posed** Indisposed, ill, sick Tro 2.3.77 *Within his tent, but ill-dispos'd*. **ill-erected** Built for evil pur-poses or under evil auspices R2 5.1.2 *ill-erected tower*. **ill-inhabited** Meanly lodged AYL 3.3.10. **ill-nurtured** Ill-bred, rude 2H6 1.2.42, Ven 134. **ill-roasted** Not properly or well cooked AYL 3.2.37 *an ill-roasted egg*. **ill-taken** Wrongly conceived, mistaken WT 1.2.460 *his ill-ta'en suspicion*.
4 (parasynthetic) **ill-favoured** Ill-looking, un-comely, ugly Wiv 1.1.299 *very ill-favour'd rough things*, Tit 3.2.66, AYL 3.5.53. **ill-favouredly** Badly, in an uncomely manner H5 4.2.40 *Ill-fav-ouredly become the morning field*, Wiv 3.5.67, AYL 1.2.39. **ill-tuned** Unmelodious Jn 2.1.197 *these ill-tuned repetitions*.
5 (special) **ill-seeming** Of evil appearance or as-pect Shr 5.2.143 *Muddy, ill-seeming thick, bereft of beauty*.

illness *n.* Evil, wickedness Mac 1.5.20 *Art not with-out ambition, but without The illness should attend it*.

illo *interj.* (falconer's cry) Hillo Ham 1.5.115 *Illo, ho, ho, my lord!*

illume *vb.* Light up Ham 1.1.37 *t'illume that part of heaven*.

illusion *n.* Deception H8 1.2.178 *th' devil's illusions*, MND 3.2.98, Mac 3.5.28.

illustrate *vb.* Make evident H8 3.2.181 *A loyal and obedient subject is Therein illustrated*.
~ *ppl. adj.* Illustrious LLL 4.1.65 *The magnani-mous and most illustrate King Cophetua*, LLL 5.1.121.

illustrious *adj.* Lacking lustre Cym 1.6.109 *an eye Base and illustrious as the smoky light*.
⬦ Negative of 'lustrous'. Some mod. edd. *inlus-trous, unlustrous*.

ill-well *adv.* so ill-well With so successful an imi-tation of a defect Ado 2.1.117 *You could never do him so ill-well, unless you were the very man.*

image *n.*
1 Appearance, semblance, likeness WT 5.1.127 *Your father's image is so hit in you*, Jn 4.2.71, Ham 5.2.77.

2 Visible appearance or form Ham 1.1.81 *our last king, Whose image even but now appear'd to us.*
3 Counterpart, copy MM 2.4.45 *heaven's image* (i.e. mankind), Mac 2.3.78, R3 2.1.124.
4 Representation Ham 3.2.238 *this play is the image of a murder done in Vienna.*
5 Embodiment, type 2H6 1.3.176 *Image of pride, Why should I hold my peace?*; symbol, sign Lr 2.4.90 *The image of revolt.*
6 Mental picture, idea, conception TN 2.4.19 *the constant image of the creature That is belov'd*, Tмp 1.2.43, Mac 1.3.135.

imagery *n.* Hangings, tapestry R2 5.2.16 *all the walls With painted imagery.*

imaginary *adj.*
1 Of or belonging to the imagination, imaginative H5 Prol.18 *your imaginary forces*, Son 27.9, Jn 4.2.265.
2 *imaginary work* Work in which images are used to suggest to the imagination related figures Luc 1422.

imagination *n.* *unfelt imaginations* Things ima-gined but not experienced R3 1.4.80; *wrong imagi-nations* delusions Lr 4.6.283.

imagined *ppl. adj.* Of imagination MV 3.4.52 *with imagin'd speed* (i.e. as quick as thought), H5 3.Ch.1, Rom 2.6.28.

imbace See IMBAR.

imbar *vb.* Bar, rule out H5 1.2.94 *amply to imbar their crooked titles Usurp'd.*
⬦ Ff *imbar(re)*; Qq 1–2 *imbace*; Q3 *embrace*. Sev-eral editors propose *imbare* (i.e. expose).

imbecility *n.* Weakness Tro 1.3.114 *Strength should be lord of imbecility.*

imbossed, imbost (var. of) EMBOSSED¹ and ².

imbrue *vb.* Stain or dye with blood MND 5.1.344 *Come, blade, my breast imbrue!*, Tit 2.3.222; (absol., of a person) shed blood, commit bloodshed 2H4 2.4.196 *shall we imbrue?*

imitari [L.] To imitate LLL 4.2.125 *Imitari is no-thing: so doth the hound his master.*

immanity *n.* Atrocious savageness 1H6 5.1.13 *such immanity and bloody strife.*

immask *vb.* Cover, hide 1H4 1.2.180 *to immask our noted...garments.*

immaterial *adj.* Flimsy, slight Tro 5.1.31 *thou idle immaterial skein of sleave-silk.*

immediacy *n.* Direct relation in a position of auth-ority Lr 5.3.65 *Bore the commission of my place..., The which immediacy may well...call itself your brother.*

immediate *adj.*
1 Next in succession (to a throne, etc.) 2H4 5.2.71 *Th' immediate heir of England*, Ham 1.2.109; (fig.) AWW 2.3.132 *In these to nature she's immediate heir.*
2 Passing in direct succession 2H4 4.5.42 *crown... immediate from thy place and blood, Derives itself to me.*
3 Direct Ant 2.6.129 *the immediate author of their variance.*

immediately *adv.* Directly, expressly MND 1.1.45 *our law Immediately provided in that case.*

imminence *n.* Impending evil Tro 5.10.13 *I...dare all imminence that gods and men Address their dangers in.*

immodest *adj.* Moderate, excessive WT 3.2.102 *immodest hatred*, 1H6 4.1.126.

immoment *adj.* Of no importance Ant 5.2.166 *Im-moment toys.*

immortal *adj.* Pertaining to eternity or life after death Ant 5.2.281 *Immortal longings.*
⬦ Ant 5.2.247 *his biting is immortal*: error for 'mortal'.

immure n. Wall Tro Prol.8 *within whose strong immures...Helen...sleeps* (F1 *emures*).

imp n.
1 Scion (of noble stock) 2H4 5.5.42 *most royal imp of fame*, H5 4.1.45.
2 (fig., used affectedly) Child LLL 1.2.5 *dear imp*, LLL 5.2.588.

imp vb. Engraft feathers in the wing of a bird so as to make good losses and deficiencies and thus restore or improve the powers of flight R2 2.1.292 *Imp out our drooping country's broken wing*.

impaint vb. Depict 1H4 5.1.80 *And never yet did insurrection want Such water-colours to impaint his cause*.

impair See IMPAR, IMPARE.

impale vb.
1 Shut or hem in Tro 5.7.5 *Impale him with your weapons round about* (F1 *empale*).
2 Encircle (the head) with a crown 3H6 3.3.189 *Did I impale him with the regal crown?*

impanel vb. Enrol as jury Son 46.9 *To 'cide this title is impanelled A quest of thoughts*.

impar, impare adj. Inferior, unfit Tro 4.5.103 *Nor dignifies an impare thought with breath* (Q *impare*; Ff *impaire*).

impart vb.
1 Furnish, afford Luc 1039 *no tool imparteth*.
2 Communicate, make known, tell MV 3.2.253 *When I did first impart my love to you*, WT 2.1.165, Shr 3.2.130; (absol.) Ham 3.2.330 *But is there no sequel...? Impart*.

impartial adj. Indifferent MM 5.1.166 *I 'll be impartial. Be you judge Of your own cause*, Ven 748.

impartment n. Communication Ham 1.4.59 *As if it some impartment did desire To you alone*.

impasted ppl. adj. Made into a paste or crust, crusted Ham 2.2.459 *Bak'd and impasted with the parching streets*.

impawn vb. Put in pawn, pledge, commit H5 1.2.21 *take heed how you impawn our person*, 1H4 4.3.108, Ham 5.2.148 (Qq; F1 *impone*).

impeach n. Calling in question, challenge, accusation Err 5.1.270 *what an intricate impeach*, 3H6 1.4.60.
~ vb. Call in question, discredit, disparage MV 3.3.29 *impeach the justice of the state*, MND 2.1.214, R2 1.1.189.

impeachment n.
1 Hindrance H5 3.6.142 *to march on to Calais Without impeachment*.
2 Detriment, impairment TGV 1.3.15 *great impeachment to his age*.
3 Accusation, charge R3 2.2.22 *Devis'd impeachments to imprison him*.

imperator n. Absolute ruler LLL 3.1.185 *Sole imperator...Of trotting paritors*.

imperceiverant adj. Undiscerning, undiscriminating Cym 4.1.14 *this imperceiverant thing loves him*.
▷ Dyce's emendation; F *imperseverant*.

imperious adj. Imperial Ant 4.15.23 *th' imperious show Of...Caesar*, Tro 4.5.172, Ham 5.1.213.

imperiously adv. Majestically Ven 265 *Imperiously he leaps, he neighs*.

imperseverant See IMPERCEIVERANT.

impertinency n. Irrelevance, incoherence, irrelevant matter Lr 4.6.174 *matter and impertinency mix'd*.

impertinent adj. Irrelevant Tmp 1.2.138 *without the which this story Were most impertinent*.
▷ Misused for the antonym by Launcelot at MV 2.2.137 *the suit is impertinent to myself*.

impeticos vb. Impocket, put in one's pocket TN 2.3.26 *I did impeticos thy gratillity*.

▷ Humorous corr., perh. intended to suggest also 'impeticot' (i.e. 'impetticoat'), referring either to his (clown's) long coat or to a woman.

impierced See ENPIERCED.

impious adj. Irreverent Cym 3.3.6 *keep their impious turbans on*.

impiteous adj. Pitiless Ham 4.5.101 *The ocean ...Eats not the flats with more impiteous haste*.

impleached ppl. adj. Intertwined LC 205 *their hair, With twisted metal amorously impleach'd*.

implorator n. One who implores or supplicates Ham 1.3.129 *implorators of unholy suits*.

imply vb. Involve AWW 1.3.216 *to find that her search implies*, Per 4.1.81.

impone See IMPAWN.

import vb.
1 Bring about, carry with it, involve as a consequence R3 3.7.68 *in matter...No less importing than our general good*, Lr 4.3.4, MM 5.1.108.
2 Imply, indicate, denote WT 1.2.57 *To be your prisoner should import offending*, Rom 5.1.28, Ham 3.2.139.
3 Express, state Oth 2.2.2 *tidings...importing the mere perdition of the Turkish fleet*, Tim 5.2.11, Ham 1.2.23; (absol.) Jn 4.3.17 *more general than these lines import*, 1H4 1.1.51.
4 Portend 1H6 1.1.2 *Comets, importing change of times and states*.
5 Matter, be important Ant 1.2.121 *what else...Importeth thee to know*, 1H4 4.4.5, Tro 4.2.50.
6 Relate to, concern LLL 4.1.57 *This letter is mistook; it importeth none here*, Oth 1.3.283 (Q1 *concerne*).

importance n.
1 Matter, affair (of importance) Cym 1.4.41 *upon importance of so slight...a nature*.
2 Importunity, solicitude Jn 2.1.7 *At our importance hither is he come*, TN 5.1.363.
3 Import, meaning WT 5.2.18 *if th' importance were joy or sorrow*.

importancy n. Significance Oth 1.3.20 *Th' importancy of Cyprus to the Turk*.

important adj. Urgent, pressing, importunate Ado 2.1.71 *If the Prince be too important, tell him there is measure in everything*, AWW 3.7.21, Lr 4.4.26 (Ff *importun'd*).

importantly adv. With weighty business Cym 4.4.19 *ears so cloy'd importantly*.

importing ppl. adj. Significant, full of import AWW 5.3.136 *Her business looks in her With an importing visage*.

importless adj. Unimportant, meaningless Tro 1.3.71 *matter...of importless burden, Divide thy lips*.

importunacy n. Importunity Tim 2.2.41 *Your importunacy cease till after dinner*, TGV 4.2.111.

importune vb.
1 Impel, urge MM 1.1.56 *As time and our concernings shall importune*.
2 Trouble, worry Ant 4.15.19 *I here importune death awhile*.

importuned ppl. adj. Importunate Lr 4.4.26 *great France My...importun'd tears hath pitied* (Ff; Qq *important*).

impose n. Command, injunction TGV 4.3.8 *According to your ladyship's impose*.
~ vb.
1 Lay (a crime, etc.) to the account of H5 4.1.150 *the imputation of his wickedness...should be impos'd upon his father*.
2 Subject (to a penalty) Ado 5.1.273 *Impose me to what penance your invention Can lay upon my sin*.

imposition n.
1 Imputation, accusation, charge MM 1.2.189 *stand under grievous imposition*, WT 1.2.74.
2 Injunction, command, charge laid upon one MV 3.4.33 *this imposition, The which my love...lays upon you*, R3 3.7.232, Luc 1697.
3 Attachment, affixation, attribution OTH 2.3.269 *Reputation is an idle and most false imposition*.

impossible adj. Extravagant, incredible, inconceivable ADO 2.1.138 *in devising impossible slanders*, TN 3.2.72.

imposthume, impostume n. Purulent swelling, abscess HAM 4.4.27 *th' impostume of much wealth and peace*, TRO 5.1.21, VEN 743.

imprese n. [It.] Heraldic device consisting of an allegorical picture and a motto R2 3.1.25 *Ras'd out my imprese, leaving me no sign* (Ff *impress(e)*, Qq *impre(e)se*).

impress n.[1] Impression TGV 3.2.6 *weak impress of love*.
~ vb.[1]
1 Produce (a mark) *upon* or *in* something by pressure AWW 1.3.133 *It is the...seal of nature's truth Where love's strong passion is impress'd in youth*, COR 5.6.107.
2 Mark or stamp LLL 2.1.236 *His heart like an agate with your print impressed*, MAC 5.8.10.

impress n.[2] Enforced levy or service TRO 2.1.97 *Ajax was here the voluntary, and you as under an impress*, HAM 1.1.75, ANT 3.7.36.
~ vb.[2] Compel into service MAC 4.1.95 *Who can impress the forest...?*; (fig.) LC 267 *When thou impressest*.

impress n.[3] See IMPRESE.

impressed ppl. adj. Enlisted, compelled to serve LR 5.3.50 *our impress'd lances*.

impressure n. Impression AYL 3.5.23 *lean upon a rush, The...capable impressure Thy palm...keeps*, TN 2.5.92, TRO 4.5.131.

imprimis, inprimis [L.] In the first place TGV 3.1.275 *Inprimis, She can fetch and carry* (F1), SHR 4.1.66 (F4 *Imprim's*).

improve vb. Make good use of, employ to advantage JC 2.1.159 *his means, If they improve them, may well stretch*.

improvident adj. Unwary, careless 1H6 2.1.58 *Improvident soldiers, had your watch been good...*, WIV 2.2.289.

imputation n.
1 Reputation, prestige TRO 1.3.339 *Our imputation shall be oddly pois'd In this wild action* (i.e. the honour or discredit imputed to us).
2 Report, opinion MV 1.3.13 *Have you heard any imputation to the contrary?*, OTH 3.3.406.

impute vb. Reckon, regard SON 83.9 *This silence for my sin you did impute*.

in adv.
1 Within TRO 3.3.97 *or without or in*.
2 Engaged, involved TN 2.5.42 *now he's deeply in*, LLL 4.3.18, R3 4.2.64.
3 In prison 2H4 5.5.38 *Doll is in*.
4 In office, in power LR 5.3.15 *who's in, who's out*.
5 In drink, drunk ANT 2.7.32 *you'll be in till then*.
~ prep.
1 At OTH 1.2.94 *In this time of the night*, COR 5.3.21, MV 2.4.1.
2 On 2H4 1.2.208 *in a hot day*, WIV 1.3.87, R3 1.4.28.
3 (used redundantly with gerunds) COR 4.6.131 *cast Your...caps in hooting at Coriolanus' exile*, R2 5.5.54, 1H6 5.3.43.
4 (used where no prep. is now expressed) MM 4.4.8 *why should we proclaim it in an hour before his ent'ring*, LLL 1.1.39, TMP 1.2.262.
5 *in(-)a(-)door* Indoors, at home LR 1.4.125 *keep in a door*.

6 *in his beard* To his face H5 3.2.71 *I will verify as much in his beard*.

in, inn vb. Get (a crop) in AWW 1.3.45 *He that ears my land...gives me leave to inn the crop* (F1 *inne*).

inaidible adj. Helpless, incurable AWW 2.1.119 *her inaidible estate*.

incaged ppl. adj. Confined R2 2.1.102 *incaged in so small a verge* (F1; Qq 1–5 *inraged*), 3H6 4.6.12, VEN 582.

incapable adj.
1 Unable to contain SON 113.13 *Incapable of more, replete with you*.
2 Insensible (to one's condition) HAM 4.7.178 *incapable Of her own distress*.
3 Not admitting *of* COR 4.6.120 *incapable of help*.
4 Lacking the capacity or fitness (for) WT 4.4.397 *incapable Of reasonable affairs*, TMP 1.2.111.
5 Unintelligent R3 2.2.18 *Incapable...innocents*.

in capite [L.] As tenant in chief, directly from the crown 2H6 4.7.123 *Men shall hold of me in capite*.

incardinate, incarnal, incarnation adj. (blunders for) Incarnate TN 5.1.182 *the very devil incardinate*; MV 2.2.27 *the very devil incarnation* (Q1 *incarnal*).

incarnadine vb. Tinge with red MAC 2.2.59 *The multitudinous seas incarnadine* (Ff *incarnardine*).

incarnal See INCARDINATE....

incarnate adj. In human shape H5 2.3.32 *they were dev'ls incarnate*, TIT 5.1.40.

incarnation See INCARDINATE.

incense vb. Incite, provoke *to*, WIV 1.3.100 *I will incense Page*, JC 1.3.13, WT 5.1.61.
▷ See also INSENSE.

incertain adj. Uncertain (in various senses) MM 3.1.126 *those that lawless and incertain thought Imagine howling*, AWW 3.1.15; 'not knowing what to think or do' (Schmidt) WT 5.1.29 *Incertain lookers-on*.

incessantly See SUCCESSANTLY.

inch n.[1]
1 *the furthest inch* The most distant part ADO 2.1.267.
2 *the very extremest inch* The very utmost 2H4 4.3.35.
3 *at an inch* In immediate readiness 2H6 1.4.42.
4 *even to his inches* From top to toe TRO 4.5.111.
5 (pl.) Stature ANT 1.3.40 *I would I had thy inches*.

inch n.[2] Small island MAC 1.2.61 *Saint Colme's inch*.

inch-meal n. *by inch-meal* Little by little TMP 2.2.3 *make him By inch-meal a disease!*

inch-thick adj. (fig.) Solid (and so beyond all doubt) WT 1.2.186 *Inch-thick, knee-deep, o'er head and ears a fork'd one!*
▷ Prob. refers to the inch board, the thickest normal plank.

incidency n. Happening, occurrence WT 1.2.403 *declare What incidency thou dost guess of harm Is creeping toward me*.

incision n.
1 Cutting for the purpose of letting blood LLL 4.3.95 *A fever in your blood! Why then incision Would let her out in saucers*, MV 2.1.6, H5 4.2.9.

incivil adj. Unmannerly, rude CYM 5.5.292 *He was a prince?—A most incivil one*.

incivility n. Rudeness ERR 4.4.46 *His incivility confirms no less*.

inclination n. Natural disposition, character, tendency of the mind JN 5.2.158 *fierce and bloody inclination*, ANT 2.5.113.

incline vb. (intr. and refl. with *to*) Side with ANT 4.6.12 *did dissuade Great Herod to incline himself to Caesar*, COR 2.3.38, LR 3.3.14.

inclining n. Party, following OTH 1.2.82 *you of my inclining*.

inclining *ppl. adj.* Compliant, sympathetic OTH 2.3.340 *'tis most easy Th' inclining Desdemona to subdue.*

inclip *vb.* Enclose, embrace ANT 2.7.68 *What e'er the...sky inclips.*

include *vb.* Bring to a close, conclude TGV 5.4.160 *we will include all jars With triumphs;* (refl.) terminate, resolve (into) TRO 1.3.119 *Then every thing include itself in power.*

inclusive *adj.*
1 Enclosing, encircling R3 4.1.58 *the inclusive verge Of golden metal.*
2 Comprehensive AWW 1.3.226 *notes whose faculties inclusive were.*

income *n.* Arrival, advent LUC 334 *Pain pays the income of each precious thing* (quibble on the sense 'financial gain').

incomprehensible *adj.* Boundless, unlimited 1H4 1.2.187 *the incomprehensible lies that this same fat rogue will tell us.*

inconsiderate *n.* Unthinking person, dull-witted person LLL 3.1.78 *Doth the inconsiderate take salve for l'envoy...?*

incontinent *adv.* At once AYL 5.2.38 *stairs...which they will climb incontinent* R2 5.6.48, OTH 4.3.12.

incontinently *adv.* At once OTH 1.3.305 *I will incontinently drown myself.*

inconvenience *n.* Mischief, harm H5 5.2.66 *expel these inconveniences,* 1H6 1.4.14.

inconvenient *adj.* Unfitting, inappropriate AYL 5.2.66 *if it appear not inconvenient to you.*

incony *adj.* (cant expression) Rare, fine, delicate LLL 4.1.142 *most incony vulgar wit!,* LLL 3.1.135.

incorporal *adj.* Incorporeal HAM 3.4.118 *th' incorporal air.*

incorporate *ppl. adj.*
1 United in one body, closely united or combined, intimately bound up (with) JC 1.3.135 *one incorporate To our attempts* (i.e. a member of the conspiracy), MND 3.2.208, COR 1.1.130.
2 Associated with another ERR 2.2.122 *me, That, undividable incorporate, Am better than thy dear self's better part.*
3 That constitutes a close union H5 5.2.366 *their incorporate league.*

incorpsed *adj.* Incorporated, made into one body with HAM 4.7.87 *As had he been incorps'd and deminatur'd With the brave beast* (Q *incorp'st,* Ff *encorp'st*).

incorrect *adj.* Uncorrected, unchastened HAM 1.2.95 *a will most incorrect.*

increase *n.*
1 Reproduction, procreation LR 1.4.279 *the organs of increase.*
2 Offspring, progeny COR 3.3.114 *her womb's increase,* TIT 5.2.191, R3 4.4.297.
3 Multiplication of crops, etc., produce R3 5.5.38 *to taste this land's increase,* TMP 4.1.110, SON 97.6.
~ *vb.* Cause to thrive COR 4.5.219 *This peace is nothing but to...increase tailors.*

increaseful *adj.* Fruitful LUC 958 *increaseful crops.*

incredulous *adj.* Incredible TN 3.4.80 *no incredulous or unsafe circumstance.*

indent *n.* Indentation 1H4 3.1.103 *it shall not wind with such a deep indent.*
~ *vb.*
1 Move in a zig-zag line, double VEN 704 *Turn, and return, indenting with the way.*
2 Enter into a compact or agreement *with,* come to terms *with* 1H4 1.3.87 *Shall we...indent with fears, When they have lost...themselves?*

indenture *n.* Agreement between two or more parties, executed in two or more copies, all having their tops or edges correspondingly serrated; orig.

written on one sheet, the copies being severed by a zig-zag line so that when brought together again the edges exactly tallied HAM 5.1.110 *a pair of indentures,* PER 4.6.176; (hence) apprentice's contract 1H4 2.4.47 *play the coward with thy indenture, and ...run from it;* (fig.) JN 2.1.20 *this...kiss As seal to this indenture of my love.*

index *n.* Table of contents prefixed to a book TRO 1.3.343 *in such indexes...to their subsequent volumes;* (fig.) argument, preface, prologue R3 2.2.149 *As index to the story we late talk'd of,* HAM 3.4.52, OTH 2.1.257.

indifferency *n.*
1 Impartiality JN 2.1.579 *take head from all indifferency.*
2 Moderate size 2H4 4.3.21 *a belly of any indifferency.*

indifferent *adj.*
1 Impartial H8 2.4.17 *No judge indifferent,* R2 2.3.116, H5 1.1.72.
2 Neither good nor bad, ordinary TGV 3.2.44 *the office is indifferent,* SHR 4.1.92, HAM 2.2.227.
~ *adv.*
1 Tolerably, fairly TN 1.3.134 *indifferent well,* HAM 3.1.121, H5 4.7.33.
2 Equally SHR 1.2.180 *news indifferent good for either.*

indifferently *adv.*
1 Impartially JC 1.2.87 *Set honour in one eye and death i' th' other And I will look on both indifferently* (perh. also with the suggestion of 'unconcernedly').
2 Neutrally COR 2.2.17 *he wav'd indifferently 'twixt doing them neither good nor harm.*
3 Moderately, tolerably, fairly H5 2.1.55 *I have a humour to knock you indifferently well;* fairly well HAM 3.2.36 *we have reform'd that indifferently with us.*

indigest *n.* Formless confusion, shapeless mess JN 5.7.26 *that indigest Which he hath left so shapeless.*
~ *adj.* Shapeless, unformed SON 114.5 *To make of...things indigest Such cherubins.*

indigested *ppl. adj.* Shapeless, formless 2H6 5.1.157 *foul indigested lump,* 3H6 5.6.51 (Ff; Qq *undigest*).

indign *adj.* Unworthy, shameful OTH 1.3.273 *all indign and base adversities.*

indignity *n.* Unworthy trait or act 1H4 3.2.146 *exchange His glorious deeds for my indignities.*

indirect *adj.* Irregular, wrong, unjust R3 1.4.218 *no indirect or lawless course,* AYL 1.1.152, OTH 1.3.111.

indirection *n.*
1 Devious course, roundabout means HAM 2.1.63 *By indirections find directions out.*
2 Irregular or unjust means, malpractice JC 4.3.75 *to wring From the hard hands of peasants their vile trash By any indirection,* JN 3.1.276.

indirectly *adv.*
1 Wrongly, unjustly JN 2.1.49 *blood That hot rash haste so indirectly shed,* H5 2.4.94.
2 Evasively MM 4.6.1 *To speak so indirectly,* 1H4 1.3.66, SON 67.7.
3 Not in express terms R3 4.4.226 *Thy head (all indirectly) gave direction.*
4 Inattentively 1H4 1.3.66 *I answered indirectly.*

indisposition *n.* Disinclination (to listen) TIM 2.2.130 *When my indisposition put you back.*

indistinguishable *adj.* Of indeterminate shape; (hence) not true-bred TRO 5.1.29 *you whoreson indistinguishable cur.*

indistinguished See UNDISTINGUISHED.

indite *vb.* (misused for) Invite 2H4 2.1.28 *he is indited to dinner,* ROM 2.4.129.

individable *adj.* (?) (1) Where the unity of place, or

of time and place, is observed (Aldis Wright); (2) 'unclassifiable' (Jenkins) HAM 2.2.399 *scene indivi-dable*.

indrenched *ppl. adj.* Immersed TRO 1.1.51 *in how many fathoms deep They lie indrench'd.*

indubitate *ppl. adj.* Undoubted LLL 4.1.66 *the...indubitate beggar.*

inducement *n.* Action of inducing, instigation, influence AWW 3.2.89 *My son corrupts a well-derived nature With his inducement.*

induction *n.* Initial step in an undertaking 1H4 3.1.2 *And our induction full of prosperous hope,* R3 1.1.32.

indue, endue *vb.*
1 Furnish, supply, endow HAM 4.7.179 *indued Unto that element* (i.e. endowed with qualities fitting her for living in the water), TGV 5.4.153, JN 4.2.43.
2 Bring (*to a certain condition*) OTH 3.4.146 *let our finger ache, and it endues Our other...members...to a sense of pain.*

indurance See ENDURANCE.

industrious *adj.* Clever, ingenious JN 2.1.376 *your industrious scenes and acts of death.*

industriously *adv.* Of set purpose WT 1.2.256 *if industriously I play'd the fool.*

industry *n.* (Armado's speech) (?) Zealous gallantry LLL 4.1.86 *in the dearest design of industry.*

inequality *n.* Disparity, want of adequacy MM 5.1.65 *do not banish reason For inequality.*

inexecrable *adj.* That cannot be sufficiently execrated or cursed enough MV 4.1.128 *inexecrable dog!* (Ff 3–4 *inexorable*).

infallible *adj.* Undoubted, certain MM 3.2.112 *he is a motion generative, that's infallible,* AWW 1.1.137, WT 1.2.287.

infamonize *vb.* (Armado's perversion of 'Infamize') Defame LLL 5.2.678 *Dost thou infamonize me among potentates?*

infant *n.* (fig.) Young plant HAM 1.3.39 *The canker galls the infants of the spring.*

infect *vb.* Affect *with* some feeling WT 1.2.262 *a fear Which oft infects the wisest,* JN 4.3.69, COR 5.6.71.

infect *ppl. adj.* Contaminated TRO 1.3.187 *many are infect.*

infected *ppl. adj.* Affected, factitious LC 323 *that infected moisture of his eye,* TIM 4.3.202.

infection *n.* (malapropism for) Affection WIV 2.2.115 *Her husband has a marvellous infection to the little page,* MV 2.2.125.

infectious *adj.* Infected with disease WT 3.2.98 *from his presence I am barr'd, like one infectious,* OTH 4.1.21 (Qq *infected*).

infer *vb.*
1 Bring about, cause R3 4.4.343 *Infer fair England's peace by this alliance.*
2 Adduce, assert, allege R3 3.5.75 *Infer the bastardy of Edward's children,* 3H6 2.2.44, TIM 3.5.72.
3 Prove, demonstrate 2H4 5.5.14 *this doth infer the zeal I had to see him,* JN 3.1.213.

inference *n.* Allegation OTH 3.3.183 *such exsufflicate ...surmises Matching thy inference.*

infest *vb.* Harass TMP 5.1.246 *Do not infest your mind with beating on The strangeness of this business.*

infinite *n.* Infinity TGV 2.7.70 *instances of infinite of love,* ADO 2.3.101, TRO 2.2.29.

infirm *adj.* Diseased AWW 2.1.167 *What is infirm from your sound parts shall fly.*

infirmity *n.*
1 Illness, disease AWW 2.1.69 *will you be cur'd Of your infirmity?,* JC 1.2.271, MAC 3.4.85.
2 Impotence PHT 60 *'Twas not their infirmity.*

inflammation *n.* Excitement with liquor 2H4 4.3.96 *fools and cowards, which some of us should be too, but for inflammation.*

inflict *vb.* Send an infliction or visitation upon, afflict PER 5.1.61 *so inflict our province.*

infliction *n.* Fact of being inflicted MM 1.3.28 *our decrees, Dead to infliction, to themselves are dead* (i.e. dead as far as their execution goes).

influence *n.*
1 Supposed flowing from the stars or heavens of an ethereal fluid acting upon the character and destiny of men HAM 1.1.119 *the moist star Upon whose influence Neptune's empire stands,* TMP 1.2.182, LR 1.2.125; (hence) exercise of personal power regarded as something akin to astral influence TGV 3.1.183 *If I be not by her fair influence Foster'd.*
2 Inspiration SON 78.10 *that which I compile Whose influence is thine,* LLL 5.2.859.

in folio *phr.* In the form of a full-sized sheet folded once LLL 1.2.185 *whole volumes in folio.*

inform *vb.*
1 Take shape MAC 2.1.48 *It is the bloody business which informs Thus to mine eyes.*
2 Imbue, inspire COR 5.3.71 *The god...inform Thy thoughts with nobleness.*
3 Instruct, teach ANT 3.2.48 *nor can Her heart inform her tongue,* COR 3.3.18, CYM 1.1.79.
4 (refl.) Learn, know WT 2.1.167 *inform yourselves We need no more of your advice.*
5 Give information MAC 1.5.33 *who...Would have inform'd for preparation,* AWW 4.1.93.
6 Report, tell (a fact) COR 1.6.42 *He did inform the truth,* AWW 4.1.82, MM 3.2.128.

informal *adj.* Disordered in mind, crazy MM 5.1.236 *These poor informal women.*

infuse *vb.*
1 Shed, diffuse 1H6 1.2.85 *those clear rays which she infus'd on me.*
2 Imbue, inspire *with* JC 1.3.69 *heaven hath infus'd them with these spirits,* TMP 1.2.154, R2 3.2.166.

infusion *n.* (term of alchemy or medicine) Essence; (hence) infused temperament, character imparted by nature HAM 5.2.117 *his infusion of such dearth and rareness.*

ingage See ENGAGE.

ingener See ENGINEER, ENGINER.

ingenious *n.* Clever or intelligent person LLL 3.1.57 *The meaning, pretty ingenious?*
~ *adj.*
1 Able, talented R3 3.1.155 *Bold, quick, ingenious.*
2 Intelligent, quick of apprehension, sensitive in mind or feeling HAM 5.1.248 *thy most ingenious sense* (i.e. sensitivity of mind), LR 4.6.280.
3 Clever at contriving, skilful LLL 1.2.27 *that an eel is ingenious?* (Q1, F4; Ff 1–3, Q2 *ingenuous*), CYM 5.5.215.
4 Skilfully contrived CYM 4.2.186 *My ingenious instrument* (F1 *ingenuous*), LLL 3.1.58 (Q2 *ingenuous*).
5 (used for 'ingenuous') Befitting a well-born person, 'liberal' SHR 1.1.9 *A course of learning and ingenious studies.*

ingeniously *adv.* Ingenuously, frankly TIM 2.2.221 *ingeniously I speak.*

ingenuous Used freq. in 17C for INGENIOUS.

ingraffed, ingraft, ingrafted See ENGRAFFED, ENGRAFTED.

ingrate *adj.* Ungrateful, unthankful 1H4 1.3.137 *this ingrate and cank'red Bullingbrook,* SHR 1.2.268, TN 5.1.113.

ingredience *n.* Ingredients; the composition of a drug or poison MAC 1.7.11 *th' ingredience of our poison'd chalice,* MAC 4.1.34.

ingredient *n.* Chief component OTH 2.3.308 *the ingredient is a devil* (Ff; Qq *ingredience*), WT 2.1.43.

ingross See ENGROSS.

inhabit vb. (fig.) Dwell in, take up (one's abode in) MAC 3.4.104 *If trembling I inhabit* (i.e. if I tremble).

inhabitable adj. Uninhabitable R2 1.1.65 *any other ground inhabitable.*

inhabited See ILL-INHABITED.

in hac spe vivo [L.] In this hope I live PER 2.2.44.

inhearse vb. Lay as in a coffin SON 86.3 *did my ripe thoughts in my brain inhearse,* 1H6 4.7.45.

inherent adj. Permanently indwelling COR 3.2.123 *A most inherent baseness.*

inherit vb.
1 Put (a person) in possession *of* R2 1.1.85 *that can inherit us So much as of a thought of ill in him.*
2 Enjoy the possession of, receive, hold as one's portion R2 2.1.83 *a grave, Whose hollow womb inherits nought but bones,* ROM 1.2.30, TMP 4.1.154.

inheritance n. Possession, ownership COR 3.2.68 *the inheritance of their loves,* HAM 1.1.92, AWW 4.3.279.

inheritor n. Possessor, owner LLL 2.1.5 *the sole inheritor Of all perfections,* HAM 5.1.112, R3 4.3.34.

inhibited ppl. adj. Forbidden, as by ecclesiastical law AWW 1.1.145 *the most inhibited sin in the canon,* OTH 1.2.79.

inhibition n. Formal prohibition HAM 2.2.332 *their inhibition comes by the means of the late innovation.*

inhooped ppl. adj. (of fighting cocks or quails) Enclosed in a hoop in which the birds were kept fighting close together ANT 2.3.39 *and his quails ever Beat mine, inhoop'd.*

inhuman, inhumane Cf. HUMAN.

Iniquity n. Comic character in the old morality plays, also called VICE R3 3.1.82 *like the formal Vice, Iniquity;* (allusion) 1H4 2.4.454 *that reverent Vice, that grey Iniquity, that father ruffian,* MM 2.1.172.

initiate adj. Of a novice MAC 3.4.142 *the initiate fear that wants hard use.*

injoint vb. Join, unite OTH 1.3.35 *Have there injointed them with an after fleet.*

injurious adj.
1 Insulting, slanderous COR 3.3.69 *Call me their traitor, thou injurious tribune!,* 2H6 1.4.48, CYM 4.2.86.
2 Malicious or insolent in wrong-doing CYM 3.1.47 *the injurious Romans did extort,* TGV 1.2.103, R2 1.1.91.

injury n.
1 Reviling, insult, calumny, affront 3H6 4.1.107 *what said Warwick to these injuries?,* ERR 5.1.200, MND 2.1.147.
2 Bodily wound or sore H5 3.6.122 *not good to bruise an injury till it were full ripe.*

inkhorn n.
1 Inkstand made of horn 2H6 4.2.110 *with his pen and inkhorn about his neck.*
2 (attrib.) *inkhorn mate* (term of contempt) Scribbler 1H6 3.1.99.

inkle n. Kind of linen tape LLL 3.1.139 *What's the price of this inkle?,* WT 4.4.207; linen or yarn from which it is made PER 5. Gower.8 *Her inkle, silk.*

inland n. Districts of a country near the capital and centres of population and culture, as opposed to the remote or outlying wild parts H5 1.2.142 *to defend Our inland from the pilfering borderers* (Qq *your England*).
~ adj. Cultured, refined AYL 3.2.345 *an inland man, one that knew courtship too well.*
~ adv. *inland bred* Reared in a centre of civilized behaviour AYL 2.7.96.

inly adj. Inward TGV 2.7.18 *the inly touch of love,* 3H6 1.4.171.
~ adv. Inwardly TMP 5.1.200 *I have inly wept,* H5 4.Ch.24.

inn n. Place of residence for law students, often named after the person from whom they were first rented or acquired 2H4 3.2.14 *Clement's Inn* (an Inn of Chancery, formerly a centre of legal studies preparatory to the Inns of Court); *inns of court* the four sets of buildings in London (the Inner Temple, the Middle Temple, Lincoln's Inn, and Gray's Inn) belonging to the four societies which have the exclusive right of calling persons to the Bar 2H6 2H4 3.2.13.

innocent n. Idiot, half-wit, simpleton AWW 4.3.187 *a dumb innocent,* LR 3.6.7, PER 4.3.17.
~ adj. Silly ADO 5.2.38 *an innocent rhyme.*

innovation n. Disturbance, commotion OTH 2.3.40 *behold what innovation it makes here;* revolution, rebellion 1H4 5.1.78 *hurly-burly innovation.*
▷ HAM 2.2.333 *their inhibition comes by the means of the late innovation:* an allusion either to some earlier disturbance or to some new law altering the condition of theatre companies for the worse.

innovator n. Revolutionary, rebel COR 3.1.174 *a traitorous innovator.*

inobled See MOBLED.

inoculate vb. Engraft HAM 3.1.117 *inoculate our old stock.*

inprimis See IMPRIMIS.

inquire n. Inquiry PER 3. Gower.22 *answering the most strange inquire,* HAM 2.1.4 (Qq; Ff *inquiry*).

insane adj. Causing madness MAC 1.3.84 *the insane root, That takes the reason prisoner.*

insanie n. Madness LLL 5.1.25 *it insinuateth me of insanie.*

insconce See ENSCONCE.

inscroll vb. Describe on a scroll MV 2.7.72 *Your answer had not been inscroll'd.*

insculp vb. Carve, engrave MV 2.7.57 *but that's insculp'd upon.*

insculpture n. Carved inscription TIM 5.4.67 *on his grave-stone this insculpture.*

insense vb. Make (a person) understand H8 5.1.43 *I have Insens'd the lords...that he is...A most arch-heretic* (F1 *incenst*).

insensible adj. Not perceptible by the senses 1H4 5.1.137 *Doth he hear it? No. 'Tis insensible then?*

inshipped pa. pple. Embarked 1H6 5.1.49 *safely brought to Dover, where inshipp'd* (F4; F12 *where-in shipp'd*).

insinewed See ENSINEWED.

insinuate vb.
1 (intr.) Wheedle oneself into a person's favour, ingratiate oneself *with* R3 1.4.148 *He would insinuate with thee but to make thee sigh,* R2 4.1.165, TIT 4.2.38.
2 Suggest or imply something to (a person) LLL 5.1.25 *it insinuateth me of insanie.*
▷ A doubtful passage, spoken by Holofernes. See similarly INSINUATION sense 2.

insinuation n.
1 Self-ingratiation JN 5.1.68 *make compromise, Insinuation, parley, and base truce;* 'artful intrusion into the business' (Clark and Wright) HAM 5.1.59 *Their defeat Does by their own insinuation grow.*
2 Suggestion, hint LLL 4.2.14 *a kind of insinuation,...in way, of explication.*
▷ A doubtful passage, spoken by Holofernes. See INSINUATE sense 2.

insisture n. [?] Steady continuance in their path TRO 1.3.87 *The heavens...Observe degree, priority, ...Insisture.*
▷ A word of obscure use: Schmidt 'persistency, constancy'; Nares 'regularity, or perhaps station'.

insociable adj. Unsociable, not companionable LLL 5.2.799 *this austere insociable life,* LLL 5.1.18.

insolence n. Pride, overbearing nature COR 1.1.262

I do wonder His insolence can brook to be commanded.

insomuch *conj.* Inasmuch as AYL 5.2.55 *insomuch I say I know you are.*

instalment *n.* Place or seat in which a person is installed WIV 5.5.63 *Each fair instalment, coat, and sev'ral crest.*

instance *n.*
1 Motive, cause R3 3.2.25 *his fears are shallow, without instance* (QQ 2-8 *instancy*), AWW 4.1.40, HAM 3.2.182.
2 Being present, presence 2H4 4.1.83 *the examples Of every minute's instance* (i.e. presented every minute).
3 Evidence, proof, sign, token 2H4 3.1.103 *I have received A certain instance that Glendower is dead,* TGV 2.7.70, ERR 1.1.64; *familiar instances* marks of familiarity JC 4.2.16; *no guilty instance* no sign of guilt LUC 1511.

instancy See INSTANCE sense 1.

instant *n.* upon, on, o' th' *instant* Immediately TIM 2.2.198 *send o' th' instant A thousand talents,* OTH 1.2.38, LLL 3.1.41.
~ *adj.*
1 Now present, existing, happening H8 1.1.225 *this instant cloud; the instant way* the path now ahead TRO 3.3.153; *the instant army* the force at present available COR 5.1.37.
2 Immediate AWW 2.4.48 *take your instant leave,* 1H4 4.4.20, LR 1.4.247.
~ *adv.* Immediately TIM 2.2.230 *'tis instant due,* HAM 1.5.94.

instantly *adv.* Simultaneously 1H4 5.2.64 *Of teaching and of learning instantly.*

instate See ENSTATE.

insteeped *ppl. adj.* Steeped *in,* imbrued H5 4.6.12 *in gore he lay insteeped.*

instigation *n.* Incentive, stimulus JC 2.1.49 *Such instigations have been often dropp'd.*

instinct *n.* Impulse, prompting R3 2.3.42 *By a divine instinct.*

instinctively See INTENTIVELY.

instruct *vb.* Inform CYM 4.2.360 *He'll then instruct us of this body,* MM 1.1.80, SHR 4.2.120.

instruction *n.* Information ANT 5.1.54 *Of thy intents desires instruction.*

instrument *n.*
1 (fig.) Means, agent 1H6 3.3.65 *that instrument of ill,* TN 5.1.122, OTH 4.2.45.
2 Document OTH 4.1.218 *I kiss the instrument of their pleasures* (i.e. the document in which their desires are communicated).

instrumental *adj.* Serviceable HAM 1.2.48 *The hand* (is not) *more instrumental to the mouth, Than is the throne...to thy father.*

insubstantial *adj.* Unreal, imaginary TMP 4.1.155 *this insubstantial pageant.*

insufficiency, insufficiency *n.* Inability, incompetence SON 150.2 *With insufficiency my heart to sway,* MND 2.2.128, WT 1.1.15 *unintelligent of our insufficience.*

insult *vb.* Exult proudly or contemptuously, triumph scornfully *over, on* SON 107.12 *While he insults o'er dull and speechless tribes,* AYL 3.5.36, TIT 3.2.71.

insulter *n.* Triumphing power VEN 550 *what ransom the insulter willeth.*

insulting *ppl. adj.* Exulting contemptuously, triumphing scornfully 1H6 4.7.19 *thy insulting tyranny,* R2 4.1.254, 3H6 2.1.168.

insultment *n.* Contemptuous triumph CYM 3.5.140 *my speech of insultment.*

insuppressive *adj.* Insuppressible JC 2.1.134 *th' insuppressive mettle of our spirits.*

Integer vitae, scelerisque purus, Non eget Mauri jaculis, nec arcu [L.] A man of spotless life and free from crime needs not the bow and arrows of the Moor TIT 4.2.20.

intellect *n.* Meaning, import LLL 4.2.133 *the intellect of the letter.*

intelligence *n.*
1 Communication, intercourse AYL 1.3.47 *If with myself I hold intelligence,* CYM 4.2.347, SON 86.10.
2 Obtaining of secret information 1H4 4.3.98 *to entrap me by intelligence;* agency by which it is obtained JN 4.2.116 *where hath our intelligence been drunk?* (i.e. our spies).

intelligencer *n.* Informer, spy, secret agent R3 4.4.71 *hell's black intelligencer,* 2H4 4.2.20.

intelligencing *ppl. adj.* Conveying intelligence or information WT 2.3.69 *A most intelligencing bawd!*

intelligent *adj.* 'Bearing intelligence, giving information, communicative' (Schmidt) LR 3.7.11 *Posts shall be swift and intelligent betwixt us,* LR 3.1.25, WT 1.2.378.

intemperature *n.* Intemperance, intemperateness 1H4 3.2.156 *The long-grown wounds of my intemperature* (Ff; QQ *intemperance*).

intend *vb.*
1 Purpose making (a journey) SON 27.6 *Intend a zealous pilgrimage,* ANT 5.2.201, PER 1.2.116; (intr.) 1H4 4.1.92 *The King...hitherwards intended speedily.*
2 Design to express, signify by one's words, mean 3H6 3.2.94 *I speak no more than what my soul intends,* 1H6 3.1.141, ANT 2.2.40.
3 Pretend, make a pretence of ADO 2.2.35 *intend a kind of zeal,* R3 3.5.8, SHR 4.1.203.
4 Tend, incline 2H4 1.2.8 *any thing that intends to laughter* (Q; Ff *tends*), MND 3.2.333.

intendment *n.* Purpose, intent, design H5 1.2.144 *But fear the main intendment of the Scot,* AYL 1.1.133, OTH 4.2.203.

intenible *adj.* Incapable of holding AWW 1.3.202 *this captious and intenible sieve* (F2 *intenible;* F1 *intenible*).

intent *n.*
1 Aim, bent LUC 46 *with swift intent,* TN 2.4.77.
2 Meaning, import, purport ANT 2.2.41 *to catch at mine intent,* MV 4.1.247, 2H4 4.1.9.

intention *n.* INTENT sense 1 WIV 1.3.66 *with such a greedy intention,* WT 1.2.138.

intentively *adv.* Intently, with earnest application or attention OTH 1.3.155 *by parcels she had something heard, But not intentively* (Q1; F1 *instinctiuely;* Ff 2-4 *distinctively*).

intercept *vb.* Interrupt TIT 3.1.40 *they will not intercept my tale.*

interchained *ppl. adj.* Linked with one another MND 2.2.49 *Two bosoms interchained with an oath* (QQ; Ff *interchanged*).

interchange *n.* Alternation, vicissitude SON 64.9 *such interchange of state.*
~ *vb.* Exchange 3H6 4.7.3 *interchange My waned state for Henry's regal crown.*

interchangeably *adv.* (in phr. based on the wording of legal agreements) mutually, reciprocally 1H4 3.1.80 *sealed interchangeably,* R2 5.2.98, TRO 3.2.58.

interdiction *n.* Restraint, exclusion MAC 4.3.107 *By his own interdiction stands accus'd.*

interessed *ppl. adj.* Invested with a right or share LR 1.1.85 *Strive to be interess'd* (F1 *interest*).

interest *n.*
1 Legal concern (in), right or title (to possessions or the enjoyment of them) LR 1.1.50 *we will divest us...of...Interest of territory,* 1H4 3.2.98, JN 4.3.147; (fig.) TIT 3.1.249 *Where life hath no more interest but to breathe!,* AYL 5.1.8, LUC 1067.

2 Right or title to share in, part R3 2.2.47 *so much interest have [I] in thy sorrow*, 1H6 5.4.167, ROM 3.1.188.
3 Advantageous concern (*in* a thing) CYM 4.2.365 *What's thy interest In this sad wrack?*; profit, advantage MAC 1.2.64 *deceive Our bosom interest*, LR 5.3.85.

inter'gatory *n.* (syncopated form of) INTERROGATORY MV 5.1.298 *charge us there upon inter'gatories*, AWW 4.3.183.

interim *n.* Interlude LLL 1.1.171 *This child...For interim to our studies shall relate; by interims* at intervals COR 1.6.5.

interjoin *vb.* Join mutually COR 4.4.22 *interjoin their issues.*

interlace *vb.* Interweave, place at intervals LUC 1390 *here and there the painter interlaces Pale cowards.*

interlude *n.* (orig.) Dramatic or mimic representation, of light or humorous character, such as was introduced between the acts of the long mystery or morality plays; (in 16C–17C) stage-play, esp. of a popular kind, comedy, farce MND 1.2.6 *to play in our interlude*, LR 5.3.89, TN 5.1.372.
▷ F1, Q1 *enterlude* on all three occasions.

intermission *n.* Delay MAC 4.3.232 *Cut short all intermission*, AYL 2.7.32, MV 3.2.199.

intermissive *adj.* Coming at intervals, having a temporary cessation or breach of continuity 1H6 1.1.88 *their intermissive miseries.*

intermit *vb.* Discontinue, suspend JC 1.1.54 *Pray to the gods to intermit the plague.*

interpret *vb.* (used with ref. to the puppet-show) Supply explanatory comment on the action (as a puppeteer did) TGV 2.1.95 *O excellent motion! O exceeding puppet! Now will he interpret to her*, HAM 3.2.246, LUC 1325.

In terram Salicam mulieres ne succedant [L.] That women shall not succeed to Salic land H5 1.2.38.

interrogatory *n.* Question formally put, or drawn up in writing to be put, to an accused person or a witness to be answered as upon oath JN 3.1.147 *What earthy name to interrogatories Can taste the...breath of a...king?*, CYM 5.5.392.

intertissued *ppl. adj.* Interwoven H5 4.1.262 *The intertissued robe of gold and pearl.*
▷ See TISSUE.

intervallum *n.* Interval, break; vacation at the law-courts 2H4 5.1.81 *six fashions, which is four terms, or two actions, and 'a shall laugh without intervallums.*

intestate *adj.* Not having made a will; (fig.) R3 4.4.128 *Aery succeeders of intestate joys* ('mere words succeed as next of kin to an empty inheritance' (Wright); Ff *intestine*).

intil *prep.* [Northern dial.] Into HAM 5.1.73 *hath shipped me intil the land.*

intitled See ENTITLED.

intituled *ppl. adj.*
1 Designated LLL 5.1.7 *who is intituled...Don Adriano.*
2 Having a claim LUC 57 *in that white intituled From Venus' doves* (Q1 *entituled*).

into *prep.* Unto, to AWW 1.3.254 *pray God's blessing into thy attempt*, TN 5.1.84, TMP 1.2.100.

intolerable *adj.* Excessive, exceedingly great 1H4 2.4.541 *intolerable deal of sack*, WIV 5.5.153.
~ *adv.* Exceedingly SHR 1.2.89 *she is intolerable curst.*

intreasured See ENTREASURED.

intrenchant *adj.* Incapable of being cut MAC 5.8.9 *the intrenchant air.*

intrince, intrinse *adj.* Entangled, involved LR 2.2.75 *Which are t' intrinse t' unloose.*

intrinsicate *adj.* Intricate, entangled ANT 5.2.304 *this knot intrinsicate.*
▷ App. from It. 'intrinsicato' (i.e. familiar) but confused in sense with 'intricato' (i.e. intricate).

intrude *vb.* Enter forcibly LUC 848 *Why should the worm intrude the maiden bud?*

inurned *pa. pple.* Interred HAM 1.4.49 *we saw thee quietly inurn'd* (F1 *enurn'd*; Q1 *interr'd*).

invasive *adj.* Invading JN 5.1.69 *make...truce To arms invasive?*

invectively *adv.* With denunciation, in abusive language AYL 2.1.58 *most invectively he pierceth through The body of the country.*

invention *n.*
1 Power of mental creation or construction, inventiveness, imagination LLL 4.2.125 *The jerks of invention*, ADO 5.1.283, OTH 2.1.125.
2 Work or writing produced by the mind or imagination, literary composition TN 5.1.333 *Or say 'tis not your seal, not your invention.*
3 Device, design, plan 1H6 3.1.5 *Do it without invention, suddenly*, LR 1.2.20, SHR 1.1.190.

inventorially *adv.* In detail, item by item HAM 5.2.113 *to divide him inventorially.*

invest *vb.*
1 Endow, furnish 2H4 4.5.72 *to invest Their sons with arts and martial exercises.*
2 Accompany, attend H5 4.Ch.26 *their gesture sad, Investing lank-lean cheeks and war-torn coats.*

investments *n.* (pl.) Clothes 2H4 4.1.45 *Whose white investments figure innocence*, HAM 1.3.128.

in via [L.] In the way LLL 4.2.14.

invincible *adj.* (perh. an error for) Invisible 2H4 3.2.313 *his dimensions to any thick sight were invincible* (F1, Q).

invised *ppl. adj.* (?) Invisible, unseen LC 212 *his invis'd properties.*

invisible *adj.*
1 (?) Subtle ANT 2.2.212 *A strange invisible perfume.*
2 (?) Secret CYM 4.2.177 *an invisible instinct.*

invitation *n.* Inducement, allurement WIV 1.3.46 *the leer of invitation.*

inviting *ppl. adj.* Attractive, alluring OTH 2.3.24 *An inviting eye.*

Invitis nubibus [L.] In spite of (the) clouds 2H6 4.1.99.

inward *n.*
1 The inside, internal part SON 128.6 *the tender inward of thy hand*, CYM 3.4.6.
2 Intimate friend MM 3.2.130 *I was an inward of his.*
~ *adj.*
1 Familiar *with* R3 3.4.8 *Who is most inward with the noble Duke?*
2 Private, secret ADO 4.1.12 *any inward impediment*, LLL 5.1.97.
3 Pertaining to the country itself, domestic 2H4 3.1.107 *these inward wars.*
~ *adv.* Inwardly, internally MV 3.2.86 *Hercules and...Mars, Who inward search'd, have livers white as milk*, HAM 4.4.28, SON 62.4.

inwardness *n.* Close friendship ADO 4.1.245 *my inwardness and love.*

Iris *n.*
1 Messenger 2H6 3.2.407 *I 'll have an Iris that shall find thee out.*
2 Rainbow TRO 1.3.379 *His crest that prouder than blue Iris bends.*
▷ In Gk. mythology Iris was the messenger of the gods, who displayed as her sign, or appeared as, the rainbow.

iron n.
1 Metal of which arms and armour are made; (hence) armour ANT 4.4.3 *put thine iron on*, 2H4 1.1.150; sword TN 4.1.39 *put up your iron*, R3 5.3.110, TRO 2.3.17; offensive weapons ADO 5.1.245 *Runs not this speech like iron through your blood?*, 1H6 4.3.20.
2 Symbol of hardness (esp. of heart) H8 3.2.424 *all that have not hearts of iron*, MND 2.1.196, 3H6 2.2.139.
~ *adj.* Harsh, cruel, merciless JN 4.1.60 *in this iron age*.

iron-witted *adj.* Harsh-minded, unfeeling R3 4.2.28 *iron-witted fools*.

irreconciled *ppl. adj.* Not atoned for H5 4.1.153 *die in many irreconcil'd iniquities*.

irregular *adj.* Lawless JN 5.4.54 *our...irregular course*, 1H4 1.1.40.

irregulous *adj.* Lawless CYM 4.2.315 *that irregulous devil Cloten*.

irreligious *adj.* Believing in a false religion TIT 5.3.121 *an irreligious Moor*.

ise See ICE.

Isebrooke See ICE-BROOK.

issue n.
1 Outcome, product (of a practice or condition) AWW 2.1.106 *the dearest issue of his practice*, JN 3.4.21, LR 1.1.17.

2 Action, deed JC 3.1.294 *The cruel issue of these bloody men*, MM 1.1.36, CYM 2.1.47.
3 Fortune, luck ANT 1.2.93 *better issue*.
4 Outcome or upshot of an argument, evidence, etc.; (hence) conclusion OTH 3.3.219 *grosser issues*.
5 (orig. legal use) Matter ripe for decision, point at which decision becomes possible JN 1.1.38 *With fearful bloody issue arbitrate*, ROM 4.1.65, MAC 5.4.20.
~ *vb.* Shed tears H5 4.6.34 *eyes...will issue too*.

issued *ppl. adj.* Born, descended 1H6 5.4.38 *But issued from the progeny of kings*, TMP 1.2.59.

issuing *ppl. adj.* Pouring or gushing out TIT 2.4.30 *their issuing spouts*, 3H6 2.6.82.

it *pron.*
1 There TGV 4.4.66 *For 'tis no trusting to yond foolish lout.*
2 Its LR 1.4.216 *it had it head bit off by it young*, ROM 1.3.52 (Qq, Ff 1-2; Ff 3-4 *its*), TMP 2.1.164 (Ff 1-2; Ff 3-4 *its*).

iterance n. Iteration OTH 5.2.150 *What needs this iterance, woman?* (Qq *iteration*).

iwis *adv.* Certainly, assuredly R3 1.3.101 *Iwis your grandam had a worser match*, SHR 1.1.62, MV 2.9.68.
▷ Often spelt *I wis* and erroneously understood as 'I know'.

J

Jack, jack n.[1]
1 familiar var. of the name (John); (hence) a generic proper name for any man of the common people MND 3.2.461 *Jack shall have Jill* (proverb), LLL 5.2.875.
2 Low-bred or ill-mannered fellow, knave MV 3.4.77 *these bragging Jacks*, SHR 2.1.288, R3 1.3.53.
3 *play the Jack* Play the knave, do a mean trick TMP 4.1.197 *your fairy...has done little better than play'd the Jack with us* (quibble on 'jack-o'-lantern', i.e. will-o'-the-wisp), ADO 1.1.184.
4 Figure of a man which strikes the bell on the outside of a clock R3 4.2.114 *like a Jack thou keep'st the stroke Betwixt thy begging and my meditation*, TIM 3.6.97, R2 5.5.60.
5 In the virginal, an upright piece of wood fixed to the key-lever and fitted with a quill which plucked the string as the jack rose when the key was pressed down SON 128.5 *those jacks that nimble leap To kiss the tender inward of thy hand* (erroneously applied here to the key).
6 Measure for drink; vessel used either for holding liquor or for drinking from SHR 4.1.49 *Be the Jacks fair within, the Gills fair without* (quibble on sense 1; see GILL).
7 (attrib.) Used as a kind of proper name or nickname, in contempt WIV 1.4.117 *I vill kill de Jack priest*, CYM 2.1.20.

jack n.[2] Short and close fitting upper garment, jacket, usu. of quilted leather 1H4 4.2.49 *How now, blown Jack? how now, quilt?* (with quibble on Falstaff's name).

Jack-a-Lent n.
1 Figure of a man set up to be pelted, an ancient form of the sport of Aunt Sally practised during Lent; (hence, fig.) butt for everyone to throw at WIV 5.5.127 *See now how wit may be made a Jack-a-Lent.*
2 (transf.) Puppet, contemptible person WIV 3.3.27 *You little Jack-a-Lent.*

jack-an-apes, jack-a-nape, jack-an-ape, jack'nape n.
1 Ape H5 5.2.142 *sit like a jack-an-apes, never off.*
2 Pert, conceited fellow CYM 2.1.3 *and then a whoreson jack-an-apes must take me up for swearing*, WIV 2.3.83, AWW 3.5.85.
3 (attrib.) Term of contempt WIV 1.4.109 *a scurvy jack-a-nape priest.*

Jack of the clock n. phr. See JACK n.[1] sense 4.

Jack-dog n. Term of contempt; (attrib.) WIV 2.3.63 *Scurvy Jack-dog priest!*

Jack sauce n. Saucy Jack, impudent fellow H5 4.7.141 *his reputation is as arrant a villain and a Jack sauce, as ever...trod upon God's ground.*

jade n.
1 Ill-conditioned horse MM 2.1.255 *let carman whip his jade*, H5 4.2.46, MAC 3.2.242; vicious horse TRO 2.1.20 *A red murrion a' thy jade's tricks!*, SHR 1.2.247, AWW 4.5.61.
2 Term of contempt (usu. applied to a woman) H5 3.7.59 *I had as live have my mistress a jade*, SHR 2.1.201; (applied to men) JN 2.1.385 *I'll play incessantly upon these jades.*
~ *vb.*
1 (lit.) Make a jade of (a horse); (hence) drive to exhaustion, weary ANT 3.1.34 *The ne'er-yet-beaten horse of Parthia We have jaded out o' th' field.*
2 Befool, make ridiculous, jape TN 2.5.164 *I do not now fool myself, to let imagination jade me*, H8 3.2.280.

jaded *ppl. adj.* Contemptible, ignoble 2H6 4.1.52 *such a jaded groom* (Qq *jady*).

jady See JADED.

jakes n. Privy LR 2.2.67 *daub the wall of a jakes with him.*

jangle *vb.* Dispute, wrangle LLL 2.1.225 *Good wits will be jangling.*

jangling n. Wrangling, noisy altercation MND 3.2.353 *this their jangling I esteem a sport.*

jar *n.*

1 Discord in music AYL 2.7.5 *If he, compact of jars, grow musical.*

2 Quarrel, quarrelling ERR 1.1.11 *the...jars 'Twixt thy seditious countrymen and us,* TGV 5.4.160, VEN 100; *at jars* into contention 2H6 1.1.253 *And Humphrey with the peers be fall'n at jars.*

3 Tick (of the clock) WT 1.2.43 *not a jar o' th' clock.*

~ *vb.*

1 Make a musical discord, be out of tune SHR 3.1.39 *the treble jars,* 4.2.67, 2H6 2.1.55.

2 Quarrel TIT 2.1.103 *be friends, and join for that you jar,* 1H6 3.1.70.

3 Cause (a watch) to tick R2 5.5.51 *My thoughts are minutes, and with sighs they jar Their watches on unto mine eyes.*

jarring *ppl. adj.* Discordant, inharmonious; (fig.) SHR 5.2.1 *our jarring notes agree,* LR 4.7.15, AWW 1.1.172.

jaunce *n.* See JAUNT.

~ *vb.* Prance (as a horse), run to and fro ROM 2.5.52 *To catch my death with jauncing up and down* (Qq 2–3; Ff, Qq 4–5 *jaunting, iaunting*).

jauncing *ppl. adj.* (fig.) Prancing R2 5.5.94 *Spurr'd, gall'd, and tir'd by jauncing Bullingbrook.*

jaunt *n.* Running to and fro, trudging about ROM 2.5.26 *Fie, how my bones ache! What a jaunt have I!* (Ff, Qq 4–5; Qq 2–3 *iaunce*).

~ *vb.* See JAUNCE.

jay *n.* Flashy or loose woman CYM 3.4.49 *Some jay of Italy...hath betray'd him,* WIV 3.3.42.

jealous *adj.*

1 Suspiciously careful, watchful, concerned (about) H5 4.1.285 *jealous of your absence,* ROM 2.2.181.

2 Apprehensive of evil, fearful LR 5.1.56 *jealous ...as the stung Are of the adder,* TGV 3.1.28, JC 1.2.71.

3 Mistrustful, doubtful JC 1.2.162 *That you do love me, I am nothing jealous,* TN 4.3.27, SHR 4.5.76.

◊ Sometimes spelt *iealious* in Ff and Qq, a spelling retained as *jealious* in some mod. edd.

ROM 4.4.13: in Ff123 *jealous hood* where *hood* may = woman, or possibly with allusion to the use of the hood as a disguise for a spy; but in F4 *jealous-hood* 'jealousy', 'hood' being the suffix forming abstract nouns.

jealousy *n.* Suspicion, apprehension of evil, mistrust ADO 2.2.49 *jealousy shall be call'd assurance,* TN 3.3.8, OTH 3.3.147.

~ *adj.* Jealous WIV 2.2.90 *He's a very jealousy man.*

jennet, gennet *n.* Small Spanish horse VEN 260 *A breeding jennet,* OTH 1.1.113 (F1 *Gennets*).

jerk *n.* Short, sharp, witty speech, sally LLL 4.2.125 *the jerks of invention.*

jerkin *n.* Short, close-fitting jacket, sometimes sleeveless, worn over, or instead of, the doublet, often made of leather TGV 2.4.20 *My jerkin is a doublet,* TRO 3.3.265, 1H4 1.2.42.

Jerusalem *n.* Paradise 3H6 5.5.8 *To meet with joy in sweet Jerusalem.*

jesses *n.* (pl.) Short straps of leather, silk, or other material fastened round the legs of a trained hawk OTH 3.3.261 *If I do prove her haggard, Though that her jesses were my dear heart-strings.*

jest *n.*

1 Merriment HAM 5.1.185 *a fellow of infinite jest.*

2 Prank, practical joke MND 3.2.239 *hold the sweet jest up.*

3 Object of ridicule WIV 3.3.151 *let me be your jest.*

~ *vb.* Amuse oneself, make merry R2 1.3.95 *As gentle and as jocund as to jest Go I to fight* (with quibble on 'act in a play or masque').

jet *vb.*¹ Walk pompously, strut, swagger TN 2.5.31

How he jets under his advanc'd plumes!, CYM 3.3.5, PER 1.4.26.

jet *vb.*² Encroach *upon* TIT 2.1.64 *how dangerous It is to jet upon a prince's right* (Ff *set*), ERR 2.2.28 (F1 *iest*), R3 2.4.51 (F1 *Iutt, jut*).

Jew's, Jewess' eye *n. phr.* (proverbial expression) Something valued highly MV 2.5.43 *There will come a Christian by, Will be worth a Jewess' eye.*

◊ F1, Qq 1–2 *Iewes*; Pope *Jewess'*.

jig *n.*

1 Lively, rapid kind of dance TN 1.3.129 *My very walk should be a jig,* ADO 2.1.74; music for such a dance LLL 4.3.166 *to tune a jig.*

2 Song or ballad of a lively, jocular character PP 17.5 *All my merry jigs are quite forgot.*

3 Lively, comic, or farcical performance given at the end or in an interval of a play HAM 2.2.500 *he's for a jig or a tale of bawdry.*

~ *vb.*

1 Sing as in a jig LLL 3.1.11 *to jig off a tune.*

2 Move with a rapid jerky motion HAM 3.1.144 *You jig and amble* (Ff *gidge;* Qq *gig*).

jigging *ppl. adj.* Engaged in composing jigs JC 4.3.137 *What should the wars do with these jigging fools* (Wright 'these foolish writers of doggerel').

Jill See GILL.

Joan *n.* Generic name for a female rustic LLL 3.1.205 *Some men must love my lady, and some Joan,* JN 1.1.184, SHR Ind.2.110.

Jockey *n.* (pet form of) JOCK (i.e. JACK) R3 5.3.304 *Jockey of Norfolk.*

John-a-dreams *n.* Dreamy fellow HAM 2.2.568 *peak Like John-a-dreams.*

join *vb.* (short for) Join battle, meet in conflict 1H4 5.1.85 *If once they join in trial,* 3H6 1.1.15, R3 5.3.312.

joinder *n.* Joining, conjunction, union TN 5.1.157 *Confirm'd by mutual joinder of your hands.*

join-stool, joined stool See JOINT-STOOL.

jointress *n.* Widow who holds a jointure, dowager HAM 1.2.9 *Th' imperial jointress to this warlike state.*

joint-ring *n.* Finger-ring made in separable halves OTH 4.3.73 *I would not do such a thing for a joint-ring.*

joint-stool *n.* Stool expertly made by a joiner as distinguished from one of rough make 2H4 2.4.247 *jumps upon joint-stools* (F1 *Ioyn'd-*), ROM 1.5.6, SHR 2.1.198.

jointure *n.* Marriage portion ROM 5.3.297 *This is my daughter's jointure,* SHR 3.1.370.

joll See JOWL.

jollity *n.* Finery SON 66.3 *needy nothing trimm'd in jollity.*

jolly *adj.*

1 Arrogant, overbearing SHR 3.2.213 *a jolly surly groom.*

2 Amorous R3 4.3.43 *a jolly thriving wooer;* licentious CYM 1.6.67 *the jolly Britain.*

jolthead *n.* Blockhead SHR 4.1.166 *You heedless joltheads...!,* TGV 3.1.290.

jordan *n.* Chamber-pot 1H4 2.1.19 *ne'er a jordan,* 2H4 2.4.34.

journal *adj.* Daily MM 4.3.88 *Ere twice the sun hath made his journal greeting,* CYM 4.2.10.

journey-bated *adj.* Wearied with travel 1H4 4.3.26 *So are the horses...journey-bated.*

journeyman *n.* (used depreciatively) One who is not a master of his trade HAM 3.2.33 *I have thought some of Nature's journeymen had made men, and not made them well.*

joul See JOWL.

Jovial *adj.* Of Jupiter CYM 5.4.105 *Our Jovial star reign'd at his birth;* Jove-like, majestic CYM 4.2.311 *his Jovial face.*

jowl *vb.* Dash, knock AWW 1.3.54 *they may jowl horns together like any deer i' th' herd* (F1 *ioule*), HAM 5.1.76.

joy *n.*
1 *take joy* Be pleased or glad AYL 4.1.89 *I take some joy to say you are*, WT 5.1.80.
2 Source or object of gladness MND 2.1.27 *makes him all her joy*, AWW 1.3.73, TIT 1.1.382.
3 (term of endearment for sweetheart or child) Darling MND 4.1.4 *my gentle joy*, LR 1.1.82.
~ *vb.*
1 Gladden, delight R3 1.2.219 *it joys me*, CYM 5.5.424, PER 1.2.9.
2 Enjoy 2H6 3.2.365 *live thou to joy thy life*, R2 5.6.26, R3 2.4.59.

judge *vb.* Think, suppose TGV 1.2.136 *although you judge I wink*, TGV 3.1.25, 2H6 3.2.67.

judgement *n.*
1 *in my judgement* In my opinion, estimation TGV 4.4.151, R3 3.4.43; (with *to*) LR 1.4.58; (similarly) *in my judgement's place* SON 131.12 *Thy black is fairest in my judgement's place.*
2 Competent critic TRO 1.2.192 *He's one o' th' soundest judgements in Troy.*
3 *judgement by* (blunder by Evans) Governed by the judgement of WIV 3.1.95 *I'll be judgement by mine host of the Garter.*

judicious *adj.*
1 Judicial, proper to a court of law or legal tribunal COR 5.6.126 *His last offences...Shall have judicious hearing.*
2 Just LR 3.4.74 *Judicious punishment.*

Jug *n.* (pet form of, or familiar substitute for, the name of) Joan; (applied to a homely woman, a maidservant, or a mistress) LR 1.4.225 *Whoop, Jug! I love thee.*

juggle *vb.* Play tricks, cheat, deceive H8 1.3.1 *juggle Men into such strange mysteries*, 1H6 5.4.68, HAM 4.5.131.

juggler *n.* Deceiver, trickster, imposter MND 3.2.282 *you juggler,...You thief of love!*

juggling *n.* Trickery, deception TRO 2.3.71 *such juggling, and such knavery!*
~ *ppl. adj.* Beguiling, deceiving MAC 5.8.19 *be these juggling fiends no more believ'd*, JN 3.1.169.

jump *n.* Hazard, venture ANT 3.8.6 *Our fortune lies Upon this jump.*
~ *vb.*
1 Agree, tally, coincide MV 2.9.32 *I will not jump with common spirits*, SHR 1.1.190, 1H4 1.2.69.
2 Hazard, risk MAC 1.7.7 *We'ld jump the life to come*, CYM 5.4.182; (by extension) apply a desperate remedy to COR 3.1.154 *To jump a body with a dangerous physic.*
~ *adv.* Exactly, precisely, at the precise moment OTH 2.3.386 *bring him jump when he may Cassio*

find Soliciting his wife, HAM 1.1.65 (Ff *just*), HAM 5.2.375.

junket *n.* Sweetmeats SHR 3.2.248 *there wants no junkets at the feast.*

jure *vb.* (used contextually in connection with 'juror') Make jurors of (you) 1H4 2.2.91 *You are grandjurors, are ye? We'll jure ye, faith.*

just *n.* (var. of) Joust, tilting match R2 5.2.52 *Do these justs and triumphs hold?*
~ *vb.* Tilt, engage in a 'just' or tournament PER 2.1.110 *to just and tourney for her love.*

just *adj.*
1 Honourable, loyal JC 3.2.85 *faithful and just to me.*
2 Exact MV 4.1.327 *a just pound*, ADO 2.1.360, OTH 1.3.5.
3 Corresponding exactly in amount, equal 2H4 4.1.224 *just distance 'tween our armies* (i.e. halfway).
~ *adv.* (in replies and expressions of assent) Exactly so, just so, right! MM 5.1.202 *Why, just, my lord*, ADO 2.1.27, AYL 3.2.264.

just-borne *adj.* Carried in a just cause JN 2.1.345 *our just-borne arms.*

justice *n.* do (*a person*) *justice* Pledge in drinking OTH 2.3.87 *I am for it, lieutenant; and I'll do you justice.*

justicer *n.* Judge, magistrate LR 3.6.21 *most learned justicer* (Qq 1-2 *Iustice*), CYM 5.5.214.

justify *vb.*
1 Show to be righteous, innocent, or in the right, vindicate MM 5.1.159 *To justify this worthy nobleman, So vulgarly...accus'd*, WT 1.1.9, SON 139.1.
2 Prove, confirm, verify TMP 5.1.128 *justify you traitors*, H8 1.2.6, CYM 2.4.79.

justle *vb.* Jostle TMP 5.1.158 *justled from your senses.*

justly *adv.*
1 Uprightly OTH 4.2.173 *I do not find that thou deal'st justly with me.*
2 Exactly, precisely PER 5.1.88 *justly weigh'd*, AYL 1.2.244, ROM 3.2.78.

justness *n.* Rightfulness, propriety TRO 2.2.119 *We may not think the justness of each Such and no other than event doth form it.*

jut *vb.* Encroach R3 2.4.51 *tyranny begins to jut Upon the...throne* (Qq *iet*).

jutting-out *n.* Thrusting out TIM 1.2.231 *jutting-out of bums.*

jutty *n.* Projecting part of a wall or building MAC 1.6.6 *no jutty, frieze, Buttress, nor coign of vantage.*
~ *vb.* Project beyond, overhang H5 3.1.13 *As fearfully as doth a galled rock...jutty his confounded base.*

juvenal *n.* (affected or jocular) Youth, juvenile LLL 3.1.66 *A most acute juvenal*, MND 3.1.95, 2H4 1.2.19.

K

Kad *n.* (Evans' speech) God WIV 1.1.185 *So Kad udge me* (Q; F1 *got-udge*).

kam *adj.* Crooked, twisted, wrong COR 3.1.302 *This is clean kam.*

kate See CATES.

kecksy *n.* [dial.] Umbelliferous plant with hollow stem, hemlock-like weed (e.g. Cow Parsnip) H5 5.2.52 *But hateful docks, rough thistles, kecksies, burrs Losing both beauty and utility.*

keech *n.* Fat of a slaughtered animal rolled into a lump, lump of suet; (fig.) applied to a butcher or

members of his family H8 1.1.55 *I wonder That such a keech can with his very bulk Take up the rays o' th' beneficial sun.*

keel *vb.* Prevent (a pot) boiling over by stirring, skimming, or pouring in something cold LLL 5.2.920 *While greasy Joan doth keel the pot.*

keen *adj.* Bitter, sharp, severe JN 3.1.182 *cry thou amen To my keen curses*, MND 2.2.123, LLL 5.2.399.

keep *n.* Keeping, custody SHR 1.2.118 *For in Baptista's keep my treasure is.*

~ vb.

1 Dwell, lodge HAM 2.1.8 *Inquire me first what Danskers are in Paris,...and where they keep,* MV 3.3.19, TRO 4.5.278; *dwell in* ROM 3.2.74 *Did ever dragon keep up such a cave?,* CYM 3.3.1.

2 (refl.) Restrain oneself TGV 4.4.10 *O, 'tis a foul thing when a cur cannot keep himself in all companies!*

3 Continue to make, carry on ERR 3.1.61 *Who is that at the door that keeps all this noise?,* TN 2.3.72.

4 *keep the deck* Remain on deck CYM 1.3.10 *he did keep The deck; keep the wind* remain to windward of 3H6 3.2.14 *how true he keeps the wind!*

5 *kept short* Kept rigidly confined or under strict discipline HAM 4.1.18 *whose providence Should have kept short, restrain'd, and out of haunt This mad young man.*

keeper *n.*

1 Gaoler 1H6 2.5.17 *tell me, keeper, will my nephew come,* WT 2.2.1, R3 1.4.73.

2 One who tends the sick, nurse 2H4 1.1.143 *breaks like a fire Out of his keeper's arms.*

⋄ ROM 5.3.89 *How oft when men are at the point of death Have they been merry, which their keepers call A lightning before death!* could be either sense 1 or 2.

3 Guardian angel TMP 3.3.20 *Give us kind keepers, heavens!*

Keisar, keiser *n.* (old form of) Kaiser, emperor WIV 1.3.9 *Thou'rt an emperor—Caesar, Keiser, and Pheazar.*

ken *n.*

1 Distance that bounds the range of ordinary vision, esp. at sea (about 30 km) 2H4 4.1.149 *within a ken our army lies,* CYM 3.6.6.

2 Sight or view (of a place) 2H6 3.2.113 *For losing ken of Albion's wished coast,* LUC 1114.

~ vb.

1 See 2H6 3.2.101 *As far as I could ken thy chalky cliffs.*

2 Recognize TRO 4.5.14 *I ken the manner of his gait.*

3 Know (a person) WIV 1.3.37 *I ken the wight.*

Kendal green *n.* Kind of green woollen cloth made at Kendal in Westmoreland 1H4 2.4.222 *three misbegotten knaves in Kendal green.*

kennel *n.*[1] Street gutter, channel SHR 4.3.98 *Go hop me over every kennel home,* 2H6 4.1.71.

kennel *n.*[2] Pack (of dogs) 1H6 4.2.47 *Maz'd with a yelping kennel of French curs!*

~ vb. Lodge as in a kennel VEN 913 *Here kennell'd in a brake she finds a hound.*

kerchief *n.*

1 Cloth worn by women to cover the head WIV 4.2.71 *There is no woman's gown big enough for him; otherwise he might put on a hat, a muffler, and a kerchief, and so escape.*

2 Head-cloth worn in time of sickness; *wear a kerchief* be ill JC 2.1.315 *O, what a time...To wear a kerchief! Would you were not sick!*

kern, kerne *n.* (often used with contempt) Light-armed Irish foot-soldier MAC 1.2.30 *Compell'd these skipping kerns to trust their heels,* R2 2.1.156, 2H6 3.1.361.

kernel *n.* Pip seed AWW 2.3.259 *for picking a kernel out of a pomegranate,* TMP 2.1.93; used as type of something insignificant WT 1.2.159 *How like, methought, I was to this kernel.*

kersey *n.* Kind of coarse cloth MM 1.2.33 *I had as lief be a list of an English kersey as be pil'd...for a French velvet.*

~ adj.

1 Made of kersey SHR 3.2.67 *a kersey boot-hose on the other.*

2 (fig.) Plain LLL 5.2.413 *In russet yeas and honest kersey noes.*

keth, ke-tha See QUOTHA.

kettle *n.* (shortened form of) Kettle-drum HAM 5.2.275 *And let the kettle to the trumpet speak.*

key *n.*

1 (transf.) Control, mastery MAC 3.6.18 *had he Duncan's sons under his key,* 2H6 1.1.114, H5 2.2.96.

2 Tuning-key, the tool for tuning stringed instruments TMP 1.2.83 *having both the key Of officer and office, set all hearts...To what tune pleas'd his ear* (with quibble on sense 1).

key-cold *adj.* Stone-cold, cold in death R3 1.2.5 *Poor key-cold figure of a holy king,* LUC 1774.

kibe *n.* Chapped or ulcerated chilblain on the heel HAM 5.1.141 *the toe of the peasant comes so near the heel of the courtier, he galls his kibe,* TMP 2.1.276, LR 1.5.9.

kickshaws *n.* Fancy dish 2H4 5.1.28 *a joint of mutton, and any pretty little tiny kickshaws, tell William cook*; (fig.) trifle TN 1.3.115 *Art thou good at these kickshawses, knight?*

⋄ Corr. of Fr. 'quelque chose'.

kicksy-wicksy, kicky-wicky *n.* (jocular) Wife AWW 2.3.280 *That hugs his kicky-wicky here at home* (Ff 2–3 *kicksie wicksie*).

kid-fox *n.* Cub-fox ADO 2.3.42 *We'll fit the kid-fox with a pennyworth.*

⋄ Some edd. read *hid-fox* and propose allusion to the game of hide-and-seek. See HIDE sense 3.

kill *n.* Kiln WIV 3.3.79 *which is as hateful to me as the reek of a lime-kill.*

kill *vb.*

1 Destroy, break 3H6 2.5.87 *that kill mine eyes and heart!*

2 Subdue ADO 3.1.106 *Some Cupid kills with arrows.*

3 *kill up* Exterminate AYL 2.1.62 *To fright the animals and to kill them up.*

killen *vb.* (archaic infin. of) Kill PER 2. Gower.20 *though we strive To killen bad.*

kill-hole *n.* Fire-hole of a kiln, opening of an oven WT 4.4.245 *Is there not milking-time? when you are going to bed? or kill-hole? to whistle off these secrets?,* WIV 4.2.58.

kind *n.*

1 Natural disposition or character AYL 4.3.59 *thy youth and kind,* LUC 1147; *of it own kind of itself* TMP 2.1.164; *do his kind* act according to its nature ANT 5.2.263.

2 Nature in general or in the abstract, established order of things MV 1.3.85 *the deed of kind; by kind* by nature, naturally AWW 1.3.63 *Your cuckoo sings by kind,* TIT 2.1.116; *from kind* contrary to nature JC 1.3.64.

3 (qualified by a demonstrative or a possessive) Manner, way, fashion TGV 3.1.90 *in their silent kind,* R2 3.3.143, LR 4.6.162.

4 Race, class MND 4.1.119 *bred out of the Spartan kind,* TMP 5.1.23, TRO 5.4.14.

5 Family, ancestral stock PER 5.1.68 *Came of a gentle kind and noble stock.*

~ adj.

1 Natural, appropriate, proper ADO 1.1.26 *A kind overflow of kindness,* LUC 1423.

2 Favourable, gracious TMP 3.1.69 *kind event,* TIM 1.2.148, SON 10.11.

3 Affectionate, loving, fond ERR 1.1.43 *kind embracements,* AWW 5.3.310, HAM 4.5.147.

kindle *vb.*[1] Incite AYL 1.1.172 *I kindle the boy thither.*

kindle *vb.*[2] (used of rabbits) Be born, bring forth AYL 3.2.340 *dwell where she is kindled.*

kindless *adj.* Unnatural HAM 2.2.581 *kindless villain!*

kindly *adj.*
1 Innate, inherent TIM 2.2.217 *kindly warmth.*
2 Natural ADO 4.1.74 *fatherly and kindly power.*
3 Appropriate, fitting 1H6 3.1.131 *the Bishop hath a kindly gird,* AYL 2.3.53.
4 Benign ANT 2.5.78 *kindly creatures.*
5 Unfeigned 2H4 4.5.83 *Washing with kindly tears his gentle cheeks.*
~ *adv.*
1 Naturally (as of the same kin) TMP 5.1.24 *kindlier mov'd.*
2 Easily, spontaneously SHR Ind.1.66 *and do it kindly.*
3 Exactly ROM 2.4.55 *Thou hast most kindly hit it.*
4 By all means SHR Ind.1.15 *Let him come, and kindly.*

kindred, kinred *adj.*
1 Of or belonging to relatives R2 2.1.182 *His hands were guilty of no kinred blood,* R3 2.2.63.
2 Cognate JN 3.4.14 *any kindred action like to this?* (Ff *kindred-action*).

kine *n.* (pl.) [dial.] Cows 1H4 2.4.473 *Pharaoh's lean kine.*

king *vb.*
1 Make a king R2 5.5.36 *Then am I king'd again.*
2 Govern, rule H5 2.4.26 *she is so idly king'd,* JN 2.1.371 (F *Kings of our fears*).

kingdom *n.*
1 Sovereignty SON 64.6 *the hungry ocean gain Advantage on the kingdom of the shore.*
2 Microcosm 2H4 4.3.109 *the rest of this little kingdom,* JN 4.2.246.

kingdomed *adj.* Having the characteristics of a kingdom, like a kingdom TRO 2.3.175 *Kingdom'd Achilles in commotion rages.*

kirtle *n.* Woman's gown, skirt or petticoat 2H4 2.4.274 *What stuff wilt have a kirtle of?,* PP 19.11; *half kirtle* skirt 2H4 5.4.21 *I'll forswear half-kirtles.*

kiss *vb.* (said of balls in the game of bowls) Touch CYM 2.1.2 *when I kiss'd the jack.*

kissing-comfit *n.* Perfumed confection for sweetening the breath WIV 5.5.20 *let it...hail kissing-comfits.*

kit See KITE[2].

kitchen *vb.* Furnish with kitchen-fare ERR 5.1.416 *That kitchen'd me for you to-day at dinner.*

kite *n.*[1] (fig.) Rapacious person; (indefinitely as a term of reproach) LR 1.4.262 *Detested kite, thou liest,* ANT 3.13.89, 2H6 3.2.196.

kite *n.*[2] (shortened form of) Kitten H5 2.1.76 *the lazar kite of Cressid's kind* (i.e. whore; F4 *kit*).

knack *n.* Trifle, knick-knack MND 1.1.34 *Knacks, trifles, nosegays, sweetmeats,* SHR 4.3.67, WT 4.4.349.

knap *vb.*
1 Bite noisily, chew MV 3.1.9 *as lying a gossip...as ever knapp'd ginger.*
2 Strike, hit LR 2.4.123 *she knapp'd 'em...with a stick.*

knave *n.* Boy employed as a servant, male servant in general WIV 3.5.98 *a couple of Ford's knaves, his hinds,* LR 1.4.94, 2H4 1.2.72; (opposed to knight) TN 2.3.66 *To call thee knave, knight,* JN 1.1.243.

knavery *n.*
1 (pl.) Roguish tricks H5 4.7.49 *He was full of jests, and gipes, and knaveries, and mocks,* MND 3.2.346, AWW 3.3.12.
2 (nonce use for rhyme) Tricks of dress or ornament SHR 4.3.58 *amber bracelets, beads, and all this knav'ry.*

knee *n.* Kneeling, prostration, curtsey TIM 4.3.37 *give them title, knee, and approbation,* R2 2.3.83,
OTH 2.1.84.
⇨ See also CAP-AND-KNEE.
~ *vb.* Kneel before, bend the knee before LR 2.4.214 *To knee his throne.*

knit *n.* Knitted work, texture SHR 4.1.92 *their garters of an indifferent knit.*
~ *vb.* Tie in or with a knot JN 4.1.42 *I knit my handkercher about your brows*; (with *up*) ROM 4.2.24 *I'll have this knot knit up*; (fig.) bind or unite closely MND 1.1.172 *that which knitteth souls*; (with *up*) TMP 3.3.89 *all knit up In their distractions.*

knob *n.* Pimple H5 3.6.102 *His face is all bubukles, and whelks, and knobs.*

knock *vb.* knock it Strike up H8 1.4.108 *Let the music knock it.*

knoll *vb.* Ring, toll AYL 2.7.114 *bells have knoll'd to church*; MAC 5.9.16, 2H4 1.1.103 (Q *tolling*).

knot *n.*
1 Folding (of the arms) TMP 1.2.224 *His arms in this sad knot,* TIT 3.2.4.
2 Flower-bed laid out in fanciful or intricate design; (hence) any laid-out garden plot R2 3.4.46 *Her knots disordered.*
3 Lump or knob TRO 5.3.33 *Let grow thy sinews till their knots be strong.*
4 Group, band, company JC 3.1.117 *So often shall the knot of us be call'd,* WIV 4.2.118, R3 3.1.182.
~ *vb.* Gather into a knot or cluster OTH 4.2.62 *for foul toads To knot and gender in!*

knot-grass *n.* Common weed, Polygonum aviculare, an infusion of which was formerly supposed to stunt the growth MND 3.2.329 *You minimus, of hind'ring knot-grass made.*

knotted *adj.*
1 Laid out in intricate designs LLL 1.1.246 *thy curious-knotted garden.*
2 Gnarled TRO 1.3.50 *knotted oaks.*

knotty *adj.* Gnarled JC 1.3.6 *knotty oaks.*

knotty-pated *adj.* Thick-headed 1H4 2.4.227 *thou knotty-pated fool.*

know *n.* See KNOWING sense 1.
~ *vb.*
1 Admit the claims or authority of JC 4.3.136 *I'll know his humour, when he knows his time.*
2 Be acquainted ANT 2.6.83 *You and I have known, sir,* CYM 1.4.35.
3 more known Better acquainted WT 4.4.66 *better friends, more known.*
4 be not you know on't Have no knowledge of it OTH 3.3.319 (Ff *acknown(e)*).
5 know for Be aware of 2H4 1.2.5 *moe diseases than he knew for.*
6 know of Ascertain from MM 1.4.8 *know his business of him,* AYL 4.3.95, H5 3.6.115.

knowing *n.*
1 Knowledge HAM 5.2.44 *on the view and knowing of these contents* (Ff *know*), TIM 3.2.67, CYM 1.4.29.
2 Experience MAC 2.4.4 *this sore night Hath trifled former knowings.*

knowingly *adv.* From experience CYM 3.3.46 *Did you but know the city's usuries, And felt them knowingly,* AWW 1.3.250.

knowledge *n.*
1 Consciousness (of what one is) JN 5.2.35 *The knowledge of thyself,* LR 4.6.284, ANT 2.2.91.
2 Carnal knowledge, sexual intimacy (with) CYM 2.4.51 *The knowledge of your mistress.*
3 Notice HAM 2.1.13 *Take...some distant knowledge of him.*
4 Personal acquaintance MM 3.2.150 *Love talks with better knowledge,* AYL 1.2.285.

L

la *interj.*

1 Exclamation used to introduce or accompany a conventional phrase or an address, or to call attention to an emphatic statement WIV 1.1.85 *I thank you always with my heart, la! with my heart,* TRO 3.1.75; *la you* look you TN 3.4.100 *La you, and you speak ill of the devil, how he takes it at heart!,* WT 2.3.50.

2 Repeated, as an expression of derision TIM 3.1.21 *La, la, la, la! 'nothing doubting', says he?*

la fin couronne les oeuvres [Fr.] The end crowns the works 2H6 5.2.28.

label *n.*

1 Slip of paper CYM 5.5.430 *I found This label on my bosom.*

2 Slip of paper, parchment or material for appending a seal to a document; (fig.) ROM 4.1.57 *And ere this hand, by thee to Romeo's seal'd, Shall be the label to another deed.*

~ *vb.* Add as a codicil TN 1.5.246 *It shall be inventoried, and every particle and utensil labell'd to my will.*

labour *n.* Trouble or pains taken TGV 2.1.133 *take it for your labour,* R2 5.6.41, H5 3.6.158.

~ *vb.*

1 (trans.) Endeavour to bring about, strive for R3 1.4.246 *That he would labour my delivery,* SHR 1.1.118; perform ADO 5.1.283 *if your love Can labour aught in sad invention.*

2 (intr.) Endeavour, strive ERR 3.2.37 *Against my soul's pure truth why labour you, To make it wander...?*

3 Travail, suffer the pains of childbirth; (fig.) OTH 2.1.127 *my Muse labours, And thus she is deliver'd,* TIM 3.4.8; (also said of what is 'brought forth') LLL 5.2.520 *When great things labouring perish in their birth.*

laboured *adj.*

1 Oppressed with labour or pain JN 2.1.232 *whose labour'd spirits, Forewearied in this action.*

2 Highly wrought, perfected PER 2.3.17 *you are her labour'd scholar.*

laboursome *adj.* Laborious, elaborate CYM 3.4.164 *Your laboursome and dainty trims,* HAM 1.2.59.

labras *n.* (pl.) [blunder for L. 'labra'] Lips WIV 1.1.163 *Word of denial in thy labras here!*

lace *n.* Cord for fastening up the bodice, etc. WT 3.2.173 *O, cut my lace, lest my heart, cracking it, Break too!,* R3 4.1.33, ANT 1.3.71.

~ *vb.* Trim with ornamental braid ADO 3.4.19 *lac'd with silver;* (fig.) streak or stripe with colour CYM 2.2.22 *white and azure lac'd With blue of heaven's own tinct,* ROM 3.5.8, MAC 2.3.112; (hence) adorn SON 67.4 *lace itself with his society?*

laced mutton See MUTTON.

lack *vb.*

1 Be wanting TIT 4.2.44 *Here lacks but your mother for to say amen,* HAM 1.4.3, HAM 1.5.186.

2 (with cannot) Do or go without ADO 4.1.179 *Alas, dear love, I cannot lack thee two hours!;* (hence) perceive the absence of, miss MAC 3.4.83 *Your noble friends do lack you,* COR 4.1.15, ANT 1.4.44.

~ in combination: Wanting, lacking.

lack-beard ADO 5.1.192. **lack-brain** 1H4 2.3.16. **lack-linen** (i.e. shirtless) 2H4 2.4.124. **lack-love** MND 2.2.77. **lack-lustre** AYL 2.7.21.

'lack *interj.* (short for) Alack.

lackey *n.* Footman AWW 4.3.290 *he outruns any lackey,* SHR 3.2.65.

~ *vb.* Follow closely (like a lackey) ANT 1.4.46 *Goes to and back, lackeying the varying tide* (Ff *lacking*).

lacquey (var. of) LACKEY.

lade *vb.* Empty, e.g. by baling 3H6 3.2.139 *he'll lade it dry.*

lading *n.* Cargo MV 3.1.3 *a ship of rich lading,* TIT 1.1.72, PER 1.2.49.

lady *n.*

1 Wife WIV 3.3.51 *I would make thee my lady,* MND 2.1.64, 2H6 2.1.175.

2 (usu. *our Lady*, occas. *God's lady*) The Virgin Mary 1H6 1.2.74 *Heaven and our Lady gracious hath it pleas'd,* H5 2.1.36.

3 Proper name given to female hounds 1H4 3.1.235 *Lady, my brach,* LR 1.4.112.

4 *lady* walled about with diamonds Brooch or pendant, often ornamented with a minute nude figure set in enamelled work studded with precious stones, and bearing on the obverse side a miniature portrait LLL 5.2.3.

~ *adj.*

1 Feminine, ladylike ANT 5.2.165 *I some lady trifles have reserv'd,* 1H4 1.3.46.

2 High-born, of high rank WT 1.2.44 *I love thee not a jar o' th' clock behind What lady she her lord.*

ladybird *n.* Sweetheart ROM 1.3.3 *What, lamb! What, ladybird!*

lady-smock *n.* A flower, possibly cuckoo-flower or stitchwort LLL 5.2.895 *And lady-smocks all silver-white And cuckoo-buds of yellow hue.*

lag *n.* Lowest class TIM 3.6.81 *together with the common lag of people.*

▷ F *legge;* Rowe *lag.*

~ *adj.* Late R3 2.1.91 *came too lag to see him buried;* *lag of* behind, later than LR 1.2.6 *I am...Lag of a brother?*

lag-end *n.* Latter part, fag-end 1H4 5.1.24 *the lag-end of my life,* H8 1.3.35.

lagging *ppl. adj.* Tardy R2 1.3.214 *Four lagging winters,* LUC 1335.

lakin *n.* (var. of) Ladykin [diminutive of LADY] MND 3.1.13 *By'r lakin,* TMP 3.3.1.

lambkin *n.* (diminutive of) Lamb; (fig., term of endearment) 2H4 5.3.116 *thy tender lambkin now is king,* H5 2.1.127.

lamentable *adj.* Of sorrow, sad JN 3.1.22 *that lamentable rheum.*

lamp *n.*

1 Torch TMP 4.1.23 *As Hymen's lamps shall light you.*

2 Eye ERR 5.1.316 *Yet hath...My wasting lamps some fading glimmer left,* VEN 489.

lampass *n.* Disease in horses, consisting in a swelling of the fleshy lining of the roof of the mouth behind the front teeth SHR 3.2.51 *his horse...troubled with the lampass.*

lance, lanch *vb.*

1 Pierce LR 2.1.52 *With his prepared sword he... lanc'd mine arm* (Qq *lancht, launcht;* Ff *latch'd*), R3 4.4.225.

2 Cut surgically R2 1.3.303 *lanceth not the sore* (Ff, Q5; Q1 *launceth,* Qq 2–4 *la(u)ncheth*), ANT 5.1.36.

land *n.* (fig.) Human body JN 4.2.245 *this fleshly land,* LUC 439.

land-carrack See CARRACK.

land-damn *vb.* (?) Give (one) hell on earth, berate sharply WT 2.1.143 *I would land-damn him.*

land-fish *n.* (lit.) Fish that lives on land; (hence)

unnatural creature TRO 3.3.263 *a very land-fish, languageless, a monster.*

land-raker See FOOT-LAND-RAKER.

land-service *n.* Military, as opposed to naval, service 2H4 1.2.135 *the laws of this land-service*, WT 3.3.94.

lane of children See LAW.

language *n.*
1 Power of speech TMP 2.2.83 *here is that which will give language to you, cat.*
2 Ability to speak a foreign tongue AWW 4.1.70 *I shall lose my life for want of language.*

languish *n.* Languishment, lingering disease or suffering ANT 5.2.42 *death...That rids our dogs of suffering*, ROM 1.2.48.
~ *vb.* Lose in a wasting disease CYM 1.1.156 *let her languish A drop of blood a day.*

languishing *n.* Lingering disease AWW 1.3.229 *cure the desperate languishings.*
~ *ppl. adj.* Lingering CYM 1.5.9 *a languishing death.*

languishment *n.* Distress, pining LUC 1130 *As the dank earth weeps at thy languishment*, TIT 2.1.110.

languor *n.* Sorrow, pining TIT 3.1.13 *My heart's deep languor.*

lank *vb.* Grow thin, become shrunken ANT 1.4.71 *that thy cheek So much as lank'd not.*

lanthorn *n.* Window-turret, tower-room glassed on all sides ROM 5.3.84 *A grave? O no, a lanthorn.*

lap *vb.* Wrap, clothe R3 2.1.116 *he did lap me Even in his own garments*, MAC 1.2.54, CYM 5.5.360.

lapis *n.* [L.] Stone WIV 4.1.31 *What is lapis, William?*

lapse *n.* Moral slip AWW 2.3.163 *the careless lapse Of youth and ignorance.*
~ *vb.*
1 Fall into sin or error, slip COR 5.2.19 *all the size that verity Would without lapsing suffer*, CYM 3.6.12.
2 Fall away HAM 3.4.107 *laps'd in time and passion* (i.e. 'having suffered time to go by and passion to cool' Johnson).
3 Apprehend TN 3.3.36 *if I be lapsed in this place I shall pay dear.*
▷ *Lapse* could be connected here with 'laps', with the sense of 'fall into the lap of, come within the power of '.

lapwing *n.* Peewit; always with allusion to its habits, e.g. its wiliness in drawing away a visitor from its nest, its supposed practice when newly hatched of running about with its head in the shell ERR 4.2.27 *Far from her nest the lapwing cries away*, HAM 5.2.185 *This lapwing runs away with the shell on his head*, ADO 3.1.24.

lard *vb.*
1 Fatten 1H4 2.2.109 *Falstaff...lards the lean earth as he walks along*; enrich (with blood) H5 4.6.8 *doth he lie, Larding the plain.*
2 (fig.) Intersperse (speech) WIV 4.6.14 *The mirth whereof so larded with my matter*, TRO 5.1.57, HAM 5.2.20.
3 Garnish HAM 4.5.38 *Larded all with sweet flowers*, H5 4.6.8.

large *n.*
1 Largeness, amplitude, great size JN 2.1.101 *This little abstract doth contain that large Which died in Geffrey.*
2 *at large* In full size, on a large scale AYL 5.4.169 *A land itself at large*, TRO 1.3.346; at length, in full, in detail TGV 3.2.61 *Where you with Silvia may confer at large*, H5 1.1.78, 1H6 1.1.109; as a whole, in general LLL 1.1.155 *So to the laws at large I write my name*, H5 2.4.121.

~ *adj.*
1 Extensive, far-reaching JN 1.1.105 *Large lengths of seas and shores*, TMP 1.2.110, SON 135.5.
2 Liberal, generous, lavish WT 4.4.147 *Your praises are too large*, LR 1.1.52, 2H6 1.1.111.
3 Unrestrained MAC 3.4.11 *Be large in mirth*; licentious, gross ADO 2.3.198 *some large jests*, ROM 2.4.97, ANT 3.6.93.

large-handed *ppl. adj.* Grasping TIM 4.1.11 *Large-handed robbers your grave masters are.*

largely *adv.*
1 Bountifully, copiously, abundantly WIV 2.2.199 *have given largely to many*, 2H4 1.3.12, PER 1.4.53.
2 At length, in full ADO 5.4.69 *I 'll tell you largely of fair Hero's death.*

largess *n.* Liberal bestowal of a gift or gifts MAC 2.1.14 *Sent forth great largess to your offices*, SHR 1.2.150, H5 4.Ch.43; lavish expenditure R2 1.4.44 *with too great a court And liberal largess.*

laroon, laroone, larron *n.* Thief, robber WIV 1.4.68 *vat is in my closet? Villainy! laroon!*

larum, 'larum See ALARM, ALARUM.

larum-bell See ALARM-BELL.

'las *interj.* (aphetic form of) Alas OTH 5.1.111 *'Las, what is the matter* (Q1; Ff *Alas*).

lass-lorn *adj.* Forsaken by one's sweetheart TMP 4.1.68 *the dismissed bachelor...Being lass-lorn.*

last *n.*
1 Conclusion, end TMP 1.2.170 *hear the last of our sea-sorrow*, JC 3.2.12, ANT 5.2.335; *try the last* fight to the finish MAC 5.8.32; *at the last* at the end, in the end, at last SHR 5.1.127, COR 5.6.37; *in the last* in the end, finally COR 5.6.41.
2 Last time AWW 5.3.79 *The last that e'er I took her leave at court.*
3 Last breath R2 2.1.1 *I may breathe my last*, TIM 3.6.90, LC 168.
~ *adj. last morning* Yesterday morning TGV 2.1.79.

lasting *ppl. adj.* Everlasting TMP 5.1.208 *With gold on lasting pillars*, TN 1.1.31, SON 122.2.

latch *vb.*
1 Catch LR 2.1.52 *With his prepared sword he... latch'd mine arm* (Qq *la(u)ncht*; see LANCE, LANCH).
2 Catch sight or sound of MAC 4.3.195 *Where hearing should not latch them*, SON 113.6.
3 Catch and hold fast as by a charm or spell MND 3.2.36 *hast thou yet latch'd the Athenian's eyes With the love-juice...?*
▷ Possibly var. of 'leach' i.e. water, wet.

late *adj.*
1 Recent in date LLL 1.1.11 *Our late edict shall strongly stand in force*; recently appointed, made, performed, completed H5 2.2.61 *Who are the late commissioners?*, H5 2.4.31, MAC 1.6.19.
2 *latest* Last 3H6 2.1.108 *breath'd his latest gasp.*
~ *adv.* Recently, lately ANT 4.1.13 *those that serv'd Mark Antony but late*, TN 5.1.215, R3 3.1.99; (with ppl. adj.) 1H6 3.2.82 *late-betrayed*, TIT 1.1.184, VEN 818.

lated *ppl. adj.* Belated MAC 3.3.6 *Now spurs the lated traveller apace*, ANT 3.11.3.

late-walking *n.* Keeping late hours WIV 5.5.144 *This is enough to be the decay of lust and late-walking.*

lath *n.*
1 The material of a counterfeit weapon ROM 1.4.5 *no Cupid...Bearing a Tartar's painted bow of lath.*
▷ See also DAGGER.
2 (fig., contemptuously) Sword TIT 2.1.41 *have your lath glued within your sheath, Till you know better how to handle it.*

latten *adj.* Mixed metal of yellow colour, identical with or closely resembling brass WIV 1.1.162 *this latten bilbo* (F1 *Latine*).

latter *adj.* Last 1H6 2.5.38 *And in his bosom spend my latter gasp*, H5 4.1.137, MV 1.1.151.

lattice *n.* red lattice Window of lattice-work painted red (the sign of an alehouse) 2H4 2.2.80 *through a red lattice*; (hence, attrib.) *red-lattice phrases* tavern talk WIV 2.2.27.

laud *n.* Hymn HAM 4.7.177 *snatches of old lauds* (Q1; Ff *tunes*).

laughter *n.*
1 Subject for merriment JC 4.3.114 *Hath Cassius liv'd To be but mirth and laughter to his Brutus?*, 1H4 2.2.95.
2 A laugh TMP 2.1.33 *The wager?—A laughter* (prob. also a pun on the dial. sense 'the whole number of eggs laid by a fowl before it is ready to sit').

launce See LANCE, LANCH.

launch See LANCE, LANCH.

laund, lawnd *n.* Glade 3H6 3.1.2 *through this laund anon the deer will come*, VEN 813.

laundry *n.* (blunder for) Laundress WIV 1.2.4 *his dry nurse—or his cook—or his laundry.*

laurel *adj.* Wreathed with laurel ANT 1.3.100 *Upon your sword Sit laurel victory* (F1 *lawrell*; Ff 2-4 *Lawrell'd*).

Laus Deo, bone, intelligo [L.] Praise to God, good sir, I understand LLL 5.1.27.

lave *vb.* Wash, bathe SHR 2.1.348 *Basins and ewers to lave her dainty hands*, TIT 4.2.103; (fig.) keep clean or unsullied MAC 3.2.33 *we Must lave our honours in these flattering streams.*

lavish *adj.* Unrestrained, wild, insolent, licentious MAC 1.2.57 *Curbing his lavish spirit*, 2H4 4.4.64.

lavishly *adv.* Wildly, excessively 2H4 4.2.57 *And some about him have too lavishly Wrested his meaning and authority.*

lavolt, lavolta *n.* Lively dance for two persons TRO 4.4.86 *Nor heel the high lavolt*, H5 3.5.33.

law *n.*
1 What the law awards 2H6 1.3.196 *Let him have all the rigour of the law.*
2 Justice ERR 4.1.83 *I shall have law in Ephesus.*
3 System of divine commands and of penalties imposed for disobedience contained in Holy Scripture LLL 4.3.361 *It is religion to be thus forsworn: For charity itself fulfils the law*, JN 2.1.180, R3 1.4.196.
4 *law of writ* HAM 2.2.401 see WRIT.
5 *law of children* JC 3.1.39: F1 *lane*, a possible var. pronunciation of 'line' (i.e. rule, canon, precept).

law *interj.* La LLL 5.2.414 *so God help me law!*

law-day *n.* Day for the sitting of a court of law, session of such a court OTH 3.3.140 *uncleanly apprehensions Keep leets and law-days.*

lay *n.* Wager 2H6 5.2.27 *My soul and body on the action both!—A dreadful lay!*, OTH 2.3.324, CYM 1.4.147.
~ *vb.*
1 Bury TN 2.4.52 *And in sad cypress let me be laid*, H8 4.2.22, CYM 4.2.233.
2 Beset with traps 2H6 4.10.4 *all the country is laid for me.*
3 Lie LC 4 *And down I laid to list the sad-tun'd tale.*
4 Put (in confinement, prison) H8 5.3.78 *I'll lay ye all By th' heels* (i.e. put in the stocks), TN 4.2.29, R3 1.3.325 (Ff *cast*).
5 Stake, wager LLL 1.1.308 *I'll lay my head to any good man's hat*, HAM 5.2.102, TRO 3.1.87.
~ in combination
lay…aboard 1 Place one's ship alongside another in order to attack or board it 2H6 4.1.25 *laying the prize aboard.* 2 *lay knife aboard* Make an attack;

(fig.) press one's claim ROM 2.4.202 *Paris, that would fain lay knife aboard.* **lay a hold** See A-HOLD. **lay apart, aside** Put away from one AYL 4.3.44 *thy godhead laid apart*, R2 2.2.3, WT 4.2.51. **lay by** 1 Put aside or away from one, waive H5 1.2.276 *I have laid by my majesty*, ADO 5.1.64, TRO 2.3.79. 2 Stop, come to a standstill 1H4 1.2.36 *got with swearing 'Lay by'.* **lay down** 1 Calculate, formulate H5 1.2.137 *lay down our proportions*, ADO 4.1.236, 2H4 1.3.35. 2 Wager OTH 4.2.13 *Lay down my soul at stake.* 3 Bring to bed of a child, make pregnant H8 1.3.40 *a speeding trick to lay down ladies.* **lay for** Lie in wait for; (fig.) strive to captivate TIM 3.5.114 *I'll cheer up My discontented troops, and lay for hearts.* **lay forth** 1 Bring out and display SHR 4.3.62 *Lay forth the gown.* 2 Dress in graveclothes and prepare for burial H8 4.2.171 *Embalm me, Then lay me forth.* **lay home to** Berate, attack HAM 3.4.1 *Look you lay home to him.* **lay it on** Do it in good style TMP 3.2.151 *I would I could see this taborer; he lays it on*, WT 4.3.40. **lay off** Steer away from shore TMP 1.1.50 *Set her two courses off to sea again! Lay her off.* **lay on** 1 (always fig.) Apply a coat of (paint) TN 1.5.240 *beauty…whose red and white Nature's own…hand laid on*, AYL 1.2.106, WT 5.3.49. 2 Hit hard TRO 1.2.207 *Look you what hacks are on his helmet!…there's laying on*, MAC 5.8.33. **lay out** Expend CYM 2.3.87 *You lay out too much pains For purchasing but trouble*, TN 3.4.202 (F *laid…on't*). **lay to** Bring into action TMP 4.1.250 *lay to your fingers.* **lay up** 1 Put away 2H4 5.1.85 *like a wet cloak ill laid up.* 2 Incapacitate AYL 1.3.7 *Then there were two cousins laid up, when the one should be lam'd with reasons.*

layer-up *n.* Storer, preserver H5 5.2.230 *old age, that ill layer-up of beauty.*

lazar *n.* Poor person afflicted with a loathsome, infectious disease, esp. a leper H5 1.1.15 *to relief of lazars*, TRO 2.3.33, HAM 1.5.72.
~ *adj.* Leprous H5 2.1.76 *the lazar kite of Cressid's kind.*

lazy *adj.* Sluggish MND 5.1.41 *How shall we beguile The lazy time…?*, AYL 3.2.304, 3H6 2.1.130.
~ *adv.* Sluggishly, slowly ROM 2.2.31 *the lazy puffing clouds.*

le cheval volant chez les narines de feu [Fr.] The winged horse with fiery nostrils H5 3.7.14.
⬦ Some edd. read 'qui a' instead of *chez*.

le chien est retourné à son propre vomissement, et la truie lavée au bourbier [Fr.] The dog has returned to his own vomit, and the washed sow to the mire (2 Pet. 2.22) H5 3.7.64.

lea *n.* Arable land TIM 4.3.193 *Dry up thy marrows, vines, and plough-torn leas*, TMP 4.1.60, H5 5.2.44.

lead *n.*
1 Bullets, shot LLL 3.1.57 *As swift as lead, sir*, 1H4 5.3.34.
2 (pl.) Flat, lead-covered roof R3 3.7.55 *Go, go up to the leads.*
3 The lead lining of a coffin; (hence) coffin 1H6 1.1.64 *burst his lead and rise from death*, PP 20.24, MV 2.7.49.

lead *vb.*
1 Carry AWW 4.3.266 *h'as led the drum before the English tragedians*; (fig.) MV 4.1.18 *thou but leadest this fashion of thy malice To the last hour of act*, TN 1.5.242.
2 Take the first steps in (a dance with a person) AWW 2.3.43 *he's able to lead her a coranto*, H8 1.4.107.
3 Go forward TMP 2.1.323 *Lead off this ground*, ANT 2.6.81, CYM 4.4.53.

~ in combination

lead away Lead astray, seduce Son 96.11 *How many gazers mightst thou lead away.* **lead on** 1 Conduct Cor 1.2.15 *These three lead on this preparation Whither 'tis bent.* 2 Entice or beguile into going to greater lengths Wiv 2.1.95 *let's...lead him on with a fine-baited delay.*

leaden *adj.*

1 Inert, sluggish, spiritless Ven 34 *leaden appetite,* 1H6 4.6.12, LLL 4.3.318.

2 Depressing Oth 3.4.177 *leaden thoughts.*

3 (of sleep) Heavy, dulling JC 4.3.268 *O murd'rous slumber! Layest thou thy leaden mace upon my boy...?,* MND 3.2.365, Luc 124.

4 *leaden dagger* Ineffectual weapon 1H4 2.4.381 *Thy state is taken for a joint-stool, thy golden sceptre for a leaden dagger.*

leading *n.*

1 Command H5 4.3.131 *I beg The leading of the vaward,* R3 5.3.297.

2 Direction Cor 4.5.137 *The leading of thine own revenges,* Luc 436.

3 Leadership, generalship 1H4 4.3.17 *men of such great leading as you are.*

league *n.*[1] Measure of distance, about five kilometres JC 3.1.286 *within seven leagues of Rome,* Err 1.1.62, Tmp 1.2.145.

league *n.*[2] Alliance, friendship, truce R3 1.3.280 *In sign of league and amity with thee,* Wiv 3.2.25, Tit 5.3.23.

~ *vb.*

1 Join in a league or alliance, ally Oth 2.3.218 *If partially affin'd, or leagu'd in office* (Ff, Qq *league*).

2 (fig.) Cross Cym 4.2.213 *His arms thus leagu'd.*

leaguer *n.* Camp AWW 3.6.26 *he is carried into the leaguer of the adversaries.*

leak *vb.* Make water 1H4 2.1.20 *we leak in your chimney.*

lean *vb.*

1 Defer Cym 1.1.78 *'twere good You lean'd unto his sentence.*

2 Rely, depend *on* Tro 3.3.85 *The love that lean'd on them,* MM 2.1.48 (with quibble), 2H4 1.1.164.

lean *adj.* (fig.)

1 Poor, meagre, mean Err 3.2.92 *I have but lean luck,* Ant 2.2.19, TN 3.4.344.

2 Barren 2H4 4.3.119 *like lean, sterile, and bare land,* 1H4 2.2.109.

lean-witted *adj.* Poor in intellect R2 2.1.115 *A lunatic lean-witted fool.*

leaping-house *n.* Brothel 1H4 1.2.9 *unless...clocks* [*were*] *the tongues of bawds, and dials the signs of leaping-houses.*

leaping time *n.* Youth Cym 4.2.200 *To have turn'd my leaping time into a crutch.*

learn *vb.* Teach H5 3.6.71 *they will learn you by rote,* TGV 2.6.13, Ham 5.2.9; (*refl.*) Rom 4.2.17 *Where I have learnt me to repent the sin*; (hence) inform (of something) Tro 2.1.21 *learn me the proclamation.*

learning *n.*

1 Lesson, instruction Cym 1.1.43 *Puts to him all the learnings that his time Could make him the receiver of,* Son 77.4.

2 Information Ant 2.2.47 *have my learning from some true reports.*

3 Acquirement, accomplishment Ham 5.2.35 *labour'd much How to forget that learning.*

learning-place *n.* Place of instruction AWW 1.1.177 *The court's a learning-place.*

lease *n.*

1 *in lease* On a lease Son 13.5 *So should that beauty which you hold in lease Find no determination.*

2 *lease of nature* Term of the natural life Mac 4.1.99 *Shall live the lease of nature.*

leash *n.* Set of three 1H4 2.4.7 *I am sworn brother to a leash of drawers.*

▷ Three was the usual number of hounds coupled in one leash.

~ *vb.* Couple together (in a set of three) H5 Prol.7 *at his heels, Leash'd in like hounds, should famine, sword, and fire Crouch.*

leasing *n.* Lying TN 1.5.97 *Mercury indue thee with leasing*; lie Cor 5.2.22 *I...Have (almost) stamp'd the leasing* (i.e. given the stamp of truth to a lie).

least *n. in the least* At the lowest estimate Lr 1.1.191 *What, in the least, Will you require in present dower with her...?*; in the smallest degree Lr 2.4.141 *in the least Would fail her obligation.*

leather-coat *n.* Russet apple 2H4 5.3.41 *There's a dish of leather-coats for you.*

leathren *adj.* Leathern MND 2.2.4 *their leathren wings* (F1).

leave *n.*

1 Permission Err 1.1.35 *I'll utter what my sorrow gives me leave,* 3H6 3.2.34, Ven 568.

2 Permission to depart WT 2.1.124 *My women, come, you have leave; take leave* bid farewell AWW 5.3.79 *The last that e'er I took my leave at court.*

▷ Used in polite forms of (1) bidding farewell: MV 2.4.15 *By your leave, sir.—Whither goest thou?,* Wiv 3.2.28; (2) dismissal: Rom 1.3.7 *Nurse, give leave a while,* Jn 1.1.230, 3H6 3.2.33.

3 Departure Mac 4.3.237 *Our lack is nothing but our leave*; leave-taking Ham 1.3.54 *Occasion smiles upon a second leave.*

leave *vb.*

1 Abandon, forsake, give up Ham 3.4.91 *such black and grained spots As will not leave their tinct,* TGV 5.4.138, MV 5.1.172.

2 Stop, discontinue, 'leave off' 2H4 4.3.71 *Now, have you left pursuit?,* MM 4.2.6, Cor 4.1.1.

3 Break off (in a narrative, reading or conversation) Cym 2.2.4 *Fold down the leaf where I have left,* Shr 3.1.24, Ham 2.1.51.

4 Die Ham 5.2.224 *no man...knows what is't to leave betimes.*

5 *leave out* Except, exclude Cym 2.4.85 *Motion and breath let out.*

6 *leave on the left hand* See LEFT HAND.

leaven *n. lay the leaven on* (fig.) Taint Cym 3.4.62.

leavened *ppl. adj.* (fig.) Well-considered MM 1.1.51 *a leaven'd and prepared choice.*

leavy *adj.* Leafy, abounding in foliage Ado 2.3.73 *Since summer first was leavy.*

lecture *n.*

1 Discourse given before an audience for the purpose of instruction Cor 2.3.235 *Say we read lectures to you, How youngly he began to serve his country,* AYL 3.2.347.

2 Course of instruction, lesson Shr 3.1.23 *His lecture will be done ere you have tun'd,* Shr 3.1.24; (fig.) instructive example Luc 618 *Must he in thee read lectures of such shame?* (F1 *lector*).

ledger See LEIGER.

leer *n.* Complexion, countenance AYL 4.1.67 *he hath a Rosalind of a better leer than you,* Tit 4.2.119.

leese *vb.* Lose Son 5.14 *But flowers distill'd...Leese but their show.*

leet *n.* Special court of record which the lords of certain manors were empowered to hold yearly or half-yearly Shr Ind.2.87 *present her at the leet,* Oth 3.3.140 (used with tautology).

left hand *n. phr. leave on the left hand* Ignore, disregard Wiv 2.2.24.

leg *n.*[1] Obeisance made by drawing back one leg and bending the other AWW 2.2.10 *He that cannot make a leg...were not for the court,* 1H4 2.4.388, Cor 2.1.69.

leg *n.*² See LAG.

legative *adj.* Pertaining to a legate, legatine H8 3.2.339 *By your power legative within this kingdom* (F1).

lege, 'lege *vb.* (aphetic form of 'allege') Bring forward SHR 1.2.28 *what he 'leges in Latin.*

lege, domine [L.] Read, sir LLL 4.2.104.

legend *n.* (misused for) Legion WIV 1.3.53 *a legend of angels* (Ff, Q3; Q1 *legians,* Q2 *legions*).

legerity *n.* Nimbleness H5 4.1.23 *move With casted sloth and fresh legerity.*

legion *n.*
1 With the ancient Romans, a body of infantry of about six thousand men JC 4.3.76 *to pay my legions;* (hence) any military force JN 2.1.59 *To land his legions,* H5 2.2.124.
2 Host, esp. of devils TMP 3.3.103 *But one fiend at a time, I'll fight their legions o'er;* (treated as a proper noun to denote a compound of all devils) TN 3.4.85 *If all the devils of hell be drawn in little, and Legion himself possess'd him* (with allusion to Mark 5:9).

legitimate *adj.* Logical, logically inferred TN 3.2.14 *I will prove it legitimate.*

legitimation *n.* Legitimacy JN 1.1.248 *Legitimation, name, and all is gone.*

leiger, lieger *n.* Ambassador, representative or agent MM 3.1.58 *Where you shall be an everlasting leiger,* CYM 1.5.80.
⟡ F1 *Leidgers;* Hanmer *liegers.*

leisure *n.*
1 (pl.) Times of pleasure, leisure moments LC 193 *Not one...any of my leisures ever charmed.*
2 *attend, stay (upon), tarry, wait for (a person's) leisure* Wait until he is unoccupied, wait his time ADO 1.3.15 *wait for no man's leisure,* MV 1.1.68, JN 2.1.58.
3 *spiritual leisure* Time devoted to religious duties and meditation H8 3.2.140 *You have scarce time To steal from spiritual leisure a brief span.*
4 *by leisure* Not at all, barely TIT 1.1.301 *I'll trust by leisure that mocks me once.*

leman *n.* Sweetheart 2H4 5.3.47 *And drink unto thee, leman mine,* TN 2.3.25; paramour, lover WIV 4.2.164 *search'd...for his wife's leman.*

lend *vb.* Give H8 3.2.151 *As I will lend you cause;* (fig.) JC 3.2.73 *lend me your ears!,* WT 4.3.68.

lendings *n.* (pl.)
1 Superfluous articles not given by nature LR 3.4.108 *Off, off, you lendings!*
2 Money advanced to soldiers when the regular pay cannot be given R2 1.1.89 *Mowbray hath receiv'd eight thousand nobles In name of lendings for your Highness' soldiers.*

length *n.*
1 Prolixity, lengthiness R2 5.1.94 *there is such length in grief,* ANT 4.14.46.
2 Reach, range MAC 4.3.234 *Within my sword's length set him,* HAM 1.2.204, PER 1.1.166.
3 Extent, stretch JN 1.1.105 *Large lengths of seas and shores,* SON 44.10.
4 *of length* Long R2 4.1.11 *Is not my arm of length...?,* TRO 1.3.136.
5 *draw out in length* Prolong, protract MV 3.2.23.
~ *vb.* Lengthen PP 14.30 *length thyself.*

leno *n.* Pimp, pander H5 4.5.14 *Like a base leno hold the chamber door Whilst...His fairest daughter is contaminated* (Q F *pander*).

lenten *adj.*
1 (fig.) Meagre, scanty TN 1.5.9 *A good lenten answer* (i.e. meagre in wit), HAM 2.2.316.
2 *lenten pie* Pie that should contain no meat ROM 2.4.132 *unless a hare, sir, in a lenten pie.*

lenvoy, l'envoy *n.* Concluding part of a poem, epi-

logue LLL 3.1.72 *Some enigma, some riddle—come, thy l'envoy—begin.*

leperous, leprous *adj.* Causing leprosy HAM 1.5.64 *And in the porches of my ears did pour The leprous distilment.*

less *adj.*
1 *less in* Inferior in point of R2 2.3.15 *And hope to joy is little less in joy Than hope enjoyed.*
2 (occas. with words expressing or implying a negative) More WT 3.2.56 *wanted Less impudence to gainsay what they did,* CYM 1.4.23; (adv.) TRO 1.1.28 *Doth lesser blench at suff'rance than I do,* COR 1.4.14.

lesson *n.* Musical piece or exercise SHR 3.1.60 *My lessons make no music in three parts.*
~ *vb.* Teach, instruct R3 1.4.240 *as he lesson'd us to weep,* TGV 2.7.5, TIT 5.2.110.

let *n.* Hindrance H5 5.2.65 *That I may know the let,* LUC 330, LUC 646.
~ *vb.*¹ Hinder TGV 3.1.113 *What lets but one may enter at her window?,* ERR 2.1.105, TN 5.1.249.

let *vb.*²
1 Allow to remain WT 1.2.41 *To let him there a month behind the gest Prefix'd for's parting.*
2 Forbear LUC 10 *did not let To praise.*
3 Cause HAM 4.6.12 *if your name be Horatio, as I am let to know it is.*
4 (with ellipsis of 'go' chiefly in the imper.) TGV 3.2.90 *Let us into the city presently,* MV 3.2.39, 1H4 1.1.91.
5 (imper.) *let me alone for* Trust me for TN 3.4.183 *let me alone for swearing.*
~ in combination
let be 1 Let it alone ANT 4.4.6 *Ah, let be! let be!* **2** No matter HAM 5.2.224. **let blood** Bleed; (hence) kill R3 3.1.183 *his...adversaries Tomorrow are let blood at Pomfret Castle.* **let down the wind** (falconry) Allow to fly free OTH 3.3.262. **let forth** Allow to pass forth, give passage to MND 5.1.381 *Every one lets forth his sprite,* LUC 1029. **let go** Say no more COR 3.2.18. **let loose 1** Unfold H5 4.2.41 *Their ragged curtains poorly are let loose.* **2** Abandon TMP 2.2.34 *I do now let loose my opinion, hold it no longer.* **3** Relax one's hold, let go MND 3.2.260 *let loose; Or I will shake thee from me.* **let out** Lend at interest TIM 3.5.106 *let out Their coin upon large interest.* **let slip** Unleash (dogs) 1H4 1.3.278 *Before the game is afoot thou still let'st slip.*

let-alone *n.* Forbearance, abstention from interference; (hence) permission LR 5.3.79 *The let-alone lies not in your good will.*

lethargied *ppl. adj.* Dulled, blunted LR 1.4.229 *his notion weakens, his discernings Are lethargied.*

Lethe *n.*
1 River in Hades, the drinking of whose water caused forgetfulness; (hence) oblivion ANT 2.7.108 *Till that the conquering wine hath steep'd our sense In soft and delicate Lethe,* TN 4.1.62, R3 4.4.251.
2 Death JC 3.1.206 *crimson'd in thy lethe* (F1 *Lethee*).

Lethe'd, Lethied *adj.* Oblivious ANT 2.1.27 *a Lethe'd dullness.*

letter *n.*
1 *no letter* Not a word CYM 4.3.36 *I heard no letter from my master.*
2 *affect the letter* Practise alliteration LLL 4.2.55.
3 (pl. with sing. sense) Formal communication, epistle 1H6 5.4.95 *letters of commission from the King,* ADO 1.1.20, OTH 4.1.275; letter of recommendation ERR 5.1.138 *your important letters.*
4 Literal meaning, literalness CYM 5.5.450 *Answering the letter of the oracle,* OTH 1.3.68.
5 Learning, scholarship 2H4 4.1.44 *Whose learning*

and good letters peace hath tutor'd, Per 4. Gower.8, Tmp 2.1.151.

lettered *adj.* Learned, literate LLL 5.1.45 *are you not lett'red?*

lettice *n.* (var. of) Lattice; (fig.) wrinkles LC 14 *Some beauty peep'd through lettice of sear'd age.*

level *n.*
1 Equal elevation, state of equality 1H4 3.2.17 *hold their level with thy princely heart.*
2 (fig.) The aim or range of a missile Son 117.11 *Bring me within the level of your frown*, WT 3.2.81, Rom 3.3.103.
~ vb.
1 *level with* Be equal, be on a par with Oth 1.3.239 *As levels with her breeding.*
2 *level at* Come close to, guess at Ant 5.2.336 *she levell'd at our purposes*, MV 1.2.38.
~ adj.
1 'Equipoised, steady' (Schmidt) 2H4 2.1.113 *thrust me from a level consideration.*
2 Readily accessible Ham 4.5.152 *It shall as level to your judgement 'pear As day does to your eye*, 2H4 4.4.7.
3 Direct, straight, in a right line Tim 4.3.19 *All's obliquy; There's nothing level in our cursed natures But direct villainy.*
~ adv.
1 In a steady manner TN 2.4.31 *So sways she level in her husband's heart.*
2 With direct aim Ham 4.1.42 *Whose whisper...*, *As level as the cannon to his blank, Transports his pois'ned shot.*

leven, 'leven *n.* (clipped form of) Eleven Tro 3.3.295 *by a leven of the clock* (F1).
~ adj. (clipped form of) Eleven WT 4.3.32 *every 'leven wether tods*, MV 2.2.162, LLL 3.1.171.

levy *vb.* (app. misused for) Level (i.e. aim) Per 2.5.52 *Never did thought of mine levy offence.*

lewd *adj.* Bad, vile, worthless 1H4 3.2.13 *such lewd, such mean attempts*, Ado 5.1.332, Shr 4.3.65.

lewdly *adv.* Wickedly 2H6 2.1.163 *naughty persons, lewdly bent.*

lewdness *n.* Wickedness H8 1.3.35 *The lag end of their lewdness.*

lewdster *n.* Lascivious person Wiv 5.3.21 *Against such lewdsters, and their lechery.*

liable *adj.*
1 *liable to* Subject to the operation of Per 4.6.168 *To the choleric fisting of every rogue Thy ear is liable*, JC 1.2.199.
2 Subservient *to*, attached or belonging *to* Jn 5.2.101 *such as to my claim are liable*, JC 2.2.104, Jn 2.1.490.
3 Fit LLL 5.1.92 *The posterior of the day...is liable...for the afternoon*, Jn 4.2.226.

libbard *n.* (var. of) Leopard LLL 5.2.548 *With libbard's head on knee.*

libel *n.* Defamatory pamphlet or bill R3 1.1.33 *drunken prophecies, libels, and dreams.*

liberal *adj.*
1 Having the habits, attributes, or character of a gentleman 3H6 1.2.43 *Witty, courteous, liberal*, 2H6 4.7.63; of, pertaining to, or befitting a man of free or noble birth Ham 5.2.153 *most delicate carriages, and of very liberal conceit*, LLL 2.1.167.
◇ Applied as the distinctive epithet of those arts and sciences that were considered worthy of a free man or person of noble birth Tmp 1.2.73 *the liberal arts.*
2 Free in speech R2 2.1.229 *My heart...must break with silence, Ere't be disburdened with a liberal tongue*, Oth 5.2.220 (Q).
3 Unrestrained by prudence or decorum, gross,

licentious Ado 4.1.92 *most like a liberal villain*, LLL 5.2.733, MV 2.2.185.
~ adv. Freely, unrestrainedly Oth 5.2.220 *I will speak as liberal as the north.*

libertine *n.* One who follows his own inclinations H5 1.1.48 *The air, a charter'd libertine, is still.*

liberty *n.*
1 *the liberty of* Unrestricted access to MM 4.2.148 *He hath evermore had the liberty of the prison.*
2 Improper freedom, licence Tim 4.1.25 *Lust, and liberty, Creep in the minds and marrows of our youth*, MM 1.3.29, Err 1.2.102.
3 (pl.) Privileges, rights Cor 2.3.215 *a consul that will from them take Their liberties*, JC 5.1.75, Per 1.2.112.
4 *the liberty* See writ.

licence, license *n.* Leave, permission, liberty of action MM 2.4.145 *your virtue hath a licence in't*, H5 4.7.71, Ham 4.4.2.
~ vb. Permit 1H4 1.3.123 *We license your departure with your son.*

licourish See liquorish.

lictor *n.* Official who attended upon a Roman magistrate Ant 5.2.214 *Saucy lictors Will catch at us.*

lid *n.* Eyelid Tro 1.2.211 *By God's lid.*

lie *vb.*
1 Be or remain in bed (asleep) Tro 4.1.4 *to lie long*, Mac 2.3.23.
2 Be still Per 3.1.47 *the wind is loud, and will not lie till the ship be clear'd of the dead.*
3 Be confined in prison 1H4 4.3.96 *There without ransom to lie forfeited*, R3 1.1.115.
4 Dwell, lodge, (esp.) sleep or pass the night somewhere Wiv 2.1.180 *Does he lie at the Garter?*, 1H6 2.2.41, Cor 1.9.82; be encamped R2 3.2.63 *How far off lies your power?*
5 Be in a certain posture of defence Tro 1.2.263 *at all these wards I lie, at a thousand watches*, 1H4 2.4.195.
~ in combination
lie along Lie prostrate, lie outstretched upon the ground AYL 2.1.30 *as he lay along Under an oak.*
lie by Sink to rest H8 3.1.11 *Hung their heads, and then lay by.* **lie in 1** Reside in, depend upon Wiv 5.1.2 *good luck lies in odd numbers*, MM 3.1.261, R2 1.2.4. **2** Be in childbed, be confined Cor 1.3.77 *the good lady that lies in.* **lie low** Be struck down, be dead Ado 5.1.52 *Some of us would lie low.* **lie off** Stand some distance away *from* (a place) 1H4 3.1.78 *The remnant northward lying off from Trent.* **lie on, upon 1** Rest as an obligation upon 1H4 5.2.47 *would the quarrel lay upon our heads!*, Cor 3.2.52. **2** Depend on AWW 3.7.43 *As if his life lay on't*, Tro 4.4.147, Son 92.10. **3** Belong to, be incident to Jn 1.1.119 *Which fault lies on the hazards of all husbands That marry wives.* **lie under** Be subject to (some disadvantage) Ado 4.1.169 *If this sweet lady lie not guiltless here Under some biting error*, Tro 2.3.135. **lie upon** See lie on.

lief *adj.*
1 Dear 2H6 3.1.164 *My liefest liege.*
2 *had as lief* Should like as much MM 1.2.33 *I had as lief be a list of an English kersey*, AYL 1.1.146, TN 3.2.31.

liege *n.* Sovereign lord, superior to whom allegiance is due WT 2.3.144 *My royal liege*, Tmp 5.1.245, Err 5.1.278; (fig.) LLL 3.1.183 *Liege of all loiterers.*

liegeman *n.* Vassal, subject WT 2.3.174 *As thou art liegeman to us*, Ham 1.1.15, 1H4 2.4.338.

lieger See leiger.

lieutenantry *n.*
1 Lieutenancy Oth 2.1.172 *If such tricks as these strip you out of your lieutenantry.*

2 *on lieutenantry* By deputy, by proxy ANT 3.11.39 *He alone Dealt on lieutenantry, and no practice had In the brave squares of war.*

lieve (var. of) LIEF.

life *n.*
1 *lines of life* Lines of living, i.e. offspring SON 16.9 *So should the lines of life that life repair.*
2 Continuance of (one's) lifetime WT 1.1.40 *They that went on crutches ere he was born desire yet their life to see him a man,* WT 5.1.137.
3 Living being MAC 5.8.2 *Whiles I see lives.*
4 Essence, soul JN 5.7.1 *the life of all his blood Is touch'd corruptibly,* TRO 1.3.384, LUC 780.
5 Living form or model, living semblance, reality ADO 2.3.105 *There was never counterfeit of passion came so near the life of passion as she discovers it,* WT 5.3.19, H5 5.Ch.5; *to the life* with faithful or exact presentation or reproduction PER 5.1.246 *call And give them repetition to the life* (i.e. reproduce them exactly as they occurred), COR 3.2.106.

life-blood *n.* Life-giving or vital blood MV 3.2.266 *a gaping wound Issuing life-blood,* 1H6 4.6.43, TIT 4.4.37; (fig.) vital part 1H4 4.1.29 *The very life-blood of our enterprise.*

lifeless See LIVELESS.

lifelings *n.* (pl.) (part of a trivial oath) Little lives TN 5.1.184 *'Od's lifelings, here he is!'*

life-rendering *adj.* Self-sacrificing HAM 4.5.147 *And like the kind life-rend'ring pelican, Repast them with my blood.*

lifter *n.* Thief TRO 1.2.117 *so young a man and so old a lifter* (with quibble).

lifting up *n.* Rising, dawning 2H4 4.4.93 *The lifting up of day.*

lig *vb.* [Northern dial.] Lie H5 3.2.115 *or I 'll lig i' th' grund for it.*

liggens *n.* (pl.) (in oath; perh. derived from) lidkin, a diminutive of lid (i.e. eyelid) 2H4 5.3.65 *By God's liggens.*

light *n.*
1 Enlightenment, information TGV 3.1.49 *That I had any light from thee of this,* PER 1.3.17, JN 4.3.61.
2 The brightness of the eye, power of seeing LUC 1378 *And dying eyes gleam'd forth their ashy lights,* TGV 2.1.71, CYM 2.2.21.
~ *vb.*[1]
1 Give light VEN 163 *Torches are made to light,* ROM 3.4.33, TMP 4.1.23.
2 Grow light, brighten, break 1H4 3.2.138 *And that shall be the day, when e'er it lights.*
3 Shine TRO 1.1.37 *as when the sun doth light a-scorn.*

light *vb.*[2] Fall, descend (lit. and fig.) PER 4.2.72 *You are light into my hands,* MAC 2.3.142, R3 3.4.93.

light *adj.*
1 Unimportant, trivial H5 2.2.89 *for a few light crowns,* MND 3.2.133, TMP 1.2.453; *hold, set, weigh light* treat as of little consequence, estimate at a low rate OTH 2.3.174 *Holds his soul light,* R2 1.3.293, AWW 3.4.32.
2 Frivolous, full of levity ROM 2.2.99 *thou mayest think my behaviour light,* SHR 2.1.203, LR 3.4.92.
3 Wanton, unchaste 2H4 2.4.295 *By this light flesh and corrupt blood,* ERR 4.3.52, MV 2.6.42.
✧ ADO 3.4.47 *Ye light a' love with your heels* i.e. light-heeled, euphemism for 'unchaste'. See HEEL.
4 Swift, nimble ROM 2.2.66 *love's light wings,* SHR 2.1.204, VEN 150.
5 Easy TMP 1.2.452 *too light winning.*
6 Cheerful, merry OTH 4.1.102 *smiles, gestures, and light behaviours,* TGV 1.2.81, 2H4 4.2.85.
7 Delirious, light-headed OTH 4.1.269 *Is he not light of brain?,* ERR 5.1.72, CYM 5.4.164.

lighten *vb.*
1 Enlighten 2H4 2.1.194 *the Lord lighten thee!*
2 Flash R2 3.3.69 *his eye...lightens forth Controlling majesty,* ROM 2.2.120, JC 1.3.74.

lightening See LIGHTNING.

light-foot *adj.* Light-footed, nimble R3 4.4.440 *Some light-foot friend.*

lightly *adv.*
1 Slightly, not highly R3 1.3.45 *they love his Grace but lightly,* LLL 1.2.152.
2 Cheerfully ANT 4.14.138 *we punish it Seeming to bear it lightly,* ROM 5.1.3.
3 Easily, readily ERR 4.4.5 *will not lightly trust the messenger,* TIT 2.3.289.
4 Nimbly, quickly TGV 3.1.142 *could their master come and go as lightly.*
5 Usually, often R3 3.1.94 *Short summers lightly have a forward spring.*
6 Thoughtlessly COR 4.1.29 *Believe't not lightly.*

lightness *n.*
1 Lightheadedness HAM 2.2.149 *Thence to a lightness, and...Into the madness wherein now he raves.*
2 Levity, frivolity, light behaviour, fickleness MM 2.2.169 *Can it be That modesty may more betray our sense Than woman's lightness?,* SHR 4.2.24, 2H4 1.2.46.

lightning, lightening *n. lightning before death* Exhilaration which is supposed to occur in some instances just before death ROM 5.3.90.

like *vb.*[1]
1 Please TGV 4.2.55 *The music likes you not,* TRO 5.2.102; (esp. in conventional phr.) TMP 4.1.239 *and't like your Grace,* H8 1.1.100, CYM 2.3.54.
2 *like of* Be pleased with, approve of, be fond of ADO 5.4.59 *I am your husband if you like of me,* ROM 1.3.96, R3 4.4.354.
3 Feel affection ERR 3.2.7 *Or if you like elsewhere, do it by stealth,* JN 2.1.511.
4 Be in good condition 2H4 3.2.83 *By my troth, you like well.*

like *vb.*[2]
1 Liken, compare 1H6 4.6.48 *And like me to the peasant boys of France,* 2H4 2.1.90.
2 *had liked to* Came near to, were near to ADO 5.1.115 *We had lik'd to have had our two noses snapp'd off.*
~ *adj.*
1 Probable, likely, in accordance with appearances MM 5.1.104 *O that it were as like as it is true!,* SHR 3.2.213, ROM 4.3.45.
2 *like to* Likely to 1H4 3.2.124 *Thou that art like enough...To fight against me,* MND 5.1.117, COR 3.1.48; apparently on the point of WIV 4.5.116 *I was like to be apprehended,* ADO 5.4.110, AYL 5.4.47.
~ *adv.*
1 Equally, similarly, alike TMP 3.3.66 *My fellow-ministers Are like invulnerable,* ERR 1.1.82, SON 132.12.
2 As well as, as also R3 3.5.9 *like enforced smiles.*
3 Likely, probably 2H6 3.1.379 *as 'tis great like he will* (i.e. very likely), TMP 5.1.265, CYM 5.5.259.
4 *like as* Even as SON 60.1 *Like as the waves make towards the pebbled shore, So do our minutes hasten to their end.*

likelihood *n.*
1 Ground of probable inference, indication, sign AWW 1.3.123 *Many likelihoods inform'd me of this,* TGV 5.2.43, OTH 1.3.108.
2 Promise, indication of future excellence or achievement 1H4 3.2.45 *A fellow of no mark nor likelihood.*

likely *adj.* Handsome, comely 2H4 3.2.175 *a likely fellow,* MV 2.9.92, 2H4 3.2.255.

liking *n.* Bodily condition 1H4 3.3.6 *while I am in some liking,* WIV 2.1.57.

lily-livered adj. Cowardly Mac 5.3.15 lily-liver'd boy.

limb n. (fig.) Member H8 1.1.220 the limbs o' th' plot, 2H4 5.2.135.

limbeck n. Alembic (properly the cap only of a distilling apparatus, the beak of which conveyed the products to the receiver), still Mac 1.7.67 the receipt of reason A limbeck only, Son 119.2.

limber adj. (fig.) Flexible WT 1.2.47 limber vows.

limb-meal adv. Limb from limb Cym 2.4.147 to tear her limb-meal!

limbo n. (properly) Abode of the just who died before Christ's coming ('Limbo patrum') or of infants who have died unbaptized ('Limbo infantum'); (used vaguely) Hell AWW 5.3.261 talk'd of Satan and of Limbo and of Furies, Tit 3.1.149; (fig.) prison H8 5.3.64 I have some of 'em in Limbo Patrum, Err 4.2.32.

lime vb.
1 Cement 3H6 5.1.84 Who gave his blood to lime the stones together.
2 Catch or trap with birdlime 3H6 5.6.13 The bird that hath been limed in a bush, Ado 3.1.104, AWW 3.5.24.
3 Put lime into liquor (to mask sour taste) Wiv 1.3.14 Let me see thee froth and lime (Qq 1–2 lyme; Ff, Q3 liue).

limed ppl. adj. Trapped (as with birdlime), ensnared Ham 3.3.68 O limed soul, that struggling to be free Art more engag'd.

lime-kill, lime-kiln n. Furnace in which stones are burned to lime Tro 5.1.21 lime-kilns i' th' palm (i.e. burning sensations; F1 lime-kills), Wiv 3.3.79.

lime-twig n. Twig smeared with bird-lime or some other sticky substance 2H6 3.3.16 Like lime-twigs set to catch my winged soul.

limit n.
1 Prescribed time or period MM 3.1.215 between which time of the contract and limit of the solemnity, R3 3.3.8, R2 1.3.151; period of rest after childbearing WT 3.2.106 before I have got strength of limit.
2 Tract, region 1H4 3.1.72 divided it Into three limits, Ven 235, Son 44.4.
~ vb.
1 Appoint (a time) MM 4.2.166 having the hour limited, Err 1.1.150.
2 Appoint (a person to an office), assign (a duty to a person) R3 5.3.25 Limit each leader to his several charge.

limitation n. Allotted time Cor 2.3.138 You have stood your limitation.

limited ppl. adj.
1 Restricted, regulated Tim 4.3.428 there is boundless theft In limited professions.
2 Appointed Mac 2.3.52 'tis my limited service.

limn vb. Paint Ven 290 Look when a painter would surpass the life In limning out a well-proportioned steed, AYL 2.7.194.

line n.[1] Linden, lime-tree Tmp 4.1.193 hang them on this line.

line n.[2]
1 Fishing-line 2H4 2.4.158 Hold hook and line; (fig.) full play, scope WT 1.2.181 I am angling now, Though you perceive me not how I give line, 2H4 4.4.39, MM 1.4.56.
2 Plumb-rule, plumb-line; by line and level by means of instruments used for determining exactly vertical and horizontal position; (hence, fig.) with methodical accuracy Tmp 4.1.239 we steal by line and level.
3 Lineament, contour AWW 1.1.96 every line and trick of his sweet favour, Cym 4.1.9, WT 1.2.153.
4 line of life (in palmistry) The line on the hand

which is supposed to indicate the nature or duration of one's life MV 2.2.160 here's a simple line of life!
5 The Equator Tmp 4.1.236 Now is the jerkin under the line.
6 Degree, rank, station 1H4 1.3.168 To show the line and the predicament Wherein you range, 1H4 3.2.85.
7 (pl.) Caprices, fits of temper Tro 2.3.130 His pettish lines, his ebbs, his flows, Wiv 4.2.22.
◇ Some mod. edd. read 'lunes' in these two contexts in sense 7.
~ vb.[1] Draw, delineate, sketch AYL 3.2.92 All the pictures fairest lin'd.

line vb.[2]
1 Reinforce, garrison, support H5 2.4.7 To line and new repair our towns of war With men of courage and with means defendant, 1H4 2.3.83, Jn 2.1.352.
2 Supply, ply (with money, gifts, food) AYL 2.7.154 with good capon lin'd, Per 4.6.58; (hence, fig.) bribe Cym 2.3.67 what If I do line one of their hands?

lineal adj.
1 Lineally descended (from) H5 1.2.82 Queen Isabel…Was lineal of the Lady Ermengare.
2 Due by right of descent Jn 2.1.85 Our just and lineal entrance to our own.

lined ppl. adj. Padded, stuffed Tim 4.1.14 the lin'd crutch.

line-grove n. Grove of lime-trees Tmp 5.1.10 In the line-grove which weather-fends your cell.

linen adj. Pale, white Mac 5.3.16 linen cheeks.

ling n.[1] Fish of the cod kind AWW 3.2.14 old ling (i.e. salted ling).

ling n.[2] Heather Tmp 1.1.66 ling, heath, broom, furze.
◇ Emendation adopted by some mod. edd.; F1 Long heath, Browne Firrs. See LONG HEATH.

linger vb.
1 Prolong, draw out Oth 4.2.226 unless his abode be ling'red here by some accident, R2 2.2.72; (with on, out) Tro 5.10.9 linger not our sure destructions on, 2H4 1.2.237, Son 90.8.
2 Delay the fulfilment of MND 1.1.4 She lingers my desires.

lingering ppl. adj. (of poison, etc.) Slow WT 1.2.320 no rash potion, But with a ling'ring dram, Ant 2.5.66, Cym 1.5.34.

link n.
1 Torch of tow and pitch 1H4 3.3.42 Thou has sav'd me a thousand marks in links and torches.
2 The smoke from links, or the material of links used as blacking Shr 4.1.134 There was no link to colour Peter's hat.

linsey-woolsey n. Cloth made of flax and wool; (fig.) strange medley (of words), nonsense AWW 4.1.11 But what linsey-woolsey hast thou to speak to us again?

linstock n. Staff about 1 metre long, having a forked head to hold a lighted match for igniting the priming powder in a cannon H5 3.Ch.33 the nimble gunner With linstock now the devilish cannon touches.

lioness n. (slang) Harlot, prostitute Jn 2.1.291 At your den, sirrah, with your lioness.

lion-sick adj. Sick (like a lion) with pride Tro 2.3.86 Yes, lion-sick, sick of proud heart.

lip n.
1 falling a lip of much contempt Expressing great contempt by a movement of the lip WT 1.2.373.
2 make a lip at Make a contemptuous face at Cor 2.1.115.
~ vb. Kiss Ant 2.5.30 a hand that kings Have lipp'd, Oth 4.1.71.

liquor n. grand liquor Elixir, i.e. a substance once supposed to have the power of indefinitely pro-

moting life or of transmuting metals TMP 5.1.280
*Where should they Find this grand liquor that hath
gilded 'em?*
~ *vb.* Oil, grease WIV 4.5.98 *they would melt me out
of my fat…and liquor fishermen's boots with me;*
(fig.) grease the palm, bribe 1H4 2.1.85 *justice hath
liquor'd her* (with quibble on the meaning 'fill with
drink, make drunk').

liquorish *adj.* Lickerish, pleasing to the palate, delightful, tempting TIM 4.3.194 *liquorish draughts*
(Ff 3–4; Ff 1–2 *Licourish*).

list *n.¹*
1 Selvage of cloth MM 1.2.33 *a list of an English
kersey.*
2 Strip of cloth SHR 3.2.68 *gart'red with a red and
blue list.*
3 (chiefly fig.) Limit, boundary, utmost bound TN
3.1.77 *she is the list of my voyage*, MM 1.1.6, AWW
2.1.51.
4 Palisades enclosing a space set apart for tilting
R2 1.3.43 *so…daring-hardy as to touch the lists;*
(also pl.) the space thus enclosed MAC 3.1.70 *come
fate into the list;* (fig.) VEN 595 *in the very lists of
love.*

list *n.²* Catalogue of the soldiers of a force, muster
LR 5.3.111 *any man…within the lists of the army,*
HAM 1.2.32, ANT 3.6.76; (hence) any catalogue H8
4.1.14 *the list Of those that claim their offices this
day.*

list *n.³* Desire OTH 2.1.104 *when I have list to sleep*
(Q1; Ff *leaue*).
~ *vb.¹* Please, choose, like WIV 2.2.119 *go to bed
when she list, rise when she list,* TMP 3.2.129, R3
3.5.84 (Qq).

list *vb.²*
1 (intr.) Listen HAM 1.5.22 *List, list, O, list!,* ANT
4.3.12, TRO 5.2.17; (with *to*) SHR 2.1.363 *Sir, list to
me,* WT 4.4.541, 1H4 3.3.95.
2 (trans.) Listen to, WIV 5.5.42 *Elves, list your
names,* H5 1.1.43, ERR 4.1.101.

listen *vb. listen after* Endeavour to hear of 2H6
1.3.149 *listen after Humphrey, how he proceeds*, 2H4
1.1.29.

literatured *adj.* Learned H5 4.7.150 *literatured in
the wars.*

lither *adj.* Yielding 1H6 4.7.21 *winged through the
lither sky.*

litigious *adj.* Questionable PER 3.3.3 *Tyrus stands
In a litigious peace.*

litter *vb.* Bring forth; (contemptuously of human
beings) TMP 1.2.282 *the son that she did litter here,*
COR 3.1.238.

little *n.*
1 *but a little* But little, not much SHR 1.2.61
Thou'dst thank me but a little for my counsel.
2 *in a little* In a few words, briefly H8 2.1.11 *I'll
tell you in a little.*
3 *in little* On a small scale, in miniature AYL
3.2.140 *The quintessence of every sprite Heaven
would in little show,* HAM 2.2.366, LC 90.
~ *adj.*
1 A little 2H4 3.1.43 *Which…may be restored With
good advice and little medicine,* TN 5.1.171.
2 High-pitched MND 1.2.52 *I'll speak in a monstrous little voice.*
3 *little world* Microcosm LR 3.1.10 *his little world
of man* (Qq).

liveless *adj.* (var. in F and Q of) Lifeless AYL
1.2.251 *a mere liveless block,* H5 4.2.55, 2H6 4.1.142.

livelihood *n.* Animation, life AWW 1.1.51 *takes all
livelihood from her cheek,* R3 3.4.55 (Ff; Qq *likelihood*), VEN 26.

lively *adj.*
1 Living, animate SON 67.10 *lively veins,* TIT 5.3.44.

2 Lifelike TIM 1.1.38 *livelier than life,* AYL 5.4.27.
3 Vivid, intense TN 5.1.246 *that record is lively in
my soul,* VEN 498, SON 153.6.
4 Vivid, brilliant, fresh LUC 1593 *Her lively colour,*
TIM 1.2.156.
~ *adv.* In a lifelike manner, very naturally TIM
5.1.82 *Thou counterfeit'st most lively,* TGV 4.4.169.

liver *n.¹*
1 Supposed seat of love and violent passion ADO
4.1.231 *If ever love had interest in his liver,* TN
1.1.36.
2 *white, pale liver* Symbol of cowardice MV 3.2.86
livers white as milk, TRO 2.2.50.

liver *n.²* Living creature CYM 3.4.140 *There's livers
out of Britain.*

liver-vein *n.* In anatomy, old name for the basilic
vein; used allusively for 'the style and manner of
men in love' (Schmidt) LLL 4.3.72 *This is the liver-
vein, which makes flesh a deity.*
⇨ See LIVER *n.¹* sense 1.

livery *n.* Legal delivery of property into one's possession; *sue one's livery* institute a suit as heir to
obtain possession of lands which are in the hands
of the court of wards R2 2.1.204, 1H4 4.3.62.
~ *vb.* Dress (in a livery); (fig.) LC 105 *His rudeness…Did livery falseness in a pride of truth.*

living *n.*
1 Lifetime LC 238 *To spend her living in eternal
love.*
2 Property, fortune MV 5.1.286 *life and living,* ROM
4.5.40, WT 4.3.98; (pl.) possessions MV 3.2.156 *virtues, beauties, livings, friends.*
~ *ppl. adj.*
1 During one's life or lifetime, while one is or was
alive TGV 3.1.170 *death, rather than living torment,* R2 5.1.39, SON 67.6.
2 Real AYL 3.2.419 *a living humour of madness,*
OTH 3.3.409 (with play on sense 3).
3 Lasting HAM 5.1.297 *This grave shall have a living monument.*
⇨ In LLL 1.1.14 *living art* perh. allusion also to
the *ars vitae* or *ars vivendi* of Stoic philosophy.
4 Life-giving MAC 2.4.10 *living light.*

loach *n.* Small freshwater fish, reputed to breed
prolifically 1H4 2.1.21 *your chamber-lye breeds
fleas like a loach.*

load *vb.* Supply in excess, reward CYM 1.5.74 *To load
thy merit richly.*

loathed *ppl. adj.* Loathsome R3 1.3.231 *Thou loathed
issue of thy father's loins!,* ROM 3.5.31, VEN 19.

loathly *adv.* With abhorrence LR 2.1.49 *how loathly
opposite I stood.*

loathness *n.* Reluctance TMP 2.1.131 *Weigh'd between loathness and obedience,* CYM 1.1.108, ANT
3.11.18.

lob *n.* Country bumpkin MND 2.1.16 *Farewell, thou
lob of spirits.*
~ *vb.* Hang heavily, droop H5 4.2.47 *and their poor
jades Lob down their heads.*

lock *n.* Lovelock ADO 3.3.170 *'a wears a lock.*

lockram *n.* Linen or hempen fabric, often coarse
COR 2.1.209 *Her richest lockram.*

locust *n.* Fruit of the carob-tree, locust-bean OTH
1.3.348 *The food that…is as luscious as locusts.*

lodestar *n.* Guiding-star MND 1.1.183 *Your eyes are
lodestars.*

lodge *n.* Gamekeeper's hut ADO 2.1.215 *a lodge in a
warren.*
~ *vb.*
1 Harbour, entertain (feelings) 2H4 4.5.207 *I well
might lodge a friend.*
2 (of rain or wind) Beat down (crops) R2 3.3.162
they shall lodge the summer corn, 2H6 3.2.176, MAC
4.1.55.

lodged *ppl. adj.* Settled, abiding MV 4.1.60 *a lodg'd hate.*

lodging *n.*
1 Accommodation for rest at night or for residence LLL 5.2.801 *hard lodging*, H5 4.1.16.
2 Residence, dwelling place MV 2.2.118 *to come anon to my lodging*, AYL 2.3.23, OTH 1.2.45; (fig.) the stocks LR 2.2.172 *This shameful lodging.*
3 Apartment, room 2H4 4.5.233 *Doth any name particular belong Unto the lodging where I first did swound?*, R2 1.2.68, SHR Ind.1.49.

loff(e) *vb.* Laugh MND 2.1.55 *the whole quire hold their hips and loff.*

loggats, loggets *n.* Game in which thick sticks were thrown to lie as near as possible to a stake fixed in the ground or a block of wood on the floor HAM 5.1.92 *Did these bones cost no more the breeding, but to play at loggats with them?*

loggerhead *n.* Stupid person, blockhead LLL 4.3.199 *Ah, you whoreson loggerhead*, ROM 4.4.21, 1H4 2.4.4.

loggerheaded *adj.* Stupid SHR 4.1.125 *You loggerheaded and unpolish'd grooms!*

long, 'long *vb.* Belong, pertain SHR 4.4.7 *such austerity as 'longeth to a father*, H8 1.2.32, MM 2.2.59.

long *adj.*[1]
1 *before, ere it be long* Before long, shortly MM 4.2.76, 1H6 3.2.75, 3H6 3.3.232.
2 *think long* Grow weary or impatient LUC 1359 *But long she thinks till he return again*, ROM 4.5.41.
~ *in combination*
long-engraffed, long-engraffed See ENGRAF-FED, ENGRAFFED. **long-tail** See CUT AND LONG-TAIL.
long-winded Capable of continuing in action for a long time without getting out of breath 1H4 3.3.160 *one poor pennyworth of sugar-candy to make thee long-winded.*
~ *adv.* After a long time SHR 5.2.1 *At last, though long, our jarring notes agree.*

long *adj.*[2] *long of* Owing to, on account of LLL 2.1.118 *'Tis long of you*, 1H6 4.3.33, COR 5.4.29.

long heath *n.* Common heath, heather, or ling, *Erica vulgaris* TMP 1.1.66 *long heath, brown furze, any thing.*

longing *adj.* Prompted by strong desire TGV 2.7.85 *my longing journey.*

longly *adv.* For a long while SHR 1.1.165 *you look'd so longly on the maid.*

long purples *n.* Early purple orchis, *Orchis mascula* HAM 4.7.169 *nettles, daisies, and long purples.*

long sword *n.* Old-fashioned two-handed sword ROM 1.1.75 *Give me my long sword.*

'loo, loo, low *interj.* Cry to incite a dog to the chase TRO 5.7.10 *Now, bull! now, dog! Low, Paris, low!* (F4 *'loo*), LR 3.4.77.

loof *vb.* (old form of) Luff, bring the head of (a vessel) nearer to the wind ANT 3.10.17 *She once being loof'd...Antony, Claps on his sea-wing.*

look *n. have a look of* Be looked at by TGV 2.4.108 *To have a look of such a worthy mistress.*
~ *vb.*
1 Take care, see TMP 4.1.51 *Look thou be true*, OTH 4.3.9, R3 3.4.78.
2 Expect WT 4.4.358 *The gifts she looks from me*; (with infin.) TMP 5.1.293 *you look To have my pardon*, MM 1.1.57, MAC 5.3.26; (with clause) R2 1.3.243 *I look'd when some of you should say I was too strict*, SON 22.4, H8 5.1.117.
3 (prefixed to an interr. or rel. pron. or adv. to form indefinite relatives) Just as, whoever, whatever, whenever, however, etc. ERR 2.1.12 *Look when I serve him so, he takes it ill*, TRO 1.3.79, SON 37.13.

4 Seek, look for WIV 4.2.81 *I will look some linen for your head*, AYL 2.5.33, LR 3.3.14 (Qq *seeke*).
5 Bring by one's looks into a certain condition CYM 5.5.94 *Thou hast looked thyself into my grace.*
6 Give promise to, show a likelihood to, seem likely to COR 3.3.29 *that is there which looks With us to break his neck.*
~ *in combination*
look about Be on the watch ROM 3.5.40 *be wary, look about*, 2H4 5.1.52. **look after 1** Seek (a person) CYM 3.5.55 *Go, look after.* **2** Demand OTH 2.1.247 *those requisites...that folly and green minds look after.* **3** Keep watch upon MM 1.2.144 *Is lechery so looked after?* **look against** Look at (something dazzling) WIV 2.2.245 *too bright to be looked against.* **look back** Look back to ANT 3.11.53 *By looking back what I have left behind.* **look beyond** Misjudge 2H4 4.4.67 *you look beyond him quite.* **look on** Hold in esteem, respect 3H6 5.7.22 *For yet I am not look'd on in the world*, ANT 3.13.109, PER 4.3.32. **look out 1** Appear, show itself TIM 3.2.73 *man When he looks out in an ungrateful shape*, ANT 5.1.50, TRO 4.5.56. **2** Find out by looking TIM 3.2.60 *I'll look you out a good turn.* **look through 1** Be visible 2H4 4.4.120 *life looks through and will break out.* **2** Be or become visible through HAM 4.7.151 *that our drift look through our bad performance*, SHR Ind.2.12. **look to** Look at HAM 1.4.77 *looks so many fathoms to the sea*, ADO 5.4.116. **look up** Take courage 2H4 4.4.113 *My sovereign lord, cheer up yourself, look up*, HAM 3.3.50, WT 5.1.215. **look upon 1** Look on, be a spectator WT 5.3.100 *look upon with marvel*, 3H6 2.3.27, TRO 5.6.10. **2** LOOK ON 2H6 2.4.38 *I'll look upon the world.*

loon, lown *n.*
1 Stupid fellow MAC 5.3.11 *The devil damn thee black, thou cream-fac'd loon!*, OTH 2.3.92.
2 Man of low birth PER 4.6.18 *We should have both lord and lown.*

loop *n.*[1] Part of a hinge OTH 3.3.365 *no hinge nor loop To hang a doubt on.*

loop *n.*[2] Loop-hole, opening 1H4 4.1.71 *And stop all sight-holes, every loop from whence The eye of reason may pry in upon us.*

looped *adj.* Having loop-holes LR 3.4.31 *Your loop'd and window'd raggedness.*

loose *n.*
1 Moment of discharge of an arrow; (hence, fig.) *at time's very loose* at the last moment LLL 5.2.742.
2 *fast and loose* See FAST AND LOOSE.
~ *vb.*
1 (of an arrow) Discharge, let fly MND 2.1.159 *And loos'd his love-shaft smartly from his bow*, H5 1.2.207, TIT 4.3.59.
2 Give vent to AYL 3.5.103 *Loose now and then A scatt'red smile*, AWW 2.3.165.
3 Let go one's hold TIT 2.3.243 *Thy hand once more; I will not loose again.*
4 Release, remit MV 4.1.24 *loose the forfeiture.*
~ *adj.*
1 *loose shot* Marksmen not attached to a company H8 5.3.56 *a file of boys behind 'em, loose shot.*
2 Wanting in restraint, undisciplined OTH 3.3.416 *so loose of soul, That in their sleeps will mutter their affairs*, H8 2.1.127, LLL 5.2.766.
3 Careless TRO 3.3.41 *Lay negligent and loose regard upon him.*

loosen *vb.* Make a breach between LR 5.1.19 *I had rather lose the battle than that sister Should loosen him and me.*

loose-wived *adj.* Having a wanton wife ANT 1.2.72 *to see a handsome man loose-wiv'd.*

lop *n.* Smaller branches and twigs H8 1.2.96 *From every tree, lop, bark, and part o' th' timber.*

lord *vb.* Raise to a position of power TMP 1.2.97 *He being thus lorded.*

lording *n.*
1 Lord PP 15.1 *a lording's daughter;* (pl.) Sirs 2H6 1.1.145 *Lordings, farewell.*
2 Lordling, petty lord WT 1.2.62 *You were pretty lordings then?*

lordliness *n.* Lordly state or office ANT 5.2.161 *Doing the honour of thy lordliness To one so meek.*

lordship *n.* Authority of a husband MND 1.1.81 *yield my virgin patent up Unto his lordship,* AWW 5.3.156.

lose *vb.*
1 Destroy, ruin 1H4 1.3.88 *When they have lost and forfeited themselves?,* HAM 3.2.195, H8 3.1.107; ruin in estimation LR 1.1.233 *though not to have it Hath lost me in your liking.*
2 Forget H8 2.1.57 *Hear what I say, and then go home and lose me,* LLL 4.3.71, MND 1.1.114.
3 Cause (a person) the loss of LR 1.2.115 *it shall lose thee nothing,* TN 2.2.20.
4 Miss (one's aim) ANT 4.14.71 *all the Parthian darts…lost aim.*
5 (refl.) Lose one's wits ANT 1.2.117 *lose myself in dotage.*

losing *ppl. adj.* Resulting in loss MV 4.1.62 *A losing suit,* JC 5.5.36, 2H4 1.1.101.

loss *n.*
1 Ruin, destruction, perdition ANT 4.12.29 *Beguil'd me to the very heart of loss,* AWW 3.2.41, LR 3.6.95.
2 Failure to make good use of (time, etc.) TGV 1.3.19 *his loss of time,* LUC 1420, TRO 2.2.4.
3 Default, lack MM 2.4.90 *in the loss of question* (i.e. in the absence of matter for argument).

lost *ppl. adj.*
1 Brought to destruction or death, perished LR 5.3.191 *Met I my father with his bleeding rings, Their precious stones new lost,* MAC 1.3.24, WT 5.3.135.
2 Spent to no advantage; (hence) vain, groundless OTH 5.2.269 *a lost fear,* R3 2.2.11.
3 Bewildered, perplexed HAM 4.7.54 *Can you devise me?—I am lost in it, my lord,* MAC 2.2.68.

lot *n.*
1 Object used in determining results; sometimes in games of chance or lotteries, the one containing marks indicating a winning lot, as opposed to losing lots which were unmarked or blank COR 5.2.10 *it is lots to blanks* (i.e. winning tickets to non-winning tickets, or more than an even chance).
2 *scot and lot* See SCOT.

lottery *n.*
1 Decision by casting or drawing of lots TRO 2.1.128 *I know not, 'tis put to lott'ry;* by chance JC 2.1.119 *Till each man drop by lottery.*
2 What falls to one by lot, prize ANT 2.2.242 *Octavia is A blessed lottery to him.*

loud *adj.*
1 Noisy, boisterous, turbulent JN 5.4.14 *this loud day,* WT 3.3.11, HAM 4.7.22.
2 Pressing, urgent OTH 1.1.150 *he's embarked With such loud reason to the Cyprus wars,* TRO 5.3.9.
3 *to the loudest* At the top of my voice WT 2.2.37 *undertake to be Her advocate to th' loudest.*

louse *vb.* Be infested with lice LR 3.2.29 *The head and he shall louse.*

lousy *adj.* (fig.) Contemptible H5 4.8.34 *what an arrant, rascally, beggarly, lousy knave it is,* 2H6 4.1.50 (Ff *lowsie;* Qq *lowly).*

lout *vb.* Treat with contumely, mock, make a fool of 1H6 4.3.13 *I am louted by a traitor villain.*
⋄ Perh. dial. *lout, lowt* 'delay' (Hulme).

love *n.*
1 Act of kindness JN 4.1.49 *What good love may I perform for you?,* PER 2.4.49.
2 Dear friend MV 4.1.277 *Whether Bassanio had not once a love,* SON 13.1, SON 66.14.
3 Lover, paramour WIV 3.5.78 *to search the house for his wife's love,* VEN 867, TGV 1.2.76.
4 *for (one's) love* For (one's) sake, on (one's) account MM 4.2.113 *for the fault's love is th' offender friended,* LLL 5.2.840.
5 Protestation of love LR 5.3.88 *If you will marry, make your loves to me.*
6 *of all loves* Expression of strong adjuration or entreaty MND 2.2.154 *Speak, of all loves!,* WIV 2.2.114, OTH 3.1.13 (Ff *for love's sake).*
7 *out of love with* Disinclined to, disgusted with 2H4 2.2.12 *these humble considerations make me out of love with my greatness,* MM 3.1.172, TGV 4.4.205.
~ in combination
love-book Book treating of love TGV 1.1.19. **love-broker** One who acts as agent between lovers TN 3.2.37. **love-cause** Love-affair AYL 4.1.97. **love-day** Day of reconciliation, day appointed for a meeting to settle a dispute TIT 1.1.491. **love-feat** Act of courtship, exploit prompted by love LLL 5.2.123. **love-in-idleness** Pansy, heartsease, Viola tricolor MND 2.1.168. **love-juice** Juice used as a philtre, love-potion MND 3.2.89. **love-line** Letter of courtship, love-letter AWW 2.1.78. **love-monger** One who deals in affairs of love LLL 2.1.254. **love-performing** Ministering to the works of love ROM 3.2.5. **love-prate** Trifling talk about love AYL 4.1.201. **love-shaked** Shaken with an amorous fever AYL 3.2.367. **love-spring** Tender 'shoot' of love ERR 3.2.3.
~ *vb.* Love one another JC 4.3.131 *Love, and be friends,* AYL 1.1.112, ANT 1.3.49.

lovely *adj.* Loving, tender SHR 3.2.123 *And seal the title with a lovely kiss!,* PP 4.3.
~ *adv.* Lovably, beautifully OTH 4.2.68 *so lovely fair,* 1H4 3.1.122.

lover *n.*
1 Friend, well-wisher JC 3.2.13 *Romans, countrymen, and lovers,* MV 3.4.17, COR 5.2.14.
2 Sweetheart, mistress MM 1.4.40 *Your brother and his lover,* AYL 3.4.43, CYM 5.5.172.

lovered *adj.* Having (such) a lover LC 320 *Who…would not be so lover'd?*

loving *ppl. adj.* Of love AYL 5.4.191 *thy loving voyage,* LUC 480; desired of love H5 5.Ch.29 *loving likelihood.*

low *adj.*
1 Short, not tall MND 3.2.295 *so dwarfish and so low,* ADO 1.1.171, AYL 4.3.87.
2 Mean, base 1H4 3.2.12 *low desires,* LR 2.3.17, 2H4 2.2.174.
3 Lowly, humble, meek CYM 4.2.249 *distinction Of place 'tween high and low,* MV 1.3.43, TN 3.4.344.
4 Not flourishing MV 3.2.317 *my estate is very low,* PER 2.1.142, 1H4 4.3.57.
5 Not loud LR 5.3.274 *Her voice was ever soft, Gentle, and low,* SHR Ind.1.114, ANT 3.3.12.
6 *lower world* The earth TMP 3.3.54, R2 3.2.38.

low See LOO.

low-crooked *adj.* Bent low JC 3.1.43 *Low-crooked curtsies.*

lower *vb.*[1] (var. of) Lour, look sullen or angry R2 1.3.235 *Why at our justice seem'st thou then to low'r?,* ERR 2.1.86, ROM 4.5.94.

lowering *ppl. adj.* Sullen, angry-looking, gloomy, threatening R2 1.3.187 *This low'ring tempest,* ROM 2.5.6, 2H6 3.1.206.

lowliness *n.* Low or mean condition, low estate LLL

4.1.80 *thou the beggar, for so witnesseth thy lowli-ness*, H5 4.8.52.

lowly *adj.*
1 Enfeebled, lying low (in death) 1H6 3.3.47 *As looks the mother on her lowly babe When death doth close his tender-dying eyes.*
2 Mean, base JC 3.1.36 *These couchings and these lowly courtesies*, SHR Ind.2.32, R3 3.7.134.
~ *adv.* In a mean condition, meanly AWW 2.2.3 *highly fed and lowly taught.*

lown See LOON.

lowness *n.*
1 Abasement, abject condition LR 3.4.71 *nothing could have subdu'd nature To such a lowness but his unkind daughters.*
2 Baseness, meanness ANT 3.11.63 *dodge And palter in the shifts of lowness.*

loyal *adj.* Legitimate LR 2.1.84 *Loyal and natural boy.*

lozel *n.* Rascal WT 2.3.109 *And, lozel, thou art worthy to be hang'd.*

lubber *n.* Clumsy stupid fellow, lout TN 4.1.14 *I am afraid this great lubber the world will prove a cock-ney*, LR 1.4.91, TRO 3.3.139.

lubberly *adj.* Loutish WIV 5.5.184 *A great lubberly boy.*

luce *n.* Pike, as a heraldic bearing WIV 1.1.16 *the dozen white luces in their coat.*

lucre *n.* Acquisition (of something), greed for gain 1H6 5.4.141 *for lucre of the rest* (i.e. in a desire to gain the rest), CYM 4.2.324.

luggage *n.* Heavy stuff to be carried, lumber TMP 4.1.231 *To dote thus on such luggage*, 1H4 5.4.156; military baggage H5 4.4.75 *the luggage of our camp*, H5 4.7.1.

lugged *ppl. adj.* (of bears or bulls) Baited 1H4 1.2.74 *as melancholy as...a lugg'd bear.*

lull *vb.* (var. of) Loll R3 3.7.72 *lulling on a lewd love-bed.*

lullaby *interj.* Farewell, goodnight TN 5.1.45 *sir, lullaby to your bounty till I come again*, PP 15.15.

lump *n.* Piece of clay taken up by a potter or sculp-tor for one operation H8 2.2.48 *All men's honours Lie like one lump before him, to be fashion'd Into what pitch he please.*

lumpish *adj.* Low-spirited, dejected TGV 3.2.62 *she is lumpish, heavy, melancholy.*

lunes *n.* (pl.) Fits of frenzy or lunacy WT 2.2.28 *These...unsafe lunes i' th' King.*
◇ See LINE n. sense 7.

lurch *vb.*
1 Lurk about with evil design WIV 2.2.25 *to shuffle, to hedge, and to lurch.*
2 Cheat, rob COR 2.2.101 *He lurch'd all swords of the garland.*

lure *n.* Dummy bird used to recall a falcon SHR 4.1.192 *she never looks upon her lure*, VEN 1027.
~ *vb.* Recall (hawk) to the lure ROM 2.2.159 *To lure this tassle-gentle back again!*

lust *n.*
1 Pleasure, delight TIM 4.3.485 *mankind, whose eyes do never give But thorough lust and laughter*, LUC 1384.
2 Desire TRO 4.4.132 *I 'll answer to my lust* (i.e. I shall be answerable for what I please to do).

lust-breathed *adj.* Inspired by lust LUC 3 *Lust-breathed Tarquin.*

lust-dieted *adj.* Feeding gluttonously, surfeited LR 4.1.67 *the superfluous and lust-dieted man.*

lustful *adj.* Provocative of lust, provoking sexual desires SHR Ind.2.38 *the lustful bed.*

lustick, lustique *adv.* [Dutch 'lustig'] Merrily, jovi-ally AWW 2.3.41 *Lustick, as the Dutchman says.*

lustihood *n.* Bodily vigour ADO 5.1.76 *His May of youth and bloom of lustihood*, TRO 2.2.50.

lusty *adj.*
1 Merry AYL 4.2.17 *The horn, the horn, the lusty horn*, JN 1.1.108, SHR 4.2.50.
2 Lustful OTH 2.1.295 *I do suspect the lusty Moor Hath leap'd into my seat* (Qq *lustfull*).

lute *n.* Stringed musical instrument, in vogue 14-17C 1H6 1.4.96 *Play on the lute*, SHR 2.1.106, TIT 2.4.45; (attrib.) H5 3.2.43 *a lute case*, ADO 3.2.60.

lux tua vita mihi [L.] Thy light is life to me PER 2.2.21.

luxurious *adj.* Lascivious, lustful H5 4.4.19 *Thou damned and luxurious mountain goat*, ADO 4.1.41, TIT 5.1.88.

luxuriously *adv.* Lasciviously ANT 3.13.120 *what hotter hours...you have Luxuriously pick'd out.*

luxury *n.* Lasciviousness, lust HAM 1.5.83 *A couch for luxury and damned incest*, WIV 5.5.94, LC 314.

lym *n.* Bloodhound LR 3.6.69 *Hound or spaniel, brach or lym.*
◇ Proposed by Hanmer as a rare form of 'lyam' (i.e. lyam-hound an earlier word for bloodhound); Q *him*, Ff *Hym.*

M

ma foi [Fr.] My word, in faith H5 3.4.9.

ma foi, il fait fort chaud. O, je m'en vois à la cour—la grande affaire [Fr.] My word, it is very hot. Oh, I am going to court—how about that! WIV 1.4.51.

mace *n.* Staff of office; (fig., of sleep) JC 4.3.268 *thy leaden mace*; sceptre of sovereignty Hr 4.1.261 *The sword, the mace, the crown imperial*, 2H6 4.7.135.

Machivel, Machiavel *n.* One who acts on the prin-ciples of Machiavelli, intriguer, unscrupulous schemer WIV 3.1.101 *Am I politic? Am I subtle? Am I a Machivel?*, 1H6 5.4.74, 3H6 3.2.193.

machine *n.* Body HAM 2.2.124 *Thine evermore... whilst this machine is to him.*

maculate *ppl. adj.* Stained, impure LLL 1.2.92 *Most maculate thoughts.*

maculation *n.* Stain (of impurity or inconstancy) TRO 4.4.64 *no maculation in thy heart.*

mad *vb.* Make mad, madden ERR 4.4.126 *wherefore dost thou mad me?*, LR 4.2.43.
~ *adj.*
1 Extravagant, unrestrained TRO 5.5.38 *Troilus, who hath done to-day Mad and fantastic execution.*
2 Wild, wanton OTH 4.3.27 *he she lov'd prov'd mad, And did forsake her.*

madam *n.* Lady of rank H8 1.1.23 *The madams too, Not us'd to toil*, H5 3.5.28.

mad-bred *adj.* Produced by madness 2H6 3.1.354 *this mad-bred flaw.*

madding *n.* Madness, mad behaviour CYM 2.2.37 *witness...To th' madding of her lord.*
~ *ppl. adj.*
1 Acting madly, frenzied 2H6 3.2.117 *madding Dido.*
2 That makes mad, maddening SON 119.8 *the dis-traction of this madding fever.*

made-up *ppl. adj.* Consummate, accomplished TIM 5.1.98 *he's a made-up villain.*

madonna *n.* [It.] My lady, madam TN 1.5.43 *Two faults, madonna, that drink and good counsel will amend.*

madrigal *n.* Short lyrical poem, kind of part-song forming a musical setting to such poems; (hence) song, ditty WIV 3.1.18 *Melodious birds sing madrigals,* PP 19.8.

maggot-pie *n.* Magpie MAC 3.4.124 *maggot-pies and choughs and rooks.*

magnanimity *n.* Courage, fortitude 3H6 5.4.41 *Infuse his breast with magnanimity.*

magnanimous *adj.* Great in courage, nobly brave, valiant TRO 2.2.200 *valiant and magnanimous deeds,* H5 3.6.6, AWW 3.6.67.

Magni dominator poli, Tam lentus audis scelera? tam lentus vides? [L.; alteration of Seneca, Hippolytus 671 'Magne regnator deum,...'] Ruler of the great heavens, are you so slow to hear the crimes that are committed? so slow to see them? TIT 4.1.81.

magnificent *adj.* Vainglorious, arrogant LLL 3.1.178 *A domineering pedant o'er the boy, Than whom no mortal so magnificent!,* LLL 1.1.191.

magnifico *n.* Title given to magnates of Venice OTH 1.2.12 *The magnifico is much belov'd,* MV 3.2.280.

maid-child *n.* Female child PER 5.3.6 *brought forth A maid-child call'd Marina.*

maiden *adj.*
1 Virgin 1H6 4.7.38 *Thou maiden youth.*
2 Belonging to or befitting a maiden TN 5.1.255 *my maiden weeds,* 1H6 2.4.47, ROM 2.2.86.
3 (of a fortress, etc.) That has never been taken, unconquered LUC 408 *maiden worlds unconquered.*
4 Untried in warfare or bloodshed 1H4 5.4.131 *full bravely hast thou flesh'd Thy maiden sword;* (hence) innocent, bloodless JN 4.2.252 *This hand of mine Is yet a maiden and an innocent hand; maiden battle* fight not carried to the bloody outcome TRO 4.5.87.

maidenhead *n.* Virginity; (hence) early phase, first stage 1H4 4.1.59 *the maidenhead of our affairs.*

maiden-widowed *adj.* Widowed while still a virgin ROM 3.2.135 *But I, a maid, die maiden-widowed.*

maidhood *n.* Virginity, maidenhood TN 3.1.150 *By maidhood, honour, truth,* OTH 1.1.172.

Maid Marian *n.* Disreputable female personage in the May-game and morris-dance 1H4 3.3.114 *Maid Marian may be the deputy's wife of the ward to thee.*

maid-pale *adj.* White-complexioned; (fig.) R2 3.3.98 *Change the complexion of her maid-pale peace To scarlet indignation.*

mail *n.*[1] Piece or suit of mail-armour TRO 3.3.152 *like a rusty mail In monumental mock'ry.*

mail *n.*[2] Pouch, bag LLL 3.1.73 *no salve in the mail.*

mail *vb.* Wrap, envelop 2H6 2.4.31 *Mail'd up in shame.*

mailed *ppl. adj.* Armoured 1H4 4.1.116 *mailed Mars;* (of a hand) gauntleted COR 1.3.35 *With his mail'd hand.*

maim *n.* Mutilation or mutilating wound; (hence, fig.) grave defect or disablement COR 4.5.86 *stop those maims Of shame seen through thy country,* R2 1.3.156, 1H4 4.1.42.

main *n.*[1] In the game of hazard, a number (from five to nine) called by the 'caster' before the dice are thrown; (fig.) stake 1H4 4.1.47 *to set so rich a main On the nice hazard of one doubtful hour;* (hence) the most important matter at stake, principal concern 2H6 1.1.208 *look unto the main.*
▷ See MAIN CHANCE.

main *n.*[2]
1 Chief or main part, main body (of something) MV 5.1.97 *Empties itself, as doth an inland brook Into the main of waters* (i.e. the ocean), HAM 4.4.15, SON 60.5.
2 Principal point, chief concern, main cause HAM 2.2.56 *I doubt it is no other but the main, His father's death and our o'erhasty marriage.*
3 Mainland LR 3.1.6 *swell the curled waters 'bove the main.*
4 Ocean R3 1.4.20 *the tumbling billows of the main,* JN 2.1.26, OTH 2.1.3.
~ *adj.*
1 Exerted to the full, overpowering 2H6 1.1.210 *by main force,* H8 2.2.6.
2 Highly important, momentous H8 3.2.215 *this main secret.*
3 Very great in degree AWW 3.6.15 *a main danger.*
4 Chief in size or extent, chief part of AYL 3.5.103 *the main harvest; main battle* the body of troops forming the bulk of an army 3H6 1.1.8, R3 5.3.299.
5 General H8 4.1.31 *by the main assent Of all these learned men,* JC 2.1.196, H5 1.2.144.
6 Principal, chief COR 4.3.20 *The main blaze of it is past,* H8 2.2.40, ANT 1.2.191.
7 *main flood* High tide MV 4.1.72.

main *vb.* (old form of) Maim 2H6 4.2.163 *thereby is England main'd, and fain to go with a staff,* OTH 1.3.99.

main chance *n.*
1 General probability with regard to a future event 2H4 3.1.83 *prophesy...of the main chance of things.*
2 Most important matter risked or at stake 2H6 1.1.212 *Main chance, father, you meant.*
▷ A term in the game of hazard. See MAIN *n.*[1].

main-course *n.* Mainsail TMP 1.1.35 *bring her to try with main-course.*

mainly *adv.*
1 Forcibly, violently 1H4 2.4.200 *These four... mainly thrust at me.*
2 Entirely LR 4.7.64 *I am mainly ignorant What place this is.*
3 Greatly, very much HAM 4.7.9 *You mainly were stirred up; so mainly* so much TRO 4.4.85 *I do not call your faith in question So mainly as my merit.*

maintain *vb.*
1 Carry on, keep up (conversation) TN 4.2.99 *Maintain no words with him,* ADO 4.1.205, LR 3.3.15.
2 Afford, bear the cost of SHR 5.1.76 *I am able to maintain it,* TIM 2.2.2.
3 Sustain (a part) LLL 5.2.892 *the one maintained by the owl, th' other by the cuckoo.*

maintenance *n.* Bearing, demeanour 1H4 5.4.22 *lustier maintenance than I did look for.*

major *n.* (elliptical for) Major premiss (of a syllogism) 1H4 2.4.495 *I deny your major.*
~ *adj.* Paramount to all other claims TRO 5.1.44 *My major vow lies here.*

majority *n.* Superiority, pre-eminence 1H4 3.2.109 *whose high deeds...Holds from all soldiers chief majority.*

make *n.* Mate, spouse LR 4.3.34 *Else one self mate and make could not beget Such different issues* (Q1; Q2 *mate*).

make *vb.*
1 Muster, raise (a force) R3 4.4.450 *Bid him levy straight The greatest strength and power he can make,* COR 5.1.37; *make head* raise a force 1H4 3.1.63 *Three times hath Henry Bullingbrook made head Against my power.*
2 Shut, close ERR 3.1.93 *the doors are made against you,* AYL 4.1.161.

3 Do, have to do OTH 3.4.169 *What make you from home?*, WIV 2.1.236, R3 1.3.163.

4 Go, move ERR 1.1.92 *Two ships from far, making amain to us*, LR 1.1.143, VEN 5.

5 Have to do (*with* a person or *in* a matter) ADO 3.3.52 *the less you meddle or make with them*, TRO 1.1.14, WIV 1.4.110.

6 Give (a dinner, etc.) H8 1.3.52 *This night he makes a supper*, 3H6 5.5.85.

7 Regard, consider, represent (a thing as so-and-so) AWW 5.3.5 *to make it Natural rebellion*, MM 5.1.51, SHR 3.2.191.

8 Amount to 1H4 4.2.6 *This bottle makes an angel* (i.e. costs).

9 Prove, show that something is the case LR 5.3.93 *I'll make it on thy heart...thou art in nothing less Than I have here proclaim'd thee* (Qq 1–2 *prove*).

10 *make all split* See SPLIT.

11 *make one* Join in, be one of the party WIV 2.3.46 *if I see a sword out, my finger itches to make one*, SHR 1.2.244, TN 1.5.201.

~ in combination

make against 1 Provide evidence against ROM 5.3.225 *as the time and place Doth make against me.* **2** Militate against H5 1.2.36 *no bar To make against your Highness' claim.* **make away** Put an end to, destroy 2H6 3.1.167 *make away my guiltless life*, VEN 763, SON 11.8. **make forth** Advance JC 5.1.25, H5 2.4.5. **make from** Get out of the way of LR 1.1.143 *The bow is bent and drawn; make from the shaft.* **make out** Go forth TN 2.5.59 *Seven of my people...make out for him.* **make to** Approach JC 3.1.18 *Look how he makes to Caesar.* **make up 1** Complete R3 1.1.21 *scarce half made up*, CYM 4.2.109. **2** Collect, get together 2H6 2.1.39 *Make up no factious numbers*, JC 4.3.208. **3** Compile H8 1.1.75 *He makes up the file Of all the gentry.* **4** Piece together, solve, work out TN 2.5.121 *O ay, make up that.* **5** Advance, go to the front 1H4 5.4.5 *make up, Lest your retirement do amaze your friends.* **6** Come to (a decision) LR 1.1.206 *Election makes not up in such conditions* (i.e. does not come to a decision), TRO 2.2.170, JN 2.1.541.

makeless *adj.* Without a mate, husbandless SON 9.4 *a makeless wife.*

make-peace *n.* Peacemaker R2 1.1.160 *To be a make-peace shall become my age.*

making *n.*

1 Form, shape, build MND 2.1.32 *your shape and making*, ERR 4.2.22.

2 *the makings of* The materials that go to make H8 4.1.87 *She had all the royal makings of a queen.*

malapert *adj.* Impudent, saucy TN 4.1.44 *this malapert blood*, R3 1.3.254, 3H6 5.5.32.

malecontent *n.* (usual 16C spelling of) Malcontent LLL 3.1.183 *Liege of all loiterers and malecontents*, TGV 2.1.20, WIV 1.3.104.

~ *adj.* Discontented 3H6 4.1.60 *thou art malecontent*, 3H6 4.1.10.

malefaction *n.* Evil-doing HAM 2.2.592 *They have proclaim'd their malefactions.*

malevolent *adj.* (fig., of a star) Exercising a baleful influence 1H4 1.1.97 *Malevolent to you in all aspects.*

malice *n.*

1 Power to harm, harmfulness JN 2.1.251 *Our cannons' malice.*

2 Malicious act COR 2.2.32 *to report otherwise were a malice.*

3 (as a form of address) Wickedness TMP 1.2.367 *Shrug'st thou, malice?*

malicious *adj.* Violent JN 2.1.314 *this hot malicious day.*

maliciously *adv.* Violently ANT 3.13.178 *I will be treble-sinew'd,...And fight maliciously*, WT 1.2.321.

malign *vb.* Deal malignantly with, regard with hatred PER 5.1.89 *wayward fortune did malign my state*, COR 1.1.113.

malignancy *n.* Unpropitiousness, baleful character TN 2.1.4 *the malignancy of my fate.*

malignant *adj.*

1 Rebellious against God OTH 5.2.353 *a malignant-...Turk.*

2 (of a disease) Virulent AWW 2.1.111 *that malignant cause.*

3 Of evil or baleful influence 1H6 4.5.6 *But O malignant and ill-boding stars!*, TGV 3.1.240.

malkin, mawkin *n.* Slattern, untidy female servant COR 2.1.208 *the kitchen malkin*, PER 4.3.34.

◇ A diminutive of 'Malde' (i.e. Maud, Matilda).

mallecho, malicho *n.* (?) Mischief, misdeed HAM 3.2.137 *this' miching mallecho, it means mischief.*

◇ Fl *Malicho*, Qq 1–2 *Mallico.* Usu. taken to represent Sp. 'malhecho' (=misdeed), but form, origin and meaning are uncertain.

malmsey-nose *adj.* Red-nosed 2H4 2.1.39 *that arrant malmsey-nose knave.*

malt-horse *n.* Heavy kind of horse used by brewers; (term of abuse) ERR 3.1.32 *Mome, malt-horse, capon, coxcomb, idiot, patch!*, SHR 4.1.129.

malt-worm *n.* (transf.) Toper, hard-drinker, drunkard 1H4 2.1.75 *these mad mustachio purple-hu'd malt-worms*, 2H4 2.4.334.

mammer *vb.* (orig.) Mutter, stammer; (hence) hesitate, waver OTH 3.3.70 *Or stand so mamm'ring on* (Q1 *muttering*).

mammet *n.* Doll, puppet ROM 3.5.184 *a whining mammet*, 1H4 2.3.92.

mammock *vb.* Break into fragments, tear to pieces COR 1.3.65 *how he mammock'd it!*

man *n.*

1 *since I was man* Since I was born LR 3.2.45.

2 *I write man* I style myself 'man', claim manhood AWW 2.3.198.

3 *never mine own man since* Not what I used to be 2H6 4.2.83.

4 *no man was his own* No man was in his senses TMP 5.1.213.

5 *man of this world* Ordinary mortal 2H4 5.3.97.

~ *vb.*

1 Provide (one) with attendants 2H4 1.2.16 *I was never mann'd with an agot till now*, 2H4 1.2.54.

2 Accustom (a hawk) to the presence of men, tame SHR 4.1.193 *to man my haggard.*

3 (prob. from the metaphor 'man a gun') Aim, direct OTH 5.2.270 *Man but a rush against Othello's breast.*

manage *n.*

1 Training of a horse in its paces R2 3.3.179 *The manage of unruly jades*, 1H4 2.3.49, PER 4.6.64.

2 Action and paces to which a horse is trained AYL 1.1.13 *His horses are bred better, for...they are taught their manage.*

3 Short gallop at full speed LLL 5.2.482 *Full merrily Hath this brave manage, this career, been run.*

◇ Theobald's emendation; Q1 *nuage*; Ff, Q2 *manager.*

4 Management, conduct, administration TMP 1.2.70 *The manage of my state*, MV 3.4.25, R2 1.4.39; bringing about, contrivance ROM 3.1.143 *The unlucky manage of this fatal brawl.*

~ *vb.*

1 Wield, handle ROM 1.1.69 *Put up thy sword, Or manage it to part these men with me*, TGV 3.1.249, R2 3.2.118; (fig.) LR 1.3.17 *still would manage those authorities.*

2 Bring about, contrive OTH 2.3.215 *To manage private and domestic quarrel?*
3 Train, break in (a horse) VEN 598 *He will not manage her, although he mount her.*

manager *n.* Wielder (of a weapon, etc.) LLL 1.2.182 *Adieu, valour, rust, rapier, be still, drum, for your manager is in love.*

manakin See MANIKIN.

mandragora *n.* mandrake OTH 3.3.330 *Not poppy, nor mandragora, Nor all the drowsy syrups of the world,* ANT 1.5.4.

mandrake *n.* Poisonous plant of the genus Mandragora, native to Southern Europe and the East, having emetic and narcotic properties; its forked root is thought to resemble the human form and when pulled up was fabled to utter a shriek causing death or insanity 2H6 3.2.310 *the mandrake's groan,* ROM 4.3.47; (a term of abuse) 2H4 1.2.14 *Thou whoreson mandrake,* 2H4 3.2.315.

mane *n.* Growth of hair on the back of the neck and shoulders, esp. of lions and horses; (transf., to the crests of waves) OTH 2.1.13 *wind-shak'd surge, with high and monstrous mane.*
⇨ F1 *Maine*; Q1 *mayne*. Some edd. prefer 'main' (i.e. power).

mangle *vb.* Hack, cut, lacerate, wound by repeated blows H5 4.4.39 *mangled shalt thou be by this my sword,* OTH 5.1.79.

mangled *ppl. adj.* Cut, lacerated, wounded ROM 4.3.52 *the mangled Tybalt,* 3H6 5.2.7, 1H4 5.4.96.

mangling *ppl. adj.* Cutting, wounding VEN 1065 *her mangling eye.*

manhood *n.* Condition of being a man; (as opposed to childhood) R3 4.4.171 *Thy school-days...furious, Thy prime of manhood daring,* MAC 5.2.11; (as opposed to womanhood) CYM 3.4.192 *fit you to your manhood.*

manikin, manakin *n.* Little man TN 3.2.53 *This is a dear manikin to you, Sir Toby.*

mankind *n.* The male sex TIM 4.3.484 *Because thou art a woman, and disclaim'st Flinty mankind,* WIV 4.2.23, WT 1.2.199.
~ *adj.* Masculine, virago-like WT 2.3.68 *A mankind witch!,* COR 4.2.16.

manly *adv.* Gallantly, bravely MAC 4.3.235 *This tune goes manly.*

manner *n.*[1]
1 Usage, custom, fashion HAM 1.4.15 *to the manner born* (i.e. familiar from birth with the usage), MM 4.2.134, ERR 1.2.12.
2 (pl.) Moral character, morals LUC 1397 *Their face their manners...told,* MV 2.3.19, H5 1.2.49.
3 (pl.) Good way of living, good breeding, civility 1H4 3.1.182 *Defect of manners, want of government,* AYL 4.3.15, TN 2.3.87.
4 (pl.) Forms of politeness SHR 1.1.227 *frame your manners to the time,* AWW 4.5.88.
5 *in, with manners* Decently, becomingly TN 2.1.15 *It charges me in manners the rather to express,* CYM 1.4.52 *Can we, with manners, ask,* SON 39.1.

manner *n.*[2] *taken with the manner* Taken with the thing stolen in one's possession 1H4 2.4.315 *thou stolest a cup of sack...and wert taken with the manner;* (hence) taken in the very act LLL 1.1.203 *I was taken with the manner.*
⇨ Term of Anglo-French law, orig. 'mainoure' (Fr. 'manœuvre', lit. hand-work), which acquired the concrete sense of 'thing stolen'.

mannerly *adj.* Seemly, decent TGV 2.7.58 *let me have What...is most mannerly,* WT 2.1.86, ROM 1.5.98.
~ *adv.* Decently, civilly CYM 3.6.91 *We'll mannerly demand thee of thy story,* ADO 2.1.76, MV 2.9.100.

man-queller *n.* Man-slayer, murderer 2H4 2.1.53 *thou art a honeyseed, a man-queller.*

mansion *n.* Dwelling TIM 5.1.215 *his everlasting mansion* (i.e. grave).

mansionry *n.* Abode MAC 1.6.5 *By his lov'd mansionry.*
⇨ Ff *mansonry*; perh. misprint for 'masonry'.

mantle *n.* Scum, vegetable coating on surface of stagnant water LR 3.4.133 *drinks the green mantle of the standing pool.*
~ *vb.*
1 Cover, envelop TMP 5.1.67 *the ignorant fumes that mantle Their clearer reason,* COR 1.6.29.
2 Become covered with a coating MV 1.1.89 *whose visages Do cream and mantle like a standing pond.*

mantled *ppl. adj.* Covered with a scum TMP 4.1.182 *th' filthy mantled pool* (some mod. edd. *filthy-mantled*).

manu cita [L.] With swift hand, with ready hand LLL 5.1.69.
⇨ Dover Wilson conjecture; F1 *vnum cita.*

manual seal *n.* 'Seal manual', seal affixed by one's own hand R2 4.1.25 *There is my gage, the manual seal of death* (i.e. death warrant).

manure *vb.* Till, cultivate OTH 1.3.324 *sterile with idleness or manur'd with industry.*

manus [L.] Hand(s) LLL 5.2.591 *Thus did he strangle serpents in his manus.*

many *n.* Multitude 2H4 1.3.91 *thou fond many,* COR 3.1.66 (F4; Ff 1–3 *Meyny, Meynie*).
~ *adj.*
1 *many a day* A long time ago H8 5.2.21 *I think your Highness saw this many a day.*
2 *for this many a day* All this long time HAM 3.1.90 *How does your honour for this many a day?*
3 *many a many* Many and many a JN 1.1.183 *many a many foot of land.*

map *n.* (fig.) Detailed representation in epitome, embodiment, very picture or image (of something) R2 5.1.12 *Thou map of honour,* COR 1.2.62, TIT 3.2.12.

mappery *n.* Mere drawing of charts and diagrams TRO 1.3.205 *They call this bed-work, mapp'ry, closet-war.*

marble *adj.*
1 Hard-hearted, pitiless WT 5.2.90 *Who was most marble there chang'd colour,* 3H6 3.1.38.
2 (of the heavens) Radiant, shining OTH 3.3.460 *yond marble heaven.*

marble-breasted *adj.* Stony-hearted, hard-hearted, pitiless TN 5.1.124 *the marble-breasted tyrant.*

marble-constant *adj.* Firm as marble ANT 5.2.240 *I am marble-constant.*

marbled *ppl. adj.* Radiant, shining like marble TIM 4.3.191 *the marbled mansion all above* (i.e. the heavens).

marcantant *n.* (corr. of It. 'mercatante') Merchant SHR 4.2.63 *a marcantant, or a pedant* (F1).

March-chick *n.* Chick which has hatched prematurely; (hence, fig.) precocious youth ADO 1.3.56 *A very forward March-chick!*

marches *n.* (pl.) The portions of England bordering respectively on Scotland and on Wales H5 1.2.140 *They of those marches...Shall be a wall sufficient to defend Our inland,* 3H6 2.1.140.

marchpane *n.* Marzipan ROM 1.5.8 *save me a piece of marchpane.*

mare *n.*[1]
1 *The man shall have his mare again* All will come right in the end MND 3.2.463.
2 *wild-mare* See-saw 2H4 2.4.247 *rides the wild-mare.*
3 *Whose mare's dead?* What is amiss? 2H4 2.1.43.

mare n.² Nightmare 2H4 2.1.77 *I will ride thee a'*
nights like the mare.

margent n.

1 Edge, border, brink MND 2.1.85 *the beached mar-*
gent of the sea, LC 39.

2 Margin of a page of a book LLL 5.2.8 *Writ o' both*
sides the leaf, margent and all; (hence) commentary (from the fact that the margin is used for a
commentary on the text) HAM 5.2.155 *I knew you*
must be edified by the margent; (esp. of the eyes as
providing a commentary on or indication of a person's thoughts or feelings) ROM 1.3.86 *written in*
the margent of his eyes, LLL 2.1.246, LUC 102.

marish See NOURISH.

mark n.¹

1 Target, butt LLL 4.1.129 *A mark marvellous well*
shot, for they both did hit it, SON 70.2, ADO 2.1.246;
(fig.) *beyond the mark of* beyond the reach of ANT
3.6.87, COR 2.2.89.

2 *God bless, save the mark* Orig. perh. a formula
invoking a blessing on the mark of the cross made
to avert evil, and hence used to qualify apologet-
ically or scornfully some remark ROM 3.2.53 *I saw*
the wound...God save the mark!, OTH 1.1.33, 1H4
1.3.56.

3 Attention, notice, observance MM 5.1.322 *As*
much in mock as mark, OTH 2.3.317; importance
1H4 3.2.45 *of no mark.*

4 Object serving to mark a spot at sea SON 116.5 *it*
is an ever-fixed mark That looks on tempests and
is never shaken; (fig.) guiding object, 'example,
pattern' (Schmidt) 2H4 2.3.31 *He was the mark and*
glass...That fashioned others, WT 4.4.8.

mark n.² Sum of money, approx. two thirds of a
pound (not a coin) H8 5.1.170 *Give her an hundred*
marks, MM 4.3.7, ERR 1.1.21.

market n.

1 *I run before my horse to market* I count the gain
before the bargain is made R3 1.1.160.

2 *market of his time* (lit.) Marketing or selling of
his time; (hence, fig.) the use to which he devotes
his time HAM 4.4.34 *If his chief good and market of*
his time Be but to sleep...

market-bell n. Bell rung to announce the opening
of a market 1H6 3.2.16 *the market-bell is rung.*

mark-man n. Marksman ROM 1.1.206 *A right good*
mark-man! (F1; Ff 3–4 *Marksman*).

marl n. Clay, earth ADO 2.1.63 *a clod of wayward*
marl (i.e. a man).

marlet See MARTLET.

marmazet n. (var. of) Marmoset, small monkey
TMP 2.2.170 *snare the nimble marmazet.*

marquess n.

1 (var. of) Marquis 3H6 3.3.164 *Marquess Monta-*
gue, 2H6 1.1.44, R3 1.3.254.

2 Marchioness H8 5.2.203 *Lady Marquess Dorset.*

marry vb. (fig.) Unite intimately, join closely JN
3.1.228 *Married in league*, ROM 1.3.63, SON 8.6.

marry interj.

1 (used as an oath of affirmation or invocation)
Indeed, to be sure ERR 2.2.102 *Marry, and did, sir*,
AWW 2.3.58, R3 1.3.260; (often with asseverative
words or invocations) TN 4.2.101 *Marry, amen*, R2
4.1.114 *Marry, God forbid!*

2 (in answering a question, when it often implies
surprise that it should have been asked) Why, to
be sure TGV 2.1.18 *how know you that I am in*
love?—Marry, by these special marks, JC 1.2.229,
R3 1.3.97.

3 *marry, come up* (in expressions of indignant or
amused surprise or contempt) 'Come off it' PER
4.6.150 *Marry, come up, my dish of chastity with*
rosemary and bays, ROM 2.5.62.

4 *marry trap* (perh. a term from a game) 'You are

caught' (Nares) WIV 1.1.167 *I will say 'marry trap'*
with you, if you run the nuthook's humour on me.

marshal n.

1 High officer of state in England, now called 'earl
marshal' 1H4 4.4.2 *the Lord Marshal*, H8 4.1.19.

2 Officer charged with arrangement of ceremonies, esp. with the regulation of combats in the lists
and with the establishment of rank and order at
feasts and processions MM 2.2.61 *The marshal's*
truncheon, nor the judge's robe, R2 1.1.204, 2H4
1.3.4; (fig.) leader MND 2.2.120 *Reason becomes the*
marshal to my will.

3 General officer of the highest rank in the French
army LR 4.3.8 *The Marshal of France.*

~ vb. Guide, lead, conduct MAC 2.1.42 *Thou mar-*
shal'st me the way that I was going, HAM 3.4.205,
OTH 2.1.261.

mart n.

1 A periodical gathering of people for the purpose
of buying or selling ERR 1.1.17 *any Syracusian*
marts and fairs, PER 4.2.4.

2 A public place for buying and selling, market
place ERR 1.2.27 *I'll meet with you upon the mart*,
MV 3.1.47.

3 Buying and selling, traffic, bargaining HAM
1.1.74 *foreign mart for implements of war*; bargain
SHR 2.1.327 *venture madly on a desperate mart.*

~ vb.

1 (intr.) Traffic, bargain CYM 1.6.151 *to mart As in*
a Romish stew.

2 (trans.) Traffic in, buy or sell JC 4.3.11 *To sell*
and mart your offices for gold.

Martial adj. Like that of the war-god Mars CYM
4.2.310 *His foot Mercurial, his Martial thigh.*

Martin n. *Saint Martin's summer* Season of fine
mild weather occurring about Martinmas, Nov.
11; (fig.) season of prosperity after adversity 1H6
1.2.131 *Expect Saint Martin's summer, halcyon*
days.

martlet n. House-martin, marlet MV 2.9.28 *like the*
martlet Builds in the weather on the outward wall,
MAC 1.6.4 (Ff *Bartlet*).

martyr vb.

1 Inflict grievous pain upon, torment, torture ROM
4.5.59 *hated, martyr'd, kill'd!*

2 Mutilate, disfigure TIT 3.1.107 *Nor tongue to tell*
me who hath mart'red thee, TIT 5.2.180, LUC 802.

martyred ppl. adj. Mutilated; (hence) defective or
imperfect (because of the mutilation of limbs) TIT
3.2.36 *I can interpret all her martyr'd signs.*

marvailes, marvail's adv. (old forms of) MARVEL-
LOUS MND 4.1.24 *I am marvail's hairy about the*
face, 2H4 5.1.35, MND 3.1.2.

marvel n.

1 Astonishment, wonder CYM 3.1.10 *And to kill the*
marvel, Shall be so ever, WT 5.1.188, WT 5.3.100.

2 *it is marvel* It is a wonder MV 2.6.3 *it is marvel*
he out-dwells his hour, SHR 4.2.86; *no marvel*
(though) no wonder (if) VEN 390 *no marvel though*
thy horse be gone, MND 2.2.96, LR 2.1.98.

marvellous adv. Wonderfully, extremely AWW
4.3.157 *The rogues are marvellous poor*, TMP 3.3.19,
ERR 4.3.58.

Mary-bud n. Bud of the marigold CYM 2.3.24 *And*
winking Mary-buds begin to ope their golden eyes.

mash vb. Mix malt with water to form wort; (hence)
brew; (fig.) TIT 3.2.38 *no other drink but tears,*
Brew'd with her sorrow, mash'd upon her cheeks
(Ff, Qq *mesh'd*).

mask vb. Take part in a masque or masquerade
ROM 1.5.37 *then we mask'd.*

masking, masquing ppl. adj.

1 Taking part in a masque or masquerade MV
2.6.59 *Our masquing mates.*

2 Used in, appropriate to masques or masquerades SHR 4.3.87 *what masquing stuff is here?*

mass *n.*

1 Solid bulk, massiveness TRO 1.3.29 *what hath mass or matter*, HAM 4.4.47; (applied to the earth) HAM 3.4.49 *this solidity and compound mass.*

2 Large amount or quantity TRO 2.2.107 *that mass of moan to come*, WIV 2.2.272, 2H6 1.3.131.

mast *n.* Fruit of the beech, oak or chestnut, serving as food for pigs TIM 4.3.419 *The oaks bear mast.*

master *n.*

1 Leader, chief TIT 5.1.15 *bees...Led by their master*, TMP 1.2.163, H5 4.8.94.

2 Captain of a merchant vessel TMP 2.2.46 *The master, the swabber, the boatswain*, MAC 1.3.7; officer having the navigation of a ship of war 2H6 4.1.SD *a Captain, a Master, a Master's-Mate.*

3 Owner TMP 2.1.5 *The masters of some merchant.*

4 *good master* Patron LLL 4.1.104 *my Lord Berowne, a good master of mine*, WT 5.2.174.

5 *great master* Chief officer of a royal household H5 4.8.95 *Great Master of France.*

6 (used vocatively as a polite form of address) (sing.) Sir 2H6 2.1.95 *A plum-tree, master*; (pl.) sirs, gentlemen HAM 2.2.429 *Masters, you are all welcome*, COR 1.1.62, SHR 1.2.188.

7 Title prefixed to a man's name WIV 1.1.80 *Master Shallow*; prefixed to a designation of office or profession ADO 3.3.17 *Master Constable*, TIM 4.2.1.

8 Title applied by inferiors to the boys and young men of the families of their superiors MV 2.2.48 *Talk you of young Master Launcelot?*, LR 2.2.46.

~ *vb.*

1 Rule as a master, be the master of CYM 4.2.395 *rather father thee than master thee.*

2 Own, possess MV 5.1.174 *the wealth That the world masters*, 1H4 5.2.63, SON 106.8.

~ *adj.* Main, principal, chief JC 3.1.163 *The choice and master spirits of this age*, OTH 2.1.262, PER 4.6.8.

masterdom *n.* Absolute control MAC 1.5.70 *solely sovereign sway and masterdom.*

masterly *adj. a masterly report* A report of one's mastery in a particular activity HAM 4.7.96 *a masterly report For art and exercise in your defence.*

master-mistress *n.* Man occupying the position of a mistress SON 20.2 *the master-mistress of my passion.*

mastership *n.*

1 (with possessive pron.) Form of address acknowledging authority or superiority MV 2.2.59 *an't please your mastership*, TGV 3.1.281.

2 Masterly skill, capacity COR 4.1.7 *all boats alike Show'd mastership in floating.*

mastic *adj.* (?) (1) Misprint for 'mastis, mastice', dial. form of 'mastiff'; (hence) massive; or (2) 'gummy' (Stokes) TRO 1.3.73 *When rank Thersites opes his mastic jaws.*

match *n.*

1 Opponent, antagonist, rival 2H6 5.2.10 *match to match I have encount'red him.*

2 A matching of adversaries against each other; contest viewed with regard to the equality or inequality of the parties TRO 4.5.46 *It were no match, your nail against his horn*, HAM 2.2.471 (Qq *matcht*); *for Hector's match* a match for Hector TRO 5.4.26.

3 *cry a match* Claim a win ROM 2.4.70 *swits and spurs, or I'll cry a match.*

4 Agreement, compact, bargain TRO 4.5.270 *Thy hand upon that match*, MV 3.1.44, WIV 2.2.290; *a match!* Agreed! TMP 2.1.34 *The wager?—A laughter.—A match!*, SHR 5.2.74.

5 *set a match* See SET.

~ *vb.*

1 Ally oneself in marriage ADO 2.1.64 *to match in my kindred*, TN 1.3.109, 2H6 1.1.131.

2 Associate or join (one) *with* another LLL 2.1.49 *a sharp wit match'd with too blunt a will*, ADO 2.1.107.

3 Oppose, esp. with equal power, be a match for MND 3.2.305 *You perhaps may think...That I can match her*, CYM 2.2.25, HAM 4.7.100.

4 (intr.) Meet in combat, fight JN 2.1.330 *Strength match'd with strength.*

5 Compare, place in competition *with* ROM 2.Ch.4 *With tender Juliet match'd*, TRO 1.3.194, OTH 3.3.237.

6 Be suitable *to* H5 2.4.130 *As matching to his youth and vanity.*

7 Procure as a match MV 3.1.78 *Here comes another of the tribe; a third cannot be match'd.*

mate *n.* Fellow 2H4 2.4.125 *you poor, base, rascally, cheating, lack-linen mate!*, SHR 1.1.58, R3 1.3.339.

~ *vb.*[1]

1 Join in or couple with VEN 909 *Her more than haste is mated with delays.*

2 Rival, vie with H8 3.2.274 *You...that in the way of loyalty and truth...dare mate a sounder man than Surrey can be.*

mate *vb.*[2]

1 Checkmate, outwit; (fig.) 2H6 3.1.265 *that is good deceit Which mates him first that first intends deceit.*

2 Stupefy, confound ERR 5.1.282 *I think you are all mated, or stark mad*, MAC 5.1.78.

material *adj.*

1 Forming the essential substance of a thing LR 4.2.35 *She that herself will...disbranch from her material sap.*

2 Full of 'matter' or sense AYL 3.3.32 *A material fool!*

matin *n.* Morning HAM 1.5.89 *The glow-worm shows the matin to be near.*

matter *n.*

1 Subject, affair, business ANT 2.2.25 *Touch you the sourest points with sweetest terms, Nor curstness grow to th' matter*, WIV 1.1.215, MM 3.1.196; *to the matter* to the point CYM 5.5.169, HAM 2.3.324; *off the matter* off the point, irrelevantly ADO 3.5.10.

2 Sense, substance (as opposed to nonsense or triviality) LR 4.6.174 *matter and impertinency mix'd*, ADO 2.1.330, AYL 2.1.68.

3 Reason, cause WT 1.1.34 *there is not...either malice or matter to alter it; ground for complaint* H8 3.2.21 *The King hath found Matter against him*, COR 3.3.76, 2H4 1.2.132.

4 *There is matter in it* There is some importance attaching to it OTH 3.4.139, WT 4.4.842; *'Tis no matter for* there is no importance attaching to H5 5.1.16; *it's no matter for that* that does not matter COR 4.5.165, TGV 3.1.330.

5 *no such matter* (used to give emphatic negative to a previous statement or implication) Nothing of the kind ADO 2.3.217, TN 3.1.5, TRO 3.1.88.

mature *adj.*

1 Ripe, ready *for* COR 4.3.25 *is almost mature for the violent breaking out.*

2 Pertaining to maturity or manhood WT 1.1.25 *their more mature dignities.*

3 (of time) Due LR 4.6.275 *in the mature time.*

maugre *prep.* In spite of TN 3.1.151 *maugre all thy pride*, TIT 4.2.110, LR 5.3.132.

maund *n.* Woven wicker basket with handles LC 36 *A thousand favours from a maund she drew.*

May *n.* (fig.) Bloom, prime, heyday ADO 5.1.76 *His May of youth.*

May-morn *n.* (fig.) Bloom, prime, heyday H5 1.2.120 *the very May-morn of his youth.*

may *vb.*

1 Can, have power or ability to 2H4 3.1.66 *as I may remember*, TMP 1.2.345, H5 1.2.292.

2 *you may*, *you may* Go on, go on COR 2.3.35, TRO 3.1.109.

mazard, mazzard *n.* (jocular) Head OTH 2.3.154 *I'll knock you o'er the mazzard*, HAM 5.1.89.

mazed *ppl. adj.* Bewildered, confused MND 2.1.113 *the mazed world...knows not which is which*, H8 2.4.186, 1H6 4.2.47.

Me pompae provexit apex [L.] The crown of triumph has led me on high PER 2.2.30.

meacock *adj.* Timid, effeminate SHR 2.1.313 *A meacock wretch*.

mead *n.* Meadow SHR 5.2.139 *as frosts do bite the meads*, H5 5.2.48, TIT 2.4.54.

meadow *n.* Low, well-watered ground TIT 3.1.125 *like meadows yet not dry, With miry slime left on them by a flood*, LLL 5.2.897, SON 33.3.

meagre *adj.* Poor, barren JN 3.1.80 *The meagre cloddy earth*, MV 3.2.104.

mealed *ppl. adj.* Spotted, stained MM 4.2.83 *Were he meal'd with that Which he corrects.*

mealy *adj.* Covered with fine dust or powder TRO 3.3.79 *for men, like butterflies, Show not their mealy wings.*

mean *n.*

1 Middle position, medium MV 1.2.8 *seated in the mean*, ANT 2.7.19; moderation 1H6 1.2.121 *he keeps no mean.*

2 Middle part, tenor or alto (intermediate between treble and bass) LLL 5.2.328 *he can sing A mean most meanly*, TGV 1.2.93; singer of such a part WT 4.3.43 *they are most of them means and bases.*

3 Something interposed or intervening 3H6 3.2.141 *the means that keeps me from it*, ANT 3.2.32.

4 *make means* Take steps, use efforts R3 5.3.40 *make some good means to speak with him*, TGV 5.4.137, CYM 2.4.3.

5 Instrument, agent, method ANT 4.6.34 *a swifter mean Shall outstrike thought*, ROM 3.3.45.

6 Opportunity of doing something, of access to a person, etc. R3 4.2.76 *Let me have open means to come to them*, ERR 1.2.18, HAM 4.6.14.

7 Instrumentality, influence, instigation 2H6 3.2.124 *murd'red By Suffolk and the Cardinal Beauford's means*, R3 1.3.77, MM 2.4.95.

8 Sum of money ERR 1.2.18 *Many a man would...go indeed, having so good a mean*; (pl.) money, wealth LR 4.1.20 *Our means secure us.*

mean *vb.* Lament, complain MND 5.1.323 *And thus she means.*

mean *adj.*

1 Of low degree, station, or position AWW 3.5.60 *she is too mean To have her name repeated*, TGV 2.4.107, TMP 3.3.87.

2 Undignified, base, contemptible 1H4 3.2.13 *Such poor, such bare,...such mean attempts*, ROM 3.3.45, 2H6 3.2.146.

meaning *n.* Intention, purpose SHR 3.2.124 *He hath some meaning in his mad attire*, LR 1.2.173, R3 3.5.55.

meanly *adv.*[1]

1 Poorly, badly LLL 5.2.328 *he can sing A mean most meanly.*

2 Basely, in a lowly way R3 4.3.37 *His daughter meanly have I match'd in marriage*, CYM 3.3.82.

meanly *adv.*[2] In the mean or middling degree, moderately; (hence) *not meanly* in no small degree ERR 1.1.58 *My wife, not meanly proud of two such boys.*

measle *n.* Scab, loathsome disease; (hence, fig.) scurvy wretch COR 3.1.78 *those measles Which we disdain should tetter us.*

measurable *adj.* Suitable LLL 5.1.92 *The posterior of the day...is...measurable for the afternoon.*

measure *n.*

1 Distance of a fencer from his opponent; (fig.) reach TGV 5.4.127 *Come not within the measure of my wrath.*

2 Something commensurate or adequate COR 2.2.123 *He cannot but with measure fit the honours Which we devise him*; satisfaction (of desire) 3H6 2.3.32 *Or fortune give me measure of revenge.*

3 Limit, restricted extent, ascertained quantity ROM 3.2.125 *There is no end, no limit, measure, bound*, MAC 5.9.39, ANT 3.4.8; *above, beyond all, out of measure* excessively CYM 2.4.113 *O, above measure false!*, SHR 1.2.90, ADO 1.3.2.

4 Moderation MV 3.2.112 *In measure rain thy joy*, R2 3.4.8, ADO 2.1.71 (with quibble).

5 Treatment meted out MM 3.2.243 *receiv'd no sinister measure from his judge*, AWW 2.3.257, 3H6 2.6.55.

6 Metre H5 5.2.134 *neither words nor measure.*

7 Music (esp. accompanying and regulating motion) JN 3.1.304 *Shall braying trumpets and loud churlish drums...be measures to our pomp?*

8 Rhythm or time of a piece of music TN 5.1.38 *The triplex, sir, is a good tripping measure.*

9 Dance, esp. grave or stately dance ADO 2.1.77 *a measure, full of state and ancientry*, ROM 1.4.10, VEN 1148.

10 Stately manner of walking WT 4.4.732 *Hath not my gait in it the measure of the court?*, MV 2.6.11.

11 Unit of capacity, length, volume MAC 3.4.11 *we'll drink a measure* (i.e. a toast), OTH 2.3.32, OTH 4.3.73.

~ *vb.*

1 *measure one's length* Fall or lie full length on the ground MND 3.2.429 *To measure out my length on this cold bed*, LR 1.4.90.

2 *measure swords* Fight, prepare for duelling AYL 5.4.87 *we measur'd swords.*

3 Mark *out* the bounds of AYL 2.6.2 *measure out my grave.*

4 Judge, estimate H5 1.2.268 *Not measuring what use we made of them*, WT 2.1.114, ROM 1.1.126.

5 Traverse MV 3.4.84 *For we must measure twenty miles to-day*, TGV 2.7.10; go back upon (one's steps), retrace (a path) TMP 2.1.259 *How shall that Claribel Measure us back to Naples?*, JN 5.5.3.

6 Tread, pace out (a 'measure') ROM 1.4.10 *We'll measure them a measure and be gone* (quibble).

meat *n.* Food in general MM 1.2.15 *the thanksgiving before meat*, ADO 2.3.239, WIV 1.1.294.

mechanic *n.* Manual worker, handicraftsman COR 5.3.83 *Do not bid me...capitulate Again with Rome's mechanics.*

~ *adj.* Engaged in a manual occupation H5 1.2.200 *The poor mechanic porters*, ANT 5.2.209; (hence) low, vulgar ANT 4.4.32 *to stand On more mechanic compliment.*

mechanical *n.* MECHANIC *n.* MND 3.2.9 *A crew of patches, rude mechanicals*, 2H6 1.3.193.

~ *adj.* MECHANIC *adj.* WIV 2.2.278 *mechanical salt-butter rogue!*, 2H4.5.5.36, JC 1.1.3.

medal *n.* Metal disk used as trinket, medallion, locket WT 1.2.307 *he that wears her like her medal hanging About his neck.*

meddle *vb.*

1 Mingle TMP 1.2.22 *More to know Did never meddle with my thoughts.*

2 Mingle in fight, engage in conflict TN 3.4.280 *I'll not meddle with him.*

3 Have dealings, concern oneself *with* ROM 1.2.39 *the shoemaker should meddle with his yard*, ADO 3.3.33, AWW 4.3.35.

Medice, teipsum [L.; *cura* omitted] Physician, [heal] thyself 2H6 2.1.51.

medicinable *adj.* Medicinal, healing, restorative OTH 5.2.351 *medicinable gum*, TRO 1.3.91, CYM 3.2.33.

medicine *n.*[1] Physician AWW 2.1.72 *a medicine That's able to breathe life into a stone*; (fig.) WT 4.4.587 *The medicine of our house*, MAC 5.2.27.

medicine *n.*[2]
1 Philosopher's stone or grand elixir sought by alchemists as the means of turning base metals into gold AWW 5.3.102 *the tinct and multiplying med'cine*; (fig.) 1H4 1.5.36 *that great med'cine hath...gilded thee; med'cine potable* drug containing gold, supposed to be like the elixir of life 2H4 4.5.162 *Preserving life in med'cine potable.*
2 Poison LR 5.3.96 *Sick, O, sick!—If not, I'll ne'er trust medicine*; (fig.) OTH 4.1.45 *Work on, My medicine, work!*
3 Love-philtre OTH 1.3.61 *corrupted By spells and medicines*, 1H4 2.2.18.
~ *vb.* 1 Cure CYM 4.2.243 *Great griefs...med'cine the less*; bring by medicinal means *to* OTH 3.3.332 *Nor all the drowsy syrups of the world Shall ever medicine thee to that sweet sleep.*

medlar *n.* The tree Mespius germanica, or its fruit which is like a small brown-skinned apple and is eaten when decayed to a soft, pulpy state TIM 4.3.304 *There's a medlar for thee, eat it*, ROM 2.1.34, MM 4.3.174.
⟡ Often with quibble on 'meddler'.

meed *n.*
1 Wages, reward, recompense TGV 2.4.112 *duty never yet did want his meed*, R3 1.4.228, AYL 2.3.58; *meed for meed* measure for measure TIT 5.3.66.
2 Merit, worth 3H6 4.8.38 *my meed hath got me fame*, HAM 5.2.142; act or service of merit TIM 1.1.277 *No meed but he repays Sevenfold above itself.*

meek *adj.*
1 Mild, merciful, gentle TIM 3.6.95 *affable wolves, meek bears*, JC 3.1.255, H8 2.4.107.
2 Subdued, spiritless, tame LUC 710 *Feeble Desire, all recreant, poor, and meek*, ANT 5.2.162.
~ *adv.* Mercifully, with gentleness MAC 1.7.17 *Duncan Hath borne his faculties so meek.*

meered See MERED.

meet *vb.*
1 Encounter, experience, receive, gain TGV 1.1.15 *When thou dost meet good hap*, 1H4 5.5.42, LR 3.7.101.
2 *meet with* (1) Come face to face with or into the company of ERR 1.2.27 *I'll meet with you upon the mart*, MAC 1.1.7, TGV 5.2.45; (2) encounter (an enemy, etc.) 2H4 3.2.48 *I must go and meet with danger there*, 1H4 4.4.13, TMP 4.1.166.
3 Come to a meeting, keep an appointment WIV 2.3.5 *the hour...that Sir Hugh promis'd to meet*, MM 4.1.18, AYL 5.2.112.

meet *adj.*
1 Proper, fit TGV 2.7.58 *let me have What thou think'st meet*, WIV 1.1.36, MV 3.5.73.
2 *be meet with* Be quits with ADO 1.1.47 *he'll be meet with you.*
~ *adv.* Fitly AWW 5.3.333 *if it end so meet*, MM 5.1.539 (F1).

meeting *n.* Meeting-place 1H4 3.2.174 *Our meeting Is Bridgenorth.*

meetly *adj.* Fairly good ANT 1.3.81 *You can do better yet; but this is meetly.*

meetness *n.* Fitness SON 118.7 *sick of welfare, found a kind of meetness To be diseas'd ere that there was true needing.*

mehercle [L.] By Hercules LLL 4.2.78.

meinie, meiny *n.*
1 Body of retainers LR 2.4.35 *They summon'd up their meiny* (Qq *men*).
2 Common herd COR 3.1.66 *the mutable, rank-scented meiny* (F4 *many*).

melancholy *n.* Ill-temper, sullenness JN 3.3.42 *that surly spirit, melancholy.*

mell *vb.* Have dealings, concern oneself *with* AWW 4.3.228 *Men are to mell with, boys are not to kiss.*

melt *vb.* Weaken, enervate ADO 4.1.319 *But manhood is melted into cur'sies*, TIM 4.3.256.

melting *ppl. adj.* Yielding or softening to emotion, tender JC 2.1.122 *The melting spirits of women*, 3H6 2.2.41, TIT 3.1.213; (hence of eyes) tearful LUC 1227 *moist'ned like a melting eye.*

member *n.*
1 Person MM 5.1.237 *instruments of some more mightier member That sets them on.*
2 One who has a part or share (in something) OTH 3.4.112 *be a member of his love*, 2H4 4.1.169, TRO 1.3.198.

memento mori [L.] Remember [that you are] to die; (used concretely) a symbolic reminder of death, such as the skull-and-crossbones 1H4 3.3.30 *I make as good use of it as many a man doth of a death's-head or a memento mori.*

memorable *adj.*
1 Easily remembered H5 2.4.53 *our too much memorable shame.*
2 Commemorative H5 4.7.104 *I wear it for a memorable honour*, H5 5.1.72.

memorial *n.* Something to preserve remembrance, souvenir, monument TRO 5.1.55 *the bull, the primitive statue and oblique memorial of cuckolds*, TN 3.3.23, SON 74.4.
~ *adj.* Of remembrance, given in memory of something TRO 5.2.80 *memorial dainty kisses.*

memorize *vb.* Cause to be remembered, make memorable H8 3.2.52 *from her Will fall some blessing to this land, which shall In it be memoriz'd*, MAC 1.2.40.

memory *n.*
1 Memorial, memento, reminder COR 4.5.71 *that surname—a good memory...of the...displeasure Which thou shouldst bear me*, LR 4.7.7, JC 3.2.134.
2 *of memory* Remembered 1H6 4.3.51 *That ever-living man of memory, Henry the Fifth*, HAM 5.2.389.
3 *of as little memory* As soon forgotten TMP 2.1.233 *this lord of weak remembrance, this Who shall be of as little memory When he is earth'd.*
4 *book of memory* Memorandum-book 1H6 2.4.101 *I'll note you in my book of memory*, 2H6 1.1.100.

mend *vb.*
1 Reform H8 3.1.105 *hollow hearts I fear ye. Mend 'em for shame...!;* (refl.) TN 1.5.45 *bid the dishonest man mend himself*; (intr. = refl.) TN 1.5.46 *if he mend, he is no longer dishonest*, MM 3.2.27, LR 2.4.229.
2 Make amends for, atone for COR 3.2.26 *You must return and mend it*; (hence) remedy, help R2 3.2.100 *Revolt our subjects? That we cannot mend*, R2 2.3.153.
3 Adjust, set right ANT 5.2.319 *Your crown's awry, I'll mend it*, AWW 3.2.7.
4 Restore to health 2H4 1.2.109 *God mend him!*
5 (intr.) Get better, recover one's health ADO 5.2.93 *Serve God, love me, and mend*; (of an illness) abate TIM 5.1.187 *My long sickness Of health and living now begins to mend.*
6 Improve by addition, increase the value of SHR 1.2.150 *I'll mend it with a largess*, TIM 1.1.172, ANT 1.5.45.

7 Supplement, supply the deficiency of ERR 4.3.59 *we'll mend our dinner here*, H8 1.4.61.
8 Do better, improve, grow better in quality COR 1.4.38 *Mend and charge home*, TN 1.5.74, ANT 1.3.82.
9 Improve upon, better LLL 5.2.329 *in hushering Mend him who can*, AYL 3.2.68.
10 (in asseverations and pious wishes) Improve, make one's condition better AYL 4.1.189 *and so God mend me*, ROM 1.5.79, CYM 5.5.68.

mends *n.* Means of reparation, remedy TRO 1.1.68 *she has the mends in her own hands.*

mercatante See MARCANTANT.

merchandise, merchandize *n.* Trade MV 3.1.128 *make what merchandise I will*, ANT 2.5.104 (construed as a pl.).
~ *vb.* Traffic in SON 102.3 *That love is merchandiz'd whose rich esteeming The owner's tongue doth publish.*

merchant *n.*
1 Fellow ROM 2.4.145 *what saucy merchant was this…?*, 1H6 2.3.57.
2 Ship of trade, merchantman TMP 2.1.5 *the masters of some merchant*, 2H4 2.4.63.

Mercurial *adj.* Fleet, resembling Mercury's CYM 4.2.310 *His foot Mercurial.*

Mercury *n.* In Roman mythology, the messenger of the gods depicted with winged sandals; (hence) fast messenger R3 2.1.89 *your first order…a winged Mercury did bear; she-Mercury* female messenger WIV 2.2.80.

mercy *n.*
1 *cry mercy* Beg for pardon or forgiveness TGV 5.4.94 *O, cry you mercy, sir, I have mistook*, AYL 3.5.61, OTH 4.2.88.
2 *by mercy* According to the law or standards of mercy TIM 3.5.55 *To kill…But in defence, by mercy, 'tis most just.*
3 Clemency of an absolute lord or conqueror, discretion 3H6 1.4.30 *Yield to our mercy*, MV 4.1.355, H5 3.3.3; *at mercy, in mercy, within the mercy* absolutely in the power (of the victor) COR 1.10.7 *I' th' part that is at mercy*, LR 1.4.327, LLL 5.2.846.

mere *adj.* Absolute, sheer, downright H8 3.2.329 *the mere undoing Of all the kingdom*, WIV 4.5.63, LLL 1.2.33.
~ *adv.* Absolutely AWW 3.5.55 *mere the truth.*

mered *ppl. adj. mered question* The matter to which the dispute is limited ANT 3.13.10 *he being The mered question.*
⇨ Some interpret as a corr. of 'mere' to give some such reading as 'the sole subject at issue'.

merely *adv.* Absolutely, entirely TMP 1.1.56 *We are merely cheated of our lives by drunkards*, HAM 1.2.137, JC 1.2.39.

merit *n.* Due reward, recompense R2 1.3.156 *A dearer merit, not so deep a maim…Have I deserved*, LLL 4.1.21.

mermaid *n.* Siren ERR 3.2.45 *train me not, sweet mermaid, with thy note*, VEN 777, LUC 1411.

merriment *n.*
1 Jest, piece of fooling SHR 4.5.76 *our first merriment hath made thee jealous*, 2H4 2.4.298.
2 Entertainment, amusement MND 3.2.146 *To set against me for your merriment.*

merry *adj.*
1 Pleasant, agreeable, bright ERR 2.1.88 *Whilst I at home starve for a merry look.*
2 Happy OTH 3.3.340 *fed well, was free and merry.*
3 (of a wind) Favourable ERR 4.1.90 *the merry wind.*
4 Amusing, funny TIT 5.2.174 *my hand cut off and made a merry jest.*
5 Facetious TIM 3.2.37 *merry with me* (i.e. mocking me).

6 *merry men* Companions in arms or followers of a knight or outlaw chief AYL 1.1.115 *he is already in the forest of Arden, and a many merry men with him*, TN 2.3.76.
7 *rest you merry* Conventional phrase of farewell ROM 1.2.62, AYL 5.1.59.

mervailous, mervilous *adj.* (old form of) Marvellous H5 2.1.47 *The 'solus' in thy most mervailous face.*

mesh See MASH.

mess *n.*
1 Dish (of food), course of dishes WIV 3.1.63 *a mess of porridge*, SHR 4.4.70, LR 1.1.117.
2 Portion (of food) 2H4 2.1.95 *to borrow a mess of vinegar.*
3 One of the groups of persons, normally four, into which the company at a banquet was divided WT 1.2.227 *Lower messes* (those dining lower at the dining table, i.e. lower in rank), JN 1.1.190, HAM 5.2.87.
4 Set of four LLL 4.3.203 *That you three fools lack'd me fool to make up the mess*, 3H6 1.4.73.

message *n.*
1 Errand 2H6 4.1.114 *I go of message* (i.e. on an errand), TGV 4.4.112, 1H6 4.7.53.
2 (sing. for pl.) HAM 1.2.22 *pester us with message* (i.e. trouble me with persistent messages).

messenger *n.* Common name for a pursuivant, a kind of police officer AYL 1.2.59 *Were you made the messenger?* (i.e. 'were you sent to arrest me?').

metal, mettle *n.*
1 Material of which arms are made; (hence) sword JN 5.2.16 *I must draw this metal from my side.*
2 Precious metal, gold ERR 4.1.82 *all the metal in your shop*, MV 1.3.134, R3 4.4.382; (fig.) TN 2.5.14 *How now, my metal of India?* (i.e. girl worth her weight in gold; Ff 2–4 *Nettle*).
3 (fig.) Substance AYL 2.7.82 *the mettle of my speech*, H5 3.1.27; stuff of life, substance out of which man is made AWW 1.1.130 *That you were made of is metal to make virgins;* (with ref. to a person's character) H8 3.2.239 *Of what coarse metal ye are moulded*, MM 1.1.48, LR 1.1.69.
4 Disposition, temperament TMP 2.1.182 *gentlemen of brave mettle*, TN 3.4.272, JN 2.1.401.
5 (of a horse) Spirit, natural vigour 1H4 4.3.22 *Worcester's horses…their…mettle is asleep*, LC 107.
6 Ardent temperament, spirit, courage ADO 5.1.133 *thou hast mettle enough in thee to kill care*, OTH 4.2.204, 1H4 2.4.12.
⇨ Differentiated spellings of the same word are used without distinction in Ff and Qq, but in mod. edd. *mettle* is usu. restricted to senses 4, 5, and 6.

metaphysical *adj.* Supernatural MAC 1.5.29 *metaphysical aid.*

mete *vb.*
1 Measure, estimate 2H4 4.4.77 *a measure…By which his Grace must mete the lives of other.*
2 Aim (*at*) LLL 4.1.132 *Let the mark have a prick in't, to mete at.*

meteor *n.* Luminous body or appearance of any kind seen temporarily in the sky, belonging to a lower region than that of the heavenly bodies, and supposedly engendered from vapours drawn up by the sun and then ignited ROM 3.5.13 *It is some meteor that the sun exhal'd*, R2 2.4.9; (fig.) ERR 4.2.6 *his heart's meteors tilting in his face.*

mete(-)yard *n.* Measuring-rod SHR 4.3.152 *give me thy mete-yard.*

metheglin *n.* Spiced drink made from wort and honey WIV 5.5.159 *sack, and wine, and metheglins*, LLL 5.2.233.

methinks *vb. phr.* It seems to me TMP 2.1.269 *Methinks I do*, TGV 1.2.87, MAC 4.2.70.

method *n.* Summary of the contents of a book; (fig.) TN 1.5.226 *In what chapter of his bosom?—To answer by the method, in the first of his heart.*

methought, methoughts *vb. phr.* (pa. t. of ME-THINKS) It seemed to me WT 1.2.154 *methoughts I did recoil Twenty-three years,* R3 1.4.9, MND 2.2.149.

mettle See METAL.

mew *vb.* Coop up, shut up SHR 1.1.87 *Why will you mew her up…?,* MND 1.1.71, ROM 3.4.11.
◇ Term from falconry, the 'mew' being the cage where the hawk was kept during the period of moulting or 'mewing'.

mewl *vb.* Cry feebly, whimper AYL 2.7.144 *the infant, Mewling and puking in the nurse's arms.*

mi perdonato [It.] Pardon me SHR 1.1.25 *Mi perdonato, gentle master mine.*

micher *n.* Truant 1H4 2.4.408 *Shall the blessed sun of heaven prove a micher and eat blackberries?*
◇ 'Mitch, mich' (*vb.*) 'play truant, esp….in order to gather blackberries' (edd).

miching *ppl. adj.* Sneaking, skulking HAM 3.2.137 *this' miching mallecho* (F1, Q1; Q2 *munching*).

mickle *adj.* Great, much H5 2.1.66 *An oath of mickle might,* ERR 3.1.45, ROM 2.3.15.

microcosm *n.* Man viewed as an epitome of the universe or macrocosm COR 2.1.63 *the map of my microcosm* (i.e. my face).

mid *n.* Middle R3 5.3.77 *the mid of night.*

middle *adj.* Mid MND 2.1.82 *the middle summer's spring.*

middle earth *n.* The earth, viewed as being between heaven and hell, or occupying the centre of the universe WIV 5.5.80 *I smell a man of middle earth.*

mid season *n.* Noon TMP 1.2.239 *Past the mid season.*

midway *n.* Middle course, medium ADO 2.1.7 *in the midway between him and Benedick,* ANT 3.4.19.
~ *adj. midway air* Mid air LR 4.6.13 *crows and choughs that wing the midway air.*
~ *adv.* Half-way TRO 1.3.278 *Midway between your tents and walls of Troy,* PER 5.1.48.

might *n.*
1 Power (to do a thing) TRO 3.2.157 *for to be wise and love Exceeds men's might,* MND 5.1.92.
2 Efficacy, virtue AYL 3.5.81 *thy saw of might,* H5 2.1.66, SON 56.4.
3 Bodily strength JC 2.4.8 *I have a man's mind, but a woman's might.*

mightily *adv.*
1 Greatly, very much 3H6 3.2.74 *thou wrong'st thy children mightily,* ADO 2.2.24, AWW 4.3.65.
2 With great effort, vigorously SHR 1.2.277 *Strive mightily.*

milch *adj.* Giving milk, in milk SHR 2.1.357 *milch kine,* VEN 875, WIV 4.4.33; (transf., applied to the eyes when weeping) tearful HAM 2.2.517 *Would have made milch the burning eyes of heaven.*

mild *adj.* Calm, not rough or stormy PER 3.1.27 *Now, mild may be thy life! For a more blusterous birth had never babe.*

militarist *n.* Soldier AWW 4.3.141 *Monsieur Parolles, the gallant militarist.*

milk *n.* Type of what is pleasant and nourishing ROM 3.3.55 *Adversity's sweet milk, philosophy,* MAC 1.5.17, MAC 4.3.98.

milk-livered *adj.* Cowardly LR 4.2.50 *Milk-liver'd man.*

milky *adj.* Timorous, weak TIM 3.1.54 *a faint and milky heart,* HAM 2.2.478, LR 1.4.341.

milliner *n.* Seller of haberdashery, gloves and fancy articles WT 4.4.192 *no milliner can so fit his customers with gloves,* 1H4 1.3.36.

millioned *adj.* Countless, multiplied into millions SON 115.5 *Time, whose million'd accidents.*

mill-sixpence *n.* Sixpence stamped by means of the mill and press, and having fluted edges WIV 1.1.155 *seven groats in mill-sixpences.*

millstone *n. drop, weep millstones* Said of a hardhearted person R3 1.3.352 *Your eyes drop millstones, when fools' eyes fall tears,* R3 1.4.240; (similarly) TRO 1.2.144 *Queen Hecuba laughed that her eyes ran o'er.—With millstones.*

mimic *n.* Burlesque actor, mime MND 3.2.19 *And forth my mimic comes.*
◇ Ff 1–3 *Mimmick;* Q1 *Minnick;* Q2 *Minnock.* See MINNICK.

mince *vb.*
1 Extenuate, make light of OTH 2.3.247 *Thy honesty and love doth mince this matter.*
2 Report (what is said) euphemistically ANT 1.2.105 *mince not the general tongue.*
3 Affect coyly LR 4.6.120 *yond simp'ring dame… That minces virtue.*

minced *ppl. adj.* Affected, effeminate TRO 1.2.256 *a minced man.*

mincing *n.* Affectation H8 2.3.31 *Saving your mincing.*

mind *n.*
1 Judgement, opinion MV 4.1.407 *in my mind you are much bound to him; to my mind* in my judgement HAM 1.4.14.
2 Purpose, intention, desire, wish ERR 4.1.113 *For servants must their masters' minds fulfil,* MV 2.8.42, TIT 5.3.1.
3 Way of thinking and feeling with respect to moral qualities TGV 5.3.13 *he bears an honourable mind, And will not use a woman lawlessly,* JC 1.2.291.
4 Disposition, intention towards others TGV 1.2.33 *I would I knew his mind,* AYL 1.2.236, 2H6 3.1.374.
5 Person (regarded abstractly as the embodiment of mental qualities) SON 117.5 *I have frequent been with unknown minds.*
~ *vb.*
1 Remind COR 5.1.18 *I minded him how royal 'twas to pardon,* WT 3.2.225, H5 4.3.13.
2 Call to mind H5 4.Ch.53 *Minding true things by what their mock'ries be.*
3 Perceive, notice, be aware of TMP 2.2.17 *I 'll fall flat, Perchance he will not mind me.*
4 Attend to, heed SHR 1.1.249 *you do not mind the play,* ROM 4.1.13, PER 2.5.20.
5 Be inclined, intend MND 5.1.113 *as minding to content you, Our true intent is,* PER 2.4.3, 3H6 4.1.106.

minded *ppl. adj.* Disposed, inclined H8 3.1.58 *to know How you stand minded,* LR 3.1.2, TMP 5.1.126.

mindless *adj.* Unmindful, careless TIM 4.3.94 *mindless of thy worth,* WT 1.2.301.

mine *n.* Subterranean cavity OTH 4.2.79 *The bawdy wind…Is hush'd within the hollow mine of earth.*

mine *pron.*
1 My property SHR 2.1.383 *she shall have me and mine,* WT 1.2.134, SON 134.3.
2 My affair, business or responsibility MM 2.2.12 *Go to; let that be mine.*

mineral *n.*
1 Mine HAM 4.1.26 *Among a mineral of metals base.*
2 Mineral medicine or poison OTH 2.1.297 *a poisonous mineral,* OTH 1.2.74, CYM 5.5.50.

mingle *n.* Mixture ANT 1.5.59 *He was not sad…; he was not merry…; but between both. O heavenly mingle!,* ANT 4.8.37.
~ *vb.*
1 Pool, throw into a common fund, put together

so as to make one CYM 1.6.186 *Some...of us and your lord...have mingled sums To buy a present.*
2 Join (faith, friendship) WT 1.2.109 *To mingle friendship far,* WT 4.4.460; *mingle eyes* look into each other's eyes, exchange friendly and knowing looks ANT 3.13.156 *To flatter Caesar, would you mingle eyes With one that ties his points.*

minikin *adj.* Shrill LR 3.6.43 *one blast of thy minikin mouth.*

minim *n.* Musical note, in ancient music the shortest; (attrib.) ROM 2.4.22 *he rests his minim rests* (F1 *rests his minum*).

minime [L.] Not at all LLL 3.1.60 *Is not lead a metal heavy...?—Minime.*

minimus *n.* Diminutive creature MND 3.2.329 *you dwarf; You minimus.*

minion *n.*
1 Darling, favourite TN 5.1.125 *your minion, whom I know you love,* MAC 1.2.19, TMP 4.1.98.
2 Saucy woman, hussy OTH 5.1.33 *Minion, your dear lies dead,* ERR 3.1.54, 2H6 1.3.138.

minister *n.*
1 Agent AWW 2.1.137 *He that of greatest works is finisher Oft does them by the weakest minister,* TMP 1.2.131, HAM 3.4.175.
2 Angel (messenger of God) HAM 1.4.39 *Angels and ministers of grace defend us!,* MM 5.1.115.
3 Servant (not necessarily animate) OTH 5.2.8 *thou flaming minister.*
~ *vb.*
1 Supply, furnish ADO 2.1.369 *minister such assistance as I shall give you direction,* R2 2.3.105, OTH 2.1.270.
2 Give occasion, prompt, suggest MM 4.5.6 *As cause doth minister.*
3 Perform (a ceremony) TMP 4.1.17 *before All... ceremonies may...be minist'red.*
4 Apply, administer (something healing or the reverse) TGV 2.4.150 *you gave me bitter pills, And I must minister the like to you,* JN 5.1.15, ROM 4.3.25; (absol.) MAC 5.3.40 *minister to a mind diseas'd.*

ministration *n.* Service AWW 2.5.60 *The ministration and required office.*

minnick, minnock *n.* One who apes or fools about MND 3.2.19 *And forth my minnick comes.*
◊ Q1; Q2 *Minnock.* Dial. 'minnock' (vb.) affect delicacy, ape, fool about; 'minnock' (*n.*) affected person. Ff 1–3 *Mimmick.* See MIMIC.

minnow *n.* Small fish; (fig.) contemptible little object LLL 1.1.248 *that base minnow of thy mirth,* COR 3.1.89.

minority *n.* Infancy, earliest age LUC 67 *from world's minority.*

minstrel *n.* One whose profession was to entertain, usu. with music and story-telling SHR 3.2.183 *I hear the minstrels play,* ROM 3.1.46, LUC 817.

minstrelsy *n.*
1 Company of minstrels LLL 1.1.176 *I will use him for my minstrelsy.*
2 Music made by minstrels PER 5.2.7 *What minstrelsy, and pretty din,* TIM 2.2.161.

minute *n.*
1 *minute while* Minute 1H6 1.4.54.
2 *by th' minute* Every moment, incessantly ANT 3.1.20, CYM 5.5.51.

minute-jack *n.* Time-server, one who changes his mind to suit the fashions of the minute TIM 3.6.97 *Cap-and-knee slaves, vapours, and minute-jacks!*
◊ A jack was the figure striking the bell in a clock; see JACK sense 4.

minutely *adj.* Happening every minute MAC 5.2.18 *Now minutely revolts upbraid his faith-breach.*

minx *n.*
1 Wanton woman OTH 3.3.476 *Damn her, lewd minx!,* OTH 4.1.153.
2 Impudent woman TN 3.4.120 *My prayers, minx!*

mirable *adj.* Worthy of admiration TRO 4.5.142 *Not Neoptolemus so mirable.*

miracle *vb.* (refl.) (?) 'Make itself a miracle' (Schmidt) CYM 4.2.29 *I 'm not their father, yet who this should be Doth miracle itself, lov'd before me.*

mire *vb.*
1 Bespatter, defile ADO 4.1.133 *mir'd with infamy.*
2 Sink as in mire TIM 4.3.147 *Paint till a horse may mire upon your face.*

mirror *n.* Model, paragon H5 2.Ch.6 *the mirror of all Christian kings,* 1H6 1.4.74, H8 2.1.53.

mirth *n.*
1 Fun ADO 2.1.330 *to speak all mirth and no matter,* WIV 4.6.14, MND 5.1.57; jest ANT 1.4.18 *give a kingdom for a mirth.*
2 Object of merriment or ridicule JC 4.3.49 *I 'll use you for my mirth,* WT 1.2.166.
3 *make yourself mirth* Amuse yourself H8 2.3.101 *Good lady, Make yourself mirth with your particular fancy.*

misadventured *adj.* Unfortunate ROM 1.Ch.7 *misadventur'd piteous overthrows.*

Misanthropos *n.* Hater of mankind TIM 4.3.54 *I am Misanthropos, and hate mankind.*

misbecome *vb.* Be unbecoming to LLL 5.2.768 *misbecom'd our oaths and gravities.*

misbehaved See MISHAVED.

miscarry *vb.*
1 Come to harm or destruction, perish MV 3.2.316 *my ships have all miscarried,* LR 5.1.5, H5 4.1.148.
2 Go wrong, prove unsuccessful COR 1.1.266 *what miscarries Shall be the general's fault,* ROM 5.3.267.
3 Be abortive, fail LLL 4.1.112 *if horns that year miscarry;* (of a child) be born prematurely 2H4 5.4.9 *and the child I go with do miscarry.*
4 Get into wrong hands H8 3.2.30 *The Cardinal's letters to the Pope miscarried,* LLL 4.2.140.

mischief *n.*
1 Misfortune, calamity 1H6 5.3.39 *A plaguing mischief light on Charles,* WIV 4.3.2, PER 1.4.8.
2 Harm, injury JC 3.1.93 *lest that the people... should do your age some mischief,* MND 2.1.237, 2H4 2.1.15; *nature's mischief evil done in nature* MAC 1.5.50.
3 Disease ADO 1.3.12 *apply a moral medicine to a mortifying mischief.*
4 Evil deed TMP 1.2.264 *For mischiefs manifold.*

misconceived *ppl. adj.* Having a wrong idea, being mistaken 1H6 5.4.49 *No, misconceived!*

misconster *vb.* (var. in 16–17C of) Misconstrue 1H6 2.3.73 *nor misconster the mind of Talbot,* R3 3.5.61, AYL 1.2.265.
◊ Occurs in F and Q. See CONSTRUE.

miscreant *n.* Infidel; (hence) villain 1H6 5.3.44 *Curse, miscreant, when thou com'st to the stake,* LR 1.1.161, R2 1.1.39.

miscreate *ppl. adj.* Illegitimate, spurious H5 1.2.16 *titles miscreate, whose right Suits not in native colours with the truth.*

misdoubt *n.* Mistrust, suspicion 2H6 3.1.332 *change misdoubt to resolution,* 2H4 4.1.204.
~ *vb.*
1 Have doubts as to ANT 3.7.62 *Do you misdoubt This sword, and these my wounds?,* AWW 3.7.1; (absol.) AWW 1.3.125 *so tott'ring in the balance that I could neither believe nor misdoubt.*
2 Be mistrustful or suspicious of (a person) WIV 2.1.185 *I do not misdoubt my wife.*
3 Have misgivings or suspicions in regard to (a thing) R3 3.2.87 *This sudden stab of rancour I misdoubt,* LLL 4.3.192, 3H6 5.6.14.

misdread n. Dread of evil PER 1.2.12 *the passions of the mind, That have their first conception by misdread.*

miser n. Wretch 1H6 5.4.7 *Decrepit miser! base ignoble wretch!*

misery n. *noble misery* Wretchedness in noble estate CYM 5.3.64 *This is a lord! O noble misery, To be i' th' field, and ask 'what news?' of me!*

misgoverned ppl. adj. Unruly R2 5.2.5 *rude misgovern'd hands.*

misgovernment n. Evil conduct ADO 4.1.99 *I am sorry for thy much misgovernment.*

misgraff vb. Graft amiss; (fig.) match badly MND 1.1.137 *misgraffed in respect of years.*

mishaved ppl. adj. Misbehaved, badly behaved ROM 3.3.143 *like a mishaved and sullen wench* (Q2; F1 *mishaped*).

mislike n. Dislike, distaste, aversion 3H6 4.1.24 *Setting your scorns and your mislike aside.*
~ vb. Dislike, disapprove of, be displeased or offended at 2H6 1.1.140 *'Tis not my speeches that you do mislike,* MV 2.1.1, ANT 3.13.147.

misorder vb. Confuse, disturb 2H4 4.2.33 *The time misord'red doth...Crowd us.*

misplace vb. Use words in a wrong place, transpose MM 2.1.88 *Do you hear how he misplaces?*

misprise, misprize vb. Undervalue, despise ADO 3.1.52 *Disdain and scorn...Misprising what they look on,* AYL 1.1.171, TRO 4.5.74 (Ff *disprising*).

misprised, misprized ppl. adj. Mistaken MND 3.2.74 *You spend your passion on a mispris'd mood.*

misprising n. MISPRISION n.², contempt, scorn, undervaluation AWW 3.2.31 *By the misprising of a maid too virtuous For the contempt of empire.*

misprision n.¹ Mistake, misunderstanding ADO 4.1.185 *There is some strange misprision in the princes,* MND 3.2.90, TN 1.5.55 (perh. with play on the sense of wrongful imprisonment).

misprision n.² Contempt, scorn, undervaluation AWW 2.3.152 *in vile misprision shackle up My love and her desert.*

misproud adj. Arrogant 3H6 2.6.7 *misproud York.*

misreport vb. Speak ill of MM 5.1.148 *a man that never yet Did...misreport your Grace.*

miss n.
1 Disadvantage caused by the loss *of* (a person) 1H4 5.4.105 *I should have a heavy miss of thee.*
2 Wrong-doing, offence VEN 53 *blames her miss.*
~ vb.
1 Do without TMP 1.2.311 *We cannot miss him.*
2 Fail (a person) WIV 3.5.55 *I will not miss her.*
3 Be wanting or lacking ROM 1.Ch.14 *What here shall miss, our toil shall strive to mend,* SON 122.8, TIM 1.1.136.

mis-sheath vb. Sheath by mistake ROM 5.3.205 *This dagger...mis-sheathed in my daughter's bosom.*

missing n. Absence CYM 5.5.275 *Upon my lady's missing.*

missingly adv. With a sense of loss WT 4.2.31 *I have (missingly) noted, he is of late much retir'd from court.*

missive n. Messenger ANT 2.2.74 *and with taunts Did gibe my missive out of audience,* MAC 1.5.6.

misspeak vb. Speak wrongly JN 3.1.4 *thou hast misspoke, misheard.*

mist n. (fig.) State of uncertainty ERR 2.2.216 *in this mist at all adventures go.*
~ vb. Bedim LR 5.3.262 *If that her breath will mist or stain the stone.*

mistake vb.
1 Take wrongly, falsely, or improperly WIV 2.2.216 *I have lost my edifice by mistaking the place where I erected it,* JN 3.1.274, HAM 3.2.252 (Q1 *must take*);

take to a wrong person or place LLL 4.1.57 *This letter is mistook.*
2 Misjudge AYL 1.3.64 *mistake me not so much To think my poverty is treacherous,* H8 1.1.195, TIM 1.2.9.
3 (refl.) Make a mistake TIM 3.2.23 *yet had he mistook him and sent to me.*
4 (intr.) Go astray ROM 5.3.203 *This dagger hath mista'en.*

mistaking n. Mistake, error TMP 1.2.248 *made thee no mistakings,* MM 3.2.141, SHR 4.5.49.

mistempered ppl. adj.
1 Disordered, deranged JN 5.1.12 *This inundation of mistemp'red humour.*
2 Tempered for an evil purpose ROM 1.1.87 *Throw your mistempered weapons to the ground.*

mistership See MISTRISHIP.

mistful adj. Obscured as with mist H5 4.6.34 *mistful eyes* (i.e. close to tears).
◊ Warburton conjecture; F1 *mixtfull.*

misthink vb. Think ill of, have an unfavourable opinion of ANT 5.2.176 *we, the greatest, are misthought For things that others do,* 3H6 2.5.108.

mistreading n. Misdeed 1H4 3.2.11 *To punish my mistreadings.*

mistress n.
1 Woman having a protecting or guiding influence LR 2.1.40 *conjuring the moon To stand auspicious mistress,* SON 126.5, MAC 3.5.6.
2 Female possessor or owner TGV 4.4.202 *I 'll use thee kindly for thy mistress' sake; mistress of* possessor of AYL 1.2.4 *I show more mirth than I am mistress of,* WT 3.2.59.
3 (as a title or prefix) Madam LLL 5.2.837 *Mistress, look on me*; Mrs WIV 4.2.129 *Mistress Ford*; Miss WIV 1.1.190 *Mistress Anne Page.*
4 (in bowls) Small ball, jack TRO 3.2.50 *kiss the mistress.*
5 Authoress, creator or patroness of an art H5 1.1.52 *So that the art and practic part of life Must be the mistress to this theoric.*
6 Chief, first H8 3.1.152 *the lily, That once was mistress of the field.*
~ adj. Chief, first H5 2.4.133 *the mistress court of mighty Europe.*

mistriship n. (var. of) Mistress-ship, condition of mistress or head of a household, etc. TIT 4.4.40 *and your mistriship be emperial* (Q2 *mistership*).

mistrust n. *mistrust of* Doubt as to JC 5.3.65 *Mistrust of my success.*
~ vb. Suspect the existence of or anticipate the occurrence of (something evil) ADO 2.1.182 *an accident of hourly proof, Which I mistrusted not,* WT 2.1.48, R3 2.3.42.

mistrustful adj. Causing suspicion, arousing anxiety or fear VEN 826 *some mistrustful wood.*

misuse n.
1 Ill-usage, ill-treatment 1H4 1.1.43 *Upon whose dead corpse there was such misuse.*
2 Offence, evil conduct OTH 4.2.109 *my least misuse.*
~ vb.
1 Revile ADO 2.1.239 *she misus'd me past the endurance of a block,* AYL 4.1.201, SHR 2.1.159.
2 'Speak falsely of, misrepresent' (Schmidt) SON 152.7 *I am perjur'd most, For all my vows are oaths but to misuse thee.*
3 Impose upon, cheat, deceive ADO 2.2.28 *Proof enough to misuse the Prince.*

mite n. Minute particle PER 2.Gower.8 *Losing a mite, a mountain gain.*

mo, moe n. More in number MM 5.1.200 *Charges she moe than me,* TIM 4.3.433, JC 2.1.72.

moan ~ *adj.* More, more in number Apo 2.3.70 *no moe* [*ditties*], Mac 5.3.35, Cor 2.3.125.

▷ In TMP 5.1.234 *moe diversity of sounds*, qualifying a sing. noun but with pl. implication.

moan *n.* Lamentation, grief 1H6 2.3.44 *Thy mirth shall turn to moan*, Apo 5.3.16, Cym 4.2.273.

~ *vb.* Lament aloud Luc 977 *To make him moan*, Son 30.8.

mobled *ppl. adj.* Muffled Ham 2.2.502 *the mobled queen* (Qq; F1 *inobled*).

mock *n.*
1 *in mock* Derided MM 5.1.322 *As much in mock as mark.*
2 *made mocks with* Played with, made sport of Oth 5.2.151 *villainy hath made mocks with love.*

~ *vb.*
1 Defy, set at nought MV 2.1.30 *mock the lion when 'a roars for prey*, Mac 2.2.6, Ant 3.13.184.
2 *mock with* Ridicule Son 71.14 *mock you with me after I am gone.*
3 Simulate, make a false pretence of 3H6 3.3.255 *For mocking marriage*, Ant 5.1.2.

mockable *adj.* Deserving ridicule AYL 3.2.48 *the behaviour of the country is most mockable at the court.*

mocker *n.* One who deceives or disappoints AYL 2.6.13 *thou art a mocker of my labour.*

mockery *n.*
1 Imitation, counterfeit representation, unreal appearance H5 4.Ch.53 *Minding true things by what their mock'ries be*, R3 3.2.27, Mac 3.4.106; (attrib.) R2 4.1.260 *O that I were a mockery king of snow...!*
2 Ludicrously futile action Ham 1.1.146 *our vain blows [are] malicious mockery* (perh. sense 1 'imitation or outward appearance of malice').

mode See MOOD.

model *n.*
1 Architect's design for a building 2H4 1.3.42 *We first survey the plot, then draw the model*; (fig.) Apo 1.3.46 *Will it serve for any model to build mischief on?*
2 Sketch on a small scale, ground-plan, plan R3 5.3.24 *I'll draw the form and model of our battle*, R2 3.4.42, 2H4 1.3.51.
3 Exact likeness or image (of something), something representing on a small scale the qualities (of another) Per 2.2.11 *princes are A model which heaven makes like to itself*, R2 1.2.28, Ham 5.2.50.
4 Something that envelops closely, mould R2 3.2.153 *that small model of the barren earth Which serves as paste and cover to our bones*, H5 2.Ch.16 (or sense 3).

modern *adj.* Ordinary, commonplace, insignificant, trite Mac 4.3.170 *where violent sorrow seems A modern ecstasy* (i.e. commonplace emotion), Jn 3.4.42, AYL 2.7.156.

modest *adj.* Moderate, marked by moderation, becoming, appropriate H8 5.2.104 *I could say more, But reverence to your calling makes me modest*, Lr 2.4.25, TN 1.3.9.

modestly *adv.* Without exaggeration, without presumption, with due moderation Tro 4.5.222 *modestly I think The fall of every Phrygian stone will cost A drop of Grecian blood*, JC 1.2.69.

modesty *n.* Moderation, restraint JC 3.1.213 *in a friend, it is cold modesty*, Shr Ind.1.68.

modicum *n.* Small quantity Tro 2.1.68 *what modicums of wit he utters!*

module *n.* Mere image or counterfeit Jn 5.7.58 *but a clod And module of confounded royalty*, AWW 4.3.99.

moe See MO.

moiety *n.*
1 Half H8 1.2.12 *you have half our power. The other moi'ty ere you ask is given*, Ant 5.1.19.
2 Share, portion Ham 1.1.90 *a moi'ty competent Was gaged*, Lr 1.1.7, 1H4 3.1.95; small part, lesser share or portion WT 2.3.8 *say that she were gone,...a moi'ty of my rest Might come to me again*, Luc Ded.2.

moist *adj.*
1 Wet Ham 4.3.223 *these moist trees*; (of the eyes) wet with tears 1H6 1.1.49 *moist eyes*, 2H4 4.5.139; watery, rheumy (as one of the signs of old age) 2H4 1.2.180 *a moist eye, a dry hand.*
2 Bringing rain AWW 2.1.164 *Moist Hesperus*, Ham 1.1.118.

~ *vb.* Moisten Ant 5.2.282 *no more The juice of Egypt's grape shall moist this lip.*

moisture *n.* Bodily humours, liquid part or constituent of a body 3H6 2.1.79 *I cannot weep; for all my body's moisture Scarce serves to quench my furnace-burning heart.*

moldwarp *n.* Mole (the animal) 1H4 3.1.147 *the moldwarp and the ant.*

molestation *n.* Turbulence Oth 2.1.16 *I never did like molestation view On the enchafed flood.*

mollis aer [L.] Tender air Cym 5.5.447 *The piece of tender air, thy virtuous daughter, Which we call mollis aer.*

mome *n.* Blockhead, dolt Err 3.1.32 *Mome, malt-horse,...idiot, patch!*

moment *n.*
1 *on, upon the moment* Immediately, instantly LC 248 *The accident which brought me to her eye Upon the moment did her force subdue*, Tim 1.1.79.
2 *in a moment* At one and the same time Mac 2.3.109 *Who can be wise, amaz'd,...Loyal, and neutral, in a moment?*
3 Cause or motive of action Ant 1.2.142 *I have seen her die twenty times upon far poorer moment.*

momentany *adj.* Momentary, lasting but a moment MND 1.1.143 *momentany as a sound* (Q1; F1 *momentarie*).

momentary-swift *adj.* Rapid as a moment Tro 4.2.14 *wings more momentary-swift than thought.*

Monarcho *n.* Title assumed by an insane Italian who fancied himself emperor of the world; (hence, applied to one who is the object of ridicule for his absurd pretensions) LLL 4.1.99 *This Armado is a Spaniard..., a Monarcho, and one that makes sport To the Prince and his book-mates.*

Monmouth cap *n.* Flat, round cap formerly worn by soldiers and sailors H5 4.7.100 *wearing leeks in their Monmouth caps.*

mons [L.] Mountain LLL 5.1.84 *mons, the hill.*

monster *vb.*
1 Make a monster of Lr 1.1.220 *her offence Must be of such unnatural degree That monsters it.*
2 Point at as something wonderful, put out of the common order of things, exhibit as a monster Cor 2.2.77 *to hear my nothings monster'd.*

monstrous *adj.* (as an exclamation) Astounding, outrageous, greatly to be marvelled at MND 3.1.104 *O monstrous! O strange! We are haunted*, Lr 5.3.160, 1H4 2.4.540.

~ *adv.* Exceedingly, wonderfully AWW 2.1.184 *monstrous desperate*, MND 1.2.52.

monstruosity *n.* Monstrosity, marvel, something unnatural Tro 3.2.81 *the monstruosity in love.*

montant *n.* 'An upright blow, or thrust' (Cotgrave) Wiv 2.3.27 *to see thee pass thy puncto,...thy montant.*

▷ Cf. Apo 1.1.30 *Signior Mountanto* applied to Benedick to imply that he is a professional fencer.

month's mind *n. phr.* Inclination, liking TGV 1.2.134 *I see you have a month's mind to them.*

monument *n.*
1 Place of burial, grave, sepulchre ROM 3.5.201 *that dim monument where Tybalt lies,* ADO 4.1.206, ANT 4.13.3.
2 Portent SHR 3.2.95 *some wondrous monument, Some comet or unusual prodigy.*
3 Statue, effigy MM 5.1.233 *Let me...else...be confixed here, A marble monument!,* AWW 4.2.6, CYM 2.2.32.

monumental *adj.*
1 Sepulchral OTH 5.2.5 *smooth as monumental alabaster.*
2 Serving as a memento or as a proof of identity AWW 4.3.17 *He hath given her his monumental ring.*
3 Having the aspect of a monument, like a monument TRO 3.3.153 *to have done is to hang Quite out of fashion, like a rusty mail In monumental mock'ry* (perh. with the sense 'a mocking memorial').

mood *n.*[1]
1 Anger, displeasure TGV 4.1.49 *Who, in my mood, I stabb'd unto the heart,* AWW 5.2.4, ROM 3.1.12; look of anger, angry cast of countenance SON 93.8 *the false heart's history Is writ in moods and frowns.*
2 Form, shape, mode HAM 1.2.82 *all forms, moods, shapes of grief* (Q1695 and some mod. edd. *modes*), LC 201.

mood *n.*[2] Key in which music is written; (fig.) 2H4 4.5.199 *And now my death Changes the mood* (Q; Ff 1–2 *moode*; Ff 3–4 *mode*).
▷ The sense 'state of mind' is also present.

moody *adj.* Angry, peevish R3 5.1.7 *your moody discontented souls,* TMP 1.2.244, ROM 3.1.12.

moon *n.*
1 Month PER 2.5.10 *One twelve moons more she'll wear Diana's livery,* PP 14.27, ANT 3.12.6.
2 *moon's men,* minions of the moon People who walk about by night, esp. with criminal intentions, 'night-walker' 1H4 1.2.31, 1H4 1.2.26; *go by the moon* to be a 'night-walker' 1H4 1.2.14 *We that take purses go by the moon and the seven stars, and not by Phoebus.*
3 *beneath, under the moon* On earth LR 4.6.26, HAM 4.7.145; *below the moon* worldly, earthly H8 3.2.134 *His thinkings are below the moon.*
4 Symbol of or identified with Diana, goddess of chastity COR 1.1.257 *Bemock the modest moon,* MND 1.1.73, 1H4 1.2.29.

moon-calf *n.* Creature born mis-shapen because of lunar influence TMP 2.2.106 *under the dead mooncalf's gaberdine,* TMP 3.2.21.

moonish *adj.* Changeable (as the moon), fickle AYL 3.2.410 *I, being but a moonish youth,...be...changeable.*

moonshine *n.*
1 Month LR 1.2.5 *I am some twelve or fourteen moonshines Lag of a brother.*
2 *moonshine in the water* Appearance without substance, something unsubstantial or unreal LLL 5.2.208 *Thou now requests but moonshine in the water.*
3 *make a sop o' th' moonshine of* (?) (1) Kill him and leave his body lying on the ground where it can soak up moonlight as a sop soaks up a liquid; or (2) make a 'mess' of (with ref. to the 16-17C dish called 'eggs in moonshine') LR 2.2.32 *I'll make a sop o' th' moonshine of you,...draw!*

Moor *n.* Negro, Negress MV 3.5.39 *the Moor is with child by you,* OTH 1.1.40, TIT 2.3.51.

mop *n.* Grimace TMP 4.1.47 *with mop and mow.*

mope *vb.* Be in a state of bewilderment, go about or act aimlessly H5 3.7.133 *to mope...so far out of his knowledge!,* TMP 5.1.240, HAM 3.4.81.

mopping *n.* Grimacing LR 4.1.61 *of mopping and mowing.*

moral *n.*
1 Hidden meaning, signification ADO 3.4.78 *You have some moral in this benedictus,* SHR 4.4.79, H5 3.6.33.
2 Symbolical figure H5 3.6.38 *Fortune is an excellent moral.*
~ *vb.* Moralize AYL 2.7.29 *When I did hear The motley fool thus moral on the time.*
~ *adj.*
1 Enunciating moral precepts, moralizing LR 4.2.58 *a moral fool,* ADO 5.1.30.
2 Allegorical TIM 1.1.90 *A thousand moral paintings.*
3 Hidden ADO 3.4.79 *I have no moral meaning.*

moralize *vb.* Draw out the hidden meaning of, interpret, explain AYL 2.1.44 *Did he not moralize this spectacle?,* SHR 4.4.81, R3 3.1.83; (intr.) VEN 712 *thou hear'st me moralize.*

moraller *n.* Moralizer OTH 2.3.299 *you are too severe a moraller.*

more *adj.*
1 Of higher class; *more and less* persons of all ranks MAC 5.4.12 *Both more and less have given him the revolt,* 1H4 4.3.68, SON 96.3.
2 (with nouns of quality, condition or action) Greater in degree or extent JN 2.1.34 *To make a more requital to your love!,* TGV 5.3.3, COR 3.2.124.

more above *adv. phr.* Moreover HAM 2.2.126 *This... hath my daughter shown me, And more above, hath his solicitings,...All come to mine ear* (F1; Qq2-4 *about*).

moreover *adv.* (used prepositionally, governing a clause) Besides the fact *that* HAM 2.2.2 *Moreover that we much did long to see you, The need we have to use you did provoke Our hasty sending.*

Morisco *n.* Morris-dancer 2H6 3.1.365 *caper upright like a wild Morisco.*

morris, morris-dance *n.*[1] Fantastic dance performed by persons in costume, usu. representing characters from the Robin Hood legend AWW 2.2.24 *As fit as...a morris for May-day,* H5 2.4.25.

morris *n.*[2] (corr. of 'merels') *nine men's morris* Game between two players, each with nine pebbles, disks, pegs or 'pins', played on a board or on squares cut in the turf; the turf on which the game is played MND 2.1.98 *The nine men's morris is fill'd up with mud.*

morris-pike *n.* Pike supposed to be of Moorish origin ERR 4.3.28 *to do more exploits with his mace than a morris-pike.*

mort *n.* Note sounded on a horn at the death of the deer WT 1.2.118 *The mort o' th' deer.*

mort de ma vie [Fr.] (an oath; lit.) Death of my life H5 3.5.11 (F1).

mort Dieu [Fr.] (an oath) 'Sdeath! 2H6 1.1.123.

mort du vinaigre [Fr.] (a meaningless oath; lit.) Death of the vinegar AWW 2.3.44.

mortal *adj.*
1 Causing death, deadly, fatal TRO 4.5.134 *my mortal sword,* LUC 364, OTH 3.3.355.
2 Of or for death AWW 3.6.76 *my mortal preparation,* MAC 4.1.100.
3 Belonging to or common to mankind, human MAC 1.5.3 *mortal knowledge,* H5 4.1.242; *mortal times* the lifetime of men R2 1.1.177; *mortal breathing* human existence R2 4.1.48.
4 Extreme, excessive AYL 2.4.56 *mortal in folly* (sense 2 also).
~ *adv.* Fatally COR 5.3.189 *Most dangerously you have with him prevail'd, If not most mortal to him.*

mortal-breathing *adj.* Breathing like a human being MV 2.7.40 *this mortal-breathing saint.*

mortality *n.*
1 Human or mortal life H5 1.2.28 *brief mortality*, MM 3.2.185, MAC 2.3.93.
2 Death JN 4.2.82 *We cannot hold mortality's strong hand*, 1H6 4.5.32, MM 1.1.44.
3 Deadliness H5 4.3.107 *Killing in relapse of mortality.*

mortal-living *adj.* Doomed to life R3 4.4.26 *Dead life, blind sight, poor mortal-living ghost.*

mortally *adv.* In the manner of mortals, of human parents PER 5.1.104 *I was mortally brought forth.*

mortal-staring *adj.* Having a deadly glare R3 5.3.90 *put thy fortune to the arbitrement Of bloody strokes and mortal-staring war.*

mortar-piece *n.* Short piece of ordnance with a large bore H8 5.3.46 *he stands there like a mortar-piece to blow us.*

mortgage *vb.* (fig.) Pledge SON 134.2 *I myself am mortgag'd to thy will.*

mortified *ppl. adj.*
1 Destroyed, dead H5 1.1.26 *his wildness, mortified in him, Seem'd to die too.*
2 Dead to worldly pleasures LLL 1.1.28 *Dumaine is mortified.*
3 Deadened, numbed, insensible JC 2.1.324 *Thou... hast conjur'd up My mortified spirit*, LR 2.3.15, MAC 5.2.5.

mortifying *ppl. adj.* Deadly, mortal, depriving of life or vigour ADO 1.3.12 *a mortifying mischief*, MV 1.1.82.

mortise *n. hold the mortise* Hold together at the joints OTH 2.1.9.

mose *vb. mose in the chine* Suffer from GLANDERS SHR 3.2.51.

most *n.*
1 Greatest amount or quality SON 85.10 *to the most of praise add something more*, MV 3.2.91, LR 5.3.70; greatest number, the majority TMP 1.2.481 *To th' most of men this is a Caliban*, TN 3.3.35, WT 4.4.404.
2 *for the most* For the most part MM 5.1.440 *They say best men are moulded out of faults, And for the most, become much more the better For being a little bad.*
~ *adj.*
1 Greatest in degree or extent MM 3.1.77 *The sense of death is most in apprehension*, ANT 2.2.166, HAM 1.5.180.
2 *most master* The one most masterful, the greatest master 2H6 1.3.146 *Though in this place most master wear no breeches.*

mot *n.* Motto LUC 830 *may read the mot afar.*

mote *n.*
1 Particle of dust in a sunbeam PER 4.4.21 *like motes and shadows see them move a while.*
2 Minute particle of anything, atom MND 5.1.318 *A mote will turn the balance*, HAM 1.1.112, JN 4.1.91.
3 Spot, blemish H5 4.1.179 *wash every mote out of his conscience.*
◇ In F and Q in sense 1 *mote, moat*, in senses 2 and 3 chiefly *moth, moath.*

moth *n.* (fig.) Parasite OTH 1.3.256 *A moth of peace*, COR 1.3.84 (pun); (as a proper name, applied to small persons) MND 3.1.162 *Cobweb! Moth! and Mustardseed!*, LLL 1.2.76.
◇ In applied sense perh. a form of MOTE.

mother *n.*
1 Womanish qualities H5 4.6.31 *And all my mother came into mine eyes* (i.e. tears).
2 Term of address to an elderly woman of the lower class WIV 4.2.182 *Come, Mother Prat*, 2H6 1.4.10.

3 (fig.) Source, cause R3 2.2.80 *Alas! I am the mother of these griefs*, CYM 3.4.50.
4 Head of a female religious community MM 1.4.86 *to give the Mother Notice of my affair.*
5 (lit.) Womb; (hence, fig.) hysteria LR 2.4.56 *O how this mother swells up toward my heart!*
◇ According to old physiology, hysteria was the rising or swelling upward of the womb, or vapours from it.

mother-queen *n.* Queen-mother JN 2.1.62 *With him along is come the mother-queen.*

motion *n.*
1 Power of movement ROM 3.2.59 *Vile earth, to earth resign, end motion here*, MM 3.1.119.
2 Bodily exertion HAM 4.7.157 *When in your motion you are hot and dry.*
3 Movement of the body acquired by drill and training, thrusting movement in fencing HAM 4.7.101 *The scrimmers of their nation...had neither motion, guard, nor eye*, TN 3.4.276.
4 Request, proposal, offer H8 2.4.234 *an earnest motion Made to the Queen to call back her appeal*, WIV 1.1.54, TIT 1.1.243.
5 Instigation, prompting WIV 3.2.35 *he gives her folly motion and advantage*, ERR 3.2.24; influence COR 2.2.53 *We do request your kindest ears, and after, Your loving motion toward the common body To yield what passes here.*
6 Inward prompting; (hence) desire, inclination, emotion MM 1.4.59 *The wanton stings and motions of the sense*, MV 5.1.86, JC 2.1.64.
7 Motive, reason H8 1.1.153 *From sincere motions*, COR 2.1.51.
8 Intuition, insight ANT 2.3.14 *I see it in my motion, have it not in my tongue.*
9 Puppet-show WT 4.3.96 *he compass'd a motion of the Prodigal Son*, LUC 1326; puppet TGV 2.1.94 *O excellent motion! O exceeding puppet!*, MM 3.2.111.
10 The action of a musical instrument, movement, tempo SON 128.2 *that blessed wood whose motion sounds With thy sweet fingers.*
11 *upon the foot of motion* Ready to manifest itself MAC 2.3.125.
~ *vb.* Propose 1H6 1.3.63 *One that still motions war and never peace.*

motive *n.*
1 Mover, promoter, instigator TIM 5.4.27 *Who were the motives that you first went out*, ANT 2.2.96, OTH 4.2.43; that which promotes H5 2.2.156 *Although I did admit it as a motive.*
2 Means, instrument AWW 4.4.20 *As it hath fated her to be my motive And helper to a husband.*
3 Moving limb or organ R2 1.1.193 *The slavish motive of recanting fear* (i.e. the tongue, with quibble on sense 2), TRO 4.5.57.

motley *n.* Parti-coloured dress of a professional jester AYL 2.7.34 *A worthy fool! Motley's the only wear*, LR 1.4.146, TN 1.5.57; (attrib.) AYL 2.7.29 *The motley fool*, H8 Prol.16; (hence) jester, fool AYL 3.3.78 *Will you be married, motley?*, SON 110.2.

motley-minded *adj.* Foolish AYL 5.4.41 *the motley-minded gentleman.*

mought *vb.* (past tense of MAY] Could 3H6 5.2.45 *in a vault, That mought not be distinguish'd.*

mould *n.*[1] Earth; *men of mould* mortal men H5 3.2.22.

mould *n.*[2]
1 Object of imitation, model, pattern HAM 3.1.153 *The glass of fashion and the mould of form.*
2 (transf.) The body with ref. to the clothes fashioned for it MAC 1.3.145 *our strange garments, cleave not to their mould But with the aid of use.*
3 Bodily form COR 3.2.103 *this single plot...This mould of Martius* (with quibble on MOULD *n.*[1]).

~ *vb. mould up* Go to form, compose H8 5.5.26 *All princely graces That mould up such a mighty piece as this.*

moulten *ppl. adj.* Having moulted 1H4 3.1.150 *A clip-wing'd griffin and a moulten raven.*

mounch *vb.* (var. of) Munch MAC 1.3.4 *A sailor's wife had chestnuts...And mounch'd.*

mount *n. on mount* Pre-eminent, set up on high HAM 4.7.28 *challenger on mount of all the age.*

~ *vb.*

1 Cause to rise, elevate H8 1.1.144 *The fire that mounts the liquor till't run o'er,* 2H6 1.4.37; erect, set up 2H6 1.4.37 *where castles mounted stand,* TMP 2.2.11; (fig.) to excite to a higher degree AWW 1.1.220 *which mounts my love so high,* H5 4.1.106.

2 Set (guns) into position JN 2.1.211 *And ready mounted are they to spit forth Their iron indignation;* (fig.) LLL 5.2.82 *encounters mounted are Against your peace,* H8 1.2.205.

mountant *adj.* Rising TIM 4.3.136 *Your aprons mountant.*

Mountanto See MONTANT.

mountebank *vb.* Win by glib talk (like an itinerant quack cajoling his hearers into buying his remedies) COR 3.2.132 *I 'll mountebank their loves.*

mouse *n.* Playful term of endearment to a woman TN 1.5.63 *Good my mouse of virtue, answer me,* LLL 5.2.19, HAM 3.4.183.

~ *vb.* Tear, bite, gnaw JN 2.1.354 *he feasts, mousing the flesh of men,* MND 5.1.269.

mouse-hunt *n.* Woman-hunter ROM 4.4.11 *you have been a mouse-hunt in your time.*

mouth *n.*

1 *a sweet mouth* (?) A taste for sweet things, 'sweet tooth' TGV 3.1.327 *Item, She hath a sweet mouth.*

2 *in the mouth(s) of* Spoken of by MV 1.3.60 *Your worship was the last man in our mouths,* JN 4.2.187, 1H6 3.1.196.

3 (of hounds) Bark 1H6 2.4.12 *Between two dogs, which hath the deeper mouth,* MND 4.1.123; *spend his mouth* bark H5 2.4.70 *for coward dogs Most spend their mouths* (i.e. bark the loudest), VEN 695; (fig.) TRO 5.1.91 *he will spend his mouth and promise.*

4 Spokesman 3H6 5.5.18 *I am now my father's mouth,* COR 3.1.36.

5 *make mouths* Grimace MND 3.2.238 *Make mouths upon me when I turn my back.*

6 *i' th' mouth* Face to face, head on LR 3.4.11 *meet the bear i' th' mouth.*

~ *vb.*

1 Take into the mouth HAM 4.2.19 *first mouth'd, to be last swallow'd.*

2 Join lips *with* MM 3.2.183 *he would mouth with a beggar.*

3 Rant, talk bombast HAM 5.1.283 *and thou'lt mouth, I 'll rant as well as thou;* (trans.) HAM 3.2.2 *Speak the speech...but if you mouth it...*

mouthed *adj.* Gaping 1H4 1.3.97 *mouthed wounds,* SON 77.6.

mouth-friend *n.* One who professes friendship insincerely TIM 3.6.89 *You knot of mouth-friends! ...trencher-friends...!*

mouth-honour *n.* Respect expressed without sincerity MAC 5.3.27 *Curses, not loud but deep, mouth-honour.*

mouth-made *adj.* Insincere, made with the lips but not with the heart ANT 1.3.30 *those mouth-made vows.*

move *vb.*

1 Make angry, exasperate SHR 5.2.142 *A woman mov'd is like a fountain troubled,* WIV 1.4.90, ROM 1.1.7.

2 Urge, incite, instigate, persuade, make a proposal to, appeal or apply to (a person) CYM 1.1.103 *I 'll move him To walk this way,* OTH 3.4.19, ERR 2.2.181.

3 Propose, suggest (something) ADO 4.1.73 *Let me but move one question to your daughter,* HAM 3.2.182, OTH 3.4.166.

mover *n.*

1 He who gives motion; (applied to God as moving the universe) 2H6 3.3.19 *O thou eternal Mover of the Heavens.*

2 Cause CYM 1.5.9 *poisonous compounds, Which are the movers of a languishing death.*

3 Living creature VEN 368 *O fairest mover on this mortal round.*

4 Active person; (ironically of loiterers for plunder) COR 1.5.4 *See here these movers.*

moving *n.*

1 Motion (of a heavenly body) 1H6 1.2.1 *Mars his true moving...is not known.*

2 Bodily movement HAM 2.2.305 *how infinite in faculties, in form and moving.*

~ *ppl. adj.* Exciting the feelings MM 2.2.36 *Heaven give thee moving graces,* R2 5.1.47.

◊ ADO 4.1.228: in Ff and Qq *More moving, delicate and full of life;* in some mod. edd. *moving-delicate,* in which *moving* acts as an adv.

mow *n.* Derisive grimace TMP 4.1.47 *with mop and mow,* HAM 2.2.364 (Qq *mouths*), CYM 1.6.41.

~ *vb.* Grimace TMP 2.2.9 *like apes that mow and chatter at me,* LR 4.1.62.

moy *n.* Imaginary name of a coin evolved by Pistol from a misunderstanding of the Fr. 'moy' (i.e. me) in his prisoner's speech H5 4.4.13 *Moy shall not serve, I will have forty moys.*

much *adj.*

1 Used ironically where 'no' would be used in serious language AYL 4.3.2 *And here much Orlando!*

2 *'tis much* It is a great or difficult thing or a serious matter OTH 4.1.243 *'Tis very much,* CYM 1.6.79, R3 3.7.93; *think* (*it*) *much* regard as important or onerous, be shy of (doing something) 2H6 4.1.18 *think you much to pay two thousand crowns...?,* TMP 1.2.252.

~ *adv.*

1 Very OTH 1.1.1 *I take it much unkindly,* AYL 1.2.184, WT 5.2.118.

2 Not at all 2H4 2.4.133 *God's light, with two points on your shoulder? Much!*

3 Pretty nearly, almost, approximately H5 5.2.192 *much at one* (i.e. very much the same), ROM 1.3.72, MM 3.2.228.

4 *by so much the more...by how much* The more ...the more AYL 5.2.45 *By so much the more shall I to-morrow be at the height of heart-heaviness, by how much I shall think my brother happy.*

mud *vb.* Bury in mud TMP 5.1.151 *I wish Myself were mudded in that oozy bed,* TMP 3.3.102.

muddy *adj.* Disturbed or confused in mind WT 1.2.325 *Dost think I am so muddy, so unsettled...?*

muddy-mettled *adj.* Dull-spirited HAM 2.2.567 *a muddy-mettled rascal.*

muffled *ppl. adj.* Blindfolded ROM 1.1.171 *that love, whose view is muffled still,* AWW 4.1.90.

muffler *n.*

1 Bandage for blindfolding H5 3.6.31 *Fortune is painted blind, with a muffler afore his eyes.*

2 Sort of kerchief or scarf worn by women in 16–17C to cover part of the face and neck either for partial concealment when in public or as a protection against wind and sun WIV 4.2.194 *I spy a great peard under his muffler,* WIV 4.2.71.

muleter *n.* (var. of) Muleteer 1H6 3.2.68 *Base muleters of France,* ANT 3.7.35 (F1 *milites*).

mulier [L.] Woman CYM 5.5.448 *The piece of tender air, thy virtuous daughter,...We term it mulier.*

mulled *ppl. adj.* Dispirited, dull COR 4.5.224 *Peace is a very apoplexy, lethargy, mull'd, deaf.*

multiply *vb.* Increase, enlarge 2H6 1.2.73 *Your Grace's title shall be multiplied,* 2H6 2.1.69.

multiplying medicine *n.* The substance with which alchemists claimed to 'multiply' or increase the number of the precious metals by transmuting the baser metals AWW 5.3.102 *Plutus himself, That knows the tinct and multiplying med'cine.*

multipotent *adj.* Most mighty TRO 4.5.129 *by Jove multipotent.*

multitudinous *adj.*
1 Vast MAC 2.2.59 *The multitudinous seas.*
2 Of the multitude or common people COR 3.1.156 *The multitudinous tongue.*

mum *n.* An inarticulate sound made with closed lips, indicating unwillingness to speak; (in negative or hypothetical context) 'not the slightest word' 2H6 1.2.89 *Seal up your lips, and give no words but mum,* TMP 3.2.51.
~ *vb.* Be silent SHR 1.1.73 *mum, and gaze your fill.*
~ *adj.* Silent R3 3.7.3 *The citizens are mum.*
~ *interj.* Silence! SHR 1.2.162 *Grumio, mum!,* MM 5.1.287.
✧ WIV 5.2.6 *I...cry 'mum'; she cries 'budget':* the two elements of the 16–17C 'mumbudget', which was used like *mum.*

mumble-news *n.* Tale-bearer LLL 5.2.464 *Some mumble-news...Told our intents before.*

mummy *n.*
1 Medicinal or magical preparation of the flesh of dead bodies MAC 4.1.23 *Witch's mummy,* OTH 3.4.74.
2 Dead flesh WIV 3.5.18 *a mountain of mummy.*

muniment *n.* Anything serving as a means of defence or protection COR 1.1.118 *the arm our soldier, Our steed the leg, the tongue our trumpeter, With other muniments.*

munition *n.* Military stores JN 5.2.98 *what munition sent, To underprop this action?;* (spec.) ammunition 1H6 1.1.168 *To view th' artillery and munition.*

mural *n.* (used for) MURE, wall MND 5.1.206 *Now is the mural down.*
✧ Pope's conjecture; Hanmer *Now is the mure all down;* Ff *mor all,* Qq *Now is the moon used.*

murdering-piece *n.* Small cannon or mortar, firing a scattering charge HAM 4.5.95 *this, Like to a murd'ring-piece, in many places Gives me superfluous death.*

mure *n.* Wall 2H4 4.4.119 *the mure that should confine it in.*

murk *n.* Darkness AWW 2.1.163 *in murk and occidental damp.*

murmur *n.* Rumour; *in murmur* whispered about TN 1.2.32 *'twas fresh in murmur...That...*

murrain, murrion *n.* (lit.) A disease of cattle; (in imprecations) plague TMP 3.2.80 *A murrain on your monster,* COR 1.5.3, TRO 2.1.19.
~ *adj.* Diseased MND 2.1.97 *crows are fatted with the murrain flock.*

murther, murtherous Var. in Ff and Qq of 'murder, murderous'.

muscadel *n.* Strong, sweet wine made from the muscatel or similar grape SHR 3.2.172 *quaff'd off the muscadel.*

muscat (var. of) MUSK-CAT.

muse *vb.*
1 Wonder, marvel AWW 2.5.65 *And rather muse than ask why I entreat you,* MAC 3.4.84, R3 1.3.304;

(trans.) wonder at, marvel at TMP 3.3.36 *I cannot too much muse Such shapes.*
2 Grumble, complain, murmur discontentedly WIV 5.5.239 *I will muse no further.*

muset *n.* Gap in a hedge or fence through which hares habitually run, when hunted, for relief VEN 683 *The many musets through the which he goes Are like a labyrinth* (Q *musits*).

music *n.* Band of musicians H8 4.2.94 *Bid the music leave,* ROM 4.4.22, LLL 5.2.211.
~ *adj.* Pleasing, delightful HAM 3.1.156 *the honey of his music vows* (F1 *Musicke*; Qq 2–3 *musickt*).

musit (var. of) MUSET.

musk-cat *n.* Musk-deer, Moschus moschiferus, from which musk is got AWW 5.2.20 *Fortune's cat—but not a musk-cat.*

musk-rose *n.* Large rambling rose with large fragrant flowers MND 2.1.252 *over-canopied...With sweet musk-roses,* MND 2.2.3.

muss *n.* Game in which small objects are thrown down to be scrambled for ANT 3.13.91 *Like boys unto a muss.*

mussel-shell *n.* One who gapes (like a mussel-shell) WIV 4.5.28 *Ay, marry, was it, mussel-shell.*

must *vb.* (as a past tense, with expression of regret with regard to an untoward event) Had to MAC 4.3.212 *And I must be from thence!*
✧ Ellipsis of a *vb.* of motion very freq. after must, e.g. R2 1.2.56 *I must to Coventry.*

muster *vb.*
1 Exhibit, set an example of AWW 2.1.54 *they...do muster true gait.*
2 Enrol CYM 4.4.10 *not muster'd Among the bands.*

muster-book *n.* Book in which military forces are registered 2H4 3.2.135 *we have a number of shadows fill up the muster-book.*

muster-file *n.* Muster-roll AWW 4.3.166 *the muster-file...amounts not to fifteen thousand pole.*

mute *n.*
1 Silent spectator, actor who has no speaking part HAM 5.2.335 *That are but mutes, or audience to this act.*
2 In Oriental countries, dumb house-servant or janitor H5 1.2.232 *our grave, Like Turkish mute, shall have a tongueless mouth,* TN 1.2.62, CYM 3.5.153.

mutine *n.* Mutineer JN 2.1.378 *Do like the mutines,* HAM 5.2.6.
~ *vb.* Rebel; (fig.) HAM 3.4.83 *If thou canst mutine in a matron's bones.*

mutiny *n.* Discord, contention LUC 1153 *So with herself is she in mutiny,* LLL 1.1.169, H8 3.2.120.
~ *vb.* Contend, strive, quarrel R2 2.1.28 *Where will doth mutiny with wit's regard,* OTH 2.1.275, ANT 3.11.13.

mutton *n.*
1 Sheep TGV 1.1.96 *a lost mutton,* AYL 3.2.56, MV 1.3.167.
2 Food for lust; (hence) loose woman or women TGV 1.1.97 *I* (*a lost mutton*) *gave your letter to her* (*a lac'd mutton*), MM 3.2.181.

mutual *adj.*
1 Intimate MM 1.2.154 *The stealth of our most mutual entertainment,* 2H6 1.1.25.
2 Common MND 4.1.117 *one mutual cry,* MV 5.1.77, TIT 5.3.71.

mutuality *n.* Intimacy OTH 2.1.261 *When these mutualities so marshal the way* (F1 *mutabilities*).

mutually *adv.*
1 In return WIV 4.6.10 *Who mutually hath answer'd my affection.*
2 Jointly, in common WIV 5.5.99 *Pinch him, fairies, mutually!,* MM 2.3.27.

mynheer [Du.] Sir WIV 2.1.220 *Will you go Mynheers?*
▷ Theobald's conjecture; F1 *An-heires.*

mystery *n.*[1]
1 Personal secret HAM 3.2.366 *you would pluck out the heart of my mystery.*

2 Religious rite (often secret) LR 1.1.110 *The mysteries of Hecate and the night.*

mystery *n.*[2]
1 Craft, trade, profession MM 4.2.36 *Painting...is a mystery*, OTH 4.2.30, TIM 4.1.18.
2 Skill, art AWW 3.6.65 *your mystery in stratagem.*

N

nag *n.* (fig.) Wanton woman ANT 3.10.10 *Yon ribaudred nag of Egypt.*

nail *n.*
1 Measure of length for cloth, 6cm SHR 4.3.108 *Thou...half-yard, quarter, nail.*
2 *blow (one's) nails* Blow on one's fingers to warm them LLL 5.2.913 *Dick the shepherd blows his nail*, 3H6 2.5.3; (fig.) exercise patience SHR 1.1.108 *we may blow our nails together.*

naked *adj.*
1 Destitute, unprovided, unfurnished LLL 5.2.795 *some forlorn and naked hermitage*, HAM 4.7.44, R2 1.2.31.
2 Unarmed 2H6 3.2.234 *and he but naked, though lock'd up in steel, Whose conscience...is corrupted*, COR 1.10.20, OTH 5.2.258.
3 Mere, bare TGV 2.4.142 *the very naked name of love.*
4 *naked bed* Phrase used with reference to the custom of sleeping entirely naked VEN 397 *in her naked bed.*

nakedness *n.* Bareness, destitution, state of being unfurnished with some particular thing H5 4.1.105 *His ceremonies laid by, in his nakedness he appears but a man*, TIM 4.1.33, ADO 4.1.175.

name *n.*
1 Family, stock TIT 2.3.183 *our general name* (i.e. the human race), AWW 1.3.156.
2 Distinguished or honourable repute, honour, renown MM 1.2.169 *for a name* (i.e. for the sake of his own reputation), 1H6 4.4.9, COR 2.1.135; famous person COR 4.6.125 *Tullus Aufidius, The second name of men* (i.e. the man second in renown).
3 Title, appellation TIT 4.4.81 *King, be thy thoughts imperious, like thy name*, 1H4 3.2.64, TMP 2.1.150; *in (the) name of* under the title or designation of, in the character of WIV 3.5.99 *to carry me in the name of foul clothes*, ADO 2.1.172, WT 3.2.60; *by the name of* in the quality of, as H5 2.2.146 *I arrest thee...,by the name of Richard Earl of Cambridge*, H8 2.1.59, MAC 2.1.16.
~ *vb.* Utter, say TIT 3.2.33 *name the word of hands*, LLL 5.2.239, 3H6 5.5.58.

nameless *adj.*
1 Of unknown name TGV 2.1.105 *the secret, nameless friend of yours.*
2 Bearing no legitimate name LUC 522 *nameless bastardy.*
3 Too small to be worth detailed description, insubstantial TGV 3.1.317 *nameless virtues*, R2 2.2.40.

napkin *n.* Handkerchief LC 15 *Oft did she heave her napkin to her eyne*, HAM 5.2.288, OTH 3.3.287.

Naples *n.* City said to be the place of origin of syphilis OTH 3.1.4 *have your instruments been in Naples, that they speak i' th' nose thus?*

napless *adj.* Threadbare, with the nap worn off COR 2.1.234 *the napless vesture of humility.*

narrow *adj.* Small ANT 3.4.8 *most narrow measure lent me.*
~ *adv.* Closely SHR 3.2.146 *the narrow prying father* (F!).

narrowly *adv.* Carefully, closely PER 4.2.3 *Search the market narrowly*, ADO 5.4.116, SHR 3.2.139.

narrow-prying *adj.* Closely watching SHR 3.2.146 *the narrow-prying father.*
▷ Pope's emendation; F1 *narrow prying.* See NARROW.

nasty *adj.* Dirty, filthy, foul HAM 3.4.94 *the nasty sty*, H5 2.1.50.

native *n.* Origin, source, that which gives birth (to) COR 3.1.129 *Th' accusation...could never be the native Of our so frank donation.*
▷ F1; Heath's conjecture *motive.*
~ *adj.*
1 Natural JN 3.4.83 *native beauty*, LLL 4.3.259, ROM 4.1.97; (with *to*) OTH 2.1.217 *native to them.*
2 Closely connected, related (*to*) HAM 1.2.47 *The head is not more native to the heart*, AWW 1.1.223.
3 Entitled to a certain position by birth, proper, rightful R2 3.2.25 *her native king*, H5 2.4.95, 3H6 3.3.190.

nativity *n.* Newborn child SON 60.5 *Nativity...Crawls to maturity.*

natural *n.* Idiot, half-wit TMP 3.2.33 *That a monster should be such a natural!*, AYL 1.2.49, ROM 2.4.92.
~ *adj.*
1 That is so by birth, having a certain relative status by birth 3H6 1.1.82 *Whom should he follow but his natural king*, LR 4.6.191.
2 Related by blood AYL 1.1.145 *his natural brother*, TIM 4.3.382, CYM 3.3.107.
3 Having natural feelings or kindness MM 3.1.221 *ever most kind and natural*, LR 2.1.84, H5 2.Ch.19.
4 Half-witted TN 1.3.29 *hath all the good gifts of nature.—He hath indeed, almost natural* (i.e. almost like a half-wit).

naturalize *vb.* Familiarize AWW 1.1.208 *My instruction shall serve to naturalize thee.*

naturally *adv.* In a life-like manner SHR Ind.1.87 *that part Was...naturally perform'd.*

nature *n.*
1 Natural feeling or affection 2H4 4.5.39 *nature, love, and filial tenderness*, TMP 5.1.76, MAC 1.5.45.
2 *of nature* Natural (in various senses) HAM 1.4.54 *Making...we fools of nature...to shake our disposition*, TRO 5.1.34; *bias of nature natural affection* LR 1.2.111 *the King falls from bias of nature.*

naught *n.*
1 Wickedness, wrong R3 1.1.99 *He that doth naught with her; thing of naught* something wicked MND 4.2.14 *A paramour is...a thing of naught.*
2 *be naught* Efface yourself, withdraw AYL 1.1.35 *be better employ'd, and be naught a while.*
3 *call all to naught* Abuse or decry vehemently VEN 993 *It was not she that call'd him all to naught.*
4 *set at naught* Slight, despise COR 3.1.269 *the public power, Which he so sets at naught*, TGV 1.1.68, 2H4 5.2.85.
▷ Senses 2, 3, and 4 sometimes spelt 'nought'.
~ *adj.*
1 Wicked, naughty LR 2.4.134 *thy sister's naught*, ROM 3.2.87, MAC 4.3.225.
2 Lost, ruined COR 3.1.230 *be gone, away! All will be naught else*, ANT 3.10.1.
3 Worthless, useless H5 1.2.73 *his title...was corrupt and naught*, ADO 5.1.156, AYL 3.2.15.

naughty adj.
1 Worthless AWW 5.3.253 a good drum,...but a naughty orator.
2 Wicked ADO 4.2.72 Thou naughty varlet, MV 3.3.9, 2H6 2.1.163.
3 (of weather) Bad, nasty LR 3.4.110 'tis a naughty night to swim in.

nave n.
1 Hub (of a wheel) HAM 2.2.496 Break all the spokes and fellies from her wheel, And bowl the round nave down the hill, 2H4 2.4.255 (with quibble on 'knave').
2 Navel MAC 1.2.22 from the nave to th' chops.

navel n. (fig.) Centre COR 3.1.123 the navel of the state.

navigation n. Vessels, shipping MAC 4.1.54 swallow navigation up.

nay adv. As a negative, its most freq. use is to correct, amplify, or emphasize something that precedes, or to express a mild protest ERR 4.2.36 A wolf, nay worse, a fellow all in buff, TMP 1.1.15, MM 3.1.147.

nayward n. to the nayward Towards denial or disbelief WT 2.1.64 lean to th' nayward.

nayword, nay-word n.
1 Watchword, password WIV 5.2.5 we have a nayword how to know one another.
2 Byword, proverb TN 2.3.135 if I do not gull him into a nayword.
▷ Rowe's emendation; F1 an ayword.

ne conj. And not, nor PER 2.Gower.36 Ne aught escapend but himself, AWW 2.1.173.

ne intelligis, domine? [L.] Do you understand, master? LLL 5.1.25.

neaf n. Fist MND 4.1.19 Give me your neaf, 2H4 2.4.186.

Neapolitan bone-ache n. Venereal disease TRO 2.3.18 the Neapolitan bone-ache...is the curse...on those that war for a placket.
▷ Cf. NAPLES.

near adj. Closely affecting or touching one TIM 3.6.10 many my near occasions, TRO 2.2.175; (absol.) MAC 3.1.117 my near'st of life (i.e. my very inmost being).
~ adv.[1] and prep.
1 Intimately, deeply, closely TGV 3.1.60 some affairs That touch me near, 1H6 3.1.58, TIM 1.2.177; (also as prep., esp. in the phr. come near) closely touching or affecting TGV 4.3.19 No grief did ever come so near thy heart, AYL 5.2.62, OTH 4.1.198.
2 Intimate with 2H4 5.1.73 being near their master.
3 come near the house, come near, draw near Enter WIV 1.4.132 Come near the house, TMP 5.1.319, MV 5.1.223.
4 near upon Close at hand MM 4.6.14 and very near upon The Duke is ent'ring.
5 go near to Be on the point of, almost succeed in (doing something) 2H6 1.2.102 if you take not heed, you shall go near To call them both a pair of crafty knaves, TMP 2.2.75.

near adv.[2] Nearer R2 3.2.64 Nor near nor farther off...Than this weak arm, MAC 2.3.140; ne'er the near no nearer the object in view R2 5.1.88 Better far off than, near, be ne'er the near.

near-legged adj. near-legged before Going with the forelegs close together SHR 3.2.56 his horse...near-legg'd before.

neat n. Animal of the ox kind SHR 4.3.17 a neat's foot, 3H6 2.1.14, MV 1.1.112; cattle WT 1.2.125 the steer, the heifer, and the calf Are all call'd neat.

neat adj.
1 Elegant 1H4 1.3.33 a certain lord, neat, and trimly dress'd, WT 1.2.123, TGV 1.2.10; dandified LR 2.2.42 you neat slave.
2 Dainty CYM 4.2.49 his neat cookery.

neat-herd n. Cowherd WT 4.4.325 three shepherds, three neat-herds, three swine-herds, CYM 1.1.149.

neb n. Beak; (hence) mouth WT 1.2.183 How she holds up the neb...to him!

necessary adj.
1 Rendering useful service COR 2.1.82 a necessary bencher in the Capitol.
2 Inevitable SON 108.11 necessary wrinkles, JC 2.2.36, HAM 3.2.192.

necessitied adj. necessitied to In need of AWW 5.3.85 Her fortunes ever stood Necessitied to help.

neck n.
1 in, on the neck of Immediately after SON 131.11 A thousand groans,...One on another's neck (i.e. one immediately after the other), 1H4 4.3.92.
2 on one's neck Phrase denoting the laying of a charge on a person OTH 5.2.170 men must lay their murders on your neck.

need n.
1 for a need In case of necessity, at a pinch 3H6 1.2.67 with five hundred...for a need, R3 3.5.85, HAM 2.2.541.
2 had need Would do well (to), ought (to) H8 2.2.44 We had need pray, AYL 2.7.169, TN 2.3.182.
~ vb.
1 it needs It is necessary, there is necessity ERR 5.1.391 It shall not need, thy father hath his life, 3H6 1.4.125, MAC 5.2.29.
2 what need(s)...? What necessity is there for...? TIM 1.2.242 What needs these feasts...?, ERR 3.1.60, ANT 2.7.125.

needful adj. Wanting supplies of (men) 3H6 2.1.147 With aid of soldiers to this needful war.

needless adj. Not in need AYL 2.1.46 his weeping into the needless stream.

needly adv. Of necessity ROM 3.2.117 needly will be rank'd with other griefs.

needy adj. Necessary for your sustenance PER 1.4.95 your needy bread.

neele n. Needle PER 5.Gower.5 with her neele composes Nature's own shape (Qq).

neeze vb. Sneeze MND 2.1.56 The whole quire... waxen in their mirth, and neeze.

negation n. Denial TRO 5.2.127 my negation hath no taste of madness.

negative adj. Denying WT 1.2.274 If thou wilt confess, Or else be impudently negative.

neglect vb. Cause neglect of R3 3.4.24 My absence doth neglect no great design.

neglected ppl. adj. Despised, disregarded H5 2.4.13 the fatal and neglected English.

neglectingly adv. Negligently 1H4 1.3.52 Answer'd neglectingly.

neglection n. Negligence, neglect 1H6 4.3.49 Sleeping neglection, TRO 1.3.127, PER 3.3.20.

negligence n. Disregard, contempt HAM 4.5.135 both the worlds I give to negligence.

negligent adj. Due to negligence ANT 3.6.81 we in negligent danger (i.e. a danger arising from our continued negligence).

neighbour n. the neighbour to Privy to R3 4.2.43 No more shall be the neighbour to my counsels.
~ vb. Lie near VEN 259 a copse that neighbours by; (trans.) be near, have as a neighbour WT 1.2.449 thy places shall Still neighbour mine, H5 1.1.62.
~ adj. Neighbouring HAM 3.4.212 the neighbour room, ROM 2.6.27, VEN 830.

neighboured ppl. adj. Closely connected or associated HAM 2.2.12 so neighboured to his youth, LR 1.1.119.

neighbourhood n. Friendly relations, neighbourly feeling H5 5.2.353 neighbourhood and Christian-like accord, TIM 4.1.17.

neither *adv.*
1 Nor that either TGV 2.5.17 *shall she marry him?—No.—How then? shall he marry her?—No, neither*, ERR 5.1.94, 1H4 3.1.240.
2 Either TGV 2.3.16 *Nay, that cannot be so neither*, TMP 3.2.19.
3 For all that, nevertheless WT 2.3.158 *let it live. It shall not neither*, AYL 1.1.87, TMP 3.2.20; (after *but*) AWW 2.2.34 *But a trifle neither*, MV 3.5.8, ADO 1.1.287.
4 *not so neither* By no means ADO 3.3.144 *But art not thou thyself giddy with the fashion too...?—Not so neither*, MND 3.1.149, COR 4.5.167.

nephew *n.*
1 Cousin 1H6 2.5.64 *Depos'd his nephew Richard*, TRO 1.2.13.
2 Grandson OTH 1.1.112 *You'll have your nephews neigh to you.*

Neptune *n.* God of the sea; (hence) the sea TMP 5.1.35 *the ebbing Neptune*, PER 3.3.36, MND 2.1.126.

nerve *n.*
1 Sinew, tendon HAM 1.4.83 *this body As hardy as the Nemean lion's nerve.*
2 (esp. pl.) The parts of the body in which the chief strength lies CYM 3.3.94 *Strains his young nerves*, TMP 1.2.485, COR 1.1.138; (fig.) MM 1.4.53 *the very nerves of state*; (applied to a person) TRO 1.3.55 *Thou great commander, nerves and bone of Greece* (Q; F1 *nerve*).

nervy *adj.* Vigorous, sinewy COR 2.1.160 *in 's nervy arm.*

net *n.* (fig.) Intricate, sophistical argument H5 1.2.93 *hide them in a net.*

nether *adj.* Committed here below LR 4.2.79 *our nether crimes.*

nether-stock *n.* Stocking, covering the foot and leg to, or slightly above, the knee (in contrast to breeches or other hose) 1H4 2.4.116 *I'll sew nether-stocks*; (transf.) LR 2.4.11 *wooden nether-stocks* (i.e. the stocks).

neuter *adj.* Neutral R2 2.3.159 *I do remain as neuter.*

new *adv.*
1 Newly, freshly, recently, lately JN 3.1.233 *even before this truce, but new before*, TIM 1.2.78, SON 56.10.
2 Anew, afresh, over again H5 4.1.295 *I Richard's body have interred new*, CYM 1.6.165, R2 1.3.76.
~ in combination A. Sense 1.
new-added Reinforced JC 4.3.209 *refresh'd, new-added, and encouraged.* **new-adopted** LR 1.1.203. **new-apparelled** ERR 4.3.13. **new-appearing** R3 4.4.10, SON 7.3. **new-beloved** ROM 2.Ch.12. **new-bleeding** LC 153. **new-built** SHR 5.2.118, CYM 1.5.59. **new-come** R2 5.2.47, 1H6 2.2.20. **new-create(d)** OTH 4.1.276, TMP 1.2.81, H8 5.4.41. **new-crowned** MV 3.2.50. **new-dated** Recently written 2H4 4.1.8. **new-delivered** Recently released R3 1.1.121. **new-devised** LLL 1.2.63. **new-dyed** TMP 2.1.64. **new-fallen 1** Recently acquired 1H4 5.1.44 *your new-fall'n right, The seat of Gaunt*, AYL 5.4.176. **2** Freshly fallen VEN 354. **new-fangled 1** Fond of novelty or of new things AYL 4.1.152 *more new-fangled than an ape*, LLL 1.1.106. **2** New-fashioned SON 91.3 *Some in their garments, though new-fangled ill.* **new-found** TGV 4.4.130, SON 76.4. **new-hatched** HAM 1.3.65, MAC 2.3.59. **new-healed** 2H4 1.2.147, R3 2.2.125. **new-killed** LUC 457. **new-made** JN 1.1.187, ROM 4.1.84, TIT 2.1.20. **new-married** MM 5.1.400, H5 5.2.179, TIT 2.2.15. **new-planted** JC 3.2.248. **new-sad** LLL 5.2.731. **new-shed** TIT 2.3.200. **new-sprung** VEN 1171. **new-taken** TRO 3.2.34. **new-transformed** TIT 2.3.64. **new-trothed** ADO 3.1.38. **new tuned** H5 3.6.76. B. Sense 2.

new-crowned JN 4.2.35. **new-enkindled** JN 4.2.163. **new-fired** JC 2.1.332. **new-made** SON 2.13, MM 2.2.79. **new pay** SON 30.12. **new-store** H5 3.5.31 (see STORE). **new-varnished** MV 2.9.49. **new woo** WT 3.2.156.

newly *adv.* Anew LUC 490 *reason beat it dead, By thy bright beauty was it newly bred*, LLL 1.2.115, ADO 1.3.22.

next *adj.*, or absol. as *n.*
1 Nearest (in place) TMP 3.2.36 *If you prove a mutineer—the next tree!*, WT 1.2.195, MAC 5.5.38; *the next way* the nearest way (lit.) WT 3.3.127 *Come, good boy, the next way home*, 1H4 3.1.259; (fig.) AWW 1.3.59 *I speak the truth the next way* (i.e. openly, in a straightforward way).
2 The nearest in relationship 1H6 2.5.73 *the next by birth*, 1H4 1.3.146, SON 133.6.
3 *the next* What comes next or afterwards 2H6 3.1.383 *Humphrey being dead,...And Henry put apart, the next for me*, JN 5.2.69; (with *my*) MND 4.1.201 *My next is...*

nice *adj.*
1 Wanton, lascivious LLL 3.1.23 *nice wenches*, ANT 3.13.179.
2 Not able to bear much, delicate 2H4 1.1.145 *Hence therefore, thou nice crutch!*
3 Shy, coy LLL 5.2.219 *We'll not be nice; take hands*, TGV 3.1.82.
4 Scrupulous, cautious, hesitant, or meticulous in acting LC 97 *nice affections wavering stood in doubt; make nice of* be scrupulous about JN 3.4.138 *he that stands upon a slipp'ry place Makes nice of no vile hold to stay him up.*
5 Fastidious, dainty, punctilious MV 2.1.14 *nice direction of a maiden's eyes*, SHR 3.1.80, AWW 5.1.15.
6 Minute, subtle 1H6 2.4.17 *these nice sharp quillets of the law*, 3H6 4.7.58, LLL 5.2.232.
7 Meagre OTH 3.3.15 *such nice and waterish diet.*
8 Unimportant, trivial JC 4.3.8 *every nice offence*, R3 3.7.175, ROM 3.1.154.
9 Precarious 1H4 4.1.48 *the nice hazard of one doubtful hour.*
10 Minutely accurate, precise TRO 4.5.250 *to prenominate in nice conjecture Where thou wilt hit me dead*, MAC 4.3.174, LUC 1412.

nicely *adv.*
1 Elegantly, daintily COR 2.1.217 *their nicely gawded cheeks*, TN 3.1.14.
2 Triflingly R2 2.1.84 *Can sick men play so nicely with their names?*
3 Scrupulously, punctiliously, with technical correctness LR 5.3.145 *What safe and nicely I might well delay*, PER 4.1.6; with great particularity H5 5.2.94 *articles too nicely urged.*
4 Subtly, ingeniously, sophistically TN 3.1.14 *dally nicely with words*, H5 1.2.15.
5 With exact correspondence CYM 2.4.90 *two... Cupids...nicely Depending on their brands.*

niceness *n.* Coyness, fastidiousness CYM 3.4.155 *fear and niceness.*

nice-preserved *adj.* Coyly guarded TIT 2.3.135 *That nice-preserved honesty.*

nicety *n.* Reserve, coyness MM 2.4.162 *Lay by all nicety.*

Nicholas *n.* *Saint Nicholas'* clerks Highwaymen 1H4 2.1.61.
▷ In Eliz. underworld slang St. Nicholas sometimes appears as the patron saint of thieves. There is a possible play on 'Old Nick' (the Devil). In standard usage St. Nicholas was the patron saint of scholars (cf. TGV 3.1.300), hence the punning pertinence in 1H4 of *clerks* (= 'scholar').

nick n.
1 *out of all nick* Beyond all reckoning; (hence) exceedingly TGV 4.2.76 *he lov'd her out of all nick.*
2 *in the nick* At the right moment OTH 5.2.317 *Iago in the nick Came in* (Q1; F1 *interim*).

~ *vb.*
1 Cut in nicks or notches ERR 5.1.175 *His man with scissors nicks him.*
2 Cut short ANT 3.13.8 *The itch of his affection should not then Have nick'd his captainship* (with prob. quibble on use of *nick* in the game of hazard 'win against').

nickname vb.
1 Name wrongly HAM 3.1.144 *you nickname God's creatures.*
2 Mention by mistake LLL 5.2.349 *You nickname virtue; vice you should have spoke.*

niece n. Granddaughter R3 4.1.1 *My niece Plantagenet.*

niesse n. (var. of) Nyas, young hawk ROM 2.2.167 *My niesse?*
◇ Duthie-Wilson; F1, Qq 2–3 *Neece*; Q1 *Madame*; F2 *sweete*; Q4 *deere.*

niggard vb.
1 Act like a niggard or miser, hoard SON 1.12 *mak'st waste in niggarding.*
2 Put off (*with* a small amount of something) JC 4.3.228 *necessity, Which we will niggard with a little rest.*

niggardly adv. Sparingly WIV 2.2.197 *every slight occasion that could but niggardly give me sight of her.*

night n.
1 *What is the night?* What time of night is it? MAC 3.4.125.
2 *good night* Farewell TMP 4.1.54 *good night your vow*, SHR 2.1.301, R3 4.3.39; (with *to*) MM 5.1.299 *Good night to your redress!*
3 *the night* During the night, by night 2H4 4.5.125 *Revel the night*, R3 4.4.118.
4 *on, a' night*(s) By night 2H4 2.4.232 *fighting a' days and foining a' nights*, 2H4 2.1.77, ERR 5.1.210.
5 *of the night* At night MND 2.1.253 *There sleeps Titania sometime of the night.*

night-bird n. Nightingale PER 4. Gower.26 *She sung, and made the night-bird mute* (Q1 *night bed*).

night-cap, night-cape n. (fig.) Wife OTH 2.1.307 *I fear Cassio with my night-cap* (Q1; F1 *Night-Cape*).

night-crow n. (?) (1) Owl; or (2) nightjar 3H6 5.6.45 *The night-crow cried, aboding luckless time.*

nighted adj. Dark or black as night LR 4.5.13 *to dispatch His nighted life*, HAM 1.2.68 (Qq; Ff *nightly*).

night-gown n. Kind of dressing-gown worn at night MAC 2.2.67 *Get on your night-gown*, ADO 3.4.18, OTH 4.3.34.

nightly adj.
1 Belonging to the night, used by night, active at night TIT 2.3.97 *the nightly owl*, TGV 2.4.132, MND 5.1.370.
2 Dark HAM 1.2.68 *cast thy nightly colour off* (Ff; Qq *nighted*).
~ *adv.* At night ROM 4.1.81 *hide me nightly in a charnel-house*, MND 2.2.6.

night-rule n. Diversion of the night MND 3.2.5 *What night-rule now about this haunted grove?*

nill vb. Will not HAM 5.1.17 *will he, nill he*, SHR 2.1.271, PER 3. Gower.55.

nimble-pinioned adj. Swift-winged ROM 2.5.7 *nimble-pinion'd doves.*

nimbly adv. Briskly MAC 1.6.2 *the air Nimbly...recommends itself Unto our...senses.*

ninefold n. Attendant company of nine LR 3.4.121 *He met the night-mare and her nine-fold.*

nine men's morris See MORRIS².

nip vb.
1 Arrest the attention of PER 5.1.234 *music...nips me unto list'ning.*
2 Affect injuriously; (fig.) TIT 4.4.70 *These tidings nip me, and I hang the head As flowers with frost*, LLL 5.2.802.
3 *nip in the head* Give a decisive or final check to MM 3.1.90 *This outward-sainted deputy...Nips youth i' th' head.*

nit n. Egg of a louse; (applied to a person as a term of contempt) LLL 4.1.148 *most pathetical nit*, SHR 4.3.109.

noble n. A gold coin, equivalent to twenty groats or one third of a pound R2 1.1.88 *receiv'd eight thousand nobles*, H5 2.1.107, R3 1.3.81.

noblesse n. Nobility R2 4.1.119 *true noblesse would Learn him forbearance.*

nod n.
1 Oscillation R3 3.4.100 *like a drunken sailor on a mast, Ready with every nod to tumble down.*
2 noddy, fool TRO 1.2.196 *Will he give you the nod?* (i.e call you fool; with quibble on sense 'sign of recognition').
~ *vb.* Beckon (a person) ANT 3.6.66 *Cleopatra Hath nodded him to her.*

noddy n. Simpleton TGV 1.1.124 *having nothing but the word 'noddy' for my pains.*

noise n.
1 Rumour, report ANT 1.2.141 *the least noise of this*, TRO 1.2.12, LR 3.6.111.
2 Musical sound, music TMP 3.2.135 *the isle is full of noises*, ANT 4.3.12, MAC 4.1.106.
3 Band of musicians 2H4 2.4.11 *see if thou canst find out Sneak's noise. Mistress Tearsheet would fain hear some music.*
~ *vb.*
1 Rumour, spread (*abroad*) TIM 4.3.402 *It is nois'd he hath a mass of treasure*, H8 1.2.105, LLL 2.1.22.
2 *noise it* Raise a disturbance, make a clamour ANT 3.6.96 *gives his...regiment to a trull That noises it against us.*

nole, nowl n. Head MND 3.2.17 *An ass's nole I fixed on his head.*

nominate vb.
1 Name, call AYL 5.4.88 *Can you nominate...the degrees of the lie?*, LLL 1.2.15, 2H6 2.1.128.
2 Appoint, specify MV 4.1.259 *Is it so nominated in the bond?*, MV 1.3.149.

nomination n.
1 Naming, mention HAM 5.2.127 *What imports the nomination of this gentleman?*, LLL 4.2.134.
2 Specifying, appointing R3 3.4.5 *the royal day...wants but nomination.*

nonage n. Minority, period of being under age R3 2.3.13 *in his nonage.*

nonce n. *for the nonce*
1 For the purpose in hand, on purpose, expressly 1H4 1.2.180 *I have cases of buckrom for the nonce*, HAM 4.7.160.
2 A tag with no special meaning 1H6 2.3.57 *This is a riddling merchant for the nonce.*

noncome n. (?) Abbreviation of 'non compos mentis' (i.e. not of sound mind) ADO 3.5.62 *drive some of them to a noncome.*
◇ Nonsensical use; perh. Dogberry intended it as a substitute for 'nonplus'.

none adj. Not any, no JN 3.4.151 *none so small advantage* (i.e. no advantage, however small), H8 4.1.33, CYM 1.4.94.

nonino See NONNY.

nonny interj. Meaningless refrain ADO 2.3.69 *hey nonny nonny*, HAM 4.5.166; (also) *nonino, nonny no* AYL 5.3.17 *a hey nonino.*

nonpareil *n.* One that has no equal TN 1.5.254 *The nonpareil of beauty,* TMP 3.2.100, MAC 3.4.18.

non-regardance *n.* Disregard TN 5.1.121 *Since you to non-regardance cast my faith.*

non(-)suit *vb.* Reject the suit of OTH 1.1.16 *Nonsuits my mediators.*

nook *n.* Inlet, sheltered creek TGV 2.7.31 *by many winding nooks he strays,* TMP 1.2.227.

▷ A play on this sense in AYL 3.2.420 *forswear the full stream of the world, and to live in a nook merely monastic.*

nooked See THREE-NOOKED.

nook-shotten *adj.* Running out into corners, highly indented H5 3.5.14 *that nook-shotten isle of Albion.*

north *n.*
1 North wind OTH 5.2.220 *I will speak as liberal as the north* (i.e. as the north wind blows; Q1 *ayre*), CYM 1.3.36.
2 *into the north of* 'Out of the sunshine of ' (Wright) TN 3.2.26 *sail'd into the north of my lady's opinion.*
3 *north pole* Pole star LLL 5.2.693 *By the north pole, I do challenge thee.*

northern star *n.* North or pole star JC 3.1.60 *I am constant as the northern star.*

nose *n.*
1 *by, to (one's) nose* Before one's very eyes TIT 2.1.94 *borne her cleanly by the keeper's nose,* COR 4.6.83 *see your wives dishonour'd to your noses.*
2 *bite, pluck, tweak by the nose* Treat with contempt MM 1.3.29 *liberty plucks justice by the nose,* HAM 2.2.574 *Tweaks me by the nose,* MM 3.1.107.
3 *speak i' th' nose* Sound like a man whose nose has been affected by syphilis OTH 3.1.4.
4 *Down with the nose* May the nasal bone decay TIM 4.3.157.

▷ Symptom of syphilis.

nose-herb *n.* Plant grown for its perfume, scented herb AWW 4.5.19 *They are not herbs,...they are nose-herbs.*

nose-painting *n.* Colouring of the nose red MAC 2.3.28 *What...things does drink especially provoke?—nose-painting.*

not *adv.*
1 Not only MM 4.1.66 *It is not my consent, But my entreaty too,* COR 3.2.71, PER 3.2.46.
2 Not even ANT 2.2.170 *Not sickness should detain me.*

notable *adj.* Observable, noticeable, perceptible OTH 4.1.82 *notable scorns That dwell in...his face.*

not-answering *n.* Refusal to answer TRO 3.3.269 *He professes not-answering.*

not-appearance *n.* Non-appearance in court H8 4.1.30 *for not-appearance and The King's late scruple,...she was divorc'd.*

notary *n.* Clerk, secretary; (fig.) LUC 765 *Dim register and notary of shame.*

note *n.*
1 Sign, token, indication WT 1.2.287 *a note infallible Of breaking honesty,* CYM 2.2.28, ADO 3.2.54.
2 Stigma, reproach, brand LUC 208 *my posterity, sham'd with the note,* R2 1.1.43, LLL 4.3.123.
3 Comment, remark TN 3.4.153 *A good note, that keeps you from the blow of the law*; marginal comment (fig.) ROM 1.1.235 *What doth her beauty serve but as a note Where I may read...?*
4 Notice, attentive regard ANT 1.1.11 *Take but good note; upon our note* on observing us CYM 4.4.20.
5 List, brief record WT 4.3.46 *dates, none—that's out of my note* (i.e. not on my list).
6 Bill, account 2H4 5.1.18 *the smith's note for shoeing and plough-irons,* TIM 2.2.16, SHR 1.2.144.
7 Distinction, importance, eminence CYM 2.3.122

foil The precious note of it with a base slave, MAC 3.2.44, LC 233.
8 Knowledge, information, intimation TMP 2.1.248 *she that from Naples Can have no note,* LR 2.1.83, WT 1.1.36; *in note* known AWW 1.3.227 *More than they were in note; take note of it* know about it TN 3.2.36.
9 Tune, melody, music CYM 4.2.237 *use like note and words,* TGV 1.2.78, 2H6 3.2.40.

~ *vb.*
1 Indicate HAM 1.5.178 *to note That you know aught of me.*
2 Stigmatize, brand JC 4.3.2 *You have condemn'd and noted Lucius Pella For taking bribes.*
3 Set music to, provide with notes ROM 4.5.120 *An you 're' us and 'fa' us, you note us* (with quibble on sense 2), TRO 5.2.11.

notedly *adv.* Particularly MM 5.1.332 *Do you remember what you said...?—Most notedly.*

nothing *n.*
1 Nothingness WT 4.4.613 *admiring the nothing of it.*
2 *be nothing of* Be irrelevant to, have no place in ANT 2.2.80 *Let this fellow Be nothing of our strife.*
~ *adv.* Not at all JC 1.2.162 *That you do love me, I am nothing jealous,* MM 2.4.113, ANT 2.6.79.

nothing-gift *n.* Worthless gift CYM 3.6.85 *That nothing-gift of differing multitudes.*

notice *n.*
1 Information JC 3.2.270 *they had some notice* (i.e. they learned), TGV 2.6.36, H5 4.7.117.
2 Observation COR 2.3.158 *To my poor unworthy notice.*

notify *vb.*
1 Take note, notice WIV 2.2.83 *she gives you to notify that her husband will be absence* (Quickly's speech).
2 Give information OTH 3.1.29 *I shall seem to notify unto her.*

notion *n.* Understanding, mind LR 1.4.228 *his notion weakens,* COR 5.6.106, MAC 3.1.82.

notorious *adj.* Well-known, notable, manifest TN 5.1.329 *you have done me wrong, Notorious wrong,* TIT 5.1.127, SHR 5.1.52.

not-pated *adj.* Close-cropped, short-haired 1H4 2.4.70 *Wilt thou rob this...not-pated,...Spanish-pouch?*

Notre très cher fils Henri, Roi d'Angleterre, Heritiér de France [Fr.] Our very dear son Henry, King of England, Heir of France H5 5.2.339.

nouns *n.* (pl.) (perversion of) Wounds WIV 4.1.24 *Od's nouns.*

nourish *n.* Nurse; (fig.) 1H6 1.1.50 *Our isle be made a nourish of salt tears.*
▷ F1; Fr. 'nourrice'. Pope's doubtful conjecture: *marish* 'marsh, swamp'.
~ *vb.* Support, maintain 2H6 3.1.348 *Whiles I in Ireland nourish a mighty band.*

nousle (var. of) NUZZLE *vb.*[1].

nouzell (var. of) NUZZLE *vb.*[2].

no-verb *n.* Word that does not exist WIV 3.1.105 *He gives me the proverbs and the no-verbs.*

novum *n.* Old game at dice played by five or six players, the two principal throws being five and nine LLL 5.2.544 *Abate throw at novum.*

now-born *adj.* (?) Produced at this juncture AWW 2.3.179 *whose ceremony Shall seem expedient on the now-born brief* (F1 *now borne*).

nowl See NOLE.

noyance *n.* Harm HAM 3.3.13 *To keep itself from noyance.*

numb *adj.* Causing numbness, numbing R3 2.1.118 *the numb cold night.*

number *n.*
1 Collection or company of persons COR 3.1.72 *us, the honour'd number*; (pl.) Multitude, populace JC 3.2.4 *go into the other street, And part the numbers.*
2 Metrical foot; (hence) metre, verse TN 2.5.100 *The numbers alter'd!*, SON 17.6, ROM 2.4.38.
~ *vb.* Celebrate in 'numbers' or verse ANT 3.2.17 *scribes, bards, poets, cannot...write, sing, number.*
numbered *ppl. adj.* Abounding in stones or sand CYM 1.6.36 *the twinn'd stones Upon the number'd beach* (see UNNUMBERED).
nuncio, nuntio *n.* Messenger TN 1.4.28 *in a nuncio's of more grave aspect.*
nuncle *n.* (var. of) Uncle, 'the customary appellation of the licensed fool to his superiors' (Nares) LR 1.4.117 *Mark it, nuncle*, LR 1.4.131.
▷ Developed by metanalysis from 'mine uncle'.
nurse *n.*
1 (fig.) That which fosters or promotes something TGV 3.1.245 *Time is the nurse and breeder of all good*, H5 5.2.35, ANT 5.2.8.
2 (transf.) One who takes care of, looks after another; (hence) housekeeper WIV 1.2.3 *Mistress Quickly, which is in the manner of his nurse.*
~ *vb.* Foster or promote H8 5.4.28 *Truth shall nurse her*, MM 3.1.15, LUC 141.
nurser *n.* (fig.) NURSE sense 1 1H6 4.7.46 *the most bloody nurser of his harms.*
nursery *n.* Nursing LR 1.1.124 *set my rest On her kind nursery.*
nurture *n.* Education, training AYL 2.7.97 *I...know some nurture*, TMP 4.1.189.
nut *n.* Type of something of trifling value ERR 4.3.73 *a pin, A nut, a cherry-stone.*
nut-hook *n.* Beadle, constable WIV 1.1.168 *if you run the nut-hook's humour on me* (i.e. if you accuse me of stealing), 2H4 5.4.7.
nuzzle *vb.*[1] Push or poke with the nose VEN 1115 *nuzzling in his flank* (Qq *nousling*).
nuzzle *vb.*[2] Train, nurture PER 1.4.42 *to nuzzle up their babes.*
▷ Steevens; Q1 *nouzell.*
nymph *n.* Young and beautiful woman HAM 3.1.88 *Nymph, in thy orisons Be all my sins rememb'red*, TGV 5.4.12, MND 2.1.245.

O

O *n.*[1]
1 Cipher, mere nothing LR 1.4.192 *thou art an O without a figure.*
2 Circle, round spot LLL 5.2.45 *O, that your face were not so full of O's!* (i.e. smallpox marks); (applied to stars) MND 3.2.188 *yon fiery oes*; (applied to the Globe Theatre, London) H5 Prol.13 *this wooden O.*
O *n.*[2] Lament, sigh ROM 3.3.90 *Why should you fall into so deep an O?*
o' *prep.*
1 Of TMP 1.2.226 *the rest o' th' fleet*, OTH 1.1.123, H5 2.3.13.
2 On AYL 4.1.48 *clapp'd him o' th' shoulder*, WT 4.4.60, WIV 1.1.40.
O diable, diable! [Fr.] O devil, devil! WIV 1.4.67.
O Dieu vivant! [Fr.] O living God! H5 3.5.5.
oak *n.*
1 The wood of the tree OTH 3.3.210 *seal...close as oak.*
▷ Ref. to the close grain of the wood.
2 Oak-leaves used as a garland COR 1.3.15 *his brows bound with oak.*
oar *vb.* Row TMP 2.1.119 *he...oared Himself...To th' shore.*
oathable *adj.* Fit to take an oath TIM 4.3.136 *You are not oathable, Although I know you'll swear.*
ob *n.* (abbreviation of) 'Obolus' (i.e. halfpenny) 1H4 2.4.539 *Item, bread...ob.*
obedient *adj.*
1 Respectful PER 1.2.42 *reproof, obedient, and in order*, LLL 4.3.221.
2 Of obedience AWW 2.3.160 *that obedient right Which...thy duty owes; obedient orb* sphere of obedience 1H4 5.1.17.
object *n.*
1 Someone or something that on being seen excites love, hate, pity, or cruelty MND 4.1.170 *The object and the pleasure of mine eye Is only Helena*, TRO 4.5.106, TIM 4.3.123; (hence) spectacle TIT 3.1.64 *this object kills me!*; curiosity, gazing stock JC 4.1.37 *one that feeds On objects, arts and imitations.*
2 Presentation (of something) to the eye or the perception TRO 2.2.41 *reason flies the object of all harm*, COR 1.1.20.

~ *vb.* Urge 1H6 2.4.43 *it is well objected.*
objection *n.* Charge, accusation 2H6 1.3.155 *your spiteful false objections*, 1H6 4.1.129, H8 3.2.307.
obligation *n.* Bond, contract 2H6 4.2.93 *he can make obligations, and write court-hand*, WIV 1.1.10.
obliged *ppl. adj.* Pledged MV 2.6.7 *To keep obliged faith unforfeited.*
oblique *adj.* Indirect TRO 5.1.55 *oblique memorial of cuckolds.*
obliquy *n.* Obliquity, moral divergence TIM 4.3.18 *All's obliquy.*
oblivious *adj.* Causing forgetfulness MAC 5.3.43 *some sweet oblivious antidote.*
obloquy *n.* Reproach, disgrace AWW 4.2.44 *Which were the greatest obloquy i' th' world In me to lose*, 1H6 2.5.49, LUC 523.
obscene *adj.* Disgusting, repulsive R2 4.1.131 *so...obscene a deed*, LLL 1.1.241, 1H4 2.4.228.
obscenely *adv.* (Misused by Costard at) LLL 4.1.143 *When it comes so smoothly off, so obscenely*; (and by Bottom at) MND 1.2.108 *there we may rehearse most obscenely.*
obscure *adj.*
1 Dark, dim MV 2.7.51 *the obscure grave*, VEN 237; loving the darkness MAC 2.3.59 *The obscure bird.*
2 Retired, remote TIT 2.3.77 *wand'red...to an obscure plot.*
3 Lowly, mean, undistinguished 1H6 4.1.50 *Obscure...swain*, HAM 4.5.214, R2 3.3.154.
4 Not clear or plain LLL 3.1.82 *Some obscure precedence*, TN 2.1.257.
obscured *ppl. adj.* Disguised LR 2.2.168 *my obscured course.*
obscurely *adv.* In the dark LUC 1250 *evils that obscurely sleep*; not openly JC 1.2.319 *wherein obscurely Caesar's ambition shall be glanced at.*
obscurity *n.* Dark place, place removed from view TIT 5.2.36 *There's...No vast obscurity...Where...murder...Can couch for fear.*
obsequious *adj.*
1 Dutiful, obedient, devoted WIV 4.2.2 *I see you are obsequious in your love*, MM 2.4.28.
2 Dutiful in manifesting regard for the dead HAM 1.2.92 *To do obsequious sorrow*, TIT 5.3.152, SON 31.5.

obsequiously *adv.* Mournfully, as a dutiful mourner R3 1.2.3 *Whilst I awhile obsequiously lament.*

obsequy *n.*
1 Funeral rite or ceremony PhT 12 *Keep the obsequy so strict;* (pl.) TIT 1.1.160 *my tributary tears I render for my brethren's obsequies,* HAM 5.1.226.
2 (pl.) Commemorative rites or services, dutiful acts performed in memory of one departed 2H6 3.2.146 *all in vain are these mean obsequies,* 3H6 1.4.147, ROM 5.3.16.

observance *n.*
1 Respectful attention, dutiful service, reverence WIV 2.2.196 *followed her with a doting observance,* AYL 5.2.96, TRO 1.3.31.
2 Observant care HAM 3.2.18 *with this special observance, that you o'erstep not the modesty of nature,* LUC 1385.
3 Observation, action of paying attention OTH 3.3.151 *his scattering and unsure observance,* AYL 3.2.234, AWW 3.2.5; perception ANT 3.3.22 *Is this certain?—Or I have no observance.*

observancy *n.* OBSERVANCE sense 1 OTH 3.4.149 *such observancy As fits the bridal* [F1; FF 2–4 *observance,* Qq *obseruances*].

observant *n.* Obsequious attendant LR 2.2.103 *twenty…observants That stretch their duties nicely.*

observation *n.*
1 Observance (of rites) MND 4.1.104 *our observation is perform'd.*
2 Observing of the wishes of others, paying court, obsequiousness JN 1.1.208 *he…That doth not smack of observation.*
3 Observant care TMP 3.3.87 *with good life, And observation strange* (i.e. exceptional care).
4 Something learned by observing, knowledge, experience AYL 2.7.41 *in his brain…he hath strange places cramm'd With observation,* ADO 4.1.165, LR 1.1.289.

observe *vb.* Show respectful attention to, pay court to, humour, gratify 2H4 4.4.30 *he is gracious if he be observ'd,* TIM 4.3.212.

observed *n.* One who receives respect and attention HAM 3.1.154 *Th' observ'd of all observers.*

observing *ppl. adj.* Obsequious, deferential TRO 2.3.128 *in an observing kind.*

obsque hoc nihil est [L.] Apart from this there is nothing 2H4 5.5.28.

obstacle *adj.* Obstinate 1H6 5.4.17 *that thou wilt be so obstacle.*

obstruct See ABSTRACT *n.* sense 4.

obstruction *n.*
1 Shutting out of light TN 4.2.39 *complainest thou of obstruction?*
2 Stagnation (of the blood) TN 3.4.21 *This does make some obstruction in the blood, this crossgartering;* cold obstruction cessation of the vital functions MM 3.1.118 *to die…To lie in cold obstruction, and to rot.*

occasion *n.*
1 Opportunity for attacking or fault-finding TRO 4.1.17 *when contention and occasion meet.*
2 Cause, reason, circumstance LR 2.1.120 *Occasions …of some prize;* (hence) cause of being occupied or detained, business ADO 1.1.150 *he heartily prays some occasion may detain us,* TIM 3.6.10; *on…occasion* for (a)…reason LUC 1270 *on what occasion break Those tears from thee?,* TN 2.1.41, OTH 4.1.58.
3 That which is occasioned or caused AYL 4.1.175 *that woman that cannot make her fault her husband's occasion* (i.e. 'represent her fault as occasioned by her husband', Johnson; perh. with quibble on sense 1).
4 Particular personal need or requirement, convenience ANT 2.6.131 *he married but his occasion here* (i.e. to further his interests), MV 1.1.139, CYM 5.5.87.
5 Course of events 2H4 4.1.72 *the rough torrent of occasion,* JN 4.2.125.
6 That which gives rise to discussion or consideration, subject debated, matter JN 4.2.62 *That…enemies may not have this To grace occasions,* MV 3.5.55.

occulted *ppl. adj.* Hidden, concealed HAM 3.2.80 *his occulted guilt.*

occupation *n.* Handicraft, trade, business COR 4.6.97 *the voice of occupation* (i.e. the vote of working men), ANT 4.4.17, MM 4.2.34.

occupy *vb.* Have to do with sexually ROM 2.4.100 *to occupy the argument no longer* (with quibble).
   ◇ In consequence of its use in this sense, this verb was not freq. used in literature in S.'s time; cf. 2H4 2.4.149 *as odious as the word 'occupy'.*

occurrent *n.* Event, incident HAM 5.2.357 *th' occurrents more and less.*

Od *n.* (used in oaths; minced form of) God WIV 3.4.57 *Od's heartlings,* TN 5.1.184, CYM 4.2.293.
   ◇ *Od's* in WIV 1.4.62 *Od's me,* AYL 3.5.43 *Od's my little life* and AYL 4.3.17 *Od's my will* either originates from the minced form through some confusion, or perh. ''s' is short for 'save'.

odd *adj.*
1 At variance *with* TRO 4.5.265 *to be odd with him.*
2 Unconnected, irregular, casual ADO 2.3.236 *some odd quirks and remnants of wit,* MV 2.2.62, R3 1.3.336.
3 Out of the way TMP 1.2.223 *In an odd angle of the isle.*
4 Extra, received over and above HAM 5.2.178 *nothing but my shame and the odd hits.*
5 Extraordinary, unexampled LUC 1433 *such odd action.*

odd-conceited *adj.* Strangely devised TGV 2.7.46 *twenty odd-conceited true-love knots.*

odd-even *n.* (?) Midnight or thereabouts OTH 1.1.123 *At this odd-even and dull watch o' th' night.*

oddly *adv.* Unevenly TRO 1.3.339 *Our imputation shall be oddly pois'd In this wild action.*

odds *n.*
1 Variance, strife OTH 2.3.185 *this peevish odds,* H5 2.4.129, TIM 4.3.43.
2 Balance of advantage, superiority (one way or another) TIT 5.2.19 *Thou hast the odds of me,* H5 4.3.5, AYL 1.2.159; *at (the) odds* with the balance of advantage in one's favour HAM 5.2.212 *I shall win at the odds,* ANT 2.3.39; *take (the) odds* take advantage 2H6 4.10.44 *Took odds to combat a poor famish'd man,* 1H4 5.1.97.
3 Chances, balance of probability WT 5.1.207 *The odds for high and low's alike,* SHR 4.3.154, CYM 5.2.9.
4 *make odds all even* Level inequalities MM 3.1.41 *death…That makes these odds all even.*

oeillade *n.* Amorous glance, ogle WIV 1.3.61 *examin'd my parts with most judicious oeillades* (F1 *illiads*), LR 4.5.25 (F1 *eliads*).

o'erbear *vb.* Overwhelm PER 5.1.193 *O'erbear the shores of my mortality.*

o'erbeat *vb.* Overwhelm COR 4.5.131 *Like a bold flood o'erbeat.*

o'erblow *vb.* Blow away H5 3.3.31 *the…wind of grace O'erblows the…clouds Of…villainy.*

o'ercloyed *ppl. adj.* Filled to satiety R3 5.3.318 *peasants Whom their o'ercloyed country vomits forth.*

o'ercome *ppl. adj.* Overrun, covered TIT 3.3.95 *O'ercome with moss* (F1 *Ore-come,* Q1 *Overcome*).

o'ercount *vb.* Outnumber ANT 2.6.26 *thou know'st How much we do o'ercount thee.*

o'er-crow *vb.* Overpower HAM 5.2.353 *The potent poison quite o'er-crows my spirit.*

o'er-dyed *ppl. adj.* Dyed with a second colour WT 1.2.132 *false As o'er-dy'd blacks* (i.e. black things).

o'er-eaten *ppl. adj.* Eaten away on all sides; (fig.) TRO 5.2.160 *greasy relics Of her o'er-eaten faith.*

o'er-eye *vb.* Observe LLL 4.3.78 *wretched fools' secrets heedfully o'er-eye.*

o'erflourish *vb.* Cover with blossom or verdure TN 3.4.370 *empty trunks o'erflourish'd by the devil* (i.e. given a deceptive appearance).

o'erflow *vb.* Pour out WIV 2.2.151 *Such Brooks are welcome to me, that o'erflow such liquor.*

o'ergall *vb. Make very sore, injure greatly* TRO 5.3.55 *Their eyes o'ergalled with recourse of tears.*

o'er-green *vb.* (fig.) Cover (a defect) with something pleasing, embellish SON 112.4 *So you o'er-green my bad.*
  ◇ Perh. ref. to Robert Greene, against whose criticisms the Earl of Southampton had defended S.

o'ergrown *ppl. adj.*
  1 (?) (1) Covered with hair; or (2) (fig.) hidden by the growth of other concerns; or (3) grown out of thought or memory CYM 4.4.33 *yourself So out of thought, and thereto so o'ergrown.*
  2 Very big MM 1.3.22 *an o'ergrown lion.*

o'erleap *vb.*
  1 Leap over or across MAC 1.4.49 *a step...I must ...o'erleap;* (fig.) pass over, omit COR 2.2.136 *Let me o'erleap that custom.*
  2 (refl.) Leap too far, overreach (itself) MAC 1.7.27 *Vaulting ambition, which o'erleaps itself.*

o'er-leaven *vb.* (lit.) Put too much leaven in bread; (hence, fig.) imbue to excess with some modifying element HAM 1.4.29 *some habit, that too much o'er-leavens The form of...manners.*

o'erlook *vb.*
  1 Examine, inspect, survey R3 3.5.17 *O'erlook the walls,* PER 1.2.48; peruse, read TGV 1.2.50 *I would I had o'erlook'd the letter,* MND 2.2.121, SON 82.2.
  2 Despise, slight JN 5.4.55 *We will...Stoop low within those bounds we have o'erlook'd.*
  3 Look upon with the evil eye, bewitch MV 3.2.15 *Beshrew your eyes, They have o'erlook'd me,* WIV 5.5.83.

o'erlooking *n.* Perusal, reading LR 1.2.39 *not fit for your o'erlooking.*

o'ermaster *vb.* Have in cne's power JN 2.1.109 *the crown that thou o'ermasterest.*

o'ermatched *ppl. adj.* Outmatched, oppressed by superior force 1H6 4.4.11 *our o'ermatch'd forces,* 3H6 1.4.64.

o'er-office *vb.* Lord it over (someone) by irtue of one's office HAM 5.1.79 *the pate of a politician, which this ass now o'er-offices* (F1; Q2 *ore-reaches*).

o'erparted *adj.* Having too difficult a part to play LLL 5.2.584 *for Alisander...a little o'erparted.*

o'erpeer *vb.* OVERPEER sense 1 COR 2.3.121 *mountainous error be too highly heap'd For truth to o'erpeer.*

o'erperch *vb.* Fly over ROM 2.2.66 *With love's light wings did I o'erperch these walls.*

o'er-picture *vb.* Surpass the picture of ANT 2.2.200 *she did lie...O'er-picturing that Venus.*

o'erpost *vb.* Get over quickly and easily 2H4 1.2.150 *You may thank th' unquiet time for your quiet o'erposting that action.*

o'erpressed *ppl. adj.* Overwhelmed COR 2.2.93 *bestrid An o'erpress'd Roman, and...Slew three opposers;* (fig.) weighed down (with pain or grief) PER 3.2.84 *kindle again The o'erpress'd spirits.*

o'er-prize *vb.* Exceed, surpass TMP 1.2.92 *that which...O'er-priz'd all popular rate.*

o'erreach *vb.*
  1 Overtake HAM 3.1.17 *certain players We o'erraught on the way.*
  2 Get the better of, gain an advantage over, cheat ERR 1.2.96 *by some device...The villain is o'erraught of all my money,* TIT 5.2.143, HAM 5.1.79.

o'erreaching *n.* Outwitting, cheating WIV 5.5.136 *to prevent so gross o'erreaching.*

o'errun *vb.*
  1 Flow over, overflow SHR Ind.2.65 *the tears...Like envious floods o'errun her lovely face,* MM 5.1.319, TIT 2.3.212.
  2 Pass in review 3H6 1.4.45 *in thy thought o'errun my former time.*
  3 Run over TRO 3.3.163 *O'errun and trampled on;* (fig.) overwhelm AYL 5.1.56 *I will o'errun thee with policy.*

o'erset *ppl. adj.* Overwhelmed, pressed hard 2H4 1.1.185 *since we are o'erset, venture again.*

o'ershoot *vb.* (refl.) Go too far JC 3.2.150 *I have o'ershot myself to tell you of it.*

o'ershot *ppl. adj.* OVERSHOT LLL 4.3.158 *are you not asham'd...to be thus much o'ershot?*

o'ersize *vb.* Cover as with something like size HAM 2.2.462 *o'er-sized with coagulate gore.*

o'erskip *vb.* Ignore, pass lightly over without heeding LR 3.6.106 *the mind much sufferance doth o'erskip.*

o'erslip *vb.* OVERSLIP TGV 2.2.9 *when that hour o'erslips me in the day.*

o'erstare *vb.* Outstare MV 2.1.27 *I would o'erstare the sternest eyes* (Q1 *outstare*).

o'erstink *vb.* Stink more than TMP 4.1.184 *the foul lake O'erstunk their feet.*

o'erstrawed *pa. pple.* Strewn over VEN 1143 *o'erstraw'd With sweets.*

o'ersway *vb.*
  1 Domineer over LLL 5.2.67 *So...would I... o'ersway his state.*
  2 Prevail over by superior authority or power SON 65.2 *mortality o'ersways their power,* HAM 5.1.228.
  3 Influence, prevail upon JC 2.1.203 *If he be so resolv'd, I can o'ersway him.*

o'er-teemed *ppl. adj.* Exhausted by excessive production HAM 2.2.508 *her...o'er-teemed loins.*

o'ertake *vb.* Overcome by drink HAM 2.1.56 *There was 'a gaming, there o'ertook in 's rouse.*

o'ertop *vb.* (fig.) Surpass, be superior to H8 2.4.88 *wisdom O'ertopping woman's pow'r,* TRO 3.3.164.

o'ertrip *vb.* Trip over, move lightly over MV 5.1.7 *o'ertrip the dew.*

o'ervalue *vb.* Surpass in value CYM 1.4.109 *pawn the moi'ty of my estate to your ring, which...o'ervalues it something.*

o'erwatched *ppl. adj.* Exhausted with much watching LR 2.2.170 *All weary and o'erwatch'd,* JC 4.3.241.
  ◇ See OVERWATCH.

o'erween *vb.* OVERWEEN WT 4.2.8 *I o'erween to think so.*

o'erwhelm *vb.* (of the brows) Overhang so as to cover H5 3.1.11 *let the brow o'erwhelm it,* VEN 183.

o'erworn *ppl. adj.*
  1 The worse for wear, faded R3 1.1.81 *The jealous o'erworn widow.*
  2 Worn out, exhausted SON 63.2 *crush'd and o'erworn,* VEN 135.
  3 Spent, passed away, advanced VEN 866 *the morning is so much o'erworn.*

o'er-wrested *ppl. adj.* Strained TRO 1.3.157 *o'erwrested seeming* (F1, Q1 *ore-rested*).

of *prep.*
  1 From, away from AWW 3.4.1 *take the letter of her,* ERR 2.2.136, COR 5.6.14.
  2 From (a certain point of time), from (a certain

stage of existence) TGV 4.4.3 *one that I brought up of a puppy*, HAM 2.2.11.

3 From (a person or thing as the origin or source) 1H4 5.4.23 *lustier maintenance than I did look for Of such an ungrown warrior*; by reason of, through 2H6 2.1.86 *cam'st thou here by chance, Or of devotion...?*, TMP 5.1.230, CYM 4.3.3.

4 (introducing the agent after a pass. vb.) By ADO 1.3.29 *to be disdain'd of all*, R3 4.4.418, HAM 1.1.25.

5 (introducing the means or instrument) With MV 5.1.297 *you are not satisfied Of these events*, HAM 5.1.211, MAC 1.2.13.

6 In, in the person of AWW 5.3.1 *We lost a jewel of her*, AWW 1.1.6.

7 In respect of (freq. in dependence on an adj.) 2H4 2.2.68 *a proper fellow of my hands*, MV 2.2.181, OTH 1.3.63.

8 During (a space of time) SHR Ind.2.82 *did I never speak of all that time?*, H8 2.1.147, LLL 1.1.43.

9 On MV 2.2.97 *he had more hair of his tail than I have of my face*, LR 1.5.22, H5 2.3.27.

10 (forming with abstract nouns equivalents of adjs. or ppl. adjs.) *of bounty* Bountiful TIM 1.1.6 *Magic of bounty*; *of danger* dangerous LR 1.2.88; *of earnest* serious AYL 4.3.171; *of expectation* expected MAC 3.3.10; *of health* saved HAM 1.4.40; *of life* living SON 16.9; *of scorn* scornful OTH 4.2.54.

off *adv.*

1 Beside the mark, beside the point COR 2.2.60 *that's off.*

2 *be off* Take off one's hat COR 2.3.100 *I will...be off to them.*

3 *off of* From 2H6 2.1.94 *A fall off of a tree.*

4 *off and on* To and fro TMP 3.2.14 *I swam...off and on.*

5 *go off* Die MAC 5.9.2 *Some must go off.*

~ *prep. off the matter* Irrelevantly ADO 3.5.9 *Goodman Verges, sir, speaks a little off the matter* (F1 *of*).

off-cap *vb.* Doff the cap OTH 1.1.10 *Off-capp'd to him.*

offence *n.*

1 Hurt, harm, injury JN 2.1.75 *To do offence and scathe*, MND 2.2.23, AYL 3.5.117; *sick offence* 'cause of harmful malady' (Aldis Wright) JC 2.1.268 *You have some sick offence within your mind.*

2 Disfavour, disgrace TN 4.2.69 *I am...in offence with my niece.*

3 Offensive object AWW 2.3.254 *thou art a general offence.*

4 Resentment, displeasure JN 3.4.180 *their souls are topful of offence*, 1H6 1.2.49, MV 4.1.68.

5 *slow offence* See SLOW.

offenceful *adj.* Sinful MM 2.3.26 *your most offenceful act.*

offenceless *adj.* Harmless OTH 2.3.275 *beat his offenceless dog.*

offend *vb.*

1 (intr.) Do amiss, transgress MM 2.1.29 *When I, that censure him, do so offend*; (trans.) sin against JN 3.4.173 *Ransacking the Church, Offending charity*, ANT 3.11.49; wrong (a person) OTH 5.2.59 *I never did Offend you*, AYL 1.3.52, LR 1.2.160; violate (a law) MM 3.2.15 *he hath offended the law.*

2 Harm, hurt, injure MV 4.1.140 *Thou but offend'st thy lungs to speak so loud*, JN 4.1.131, AWW 5.3.55; afflict OTH 3.4.51 *a...rheum offends me*; (absol.) TIT 3.1.46 *A stone is silent, and offendeth not.*

3 Be an obstacle or hindrance to ERR 1.1.89 *Dispers'd those vapours that offended us*, TIM 5.4.60.

offender *n.* One who wrongs another SON 34.11 *Th' offender's sorrow lends but weak relief To him that bears the strong offence's cross.*

offending *n.* Transgression OTH 1.3.80 *The very head...of my offending.*

offer *vb.*

1 Act on the offensive, make an attack 2H4 4.1.217 *his power...May offer, but not hold.*

2 Venture, dare, presume (to do a thing) SHR 5.1.63 *what are you that offer to beat my servant?*, PER 4.2.107, WT 4.4.777.

offering *n.* Act of worship, ritual MAC 2.1.52 *witchcraft celebrates Pale Hecat's off 'rings*; sacrifice, oblation JC 2.2.39 *the entrails of an offering*, TRO 5.3.17.

~ *ppl. adj.* Attacking 1H4 4.1.69 *we of the off 'ring side.*

office *n.*

1 Proper function or action OTH 3.4.113 *with all the office of my heart* (i.e. devotion).

2 People holding official position HAM 3.1.72 *The insolence of office*, H8 1.1.44.

3 (pl.) Parts of house-buildings devoted to purely household matters, esp. kitchen, etc. TIM 2.2.158 *our offices have been oppress'd With riotous feeders*, MAC 2.1.14, OTH 2.2.8; (fig.) COR 1.1.137 *the cranks and offices of man.*

~ *vb.*

1 Perform as a service, act as a servant AWW 3.2.126 *angels offic'd all.*

2 Drive by virtue of one's office COR 5.2.62 *a Jack guardant cannot office me from my son* (i.e. an officious fellow cannot keep me from my son).

officed *ppl. adj.* Appointed to an office, having a particular function WT 1.2.172 *So stands this squire Offic'd with me*, OTH 1.3.270.

officer *n.*

1 One who performs a service, agent ANT 3.1.17 *Caesar and Antony have ever won More in their officer than person*, SHR 5.2.37, JC 4.2.7.

2 Person engaged in the management of the domestic affairs of a (great) household, servant CYM 3.1.64 *hath moe kings his servants than Thyself domestic officers*, SHR 4.1.48, TN 2.5.47.

3 *officer-at-arms* Herald, poursuivant R2 1.1.204 *command our officers-at-arms.*

officious *adj.* Zealous in one's duty WT 2.3.159 *so tenderly officious...To save this bastard's life*, TIT 5.2.201.

oft *adj.* Frequent SON 14.8 *By oft predict.*

often *adj.* Frequent AYL 4.1.19 *by often rumination.*

'old *n.* Wold, upland plain LR 3.4.120 *Swithold footed thrice the 'old.*

old *n.* Old age TRO 2.2.104 *mid-age and wrinkled old.*
◇ F1; Q *elders*; Theobald *eld.*

~ *adj.*

1 Belonging to or characteristic of advanced age TMP 1.2.369 *old cramps*, LR 1.1.187, SON 2.11.

2 That has been so (a certain number of months, years, etc.) MM 4.2.131 *a prisoner nine years old*, ERR 1.1.44, HAM 4.6.16; *of many years'* standing ROM 3.3.94 *an old murderer.*

3 In old clothes, shabby SHR 4.1.137 *The rest were ragged, old, and beggarly.*

4 Great, plentiful, abundant WIV 1.4.5 *an old abusing of God's patience*, MV 4.2.15, MAC 2.3.2.

5 *old-fac'd* See FEAZED.

~ *adv.* Long ago PER 1.Gower.1 *a song that old was sung.*

omen *n.* Event foretold by an omen HAM 1.1.123 *prologue to the omen coming on.*

omit *vb.*

1 Take no notice of, disregard MM 4.3.73 *omit This reprobate*, 2H4 4.4.27, 2H6 3.2.382.

2 Cease to retain, let go OTH 2.1.71 *omit Their moral natures.*

omittance *n.* Omission AYL 3.5.133 *omittance is no quittance.*

omnipotent *adj.* (jocular) 'Mighty', unparalleled, arrant 1H4 1.2.109 *omnipotent villain.*

on *prep.*
1 Against or over LR 5.3.166 *what art thou That hast this fortune on me?*
2 Of TMP 4.1.157 *such stuff As dreams are made on,* MAC 2.3.38, CYM 4.2.198; *on's* of his H8 3.2.106 *The master cord on's heart,* LR 1.5.20, COR 1.3.66; *on't* of it TMP 1.2.457 *the lord on't,* WIV 5.5.181, TN 3.4.289.
4 At or just about (a certain time) TMP 5.1.4 *How's the day?—On the sixt hour.*

once *adv.*
1 At any time, ever, at all 1H6 5.3.58 *if this servile usage once offend,* ADO 5.1.208, CYM 5.3.78; *when...once whenever, every time* SON 57.8 *When you have bid your servant once adieu.*
2 For once 1H4 1.2.142 *once in my days I'll be a madcap,* TMP 3.2.21, MND 3.2.68.
3 Once for all COR 2.3.1 *Once if he do require our voices;* (hence) *once this, 'tis once* to be brief, in short ADO 1.1.318 *'tis once, thou lovest,* ERR 3.1.89.
4 *at once* (elliptic) Let us proceed without more ado 2H6 3.1.66 *My lords, at once,* R3 3.4.1.

one-trunk-inheriting *adj.* Possessing only one trunkful of effects LR 2.2.19 *one-trunk-inheriting slave.*

oneyer *n.* (?) (1) Sheriff accountable to the king for money due (Malone: derived from 'o.ni', a fiscal term); or (2) one 1H4 2.1.76 *I am join'd...with nobility and tranquillity, burgomasters and great oneyers.*

onion-eyed *adj.* Ready to weep, tearful ANT 4.2.35 *they weep; and I...am onion-ey'd.*

onset *n.* Beginning, start TGV 3.2.93 *give the onset to thy good advice,* SON 90.11, TIT 1.1.238.

open *vb.*
1 Unlock, provide free access to; (fig.) H8 3.2.184 *my hand has open'd bounty to you.*
2 Disclose, reveal (a matter) TGV 1.1.127 *open the matter,* H5 1.1.78, HAM 2.2.18.
3 Expound, explain H5 1.2.16 *charge your...soul With opening titles miscreate.*
4 (of hounds) Give tongue WIV 4.2.197 *If I cry out thus upon no trail, never trust me when I open again.*
~ *adj.*
1 Public MM 2.1.131 *an open room,* H8 2.1.168, ROM 5.3.193; *in open* in public H8 3.2.404 *Lady Anne...This day was view'd in open as his queen.*
2 Patent, evident H5 2.2.142 *Their faults are open,* R3 3.5.30, MM 1.2.21.
3 Generous, liberal TIM 5.1.58 *open bounty,* 2H4 4.4.32.
~ *adv.* Publicly TN 3.3.37 *Do not then walk too open.*

open-arse See OPEN ET CETERA.

opener *n.* One who reveals, interpreter 2H4 4.2.20 *The very opener and intelligencer Between the...sanctities of heaven, And our dull workings.*

open et cetera *n.* (substitute for) open-arse, the old name of the medlar (fruit and tree) ROM 2.1.38 *O that she were An open et cetera.*
◇ Q1; F1, Qq 2-3 *open, or;* Duthie *open-arse.*

open-eyed *adj.* Vigilant TMP 2.1.301 *Open-ey'd conspiracy.*

operant *adj.* Active HAM 3.2.174 *My operant powers;* potent TIM 4.3.25 *thy most operant poison.*

operation *n.* Efficacy ANT 4.15.26 *if knife, drugs, serpents have Edge, sting, or operation.*

operative *adj.* Effective, efficacious LR 4.4.14 *many simples operative.*

opinion *n.*
1 Censure OTH 4.2.109 *The small'st opinion on my least misuse.*

2 Public judgement 1H4 3.2.42 *Opinion, that did help me to the crown,* 2H4 5.2.128, OTH 1.3.224.
3 (one's) Reputation, credit 1H4 5.4.48 *Thou hast redeem'd thy lost opinion,* MV 1.1.91, OTH 2.3.195.
4 Favourable estimate of oneself; (in a bad sense) self-conceit, arrogance LLL 5.1.5 *learned without opinion,* TRO 3.3.264, 1H4 3.1.183; (in a good sense) self-confidence TRO 1.3.353 *To steel a strong opinion to themselves,* ANT 2.1.36.

opportunity *n.* (misused for) Importunity WIV 3.4.20 *If opportunity and humblest suit Cannot attain it.*

oppose *vb.*
1 Expose H8 4.1.67 *opposing freely The beauty of her person to the people,* LR 4.7.31 (Qq *exposd*).
2 Offer resistance (*to*), contend (*against*) (refl.) TGV 3.2.26 *How she opposes her against my will,* R2 3.3.18; (intr.) WT 5.1.46 *Oppose against their wills,* LR 4.2.74, HAM 3.1.59.
3 Set over against; (hence) compare TIT 1.1.132 *Oppose not Scythia to ambitious Rome.*

opposed *n.* Adversary HAM 1.3.67 *th' opposed may beware of thee.*
~ *ppl. adj.*
1 Opposite, contrary MV 2.9.62 *To offend and judge are distinct offices, And of opposed natures,* 1H4 3.1.109.
2 In antagonism, hostile 1H4 1.1.9 *those opposed eyes.*

opposeless *adj.* Irresistible LR 4.6.38 *your great opposeless wills.*

opposing *adj.* Opposite PER 3.Gower.17 *the four opposing coigns.*

opposite *n.* Antagonist, adversary, opponent LR 5.3.42 *the opposites of this day's strife,* R3 5.4.3, TN 3.4.267.
~ *adj.* Hostile, antagonistic, adverse TIM 1.1.273 *He's opposite to humanity,* R3 4.4.216, OTH 1.2.67; (with *with*) TN 2.5.149 *Be opposite with a kinsman,* R3 2.2.94.

opposition *n.*
1 Offering for combat HAM 5.2.171 *the opposition of your person in trial.*
2 What is opposed 1H4 2.3.14 *too light for the counterpoise of so great an opposition.*
3 Antagonism, hostility LLL 5.2.733 *The liberal opposition of our spirits,* CYM 2.5.17, ROM 4.2.18.
4 Encounter, combat 1H4 1.3.99 *In single opposition hand to hand,* OTH 2.3.184, CYM 4.1.13.

oppress *vb.*
1 Suppress PER 3.Gower.29 *The mutiny...t' oppress.*
2 Trouble, harass, distress AWW 1.3.147 *You ne'er oppress'd me,* LR 5.3.5, CYM 5.4.99.
3 Burden, strain, reduce to straits TIM 2.2.158 *When all our offices have been oppress'd With riotous feeders.*

oppressed *ppl. adj.* Distressed, troubled HAM 1.2.203 *their oppress'd and fear-surprised eyes.*

oppression *n.*
1 Pressure, burden R2 3.4.31 *oppression of their...weight,* NUM 1.4.24.
2 Distress, trouble ROM 1.1.184 *thy good heart's oppression,* R2 1.4.14, H8 2.4.209.

oppugnancy *n.* Conflict TRO 1.3.111 *Each thing meets In mere oppugnancy.*

or *conj.*[1] Before HAM 5.2.30 *Or I could make a prologue* (Ff *Ere*), CYM 2.4.14; (esp.) *or e'er, or ere, or ever* HAM 1.2.183 *Would I had met my dearest foe in heaven Or ever I had seen that day,* TMP 1.2.11, JN 4.3.20.

or *conj.*[2]
1 *or...or* Either...or SON 81.1 *Or I shall live your epitaph to make, Or you survive when I...am rotten,*

TMP 4.1.30, COR 1.3.37; (introducing alternate questions) MV 3.2.64 *Tell me where is fancy bred, Or in the heart or in the head,* CYM 4.2.356, SON 114.1.

2 (loose use where no alternative is in question, approx. equivalent to) And VEN 10 *More white and red than doves or roses are,* TIM 2.2.155 *my husbandry or falsehood* (perh. hendiadys; i.e. dishonest husbandry).

orange-tawny *adj.* A dull yellowish-brown MND 1.2.94 *your orange-tawny beard,* MND 3.1.126.

orange-wife *n.* Woman who sells oranges COR 2.1.70 *a cause between an orange-wife and a faucet-seller.*

orator *n.* Advocate LUC 30 *Beauty...doth...persuade The eyes of men without an orator.*

orb *n.*
1 Circle MND 2.1.9 *her orbs upon the green* (i.e. fairy rings).
2 (in old astronomy) Each of the concentric spheres which carry the planets and stars with them in their revolutions ANT 3.13.146 *my good stars...Have empty left their orbs,* ROM 2.2.110, ADO 4.1.57.
3 Sphere, globe, anything of spherical or globular shape LC 289 *orb of one particular tear.*
4 Heavenly body CYM 1.6.35 *The fiery orbs above,* MV 5.1.60, LR 1.1.111.
5 The earth, the world ANT 5.2.85 *To shake the orb,* TN 3.1.38, HAM 2.2.485.
6 Sphere of action 1H4 5.1.17 *move in that obedient orb again,* PER 1.2.122.

orbed *ppl. adj.* Spherical LC 25 *th' orbed earth,* HAM 3.2.156, TN 5.1.271.

orchard *n.* Garden for herbs and fruit-trees LC 171 *his plants in others' orchards grew,* ADO 3.1.5, SHR 2.1.111.

ordain *vb.*
1 Establish, found, institute SHR 3.1.10 *why music was ordain'd,* 1H6 4.1.33, CYM 3.1.55.
2 Design ROM 4.5.84 *All things that we ordained festival,* TIT 5.3.22.

order *n.*
1 Suitable measures for the accomplishment of a purpose MM 2.2.25 *There shall be order for't; take order* take measures or steps, make necessary arrangements R2 5.1.53 *there is order ta'en for you,* AWW 4.2.55, OTH 5.2.72.
2 Plan (of action), arrangement H5 3.2.65 *the order of the siege,* MAC 5.6.6, JN 5.2.4.
3 The way in which something takes place 2H6 3.2.129 *hear the order of his death,* 2H4 4.4.100, JC 1.2.25; course JC 3.1.230 *Speak in the order of his funeral.*

orderly *adv.* Properly, duly, according to rule MV 2.2.170 *These things being bought and orderly bestowed,* HAM 3.2.210, SHR 4.3.94.

ordinance *n.*
1 Dispensation of providence, decree of destiny CYM 4.2.145 *let ord'nance Come as the gods foresay it,* LR 4.1.68, R3 4.4.184.
2 Practice, usage, established rule JC 1.3.66 *all these things change from their ordinance,* H5 2.4.83.
3 Rank, order COR 3.2.12 *one but of my ordinance.*
4 Ordnance, cannon JN 2.1.218 *the compulsion of their ordinance,* H5 2.4.126.

ordinant *adj.* Directing, controlling, provident HAM 5.2.48 *even in that was heaven ordinant.*
▷ Qq; F1 *ordinate.* See ORDINATE.

ordinary *n.*
1 Public meal regularly provided at a fixed price in an eating-house or tavern AWW 2.3.201 *I did think thee, for two ordinaries, to be a pretty wise fellow;* (used vaguely) meal ANT 2.2.225 *for his ordinary pays his heart.*

2 'Ordinary condition, run', what is customary or usual AYL 3.5.42 *I see no more in you than in the ordinary Of nature's sale-work.*

ordinate *ppl. adj.* Orderly, observant of due order or providential control HAM 5.2.48 *even in that was heaven ordinate.*
▷ F1. Perh. a ref. to the phr. 'ordinate power' (of God), i.e. the divine power as exhibited in the order of mundane things. Qq *ordinant* q.v.

organ *n.*
1 Musical instrument HAM 3.2.368 *there is much music...in this little organ* (i.e. a recorder).
2 'Vocal organs', voice TN 1.4.33 *as the maiden's organ, shrill and sound,* AWW 2.1.176.
3 Means of action or operation, instrument, agent MM 1.1.20 *given his deputation all the organs Of our own pow'r,* HAM 4.7.70.
4 Mental faculty (regarded as the instrument of the mind) WIV 5.5.51 *the organs of her fantasy.*

organ-pipe *n.* (fig.) ORGAN sense 2 JN 5.7.23 *from the organ-pipe of frailty sings,* TMP 3.3.98.

orgillous, orgulous *adj.* Proud TRO Prol.2 *The princes orgillous* (F1).

orient *adj.* Orig. applied to pearls of superior value as coming from the East; (hence) excellent, lustrous MND 4.1.54 *like round and orient pearls,* R3 4.4.322, ANT 1.5.41; (applied to a tear) VEN 981 *an orient drop.*

orifex *n.* (var. of) Orifice, aperture TRO 5.2.151 *no orifex for a point...to enter.*

original *n.* Origin MND 2.1.117 *We are their parents and original,* 2H4 1.2.115.

orison *n.* Prayer HAM 3.1.88 *in thy orisons Be all my sins rememb'red,* ROM 4.3.3, CYM 1.3.32.

ornaments *n.* (pl.) Equipment, attire 1H6 5.1.54 *For clothing me in these grave ornaments,* SHR 4.3.61, ROM 1.1.93.

orphan *adj.* Without parents WIV 5.5.39 *You orphan heirs of fixed destiny* (i.e. the fairies).
▷ Fairies were supposed to be of spontaneous birth and hence would be without parents like orphans. there was also a popular superstition connecting fairies with the souls of dead children. Theobald proposed *ouphen* (i.e. elfin). See OUPH.

ort *n.* Fragment of food LUC 985 *a beggar's orts;* (fig.) TRO 5.2.158 *The fractions of her faith, orts of her love,* TIM 4.3.399.

orthography, ortography *n.* (app. error for) Orthographer ADO 2.3.20 *now is he turn'd orthography* (i.e. pedantic in his use of words).

osprey *n.* Fish-hawk, to which, it was said, fish surrendered themselves without attempting an escape COR 4.7.34 *As is the osprey to the fish, who takes it By sovereignty of nature* (Ff *aspray*).

ostent *n.* Manifestation, show, display MV 2.2.196 *well studied in a sad ostent,* H5 5.Ch.21, PER 1.2.25.

ostentare [L.] To show LLL 4.2.15 *ostentare, to show, as it were, his inclination.*

ostentation *n.*
1 Show, exhibition, display R2 2.3.95 *ostentation of despised arms,* ANT 3.6.52, ADO 4.1.205.
2 Spectacular show LLL 5.1.112 *some delightful ostentation.*

other *n., pron., and adj.*
1 Each preceding (one) MM 4.4.2 *Every letter he hath writ hath disvouch'd other,* R2 1.1.27, JC 1.2.230.
2 Used to characterize a thing as being of a different kind from something before mentioned or contemplated OTH 4.2.84 *to preserve this vessel for my lord From any other foul unlawful touch,* R2 1.1.33, MAC 4.3.90.
3 *no other cause* No cause to be otherwise ERR 2.1.33 *They can be meek that have no other cause.*

~ *adv.* Otherwise COR 4.6.102 *you'll look pale Before you find it other*, H8 1.3.58, MAC 1.7.77.

othergates *adv.* In another and different way TN 5.1.194 *he would have tickled you othergates than he did.*

otherwhere *adv.* Elsewhere H8 2.2.59 *The King has sent me otherwhere*, ERR 2.1.104.

otherwhiles *adv.* At times 1H6 1.2.7 *Otherwhiles the famish'd English...Faintly besiege us one hour in a month.*

ouch *n.* Brooch; (pl., used vaguely) gems, jewels 2H4 2.4.48 *Your brooches, pearls, and ouches.*

ought *vb.* (early pa. t. form) Owed 1H4 3.3.134 *you ought him a thousand pound.*

Oui, mettez-le au mon pocket; dépêchez [Fr.] Yes, put it in my pocket; be quick. WIV. 1.4.54.

ounce *n.* Lynx MND 2.2.30 *Be it ounce, or cat, or bear.*

ouph *n.* Elf, goblin WIV 4.4.50 *dress Like urchins, ouphes, and fairies*, WIV 5.5.57.

ousel See OUZEL.

out *adv.*
1 Without, outside WIV 5.5.56 *Search...within and out.*
2 Abroad TGV 1.3.7 *seek preferment out*, LR 1.1.32; in the field (for war), in arms MAC 4.3.183 *many worthy fellows that were out.*
3 In other hands or occupation TGV 5.2.29 *my possessions—they are out by lease.*
4 At variance, not friends JC 1.1.16 *be not out with me*, MV 3.5.32.
5 Fully, quite TMP 1.2.41 *thou wast not Out three years old*, TMP 4.1.101, COR 4.5.121.
6 At an end, finished ANT 4.9.32 *Our hour Is fully out*, R3 3.3.8, TMP 3.2.1.
7 Out at heel JC 1.1.17 *if you be out, sir, I can mend you.*
8 At a loss from failure of memory or self-possession, nonplussed, off balance, put off COR 5.3.41 *I have forgot my part, and I am out*, LLL 5.2.152, AYL 4.1.76.
9 Excluded, not involved H8 1.1.79 *The honourable board of council out.*
10 Out of pocket TN 2.3.185 *I am a foul way out.*

~ *prep.*
1 Outside TIM 4.1.38 *within and out that wall.*
2 Out of, from within COR 5.2.39 *push'd out your gates*, MV 3.4.21, 2H4 2.2.23.

~ *interj.* Exclamation of abhorrence, reproach or indignation TGV 2.7.54 *Out, out, Lucetta, that will be ill-favour'd*, MND 3.2.65, R3 1.3.117; (with *upon*) WIV 1.4.165 *Out upon't! what have I forgot?*, ERR 3.1.77, WT 4.3.101; (with words of lamentation) WIV 1.4.36 *Out, alas!*, OTH 5.2.119, SON 33.11.

outbrag *vb.* 'Exceed in pride of beauty' (Schmidt), surpass in appearance LC 95 *Whose bare outbragg'd the web it seem'd to wear.*

outbrave *vb.*
1 Surpass in valour MV 2.1.28 *Outbrave the heart most daring on the earth.*
2 Excel in beauty SON 94.12 *The basest weed outbraves his dignity* (i.e. the flower's).

outbreathed *ppl. adj.* Out of breath 2H4 1.1.108 *wearied and outbreath'd.*

out-burn *vb.* Burn away PP 7.14 *as soon as straw out-burneth.*

outcrafty *vb.* Excel in craft, overcome by craft CYM 3.4.15 *That drug-damn'd Italy hath outcraftied him.*

outdare *vb.*
1 Brave, defy 1H4 5.1.40 *did outdare The dangers of the time*, R2 1.1.190.
2 Surpass in daring COR 1.4.53 *sensibly outdares his senseless sword.*

out-dwell *vb.* Stay beyond MV 2.6.3 *he out-dwells his hour.*

outface *vb.*
1 Stare down; (hence) put out of countenance ERR 5.1.245 *with no face, as 'twere, outfacing me*, MV 4.2.17, HAM 5.1.278; browbeat, intimidate JN 2.1.97 *thou hast...Outfaced infant state* (i.e. intimidated the child-king); frighten away from 1H4 2.4.256 *outfac'd you from your prize.*
2 Brave, defy LR 2.3.11 *outface The winds.*
3 Put a bold face on, brazen out PP 1.8 *Outfacing faults.*

outfacing *ppl. adj.* Swaggering, brow-beating ADO 5.1.94 *outfacing, fashion-monging boys.*

outfly *vb.* Exceed in flight; (fig.) TRO 2.3.115 *his evasion...Cannot outfly our apprehensions* (i.e. our understanding of the truth).

outgo *vb.*
1 Go beyond, exceed, surpass TIM 1.1.274 *he outgoes The very heart of kindness*, CYM 2.4.84, H8 1.2.207.
2 Go beyond in duration, outlast ANT 3.2.61 *the time shall not Outgo my thinking on you.*

out-Herod *vb.* *out-Herod Herod* Outdo Herod (represented in the old mystery plays as a blustering tyrant) in violence, be more outrageous than the most outrageous HAM 3.2.14 *it out-Herods Herod.*

outjest *vb.* Dispel by means of jesting LR 3.1.16 *the fool, who labours to outjest His heart-struck injuries.*

outlaw *n.* (used vaguely) Exile 1H4 4.3.58 *A poor unminded outlaw sneaking home.*

outlawed *ppl. adj.* Banished LR 3.4.167 *I had a son, Now outlaw'd from my blood.*

outlive *vb.* (intr.) Survive TIT 2.3.132 *Let not this wasp outlive, us both to sting.*

outlook *vb.* Look or stare down JN 5.2.115 *To outlook conquest and to win renown.*

outnight *vb.* Outdo in mentioning nights MV 5.1.23 *I would out-night you, did nobody come.*

out of *prep. phr.*
1 Made from WT 1.2.122 *They say it is a copy out of mine*, TRO 1.1.15.
2 As a result of TGV 5.4.89 *out of my neglect.*
3 Beyond VEN 567 *Things out of hope*, LLL 4.1.30, 1H4 4.1.135; outside the limits of H8 3.2.13 *When did he regard The stamp of nobleness in any person Out of himself?* (i.e. except himself).

outpeer *vb.* Surpass CYM 3.6.86 *Great men...Could not outpeer these twain.*

outprize *vb.* Exceed in value CYM 1.4.81 *She's outpriz'd by a trifle.*

outrage *n.* Violent conduct or language, fury 1H6 4.1.126 *this immodest clamorous outrage*, JN 3.4.106, ROM 5.3.216.

outrageous *adj.* Excessive, unrestrained TIT 3.2.13 *thy poor heart beats with outrageous beating.*

outsell *vb.* (fig.) Exceed in value CYM 2.4.102 *Her pretty action did outsell her gift*, CYM 3.5.74.

outside *n.* Outer garments WT 4.4.632 *for the outside of thy poverty we must make an exchange*; (fig.) TIM 3.5.33 *make his wrongs His outsides, to wear them like his raiment.*

outsleep *vb.* Sleep beyond MND 5.1.365 *outsleep the coming morn.*

outspeak *vb.* Describe what is more than (something), utter more than H8 3.2.127 *an inventory... which...outspeaks Possession of a subject.*

outsport *vb.* Go beyond limits (in revelling) OTH 2.3.3 *Not to outsport discretion.*

outstand *vb.* Overstay, stay beyond CYM 1.6.207 *I have outstood my time.*

outstretch *vb.* Stretch to its limit TIM 5.3.3 *Timon is dead, who hath outstretch'd his span.*

outstretched *ppl. adj.* Strained to the limit, 'puffed up' (Schmidt) HAM 2.2.264 *Then are our beggars bodies, and our monarchs and outstretch'd heroes the beggars' shadows.*

outstrike *vb.* Deal swifter blows than ANT 4.6.35 *a swifter mean Shall outstrike thought.*

outswear *vb.* Overcome with swearing LLL 1.2.64 *methinks I should outswear Cupid.*

outsweeten *vb.* Surpass in fragrance or sweetness CYM 4.2.224 *eglantine...Outsweet'ned not thy breath.*

out-wall *n.* Exterior LR 3.1.45 *I am much more Than my out-wall.*

outward *n.* Outward appearance, exterior SON 69.5 *Thy outward thus...is crown'd,* CYM 1.1.23, TRO 3.2.162; (pl.) LC 80 *one by nature's outwards so commended.*

~ *adj.* Not having an intimate knowledge of things AWW 3.1.11 *a common and an outward man.*

~ *adv.* Externally ADO 1.2.8 *They show well outward,* MM 3.1.88, HAM 2.2.374 (F1).

outwards *adv.* Externally HAM 2.2.374 *my extent to the players...must show fairly outwards* (Qq; F1 *outward*).

outwork *vb.* Excel in workmanship ANT 2.2.201 *we see The fancy outwork nature.*

outworth *vb.* Be worth more than H8 1.1.123 *A beggar's book Outworths a noble's blood.*

ouzel, ousel *n.* Blackbird MND 3.1.125 *The ouzel cock so black of hue* (Q1 *woosel*); (applied to a person of dark hair or complexion) 2H4 3.2.8 *Alas, a black ouzel* (Q *woosel*).

overbear *vb.* Overwhelm MND 2.1.92 *every pelting river...they have overborne their continents;* overrule JN 4.2.37 *it pleas'd your Highness To overbear it;* suppress, subdue H5 4.Ch.39 *overbears attaint With cheerful semblance,* ADO 2.3.151, TIT 4.4.2.

overblown *ppl. adj.* Blown over TMP 2.2.110 *Is the storm overblown?;* (chiefly fig.) past SHR 5.2.3 *perils overblown,* R2 3.2.190, 2H6 1.3.152.

overbulk *vb.* Surpass TRO 1.3.320 *a nursery of like evil, To overbulk us all.*

overbuy *vb.* Buy at a higher price, pay too much for CYM 1.1.146 *overbuys me Almost the sum he pays.*

overcome *vb.*
1 Come over suddenly, take by surprise MAC 3.4.110 *overcome us like a summer's cloud.*
2 Overrun TIT 2.3.95 *trees...Overcome with moss.*

over-eye *vb.* Observe SHR Ind.1.95 *over-eyeing of his odd behaviour.*

overflow *n.* Excess, superfluity R2 5.3.64 *Thy overflow of good converts to bad,* ADO 1.1.26.

~ *vb.* Submerge, spread over MND 4.1.16 *I would be loath to have you overflown with a honey-bag.*

overfly *vb.* Fly faster than, outsoar VEN 324 *Outstripping crows that strive to overfly them.*

overglance *vb.* Cast the eye over LLL 4.2.131 *I will overglance the superscript.*

overgo *vb.*
1 Go beyond, exceed SON 103.7 *a face That overgoes my blunt invention,* R3 2.2.61.
2 Oppress, overcome 3H6 2.5.123 *Sad-hearted men, much overgone with care.*

over-handled *ppl. adj.* Employed to excess VEN 770 *your idle over-handled theme.*

overhear *vb.* Hear over again LLL 5.2.95 *overheard what you shall overhear.*

overhold *vb.* Over-estimate TRO 2.3.133 *if he overhold his price so much.*

overleather *n.* Upper leather SHR Ind.2.12 *such shoes as my toes look through the overleather.*

overlive *vb.* Survive, outlive 2H4 4.1.15 *prayers That your attempts may overlive the hazard.*

overlook *vb.*
1 Overtop H5.3.5.9 *shall...Our scions...Spurt up ...And overlook their grafters?*
2 Look down on from above JN 2.1.344 *this hand... That sways the earth this climate overlooks,* 3H6 1.4.180, TIT 2.1.8.
3 Peruse HAM 4.6.14 *when thou shalt have overlook'd this,* H5 2.4.90.
⊳ See O'ERLOOK.

overlooking *n.* Superintendence AWW 1.1.39 *bequeath'd to my overlooking.*

overlusty *adj.* Too lively H5 4.Ch.18 *The confident and overlusty French,* LR 2.4.10.

overmatching *ppl. adj.* Superior in power 3H6 1.4.21 *swim against the tide, And spend her strength with overmatching waves.*

overnight *n.* Before the night (as considered in relation to the following day), preceding evening AWW 3.4.23 *If I had given you this at overnight* (i.e. yesterday evening).

overpass *vb.* Pass, spend 1H6 2.5.117 *like a hermit overpass'd thy days.*

overpeer *vb.*
1 Look over or down upon 1H6 1.4.11 *to overpeer the city, And thence discover how...*
2 Rise or tower above MV 1.1.12 *your argosies...Do overpeer the petty trafickers,* 3H6 5.2.14; (fig.) HAM 4.5.100 *The ocean, overpeering of his list.*

overplus *n.* Surplus ANT 3.7.50 *Our overplus of shipping; in overplus in excess* SON 135.2 *And will to boot, and will in overplus.*

~ *adv.* In addition ANT 4.6.21 *Hath...sent all thy treasure, with His bounty overplus.*

overreach *vb.* O'ERREACH sense 2 SHR 3.2.145 *We'll overreach the greybeard Gremio.*

over-read *vb.* Read through MM 4.2.197 *You shall anon over-read it.*

over-red *vb.* Redden over, cover over with red MAC 5.3.14 *Go prick thy face, and over-red thy fear.*

override *vb.* Overtake in riding, outride 2H4 1.1.30 *I overrode him on the way.*

overscutched *ppl. adj.* (lit.) Well-whipped, beaten; (hence) worn, haggard, hardened (to the trade) 2H4 3.2.317 *overscutch'd huswives.*

oversee *vb.* Supervise, superintend, attend to the execution of LUC 1205 *Thou, Collatine, shalt oversee this will.*

overseen *ppl. adj.* Deceived, deluded, in error LUC 1206 *How was I overseen.*

overset *vb.* Capsize, overturn ROM 3.5.136 *will overset Thy tempest-tossed body.*

overshine, over-shine *vb.*
1 Illumine 3H6 2.1.38 *join our lights..., And overshine the earth.*
2 Outshine, excel TIT 1.1.317 *Dost overshine the gallant'st dames of Rome,* TRO 3.1.158.

overshoot *vb.* Run beyond; (hence) escape from VEN 680 *to overshoot his troubles, How he outruns the wind* (Q1 *overshut*).

overshot *ppl. adj.* Wide of the mark, in error LLL 1.1.142 *So study evermore is overshot.*

overshut (var. of) OVERSHOOT.

overslip *vb.* Pass unnoticed by LUC 1576 *Which... hath overslipp'd her thought.*

oversway *vb.* O'ERSWAY sense 2 VEN 109 *he that overrul'd I oversway'd.*

overswear *vb.* Swear over again TN 5.1.269 *And all those sayings will I overswear.*

overthrow *n.*
1 *have the overthrow* Be defeated 1H6 3.2.106 *We are like to have the overthrow again.*

2 *give the overthrow* Defeat, overthrow JC 5.2.5 *sudden push gives them the overthrow.*

overtopping *n.* Rising too high (esp. in power) TMP 1.2.81 *who To trash for overtopping.*

overture *n.* Disclosure LR 3.7.89 *made the overture of thy treasons to us,* WT 2.1.172.
▷ COR 1.9.46 *Let him be made an overture for th' wars!:* (?) (1) old spelling of 'ovator', one who receives an ovation (Hulme); or (2) misreading of COVERTURE (Steevens' conjecture).

over-view *n.* Inspection LLL 4.3.173 *Are we betrayed thus to thy over-view?*

overwatch *vb.* Watch all through (a night) MND 5.1.366 *As much as we this night have overwatch'd.*
▷ See O'ERWATCH'D.

over-weathered *ppl. adj.* Weatherbeaten MV 2.6.18 *with over-weather'd ribs and ragged sails* (F1 *ouer-wither'd*).

overween *vb.* Be arrogant or presumptuous 2H4 4.1.147 *you overween to take it so,* TIT 2.1.29.

overwhelming *ppl. adj.* Overhanging ROM 5.1.39 *overwhelming brows.*

overworn *ppl. adj.* Stale TN 3.1.59 *the word is overworn.*

owd *adj.* [northern dial. form] Old OTH 2.3.96 *take*

thy owd cloak about thee (Q1; Qq 2–3 *auld*; Ff *awl'd*).

owe *vb.*
1 Possess, own, have TMP 1.2.455 *Thou dost here usurp The name thou ow'st not,* JN 4.2.99, MAC 1.3.76.
2 (transf.) Have or cherish toward another, bear (love or hate) VEN 523 *if any love you owe me,* AYL 3.2.74, TN 2.4.105.

own *vb.* Have (a certain function) WT 4.4.143 *own no other function.*
~ *adj.* be (one's) *own* Be master of oneself, have full control over one's senses TMP 5.1.213 *no man was his own.*

ox *n.* (fig.) Fool WIV 5.5.120 *I am made an ass.—Ay, and an ox too,* TRO 5.1.59.

oxhead *n.* (transf.) Symbol of cuckoldry JN 2.1.292 *with your lioness, I would set an ox-head to your lion's hide* (i.e. make you a cuckold).

oxlip *n.* Flowering herb uniting features of the cowslip and the primrose MND 2.1.250 *Where oxlips and the nodding violet grows,* WT 4.4.125.

oyes *n.* Call of 'Oyez' (the call of the public crier or court official) WIV 5.5.41 *Crier Hobgoblin, make the fairy Oyes,* TRO 4.5.143.

P

pace *n.*
1 Manner of walking, gait PER 5.1.111 *in pace another Juno,* VEN 294, R2 5.2.10.
2 Gait of a horse when trained; (fig.) AWW 4.5.67 *he has no pace, but runs where he will* (i.e. he is under no discipline or restraint).
3 *hold me pace* Keep pace with me 1H4 3.1.48 *hold me pace in deep experiments.*
~ *vb.* Train (a horse) to pace H8 5.2.57 *those that tame wild horses Pace 'em not in their hands* (i.e do not train them by leading them); (fig.) ANT 2.2.64 *The third o' th' world is yours, which with a snaffle you may pace easy, but not such a wife,* MM 4.3.132, PER 4.6.63.

pack *n.* Confederacy, conspiring gang WIV 4.2.118 *there's a...pack, a conspiracy against me,* R3 3.3.4, ERR 4.4.102.
~ *vb.*[1]
1 Conspire TIT 4.2.155 *Go pack with him.*
2 (pass.) Be a confederate in a plot ERR 5.1.219 *were he not pack'd with her,* ADO 5.1.299.
3 Shuffle (cards) so as to cheat; (fig.) ANT 4.14.19 *she, Eros, has Pack'd cards with Caesar's* (i.e. stacked the cards in Caesar's favour).

pack *vb.*[2]
1 Load 2H4 4.5.76 *Our thighs pack'd with wax, our mouths with honey, We bring it to the hive,* 1H4 2.1.3.
2 Take oneself off, depart ERR 3.2.153 *'Tis time...to trudge, pack, and be gone,* WIV 1.3.82, H8 1.3.33.

pack-horse *n.* (fig.) Drudge R3 1.3.121 *I was a packhorse in his great affairs,* LUC 928.

packing *n.* Plotting SHR 5.1.118 *Here's packing, with a witness, to deceive us all,* LR 3.1.26.

paction *n.* Compact, agreement H5 5.2.365 *Thrust in between the paction of these kingdoms.*
▷ Theobald; Ff 1–2 *Pation*; Ff 3–4 *Passion.*

paddle *vb.* Toy, play fondly (with the fingers) HAM 3.4.185 *paddling in your neck with his damn'd fingers,* OTH 2.1.254; (trans.) finger fondly, fondle, caress WT 1.2.115 *to be paddling palms.*

paddock *n.* A kind of toad, generally believed to be highly poisonous HAM 3.4.190 *from a paddock,*

from a bat, a gib; (?) 'familiar spirit, in the shape of a toad' (Schmidt) MAC 1.1.9 *Paddock calls.*

pagan *n.* Prostitute 2H4 2.2.154 *What pagan may that be?*

page *vb.* Attend, follow like a page TIM 4.3.224 *page thy heels.*

pageant *n.*
1 Theatrical representation; (hence) show, spectacle, sight MND 3.2.114 *Shall we their fond pageant see?* (i.e. the foolish spectacle they present), H8 4.1.11, TMP 4.1.155; false show OTH 1.3.18 *a pageant To keep us in false gaze.*
2 A movable stage or platform on which scenes were acted, (esp. mystery plays), device, or tableau on a moving cart exhibited as a feature of a public show; (fig., applied to a ship) MV 1.1.11 *as it were the pageants of the sea*; (applied to clouds) ANT 4.14.8 *They are black vesper's pageants.*
~ *vb.* Imitate as in a pageant, mimic TRO 1.3.151 *He pageants us.*

pageantry *n.* Theatrical exhibition PER 5.2.6 *What pageantry, what feats, what shows...The regent made...To greet the King.*

pain *n.*
1 Punishment, penalty MM 2.4.86 *his offence is so, as it appears, Accountant to the law upon that pain*; (esp. in the phr.) *on pain of* LR 3.3.4 *on pain of perpetual displeasure,* LLL 1.1.123, R2 1.3.42; *in pain of* 2H6 3.2.257 *In pain of your dislike.*
▷ In Eliz. English the expression *on pain of* could be followed by the thing to be forfeited (e.g. R2 1.3.140 *upon pain of life*) as well as the penalty incurred (e.g. LLL 1.1.123 *on pain of losing her tongue*).
2 Trouble, labour, effort to accomplish something MND 5.1.80 *conn'd with cruel pain,* LR 3.1.53, R3 4.4.303.
~ *vb.* Put to trouble MM 5.1.386 *I...have employ'd and pain'd Your unknown sovereignty.*

pained *ppl. adj.* Troubled, tormented PER 4.6.163 *the pained'st fiend Of hell,* LLL 5.2.854; (absol.) LUC 901 *Give...ease to the pained.*

painful *adj.*
 1 Laborious, toilsome (of actions, etc.) LLL 2.1.23 *painful study*, H5 4.3.111, COR 4.5.68.
 2 Toiling SON 25.9 *The painful warrior.*
painfully *adv.* Laboriously LLL 1.1.74 *painfully to pore upon a book*, JN 2.1.223.
paint *vb.* Flatter with specious words LLL 4.1.16 *never paint me now.*
painted *ppl. adj.*
 1 *painted cloth* Hanging for a room, painted or worked with figures, mottoes, or texts, tapestry LLL 5.2.576 *You will be scrap'd out of the painted cloth for this*, 1H4 4.2.25, LUC 245; (used as adv.) in a style resembling the mottoes or the brief inscriptions in tapestries AYL 3.2.273 *I answer you right paint'd cloth, from whence you have studied your questions.*
 2 Specious, feigned, unreal JN 3.1.105 *painted peace*, AYL 2.1.3, HAM 3.1.52.
 ⟡ In R3 1.3.240 *Poor painted queen*, there could also be a ref. to the painted wooden or wax figure of a dead queen sometimes carried in funeral processions.
painting *n.* Paint; (hence) cosmetics CYM 3.4.50 *Some jay of Italy (Whose mother was her painting)* (i.e. cosmetics made her what she was), WT 5.3.83; H8 1.1.26 *their very labour Was to them as a painting* (i.e. as good as using cosmetics for heightening the colour).
pair *n. pair of stairs* Flight of stairs AYL 5.2.37.
pajock *n.* (?) (1) Peacock (associated with vicious qualities in Eliz. times); or (2) PADDOCK; or (3) (var. of) patchock, base, contemptible fellow, savage (Jenkins) HAM 3.2.284 *...now reigns here A very, very—pajock.*
 ⟡ F1, Qq 2-6 *paiock(e)*, Ff 2-4 *pajock(e)*. The rhyme demands *ass*, but Hamlet prob. intended something worse by this substitute. In HAM 3.4.190 he uses 'paddock' in ref. to Claudius.
palabras [Sp.] Words ADO 3.5.16 *Comparisons are odorous—palabras, neighbour Verges.*
palate *vb.*
 1 Enjoy the taste of, relish TRO 4.1.60 *Not palating the taste of her dishonour*, ANT 5.2.7.
 2 Savour of COR 3.1.104 *the great'st taste Most palates theirs.*
pale *n.*[1]
 1 (pl.) Palings H8 5.3.90 *I 'll peck you o'er the pales.*
 2 Fence, paling ERR 2.1.100 *too unruly deer, he breaks the pale*, R2 3.4.40, TRO 2.3.249; (fig.) HAM 1.4.28 *the pales and forts of reason.*
 3 Fenced area, enclosure 1H6 4.2.45 *bounded in a pale*, VEN 230, MND 2.1.4; (fig.) WT 4.3.4 *the red blood reigns in the winter's pale* (perh. with quibble on PALE *n.*[2]).
 ~ *vb.* Enclose, encircle ANT 2.7.68 *What e'er the ocean pales, or sky inclips*, CYM 3.1.19, 3H6 1.4.103.
pale *n.*[2] Paleness, pallor VEN 589 *a sudden pale... Usurps her cheek*, WT 4.3.4 (see PALE *n.*[1] SENSE 3).
 ~ *vb.* Make, cause to become pale HAM 1.5.90 *to pale his uneffectual fire.*
 ~ *adj.*
 1 Causing paleness VEN 739 *agues pale and faint.*
 2 *pale at mine heart* PALE-HEARTED MM 4.3.151.
paled See PALLID.
pale-hearted *adj.* Cowardly MAC 4.1.85 *pale-hearted fear.*
palfrey *n.* A saddle-horse for ordinary riding, as distinct from a war horse 2H6 4.2.69 *in Cheapside shall my palfrey go to grass*, H5 3.7.33, TIT 5.2.50.
palisado *n.* Fence made of stakes, palisade 1H4 2.3.52 *palisadoes, frontiers, parapets.*
pall *vb.*[1] Shroud, cover as with a pall or mantle MAC 1.5.51 *pall thee in the dunnest smoke of hell.*
pall *vb.*[2] Fail HAM 5.2.9 *When our deep plots do pall.*

palled *ppl. adj.* Weakened, impaired ANT 2.7.82 *Thy pall'd fortunes* (F1 *paul'd*).
pallet *n.* Straw bed, small, poor or mean bed 2H4 3.1.10 *Upon uneasy pallets.*
 ⟡ Q1; Ff *pallads*, a common var. in 16–18C.
palliament *n.* White gown of a candidate for the Roman consulship TIT 1.1.182 *This palliament of white and spotless hue.*
pallid *adj.* Lacking depth or intensity of colour LC 198 *pallid pearls* (Q *palyd*).
palm *n.*
 1 (fig.) Emblem of victory COR 5.3.117 *bear the palm*, TRO 3.1.157, JC 1.2.131.
 2 (fig., applied to a man) Conspicuous person TIM 5.1.10 *You shall see him a palm in Athens again.*
palmer *n.* Pilgrim (properly one from the Holy Land, bearing a palm leaf) ROM 1.5.101 *Have not saints lips, and holy palmers too?*, R2 3.3.151, 2H6 5.1.97.
palm tree *n.* Any species of willow, esp. goat willow (Salix caprea), the branches or sprigs of which were used instead of palm-branches in northern countries AYL 3.2.175 *look here what I found on a palm tree.*
palmy *adj.* Triumphant, flourishing HAM 1.1.113 *In the most high and palmy state of Rome.*
palsy *n. cold palsies* Paralysis induced by cold phlegm TRO 5.1.20 *the rotten diseases of the south, the guts-griping,...cold palsies...*
 ~ *adj.* Palsied, shaking as if with palsy TRO 1.3.174 *with a palsy fumbling.*
palter *vb.* Shuffle, use trickery, equivocate MAC 5.8.20 *fiends...That palter with us in a double sense*, ANT 3.11.63, JC 2.1.126.
paly *adj.* Pale 2H6 3.2.141 *chafe his paly lips*, H5 4.Ch.8.
palyd See PALLID.
pamphlet *n.* Small treatise or composition in writing 1H6 3.1.2 *written pamphlets studiously devis'd*, LUC Ded.1.
pancake *n.* Fritter, perh. containing meat AYL 1.2.66 *the pancakes were naught, and the mustard was good*, AWW 2.2.23.
pander *n.* Go-between in clandestine amours, one who supplies another with the means of gratifying lust, male bawd, pimp, procurer H5 4.5.14 *Like a base pander hold the chamber door*, ADO 5.2.31, TRO 3.2.204.
 ~ *vb.* Minister to the gratification of HAM 3.4.88 *reason panders will* (F1; Qq 2–4 *pardons*).
panderly *adj.* Bawdy WIV 4.2.117 *you panderly rascals.*
pang *vb.* Cause pangs, penetrate or afflict with pain H8 2.3.15 *'tis a sufferance panging As soul and body's severing*, CYM 3.4.95.
pannel *vb.* (?) (No direct explanation) ANT 4.12.21 *The heart's That pannelled me at heels.*
 ⟡ Ff *pannelled*; Hanmer conjecture *spaniel'd.* See SPANIEL. Hulme proposes a connection with 'panele' (brown unpurified sugar from the Antilles) with a sense related to 'sweeten', hence 'flatter, fawn'.
pant *n.* Palpitation of the heart ANT 4.8.16 *leap thou...to my heart, and there Ride on the pants triumphing*, OTH 2.1.80.
pantaloon *n.* The Venetian character in Italian comedy, represented as a lean and foolish old man, wearing spectacles, pantaloons, and slippers; (hence) foolish, enfeebled old man AYL 2.7.158 *the lean and slipper'd pantaloon*, SHR 3.1.37.
pantler *n.* Servant who had charge of the pantry 2H4 2.4.238 *'A would have made a good pantler, 'a would 'a' chipp'd bread well*, CYM 2.3.124, WT 4.4.56.

paper *n.* Note fastened on the back of a criminal undergoing punishment, specifying his offence LLL 4.3.46 *Why, he comes in like a perjure, wearing papers*, 2H6 2.4.31.
~ *vb.* Set down on paper, write in a list H8 1.1.80 *his own letter...Must fetch him in he papers.*

paper-faced *adj.* Having a face as pale or as thin as paper 2H4 5.4.10 *thou paper-fac'd villain!*

paradox *n.* Statement or tenet contrary to received opinion HAM 3.1.113 *This was sometime a paradox, but now the time gives it proof.*

paragon *vb.*
1 Compare ANT 1.5.71 *If thou with Caesar paragon again My man of men.*
2 Surpass OTH 2.1.62 *a maid That paragons description and wild fame.*
3 Set forth as a paragon or perfect model H8 2.4.231 *the primest creature That's paragon'd o' th' world.*

parallel *n.* (pl.) Parallel lines TRO 1.3.168 *the extremest ends Of parallels*; (transf.) furrows, wrinkles SON 60.10 *delves the parallels in beauty's brow.*
~ *vb.*
1 Bring into conformity with MM 4.2.79 *his life is parallel'd Even with the stroke and line of his great justice.*
2 Present as a parallel or equal MAC 2.3.62 *My young remembrance cannot parallel A fellow to it.*
3 Equal TRO 2.2.162 *her whom...The world's large spaces cannot parallel*, AWW 4.3.251.
~ *adj.* (fig.) Having the same tendency or purport, coinciding with a person's wish or purpose OTH 2.3.349 *To counsel Cassio to this parallel course.*

paraquito *n.* (var. of) Parakeet 1H4 2.3.85 *Come, come, you paraquito, answer me.*

parcel *n.*
1 Part, portion WIV 1.1.230 *that the lips are parcel of the mouth*, ERR 5.1.106, COR 1.2.32; *by parcels* by parts, piecemeal OTH 1.3.154 *my pilgrimage... Whereof by parcels she had something heard.*
2 Item, detail, particular 2H4 4.2.36 *The parcels and particulars of our grief*, AWW 4.3.90.
3 Small party, company, group, or set MV 1.2.108 *this parcel of wooers*, LLL 5.2.160, AWW 2.3.52.
~ *vb.* (?) (1) Make up into a parcel; (hence, fig.) 'make up into a mass' (Johnson); or (2) 'specify' (Schmidt) ANT 5.2.163 *that mine own servant should Parcel the sum of my disgraces by Addition of his envy!*

parcel-bawd *n.* Part-time bawd MM 2.1.63 *A tapster, sir; parcel-bawd.*

parcel-gilt *adj.* Partly gilded 2H4 2.1.87 *a parcel-gilt goblet.*

parcelled *ppl. adj.* Divided into parcels or separate portions; (hence) particular R3 2.2.81 *Their woes are parcell'd, mine is general.*

pard *n.* Panther or leopard TMP 4.1.261 *more pinch-spotted make them Than pard or cat o' mountain*, MND 2.2.31, AYL 2.7.150.

pardie See PERDIE.

pardon *n.* Leave, permission ANT 3.6.60 *I begg'd His pardon for return*, LLL 4.2.101, HAM 4.7.46.
~ *vb.*
1 Remit (a penalty) MV 4.1.369 *I pardon thee thy life*, LR 4.6.109.
2 Excuse ADO 2.1.126 *Will you not tell me...?—No, you shall pardon me*, TGV 3.2.97.

pardona-mee [It. 'perdonami'] See PARDON-ME.

pardon-me *n.* One who is always excusing himself ROM 2.4.33 *these fashion-mongers, these pardon-me's.*
◇ F1 *pardon-mees*, Qq 2-3 *pardons mees*, Qq 4-5 *pardona-mees*; Theobald *pardonnez-moys.*

pardonne moy, pardonnez(-)moi [Fr.] Pardon me R2 5.3.119, H5 4.4.21.

'parel *n.* (apheptic form of) Apparel LR 4.1.49 *I'll bring him the best 'parel that I have.*

parfect *vb.* (malapropism for) Perform LLL 5.2.501 *to parfect one man in one poor man.*

Paris ball *n.* Tennis ball H5 2.4.131 *I did present him with the Paris balls.*

parish-top *n.* Whipping-top kept for the exercise of parishioners TN 1.3.42 *till his brains turn o' th' toe like a parish-top.*

Paris-ward *n.* unto Paris-ward Towards Paris 1H6 3.3.30 *Their powers are marching unto Paris-ward.*

paritor *n.* Apparitor, summoning officer of an ecclesiastical court LLL 3.1.186 *great general Of trotting paritors* (Q2; F1, Q1 *Parretors*).

park *n.* Enclosed tract of land, often for keeping beasts of chase MND 2.1.4 *Over park, over pale*, LLL 1.1.208, WIV 5.1.11.

parked *ppl. adj.* Enclosed (like a park) 1H6 4.2.45 *How are we park'd and bounded in a pale...!*

park-ward *n.* the park-ward Toward the park WIV 3.1.5 *have you look'd for Master Caius...?—Marry, sir, the pittie-ward, the park-ward, every way.*

parle *n.* Parley, conversation, conference, esp. meeting to discuss terms under a truce JN 2.1.205 *call'd you to this gentle parle*, TGV 1.2.5, H5 3.3.2; trumpet-call to such a meeting 3H6 5.1.16 *Go, trumpet,...and sound a parle.*

parling *ppl. adj.* Speaking LUC 100 *their parling looks.*

parlous *adj.*
1 Perilous, dangerous AYL 3.2.44 *in a parlous state.*
2 Dangerously cunning, shrewd R3 2.4.35 *A parlous boy!* (F4; Qq 7-8 *perlous*; Ff 1-3, Qq 1-6 *peril(l)ous).*
3 Alarming, dreadful, shocking MND 3.1.13 *a parlous fear.*

parmaceti, parmaciti *n.* (16C corr. of) Spermaceti 1H4 1.3.58 *the sovereignest thing on earth Was parmaciti for an inward bruise.*

part *n.*
1 *the better part* The greater part AYL 3.1.2 *were I not the better part made mercy*, MV 1.1.16, 2H4 1.2.156; *a little part* a little TIM 3.2.47 *purchase...for a little part; no part* not at all AWW 2.1.132 *what at full I know, thou know'st no part.*
2 Member of the body or of the whole man TRO 2.3.174 *'twixt his mental and his active parts*, MM 2.4.22, SON 74.6; (with appropriate modifier) the soul 2H4 2.2.104 *the immortal part*, H8 4.2.30, SON 74.8.
3 Personal quality or attribute HAM 5.2.111 *the continent of what part a gentleman would see*, ADO 5.2.60, WT 5.1.64; (usu. pl.) abilities, capacities, talents AYL 1.1.144 *an envious emulator of every man's good parts*, SON 17.4, LLL 4.2.114.
4 Piece of conduct, act, action 2H4 4.5.63 *This part of his conjoins with my disease, And helps to end me*, TN 5.1.361, OTH 1.2.31.
5 Side in a contest, party, faction JN 5.6.2 *Of the part of England* (i.e. on the side of), H5 4.7.118, CYM 5.1.25; *on part and part* (some) on one side and (some) on the other ROM 1.1.114 *Came more and more, and fought on part and part.*
6 (pl.) (?) Divisions of a heraldic shield in which charges are borne SON 37.7 *whether beauty, birth, or wealth...Intitled in their parts do crowned sit* (Q; Capell thy).
7 *in, on, upon the part of* On behalf of ERR 3.1.91 *Plead on her part some cause to you unknown*, COR 3.1.209, SON 49.12; in recognition of TIT 1.1.236 *I give thee thanks in part of thy deserts.*

~ *vb.*

1 *part from* Part with, give up MV 3.2.172 *this ring, Which when you part from, lose, or give away.*

2 *part with* Part from, go away from, leave ERR 5.1.221 *who parted with me to go fetch a chain,* AYL 3.2.223, ROM 3.3.174.

3 Depart, go away TGV 1.1.71 *But now he parted hence,* 2H4 4.2.70, TIT 1.1.488.

4 Depart this life, die H5 2.3.12 *'A parted...between twelve and one,* R3 2.1.5, MAC 5.9.18.

5 Depart from, leave PER 5.3.38 *When we...parted Pentapolis,* R2 3.1.3.

partake *vb.*

1 Take (some) of WT 2.1.41 *one may drink, depart, And yet partake no venom.*

2 Impart, communicate WT 5.3.132 *your exultation Partake to every one,* PER 1.1.152.

3 Take sides *with* SON 149.2 *When I against myself with thee partake.*

partaker *n.* Supporter, adherent 1H6 2.4.100 *your partaker Pole.*

parted *ppl. adj.*

1 Divided; (hence) out of focus MND 4.1.189 *with parted eye, When every thing seems double.*

2 Endowed, gifted TRO 3.3.96 *man, how dearly ever parted.*

▷ See TIMELY-PARTED.

partial *adj.* nothing...partial No partiality MM 2.1.31; *A partial slander* an imputation of partiality R2 1.3.241.

partialize *vb.* Render partial or one-sided R2 1.1.120 *nearness to our...blood Should nothing privilege him nor partialize The unstooping firmness of my-...soul.*

partially *adv.* With undue favour OTH 2.3.218 *If partially affin'd, or leagu'd in office,* LUC 634.

participate *vb.* Share with others TN 5.1.238 *that dimension...Which from the womb I did participate.*

~ *pa. pple.* Participating COR 1.1.103 *And, mutually participate, did minister.*

parti-coated *adj.* Clad in a parti-coloured or motley coat LLL 5.2.766 *parti-coated presence of loose love Put on by us.*

parti-coloured *adj.* Partly of one colour and partly of another, variegated in colour MV 1.3.88 *parti-colour'd lambs.*

particular *n.*

1 Detail 2H4 4.4.90 *With every course in his particular* (i.e. with the details fully set forth), HAM 2.2.239, AWW 4.3.182; *by particulars* one by one, in detail COR 2.3.43 *He's to make his requests by particulars.*

2 Personal interest or concern COR 4.7.13 *for your particular* (i.e. as far as you are concerned), ANT 1.3.54, AWW 2.5.61.

3 Close relation, intimacy COR 5.1.3 *who loved him In a most dear particular,* H8 3.2.189.

~ *adj.* Private, personal H5 3.2.78 *particular knowledge,* MM 4.4.27, LR 5.1.30; referring to one special person 2H4 4.3.48 *particular ballad;* belonging to one lover H5 3.7.47 *a good and particular mistress.*

particularities *n.* (pl.) Individual affairs or matters H5 3.2.130 *the derivation of my birth, and in other particularities,* 2H6 5.2.66.

particularly *adv.* Individually TIM 1.1.46 *my free drift Halts not particularly* (i.e. at any individual person), COR 4.5.66.

parti-eyed *adj.* With his eyes 'motley' (i.e. bleeding) LR 4.1.10 *My father, parti-ey'd?*

▷ F1, Q2 *poorly led,* Q1(u) *poorlie, leed;* Q1(c) *parti, eyd;* Davenport conjecture *parti-ey'd.*

partisan, partizan *n.* Weapon used by infantry in the 16–17C, consisting of a long-handled spear and a blade having one or more lateral cutting projections ROM 1.1.73 *Clubs, bills, and partisans!,* HAM 1.1.140.

Partlet *n.* Traditional proper name for a hen (often 'Dame Partlet'); (applied, like 'hen', to a woman) 1H4 3.3.52 *How now, Dame Partlet the hen? have you inquir'd yet who pick'd my pocket?,* WT 2.3.76.

partner *n.*

1 Fellow-sponsor H8 5.4.5 *My noble partners,* H8 5.2.202.

2 Accomplice MM 2.3.37 *Your partner...Must die to-morrow.*

~ *vb.* Associate CYM 1.6.121 *A lady...to be partner'd With tomboys.*

party *n.*

1 Side in a contest, (a particular) cause or interest R3 4.4.526 *they came from Buckingham Upon his party,* JN 1.1.34, LR 2.1.26.

2 Faction COR 3.1.313 *Lest parties...break out.*

3 Partner, ally 1H4 3.1.1 *These promises are fair, the parties sure,* WT 2.3.21, COR 5.6.13.

party-verdict *n.* One person's share in a joint verdict R2 1.3.234 *Thy son is banish'd upon good advice, Whereto thy tongue a party-verdict gave.*

pash *n.* Head WT 1.2.128 *Thou want'st a rough pash and the shoots that I have* (i.e. a bull's shaggy head and horns).

pash *vb.* Strike violently TRO 2.3.203 *I'll pash him o'er the face* (F1; Q *push*).

pashed *ppl. adj.* Crushed, smashed to pieces TRO 5.5.10 *the pashed corses of the kings.*

pass *n.*

1 Passage HAM 2.2.77 *to give quiet pass,* H5 2.Ch.39.

2 Act of going beyond the bounds or limits prescribed, transgression MM 5.1.370 *your Grace ...Hath look'd upon my passes.*

3 Reputation, estimation AWW 2.5.53 *common speech Gives him a worthy pass.*

4 Issue, end SON 103.11 *to no other pass my verses tend.*

5 Critical position, juncture, predicament ERR 3.1.17 *being at that pass, You would keep from my heels,* SHR 5.2.124, LR 3.4.63.

6 Permission to act, licence MM 1.3.38 *When evil deeds have their permissive pass.*

7 Lunge or thrust in fencing HAM 5.2.61 *Between the pass and fell incensed points Of mighty opposites;* bout of fencing TN 3.4.274 *I had a pass with him, rapier, scabbard, and all.*

8 *pass of pate* Sally of wit TMP 4.1.244 *'Steal by line and level' is an excellent pass of pate,* WIV 2.1.225, HAM 5.2.166.

~ *vb.*

1 Die, pass away 2H6 3.3.25 *let him pass peaceably,* LR 4.6.47.

2 Go through JC 1.1.42 *see great Pompey pass the streets of Rome;* go through point by point MAC 3.1.79 *In our last conference, pass'd in probation with you;* (fig.) experience, suffer TRO 2.2.139 *to pass the difficulties,* PER 2.Gower.6, OTH 1.3.131.

3 Go beyond, exceed LLL 4.3.237 *She passes praise,* WIV 1.1.179, HAM 1.2.85.

4 (intr.) Go beyond all bounds, beggar description, excel TIM 1.1.12 *breath'd, as it were, To an untirable...goodness; He passes,* TRO 1.2.167, WIV 1.1.297.

5 Neglect, disregard JN 2.1.258 *If you fondly pass our...offer,* MM 4.6.12, COR 2.2.139.

6 Transfer, hand over SHR 4.4.45 *pass my daughter a sufficient dower.*

7 Transact SHR 4.4.57 *pass the business privately and well.*

8 Pass for; (hence) be suitable for the part of LLL 5.1.128 *this swain, because of his great limb..., shall pass Pompey the Great.*

9 Pass sentence, give judgement LR 3.7.24 *pass upon his life*, MM 2.1.19.
10 Receive the approval of COR 3.1.29 *Hath he not pass'd the noble and the common?*
11 Pledge TN 1.5.80 *he will not pass his word*, LLL 1.1.19, R2 5.3.51.
12 Make a thrust HAM 5.2.298 *I pray you pass with your best violence*; (fig.) make a witty sally TN 3.1.42 *and thou pass upon me*, LR 3.7.24; (trans.) make (a pass) WIV 2.3.26 *see thee pass thy puncto*.
13 Care 2H6 4.2.128 *As for these silken-coated slaves, I pass not*.
14 *pass upon* Impose upon TN 5.1.352 *This practice hath most shrewdly pass'd upon thee*.

passable *adj.*
1 Current (like coin) COR 5.2.13 *the virtue of your name Is not here passable*.
2 Affording passage CYM 1.2.9 *His body's a passable carcass...it is a thoroughfare for steel*.

passado *n.* Forward thrust with the sword, one foot being advanced at the same time ROM 2.4.26 *ah, the immortal passado, the punto reverso*, ROM 3.1.85, LLL 1.2.178.

passage *n.*
1 Passing of people, people passing by ERR 3.1.99 *Now in the stirring passage of the day* (i.e. the busy period when there are a lot of passers-by), OTH 5.1.37.
2 Death HAM 3.3.86 *fit and season'd for his passage*, HAM 5.2.398.
3 Procedure, course ROM Prol.9 *The fearful passage of their death-mark'd love*, WT 3.2.90, TRO 2.3.131.
4 Occurrence, incident HAM 4.7.112 *in passages of proof* (i.e. by actual examples), AWW 1.1.18, CYM 3.4.91.
5 Act, proceeding 1H4 3.2.8 *thy passages of life* (i.e. the actions of thy life), TN 3.2.72, H5 3.6.93.
6 Journey, travel R2 1.3.272 *Must I not serve a long apprenticehood To foreign passages*.

passant *adj.* (heraldic term) Walking WIV 1.1.20 *The dozen white louses do become an old coat well; it agrees well, passant*.

passed *ppl. adj.* Uttered 2H6 3.2.221 *thy passed speech*.

passenger *n.* Traveller on foot, wayfarer, passer-by VEN 91 *Never did passenger...More thirst*, R2 5.3.9, TGV 4.1.1.

passing *ppl. adj.* Surpassing, extreme 3H6 5.1.106 *O passing traitor...!*, TGV 1.2.17, TGV 2.1.75.
~ *adv.* Pre-eminently, exceedingly SHR 2.1.242 *I find you passing gentle*, ADO 2.1.81, SHR 2.1.112.

passing-bell *n.* Bell which rings at the hour of death, to obtain prayers for the passing soul VEN 702 *To one sore sick that hears the passing-bell*.

passion *n.*
1 Any kind of feeling by which the mind is powerfully moved JN 3.3.47 *idle merriment—A passion hateful to my purposes*, H5 2.2.132, TMP 4.1.143.
2 Malady or disorder of the body or mind ERR 5.1.47 *But till this afternoon his passion brake into extremity of rage*, MAC 3.4.56, 1H4 3.1.34.
3 Sorrowful emotion, lamentation TIT 1.1.106 *A mother's tears in passion for her son*, VEN 832, 1H4 2.4.416.
4 (pl.) Feelings or desires of love TIT 2.1.36 *plead my passions for Lavinia's love*, LUC Arg.23.
5 Passionate speech or outburst, poem of emotion MND 5.1.315 *her passion ends the play*.
6 The sufferings of Christ WIV 3.1.62 *God's will, and his passion of my heart!*, SHR 4.1.118.
~ *vb.* Sorrow, grieve VEN 1059 *Dumbly she passions*, TMP 5.1.24, LLL 1.1.260.

passionate *vb.* Express with passion TIT 3.2.6 *cannot passionate our tenfold grief*.
~ *adj.*
1 Grieved, sorrowful JN 2.1.544 *She is sad and passionate*, TGV 1.2.121, LLL 3.1.1.
2 Compassionate R3 1.4.118 *this passionate humour of mine* (Qq *my holy humour*).

passy-measures pavin *n. phr.* [It. 'passamezzo pavana'] A dance of Italian origin, a version of the pavan but played more quickly and less solemnly TN 5.1.200.

past-proportion *n.* That which is beyond measure TRO 2.2.29 *will you with counters sum The past-proportion of his infinite* (i.e. the immeasurableness of his infinite greatness).

pastry *n.* Place where pastry is made ROM 4.4.2 *They call for dates and quinces in the pastry*.

pasture *n.* the mettle of your pasture The quality of your rearing H5 3.1.27.

patch *n.* Fool, dolt LLL 4.2.31 *a patch set on learning*, TMP 3.2.63, MV 2.5.46.

patch *vb.*
1 Make up with patches ANT 2.2.52 *patch a quarrel* (i.e. make a cause for quarrel out of bits and pieces).
2 Mark (a surface) as patches of different material do JN 3.1.47 *Patch'd with foul moles*.

patched *ppl. adj. patch'd fool* Motley fool, professional jester MND 4.1.209 *man is but a patch'd fool* (F1; Qq 1-2 *patcht a fool*).

patchery *n.* Roguery, trickery TRO 2.3.71 *Here is such patchery, such juggling, and such knavery!*, TIM 5.1.96.

paten *n.* Thin plate (of metal) MV 5.1.59 *Look how the floor of heaven Is thick inlaid with patens of bright gold* (F1, Qq 2-4 *pattens*; Q1 *pattents*; later Ff *patterns*).

patent *n.* Authority, leave, title, licence, privilege OTH 4.1.198 *give her patent to offend*, MND 1.1.80 *my virgin patent* (i.e. title to virginity), AWW 4.5.66.

path *vb.* (intr.) Go about JC 2.1.83 *if thou path, thy native semblance on*.
◊ F1 *path thy*; F2 *path, thy*; Coleridge conjecture *put thy*.

pathetical *adj.*
1 Moving, affecting LLL 1.2.98 *Sweet invocation of a child, most pretty and pathetical!*, LLL 4.1.148.
2 (derogatory) Pitiable, despicable, contemptible, AYL 4.1.192 *the most pathetical break-promise, and the most hollow lover*.

patience *n.* Indulgence, leave, permission 1H6 2.3.78 *But only, with your patience, that we may Taste of your wine*, HAM 3.2.107, TMP 3.3.3.

patient *vb.* (refl.) Be patient, calm yourself TIT 1.1.121 *Patient yourself*.

patine See PATEN.

patron *n.* Example or model deserving imitation TIT 1.1.65 *Patron of virtue, Rome's best champion*.
◊ Var. of *pattern*. During 17C *patron* and *pattern* became differentiated in form and sense.

patronage *vb.* Uphold, defend 1H6 3.1.48 *as an outlaw in a castle keeps And useth it to patronage his theft*, 1H6 3.4.32.

patten See PATEN.

pattern *n.*
1 Precedent, instance appealed to JN 3.4.16 *find some pattern of our shame*, TIT 5.3.44.
2 (lit. the model from which something is made) 'Something made after a model, an example, an instance' (Schmidt) H5 2.4.61 *The patterns that by God and by French fathers Had twenty years been made*, 1H6 5.5.65, LUC 1350.
~ *vb.*
1 Be a pattern for, provide a precedent for MM

2.1.30 *Let mine own judgement pattern out my death*, Tɪᴛ 4.1.57, Lᴜᴄ 629.
2 Match WT 3.2.36 *more Than history can pattern.*
paucas pallabris (blunder for Sp. 'pocas palabras') Few words Sʜʀ Ind.1.5 *Therefore paucas pallabris, let the world slide.*
pauca [L.] Few H5 2.1.79 *and—pauca, there's enough too!; pauca verba* few words Wɪᴠ 1.1.120 *Pauca verba; Sir John, good worts.*
paunch n. Stab in the paunch Tᴍᴘ 3.2.90 *Batter his skull, or paunch him with a stake.*
pause n. Hesitation, suspense Hᴀᴍ 4.3.9 *This sudden sending him away must seem Deliberate pause*, MV 2.9.53, Tʀᴏ 4.4.35; *in pause* hesitating, deliberating Hᴀᴍ 3.3.42 *I stand in pause where I shall first begin; give (one) pause* cause one to hesitate Hᴀᴍ 3.1.67 *what dreams may come...Must give us pause.*
~ *vb.* (refl.) Make a pause, delay action 2H4 4.4.9 *And pause us till these rebels...Come underneath the yoke of government.*
pauser n. One who pauses, hesitater, more deliberate mover Mᴀᴄ 2.3.111 *Th' expedition of my violent love Outrun the pauser, reason.*
paved bed n. phr. A grave with the top paved in stone MM 5.1.435 *Her brother's ghost his paved bed would break.*
pavement n.
1 Paved thoroughfare (for all traffic) Tʀᴏ 3.3.162 *Or like a...horse fall'n in first rank, Lie there for pavement to the abject rear.*
2 *the marble pavement* The sky Cʏᴍ 5.4.120 *The marble pavement closes, he is enter'd His radiant roof.*
pavilion n. A tent, chiefly applied to one of large or stately kind, rising to a peak above Tʀᴏ 1.3.305 *To our pavilion shall I lead you*, H5 4.1.27, Aɴᴛ 2.2.199.
pavilioned adj. Tented, encamped H5 1.2.129 *lie pavilion'd in the fields of France.*
pavin See ᴘᴀssʏ-ᴍᴇᴀsᴜʀᴇs ᴘᴀᴠɪɴ.
pawn n.
1 Gage of battle R2 1.1.74 *to take up mine honour's pawn.*
2 Stake Lʀ 1.1.155 *My life I never held but as a pawn To wage against thine enemies.*
~ *vb.*
1 Stake, wager, risk WT 2.3.166 *what will you adventure...?—I'll pawn the little blood which I have left To save the innocent*, MV 3.5.82, Lᴜᴄ 156.
2 Forfeit R3 4.4.370 *Thy Garter, blemish'd, pawn'd his knightly virtue*, Aɴᴛ 1.4.32.
3 'Secure by a pledge' (Schmidt) Tʀᴏ 1.3.301 *I'll pawn this truth with my three drops of blood* (F1; Q *proue*).
pax n. Tablet with a projecting handle behind, bearing a representation of the Crucifixion or other sacred subject, which was kissed by the priest and then by the people at mass H5 3.6.40 *he hath stol'n a pax.*
pay vb.
1 'Subdue by liquor' (Steevens) Cʏᴍ 5.4.163 *sorry that you are paid too much.*
2 *pay home* Fully repay WT 5.3.4 *All my services You have paid home;* (with quibble on the fencing sense 'give a home thrust') 1H4 1.3.288 *Till he hath found a time to pay us home.*
peace n.
1 *the peace* The king's peace, the general peace and order of the realm under the king's authority Wɪᴠ 2.3.45 *though I now be...of the peace* (i.e. an officer of the public peace), 2H4 3.2.90; *sworn of the peace made a justice of the peace* Wɪᴠ 2.3.53.
2 *keep peace between* Keep apart Mᴀᴄ 1.5.46 *keep peace between Th' effect and it.*
3 *take peace with* Make peace with H8 2.1.85 *those*

numberless offences 'Gainst me, that I cannot take peace with.
~ *vb.* Be silent Lʀ 4.6.102 *when the thunder would not peace at my bidding*, R2 5.2.81, Tᴍᴘ 2.1.9.
peaceful adj. Free from strife; (hence) unopposed R2 3.2.125 *let the dangerous enemy Measure our confines with such peaceful steps.*
peace-parted adj. Departed this life in peace Hᴀᴍ 5.1.238 *such rest to her As to peace-parted souls.*
peach (aphetic form of) ᴀᴘᴘᴇᴀᴄʜ
1 (trans.) Denounce (one) as being (something) MM 4.3.11 *peaches him a beggar.*
2 (intr.) Turn informer, turn king's evidence 1H4 2.2.44 *If I be ta'en, I'll peach for this.*
peak vb.
1 Mope about Hᴀᴍ 2.2.567 *Yet I...peak...And can say nothing.*
2 Waste away Mᴀᴄ 1.3.23 *dwindle, peak, and pine.*
peaking ppl. adj. Sneaking, skulking Wɪᴠ 3.5.70 *the peaking cornuto her husband.*
pearl n.
1 Cataract in the eye TGV 5.2.13 *such pearls as put out ladies' eyes.*
2 Finest part; (hence) nobility Mᴀᴄ 5.9.22 *I see thee compass'd with thy kingdom's pearl.*
peasant n. Low fellow, rascal TGV 5.2.35 *She's fled unto that peasant Valentine*, Wɪᴠ 2.2.282, Eʀʀ 2.1.81; (attrib.) Hᴀᴍ 2.2.550 *O, what a rogue and peasant slave am I!* (i.e. base).
peasantry n. Low birth, baseness MV 2.9.46 *How much low peasantry would then be gleaned From the true seed of honour?*
peascod-time n. Early summer (when peas are in pod) 2H4 2.4.383 *I have known thee these twenty-nine years, come peascod-time.*
peat n. Pet, darling Sʜʀ 1.1.78 *A pretty peat!*
peck n. Round vessel used as a measure of a peck Wɪᴠ 3.5.111 *in the circumference of a peck.*
peck vb. Pitch, fling H8 5.3.90 *I'll peck you o'er the pales else.*
peculiar adj.
1 Appropriated to an individual, own particular, private MM 1.2.90 *a peculiar river*, Oᴛʜ 1.1.60, Lᴜᴄ 14; *the single and peculiar life* the private individual Hᴀᴍ 3.3.11; *my peculiar care* my concern for myself Cʏᴍ 5.5.83.
pedant n. Schoolmaster, tutor TN 3.2.75 *like a pedant that keeps a school i' th' church*, LLL 3.1.177, Sʜʀ 3.1.4.
pedantical adj. Schoolmasterly LLL 5.2.408 *Three-pil'd hyperboles,...Figures pedantical.*
pedascule n. [vocative of a coined L. 'pedasculus'] Tutor Sʜʀ 3.1.50 *Pedascule, I'll watch you.*
peeled ppl. adj. Tonsured 1H6 1.3.30 *Peel'd priest* (Ff *Piel'd*).
peep n. (early form of) Pip, a spot on a playing card Sʜʀ 1.2.33 *two and thirty, a peep out* (i.e. 32 when 31 is needed).
◇ A ref. to the card game of one-and-thirty or bone-ace. The name of the game was a slang expression to denote someone drunk.
peer vb.¹
1 Come in sight, be seen, appear H5 4.7.85 *a many of your horsemen peer*, WT 4.4.3, Vᴇɴ 86.
2 Let be seen, make to peep out Lᴜᴄ 472 *Who o'er the white sheet peers her whiter chin.*
peer vb.² peer over Rise above, ᴏᴠᴇʀᴘᴇᴇʀ sense 2 Jɴ 3.1.23 *Like a proud river peering o'er his bounds.*
peevish adj.
1 Silly, senseless JC 5.1.61 *A peevish schoolboy*, Wɪᴠ 1.4.14, AYL 3.5.110.
2 Perverse, refractory, obstinate 1H4 3.1.196 *A peevish self-will'd harlotry*, TGV 5.2.49, Cʏᴍ 1.6.54.

peevish-fond adj. Obstinately foolish R3 4.4.417 *be not peevish-fond in great designs.*

▷ Malone; Ff *peeuish found*; Q1 *pieuish, fond*; Qq 3-4 *peeuish fond.*

Peg-a-Ramsey n. The type of a hovering, spoilsport woman in yellow stockings (prob. based on a ballad headed and sung to the tune of 'Pegge of Ramsey') TN 2.3.76 *Malvolio's a Peg-a-Ramsey.*

peise, peize vb.

1 Keep in equilibrium, poise JN 2.1.575 *The world, who of itself is peized well.*

2 Weigh down R3 5.3.105 *Lest leaden slumber peize me down.*

3 *peize the time* 'Weight the time that it may pass slowly' (Steevens) MV 3.2.22 *'tis to peize the time,...to draw it out in length.*

▷ Peise, peize was the name for the weights used in winding a clock.

pelf n. Property, possessions TIM 1.2.62 *Immortal gods, I crave no pelf*, PER 2.Gower.35, PP 14.12.

pelican n. (attrib.) Feeding on their parent's blood LR 3.4.75 *Those pelican daughters.*

▷ Ref. to the fable that the pelican revives or feeds her young with her own blood, cf. R2 2.1.126, HAM 4.5.147.

pellet vb. Form into small globules LC 18 *the brine That seasoned woe had pelleted in tears.*

pelleted ppl. adj. Consisting of pellets (of hail) ANT 3.13.165 *this pelleted storm.*

pell-mell adv. Without keeping ranks; (hence) at close quarters, hand to hand JN 2.1.406 *defy each other, and pell-mell Make work upon ourselves*, LLL 4.3.365, LR 4.6.117.

pelt vb. (fig.) Assail with angry words LUC 1418 *to pelt and swear.*

pelting adj. Paltry, petty R2 2.1.60 *Like to a tenement or pelting farm*, TRO 4.5.267, MM 2.2.112.

Pene gelidus... See PINE GELIDUS...

pencil n. Artist's paintbrush JN 3.1.237 *they were besmear'd...With slaughter's pencil*, SON 16.10, ROM 1.2.41; (used for applying make-up) LLL 5.2.43 *'Ware pencils, ho!*

pencilled ppl. adj. Painted LUC 1497 *sad tales doth tell To pencill'd pensiveness and colour'd sorrow*, TIM 1.1.159.

pendant adj. Hanging unsupported in space MM 3.1.125 *round about The pendant world.*

pendulous adj. Hanging overhead LR 3.4.67 *all the plagues that in the pendulous air Hang.*

penetrate vb. (intr.) Touch the heart CYM 2.3.12 *give her music a' mornings;...it will penetrate.*

penetrative adj. That sounds the depths of the feelings ANT 4.14.75 *penetrative shame.*

pennon n. Flag, banner H5 3.5.49 *pennons painted in the blood of Harfleu.*

pennyworth n.

1 Bargain ADO 2.3.42 *We'll fit the hid-fox with a pennyworth* (i.e. sell him a bargain in which he gets the worst of it), WT 4.4.635.

2 *pennyworth of sugar* Small packet of sugar sold by the tapster to sweeten sack 1H4 2.4.23.

pensioners n. (pl.) Body of gentlemen instituted by Henry VIII to be a bodyguard to the sovereign within the royal palace WIV 2.2.77 *earls, nay, which is more, pensioners;* (transf.) MND 2.1.10 *The cowslips tall her pensioners be.*

pensived adj. Saddened LC 219 *Of pensiv'd and subdued desires.*

penthouse lid n. Eyelid MAC 1.3.20 *Sleep shall neither night nor day Hang upon his penthouse lid.*

penurious adj. Needy TIM 4.3.93 *The want whereof doth daily make revolt In my penurious band.*

peonied See PIONED.

pepper vb. Punish decisively, trounce, make an end

of 1H4 2.4.191 *I have pepper'd two of them*, ROM 3.1.99, 1H4 5.3.36.

pepper-gingerbread n. Hot-spiced gingerbread 1H4 3.1.255 *such protest of pepper-gingerbread* (i.e. namby-pamby protestations).

per se [L.] By himself TRO 1.2.15 *They say he is a very man per se and stands alone.*

Per Styga, per manes vehor [L.] I am carried through Stygian regions, through (the realm of) the shades TIT 2.1.135.

peradventure adv.

1 By chance, by accident MM 3.1.203 *if peradventure he shall ever return*, ADO 1.2.23, MM 4.6.5.

2 Perhaps, maybe 2H4 3.2.295 *Peradventure I will with ye to the court*, AYL 1.2.51, JN 5.6.31.

peradventures adv. Perhaps, maybe WIV 1.1.77 *that peradventures shall tell you another tale.*

perceive vb.

1 (fig.) See through H8 3.2.38 *The King in this perceives him, how he coasts And hedges his own way*, TRO 1.1.36, TRO 4.5.87.

2 Receive TGV 1.1.136 *I could perceive nothing ...from her; no, not so much as a ducat.*

perch n. Measure of land, about 5 metres PER 3.Gower.15 *By many a dern and painful perch.*

perchance adv.

1 By chance, by accident TN 1.2.6 *It is perchance that you yourself were sav'd.*

2 Perhaps TMP 2.2.17 *I'll fall flat, Perchance he will not mind me*, ERR 1.2.86, ROM 2.5.3.

perdie, perdy interj. (lit.) 'By God!'; (hence) certainly, indeed TN 4.2.75 *My lady is unkind, perdie*, ERR 4.4.71, HAM 3.2.294.

perdition n.

1 Destruction, complete ruin OTH 2.2.3 *the mere perdition of the Turkish fleet*, WT 4.4.378, TMP 3.3.77.

2 Loss, diminution TMP 1.2.30 *not so much perdition as an hair*, H5 3.6.98, HAM 5.2.112.

perdu n. Soldier placed in a position of special danger LR 4.7.34 *to watch—poor perdu!—With this thin helm?*

perdurable adj. Lasting, eternal H5 4.5.7 *O perdurable shame!*, OTH 1.3.338.

perdurably adv. Eternally MM 3.1.114 *for the momentary trick Be perdurably fin'd.*

perdy See PERDIE.

peregrinate adj. Having the air of one who has travelled abroad LLL 5.1.14 *he is...too peregrinate.*

peremptorily adv. Decisively 1H4 2.4.429 *peremptorily I speak it.*

peremptory adj.

1 Conclusive, final H5 5.2.82 *our accept and peremptory answer.*

2 Resolved, determined COR 3.1.284 *we are peremptory to dispatch This viperous traitor*, JN 2.1.454.

3 Overbearing 1H4 1.3.17 *your presence is too bold and peremptory*, LLL 4.3.222, 2H6 3.1.8.

perfect vb.

1 Carry through, accomplish AWW 4.4.4 *Ere I can perfect mine intents*, H5 1.1.69.

2 Instruct or inform completely MM 4.3.141 *Her cause and yours I'll perfect him withal*, TMP 1.2.79, PER 3.2.67.

~ adj.

1 Full, mature LR 1.2.72 *sons at perfect age.*

2 Fully prepared MM 5.1.82 *when you have A business for yourself, pray heaven you then Be perfect*, OTH 1.2.31.

3 Thorougly learnt VEN 408 *the lesson...once made perfect, never lost again*; (with in) expert, extremely knowledgeable TIT 3.2.40 *In thy...action will I be as perfect As...hermits in their...prayers*, 1H4 3.1.200, MAC 4.2.66.

4 Sound, sane ERR 5.1.42 *not in his perfect wits*, LR 4.7.62.

5 Correct 2H4 3.1.88 *a perfect guess*, JN 5.6.6, MAC 3.1.129.

6 Completely assured, certain WT 3.3.1 *Thou art perfect then, our ship hath touch'd upon The deserts...?*, CYM 3.1.72; (of statement) accurate, reliable MAC 1.5.2 *the perfect'st report.*

7 Satisfied, contented TIM 1.2.87 *Might we but have that happiness...we should think ourselves for ever perfect*, MAC 3.4.20.

perfection *n.*

1 Accomplishment, performance, execution TRO 3.2.86 *vowing more than the perfection of ten and discharging less than the tenth part of one*, LUC 837, MM 3.1.260.

2 Completed state, final state, highest state TIM 3.6.90 *Smoke and luke-warm water Is your perfection.*

perfectness *n.*

1 Fullness (of time) 2H4 4.4.74 *The Prince will in the perfectness of time Cast off his followers.*

2 Skill, mastery LLL 5.2.174 *Is this your perfectness?*

perfit *adj.* (var. of) PERFECT H5 3.6.70 *perfit in the great commanders' names* (FF).

perfitly *adv.* (var. of) Perfectly H5 3.6.75 *this they con perfitly in the phrase of war.*

perforce *adv.* By violence or constraint, forcibly ERR 4.3.94 *He...took perforce My ring away*, LR 1.4.298, R2 2.3.121.

perform *vb.* (intr.) Do one's part COR 1.1.267 *though he perform To th' utmost of a man*, H8 1.1.35.

performer *n.* Doer, agent TIT 4.1.80 *Performers of this...bloody deed*, AWW 3.6.61, CYM 5.3.30.

perfume *n.* *diseas'd perfume* Perfumed mistress, prostitute TIM 4.3.207 *Hug their diseas'd perfumes.*

perfumer *n.* One employed to perfume rooms ADO 1.3.58 *Being entertain'd for a perfumer.*

perge [L.] Go on, proceed LLL 4.2.53 *perge, so it shall please you to abrogate squirility.*

periapt *n.* Amulet 1H6 5.3.2 *ye charming spells and periapts.*

peril *n.*

1 *at peril* At the risk (of), under the penalty (of) MM 2.4.67 *Pleas'd you to do't at peril of your soul*, LR 3.7.52, MV 4.1.344.

2 *in peril of* Exposed to danger in regard to MV 2.2.164 *to be in peril of my life*; at the risk of, under the penalty of COR 3.3.102 *In peril of precipitation From off the rock Tarpeian.*

3 *in peril to* At the risk of (doing something) SHR Ind.2.122 *In peril to incur your former malady.*

4 *without the peril of* Beyond the dangerous reach of MND 4.1.153 *Without the peril of the Athenian law.*

perilous *adj.*

1 PARLOUS sense 2 R3 3.1.154 *a perilous boy, Bold, quick, ingenious.*

2 Alarming, dreadful, PARLOUS sense 3 ROM 1.3.54 *A perilous knock.*

period *n.*

1 Termination, conclusion 1H6 4.2.17 *The period of thy tyranny approacheth*, R3 1.3.237, OTH 5.2.357.

2 Highest point, acme ANT 4.14.107 *time is at his period.*

3 End, goal WIV 3.3.45 *This is the period of my ambition*, WIV 4.2.221, H8 1.2.209.

4 Pause such as is properly made at the end of a sentence MND 5.1.96 *Make periods in the midst of sentences*, TGV 2.1.116, LUC 565.

~ *vb.* Bring to an end TIM 1.1.99 *Your...letter he desires...which failing, Periods his comfort.*

perish *vb.* Destroy, cause to perish 2H6 3.2.100 *Because thy flinty heart...Might in thy palace perish.*

periwig-pated *adj.* Wearing a wig (the mark of an actor) HAM 3.2.9 *to hear a robustious periwig-pated fellow tear a passion to tatters.*

perjure *n.* One guilty of perjury, perjurer LLL 4.3.46 *like a perjure, wearing papers.*

~ *vb.* Make perjured, corrupt ANT 3.12.30 *want will perjure The ne'er-touch'd vestal.*

perjured note *n.* Paper attached to a perjurer announcing his guilt LLL 4.3.123 *from my forehead wipe a perjur'd note.*

perk *vb.* perk up Trim out H8 2.3.21 *to be perk'd up in a glist'ring grief And wear a golden sorrow.*

pernicious *adj.* Wicked, villainous R2 1.3.82 *thy adverse pernicious enemy*, MM 2.4.150, LR 3.2.22.

perniciously *adv.* 'So as to desire his death' (Wright) H8 2.1.50 *all the commons Hate him perniciously.*

peroration *n.* Rhetorical discourse 2H6 1.1.105 *what means this passionate discourse, This peroration...?*

perpend *vb.* Consider H5 4.4.8 *Perpend my words*, WIV 2.1.115, TN 5.1.299.

persecute *vb.* Harass, trouble, afflict, torture AWW 1.1.14 *persecuted time with hope* (i.e endured pain in the present time in the hope of cure).

persisted *ppl. adj.* Persisted in ANT 5.1.30 *to lament Our most persisted deeds* (i.e. our deeds most persisted in).

persistive *adj.* Steadfast TRO 1.3.21 *find persistive constancy in men.*

person *n.*[1]

1 Bodily figure, personal appearance, bearing HAM 1.2.243 *If it assume my noble father's person*, MND 4.2.11, ANT 2.2.197; *a proper man of person* a fine figure of a man TRO 1.2.193.

2 Personal presence MAC 3.4.127 *Macduff denies his person At our great bidding.*

person *n.*[2] Parson, clergyman LLL 4.2.82 *God give you good morrow, Master Person.*

personage *n.* Personal appearance, figure MND 3.2.292 *her tall personage*, TN 1.5.155.

personal *adj.* Bodily, physical 2H4 4.4.8 *a little personal strength*, JC 1.3.77.

personate *vb.* Represent, typify CYM 5.5.454 *The lofty cedar...Personates thee*, TN 2.3.159, TIM 1.1.69.

perspective *n.*

1 Optical device for producing fantastic images AWW 5.3.48 *Contempt his scornful perspective did lend me*, SON 24.4.

2 Picture or figure constructed so as to produce some fantastic effect, e.g., appearing distorted except from one particular point of view, or presenting totally different aspects from different points R2 2.2.18 *Like perspectives, which rightly gaz'd upon Show nothing but confusion, ey'd awry, Distinguish form*, TN 5.1.217.

perspectively *adv.* As through a PERSPECTIVE (sense 1) H5 5.2.320 *you see them perspectively.*

perspicuous *adj.* Easily seen, conspicuous TRO 1.3.324 *the purpose is perspicuous as substance.*

persuade *vb.*

1 Urge (a person), plead with, advise strongly R3 1.4.146 *persuading me not to kill the Duke*, WIV 1.1.1, LR 2.4.216; *persuade from* dissuade from 2H6 5.3.10 *Persuaded him from any further act*, AYL 1.2.206.

2 Urge (something upon a person) 3H6 3.3.176 *to persuade me patience*, HAM 4.5.169.

3 Use persuasion MM 5.1.93 *How I persuaded, how I pray'd*, MV 3.2.281.

persuading *ppl. adj.* Persuasive H8 4.2.52 *wise, fair-spoken, and persuading.*

persuasion   **pie**

persuasion *n.*

1 Persuasiveness TN 3.4.349 *Is't possible that my deserts to you Can lack persuasion?*

2 Belief, opinion CYM 1.4.114 *too bold a persuasion,* MM 4.1.46, MND 1.1.156.

pert *adj.* Lively, brisk LLL 5.2.272 *This pert Berowne was out of count'nance,* MND 1.1.13.

pertain *vb.* pertain to life Live WT 5.3.113 *If she pertain to life.*

pertaunt *n.* (?) 'Pair-taunt', four cards of a sort (i.e. four kings, etc.) being the winning hand in the game of post and pair LLL 5.2.67 *So pertaunt like would I o'ersway his state* (i.e. overwhelmingly).

◇ F1, Q1 *pert(t)aunt like.* Dover Wilson adopted Moore Smith's emendation *planet-like* which has strong support from the context; cf. 2H6 4.4.16.

pertly *adv.* Briskly, promptly TMP 4.1.58 *Appear, and pertly!*

perturbation *n.* Cause of agitation 2H4 4.5.23 *O polish'd perturbation! golden care!*

perusal *n.*

1 Scrutiny HAM 2.1.87 *He falls to such perusal of my face.*

2 Reading over SON 38.6 *aught in me Worthy perusal.*

peruse *vb.*

1 Survey, inspect ROM 5.3.74 *Let me peruse this face,* ERR 1.2.13, CYM 1.4.6.

2 *peruse over* Read over JN 5.2.5 *we, perusing o'er these notes.*

pervert *vb.* Turn, divert CYM 2.4.151 *Let's...pervert the present wrath He hath against himself.*

pester *vb.* Clog, crowd, obstruct by crowding COR 4.6.7 *behold Dissentious numbers pest'ring streets.*

petar *n.* Small engine of war used to blow in a door or to make a breach HAM 3.4.207 *to have the enginer Hoist with his own petar.*

petition *n.* Clause of a prayer MM 1.2.15 *do relish the petition well that prays for peace.*

~ *vb.* Solicit, beg (for a thing) ANT 1.2.183 *Petition us at home* (i.e. beg for my presence at home).

petitionary *adj.* Suppliant, intreating AYL 3.2.189 *with most petitionary vehemence,* COR 5.2.76.

petitioner *n.* Plaintiff in an action commenced by petition 2H6 1.3.23 *I am but a poor petitioner of our whole township.*

pettiness *n.* Insignificance H5 3.6.129 *losses...which in weight to re-answer, his pettiness would bow under.*

pettish *adj.* Ill-humoured TRO 2.3.130 *watch His pettish lines, his ebbs, his flows* (F1).

pettitoes *n.* (pl.) Feet of a pig, esp. as article of food, pig's trotters; (hence, as term of contempt applied to humans) WT 4.4.607 *he would not stir his pettitoes.*

pew-fellow *n.* Associate (i.e. fellow-mourner). R3 4.4.58 *makes her pew-fellow with others' moan.*

phantasime *n.* Fantastic being LLL 5.1.18 *I abhor such fanatical phantasimes,* LLL 4.1.99.

◇ ROM 2.4.29: see FANTASTICO.

phantasma *n.* Nightmare JC 2.1.65 *Like a phantasma or a hideous dream.*

Phebe *vb.* Treat cruelly, like Phoebe AYL 4.3.39 *She Phebes me.*

Pheezar, Pheazar *n.* Jocular derivative of PHEEZE invented to jingle with *Caesar, Keiser* WIV 1.3.10 *Thou'rt an emperor—Caesar, Keiser, and Pheazar.*

pheeze (var. of) FEEZE.

phil-horse See FILL-HORSE.

Philip *n.* (popular name for) sparrow JN 1.1.231 *Philip? sparrow!*

Philip and Jacob *n.* Festival of St. Philip and St. James, 1st May MM 3.2.202 *a year and a quarter old come Philip and Jacob.*

Philippan *adj.* sword Philippan The sword that triumphed over Brutus and Cassius at Philippi ANT 2.5.23 *I wore his sword Philippan.*

◇ Taken by some as a n., the proper name of the sword.

Philomel(a) *n.* Nightingale MND 2.2.13 *Philomel, with melody, Sing in our sweet lullaby,* LUC 1079, PP 14.17.

philosopher *n. philosopher's stone* Reputed substance supposed by the alchemists to have the property of changing other metals into gold; (alluded to quibblingly) 2H4 3.2.329 *I'll make him a philosopher's two stones,* TIM 2.2.110.

phoenix *n.* (fig.) Unique or matchless person AWW 1.1.168 *Thou shalt your master have...A phoenix;* (attrib.) LC 93 *His phoenix down began but to appear...on that termless skin* (i.e. matchless down).

phrase *n.*

1 Word, expression WIV 1.3.30 *'Steal'? foh! a fico for the phrase!,* 2H4 3.2.72, HAM 2.2.112.

2 Language, phraseology HAM 2.2.443 *no sallets in the lines...nor no matter in the phrase.*

~ *vb.* Describe (a thing) by a name, call, designate H8 1.1.34 *these suns (For so they phrase 'em).*

phraseless *adj.* Beyond description, which there is no word to describe LC 225 *that phraseless hand.*

physic *n.*

1 The healing art PER 3.2.32 *I ever Have studied physic,* LLL 2.1.188; (transf.) ROM 2.3.52 *holy physic.*

2 Medical faculty, physicians CYM 4.2.268 *The sceptre, learning, physic, must All follow this and come to dust.*

~ *vb.* Do (a thing) good, keep in health or vigour CYM 3.2.34 *Some griefs are med'cinable, that is one of them, For it doth physic love,* WT 1.1.38; cure MAC 2.3.50 *The labour we delight in physics pain,* TRO 1.3.377.

physical *adj.* Curative, remedial, beneficial JC 2.1.261 *is it physical To walk unbraced and suck up the humours Of the dank morning?,* COR 1.5.18.

physiognomy *n.* Art of judging character by the features of the face LUC 1395 *In Ajax and Ulysses, O what art Of physiognomy might one behold.*

pia mater *n.* The membrane that covers the brain; (hence, used loosely) the brain TRO 2.1.71 *his pia mater is not worth the ninth part of a sparrow.*

pibble *n.* (var. of) Pebble TGV 2.3.10 *He is...a very pibble stone, and has no more pity in him than a dog.*

pick *vb.* Pitch, throw COR 1.1.200 *as high As I could pick my lance.*

picked *ppl. adj.* Refined, exquisite, fastidious JN 1.1.193 *I suck my teeth, and catechize My picked man of countries* (quibble on the sense 'pick one's teeth'), LLL 5.1.13, HAM 5.1.140.

picker *n. pickers and stealers* Hands HAM 3.2.336.

◇ From Catechism, Book of Common Prayer, 'keep my hands from picking and stealing'.

picking *ppl. adj.* Fastidious 2H4 4.1.196 *such picking grievances.*

pick-thank *n.* Flatterer, sycophant 1H4 3.2.25 *smiling pick-thanks and base newsmongers.*

Pick-hatch *n.* Area of London noted in Eliz. times for brothels, the houses having hatches or half-doors guarded with spikes WIV 2.2.18 *Go...to your manor of Pickt-hatch!*

picture *n.*

1 Statue, image WT 5.2.174 *to see the Queen's picture.*

2 *picture of 'we three'* Picture of two fools or two ass-heads and inscribed 'we three', the spectator being the third TN 2.3.17.

3 *picture in little* Miniature HAM 2.2.366.

pie *n.*¹ Magpie 3H6 5.6.48 *chatt'ring pies.*

pie *n.*² (euphemism) Directory of divine service WIV 1.1.303 *By cock and pie* (i.e. By God and the divine services).

piece *n.*
1 Cask of liquor; (fig.) TRO 4.1.63 *The lees and dregs of a flat tamed piece.*
2 Person, personage, individual; (applied to a woman or girl) TMP 1.2.56 *Thy mother was a piece of virtue*, H8 5.4.26; (sometimes derogatory) TIT 1.1.309 *give that changing piece To him that flourish'd for her with his sword*, PER 4.2.43.
3 Specimen, masterpiece HAM 2.2.303 *What a piece of work is man.*
4 Piece of printing or sculpture, painting, statue WT 5.2.96 *her mother's statue...a piece many years in doing*, TIM 1.1.28, LUC 1443.
5 Piece of money, coin 1H4 2.4.491 *Never call a true piece of gold a counterfeit*, TMP 2.2.29, COR 3.3.32.
~ *vb.* Add to, eke out, augment LC 119 *their purpos'd trim Piec'd not his grace but were all grac'd by him;* (esp. with *out*) TRO 3.1.51 *you shall make it whole again—you shall piece it out with a piece of your performance*, WIV 3.2.34, LR 3.6.2; (with *up*) WT 5.3.56 *so much grief from you as he Will piece up in himself.*

pied *ppl. adj.* Parti-coloured, variegated in colour MV 1.3.79 *all the eanlings which were streak'd and pied*, LLL 5.2.894, TMP 3.2.63.

piedness *n.* The quality of being pied or multi-coloured, variegated colour WT 4.4.87 *an art which in their piedness shares With great creating Nature.*

pigeon-egg *n.* Type of something small LLL 5.1.74 *thou pigeon-egg of discretion.*

pigeon-livered *adj.* Meek, gentle HAM 2.2.577 *I am pigeon-liver'd, and lack gall To make oppression bitter.*
◇ It was a popular belief that pigeons were mild because they lacked gall.

pight *ppl. adj.* (pa. pple. of 'pitch')
1 Pitched TRO 5.10.24 *tents, Thus proudly pight* (F1; Q *pitcht*).
2 Determined, resolved LR 2.1.65 *found him pight to do it.*

pig-nut *n.* Earth-nut, Bunium flexuosum TMP 2.2.168 *I with my long nails will dig thee pig-nuts.*

pike *n.*
1 Spike in the centre of a buckler ADO 5.2.21 *you must put in the pikes with a vice.*
2 Stake about 1.75 metres long, bound with iron, sharp at both ends, driven into the ground as a defence in front of archers 1H6 1.1.116 *He wanted pikes to set before his archers.*
3 Type of lance used in war 3H6 1.1.244 *The soldiers should have toss'd me on their pikes*, 2H4 2.4.50, H5 4.1.40.
4 Pitchfork COR 1.1.23 *Let us revenge this with our pikes, ere we become rakes* (perh. with quibble on sense 3).

Pilch *n.* Outer garment of skin or leather; (used jocularly as a proper name) PER 2.1.12 *What ho, Pilch!*
◇ Malone; Q1 *to pelch?*

pilcher *n.*¹ (var. of) Pilchard TN 3.1.34 *fools are as like husbands as pilchers are to herrings.*

pilcher *n.*² Scabbard ROM 3.1.80 *pluck your sword out of his pilcher.*

pile *n.* The downy nap on velvet or other fabrics; (applied to the cheek) AWW 4.5.97 *a cheek of two pile and a half.*
◇ Velvets were cut in three heights, 'two pile' being double the ordinary closeness, and 'three pile' the best.

piled *adj.* Having a pile like velvet MM 1.2.34 *pil'd, for a French velvet.*

◇ Perh. a play here on 'pilled' (i.e bald) and the connection between baldness and venereal disease, or the 'French disease'.

pill *vb.*
1 Plunder, rob R2 2.1.246 *The commons hath he pill'd with grievous taxes*, R3 1.3.158, TIM 4.1.12.
2 Strip, strip off MV 1.3.84 *The skilful shepherd pill'd me certain wands*, LUC 1167.

pillage *n.* Booty, plunder H5 1.2.195 *Which pillage they with merry march bring home*, 1H6 4.7.41, LUC 428.

pillar *n.* Portable ensign of office in the form of a pillar borne before Wolsey as cardinal H8 2.4.SD *two Gentlemen bearing two great silver pillars.*

pilled *ppl. adj.* Bare; (hence, fig.) beggarly 1H6 1.4.33 *I would be so pill'd esteem'd.*

pillicock *n.* Penis LR 3.4.76 *Pillicock sat on Pillicock-Hill.*

pin *n.*
1 Peg, nail, or stud fixed in the centre of a target LLL 4.1.136 *cleaving the pin* (F2); (fig.) ROM 2.4.15 *the very pin of his heart;* pin-auger, auger for boring holes for pins or pegs R2 3.2.169 *with a little pin Bores through his castle wall.*
2 Type of something insignificant; (hence, used as interj. to express impatience at trifles) WIV 1.1.114 *Tut, a pin!*, TRO 5.2.22.
3 *pin and web* A disease of the eye WT 1.2.291 *Blind with the pin and web*, LR 3.4.117.

pin-buttock *n.* Narrow or sharp buttock AWW 2.2.18 *the pin-buttock, the quatch-buttock,...or any buttock.*

pinch *n.*
1 Bite 1H6 4.2.49 *Not rascal-like, to fall down with a pinch.*
2 Pang (of remorse, sorrow, etc.) TMP 5.1.77 *inward pinches*, CYM 1.1.130, LR 2.4.211.
~ *vb.*
1 Bite 3H6 2.1.16 *a bear...having pinch'd a few dogs.*
2 Gripe 1H4 3.1.28 *with a kind of colic pinch'd;* torment 2H4 1.2.231 *the pox pinches the other.*
3 Distress, afflict, harass, cause discomfort to ANT 2.7.6 *As they pinch one another by the disposition*, TMP 5.1.74, 1H4 1.3.229.

pinched *ppl. adj.* Afflicted, harassed, straitened WT 2.1.51 *I Remain a pinch'd thing* (with quibble on the senses of 'squeezed' and 'made ridiculous').

pinching *ppl. adj.* Distressingly cold CYM 3.3.38 *our pinching cave.*

pinch-spotted *adj.* Discoloured with marks of pinching TMP 4.1.260 *more pinch-spotted make them Than pard or cat o' mountain.*

pine *vb.*
1 Deprive of food, starve VEN 602 *pine the maw.*
2 Consume, wear away R2 5.1.77 *the north, Where shivering cold and sickness pines the clime.*

Pine gelidus timor occupat artus [L.] Cold fear takes hold of the limbs 2H6 4.1.117.
◇ F1; Malone *Pene.*

pinfold *n.* Pound for stray cattle TGV 1.1.107 *I mean the pound—a pinfold*, LR 2.2.9.

pinion *n.* Flight-feather of a wing ANT 3.12.4 *so poor a pinion of his wing.*

pink *n.* The 'flower', acme, finest example ROM 2.4.57 *I am the very pink of courtesy* (with quibble on senses of 'rapier thrust' and the common name of the species Dianthus).

pink *adj.* Winking, half-shut ANT 2.7.114 *Bacchus with pink eyne!*

pinked *ppl. adj.* Ornamented with perforations H8 5.3.48 *her pink'd porringer.*

pinnace *n.* Small light vessel, generally two-masted

2H6 4.1.9 *our pinnace anchors in the Downs*, 2H6 4.1.107, WIV 1.3.80.

pinse *vb.* Put to pain or torture, torment WIV 5.5.130 *fairies will not pinse you*.

pioned *adj.* (?) Excavated, trenched TMP 4.1.64 *Thy banks with pioned and twilled brims*.

pioner *n.* (military) Digger, miner, one employed in minor engineering works H5 3.2.87 *Have you quit the mines? have the pioners given o'er?*, HAM 1.5.163, OTH 3.3.346.

pip See PEEP.

pipe *n. put up one's pipes* Put one's instruments away, cease playing ROM 4.5.96 *we may put up our pipes and be gone*, OTH 3.1.19.

~ *vb. pipe for* Look for in vain, 'whistle for' TIT 4.3.24 *we may go pipe for justice*.

pipe-wine *n.* Wine from the pipe, cask, or 'wood' WIV 3.2.89 *I shall drink in pipe-wine first with him* (with quibble).

piping times *n.* Peaceful times in which the music of the pastoral pipe is heard, instead of that of the martial fife R3 1.1.24 *this piping time of peace*.

pire *vb.* (var. of) peer, pry MV 1.1.19 *Piring in maps for ports and piers and roads* (Q2; F1 *Peering*; Q1 *Piering*).

pismire *n.* ANT 1H4 1.3.240 *stung with pismires*.

pissing-conduit *n.* Popular name of a conduit near the Royal Exchange, which ran with a very small stream 2H6 4.6.3 *I...command that...the pissing-conduit run nothing but claret wine*.

pissing-while *n.* Very short time TGV 4.4.19 *He had not been there...a pissing-while*.

pit *n.*
1 (applied to) Dimple VEN 247 *these round enchanting pits*.
2 Excavation, covered or otherwise hidden to serve as a trap for game or for enemies JC 5.5.23 *Our enemies have beat us to the pit* (i.e. have driven us to the last ditch).

pitch *n.*¹ Type of something foul OTH 2.3.360 *So will I turn her virtue into pitch*.

pitch *n.*² The height to which a falcon soars before stooping or swooping down on its prey 1H6 2.4.11 *Between two hawks, which flies the higher pitch*, 2H6 2.1.12; (fig.) R3 3.7.188 *Seduc'd the pitch and height of his degree To base declension*, TN 1.1.12, R2 1.1.109.

pitch *vb.*
1 Drive (stakes into the ground as a defence against the enemy cavalry) 1H6 1.1.118 *sharp stakes...They pitched in the ground*; (hence) set in order for fighting 3H6 5.4.66 *Here pitch our battle*, 1H6 4.2.23.
2 *pitch and pay* Pay cash H5 2.3.49 *the word is 'Pitch and pay'*.

pitchy *adj.* Pitch-dark, very dark 1H6 2.2.2 *night ...Whose pitchy mantle over-veil'd the earth*, AWW 4.4.24, 3H6 5.6.85.

piteous *adj.* Full of pity, compassionate TMP 1.2.14 *your piteous heart*, R2 5.3.126, Ven 504.

piteously *adv.* So as to excite pity ANT 4.13.9 *word it...piteously*, TIT 5.1.66.

pitfall *n.* Fowler's snare MAC 4.2.35 *never fear the net nor lime, The pitfall nor the gin*.

pith *n.*
1 Strength, vigour, mettle H5 3.Ch.21 *not arriv'd to pith and puissance*, OTH 1.3.83, VEN 26.
2 Importance, gravity HAM 3.1.85 *enterprises of great pith and moment* (F1; Q *pitch*).

pithless *adj.* Weak 1H6 2.5.11 *pithless arms*.

pittance *n.* Scanty meal SHR 4.4.61 *You are like to have a thin and slender pittance*.

pittie-ward *adv.* (?) Towards the Petty or Little

Park in Windsor WIV 3.1.5 *the pittie-ward, the park-ward—every way*.

pittikins *n.* Diminutive of 'pity' CYM 4.2.293 *'Ods pittikins*.

pity *n.*
1 *of pity* Compassionate MV 4.1.27 *an eye of pity*, WT 3.2.123; exciting pity, to be pitied CYM 5.4.47 *A thing of pity!*
2 *it is pity of* It is a sad thing for MND 3.1.43 *If you think I come hither as a lion, it were pity of my life*, MM 2.1.77, OTH 2.3.125.

Piu per dolcera que per forca [It.-Sp.-Portuguese] More by gentleness than by force PER 2.2.27.
◊ Q1 *Pue* PER *doleera kee per forsa*; Malone *Piu*; Rowe (Wilkins) *dolcera*; Malone *que*; Maxwell *forca*.

pizzle *n.* bull's *pizzle* Type of something very thin 1H4 2.4.245 *you starveling,...you bull's pizzle...!*

place *n.*
1 Residence, dwelling AYL 2.3.27 *This is no place, this house is but a butchery*, R3 3.1.69, OTH 1.3.237.
2 Pitch attained by a falcon before swooping on her quarry MAC 2.4.12 *A falcon, tow'ring in her pride of place*.
3 *in place* Present, at hand 3H6 4.1.103 *she was there in place*, MM 5.1.499, SHR 1.2.156.
4 *keep place* Be in agreement or accord WIV 2.1.62 *they do no more adhere and keep place together than...*, TRO 3.3.199.
5 *take place* Find acceptance AWW 1.1.103 *evils ...take place when virtue's steely bones Looks bleak*.
~ *vb.* Put in office, appoint to a place or post, give position to TIM 4.3.36 *place thieves, And give them title*, PER 4.6.193.

placket *n.* Petticoat, skirt, apron; opening or slit in a skirt or petticoat; (hence, transf.) pudendum LR 3.4.97 *Keep thy foot out of brothels, thy hand out of plackets*, TRO 2.3.20, WT 4.4.243.

plague *vb.*
1 Punish, torment JN 2.1.184 *he is not only plagued for her sin*, AWW 1.1.90, R2 3.1.34.
2 Bother, annoy TRO 5.2.105 *I shall be plagued* (i.e. this is a nuisance!).

plain *n.* Field of battle R3 5.3.291 *I will lead forth my soldiers to the plain*, JN 2.1.295, H5 4.6.8.
~ *adj.*
1 Flat, level MND 3.2.404 *Follow me then To plainer ground*, MV 3.1.12, AWW 2.1.31.
2 Smooth ERR 2.2.69 *the plain bald pate of Father Time*, WT 4.4.721.
3 Open, honest LUC 1532 *Such signs of truth in his plain face*, R3 1.1.118, TMP 3.1.82; *plain dealer* one who is open, straightforward and candid ERR 2.2.87 *thou didst conclude hairy men plain dealers without wit*.

plain *vb.*¹ Complain LR 3.1.39 *Of how unnatural and bemadding sorrow The King hath cause to plain*.

plain *vb.*² Explain PER 3.Gower.14 *What's in dumb show I'll plain with speech*.

plaining *n.* Lamentation, complaint LUC 559 *his heart granteth No...entrance to her plaining*, ERR 1.1.72, R3 1.3.175.

plainness *n.* Frankness, openness, honesty, plain-speaking 2H6 1.1.191 *Thy deeds, thy plainness, and thy house-keeping*, SHR 4.4.39, H5 1.2.244.

plain-song *n.* Simple melody or theme H8 1.3.45 *An honest country lord...may bring his plain-song*; (fig.) H5 3.2.6 *the very plain-song* (i.e. the simple truth); (attrib.) MND 3.1.131 *The plain-song cuckoo* (i.e. which sings a plain tune).

plaint *n.* Lamentation R2 5.3.127 *our plaints and prayers*, LUC 1364, 3H6 2.6.23.

plaintful *adj.* Mournful LC 2 *A plaintful story*.

plait See PLEAT.

plaited See PLEATED.

planched ppl. adj. Boarded MM 4.1.30 a planched gate.

plant n. Sole of the foot ANT 2.7.1 Some o' their plants are ill-rooted already (with quibble on the sense 'vegetable').
~ vb. Set up, establish R2 5.1.63 To plant unrightful kings, 1H6 2.5.80, LLL 1.1.164.

plantage n. Plants TRO 3.2.177 As true as steel, as plantage to the moon.
▷ 'Plants were supposed to improve as the moon increases' (Nares).

plantain n. Plant or herb of the genus Plantago, supposed to possess healing powers LLL 3.1.74 no salve, sir, but a plantain (F1, Q1 plantan); (attrib.) ROM 1.2.51 Your plantain leaf is excellent for that (F1 plantan).

plantan See PLANTAIN.

plantation n. Settlement, colonization TMP 2.1.144 Had I plantation of this isle.

plash n. Pool SHR 1.1.23 A shallow plash.

plat n. Plait LC 29 Her hair, nor loose nor tied in formal plat.

plate n. Piece of money, silver coin ANT 5.2.92 realms and islands were As plates dropp'd from his pocket.
~ vb. Clothe in armour R2 1.3.28 plated in habiliments of war; (fig.) LR 4.6.165 Plate sin with gold, And the...lance of justice...breaks.
▷ Pope; F1 Place sinnes.

plated ppl. adj. Clothed in armour ANT 1.1.4 plated Mars.

platform n.
1 Plan 1H6 2.1.77 lay new platforms to endamage them.
2 Level place constructed for mounting guns in a fort HAM 1.2.213 upon the platform where we watch, HAM 1.2.251, OTH 2.3.120.

plausible adj. Such as to be received with favour, agreeable, winning MM 3.1.244 answer his requiring with a plausible obedience.

plausibly adv. Approvingly LUC 1854 The Romans plausibly did give consent To Tarquin's ...banishment.

plausive adj.
1 Deserving of applause or approval, laudable, praiseworthy AWW 1.2.53 his plausive words, HAM 1.4.30.
2 Plausible, specious AWW 4.1.26 a very plausive invention.

play vb. play off Toss off (liquor) 1H4 2.4.17 bid you play it off.

plea n. That which is claimed MV 4.1.198 Though justice be thy plea, MV 3.2.282, LLL 2.1.7.

pleached ppl. adj.
1 (of the arms) Folded ANT 4.14.73 with pleach'd arms.
2 Formed by or fenced with intertwining boughs ADO 3.1.7 the pleached bower, ADO 1.2.9.
▷ See also EVEN-PLEACHED.

plead vb. Utter by way of plea or argument 1H6 2.4.29 If he suppose that I have pleaded truth, MND 1.1.61.

pleasance n. Delight, joy OTH 2.3.292 with joy, pleasance, revel, and applause.

pleasant adj. Jocular, facetious SHR 3.1.58 I have been thus pleasant with you both, LLL 5.1.3, H5 1.2.281.

pleasant-spirited adj. Light-hearted, playful, humorous, jocose ADO 2.1.341 a pleasant-spirited lady.

please vb. (impersonal, in courteous reply) May it

(so) please (you) AYL 4.3.37 Will you hear the letter?—So please you, CYM 2.2.1, R3 4.2.70.

please-man n. Sycophant LLL 5.2.463 Some carrytale, some please-man, some slight zany.

pleaseth (alteration of) please it May it please 2H4 4.1.223 Pleaseth your lordship To meet his Grace, ERR 4.1.12, H5 5.2.78.
An alteration of 'please it'.

pleasing n. Agreeableness R3 1.1.13 the lascivious pleasing of a lute.
~ ppl. adj. Willing (to listen), approving LUC 1126 Relish your nimble notes to pleasing ears.

pleasure n.
1 (one's) Will, desire, choice LLL 1.2.127 the Duke's pleasure is that you keep Costard safe, TMP 1.2.190, MM 1.1.26; of pleasure voluntarily 2H6 5.1.16 Art thou a messenger, or come of pleasure?
2 speak one's pleasure Give free expression to one's thoughts H8 3.2.13 My lords, you speak your pleasures, TRO 3.1.48, TIM 3.1.33.
3 (pl.) Pleasure-grounds JC 3.2.250 common pleasures, To walk abroad and recreate yourselves.
~ vb. Give pleasure to, gratify TIM 3.2.56 I cannot pleasure such an honourable gentleman, 3H6 3.2.22, MV 1.3.7.

pleat n. Fold LUC 93 Hiding base sin in pleats of majesty.

pleated ppl. adj. Wrapped as in pleats, folded; (fig.) concealed LR 1.1.280 Time shall unfold what pleated cunning hides (Qq 1–2; Ff plighted).

plebeii [L.] Plebeians COR 2.3.184 Fast foe to th' plebeii.

pledge n.
1 Bail, surety SHR 1.2.45 I am Grumio's pledge, R2 5.2.44, TIT 3.1.291.
2 Drinking to a person's health, toast JC 4.3.160 My heart is thirsty for that noble pledge, HAM 1.4.12, MAC 3.4.91.
~ vb. Drink to the health of, drink a toast to 2H6 2.3.66 I 'll pledge you all, TIM 1.2.47, ANT 2.7.85.

plenty n. (pl.) Necessaries and comforts of life H5 5.2.35 Dear nurse of arts, plenties, and joyful births.
~ adj. Abundant, plentiful TMP 4.1.110 Earth's increase, foison plenty, 1H4 2.4.239 (F1; Q1 plentifull).

pleurisy n. Abundance, excess HAM 4.7.117 goodness, growing to a pleurisy, Dies in his own too much (F, Q plurisy).

pliant adj. That lends itself to the purpose; (hence) suitable OTH 1.3.151 a pliant hour.

plight n. Pledge, plighting LR 1.1.101 That lord whose hand must take my plight.
~ vb. Give in pledge, pledge TN 4.3.26 Plight me the full assurance of your faith, LR 3.4.123, LLL 5.2.283.

plighted ppl. adj.[1] Pledged 1H6 5.3.162 sign of plighted faith.

plighted ppl. adj.[2] See PLEATED.

plot n. Piece of earth; (hence, fig.) body COR 3.2.102 were there but this single plot to lose.

pluck vb.
1 Draw in a particular direction, draw or bring down, take away AWW 1.1.69 What...my prayers pluck down, R2 5.2.92, H5 4.Ch.42; draw on, incite JN 3.1.57 with her golden hand hath pluck'd on France To tread down...respect, R3 4.2.64; derive SON 14.1 Not from the stars do I my judgement pluck.
2 pluck a crow together Settle accounts, pick a bone together ERR 3.1.83.
3 pluck off Disrobe; (fig.) descend to a lower rank H8 2.3.40 pluck off a little.
4 pluck up (intr.) Rouse yourself, collect yourself ADO 5.1.203 Pluck up, my heart, and be sad.

plume *n.* (?) Plumage TMP 3.3.65 *One dowle that's in my plume* (F1 *plumbe*).

~ *vb.* **plume up** Adorn with feathers; (fig.) trick out, glorify, dress up OTH 1.3.393 *to plume up my will In double knavery* (F1; Q1 *make*).

plume-plucked *adj.* Humbled R2 4.1.108 *plume-pluck'd Richard, who...his high sceptre yields.*

plummet *n.* Plumb-line WIV 5.5.163 *I am not able to answer the Welsh flannel; ignorance itself is a plummet o'er me* (i.e. has sounded me, with a quibble on 'plumbet', a woollen fabric), TMP 3.3.101.

plumpy *adj.* Plump ANT 2.7.114 *Plumpy Bacchus.*

plurisy See PLEURISY.

pocket *vb.* (with *up*)
1 Put away out of sight; (hence) conceal or leave unheeded TMP 2.1.68 *falsely pocket up his report*, ANT 2.2.73.
2 Submit to, put up with JN 3.1.200 *I must pocket up these wrongs*, 1H4 3.3.163.

pocketing *n.* (with *up*) Submission, endurance H5 3.2.51 *it is plain pocketing up of wrongs.*

pocky *adj.* Infected with the pox, usu. syphilis HAM 5.1.166 *many pocky corses.*

point *n.*
1 Highest elevation, summit MND 2.2.119 *the point of human skill.*
2 Conclusion MND 1.2.10 *and so grow to a point.*
3 Order, direction COR 4.6.125 *obeys his points As if he were his officer.*
4 Point of the sword HAM 4.7.146 *I'll touch my point With this contagion*, 1H4 2.4.195, ROM 3.1.160.
5 Tagged lace for attaching hose to the doublet and fastening various parts where buttons are now used ANT 3.13.157 *one that ties his points*, SHR 3.2.48, 2H4 1.1.53.
6 Advantageous position from which the hawk swoops on prey 2H6 2.1.5 *what a point...your falcon made.*
7 *point of war* Short phrase sounded on an instrument as a signal 2H4 4.1.52 *a loud trumpet and a point of war.*
8 *full point* Full stop 2H4 2.4.184 *Come we to full points here?* (with quibble).

~ in phrases
at (a) point 1 In readiness LR 1.4.324 *keep At point a hundred knights*, MAC 4.3.135. 2 Ready *to*, just about *to* COR 3.1.193 *You are at point to lose your liberties*, LR 3.1.33, CYM 3.1.30. 3 Appropriately HAM 1.2.200 *Armed at point exactly* (i.e. in every particular). **at ample point** To the full TRO 3.3.89. **at some hard point** In a tight corner CYM 3.4.16. **no point** Not at all LLL 2.1.190 *Will you prick't with your eye?—No point, with my knife.* **stand on, upon (nice) points** Be overscrupulous MND 5.1.118 *This fellow doth not stand upon points*, 3H6 4.7.58. **to (the) point** To the smallest detail, exactly MM 3.1.245 *agree with his demands to the point*, TMP 1.2.194.

~ *vb.*[1]
1 Indicate to, direct (a person) WT 4.4.561 *The which shall point you forth...What you must say*, HAM 1.5.129, LLL 2.1.245.
2 *point on* Direct (its) rays on R2 1.3.147 *those his golden beams...Shall point on me*; (hence with astrological connotations) direct an influence towards JC 1.3.32 *portentous things Unto the climate that they point upon*, SON 26.10.

point, 'point *vb.*[2] (aphetic form of) APPOINT LUC 879 *thou 'point'st the season*, LUC 2.1.15, SON 14.6.

point-blank *n.* (fig.) Range, reach 2H6 4.7.26 *within point-blank of our jurisdiction.*

point-device, point-devise *adj.* Extremely precise

LLL 5.1.18 *such insociable and point-device companions*, AYL 3.2.382.

~ *adv.* Precisely TN 2.5.163 *I will be point-devise the very man.*

pointed *ppl. adj.* (aphetic form of) Appointed SHR 3.1.19 *I'll not be tied to hours nor pointed times*, SHR 3.2.1.

pointing-stock *n.* Object of ridicule 2H6 2.4.46 *a pointing-stock To every idle rascal follower.*

poise *n.*
1 Weight; (fig.) 3H6 2.5.13 *the equal poise of this fell war* (i.e. equipoise, balance), MM 2.4.68, OTH 3.3.82.
2 Impact, heavy blow TRO 1.3.207 *the great swinge and rudeness of his poise.*

~ *vb.*
1 Weigh, estimate AWW 2.3.154 *We poising us in her defective scale*, TRO 1.3.339, ROM 1.2.95.
2 Counterbalance OTH 1.3.327 *one scale of reason to poise another of sensuality.*

poison *vb.* empoison, destroy OTH 5.2.364 *The object poisons sight*, ROM 3.2.46, LLL 4.3.301.

poisoned *ppl. adj.* Empoisoned, destroyed 1H6 5.4.121 *The hollow passage of my poison'd voice.*

poisonous *adj.* Destructive of COR 5.3.135 *poisonous of your honour.*

poke *n.* Pocket AYL 2.7.20 *he drew a dial from his poke.*

poking-stick *n.* Rod used for stiffening the plaits of ruffs WT 4.4.226 *poking-sticks of steel.*

Polack *n.* Pole HAM 4.4.23 *the Polack never will defend it.*

~ *adj.* Polish HAM 5.2.376 *from the Polack wars.*

pole *n.*[1] Pole star OTH 2.1.15 *th' ever-fixed Pole*, HAM 1.1.36; (fig., symbol of constant determination) lodestar, guiding star ANT 4.15.65 *The soldier's pole is fall'n!*

pole *n.*[2] See POLL.

polecat, poulcat *n.* (term of contempt) Prostitute WIV 4.2.185 *you baggage, you polecat, you runnion!* (F1 *poulcat*).

pole-clipt *adj.* Hedged in with poles TMP 4.1.68 *thy pole-clipt vineyard.*
◇ Perh. var. of *poll-clipt*, i.e. pruned, pollarded.

policy *n.*
1 Prudence in the conduct of affairs ADO 4.1.198 *Both strength of limb, and policy of mind*, R2 5.1.84, SON 118.9.
2 Form of government, established regime LR 1.2.46 *This policy and reverence of age.*
3 Conduct of affairs, administration of government H5 1.1.45 *Turn him to any cause of policy*, TRO 1.3.197.
4 Contrivance, crafty device, stratagem COR 3.2.42 *Honour and policy...I' th' war do grow together*, AWW 1.1.121, 1H6 3.2.2.

politic *adj.* Dealing with political science TN 2.5.161 *I will read politic authors.*

politician *n.* Schemer, crafty intriguer LR 4.6.171 *a scurvy politician*, 1H4 1.3.241, TN 3.2.32.

poll *n.*
1 Head HAM 4.5.196 *flaxen was his poll*, 2H4 2.4.259.
2 (in numbering) Unit AWW 4.3.167 *fifteen thousand poll.*
3 Number of persons, muster COR 3.1.134 *We are the greater poll; by the poll* by counting of heads COR 3.3.10.
◇ *pole*: var. spelling in all senses.

polled *ppl. adj.* Stripped (properly, of branches or foliage) COR 4.5.202 *He will mow all down...and leave his passage poll'd* (F1, *poul'd*).

pomander *n.* Perfumed ball WT 4.4.598 *not a ribbon, glass, pomander, brooch.*

pomewater *n.* Large juicy kind of apple LLL 4.2.4 *ripe as the pomewater.*

pomp *n.* Triumphal or ceremonial procession, pageant TIM 1.2.242 *these feasts, pomps, and vainglories,* MND 1.1.15, TIT 1.1.176.

Pompion *n.* (var. of) PUMPION LLL 5.2.502 *I am...Pompion the Great* (error for 'Pompey').

pompous *adj.* Invested or attended with pomp or splendour AYL 5.4.182 *the pompous court,* PER 3.Gower.4, R2 4.1.250.

ponderous *adj.* (fig.) Weighty LR 1.1.78 *my love's More ponderous than my tongue,* WT 4.4.524.

poniard *n.* Dagger 3H6 2.1.98 *Stab poniards in our flesh,* AWW 4.1.76, HAM 5.2.149; (fig.) ADO 2.1.247 *She speaks poniards, and every word stabs.*

poop *vb.* Cause to founder, swamp, overwhelm PER 4.2.24 *she quickly poop'd him, she made him roast-meat for worms* (i.e. by infecting with syphilis).

poor-John *n.* Salted hake (a cheap fish) ROM 1.1.31 *'Tis well thou art not fish; if thou hadst, thou hadst been poor-John,* TMP 2.2.27.

poorly *adv.* Meanly, unworthily MAC 2.2.69 *Be not lost So poorly in your thoughts,* R2 3.3.128, H5 4.2.41.

poother See POTHER.

poperin *adj.* Variety of pear ROM 2.1.38 *a pop'rin pear.*

popingay, popinjay *n.* Parrot; (hence) prattler 1H4 1.3.50 *pest'red with a popingay.*

popular *adj.* Belonging to the common people; (hence) plebeian, low, vulgar H5 4.1.38 *art thou officer, Or art thou base, common, and popular?,* TMP 1.2.92, COR 2.3.101.

popularity *n.* Keeping company with the common people, vulgarity H5 1.1.59 *sequestration From open haunts and popularity,* 1H4 3.2.69.

populous *adj.* Numerous ANT 3.6.50 *your populous troops.*

porch *n.* Portico JC 1.3.126 *stay for me In Pompey's Porch* (i.e. the portico of a theatre built by Pompey).

poring *ppl. adj.* Looking closely as if short-sighted, peering H5 4.Ch.2 *the poring dark.*
⋄ Perh. 'the dark which causes men to strain their eyes to see'.

porpentine *n.* Porcupine HAM 1.5.20 *quills upon the...porpentine,* 2H6 3.1.363; (applied as a term of reproach to a person) TRO 2.1.26 *Do not, porpentine, do not, my fingers itch;* name of an inn ERR 3.1.116.

porridge *n.* Pottage, soup ERR 2.2.99 *at dinner they should not drop in his porridge,* LR 3.4.55, TMP 2.1.10.

porringer *n.* Basin from which soft or liquid food is eaten SHR 4.3.64 *this was moulded on a porringer;* (applied humorously to a cap) H8 5.3.48 *her pink'd porringer fell off her head.*

port *n.*¹ Gate COR 5.6.6 *Him I accuse The city ports by this hath enter'd,* AWW 3.5.36, ANT 4.4.23; (fig.) 2H4 4.5.24 *the ports of slumber.*

port *n.*²
1 Bearing, carriage, demeanour H5 Prol.6 *Assume the port of Mars,* 2H6 4.1.19, ANT 4.14.52.
2 Style of living, state, social station SHR 1.1.203 *Keep house and port and servants, as I should,* MV 1.1.124, MV 3.2.281.

portable *adj.* Bearable, endurable LR 3.6.108 *How light and portable my pain seems now,* MAC 4.3.89.

portage *n.*¹ The freight or cargo, which a sailor was entitled to put on board, if he took part in the common adventure and did not receive wages, or which formed part of his wages; (fig.) PER 3.1.35 *Thy loss is more than can thy portage quit With all thou canst find here.*

portage *n.*² Port-holes; (fig.) H5 3.1.10 *through the portage...Like the...cannon.*

portance *n.* Behaviour COR 2.3.224 *his present portance, Which...he did fashion After the...hate he bears you,* OTH 1.3.139.

portcullis *vb.* Enclose as with a portcullis (a grating made to slide up and down vertical grooves at each side of a gateway) R2 1.3.167 *portcullis'd my tongue, Doubly portcullis'd with my teeth and lips.*

portend *vb.* Signify TN 2.5.119 *what should that alphabetical position portend?*

portly *adj.* Stately, dignified, majestic MV 1.1.9 *with portly sail,* ROM 1.5.66, 1H4 1.3.13.

posied *adj.* Inscribed with a motto LC 45 *many a ring of posied gold and bone.*

position *n.* Affirmation, affirmative assertion OTH 3.3.234 *I do not in position Distinctly speak of her,* OTH 2.1.236, TRO 3.3.112.

positive *adj.*
1 Admitting no question, certain WIV 3.2.48 *it is as positive as the earth is firm that Falstaff is there,* H5 4.2.25.
2 Absolute TRO 2.3.65 *Patroclus is a fool positive.*

positively *adv.* With assurance or confidence R3 4.2.25 *Before I positively speak in this,* HAM 2.2.154.

possess *vb.*
1 Be in occupation CYM 1.5.48 *let instructions enter Where folly now possesses.*
2 Take possession of, seize, take TMP 3.2.92 *Remember First to possess his books,* 3H6 1.1.26, ROM 3.2.27.
3 (with *of* or *with*) Put in possession *of,* endow with ANT 3.11.21 *I will possess you of that ship;* (refl.) take possession *of* LUC Arg.5 *Lucius...had possessed himself of the kingdom;* (pass.) be in possession of R2 2.1.162 *Whereof our uncle Gaunt did stand possess'd,* JN 4.2.9, SON 29.6.
4 Inform, acquaint TRO 4.4.112 *I'll...possess thee what she is,* MM 4.1.43, TN 2.3.138.

possessed *ppl. adj.* Seized with a passion to R2 2.1.108 *thou...art possess'd now to depose thyself.*

possession *n.* The condition of being possessed by a spirit or demon ERR 5.1.44 *How long hath this possession held the man?*

posset *n.* Drink composed of hot milk curdled with ale, wine, etc., used as a delicacy and as a remedy WIV 1.4.8 *we'll have a posset for't soon,* MAC 2.2.6, WIV 5.5.171 *(eat a posset).*
~ *vb.* Curdle like a posset HAM 1.5.68 *it doth posset And curd* (F1; Qq 2–4 *posesse*).

possibility *n.*
1 Capability, capacity AWW 3.6.82 *I...to the possibility of thy soldiership will subscribe for thee,* 2H4 4.3.35; chance (of having something) 1H6 5.4.146 *I'll rather keep That which I have than...Be cast from possibility of all.*
2 Pecuniary prospects, 'expectations' WIV 1.1.64 *Seven hundred pounds, and possibilities, is goot gifts.*
3 *speak with possibility* Speak of things within the range of possibility TIT 3.1.214 (Q1; F1 *possibilities*).

post *n.*¹
1 Pole, column, etc., set up in the ground and used to display public notices WT 3.2.101 *myself on every post Proclaim'd a strumpet;* pole set up by the door of a sheriff TN 1.5.148 *he'll stand at your door like a sheriff's post.*
2 Doorpost on which the reckoning at a tavern was kept ERR 1.2.64 *I shall be post indeed, For she will score your fault upon my pate.*

post *n.²*
1 Courier MV 5.1.46 *there's a post come...with his horn full of good news*, MAC 1.3.98, 2H4 Ind.37.
2 Post-horse, a horse for rapid travel, available for hire at a post-house or inn 2H4 4.3.36 *I have found'red ninescore and odd posts; take post* start on a journey with post-horses ROM 5.1.21 *I...presently took post to tell it you.*
3 *in post* In haste ERR 1.2.63 *I from my mistress come to you in post* (i.e. at express speed), WT 2.1.182; (similarly with *such*) 3H6 1.2.48 *in such post.*
~ *vb.*
1 Go with haste, speed, hasten CYM 5.5.283 *away he posts*, R2 1.1.56, LR 3.7.1.
2 Convey swiftly CYM 2.4.27 *The swiftest harts have posted you by land.*
3 *post over* Hurry over, pass off easily 2H6 3.1.255 *His guilt should be but lightly posted over.*
4 *post off* Put off 3H6 4.8.40 *I have not...posted off their suits with slow delays.*
~ *adv.* In haste R2 5.2.112 *Spur post, and get before him to the king*, 2H4 2.4.378, AWW 4.5.80.

poster *n.* Swift traveller MAC 1.3.33 *The weird sisters, ...Posters of the sea and land.*

postern *n.* Small back or side door TGV 5.1.9 *Go on...Out at the postern by the abbey wall*, MM 4.2.89, WT 1.2.438; (fig.) R2 5.5.17 *as for a camel To thread the postern of a...needle's eye.*

post-haste *n.* Great expedition HAM 1.1.107 *this post-haste and romage in the land.*
~ *adv.* With all possible haste R2 1.4.55 *hath sent post-haste.*
▷ See HASTE-POST-HASTE and POST-POST-HASTE.

posting *n.* Speedy travelling, haste AWW 5.1.1 *this exceeding posting*, SON 51.4.
~ *ppl. adj.* Swift, hurrying, fleeting CYM 3.4.36 *the posting winds.*

post-post-haste *adv.* (emphatic form of) POST-HASTE OTH 1.3.46 *Write from us to him, post-post-haste. Dispatch!*
▷ Steevens; F1 *Post, Post-haste*; Q1 *wish him post post-haste.*

posture *n.* Particular position of a weapon in drill or warfare JC 5.1.33 *The posture of your blows are yet unknown.*

posy *n.* (syncopation of) Poesy, motto, orig. a line or verse of poetry, inscribed on the inside of a finger-ring HAM 3.2.152 *Is this a prologue, or the posy of a ring?*, MV 5.1.148, MV 5.1.151.

pot *n.* *to the pot* To destruction COR 1.4.47.

potato *n.* The Spanish or sweet potato, Batatas edulis, in 16–17C thought to have aphrodisiac qualities, WIV 5.5.19 *Let the sky rain potatoes;* (attrib.) TRO 5.2.56 *potato finger.*

potch *vb.* Thrust at COR 1.10.15 *I 'll potch at him.*

potent *n.* Potentate JN 2.1.358 *You equal potents, fiery kindled spirits!*

potential *adj.* Powerful LR 2.1.76 *potential spirits*, LC 2.04, OTH 1.2.13.

pothecary *n.* (apheticform of) Apothecary, pharmacist ROM 5.3.289 *he did buy a poison Of a poor pothecary*, PER 3.2.9.

pother *n.* Disturbance, commotion, turmoil COR 2.1.218 *such a pother* (Ff *poother*), LR 3.2.50 (Q1 *Powther*; Ff *pudder*; Qq 2–3 *Thundring*).

potting *n.* Tippling OTH 2.3.77 *they are most potent in potting.*

pottle *n.* Measure of capacity for liquids, two (Imperial) quarts (2.27 litres) WIV 3.5.29 *a pottle of sack*; pot or tankard containing this capacity OTH 2.3.84 *ere the next pottle can be fill'd.*

pottle-deep *adv.* To the bottom of the tankard OTH 2.3.54 *carous'd Potations pottle-deep.*

pottle-pot *n.* Pot or tankard containing a POTTLE 2H4 5.3.64 *you'll crack a quart together...?—Yea, sir, in a pottle-pot*, 2H4 2.2.78.

pouch *n.* Purse WIV 1.3.87 *Tester I 'll have in pouch when thou shalt lack*, AYL 2.7.159.

poulcat See POLECAT.

poulter *n.* Poulterer 1H4 2.4.437 *hang me up by the heels for...a poulter's hare.*

pouncet-box *n.* Small box for perfumes 1H4 1.3.38 *he held A pouncet-box, which ever and anon He gave his nose.*

pound *n.¹* Pound-weight COR 3.1.312 *Tie leaden pounds to 's heels.*

pound *n.²* Public enclosure for stray cattle, pinfold TGV 1.1.107 *I mean the pound—a pinfold.*
~ *vb.* Shut up as in a pound TGV 1.1.104 *you are astray; 'twere best pound you*, COR 1.4.17.

pourquoi [Fr.] Why TN 1.3.90 *Pourquoi, my dear knight?*

poverty *n.* Poor stuff SON 103.1 *what poverty my Muse brings forth*, SON 40.10.

pow *interj.* (var. of) Pooh. See POW WAW.

powder *vb.* Salt 1H4 5.4.112 *to powder me and eat me.*

powdered *ppl. adj.* (lit.) Salted; (hence) subjected to the sweating-tub treatment MM 3.2.59 *your fresh whore and your powder'd bawd.*

powdering-tub *n.* (lit.) Pickling-vat; (humorously applied to) sweating-tub used for the 'cure' of venereal disease H5 2.1.75 *the powd'ring-tub of infamy.*

power *n.*
1 Person of rank or influence H8 2.4.113 *Where pow'rs are your retainers.*
2 Body of armed men, fighting force LUC 1368 *the power of Greece*, JN 4.2.110, LR 3.1.30; (pl.) forces JC 4.1.42 *Brutus and Cassius Are levying powers.*
3 Faculty HAM 3.2.174 *My operant powers their functions leave to do*, MV 3.2.177, MND 2.2.143.

pow, waw *interj.* (var. of) Pow wow, pooh pooh, nonsense! COR 2.1.142 *The gods grant them true!—True? pow, waw.*

pox *n.*
1 Syphilis, venereal disease PER 4.6.16 *the way to the pox*, 2H4 1.2.231.
2 (in imprecations and exclamations of irritation (esp. with *on, upon*)) Plague upon, curse upon TMP 1.1.40 *A pox o' your throat*, AWW 3.6.46, PER 4.6.13.

prabble *n.* (Welsh characters' pronunciation of) BRABBLE WIV 1.1.55 *if we leave our pribbles and prabbles* (Evans' speech), H5 4.8.65 (Fluellen).

practic *adj.* Practical H5 1.1.51 *the art and practic part of life.*

practice *n.*
1 Execution ADO 5.1.248 *paid me richly for the practice of it; put in practice* put into execution TGV 3.2.88 *thy advice this night I 'll put in practice*, LLL 1.1.306, PP 15.7.
2 Stratagem, conspiracy, trickery, plot, intrigue TN 5.1.352 *This practice hath most shrewdly pass'd upon thee*, MM 5.1.107, HAM 4.7.138.

practisant *n.* One who carries out a stratagem, conspirator, plotter, intriguer, schemer 1H6 3.2.20 *Pucelle and her practisants.*

practise *vb.*
1 Perform, carry on 1H6 2.3.47 *aught...Whereon to practise your severity*, JC 4.3.88.
2 Use stratagem or artifice, scheme, plot (with *against, on, upon*) AYL 1.1.150 *he will practise against thee by poison*, H5 2.2.99, OTH 1.2.73.
3 Plot (some evil) JN 4.1.20 *My uncle practises more harm to me*, ROM 3.5.209.

practiser *n.* Practitioner, physician AWW 2.1.185 *Sweet practiser, thy physic I will try.*

Praeclarissimus filius noster Henricus, Rex Angliae, et Heres Franciae [L.] Our most renowned son Henry, king of England and heir to France H5 5.2.341.

praemunire *n.* (more fully 'praemunire facias') A writ by which the sheriff is charged to summon a person accused of maintaining papal jurisdiction in England H8 3.2.340 *Fall into th' compass of a praemunire.*

praetor *n.* Magistrate in ancient Rome, subordinate to the consuls JC 2.4.35 *The throng...Of senators, of praetors.*

praise *n.* That for which a person or thing deserves to be praised, desert, virtue TRO 2.2.145 *So to be valiant is no praise at all,* MV 5.1.108, PER 1.1.15; *praise in departing* (var. of proverbial phr. 'praise at parting') praise given not too soon, not till entertainment is over TMP 3.3.39.

~ *vb.* Appraise, value TN 1.5.249 *Were you sent hither to praise me?*, TRO 3.2.90.

praised *ppl. adj.* Esteemed PER 3.2.101 *The diamonds Of a most praised water.*

praiseful *adj.* Laudable LLL 4.2.56 *The praiseful Princess pierc'd...a...pricket.*

◊ F2 *praysfull*, Ff 3–4 *prais(e)full*; F1, Qq *prayful*; Collier *preyful*. See PREYFUL.

prank *n.* Malicious or mischievous deed or trick OTH 2.1.142 *foul pranks,* HAM 3.4.2, ERR 2.2.208.

prank *vb.* Dress up, adorn TN 2.4.86 *that miracle and queen of gems That nature pranks her in,* WT 4.4.10; (fig.) COR 3.1.23 *they do prank them in authority.*

prat *vb.* Beat about the buttocks WIV 4.2.184 *Come, Mother Prat...- I 'll prat her.*

prate *n.* Prattle, chatter JN 4.1.25 *his innocent prate,* 1H6 4.1.124.

~ *vb.*

1 Prattle, chatter, talk idly R3 1.3.349 *Tut, tut, my lord, we will not stand to prate,* WIV 1.4.121, ERR 2.2.193.

2 Speak insolently OTH 1.2.6 *he prated, And spoke such scurvy and provoking terms,* OTH 2.3.150; speak boastfully 2H4 3.2.305 *prate to me of the wildness of his youth,* TMP 2.1.263.

pray *vb.*

1 Invite MM 2.1.278 *I pray you home to dinner with me.*

2 *pray in aid* (legal term) Beg for assistance ANT 5.2.27 *A conqueror that will pray in aid for kindness.*

preachment *n.* Obstrusive or wearisome discourse 3H6 1.4.72 *made a preachment of your high descent?*

preambulate *vb.* Walk in front LLL 5.1.81 *Artsman, preambulate.*

precedence *n.* Something said before LLL 3.1.82 *an epilogue...to make plain Some obscure precedence,* ANT 2.5.51.

precedent *n.*

1 Sign, token VEN 26 *The precedent of pith and livelihood* (Q1 *president*).

2 Original from which a copy is made JN 5.2.3 *let this be copied out,...Return the precedent to these lords again* (F1 *president*), R3 3.6.7.

~ *adj.* Former HAM 3.4.98 *your precedent lord,* TIM 1.1.133, ANT 4.14.83.

precept *n.*

1 Instruction, direction TMP 3.1.58 *my father's precepts,* LC 267, HAM 2.2.142 (Qq 2–4 *prescripts*).

2 Writ requiring something to be done H5 3.3.26 *send precepts to the leviathan To come ashore,* 2H4 5.1.13.

preceptial *adj.* Consisting of precepts ADO 5.1.24 *give preceptial med'cine to rage.*

precinct *n.* Quarter over which a person has control 1H6 2.1.68 *Within her quarter and mine own precinct.*

precious *adj.*

1 Egregious, arrant, complete CYM 3.5.81 *you precious pandar!*, OTH 5.2.235.

2 Fastidious, sensitive CYM 1.6.37 *spectacles so precious.*

~ *adv.* Preciously JN 4.3.40 *too precious princely for a grave,* TRO 5.3.28, ROM 2.3.8.

◊ Freq. spelt with hyphen in mod. edd.

preciously *adv.* As a valuable thing TMP 1.2.241 *The time...Must...be spent most preciously.*

precipit *n.* Precipice H8 5.1.139 *You take a precipit for no leap of danger* (F1 *Precipit*).

precipitate *vb.* Fall headlong LR 4.6.50 *So many fathom down precipitating.*

precipitation *n.* Steepness of descent, precipitousness COR 3.2.4 *That the precipitation might down stretch Below the beam of sight.*

precise *adj.* Strict in the observance of rule or form, punctilious MM 1.3.50 *Lord Angelo is precise,* WIV 2.2.22, 2H4 2.3.40.

preciseness *n.* Scrupulousness, propriety 1H6 5.4.67 *Is all your strict preciseness come to this?*

precisian *n.* One who is precise in the observance of forms, religion, etc. WIV 2.1.5 *though Love use Reason for his precisian, he admits him not for his counsellor* (i.e. punctilious instructor).

pre-contract *n.* Previous engagement of marriage MM 4.1.71 *He is your husband on a pre-contract.*

precurrer *n.* Forerunner PHT 6 *Foul precurrer of the fiend.*

precurse *n.* Heralding HAM 1.1.121 *the like precurse of fear'd events.*

predeceased *ppl. adj.* Previously extinct, by now extinct H5 5.1.72 *worn as a memorable trophy of predeceased valour.*

predecessor *n.* Ancestor H5 1.2.248 *your great predecessor, King Edward the Third,* COR 2.1.91, MAC 2.4.34.

predicament *n.* Condition, situation 1H4 1.3.168 *the line and the predicament Wherein you range,* MV 4.1.357, ROM 3.3.86.

predict *n.* Prediction SON 14.8 *By oft predict that I in heaven find* (i.e. frequent signs).

predominance *n.* Ascendancy of a planet LR 1.2.123 *thieves and treachers by spherical predominance.*

predominant *adj.* In the ascendant, ruling AWW 1.1.197 *you must needs be born under Mars.— When he was predominant,* WT 1.2.202.

predominate *vb.*

1 Have ascendancy (like a planet) WIV 2.2.282 *I will predominate over the peasant.*

2 (trans.) Prevail over TIM 4.3.143 *Let your close fire predominate his smoke.*

prefer *vb.*

1 Place or put before a person, put forward, present, offer 1H6 3.1.10 *in writing I prefer'd The manner of thy...crimes,* JC 3.1.28, OTH 1.3.109.

2 Introduce, recommend 2H6 4.7.72 *my book prefer'd me to the King,* TGV 2.6.15, SHR 1.1.97.

preferment *n.*

1 Advancement, promotion 2H6 1.1.181 *these do labour for their own preferment,* OTH 1.1.36, R3 1.3.94.

2 Preference for, priority given to SHR 2.1.93 *the preferment of the eldest sister.*

preformed *ppl. adj.* Formed beforehand; (hence) innate, inherited JC 1.3.67 *all these things change from their...preformed faculties.*

pregnancy *n.* Readiness or quickness (of wit) 2H4 1.2.170 *pregnancy is made a tapster, and his quick wit wasted in giving reckonings.*

pregnant adj.[1]
1 Clear, obvious MM 2.1.23 *'Tis very pregnant, The jewel that we find, we stoop and take't*, WT 5.2.30, ANT 2.1.45.
2 Pressing, cogent, compelling LR 2.1.76 *the profits of my death Were very pregnant and potential spurs To make thee seek it* (Q1 *spurres*; F1 *spirits*: see PREGNANT adj.[2] sense 2.

pregnant adj.[2]
1 Resourceful, ready, apt TN 2.2.28 *the pregnant enemy*, MM 1.1.11, HAM 2.2.209.
2 Receptive TN 3.1.89 *your own most pregnant and vouchsafed ear*; (hence) disposed, inclined LR 4.6.223 *pregnant to good pity*, HAM 3.2.61.
▷ In F reading of LR 2.1.76 *pregnant* prob. has this sense. See PREGNANT adj.[1] sense 2.

pregnantly adv. Cogently, clearly TIM 1.1.92 *paintings...That shall demonstrate these...blows...More pregnantly than words.*

prejudicate vb. Pass judgement upon beforehand AWW 1.2.8 *our dearest friend Prejudicates the business.*

prejudice n. Injury, detriment H8 1.1.182 *the interview...might...Breed him some prejudice*, H8 2.4.155.
~ vb. Injure 1H6 3.3.91 *how we may prejudice the foe.*

premise n. (pl.)
1 Conditions, stipulations AWW 2.1.201 *the premises observ'd*, TMP 1.2.123.
2 Previous circumstances H8 2.1.63 *'T has done, upon the premises, but justice* (i.e. given the previous circumstances).

premised ppl. adj. Sent before the time 2H6 5.2.41 *the premised flames of the last day.*

prenominate vb. Name beforehand TRO 4.5.250 *to prenominate...Where thou wilt hit me dead.*
~ ppl. adj. Aforesaid, mentioned earlier HAM 2.1.43 *the prenominate crimes.*

prenzie n. and adj. (?) (doubtful word; prob. error) MM 3.1.93 *The prenzie Angelo?*; MM 3.1.96 *to invest and cover In prenzie guards.*

pre-ordinance n. Previously established ordinance JC 3.1.38 *turn pre-ordinance and first decree Into the law of children.*

preparation n.
1 Force or fleet equipped for fight OTH 1.3.14 *The Turkish preparation makes for Rhodes*, COR 1.2.15, 1H4 4.1.93.
2 Accomplishment WIV 2.2.228 *Your many warlike...and learned preparations.*

prepare n. Preparation 3H6 4.1.131 *make prepare for war.*

preposterous adj. Inverting the natural order of things SHR 3.1.9 *Preposterous ass.*

preposterously adv. Unnaturally H5 2.2.112 *wrought upon thee so preposterously*, MND 3.2.121, OTH 1.3.62.

prerogative n. Precedence, pre-eminence TMP 1.2.105 *executing th' outward face of royalty With all prerogative*, SHR 3.1.6, AWW 2.4.41.

prerogatived adj. Privileged OTH 3.3.274 *Prerogativ'd are they less than the base.*

presage n.
1 Omen, portent JN 1.1.28 *sullen presage of your own decay*, JN 3.4.158, VEN 457.
2 Prognostication SON 107.6 *the sad augurs mock their own presage.*
3 Presentiment, foreboding R2 2.2.142 *heart's presages.*

presager n. That which indicates SON 23.10 *let my books be...dumb presagers of my speaking breast.*

prescribe vb. Limit, restrict LR 1.2.24 *Prescrib'd his pow'r...?* (Qq *subscribed*).

prescript n. Direction, instruction ANT 3.8.5 *Do not exceed The prescript of this scroll.*
~ adj. Prescribed, laid down H5 3.7.46 *the prescript praise...of a good...mistress.*

prescription n. Claim founded upon long use 3H6 3.3.94 *a silly time To make prescription for a kingdom's worth.*

presence n.
1 Presence-chamber, reception-room in which a sovereign receives guests or others entitled to see him H8 3.1.17 *the two great Cardinals Wait in the presence*, R2 1.3.289, ROM 5.3.86.
2 Assembly, company HAM 5.2.228 *This presence knows*, LLL 5.2.533, R2 4.1.32.
3 (with possessive) Person, personality 1H4 3.2.56 *My presence...Ne'er seen but wond'red at*, JN 1.1.137, R2 3.3.76.
4 *in presence* Present 2H4 4.4.17 *he is in presence here*, H5 1.2.2, R2 4.1.62.

present n.
1 Present document, writing LLL 4.3.187 *What present hast thou there?* (with quibble on sense 2), AYL 1.2.124.
2 Affair in hand, present occasion or purpose COR 1.6.60 *that you not delay the present*, MM 4.2.25, ANT 2.6.30; thing present TN 3.4.346 *I'll make division of my present with you* (i.e. the money I have on me).
3 *this present* The present time or moment CYM 4.3.8 *her son gone, So needful for this present!*, WT 1.2.192, H8 5.2.44; (adverbially) TN 1.5.234 *such a one I was this present* (i.e. just now).
4 *in, on the present* At present, now TRO 3.2.93 *shall have a praise in present*, TRO 3.3.163, TIM 1.1.141 *on the present.*
~ vb.
1 Set forth, describe, relate OTH 1.3.124 *to your grave ears I'll present...*
2 Represent (a character) TMP 4.1.167 *When I presented Ceres*, WIV 4.6.20, MND 3.1.67.
3 Bring a charge against SHR Ind.2.87 *rail upon the hostess...And say you would present her at the leet.*
~ adj.
1 (of money) Immediately available, ready at hand ERR 4.1.34 *I am not furnish'd with the present money*, MV 1.1.179, MV 3.2.273; *present debts, dues* debts due now, debts to be paid immediately TIM 2.2.145, TIM 2.2.148.
2 Immediate, instant H8 1.2.211 *Call him to present trial*, ANT 2.2.137, ROM 4.1.61.
3 Urgent, pressing TIM 3.2.34 *H'as only sent his present occasion.*

presentation n.
1 Display, show AYL 5.4.107 *He uses his folly like a stalking-horse, and under the presentation of that he shoots his wit.*
2 Semblance, image R3 4.4.84 *poor shadow, painted queen, The presentation of but what I was.*

presently adv. Immediately, instantly TN 5.1.173 *For the love of God, a surgeon! Send one presently*, MV 1.1.183, R3 3.2.16.

presentment n.
1 Dedication of a book TIM 1.1.27 *When comes your book forth?—Upon the heels of my presentment.*
2 Picture, portrait HAM 3.4.54 *The counterfeit presentment of two brothers.*

president n. Head, sovereign ANT 3.7.17 *the president of my kingdom.*

press n.[1] Warrant or commission giving authority to impress recruits 1H4 4.2.12 *I have misus'd the King's press.*
~ vb.[1] Conscript, impress into military or naval service COR 1.2.9 *They have press'd a power*, 1H4 4.2.14, R2 3.2.58.

press n.²
1 Crowd, throng JC 1.2.15 *Who is it in the press that calls on me?*, H8 4.1.78, LUC 1301.
2 Crowding or thronging together JN 5.7.19 *in their throng and press...Confound themselves.*
3 Printing-press WIV 2.1.78 *He will print them...; for he cares not what he puts into the press* (with quibble).
4 Clothes-press WIV 4.2.61 *press, coffer, chest, trunk*, WIV 3.3.212.
~ vb.²
1 Oppress, weigh down OTH 3.4.177 *I have...with leaden thoughts been press'd*, LR 4.3.26, ROM 1.1.187.
2 Crowd, throng JC 2.4.15 *what suitors press to him*, 3H6 3.1.19, H8 2.4.187.
3 Push or strain forward TIT 4.3.91 *to press to heaven*, ROM 5.3.215.
4 *press to death* Subject to the ancient torture called the 'peine forte et dure', i.e. the pressing to death with weights placed on the chest of an accused person who would not plead MM 5.1.522 *pressing to death, whipping, and hanging*; (fig.) R2 3.4.72 *O, I am press'd to death through want of speaking!*, ADO 3.1.76, TRO 3.2.209.
press-money n. Money paid to a soldier or sailor on his being 'pressed' into the service as evidence of his enlistment LR 4.6.87 *There's your press-money.*
pressure n. Impressed character, impression, stamp HAM 3.2.24 *to show...the very age and body of the time his...pressure*, HAM 1.5.100.
prest adj. Ready PER 4.Gower.45 *The pregnant instrument of wrath Prest for this blow*, MV 1.1.160.
presuppose vb. Suggest beforehand (for one's adoption) TN 5.1.350 *such forms which here were presuppos'd Upon thee in the letter.*
pretence n.
1 Intention, purpose, design MAC 2.3.131 *the undivulg'd pretence...Of treasonous malice*, WT 3.2.17, LR 1.2.87.
2 Pretext H8 1.1.177 *Under pretence to see the Queen*, AWW 3.4.48, CYM 3.4.103.
pretend vb.
1 Offer, hold out LUC 576 *such black payment as thou hast pretended.*
2 Profess, assert TIT 1.1.42 *Whom you pretend to honour and adore.*
3 Claim 3H6 4.7.57 *if you pretend no title.*
4 Allege falsely, use as a pretext MM 3.1.227 *swallow'd his vows whole, pretending in her discoveries of dishonour*, CYM 2.3.113, CYM 5.5.250.
5 Intend, purpose, design MAC 2.4.24 *What good could they pretend?*, 1H6 4.1.6.
6 Indicate, import, signify 1H6 4.1.54 *doth this churlish superscription Pretend some alteration in good will?*
pretended ppl. adj. Intended, purposed TGV 2.6.37 *their...pretended flight.*
prettily adv. Ingeniously, skilfully, neatly MND 2.2.53 *Lysander riddles very prettily*, R3 3.1.134.
prettiness n. Pleasantness HAM 4.5.189 *hell itself She turns to...prettiness.*
pretty adj.
1 Ingenious, cleverly made H5 1.2.177 *pretty traps to catch the petty thieves.*
2 Considerable LUC 1233 *A pretty while.*
prevail vb. Avail, have effect H5 3.2.15 *If wishes would prevail with me*, ROM 3.3.60.
prevailment n. Superior power or influence MND 1.1.35 *messengers Of strong prevailment in unhardened youth.*
prevent vb.
1 Anticipate (an event) JC 5.1.104 *so to prevent The time of life*, HAM 2.2.294.

2 Be beforehand with, forestall, anticipate (a person), act before or more quickly than (another person) JC 3.1.35 *I must prevent thee*, MV 1.1.61, TN 3.1.83.
3 Escape, avoid by timely action R2 3.2.179 *wise men ne'er sit and wail their woes, But presently prevent the ways to wail*, 2H4 1.2.232.
4 (intr.) Use preventive measures JC 2.1.28 *So Caesar may; Then lest he may, prevent.*
prevention n.
1 Action of forestalling another in the execution of his designs by previous action JC 3.1.19 *be sudden, for we fear prevention*, R2 2.1.167, 2H6 2.4.57.
2 Precaution TRO 1.3.181 *Achievements, plots, orders, preventions.*
prey n. Action of preying LR 3.4.94 *wolf in greediness, dog in madness, lion in prey*, H5 1.2.169, MND 2.2.150.
preyful adj. Killing much prey LLL 4.2.56 *The preyful Princess pierc'd...a...pricket.*
▷ See PRAISEFUL.
pribble n. (weakened echo of) PRABBLE, quarrel, squabble; *pribbles and prabbles* petty disputing, vain chatter WIV 5.5.160 *swearings and starings, pribbles and prabbles*, WIV 1.1.55.
price, prize n.
1 Value, worth 2H4 5.3.96 *happy news of price* (i.e. worth much), LR 1.1.197, TRO 2.2.82.
2 Esteem, estimation TN 1.1.13 *falls into...low price*, MM 1.3.9, AWW 5.3.61.
3 Valuation, appraisement ANT 5.2.183 *to make prize with you Of things*, LR 2.1.120, CYM 3.6.76 (with play on sense of captured ship).
▷ *Prize*, a var. form from 16–18 C, is the regular spelling in F and Q for sense 3, and is retained in some mod. edd.
prick n.
1 Each of the marks by which the circumference of a dial is divided 3H6 1.4.34 *at the noontide prick*, ROM 2.4.113, LUC 781.
2 Mere point TRO 1.3.343 *small pricks To their subsequent volumes.*
3 Spot in the centre of a target LLL 4.1.132 *Let the mark have a prick in't*; *at pricks* shooting at a target having such a mark fixed at a certain distance (opposed to shooting 'at the butts') LLL 4.1.138 *She's too hard for you at pricks.*
4 Prickle of a hedgehog TMP 2.2.12 *hedgehogs which...mount Their pricks at my footfall*; thorn AYL 3.2.112 *He that sweetest rose will find, Must find love's prick*; skewer LR 2.3.16 *Pins, wooden pricks, nails.*
~ vb.
1 Spur, goad MAC 1.7.26 *I have no spur To prick the sides of my intent*; (hence) urge, incite TGV 3.1.8 *My duty pricks me on to utter that*, SHR 3.2.72, 1H4 5.1.129.
2 Mark or indicate by a 'prick' or tick, mark or tick off JC 3.1.216 *Will you be prick'd in number of our friends...?*, JC 4.1.1, 2H4 2.4.332; choose or pick out SON 20.13 *she prick'd thee out*, LLL 5.2.545 (Q1 picke).
3 Attire elaborately, dress up 2H4 3.2.153 *if he had been a man's tailor, he'd 'a' prick'd you*, 2H4 3.2.145.
4 Fasten with a pin SHR 3.2.69 *the humour of forty fancies prick'd in't for a feather.*
5 Remove by pricking ROM 1.4.69 *a...worm Prick'd from the lazy finger.*
prick-eared adj. Having erect ears H5 2.1.42 *thou prick-ear'd cur...!*
pricket n. Buck in its second year LLL 4.2.12 *it was a buck of the first head.—...'twas a pricket.*

pricking n. Tingling MAC 4.1.44 *By the pricking of my thumbs.*
~ *ppl. adj.* Goading VEN 285 *The pricking spur.*
prick-song n. Descant or accompanying melody to a plainsong or simple theme 'pricked' or noted down ROM 2.4.21 *He fights as you sing prick-song, keeps time, distance, and proportion.*
pride n.
1 Magnificence, pomp, splendour SON 80.12 *He of tall building and of goodly pride,* ROM 1.2.10, OTH 3.3.354.
2 Love of display LUC 864 *in their pride do presently abuse it.*
3 Magnificent or ostentatious adornment H8 1.1.25 *the madams...did almost sweat to bear The pride upon them,* LUC 1809, SON 76.1.
4 Honour, glory 1H6 4.6.57 *let's die in pride.*
5 Best condition, prime 1H4 1.1.60 *in the very heat And pride of their contention,* 1H6 4.7.16.
6 Mettle in a horse VEN 420 *The colt that's back'd and burden'd being young, Loseth his pride,* 1H4 4.3.22.
7 Sexual desire OTH 3.3.404 *As salt as wolves in pride,* LLL 2.1.237, SON 144.8.
8 *pride of place* See PLACE n. sense 2.
priest n.
1 Priestess PER 5.1.242 *my maiden priests,* CYM 1.6.133.
2 *be one's priest* Kill him (in allusion to the priest's performing the last offices to the dying) 2H6 3.1.272 *Say but the word, and I will be his priest.*
priesthood n. (with possessive) Used as a mock title for a priest 2H6 2.1.23 *What, Cardinal? is your priesthood grown peremptory?*
prig n. (slang) Thief WT 4.3.101 *prig, for my life, prig!*
primal adj. Primitive, primeval ANT 1.4.41 *from the primal state,* HAM 3.3.37.
primater n. (error for) PIA MATER, LLL 4.2.69 *begot in the ventricle of memory, nourish'd in the womb of primater.*
⇨ F1; Q1 *prima, primater;* Rowe *pia mater.*
prime n. 1 Spring LUC 332 *frosts that sometime threat the spring To add a more rejoicing to the prime,* SON 97.7.
~ *adj.*
1 First in time R3 4.3.19 *the prime creation.*
2 First in rank or dignity TMP 1.2.72 *Prospero the prime duke,* H8 3.2.162.
3 First in importance or excellence H8 1.2.67 *There is no primer business* (F1 *baseness*), H8 2.4.230, TMP 1.2.426.
4 Sexually excited OTH 3.3.403 *as prime as goats.*
primero n. Gambling card-game very fashionable from about 1530 to 1640 WIV 4.5.102 *I forswore myself at primero,* H8 5.1.7.
primo, secundo, tertio [L.] Firstly, secondly, thirdly TN 5.1.36 *Primo, secundo, tertio, is a good play, and...the third pays for all.*
primogenitive, primogenity n. The right of succession belonging to the first-born TRO 1.3.106 *The primogenity and due of birth* (Q1; F1 *primogenitive*).
primrose n. *primrose path, way* Path of pleasure MAC 2.3.19 *go the primrose way to th' everlasting bonfire,* HAM 1.3.50.
primy adj. That is in its prime HAM 1.3.7 *A violet in the youth of primy nature.*
prince n.
1 Sovereign ruler ROM 1.1.88 *the sentence of your moved prince,* ERR 5.1.197, MM 1.3.45.
2 Male member of a royal family TRO 3.3.26 *Give us a prince of blood, a son of Priam,* WT 2.1.17, JN 2.1.248.

3 (pl.) Royal pair JN 2.1.445 *these two princes, if you marry them.*
~ *vb.* (with *it*) Play the prince CYM 3.3.85 *nature prompts them...to prince it much.*
princess n. Female sovereign ruler H8 5.4.57 *She shall be...An aged princess,* LR 4.7.28, ANT 5.2.326.
principal n.
1 Employer PER 4.6.82 *hath your principal made known unto you who I am?*
2 (legal term) One who is directly responsible for a crime, or aids and abets it WT 2.1.92 *with her most vile principal.*
3 Principal rafter of a house PER 3.2.16 *The very principals did seem to rend, And all to topple.*
principality n. A spiritual being or angel of a high order TGV 2.4.152 *if not divine, Yet let her be a principality.*
princox n. Pert saucy boy ROM 1.5.86 *You are a princox, go, Be quiet.*
print n. *in print* With exactness, to a nicety LLL 3.1.172 *I will do it, sir, in print,* TGV 2.1.169.
~ *vb.* Commit to writing TIT 4.1.75 *Heaven guide thy pen to print thy sorrows plain.*
Priscian n. Famous Roman grammarian LLL 5.1.28 *Priscian a little scratch'd* (i.e. your Latin grammar is a little faulty).
⇨ A mild var. of the common phr. 'break Priscian's head', i.e. violate the rules of grammar.
prison vb. Imprison, confine; (always fig.) SON 133.9 *Prison my heart in thy steel bosom's ward,* VEN 362, LLL 4.3.301 (F1 *poysons*).
pristine adj. Ancient H5 3.2.81 *the pristine wars of the Romans;* former, original MAC 5.3.52 *to a sound and pristine health.*
prithee interj. phr. (I) pray thee TRO 4.2.15 *Prithee tarry,* WIV 5.1.1, AYL 4.1.1.
privacy n. Secrecy WIV 4.5.23 *Let her descend...; my chambers are honourable. Fie, privacy?*
private n.
1 One not holding a public position H5 4.1.237 *what have kings, that privates have not too...?*
2 Intimate, favourite HAM 2.2.234 *Faith, her privates we* (with quibble).
3 Private communication JN 4.3.16 *Whose private with me of the Dauphin's love Is much more general than these lines import.*
4 Privacy TN 3.4.89 *Let me enjoy my private.*
~ *adj.* By oneself, alone ROM 1.1.138 *And private in his chamber pens himself,* H8 2.2.14.
privilege n.
1 Advantage yielded, superiority, favour 1H6 3.1.121 *I would see his heart out ere the priest Should ever get that privilege of me.*
2 'Favourable circumstance' (Schmidt) TGV 3.1.160 *my patience...Is privilege for thy departure hence,* MND 2.1.220, SON 95.13.
3 Right of asylum or sanctuary R3 3.1.41 *the holy privilege Of blessed sanctuary.*
~ *vb.* Authorize, license LUC 621 *To privilege dishonour,* SON 58.10.
privity n. Private cognizance H8 1.1.74 *Without the privity o' th' King.*
prize n.¹ Booty, plunder R3 3.7.187 *Made prize and purchase of his wanton eye* (i.e. took possession of), 1H4 3.1.101, JC 5.4.27; a vessel captured at sea 2H6 4.1.25 *I lost mine eye in laying the prize aboard.*
prize n.²
1 Advantage, privilege 3H6 1.4.59 *It is war's prize to take all vantages,* 3H6 2.1.20.
2 Contest, match MV 3.2.141 *Like one of two contending in a prize; play one's prize* engage in one's contest, play one's part (and hence deserve a reward) TIT 1.1.399 *you have play'd your prize.*
⇨ See also PRICE, PRIZE.

~ vb.

1 Value, esteem TMP 1.2.168 *volumes that I prize above my dukedom*, COR 1.5.4, TIM 1.1.171.

2 Rate, appraise ADO 3.1.90 *so swift...a wit As she is priz'd to have*, TRO 4.4.134.

3 (with negative) Care nothing for SON 143.8 *Not prizing her poor infant's discontent*, TN 2.4.82, WT 4.4.357.

prizer *n.*[1] One who values a thing TRO 2.2.56 *'tis precious of itself As in the prizer.*

prizer *n.*[2] One who fights in a 'prize' or match AYL 2.3.8 *to overcome The bonny prizer of the...Duke* (F1 *priser*).

probable *adj.* Worthy of acceptance or belief, plausible 2H6 3.2.178 *The least of all these signs were probable*, AWW 2.4.51, COR 4.6.66.

probal *adj.* PROBABLE OTH 2.3.338 *this advice is...honest, Probal to thinking.*

probation *n.*

1 Trial, investigation TN 2.5.130 *there is no consonancy in the sequel that suffers under probation*; testing of vocation MM 5.1.72 *in probation of a sisterhood.*

2 Proof HAM 1.1.156 *of the truth herein This present object made probation*, MAC 3.1.79, OTH 3.3.365.

proceed *vb.*

1 Take place AWW 4.2.62 *what in time proceeds*, R3 3.2.23, JC 1.2.181.

2 Arise, be caused CYM 3.5.58 *I pray his absence Proceed by swallowing that drug*, H5 2.2.54.

3 Advance (in one's university course) from one degree to a higher one; (fig.) TIM 4.3.252 *Hadst thou...proceeded The sweet degrees that this brief world affords.*

proceeder *n.* One who proceeds to a university degree SHR 4.2.11 *And may you prove, sir, master of your art!—While you, sweet dear, prove mistress of my heart!—Quick proceeders, marry!* (with quibble).

proceeding *n.* Advancement, progress JC 2.2.103 *my...love To your proceeding bids me tell you this.*

process *n.*

1 Drift, tenor, gist TRO 4.1.9 *the process of your speech.*

2 Narrative, story, account HAM 1.5.37 *a forged process of my death*, MV 4.1.274, R3 4.3.32.

3 Succession of events, proceeding H8 2.3.9 *after this process, To give her the avaunt, it is a pity Would move a monster*, AWW 1.1.15.

4 Formal command or mandate HAM 4.3.63 *thou mayst not coldly set Our sovereign process*, ANT 1.1.28.

process-server *n.* Officer of justice under a sheriff, who executes writs, distrains, and arrests, bailiff WT 4.3.96 *he hath been since an ape-bearer, then a process-server, a bailiff.*

proclaim *vb.*

1 (intr.) Make a public announcement MM 4.4.24 *Will not proclaim against her maiden loss.*

2 (short for) Proclaim (a person) as a rebel or outlaw LR 2.3.1 *I heard myself proclaim'd*, OTH 1.1.69; (hence) denounce MM 2.4.151 *I will proclaim thee, Angelo.*

proclamation *n.* Open declaration, manifestation MM 3.2.144 *The very stream of his life...must...give him a better proclamation* (i.e. proclaim him to be a better man), AWW 1.3.174.

procreant *n.* Generator, one who procreates OTH 4.2.28 *Leave procreants alone.*

~ adj. Pertaining to procreation MAC 1.6.8 *this bird Hath made his...procreant cradle.*

procurator *n.* One authorized to act in behalf of another in any business, agent, deputy 2H6 1.1.3

As procurator to your Excellence, To marry Princess Margaret for your Grace.

procure *vb.*

1 Cause, bring about MM 5.1.474 *I am sorry that such sorrow I procure*, LR 2.4.303, 2H6 2.4.62.

2 Get (a person to do something) WIV 4.6.48 *you'll procure the vicar To stay for me*, ROM 2.2.145, 1H6 5.5.88.

3 Bring (a person to a place) ROM 3.5.67 *What... cause procures her hither?*

4 Manage or contrive (to do something) PP 17.21 *With sighs so deep procures to weep.*

prodigal *adj.* (transf. from the agent to an attribute) Wastefully lavish AYL 1.1.38 *What prodigal portion have I spent...?*, TIM 2.2.165, LLL 5.2.64.

~ adv. Lavishly HAM 1.3.116 *how prodigal the soul Lends the tongue vows.*

prodigious *adj.*

1 Of the nature of a prodigy, ominous, portentous MND 5.1.412 *Never mole, hare-lip,...Nor mark prodigious*, TRO 5.1.93, ROM 1.5.140.

2 Abnormal, unnatural, monstrous R3 1.2.22 *If ever he have child, abortive be it, Prodigious*, JN 3.1.46.

3 (blunder by Launce for) Prodigal TGV 2.3.3 *like the prodigious son.*

prodigiously *adv.* By prodigies JN 3.1.91 *let wives with child Pray that their burdens may not fall this day, Lest that their hopes prodigiously be cross'd* (i.e. by the birth of monsters).

prodigy *n.*

1 Omen, portent 1H4 5.1.20 *A prodigy of fear, and a portent Of...mischief*, JC 1.3.28, VEN 926.

2 Something abnormal, monster R2 2.2.64 *Now hath my soul brought forth her prodigy.*

proditor *n.* Traitor 1H6 1.3.31 *thou most usurping proditor.*

product *vb.* Produce OTH 1.1.146 *To be producted... Against the Moor* (Ff; Qq *produced*).

proface [L.] May it do you good 2H4 5.3.28 *Proface! What you want in meat, we'll have in drink.*

▷ Formula of welcome at a meal, in frequent use from early 16C to mid-17C.

profane *adj.* Coarse in language, foul-mouthed OTH 1.1.114 *What profane wretch art thou?*, 2H4 5.5.50, CYM 2.3.124.

profess *vb.*

1 Declare openly, affirm, acknowledge H8 2.4.84 *I do profess You speak not like yourself*, MM 4.2.100, LR 1.1.72.

2 (refl.) Make a profession, (esp.) profess friendship JC 1.2.77 *That I profess myself in banqueting To all the rout*; (intr.) WT 1.2.456 *a man which ever Profess'd to him.*

3 Claim to have knowledge of or skill in (an art or science), declare oneself expert or proficient in 1H4 5.2.91 *I profess not talking*, AYL 3.2.404, SHR 4.2.8; make (a thing) one's business MM 2.1.65 *she professes a hot-house.*

professed *ppl. adj.* Openly declared or avowed ADO 1.1.169 *a profess'd tyrant to their sex*, TIM 4.3.426, ROM 3.3.50.

professor *n.* One who professes a religion WT 5.1.108 *the zeal Of all professors*, 1H6 5.1.14; one who makes an open declaration of his sentiments or allegiance H8 3.1.115 *Woe upon...all such false professors!*

proficient *n.* Learner who makes progress 1H4 2.4.18 *I am so good a proficient in one quarter of an hour.*

profit *n.*

1 Something advantageous, that which is to the benefit of someone or something OTH 3.3.379 *I* *thank you for this profit* (i.e. profitable lesson), MM 1.4.61.

2 Progress, proficiency AYL 1.1.6 *report speaks goldenly of his profit* (i.e. at school), SHR 1.1.39.

~ *vb.* Make progress, improve WIV 4.1.15 *my son profits nothing in the world at his book*, SHR 4.2.6.

profited *ppl. adj.* Proficient 1H4 3.1.164 *profited In strange concealments.*

profiting *n.* Improvement, progress 1H4 1.2.153 *God give...him the ears of profiting.*

profound *adj.* Of deep significance MAC 3.5.24 *hangs a vap'rous drop profound.*

progeny *n.*
1 Race, stock, family COR 1.8.12 *the Hector That was the whip of your bragg'd progeny*, 1H6 5.4.38.
2 Lineage, descent 1H6 3.3.61 *Doubting thy birth and lawful progeny.*

prognostication *n.*
1 Forecast for the year published in or as an almanac WT 4.4.788 *in the hottest day prognostication proclaims.*
2 Sign, token ANT 1.2.53 *if an oily palm be not a fruitful prognostication.*

progress *n.*
1 State journey made by a king 2H6 1.4.72 *The King is now in progress towards Saint Albans*; (jocularly) HAM 4.3.31 *how a king may go a progress through the guts of a beggar.*
2 Onward movement in space, course JN 2.1.340 *A peaceful progress to the ocean*, JC 2.1.2, 1H4 3.1.219.
3 Course or process (of action, etc.) H8 5.2.67 *in all the progress Both of my life and office*, H8 2.4.176.
~ *vb.* Move onward, advance, proceed JN 5.2.46 *dew, That silverly doth progress on thy cheeks.*

prohibit *vb.* (malapropism by Dogberry) Permit ADO 5.1.326 *A merry meeting may be wish'd, God prohibit it.*

project *n.* Conception, idea, notion ADO 3.1.55 *She cannot...take no shape nor project of affection*, 2H4 1.3.29.
~ *vb.* Put forth, exhibit ANT 5.2.121 *I cannot project mine own cause so well.*

projection *n.* Scheme, design H5 2.4.46 *of a weak and niggardly projection.*

prolixious *adj.* Tedious MM 2.4.162 *prolixious blushes.*

prologue *n.* One who speaks the prologue to a play H5 Prol.SD *Enter Prologue.*
~ *vb.* Introduce, preface AWW 2.1.92 *Thus he his special nothing ever prologues.*

prolong *vb.* Defer ADO 4.1.254 *this wedding-day Perhaps is but prolong'd*, R3 3.4.45.

Promethean *adj.* (used allusively) Inspiring or infusing life LLL 4.3.300 *Promethean fire*, OTH 5.2.12.

promise *n.* (with *claim*) Fulfilment of a promise TGV 4.4.87 *I claim The promise for her heavenly picture.*
~ *vb.* I promise thee, you I assure you, I can tell you ADO 4.2.45 *I do not like thy look, I promise thee*, LR 1.2.143, WIV 3.2.71.

promised *ppl. adj.* be promised Be engaged, have an engagement JC 1.2.289 *Will you sup with me...?—No, I am promis'd forth.*

prompt *vb.*
1 Incite, move TN 3.4.139 *till our...pastime... prompt us to have mercy*, HAM 2.2.584, TRO 3.3.2.
2 Inspire TMP 3.1.82 *prompt me, plain and holy innocence!*
3 Suggest (a thing to a person) COR 3.2.54 *th' matter which your heart prompts you.*
4 Remind ADO 1.1.304 *All prompting me how fair young Hero is.*
~ *adj.* Inclined, disposed TRO 4.4.88 *virtues...To which the Grecians are most prompt.*

prompted *ppl. adj.* Ready TRO 5.2.175 *my prompted sword.*

prompting *ppl. adj.* Inspiring LLL 4.3.319 *the prompting eyes Of beauty's tutors.*

prompture *n.* Prompting, urging MM 2.4.178 *he hath fall'n by prompture of the blood.*

promulgate *vb.* Publish OTH 1.2.21 *Which, when I know that boasting is an honour, I shall promulgate* (F1; Q1 *provulgate*).

prone *adj.* Ready, eager CYM 5.4.199 *I never saw one so prone*, LUC 684.
▷ In MM 1.2.183 *in her youth There is a prone and speechless dialect* there is possibly hendiadys: 'speechlessly prone, speaking eagerly without words'.

pronounce *vb.* Deliver, declaim, recite HAM 3.2.1 *Speak the speech...as I pronounc'd it to you*, MV 1.2.10; (intr.) HAM 3.2.310 *Pronounce.*

proof *n.*
1 Test, trial, experiment TRO 1.2.129 *stand to the proof*, OTH 5.1.26, HAM 4.7.154.
2 Experience CYM 3.3.27 *Out of your proof you speak*, ADO 2.1.181, R3 2.3.43.
3 Issue, result, fulfilment SHR 4.3.43 *all my pains is sorted to no proof* (i.e. come(s) to nothing), 2H4 4.3.91.
4 Proved or tested strength of armour or arms, impenetrability SHR 2.1.140 *be thou arm'd...· Ay, to the proof* (i.e. so as to be proof against attack), VEN 626, R2 1.3.73.

propagate *vb.* (fig.) Cause to increase or multiply TIM 1.1.67 *To propagate their states*, ROM 1.1.187.

propagation *n.* Increase MM 1.2.150 *propagation of a dow'r.*

propend *vb.* Incline TRO 2.2.190 *I propend to you In resolution to keep Helen still* (i.e. I incline to your resolve).

propension *n.* Inclination TRO 2.2.133 *your full consent Gave wings to my propension.*

proper *adj.*
1 (one's, its) Own 2H4 5.2.109 *my proper son*, TMP 3.3.60, HAM 5.2.66.
2 Belonging distinctly or exclusively (*to*), peculiar MM 5.1.110 *Faults proper to himself*, H5 5.Ch.5, JC 1.2.41.
3 (ironically) Fine, excellent 2H6 1.1.132 *A proper jest*, ADO 4.1.309, MAC 3.4.59.
4 Honest, respectable AWW 4.3.213 *a proper maid*, 2H4 2.2.155.
5 Good-looking, handsome, elegant TRO 1.2.193 *a proper man of person*, TMP 2.2.60, TGV 4.1.10.
~ *adv.* Appropriately TIM 1.2.102 *what better or properer can we call our own...?*

proper-false *n.* Handsome, but false-hearted TN 2.2.29 *How easy is it for the proper-false In women's waxen hearts to set their forms!*

properly *adv.*
1 For oneself COR 5.2.84 *though I owe My revenge properly, my remission lies In Volscian breasts*, WT 2.1.170.
2 In accordance with fact, strictly AYL 1.1.8 *to speak more properly*, JN 2.1.514.

propertied *adj.* Possessed of qualities ANT 5.2.83 *his voice was propertied As all the tuned spheres.*

property *n.*
1 Exclusive right of possession, ownership, proprietorship PhT 37 *Property was thus appalled, That the self was not the same.*
2 Means to an end, tool WIV 3.4.10 *'tis a thing impossible I should love thee but as a property*, JC 4.1.40.
~ *vb.*
1 Make a 'property' or tool of, use for one's own

end JN 5.2.79 *to be propertied, To be a...servingman and instrument*, TN 4.2.91.
2 Appropriate TIM 1.1.57 *His large fortune ...properties to his love...All sorts of hearts.*

prophesy *vb.* Foreshow, indicate beforehand LR 5.3.176 *thy very gait did prophesy A royal nobleness.*

prophet *n.* Omen, portent 1H6 3.2.32 *a comet of revenge, A prophet to the fall of all our foes!*

proportion *n.*
1 Size 1H4 4.4.15 *Whose power was in the first proportion* (i.e. of the first magnitude), 2H4 4.1.23.
2 The act of making proportionate, proportionate adjustment MAC 1.4.19 *That the proportion both of thanks and payment Might have been mine!* (i.e. in my power to perform).
3 Estimate of forces or supplies required for war HAM 1.2.32 *the levies, The lists, and full proportions are all made Out of his subject*; (hence) the forces or supplies themselves H5 1.2.137 *lay down our proportions to defend Against the Scot*, H5 2.4.45.
4 Configuration, form, shape 2H6 1.3.54 *King Henry had resembled thee In...proportion*, MV 3.4.14, R3 1.1.18.
5 Metrical or musical rhythm R2 5.5.43 *How sour sweet music is When time is broke, and no proportion kept!*, MM 1.2.22.
6 Portion, amount MM 5.1.219 *her promised proportions* (i.e. dowry), PER 4.2.27, TGV 2.3.3.
~ *vb.*
1 Be in proportion to H5 3.6.126 *his ransom, which must proportion the losses we have borne.*
2 Adjust in due proportion, measure, or relation ANT 4.15.5 *our size of sorrow, Proportion'd to our cause, must be as great As that which makes it.*

proportioned *ppl. adj.*
1 Assigned, allotted LUC 774 *proportion'd course of time.*
2 Formed, fashioned ROM 3.5.182 *Proportion'd as one's thought would wish a man.*

propose *n.* Subject (of conversation or discussion) ADO 3.1.12 *To listen our propose* (Ff *purpose*).
~ *vb.*
1 Set before one's mind as something to be expected TRO 2.2.146 *I propose not merely to myself The pleasures*; 'look forward to, be ready to meet' (Schmidt) TIT 2.1.80 *a thousand deaths Would I propose to achieve her.*
2 Contemplate as a supposition, imagine 2H4 5.2.92 *Be now the father and propose a son.*
3 Converse, discourse ADO 3.1.3 *Proposing with the Prince and Claudio*, OTH 1.1.25.

proposer *n.* One who propounds something for consideration HAM 2.2.286 *a better proposer.*

proposition *n.*
1 Offer, promise TRO 1.3.3 *The ample proposition that hope makes In all designs.*
2 Question proposed for resolution AYL 3.2.233 *to resolve the propositions of a lover.*

propriety *n.*
1 Individuality, identity TN 5.1.147 *it is the baseness of thy fear That makes thee strangle thy propriety.*
2 Proper state or condition OTH 2.3.176 *it frights the isle From her propriety.*

propugnation *n.* Defence TRO 2.2.136 *What propugnation is in one man's valour To stand...push and enmity...?*

prorogue *vb.*
1 Prolong ANT 2.1.26 *That sleep and feeding may prorogue his honour*, PER 5.1.26.
2 Defer ROM 4.1.48 *nothing may prorogue it*, ROM 2.2.78.

prosecution *n.* Pursuit ANT 4.14.65 *behind me Th' inevitable prosecution of Disgrace.*

prospect *n.*
1 Range or scope of vision ADO 4.1.229 *the eye and prospect of his soul*, JN 2.1.208.
2 What is seen, scene, view 2H6 3.2.324 *Their chiefest prospect murd'ring basilisks.*
3 Appearance presented by anything, aspect OTH 3.3.398 *It were a tedious difficulty...To bring them to that prospect* (i.e. so that they can be witnessed in the act).

prosperous *adj.*
1 Propitious, favourable WT 5.1.161 *A prosperous south-wind*, TIM 5.1.183, OTH 1.3.244.
2 Promoting success, bringing prosperity, profitable MAC 3.1.21 *good advice* (*Which still hath been ...prosperous*).

protect *vb.* Act as Protector (of a king) 2H6 1.1.165 *Why should he then protect our sovereign...?*, 2H6 2.3.29, R3 2.3.21.

protest *n.* Protestation TRO 3.2.175 *their rhymes, Full of protest* (i.e. with many vows), 1H4 3.1.255.
~ *vb.*
1 Assert publicly, proclaim ADO 5.1.147 *I will protest your cowardice*, OTH 4.2.202.
2 Vow, promise TIM 4.3.434 *since you protest to do't*, MND 1.1.89.

protestation *n.* Solemn declaration, affirmation, or promise AWW 5.3.139 *his many protestations to marry me*, LLL 1.1.33, H5 5.2.144.

protester *n.* One who makes solemn declarations, one who professes something (e.g. friendship) JC 1.2.74 *every new protester.*

protract *vb.* Delay CYM 4.2.232 *not protract with admiration what Is now due debt.*

protractive *adj.* Long drawn out TRO 1.3.20 *the protractive trials.*

proud *adj.*
1 Elated, gratified, pleased LLL 2.1.17 *I am less proud to hear you tell my worth*, R2 5.5.84, VEN 309.
2 Exalted, lofty ADO 3.1.50 *nature never fram'd a woman's heart Of prouder stuff than that of Beatrice*, H8 3.2.127.
3 Magnificent, splendid JN 3.3.34 *the proud day*, LR 3.4.83, SON 2.3.
4 (of animals) Spirited, high-mettled, vigorously or fearlessly active TIT 2.2.21 *the proudest panther in the chase*, VEN 260, VEN 884.
5 (of waters) Swelling, swollen MND 2.1.91 *Hath every pelting river made so proud*; (of plants) exuberant, luxuriant R2 3.4.59 *over-proud in sap.*
6 Sensually excited, lascivious LUC 712 *The flesh being proud.*

proudly *adv.*
1 Magnificently, splendidly JN 2.1.70 *Bearing their birthrights proudly on their backs.*
2 With force, vigour 2H4 5.2.130 *The tide of blood in me Hath proudly flow'd.*

proud-pied *adj.* Splendidly variegated SON 98.2 *proud-pied April.*

provand *n.* Provender, fodder COR 2.1.251 *camels ...who have their provand Only for bearing burdens.*

prove *vb.*
1 Try, test 1H6 2.2.58 *I mean to prove this lady's courtesy*, CYM 1.5.38; (with infin.) VEN 40 *To tie the rider she begins to prove*; (with clause) ADO 1.3.73 *Shall we go prove what's to be done?*, MV 2.1.7, HAM 3.2.202.
2 Find out by experience JN 3.1.28 *give you cause to prove my saying true*, OTH 3.3.260, LUC 613; *prove* (*you*) *that* if you discover PER 4.6.189 *Prove that I cannot, take me home again*, ADO 1.1.250, 2H4 2.4.279.

3 Have experience of, experience ANT 1.2.33 *You have seen and prov'd a fairer..fortune*, HAM 3.1.46, SON 129.11.

prover *n.* One who tries or tests another TRO 2.3.67 *Why am I a fool?—Make that demand of the prover* (Q1; F1 *to the Creator*).

proverb *vb.* Provide with a proverb ROM 1.4.37 *I am proverb'd with a grandsire phrase.*

provide *vb.*
1 Prepare or make ready for ANT 3.4.36 *Provide your going.*
2 (refl.) Equip or prepare oneself HAM 3.3.7 *Therefore prepare you...- We will ourselves provide*, AYL 1.3.87.

provided *ppl. adj.* Prepared, ready TGV 1.3.72 *I cannot be so soon provided*, R3 3.1.132, LR 2.4.232.

providence *n.* Foresight TRO 3.3.196 *The providence that's in a watchful state*, HAM 4.1.17.

provincial *adj.* Subject to a certain province MM 5.1.316 *His subject am I not, Nor here provincial.*

Provincial rose *n.* Rosette imitating the damask rose HAM 3.2.276 *with two Provincial roses on my raz'd shoes.*

provoke *vb.* Incite, urge, stimulate to action AYL 1.3.110 *Beauty provoketh thieves sooner than gold*, R3 1.2.97, SON 50.9; (absol.) JN 2.1.246 *no further enemy to you Than the constraint of hospitable zeal...provokes.*

provost *n.* Officer charged with the apprehension, custody, and punishment of all offenders MM 1.2.115 *led by the Provost to prison*, MM 1.4.73.

provulgate See PROMULGATE.

pruin *n.* Prune WT 4.3.48 *four pounds of pruins* (F1).

prune *vb.* (term from falconry; of a bird) Preen (its feathers) CYM 5.4.118 *His royal bird Prunes the immortal wing*, 1H4 1.1.98; (of a person) trim, dress up LLL 4.3.181 *see me...spend a minute's time In pruning me?*

psaltery *n.* Stringed instrument resembling the dulcimer, but played by plucking the strings with the fingers or a plectrum COR 5.4.49 *trumpets, sackbuts, psalteries, and fifes.*

publican *n.* Tax-gatherer MV 1.3.41 *fawning publican.*

publication *n.* The action of making a thing generally known, public announcement TRO 1.3.326 *in the publication.*

publish *vb.* Proclaim (a person) publicly as being of a certain character TN 2.1.28 *thus far I will boldly publish her*; (depreciatively) denounce WT 2.1.98 *that You thus hath publish'd me.*

published *ppl. adj.* Publicly proclaimed LR 4.6.232 *a publish'd traitor.*

publisher *n.* One who brings to light or makes public LUC 33 *the publisher Of that rich jewel*, TGV 3.1.47.

Pucelle See PUZEL.

Puck *n.* Mischievous spirit MND 5.1.431 *as I am an honest Puck*; name of a fancied mischievous sprite or goblin, also called Robin Goodfellow and Hobgoblin MND 2.1.40 *Those that Hobgoblin call you, and sweet Puck.*

pudder See POTHER.

pudding *n.* (orig.) Mixture of meat, herbs, etc. stuffed into an animal's stomach or intestine and boiled, kind of sausage WIV 2.1.32 *his guts are made of puddings*, OTH 2.1.253; (hence) stuffing for a roasted animal 1H4 2.4.453 *that roasted...ox with the pudding in his belly.*

puddle *vb.* Sully the purity of OTH 3.4.143 *Something...Hath puddled his clear spirit.*

puddled *ppl. adj.* Made muddy, foul ERR 5.1.173 *pails of puddled mire.*

pudency *n.* Modesty CYM 2.5.11 *did it with A pudency so rosy the sweet view on't Might...have warm'd...Saturn.*

pueritia [L.] Boyhood LLL 5.1.49 *Ba, pueritia, with a horn added.*

pugging *ppl. adj.* (?) Thieving, thievish WT 4.3.7 *The white sheet bleaching on the hedge...Doth set my pugging tooth on edge.*

puisne, puisny *adj.* Junior; (hence) that is a novice, inexperienced AYL 3.4.43 *a puisny tilter, that spurs his horse but on one side.*

puissance *n.*
1 Power, strength H5 3.Ch.21 *not arriv'd to pith and puissance*, 2H6 4.2.163.
2 Armed force JN 3.1.339 *draw our puissance together*, H5 2.2.190, 2H4 1.3.9.

puissant *adj.* Powerful, strong H5 1.2.116 *your puissant arm*, LR 5.3.217, 2H6 4.9.25.

puke *n.* Superior kind of dark woollen cloth (attrib.) 1H4 2.4.70 *this leathern-jerkin,...puke-stocking.*

puke *vb.* Vomit AYL 2.7.144 *the infant, Mewling and puking.*

pulcher [L.] Beautiful WIV 4.1.27 *What is 'fair', William?—Pulcher.*

pull *n.* Wrench 2H6 2.3.41 *two pulls at once—His lady banish'd, and a limb lopp'd off.*
~ *vb.* Pluck out (feathers) 1H6 3.3.7 *We'll pull his plumes.*
~ in combination
pull down 'Bring low', humiliate 2H6 1.1.259 *Whose bookish rule hath pull'd fair England down*, OTH 2.3.95. **pull in** *Rein in* MAC 5.5.41 *I pull in resolution, and begin To doubt.*

pulpit *n.* (applied to) The rostra in the Forum of ancient Rome JC 3.1.80 *Some to the common pulpits, and cry out.*

pulpiter *n.* Preacher AYL 3.2.155 *O most gentle pulpiter, what tedious homily of love have you wearied your parishioners withal.*
◇ Spedding's conjecture; Ff *Iupiter.*

pulsidge *n.* (blunder for) Pulse 2H4 2.4.23 *Your pulsidge beats.*

pumpion *n.* Pumpkin WIV 3.3.41 *this gross wat'ry pumpion.*

pun *vb.* Pound TRO 2.1.39 *He would pun thee into shivers.*

puncto See PUNTO.

punk *n.* Prostitute, harlot MM 5.1.522 *Marrying a punk...is pressing to death, whipping, and hanging*, WIV 2.2.135, AWW 2.2.22.

punto *n.* (in fencing) Stroke or thrust with the point of the sword WIV 2.3.26 *pass thy punto, thy stock, thy reverse* (F1 *puncto*); *punto reverso* back-handed thrust ROM 2.4.26.

puny *adj.* Raw, inexperienced 1H6 4.7.36 *Did flesh his puny sword.*

puppy-headed *adj.* Stupid TMP 2.2.154 *this puppy-headed monster.*

pur See PURR.

purblind *adj.*
1 Quite blind LLL 3.1.179 *This...purblind, wayward boy,...Dan Cupid*, WT 1.2.228, ROM 2.1.12.
2 Partially blind, dimsighted 1H6 2.4.21 *The truth appears so naked on my side That any purblind eye may find it out*, VEN 679.

purblinded *adj.* PURBLIND sense 1 TRO 1.2.29 *purblinded Argus, all eyes and no sight* (F1; Q1 *purblinde*).

purchase *n.*
1 Obtaining, acquisition JN 3.1.205 *purchase of a heavy curse*, PER 1.2.72.
2 Spoil, booty R3 3.7.187 *A...widow...Made prize and purchase of his wanton eye*, 1H4 2.1.92, H5

3.2.42; advantage, gain, profit PER 1.Gower.9 *The purchase is to make men glorious.*

3 *after fourteen years' purchase* (lit.) At a price equivalent to fourteen years' annual rent; (hence) at a very high price (since the ordinary purchase price was based on twelve years' rental) TN 4.1.23.

~ *vb.*

1 Exert oneself, strive TIM 3.2.47 *that I should purchase...for a little part, and undo a great deal of honour.*

2 Acquire, obtain, gain LLL 3.1.26 *How hast thou purchased this experience?*, TMP 4.1.14, CYM 2.3.88.

3 (legal term) Acquire otherwise than by inheritance or descent ANT 1.4.14 *His faults...hereditary, Rather than purchas'd*, 2H4 4.5.199.

4 Acquire as a result of something, earn, win, deserve ADO 3.1.70 *that Which simpleness and merit purchaseth.*

5 *purchase out* Buy out, redeem ROM 3.1.193 *Nor tears nor prayers shall purchase out abuses.*

purchasing *n.* Deserved acquisition COR 2.1.140 *not without his true purchasing.*

pure *adv.* Merely, simply TN 5.1.83 *expose myself (pure for his love) Into the danger.*

purely *adv.* Without mixture of anything deteriorating or debasing, without blemish or corruption, so as to be pure TRO 4.5.169 *faith and troth, Strain'd purely from all hollow bias-drawing.*

purgation *n.* Action of clearing (oneself) from the accusation or suspicion of guilt AYL 1.3.53 *If their purgation did consist in words, They are as innocent as grace itself*, WT 3.2.7, H8 5.2.187; *put to (one's) purgation* submit (a person) to the test of clearing (himself), give (a person) an opportunity to clear (himself) AYL 5.4.44 *If any man doubt that, let him put me to my purgation*, HAM 3.2.306 (with play on sense 'purging by evacuation of excrement').

◇ Canonical purgation was by oath; popular purgation was by the ordeal of fire or water, or by wager of battle.

purge *n.* Act of purging, purgation, ridding of objectionable elements MAC 5.2.28 *pour we, in our country's purge, Each drop of us* (with play on sense of 'purgative, aperient medicine').

~ *vb.*

1 Clear (oneself) of guilt COR 5.6.8 *hoping To purge himself with words*, ROM 5.3.226, 1H4 3.2.20.

2 (fig.) Become pure 1H4 5.4.164 *I'll purge and leave sack.*

3 Discharge HAM 2.2.198 *their eyes purging...gum.*

4 (intr.) Be restored to a state of activity (as by medicinal purgation) ANT 1.3.53 *quietness, grown sick of rest, would purge By any desperate change.*

purl *vb.* (of breath) Flow with a whirling motion LUC 1407 *Thin winding breath, which purl'd up to the sky.*

purlieu *n.* Tract of land on the border of a forest AYL 4.3.76 *in the purlieus of this forest.*

purple *n.* See LONG PURPLES.

~ *adj.* Used poetically to describe the colour of blood (properly said of the crimson venous blood, the arterial blood being scarlet) ROM 1.1.85 *purple fountains issuing from your veins*, R2 3.3.94, LUC 1734.

purpled *ppl. adj.* Blood-stained JN 2.1.322 *with purpled hands*, JC 3.1.58.

purport *n.*

1 Meaning HAM 2.1.79 *a look so piteous in purport.*

2 Intention LR 1.4.70 *a very pretence and purport of unkindness* (Qq 1-2; F1 *purpose*).

purpose *n.*

1 That which one sets before oneself as a thing to be done, object, intention; (with vb. of motion

implied) 1H4 1.1.102 *Our holy purpose to Jerusalem*, MND 4.1.161.

2 Proposition, proposal 1H4 4.3.111 *shall mine uncle Bring him our purposes*, 1H6 5.1.36, ANT 2.6.4.

3 Discourse, conversation ADO 3.1.12 *To listen our purpose* (F1; Q1 *propose*).

4 Meaning, import MM 2.4.148 *My words express my purpose*; effect TRO 1.3.264 *He bade me...to this purpose speak.*

5 *to such a purpose* With such an end in view, with regard to this WIV 2.2.212 *Have you importun'd her to such a purpose?*, MM 1.2.78; *of this war's purpose* with regard to this war CYM 4.2.345 *What have you dream'd of late of this war's purpose?*

6 *to any purpose* Of any importance ADO 5.4.106 *I will think nothing to any purpose that the world can say against it.*

~ *vb.*

1 Intend (with verb of motion implied) ANT 3.1.35 *He purposeth to Athens.*

2 (pass.) Be (so) resolved LR 2.4.293 *So am I purpos'd.*

purr *n.* Type of fish, small codlin AWW 5.2.19 *Here is a purr of Fortune's.*

◇ Prob. with play on other senses: (1) piece of dung; (2) jack or knave of cards; (3) soft murmuring sound of cat.

purse *vb.* Pocket MV 1.3.174 *I will go and purse the ducats straight*; (hence, fig.) take possession of ANT 2.2.187 *she purs'd up his heart.*

purse-bearer *n.* One who has charge of another's money TN 3.3.47 *I'll be your purse-bearer.*

purse-taking *n.* Robbing of purses on the highway, stealing 1H4 1.2.103 *from praying to purse-taking.*

pursue *vb.*

1 Follow with hostility, persecute TRO 4.5.69 *Will you the knights Shall to the edge of all extremity Pursue each other...?*, WIV 4.2.208; follow with punishment MM 5.1.109 *pursue Faults.*

2 Follow as an attendant or suppliant ANT 3.12.25 *Fortune pursue thee!*, TRO 5.3.10, HAM 3.2.222.

3 Ensue R3 2.3.43 *mistrust Pursuing danger* (Ff; Qq *ensuing*).

4 Proceed with MV 4.1.298 *pursue sentence*, HAM 1.5.84, ANT 5.2.355.

pursuit *n.* Endeavour TRO 4.1.19 *With all my force, pursuit, and policy*, TRO 2.2.142.

pursuivant *n.* One of the junior officers attendant on the heralds R3 5.3.59 *Send out a pursuivant-at-arms*, H8 5.2.24, 2H6 1.3.34; (fig.) messenger 1H6 2.5.5 *these grey locks, the pursuivants of death.*

pursy *adj.*

1 Short-winded TIM 5.4.12 *breathless wrong...And pursy insolence.*

2 Fat, corpulent (fig.) HAM 3.4.153 *in the fatness of these pursy times.*

purveyor *n.* Domestic officer who provided lodging and necessaries in advance for a great personage MAC 1.6.22 *We cours'd him at the heels, and had a purpose To be his purveyor.*

push *n.*

1 Attack, onset JC 5.2.5 *sudden push gives them the overthrow*; *stand the push of* withstand the attack of, face, meet 1H4 3.2.66 *stand the push Of every beardless vain comparative*, 2H4 2.2.37, TRO 2.2.137.

2 Effort, attempt MAC 5.3.20 *This push Will cheer me ever, or disseat me now*; impulse WT 5.3.129 *Lest they desire (upon this push) to trouble Your joys.*

3 *put...to the present push* Put...to immediate trial HAM 5.1.295.

~ *vb.* Thrust with a weapon H5 2.1.98 *Push home.*

push-pin *n.* Child's game in which each player pushes his pin with the object of crossing that of

another player LLL 4.3.167 *great Hercules whipping a gig,...And Nestor play at push-pin with the
boys.*
put *vb.*
1 Thrust (a weapon) *home* OTH 5.1.2 *Wear thy good
rapier bare, and put it home.*
2 Stake (something) *on* CYM 1.4.123 *Would I had
put my estate...on th' approbation of what I have
spoke!*
3 Foist (a trick) *upon* (a person) TMP 2.2.58 *Do you
put tricks upon's...?,* AWW 4.5.60.
4 Pass off (news, unwelcome speech) *upon* (a person), communicate, impart MM 2.2.133 *Why do you
put these sayings upon me?,* TN 5.1.67, HAM 1.3.94.
5 Lay the guilt or blame (of something) *on* (a person), impute *to* HAM 2.1.19 *put upon him What
forgeries you please,* MAC 1.7.70, MAC 2.4.26.
6 Urge or incite (to do something) 2H6 3.1.43 *had I
first been put to speak my mind,* LR 2.1.99, COR
2.1.256.
7 Oblige, compel, force CYM 2.3.105 *You put me to
forget a lady's manners,* MM 1.1.5, 2H6 3.1.43.
8 Assert, affirm TIM 5.1.193 *As common bruit doth
put it.*
9 *put to* (one's) *books* Place or enter in (one's)
books; (hence) mortgage TIM 1.2.200 *his land's put
to their books.*
~ in combination
put apart, away Send away, dismiss, get rid of
WT 2.2.13 *To put apart these your attendants,* ROM
2.4.197, LR 1.4.220. **put back** Repulse, reject 3H6
5.5.80 *Petitioners for blood thou ne'er put'st back,*
TRO 4.4.34, LUC 843. **put by 1** Thrust aside JC
1.2.222 *he put it by with the back of his hand.* **2**
Desist from, give up OTH 2.3.172 *put by this barbarous brawl,* R3 3.7.183 (Qq; F1 *put off*). **put down 1**
Abolish MM 3.2.103 *till eating and drinking be put
down.* **2** Depose from office 3H6 1.1.200 *to put me
down and reign thyself.* **3** Lower the self-esteem
of, take down, put to silence, make a fool of LLL
4.1.141 *how the ladies and I have put him down!,*
TN 1.5.84, 1H4 2.4.255. **4** Subdue, overthrow JN
2.1.346 *We'll put them down, 'gainst whom these
arms we bear,* 2H6 4.4.40; make incapable (with
drink) TN 1.3.83 *unless you see canary put me
down.* **5** Make away with, destroy 1H4 1.3.175 *To
put down Richard, that sweet lovely rose.* **put forth
1** Extend (one's hand) 2H6 1.2.11 *Put forth thy
hand, reach at the glorious gold,* H5 1.2.292. **2** Send
out TGV 1.3.7 *Put forth their sons to seek preferment out.* **3** Lend out (money) SON 134.10 *Thou
usurer, that put'st forth all to use.* **4** (fig.) Burst
forth, sprout WT 1.2.254 *his negligence, his folly,
fear,...Sometime puts forth.* **put in 1** Advance
one's claim TIM 3.4.84 *Put in now, Titus.* **2** Plead,
intercede MM 1.2.100 *They had gone down too, but
that a wise burgher put in for them.* **3** Enter the
harbour OTH 2.1.65 *who has put in?* **put o'er** See
PUT OVER. **put off 1** Dismiss from one's mind or
thought TMP 3.3.7 *here I will put off my hope,* WIV
2.1.234. **2** Set aside (scornfully) AWW 2.2.6 *when
you put off that with such contempt.* **3** Dismiss from
service or employment H8 1.2.32 *The cloth-
iers...have put off The spinsters, carders, fullers,*

weavers, H8 2.4.21. **4** Avert PER 1.1.140 *Poison and
treason are...the targets to put off the shame.* **5** Refuse (an invitation) TIM 3.6.11 *an earnest inviting,
which many my near occasions did urge me to put
off.* **6** Postpone, defer AWW 2.4.43 *The...
prerogative...he does acknowledge, But puts it off
to a compell'd restraint.* **7** Refer (a person) to a
later time for payment of debts TIM 2.2.19 *he hath
put me off To the succession of new days this month.*
8 *put it off* Pull it off, carry it off AWW 2.2.9 *if God
have lent a man any manners, he may easily put it
off at court.* **9** Repulse, baffle LLL 4.1.110 *Finely put
off!* **10** (of a ship) Leave the land or a jetty ANT
2.7.72 *Let me cut the cable, And when we are put
off, fall to their throats.* **11** See PUT BY. **put on 1**
'Lay on, as a blow' (Schmidt) LLL 4.1.113 *Finely
put on!* **2** Set to work, or to perform an office HAM
5.2.397 *he was likely, had he been put on, To have
prov'd most royal,* HAM 5.2.397, MAC 4.3.239. **3** Assume AYL 5.4.181 *The Duke hath put on a religious
life.* **4** Encourage the performance of (an evil
deed), promote (an evil state of things) LR 1.4.208
*That you protect this course and put it on By your
allowance,* CYM 5.1.9, HAM 3.1.2. **5** Clothe oneself
with, don; (hence) reveal JC 2.1.225 *Let not our
looks put on our purposes.* **put out** Put in exercise,
exert, extend ROM 4.5.121 *put out your wit.* **put
over** Hand over, refer JN 1.1.62 *But for the certain
knowledge of that truth I put you o'er to heaven
and to my mother.* **put to** Copulate, indulge in
sexual intercourse, 'go to it' WT 1.2.277 *any flax-
wench that puts to Before her troth-plight.* **put to
it** Force (one) to do one's utmost; (hence) reduce
to straits, drive to extremities MM 3.2.95 *he puts
transgression to't,* AWW 3.6.1, WT 1.2.16. **put up**
Submit to, suffer quietly, endure, put up with OTH
4.2.179 *to put up in peace what already I have foolishly suff'red,* TIT 1.1.433.
putter-on *n.* Instigator H8 1.2.24 *putter-on Of these
exactions,* WT 2.1.141.
putter-out *n.* One who invests money at interest
TMP 3.3.48 *Each putter-out of five for one.*
◇ A traveller could deposit a sum of money in
London before departure; the sum was forfeit if
the traveller failed to return, but was repaid
fivefold if he returned and produced proof of his
having reached his destination.
putting *n.*
1 (with *down*) Destruction, extermination WIV
2.1.29 *the putting down of men.*
2 (with *on*) Incitement, urging MM 4.2.117 *this un-
wanted putting on,* OTH 2.1.304, COR 2.3.252.
puttock *n.* Bird of prey of the kite kind CYM 1.1.140
I chose an eagle, And did avoid a puttock, TRO
5.1.62, 2H6 3.2.191.
puzzel *n.* (var. of) PUCELLE, maid; (hence) slut,
huzzy 1H6 1.4.107 *Pucelle or puzzel* (F1 *Puzel or
Pussel*).
puzzle *vb.* Bewilder, perplex, confound TN 4.2.43
*thou art more puzzled than the Egyptians in their
fog,* HAM 3.1.79, ANT 3.7.10.
pyramis *n.* Pyramid ANT 2.7.35 *the Ptolomies' pyra-
mises,* ANT 5.2.61, 1H6 1.6.21.

Q

Q *n.* (var. form of) Cue R3 3.4.7 *Had you not come
upon your Q* (Ff).
Qu'ai-je oublié [Fr.] What have I forgotten WIV
1.4.63.

quail *n.* Prostitute TRO 5.1.52 *one that loves quails.*
quail *vb.*
1 Slacken, become feeble AYL 2.2.20 *let not search
and inquisition quail.*

2 Overpower, ANT 5.2.85 *he meant to quail and shake the orb*; (absol.) MND 5.1.287 *O Fates,... Quail, crush,...and quell!*

quaint *adj.*
1 Skilled, clever 2H6 3.2.274 *how quaint an orator*, SHR 3.2.147.
2 Ingeniously or cunningly contrived, elaborate MND 2.1.99 *quaint mazes.*
3 (of speech, modes of expression, etc.) Carefully or ingeniously elaborated MV 3.4.69 *quaint lies*, 1H6 4.1.102.
4 (of persons) Pretty, fine, dainty, handsome MND 2.2.7 *wonders At our quaint spirits*, TMP 1.2.317.
5 (of appearance, dress) Beautiful, fine, elegant WIV 4.6.41 *quaint in green she shall be loose enrob'd*, SHR 4.3.102, ADO 3.4.22.

quaintly *adv.*
1 Skilfully, cleverly, ingeniously TGV 3.1.117 *a ladder, quaintly made of cords*, HAM 2.1.31, 3H6 2.5.24.
2 Elegantly, daintily TGV 2.1.122 *the lines are very quaintly writ*, MV 2.4.6.

quake *vb.* Cause to quake or tremble, agitate COR 1.9.6 *frighted, And...quak'd.*

qualification *n.* Determining or distinctive quality of a person or thing condition, nature, character OTH 2.1.275 *will I cause these...to mutiny, whose qualification shall come into no true taste again but by the displanting of Cassio.*

qualified *ppl. adj.*
1 *so qualified* Of such qualities SHR 4.5.66 *so qualified as may beseem The spouse of any noble gentleman*, WT 2.1.113.
2 *qualified in* Fit or competent for LR 1.4.35 *That which ordinary men are fit for, I am qualified in.*

qualify *vb.*
1 Moderate, mitigate so as to reduce to a more satisfactory condition MM 1.1.65 *So to enforce or qualify the laws As to your soul seems good*, JN 5.1.13, LR 1.2.161.
2 Appease, pacify WT 4.4.532 *Your discontenting father strive to qualify.*
3 Control, regulate TRO 2.2.118 *no discourse of reason, No fear...Can qualify the same* (i.e. your hot blood).
4 Dilute OTH 2.3.40 *one cup...and that was craftily qualified.*
5 Abate, diminish (something good) HAM 4.7.113 *Time qualifies the spark and fire of it*, SON 109.2.

quality *n.*
1 Character, nature, disposition MV 4.1.184 *The quality of mercy*, TIM 1.1.54, LR 2.4.92; *stream of quality* natural inclination 2H4 5.2.34.
2 Excellence of disposition, good natural gifts TRO 4.4.76 *The Grecian youths are full of quality*, TGV 3.1.65.
3 Accomplishment, attainment TIM 1.1.125 *I have bred her at my dearest cost In qualities of the best*, TGV 3.1.272, PER 4.2.46.
4 Rank, position AWW 1.3.113 *where qualities were level*, LR 5.3.120, 2H4 4.1.11; high rank H5 4.8.90 *gentlemen of blood and quality*, LR 5.3.110.
5 Profession, occupation, business TGV 4.1.56 *a man of such perfection As we do in our quality much want*, MM 2.1.58, HAM 2.2.432.
6 Party, side 1H4 4.3.36 *Because you are not of our quality.*
7 Manner, style MV 3.2.6 *Hate counsels not in such a quality*, H8 1.2.84, LR 2.4.137.
8 Nature, with reference to origin; (hence) cause, occasion TRO 4.1.45 *note of our approach, With the whole quality wherefore*, TIM 3.6.107.

Qualtitie! Calen o custere me! [Macaronic] The last word, *qualité*, of the preceding speech of the French soldier to which Pistol adds *Calen o custere me*, the burden of an Eliz. song (also appearing as the name of a tune 'Callino castura-me'), intended to represent Irish 'cailin oc astoir' i.e. young girl, my treasure; prob. meaningless H5 4.4.4.
▷ Malone conjecture; F1 *Qualtitie calmie custure me.*

quantity *n.*
1 Proportion HAM 3.2.167 *women's fear and love hold quantity* (i.e. are related in direct proportion), MND 1.1.232.
2 Fragment SHR 4.3.111 *thou quantity, thou remnant*, JN 5.4.23, 2H4 5.1.62.

quare [L.] Why LLL 5.1.33 (F2; F1, Q1 *Quari*).

quarrel *n.*
1 *have a quarrel to* Have a difference with ADO 2.1.236 *The Lady Beatrice hath a quarrel to you*, TN 3.4.227, COR 4.5.127.
2 Ground or occasion of complaint or dispute R2 1.3.33 *what's thy quarrel?*, HAM 4.4.55; (with possessive) cause, side, or party in a contest TIT 3.1.4 *my blood in Rome's great quarrel shed*, 2H6 3.2.233.
3 Quarrelsomeness OTH 2.3.50 *full of quarrel and offence.*
4 (?) (abstract for concrete) 'Quarreller' (Johnson) H8 2.3.14 *that quarrel, fortune.*
~ *vb.* Be at variance *with* TMP 3.1.45 *some defect in her Did quarrel with the noblest grace she ow'd*, JN 5.1.9.

quarrelling *n.* Cavilling, captious carping MV 3.5.55 *Yet more quarrelling with occasion* (i.e. cavilling on every opportunity).

quarrellous *n.* Quarrelsome CYM 3.4.159 *As quarrellous as the weasel.*

quarry *n.* Heap made of the deer killed at a hunt MAC 4.3.206 *the quarry of these murder'd deer*; heap of dead men COR 1.1.198 *I'd make a quarry With thousands of these quarter'd slaves*, HAM 5.2.364.

quarter *n.*
1 One of the four principal points of the compass; (hence) region of the world MAC 1.3.16 *All the quarters...I' th' shipman's card.*
2 Part of an army or camp 1H6 2.1.63 *Had all your quarters been as safely kept*; soldiers' lodging, billet, assigned area AWW 3.6.66 *bring this instrument of honour again into his native quarter*, TIM 5.4.60, ANT 4.3.21; *keep good quarter* keep good watch JN 5.5.20.
3 Relations with, or conduct towards, another ERR 2.1.208; *So he would keep fair quarter with his bed* (i.e. be true to the marriage), OTH 2.3.180.
~ *vb.* (esp. of a traitor or criminal) Cut into quarters JN 2.1.508 *Hang'd and drawn and quarter'd*; (hence) slaughter JC 3.1.268 *behold Their infants quartered with the hands of war.*

quartered *ppl. adj.*
1 (lit.) Cut into quarters; (hence) slaughtered COR 1.1.199 *these quarter'd slaves.*
2 Belonging to military quarters CYM 4.4.18 *their quarter'd fires.*

quartering *ppl. adj.* That cuts into quarters, slaughtering 1H6 4.2.11 *quartering steel.*

quasi [L.] As if LLL 4.2.83 *Master Person, quasi persone.*

quat *n.* Pimple, pustule; (applied contemptuously to a young person) OTH 5.1.11 *I have rubb'd this young quat almost to the sense.*

quatch *adj.* (?) Squat AWW 2.2.18 *chair that fits...the pin-buttock, the quatch-buttock.*

quean *n.* Bold, impudent, or ill-behaved woman, hussy, harlot WIV 4.2.172 *A witch, a quean, an old cozening quean!*, AWW 2.2.26, 2H4 1.4.47.

queasiness n. Squeamishness 2H4 1.1.196 *did fight with queasiness.*

queasy adj.
1 Hazardous, ticklish LR 2.1.17 *of a queasy question.*
2 Inclined to nausea, squeamish ADO 2.1.383 *queasy stomach.*
3 *queasy with* Disgusted with ANT 3.6.20 *queasy with his insolence.*

quell n. Murder MAC 1.7.72 *our great quell.*
~ vb. (intr.) Slay, kill MND 5.1.287 *Quail, crush, conclude, and quell!*

queller n. Destroyer, killer, murderer 2H4 2.1.53 *Murder, murder! ...thou art...a man-queller, and a woman-queller,* TRO 5.5.45.

quench vb.
1 Suppress a feeling in (a person) WT 5.1.107 *might quench the zeal,* ADO 4.1.239; (with personal object) CYM 5.5.195 *Being thus quench'd Of hope.*
2 (intr.) Cool down CYM 1.5.47 *Dost thou think in time She will not quench...?*

quern n. Hand-mill MND 2.1.36 *Skim milk, and sometimes labour in the quern.*

quest n.
1 Body of persons appointed to hold an inquiry R3 1.4.184 *What lawful quest have given their verdict up Unto the...judge,* HAM 5.1.22; (fig.) SON 46.10 *A quest of thoughts.*
2 Person or persons sent out to search OTH 1.2.46 *The Senate hath sent about three several quests To search you out.*
~ vb. (of hunting dogs) Break out into a peculiar bark at the sight of game, give tongue, yelp; (fig.) MM 4.1.61 *Volumes of report Run with these false, and most contrarious quest Upon thy doings.*

questant n. Seeker AWW 2.1.16 *The bravest questant shrinks.*

question n.
1 Talk, conversation LR 4.3.24 *Made she no verbal question?* (i.e. did she not speak?), HAM 3.1.13, 2H4 1.1.48.
2 Trial by arms OTH 1.3.23 *So may he with more facile question bear it* (i.e. capture it more easily).
3 *in question* Under judicial examination, on trial 2H4 1.2.60 *He that was in question for the robb'ry?,* ADO 3.3.179, WT 5.1.198; under consideration, to be considered MM 1.1.46 *Old Escalus, Though first in question, is thy secondary,* CYM 1.1.34, H5 1.1.5.
4 *call in question* Enquire into, examine, consider JC 4.3.165 *call in question our necessities,* AYL 5.2.5, HAM 4.5.218.
5 (in negative expressions) No doubt, without doubt; (with *no*) MM 3.2.138 *Why, no question but he was,* 2H6 4.2.57, OTH 4.3.63; (with *out of*) H5 5.1.46 *out of doubt and out of question too,* ADO 2.1.332; (with *past*) TN 1.3.98 *would that have mended my hair?—Past question;* (with *sans*) LLL 5.1.86 *I do, sans question;* (with *in contempt of*) TN 2.5.88 *It is, in contempt of question, her hand.*
~ vb.
1 Ask about, inquire into, investigate H5 2.4.142 *to question our delay,* MND 1.1.67, MAC 2.3.128.
2 Debate, talk, converse WIV 3.1.76 *Disarm them, and let them question,* CYM 2.4.52, LUC 122; (trans.) talk to 1H4 1.3.47 *With many holiday...terms He questioned me,* HAM 1.1.45 (Qq *Speak to it*).
3 (with *with*) Discuss, dispute *with* H8 1.1.130 *let your reason with your choler question,* SON 57.9.

questionable adj. Inviting question or conversation HAM 1.4.43 *Thou com'st in such a questionable shape That I will speak to thee.*

questrist n. One who goes in quest of another LR 3.7.17 *Hot questrists after him.*

quick adj.
1 Living, alive H5 2.2.79 *The mercy that was quick in us...is...kill'd,* HAM 5.1.126, WIV 3.4.86.
2 Pregnant, 'quick with child' LLL 5.2.681 *Jaquenetta that is quick by him,* LLL 5.2.676; fertile, potentially fertile ANT 1.2.110 *we bring forth weeds When our quick winds lie still.*
3 (of springs) Running, flowing TMP 3.2.67 *the quick freshes.*
4 (of air) Sharp, piercing PER 4.1.27 *the air is quick there, And it pierces and sharpens the stomach.*
5 Hasty, impatient R3 4.4.361 *Your reasons are too shallow and too quick,* LLL 2.1.117.
6 Lively LLL 1.1.161 *quick recreation,* AWW 4.2.5.

quicken vb.
1 Make alive TMP 3.1.6 *quickens what's dead,* AWW 2.1.74, ANT 1.3.69; become living ANT 4.15.39 *Die when thou hast liv'd, Quicken with kissing,* LR 3.7.39, OTH 3.3.277.
2 Enliven, stimulate, refresh MV 2.8.52 *quicken his...heaviness,* R3 4.4.124, SHR 1.1.36.

quick-answered adj. Sharp in reply CYM 3.4.158 *Ready in gibes, quick-answer'd, saucy.*

quickening n. Revival of life MM 5.1.495 *I see a quick'ning in his eye.*
~ ppl. adj. That quickens, life-giving TIM 4.3.184 *Hyperion's quick'ning fire.*

quid 'for' quo [L.] *Quid pro quo, tit for tat* 1H6 5.3.109.

quiddity n. Subtlety, quibble HAM 5.1.99 *Where be his quiddities now,...his tricks?* (Q2; F1 *Quiddits;* Q1 *Quirkes*), 1H4 1.2.45.

quiet n. *out of quiet* Disquieted TN 2.3.133.

quietus n.
1 Discharge or acquittance given on payment of sums due, settlement of accounts SON 126.12 *Time...her quietus is to render thee.*
2 Discharge or release from life HAM 3.1.74 *his quietus make With a bare bodkin.*

quill n. *in the quill* In a body 2H6 1.3.3 *we may deliver our supplications in the quill.*

quillet n. Verbal nicety or subtle distinction 1H6 2.4.17 *these nice sharp quillets of the law,* OTH 3.1.23, HAM 5.1.100 (F1; Qq 3–4 *quillities*).

quilt n. (transf.) Thick covering; (humorously applied to a fat person, Falstaff) 1H4 4.2.49 *How now, blown Jack? how now, quilt?*

quintain n. Stout post or plank or some object mounted on such a support, set up as a mark to be tilted at; (fig.) AYL 1.2.251 *that which here stands up Is but a quintain, a mere lifeless block.*

quintessence n. (lit.) The 'fifth essence' of ancient and medieval philosophy, supposed to be the substance of which the heavenly bodies were composed, and to be actually latent in all things; (hence) pure essence or extract, essential part (of a thing), the purest or most perfect form or manifestation HAM 2.2.308 *this quintessence of dust,* AYL 3.2.139.

quip n. Sharp or sarcastic remark TGV 4.2.12 *notwithstanding all her sudden quips,* 1H4 1.2.45, WIV 1.3.41.

quire n. Company MND 2.1.55 *the whole quire.*
~ vb. Make music COR 3.2.113 *Which quir'd with my drum* (F1 *quier'd*), MV 5.1.62.

quirk n.
1 Verbal subtlety, quibble PER 4.6.7 *she has me her quirks, her reasons.*
2 Clever or witty turn of expression or conceit OTH 2.1.63 *excels the quirks of blazoning pens* (perh. with quibble on sense of 'flourish'), ADO 2.3.236.
3 Trick or peculiarity of behaviour TN 3.4.245 *a man of that quirk.*
4 Fit, start AWW 3.2.49 *quirks of joy and grief.*

quis [L.] Who LLL 5.1.52.

quit vb.
1 Set free TN 5.1.321 *Your master quits you.*
2 Rid, free (one of a thing) H8 5.1.70 *God safely quit her of her burden*, H5 3.5.47, 2H6 3.2.218.
3 Prove innocent, clear, acquit, absolve H5 2.2.166 *God quit you in his mercy!*, AYL 3.1.11, 1H4 3.2.19.
4 (refl.) Acquit oneself in action LR 2.1.30 *quit you well.*
5 Play (one's part) MM 2.4.28 *The general subject to a well-wish'd king Quit their own part.*
6 Remit (a penalty, etc.) MV 4.1.381 *To quit the fine*, MM 5.1.483.
7 Repay, reward, requite ROM 2.4.192 *be trusty, and I'll quit thy pains*, LR 3.7.87, MM 5.1.411.
8 (refl.) Be quits (with) ADO 4.1.200 *To quit me of them.*
9 Pay or clear off ERR 1.1.22 *To quit the penalty.*
~ adj. Quits SHR 3.1.92 *Hortensio will be quit with thee; quit of* revenged upon COR 4.5.83 *To be full quit of those.*

quite vb. (var. of) QUIT ROM 2.4.192 [FF], R2 5.1.43 [QQ 1–4], PER 3.2.18 [QQ].

quittal n. Requital LUC 236 *in revenge or quittal of such strife.*

quittance n.
1 Discharge from debt AYL 3.5.133 *omittance is no quittance* (i.e. failure to assert a claim does not imply renunciation of the claim), WIV 1.1.10.
2 Return, requital, recompense, repayment, reprisal H5 2.2.34 *quittance of desert and merit*, 2H4 1.1.108, TIM 1.1.280.
~ vb. Requite 1H6 2.1.14 *to quittance their deceit.*

quiver adj. Active, nimble 2H4 3.2.281 *a little quiver fellow.*

Quod me alit, me extinguit [L.] That which feeds my flame puts out my light PER 2.2.33 (Q1 *Qui*).

quoif n. (var. of) Coif, close-fitting cap WT 4.4.224 *Golden quoifs...For my lads to give their dears*, 2H4 1.1.147 (F1).

quoit vb. Throw like a quoit 2H4 2.4.192 *Quoit him down...like a shove-groat shilling* (F1; Q *Quaite*).

quondam adj. That formerly was or existed, former 3H6 3.1.23 *the quondam king*, TRO 4.5.179, H5 2.1.78; *this quondam day the other day* LLL 5.1.6.

quoniam [L.] Because LLL 5.2.592.

quote vb.
1 Give the reference to (a passage in a book); (fig.) indicate LLL 2.1.246 *His face's own margent did quote such amazes.*
2 Set down as in writing JN 4.2.222 *A fellow by the hand of nature mark'd, Quoted, and sign'd to do a deed of shame.*
3 Notice, observe, examine closely TRO 4.5.233 *I have with exact view perus'd thee...And quoted joint by joint*, ROM 1.4.31, HAM 2.1.109.
4 Regard or set down as being so-and-so LLL 4.3.85 *Her amber hairs for foul hath amber quoted* (i.e. her amber-coloured hair has made amber seem ugly by comparison), AWW 5.3.205, LLL 5.2.786.
▷ Also spelt *coat(e)*, *cote* in Ff and Qq.

quoth vb.
1 (used with nouns, or pronouns of the first and third persons, to indicate that the words of a speaker are being repeated) Said ERR 2.1.62 ' '*Tis dinner-time', quoth I: 'My gold!' quoth he*, 1H4 2.1.48, MAC 1.3.5.
2 (with a pronoun of the second person used with contemptuous or sarcastic force) Indeed LLL 4.3.217 *Did they, quoth you?*

quotha, quoth'a interj. (used with contemptuous or sarcastic force in repeating something said by another) Said he; (hence) indeed, forsooth WIV 2.1.138 '*The humour of it', quoth 'a!*, AWW 1.3.85, 2H4 5.3.16.
▷ From 'quoth' plus 'a'. See 'A.

quotidian n. (short for) Quotidian fever, fever or ague recurring every day H5 2.1.119 *a burning quotidian tertian* (i.e. a mixture of different types of fever); (fig.) AYL 3.2.365 *the quotidian of love.*

R

rabato See REBATO.

rabbit-sucker n. Sucking rabbit, very young rabbit 1H4 2.4.437 *hang me up by the heels for a rabbit-sucker.*

rabblement n. The common, low, or disorderly part of the populace JC 1.2.244 *the rabblement howted.*

race n.[1] Course (of time) JN 3.3.39 *the drowsy race of night.*

race n.[2]
1 Herd or stud (of horses) MV 5.1.72 *herd Or race of...unhandled colts.*
2 Natural or inherited disposition MM 2.4.160 *I give my sensual race the rein*, TMP 1.2.358.
3 Flavour ANT 1.3.37 *none of our parts so poor But was a race of heaven* (with quibble on senses 1 and 2).

race, raze n.[3] Root (of ginger) WT 4.3.47 *a race or two of ginger*, 1H4 2.1.24 (Q1 *raze*).

race vb. See RASE, RAZE vb.

raced See RASED, RAZED.

rack n. Clouds, or mass of cloud, driven before the wind in the upper air HAM 2.2.484 *A silence in the heavens, the rack stand still*, SON 33.6; (fig.) TMP 4.1.156 *the great globe itself...shall dissolve, And...leave not a rack behind*; driving mist or fog ANT 4.14.10 *That which is now a horse...The rack dislimns.*

rack vb.
1 Stretch the joints of (a person) by pulling, esp. with intention to cause severe pain, and specifically by means of a special apparatus (the rack), torture on the rack 2H6 3.1.376 *Say he be taken, rack'd, and tortured*, MM 5.1.315; (hence) affect with pain similar to that caused by use of the rack, torment, torture TMP 1.2.369 *I'll rack thee with old cramps, Fill all thy bones with aches*; inflict mental torture on TN 5.1.219 *How have the hours rack'd and tortur'd me...!*
2 Stretch or strain beyond the normal extent MV 1.1.181 *my credit...shall be rack'd, even to the uttermost*, LLL 5.2.818, ADO 4.1.220.
▷ Perh. intr. use in COR 5.1.16 *A pair of tribunes that have rack'd for Rome To make coals cheap!* (F1 *wrack'd*).
3 Oppress by extortions or exactions 2H6 1.3.128 *The commons hast thou rack'd.*

racker n. Tormentor, torturer, 'murderer' LLL 5.1.19 *such rackers of orthography.*

racking ppl. adj. Driving before the wind, scudding 3H6 2.1.27 *racking clouds.*

raddock See RUDDOCK.

rag n.
1 Scrap ERR 4.4.86 *not a rag of money.*
2 (term of contempt) Tattered, shabby, worthless

person R3 5.3.328 *these overweening rags of France*, WIV 4.2.185, SHR 4.3.111.

rage *n.*
1 Madness, insanity LR 4.7.77 *the great rage...is kill'd in him*, ERR 4.3.87, ROM 4.3.53.
2 Angry disposition MV 5.1.81 *stockish, hard, and full of rage*, 1H4 3.1.181, LUC 1398.
3 Violent passion or appetite, height (*of* a feeling), vehement desire 2H4 4.4.63 *rage and hot blood are his counsellors*, LUC 424, LUC 468; sexual passion HAM 3.3.89 *When he is drunk asleep, or in his rage*.
4 Violence, violent operation or action, 'fury' (of things, the wind, the sea, fire, etc.) VEN 332 *river stay'd...swelleth with more rage*; (fig.) TGV 2.7.22 *the fire's extreme rage* (i.e. the fire of love), R2 3.3.59; a flood, high tide, rising of the sea (fig.) R2 3.2.109 *So high above his limits swells the rage Of Bullingbrook*.
5 Poetic enthusiasm or inspiration SON 17.11 *your true rights be term'd a poet's rage*.
6 Martial spirit, ardour, fervour JN 2.1.265 *shall we give the signal to our rage, And stalk in blood to our possession*, R2 2.4.14, 1H4 1.3.31.
~ *vb.*
1 Behave wantonly or riotously ADO 4.1.61 *rage in savage sensuality*, LC 160.
2 Act with fury or vehemence 3H6 2.3.26 *whiles the foe doth rage*.
3 Enrage R2 2.1.70 *young hot colts being rag'd*, R2 2.1.173.

ragged(-)staff *n.* Staff with projecting stumps or knobs 2H6 5.1.203 *The rampant bear chain'd to the ragged staff*.

raging *ppl. adj.* Wanton, lustful R3 3.5.83 *his raging eye*, OTH 1.3.330, TRO 2.2.281.

raging(-)wood *adj.* Raving mad 1H6 4.7.35 *the young whelp of Talbot's, raging wood*.

rainy *adj.* Done in the rain H5 4.3.111 *rainy marching*.

raise *vb.* Originate (a rumour) COR 4.6.70 *Rais'd only that the weaker sort may wish Good Martius home again*.

raised *ppl. adj.*
1 Roused up OTH 1.2.29 *the raised father*.
2 Set on foot, instituted OTH 1.1.158 *the raised search*.

raising *n.* Report, rumour, fabrication COR 4.6.61 *his raising, Nothing but his report*.

raisins o' th' sun *n. phr.* Sun-dried grapes WT 4.3.48 *four pounds of pruins, and as many of raisins o' th' sun*.

rake *n.* Very lean person COR 1.1.23 *ere we become rakes*.

rake *vb.* (with *up*) Cover up, bury LR 4.6.274 *Thee I'll rake up*.

ram *vb.* Block *up* JN 2.1.272 *Have we ramm'd up our gates against the world*.

ramp *n.* Bold, ill-behaved woman, prostitute CYM 1.6.134 *variable ramps*.

rampallian, rampallion *n.* Ruffian, scoundrel; (applied to a woman) 2H4 2.1.59 *you scullion! you rampallian!* (F1).

ramping *ppl. adj.*
1 Rearing on the hind legs and showing fierceness 1H4 3.1.151 *A couching lion and a ramping cat*; (hence) of a fierce disposition 3H6 5.2.13 *Under whose shade the ramping lion slept*.
2 Unrestrained JN 3.1.122 *A ramping fool*.

rampired *ppl. adj.* Fortified against attack, as by ramparts, blocked up, stopped up by having earth piled behind (them) TIM 5.4.47 *our rampir'd gates*.

random, randon *n. at random* Untended, unattended, neglected ERR 1.1.42 *goods at random left* (F1 *randon*).

range *n.* Rank, row ANT 3.13.5 *that great face of war, whose several ranges Frighted each other* (i.e. battle lines).
~ *vb.*
1 Stretch out in a line COR 3.1.205 *bury all, which yet distinctly ranges, In heaps and piles of ruin* (i.e. which clearly has a recognized position).
2 Extend or lie in the same plane *with* ADO 2.2.7 *whatsoever comes athwart his affection ranges evenly with mine*.
3 Occupy a position, rank H8 2.3.20 *range with humble livers in content*, 1H4 1.3.169.
4 Rove, roam AYL 1.3.68 *Else had she with her father rang'd along*, HAM 3.3.2.
5 Be inconstant SHR 3.1.91 *if once I find thee ranging*, SON 109.5.
6 Traverse, go about TN 4.3.7 *range the town to seek me out*.

ranged *ppl. adj.* Ordered ANT 1.1.34 *the rang'd empire*.

ranger *n.* Gamekeeper CYM 2.3.69 *Diana's rangers*.

rank *n.* Movement in line or file AYL 3.2.98 *the right butter-women's rank to market*.
▷ Hanmer's conjecture *rate*; Aldis Wright *rack* (i.e. ambling gait).
~ *vb.* Surround, occupy *with* (ranks or rows) TIM 1.1.65 *The base o' th' mount Is rank'd with all deserts, all kind of natures* (i.e. with all kinds of men).

rank *adj.*
1 Coarsely luxuriant H5 5.2.50 *Wanting the scythe..., uncorrected, rank*, HAM 3.4.152; (hence, fig.) TRO 1.3.318 *the seeded pride That hath to this maturity blown up In rank Achilles*, AYL 2.7.46; high or excessive in amount HAM 4.4.22 *Nor will it yield...A ranker rate, should it be sold in fee*, AYL 4.1.84.
2 Puffed up, swollen, grossly fat JC 3.1.152 *Who else must be let blood, who else is rank*; (hence, fig.) exuberant, over-full 2H4 4.1.64 *To diet rank minds*, SON 118.12.
3 Copious, full VEN 71 *a river that is rank*.
4 Of offensively strong smell, rancid TN 2.5.124 *as rank as a fox*, WIV 3.5.92, ANT 5.2.212; (fig.) HAM 3.3.36 *O, my offence is rank, it smells to heaven*.
5 Lustful, in heat MV 1.3.80 *the ewes being rank*; lascivious CYM 2.5.24 *rank thoughts*, LC 307, OTH 2.1.306 (Q1; F1 *right*).
6 Corrupt, foul 2H4 3.1.39 *rank diseases*, HAM 3.4.148, TRO 1.3.73.
~ *adv.* Abundantly WIV 4.6.22 *other jests are something rank on foot*; excessively TRO 1.3.196 *How rank soever rounded in with danger*.

rankle *vb.* Cause a festering wound R3 1.3.290 *His venom tooth will rankle to the death* (F1; Q1 *rackle thee to death*), R2 1.3.302.

rankness *n.*
1 Flooding, 'fulness to overflowing' (Wright) JN 5.4.54 *like a bated...flood, Leaving our rankness and irregular course*; (fig.) exuberance H8 4.1.59 *the mere rankness of their joy*.
2 Insolence AYL 1.1.86 *I will physic your rankness*.

ransacked *ppl. adj.* Carried off, ravished TRO 2.2.150 *the ransack'd queen*.

ransom *n.*
1 The action of procuring the release of a prisoner or captive by paying a certain sum AWW 1.3.116 *without rescue in the first assault or ransom afterward*, 1H4 1.3.141, 1H4 4.3.96; the action of procuring one's own freedom in this way 2H6 4.1.10 *Here shall they make their ransom*, H5 4.3.80.
2 Atonement, expiation TGV 5.4.75 *if hearty sorrow Be a sufficient ransom for offence*, 2H6 3.1.127, CYM 5.3.80.

~ *vb.* Atone for SON 120.14 *Mine [trespass] ransoms yours*, SON 34.14; bring *into* by ransoming OTH 3.4.118 *nor my service past, nor present sorrows…Can ransom me into his love again.*

rap *vb.* Affect with rapture, transport (with joy, etc.) CYM 1.6.51 *What…raps you?*

rapier and dagger See DAGGER.

rapture *n.*
1 The act of seizing and carrying off as prey or plunder, plundering PER 2.1.155 *And, spite of all the rapture of the sea.*
  ⟡ Rowe conjecture; Q *rupture*.
2 Fit COR 2.1.207 *Into a rapture lets her baby cry.*

rare *interj.* Splendid! 1H4 1.2.64 *O rare!*

rarely *adv.*
1 Finely, splendidly ADO 3.1.60 *rarely featur'd*, ANT 4.4.11, MND 1.2.29.
2 Exceptionally ANT 5.2.158 *O rarely base!*, WT 5.1.150.

rareness *n.* Unusual or exceptional character, esp. in respect of excellence HAM 5.2.117 *infusion of such dearth and rareness.*

rariety See RARITY.

rarity *n.* Unusual or exceptional character, esp. in respect of excellence AWW 4.3.274 *He hath outvillain'd villainy so far, that the rarity redeems him* (i.e. the excellence of his performance), PHT 53, TMP 2.1.59 (F1 *rariety*).

rascal *n.* Lean or inferior deer of a herd AYL 3.3.58 *Horns…the noblest deer hath them as huge as the rascal*; (fig.) 2H4 5.4.30 *Come, you thin thing, come, you rascal*, 1H6 1.2.35, COR 1.1.159.
  ~ *adj.*
1 Lean, inferior, worthless TIM 5.1.115 *Out, rascal dogs!*, JC 4.3.80.
2 Belonging to, or forming, the rabble 2H6 4.4.51 *The rascal people.*

rase *vb.*[1] Pull, pluck *off* R3 3.2.11 *He dreamt the boar had rased off his helm* (Ff 1-2; Ff 3-4 *raised off*; Qq 1-4 *raste*; Qq 5-8 *cast(e)*), R3 3.4.82 (F1 *rowse*; Qq 1-6 *race*).

rase, raze *vb.*[2] Erase, obliterate MAC 5.3.42 *Raze out the written troubles of the brain*, SON 25.11; (fig.) TIT 1.1.451 *massacre them all, And rase their faction and their family* (F1 *race*), 2H6 1.1.101, CYM 5.5.70.

rased, razed *ppl. adj.*
1 Cut, slashed HAM 3.2.277 *my raz'd shoes* (Q; F1 *rac'd*).
2 'Leaving no trace behind' (Schmidt), removed in a thorough manner SON 122.7 *raz'd oblivion.*

rash *vb.* Dash LR 3.7.58 *In his anointed flesh rash boarish fangs* (Qq 1-2; F1 *sticke*).

rash *adj.*
1 (of things) Operating quickly and strongly WT 1.2.319 *with no rash potion, but with a ling'ring dram*, 2H4 4.4.48, MM 5.1.392.
2 Urgent, pressing TRO 4.2.60 *My matter is so rash.*
  ~ *adv.* Rashly, hastily, without consideration OTH 3.4.79 *Why do you speak so startlingly and rash?*

rate *n.*
1 (Estimated) quantity 2H4 4.1.22 *I judge their number Upon or near the rate of thirty thousand.*
2 (Estimated) value or worth MND 3.1.154 *a spirit of no common rate*, AWW 5.3.91, ROM 5.3.301.
3 Estimation, consideration TMP 1.2.92 *all popular rate*, TMP 2.1.110.
4 Standard of conduct or action; (hence) manner, mode, style MV 1.1.127 *such a noble rate* (i.e. style of living).
  ~ *vb.*[1]
1 Allot, apportion ANT 3.6.25 *we had not rated him His part o' th' isle.*

2 Calculate, estimate 2H4 1.3.44 *must we rate the cost of the erection*, TIM 2.2.126.
3 Reckon, esteem, consider AWW 2.1.179 *all that life can rate Worth name of life.*
4 Be of equal value with, be worth ANT 3.11.69 *Fall not a tear,…one of them rates All that is won and lost.*

rate *vb.*[2]
1 Chide, scold, reprove vehemently or angrily 2H6 3.2.56 *Why do you rate my Lord of Suffolk thus?*, JC 2.1.216, MV 1.3.107.
2 Drive away by rating SHR 1.1.160 *Affection is not rated from the heart*, 1H4 4.3.99.
3 (intr.) Utter strong or angry reproofs SHR 4.1.184 *rails, and swears, and rates*, 2H6 3.1.175.

rated *ppl. adj.*
1 Esteemed, reckoned upon 1H4 4.4.17 *a rated sinew.*
2 Assessed, estimated at its true value JN 5.4.37 *Paying the fine of rated treachery.*

rather *adv.*
1 *the rather* The more quickly MAC 1.7.62 *When Duncan is asleep (Whereto the rather shall his day's hard journey Soundly invite him)*; the more readily AWW 3.5.42 *where you shall be lodg'd, The rather for I think I know your hostess As ample as myself*, JN 5.7.87, TN 3.3.12.
2 *me rather had* I had rather R2 3.3.192.

ratherest *adv.* Most of all LLL 4.2.18 *after his…untrained, or rather unlettered, or ratherest unconfirmed fashion.*

ratify *vb.* Bring into proper metrical 'proportion' or rhythm LLL 4.2.121 *Here are only numbers ratified, but for the…golden cadence of poesy, caret.*

rational *adj.*
1 Exercising one's reason in a proper manner, sensible LLL 1.2.118 *the rational hind Costard.*
2 Agreeable to reason, reasonable AWW 1.1.128 *Loss of virginity is rational increase, and there was never virgin got till virginity was first lost.*

ratalorum, rato-lorum See CUSTALORUM.

ratsbane *n.* Rat-poison LR 3.4.55 *set ratsbane by his porridge*, 2H4 1.2.42, 1H6 5.4.29.

rattle *vb.* Assail with a rattling noise JN 5.2.172 *rattle the welkin's ear.*

raught See REACH.

ravel *vb.*
1 Become entangled TGV 3.2.52 *as you unwind her love from him, Lest it should ravel…You must provide to bottom it on me.*
2 (with *out*) Disentangle, make plain or clear R2 4.1.228 *must I ravel out My weav'd-up follies?*, HAM 3.4.186.

ravelled *ppl. adj.* Tangled MAC 2.2.34 *Sleep that knits up the ravell'd sleave of care.*

raven, ravin *vb.* Devour voraciously CYM 1.6.49 *ravening first the lamb*; (with *down*) MM 1.2.129 *Like rats that ravin down their proper bane*; (with *up*) MAC 2.4.28 *ravin up Thine own live's means.*

ravened, ravined *ppl. adj.* (?) Glutted MAC 4.1.24 *the ravin'd salt-sea shark.*

ravin *adj.* Ravenous AWW 3.2.117 *I met the ravin lion.*

ravish *vb.*
1 Spoil, corrupt LUC 778 *With rotten damps ravish the morning air.*
2 Pull out, remove by force LR 3.7.38 *These hairs which thou dost ravish from my chin.*
3 Carry away with rapture, entrance LLL 1.1.167 *the music…Doth ravish like enchanting harmony*, 1H6 5.5.15, ADO 2.3.58; (intr.) 2H6 1.1.32 *Her sight did ravish.*

ravished *ppl. adj.* Carried away by force TRO Prol.9 *The ravish'd Helen.*

ravishing *ppl. adj.* Seizing upon prey, ravenous MAC 2.1.55 *Murder,...With Tarquin's ravishing strides, towards his design Moves.*

raw *adj.* Unripe, immature R2 2.3.42 *my service,... being tender, raw and young*; inexperienced, unskilled, untrained MV 3.4.77 *raw tricks*, PER 4.2.55, AYL 3.2.72 (with quibble on sense 'excoriated').

raw-boned *adj.* Excessively lean or gaunt 1H6 1.2.35 *Lean raw-bon'd rascals!*

rawly *adv.* At an immature age H5 4.1.141 *crying... upon their children rawly left.*

rawness *n.* (fig.) Imperfection, incompleteness; (hence) unpreparedness MAC 4.3.26 *Why in that rawness left you wife and child...?*

ray *vb.* Beray, dirty, defile SHR 3.2 53 *his horse ...ray'd with the yellows*, SHR 4.1.3.

raze See RACE, RAZE.

razed See RASED, RAZED.

razorable *adj.* Capable of, or fit for, being shaved TMP 2.1.250 *till new-born chins Be rough and razorable.*

razure *n.* (fig.) Obliteration, effacement MM 5.1.13 *razure of oblivion.*

re *n.* The second note of Guido's hexachords and of the octave SHR 3.1.74 *A re, to plead Hortensio's passion*, SHR 3.1.77, LLL 4.2.100.
▷ Used jocularly as a vb. at ROM 4.5.118 *I'll re you* and ROM 4.5.120.

reach *n.* Capacity, ability, power of attainment HAM 2.1.61 *thus do we of wisdom and of reach...By indirections find directions out.*
~ *vb.* (pa. t. and pa. pple. usu. *raught*)
1 Seize in the hand, take or lay hold of ANT 4.9.29 *The hand of death hath raught him*, 2H6 2.3.43.
2 Grasp or clutch *at* 2H6 1.2.11 *Put forth thy hand, reach at the glorious gold*, 3H6 1.4.68; (fig.) R2 1.3.72 *To reach at victory above my head.*
3 Extend; (of time) last, endure LLL 4.2.40 *The moon...raught not to five weeks*; (of quantity) amount *to* 1H4 4.1.129 *What may the King's whole battle reach unto?—To thirty thousand.*
4 Attain *to* R3 1.1.159 *another...intent By marrying her which I must reach unto.*

reaching *ppl. adj.* Able to reach far 2H6 4.7.81 *Great men have reaching hands.*

read *vb.* (elliptical for) Read lessons; (hence) give instruction, lecture 1H4 3.1.45 *Which calls me pupil or hath read to me?*; teach SHR 3.1.13 *give me leave to read philosophy.*

readiness *n.*
1 Quickness in performance, facility, proficiency MM 2.1.261 *I thought, by the readiness in the office, you had continu'd in it some time.*
2 put on manly readiness Dress oneself MAC 2.3.133.

ready *adj.*
1 (used in replying to a call or summons) Here! MND 1.2.18 *Answer as I call you.* Nick Bottom the weaver.—*Ready*, MV 4.1.2, ROM 1.5.11.
2 Dressed 1H6 2.1.SD *Enter...Bastard, Alanson, Regnier, half ready and half unready*, CYM 2.3.81.

reak (var. of) RECK.

re-answer *vb.* Meet, be sufficient, compensate for H5 3.6.128 *his ransom, which must proportion the losses we have borne,...which in weight to re-answer, his pettiness would bow under.*

reap *vb.* Get in return, gain, acquire TN 3.1.133 *when wit and youth is come to harvest, Your wife is like to reap a proper man*, H8 3.2.204, AWW 2.1.147; get knowledge of CYM 2.4.86 *a thing Which you might from relation likewise reap.*

rear *n.*
1 The hindmost portion of an army or fleet TRO

3.3.162 *Or like a gallant horse fall'n in first rank, Lie there for pavement to the abject rear.*
▷ F1 *abiect, neere*; Hanmer conjecture *abject rear.*
2 *in, within the rear (of)* Behind HAM 1.3.34 *keep you in the rear of your affection*, WT 4.4.581.

rear *vb.*
1 Lift up, raise TMP 2.1.295 *When I rear my hand*, TIT 3.1.168, ANT 2.1.35.
2 Rouse, stir up R2 4.1.145 *if you rear this house against this house.*
3 Erect, construct 1H6 1.6.21 *a statelier pyramis to her I'll rear*, TIT 5.2.188.

rearmouse, rere-mouse *n.* Bat MND 2.2.4 *Some war with rere-mice for their leathren wings* (F1).

rearward *n.* Rear-guard, that part of an army (or fleet) which is stationed behind the main body 1H6 3.3.33 *in the rearward comes the Duke*; (fig.) ROM 3.2.121 *with a rearward following Tybalt's death, 'Romeo is banished'*, SON 90.6, 2H4 3.2.316.

reason *n.*
1 Observation, remark, account or explanation of something LLL 5.1.2 *Your reasons at dinner*, AYL 1.3.6, R3 4.4.361; discourse, speech MM 1.2.185 *reason and discourse*, SON 151.8.
2 Ground or cause of, or for, something ROM 4.1.15 *the reason of this haste*, JC 1.3.30; *reason, great reason* there is good reason (for it) JN 5.2.130 *and reason too he should*, R3 5.3.185, TIT 2.3.81.
3 Reasonableness, conformity of something to the dictates of reason (chiefly in phr. *in (all) reason, good reason, 'tis but reason*) MND 5.1.255 *in all reason, we must stay the time*, 3H6 3.3.147, OTH 3.3.64.
4 Reasonable behaviour or speech WIV 1.1.211 *I shall do that that is reason*, H5 5.2.330, ADO 5.1.41.
5 Reasonable quantity, amount, or degree ADO 5.4.77 *Do not you love me?—Troth no, no more than reason*, MV 3.5.41.
6 That treatment which may with reason be expected by, or required from, a person; *do reason* do justice, make satisfaction TIT 1.1.279 *To do myself this reason and this right*, TMP 3.2.119, WIV 1.1.234.
7 *have reason* Be right (esp. in making a statement) TGV 2.4.156 *Have I not reason to prefer mine own?*, MAC 3.5.2, VEN 612.
8 (with neg.) Possibility of action or occurrence TGV 2.4.212 *There is no reason but I shall be blind*, SHR 2.1.407.
~ *vb.*
1 Hold argument, carry on discussion, discourse or talk *with* (another) MV 2.8.27 *I reason'd with a Frenchman yesterday, Who told me...*, LLL 1.1.94, ROM 3.1.52.
2 Question, discuss (*what, whether, where*, etc.) R3 1.4.93 *I will not reason what is meant hereby*, 1H4 2.3.104, COR 4.6.52.
3 Discuss or argue (a matter) LR 2.4.264 *reason not the need*; explain, support, infer, deal with by (or as by) reasoning LR 1.2.105 *Though the wisdom of nature can reason it thus and thus*, COR 5.3.176; (with *with*) JC 5.1.96 *Let's reason with the worst that may befall.*

reasonable *adj.*
1 (of the soul or intellectual powers) Endowed with reason TMP 5.1.81 *the reasonable shores* (i.e. shores of reason; the mind).
▷ F1 *shore*; Malone *shores.*
2 Requiring the use of reason WT 4.4.398 *incapable Of reasonable affairs.*

reave *vb.* (pa. t. and pa. pple. *reft*)
1 Rob (a person), deprive (one) of something by force VEN 766 *butcher sire that reaves his son of life*, ERR 1.1.115, CYM 3.3.103.

2 Take away VEN 1174 *he himself is reft from her by death.*

rebate *vb.* Blunt, dull, ABATE sense 3 MM 1.4.60 *rebate and blunt his natural edge.*

rebato *n.* Kind of stiff collar worn about 1590-1630 ADO 3.4.6 *I think your other rebato were better.*

rebeck *n.* Early form of the fiddle; (used as a musician's name) ROM 4.5.133 *What say you, Hugh Rebeck?*

rebuke *vb.* Beat down or force back H5 3.6.121 *we could have rebuk'd him at Harfleur,* PER 3.1.1; repress, check MAC 3.1.55 *under him My genius is rebuk'd,* JN 2.1.9; repulse MND 3.2.43 *why rebuke you him that loves you so?*

recant *vb.* Withdraw, retract (a promise, vow, etc.) MV 4.1.391 *or else I do recant The pardon that I late pronounced here.*

recanting *ppl. adj.* That recants or retracts R2 1.1.193 *The slavish motive of recanting fear,* TIM 1.2.17.

receipt *n.*
1 That which is received; (in money) R2 1.1.126 *Three parts of that receipt I had for Calais*; (in food or other things) LUC 703 *Drunken Desire must vomit his receipt,* COR 1.1.112.
2 Place for the reception of things, receptacle MAC 1.7.66 *the receipt of reason A limbeck only.*
◊ It was believed that reason occupied a separate ventricle of the brain. It was also believed that the fumes of wine rose from the stomach to the brain and intoxicated it.
3 Capability of receiving, accommodating, or containing, capacity SON 136.7 *things of great receipt.*
4 Act of receiving or admitting, reception etc. H8 2.2.138 *such receipt of learning.*
5 Formula or prescription, statement of the ingredients (and mode of procedure) necessary for the making of some preparation, esp. in medicine and cookery, recipe AWW 2.1.105 *many receipts he gave me.*

receive *vb.*
1 Take from another by hearing or listening, attend or listen to AWW 2.1.22 *Our hearts receive your warnings,* HAM 5.2.91, LR 5.3.216.
2 Take into the mind, understand MM 2.4.82 *To be received plain, I 'll speak more gross.*
3 Give credit to, believe MAC 1.7.74 *Will it not be receiv'd...That they have done't?,* TN 3.4.193, HAM 2.2.437.
4 Take or accept (a person) in some capacity TIT 4.2.158 *be received for the Emperor's heir,* H5 5.2.368, 1H6 1.2.92.

receiving *n.*
1 Reception (with signs of attention and respect) WT 4.4.526 *you shall have such receiving As shall become your Highness.*
2 Understanding TN 3.1.120 *To one of your receiving.*

receptacle *n.* Place or space which receives persons or things; (used of grave, burial vault) TIT 2.3.235 *this fell devouring receptacle,* TIT 1.1.92, ROM 4.3.39; (used of a sewer) PER 4.6.175 *Empty Old receptacles, or common shores, of filth.*

rechate (var. of) RECHEAT.

recheat *n.* Series of notes sounded on the horn for calling the hounds together ADO 1.1.240 *I will have a recheat winded in my forehead* (with ref. to the cuckold's 'horns'; Q *rechate*).

recite *vb.* Rehearse, tell, declare SON 72.1 *to recite What merit liv'd in me.*

reck, reak *vb.*
1 (trans.) Heed, regard, care for HAM 1.3.51 *recks not his own rede,* TGV 4.3.40, VEN 283; (intr.) care,

mind, be troubled TRO 5.6.26 *I reck not though I end my life today.*
2 (with infin.) Care, desire, be willing or anxious to (do something) AYL 2.4.81 *And little recks to find the way to heaven By doing deeds of hospitality.*
◊ Ff and Qq always *reak* or *wreak.*

reckon *vb.*
1 Include in the reckoning, count among the number *of* WT 3.2.190 *trespasses...whereof I reckon The casting forth to crows thy baby daughter To be none or little.*
2 Estimate, value AWW 5.3.90 *she reckon'd it At her live's rate,* LUC 19.

reckoning *n.*
1 Bill, esp. at an inn or tavern 1H4 2.4.101 *his eloquence the parcel of a reckoning,* AYL 3.4.32, 2H4 1.2.171.
2 Way of regarding a matter SHR 4.1.85 *By this reck'ning he is more shrew than she.*
3 *be one reckoning* Be of the same value, be equivalent H5 4.7.17 *the great, or the mighty, or the huge...are all one reckonings* (Fluellen's speech).
4 Estimation, repute ROM 1.2.4 *Of honourable reckoning are you both.*

reclaim *vb.* Reduce to obedience, subdue 1H6 3.4.5 *this arm, that hath reclaim'd To your obedience fifty fortresses,* 2H6 5.2.54, ROM 4.2.47.

reclusive *adj.* Marked by reclusion or retirement ADO 4.1.242 *some reclusive and religious life.*

recognizance *n.*
1 Bond or obligation, recorded before a court or magistrate, by which a person engages himself to perform some act or observe some condition (e.g. to pay a debt) HAM 5.1.105 *This fellow might be...a great buyer of land, with his statutes, his recognizances, his fines...*
2 Token, badge OTH 5.2.214 *that recognizance...of love.*

recoil *vb.*
1 Fall away (from some state or condition), degenerate MAC 4.3.19 *A good and virtuous nature may recoil,* CYM 1.6.128.
2 Go back in memory WT 1.2.154 *methoughts I did recoil Twenty-three years.*

recollect *vb.* Collect, gather up PER 2.1.50 *from their wat'ry empire recollect All that may men approve or men detect!*

recollected *ppl. adj.* Gathered, picked up; (hence) imitated, not spontaneous or deeply felt, superficial TN 2.4.5 *light airs and recollected terms Of these...giddy-paced times.*

recomforted *ppl. adj.* Consoled; (absol.) COR 5.4.48 *Ne'er through an arch so hurried the blown tide, As the recomforted through the gates.*

recomforture *n.* Consolation, comfort R3 4.4.425 *to your recomforture* (F1; Qq 1-6 *recomfiture*).

recommend *vb.*
1 Consign, commit TN 5.1.91 *denied me mine own purse, Which I had recommended to his use Not half an hour before,* COR 2.2.151.
2 Inform OTH 1.3.41 *Your trusty...servitor...recommends you thus.*
3 (refl.) Be acceptable, make itself agreeable MAC 1.6.2 *the air...sweetly recommends itself Unto our... senses.*

recompt *vb.* (var. of) Recount 3H6 2.1.96 *if we should recompt Our baleful news.*

reconcile *vb.* Bring back to, into (a state of peace) R3.2.1.60 *I desire To reconcile me to his friendly peace*; (favour) LR 3.6.113 *When false opinion...In thy just proof repeals and reconciles thee.*

reconciliation *n.* Submission or action aimed to produce reconciliation and to restore one to favour OTH 3.3.47 *His present reconciliation take.*

record *n.*

1 *in, upon record* Committed to writing as authentic evidence of a matter having legal importance MM 2.2.40 *To fine the faults whose fine stands in record*, ADO 5.1.240, R2 4.1.230.

2 Witness R2 1.1.30 *heaven be the record to my speech.*

3 Memory, recollection TN 5.1.246 *that record is lively in my soul!*, COR 4.6.50.

~ *vb.*

1 (intr.) Sing, warble PER 4.Gower.27 *the nightbird...That still records with moan;* (trans.) sing of or about (something), render in song TGV 5.4.6 *to the nightingale's...notes Tune my distresses and record my woes.*

2 Have (a gift) properly recorded MV 4.1.388 *that he do record a gift Here in the court.*

3 (intr.) Bear witness to (a fact, etc.) TIT 1.1.255 *How proud I am of thee...Rome shall record;* (trans.) take to witness TIM 4.2.4 *Let me be recorded by the righteous gods.*

recordation *n.* Remembrance, recollection, commemorative account TRO 5.2.116 *make a recordation to my soul Of every syllable that here was spoke*, 2H4 2.3.61.

recorded *ppl. adj.* Put on record, preserved in writing MAC 5.5.21 *the last syllable of recorded time*, MM 2.4.61.

recorder *n.*[1] (orig.) Official with legal knowledge appointed by the mayor and aldermen to 'record' or keep in mind the proceedings of their courts and the customs of the city, his oral statement of these being taken as the highest evidence of fact R3 3.7.30 *the people were not used To be spoke to but by the Recorder.*

recorder *n.*[2] Wind instrument of the flute or flageolet kind MND 5.1.123 *he hath play'd on this prologue like a child on a recorder*, HAM 3.2.292.

recountment *n.* Relation, recital AYL 4.3.140 *Tears our recountments had...bath'd.*

recourse *n.*

1 Flowing TRO 5.3.55 *Their eyes o'ergalled with recourse of tears.*

2 Opportunity of resorting *to* (a person), access, admission R3 3.5.109 *that no manner person Have...recourse unto the Princes*, TGV 3.1.112, WIV 2.1.215.

recover *vb.*[1]

1 Bring back to friendship, reconcile OTH 2.3.272 *there are more ways to recover the general again.*

2 Get (the wind of, to windward of, a person) HAM 3.2.346 *why do you go about to recover the wind of me?* (i.e. outwit).

3 Get to, reach, arrive at TMP 3.2.14 *ere I could recover the shore*, TGV 5.1.12, TN 2.3.184.

4 Restore or bring back to life or consciousness AYL 4.3.150 *he fainted...I recover'd him*, WT 4.4.786, PER 2.2.9; restore to health or strength, cure, heal AWW 3.2.20 *she hath recover'd the King*, TMP 2.2.93.

5 Rescue, deliver (a person) from danger TN 2.1.38 *kill him whom you have recover'd.*

6 (malapropism for) Discover ADO 3.3.167 *We have here recover'd the most dangerous piece.*

recover *vb.*[2] Cover again, re-sole JC 1.1.24 *I am...a surgeon to old shoes;...I recover them* (with pun on RECOVER *vb.*[1] sense 4).

recoverable *adj.* Capable of being retraced TIM 3.4.13 *a prodigal course Is like the sun's, but not like his recoverable.*

recovery *n.* Process by which an entailed estate was commonly transferred from one party to another HAM 5.1.106 *his fines, his double vouchers, his recoveries*, WIV 4.2.211, ERR 2.2.74 (with quibble).

recreant *n.*

1 One who yields in combat, a cowardly or faint-hearted person MND 3.2.409 *Come, recreant, come, thou child*, TRO 1.3.287, 2H6 4.8.27.

2 One who breaks allegiance or faith, traitor, deserter, villain LR 1.1.166 *Hear me, recreant, On thine allegiance*, R2 1.2.53, COR 5.3.114.

▷ The two senses freq. merge.

~ *adj.*

1 Cowardly, faint-hearted, craven JN 3.1.129 *Thou wear a lion's hide! Doff it for shame, And hang a calve's-skin on those recreant limbs*, 2H4 5.3.92.

2 Unfaithful to duty, false, apostate R2 1.1.144 *A recreant and most degenerate traitor.*

recreation *n.*

1 Refreshment by partaking of food LLL 4.2.166 *the gentles are at their game, and we will to our recreation.*

2 One who furnishes amusement TN 2.3.135 *make him a common recreation.*

rector *n.* Ruler, governor AWW 4.3.59 *Her death ...was...confirm'd by the rector of the place.*

rectorship *n.* Government, rule COR 2.3.205 *the rectorship of judgement.*

recure *vb.*

1 Bring back to a normal state or condition, restore after loss, damage, etc. SON 45.9 *Until life's composition be recured*, R3 3.7.130.

2 Remedy VEN 465 *A smile recures the wounding of a frown.*

red *adj.* Epithet applied to one kind of the plague, marked by cutaneous eruptions and sores TRO 2.1.19 *a red murrion*, COR 4.1.13, TMP 1.2.364.

redbreast *n. redbreast teacher* One who teaches robins to sing 1H4 3.1.260.

rede *n.* Counsel, advice HAM 1.3.51 *Himself...recks not his own rede* (F1 *read*; Q2 *reed*).

redeem *vb.*

1 Regain, recover (an immaterial thing) 1H4 5.4.48 *Thou hast redeem'd thy lost opinion*, 1H4 1.3.180.

2 Go in exchange for 1H6 2.5.108 *would some part of my young years Might but redeem the passage of your age!*

3 Save (time) from being lost 1H4 1.2.217 *Redeeming time when men think least I will.*

4 Make up for WT 5.1.3 *No fault could you make Which you have not redeem'd*, TN 3.2.28, LR 5.3.267; make up to oneself for (some wrong sustained), repay 1H4 3.2.132 *I will redeem all this on Percy's head.*

5 Save (a person or thing) from some defect or blot AWW 4.3.274 *He hath out-villain'd villainy so far, that the rarity redeems him*, TIM 4.3.500.

redeliver *vb.* Repeat, report HAM 5.2.179 *Shall I redeliver you e'en so?—To this effect* (F1; Qq *deliver*).

▷ For MM 4.4.6 see RELIVER.

Redime te captum quam queas minimo [L.] Buy yourself out of captivity for as little as you can SHR 1.1.162.

red(-)lattice *n.* Lattice painted red as the mark of an alehouse or inn; (attrib.) WIV 2.2.27 *red-lattice phrases* (i.e. ale-house talk).

redoubted *ppl. adj.* Feared, dreaded MV 3.2.88 *How many cowards...assume but valour's excrement To render them redoubted!*; (in addressing sovereigns, high personages, etc.) dread, reverenced, respected R2 3.3.198 *my most redoubted lord*, H5 2.4.14, 1H6 2.1.8.

red-plague See RED.

redress *n.*

1 Remedy for, or relief from, trouble, assistance, aid, help JN 3.4.24 *that which ends all counsel, true redress*, R2 3.2.32, ROM 4.5.143; *past redress* beyond the possibility of remedy or aid R2 2.3.171.

2 (with *a* or in pl.) Means or way of redress, act or arrangement whereby a person or thing is redressed LR 1.4.206 *a safe redress*, LR 1.4.210 *the fault Would not scape censure, nor the redresses sleep*.

~ *vb.* Restore or bring back to a proper state, mend, repair PP 13.10 *broken glass no cement can redress*.

reduce *vb.*
1 Bring back, restore (state of things, time, etc.) R3 5.5.36 *Abate the edge of traitors...That would reduce these bloody days again*.
2 Bring (a thing, institution, etc.) back *into* a former state H5 5.2.63 *Which to reduce into our former favour You are assembled*.
3 Bring or draw together R3 2.2.68 *All springs reduce their currents to mine eyes...!*

reechy *adj.* Smoky; (hence) dirty, squalid, filthy ADO 3.3.134 *the reechy painting*, HAM 3.4.184, COR 2.1.209.

reed voice *n.* Squeaking voice MV 3.4.67 *speak between the change of man and boy With a reed voice*.

re-edify *vb.* Rebuild R3 3.1.71 *that place, Which, since, succeeding ages have re-edified*, TIT 1.1.351.

reek *vb.* (of smoke, vapour, perfume, etc.) Be emitted or exhaled; (hence) rise, emanate SON 130.8 *the breath that from my mistress reeks*; (fig.) LLL 4.3.138 *Saw sighs reek from you*, H5 4.3.101.

reeky *adj.* Full of rank moisture ROM 4.1.83 *dead men's rattling bones, With reeky shanks*.

reel *n.* (pl.) Revels, revelry ANT 2.7.94 *Drink thou; increase the reels*, HAM 1.4.9.

~ *vb.* Stagger through or along (a street) ANT 1.4.20 *To reel the streets*.

reeling(-)ripe *adj.* Drunk enough to be on the point of reeling TMP 5.1.279 *Trinculo is reeling ripe*.

refel *vb.* Refute MM 5.1.94 *How he refell'd me, and how I replied*.

refer *vb.*
1 (refl.) Have recourse (*to*), rely (upon) WT 3.2.115 *I do refer me to the oracle*, OTH 1.2.64, MM 3.1.245.
2 Hand over, give, transfer CYM 1.1.6 *His daughter...hath referr'd herself Unto a poor but worthy gentleman* (i.e. married).

reference *n.*
1 Submission of a matter, esp. a dispute or controversy, to a person or authority for consideration, decision, or settlement ANT 5.2.23 *Make your full reference freely to my lord*.
2 Assignment OTH 1.3.237 *Due reference of place*.
3 Relation, relationship AYL 1.3.127 *Something that hath a reference to my state*, AWW 5.3.29, H5 1.2.205.

refigure *vb.* Figure again, represent anew, reproduce the form of (a person) SON 6.10 *If ten of thine ten times refigur'd thee*.

reflect *vb.*
1 Throw or cast back again WT 4.4.734 *Reflect I not on thy baseness court-contempt?*
2 Shine, cast a light TIT 1.1.226 *whose virtues will...Reflect on Rome as Titan's rays on earth*, LUC 376.
3 Bestow attention or regard *upon*, set a value *on* CYM 1.6.23 *He is one of the noblest note...Reflect upon him accordingly, as you value your trust*.

reflection *n.* Action of turning back from some point, return MAC 1.2.25 *whence the sun gins his reflection*.

reflex *vb.* Throw, cast (beams on a place) 1H6 5.4.87 *May never glorious sun reflex his beams Upon the country*.

reform *vb.* Put a stop to (an abuse, disorder, malpractice, etc.) 1H4 4.3.78 *to reform Some...edicts*, H8 5.2.54, HAM 3.2.36.

refrain *vb.* Keep from (an action), desist from, give

up 3H6 2.2.110 *scarce I can refrain The execution of my big-swoll'n heart Upon that Clifford*.

reft See REAVE.

refuge *n.*
1 Way or means of obtaining safety, resource COR 5.3.11 *Their latest refuge Was to send him*.
2 Pretext, excuse 1H6 5.4.69 *I did imagine what would be her refuge*, LUC 1654.

~ *vb.* Find protection or consolation for shelter, protect; (fig.) R2 5.5.26 *beggars Who sitting in the stocks refuge their shame, That...others must sit there*.

refuse *vb.*
1 Decline to meet (an opponent) ANT 3.7.39 *for refusing him at sea*.
2 Decline to bear (a name) ROM 2.2.34 *Deny thy father and refuse thy name*.
3 Cast off (a person) ADO 4.1.184 *O my father,...Refuse me, hate me*.
4 Reject (a person), decline to admit to a certain position, or to some relationship H8 2.4.82 *I... Refuse you for my judge*, JN 1.1.127, ADO 4.2.63.
5 Renounce, abandon, forsake TRO 4.5.267 *since you refus'd The Grecians' cause*.

regard *n.*
1 Look, glance, gaze TN 5.1.212 *You throw a strange regard upon me*, TRO 3.3.254, MM 5.1.20.
2 Prospect, view LC 213 *in whose fresh regard Weak sights their sickly radiance do amend*.
3 Object of sight OTH 2.1.40 *till we make the main and th' aerial blue An indistinct regard*.
4 Intention, design, purpose JC 3.1.224 *Our reasons are so full of good regard That were you, Antony, the son of Caesar, You should be satisfied* (or sense 7), H5 1.1.22.
5 Repute, account, or estimation, in which anything is held H5 2.4.117 *slight regard, contempt*, 2H4 1.2.168, 1H6 4.1.145; *in* (*one's*) *regard* in (one's) opinion, estimation, or judgement 1H4 4.3.57 *Sick in the world's regard, wretched and low*, HAM 4.7.75.
6 Observant attention or care bestowed on or given to a matter, heed TIM 1.2.245 *I am sworn not to give regard to you*, MAC 3.2.12, SHR 4.1.126.
7 Thoughtful attention, consideration, deliberation R2 2.1.28 *Where will doth mutiny with wit's regard*, LUC 277, LUC 305.
8 Task of taking care of, care or charge of a person 1H6 4.5.22 *Your loss is great, so your regard should be* (i.e. 'your care of your own safety' (Johnson)).
9 Consideration, motive, thing or circumstance taken into account LR 1.1.239 *Love's not love When it is mingled with regards that stands Aloof from th' entire point* (Qq *respects*), HAM 3.1.86.
10 Condition HAM 2.2.79 *On such regards of safety and allowance As therein are set down*.

~ in prepositional phrases

in regard of 1 Out of consideration for R2 1.3.216 *I thank my liege that in regard of me He shortens four years of my son's exile*. 2 In respect of, with respect or reference to H5 1.1.77 *in regard of causes now in hand*; *in which regard* in respect to which OTH 1.1.153. **in regard** Since, because, inasmuch as, considering that 1H6 5.4.124 *in regard King Henry gives consent*.

~ *vb.*
1 Look to, consider, take into account TGV 3.1.258 *Regard thy danger*; (with clause) TGV 3.1.73 *Neither regarding that she is my child*.
2 Look after, take care of, attend to 1H6 3.2.86 *regard this dying prince*.
3 Hold (a person) in great respect or esteem COR 5.6.142 *Let him be regarded As the most noble corse that ever herald Did follow to his urn*, JC 5.3.88.

4 Have respect for or dread of 1H6 1.3.60 *Here's Beauford, that regards nor God, nor king*, 2H6 3.1.18.

5 Value or set store by TIT 5.2.130 *so let him As he regards his aged father's life*, 2H6 4.2.10.

regardfully *adv.* Attentively, respectfully TIM 4.3.82 *th' Athenian minion, whom the world Voic'd so regardfully*.

regenerate *ppl. adj.* Re-born, brought again into existence, formed anew R2 1.3.70 *Whose youthful spirit, in me regenerate*.

regent *n.* Ruler, governor R2 2.1.109 *wert thou regent of the world, It were a shame to let this land by lease*, PER 5.1.186; (fig.) LLL 3.1.181 *Regent of love-rhymes*.

regiment *n.* Rule or government over a person, people, or country ANT 3.6.95 *gives his potent regiment to a trull*.

region *n.*
1 The air, heaven HAM 2.2.487 *the dreadful thunder Doth rend the region*, ROM 2.2.21, 1H6 5.3.11; (attrib.) HAM 2.2.579 *the region kites*, SON 33.12.
2 One of the successive portions into which the air or atmosphere is theoretically divided according to height; (hence, fig.) status, rank WIV 3.2.73 *he is of too high a region, he knows too much*, CYM 5.4.93.
3 Part or division of the body or its parts OTH 4.1.83 *every region of his face*, LR 1.1.145, H8 2.4.185.

register *n.*[1] List, catalogue, record WIV 2.2.187 *as you have one eye upon my follies,...turn another into the register of your own*, SON 123.9, LC 52; in register on the list ANT 4.9.21.

register *n.*[2] Keeper of a register, one who keeps a record LUC 765 *Night...Dim register and notary of shame*.

regreet *n.* Return of a salutation or greeting JN 3.1.241 *this seizure and this kind regreet*; (pl.) greetings MV 2.9.89 *From whom he bringeth sensible regreets*.
~ *vb.*
1 Greet again or anew R2 1.3.142 *You...Shall not regreet our fair dominions*, R2 1.3.186.
2 Greet, give salutation to R2 1.3.67 *I regreet The daintiest last, to make the end most sweet*.

regress *n.* Return, re-entry WIV 2.1.218 *thou shalt have egress and regress*.

reguerdon *n.* Reward 1H6 3.1.169 *in reguerdon of that duty done*.
~ *vb.* Reward 1H6 3.4.23 *never have you...been reguerdon'd with so much as thanks*.

rehearsal *n.* Recounting, recital 2H6 1.2.24 *With sweet rehearsal of my morning's dream*.

rehearse *vb.*
1 Say, utter, speak SON 71.11 *Do not so much as my poor name rehearse*.
2 Give an account of, relate, narrate, recount, describe at length WT 5.2.62 *Like an old tale still, which will have matter to rehearse*, SON 38.4, TGV 4.1.26.

rein *n.*
1 *give (the) rein(s) to* Allow full course or scope to LLL 5.2.657 *rein thy tongue.—I must rather give it the rein*, MM 2.4.160, R2 1.1.55.
2 *take the rein* Go on without restraint WT 2.3.51 *When she will take the rein I let her run*.
3 *bear (in a, the) rein* Hold the head up high or haughtily LR 3.1.27 *the hard rein which both of them have borne Against the...King*, TRO 1.3.189.
~ *vb.*
1 Restrain (*from* something) LLL 5.2.656 *rein thy tongue*, TRO 5.3.48, LUC 706.
2 Bear, or submit to, the rein, submit to rule or control TN 3.4.324 *He...reins well*.

reinforce *vb.* (intr.) Obtain reinforcements CYM 5.2.18 *Let's reinforce, or fly*.

reins *n.* (pl.) Kidneys; region of the kidneys, loins WIV 3.5.23 *as if I had swallow'd snowballs for pills to cool the reins*.

rejoice *vb.* Feel joy on account of (an event) CYM 5.5.370 *Ne'er mother Rejoic'd deliverance more*, H5 2.2.159.

rejoicing-fire *n.* Bonfire CYM 3.1.32 *Made Lud's-Town with rejoicing-fires bright*.

rejoindure *n.* Reunion TRO 4.4.36 *beguiles our lips Of all rejoindure*.

rejourn *vb.* Put off, adjourn COR 2.1.71 *rejourn the controversy*.

relapse *n.*
1 Falling back again into an illness after a partial recovery PER 3.2.109 *her relapse is mortal*.
2 *in relapse of mortality* With a deadly rebound H5 4.3.107 *Killing in relapse of mortality*.

relation *n.*
1 The action of relating in words, expression in speech TRO 3.3.201 *a mystery (with whom relation Durst never meddle)*.
2 Narrative, account, statement, report PER 5.1.123 *make my senses credit thy relation*, MAC 4.3.173, WT 5.2.2.

relative *adj.* 'Able to be related' (Hulme); (hence) credible, substantial HAM 2.2.604 *I 'll have grounds More relative than this*.

release *vb.* Remit, surrender, give up, relinquish R2 4.1.210 *With mine own breath release all duteous oaths*, 2H6 1.1.51.

relent *vb.*
1 Dissolve, melt, soften MM 3.1.230 *he, a marble to her tears,...relents not*, VEN 200.
2 Give up a previous determination or obstinacy, yield, give way 2H6 4.8.11 *will ye relent And yield to mercy...?*, MND 1.1.91, 1H6 3.1.108.

relenting *ppl. adj.* Easily moved to pity, compassionate 2H6 3.1.227 *as the mournful crocodile With sorrow snares relenting passengers*, R3 4.4.431, LUC 1829.

relic *n.*
1 Something which serves as a memorial, memento, souvenir JC 2.2.89 *great men shall press For...relics, and cognizance*, AWW 5.3.25.
2 Object invested with interest by reason of its antiquity or associations with the past TN 3.3.19 *go see the relics of this town* (i.e. ancient remains).
3 (pl.) Remains of a meal or of food, scraps, remnants; (fig.) TRO 5.2.159 *the bits and greasy relics Of her o'er-eaten faith*.

relier *n.* One who relies (*on* a person or thing) LUC 639 *to thee, my...hands appeal, Not to seducing lust, thy rash relier*.

relieve *vb.* Lift or raise up again TMP 2.1.122 *th' shore, that...bowed As stooping to relieve him*.

religion *n.* Devotion to some principle, strict fidelity or faithfulness, conscientiousness AYL 4.1.197 *keep your promise.— With no less religion than if thou wert indeed my Rosalind*, ROM 1.2.88, CYM 1.4.137; *make religion to make a point of, be scrupulously careful (to do something)* ANT 5.2.199 *Which my love makes religion to obey*.

religious *adj.* Scrupulous, exact, strict, conscientious TN 3.4.389 *a most devout coward, religious in it*, H8 4.2.74, SON 31.6.

religiously *adv.*
1 Solemnly, ceremoniously JN 3.1.140 *I...from Pope Innocent the legate here, Do in his name religiously demand*.
2 Faithfully, conscientiously, scrupulously, strictly, exactly JN 2.1.246 *Being no further enemy*

to you Than the constraint of hospitable zeal...Religiously provokes, JN 4.3.73, H5 1.2.10.

relinquish *vb.* To give up as incurable AWW 2.3.10 *To be relinquish'd of the artists.*

relique (var. of) RELIC.

relish *n.*
1 Taste, flavour (of a thing); (fig.) TRO 3.2.19 *th' imaginary relish is so sweet*, TN 4.1.60; (hence) kind, quality H5 4.1.109 *of the same relish as ours are.*
2 Trace, tinge, suggestion 2H4 1.2.98 *some relish of the saltness of time*, MAC 4.3.95, HAM 3.3.92.
3 Individual taste or liking COR 2.1.189 *grafted to your relish.*
~ *vb.*[1]
1 Taste (a thing); (fig.) AYL 3.2.234 *take a taste of my finding him, and relish it with good observance*; feel TMP 5.1.23 *shall not myself,...that relish all as sharply Passion as they?*
2 Appreciate, understand WT 2.1.167 *Relish a truth like us.*
3 Have a taste *of* (something), savour *of*, have a touch or trace *of* HAM 3.1.117 *virtue cannot so inoculate our old stock but we shall relish of it*, CYM 3.2.30, PER 2.5.60.
4 Be agreeable or pleasant, find acceptance or favour WT 5.2.122 *had I been the finder-out of this secret, it would not have relish'd among my other discredits.*

relish *vb.*[2] Sing, warble TGV 2.1.20 *relish a love-song, like a robin-redbreast*, LUC 1126.

reliver *vb.* Give up again, restore MM 4.4.6 *reliver our authorities.*
◇ F1; Ff 2–4 *deliver*; Capell conjecture *redeliver.*

relume, relumine *vb.* Relight, rekindle, cause to burn afresh OTH 5.2.13 *that Promethean heat That can thy light relume* (Ff; Q1 *returne*; Qq 2–3 *relumine*).

remain *n.*[1] That which remains to be done CYM 3.1.85 *All the remain is 'Welcome'!*

remain *n.*[2] Stay COR 1.4.62 *Let's fetch him off, or make remain alike*, MAC 4.3.148.
~ *vb.*
1 Dwell AYL 3.2.223 *Where remains he?*, TMP 1.2.424, CYM 4.3.14.
2 Continue to belong *to* (one) LR 1.1.80 *To thee and thine hereditary ever Remain this ample third of our fair kingdom.*
3 Continue to be, be TIM 5.1.97 *remain assur'd That he's a...villain*, TIM 4.3.325, CYM 1.4.160; *let her remain let her be* CYM 3.3.16.
4 *remain with* Stick in the mind of TIM 3.6.36 *I hope it remains not unkindly with your lordship that...*

remainder *n.*
1 Residual or further interest remaining over from a particular estate, coming into effect when this has determined, and created by the same conveyance by which the estate itself was granted AWW 4.3.280 *cut th' entail from all remainders.*
2 (pl.) Those who remain, the rest CYM 1.1.129 *the good remainders of the court*, LR 1.4.250 (Ff).
3 Balance or unpaid part of a sum of money R2 1.1.130 *in my debt Upon remainder of a dear account.*
~ *adj.* Remaining, left over AYL 2.7.39 *the remainder biscuit After a voyage*, TRO 2.2.70.

remarked *ppl. adj.* Marked, conspicuous, noted H8 5.1.33 *The most remark'd i' th' kingdom.*

remediate *adj.* Remedial LR 4.4.17 *be aidant and remediate In the good man's distress!*
◇ F1; Qq *remediat.* Perh. error for 'remedial' or 'remediant'.

remedy *n.* Means of counteracting or removing an outward evil of any kind, reparation, redress, re-

lief COR 4.6.2 *His remedies are tame*, ROM 2.3.51, 2H4 1.2.236.
~ *in phrases*
there is no remedy There is no way out of it, help for it, alternative WIV 1.3.33, MM 2.1.281, TN 3.4.296. **no remedy** Unavoidably WIV 2.2.122 *You must send her your page, no remedy*, MM 2.2.48, TRO 4.4.55. **what remedy?** What help for it? What can be done? TN 1.5.51 *if it will not, what remedy?*, WIV 5.5.236, 1H6 5.3.132.

remember *vb.*
1 Record, maintain 2H4 5.2.142 *we will accite (As I before rememb'red) all our state*, H8 4.2.160.
2 Commemorate TMP 1.2.406 *The ditty does remember my drown'd father*, 1H4 5.4.101.
3 Bear (a person) in mind as entitled to a gift, recompense, or fee; (hence) reward, 'tip' MAC 2.3.20 *remember the porter.*
4 Have memory or recollection *of* (something) H8 1.2.190 *I remember Of such a time, being my sworn servant, The Duke retain'd him his.*
5 (refl.) Bethink, recollect R3 4.2.95 *I do remember me, Henry...Did prophesy*, TN 5.1.279, ROM 1.3.9; reflect upon (oneself) LR 4.6.229 *Briefly thyself remember* (i.e. think on your spiritual state).
6 Remind (a person), put (one) in mind *of* (a thing or person) TMP 1.2.243 *Let me remember thee what thou hast promis'd*, JN 3.4.96, LR 1.4.67.
7 *remember thy courtesy* Remember proper behaviour (viz., to cover your head) LLL 5.1.98 *remember thy courtesy...apparel thy head*; (absol.) HAM 5.2.104 *I beseech you remember.*
8 *be remembered* Recollect, remember SHR 4.3.96 *if you be rememb'red, I did not bid you mar it to the time*, MM 2.1.106, R3 2.4.23.

remembrance *n.*
1 Faculty or power of remembering or recalling to mind TMP 2.1.232 *this lord of weak remembrance*, CYM 2.4.93, JN 5.6.12.
2 Memorial inscription H5 1.2.229 *Tombless, with no remembrance over them.*
3 Reminder (given by one person to another) 2H4 5.2.115 *With this remembrance, that you use the same With the like...spirit As you have done 'gainst me.*
4 Article serving to remind one person of another, keepsake, souvenir, love-token TGV 2.2.5 *Keep this remembrance for thy Julia's sake*, MV 4.1.422, OTH 3.3.291.
5 Kind thought or consideration AWW 4.5.73 *out of a self-gracious remembrance*, COR 2.3.248, HAM 1.2.7.
~ *vb.* (Evans' blunder for) Remember WIV 3.3.239 *remembrance tomorrow on the lousy knave.*

remembrancer *n.* One who reminds another CYM 1.5.77 *the remembrancer of her to hold The handfast to her lord*, MAC 3.4.36.

remission *n.*
1 Inclination towards pardon MM 5.1.498 *I find an apt remission in myself; And yet here's one in place I cannot pardon.*
2 Release from a debt or payment; (fig.) COR 5.2.84 *though I owe My revenge properly, my remission lies In Volscian breasts.*

remit *vb.* Give up, resign, surrender (a right or possession) LLL 5.2.459 *I remit both twain.*

remnant *n.* (of a single person) Survivor R3 1.2.7 *Thou bloodless remnant of that royal blood.*

remonstrance *n.* Demonstration MM 5.1.392 *Make rash remonstrance of my hidden pow'r.*

remorse *n.*
1 Sorrow, pity, compassion JN 4.3.50 *the vilest stroke That ever...rage Presented to the tears of soft remorse*, TMP 5.1.76, TIM 4.3.123.

2 *without remorse* Without intermission or mitigation TN 2.3.90 *without any mitigation or remorse of voice?*

3 Solemn obligation OTH 3.3.468 *to obey shall be in me remorse.*

remorseful *adj.* Compassionate, full of pity R3 1.2.155 *remorseful tear*, TGV 4.3.13, AWW 5.3.58.

remorseless *adj.* Devoid of remorse, pitiless, cruel 3H6 1.4.142 *Thou stern, obdurate,...remorseless*, HAM 2.2.581, LUC 562.

~ *adv.* Without remorse or pity 2H6 3.1.213 *Even so remorseless have they borne him hence.*

remotion *n.* Action of removing or keeping aloof LR 2.4.114 *this remotion of the Duke and her Is practice only*, TIM 4.3.342.

remove *n.*

1 Removal from one place to another, change of place PP 17.8 *a nay is plac'd without remove* (i.e. irremovable), LLL 5.2.135.

2 Act of changing one's place, esp. one's place of residence AWW 5.3.131 *a petition from a Florentine Who hath for four or five removes come short To tender it herself*; departure to another place ANT 1.2.196 *Our quick remove from hence*, LR 2.4.4.

3 Period of absence from a place MM 1.1.43 *In our remove be thou at full ourself.*

4 Removal of a person by death HAM 4.5.81 *author Of his own just remove.*

5 Raising of a siege COR 1.2.28 *If they set down before 's, for the remove Bring up your army.*

~ *vb.*

1 Go away, depart from a place, move off to somewhere else MAC 5.3.2 *Till Birnam wood remove to Dunsinane*, AYL 3.4.56, JN 5.2.33; depart this life, die 1H6 2.5.104 *thy uncle is removing hence.*

2 Move or put (a person) out of the way, assassinate, murder 1H6 2.5.71 *young Richard thus remov'd*, WT 1.2.335, H8 2.1.42.

removed *ppl. adj.*

1 Distant in relationship by a certain degree, properly of descent, but often vaguely of consanguinity in general WT 4.4.774 *those that are germane to him* (*though remov'd fifty times*), JN 2.1.182, ROM 3.3.96; (fig.) AYL 5.4.68 *a lie seven times remov'd.*

2 Remote, retired, secluded AYL 3.2.342 *so remov'd a dwelling*, MM 1.3.8, HAM 1.4.61.

3 Separated by time or space TMP 2.1.111 *so far from Italy removed*, TN 5.1.89, SON 44.6; (transf.) SON 97.5 *this time remov'd* (i.e. this time of absence).

4 Less intimately involved, not immediately concerned 1H4 4.1.35 *To lay so dangerous...a trust On any soul remov'd, but on his own.*

removedness *n.* Absence, retirement WT 4.2.36 *eyes ...which look upon his removedness.*

remover *n.* One who constantly changes his place, restless person SON 116.4 *love is not love Which ...bends with the remover to remove.*

render *n.*

1 Surrender SON 125.12 *mutual render, only me for thee.*

2 Rendering of an account, statement, confession CYM 4.4.11 *Newness Of Cloten's death...may drive us to a render Where we have liv'd*, CYM 5.4.17, TIM 5.1.149.

~ *vb.*

1 Give back, return (a sound, image, etc.) by reflection or repercussion TRO 3.3.122 *who...like a gate of steel, Fronting the sun, receives and renders back His figure and his heat*; (fig.) 1H4 3.2.82 *rend'red such aspect As cloudy men use to their adversaries.*

2 Reproduce or represent, esp. by artistic means,

depict H5 1.1.44 *you shall hear A fearful battle rend'red you in music.*

3 Represent or describe (a person or thing) as being of a certain character or in a certain state, give or make (one) out to be AYL 4.3.122 *he did render him the most unnatural That liv'd*, CYM 3.4.150, AWW 1.3.230.

4 Hand over, deliver, grant, concede MV 3.4.49 *See thou render this Into my cousin's hands*, COR 1.9.34, TRO 4.5.36.

5 Give up, relinquish, surrender ANT 4.14.33 *She rend'red life*, MAC 5.7.24, LC 221; (refl.) HAM 1.5.4 *I to...flames Must render up myself.*

6 Declare, state CYM 5.5.135 *that this gentleman may render Of whom he had this ring*, CYM 2.4.119, H5 1.2.238.

7 Pay as a due or tribute; (fig.) TIT 1.1.160 *my tributary tears I render for my brethren's obsequies.*

8 Give as a service; (fig.) ADO 5.3.33 *this for whom we rend'red up this woe.*

rendezvous *n.* Resort, retreat, refuge 1H4 4.1.57 *A rendezvous, a home to fly unto*, H5 5.1.83 (Pistol); last resort or shift H5 2.1.16 *that is the rendezvous of it* (Nym).

renegado *n.* Renegade, apostate from any religious faith, esp. a Christian who becomes a Mohammedan TN 3.2.70 *Malvolio is turn'd heathen, a very renegado.*

◇ F1 *Renegatho*, representing the Sp. pronunciation; Rowe *renegado.*

renege, renegue *vb.*

1 (trans.) Deny, renounce, abandon, desert ANT 1.1.8 *reneges all temper.*

2 (intr.) Make denial LR 2.2.78 *Renege, affirm* (F1 misprinted *Reuenge*; Ff 2–4 *Renege*, Qq *Reneag*).

renew *vb.*

1 Repeat (an action) H5 1.2.116 *renew their feats.*

2 (intr.) Begin a fresh attack, renew the fight TRO 5.5.6 *Renew, renew! The fierce Polydamas Hath beat down Menon.*

renounce *vb.* Disclaim or disown obedience or allegiance to (a person) 3H6 3.3.194 *I here renounce him.*

renowned *ppl. adj.* (var. of) Renowned 1H4 3.2.107 *renowmed Douglas*, TIT 1.1.373, TIT 5.1.20.

renown *n.*

1 Report, rumour TMP 5.1.193 *Of whom so often I have heard renown.*

2 Reputation (good or bad) AWW 4.3.15 *of a most chaste renown*, PER 4.6.39.

3 Good name CYM 5.5.202 *his belief in her renown.*

~ *vb.* Make famous, spread the fame of TN 3.3.24 *the things of fame That do renown this city*, H5 1.2.118.

rent *vb.* Rend, tear MND 3.2.215 *will you rent our ancient love asunder...?*, R3 1.2.126 (Qq *rend*), MAC 4.3.168.

renying *n.* Renunciation PP 17.4 *Love is dying, faith's defying, Heart's renying, causer of this.*

◇ 01 *denieng*; 03 *denying*; 02 *nenying*; Malone conjecture *renying.*

repair *n.*[1] Resort, coming or going to (a place) HAM 5.2.218 *their repair hither*, MM 4.1.42, LLL 2.1.240.

~ *vb.*[1]

1 Go, betake oneself, make one's way JN 2.1.554 *bid her repair To our solemnity*, ANT 1.4.39, JC 1.3.147.

2 Return MND 4.1.67 *to Athens back again repair*, LLL 5.2.292, TIM 3.4.68.

repair *n.*[2]

1 Act of restoring to a sound or unimpaired condition, restoration CYM 3.1.56 *our laws,...whose repair and franchise Shall...be our good deed*, JN 3.4.113, WT 5.1.31.

2 *fresh repair* Healthful state SON 3.3 *that face ...Whose fresh repair.*

~ *vb.*[2]
1 Restore, renew (with immaterial object) 3H6 3.3.193 *to repair my honour lost for him,* H8 5.1.3, CYM 2.2.12.
2 Revive, refresh, recreate (a person) TGV 5.4.11 *Repair me with thy presence, Silvia,* AWW 1.2.30.
3 Remedy (an evil, etc.), set right again LR 4.1.76 *I'll repair the misery thou dost bear With something rich about me,* LR 4.7.27, PER 4.2.111.

repairing *ppl. adj.* That recovers easily 2H6 5.3.22 *'Tis not enough our foes are this time fled, Being opposites of such repairing nature.*

repast *vb.* Feed HAM 4.5.148 *like the...pelican, Repast them with my blood.*

repast *adj.* (app. misprint for) O'erpast, past, gone R3 4.4.396 *for that thou hast Misus'd ere us'd, by times ill-used repast.*
▷ F1; Maxwell conjecture *orepast.*

repasture *n.* Food, a repast LLL 4.1.93 *Food for his rage, repasture for his den.*

repeal *n.* Recall from exile JC 3.1.54 *freedom of repeal,* TGV 3.1.236, LUC 640.

~ *vb.*
1 Recall (a person) from exile R2 2.2.49 *The banish'd Bullingbrook repeals himself,* TGV 5.4.143, R2 4.1.87; (fig.) AWW 2.3.49 *this...hand, whose banish'd sense Thou hast repeal'd.*
2 Call or summon back (into favour or honour) LR 3.6.113 *When false opinion, whose wrong thoughts defile thee, In thy just proof repeals and reconciles thee;* try to get (one) restored OTH 2.3.357 *That she repeals him for her body's lust.*

repent *vb.* Live out (a time) in repentance AWW 4.3.243 *I would repent out the remainder of nature.*

repetition *n.* Recital, narration, mention AWW 5.3.22 *kill All repetition* (i.e. check any mention of what is past), JN 2.1.197, COR 1.1.46.

repine *n.* Discontent, dissatisfaction, act of repining VEN 490 *Had not his clouded with his brow's repine.*

replenish *vb.* Fill LUC 1357 *saw the blood his cheek replenish.*

replenished *ppl. adj.* Full, perfect, complete WT 2.1.79 *The most replenish'd villain in the world,* LLL 4.2.26, R3 4.3.18.

replication *n.*
1 Reply, answer HAM 4.2.13 *what replication should be made by the son of a king?,* LLL 4.2.15, LC 122.
2 Reverberation, echo JC 1.1.46 *the replication of your sounds.*

report *n.*
1 Rumour, common talk AYL 1.1.6 *report speaks goldenly of his profit,* 1H6 2.3.18, ANT 2.2.184.
2 Repute, fame, reputation MM 2.3.12 *Hath blister'd her report,* ADO 3.1.97, CYM 3.3.57.
3 Testimony, commendation *of* (a person or quality) LLL 2.1.63 *my report to his great worthiness,* SON 95.8, ANT 5.2.255.
4 Reporter, informant ANT 2.2.47 *I did...have my learning from some true reports That drew their swords with you.*
5 Resounding noise R3 4.4.153 *clamorous report of war,* MND 3.2.22, 1H4 4.2.19.
6 *suffer the report* Be told CYM 1.4.56 *a contention ...which may, without contradiction, suffer the report.*

~ *vb.*
1 (trans.) Give an account of, describe HAM 5.2.339 *Report me and my cause aright,* COR 5.4.25, PER 5.1.129; (refl.) CYM 2.4.83 *Never saw I figures So likely to report themselves.*
2 (trans.) Speak in commendation of WT 3.1.3 *I*

shall report, For most it caught me, the celestial habits...Of the grave wearers.
3 (intr.) Speak or talk in a certain way *of* AWW 3.5.57 *There is a gentleman...Reports but coarsely of her.*
4 Relate, state COR 2.2.31 *to report otherwise were a malice,* 1H4 2.4.413, MM 3.2.108.

reporter *n.* One who reports, informant ANT 2.2.188 *There she appear'd indeed; or my reporter devis'd well for her.*

reportingly *adv.* By report or hearsay ADO 3.1.116 *I Believe it better than reportingly.*

reposal, reposure *n.* Act of placing (trust), reliance LR 2.1.68 *would the reposal Of any trust...in thee Make thy words faith'd?* (F1; Qq *reposure*).

repose *vb.*
1 (fig.) Settle (oneself) with confidence *on* 3H6 4.6.47 *on thy fortune I repose myself.*
2 Confide or place one's trust in, rely on TGV 4.3.26 *Upon whose faith and honour I repose,* AWW 3.6.13.
3 Place, settle; (fig.) R2 2.4.6 *The king reposeth all his confidence in thee.*

reposure See REPOSAL.

reprieve *n.* Time during which one is reprieved MM 2.4.39 *in his reprieve, Longer or shorter.*

reprisal *n.* Prize 1H4 4.1.118 *this rich reprisal is so nigh, And yet not ours.*

reproach *vb.* Bring (a thing) into reproach or discredit MM 5.1.421 *reproach your life.*

reproachful *adj.* Abusive TIT 2.1.55 *Thrust those reproachful speeches down his throat,* TIT 1.1.308.

reproachfully *adv.* Shamefully, disgracefully 2H6 2.4.97 *shall I then be us'd reproachfully?*

reprobance *n.* State or condition of being reprobate, reprobation, rejection by God OTH 5.2.209 *curse his better angel from his side, And fall to reprobance* (F1; Qq *reprobation*).

reprobate *adj.* Depraved, degraded, morally corrupt LUC 300 *reprobate desire,* LLL 1.2.61.

reproof *n.*
1 Shame, disgrace, reproach ERR 5.1.90 *She did betray me to my own reproof,* TIM 5.4.57 (with quibble).
2 Disproof, refutation 1H4 3.2.23 *in reproof of many tales devis'd,* TRO 1.3.33, COR 2.2.33.

reprove *vb.* Prove (an idea, statement, etc.) to be false or erroneous, disprove, refute 2H6 3.1.40 *Reprove my allegation,* ADO 2.3.232, VEN 787.

repugn *vb.* Oppose, resist, contend against 1H6 4.1.94 *he did repugn the truth.*

repugnancy *n.* Resistance, opposition TIM 3.5.45 *let the foes quietly cut their throats Without repugnancy.*

repugnant *adj.* Offering resistance, refractory HAM 2.2.471 *His ...sword...lies where it falls, Repugnant to command.*

repure *vb.* Purify again TRO 3.2.22 *Love's thrice-repured nectar* (Q1; F1 *thrice reputed*).

repute *vb.* Think of, esteem, reckon, value TIT 1.1.448 *ingratitude, Which Rome reputes to be a heinous sin,* SHR 4.2.113, TGV 2.7.59; think (highly) of 2H6 3.1.48 *by reputing of his high descent.*

request *vb.* (with *off*) Ask (one) to come away ANT 2.7.120 *Let me request you off, our graver business Frowns at this levity.*
▷ F1 *of*; Rowe *off.*

require *vb.* Ask, request, desire (a person to do something) H8 2.4.145 *In humblest manner I require your Highness That it shall please you to declare,* WIV 1.2.10, COR 2.2.156.

required *ppl. adj.* Requisite LR 4.3.6 *his personal return was most requir'd and necessary,* WT 5.3.94, OTH 2.1.231.

requiring n. Request, demand H5 2.4.101 *if requiring fail he will compel*, TMP 2.2.182, MM 3.1.244.

requit vb. (var. of) Requite, repay TMP 3.3.71 *the sea (which hath requit it)*, COR 4.5.70, OTH 4.2.16 (Q1 *requite*).

reremouse See REARMOUSE.

rescue n. Forcible taking of a person out of legal custody ERR 4.4.111 *I am thy prisoner. Wilt thou suffer them To make a rescue?*, COR 3.1.275; (fig.) ANT 3.11.48 *death will seize her, but Your comfort makes the rescue.*

resemblance n. Likelihood, probability MM 4.2.188 *Not a resemblance, but a certainty.*

reservation n.
1 Action of reserving for oneself some right, privilege, etc. LR 1.1.133 *With reservation of an hundred knights*; right thus reserved LR 2.4.252 *kept a reservation to be followed With such a number.*
2 Action of keeping back or concealing from others, keeping a thing secret or to oneself AWW 2.3.245 *make some reservation of your wrongs.*
3 Action of keeping something for one's own use AWW 1.3.225 *he will'd me In heedfull'st reservation to bestow them*, COR 3.3.130.

reserve vb.
1 Retain or preserve alive, save from death MM 5.1.467 *one in the prison...I have reserv'd alive.*
2 Keep in one's possession SON 32.7 *Reserve them for my love, not for their rhyme*, OTH 3.3.295.
3 Keep safe, maintain (a person or thing) in a certain state or condition PER 4.1.39 *reserve That excellent complexion*, SON 85.3, TIT 1.1.165.
4 Retain as one's own, keep or for oneself LR 1.1.149 *Reserve thy state*, R2 1.1.128, LR 3.4.65.
5 Retain (in a certain function) R3 4.4.72 *hell's black intelligencer, Only reserv'd their factor to buy souls.*

reserved ppl. adj.
1 Excepted, with the reservation 1H6 5.4.167 *Only reserv'd, you claim no interest In any of our towns of garrison.*
2 Preserved, guarded, safely kept AWW 3.5.62 *a reserved honesty.*

residence n.
1 Residing or being resident in a place HAM 2.2.329 *How chances it they travel? Their residence...was better both ways*; (fig.) AWW 2.5.39 *my lord's displeasure...out of it you'll run again, rather than suffer question for your residence.*

resign vb. Submit, yield ROM 3.2.59 *Vile earth, to earth resign.*

resist vb. Repel, affect with distaste PER 2.3.29 *These cates resist me.*

resolute n. Resolute or determined person, desperado HAM 1.1.98 *a list of lawless resolutes.*

resolution n. Conviction, certainty, positive knowledge LR 1.2.100 *I would unstate myself to be in a due resolution.*

resolve n. Firmness, steadfastness of purpose 1H6 5.5.75 *a lady of so high resolve.*

~ vb.
1 Melt, dissolve (into some other form) LC 296 *his passion...resolv'd my reason into tears*, TIM 4.3.439; (intr.) JN 5.4.25 *as a form of wax Resolveth from his figure 'gainst the fire*; (refl.) HAM 1.2.130 *Thaw and resolve itself into a dew.*
2 Answer (a question, argument, etc.) AYL 3.2.232 *to resolve the propositions of a lover*; (with double object) SHR 4.2.7 *What, master, read you? First resolve me that*, TIT 5.3.35, R3 4.2.117 (Qq1–6); solve (a problem, riddle) PER 1.1.71 *How they may be...resolve it you.*
3 Remove, clear away, dispel (a doubt, difficulty, fear, etc.) 3H6 4.1.135 *Resolve my doubt*, JN 2.1.371.

4 Free (one) from doubt or perplexity, bring to certainty or clear understanding MM 4.2.209 *you are amaz'd, but this shall absolutely resolve you*, 3H6 2.1.9, JC 3.2.179.
5 Inform, tell (a person *of* a thing) R3 4.5.20 *My letter will resolve him of my mind*, TMP 5.1.248; (with dependent clause) LR 2.4.25 *Resolve me... which way Thou mightst deserve...this usage.*
6 (refl.) Make up one's mind MAC 3.1.137 *Resolve yourselves apart*, WT 5.3.86, 3H6 1.1.49.
7 (with *for*) Decide on setting out for (a place) 2H4 2.3.67 *I will resolve for Scotland.*
8 (with *on*) Be satisfied, convinced, sure of 1H6 1.2.91 *Resolve on this: thou shalt be fortunate.*

resolved ppl. adj.
1 Prepared in mind (esp. for some evil) MM 3.2.248 *now is he resolv'd to die*, TIT 1.1.135; (with *for*) 2H6 5.1.194 *resolv'd for death*, WT 4.4.508.
2 Resolute JN 5.6.29 *a resolved villain*, R3 1.3.339.
3 Convinced, satisfied 1H6 3.4.20 *we were resolved of your truth*, 3H6 2.2.124.
4 Fully determined upon, deliberate JN 2.1.585 *a resolv'd and honourable war*, LR 4.1.211.

resolvedly adv. So that doubt and uncertainty are removed AWW 5.3.332 *Of that and all the progress...Resolvedly more leisure shall express.*

resort n.
1 Visiting of a place or person, visit TIM 1.1.127 *to forbid him her resort*, TGV 3.1.108, HAM 2.2.143; *house, place of resort* brothel MM 1.2.101 *shall all our houses of resort in the suburbs be pull'd down?*, PER 4.6.80.
2 Assemblage, gathering throng, crowd TGV 1.2.4 *all the fair resort of gentlemen.*

resorter n. Frequenter, visitor PER 4.6.24 *'tis the better for you that your resorters stand upon sound legs.*

respect n.
1 Relationship, reference MV 5.1.99 *It is your music... —Nothing is good...without respect; Methinks it sounds much sweeter than by day* (i.e. without reference to circumstances).
2 Regard, consideration, reflection LUC 275 *Respect and reason wait on wrinkled age!*, MV 1.1.74, COR 3.1.180.
3 Discrimination TN 2.3.91 *Is there no respect of place, persons, nor time in you?*
4 Heed, care, attention R2 2.1.25 *So it be new, there's no respect how vile*, MM 2.2.86, 1H4 4.3.31.
5 Fact or motive regarding something, consideration WIV 2.1.45 *if it were not for one trifling respect*, JN 5.4.41, HAM 3.2.183.
6 Condition or state of being esteemed or honoured AWW 5.3.192 *this ring, Whose high respect...*, JN 5.7.85, MAC 3.6.29.
7 Rank, standing, station in life JC 1.2.59 *many of the best respect in Rome*, JC 5.5.45, OTH 1.3.282.

~ in phrases

in my respect As far as I am concerned MND 2.1.224, CYM 2.3.135. **in respect 1** In comparison 3H6 5.5.56 *He was a man; this, in respect, a child.* **2** (as conj. with clause foll.) Considering, seeing, since *(that)* AYL 3.2.14 *in respect that it is a shepherd's life, it is naught*, AYL 3.2.17. **in respect of 1** In comparison with LLL 5.2.636 *Hector was but a Trojan in respect of this*, ADO 3.4.18, JC 1.1.10. **2** With reference to, as relates to, in regard to MND 1.1.137 *misgraffed in respect of years*, AYL 3.2.13. **3** In view of, because of, on account of 1H4 2.3.2 *in respect of the love I bear your house*, HAM 5.2.115, TGV 3.1.324.

~ vb.

1 Regard, consider, take into account TGV 5.4.54 *In love Who respects friend?*, ERR 4.4.41, VEN 911.

2 Heed, pay attention to, care for R3 1.4.152 *Spoke like a tall man that respects thy reputation*, TGV 3.1.89, CYM 1.6.155; (with neg.) make light of, care nothing about R2 2.1.131 *thou respect'st not spilling Edward's blood*, LLL 1.2.179, JC 4.3.69.

3 Regard, consider *as*, take *for* MND 1.1.160 *I have a widowed aunt...And she respects me as her only son*, 1H4 5.4.20, COR 3.1.305.

4 Esteem, prize, value TGV 1.2.131 *If you respect them, best to take them up*, PER 2.2.13, TGV 4.4.182.

respecting *prep.*
1 Having regard to, considering 2H6 3.1.24 *Respecting what a rancorous mind he bears*, H8 2.4.181.

2 IN RESPECT OF sense 1, in comparison with WT 5.1.35 *There is none worthy, Respecting her that's gone*, SHR 5.2.32.

respective *adj.*
1 Attentive, careful MV 5.1.156 *You should have been respective and have kept it.*

2 Respectful, courteous JN 1.1.188 *'Tis too respective and too sociable For your conversion.*

3 Partial, discriminating ROM 3.1.123 *Away to heaven, respective lenity, And...fury be my conduct now!*

4 Worthy of respect or deference TGV 4.4.195 *What should it be that he respects in her But I can make respective in myself.*

respectively *adv.* Respectfully, with becoming respect, particularly TIM 3.1.8 *you are very respectively welcome.*

respice finem [L.] Look to the end ERR 4.4.41.

respite *n.*
1 Date to which something is postponed, delay, extension of time R3 5.1.19 *this...day...Is the determin'd respite of my wrongs*, MM 4.2.160, H8 2.4.178.

2 Delay in action, stay 1H6 4.1.170 *Ourself,...After some respite, will return to Calais.*

responsive *adj.* Correspondent, corresponding, suited HAM 5.2.151 *Three of the carriages...are... very responsive to the hilts.*

rest *n.*[1]
1 In primero, the stakes kept in reserve, which were agreed upon at the beginning of the game, and upon the loss of which the game terminated; (fig.) what one stands to win or lose, final stake H5 2.1.16 *when I cannot live any longer, I will do as I may; that is my rest; set up one's rest* stake, hazard, or venture one's all *on or upon* something; (hence) have or take a resolution, be resolved or determined ERR 4.3.27 *he that sets up his rest to do more exploits*, MV 2.2.103; (with allusion to 'rest' = repose) ROM 5.3.110 *here...Will I set up my everlasting rest*, LR 1.1.123.

2 *above the rest* Especially TGV 4.1.58 *Therefore, above the rest, we parley to you*, LR 4.1.48, SON 91.6.

rest *n.*[2]
1 Restored vigour or strength JC 4.3.202 *we...Are full of rest, defence, and nimbleness*, 1H4 4.3.27.

2 Stay, abode HAM 2.2.13 *your rest here in our court*, PER 2.Gower.26.

3 Quiet, tranquillity, peace of mind MV 2.5.17 *There is some ill a-brewing towards my rest*, WT 2.1.191, LR 2.4.290; *have in rest* possess quietly, have in peace of mind JN 4.2.55 *If what in rest you have in right you hold*; *do one rest* give one peace of mind TN 5.1.133 *I most...willingly, To do you rest, a thousand deaths would die.*

~ *vb.*[1]
1 Give (one) rest or repose MV 2.2.71 *God rest his soul*, ROM 1.3.18, MAC 4.3.227; (hence, in conventional phr. of salutation) AYL 5.1.59 *God rest you merry*, MV 1.3.59, ROM 1.2.62.

2 *rest in* Lie in the power of 3H6 3.2.45 *What you*

command that rests in me to do, MM 1.3.31, TIT 2.3.41.

3 *rest on* Rely on, depend upon TIT 1.1.267 *Rest on my word*, HAM 3.3.14.

rest *vb.*[2]
1 Remain 1H6 4.1.121 *let it rest where it began at first*, H8 5.1.55, MAC 1.6.20.

2 Remain to be done HAM 3.3.64 *What then? What rests? Try what repentance can*, SHR 1.1.246, 3H6 1.2.44.

rest, 'rest *vb.*[3] (aphetic form of) Arrest ERR 4.2.45 *in a suit of buff which 'rested him*, ERR 4.2.42, ERR 4.4.3.

restem *vb.* Stem again, steer again OTH 1.3.37 *and now they do restem Their backward course* (Ff *restem*; Qq 2-3 *resterne*).

resting *ppl. adj.* Stationary, unchanging, stable JC 3.1.61 *the northern star, Of whose true-fix'd and resting quality.*

restive See RESTY.

restore *vb.*
1 Make amends for (loss or damage) SON 30.14 *All losses are restor'd*; (hence) make (amends) MND 5.1.438 *And Robin shall restore amends.*

2 Bring back to mental calm H8 2.2.29 *to restore the King, He counsels a divorce.*

restrain *vb.*
1 Withhold, keep back (something *from* one) COR 5.3.167 *thou restrain'st from me the duty which To a mother's part belongs*, R3 5.3.322, TIM 5.1.148.

2 Draw tightly SHR 3.2.58 *a head-stall...which being restrain'd to keep him from stumbling.*

restrained *ppl. adj.* Forbidden, prohibited MM 2.4.48 *put a metal in restrained means.*

restraint *n.*
1 Act of restraining, stoppage ERR 3.1.97 *this strange restraint* (i.e. locking-out).

2 Abridgement of liberty, confinement JN 4.2.52 *Th' enfranchisement of Arthur, whose restraint...*, CYM 1.1.74, MM 1.2.124.

3 Constraint, reserve AWW 5.3.213 *Madding my eagerness with her restraint*, AWW 2.4.43, TN 5.1.81.

resty *adj.* Disinclined for action or exertion, inactive, lazy, sluggish CYM 3.6.34 *when resty sloth Finds the down pillow hard*, SON 100.9.

◊ In TRO 1.3.263 *Hector...Who in this dull and long-continued truce Is resty grown* (F1 *rusty*) perh. in sense of 'restive, refractory'.

resume *vb.* Assume, undertake, take TIM 2.2.4 *Takes no accompt How things go from him, nor resumes no care Of what is to continue.*

retain *vb.* Engage, have in one's service H8 1.2.192 *being my sworn servant, The Duke retain'd him his.*

retention *n.*
1 Power of retaining things in the mind, memory SON 122.9 *That poor retention could not so much hold* (with quibble on sense of a copy-book retaining impressions or marks made in it).

2 Capacity for holding or keeping something TN 2.4.96 *no woman's heart So big, to hold so much; they lack retention.*

3 Detention of persons by forcible or other means, confinement LR 5.3.47 *send the...King To some retention.*

4 Reserve, reticence, reservation TN 5.1.81 *My love, without retention or restraint, All his in dedication.*

retentive *adj.* Holding, confining, keeping firm hold TIM 3.4.81 *my retentive enemy*, JC 1.3.95.

retire *n.*
1 Withdrawal from the world or the society of

others, retirement LLL 2.1.234 *all his behaviours did make their retire To the court of his eye.*
2 Return LUC 573 *That to his borrowed bed he make retire,* JN 2.1.253.
3 Retreat, act of drawing back or yielding ground in warfare COR 1.6.3 *Nor cowardly in retire,* JN 2.1.326; (fig.) LUC 174.
~ *vb.*
1 (intr.) Return VEN 906 *now she will no further, But back retires,* TRO 1.3.281.
2 (trans.) Draw or pull (a thing) back LUC 303 *The locks...Each one by him enforc'd retires his ward,* R2 2.2.46.
3 (refl.) Withdraw or remove (oneself) R2 4.1.96 *retir'd himself To Italy,* OTH 2.3.380; retreat in battle JN 5.3.13 *The French fight coldly, and retire themselves.*
retired *ppl. adj.*
1 Withdrawn from society TMP 1.2.91 *by being so retir'd,* CYM 3.5.36, WT 4.2.32.
2 Withdrawn into oneself, reserved WT 4.4.62 *You are retired, as if you were a feasted one and not The hostess.*
3 That has receded or subsided JN 5.4.53 *like a bated and retired flood.*
retirement *n.*
1 Act of withdrawing into seclusion or privacy H5 1.1.58 *Any retirement...From open haunts.*
2 State or condition of being withdrawn from society or publicity MM 5.1.130 *certain words he spake against your Grace In your retirement.*
3 Retreat, refuge 1H4 4.1.56 *A comfort of retirement lives in this.*
retiring *ppl. adj.* Returning LUC 962 *One poor retiring minute.*
retort *vb.*
1 Reflect (heat or light) TRO 3.3.101 *Heat them, and they retort that heat again.*
2 Reject, refuse (an appeal) MM 5.1.301 *The Duke's unjust Thus to retort your manifest appeal.*
3 Repay, pay back WIV 2.2.1 *I will retort the sum in equipage* (Qq 1–2).
retrait *n.*
1 (military) Signal to retreat 1H4 5.4.159 *The trumpet sounds retrait.*
2 Retreat 2H4 3.2.267 *for a retrait, how swiftly will this Feeble...run off!*
3 See RETREAT.
retreat *n.* Recall of a pursuing force 2H4 4.3.72 *Retreat is made and execution stay'd* (F1; Q1 *Retraite*).
retrograde *adj.*
1 (of the planets) Apparently moving in a direction contrary to the order of the signs, or from east to west AWW 1.1.198 *born under Mars ...When he was retrograde.*
2 Opposed, contrary, repugnant *to* HAM 1.2.114 *It is most retrograde to our desire.*
return *n.* Reply, answer, retort H5 2.4.127 *if my father render fair return.*
~ *vb.*[1]
1 (refl.) Turn round or away 1H6 3.3.56 *Return thee therefore with a flood of tears.*
2 Say by way of answer, reply R2 3.3.121 *say thus the King returns: His noble cousin is right welcome,* PER 2.2.4, H5 3.3.46.
return *vb.*[2] Turn back again VEN 704 *see the dew-bedabbled wretch Turn, and return.*
revenge *n.*
1 Vindictive desire, desire to repay injuries by inflicting hurt in return AWW 5.3.10 *Though my revenges were high bent upon him,* ADO 5.1.292, WT 2.3.19.
2 Avenging of a person 1H6 1.5.35 *none would*

strike a stroke in his revenge, 1H6 2.2.11, 2H6 3.2.127.
3 *in revenge of* In return or retaliation for TGV 1.2.107 *in revenge of thy ingratitude,* TGV 2.4.133, LUC 236.
~ *vb.*
1 (pass.) *be revenged* Take revenge (*on* a person *for* a wrong, etc.) WIV 2.1.31 *reveng'd I will be!*; (with *on* = for) LUC 1778 *to be revenged on her death*; (with *of* = on) 2H4 2.4.154 *I 'll be reveng'd of her* (Q; Ff *on*).
2 (intr.) Take vengeance or revenge MV 3.1.67 *if you wrong us, shall we not revenge?,* 3H6 1.4.36, TIT 4.1.129.
revengement *n.* Retribution, punishment 1H4 3.2.7 *He'll breed revengement and a scourge for me.*
revengingly *adv.* In revenge, vindictively CYM 5.2.4 *the air...Revengingly enfeebles me.*
revengive *adj.* Revenging, vindictive LR 2.1.45 *the revengive gods* (Qq; Ff *revenging*).
reverb *vb.* Reverberate, re-echo LR 1.1.154 *those empty-hearted whose low sounds Reverb no hollowness.*
reverberate *adj.* Reverberating, resounding TN 1.5.272 *the reverberate hills.*
reverence *n.*
1 Condition or state of being respected or venerated; (hence, applied to venerable age) 2H6 5.2.48 *in thy reverence, and thy chair-days,* ADO 2.3.120, LR 4.7.28.
2 *save, saving (one's) reverence* Phrase of apology, introducing a criticism, contradiction, or some remark that might offend the hearer CYM 4.1.5 *saving reverence of the word,* ADO 3.4.32, 1H4 2.4.469.
⬦ Corrupted to SIR-REVERENCE.
reverend, reverent *adj.*
1 Worthy of deep respect or reverence SHR 4.5.60 *reverent age,* ERR 5.1.134 *a virtuous and a reverend lady,* PER 5.1.14.
2 Characterized by, exhibiting or feeling, reverence SHR 4.1.204 *all is done in reverend care of her,* 2H6 3.1.34 *reverent care,* 1H6 5.3.47.
⬦ The two forms were used interchangeably in 16–17C.
reverse *n.* Back-handed stroke or cut WIV 2.3.26 *thy puncto, thy stock, thy reverse.*
reversion *n.* Prospect of possessing a thing at some future time 1H4 4.1.53 *Where now remains a sweet reversion We may boldly spend; in reversion* destined to come into a person's possession or to be realized in the future R2 1.4.35 *As were our England in reversion his,* TRO 3.2.92.
revert *vb.* Return, come or go back (to or from a place or position) HAM 4.7.23 *my arrows...Would have reverted to my bow again.*
reverted *ppl. adj.* Turned backwards or the wrong way; (hence, fig.) in opposition or rebellion ERR 3.2.123 *In her forehead, arm'd and reverted, making war against her heir.*
⬦ See ARMED AND REVERTED.
review, re-view *vb.*
1 See or behold again WT 4.4.666 *I shall re-view Sicilia.*
2 Survey, take a survey of SON 74.5 *When thou reviewest this, thou dost review The very part was consecrate to thee.*
revokement *n.* Revocation H8 1.2.106 *through our intercession this revokement And pardon comes.*
revolt *n.*[1]
1 Revulsion of appetite TN 2.4.99 *suffer surfeit, cloyment, and revolt.*
2 Change of affection, inconstancy SON 92.10 *Since that my life on thy revolt doth lie,* ROM 4.1.58, OTH

3.3.188; *revolt to* relapse into LLL 5.2.74 *gravity's revolt to wantonness.*

3 *give (one) the revolt* Revolt against (one) MAC 5.4.12 *both more and less have given him the revolt.*

revolt *n.*² Revolter, rebel JN 5.2.151 *you ingrate revolts,* JN 5.4.7, CYM 4.4.6.

revolted *ppl. adj.* That has cast off allegiance, rebel, insurgent R2 2.2.57 *revolted faction,* 1H4 1.3.92; unfaithful, inconstant WT 1.2.199 *revolted wives,* WIV 3.2.39, TRO 5.2.186.

revolution *n.*
1 Alteration, change, mutation (esp. as wrought by time) 2H4 3.1.46 *the revolution of the times,* LLL 4.2.67, HAM 5.1.90.
2 *by revolution* In due course of time ANT 1.2.125 *The present pleasure, By revolution low'ring, does become The opposite of itself.*

revolve *vb.*
1 (trans.) Turn over (something) in the mind, meditate upon (something) 1H6 5.5.101 *I may revolve and ruminate my grief,* CYM 3.3.14, TRO 2.3.187.
2 (intr.) Deliberate, consider TN 2.5.143 *If this fall into thy hand, revolve.*

reward *n.* (hunting) Some part of the animal which has been caught and killed, given to the hounds on the spot; (fig.) 1H4 5.4.162 *I 'll follow, as they say, for reward,* 2H6 2.3.105.

reword *vb.*
1 Put into words again, repeat HAM 3.4.143 *the matter will reword, which madness Would gambol from.*
2 Re-echo LC 1 *a hill whose concave womb reworded A plaintful story.*

rhapsody *n.* 'String' *(of* words) HAM 3.4.48 *such a deed As from...sweet religion makes A rhapsody of words.*

rheum *n.*
1 Watery matter secreted by the mucous glands or membranes: (1) mucus from the nose ERR 3.2.128 *the salt rheum that ran between France and it* (i.e. her nose); (2) saliva H5 3.5.52 *spit and void his rheum upon,* MV 1.3.117; (3) tears JN 4.3.108 *Trust not those cunning waters of his eyes, For villainy is not without such rheum,* ADO 5.2.83, R2 1.4.8.
2 Excessive or morbid defluxion of humours (supposed to cause rheumatism), catarrh TRO 5.3.104 *I have a rheum in mine eyes,* MM 3.1.31, WT 4.4.399.
▷ See SALT.

rheumatic *adj.*
1 (of persons, their bodies, etc.) Suffering from a 'defluxion of rheum' or catarrh VEN 135 *Were I hard-favour'd,...rheumatic, and cold.*
2 (of a disease) Characterized by rheumy or catarrhal 'defluxion' MND 2.1.105 *rheumatic diseases.*
3 (of weather) Inducing or having a tendency to provoke rheum (*n.* sense 2) WIV 3.1.47 *this raw rheumatic day.*
▷ Misused at H5 2.3.38 *he was rheumatic,* 2H4 2.4.57.

rheumy *adj.* Inducing rheum, moist, damp JC 2.1.266 *the rheumy and unpurged air.*

rib *vb.* Enclose as with ribs, enclose with a strong protection MV 2.7.51 *To rib her cerecloth in the obscure grave,* CYM 3.1.19.

ribald *adj.* Offensively cacophonic TRO 4.2.9 *the ribald crows.*

ribaudred *adj.* Lewd, wanton ANT 3.10.10 *Yon ribaudred nag of Egypt.*

rich *adj.*
1 (of eyes) That have seen much AWW 5.3.17 *Whose beauty did astonish the survey Of richest eyes,* AYL 4.1.24.

2 (of the nose or face) Highly inflamed 1H4 3.3.78 *Look upon his face; what call you rich?* (with quibble).
3 *rich opinion* Good reputation OTH 2.3.195 *spend your rich opinion for the name Of a night-brawler.*

riched *ppl. adj.* Enriched LR 1.1.64 *With shadowy forests and with champains rich'd.*

riches *n.* (sing., var. of) 'richesse' Wealth, opulence PER 1.4.23 *A city on whom plenty held full hand, For riches strew'd herself even in her streets,* OTH 2.1.83, SON 87.6.

rid *vb.*
1 Remove by violence, kill, destroy TMP 1.2.364 *The red-plague rid you...!,* R2 5.4.11, 3H6 5.5.67.
2 *rid way* Cover ground quickly, make rapid progress 3H6 5.3.21 *We...Will thither straight, for willingness rids way.*

ridden *ppl. adj.* Broken-in, trained H8 2.2.2 *the horses...I saw well chosen, ridden, and furnish'd.*

ride *vb.*
1 Rest or turn *on* (something of the nature of a pivot or axle) 1H4 5.2.83 *If life did ride upon a dial's point,* TRO 1.3.67.
2 Oppress, harass, tyrannize over ERR 2.2.200 *she rides me and I long for grass,* WIV 5.5.137.
3 *ride out* (of a ship) Sustain (a gale or storm) without great damage or dragging anchor; (fig.) PER 4.4.31 *He bears A tempest, which his mortal vessel tears, And yet he rides it out.*

rider *n.* Horse-trainer AYL 1.1.13 *they are taught their manage, and to that end riders dearly hir'd.*

riding-rod *n.* Rod or switch used in riding JN 1.1.140 *if my legs were two such riding-rods.*

rife *adj.* Ready, prepared MND 5.1.42 *There is a brief how many sports are rife* (F1; Q1 *ripe*).

rift *vb.* Split WT 5.1.66 *Then I 'ld shriek, that even your ears Should rift to hear me;* (trans.) TMP 5.1.45 *rifted Jove's stout oak.*

riggish *adj.* Wanton, licentious ANT 2.2.239 *the holy priests Bless her when she is riggish.*

right *n.*¹ (erron. spelling of) Rite MND 4.1.133 *The right of May.*

right *n.*²
1 Just or equitable treatment, justice; *do (one) right* do one justice, give one satisfaction ADO 5.1.147 *Do me right, or I will protest your cowardice,* LUC 1027, TIT 1.1.203; (with ref. to pledging a person by drinking to him) 2H4 5.3.72 *now you have done me right; right for right* 'justice answering to the claim for justice' (Johnson) R3 4.4.15.
2 Justifiable claim, on legal or moral grounds, to have or obtain something, or to act in a certain way; *in (the) right of* in support or by virtue of the claim of JN 2.1.153 *In right of Arthur do I claim of thee,* 1H6 3.1.149, COR 3.3.14.
3 *the right* The direct road or way JN 1.1.170 *Something about, a little from the right.*
~ *adj.* Straight LLL 5.2.565 *Your nose...stands too right.*
~ *adv.*
1 In a direct course or line, straight; *right on* straight on JC 3.2.223 *I only speak right on,* LC 26.
2 *right out* Outright, entirely, to the full extent TMP 4.1.101 *be a boy right out.*
3 Precisely, exactly, just, quite ERR 5.1.357 *here begins his morning story right,* MND 4.2.31, TRO 1.3.170; *right now* just now 2H6 3.2.40 *Came he right now.*
4 Very JC 1.3.162 *right well,* MAC 3.6.5, LR 1.1.195.
5 In accordance with justice or righteousness R2 1.1.46 *my right drawn sword.*
6 Properly, in a proper or fitting manner, in the required or necessary way 3H6 1.4.160 *if thou tell'st the heavy story right,* JN 2.1.139, JN 3.1.183.

7 *take right* See TAKE.

right-drawn *adj.* See RIGHT *adv.* sense 5.

righteously *adv.* Correctly, rightly, aright AYL 1.2.14 *if the truth of thy love to me were so righteously temper'd as mine is to thee.*

rightful *adj.* Disposed to do right, upright, just MV 4.1.301 *Most rightful judge!*

right-hand file *n. phr.* Aristocratic party COR 2.1.23 *us a' th' right-hand file.*

rightly *adv.* Directly, straightly R2 2.2.18 *perspectives, which rightly gaz'd upon Show nothing but confusion; ey'd awry Distinguish form.*

rigol, rigoll *n.* Ring, circle 2H4 4.5.36 *this golden rigol* (i.e. the crown), LUC 1745.

rim *n.* (elliptical for) Rim of the belly, peritoneum, lining membrane of the abdomen H5 4.4.14 *I will fetch thy rim out at thy throat.*

ring *n.* Border, rim, or outer part of some circular object, esp. of a coin or a wheel; *crack'd within the ring* (of a coin) having the circle broken that surrounds the sovereign's head HAM 2.2.428.

ring-carrier *n.* Go-between AWW 3.5.92 *hang you!—And your courtesy, for a ring-carrier!*

ringlet *n.* Circular dance or course MND 2.1.86 *dance our ringlets to the whistling wind;* fairy ring (i.e. circular band of grass differing in colour from the grass around it, a phenomenon supposed in popular belief to be produced by fairies when dancing but really caused by the growth of certain fungi) TMP 5.1.37 *you demi-puppets that By moonshine do the green sour ringlets make, Whereof the ewe not bites.*

ring(-)time *n.* Time of giving or exchanging rings as love tokens AYL 5.3.19 *In spring time, the only pretty ring-time.*
▷ Steevens conjecture; F1 *rang time.*

rinsing See WRENCHING.

riot *n.* Wanton, loose, or wasteful living, debauchery, dissipation, extravagance TIM 2.2.3 *his flow of riot,* PER 1.4.54, VEN 1147.

rioter *n.* Reveller, dissolute person, one who indulges in debauchery or wanton living TIM 3.5.67 *He's a sworn rioter.*

riotous *adj.*
1 Wanton, dissolute, extravagant TIM 2.2.159 *riotous feeders,* LR 2.1.94, MM 4.4.29.
2 Noisy, tumultuous LR 1.4.244 *this our court... Shows like a riotous inn; unrestrained* ANT 1.3.29 *riotous madness,* LR 4.6.123.

ripe *vb.*
1 Grow or become ripe AYL 2.7.26 *from hour to hour, we ripe and ripe,* MND 2.2.118.
2 Make ripe, bring to ripeness 2H4 4.1.13 *to ripe his growing fortunes,* JN 2.1.472.
~ *adj.* (fig. and transf.)
1 Resembling ripe fruit, red and full MND 3.2.139 *how ripe in show Thy lips...tempting grow!,* LR 4.3.20.
2 Ready for birth R2 2.2.10 *Some unborn sorrow, ripe in fortune's womb.*
3 (of persons) Fully developed in body or mind, mature, grown-up AYL 4.3.87 *a ripe sister.*
4 Requiring immediate satisfaction MV 1.3.63 *ripe wants.*
5 Ready for action, execution, or use, arrived at the fitting stage or time for some purpose R3 3.7.158 *ripe revenue,* JC 4.3.215, MND 5.1.42 (Q1).

rivage *n.* Coast, shore, or bank H5 3.Ch.14 *You stand upon the rivage.*

rival *n.* Partner, associate HAM 1.1.13 *The rivals of my watch.*
~ *vb.* Act as a rival, be a competitor LR 1.1.191 *who with this king Hath rivall'd for our daughter.*

rivality *n.* Partnership, equality ANT 3.5.8 *Caesar... denied him rivality.*

rive *vb.*
1 Cleave, Split TRO 1.3.316 *Blunt wedges rive hard knots,* COR 5.3.153, JC 1.3.6; (fig., applied to artillery) 1H6 4.2.29 *rive their dangerous artillery* (i.e. fire it so heavily that the cannons would seem to burst); (intr.) ANT 4.13.5 *The soul and body rive not more in parting Than greatness going off,* TRO 1.1.35.
2 (of the heart) Rend with pain JC 4.3.85 *Brutus hath riv'd my heart.*

rivelled *ppl. adj.* Wrinkled, full of wrinkles or small folds, corrugated, furrowed TRO 5.1.22 *the rotten diseases...the rivell'd fee-simple of the tetter.*

rivo *interj.* Exclamation used at revels or drinking-bouts 1H4 2.4.111 *'Rivo!' says the drunkard.*

road *n.*
1 Spell of riding, journey on horseback H8 4.2.17 *At last, with easy roads, he came to Leicester.*
2 Hostile incursion by mounted men, foray, raid H5 1.2.138 *the Scot, who will make road upon us,* COR 3.1.5.
3 Sheltered piece of water near the shore where vessels may lie at anchor in safety, roadstead SHR 2.1.375 *an argosy That now is lying in Marsellis road,* TGV 1.1.53, MV 1.1.19.
4 Highway AYL 2.3.33 *enforce A thievish living on the common road?,* 1H4 2.1.15; (fig.) way, course COR 5.1.59 *the very road into his kindness,* ADO 5.2.34, 2H4 2.2.166.
5 Usual course, way, or practice PER 4.5.9 *out of the road of rutting for ever.*

roadway *n.* Highway 2H4 2.2.58 *Never a man's thought in the world keeps the roadway better than thine.*

roar *n.*
1 Confusion, tumult, disturbance TMP 1.2.2 *you have Put the wild waters in this roar.*
2 Wild outburst of mirth HAM 5.1.191 *your flashes of merriment, that were wont to set the table on a roar?*

roast *n.* *rule the roast* Have full sway or authority, be master 2H6 1.1.109.

rob *vb.* Take *away,* cut off *from* (the possibility of doing something) R2 1.3.173 *death, Which robs my tongue from breathing native breath?*

Robin Goodfellow See PUCK.

robustious *adj.* Violent, boisterous, noisy HAM 3.2.9 *a robustious periwig-pated fellow,* H5 3.7.148.

rogue *n.*
1 One belonging to a class of idle vagrants or vagabonds LR 4.7.38 *To hovel thee with swine and rogues forlorn In...straw;* roguing, vagrancy, 'occupation' of being a vagabond WT 4.3.100 *having flown over many knavish professions, he settled only in rogue.*
2 Dishonest, unprincipled person, rascal 1H4 2.4.124 *You rogue, here's lime in this sack too,* TRO 5.1.88, OTH 2.3.145; (applied abusively to servants) SHR 4.1.144 *Off with my boots, you rogues!*
3 (term of endearment) One who is of a mischievous disposition 2H4 2.4.216 *you sweet little rogue,* LR 5.3.13, OTH 4.1.111.

roguing *ppl. adj.* Wandering, vagrant PER 4.1.96 *These roguing thieves.*

roguish *adj.* Vagrant LR 3.7.104 *his roguish madness Allows itself to anything.*

roisting *ppl. adj.* Blustering, boisterous TRO 2.2.208 *I have a roisting challenge sent amongst The dull and factious nobles of the Greeks.*

roll *n.*
1 Register, list, catalogue; (fig.) 1H4 3.1.42 *the roll of common men,* ANT 5.2.181.

2 (military use) Muster-roll 2H4 3.2.96 Where's the roll?

3 *Master of the Rolls* One of the four ex-officio judges of the Court of Appeal and a member of the Judicial Committee, who has charge of the rolls, patents, and grants that pass the great seal, and of all records of the Court of Chancery H8 5.1.35 *is made Master O' th' Rolls, and the King's secretary.*

romage (var. of) RUMMAGE.

Roman *adj.*
1 (of handwriting, applied in Eliz. times to a variety of the sloping Italian hand) Round and bold TN 3.4.28 *the sweet Roman hand.*
2 (of the alphabet or its characters) Employed by the Romans TIT 5.1.139 *Roman letters.*

rondure *n.* Circle, round object SON 21.8 *all things rare That heaven's air in this huge rondure hems.*

ronyon *n.* Term of abuse applied to a woman MAC 1.3.6 *the rump-fed ronyon*, WIV 4.2.185 (Ff *runnion*).

roofed *ppl. adj.* Covered as with a roof, in one's house MAC 3.4.39 *Here had we now our country's honour roof'd.*

rook *vb.* (var. of) RUCK, squat, crouch, cower 3H6 5.6.47 *The raven rook'd her on the chimney's top.*

rooky *adj.* Full of, abounding in, rooks MAC 3.2.51 *th' rooky wood.*

room *n.*
1 Particular place assigned or appropriated to a person or thing Shr 3.2.250 *let Bianca take her sister's room*, JN 3.4.93, R2 5.5.107.
2 *in one's room* In one's place ADO 1.1.302 *now... that war-thoughts Have left their places vacant, in their rooms Come thronging soft and delicate desires.*

root *n.* (of the heart) Bottom COR 2.1.185 *at very root on 's heart*, TGV 5.4.103, ANT 5.2.105. *vb.*[1]
1 Fix or establish firmly, implant deeply TGV 2.4.162 *lest the...earth...Disdain to root the summer-swelling flower*, SON 142.11, HAM 1.5.33.
2 (of plants) (intr.) Take or strike root H5 5.2.46 *her fallow leas The darnel, hemlock, and rank femetary Doth root upon*, ROM 1.1.122; (fig.) WT 1.1.23 *there rooted betwixt them then such an affection.*

root *vb.*[2] Turn over, dig up with the snout TIM 5.1.165 *like a boar too savage, doth root up His country's peace*, VEN 636.

rooting *ppl. adj.* That roots or grubs in the earth for food R3 1.3.227 *rooting hog.*

rope *n.*[1] Cord for hanging a person, halter, the hangman's cord TMP 1.1.31 *the rope of his destiny*; (used as a derisive cry) 1H6 1.3.53 *Winchester goose, I cry, 'A rope! a rope!'*

rope *vb.*[2] Cry of distress, lamentation AWW 4.2.38 *I see that men make rope's in such a scarre* (i.e. utter cries of distress in such a plight).

ropery *n.* Trickery, knavery ROM 2.4.146 *what saucy merchant was this, that was so full of his ropery?* (F1, Q2; Q1 *roperipe*).

roping *ppl. adj.* Forming rope-like threads, running down in filaments H5 3.5.23 *Let us not hang like roping icicles*; (in combination) H5 4.2.48 *The gum down-roping from their pale dead eyes.*

rope-trick *n.* (?) Punning or illiterate distortion of 'rhetoric' SHR 1.2.112 *he'll rail in his rope-tricks* (perh. with bawdy connotations).

rose *n. cake of roses* Preparation of rose-petals in the form of a cake, used as perfume ROM 5.1.47 *old cakes of roses.*

rosed *adj.* Rendered red or rosy in colour, rose-coloured, rosy TIT 2.4.24 *a crimson river of warm blood...Doth rise and fall between thy rosed lips*, H5 5.2.295.

rote *vb.* Learn or fix by rote COR 3.2.55 *such words that are but roted in Your tongue.*

rother *n.* Ox TIM 4.3.12 *It is the pasture lards the rother's sides.*
  ◇ Ff *Brothers*; Singer conjecture *rother's*.

rotten *adj.* Putrid, tainted, foul (of air, water, etc.) COR 2.3.32 *rotten dews*, TIM 4.3.2, LUC 778; (of disease) TRO 5.1.18 *the rotten diseases of the south.*

rough-hew *vb.* Shape out roughly, give crude form to; (fig.) HAM 5.2.11 *There's a divinity that shapes our ends, Rough-hew them how we will.*

round *n.*
1 Circle, circlet, ring MAC 1.5.28 *the golden round* (i.e the crown), MAC 4.1.88, WIV 4.4.51.
2 Dance in which the performers move in a circle or ring MAC 4.1.130 *While you perform your antic round*, MND 2.1.140.
3 Movement in a circle LC 109 *What rounds, what bounds, what course.*
4 Roundabout way or course MND 3.1.106 *lead you about a round.*
5 Rung of a ladder JC 2.1.24 *when he once attains the upmost round, He then unto the ladder turns his back.*
6 *this mortal round* Earth VEN 368.
  ~ *vb.*[1]
1 Finish off, bring to completeness or to a perfect form TMP 4.1.158 *our little life Is rounded with a sleep.*
2 Surround, encircle, encompass R2 3.2.161 *the hollow crown That rounds the mortal temples of a king*, MND 4.1.51, AWW 1.3.152.
3 Become round, circular, or spherical, grow or develop to a full round form WT 2.1.16 *The Queen...rounds apace: we shall Present our services to a fine new prince One of these days.*
4 Hem in TRO 1.3.196 *How rank soever rounded in with danger.*
  ~ *adj.*
1 (of a sum of money) Large, considerable in amount H8 5.3.80 *round fines*, MV 1.3.103.
2 Plain, honest, straightforward OTH 1.3.90 *a round unvarnish'd tale.*
3 Plain-spoken, not mincing matters, uncompromising, severe in speech or dealings H5 4.1.203 *Your reproof is something too round*, LR 1.4.54, TIM 2.2.8.
  ~ *adv.*
1 Openly, in a straightforward manner HAM 2.2.139 *I went round to work.*
2 *round about* All over, on all sides, all about TIT 4.2.18 *a scroll, and written round about*, ADO 5.3.26.

round *vb.*[2] Whisper, converse or talk privately WT 1.2.217 *They're here with me already, whisp'ring*, *rounding*, JN 2.1.566.

roundel *n.* Round dance MND 2.2.1 *a roundel and a fairy song.*

rounder See ROUNDURE.

roundly *adv.*
1 To the full, completely, thoroughly 2H4 3.2.18 *I would have done any thing indeed too, and roundly too.*
2 Plainly, outspokenly, bluntly SHR 5.2.21 *Roundly replied*, SHR 1.2.59, SHR 3.2.214.
3 Without circumlocution, straight AYL 5.3.11 *Shall we clap into't roundly?*, 1H4 1.2.22, TRO 3.2.154.
4 Glibly, readily R2 2.1.122 *This tongue that runs so roundly in thy head.*

roundure *n.* Circle, circuit JN 2.1.259 *the roundure of your old-fac'd walls* (Ff *rounder*).

rouse *n.*
1 Full draught of liquor, bumper HAM 1.2.127 *the King's rouse*, HAM 1.4.8, OTH 2.3.64.

2 Carousal, bout of drinking HAM 2.1.56 *o'ertook in 's rouse*.

rouse *vb.*

1 Cause (game) to rise or issue from cover or lair 1H4 1.3.198 *To rouse a lion*, TIT 2.2.21, VEN 240; (fig.) R2 2.3.128 *To rouse his wrongs and chase them to the bay*, 3H6 5.1.65.

2 Raise, lift up 2H4 4.1.116 *Being mounted and both roused in their seats*; (refl.) H5 1.2.275 *When I do rouse me in my throne*, ANT 5.2.284, LUC 541.

3 Rise up, stand on end MAC 5.5.12 *my fell of hair Would...rouse and stir.*

4 (intr.) Get up from sleep or repose, waken up MAC 3.2.53 *night's black agents to their preys do rouse.*

rout *n.*

1 Disorderly, tumultuous, or disreputable crowd of persons 2H4 4.2.9 *a rout of rebels*, 2H4 4.1.33, 1H6 4.1.173.

2 *the* (common) *rout* The common herd, the rabble JC 1.2.78 *profess myself in banqueting To all the rout*, ERR 3.1.101 *the common rout*, SHR 3.2.181.

3 Riot, disturbance, stir, uproar OTH 2.3.210 *How this foul rout began.*

row *n.* Stanza HAM 2.2.419 *the first row of the pious chanson.*

royal *n.* Gold coin formerly current in England, originally of the value of ten shillings; (only alluded to in puns) 1H4 1.2.141 *thou cam'st not of the blood royal, if thou darest not stand for ten shillings*, 1H4 2.4.291, R2 5.5.67.

~ *adj.*

1 Of or consisting of a sovereign or sovereigns JN 2.1.347 *add a royal number to the dead*, H5 5.2.27, H8 1.4.86; *royal hope* prospect of kingship MAC 1.3.56.

2 Devoted, dedicated to the sovereign 2H4 4.1.191 *our royal faiths* (i.e fidelity), H8 4.1.8.

3 Proceeding from a sovereign, appointed by a sovereign H8 2.4.66 *this royal session*, MAC 5.3.57; performed by a sovereign or sovereigns JN 3.1.235 *this royal bargain.*

4 (of things) Befitting, appropriate to, a sovereign; (hence) magnificent, splendid TN 2.3.172 *sport royal*, TIM 3.6.49, ANT 4.8.35.

5 (of persons, their character, etc.) Having the character proper to a king LR 5.3.177 *A royal nobleness*, R3 1.2.244; (hence) noble, majestic, generous, munificent H5 4.8.101 *a royal fellowship of death*, JC 3.1.127, AYL 4.3.117.

6 Powerful and wealthy as a king MV 3.2.239 *that royal merchant*, MV 4.1.29.

royalty *n.*

1 Personality of a sovereign, royal person, (his, your) majesty WT 1.2.15 *I have stay'd To tire your royalty*, JN 5.2.129, ANT 1.3.91.

2 Sovereignty or sovereign rule (*of* a state) R3 3.4.40 *lose the royalty of England's throne.*

3 Royal persons collectively or individually, royal family H5 5.2.5 *as a branch and member of this royalty*, MAC 4.3.155.

4 Kinglike or majestic character or quality MAC 3.1.49 *his royalty of nature*, CYM 4.2.178.

5 Emblem of sovereignty, crown JN 4.2.5 *You were crown'd before, And that high royalty was ne'er pluck'd off*, 1H4 4.3.55, R3 5.5.4; (pl.) prerogatives, rights, or privileges pertaining to, or enjoyed by, the sovereign TMP 1.2.110 *temporal royalties*, JN 2.1.176; (of a noble) R2 2.1.190 *The royalties and rights of banish'd Herford.*

roynish *adj.* Scurvy, coarse, base AYL 2.2.8 *the roynish clown.*

rub *n.*

1 In bowls, an obstacle or impediment by which a

bowl is hindered in, or diverted from, its proper course; (fig.) R2 3.4.4 *'Twill make me think the world is full of rubs, and that my fortune runs against the bias.*

2 Obstacle, impediment, hindrance, or difficulty H5 2.2.188 *every rub is smoothed on our way*, JN 3.4.128, HAM 3.1.64.

3 Unevenness, inequality, roughness MAC 3.1.133 *leave no rubs nor botches in the work.*

~ *vb.*

1 Impede, hinder LR 2.2.154 *Whose disposition... Will not be rubb'd nor stopp'd.*

2 (of a bowl) Encounter some impediment which retards or diverts its course; (allusively) TRO 3.2.49 *rub on and kiss the mistress* (i.e. continue on past the rubs).

▷ 'Rub on' was a common cry during a game to encourage a bowl on its course past a 'rub'.

3 *rub the elbow* See ELBOW.

4 *rub the vein of him* See VEIN.

rubbing *n.* (in bowls) Encountering of an obstacle, impediment LLL 4.1.139 *challenge her to bowl.—I fear too much rubbing.*

rubious *adj.* Ruby-coloured TN 1.4.32 *Diana's lip Is not more smooth and rubious.*

ruby *n.* Red pimple on the face ERR 3.2.135 *her nose, all o'er embellish'd with rubies.*

ruddock *n.* Robin redbreast CYM 4.2.224 *The ruddock would...bring thee all this.*

▷ F1 *Raddocke*; Hanmer *ruddock.* It was believed that the robin redbreast covered corpses with leaves, flowers, and mosses.

rude *adj.*

1 Uneducated, unlearned, ignorant LLL 5.1.89 *the posteriors of this day, which the rude multitude call the afternoon.*

2 Devoid of or deficient in refinement, uncultured OTH 1.3.81 *Rude am I in my speech*, AYL 2.7.92, 1H4 3.2.14.

3 Uncivilized, barbarous CYM 3.6.65 *this rude place we live in*, 2H4 1.1.159, SON 78.14.

4 Ungentle, violent, harsh, brutal TGV 5.4.60 *that rude uncivil touch*, 1H4 1.1.41, R2 5.5.105.

5 Turbulent, boisterous, rough LR 4.2.30 *the rude wind*, 2H4 3.1.20, TN 5.1.78.

6 (of sounds) Discordant, harsh, unmusical TRO 1.1.89 *Peace, you ungracious clamours! peace, rude sounds!*

7 (of language, composition, etc.) Lacking polish or elegance JN 4.2.150 *rude harsh-sounding rhymes*, SON 32.4.

8 (of natural objects) Uncultivated, wild ANT 1.4.64 *the roughest berry on the rudest hedge.*

9 Big and coarse, strong but ill-shaped JN 5.7.27 *To set a form upon that indigest Which he hath left so shapeless and so rude*, JN 2.1.262, R2 3.3.32.

rude-growing *adj.* Rough TIT 2.3.199 *rude-growing briers.*

rudely *adv.*

1 With violence, roughly COR 4.5.142 *knock against the gates of Rome, Or rudely visit them in parts remote*, LUC 170, LUC 669.

2 By violent or rough behaviour 1H4 3.2.32 *Thy place in council thou hast rudely lost.*

3 Under rough or harsh conditions PER 3.1.30 *Thou art the rudeliest welcome to this world That ever was prince's child.*

4 With rough or unskilful workmanship R3 1.1.16 *I, that am rudely stamp'd.*

rudeness *n.*

1 Want of refinement, roughness of life or habits, uncouthness TRO 2.1.53 *Do, rudeness, do, camel.*

2 Roughness, harshness, or violence in action or

in the treatment of others TRO 1.3.207 *the great swinge and rudeness of his poise*, LC 104.

3 Roughness of style or workmanship CYM 4.2.214 *My clouted brogues...whose rudeness Answer'd my steps too loud.*

rudesby *n.* Insolent, unmannerly, or disorderly fellow SHR 3.2.10 *a mad-brain rudesby full of spleen*, TN 4.1.51.

rue *vb.* Regard with pity or compassion TIT 1.1.105 *Victorious Titus, rue the tears I shed.*

ruff *n.* Article of neckwear, usu. consisting of starched linen or muslin arranged in horizontal flutings and standing out all round the neck SHR 4.3.56 *With silken coats...With ruffs and cuffs and fardingales*, PER 4.2.103, 2H4 2.4.145.

ruffian *vb.* (of the wind) Act like a ruffian, rage, bluster OTH 2.1.7 *it hath ruffian'd so upon the sea.*

ruffle *n.* Ostentatious bustle or display LC 58 *a blusterer that the ruffle knew Of court, of city.*
~ *vb.*[1]

1 Swagger, bully TIT 1.1.313 *To ruffle in the commonwealth of Rome.*

2 (of winds) Be turbulent, rage, bluster LR 2.4.301 *the bleak winds Do sorely ruffle* (F1; Qq 1-2 *russel*).

3 Take or snatch rudely LR 3.7.41 *With robber's hands my hospitable favours You should not ruffle thus.*

ruffle *vb.*[2] Stir *up* to indignation JC 3.2.228 *there were an Antony Would ruffle up your spirits.*

ruffling *ppl. adj.* Forming ruffles; (hence) showy, frilly SHR 4.3.60 *The tailor stays thy leisure, To deck thy body with his ruffling treasure.*

rugged *adj.*

1 Shaggy MAC 3.4.99 *the rugged...bear*, 2H6 3.2.175, HAM 2.2.450.

2 Wrinkled with displeasure, frowning MAC 3.2.27 *sleek o'er your rugged looks.*

rug-headed *adj.* Shock-headed, shaggy-headed R2 2.1.156 *those rough rug-headed kerns.*

ruinate *ppl. adj.* Ruinous, fallen into ruin, dilapidated ERR 3.2.4 *Shall love in building grow so ruinate.*
◊ F1; many mod. edd. emend to *ruinous.*

ruinous *adj.*

1 Falling or fallen into ruin, decayed, dilapidated TRO 5.1.28 *you ruinous butt*, TGV 5.4.9, TIT 5.1.21.

2 Brought to, sunk into, ruin or decay TIM 4.3.459 *yond despis'd and ruinous man.*

rule *n.*

1 Principle, maxim, law JC 5.1.100 *the rule of that philosophy By which I did blame Cato*, R3 1.2.68, SHR 3.1.81; *rule of*, in nature natural law AWW 1.1.136 *the rule of nature*, H5 1.2.188, OTH 1.3.101.

2 Good order, discipline MAC 5.2.16 *He cannot buckle his distemper'd cause Within the belt of rule*; *out of true rule* in a state of disorder or revolt 1H4 4.3.39; *in such rule* so far in order MV 4.1.178.

3 Conduct, behaviour TN 2.3.123 *this uncivil rule.*

4 Graduated strip of metal or wood used for measuring length, measure JC 1.1.7 *where is thy leather apron and thy rule?*, ANT 5.2.210; (fig.) TRO 5.2.133 *to square the general sex By Cressid's rule*, ANT 2.3.7.

rummage *n.* Bustle, commotion, turmoil HAM 1.1.107 *this post-haste and rummage in the land* (Q *romage*).

rumour *n.*

1 Talk or report (*of* a person) 1H6 2.3.7 *Great is the rumour of this dreadful knight.*

2 Uproar, tumult, disturbance JN 5.4.45 *the noise and rumour of the field*, JC 2.4.18.

rump-fed *adj.* (?) (1) Fat-rumped; or (2) fed on the best joints, pampered MAC 1.3.6 *the rump-fed ronyon.*

run *vb.*

1 Ride (on horseback) rapidly 1H4 2.4.343 *That runs a' horseback up a hill*; (fig.) TMP 1.2.254 *To run upon the sharp wind of the north.*

2 (of the tongue) Wag freely R2 2.1.122 *This tongue that runs so roundly in thy head.*

3 Pierce or stab (a person) H5 2.1.64 *I'll run him up to the hilts.*

4 Give forth, discharge, vent, pass H5 2.1.121 *The King hath run bad humours on the knight*, WIV 1.1.167, WIV 1.3.77.

runagate *n.*

1 Deserter, fugitive, runaway CYM 1.6.137 *that runagate to your bed.*

2 Vagabond, wanderer ROM 3.5.89 *that same banish'd runagate*, CYM 4.2.62, R3 4.4.464.

runaway *n.*

1 One who runs away, fugitive AYL 2.2.21 *bring again these foolish runaways*, MV 2.6.47, MND 3.2.405.

2 Runagate, vagabond R3 5.3.316 *vagabonds, rascals, and runaways*, ROM 3.2.6.

runner *n.* Fugitive, deserter ANT 4.7.14 *'Tis sport to maul a runner.*

runnion See RONYON.

rupture *n.*

1 Breach (of harmony between two persons) MM 3.1.235 *It is a rupture that you may easily heal.*

2 Breaking of waves PER 2.1.155 *And, spite of all the rupture of the sea.*
◊ Q; Rowe conjecture *rapture.* See RAPTURE sense 1.

rush *n.*

1 Plant of the order Juncaceae, used for making a finger-ring AWW 2.2.23 *Tib's rush for Tom's forefinger.*

2 Emblem of something of no value or of no strength OTH 5.2.270 *Man but a rush against Othello's breast And he retires*, JN 4.3.129, AYL 3.2.371.

rush *vb.* Force out of place or position, brush *aside*; (fig.) ROM 3.3.26 *The kind Prince, Taking thy part, hath rush'd aside the law.*

rush-candle *n.* Candle of feeble power made by dipping the pith of a rush in tallow or other grease SHR 4.5.14 *call it a rush-candle.*

rushling *ppl. adj.* (var. of) Rustling, going about, being finely dressed *in* some material which rustles WIV 2.2.67 *so rushling...in silk and gold.*

russel *vb.* (misprint for) RUFFLE (see *vb.*[1] sense 2) LR 2.4.301 *the...winds Do sorely russel* (Qq 1-2).

russet *adj.*

1 (of garments, etc.) Made of russet cloth, a coarse homespun woollen cloth of a reddish-brown, grey, or neutral colour HAM 1.1.166 *the morn in russet mantle clad.*

2 Rustic, homely, simple LLL 5.2.413 *russet yeas and honest kersey noes.*

russet-pated *adj.* Grey-headed or red-headed MND 3.2.21 *russet-pated choughs.*

rust *n.* Corruption WT 3.2.171 *How he glisters Through my rust.*
~ *vb.* Form a rust 3H6 1.3.51 *this...blood cleaving to my blade Shall rust upon my weapon.*

ruth *n.* Compassion, pity SON 132.4 *Looking with pretty ruth upon my pain*, R2 3.4.106, COR 1.1.197.

ruthful *adj.* That excites compassion or pity, lamentable, piteous 3H6 2.5.95 *O that my death would stay these ruthful deeds!*, TIT 5.1.66, TRO 5.3.48.

rut-time *n.* Period of sexual excitement in male deer WIV 5.5.14 *Send me a cool rut-time.*

rutting *n.* Copulating, fornication PER 4.5.9 *I am out of the road of rutting for ever.*

ruttish *adj.* Lewd, lascivious AWW 4.3.216 *a foolish idle boy, but for all that very ruttish.*

S

's (reduced form)
1 Us MAC 1.3.125 *to betray 's,* ADO 5.3.32, ANT 3.13.114.
2 His MV 5.1.158 *on 's face,* LR 1.4.102, ANT 3.2.51.
3 This HAM 3.2.127 *my father died within 's two hours.*

sa *interj.* Exclamation, repeated, accompanying or inciting to sudden action LR 4.6.203 *you shall get it by running. Sa, sa, sa, sa.*

sable *n.*[1] Black colour HAM 1.2.241 *It was...A sable silver'd.*
~ *adj.* Black HAM 2.2.452 *whose sable arms, Black as his purpose,* LUC 117, SON 12.4.

sable *n.*[2] Fur of the sable, Mustela zibellina, worn on rich garments HAM 3.2.130 *let the dev'l wear black, for I'll have a suit of sables,* HAM 4.7.80.
⋄ Sable was often dyed black and thus used in more lavish suits of mourning. In HAM 3.2.130 there is prob. a quibble on SABLE *n.*[1]

sack *n.* General name for a class of white wines formerly imported from Spain and the Canaries TN 2.3.190 *I'll go burn some sack* (i.e. prepare some warm sack), 1H4 2.4.470, 2H6 2.3.60.
⋄ See SHERRIS.

sack *vb.* Plunder; (hence, used loosely) destroy ROM 3.3.107 *that I may sack The hateful mansion.*

sackbut *n.* Bass trumpet with a slide like that of a trombone for altering the pitch COR 5.4.49 *trumpets, sackbuts, psalteries, and fifes.*

sacrament *n. receive, take the sacrament* Receive Holy Communion as a confirmation of one's word; (hence) swear, bind oneself R3 1.4.203 *Thou didst receive the sacrament to fight,* AWW 4.3.136 *I'll take the sacrament on't,* R3 5.5.18.

sacred *adj.*
1 Regarded with or entitled to respect or reverence similar to that which attaches to holy things 1H6 4.1.40 *the sacred name of knight,* SHR 1.1.176, TGV 3.1.212; (as an epithet of royalty) JN 3.1.148 *a sacred king,* ERR 5.1.133, H5 1.2.7.
2 Accursed TIT 2.1.120 *our empress, with her sacred wit To villainy...consecrate* (prob. quibble on sense 1).
3 *sacred vials* See VIAL.

sacrificial *adj.* Pertaining to or connected with sacrifice TIM 1.1.81 *Rain sacrificial whisperings in his ear.*

sacrificing *ppl. adj.* Sacrificial TIT 1.1.144 *the sacrificing fire.*

sacring bell *n.* Bell rung at the consecration of the elements at Mass H8 3.2.295 *startle you Worse than the sacring bell.*

sad *adj.*
1 Grave, serious H5 4.1.301 *sad and solemn priests,* TGV 1.3.1, TN 3.4.18.
2 Morose R2 5.5.70 *that sad dog That brings me food,* MND 3.2.439; dismal-looking TIT 5.2.1 *sad habiliment.*

sad-eyed *adj.* Grave-looking H5 1.2.202 *The sad-ey'd justice.*

sadly *adv.* Gravely, seriously ROM 1.1.201 *sadly tell me, who?,* ADO 2.3.221, 2H4 5.2.125.

sadness *n.* Seriousness 3H6 3.2.77 *this merry inclination Accords not with the sadness of my suit,* CYM 1.6.62, SHR 5.2.63; *in (good) sadness* in all seriousness WIV 3.5.123, ROM 1.1.204, VEN 807.

safe *vb.*
1 Make safe ANT 1.3.55 *should safe my going.*
2 Conduct safely ANT 4.6.25 *Best you saf'd the bringer Out of the host.*
~ *adj.*
1 (mentally or morally) Sound, sane OTH 4.1.269 *Are his wits safe?,* COR 2.3.218, JC 1.1.13.
2 Sure, trustworthy OTH 2.3.205 *My blood begins my safer guides to rule,* 3H6 4.7.52.
~ *adv. safe toward* With a sure regard to MAC 1.4.27 *by doing everything Safe toward your love and honour.*

safe-conduct *vb.* Conduct safely R3 4.4.482 *Are they not...Safe-conducting the rebels...?*

safeguard *n.* Protection, safety MM 5.1.419 *consenting to the safeguard of your honour,* COR 3.2.68; *in safeguard of* for the defence or protection of 3H6 2.2.18 *doves will peck in safeguard of their brood,* R3 5.3.259; *on safeguard* under guarantee of safe-conduct COR 3.1.9 *On safeguard he came to see me.*

safely *adv.* In safe custody AWW 4.1.94 *I'll keep him dark and safely lock'd,* R2 4.1.153; *in a safe place* HAM 5.2.52 *plac'd it safely.*

safety *n.*
1 Means of safety, safeguard JN 4.3.12 *It is our safety,* MAC 3.1.53, TRO 5.3.94.
2 Safe custody JN 4.2.158 *Deliver him to safety,* ROM 5.3.183.

saffron *n.* Orange-red product of the Autumnal Crocus, Crocus sativus, used to give pastry a yellowish colour AWW 4.5.2 *whose villainous saffron would have made all the unbak'd...youth...in his colour* (with allusion to the fashionable wearing of yellow), WT 4.3.45.

sag *vb.* Droop, decline MAC 5.3.10 *the heart I bear, Shall never sag with doubt.*

sagittary *n.* Centaur; esp. the centaur who, according to medieval romance, fought in the Trojan army against the Greeks TRO 5.5.14 *The dreadful Sagittary Appals our numbers.*

sail *n.*[1] (collective sing.) Ships, vessels JN 3.4.2 *A whole armado of convicted sail,* OTH 1.3.37; (also pl.) ANT 2.6.24 *Thou canst not fear us...with thy sails.*

sail *n.*[2] Number (of vessels) sailing PER 1.4.61 *A portly sail of ships.*

sain *pa. pple.* (used chiefly in rhymes) Said LLL 3.1.82 *that hath tofore been sain.*

saint *vb.*
1 Play the saint PP 18.44 *To sin and never for to saint.*
2 Become a saint in Heaven MM 1.4.34 *a thing enskied, and sainted.*

Saint Nicholas' clerks See NICHOLAS.

sainted *ppl. adj.*
1 Enrolled among the saints, that is a saint in Heaven WT 5.1.57 *her sainted spirit.*
2 Sanctified, holy MAC 4.3.109 *a most sainted king.*
3 Befitting a saint, sacred AWW 3.4.7 *sainted vow.*

sake *n. are...for the Lord's sake* Are 'doing time' MM 4.3.19.
⋄ *For the Lord's sake* was the cry used by Ludgate prisoners when asking for alms, etc., at the grated window.

salad *n.* (attrib.) *salad days* Days of youthful inexperience ANT 1.5.73 *My salad days, When I was green in judgement.*

salamander *n.* Lizard-like animal supposed to live in fire, spirit living in fire; (applied to a fiery-red face) 1H4 3.3.47 *I have maintain'd that salamander of yours with fire.*

salary *n.* Reward, fee HAM 3.3.79 *this is hire and salary, not revenge* (F1; Qq 2–4 *base and silly*; Q1 *a benefit*).

sale *n. of sale*
1 That is to be sold, vendible, venal LLL 4.3.236 *things of sale*, PER 4.6.78.
2 For the sale of a commodity HAM 2.1.58 *'I saw him enter such a house of sale', Videlicet, a brothel.*

sale-work *n.* Ready-made work; (hence) work not of the best quality AYL 3.5.43 *the ordinary Of nature's sale-work.*

sallet *n.*[1] (a prevalent Eliz. form of) Salad; (hence) something mixed or savoury HAM 2.2.441 *no sallets in the lines to make the matter savoury,* AWW 4.5.17.

sallet *n.*[2] (in medieval armour) Light, round head-piece 2H6 4.10.11 *but for a sallet, my brain-pan had been cleft with a brown bill.*

Salique *adj.*
1 Pertaining to the Salian Franks H5 1.2.40 *Which Salique land the French unjustly gloze To be the realm of France.*
2 *Salique law* The alleged fundamental law of the French monarchy, by which females were excluded from succession to the crown H5 1.2.91 *they would hold up this Salique law To bar your Highness claiming from the female.*

salt *n.* (fig.) Tears LR 4.6.195 *a man of salt* (i.e. melting to tears), COR 5.6.92.
▷ Applied to tears because of their saline taste. See HAM 1.2.154 *the salt of most unrighteous tears.*
~ *adj.*[1]
1 Living in the sea WIV 1.1.22 *salt fish.*
2 (fig.) Bitter TRO 1.3.370 *salt scorn.*
3 *salt rheum* Irritating discharge of mucus from the nose, a running cold ERR 3.2.128, OTH 3.4.51.

salt *adj.*[2] (var. of 'saut', aphetic form of) ASSAUT, lecherous, wanton TIM 4.3.86 *thy salt hours,* MM 5.1.401, OTH 2.1.240.

Saltier *n.* (blunder for) Satyr WT 4.4.327 *They call themselves Saltiers.*

saltness *n.* (?) Rankness 2H4 1.2.98 *some relish of the saltness of time in you.*

salt-butter *n.* (attrib.) (?) Rank WIV 2.2.278 *salt-butter rogue.*

salutation *n. give salutation to* Affect, act upon SON 121.6 *why should others' false adulterate eyes Give salutation to my sportive blood?*

salute *vb.*
1 Come into contact with JN 2.1.590 *When his fair angels would salute my palm.*
2 Affect, act upon H8 2.3.103 *If this salute my blood a jot.*

salvage *n.* (var. of) Savage TMP 2.2.58 *salvages and men of Inde.*

salve *vb.* Anoint; (hence) soften, palliate ADO 1.1.315 *I would have salv'd it with a longer treatise.*

sampire *n.* Samphire, cliff plant with aromatic saline fleshy leaves LR 4.6.15 *one that gathers sampire.*

sample *n.* Example CYM 1.1.48 *A sample to the youngest.*

sancta majestas [L.] Sacred majesty 2H6 5.1.5 (Qq *santa maesta* [It.]).

sanctified *ppl. adj.*
1 Consecrated, hallowed, holy AWW 1.1.140 *buried ...out of all sanctified limit,* OTH 3.4.126, LC 233.

2 Sanctimonious AYL 2.3.13 *Your virtues...Are sanctified and holy traitors to you,* HAM 1.3.130.

sanctify *vb.*
1 Consecrate (a person) 2H4 4.5.114 *drops of balm to sanctify thy head.*
2 Honour as holy, reverence AWW 3.4.11 *His name with zealous fervour sanctify,* AWW 1.1.98.
3 Impart a blessing or virtue to, sanction AWW 1.3.245 *his good receipt Shall...be sanctified By th' luckiest stars in heaven,* COR 4.5.195; give a sanctity to TRO 3.2.183 *'As true as Troilus' shall...sanctify the numbers.*

sanctimonious *adj.* Sacred TMP 4.1.16 *All sanctimonious ceremonies.*

sanctimony *n.*
1 Holiness, sanctity, piety TRO 5.2.140 *If sanctimony be the gods' delight,* AWW 4.3.50.
2 Sacred or religious bond OTH 1.3.355 *sanctimony and a frail vow* (i.e. marriage bond).
3 (pl.) Sacred things TRO 5.2.139 *if vows be sanctimonies* (F1 *are sanctimonie*).

sanctuarize *vb.* Afford sanctuary to HAM 4.7.127 *No place...should murder sanctuarize.*

sanctuary *n.*
1 *break sanctuary* Violate the right of a sanctuary R3 3.1.47 *You break not sanctuary in seizing him.*
2 (attrib.) *sanctuary men, children* Those who have taken refuge in a privileged place of protection R3 3.1.55.

sandal *n.* (attrib.) *sandal shoon* Sandals HAM 4.5.26 *his cockle hat and staff, And his sandal shoon.*

sand-blind *adj.* Half-blind MV 2.2.36 *being more than sand-blind.*

sanded *adj.* Of a sandy colour MND 4.1.120 *My hounds are bred out of the Spartan kind; So flew'd, so sanded.*

sandy *adj.* Containing sand for measuring time MV 1.1.25 *see the sandy hour-glass run;* (hence) *sandy hour* 1H6 4.2.36.

sanguine *adj.* Blood-red 1H6 4.1.92 *the sanguine colour of the leaves,* CYM 5.5.364; red-faced 1H4 2.4.242 *This sanguine coward,* TIT 4.2.97.

sanguis [L.] Blood LLL 4.2.3.

sans *prep.* Without AYL 2.7.166 *Sans teeth, sans eyes,* HAM 3.4.79, TMP 1.2.97.

sap *n.* Juice, fluid R3 4.4.277 *did drain The purple sap from her sweet brother's body;* (fig.) H8 1.1.148 *If with the sap of reason you would quench...the fire of passion;* (hence) vigour, vitality SON 15.7 *that men as plants increase,...Vaunt in their youthful sap; there's sap in...* there is life or promise in...WT 4.4.565, ANT 3.13.191.

sapego See SERPIGO.

sarsenet, sarcenet *n.* Fine soft silk material; (attrib.) TRO 5.1.31 *green sarcenet flap for a sore eye;* (fig.) soft 1H4 3.1.251 *givest such sarcenet surety for thy oaths.*

sate See SET.

satire *n.* Satirist SON 100.11 *be a satire to decay.*

Satis quod sufficit [L.] Enough is as good as a feast LLL 5.1.1 (Ff, Qq *quid*).

satisfaction *n. in heavy satisfaction* In sorrowful acceptance of the truth AWW 5.3.100 *she ceas'd In heavy satisfaction.*

sauce *vb.*
1 Make (a person) pay dearly, overcharge WIV 4.3.9 *I'll make them pay; I'll sauce them.*
▷ 'Pay sauce' was an old phr. meaning 'pay dearly'.
2 Rebuke smartly AYL 3.5.69 *I'll sauce her with bitter words.*

saucer *n.* Dish used to receive the blood in bloodletting LLL 4.3.96 *A fever in your blood! why then incision Would let her out in saucers.*

saucily adv. Presumptuously Luc 1348 others sauc- ily Promise more speed.

sauciness n. Insolence Tit 2.3.82 that my noble lord be rated For sauciness.

saucy adj.

1 Highly seasoned, piquant; (fig.) Tn 3.4.145 Here's the challenge...there's vinegar and pepper in't.— Is't so saucy?

2 Wanton, lascivious MM 2.4.45 Their saucy sweet- ness, AWW 4.4.23, Cym 1.6.151.

3 Insolent, presumptuous Cym 5.5.325 I am too blunt and saucy, Mac 3.4.24, Oth 1.1.128.

4 (of a boat) Rashly venturing, presumptuous Tro 1.3.42 the saucy boat, Son 80.7.

savage adj.

1 Wild, untamed AYL 2.6.7 any thing savage (i.e. any wild animal), MV 5.1.78.

2 (of demeanour, noise, etc.) Wild, ungoverned WT 3.3.56 A savage clamour, Ado 4.1.61; 'uncivil' (Schmidt) Tro 2.3.126 the savage strangeness he puts on; savage cause reason to run wild Ant 3.13.128 I have savage cause.

savagery n. Wild vegetation H5 5.2.47 deracinate such savagery.

save vb.

1 save, 'save (short for) God save Lr 2.1.1 Save thee, TGV 1.1.70, Cor 4.4.6.

2 Spare (a person's life), allow to live Cym 2.3.71 makes the true man kill'd and saves the thief, JC 5.3.38, Lr 5.3.152.

3 Anticipate and so prevent 1H4 5.4.57 And sav'd the treacherous labour of your son, Tim 1.1.252, Tro 3.3.241.

4 save your reverence See REVERENCE.

save conj. save that Were it not that AWW 3.2.2 save that he comes not along with her, R3 3.7.193, Son 66.14.

~ prep. Except TN 3.1.160 save I alone, Tim 4.3.500, JC 5.5.69; save for except for Tmp 1.2.282 Save for the son.

saving prep.

1 Except Jn 1.1.201 Saving in dialogue of compli- ment.

2 Without prejudice or offence to, with all respect to H8 2.3.31 Saving your mincing, Err 4.1.27, Shr 2.1.71.

▷ See REVERENCE.

savour n.

1 Smell, perfume Tmp 2.2.52 the savour of tar, Shr Ind.2.71, Jn 4.3.112.

2 Character, style Lr 1.4.237 much o' th' savour Of other your new pranks (Q3 fauour).

~ vb.

1 Have a particular smell Per 4.6.110 The very doors and windows savour vilely; (fig.) savours no- bly has a noble quality about it TN 5.1.120; (with of) H5 1.2.295 His jest will savour but of shallow wit, TN 5.1.314, WT 2.3.119.

2 Care for, like Lr 4.2.39 Filths savour but them- selves.

sawn pa. pple. (?) (1) Seen; or (2) sown LC 91 on his visage was in little drawn What largeness thinks in Paradise was sawn.

say n.[1] Cloth of fine texture resembling serge 2H6 4.7.25 thou say, thou serge,...thou buckram lord! (punning).

say n.[2] (usu. taken as the aphetic form of) Assay, proof, sample Lr 5.3.144 thy tongue some say of breeding breathes (F1 (some say)).

~ vb.[1] ASSAY, try Per 1.1.59 Of all 'say'd yet, mayst thou prove prosperous!

say vb.[2]

1 Speak to the point Ham 5.1.26 Why, there thou say'st.

2 I have said (1) I have finished speaking, I have spoken my mind Jn 2.1.235 When I have said, make answer to us both, Ant 3.2.34; (2) I have spoken decisively H8 5.1.86 I have said. Be gone; (3) It is as I have said, that is so Mac 4.3.213 My wife kill'd too?—I have said, Ant 1.2.57.

3 you have said What you say is true TGV 2.4.29, TN 3.1.11, Oth 4.2.201.

4 say you? What is that you say? MM 5.1.274, Ham 4.5.28, Cym 2.1.25.

5 how say you by...? What do you say about...MV 1.2.54, Oth 1.3.17.

▷ See BY sense 1.

'sblood interj. God's blood H5 4.8.9 'Sblood, an ar- rant traitor...!, Ham 2.2.366, Ham 3.2.369.

▷ Occurs several times in early Qq, but only once (H5 4.8.9 'Sblud) in Ff, in which a milder oath is sometimes substituted.

scab n. Mean, low, scurvy fellow, scoundrel Tro 2.1.29 and I had the scratching of thee, I would make thee the loathsomest scab in Greece, TN 2.5.74.

▷ Possible puns in Ado 3.3.100, Cor 1.1.166, 2H4 3.2.276.

scaffoldage n. Theatrical stage Tro 1.3.156 'Twixt his...footing and the scaffoldage (F1 scaffolage).

scaffold n. Theatrical stage H5 Prol.10 On this un- worthy scaffold.

scald vb.

1 (intr.) Get burning hot with the sun 2H4 4.5.31 Like a rich armour worn in heat of day, That scald'st with safety (i.e. to the wearer).

2 (pass.) Be heated Jn 5.7.49 I am scalded with my violent motion.

scald adj. Mean, paltry, contemptible H5 5.1.5 the rascally, scald...knave, Ant 5.2.215.

scalding ppl. adj. Scorching 3H6 5.7.18 summer's scalding heat.

scale n.[1] equal scale Just balance Ham 1.2.13 In equal scale weighing delight and dole.

~ vb.[1] Weigh as in scales, compare, estimate MM 3.1.255 the corrupt deputy [is] scal'd, Cor 2.3.249.

scale n.[2] (pl.) Graduations Ant 2.7.18 they take the flow o' th' Nile By certain scales i' th' pyramid.

~ vb.[2] (intr.) Ascend Luc 440 as his hand did scale.

scaling ppl. adj. Having scales, scaly Tro 5.5.22 like scaling sculls (Q scaling, F1 scaled).

scall adj. Mean, paltry, contemptible, SCALD Wiv 3.1.120 This same scall, scurvy...companion.

scalp n. Head, crown of the head, skull TGV 4.1.36 the bare scalp of Robin Hood's fat friar, MND 4.1.64, Luc 1413.

scaly adj. (said of armour) Having small overlap- ping plates of metal or leather 2H4 1.1.146 A scaly gauntlet...with joints of steel.

scamble vb. Struggle indecorously or rapaciously to obtain something, scramble Jn 4.3.146 To tug and scamble.

scambling n. Indecorous, disorderly struggle H5 5.2.205 I get thee with scambling.

~ ppl. adj. Contentious, rapacious Ado 5.1.94 Scambling...boys, That lie and cog and flout, H5 1.1.4.

scamel n. (?) Seagull Tmp 2.2.172 I 'll get thee Young scamels from the rock.

(?) (1) a SEAMEL; or (2) STANIEL.

scan vb.

1 Estimate, judge Per 2.2.56 scan The outward habit by the inward man.

2 Examine, consider Mac 3.4.139 Which must be acted ere they may be scann'd, Err 2.2.150, Oth 3.3.245.

3 Interpret Ham 3.3.75 That would be scann'd: A villain kills my father, and for that I...do this same villain send To heaven.

scandal *n.* Disgraceful imputation HAM 2.1.29 *You must not put another scandal on him, That he is open to incontinency*, WT 1.2.330; damage to reputation ERR 5.1.15 *not without some scandal to yourself*, 2H6 2.4.65, HAM 1.4.38.

~ *vb.*

1 Bring into disrepute CYM 3.4.60 *Sinon's weeping Did scandal many a holy tear.*

2 Defame JC 1.2.76 *fawn on men...And after scandal them*, COR 3.1.44.

scandalize *vb.*

1 Discredit, disgrace TGV 2.7.61 *I fear me it will make me scandaliz'd.*

2 Defame 1H4 1.3.154 *we in the world's wide mouth live scandaliz'd and foully spoken of.*

scant *vb.*

1 Put (a person) off *with* a scanty supply, stint TRO 4.4.47 *scants us with a single famish'd kiss.*

2 Reduce, diminish the amount of, cut down ANT 4.2.21 *Scant not my cups*, LR 2.4.175.

3 Stint the supply of, refrain from giving, withhold MV 5.1.141 *I scant this breathing courtesy*, ERR 2.2.80, LR 2.4.140.

4 Limit, restrict MV 2.1.17 *had not scanted me And hedg'd me by his wit*, MV 3.2.112.

5 Treat slightingly, neglect OTH 1.3.267 *I will your...great business scant.*

~ *adj.*

1 Chary HAM 1.3.121 *Be something scanter of your maiden presence.*

2 Having a scanty or limited supply *of*, short *of* HAM 5.2.287 *He's fat, and scant of breath.*

~ *adv.* Scarcely ROM 1.2.99 *she shall scant show well that now seems best.*

scantle *n.* Piece 1H4 3.1.99 *And cuts me...a monstrous scantle out.*

⋄ Qq; Ff *cantle*, for which the Qq reading may be an error. See CANTLE.

scantling *n.* Specimen, sample TRO 1.3.341 *the success...shall give a scantling Of good or bad unto the general.*

scantly *adv.* Grudgingly ANT 3.4.6 *Spoke scantly of me.*

scape *n.*

1 Escape SHR 5.2.3 *To smile at scapes and perils overblown*, OTH 1.3.136.

2 Transgression, esp. breach of chastity WT 3.3.72 *A boy or a child, I wonder?...sure some scape*, LUC 747.

~ *vb.* Escape TGV 5.3.11 *The thicket is beset, he cannot scape*, MV 2.2.163, 3H6 1.3.1.

scarcity *n.* Penury TMP 4.1.116 *Scarcity and want shall shun you; in scarcity of* badly off for, illprovided with TIM 2.2.225 *he was...in scarcity of friends.*

scare See SCARRE.

scarf *n.*

1 Military officer's sash ADO 2.1.190 *a lieutenant's scarf*, AWW 3.5.85, AWW 4.3.324; decorative sash JC 1.2.285 *pulling scarfs off Caesar's images.*

2 Sling for a limb AYL 5.2.20 *to see thee wear thy heart in a scarf*, COR 1.9.SD.

3 Streamer used for decking out a ship AWW 2.3.203 *the scarfs...about thee did...dissuade me.*

~ *vb.*

1 Blindfold MAC 3.2.47 *Scarf up the...eye of...day.*

2 Wrap *about* one in the manner of a scarf HAM 5.2.13 *My sea-gown scarf'd about me.*

scarfed *ppl. adj.* Decorated with flags or streamers MV 2.6.15 *The scarfed bark.*

scarlet *adj.* Clothed in scarlet (the cardinal's colour) H8 3.2.255 *Thou scarlet sin* (cf. CARDINAL), 1H6 1.3.56.

scarre *n.* (?) (var. of) Scare, fright, alarm, panic

(Lancashire, JEGP LXVIII:244) AWW 4.2.38 *I see that men make rope's in such a scarre, That we'll forsake ourselves* (i.e. utter cries of distress in such a plight).

scathe *n.* Harm R3 1.3.316 *that have done scathe to us*, JN 2.1.75, 2H6 2.4.62.

~ *vb.* Injure ROM 1.5.84 *This trick may chance to scathe you* (F1 *scath*).

scatheful *adj.* Harmful TN 5.1.56 *such scatheful grapple* (F1 *scathfull*).

scattered *ppl. adj.*

1 Distracted LR 3.1.31 *this scattered kingdom.*

2 Stray AYL 3.5.104 *Loose now and then A scatt'red smile.*

scattering *ppl. adj.* Stray, erratic OTH 3.3.151 *his scattering and unsure observance.*

scene *n.* Representation of a piece on the stage, dramatic performance, play, or drama AYL 2.7.138 *the scene Wherein we play in*, WIV 4.6.17, HAM 2.2.399.

schedule *n.* Slip or scroll of paper containing writing, document LUC 1312 *this short schedule* (i.e. letter), MV 2.9.55, JC 3.1.3; (hence) tabular or classified statement, inventory 2H4 4.1.166 *this schedule...contains our general grievances*, LLL 1.1.18, TN 1.5.245.

scholar *n.* Pupil ANT 4.14.102 *Thy master dies thy scholar*, PER 2.3.17, PER 2.5.31.

scholarly *adv.* As befits a scholar WIV 1.3.2 *Speak scholarly and wisely.*

school *n.*[1]

1 University AYL 1.1.6 *My brother...he keeps at school*, HAM 1.2.113, TRO 1.3.104.

2 Schooling, learning LLL 5.2.71 *wisdom's warrant and the help of school.*

3 *set to school* Send to be taught, give instruction to 3H6 3.2.193 *And set the murderous Machevil to school*, LR 2.4.67, LUC 1820.

4 *the schools* The (medical) faculty AWW 1.3.240 *the schools...have left off The danger to itself.*

~ *vb.*

1 Reprimand, lecture 1H4 3.1.188 *Well, I am school'd.*

2 Discipline, control MAC 4.2.15 *school yourself.*

school *n.*[2] Shoal of fish TRO 5.5.22 *like scaling schools Before the...whale* (Ff *sculs*); (fig.) large number, 'crowd' 2H4 4.3.18 *I have a whole school of tongues in this belly of mine.*

schooling *n.* Reprimand, admonition MND 1.1.116 *I have some private schooling for you both.*

schoolmaster *n.* Private tutor LR 1.4.179 *keep a schoolmaster*, TMP 1.2.172, COR 1.3.56.

science *n.* Knowledge AWW 5.3.103 *Plutus himself...Hath not in nature's mystery more science Than I have in this ring*, MM 1.1.5.

scion *n.* Shoot, twig; (fig.) OTH 1.3.332 *lusts; whereof I take this that you call love to be a set or scion* (F1 *Seyen*, Q1 *syen*); slip for grafting, graft WT 4.4.93 *we marry A gentler scion to the wildest stock* (F1 *Sien*), H5 3.5.7.

scold *vb.* Quarrel noisily, brawl, rail (against), wrangle (with) ADO 2.1.242 *My...visor began to...scold with her*, TIM 4.3.156, H8 5.1.173.

scolding *ppl. adj.* Chiding, brawling, noisy JC 1.3.5 *the scolding winds.*

sconce *n.*[1] (jocular term) Head HAM 5.1.102 *knock him about the sconce*, ERR 1.2.79, COR 3.2.99.

sconce *n.*[2] Small fort or earthwork H5 3.6.72 *at such and such a sconce*; (fig.) defence ERR 2.2.37 *I must get a sconce for my head, and insconce it.*

~ *vb.* (refl.) Entrench oneself; (fig.) HAM 3.4.4 *I'll sconce me even here.*

⋄ Hanmer; F1 *silence.*

scope *n.*

1 End in view, object, aim R2 3.3.112 *His coming*

hither hath no further scope Than..., 1H4 3.1.169, HAM 3.2.219; *to scope* to the purpose, fittingly TIM 1.1.72 *'Tis conceiv'd to scope.*
2 Liberty, free course 2H6 3.1.176 *scope of speech*, MM 1.3.35, R2 3.3.141; instance of liberty MM 1.2.127 *every scope by the immoderate use Turns to restraint.*
3 *scope of nature* 'Circumstances within the limits of nature's operations' (Aldis Wright), JN 3.4.154.

scorch *vb.* Slash with a knife MAC 3.2.13 *We have scorch'd the snake, not kill'd it*, ERR 5.1.183.

score *n.*
1 Notch cut in a stick or tally used in keeping accounts 2H6 4.7.35 *our forefathers had no other books but the score and the tally.*
2 Account kept by means of tallies or marks on a door, etc. AWW 4.3.224 *he never pays the score*, MAC 5.9.18; *on my score* at my expense 2H6 4.2.73; *on the score* in debt SHR Ind.2.23.
~ *vb.*
1 Notch, cut, mark by cuts of a whip ANT 4.7.12 *Let us score their backs.*
2 Keep account by notches or marks on a stick or post SON 122.10 *Nor need I tallies thy dear love to score*; (fig.) record SHR Ind.2.24 *score me up for the lying'st knave in Christendom.*
▷ OTH 4.1.126 *Have you scor'd me?* (F1, Q2; Q1 *stor'd*): either sense 1 (i.e. branded or beaten me), or sense 2 (i.e. set down my reckoning, settled my account).
3 Run up a score, obtain goods on credit AWW 4.3.224 *After he scores, he never pays the score*, 1H4 2.4.27.

scorn *n.*
1 Derisive utterance or gesture, taunt, insult HAM 3.1.69 *the whips and scorns of time*, LLL 5.2.865, OTH 4.1.82.
2 Object of mockery or contempt ERR 4.4.103 *To make a loathsome abject scorn of me*, 1H6 4.6.49, TIT 1.1.265.
3 *take scorn, think scorn* (with infin.) Regard as disgraceful, disdain, despise 1H6 4.4.35 *take foul scorn to fawn on him*, LLL 1.2.63; *think scorn* (absol.) despise everything else CYM 4.4.53 *their blood thinks scorn Till it...show them princes born.*
~ *vb.*
1 (intr.) Mock, jeer (*at* a person) JN 1.1.228 *Why scorn'st thou at Sir Robert?*, ROM 1.5.57, LLL 4.3.145.
2 (trans.) Ridicule, deride MV 3.1.56 *He hath...mock'd at my gains, scorn'd my nation*, COR 2.3.222, ERR 4.4.75.
3 Disdain PER 2.4.12 *That all those eyes ador'd them ere their fall Scorn now their hand should give them burial*; contemptuously refuse COR 3.1.267 *law shall scorn him further trial.*

scornful *adj.* Regarded with scorn, contemptible LUC 520 *The scornful mark of every open eye.*

scot *n.* Payment, contribution, 'reckoning'; *scot and lot* tax levied by a municipal corporation in proportionate shares upon its members for the defraying of municipal expenses; *pay* (*a person*) *scot and lot* (fig.) pay out thoroughly, settle with 1H4 5.4.114 *or that hot termagant Scot had paid me scot and lot too.*

scotch *n.* Cut, gash ANT 4.7.10 *I have yet Room for six scotches more.*
~ *vb.* Cut, score, gash COR 4.5.186 *he scotch'd him and notch'd him like a carbinado.*
▷ MAC 3.2.13: Theobald *scotch'd*; F1 *scorch'd.* See SCORCH.

scour *vb.*[1]
1 Remove, get rid of, purge 1H4 3.2.137 *Which*

wash'd away shall scour my shame with it, MAC 5.3.56, H5 1.1.34.
2 Beat, punish ERR 1.2.65 *she will scour your fault upon my pate.*
3 Clean a pistol with a 'scourer', i.e. a ramrod with a wad or sponge H5 2.1.56 *If you grow foul with me, Pistol, I will scour you with my rapier* (with quibble on sense 2).

scour *vb.*[2] Hurry, move rapidly WT 2.1.35 *never Saw I men scour so on their way.*

scouring *n.* Hasty movement to and fro TIM 5.2.15 *fearful scouring Doth choke the air with dust.*

scout *vb.*[1] Keep a look-out TN 3.4.176 *scout me for him.*

scout *vb.*[2] Deride TMP 3.2.122 *scout 'em and flout 'em.*

scrape *vb.* Erase (writing, sketch) with a knife MM 1.2.9 *went to sea with the Ten Commandments, but scrap'd one out of the table*, LLL 5.2.575; (fig.) WIV 4.2.216 *to scrape the figures out of your husband's brains.*

scraping *ppl. adj.* Saving, parsimonious R2 5.3.69 *their scraping fathers' gold.*

scribe *n.* Penman, writer, clerk TGV 2.1.140 *my master, being scribe, to himself should write the letter*, TIT 2.4.4, H8 2.4.SD.

scrimer *n.* Fencer HAM 4.7.100 *The scrimers...had neither motion, guard, nor eye.*

scrip *n.*[1] Piece of paper written upon MND 1.2.3 *to call them generally, man by man, according to the scrip.*

scrip *n.*[2] Wallet, satchel, such as beggars and shepherds wore AYL 3.2.162 *though not with bag and baggage, yet with scrip and scrippage.*

scrippage *n.* Contents of a SCRIP *n.*[2] AYL 3.2.162 *though not with bag and baggage, yet with scrip and scrippage.*
▷ Coinage; *scrip and scrippage* is modelled on *bag and baggage.*

scripture *n.* (pl.) Writings CYM 3.4.81 *The scriptures of the loyal Leonatus, All turn'd to heresy?*

scrivener *n.*
1 Professional scribe R3 3.6.SD *Enter a Scrivener.*
2 Notary or drawer-up of contracts SHR 4.4.59 *My boy shall fetch the scrivener.*

scrowl *vb.* (?) (a form of) Scrawl, gesticulate TIT 2.4.5 *See how with signs and tokens she can scrowl* (with a play on 'scroll' i.e. write down; F1 *scowle*).

scroyle *n.* Scoundrel, wretch JN 2.1.373 *these scroyles...flout you.*

scrubbed *ppl. adj.* Stunted MV 5.1.162 *a little scrubbed boy*, MV 5.1.261.

scruple *n. make scruple of*
1 Stick at, entertain doubt about TRO 4.1.57 *Not making any scruple of her soil.*
2 Doubt, hesitate to believe or admit CYM 5.5.182 *I...Made scruple of his praise*, 2H4 1.2.130.

scrupulous *adj.* Cautious or hesitating in taking action ANT 1.3.48 *Equality of two domestic powers Breed scrupulous faction*, 3H6 4.7.61.

scul(l) See SCHOOL *n.*[2].

scullion *n.* Domestic servant of the lowest rank who performed the menial duties of the kitchen 2H4 2.1.59 *Away, you scullion!*, HAM 2.2.587 (Q1 *scalion;* Q2 *stallyon*).

scurril *adj.* Scurrilous, grossly or obscenely abusive TRO 1.3.148 *Breaks scurril jests.*

scuse *n.* (aphetic form of) Excuse MV 4.1.444 *That scuse serves many men to save their gifts*, OTH 4.1.79.

scut *n.* Tail of a deer WIV 5.5.18 *My doe with the black scut* (with indecent quibble).

scutcheon *n.* (var. of) Escutcheon, hatchment of arms exhibiting the armorial bearings of a deceased person, often carried at funerals 1H4 5.1.140 *honour is a mere scutcheon.*

scythe *vb.* Mow down; (fig.) LC 12 *Time had not scythed all that youth begun.*

'sdeath *interj.* (an oath) God's death COR 1.1.217 *'Sdeath, The rabble should have first unroof'd the city.*

sea *n.*

1 (fig.) Water as one of the 'elements' HAM 1.1.153 *Whether in sea or fire, in earth or air,* ERR 2.1.17, PER 1.4.34.

2 (pl. used for sing.) Sea, stretch of water MV 2.8.28 *the Narrow Seas that part the French and English,* SHR 1.2.74; *to seas* to sea PER 2.Gower.27 *put forth to seas.*

3 *at the sea* At sea PER 1.3.28 *He scap'd the land to perish at the sea,* PER 5.3.47.

sea-bank *n.* Sea-shore MV 5.1.11 *Stood Dido...Upon the wild sea-banks,* OTH 4.1.133.

sea-boy *n.* Ship's boy, 'the most junior rating in the Royal Navy' (Falconer, 1965) 2H4 3.1.27 *give then repose To the wet sea-boy* (F1; Q (second issue) *season*).

sea-cap *n.* Sailor's cap TN 3.4.330 *no sea-cap on your head.*

sea-coal *n.* Mineral coal (as distinguished from charcoal) brought by sea from Newcastle WIV 1.4.9 *a sea-coal fire,* 2H4 2.1.88.

seal *n.*

1 Something which authenticates, attests, or confirms a covenant or undertaking, final addition which completes and secures MM 4.1.6 *my kisses...Seals of love,* H5 4.1.164, TRO 4.4.122; HAM 3.2.399 *To give them seals* (i.e. to confirm them by making words into deeds).

2 Token, sign (of a thing) OTH 2.3.344 *All seals and symbols of redeemed sin,* AWW 1.3.132, MND 3.2.144.

~ *vb.*

1 (intr.) Set one's seal (to something) MV 1.3.152 *I'll seal to such a bond,* TN 2.5.93, 1H4 3.1.265; *seal under for* become surety for MV 1.2.82 *the Frenchman became his surety and seal'd under for another.*

2 Bring to completion or conclusion TIM 5.4.54 *till we Have seal'd thy full desire,* HAM 4.3.56; (absol.) ANT 4.14.49 *Seal then, and all is done.*

~ in combination

seal up 1 Confirm fully 2H4 4.5.103 *Thou hast seal'd up my expectation.* **2** Complete 1H6 1.1.130 *Here had the conquest fully been seal'd up If...3* Make up (one's mind) finally AYL 4.3.58 *seal up thy mind, Whether...*

sealed quarts *n.* (pl.) Quart measures officially marked with a stamp as a guarantee of accurate size SHR Ind.2.88 *you would present her at the leet, Because she brought...no seal'd quarts.*

sea-like *adj.* Likely to keep the sea, in sea-going trim ANT 3.13.171 *our sever'd navy too Have knit again, and fleet, threat'ning most sea-like.*

sealing-day *n.* Day of contract MND 1.1.84 *The sealing-day betwixt my love and me.*

seal manual *n.* (app. alteration of the ordinary phr.) Sign manual (i.e. an autograph signature, esp. of a sovereign, serving to authenticate a document); (fig.) VEN 516 *Set thy seal manual on my wax-red lips.*

seam *n.* Fat, grease TRO 2.3.185 *bastes his arrogance with his own seam.*

sea-maid *n.* Mermaid MM 3.2.108 *Some report a sea-maid spawn'd him,* MND 2.1.154.

sea-mall See SCAMEL.

sea-mark *n.* Conspicuous object distinguishable at sea which serves to guide or warn sailors COR

5.3.74 *Like a great sea-mark...saving those that eye thee!,* OTH 5.2.268.

sea-mel(l) Seamew, seagull TMP 2.2.172 *I'll get thee young seamels from the rack.*

⟡ Keightley's conjecture; F1 *scamel.*

sear *n.* and *adj.* (var. of) *n.* SERE[1].

~ *vb.*

1 Dry *up,* cause to wither, blight CYM 1.1.116 *sear up my embracements from a next.*

2 Brand WT 2.1.73 *calumny will sear Virtue itself,* AWW 2.1.173.

3 Burn, scorch R3 4.1.60 *to sear me to the brains,* 3H6 5.6.23, MAC 4.1.113.

search *n.* Search-party OTH 1.1.158 *Lead to the Sagittary the raised search.*

~ *vb.*

1 Seek, seek for CYM 5.5.11 *He hath been search'd among the dead and living,* 3H6 5.2.18.

2 Probe (a wound) TIT 2.3.262 *to the bottom dost thou search my wound,* TGV 1.2.113, AYL 2.4.44; (absol.) TRO 2.2.16 *the tent that searches To th' bottom of the worst.*

3 Penetrate JC 5.3.42 *with this good sword...search this bosom,* LLL 1.1.85.

searcher *n.* Official appointed to view dead bodies and report on the cause of death ROM 5.2.8 *the searchers...Seal'd up the doors.*

searching *ppl. adj.* (of words) Cutting, trenchant 2H6 3.2.311 *bitter searching terms;* (of wine) stirring, exciting the blood 2H4 2.4.27 *a marvellous searching wine.*

seared *ppl. adj.* Withered, blighted LC 14 *sear'd age,* MM 2.4.9 (F1 *feard*).

sea-room *n.* The open sea PER 3.1.45 *But sea-room, and the brine and cloudy billow kiss the moon, I care not.*

sea-sick *adj.* Weary of the sea, weary of voyaging ROM 5.3.118 *thy sea-sick weary bark.*

sea-side *n.* Seashore, edge of the sea OTH 2.1.36 *Let's to the sea-side.*

season *n.*

1 Spell of bad weather LR 3.4.32 *How shall your houseless heads...defend you From seasons such as these?*

2 Preservative, 'seasoning', that which keeps things fresh (also fig.) ADO 4.1.142 *season give To her foul tainted flesh,* MAC 3.4.140, MM 2.2.167 (with quibble).

3 Age, year CYM 3.4.172 *From youth of such a season.*

4 Opportunity ERR 4.2.58 *Time is a very bankrupt and owes more than he's worth to season* (i.e. there is never enough time for all the opportunities that present themselves).

5 *of (the) season* In season WIV 3.3.159 *buck, and of the season too,* MM 2.2.85; befitting the time of year, seasonable AWW 5.3.32 *a day of season.*

~ *vb.*

1 Mature, ripen HAM 1.3.81 *my blessing season this in thee,* TIM 4.3.86, HAM 3.2.209.

2 Temper, qualify, moderate MV 4.1.197 *When mercy seasons justice,* HAM 1.2.192, HAM 2.1.28.

3 Gratify (the palate) MV 4.1.97 *let their palates Be season'd with such viands.*

seasoned *ppl. adj.* Established or perfected by time COR 3.3.64 *you have contriv'd to take From Rome all season'd office.*

seat *n.*

1 Throne H5 1.1.88 *the crown and seat of France,* R2 3.2.119, R3 3.7.169.

2 Estate MV 1.1.171 *her seat of Belmont,* CYM 5.4.60; fief H5 3.5.47 *For your great seats now quit you of great shames,* 1H4 5.1.45.

3 Situation, site MAC 1.6.1 *This castle hath a pleasant seat.*

~ *vb.* Settle H5 1.2.62 *did seat the French Beyond the river Sala.*

seated *ppl. adj.*
1 Enthroned, on the throne 3H6 3.1.96 *If he were seated as King Edward is,* R3 4.2.4.
2 Firmly fixed MAC 1.3.136 *my seated heart.*
3 Situated LUC 1144 *Some...desert seated from the way.*

second *n.*
1 Supporter LR 4.6.194 *No seconds? All myself?,* TMP 3.3.103, CYM 5.3.90; (of a thing) support, assistance HAM 4.7.153 *this project Should have a back or second,* COR 1.8.15.
2 (pl.) Inferior matter SON 125.11 *my oblation, poor but free, Which is not mix'd with seconds.*
~ *adj.*
1 Secondary, subordinate 2H4 5.2.90 *a second body* (i.e. a deputy), 1H4 1.3.165; *in second voice* by proxy TRO 2.3.140.
2 Supportive WT 2.3.27 *be second to me* (i.e. support me).

secondary *adj.* Subordinate MM 1.1.46 *Escalus...is thy secondary,* JN 5.2.80.

secret *n.* marks *of secret* Secret marks CYM 5.5.206.
~ *adj.*
1 Belonging peculiarly to oneself, private TN 1.4.14 *my secret soul,* R3 3.5.28, HAM 2.2.235.
2 Mysterious, occult 3H6 4.6.68 *secret powers,* TMP 1.2.77, MAC 4.1.48.
3 Keeping counsel, not revealing secrets ADO 1.1.209 *secret as a dumb man,* TGV 3.1.60, JC 2.1.125.
4 *secret to* Having the confidence of (a person), in close intimacy with SHR 1.1.153 *thee That art to me as secret and as dear As...,* ROM 1.1.149.
5 *have secret feet in* Have landed secretly at LR 3.1.32.

sect *n.*[1]
1 Party, faction LR 5.3.18 *packs and sects of great ones,* TIM 3.5.30.
2 Class (of people), rank MM 2.2.5 *All sects, all ages*; sex 2H4 2.4.37 *So is all her sect*; *sect and force* faction and vehemence HAM 1.3.26 (Ff; Qq *act and place*).

sect *n.*[2] See SET *n.* sense 4.

sectary *n.*
1 Member of a (heretical) sect, schismatic H8 5.2.105 *you are a sectary...Your...gloss discovers ...words and weakness.*
2 *sectary astronomical* Student of astrology LR 1.2.150.

secure *vb.*
1 Give confidence or a sense of safety to, make careless TIM 2.2.176 *Secure thy heart* (i.e. set your heart at ease), LR 4.1.20; (refl.) OTH 1.3.10 *I do not so secure me in the error.*
2 Make safe, guard TMP 2.1.310 *securing your repose,* HAM 1.5.113, 2H6 5.2.76.
~ *adj.*
1 Free from care or apprehension, confident, over-confident, unsuspicious R2 5.3.43 *secure foolhardy King,* WIV 2.1.233, OTH 3.3.198.
2 Safe 3H6 4.4.33 *secure from force and fraud*; *secure of* safe from TIT 2.1.3.
3 Safe from doing harm 1H6 1.4.49 *In iron walls they deem'd me not secure.*
~ *adv.* Safely 1H4 1.2.131 *We may do it as secure as sleep.*

securely *adv.* Confidently, without apprehension or suspicion of evil JN 2.1.374 *stand securely on their battlements,* WIV 2.2.243, TRO 4.5.73.

security *n.* Consciousness of safety, confidence,

want of caution MAC 3.5.32 *security Is mortals' chiefest enemy,* R2 3.2.34, JC 2.3.7.

sedge *n.* Kinds of grasslike plant growing in marshes or by waterside, bed of such plants SHR Ind.2.53 *as the waving sedges play with wind,* ADO 2.1.203, TGV 2.7.29.

sedged *adj.* Made of sedges TMP 4.1.129 *sedg'd crowns.*

see *n.* the *See* Rome MM 3.2.219 *late come from the See, In special business from his holiness.*
▷ F1 *Sea*; Theobald *See.*

see *vb.*
1 (in reciprocal sense) See each other, meet H8 1.1.2 *Since last we saw in France,* TRO 4.4.57, CYM 1.1.124.
2 Attend to, provide for, 'see to' R2 2.1.217 *To see this business,* SHR 1.2.146, ANT 5.2.365.
3 *see away* Spend in seeing H8 Prol.12 *may see away their shilling Richly in two short hours.*
4 *see for* Look out for ROM 5.1.35 *Let's see for means,* OTH 2.1.95.

seeded *adj.* Arrived at maturity like a plant that has done flowering and is ready to sow itself TRO 1.3.316 *the seeded pride...must or now be cropp'd, Or, shedding, breed a nursery of like evil...,* LUC 603.

seedness *n.* Seed-time, sowing with seed MM 1.4.42 *as blossoming time That from the seedness the bare fallow brings To teeming foison.*

seedsman *n.* Sower of seed ANT 2.7.21 *the seedsman ...scatters his grain.*

seeing *n.*
1 Faculty of sight LLL 4.3.330 *It adds a precious seeing to the eye.*
2 Appearance SON 67.6 *And steal dead seeing of his living hue?,* WT 5.2.17.

seek *vb.*
1 *seek through* Seek out, follow up CYM 4.2.160 *I would revenges...would seek us through And put us to our answer.*
2 *seek to* Approach in the way of appeal LUC 293 *with a pure appeal seeks to the heart.*

seeking *n.* Suit, petition COR 1.1.188 *What's their seeking?*

seel *vb.* (in falconry) Close up a hawk's eyes when it is taken by drawing the upper eyelids down with a needle and thread which is fastened under the beak; (fig.) blind OTH 3.3.210 *To seel her father's eyes up, close as oak* (Ff 1–2 *seele*; Ff 3–4, Qq *seale*), OTH 1.3.269, ANT 3.13.112.

seeling *ppl. adj.* Blinding MAC 3.2.46 *Come, seeling night.*

seely (var. of) SILLY.

seeming *n.*
1 Outward form, appearance, or show H8 2.4.108 *in full seeming* (i.e. to all appearance), HAM 3.2.87, CYM 5.5.65.
2 False appearance or show, hypocrisy LR 3.2.56 *covert and convenient seeming,* MM 2.4.150, ADO 4.1.56.
3 Probability CYM 5.5.452 *This hath some seeming.*
~ *ppl. adj.* That is so in appearance, apparent to the senses or to the mind as distinct from what is 1H4 5.2.34 *There is no seeming mercy in the King* (i.e. no mercy even in appearance), MV 3.2.100, ANT 2.2.209; (hence) specious WIV 3.2.42 *the so-seeming Mistress Page.*
~ *adv.*
1 Seemingly, ostensibly, apparently, to external appearance HAM 1.5.46 *my most seeming virtuous queen,* LC 327.
2 Becomingly AYL 5.4.69 *bear your body more seeming.*

seen *pa. pple. well seen* Versed or skilled *in* SHR 1.2.134 *a schoolmaster Well seen in music.*

seethe *vb.* Boil TIM 4.3.430 *Till the high fever seethe your blood to froth;* (hence, fig.) be in hot haste, be urgent TRO 3.1.40 *my business seethes.*
▷ See also SOD, SODDEN.

seething *ppl. adj.* Boiling hot SON 153.7 *a seething bath;* (fig.) MND 5.1.4 *seething brains.*

segregation *n.* Dispersal OTH 2.1.10 *A segregation of the Turkish fleet.*

seize *vb.*
1 *seize on, upon* Take legal possession of (a person) LR 1.1.252 *Thee and thy virtues here I seize upon,* LR 2.1.116, ADO 5.4.53; (a thing) OTH 5.2.366 *seize upon the fortunes of the Moor.*
2 *seized of* Possessed of HAM 1.1.89 *all those his lands Which he stood seiz'd of.*

seizure *n.* Grasp, clasp TRO 1.1.57 *her hand...to whose soft seizure,* JN 3.1.241.

seld *adv.* Seldom TRO 4.5.150 *As seld I have the chance,* COR 2.1.213.

seldom *adj.* Infrequent 1H4 3.2.58 *my state, Seldom but sumptuous, show'd like a feast,* SON 52.4.
~ *adv.*
1 *seldom but* It is seldom that...not, usually PER 4.2.120 *seldom but that pity begets you a good opinion.*
2 *seldom when* Seldom that MM 4.2.86 *seldom when The steeled jailer is the friend of men,* 2H4 4.4.79.

self *adj.*
1 Of or belonging to oneself, one's own MAC 5.9.36 *self and violent hands,* ANT 5.1.21, R2 3.2.166.
2 Same, selfsame MV 1.1.148 *that self way,* 3H6 3.1.11, PHT 38.
3 *one self* One and the same TN 1.1.38 *one self king* (Ff234 *selfsame*), LR 4.3.34.
~ in combination
1 (in attrib. relation) One's own; (occas.) one's very TRO 2.3.172 *speaks not to himself but with a pride That quarrels at self-breath* (i.e. his own words), MND 1.1.113 (*self-affairs*), OTH 3.3.200 (*self-bounty*).
2 (in objective relation; usu.) Of oneself OTH 2.3.202 *Unless self-charity be sometimes a vice* (i.e. self-love), MAC 3.4.141 (*self-abuse;* see ABUSE *n.* sense 2), R2 3.2.53 (*self-affrighted*).
3 (in adv. relation) (1) (denoting the agent) By oneself SON 58.12 *to you it doth belong Your self to pardon of self-doing crime* (i.e. committed by yourself), LR 2.2.122 (*self-subdued*), CYM 2.3.119 (*self-figur'd*); (2) to oneself TRO 2.3.239 *Or strange, or self-affected!* (i.e. in love with oneself), ADO 3.1.56 (*self-endeared*), AWW 4.5.73 (*self-gracious*); (3) from or out of oneself H8 1.1.63 *spider-like Out of his self-drawing web* (i.e. drawn or spun out of his own substance); (4) of oneself SON 1.6 *Feed'st thy light's flame with self-substantial fuel* (i.e. consisting of thine own self); (5) with respect to oneself LR 4.2.62 *Thou changed and self-cover'd thing* (i.e. having the true self concealed); (6) *self-unable* impotent of one's own self AWW 3.1.13 *By self-unable motion;* (7) *self-born* 'indigenous, home-sprung' (Clark and Wright) R2 2.3.80 *fright our native peace with self-born arms* (F1 *self-borne* (q.v.)).

self-born *adj.* Self-same WT 4.1.8 *in one self-born hour To plant and o'erwhelm custom* (i.e. one and the self-same hour).
▷ F1; but perh. two words (see SELF sense 3), though with no change in interpretation.

self-borne *adj.* Borne or carried for one's own benefit (not for the king's or the country's) R2 2.3.80 *self-borne arms.*
▷ F1. Some mod. edd. *self-born* (see self in combination sense 3 (7)). In S.'s period 'born' and 'borne'

were not distinguished in spelling. Either interpretation is possible in the context.

sell *vb.*
1 *sell (one's) life, body* Die 3H6 5.1.74 *Two of thy name...Have sold their lives unto the house of York,* 1H6 5.4.106, MV 2.7.67.
2 *sell (a thing) from (oneself)* Lose (a thing) JN 3.1.167 *sells pardon from himself,* COR 1.3.9.

sellingly *adv.* Like a seller, as if selling; (hence) in favourable terms HAM 5.2.109 *to speak sellingly of him, he is...* (Q2(uncorrectdd); Q2(corrected) *feelingly;* Qq 3–4 *fellingly*).

semblable *n.* (one's) Like, fellow HAM 5.2.118 *his semblable is his mirror* (i.e. his only likeness or equal is his reflection), TIM 4.3.22.
~ *adj.* Similar, like ANT 3.4.3 *Of semblable import,* 2H4 5.1.65.

semblably *adv.* Similarly 1H4 5.3.21 *Semblably furnish'd like the King.*

semblative *prep.* Like, resembling TN 1.4.34 *all is semblative a woman's part.*

semi-circled farthingale *n. phr.* Petticoat, the hoop of which did not come round in front WIV 3.3.64 *the firm fixture of thy foot would give an excellent motion to thy gait in a semi-circled farthingale.*

semper idem [L.] Always the same 2H4 5.5.28.

send *vb.* Send acknowledgement of allegiance to ANT 5.2.29 *I send him The greatness he has got.*

seniory *n.* Seniority R3 4.4.36 *the benefit of seniory.*
▷ F1 *signeurie;* Qq 1–5 *signorie;* Q6 *signiorie;* Capell *seniory.*

sennet *n.* Set of notes played on a trumpet as a signal for the approach and departure of processions 2H6 3.1.SD *Sound a sennet,* H8 2.4.SD, LR 1.1.SD.

sennight, se'nnight *n.* Week AYL 3.2.315 *If the interim be but a se'nnight...it seems the length of seven year,* OTH 2.1.77, MAC 1.3.22 (Ff *Seu'nights*).
▷ See also SEVENNIGHT.

Senoys *n.* (pl.) Sienese AWW 1.2.1 *The Florentines and Senoys.*

sense *n.*
1 Organ of sense; (pl. without inflection) SON 112.10 *my adder's sense To critic and to flatterer stopped are* (i.e. my ears), MAC 5.1.25, OTH 4.3.94.
2 Physical perception, feeling TRO 2.1.22 *Dost thou think I have no sense, thou strik'st me thus,* HAM 4.5.156, PER 3.2.60; *to the sense* to the quick OTH 5.1.11.
3 Mental faculty, mind CYM 2.2.11 *man's o'erlabour'd sense Repairs itself by rest,* OTH 3.3.374, TN 4.1.62.
4 Opinion OTH 5.2.290 *in my sense, 'tis happiness to die.*
5 Sensual nature, sensuality, sexual desire MM 1.4.59 *The wanton stings and motions of the sense,* MM 2.2.168, PER 5.3.30.

senseless *adj.*
1 Deprived or destitute of sensation, without feeling, insensible HAM 5.2.369 *The ears are senseless that should give us hearing,* CYM 2.3.53; *senseless of* insensible to AYL 2.7.55 *seem senseless of the bob,* CYM 1.1.135.
2 Having no sensation, incapable of perception or feeling, inanimate JC 1.1.35 *You blocks, you stones, you worse than senseless things,* VEN 211, PP 20.21.
▷ R2 3.2.23 *my senseless conjuration* my conjuring of inanimate things.
~ *adv.* Unreasonably R3 3.1.44 *You are too senseless-obstinate.*

sensible *adj.*
1 Capable of physical feeling or perception, sensitive TMP 2.1.174 *sensible and nimble lungs,* MM

3.1.119, COR 1.3.85; (with *of*) JC 1.3.18 *his hand, Not sensible of fire*, 1H4 5.4.94.
2 Involving the use of the senses HAM 1.1.57 *the sensible and true avouch Of mine own eyes.*
3 Capable of emotion, 'feeling' MV 2.8.48 *with affection wondrous sensible*, HAM 4.5.151 (Ff); (with *of*) JN 3.4.53 *sensible of grief.*
4 Acutely felt, intensely felt LUC 1678 *My woe too sensible.*
5 Capable of being perceived (by a sense) MAC 2.1.36 *sensible To feeling as to sight;* tangible, palpable, substantial MV 2.9.89 *sensible regreets: To wit...Gifts of rich value.*
sensibly *adv.*
1 As a creature endowed with feeling COR 1.4.53 *Who sensibly outdares his senseless sword*, TIT 4.2.122.
2 Feelingly, with emotion LLL 3.1.113 *I will tell you sensibly*, HAM 4.5.151 (Qq 2-3).
sentence *n.* Sententious saying, maxim ADO 2.3.240 *quips and sentences*, MV 1.2.10, OTH 1.3.199.
sententious *adj.* Expressing much in few words, pithy LLL 5.1.3 *Your reasons...have been sharp and sententious*, AYL 5.4.62.
▷ In ROM 2.4.211 *she hath the prettiest sententious of it* app. a blunder for 'sentences'.
sentinel *vb.* Guard LUC 942 *To...sentinel the night.*
se offendendo [L.] *In self-'offence'* HAM 5.1.9.
▷ Comic blunder for the legal phr. 'se defendendo' (i.e. in self-defence).
separable *adj.* Causing separation SON 36.6 *a separable spite* (i.e. a spiteful separation).
Septentrion *n.* North 3H6 1.4.136 *as the south to the septentrion.*
sequel *n.* in *sequel* In due succession H5 5.2.333 *in sequel all, According to their...natures.*
sequence *n.* in *sequence* One after the other TIT 4.1.37 *Why lifts she up her arms in sequence thus?; in the sequence of degree* according to the order of rank TIM 5.1.208.
sequent *n.* Follower LLL 4.2.138 *a sequent of the stranger queen's.*
~ *adj.*
1 Consequent MM 5.1.373 *Immediate sentence... and sequent death*, LR 1.2.106, TRO 4.4.66; *sequent* to consequent upon HAM 5.2.54 *what to this was sequent Thou knowest already*, AWW 2.2.54.
2 Following one upon another OTH 1.2.41 *a dozen sequent messengers.*
sequester *n.* Sequestration, seclusion, separation OTH 3.4.40 *This hand of yours requires A sequester from liberty.*
~ *vb.* Separate TRO 3.3.8 *sequest'ring me from all That time...Made tame*, TIT 2.3.75.
sequestration *n.* Separation, disjunction, seclusion H5 1.1.58 *any sequestration From open haunts*, 1H6 2.5.25, OTH 1.3.345.
sere, sear *n.*[1] Withered state MAC 5.3.23 *fall'n into the sere, the yellow leaf.*
~ *adj.* Dry, withered ERR 4.2.19 *crooked, old, and sere*, MM 2.4.9 (F1 *feard*).
sere *n.*[2] Catch of a gun-lock which keeps the hammer at full or half cock; (fig.) HAM 2.2.324 *whose lungs are tickle a' th' sere* (i.e. ready to 'go off' at any time, readily affected by any impulse).
sergeant *n.*
1 Sheriff's officer HAM 5.2.336 *this fell sergeant, Death, Is strict in his arrest*, ERR 4.2.56, H8 1.1.198.
2 *sergeant of a band* 16C military title for an officer of higher rank than the modern 'sergeant' 1H6 2.1.SD *Enter a Sergeant of a band*, MAC 1.2.3.
serpent *n.* *serpent's tongue* Hissing MND 5.1.433 *to scape the serpent's tongue.*
serpigo *n.* Skin eruption TRO 2.3.74 *the dry serpigo*

(F4; F1 *sapego, suppeago*; Ff234 *sarpego*; F3 *serpego*), MM 3.1.31.
servant *n.* (term of gallantry) One devoted to the service of a lady, professed lover LLL 5.2.277 *my servant straight was mute*, R3 1.2.206, TGV 2.4.106.
servanted *ppl. adj.* Subject, in subjection COR 5.2.83 *My affairs Are servanted to others.*
serve *vb.*
1 Afford (one) opportunity, be opportune or favourable (*to*); (intr.) TIM 5.1.44 *When the day serves, before black-corner'd night*, 3H6 3.3.236, JC 4.3.223; (trans.) SHR 1.1.38 *as you find your stomach serves you*, 3H6 4.7.78, ROM 4.1.39.
2 Provide for, satisfy the calls or needs of AYL 2.7.89 *till necessity be serv'd*, JC 3.1.8, SHR 1.1.15; (hence) fulfil AWW 2.1.202 *Thy will by my performance shall be serv'd*, 2H4 5.1.14.
3 Suit TGV 4.4.162 *Which served me as fit...As if the garment had been made for me*, CYM 4.1.3.
4 *serve (one's) turn* Answer (one's) purpose or requirement WIV 5.5.104 *Will none but Herne the hunter serve your turn?*, R2 3.2.90, OTH 1.1.42.
5 *serve in* Bring in (meat or drink), serve up TIM 4.3.478 *all I kept were knaves, to serve in meat to villains*, MV 3.5.59, MV 3.5.61; (fig.) SHR 3.1.14 *serve in your harmony.*
6 (of tricks) Play WIV 3.5.6 *Well, and I be serv'd such another trick, I'll have my brains ta'en out and butter'd.*
service *n.*
1 All that was laid upon a table in preparation for a meal (cloth, bread, salt, etc.) MAC 1.7.SD *with dishes and service*; order of dishes at a meal, course of a meal HAM 4.3.24 *variable service.*
2 Condition of being the SERVANT (of one's lady) LLL 5.2.284 *Longaville was for my service born*, AYL 5.2.89, CYM 1.6.140.
3 Fealty, homage, allegiance JN 5.1.23 *your oath of service to the Pope*, JN 5.1.34, H8 4.2.115; (transf.) *do (one's) service* convey (one's) respects H8 3.1.179 *Pray do my service to his Majesty.*
serviceable *adj.* Active or diligent in service LR 4.6.252 *a serviceable villain*, SHR 1.1.214, CYM 3.2.15; expressing readiness to serve TGV 3.2.70 *serviceable vows.*
servile *adj.* Subject VEN 112 *Yet was he servile to my coy disdain*, VEN 1161, MM 3.1.9.
servility *n.* Servitude 1H6 5.3.113 *To be a queen in bondage is more vile Than is a slave in base servility.*
serving *n.*
1 Bowing TIM 1.2.231 *Serving of becks and jutting-out of bums.*
2 *in their serving* Assisted by them CYM 3.4.170 *Would you in their serving...Present yourself.*
servingman *n.* SERVANT LR 3.4.85 *A servingman! proud in heart and mind.*
servitor *n.*
1 Servant 3H6 3.3.196 *I am thy true servitor*, OTH 1.3.40, LUC 285.
2 Attendant MV 2.9.SD *Enter...a Servitor*, ANT 4.2.SD, R3 4.3.52.
3 One who serves in war, soldier 1H6 2.1.5 *poor servitors,...Constrain'd to watch in darkness, rain, and cold.*
sessa *interj.* (var. of sa-sa [Fr. ça ça]; in fencing and hunting) Cry of incitement LR 3.4.100 *Dolphin my boy, boy, sessa! let him trot by* (F *sesy*; Q1 *caese*; Q2 *cease*; Q3 *ceas*; Malone *sessa*), LR 3.6.74 (F *sese*).
▷ In SHR Ind.1.6 *let the world slide. Sessa!* perh. instead from Fr. 'cessez' i.e. cease.
session *n.* Sitting of a court of justice, judicial proceedings WT 2.3.202 *Summon a session*, H8 2.4.66, OTH 1.2.86; (fig.) SON 30.1 *the sessions of...thought.*

set *n.*

1 Sunset H5 4.1.272 *from the rise to set*; setting (of the sun) R3 5.3.19 *The weary sun hath made a golden set*, MAC 1.1.5.

2 Round (of the clock) OTH 2.3.130 *He'll watch the horologe a double set* (i.e. two rounds of the clock).

3 Definite number of games (of tennis, cards); match, contest (fig.) LLL 5.2.29 *a set of wit well played*, JN 5.2.107, TIT 5.1.100.

4 Sucker, slip or shoot for planting OTH 1.3.332 *a set or scion.*

◇ F, Qq *sect*; Johnson *set.*

~ *vb.*

1 (pass.) Sit H8 3.1.74 *I was set at work*, TGV 2.1.85, COR 4.5.192; (refl.) LLL 4.3.4 *set thee down*; (mixed const.) 3H6 4.3.2 *The King...is set him down.*

2 Add or impart (something) *to*, bestow *on* JN 4.3.71 *Till I have set a glory to this hand*, TIM 1.2.147, VEN 935.

3 Place (one thing) in opposition *to* another JN 3.1.264 *set'st oath to oath*, MND 3.1.134, TRO 2.1.86.

4 Close JN 5.7.51 *to set mine eye.*

5 (pass., of the eyes) Have a fixed look or expression TN 5.1.199 *his eyes were set at eight i' th' morning*, TMP 3.2.9.

6 Stake LR 1.4.123 *Set less than thou throwest*, 1H4 4.1.46, JC 5.1.74; (intr., fig.) put up a stake R2 4.1.57 *Who sets me else?* (i.e. Who challenges me?).

7 (intr.) Compose music TGV 1.2.78 *Give me a note, your ladyship can set* (taken up quibblingly in sense 8); (trans.) fit (words) to music (fig.) TMP 1.2.84 *set all hearts...To what tune pleas'd his ear.*

8 (with adverbial expressions) Regard, esteem, value R2 1.3.293 *mocks at it and sets it light*, ROM 5.3.301, HAM 4.3.62.

9 (pass.) Have gone forth or set out H5 2.Ch.34 *The King is set from London.*

10 Station, post OTH 2.3.120 *let's set the watch*, ROM 3.3.148.

11 Reject, set aside TRO 2.3.79 *He sate our messengers.*

◇ Q; a spelling of pa. t. of *set* in 15–19C. See SHENT.

~ in phrases

set...clear Place in an innocent light TIM 3.3.30 *in the end, the villainies of man will set him clear.* **set (one's) countenance** Put on a set or serious expression SHR 4.4.18 *set your countenance.* **set a form upon** Give a good appearance to SON 89.6 *To set a form upon desired change.* **set a match** (lit.) Make an appointment; (in thieves' cant) arrange a meeting between highwaymen and victims, plan a highway robbery 1H4 1.2.106. **set off his head** Not laid to his charge 1H4 5.1.88 *This present enterprise set off his head.* **set on edge** Put an edge on; (hence) excite the appetite WT 4.3.7 *Doth set my pugging tooth on edge.* **set on the proof** Put to the proof TIM 2.2.157 *Call me before th' exactest auditors, And set me on the proof.* **set spurs** 'Clap' spurs to one's horse WIV 4.5.68. **set to himself** Wrapped up in himself, completely intent on himself TIM 5.1.117 *For he is set so only to himself.* **set to't** Render (a person) lustful MM 4.3.154 *one fruitful meal would set me to't.* **set upon the head of** Treat within the category of TIM 3.5.27.

~ in combination

set abroad Stir up, set on foot TIT 1.1.192 *resign my life, And set abroad new business for you all.* **set against** Make an attack on MND 3.2.146 *bent To set against me for your merriment.* **set apart** Discard JN 3.1.159 *all reverence set apart To...his usurp'd authority.* **set aside** Discontinue, stop 1H6 3.1.93 *set this...fight aside.* **set down 1** Appoint or fix a time for R3 3.4.42 *We have not yet set down this day of triumph*, R2 4.1.319 (F1). **2** Determine

upon, settle COR 4.5.138 *set down...thine own ways*, 1H4 1.3.274, HAM 3.1.169. **3** Be encamped ANT 3.13.168 *Caesar sets down in Alexandria.* **4** *set down the pegs* Lower the pitch of the strings of a musical instrument OTH 2.1.200 *I'll set down the pegs that make this music.* **set down before** 'Sit down' before (a town) to besiege it, lay siege to, besiege COR 1.2.28 *If they set down before 's*, AWW 1.1.118, MAC 5.4.10. **set forth 1** Exhibit, show MAC 1.4.6 *set forth A deep repentance.* **2** Commend highly MV 3.5.90 *I'll set you forth* (with a ref. to serving up dishes), LUC 32. **set forward** Start on a journey, set out JN 4.3.19 *then set forward, for 'twill be Two long days' journey.* **set off 1** Show to the best advantage CYM 1.6.170 *He hath a kind of honour sets him off*, TMP 3.1.2 (F1 *set*; Rowe *sets*); (absol.) CYM 3.3.13 *it is place which lessens and sets off.* **2** Put out of consideration, remove 2H4 4.1.143 *You shall enjoy them, every thing set off That might so much as think you enemies.* **set on 1** Cause (an action) by one's instigation OTH 5.2.187 *your reports have set the murder on*, OTH 2.3.210. **2** Put (one's foot) forward JC 2.1.331 *Set on your foot*; send (an army) forward JC 4.3.307 *Bid him set on his pow'rs*, JC 5.3.108. **3** (intr.) Go forward, march CYM 5.5.484 *Set on there!*, 2H4 1.3.109, H8 2.4.242. **4** Proceed, go on JC 1.2.11 *Set on, and leave no ceremony out*, COR 3.1.58. **set apart** *for* certain treatment TIM 5.4.57 *Those enemies...Whom you...shall set out for reproof.* **set to** Set (a limb) 1H4 5.1.131 *Can honour set to a leg?* **set up 1** SET ON sense 1 CYM 3.4.88 *That didst set up my disobedience.* **2** (of a top) Start spinning COR 4.5.153 *as one would set up a top.*

~ ppl. adj.

1 Deliberate, not spontaneous; (hence) stereotyped, unoriginal TN 1.5.89 *these set kind of fools.*

2 *set hand* Style of handwriting used in legal documents R3 3.6.2 *Which in a set hand fairly is engross'd.*

setter *n.* One who 'sets matches', one who decoys persons to be robbed 1H4 2.2.51 *'tis our setter, I know his voice.*

setting *n.*

1 Set expression TMP 2.1.229 *The setting of thine eye.*

2 Downfall H8 3.2.225 *I haste now to my setting.*

settle *vb.* Become calm WT 4.4.471 *till the fury of his Highness settle*, LR 4.7.81.

settled *ppl. adj.*

1 Fixed, rooted R2 1.1.201 *your settled hate*, WT 4.3.524.

2 Congealed, stagnant ROM 4.5.26 *Her blood is settled*, 2H4 4.3.104.

3 Resolved MAC 1.7.79 *I am settled, and bend my Each corporal agent to this terrible feat.*

4 Composed, calm MM 3.1.89 *settled visage*, HAM 4.7.80, SON 49.8.

seven *adj.*

1 Typically, in expressions of time, etc., for a large number 2H6 2.1.2 *I saw not better sport these seven years' day*, WT 4.4.578, LR 3.4.139; large quantity HAM 4.5.155 *tears Seven times salt*, MV 2.9.63.

2 *seven stars* The Pleiades LR 1.5.35 *The reason why the seven stars are no moe than seven*, 1H4 1.2.14, 2H4 2.4.187.

sevennight *n.* SENNIGHT, week ADO 2.1.360 *a just sevennight* (i.e. exactly a week), WT 1.2.17.

several *n.* (only in pl.)

1 Individual persons WT 1.2.226 *By some severals Of head-piece extraordinary.*

2 Details, particulars H5 1.1.86 *The severals...Of his true titles to...*

3 Individual qualities TRO 1.3.180 *Severals and generals of grace exact.*

~ *adj.*

1 Separate, distinct, different TMP 3.1.42 *For several virtues Have I lik'd several women*, ANT 1.5.62, HAM 5.2.20; (freq. with *each* or *every*) MND 5.1.417 *each several chamber*, 2H6 3.2.363.

2 Particular, respective TMP 3.3.88 *my meaner ministers Their several kinds have done*, PER 2.3.109, CYM 1.5.23.

3 Divers, various H8 3.2.125 *The several parcels of his plate*, TMP 5.1.232, WT 4.4.184.

4 Private, privately owned (opposed to 'common') SON 137.9 *Why should my heart think that a several plot*; (hence allusively) LLL 2.1.223 *My lips are no common, though several they be* (with quibble).

severally *adv.*

1 Each in a particular way or for a particular purpose CYM 5.5.397 *the counterchange Is severally in all*, JC 3.2.10, TIM 2.2.187.

2 Separately, singly TRO 4.5.273 *Concur together, severally intreat him*, SHR 4.1.SD.

severe *adj.* (of an animal) Merciless VEN 1000 *that bloody beast, Which knows no pity, but is still severe.*

sewer *n.*[1] Drain TRO 5.1.76 *Sweet sink, sweet sewer* (F1; Q *sure*), PER 4.6.175 (Q1 *shores*).

sewer *n.*[2] Attendant at a meal who superintended the arrangement of the table, the seating of the guests, and the tasting and serving of the dishes MAC 1.7.SD *Enter a Sewer and divers Servants with dishes.*

sex *n. the general sex* See GENERAL.

sexton *n.* Church officer charged with the care of a church, its contents, the church clock and churchyard, and often with duties of ringing the bell and digging graves JN 3.1.324 *Old Time the clock-setter, that bald sexton Time!*, HAM 5.1.90, PER 2.1.36.

'sfoot *interj.* (shortened form of) God's foot TRO 2.3.5 *'Sfoot, I'll learn to conjure.*

shackle *vb.* Fetter; (only fig.) AWW 2.3.152 *That dost...shackle up My love and her desert*, ANT 5.2.6.

shade *n.*

1 (a person's) Shadow SON 53.3 *every one hath, every one, one shade.*

2 Unsubstantial image of something real SON 43.8 *thy shade shines*, SON 43.11.

3 Phantom WIV 5.5.38 *Fairies...moonshine revelers, and shades of night.*

~ *vb.*

1 Cover up LLL 4.3.42 *Sweet leaves, shade folly.*

2 Darken, cover with a shadow PP 10.3 *Bright orient pearl,...too timely shaded.*

shadow *n.*

1 Shade TMP 4.1.67 *thy broom-groves, Whose shadow the dismissed bachelor loves*, R2 3.4.25, LR 5.2.1; shady place AYL 1.1.217 *I'll go find a shadow*; obscurity, darkness MM 3.1.247 *all shadow and silence*; (pl.) SON 43.5 *whose shadow shadows doth make bright.*

2 Shelter, protection 2H4 4.2.15 *In shadow of such greatness*, TIM 5.4.6.

3 Reflected image, reflection JN 2.1.498 *The shadow of myself form'd in her eye*, JC 1.2.58, VEN 162.

4 Image, portrait, likeness 1H6 2.3.36 *Long time thy shadow hath been thrall to me, For in my gallery thy picture hangs*, MV 3.2.127, LUC 1457.

5 Delusive semblance, unsubstantial object, 'image produced by the imagination' (Schmidt) LUC 460 *Such shadows are the weak brain's forgeries*, ANT 5.2.100, R3 5.3.216.

6 Departed spirit, 'shade' R3 1.4.53 *A shadow like an angel*, TIT 1.1.100, CYM 5.4.97; (hence, transf.) corpse ANT 4.2.27 *A mangled shadow.*

7 Spectre, phantom VEN 1001 *gentle shadow* (i.e.

Death); (applied to fairies) MND 3.2.347 *king of shadows*, MND 5.1.423.

~ *vb.*

1 Conceal MAC 5.4.5 *thereby shall we shadow The numbers of our host*, TIT 2.1.130.

2 Shelter, protect JN 2.1.14 *Shadowing their right under your wings of war.*

shadowed *ppl. adj.* Dark MV 2.1.2 *The shadowed livery of the burnish'd sun.*

shadowing *ppl. adj.* Prefiguring, adumbrating OTH 4.1.40 *Nature would not invest herself in such shadowing passion without some instruction.*

shadowy *adj.* Shady TGV 5.4.2 *This shadowy desert*, LR 1.1.64 (Qq *shady*).

shady *adj.* Of a shadow SON 77.7 *thy dial's shady stealth* (i.e. slow progress of the shadow on the dial).

shaft *n.* Arrow for the long-bow WIV 3.4.24 *I'll make a shaft or bolt on't*, TN 1.1.34, ROM 1.4.19.

shag *adj.* Shaggy VEN 295 *fetlocks shag.*

shag-eared *adj.* Hairy-eared MAC 4.2.83 *thou shag-ear'd villain!*

▷ Ff 1–2 *shagge-ear'd*, Ff 3–4 *shag-ear'd*; Steevens conjecture *shag-hair'd.*

shag-haired *adj.* Shaggy-haired 2H6 3.1.367 *a shag-hair'd crafty kern*, MAC 4.2.83 (see SHAG-EARED).

shake *vb.*

1 Bestir oneself ROM 1.3.33 *Shake, quoth the dove-house.*

2 *shake (a person's) beard* Defy, beard HAM 4.7.32 *That we can let our beard be shook with danger*, LR 3.7.77.

3 *shake the ears* See EAR.

4 *shake the head* Nod (in recognition) 2H6 4.1.55 *thought thee happy when I shook my head.*

~ *in combination*

shake off Refuse to accept or entertain TN 5.1.73 *I shake off these names*, ANT 3.7.33. **shake out** Blab, reveal indiscreetly, let out AWW 2.4.24 *many a man's tongue shakes out his master's undoing.* **shake up** Berate or scold vehemently, abuse violently AYL 1.1.28 *thou shalt hear how he will shake me up.*

shale *n.* Shell H5 4.2.18 *the shales and husks of men.*

shall *vb.*

1 Will MAC 3.4.56 *If much you note him, You shall offend him*, ANT 2.1.1, TIT 4.4.107.

2 Will inevitably or assuredly, be bound to, must JN 5.2.78 *Your Grace shall pardon me*, AYL 1.1.128, LR 5.3.22.

3 (with ellipsis of verb of motion) Shall go COR 4.6.147 *Shall's to the Capitol?*, H8 3.2.304, HAM 3.3.4.

▷ Sometimes contracted to *'s, se*; ROM 1.3.9 *thou 's hear our counsel*, LR 4.6.241 *Ise try* (F1 *Ice*). See SHOULD for a treatment of its uses.

shallow *adj. shallow in* Superficial in the judgement of AWW 1.3.42 *y' are shallow, madam—in great friends.*

shallowly *adv.* without consideration, rashly 2H4 4.2.118 *Most shallowly did you these arms commence.*

shambles *n.* (pl.) Butcher's shop or stall, slaughter-house OTH 4.2.66 *as summer flies are in the shambles*; (fig.) place of carnage, scene of blood 3H6 1.1.71 *To make a shambles of the parliament house.*

shame *n.* Modesty CYM 5.3.22 *faces..fairer Than those for preservation cas'd, or shame.*

~ *vb.* Be ashamed MAC 2.2.61 *I shame To wear a heart so white*, AYL 4.3.135, HAM 3.2.145.

shame-faced, shamefast *adj.* Modest, bashful R3 1.4.138 *a blushing shame-fac'd spirit*, 3H6 4.8.52.

▷ Qq *shamefast*, the usu. spelling in 16–17C.

shape *n.*
1 Form CYM 1.5.71 *I'll move the King To any shape of thy preferment*, TRO 1.3.17, PER 5.Gower.6; form of proceeding HAM 4.7.150 *What convenience both of time and means May fit us to our shape* (i.e. the part we propose to act); *shape of likelihood* probability 1H4 1.1.58.
2 Fashion, customary dress, external appearance ADO 3.2.34 *in the shape of two countries at once*, WIV 4.4.45, H5 4.8.53.
3 Imaginary or ethereal form 2H4 4.3.100 *full of nimble, fiery, and delectable shapes*, MND 5.1.16, TN 1.1.14.
~ *vb.*
1 (trans.) Conform, adjust, proportion (one thing to another) LLL 5.2.65 *make him...shape his service wholly to my device*, TN 1.2.61, LUC 1458; (intr.) be conformable, suit, agree CYM 5.5.346 *The more of you 'twas felt, the more it shap'd Unto my end of stealing them.*
2 Form a mental image of, conceive, imagine OTH 3.3.148 *my jealousy Shapes faults that are not*, JC 4.3.277, 2H4 4.4.58.
shapeless *adj.*
1 Not shaped to any end, aimless, purposeless TGV 1.1.8 *shapeless idleness.*
2 Unshapely, ugly, misshapen ERR 4.2.20 *Ill-fac'd, worse bodied, shapeless every where*, LLL 5.2.303, LUC 973.
shaping *ppl. adj.* Given to imagining, imaginative, inventive MND 5.1.5 *Such shaping fantasies.*
shard *n.*
1 Fragment of pottery, potsherd HAM 5.1.231 *Shards, flints, and pebbles should be thrown on her.*
2 Wing-case of a beetle ANT 3.2.20 *They are his shards, and he their beetle.*
▷ *Shard* may also mean 'patch of cow-dung'; and some have seen a reference in ANT 3.2.20 to the shard-beetle, which is born and lives in dung, but this interpretation seems unlikely.
shard-born(e) *adj.* Borne or supported on scaly wings MAC 3.2.42 *The shard-borne beetle.*
▷ See note to SHARD.
sharded *adj.* Provided with wing-cases (i.e. elytra) CYM 3.3.20 *The sharded beetle.*
▷ See note to SHARD.
share *vb.* Take as one's share, receive, gain ROM 1.3.91 *That book...doth share the glory*, TRO 1.3.367, R3 5.3.268; experience LUC 1431 *many Troyan mothers, sharing joy To see...; share from* gain at the expense of H5 4.3.32 *so great an honour As one man more...would share from me*, TRO 1.3.366.
shark *vb. shark up* Collect hastily without regard to selection, get together haphazardly HAM 1.1.98 *young Fortinbras...Hath...Shark'd up a list of lawless resolutes.*
sharp *n.* Shrill high note ROM 3.5.28 *harsh discords and unpleasing sharps.*
~ *adj.*
1 Hungry, famished SHR 4.1.190 *My falcon now is sharp and passing empty*, VEN 55; keen LUC 422 *Sharp hunger*, AWW 3.2.118, MM 2.4.161.
2 Acute, subtle LLL 5.1.3 *Your reasons...have been sharp*, 1H6 2.4.17, H8 2.1.14.
3 Shrill, out of tune by being too high-pitched TGV 1.2.88 *I do not like this tune...'tis too sharp.*
sharp-ground *adj.* Sharpened ROM 3.3.44 *no sharp-ground knife.*
sharp-looking *adj.* Hungry-looking ERR 5.1.241 *A needy,...sharp-looking wretch.*
sharply *adv.* Keenly, pungently TMP 5.1.23 *myself, ...that relish all as sharply*, CYM 3.4.86, AWW 3.4.33.
sharpness *n.* Harshness, severity ANT 3.3.35 *Thou must not take my former sharpness ill*, AWW 1.2.37, LR 5.3.57.
sharp-provided *adj.* Quick and ready, keenly reasoned R3 3.1.132 *With what a sharp-provided wit he reasons!*
she *n.*
1 Woman TN 1.5.241 *the cruell'st she alive*, CYM 1.3.29, SON 130.14; *lady she* titled lady WT 1.2.44.
2 Mistress, lady-love H5 2.1.79 *I have...the quondam Quickly For the only she*, AYL 3.2.10, WT 4.4.349.
sheaf *vb.* Make corn into sheaves AYL 3.2.107 *They that reap must sheaf and bind.*
shealed *ppl. adj.* Shelled, with the peas taken out LR 1.4.200 *That's a sheal'd peascod.*
shearman *n.* One who shears woollen cloth 2H6 4.2.133 *thy father was a plasterer, And thou thyself a shearman.*
sheathing *n.* The process of having a sheath made SHR 4.1.135 *Walter's dagger was not come from sheathing.*
sheaved *ppl. adj.* Made of straw LC 31 *her sheav'd hat.*
shed *vb.* Scatter (seeds) TRO 1.3.319 *the seeded pride ...must or now be cropp'd Or, shedding, breed a nursery of like evil.*
sheep-biter *n.* Dog that bites or worries sheep; (hence, fig.) sneaking, censorious, surly fellow, thievish rogue TN 2.5.5 *the niggardly rascally sheep-biter.*
sheep-biting *adj.* (fig.) Thieving, sneaking MM 5.1.354 *Show your sheep-biting face, and be hang'd an hour!*
sheep-cote *n.* Building for sheltering sheep LR 2.3.18 *Poor pelting villages, sheep-cotes*, AYL 2.4.84, WT 4.4.779.
sheep-hook *n.* Shepherd's crook WT 4.3.420 *a sceptre's heir, That thus affects a sheep-hook!*
sheep-shearing *n.* Feast held on the occasion of the annual shearing of sheep on a farm WT 4.3.117 *I must go buy spices for our sheep-shearing.*
sheep-whistling *adj.* Whistling after sheep, tending sheep WT 4.4.776 *An old sheep-whistling rogue, a ram-tender.*
sheer *adj.* Unmixed with other matter, clear, pure R2 5.3.61 *Thou sheer, immaculate, and silver fountain*; taken alone without solid food SHR Ind.2.23 *sheer ale* (i.e. ale alone).
sheet *vb.* Cover as with a sheet ANT 1.4.65 *when snow the pasture sheets.*
sheeted *ppl. adj.* Wrapped in a shroud HAM 1.1.115 *the sheeted dead.*
shekel See SICLE.
shelf *n.* Sandbank 3H6 5.4.23 *shelves and rocks that threaten*, LUC 335.
shelving *ppl. adj.* (quasi-adv.) Projecting, so as to project TGV 3.1.115 *Her chamber is aloft,...And built so shelving that one cannot climb it...*
shelvy *adj.* Made of sandbanks WIV 3.5.15 *the shore was shelvy and shallow.*
shent *pa. pple.* Blamed, reproved, rebuked, berated TN 4.2.104 *I am shent for speaking to you*, WIV 1.4.37, HAM 3.2.398.
▷ At TRO 2.3.89 Theobald's emendation *He shent our messengers* has been generally accepted; Ff *sent*; Q *sate*: see SET *vb.* sense 11.
sherris *n.* Orig. the still white wine made near Jerez de la Frontera in Spain, SACK 2H4 4.3.113 *this valour comes of sherris*, 2H4 4.3.103, 2H4 4.3.121; (attrib.) 2H4 4.3.96 *A good sherris-sack.*
sheriff's post See POST.
shew *vb.* (apheretic form of) Eschew PER 1.1.136 *those men...Will shew no course.*
▷ Q1; Theobald *schew.*

shield vb. God, Heaven shield God, Heaven forbid MM 3.1.140 Heaven shield my mother play'd my father fair!, ROM 4.1.41; (with neg. idea repeated in the second clause) AWW 1.3.168 God shield you mean it not!

shift n.
1 Expedient, ingenious device, contrivance, stratagem JN 4.3.7 I'll find a thousand shifts to get away, ERR 3.2.182, TIT 4.1.72; expedient necessitated by stress of circumstances ANT 3.11.63 dodge And palter in the shifts of lowness; (in a bad sense) trick, fraudulent device LUC 920 treason, forgery, and shift.
2 for (a) shift As a makeshift, for want of something better SHR Ind.1.126 To rain...tears, An onion will do well for such a shift, ADO 2.3.78, 3H6 3.2.108.
3 make (a) shift Contrive, devise, attain one's end by ingenuity MV 1.2.90 I shall make shift to go without him, MAC 2.3.41, 2H6 4.8.31; make other shift manage some other way 2H4 2.1.156.
~ vb.
1 Contrive means, devise a stratagem TMP 5.1.256 Every man shift for all the rest, WIV 1.3.34, ERR 5.1.168.
2 Contrive to get (somewhere) ADO 3.3.142 thou hast shifted out of thy tale.
3 shift away (intr.) Move away, slip off unobserved MAC 2.3.145 let us not be dainty of leave-taking, But shift away; (trans.) get (a person) out of the way OTH 4.1.78 I shifted him away.
4 Exchange ANT 5.2.152 Mine will now be yours, And should we shift estates, yours would be mine.
5 Change SHR 5.2.46 Am I your bird? I mean to shift my bush (i.e. fly to another tree), 2H6 2.4.107 (with quibble on sense 6), MM 3.1.24; (absol.) pass away LUC 1104 No object but her passion's strength renews; And as one shifts, another straight ensues.
6 Change (clothing) CYM 1.2.1 I would advise you to shift a shirt, CYM 1.2.5; (refl.) put on fresh clothes 2H4 5.5.22 to ride day and night, and...not to have patience to shift me; (intr.) change into other clothes LR 5.3.187 to shift Into a madman's rags.

shifting ppl. adj. (?) (1) That shifts or changes; or (2) that uses shifts, tricks, stratagems, deceit LUC 930 injurious shifting Time.
▷ S. could have both senses in operation here.

shine n. (fig.) Brilliance, radiance, splendour, lustre PER 1.2.124 Thou show'dst a subject's shine, I a true prince.
~ vb. shine down Surpass in brilliance H8 1.1.20 the French,...all in gold,...Shone down the English.

shipboard n. to shipboard Aboard ship WT 4.4.654 that you may...to shipboard Get undescried.

shipman n. Mariner, sailor TRO 5.2.172 the dreadful spout Which shipmen do the hurricano call, PER 1.3.23, MAC 1.3.17.

shipped adj. Provided with a ship OTH 2.1.47 Is he well shipped?

shipping n. take shipping Embark 1H6 5.5.87; good shipping good voyage, fair sailing SHR 5.1.42.

ship-tire n. Woman's head-dress of extravagant form resembling a ship, fashionable in the Eliz. period WIV 3.3.57 the...beauty of the brow that becomes the ship-tire.

shive n. Slice TIT 2.1.87 easy it is Of a cut loaf to steal a shive.

shiver vb. (trans.) Break into small fragments or splinters LUC 1763 shiver'd all the beauty of my glass; (intr.) be shattered into small pieces LR 4.6.51 Thou'dst shiver'd like an egg.

shivering ppl. adj. That shatters or breaks into

fragments MND 1.2.32 The raging rocks And shivering shocks.

shivers n. (pl.) Splinters, small fragments R2 4.1.289 crack'd in a hundred shivers.

shoal n. Shallow H8 3.2.436 all the depths and shoals of honour, MAC 1.7.6.

shock vb. Meet with force JN 5.7.117 Come the three corners of the world in arms, And we shall shock them.

shoeing-horn n. Shoe-horn; (transf.) person used as a tool by another TRO 5.1.55 a thrifty shoeing-horn in a chain, hanging at his brother's leg (with allusion to cuckoldry).

shog vb. Move along, go away H5 2.1.45 Will you shog off?, H5 2.3.45.

shoon n. (pl.) Shoes HAM 4.5.26 his cockle hat and staff, And his sandal shoon, 2H6 4.2.185.

shoot n. Act of shooting, discharge of a missile, shot LLL 4.1.10 A stand where you may make the fairest shoot, 3H6 3.1.7, HAM 5.2.366 (Qq shot).

shop n.
1 (fig.) Store CYM 5.5.166 A shop of all the qualities that man Loves woman for.
2 Workshop COR 1.1.133 the store-house and the shop Of the whole body.
3 Place where something is produced; (hence) organ of generation; codpiece LLL 4.3.57 rhymes are guards on wanton Cupid's hose: Disfigure not his shop.

shore n.[1]
1 Limit MM 3.2.252 I have labour'd for the poor gentleman to the extremest shore of my modesty.
2 the high shore of this world The exalted places of the earth H5 4.1.265.
3 the varying shore o' th' world The earth, with its continual variations from land to land ANT 4.15.11.
~ vb. Put ashore WT 4.4.837 to shore them again.

shore n.[2] See SEWER n.[1].

short vb.
1 (fig.) Cut short CYM 1.6.200 I shall short my word By length'ning my return.
2 Shorten PP 14.30 good day, of night now borrow: Short night tonight, and length thyself to-morrow.
~ adj.
1 Inadequate LLL 4.3.237 She passes praise, then praise too short doth blot, TIM 1.1.16, PER 1.2.8.
2 kept short 'Kept, as it were, tethered, under control' (Clark and Wright) HAM 4.1.18 Should have kept short, restrain'd...This mad young man.
3 short'st of day Shortest day of the year R2 5.1.80.

short-armed adj. Having a short reach; (fig.) not reaching very far TRO 2.3.14 short-arm'd ignorance.

shorten vb. Render ineffectual, prejudice LR 4.7.9 Yet to be known shortens my made intent, COR 1.2.23.

shortness n. Fewness of words, straightforwardness SHR 4.4.39 Your plainness and your shortness please me well.

shot n.[1] What a person owes at an alehouse, tavern-reckoning TGV 2.5.9 one shot of five pence, 1H4 5.3.31 (with quibble on SHOT n.[2]), CYM 5.4.156.

shot n.[2] Marksman 2H4 3.2.275 a little, lean, old, chopp'd, bald shot (perh. with play on rural sense 'inferior or refuse animal left after the best of the flock or herd has been selected'); (as a collective) marksmen 1H6 1.4.53 a guard of chosen shot, H8 5.3.56.

shot-free adj. Without having to pay (the tavern bill) 1H4 5.3.30 I could scape shot-free.

shotten ppl. adj. (of a herring) That has 'shot' or shed its roe and is thin and worthless 1H4 2.4.130 if...then I am a shotten herring.

shough *n.* Shaggy-haired kind of dog MAC 3.1.93 *spaniels, curs, Shoughs.*

should *vb.*
1 Would TRO 1.3.116 *Force should be right,* MV 1.2.93, HAM 3.2.304.
2 Was likely to; (hence) might (have), could (have) TMP 5.1.279 *Where should they Find this grand liquor...?,* 1H6 2.1.71, OTH 3.4.23.
3 (in narrative or reported speech, serving as the auxiliary of the pa. t.) Did SHR 3.2.159 *when the priest Should ask...,* TGV 2.3.24, AYL 3.2.173.

shoulder *n. in the shoulder of* Behind HAM 1.3.56.

shoulder-clapper *n.* One who claps another on the shoulder (1) in a friendly way, (2) to arrest him ERR 4.2.37 *A back-friend, a shoulder-clapper* (with play on both senses).

shouldered *pa. pple.* Thrust violently, pushed unceremoniously R3 3.7.128 *almost should'red in the swallowing gulf Of dark forgetfulness.*

shoulder-shotten *adj.* Foundered in the shoulder, having a dislocated shoulder SHR 3.2.56 *his horse... shoulder-shotten.*

shove-groat-shilling *n.* A shilling coined in the reign of Edward VI commonly used in the game of shove-groat, which consisted in pushing coins towards a mark 2H4 2.4.192 *Quoit him down...like a shove-groat-shilling.*
▷ Also called EDWARD SHOVEL-BOARD.

show *n.*
1 Person or thing exhibited or gazed at as an object of admiration, curiosity, mockery, or the like MAC 5.8.24 *the show and gaze o' th' time.*
2 Sight, thing seen LR 3.6.105 *Leaving free things and happy shows behind,* R2 3.3.71, TMP 2.2.5; phantasmal appearance, apparition CYM 5.5.428 *other spritely shows Of mine own kindred.*
3 Representation, picture LUC 1580 *in shows of discontent,* LUC 1507.
~ *vb.*
1 Have (a certain) appearance, appear, seem AYL 1.3.81 *thou wilt show more bright and seem more virtuous When she is gone,* H5 4.1.103, MAC 1.3.54.
2 Exhibit as a show ANT 4.12.36 *most monster-like, be shown For poor'st diminutives.*

showing *n.*
1 *great showing* 'Distinguished appearance' (Schmidt) HAM 5.2.108.
2 *in showing* On display, visible AWW 2.3.21 *if you will have it in showing* (i.e. in print).

shrew *n.* Person given to railing or scolding or other perverse behaviour ERR 4.1.51 *like a shrew you first begin to brawl,* TN 1.3.47, SHR 2.1.313.
▷ In Ff and Qq often *shrow.*
~ *vb.* Beshrew, curse CYM 2.3.142 *Shrew me If I would lose it,* WT 1.2.281.

shrewd *adj.*
1 Malicious, mischievous, ill-natured; (of persons) 1H6 1.2.123 *shrewd tempters,* MND 2.1.33, JC 2.1.158; (of things) AWW 3.5.68 *A shrewd turn,* WIV 2.2.223, H8 5.2.211.
2 Sharp (of tongue or speech), shrewish ADO 2.1.19 *so shrewd of thy tongue,* MND 3.2.323, SHR 1.1.180.
3 (of things) Of evil import, nature, or effect, grievous, difficult to bear MV 3.2.243 *There are some shrewd contents in yond same paper* (Q1 *shrowd*), AYL 5.4.173, JN 5.5.14.

shrewdly *adv.*
1 Sharply, severely H5 3.7.49 *your mistress shrewdly shook your back,* TRO 3.3.228, HAM 1.4.1; (mentally) ADO 2.1.81 *you apprehend passing shrewdly.*
2 Grievously, intensely, highly, very much H5 3.7.152 *these English are shrewdly out of beef* (i.e. devilishly short of beef), AWW 3.5.89, JC 3.1.146.

shrieve *n.* Sheriff AWW 4.3.187 *the shrieve's fool,* 2H4 4.4.99 (F1 *Sherife*).

shrift *n.*
1 Confession and absolution 3H6 3.2.107 *done his shrift* (i.e. heard confession and given absolution), MM 4.2.207; confession R3 3.4.95 *Make a short shrift,* ROM 1.1.159, ROM 2.4.180; absolution consequent on confession ROM 2.3.56 *Riddling confession finds but riddling shrift.*
2 Confessional OTH 3.3.24 *His bed shall seem a school, his board a shrift.*

shrike *n.* Shriek TRO 2.2.97 *what shrike is this?*
~ *vb.* Shriek MND 1.2.76 *you would fright the...ladies, that they would shrike,* ROM 5.3.190, TRO 2.2.210 (Q).

shrill *vb. shrill forth* Utter loudly TRO 5.3.84 *Andromache shrills her dolours forth.*

shrill-gorged *adj.* High-voiced LR 4.6.58 *the shrill-gorg'd lark.*

shrine *n.* Image (as of a saint) MV 2.7.40 *this shrine, this mortal-breathing saint,* CYM 5.5.164, LUC 194.

shrink *vb.*
1 Shiver with cold or fear AYL 2.1.9 *I shrink with cold,* R2 2.2.32, 1H6 4.1.37.
2 Fall away, desert R3 5.3.222 *if any mean to shrink from me,* H8 4.1.107; (fig.) TIM 3.2.7 *his estate shrinks from him.*

shrinking *ppl. adj.* Shivering CYM 4.4.30 *The shrinking slaves of winter.*

shrive *vb.* Hear a person's confession and give him absolution ERR 2.2.208 *I'll...shrive you of a thousand idle pranks,* MV 1.2.131, 1H6 1.2.119.

shriver *n.* Confessor 3H6 3.2.108 *When he was made a shriver, 'twas for shrift.*

shriving *n.* (attrib.) Confession and absolution R3 3.2.115 *shriving work,* HAM 5.2.47.

shroud *n.*[1] Shelter, protection ANT 3.13.71 *had...put yourself under his shroud.*
~ *vb.* (trans.) Shelter, conceal LLL 4.3.135 *I have been closely shrouded in this bush,* MAC 3.1.1, 3H6 4.3.40; (intr.) take shelter TMP 2.2.40 *I will here shroud.*

shroud *n.*[2] (pl.) Sail-ropes JN 5.7.53 *all the shrouds wherewith my life should sail,* H8 4.1.72, 3H6 5.4.18.

shrow See SHREW.

shrowd, shrowdly (var. of) SHREWD, SHREWDLY.

shuffle *vb.*
1 Practise trickery, act in an evasive manner WIV 2.2.25 *to shuffle, to hedge.*
2 *shuffle for oneself* Shift for oneself CYM 5.5.105 *your life...Must shuffle for itself.*
3 Remove in a hurried, secret, or underhand manner WIV 4.6.29 *That he shall...shuffle her away.*
4 *shuffle off* Get rid of or evade (something difficult, arduous, or irksome), put aside, thrust off HAM 3.1.66 *When we have shuffled off This mortal coil,* TN 3.3.16.

shuffling *n.* Deceitful action, trickery, shifty conduct HAM 4.7.137 *with a little shuffling, you may choose A sword unbated,* HAM 3.3.61.

shunless *adj.* Inevitable COR 2.2.112 *shunless destiny.*

shut *vb.*
1 *shut up* Exclude, bar the way of 3H6 4.3.20 *did shut up his passage.*
2 *shut up* in Confine to AWW 1.1.183 *Whose baser stars do shut us up in wishes,* TRO 1.3.58, OTH 3.4.121 (F1, Q2; Q1 *shoote*).

Si fortune (-a) me tormente (-o), sperato (spero) me contente (-o) [Pistol's It.: variously altered in mod. edd.] If fortune torments me, hope contents me 2H4 2.4.181, 2H4 5.5.96.

Sic spectanda fides [L.] Thus is faith to be tested PER 2.2.38.

sick *adj.*

1 Oppressed with sorrow, weakness, or faintness TGV 1.1.69 *heart sick with thought*, JN 5.3.4, HAM 1.1.9.

2 Longing *for*, pining *for* AWW 1.2.16 *sick For breathing and exploit*, 2H4 5.3.135, MM 2.4.103; *sick till I see her* longing to see her WIV 3.2.28.

3 Envious (*of*) H8 1.2.82 *sick interpreters*, TRO 1.3.132.

4 Affected with a feeling of loathing, repugnance, or envy MND 2.1.212 *I am sick when I do look on thee*, ADO 2.2.5.

5 Of a sickly hue, pale ROM 2.2.8 *Her vestal livery is but sick and green*.

6 Accompanied by illness R2 2.2.84 *the sick hour that his surfeit made*; pertaining to, connected with, persons suffering from illness JN 4.1.52 *at your sick service* (i.e. attending you when you were sick).

7 Spiritually or morally ailing, corrupt H8 2.2.82 *I would not be so sick though for his place* (i.e. so sick with pride), H8 2.4.205, HAM 4.5.17.

~ *vb.* Sicken 2H4 4.4.128 *sick'd and died*.

sicken *vb.*

1 (intr.) Be nauseated (with surfeit) TN 1.1.3 *The appetite may sicken*, MAC 4.1.60; (with revulsion) AWW 5.3.207 *Whose nature sickens but to speak a truth*, ANT 3.10.16.

2 (trans.) Cause to ail; (hence, fig.) weaken, impair, impoverish H8 1.1.82 *that have...so sicken'd their estates*.

sickle See SICLE.

sicklied *adj. sicklied o'er* Cover with a faint hue; (fig.) HAM 3.1.84 *the native hue of resolution Is sicklied o'er with the pale cast of thought*.

sickly *adj.* Of sickness, pertaining to or associated with sickness or the sick 2H4 1.1.147 *sickly coif* (i.e. invalid's cap), AWW 2.3.111, HAM 3.3.96.

~ *adv.*

1 With sickness MAC 3.1.106 *Who wear our health but sickly in his life*.

2 Feebly, weakly ANT 3.4.7 *cold and sickly He vented them*.

sick-thoughted *adj.* Lovesick, oppressed with desire VEN 5 *sick-thoughted Venus*.

sicle *n.* Shekel, a coin, orig. of the Middle East MM 2.2.149 *sicles of...gold* (F *sickles*).

side *n.*

1 Interests of one person, party, etc. in contrast to that of an opposing one LR 5.1.61 *hardly shall I carry out my side* (i.e. gain my ends, win).

2 Either of the two lateral parts of the human frame (esp. that part enclosing heart and lungs) LR 2.4.197 *O sides, you are too tough!*, TN 2.4.93, CYM 1.6.69.

3 (pl.) Regions or quarters (of the globe) ANT 1.2.192 *whose quality...The sides o' th' world may danger*, WT 4.4.478.

~ *vb.*

1 (intr.) Take a side COR 4.2.2 *The nobility...whom we see have sided In his behalf*; (trans.) take sides with COR 1.1.193 *They'll ...side factions*.

2 Assign to one of two sides or parties SON 46.9 *To side this title*.

▷ Q; see 'CIDE.

~ *adj. side sleeves* 'Hanging or pendant sleeves, open from the shoulder' (Linthicum, 1936) ADO 3.4.20.

side-piercing *adj.* Heart-rending LR 4.6.85 *O thou side-piercing sight!*

siege *n.*

1 Seat MM 4.2.98 *the very siege of justice*.

2 Rank HAM 4.7.76 *Of the unworthiest siege*, OTH 1.2.22 (Qq 1–2 *height*).

3 Excrement TMP 2.2.106 *the siege of this mooncalf*.

sieve *n.*

1 Basket, receptacle for fragments TRO 2.2.71 *nor the remainder viands We do not throw in unrespective sieve*.

▷ Q *siue*; F1 *same*; Ff 2–4 *place*; Johnson *sieve*.

2 Receptacle used by witches for sailing in MAC 1.3.8 *in a sieve I'll thither sail*.

sigh *vb.* Lament SON 30.3 *I sigh the lack of many a thing I sought*.

sight *n.*

1 Eye or eyes VEN 183 *His low'ring brows o'erwhelming his fair sight*, PHT 35, MND 2.1.183; (pl.) COR 2.1.205, PER 1.1.74.

2 Gaze, look LUC 104 *his wanton sight*.

3 Appearance (as opposed to reality) PER 1.1.123 *good in nothing but in sight*.

4 Visor 2H4 4.1.119 *their beavers down, Their eyes ...sparkling through sights of steel*.

5 Sighting TIM 1.1.245 *I am joyful of your sights* (i.e. at seeing you).

sighted *ppl. adj.* Having eyes WT 1.2.388 *Make me not sighted like the basilisk*.

sight-hole *n.* Peep-hole 1H4 4.1.71 *stop all sight-holes*.

sightless *adj.*

1 Blind, not seeing SON 27.10 *my sightless view*, SON 43.12.

2 Not lit by the sun or 'eye of day', dark LUC 1013 *Poor grooms are sightless night, kings glorious day*.

3 Invisible MAC 1.5.49 *sightless substances*, MAC 1.7.23.

4 Unsightly JN 3.1.45 *sightless stains*.

sightly *adv.* Pleasing to the sight JN 2.1.143 *It lies as sightly on the back of him As great Alcides' shows upon an ass*.

sign *n.*

1 Signal JC 5.1.23 *shall we give sign of battle?*, 1H6 2.1.3, 1H6 3.2.8.

2 Banner PER 1.1.156 *a flag and sign of love*; *sign of battle*, war ensign, standard H5 2.2.192 *The signs of war advance!*, JC 5.1.14.

3 *in* (*a*) *sign* As (a) token H8 3.1.66, *in a sign of peace*, R3 1.3.280.

4 Mere appearance or semblance (*of* something) OTH 1.1.157 *a flag...Which is indeed but sign*, ADO 4.1.33, LLL 5.2.469.

▷ In CYM 1.2.30 *She's a good sign*, sense 4 but perh. with quibble on the sense of 'constellation'.

~ *vb.*

1 Mark H8 2.4.108 *You sign your place and calling...With meekness*, JC 3.1.206.

▷ In JN 4.2.222 *by the hand of nature mark'd, Quoted, and sign'd to do a deed of shame* either in this sense of 'marked' or an aphetic form of 'assigned'.

2 Bode ANT 4.3.14 *It signs well*.

signal *n.* Sign, token 1H6 2.4.121 *in signal of my love to thee*, H5 5.Ch.21, R3 5.3.21 (Qq; F1 *token*).

significant *n.* Token, sign 1H6 2.4.26 *In dumb significants*, LLL 3.1.130 (applied bombastically to a letter).

signior *n.* Gentleman, nobleman MV 1.1.10 *signiors and rich burghers*, CYM 1.4.100; (esp. as a form of address, without following name) sir MM 3.1.49 *Look, signior, here's your sister*, OTH 1.3.76, 1H6 3.2.67; (with following name) TGV 3.1.280 *Signior Launce*, ERR 3.1.1, SHR 1.1.85.

signory *n.*

1 Domain, estate R2 3.1.22 *you have fed upon my signories*, 2H4 4.1.109.

2 One of the states of northern Italy under the

rule of princes Tmp 1.2.71 *Through all the signories it was the first.*

3 Governing body of Venice Oth 1.2.18 *My services which I have done the signory.*

silence *n.* Silent one Cor 2.1.175 *My gracious silence, hail!*

~ *vb.* (used euphemistically for) Keep under restraint 2H4 5.2.97 *imagine me...in your power soft silencing your son,* H8 1.1.97.

silent *n.* Silence 2H6 1.4.16 *the silent of the night.*

silk *adj.* Silky AYL 3.5.46 *black silk hair.*

silken *adj.*

1 Worked in silk LC 17 *silken figures.*

2 Delicate, soft, effeminate Jn 5.1.70 *a beardless boy, A cock'red silken wanton,* LLL 5.2.406, R3 1.3.53.

silly *adj.*

1 Deserving of pity, 'poor', hapless R2 5.5.25 *silly beggars Who sitting in the stocks refuge their shame,* 2H6 1.1.225, Luc 1812.

2 Helpless, defenceless: (of women) TGV 4.1.70 *silly women or poor passengers,* 3H6 1.1.243; (of sheep) 3H6 2.5.43 *silly sheep,* Ven 1098.

3 Feeble, frail 1H6 2.3.22 *a child, a silly dwarf.*

4 Scanty, meagre 3H6 3.3.93 *a pedigree Of three-score and two years—a silly time.*

5 Unsophisticated, simple Luc 1345 *silly groom.*

6 Plain, unadorned TN 2.4.46 *It is silly sooth,* Cym 5.3.86, 1H6 4.7.72; (hence) petty WT 4.3.28 *my revenue is the silly cheat* (i.e. petty thievery or fraud).

◇ The earlier form *seely* occurs in Q1 versions of Luc 1345, Luc 1812, R2 5.5.25 and R2 5.6.14.

silly-ducking *adj.* Bowing ridiculously Lr 2.2.103 *silly-ducking observants.*

silverly *adv.* With silvery brightness Jn 5.2.46 *this ...dew, That silverly doth progress on thy cheeks.*

silver-shedding *adj.* Flowing in silvery streams TGV 3.1.232 *silver-shedding tears.*

simple *n.*

1 Ingredient or element in a compound, esp. a medicinal compound Luc 530 *The poisonous simple sometime is compacted In a pure compound,* AYL 4.1.16.

2 Medicinal herb Rom 5.1.40 *Culling of simples,* Wiv 1.4.63, Lr 4.4.14; (attrib.) Wiv 3.3.73 *smell like Bucklersbury in simple time* (i.e. midsummer, the time at which apothecaries were supplied with simples).

◇ Ham 4.7.144 *Collected from all simples that have virtue,* sense 2 most likely, but perh. sense 1.

~ *adj.*

1 Of poor or humble condition Shr Ind.1.135 *When they do homage to this simple peasant,* WT 4.4.745, Ant 5.2.339.

2 Uncompounded, unmixed Wiv 3.5.31 *brew me a pottle of sack finely.—With eggs, sir?—Simple of itself,* Son 125.7, PhT 44.

simpleness *n.*

1 Innocence, simplicity Ado 3.1.70 *never gives to truth and virtue that Which simpleness and merit purchaseth,* MND 5.1.83, Oth 1.3.246.

2 Integrity AWW 1.1.44 *In her they are the better for their simpleness.*

3 Piece of folly Rom 3.3.77 *What simpleness is this?*

simplicity *n.* Folly, silliness LLL 5.2.52 *profound simplicity,* MV 1.3.43, Son 66.11.

simply *adv.* Without addition, by itself Wiv 3.2.76 *let him take her simply,* AWW 4.3.333, Tro 3.3.80.

simular *n.* One who simulates or puts on a false appearance, counterfeiter Lr 3.2.54 *thou simular of virtue* (F; Qq 1–2 *simular man*).

~ *adj.* Simulated, pretended, counterfeited Cym 5.5.200 *simular proof,* Lr 3.2.54 (Qq).

since *adv.* Ago, before now Tmp 1.2.53 *Twelve year*

since, AWW 1.2.71, 1H6 3.4.20; *since night* a night ago, last night MND 3.2.275, *Since night you loved me.*

~ *conj.*

1 (with vbs. of recollection) When, the time when WT 5.1.219 *Remember since you ow'd no more to time Than I do now,* MND 2.1.149, 2H6 3.1.9.

2 *since that* Since Mac 4.3.106 *Since that the truest issue of thy throne...stands accus'd,* Lr 1.1.248, Cor 3.2.50.

sinew, sinow *n.*

1 (pl.) Nerves Lr 3.6.98 *This rest might yet have balm'd thy broken sinews,* Ven 903.

2 (pl.) Strength Cor 5.6.44 *my sinews shall be stretch'd upon him.*

3 (fig.) Main strength or support, mainstay MM 3.1.221 *the portion and sinew of her fortune,* 1H4 4.4.17, H5 1.2.223.

~ *vb.* Join fast as with sinews 3H6 2.6.91 *So shalt thou sinew both these lands together* (F1 *sinow*).

sinewed *ppl. adj.* Strengthened Jn 5.7.88 *when he sees Ourselves well sinewed to our defence.*

◇ See TREBLE-SINEWED.

sinfully *adv.* In the midst of his sins, without having repented of his sins H5 4.1.148 *do sinfully miscarry upon the sea.*

sing *vb.*

1 (of a woman) 'Allure, make advances to' (Partridge) Tro 5.2.9 *She will sing any man at first sight.*

2 (of a man) Have intercourse with Tro 5.2.10 *any man may sing her.*

◇ Quibble on musical sense of *sing* in both 1 and 2.

singing-man *n.* Man who sings in the choir of a cathedral or collegiate church 2H4 2.1.90 *a singing-man of Windsor.*

single *vb.* (in hunting) Select (an animal) from the herd to be hunted; (allusively) 3H6 2.4.1 *I have singled thee alone,* Tit 2.1.117, LLL 2.1.28; (with forth) Tit 2.3.69 *your Moor and you Are singled forth to try thy experiments,* 3H6 2.1.12.

~ *adj.*

1 Solitary, alone, by oneself Tim 2.2.56 *thou stand'st single,* AWW 2.3.296 (with quibble on the sense 'husbandless'), Ant 5.1.18; individual Ham 3.3.11 *The single and peculiar life*; unaided Lr 5.3.103 *Trust to thy single virtue,* Tro 2.2.135; *single blessedness* divine blessing accorded to a life of celibacy MND 1.1.78; *single bond* (?) (1) bond signed by the debtor alone, without the support of sureties; or (2) bond with only one condition MV 1.3.145.

2 Mere 3H6 5.1.43 *whiles he thought to steal the single ten* (i.e. not a court card).

3 Poor, weak, feeble Tmp 1.2.433 *A single thing* (with quibble on sense 1), 2H4 1.2.183, Mac 1.6.16.

4 Indivisible, undivided Mac 1.3.140 *my single state of man* (with quibble on sense 3).

5 Single-minded, sincere H8 5.2.73 *a single heart,* AWW 4.2.22 (with quibble on sense 1).

~ *adv.* Singly, by oneself Tmp 5.1.248 *single I'll resolve you.*

singleness *n.* Simplicity, silliness Rom 2.4.66 *solely singular for the singleness!*

single-soled *adj.* (fig.) Contemptible, mean, feeble Rom 2.4.65 *O single-sol'd jest!*

singly *adv.*

1 By a single individual Cor 2.2.87 *The man ...cannot in the world Be singly counterpois'd.*

2 Uniquely Tim 4.3.523 *Thou singly honest man* (perh. with quibble on sense of 'truly, sincerely').

singular *adj.* Unmatched, unique Cym 3.4.121 *singular in his art,* WT 4.4.144, Rom 2.4.65.

~ *adv.* Singularly, remarkably, unusually 2H4 3.2.108 *Very singular good.*

Singulariter, nominativo, hic, haec, hoc [L.] In the singular number, in the nominative case, this, this, this WIV 4.1.41.

singularity *n.*
1 Peculiarity, eccentricity COR 1.1.278 *More than his singularity* (i.e. apart from his eccentricity), TN 2.5.152.
2 (pl.) Rarities, curiosities WT 5.3.12 *much content In many singularities.*

singule *vb.* Single out LLL 5.1.81 *we will be singuled from the barbarous.*

sinister *adj.*
1 Situated on the left side, left AWW 2.1.44 *on his sinister cheek,* MND 5.1.163, TRO 4.5.128.
2 Unjust, unfair, illegitimate, wrong MM 3.2.242 *no sinister measure,* H5 2.4.85, TN 1.5.176.

sink *n.* Sewer, drain for carrying away dirty water or sewage 2H6 4.1.71 *kennel, puddle, sink, whose filth and dirt Troubles the...spring,* TRO 5.1.76, COR 1.1.122; (fig.) H5 3.5.59 *the sink of fear.*
~ *vb.*
1 (intr.) Perish, go to ruin ANT 3.7.15 *Sink Rome ...!,* OTH 2.3.209, PER 4.6.120.
2 (trans.) Cause to fall CYM 5.5.413 *my heavy conscience sinks my knee,* TMP 2.1.201; (hence) cause to perish, ruin H8 2.1.60 *if I have a conscience, let it sink me,* H8 2.1.131, AWW 5.3.181.

sinke-a-pace See CINQUEPACE.

sinking-ripe *adj.* Ready to sink ERR 1.1.77 *the ship, then sinking-ripe.*

sinow See SINEW.

sir *n.*
1 Lord, sovereign ANT 5.2.120 *Sole sir o' th' world.*
2 Gentleman TN 3.4.73 *some sir of note,* TMP 5.1.69, CYM 5.5.145; (used ironically) WT 1.2.212 *this great sir,* LR 2.4.78, CYM 1.1.166; *play the sir* act the fine gentleman, play the gallant OTH 2.1.174.
3 Polite form of address; (with another vocative) TMP 5.1.245 *Sir, my liege,* WT 1.2.318, CYM 3.1.16; (prefixed to a designation of rank, status, or occupation) ADO 5.1.83 *sir boy,* TMP 5.1.106, WT 1.2.135; (pl., addressed to women) ANT 4.15.85 *Good sirs;* (to a man and a woman together) LLL 4.3.208 *Hence, sirs, away!*
4 Title given to a priest TN 3.4.271 *I am one that had rather go with sir priest than sir knight;* (often prefixed to his Christian name) TN 4.2.2 *make him believe thou art Sir Topas the curate,* LLL 4.2.11, WIV 1.1.1.
▷ In R3 3.2.109 *good Sir John,* John was the name conventionally applied to a priest. See JACK sense 7.

Siren *n.* Name of certain sea-nymphs who allured sailors by their songs; (transf.) fair charmer TIT 2.1.23 *This siren that will charm Rome's Saturnine, And see his shipwrack,* ERR 3.2.47; (attrib.) SON 119.1 *Siren tears.*

sirrah *n.* Ordinary form of address to inferiors WIV 1.3.79 *Hold, sirrah, bear you these letters tightly,* TGV 2.1.7, MM 3.2.19; (addressed to a woman attendant) ANT 5.2.229 *Sirrah Iras;* (prefixed to a designation) LLL 3.1.120 *Sirrah Costard,* 1H4 2.1.41 *Sirrah carrier,* SHR 2.1.400; (addressed to a superior, implying disrespect or undue familiarity) 1H4 1.2.179 *and, sirrah, I have cases of buckrom,* JN 2.1.140, ERR 4.1.81; (addressed to an equal, both being servants) 2H4 2.4.15 *Sirrah, here will be the Prince and Master Poins anon,* ERR 3.1.83, TGV 2.5.11.
▷ In passages of soliloquy *ah sirrah* is app. addressed by the speaker to himself, e.g. AYL 4.3.165, 2H4 5.3.16, ROM 1.5.29.

sir-reverence *interj.* (corr. of) 'Save your reverence' ERR 3.2.91 *such a one as a man may not speak of without he say 'Sir-reverence';* (attrib.) ROM 1.4.42 *the mire Of this sir-reverence love* (Q1; Qq 2-4 *Or saue you reuerence;* F1 *Or saue your reuerence.* With pun on euphemism for 'dung').

sister *n. the sisters three* The three Fates or Parcae MND 5.1.336, MV 2.2.63, 2H4 2.4.199.
~ *vb.* Be near akin to PER 5.Gower.7 *even her art sisters the natural roses.*

sistering *ppl. adj.* Neighbouring LC 2 *a sist'ring vale.*

sit *vb.*
1 Sit in council, take counsel together, hold a session PER 2.3.92 *we sit too long on trifles,* H5 5.2.80, R3 3.1.173.
2 Sit or lie heavy, be oppressive MM 5.1.389 *Your brother's death...sits at your heart,* HAM 3.4.112, AWW 2.1.144 (F1 *shifts;* Theobald *fits*); (with *heavy*) R2 1.3.280 *Woe doth the heavier sit,* R3 5.3.118.
3 (of the wind) Blow from, be in, a particular direction or quarter MV 1.1.18 *Plucking the grass to know where sits the wind,* H5 2.2.12, R2 2.2.123; (fig.) ADO 2.3.98 *Sits the wind in that corner?,* LR 1.4.100.
4 Live at (a certain rate of expense) WIV 1.3.8 *I sit at ten pounds a week.*
5 *sit in* Be contained in SON 103.13 *much more than in my verse can sit.*
6 (trans.) Maintain one's seat on H8 4.2.16 *grew so ill He could not sit his mule.*
~ in combination
sit above Have a higher place than TIM 3.2.87 *policy sits above conscience.* **sit down** Lay siege COR 4.7.28 *All places yields to him ere he sits down.* **sit out** Not take part LLL 1.1.110 *Well, sit you out* (term from card-playing).

sit fas aut nefas [L.] Be it right or wrong TIT 2.1.133.

sith *adv.* Since that time HAM 2.2.12 *And sith so neighboured to his youth and haviour* (Qq; Ff *since*).
~ *conj.* Since, seeing that WIV 2.2.188 *sith you yourself know how easy it is,* LR 1.1.180, OTH 3.3.380; (with *that*) MM 4.1.73 *Sith that the justice of your title to him Doth flourish the deceit,* LR 2.4.239.
~ *prep.* Since (a specified time) 3H6 2.1.106 *things sith then befall'n.*

sithence *adv.* Since, after that time COR 3.1.47 *Have you inform'd them sithence?*
~ *conj.* Since, seeing that, as AWW 1.3.119 *sithence...it concerns you something to know it.*

sitting *n.* Interview, meeting WT 4.4.561 *at every sitting.*

sixpenny *adj.* (fig.) Paltry 1H4 2.1.74 *long-staff sixpenny strikers* (i.e. unmounted highwaymen that will knock a man down for sixpence).

size *n.*
1 (fig.) Magnitude, extent, measure, amount, quantity ANT 4.15.4 *our size of sorrow,* COR 5.2.18, TIM 5.1.66.
2 (pl.) Allowances LR 2.4.175 *to scant my sizes.*

sized *pa. pple.* Of a particular magnitude HAM 3.2.170 *as my love is siz'd, my fear is so.*

skainsmate *n.* One who works with skeins, (perh.) milliner or seamstress; (hence, term of contempt) woman of loose morals ROM 2.4.154 *I am none of his flirt-gills, I am none of his skainsmates.*

skill *n.*
1 Cunning, craft WT 2.1.166 *or stupefied Or seeming so in skill.*
2 Piece of good policy 1H4 1.2.216 *I'll so offend, to make offence a skill.*
3 Reason, cause, ground WT 4.4.152 *you have As little skill to fear as I have purpose To put you to't*

(perh. with play on sense of 'capacity, power to reason').

~ *vb. it skills not greatly, not much* It makes no great difference, it is no great matter SHR 3.2.132, TN 5.1.288, 2H6 3.1.281.

skilless, skill-less *adj. skilless in, of* Unacquainted with TMP 3.1.53 *How features are abroad I am skilless of*, TN 3.3.9 *Being skilless in these parts.*

skillet *n.* Small metal cooking-pot with long handle OTH 1.3.272 *Let housewives make a skillet of my helm.*

skimble-skamble *adj.* Nonsensical, confused, rambling 1H4 3.1.152 *skimble-skamble stuff.*

skin *vb.* Cover with or as with skin HAM 3.4.147 *skin and film the ulcerous place, Whiles...corruption...Infects unseen*, MM 2.2.136.

skin-coat *n.* Coat made of skin; (transf.) one's skin JN 2.1.139 *I'll smoke your skin-coat and I catch you right.*

skipper *n.* Flighty fellow SHR 2.1.339 *Skipper, stand back.*

skipping *ppl. adj.* Flighty, thoughtless MV 2.2.187 *Thy skipping spirit*, LLL 5.2.761, TN 1.5.201.

skirr *vb.* Move rapidly H5 4.7.61 *we will...make them skirr away*; (trans.) scour (the country) MAC 5.3.35 *Send out moe horses, skirr the country round.*

skirt *n.* (pl.) Outlying parts, border, edge AYL 3.2.336 *the skirts of the forest*, AYL 5.4.159, HAM 1.1.97.

skirted *adj.* Wearing a coat with skirts (in vogue among the French) WIV 1.3.84 *French thrift, you rogues—myself and skirted page.*

skyey *adj.* Of the atmosphere, emanating from the sky MM 3.1.9 *skyey influences.*

skyish *adj.* Reaching to the sky, lofty HAM 5.1.253 *the skyish head Of blue Olympus.*

slab *adj.* Viscous, semi-solid MAC 4.1.32 *Make the gruel thick and slab.*

slack *vb.* Be slack or remiss in OTH 4.3.87 *they slack their duties*, WIV 3.4.111; be neglectful of (a person) LR 2.4.245 *If...they chanc'd to slack ye.*

~ *adj. come slack of* Fall short of, in duteousness LR 1.3.9 *If you come slack of former services.*

slake *vb.* Abate, moderate, decrease 3H6 1.3.29 *It could not slake mine ire*, LUC 425 (Q1; Q2 *Slacked*); (intr.) LUC 1677 *no flood by raining slaketh.*

slander *n.*

1 Reproach, disgrace R2 1.3.241 *A partial slander* (i.e. reproach of partiality), ERR 4.4.67, R3 3.3.13; (applied to persons who cause disgrace or bring reproach) R2 1.1.113 *this slander of his blood*, H5 3.6.80, R3 1.3.230.

2 Evil report, ill repute CYM 1.1.71 *After the slander of most stepmothers*, ERR 3.1.105, H8 2.1.153.

~ *vb.*

1 Reproach (a person) *with* (something disgraceful) JN 1.1.74 *he slander'd me with bastardy*, 3H6 1.4.47, 1H4 1.3.112.

2 Bring disgrace or reproach upon ADO 2.3.45 *to slander music*, HAM 1.3.133, CYM 3.5.76.

slanderous *adj.*

1 That is a disgrace or reproach, discreditable, shameful JN 3.1.44 *Ugly, and sland'rous to thy mother's womb*, LUC 1001.

2 Giving cause or occasion for slander JC 4.1.20 *To ease ourselves of diverse sland'rous loads* (i.e. burdens of slander).

slaughter *n.* (transf.) Blood JN 2.1.323 *Dy'd in the dying slaughter of their foes.*

slaughterman *n.* Killer, slayer 3H6 1.4.169 *Had he been slaughterman to all my kin*, 1H6 3.3.75, CYM 5.3.49; executioner TIT 4.4.58 *For this proud mock I'll be thy slaughterman.*

slave *vb.* Make subservient to oneself LR 4.1.68 *the...man, That slaves your ordinance.*

slaver *vb.* Be befouled (with unclean lips) CYM 1.6.105 *should I...Slaver with lips as common as the stairs.*

sleave *n.* Filament of silk obtained by separating ('sleaving') a thicker thread; silk in the form of such filaments, floss silk MAC 2.2.34 *the ravell'd sleave* (i.e. tangled thread); (attrib.) TRO 5.1.31 *thou...skein of sleave-silk* (Ff *Sleyd silke*).

sledded *adj.* Conveyed in a sled or sledge HAM 1.1.63 *He smote the sledded Polacks on the ice.*

sleek *vb.* Smoothe MAC 3.2.27 *sleek o'er your rugged looks.*

~ *adj.* Oily, plausible H8 3.2.241 *how sleek and wanton Ye appear in every thing may bring my ruin!*

sleep *vb.*

1 (fig.) Be inactive or ineffectual MM 2.2.90 *The law hath not been dead, though it hath slept*, HAM 1.3.3, LR 1.4.210.

2 (fig.) Cease, die H8 5.4.39 *Nor shall this peace sleep with her.*

3 *sleep upon* Be regardless of or blind to (some evil) H8 2.2.42 *The King's eyes, that so long have slept upon This hold bad man*, TIM 3.5.43.

sleeve-hand *n.* Cuff or wristband WT 4.4.210 *the sleeve-hand and the work about the square on't.*

sleeveless *adj.* Futile TRO 5.4.8 *a sleeveless arrant* (i.e. useless errand).

sleid, sleided *ppl. adj.* (of silk) Sleaved, divided into filaments TRO 5.1.31 *thou...skein of sleid silk* (Ff; Q *sleiue silk*), LC 48 *sleided silk*, PER 4.Gower.21 (Q1 *sleded*).

sleight *n.* Cunning, trickery 3H6 4.2.20 *With sleight and manhood stole to Rhesus' tents*; precise art or method (of doing something) MAC 3.5.26 *magic sleights.*

⟡ PER 5.1.260 *I have another sleight* (Q1; Malone *suit*): prob. corrupt text.

slenderly *adv.* To a slight extent, meagrely, poorly LR 1.1.294 *yet he hath ever but slenderly known himself.*

slice *n.* (applied to Slender) Thin person WIV 1.1.132 *Slice, I say!*

'slid *interj.* (an oath; corr. of) By God's lid (i.e. eyelid) WIV 3.4.24 *'Slid, 'tis but venturing*, TN 3.4.391.

⟡ Cf. LID.

sliding *n.* Lapse, moral slip MM 2.4.115 *You...rather prov'd the sliding of your brother A merriment than a vice.*

slight *vb.*

1 Toss slightingly, throw contemptuously WIV 3.5.9 *The rogues slighted me into the river.*

2 Put off disdainfully JC 4.3.5 *my letters...was slighted off.*

~ *adj.*

1 Insignificant LLL 5.2.463 *some slight zany*, COR 5.2.104, JC 4.1.12.

2 Easy-going, careless CYM 3.5.35 *We have been too slight in sufferance*, TIM 2.1.17.

3 Unsubstantial SON 45.1 *slight air.*

'slight *interj.* (an oath; corr of) By God's light TN 2.5.33, TN 3.2.13.

slightly *adv.* Carelessly, heedlessly R3 3.7.19 *Untouch'd or slightly handled in discourse*, MV 5.1.167, TRO 3.3.166; lightly, easily H8 2.4.112 *You have...Gone slightly o'er low steps.*

slightness *n.* Trifling, triviality COR 3.1.148 *give way...To unstable slightness.*

slip *n.*

1 Leash in which greyhounds are held and from which they can be released easily H5 3.1.31 *you stand like greyhounds in the slips.*

2 Counterfeit coin ROM 2.4.48 *What counterfeit coin did I give you?—The slip*, VEN 515 (quibble).

3 (fig.) Scion, young member of (esp. noble) family TIT 5.1.9 *Brave slip, sprung from the great Andronicus*, 2H6 2.2.58, MM 3.1.141.

~ *vb.*

1 *let slip* Allow (dogs) to go from the 'slips' or leash JC 3.1.273 *let slip the dogs of war*, COR 1.6.39; (absol.) 1H4 1.3.278 *Before the game is afoot thou still let's't slip.*

2 Let slip, unleash SHR 5.2.52 *Lucentio slipp'd me like his greyhound*; let go free CYM 4.3.22 *We'll slip you for a season.*

slipper *adj.* Slippery OTH 2.1.242 *a slipper and a subtle knave* (F1; Ff 2–3 *slippery*).

slippery *adj.* Inconstant, fickle WT 1.2.273 *My wife is slippery?*, ANT 1.2.185, COR 4.4.12.

slip-shod *adj.* In 'slip-shoes' or slippers LR 1.5.12 *thy wit shall not go slip-shod.*

sliver *n.* Piece cut or split off from a tree HAM 4.7.173 *an envious sliver broke.*

~ *vb.* Tear off (a branch), cut into slivers MAC 4.1.28 *slips of yew Sliver'd in the moon's eclipse*, LR 4.2.34.

slobbery *adj.* Sloppy, slovenly H5 3.5.13 *a slobb'ry and a dirty farm.*

slop(s) *n.* Loose breeches 'of knee length or shorter' (Linthicum, 1936) 2H4 1.2.30 *the satin for my short cloak and my slops*, ADO 3.2.36, ROM 2.4.45.

slovenly *adj.* Foul, nasty 1H4 1.3.44 *a slovenly unhandsome corse.*

slovenry *n.* Slovenliness H5 4.3.114 *time hath worn us into slovenry.*

slow *adj.*

1 Heavy TGV 4.2.65 *a slow heart*; dull, sober, serious LLL 4.3.321 *slow arts*, R3 1.2.116.

2 *slow offence* 'Offence of slowness' (Schmidt) SON 51.1.

slubber *vb.*

1 Sully OTH 1.3.227 *to slubber the gloss of your new fortunes.*

2 Do in a slovenly manner, hurry over MV 2.8.39 *Slubber not business for my sake* (F, Q2; Q1 *slumber*).

slug *n.* Sluggard R3 3.1.22 *what a slug is Hastings*, ERR 2.2.194.

slug-a-bed *n.* Sluggard ROM 4.5.2 *fie, you slug-a-bed!...How sound is she asleep!*

slumber *vb.* Be inactive or ineffectual PER 1.4.16 *If heaven slumber*, AWW 3.6.73.

sluttish *adj.* Of low or lewd character, unchaste TRO 4.5.62 *sluttish spoils of opportunity* (i.e. 'corrupt wenches, of whose chastity every opportunity may make prey', Johnson).

sly *adj.* Stealthy R2 1.3.150 *The sly, slow hours.*

▷ Ff, Qq *slie slow*, *slye slow*; F2 *flye slow*. See FLY-SLOW.

small *n.*

1 Little, not much LLL 1.1.86 *Small have continual plodders ever won.*

2 Thin part of the leg below the calf LLL 5.2.641 *he is best indu'd in the small.*

3 *in the smallest* In the smallest degree, in the least MM 4.2.168 *to cross this in the smallest.*

4 *by small and small* Little by little, by degrees, gradually R2 3.2.198 *I play the torturer by small and small.*

~ *adj.*

1 Thin, fine, slender TGV 2.3.21 *as small as a wand*, ROM 1.4.64, PER 4.Gower.22; (of powder) fine TIT 5.2.198 *grind their bones to powder small*; (of rain) not heavy or violent R2 2.1.35 *Small show'rs.*

2 (of sound) Thin, shrill, piping TN 1.4.32 *thy small pipe Is as the maiden's organ*, COR 3.2.114.

3 (of time) Short R3 4.1.78 *Within so small a time*, H5 2.4.145, AYL 4.3.151.

4 (of drinks, beverages) Light, weak, inferior SHR Ind.2.1 *a pot of small ale*, 2H4 2.2.6, 2H6 4.2.68; (hence) trivial occupations, affairs, etc. OTH 2.1.160 *To suckle fools and chronicle small beer.*

~ *adv.*

1 In a 'small' voice, shrilly WIV 1.1.48 *speaks small like a woman*, MND 1.2.50.

2 To a small extent, little LUC 1273 *it small avails my mood.*

smart *adj.* Painful HAM 3.1.49 *How smart a lash that speech doth give my conscience*, 2H6 3.2.325.

smatch *n.* Smack, taste, flavour JC 5.5.46 *Thy life hath had some smatch of honour in it.*

smatter *vb.* Chatter, talk superficially ROM 3.5.171 *smatter with your gossips.*

smear *vb.* Besmirch, befoul, sully 1H6 4.7.3 *Triumphant Death, smear'd with captivity*, ADO 4.1.133 (Q1 *smirched*), LUC 945.

smell *vb.* Have the smell of, exhale the odour of, smell of TMP 4.1.199 *I do smell all horse-piss*, MM 3.2.183, WIV 3.2.68.

smile *vb.*

1 Sneer, mock at LR 2.2.82 *Smile you my speeches* (Ff, Qq *smoile*, *smoyle*); (with *at*) TRO 5.10.7 *Sit, Gods, upon your thrones, and smile at Troy.*

2 *smile (one's) cheeks in years* Laugh (one's) face into wrinkles LLL 5.2.465.

smilet *n.* Little smile LR 4.3.19 *those happy smilets That play'd on her ripe lip.*

smit *pa. pple.* (var. of) Smitten TIM 2.1.23 *my reliances on his fracted dates Have smit my credit.*

smock *n.* Woman's undergarment OTH 5.2.273 *O illstarr'd wench, Pale as thy smock*, ADO 2.3.132, WIV 3.5.90; (allusively) woman ROM 2.4.103 *a shirt and a smock* (i.e. a man and a woman), ANT 1.2.168, AWW 2.1.30.

smoke *n.*

1 Vapour, mist MAC 1.5.51 *the dunnest smoke of hell*, 1H6 2.2.27, SON 34.4.

2 (fig., denoting a clouding or obscuring influence) 'Mist' of words, mere talk, idle expressions LLL 3.1.63 *Sweet smoke of rhetoric!*, JN 2.1.229, LUC 1027.

~ *vb.*

1 Fill with smoke CYM 5.5.398 *smoke the temple with our sacrifices*; purify with smoke ADO 1.3.59 *as I was smoking a musty room.*

2 Unearth (a fox) by fire; (fig.) find a person out AWW 3.6.103 *He was first smok'd by the old Lord Lafew*, AWW 4.1.27.

3 *smoke one's skincoat* Give him a drubbing, thrash him JN 2.1.139 *I'll smoke your skincoat and I'll catch you right.*

4 Suffer, have a 'warm' time of it TIT 4.2.111 *some of you shall smoke for it in Rome.*

5 Steam LR 5.3.224 *What means this bloody knife?— 'Tis hot, it smokes.*

smoking *ppl. adj.* Giving out steam or vapour, reeking COR 1.4.11 *smoking swords*, 3H6 2.3.21.

smooth *vb.*

1 Gloss over, minimize, make less offensive R2 1.3.240 *To smooth his fault*, 3H6 3.1.48.

2 Flatter, humour R3 1.3.48 *smooth, deceive, and cog*, TIT 4.4.96, PER 1.2.78; (trans.) LR 2.2.75 *smooth every passion*, 2H6 2.1.22, TIT 5.2.140.

3 Make smooth, bland, insinuating, or plausible PP 18.8 *smooth not thy tongue with filed talk.*

~ *adj.*

1 Mild, bland, 'oily', insinuating AYL 2.7.96 *smooth civility*, 2H6 3.1.65, TIM 3.6.94.

2 Free from inequalities, asperities, or difficulties, pleasant 1H4 1.1.66 *smooth and welcome news*, 2H4 Ind.40, ANT 1.3.100.

smoothing *ppl. adj.* Flattering, plausible 2H6 1.1.156 *let not his smoothing words Bewitch your hearts*, R3 1.2.168, Luc 892.

smooth-faced *adj.* (fig.) Having a bland, ingratiating expression, plausible in manner Jn 2.1.573 *That smooth-fac'd gentleman*, LLL 5.2.828.

smooth-pate, smoothy-pate *n.* Smooth-headed person 2H4 1.2.38 *The whoreson smooth-pates do now wear nothing but high shoes* (F1; Q1 *smoothy-pates*).

smote *pa. pple.* Smitten LLL 4.3.27 *when their fresh rays have smote The night of dew*, Cor 3.1.317.

smother *n.* Suffocating smoke AYL 1.2.287 *Thus must I from the smoke into the smother*.

smug *adj.* (of persons) Spruce, smart, trim MV 3.1.46 *to come so smug upon the mart*, Lr 4.6.198 (Ff); (of river) smooth, neat 1H4 3.1.101 *the smug and silver Trent*.

snaffle *n.* Simple form of bridle-bit, having less restraining power than one provided with a curb Ant 2.2.63 *The third o' th' world is yours, which with a snaffle You may pace easy*.

snatch *n.*
1 Hasty catch, sudden grab (at something) Tit 2.1.95 *some certain snatch or so Would serve your turns*.
2 Sudden check in speech Cym 4.2.105 *The snatches in his voice*.
3 Quibble, smart repartee MM 4.2.6 *leave me your snatches*.

snatcher *n.* Thief, pilferer H5 1.2.143 *the coursing snatchers*.

sneak-cup Error for SNEAK-UP.

sneak-up *n.* One who sneaks up to a person, mean, servile person, shirk 1H4 3.3.85 *the Prince is a Jack, a sneak-up*.
◇ Vaughan's conjecture; Qq 1–2 *sneakeup*; F1, Qq3–6 *sneak-cup*.

sneap *n.* Snub, rebuke 2H4 2.1.122 *I will not undergo this sneap without reply*.

sneaped *ppl. adj.* Nipped or pinched (with cold) Luc 333 *the sneaped birds*.

sneaping *ppl. adj.* Nipping, biting WT 1.2.13 *sneaping winds*, LLL 1.1.100.

sneck *vb.* (with *up*) Go hang TN 2.3.94 *Sneck up!*

snip *n.* Small amount, portion, snatch LLL 3.1.22 *keep not too long in one tune, but a snip and away*.

snipe *n.* (term of contempt applied to persons) Fool, simpleton Oth 1.3.385 *If I would time expend with such a snipe*.

snipt-taffeta *adj.* Wearing 'snipped', slashed garments of taffeta AWW 4.5.1 *misled with a snipt-taffeta fellow*.

snort *vb.* Snore 1H4 2.4.529 *Fast asleep...and snorting like a horse*.

snorting *ppl. adj.* Snoring Oth 1.1.90 *Awake the snorting citizens*.

snuff *n.* Huff, resentment, taking offence Lr 3.1.26 *snuffs and packings of the Dukes*; *take in snuff* take offence at, resent 1H4 1.3.41 *Who therewith angry...Took it in snuff*; (with play on the sense 'burning candle-wick') LLL 5.2.22 *You'll mar the light by taking it in snuff*, MND 5.1.250.

so *adj.* Middling, so so LLL 1.1.225 *he is, in telling true—but so*.
~ *adv.*
1 (in ellipt. constr. modifying an adj.) However..., be (he, it) never so...Ham 4.7.143 *no cataplasm so rare...can save the thing from death*, MM 3.2.187, Shr 5.2.144.
2 (expression of approval, satisfaction or acquiescence) Good!, very well! Tmp 1.2.24 *So, Lie there, my art*, H8 5.2.7, Oth 5.1.82.
3 *so many* The same number (of) AWW 4.3.162

Spurio, *a hundred and fifty; Sebastian, so many*, WT 5.3.51.
4 *so as* Such as Son 131.1 *so as thou art*, Son 52.1, WT 5.1.172 *So sacred as it is* (i.e. sacred though it is).
5 *so, so* Good!, good!, that will do very well H8 1.1.219 *So, so; These are the limbs o' th' plot. No more, I hope?*, Ant 4.4.28, TGV 2.3.23; *so so so* Tmp 5.1.96, Lr 3.6.84.
~ *conj.*
1 Provided that, if only Ado 2.1.88 *will you walk about with your friend?—So you walk softly*, R3 1.2.124, Son 134.3; (with *as*) R2 5.6.27 *So as thou liv'st in peace, die free from strife*; (with *that*) AWW 2.4.20 *So that you had her wrinkles, and I her money*; (with *if*) Ham 4.7.60 *So you will not o'errule me to a peace* (Qq *So you will not*); (freq.) *so* (*it*) *please* if it please MV 4.1.380 *So please my lord...To quit the fine..., I am content*, 3H6 2.6.98, Rom 4.3.9.
2 Even though Ant 2.5.94 *So half my Egypt were submerg'd*.

soaking *ppl. adj.* Absorbent WT 1.2.224 *thy conceit is soaking*.

sob *n.* Opportunity given to a horse to recover its wind after exertion; (fig.) rest, respite Err 4.3.25 *the man, sir, that when gentlemen are tir'd, gives them a sob*.

sober *adj.*
1 Calm Tim 3.5.21 *sober and unnoted passion*, JC 4.2.40.
2 Serious Ado 1.1.170 *speak in sober judgement*, AYL 5.2.69.
3 Grave, dignified MV 2.5.36 *my sober house*, Shr 1.2.132, Luc 1403; (of women) modest, demure Err 3.1.90 *Her sober virtue*, Ham 3.4.189, Ant 5.2.54.

sober-blooded *adj.* Calm, devoid of passion 2H4 4.3.87 *this same young sober-blooded boy*.

soberly *adv.* With dignity Ant 1.5.48 *soberly did mount an arm-gaunt steed*.

sober-sad *adj.* Grave, serious Luc 1542 *even as subtle Sinon here is painted, So sober-sad, so weary*.

sober-suited *adj.* Decently, demurely dressed Rom 3.2.11 *night, Thou sober-suited matron all in black*.

sobriety *n.* Modesty Shr 1.1.71 *Maid's mild behaviour and sobriety*; decorum H5 4.1.73 *the ceremonies of the wars,...the sobriety of it*.

sociable *adj.* Sympathetic Tmp 5.1.63 *Mine eyes, ev'n sociable to the show of thine*.

society *n.*
1 Association, companionship Wiv 3.4.8 *My riots past, my wild societies*.
2 (fig.) Partnership LLL 4.3.51 *Thou makest the triumphery, the corner-cap of society*.

sod *ppl. adj.* Boiled LLL 4.2.22 *twice sod simplicity* (i.e. the essence of simplicity); (hence) scalded (with tears) Luc 1592 *Her eyes, though sod in tears*.

sodden *ppl. adj.* Boiled H5 3.5.18 *sodden water*; (transf., with allusion to brothels and the treatment of venereal disease in the sweating-tub) Tro 3.1.41 *Sodden business! There's a stew'd phrase indeed*, Per 4.2.20.

so-forth *n.* (euphemism) Such and such a thing, 'et cetera' WT 1.2.218 *Sicilia is a so-forth*.

soft *adj.* Gentle, mild, compassionate H5 3.3.48 *thy soft mercy*, Cor 3.2.82, Oth 1.3.82.
~ *adv.*
1 (short for 'go soft') Stay!, stop! Tmp 1.2.450 *Soft, sir, one word more*, Ant 2.2.83, Rom 1.1.195; (with pron.) Ado 5.1.203 *soft you*, Ham 3.1.87, Oth 5.2.338.
2 Gently 2H4 5.2.97 *soft silencing your son*, AWW 4.3.332.

softly *adv.*
1 (used interjectionally) Gently, without violence,

carefully SHR 1.2.236 *Softly, my masters!*, TN 2.5.120, WT 4.3.72.
2 Slowly, with an easy or gentle pace JC 5.1.16 *lead your battle softly on*, AYL 3.2.328, PER 4.1.48.

softly-sprighted *adj.* Having a gentle spirit, mild-mannered WIV 1.4.24 *A softly-sprighted man, is he not?* (perh. here a euphemism for 'cowardly').

soho, so ho *interj.* Hunting cry used when a hare was discovered or started ROM 2.4.130 *Soho!—What hast thou found?—No hare, sir*, TGV 3.1.189.

soil *n.*[1] Blemish, stain ANT 1.4.24 *yet must Antony No way excuse his soils* (Ff *foyl(e)s*: see FOIL *n.*[3]), ADO 3.2.5, HAM 1.3.15.
~ *vb.* Stain, tarnish, sully; (fig.) HAM 1.4.20 *with swinish phrase Soil our addition*, TIM 3.5.16, R2 1.3.125.

soil *n.*[2] Solution of a problem SON 69.14 *The soil is this.*
⇨ Q *solye*; Benson conjecture *soil*.

soiled *ppl. adj.* Fed with fresh-cut green fodder LR 4.6.122 *the soiled horse.*

soilure *n.* Defilement TRO 4.1.57 *Not making any scruple of her soilure* (Ff; Q *soyle*).

Sol *n.* The sun, viewed astrologically TRO 1.3.89 *the glorious planet Sol.*

sola *interj.* Hallo! MV 5.1.39 *Sola, sola! wo ha, ho!*, LLL 4.1.149.

solace *vb.*
1 Provide sport or amusement for, entertain LLL 4.3.374 *with some strange pastime solace them.*
2 Be happy, delight (*in*) ROM 4.5.47 *one thing to rejoice and solace in*, R3 2.3.30, CYM 1.6.86.

solder *vb.* Unite, close *up*; (fig.) ANT 3.4.32 *that slain men Should solder up the rift*, TIM 4.3.387.

soldier *n. soldier to* Enlisted in the service of, devoted to CYM 3.4.183 *This attempt I am soldier to*, PER 4.1.8.

sole *adj.*
1 Unique JN 4.3.52 *this, so sole and so unmatchable*, SON 36.7, PHT 2.
2 Mere MAC 4.3.12 *whose sole name.*
~ *adv.* Uniquely TRO 1.3.244 *that praise, sole pure.*

solely *adv.*
1 Absolutely, entirely AWW 1.1.101 *solely a coward*, MAC 1.5.70, ROM 2.4.65; *not solely* not only MV 2.1.13 *In terms of choice I am not solely led.*
2 (passing into adj.) Alone WT 2.3.17 *Leave me solely*, H5 2.Ch.4; sole SHR 2.1.117 *Left solely heir.*

solemn *adj.*
1 Belonging to or associated with a celebration, festivity, or religious observance SHR 3.2.101 *our solemn festival*, TIT 2.1.112, MAC 3.1.14.
2 Performed with due formality, ceremonious, formal AYL 4.3.77 *he hath taken a solemn leave*, SON 52.5, ANT 5.2.364.
3 Impressive, awe-inspiring VEN 1057 *This solemn sympathy poor Venus noteth.*
4 Gloomy, sombre HAM 1.2.78 *customary suits of solemn black.*
5 'Sad, melancholy' (Schmidt) LLL 5.2.118 *passion's solemn tears.*

solemnity *n.*
1 Observance of ceremony on important occasions MND 4.1.185 *hold a feast in great solemnity.*
2 Celebration of special importance, festival, festivity TGV 5.4.161 *triumphs, mirth, and rare solemnity*, ROM 1.5.57, MND 4.1.134; (esp.) celebration of nuptials ROM 4.5.61 *murder our solemnity*, JN 2.1.555, MM 3.1.216.
3 Impressiveness, grandeur 1H4 3.2.59 *my state ...won by rareness such solemnity.*

solemnly *adv.* With due formality, ceremoniously

R2 4.1.319 *we solemnly proclaim Our coronation*, H5 5.Ch.14, R3 1.2.213.

sol-fa *vb.* (jocular) Sing from a score SHR 1.2.17 *I'll try how you can sol-fa and sing it* (F1 *Sol, Fa*).

solicit *n.* Solicitation, entreaty CYM 2.3.47 *Frame yourself To orderly solicits* (F2; F1 *solicity*).
~ *vb.*
1 Move, stir 1H6 5.3.190 *Solicit Henry with her wondrous praise*, R2 1.2.2, HAM 5.2.358.
2 Urge, plead (one's suit, cause) TN 3.1.109 *would you undertake another suit, I had rather hear you to solicit that.*

solicitation *n.* Courtship OTH 4.2.199 *my unlawful solicitation.*

soliciting *n.*
1 Incitement, prompting MAC 1.3.130 *This supernatural soliciting Cannot be ill.*
2 (pl.) Courtship, wooing HAM 2.2.126 *my daughter...hath his solicitings...All given to mine ear.*

solicity See SOLICIT.

solidare *n.* Small coin TIM 3.1.43 *Here's three solidares for thee.*

solus *adj.* [L.] Alone H5 2.1.45 *I would have you solus*, 1H4 2.3.SD, R3 1.1.SD.

some *pron.* Some one R2 4.1.268 *Go some of you and fetch a looking-glass.*
~ *adj.*
1 About a(n) LR 1.1.20 *some year elder*, R3 3.1.64, LLL 5.2.90.
2 (followed by *certain* with limiting force) Certain JC 1.3.122 *Some certain of the noblest-minded Romans*, R3 1.4.121.
3 *some deal* Somewhat TIT 3.1.244 *To weep with them that weep doth ease some deal.*
4 *some other where* Somewhere else ROM 1.1.198 *This is not Romeo, he's some other where*, ERR 2.1.30.

something *adv.* Somewhat, to some extent TMP 3.1.58 *I prattle Something too wildly*, 2H4 1.2.188, HAM 1.3.121 (Ff *somewhat*); at some distance MAC 3.1.131 *something from the palace.*

sometime, sometimes *adj.* Former HAM 1.2.8 *our sometime sister, now our queen*, COR 4.1.23, LR 1.1.120.
~ *adv.*
1 Once, on a particular occasion MV 1.1.163 *Sometimes from her eyes I did receive fair speechless messages*, PER 2.1.137, 1H6 5.1.31.
2 Formerly, at one time TMP 5.1.86 *I was sometime Milan*, COR 5.1.2, HAM 1.1.49.

son *n.* Son-in-law SHR 5.2.13 *Padua affords this kindness, son Petruchio*, WIV 3.4.75, LR 1.1.41.

sonance *n.* Sound H5 4.2.35 *The tucket sonance.*

song-men See THREE-MAN-SONG-MEN.

sonnet *n.* Poem written in praise of a person, esp. a mistress ADO 5.2.4 *Will you then write me a sonnet in praise of my beauty?*, H5 3.7.41, LLL 4.3.15.

sonneting *n.* Composition of sonnets, sonnet-writing LLL 4.3.156 *none but minstrels like of sonneting.*

sonties *n.* *by God's sonties* Oath used by old Gobbo MV 2.2.45.
⇨ Either a diminutive of an old form 'sont' (i.e. saint) or a corr. of 'sante' (i.e. sanctity).

soon *adj.* Quick ANT 3.4.27 *your soonest haste*, H5 3.6.113.
~ *adv.* (with *at*) Early, before the time specified or referred to is much advanced ERR 3.2.174 *soon at supper-time I'll visit you*, R3 4.3.31, MV 2.3.5; (hence) *soon at night* towards evening WIV 1.4.8 *we'll have a posset for't soon at night*, OTH 3.4.198, MM 1.4.88.

soopstake See SWOOPSTAKE.

sooth *n.*

1 Truth MAC 1.2.36 *If I say sooth*, H5 3.6.142, H8 2.3.30; *in* (*good*) *sooth* (asseverative phr.) in truth, truly, indeed TRO 3.1.56 *in sooth, in good sooth, very rude*, TMP 2.2.147, MV 1.1.1; (with ellipsis of *in*) MND 2.2.129 *Good troth, you do me wrong* (*good sooth, you do*), TRO 2.2.109, WT 4.4.160; (with *very*) WT 1.2.17 *Very sooth, tomorrow*.

2 Flattery, smooth or plausible speech R2 3.3.136 *words of sooth*; (personified) PER 1.2.44 *When Signior Sooth here does proclaim a peace, He flatters you*.

~ *adj.* True MAC 5.5.39 *if thy speech be sooth*.

~ *adv.* Truly, indeed TN 2.1.11 *No, sooth, sir*, WT 4.4.347, OTH 3.3.52 (F1).

soothe *vb.*

1 Humour ERR 4.4.79 *to soothe him in these contraries*, R3 1.3.297, LR 3.4.177.

2 Flatter COR 2.2.73 *You sooth'd not, therefore hurt not*, JN 3.1.121.

soother *n.* Flatterer 1H4 4.1.7 *I do defy The tongues of soothers*.

soothing *n.* Flattery COR 1.9.44 *false-fac'd soothing*.

~ *ppl. adj.* Flattering R3 1.2.168 *My tongue could never learn sweet soothing word* (Ff, Qq 7–8 *smoothing*), PP 1.11.

soothsay *vb.* Make predictions, foretell future events ANT 1.2.51 *Go, you wild bedfellow, you cannot soothsay*.

soothsayer *n.* One who foretells future events JC 1.2.19 *A soothsayer bids you beware the ides of March*, ANT 1.2.3, CYM 5.5.426.

sop *n.* Bread, cake, wafer, etc. dipped or steeped in a drink before being eaten SHR 3.2.173 *threw the sops all in the sexton's face*; (fig.) R3 1.4.157 *throw him into the malmsey-butt…make a sop of him*, TRO 1.3.113, LR 2.2.32 (see MOONSHINE).

sophister *n.* Sophist, one who makes use of fallacious arguments, 'cunning, or cauilling disputer' (Cotgrave) 2H6 5.1.191 *A subtle traitor needs no sophister*.

sophisticated *ppl. adj.* Adulterated LR 3.4.106 *Here's three on 's are sophisticated*.

sore *n.*¹ Buck, deer in its fourth year LLL 4.2.57 *Some say a sore*.

sore *n.*² Sickness, disease OTH 4.2.49 *All kind of sores and shames on my bare head*, ADO 4.1.252, TIM 4.3.7.

~ *adj.* Grievous, severe, harsh TMP 3.1.11 *a sore injunction*, R3 1.4.42, LR 3.5.22.

~ *adv.* Grievously, heavily WT 5.3.49 *your sorrow was too sore laid on*, TRO 5.5.14, VEN 702.

sorel *n.* Buck, deer in its third year LLL 4.2.58 *then sorel jumps from thicket*.

sorely *adj.* Grievously, heavily MAC 5.1.53 *The heart is sorely charg'd*, WT 5.1.18, H8 4.2.14.

sorrow *n.*

1 *I am sorrow* I am sorry CYM 5.5.297 *I am sorrow for thee* (F1).

2 Outward expression of grief, lamentation, mourning, lament H8 4.2.28 *full of repentance, Continual meditations, tears, and sorrows*, TIT 3.1.119, VEN 963.

sorrowed *ppl. adj.* Sorrowful TIM 5.1.149 *their sorrowed render*.

sorrow-wreathen *adj.* Folded in grief TIT 3.2.4 *unknit that sorrow-wreathen knot*.

sorry *adj.*

1 Distressing, painful OTH 3.4.51 *a salt and sorry rheum*.

2 Full of sorrow, sorrowful, sad WT 2.1.123 *I never wish'd to see you sorry*, MAC 3.2.9, H8 2.4.26.

3 Exciting sorrow or sadness, woeful, wretched MAC 2.2.18 *This is a sorry sight*, ERR 5.1.121, 2H6 1.4.75.

sort *n.*¹ Lot TRO 1.3.375 *draw The sort*.

sort *n.*²

1 *of sorts* Of various kinds H5 1.2.190 *They have a king, and officers of sorts* (Qq *of sort*, which may belong to sense 2).

2 Rank, degree H5 4.7.136 *a gentleman of great sort*, H5 4.8.75; (hence) high rank MM 4.4.17 *men of sort and suit*, ADO 1.1.7, ADO 1.1.33.

3 Class of people TIT 1.1.230 *With voices and applause of every sort, Patricians and plebeians*, AYL 1.1.167, 1H6 2.5.123.

4 Band, company, group, set R2 4.1.246 *a sort of traitors*, MND 3.2.13, R3 5.3.316; *in sort* in a body or company, assembled together MND 3.2.21 *choughs, many in sort*.

5 Manner, way COR 1.3.2 *express yourself in a more comfortable sort*, MV 1.2.104, 3H6 4.2.28; *in a, some sort* in a, some way TMP 2.1.104 *I mean, in a sort*, WIV 1.1.103 *he doth in some sort confess it*, MM 3.2.28; *in sort* after a fashion JC 2.1.283.

6 State, condition TMP 4.1.146 *You do look my son, in a mov'd sort*; outward style, array H5 5.Ch.25 *The mayor and all his brethren in best sort*.

~ *vb.*

1 Put in the same class HAM 2.2.267 *I will not sort you with the rest of my servants*; (hence) associated with LLL 1.1.258 *sorted and consorted…· With a wench*; (intr.) consort with VEN 689 *the hare …sometime sorteth with a herd of deer*.

2 Choose, select, find *out*, contrive TGV 3.2.91 *To sort some gentleman well skill'd in music*, R3 2.2.148, ROM 3.5.109.

3 (trans.) Fit, adapt, make to agree with 2H6 2.4.68 *sort thy heart to patience*, TGV 1.3.63, LUC 1221; (intr.) fit, suit, be in accordance *with*, be fitting TRO 1.1.106 *This woman's answer sorts*, HAM 1.1.109, H5 4.1.63.

4 (of God) Dispose, ordain R3 2.3.36 *if God sort it so*, MV 5.1.132.

5 Fall out, turn out MND 3.2.352 *so far am I glad it so did sort*, 2H6 1.2.107, SHR 4.3.43 (see PROOF sense 3).

sortance *n.* Agreement, correspondence, suitableness 2H4 4.1.11 *with such powers As might hold sortance with his quality*.

sorted *ppl. adj. ill sorted* Associated with a class of evil things, in bad company 2H4 2.4.150 *which was an excellent word before it was ill sorted*.

sot *n.* Stupid person, fool, blockhead ERR 2.2.194 *thou snail, thou slug, thou sot*, TMP 3.2.93, LR 4.2.8.

sottish *adj.* Stupid, foolish ANT 4.15.79 *Patience is sottish*.

soud *interj.* (?) Onomatapoeic coinage imitating the sound made when one is either tired or impatient SHR 4.1.142 *Sit down, Kate, and welcome. Soud, soud, soud, soud.*

soul *n.*

1 Quintessence HAM 2.2.90 *brevity is the soul of wit*, MM 3.1.183, H5 4.1.245.

2 (used periphrastically) I, you, etc. WIV 2.2.244 *the folly of my soul* (i.e. my folly), MM 5.1.6 *our soul* (i.e. we), HAM 3.2.63 *Since my dear soul was mistress of her choice* (i.e. I), OTH 1.3.266 *heaven defend your good souls* (i.e. you).

3 (metaphysics) The vital, sensitive, or rational principle in plants, animals, or human beings; *three souls* allusion to the three 'souls' or principles (vegetable, animal, and rational) as combined in human beings TN 2.3.58 *Shall we rouse the night-owl in a catch that will draw three souls out of one weaver*.

◇ There was also a convention that music could draw the soul from the body.

4 Element, principle, trace (*of* something) H5 4.1.4 *There is some soul of goodness in things evil*.

soul-confirming *adj.* Confirmed, ratified by the soul TGV 2.6.16 *twenty thousand soul-confirming oaths.*

soul-fearing *adj.* Terrifying the soul JN 2.1.383 *their soul-fearing clamours.*

sound *vb.*[1] (var. in 16–17C of 'swowne') Swoon HAM 5.2.308 *She sounds to see them bleed,* ROM 3.2.56, TIT 5.1.119.
◇ Occurs in Ff and Qq.

sound *vb.*[2]
1 Utter, pronounce, proclaim R2 3.4.74 *sound this unpleasing news,* ANT 2.2.34, SHR 2.1.192 (with quibble).
2 Give a signal for (by the sound of a trumpet) LUC 471 *like a trumpet doth his tongue begin To sound a parley,* 1H4 5.4.159, OTH 2.3.22.
3 *sound out* (imper.) Blow a trumpet as a signal or salute ANT 2.7.133.

sound *adj.*
1 Honest, loyal, true H8 3.2.274 *Dare mate a sounder man than Surrey can be,* H8 5.2.116.
2 (of voice) Clear TN 1.4.33 *thy small pipe Is as the maiden's organ, shrill and sound.*
~ *adv.* Soundly, heartily WIV 4.4.62 *pinch him sound.*

soundless *adj.*[1] Without sound JC 5.1.36 *rob the Hybla bees, And leave them…soundless too.*

soundless *adj.*[2] Unfathomable SON 80.10 *Whilst he upon your soundless deep doth ride.*

soundpost *n.* Small peg of wood fixed beneath the bridge of a violin; (used as name of musician) ROM 4.5.136 *What say you, James Soundpost?*

sour *n.* That which is sour (as opposed to sweet) LUC 867 *The sweets we wish for turn to loathed sours,* OTH 4.3.95.
~ *vb.* Invest with a sour, sullen expression R2 2.1.169 *made me sour my patient cheek* (i.e. made me look sullen), VEN 185.
~ *adj.* Bitter, harsh LLL 1.1.313 *the sour cup of prosperity,* R2 4.1.241, 2H6 3.2.301.

sour-faced *adj.* Of melancholy aspect LUC 1334 *the sour-fac'd groom.*

sourly *adv.* Cruelly, in a hurtful manner SON 35.14 *To that sweet thief which sourly robs from me.*

souse *vb.* (of a bird of prey) Swoop down upon JN 5.2.150 *like an eagle…To souse annoyance that comes near his nest.*

soused *ppl. adj.* Pickled 1H4 4.2.12 *a sous'd gurnet.*

south fog *n.* Fog coming from the south, which was generally regarded as unhealthy CYM 2.3.131 *The south fog rot him!*

southward *adj.* Southern WT 4.4.789 *looking with a southward eye.*

south-west *n.* South-west wind TMP 1.2.323 *A south-west blow on ye.*

sovereign *adj.* Supreme, paramount, most notable LLL 2.1.44 *A man of sovereign parts,* LR 4.3.42, 1H4 3.2.161; (of medicines) efficacious in a superlative degree COR 2.1.116 *the most sovereign prescription in Galen,* 1H4 1.3.57, VEN 28; (fig.) TGV 1.2.113 *I search it with a sovereign kiss.*

sovereignly *adv.* Supremely WT 1.2.323 *So sovereignly being honourable.*

sovereignty *n.* Supreme excellence TGV 2.6.15 *Whose sovereignty so oft thou hast preferr'd,* LLL 4.3.230, LUC 36; (of medicines) supreme efficacy AWW 1.3.224 *prescriptions…such as his reading…had collected For general sovereignty.*

sowl *vb.* Pull by the ears COR 4.5.200 *sowl the porter of Rome gates by th' ears* (F1 *sole*).

sowter *n.* (properly) Cobbler; (used as name for a poor hound in contempt) TN 2.5.123 *Sowter will cry upon't for all this, though it be as rank as a fox.*

space *n.* Time, period or interval of time AYL 4.3.151

after some small space, ANT 2.1.31, AWW 2.3.181; *at further space* later LR 5.3.53 *they are ready Tomorrow, or at further space.*

span *n.* Short space of time H8 3.2.140 *To steal from spiritual leisure a brief span*; (esp.) short duration of human life TIM 5.3.3 *Timon is dead, who hath outstretch'd his span,* OTH 2.3.72.
~ *vb.* Limit H8 1.1.223 *My life is spann'd already.*

span-counter *n.* Boy's game in which 'one throws a counter, or piece of money, which the other wins, if he can throw another so as to hit it, or lie within a span of it' (Nares) 2H6 4.2.158 *in whose time boys went to span-counter for French crowns.*

spaniel *vb.* Follow subserviently (like a spaniel or lap-dog), fawn on ANT 4.12.21 *The hearts That spaniel'd me at heels.*
◇ Hanmer conjecture; F1 *pannelled.* See PANNEL.

Spanish pouch *n.* Pouch made of Spanish leather, part of a vintner's outfit; (hence, term of contempt applied to a vintner) 1H4 2.4.71 *Caddis garter, smooth tongue, Spanish pouch.*

spare *n.* Exercise of economy, frugality H8 5.3.21 *I made no spare.*
~ *vb.*
1 *spare for no…, spare not for…* Be liberal in respect of ADO 3.5.61 *We will spare for no wit,* ROM 4.4.6, 1H6 5.4.56.
2 Forbear TMP 2.1.25 *I prithee spare,* R3 1.3.113, COR 1.1.256; (ellipt.) forbear to give 2H4 3.2.269 *spare me the great ones.*
3 Avoid MND 2.1.142 *shun me, and I will spare your haunts.*
4 Save (one's feelings from offence, etc.) MM 2.3.33 *Showing we would not spare heaven as we love it.*
~ *adj.*
1 Thin, lean 2H4 3.2.269 *give me the spare men,* JC 1.2.201.
2 Sparing H5 2.2.131 *they are spare in diet.*

sparingly *adv.* (of speaking, etc.) With reserve or restraint, with forbearance H5 1.2.239 *Or shall we sparingly show you far off The Dauphin's meaning,* R3 3.5.93.

sparkle *vb.*
1 Send out sparks of fire; (fig.) JN 4.1.114 *it perchance will sparkle in your eyes* (i.e. send out sparks into your eyes and hurt them).
2 Emit, throw out (fire, etc.) as or like sparks LLL 4.3.348 *Women's eyes…sparkle still the right Promethean fire.*

sparrow *n.* Symbol of a lecher TRO 5.7.11 *my double-henn'd sparrow* (F1), MM 3.2.175.

Spartan dog *n.* Kind of bloodhound MND 4.1.119 *My hounds are bred out of the Spartan kind,* OTH 5.2.361.
◇ MND 4.1.114 *hounds of Sparta.*

spavin *n.* Disease of horses causing swelling of the joints SHR 3.2.53 *sped with spavins*; (applied to men) H8 1.3.12 *the spavin And springhalt reign'd among 'em.*

spay *vb.* Castrate MM 2.1.230 *to geld and spay all the youth of the city* (Ff *splay*).

speak *vb.*
1 Call for action COR 3.2.41 *when extremities speak,* HAM 5.2.201, ANT 2.2.102; (trans.) call upon, summon to action TMP 2.1.207 *Th' occasion speaks thee.*
2 Proclaim, show (a person to be so-and-so) MAC 4.3.159 *blessings…That speak him full of grace,* H8 2.4.141.
3 Tell or talk of, describe H8 4.1.61 *speak it to us,* HAM 3.2.30, 1H4 5.2.57; make mention of a person, bear witness in favour of (a person), give testimony to H8 3.1.125 *let me speak myself,* H8 2.4.167, COR 2.2.103 (see HOME *adv.*); (with *far*) say much of (a person) CYM 1.1.24 *You speak him far.*

4 *speak (oneself) of* Bespeak MV 2.4.5 *We have not spoke us yet of torchbearers.*

5 (euphemism) Exchange blows, fight ANT 2.2.164 *Would we had spoke together!*, ANT 2.6.25, COR 1.4.4.

6 (of wind) Make a sound, reverberate OTH 2.1.5 *the wind hath spoke aloud at land.*

7 (transf., of musical instruments) Emit a sound, utter a full and proper note HAM 5.2.275 *let the kettle to the trumpet speak*, MAC 5.6.9, CYM 4.2.191.

8 (with object equivalent to an adverbial expression defining the manner of speaking) OTH 2.3.279 *speak parrot* (i.e. talk nonsense), ADO 2.1.247 *speaks poniards, and every word stabs*, H5 5.2.149 *speak...plain soldier.*

~ in combination
speak for Call for, demand LR 1.4.246 *The shame itself doth speak For instant remedy.* **speak on** Speak of 2H4 2.2.65 *I am well spoke on.* **speak out** Proclaim, declare, manifest H8 2.4.141 *If thy rare qualities...could speak thee out.* **speak to 1** Make an appeal to ANT 1.2.181 *The death of Fulvia with more urgent touches, Do strongly speak to us*, OTH 1.2.23. **2** (pass.) Have an intimation (of something) H8 1.3.66 *I was spoke to, with Sir Henry Guilford, This night to be comptrollers.*

speaking *n.* Speech, talk, words H8 2.4.104 *to unthink your speaking*; instance of speech or talk CYM 5.4.147 *a speaking such As sense cannot untie.*
~ *ppl. adj.* Expressive, eloquent LR 4.5.25 *most speaking looks.*

speargrass *n.* Spearwort, one of the species of ranunculus 1H4 2.4.309 *to tickle our noses with speargrass to make them bleed.*

special *adj.* make special Indicate specially, specify AWW 2.2.6 *what place make you special.*

specialty *n.*
1 *specialty of rule* 'Particular rights of supreme authority' (Johnson) TRO 1.3.78 *The specialty of rule hath been neglected.*
2 Special contract or bond under seal for the payment of money SHR 2.1.126 *Let specialties be therefore drawn between us*, LLL 2.1.164.

speciously *adv.* [dial. var.] Specially WIV 3.4.108 *but speciously for Master Fenton*, WIV 4.5.111.

spectacle *n.* (pl.) (transf.) Organs of sight, eyes 2H6 3.2.112 *bid mine eyes be packing...And call'd them blind and dusky spectacles*, CYM 1.6.37.

spectatorship *n.* Presentation to the eyes of spectators COR 5.2.66 *If thou stand'st not i' th' state of...some death more long in spectatorship* (i.e. under the eyes of spectators).

speculation *n.*
1 Observation LR 3.1.24 *spies and speculations.*
2 Looking on H5 4.2.31 *idle speculation.*
3 Power of seeing, sight TRO 3.3.109 *speculation turns not to itself*; (esp.) intelligent or comprehending vision MAC 3.4.94 *Thou hast no speculation in those eyes.*

speculative *adj.* Having the power of vision, seeing OTH 1.3.270 *my speculative and offic'd instruments* (see OFFICED).

speechless *adj.* Without words SON 8.13 *speechless song*, MV 1.1.164, MM 1.2.183.

speed *n.*
1 *have the speed of* Outdistance, outstrip MAC 1.5.35 *One of my fellows had the speed of him.*
2 Success, prosperity, fortune SHR 2.1.138 *happy be thy speed*, CYM 3.5.161, WT 3.2.145.
3 One who promotes success or prosperity TGV 3.1.300 *Saint Nicholas be thy speed*, ROM 5.3.121, AYL 1.2.210; that which promotes success or prosperity 1H4 3.1.188 *good manners be your speed.*

~ *vb.*
1 Have (a certain) success, fare (well or ill) SHR 2.1.283 *It were impossible I should speed amiss*, JN 4.2.141, TRO 3.1.142.
2 Turn out COR 5.1.61 *Speed how it will.*
3 Be successful, succeed LR 1.2.19 *if this letter speed*, R3 4.4.358, OTH 4.1.108.
4 (trans.) Hasten AWW 3.4.37 *speed her foot*, MM 4.5.10, H5 3.5.36.
5 Be a person's 'speed' (see SPEED *n.* sense 3), prosper, cause to succeed JC 1.2.88 *let the gods so speed me*, WT 4.4.667, WIV 3.4.12; (with subject omitted) LR 4.6.208 *Sir, speed you.*
6 Bring to an infelicitous condition SHR 5.2.185 *We three are married, but you two are sped*; bring to an end, finish SHR 3.2.52 *sped with spavins*; kill (a person), dispatch ROM 3.1.91 *I am sped.*

speeding *n.*
1 Fortune, prosperity, succeeding SHR 2.1.301 *Is this your speeding?*, PER 2.3.115.
2 Lot in respect of success PP 17.16 *O cruel speeding.*
~ *ppl. adj.* Effective H8 1.3.40 *a speeding trick.*

speken *vb.* (archaic infin. of) Speak PER 2.Gower.12 *each man Thinks all is writ he speken can* (Q1 spoken).

spell *vb.* *spell backward* Misconstrue ADO 3.1.61 *she would spell him backward.*

spelling *ppl. adj.* That binds with spells, bewitching 1H6 5.3.31 *spelling charms.*

spell-stopped *adj.* Spellbound TMP 5.1.61 *there stand, For you are spell-stopp'd.*

spend *vb.*
1 Employ, make use of LUC 1457 *On this sad shadow Lucrece spends her eyes*, AWW 5.1.8, SON 80.3.
2 (speech or language) Expend, utter OTH 1.2.48 *spend a word*, 1H6 2.5.38, CYM 2.1.5; (of passion, fury, etc.) give vent to MND 3.2.74 *spend your passion*, 3H6 5.5.57, COR 2.1.53.
3 *spend (the) mouth, tongue* (of hunting dogs) Bark on finding or seeing the game H5 2.4.70, TRO 5.1.91, VEN 695.
4 Part with freely, throw away, lose, squander MAC 3.2.4 *Nought's had, all's spent*, R2 1.1.108, OTH 2.3.195.
5 Consume, exhaust, waste 3H6 1.4.21 *spend her strength*, SHR 5.1.69, ADO 1.1.271.
6 Consume, eat ROM 2.4.133 *stale and hoar ere it be spent*, 2H4 3.2.117.

spent *ppl. adj.*
1 Exhausted MAC 1.2.8 *two spent swimmers*, CYM 3.6.62.
2 Passed, gone by R2 1.3.211 *Six frozen winters spent*, SON 107.14, LUC 1589.

sperr, sperre *vb.* (var. of) Spar, fasten with a bar, shut securely TRO Prol.19 *with massy staples...Sperr up the sons of Troy.*
◇ F1 *stirre*; Theobald's conjecture *sperre.*

sphere *n.*
1 One or other of the concentric, transparent, hollow globes imagined by the older astronomers as revolving round the earth and respectively carrying with them the several heavenly bodies (moon, sun, planet, and the fixed stars); (hence) orbit of a planet MND 2.1.7 *Swifter than the moon's sphere*, JN 5.7.74, HAM 4.7.15; (allusively) ANT 4.15.10 *O sun, Burn the great sphere thou mov'st in*, AWW 1.1.89; (with ref. to the music supposed to be produced by the motion of these spheres) AYL 2.7.6 *discord in the spheres*, ANT 5.2.84, TN 3.1.110; (with ref. to the stars 'starting' from their 'spheres') MND 2.1.153 *certain stars shot madly from their spheres*; (fig.) orbit of the eye ROM 2.2.17 *do entreat*

her eyes To twinkle in their spheres, HAM 1.5.17, ANT 2.7.14.

2 Planet, star TIM 1.1.66 *all kind of natures, That labour on the bosom of this sphere* (i.e. the earth), LC 23.

~ *vb.* Place in a sphere TRO 1.3.90 *therefore is the glorious planet Sol...spher'd Amidst the other.*

sphered *ppl. adj.* Formed like a sphere, rounded TRO 4.5.8 *thy sphered bias cheek.*

spherical *adj.* Pertaining to the celestial spheres, planetary LR 1.2.123 *spherical predominance.*

sphery *adj.* Star-like MND 2.2.99 *Hermia's sphery eyne.*

spice *n.* (fig.) Taste, tincture, sample WT 3.2.184 *Thy by-gone fooleries were but spices of it*, H8 2.3.26, COR 4.7.46.

spicery *n.* (pl.) Spices R3 4.4.424 *nest of spicery* (with allusion to the nest of spices of which the phoenix made a funeral pyre).

spigot *n.* Small wooden peg inserted into and controlling the opening of a faucet of a barrel of liquor and used to regulate the flow WIV 1.3.21 *Wilt thou the spigot wield.*

spill *vb.* Destroy HAM 4.5.20 *It spills itself in fearing to be spilt*, LR 3.2.8.

spilth *n.* Spilling TIM 2.2.160 *drunken spilth of wine.*

spin *vb.* (of blood) Gush forth H5 4.2.10 *That their hot blood may spin in English eyes.*

spinner *n.* Spider, esp. one that spins a web MND 2.2.21 *Hence you long-legg'd spinners*, ROM 1.4.62.

spinster *n.* One who spins TN 2.4.44 *The spinsters and the knitters*, H8 1.2.33.

spire *n.* (fig.) Summit COR 1.9.24 *the spire and top of praises.*

spirit *n.*

1 Vital energy, life ANT 4.15.58 *Now my spirit is going*, JN 4.1.109, SON 129.1.

⇨ See also sense 5 (1).

2 Intellectual power 1H6 2.4.16 *some shallow spirit of judgement*, SON 86.5.

3 *spirit of sense* Exquisite sense, essence of sensibility TRO 3.3.106 *the eye itself, That most pure spirit of sense*, TRO 1.1.58.

4 Anger TIM 3.5.101 *not to swell our spirit.*

5 (uses of the pl.) (1) = Sense 1 TMP 1.2.487 *My spirits, as in a dream, are all bound up*, JN 2.1.232, CYM 1.5.41; (2) sentiments, feelings MAC 1.5.26 *pour my spirits in thine ear*, HAM 3.2.58, TIM 5.4.74; (3) mind, soul MM 4.2.70 *Heaven give your spirits comfort*, OTH 3.4.62, JN 3.1.17.

6 *vital spirits* Certain subtle highly-refined substances or fluids which formerly were supposed to permeate the blood and chief regions of the body 2H4 4.3.109 *the vital commoners and inland petty spirits.*

⇨ Three categories of such substances were recognized: 'natural', 'animal' and 'vital'.

~ *vb.* Make of a more active character, animate H5 3.5.21 *shall our quick blood, spirited with wine, Seem frosty.*

spiriting See SPRIGHTING.

spiritualty *n.* Body of spiritual or ecclesiastical persons, clergy H5 1.2.132 *we of the spiritualty.*

spirt *vb.* (of a plant) Shoot H5 3.5.8 *shall...Our scions, put in wild and savage stock, Spirt up so suddenly.*

spital *n.* Hospital H5 5.1.81 *my Doll is dead i' th' spital*, H5 2.1.74; (attrib.) TIM 4.3.40 *the spital-house.*

spite *n.*

1 Outrage, injury MND 3.2.420 *I'll...revenge this spite*, ROM 4.1.31.

2 Contemptuous defiance ROM 1.1.78 *Old Montague...flourishes his blade in spite of me*, ROM 1.5.62.

3 Vexation, mortification OTH 4.1.70 *the spite of*

hell, ERR 4.2.8, 1H4 3.1.190; *in spite of* to the mortification of MND 3.2.194 *To fashion this false sport, in spite of me*, 1H6 2.4.106; (*in*) *spite of spite* let the worst happen that may, notwithstanding anything 3H6 2.3.5 *And spite of spite needs must I rest awhile*, JN 5.4.5.

4 Vexatious or mortifying circumstance HAM 1.5.188 *The time is out of joint—O cursed spite* (F1 *spight*), TGV 4.2.69, ERR 2.2.189.

~ *vb.* Vex, mortify SHR 4.3.11 *that which spites me more than all these*, MAC 3.1.110.

spitting *ppl. adj.* Transfixing (as on a spit); (fig.) H8 2.4.184 *a spitting power.*

spittle See SPITAL.

splay See SPAY.

spleen *n.*

1 The organ itself viewed as the seat of emotions and passions JC 4.3.47 *digest the venom of your spleen*, MM 2.2.122, JN 2.1.68.

2 Fiery temper, fiery impetuosity or eagerness ROM 3.1.157 *the unruly spleen of Tybalt*, JN 5.7.50, 1H4 5.2.19; high spirit, courage 3H6 2.1.124 *That robb'd my soldiers of their heated spleen.*

3 Malice, hatred COR 4.5.91 *the spleen Of all the under fiends*, LR 1.4.282, H8 2.4.89.

4 Impulse, fit: (1) of anger or passion OTH 4.1.88 *y' are all in all in spleen*; (fig.) MND 1.1.146 *the lightning...That, in a spleen, unfolds both heaven and earth*; (2) of laughter, merriment, gaiety LLL 5.2.117 *That in this spleen ridiculous appears To check...passion's solemn tears*, SHR Ind.1.137, TN 3.2.68; (3) of passionate desire TRO 2.2.196 *our heaving spleens*, VEN 907.

5 Caprice, waywardness, changeable temper 1H4 2.3.78 *A weasel hath not such a deal of spleen*, 1H4 3.2.125, AYL 4.1.212.

spleenative *adj.* Passionate, impetuous, hotheaded HAM 5.1.261 *spleenative and rash.*

⇨ F1; mod. edd. *splenetive, splenitive.*

spleeny *adj.* Spleenful, splenetic, ill-humoured H8 3.2.99 *A spleeny Lutheran.*

splenitive See SPLEENATIVE.

spleet See SPLIT.

splint See SPLINTER.

splinter *vb.* Mend as with splints R3 2.2.118 *The broken rancour of your...hates, But lately splinter'd, knit, and join'd together* (Q1; Q2 *splint*), OTH 2.3.323.

split *vb.*

1 (applied to speech) Mutilate ANT 2.7.124 *mine own tongue Splits what it speaks* (F1 *spleets*), ERR 5.1.309.

2 *make all split* Cause great commotion MND 1.2.30 *a part to tear a cat in, to make all split.*

splitted *ppl. adj.* Split asunder, wrecked 2H6 3.2.411 *a splitted bark.*

splitting *ppl. adj.* Causing to split, causing wreck 2H6 3.2.97 *The splitting rocks.*

spoil *n.*

1 Prey, victim LUC 733 *Leaving his spoil perplex'd in greater pain*, TRO 4.5.62.

2 Plundering, spoliation JC 5.3.7 *His soldiers fell to spoil*, H5 3.3.25, 2H6 4.7.134; act of plundering or rapine MV 5.1.85 *fit for treasons, stratagems, and spoils.*

3 Destruction, havoc, ruin AWW 4.3.16 *the spoil of her honour*, 1H4 3.3.10, SON 100.12.

4 (in hunting) Capture of the quarry and division of rewards to the hounds; (hence) slaughter, massacre JC 3.1.206 *here thy hunters stand, Sign'd in thy spoil*, COR 2.2.120.

~ *vb.*

1 Plunder, despoil 2H6 4.4.53 *To spoil the city*, ANT 3.6.25.

2 Carry off as prey 3H6 2.2.14 *Not his that spoils her young before her face.*

3 Destroy, ruin OTH 5.1.54 *I am spoil'd*, SHR 5.1.110.

spongy *adj.*

1 Resembling a sponge in absorptive qualities; (hence) drunken MAC 1.7.71 *His spongy officers.*

2 Wet, moist TMP 4.1.65 *spongy April*, CYM 4.2.349.

spoon *n.* In allusion to the gift of a spoon to a child at its christening H8 5.2.201 *you'd spare your spoons*, H8 5.3.39.

spoon-meat *n.* Soft or liquid food for taking with a spoon, esp. by infants or invalids; (hence) delicacies ERR 4.3.60 *expect spoon-meat.*

sport *n.*

1 Pleasant pastime, amusement, diversion R2 3.4.1 *What sport shall we devise here in this garden*, WIV 2.1.197, ANT 1.1.47; (spec.) theatrical performance MND 3.2.14 *Who Pyramus presented, in their sport*, LLL 5.1.155; the chase TRO 4.5.239 *a book of sport*, LLL 4.2.1; games of chance MV 3.2.216 *We shall ne'er win at that sport*, ANT 2.3.35; amorous dalliance or intercourse OTH 2.1.227 *When the blood is made dull with the act of sport*, VEN 124; war, fighting H5 4.2.23 *for lack of sport*, 1H4 1.3.302.

2 *make sport* (1) Provide entertainment or amusement LLL 4.1.99 *one that makes sport To the Prince*, WIV 4.4.13, AWW 4.5.65; (2) amuse oneself, take one's pleasure, play ERR 2.2.30 *let foolish gnats make sport*, HAM 2.2.513, R2 2.1.85; (3) jest, mock WIV 3.3.150 *why then make sport at me*, ADO 3.1.58, AYL 1.2.26.

3 Jest, jesting ERR 3.2.27 *'Tis holy sport to be a little vain*, ADO 1.1.177, MV 1.3.145; matter for jesting ADO 2.3.156 *He would make but a sport of it*, CYM 2.4.48.

~ *vb.* (intr. and refl.) Make merry, divert oneself 3H6 2.5.34 *So many hours must I sport myself*, TMP 4.1.74, LUC 907.

sportful *adj.*

1 Amorous SHR 2.1.261 *let Kate be chaste and Dian sportful.*

2 Performed in jest TRO 1.3.335 *a sportful combat.*

sportive *adj.* Amorous, wanton R3 1.1.14 *sportive tricks*, SON 121.6.

spot *n.*

1 Stain, disgrace JN 5.2.30 *the spot of this enforced cause*, ANT 4.12.35, AWW 5.3.206.

2 Pattern, figure in embroidery or needlework COR 1.3.52 *What are you sewing here? A fine spot.*

3 Mark, dot (used to check off a name on a list) JC 4.1.6 *with a spot I damn him.*

spotted *ppl. adj.*

1 Stained, polluted R2 3.2.134 *their spotted souls*, MND 1.1.110, TIT 2.3.74; (absol.) TIM 5.4.35 *the spotted.*

2 Embroidered OTH 3.3.435 *a handkerchief Spotted with strawberries.*

spousal *n.* Marriage; (fig.) H5 5.2.362 *So be there 'twixt your kingdoms such a spousal.*

~ *adj.* Nuptial, matrimonial TIT 1.1.337 *our spousal rites.*

sprag *adj.* (Sir Hugh Evans' pronunciation of) 'Sprack', lively, alert WIV 4.1.82 *He is a good sprag memory.*

sprat *n.* Small sea fish; (fig., term of contempt) worthless creature AWW 3.6.105 *what a sprat you shall find him.*

sprawl *vb.* Struggle in the death agony TIT 5.1.51 *Hang the child, that he may see it sprawl*, 3H6 5.5.39.

spright, sprite (contractions of) SPIRIT.

▷ In Ff and Qq *spright* is used for all meanings, but in mod. edd. the spelling *sprite* is usu. restric-

ted to the meanings of 'supernatural being', 'ghost'.

sprighted, sprited *ppl. adj.* Haunted (as by a SPRIGHT) CYM 2.3.139 *I am sprighted with a fool.*

sprightful, spriteful *adj.* Spirited JN 4.2.177 *a sprightful noble gentleman.*

sprightfully *adj.* With great spirit R2 1.3.3 *The Duke of Norfolk, sprightfully and bold, Stays but the summons.*

sprighting, spriting *n.* Duties as a 'sprite' TMP 1.2.298 *do my spriting gently.*

sprightly, spritely *adj.*

1 High-spirited, lively, brisk AWW 2.1.75 *sprightly fire and motion*, ANT 4.14.52, 1H4 2.4.342.

2 Cheerful, in good spirits ANT 4.7.15 *thy sprightly comfort*, CYM 3.6.74.

3 In the form of spirits CYM 5.5.428 *spritely shows Of mine own kindred.*

~ *adv.* In a lively manner, cheerfully WT 4.4.53 *entertain them sprightly.*

spring *n.*

1 Young shoot (of a plant) LUC 869 *Unruly blasts wait on the tender spring*, LUC 950; (fig., of love) VEN 656 *This canker that eats up Love's tender spring*, ERR 3.2.3 (see LOVE: LOVE-SPRING); (of the down on the lip) VEN 127 *The tender spring upon thy tempting lip.*

2 Source; (fig.) MAC 1.2.27 *from that spring whence comfort seem'd to come*, R2 1.1.97, 1H4 5.2.23.

3 Beginning, early part MND 2.1.82 *the middle summer's spring* (i.e. the beginning of midsummer), 2H4 4.4.35 *the spring of day* (i.e. very early morning).

4 First season of the year; (fig.) first or early stage (of life, etc.) R2 5.2.50 *in this new spring of time*, LUC 49, PER 4.4.35; (esp. of love) TGV 1.3.84 *this spring of love*, ANT 3.2.43, SON 102.5.

springe *n.* Snare for birds HAM 1.3.115 *springes to catch woodcocks*, HAM 5.2.306, WT 4.3.35.

springing *ppl. adj.* Growing VEN 417 *springing things.*

springhalt *n.* Stringhalt, lameness, or affection of the hind legs of a horse which causes certain muscles to contract spasmodically H8 1.3.13 *They have all new legs, and lame ones...the spavin And springhalt reign'd among 'em.*

sprite, sprited, spriteful, spritely, spriting See SPRIGHT, SPRIGHTED, SPRIGHTFUL, SPRIGHTLY, SPRIGHTING.

spungy (var. of) SPONGY.

spur *n.*

1 *on the spur* At full speed JC 5.3.29 *With horsemen, that make to him on the spur; set spurs* started off at full speed WIV 4.5.68 *set spurs and away.*

2 (fig.) Incitement, incentive LR 2.1.76 *potential spurs To make thee seek it* (Qq; Ff *spirits*), R2 1.2.9, PER 3.3.23.

3 Root of a tree TMP 5.1.47 *by the spurs pluck'd up The pine and cedar*; (transf.) CYM 4.2.58 *grief and patience, rooted in them both, Mingle their spurs together.*

spur-galled *adj.* Chafed with the spur R2 5.5.94 *Spur-galled and tir'd by jauncing* (Ff; Qq *Spurrde*, *galld*).

spurn *n.* Contemptuous stroke or thrust TIT 3.1.101 *that which gives my soul the greatest spurn*, TIM 1.2.141; insult HAM 3.1.72 *the spurns That patient merit of th' unworthy takes.*

~ *vb.*

1 Kick 1H6 1.4.52 *spurn in pieces posts of adamant*, ERR 2.1.83 (with play on sense of 'treat contemptuously').

2 *spurn at, against* Oppose contemptuously JC

2.1.11 *I am know no personal cause to spurn at him,* Jn 3.1.142.

3 *spurn upon* Trample upon, tread underfoot R3 1.2.42 *I'll strike thee to my foot, And spurn upon thee.*

spy *n.*
1 Observer; (transf.) eye Tmp 5.1.259 *If these be true spies which I wear in my head* (i.e. accurate observers).
2 Observation Mac 3.1.129 *the perfect spy o' th' time.*

squander *vb.* Scatter recklessly MV 1.3.21 *other ventures he hath, squand'red abroad.*

squandering *ppl. adj.* Random AYL 2.7.57 *the squand'ring glances of the fool.*

square *n.*
1 Instrument or tool for measuring, footrule LLL 5.2.474 *Do not you know my lady's foot by th' square* (i.e. precisely, exactly), 1H4 2.2.12, WT 4.4.339.
2 Rule, proportion or bounds (in action) Ant 2.3.6 *I have not kept my square.*
3 (?) (1) Area, part; or (2) portion Lr 1.1.74 *the most precious square of sense* (i.e. (1) the most delicately sensitive part of my nature, or (2) feeling in its highest perfection).
4 Body of troops drawn up in a square formation, squadron H5 4.2.28 *squares of battle,* Ant 3.13.40.
5 Embroidered bosom or yoke of a garment WT 4.4.210 *the work about the square on't.*
~ *vb.*
1 Adjust, shape (to some pattern or model), rule, regulate Tit 3.2.31 *square my talk,* MM 5.1.482, WT 3.3.41.
2 Take the measure of, estimate Tro 5.2.132 *to square the general sex By Cressid's rule.*
3 Quarrel Ant 3.13.41 *Mine honesty and I begin to square,* MND 2.1.30, Tit 2.1.100; (refl.) quarrel with Tit 2.1.124 *to square yourselves.*
~ *adj.*
1 *square brows* High forehead Per 5.1.108 *My queen's square brows.*
2 Suitable, proper Tim 5.4.36 *it is not square to take On those.*
3 Corresponding faithfully to Ant 2.2.185 *if report be square to her.*

squarer *n.* Quarreller Ado 1.1.82 *Is there no young squarer now that will make a voyage with him to the devil.*

squash *n.* Unripe pea-pod TN 1.5.157 *as a squash is before 'tis a peascod,* MND 3.1.186; (term of contempt applied to a person) WT 1.2.160 *this kernel, this squash, this gentleman.*

squene (var. of) SQUINY.

squier (var. of) SQUARE.

squint *vb.* Cause to squint Lr 3.4.117 *squints the eye.*
▷ F1; Q1 *pin queues; pin squemes;* Q2 *pin queuer;* anon. and Greg conjecture *squinies.*

squiny *vb.* Look peeringly *at* Lr 4.6.137 *Dost thou squiny at me?*

squire *n.*¹ (var. of) SQUARE.

squire *n.*²
1 Gentleman next below a knight in rank H5 4.8.78 *lords and barons, knights and squires,* Cym 2.3.123, Lr 1.4.241.
2 Attendant, officer charged with personal attendance upon a sovereign or nobleman 1H4 1.2.24 *us that are squires of the night's body,* Ant 4.4.14.
3 Young man, young fellow Ado 1.3.52 *A proper squire!,* MND 2.1.131; (used with contempt) Oth 4.2.145 *Some such squire he was That turn'd your wit the seamy side without,* 1H6 4.1.23.

squire-like *adj.* Like a personal attendant or body-servant Lr 2.4.214 *To knee his throne, and, squire-like, pension beg.*

squirility *n.* Scurrility LLL 4.2.53 *abrogate squirility* (Q1; F1 *scurilitie*).

squirrel *n.* (applied to a) Small dog TGV 4.4.55 *the other squirrel was stol'n from me.*

stable *adj.* Steady TN 4.3.19 *stable bearing.*

stableness *n.* Constancy Mac 4.3.92 *justice, verity, temp'rance, stableness.*

stablish *vb.* Establish 1H6 5.1.10 *And stablish quietness on every side.*

stablishment *n.* Confirmed possession, settled occupation Ant 3.6.9 *Unto her He gave the stablishment of Egypt.*

staff *n.*
1 Shaft of a lance Jn 2.1.318 *There stuck no plume in any English crest That is removed by a staff of France,* R3 5.3.65, Mac 5.7.18; *break a shaft* tilt, contend *with* (an antagonist) AYL 3.4.44 *breaks his staff like a noble goose,* Per 2.3.35, Ado 5.1.138.
2 *set in* (one's) *staff* Make (oneself) at home, settle down in a place Err 3.1.51 *Shall I set in my staff?*
3 Strophe, stanza LLL 4.2.104 *Let me hear a staff, a stanze, a verse.*
▷ Old genitive form in TN 5.1.285 *he holds Belzebub at the stave's end.*

stage *n.* Scaffold, platform Ham 5.2.378 *that these bodies High on a stage be placed to the view,* Ham 5.2.396.
~ *vb.* Represent on the stage Ant 5.2.217 *quick comedians Extemporally will stage us,* Ant 3.13.30; (fig.) exhibit publicly MM 1.1.68 *do not like to stage me to their eyes.*

stagger *vb.* Waver, hesitate AYL 3.3.49 *A man may ...stagger in this attempt,* MM 1.2.165.

staggering *n.* Wavering, hesitation Wiv 3.3.12 *without any pause or staggering.*

staggers *n.* (pl.)
1 Giddiness Cym 5.5.233 *How comes these staggers on me;* (spec.) disease in animals attended by giddiness or staggering Shr 3.2.54 *his horse...spoil'd with the staggers.*
2 (?) (1) Giddy, wild conduct; or (2) bewilderment, perplexity, confusion AWW 2.3.163 *throw thee from my care for ever Into the staggers and the careless lapse Of youth and ignorance.*

staid *adj.* Calm, settled Cym 3.4.10 *my staider senses.*

stain *n.*
1 Disfigurement, blotch, sore Jn 3.1.45 *Full of unpleasing blots and sightless stains,* Cym 2.4.139.
2 Disgrace MM 3.1.202 *do no stain to your own gracious person,* 1H4 3.1.185, Cor 1.10.18.
3 One who causes disgrace 1H6 4.1.45 *Stain to thy countrymen.*
4 One who eclipses or casts into the shade Ven 9 *sweet above compare, Stain to all nymphs.*
5 Tinge, slight trace AWW 1.1.111 *You have some stain of soldier in you,* Tro 1.2.26.
~ *vb.*
1 Disfigure R3 4.4.207 *stain her beauty,* R2 3.1.14, Ven 797.
2 Taint, corrupt AWW 2.1.120 *stain our judgement,* Ham 4.4.57, Jn 4.2.6.
3 Make dim, eclipse Son 35.3 *Clouds and eclipses stain both moon and sun,* R2 3.3.66, Lr 5.3.263; (fig.) eclipse Ant 3.4.27 *I'll raise the preparation of a war Shall stain your brother;* (intr.) be dimmed or obscured, suffer eclipse LLL 2.1.48 *If virtue's gloss will stain with any soil,* Son 33.14.

stained *ppl. adj.*
1 Full of disgrace Luc 1059 *thou shalt not know The stained taste of violated troth,* Luc 1316, 1H6 3.3.57.
2 Disfigured Tmp 1.2.415 *he's something stain'd With grief.*

staining *ppl. adj.* Corrupting AWW 3.7.7 *any stain-ing act.*

stair-work *n.* Clandestine love affair in which the lovers either met on the stairs or had access to each other by hidden staircases WT 3.3.74 *This has been some stair-work.*

stake *n.* Post to which a bear was fastened to be baited; (fig.) JC 4.1.48 *we are at the stake, And bay'd about with many enemies,* TN 3.1.118, 2H6 5.1.144.

stale *n.*[1]

1 Decoy, bait TMP 4.1.187 *For stale to catch these thieves,* SHR 3.1.90.

2 Dupe, laughing-stock SHR 1.1.58 *To make a stale of me amongst these mates* (with play on 'stale-mate'), 3H6 3.3.260, TIT 1.1.304; a wife or mistress whose devotion is turned into ridicule for the amusement of rivals ERR 2.1.101 *poor I am but his stale.*

3 Prostitute, harlot of the lowest class, employed as a decoy by thieves; (used gen. as a term of contempt for an unchaste woman) ADO 2.2.25 *marry-ing the renown'd Claudio...to a contaminated stale,* ADO 4.1.65.

stale *n.*[2] Urine (of horses) ANT 1.4.62 *Thou didst drink The stale of horses*; (applied to Dr Caius) WIV 2.3.30 *is he dead, bully-stale?*

stale *vb.* Make stale or uninteresting ANT 2.2.234 *nor custom stale Her infinite variety,* COR 1.1.92 (F1 scale), JC 4.1.38; lower in estimation, make common or cheap JC 1.2.73 *To stale with ordinary oaths my love,* TRO 2.3.191.

stalk *vb.* Move cautiously or stealthily like a fowler in pursuit of his game, esp. by the use of a stalking-horse or some device for concealing oneself ADO 2.3.92 *stalk on, stalk on, the fowl sits*; (transf.) LUC 365 *Into the chamber wickedly he stalks.*

stalking-horse *n.* Real or artificial horse behind which a fowler hid when pursuing his game AYL 5.4.106 *He uses his folly like a stalking-horse.*

stall *vb.*

1 Put, keep in a stall VEN 39 *The steed is stalled up,* PP 18.2; (fig.) keep close AWW 1.3.126 *Stall this in your bosom.*

2 Install, invest R3 1.3.205 *Deck'd in thy rights, as thou art stall'd in mine.*

3 Dwell, lodge ANT 5.1.39 *we could not stall togeth-er.*

stalling *n.* Stall-accommodation AYL 1.1.10 *the stalling of an ox.*

stallion See SCULLION, STANIEL.

stamp *n.*

1 That with which an impression is made COR 2.2.107 *His sword, death's stamp,* SON 82.8; (spec.) instrument for stamping coin MM 2.4.46 *coin heaven's image In stamps that are forbid* (with ref. to begetting children).

2 Impression made, mark, character, imprint MV 2.9.39 *Without the stamp of merit,* CYM 5.5.366, HAM 1.4.31; (metaphor from coining) R3 1.3.255 *Your fire-new stamp of honour is scarce current,* 1H4 4.1.4.

3 That which is stamped with a certain impression TIT 4.2.69 *The empress sends it thee, thy stamp, thy seal* (with ref. to begetting children); (spec.) coin MAC 4.3.153 *a golden stamp about their necks,* WIV 3.4.16, CYM 5.4.24.

~ *vb.*

1 Mark with a stamp or character R3 1.1.16 *I, that am rudely stamp'd.*

2 (fig.) Beget CYM 2.5.5 *When I was stamp'd.*

3 Give currency to OTH 2.1.243 *has an eye can stamp and counterfeit*; give the impression of gen-uineness to COR 5.2.22 *Have almost stamp'd the leasing.*

stanch *vb.* Satiate, satisfy TIT 3.1.14 *Let my tears stanch the earth's dry appetite.*

~ *adj.* See STAUNCH.

stanchless *adj.* Insatiable MAC 4.3.78 *stanchless av-arice.*

stand *n.* Place where one stands, station MM 4.6.10 *I have found you out a stand most fit*; (esp.) *make (one's) stand* MV 2.6.2, LUC 438; *take (one's) stand* H8 4.1.2, 3H6 4.3.1, PP 9.5; (spec.) station taken up by a hunter or an archer, standing in ambush or in cover 3H6 3.1.3 *For through this laund anon the deer will come, And in this covert will we make our stand,* LLL 4.1.10, WIV 5.5.235.

~ *vb.*

1 Remain stationary, stop TGV 4.1.3 *Stand, sir,* MM 3.2.264, SHR 4.3.44.

2 Make a stand, fight MND 3.2.424 *dar'st not stand, nor look me in the face,* ROM 1.1.10.

3 (in imper.) Forbear, stop! TRO 5.6.9 *Stand, Diomed,* COR 5.6.126.

4 Continue, remain MAC 3.1.4 *it was said It should not stand in thy posterity.*

5 Remain, stay (to do something), lose time over TGV 5.2.44 *stand not to discourse,* JC 5.3.43, WIV 3.3.125.

6 (trans.) Withstand, resist 1H6 1.1.123 *none durst stand him,* LR 4.1.68 (Ff *slaves*), CYM 5.3.60.

7 *stand in act* Be in action, be under way OTH 1.1.151 *the Cyprus wars (Which even now stands in act).*

~ in combination

stand by 1 Remain inactive 2H6 2.4.45 *he stood by, whilst I...Was made a wonder and a pointing-stock.* **2** Make a stand, fight WT 1.2.444 *if you seek to prove, I dare not stand by.* **stand for** Take the side of, support, stand up for COR 4.6.45 *when Mar-tius stood for Rome,* H5 1.2.101, CYM 3.5.56. **stand in 1** Insist upon having TIT 4.4.105 *if he stand in hostage for his safety* (F4 *stand on*). **2** Be the object of OTH 1.3.70 *though our proper son Stood in your action.* **stand off 1** Stand apart AWW 2.3.120 *our bloods...stands off differences so mighty.* **2** Be prominent, stand out H5 2.2.103 *the truth of it stands off as gross As black and white.* **stand on, upon 1** Depend, rest upon LR 4.6.214 *Stands on the hourly thought* (i.e. is hourly expected), MND 1.1.139, MV 3.2.201. **2** Rely upon, take one's stand on H8 5.1.122 *The good I stand on is my truth and honesty,* WIV 2.1.233. **3** Insist on, be particular about, make much of WIV 2.1.225 *you stand on dis-tance,* MAC 3.4.118, ANT 4.4.31. **4** Value, set store by JC 2.2.13 *I never stood on ceremonies, Yet now they fright me,* COR 4.6.96. **5** Concern or trouble oneself about JC 3.1.100 *'tis but the time...that men stand upon,* ERR 1.2.80, ROM 2.3.93. **6** Be of import-ance to ERR 4.1.69 *how it stands upon my credit,* R3 4.2.58. **7** Be incumbent upon R2 2.3.138 *It stands your Grace upon to do him right,* HAM 5.2.63; (im-personal) it behoves, it is incumbent on LR 5.1.69 *for my state Stands on me to defend.* **stand out** Hold out R2 1.4.38 *Now for the rebels which stand out in Ireland.* **stand to 1** Uphold (authority) COR 3.1.207 *let us stand to our authority.* **2** Stand by (a person) COR 5.3.199 *Stand to me in this cause,* 2H4 2.1.64, 3H6 2.3.51. **3** Fall to, begin eating TMP 3.3.49 *I will stand to, and feed,* MAC 2.3.34. **stand to it 1** Make a stand COR 4.6.10 *We stood to't in good time,* AWW 2.1.29, 2H4 2.1.4. **2** Insist upon, maintain (a statement, assertion) AYL 1.2.65 *I'll stand to it, the pancakes were naught,* 1H4 3.3.162. **stand under** Be subject to H8 5.1.112 *There's none stands under more calumnious tongues Than I.* **stand up 1** Make a stand, rise up JC 2.1.167 *We all stand up against the spirit of Caesar,* COR 2.3.15, LR 3.7.80. **2**

Take one's stand as, claim to be ANT 1.1.40 *We stand up peerless*, CYM 5.4.54. **stand upon** See STAND ON. **stand with** Be consistent with AYL 2.4.91 *if it stand with honesty*, COR 2.3.85.

standard *n.*
1 Something upright or erect TMP 3.2.17 *he's no standard* (i.e. he cannot stand upright).
2 Standard-bearer TMP 3.2.16 *thou shalt be my lieutenant, monster, or my standard.*

standing *n.*
1 Continuance in existence, duration WT 1.2.431 *his folly...will continue The standing of his body* (i.e. while he lives).
2 Status, rank TIM 1.1.31 *How this grace Speaks his own standing.*
~ *ppl. adj.*
1 (of water) Still, not ebbing or flowing TMP 2.1.221 *I am standing water*, LR 3.4.133, TN 1.5.159.
2 Fixed, staring TIT 2.3.32 *my deadly standing eye.*
3 Having a support; (of a bed) having legs WIV 4.5.7 *his standing bed and truckle bed*; (of a bowl) resting on a foot or base PER 2.3.65 *we drink this standing bowl of wine to him*, H8 5.4.SD.
4 Sit on end, set in a vertical position 1H4 2.4.247 *you vile standing tuck.*

standing-bed See STANDING *ppl. adj.* sense 3.
standing-bowl See STANDING *ppl. adj.* sense 3.
staniel *n.* Inferior kind of hawk TN 2.5.113 *with what wing the staniel checks at it* (F1 *stallion*), TMP 2.2.172 (F1 *scamel*).
stanze *n.* Stanza LLL 4.2.104 *Let me hear a staff, a stanze, a verse* (F1, Q2; Ff 2–4 *stanza*).
stanzo *n.* (var. of) Stanza AYL 2.5.18 *Come, more, another stanzo*, AYL 2.5.19.
staple *n.* Fibre (of wool); (fig.) LLL 5.1.17 *He draweth out the thread of his verbosity finer than the staple of his argument.*
star *n.*
1 In astrology, used of the planets and zodiacal constellations as supposed to influence human affairs; (transf.) person's fortune, rank, position, condition, destiny, temperament, etc., viewed as determined by the stars TN 2.5.144 *In my stars I am above thee*, HAM 1.4.32; *out of thy star* above thee in position HAM 2.2.141.
2 *moist, watery star* The moon HAM 1.1.118 *the moist star*, WT 1.2.1 *the wat'ry star*; *seven stars* Pleiades or the Great Bear 1H4 1.2.14, 2H4 2.4.187, LR 1.5.35.
3 *Pole-star, lodestar* ADO 3.4.58 *there's no more sailing by the star*; (fig.) SON 116.7 *love...is the star to every wandering bark.*
4 Spot or mark resembling a star CYM 5.5.364 *Upon his neck a mole, a sanguine star.*
star-blasting *n.* Pernicious influence of malign stars LR 3.4.59 *Bless thee from whirlwinds, star-blasting.*
Star-chamber *n.* Court, chiefly of criminal jurisdiction; (attrib.) WIV 1.1.2 *I will make a Star-chamber matter of it.*
stare *n.* Condition of amazement indicated by staring TMP 3.3.94 *why stand you In this strange stare?* ~ *vb.* (of hair) Stand on end JC 4.3.280 *That mak'st...my hair to stare.*
stark *adj.* Rigid, stiff (in death) ROM 4.1.103 *Each part...Shall, stiff and stark and cold, appear like death*, CYM 4.2.209, 1H4 5.3.41.
~ *adv.* Completely, absolutely, utterly SHR 3.2.54 *stark spoiled with the staggers*, TN 3.4.251, ERR 2.1.59.
starkly *adv.* Rigidly, stiffly MM 4.2.67 *When it lies starkly in the traveller's bones.*
starred *ppl. adj.* Fated WT 3.2.99 *My third comfort (Starr'd most unluckily).*

start *n.*
1 Sudden journey, sudden flight or invasion MV 2.2.6 *use your legs, take the start, run away*, 2H6 4.8.43.
2 Sudden fit or impulse 1H4 3.2.125 *the start of spleen*, LR 1.1.300; *by, in starts* by fits and starts TN 2.2.21 *she did speak in starts distractedly*, H5 Epil.4, ANT 4.12.7; *on the start* when it suddenly appears AWW 3.2.50 *the first face of neither on the start Can woman me unto't.*
3 Advantage gained by starting first in a race or journey, etc. WIV 5.5.161 *You have the start of me*, JC 1.2.130.
~ *vb.*
1 Startle, alarm AWW 5.3.232 *every feather starts you*, MAC 5.5.15, TRO 5.2.101; disturb OTH 1.1.101 *dost thou come To start my quiet.*
2 Force an animal to leave its lair or resting place 1H4 1.3.198 *the blood more stirs To rouse a lion than to start a hare*; (transf.) rouse JC 1.2.147 *'Brutus' will start a spirit as soon as 'Caesar'*, JN 5.2.167, TN 4.1.59.
starting *ppl. adj.* Leaping, bounding, full of vigour TRO 4.5.2 *starting courage.*
starting-hole *n.* Place of refuge for a hunted animal; (fig.) subterfuge 1H4 2.4.263 *What trick? what device? what starting-hole?*
startingly *adv.* By fits and starts OTH 3.4.79 *Why do you speak so startingly and rash?*
startle *vb.* Start, be alarmed or shocked AYL 4.3.13 *Patience herself would startle at this letter*, R3 3.4.85 (F1 *started*); (trans.) alarm, shock JN 4.2.25 *startles and frights consideration*, PER 5.1.146, H8 3.2.294.
start-up *n.* Upstart ADO 1.3.66 *That young start-up hath all the glory.*
starve *vb.*
1 Die of cold CYM 1.4.167 *catch cold and starve.*
2 Nip with cold TGV 4.4.154 *The air hath starv'd the roses in her cheeks.*
3 Cause to wither or perish, disable, paralyse TIM 1.1.248 *Aches contract and starve your supple joints*, PER 1.4.38.
4 *starve out* Endure in perishing cold TRO 5.10.2 *Never go home; here starve we out the night.*
starved *ppl. adj.*
1 Benumbed with cold 2H6 3.1.343 *warm the starved snake*, TIT 3.1.251.
2 Hungry, famished MV 4.1.138 *thy desires Are wolvish, bloody, starv'd, and ravenous.*
3 Emaciated as with want of food, lean 2H4 3.2.304 *This same starv'd Justice*, 2H4 5.4.27; (fig.) feeble, miserable TRO 1.1.93 *It is too starv'd a subject for my sword.*
starve-lackey *n.* One who starves his lackeys or servants MM 4.3.14 *Master Starve-lackey the rapier and dagger man.*
state *n.*
1 Condition (of things) H8 2.4.214 *Bearing a state of mighty moment in't*, LR 2.2.169, JC 1.3.71; *the child of state* born of circumstances, merely accidental SON 124.1 *If my dear love were but the child of state.*
2 Condition in respect of worldly prosperity, fortune; (hence) estate, property MV 3.2.259 *When I told you My state was nothing*, WIV 3.4.5, 1H4 4.1.46.
3 Status or position in the world, degree, rank, (esp.) high rank or dignity; (hence) majesty, power TMP 1.2.76 *I...to my state grew stranger*, R3 3.7.205, MAC 4.2.66; (fig.) *the state of floods* the majesty of oceans 2H4 5.2.132.
4 (pl.) Persons of 'state' or rank CYM 3.4.37 *Kings, queens, and states*, JN 2.1.395, TIM 1.2.SD.
5 Outward display of one's condition, grandeur, dignity, pomp (of behaviour, equipment, furni-

ture) ADO 2.1.77 *a measure, full of state and ancien-*
try, 2H4 3.1.13, ROM 4.3.8; *keep...state* maintain a
position or demeanour of dignity LLL 5.2.594 *Keep*
some state in thy exit, JC 1.2.160, H5 1.2.273; *chair*
of state canopied chair, dais or throne for a king,
etc. H8 4.1.67 *a rich chair of state,* 3H6 1.1.51.
6 (short for) Chair of state (sense 5) TN 2.5.45 *sit-*
ting in my state, MAC 3.4.5, 1H4 2.4.378.
7 Assembly or body of the highest in rank or office
in a state or community; (hence) governing body,
government 2H4 5.2.142 *we will accite...all our*
state, COR 4.3.11, TRO 1.3.191.
8 Settled government, condition of order R2 4.1.225
Against the state and profit of this land.
9 Kingdom, commonwealth; (fig.) MAC 1.3.140
Shakes so my single state of man, JC 2.1.67.
10 Attitude, pose LLL 4.3.183 *A gait, a state.*
state-statue *n.* Mere image of a statesman H8 1.2.88
We should take root here where we sit, or sit State-
statues only.
station *n.* Manner of standing HAM 3.4.58 *A station*
like the herald Mercury, ANT 3.3.19.
statist *n.* Statesman CYM 2.4.16 *I do believe (Statist*
though I am none), HAM 5.2.33.
statua *n.* Statue JC 2.2.76 *she saw my statua,* JC
3.2.188, 2H6 3.2.80, R3 3.7.25.
▷ A spelling adopted in some mod. edd. for *statue*
in the above passages, where it requires a trisyl-
labic pronunciation (Ff, Qq *statues*).
statute *n.* Bond by which the creditor had the
power of holding the debtor's lands and goods in
case of default HAM 5.1.104 *a great buyer of land,*
with his statutes; (fig.) SON 134.9 *The statute of thy*
beauty thou wilt take.
statute-cap *n.* Woollen cap ordered by an act of
parliament of 1571 to be worn on Sundays and
holy days by all persons not of a certain social or
official rank LLL 5.2.281 *better wits have worn*
plain statute-caps.
staunch *vb.* See STANCH.
~ *adj.* Watertight; (hence) firm, firmly united ANT
2.2.115 *if I knew What hoop should hold us staunch*
from edge to edge.
staves See STAFF.
stay *n.*[1] Prop, support TRO 5.3.60 *if thou lose thy stay,*
JN 5.7.68, R3 2.2.74.
~ *vb.*[1] Prop, support, sustain R3 3.7.97 *Two*
*props...*To stay him, R3 1.4.19, JN 3.4.138.
stay *n.*[2]
1 Check, hindrance JN 2.1.455 *Here's a stay That*
shakes the rotten carcass of old Death Out of his
rags.
2 Continuance in a state SON 15.9 *the conceit of this*
inconstant stay.
~ *vb.*[2]
1 Stop R3 1.2.33 *Stay, you that bear the corse,* ROM
4.3.57, VEN 706; cease speaking ERR 5.1.365 *Stay,*
stand apart; I know not which is which, WIV 5.5.80;
(trans.) stop, cease WT 2.3.110 *That wilt not stay*
her tongue, ADO 3.3.79, TIT 3.1.192.
2 Delay (as opposed to going on), tarry, linger MM
1.4.86 *no longer staying but to give the mother No-*
tice, TGV 3.1.378, 3H6 2.5.135; (trans.) discontinue,
delay, withhold WT 1.2.9 *Stay your thanks a while,*
2H6 3.2.136.
3 Stand one's ground, stand firm 3H6 2.3.50 *give*
them leave to fly that will not stay; (trans.) stand
firm against, offer resistance to, meet the force of
ROM 1.1.212 *stay the siege of loving terms,* VEN 894,
JC 5.1.106.
4 Wait for, await TGV 2.2.13 *My father stays my*
coming, MND 2.1.235, JN 2.1.58; stay to make or
offer, remain to do (something) LLL 2.1.193 *I can-*
not stay thanksgiving, LLL 4.2.142.

5 Restrain, make to stay JC 2.2.75 *my wife, stays*
me at home, SHR 4.2.83, H8 1.1.5.
6 Allay strife, compose, bring under control LLL
3.1.98 *Until the goose came out of door, Staying the*
odds by adding four (with quibble on 'preventing
the odd number').
~ in combination
stay behind Fail to take part in (a venture), fail
to join (a person) COR 1.1.243 *Ere stay behind this*
business, AYL 1.1.110, TN 3.3.4; (absol.) ANT 3.7.19
I will not stay behind, JN 3.3.1, LR 3.6.101. **stay by**
Stand firm against, oppose COR 2.1.130 *and he had*
stay'd by him. **stay by it** Keep at it ANT 2.2.176
You stay'd well by't in Egypt. **stay for** Wait in a
place for, await the coming of TGV 3.1.373 *thy mas-*
ter stays for thee at the North-gate, MV 2.6.48, ERR
1.2.76. **stay on, upon** 1 Attend, wait upon MAC
1.3.148 *we stay upon your leisure,* TN 2.4.24, ANT
1.2.115. 2 Await MM 4.1.46 *I have a servant...that*
stays upon me, COR 5.4.8.
stead *n.* stand in little stead Be of little avail or
service 1H6 4.6.31 *The help of one stands me in little*
stead.
~ *vb.*
1 Avail, profit, help, be of use to, benefit OTH
1.3.339 *I could never better stead thee than now,*
TGV 2.1.113, AWW 3.7.41; (intr.) TMP 1.2.165 *neces-*
saries, Which since have steaded much.
2 stead up Take a person's place in (an arrangement) MM 3.1.250 *We shall advise this wrong'd*
maid to stead up your appointment.
steal *vb.* steal a marriage Get married secretly SHR
3.2.140 *'Twere good methinks to steal our marriage.*
stealing *ppl. adj.* Moving stealthily on R3 3.7.168 *the*
stealing hours of time, HAM 5.1.71.
stealth *n.*
1 Theft, stealing TIM 3.4.27 *And now ingratitude*
makes it worse than stealth, LR 3.4.93.
2 Secret or clandestine motion, stealing away
MND 3.2.310 *your stealth unto this wood,* TN
1.5.297, SON 77.7; (euphemistically) clandestine act
MM 1.2.154 *The stealth of our most mutual enter-*
tainment, LR 1.2.11.
steel *n.*
1 Metal of which arms and armour are made;
(hence, transf.) weapons (e.g., sword, axe) JC
3.2.177 *as he pluck'd his cursed steel away,* H8
2.1.76, R2 3.2.59; armour 3H6 1.1.58 *The hope thereof*
makes Clifford mourn in steel.
2 Emblem of hardness ANT 4.4.33 *a man of steel,*
TGV 1.1.141, VEN 199; (attrib.) SON 133.9 *thy steel*
bosom's ward.
~ *vb.*
1 (fig.) Make hard as steel, make unbending VEN
375 *O, give it me, lest thy hard heart do steel it,* R2
5.2.34, H5 4.1.289.
2 Engrave SON 24.1 *Mine eye hath play'd the*
painter and hath steel'd Thy beauty's form in table
of my heart.
steeled *ppl. adj.*
1 Made of steel 1H6 1.1.85 *my steeled coat;* strengthened as with steel 2H4 1.1.116 *from his metal was*
his party steeled.
2 (of a person, his attributes, etc.) Hardened like
steel, inflexible, callous MM 4.2.87 *the steeled*
gaoler, H5 2.2.36, SON 112.8.
steely *adj.* Made of steel 3H6 2.3.16 *the steely point*
of Clifford's lance; (fig.) with the strength of steel,
hard, unyielding AWW 1.1.103 *virtue's steely bones*
(i.e. uncompromised virtue).
steep *n.* Steep or precipitous place; (hence) mountain range MND 2.1.69 *the farthest steep of India.*
▷ Ff, Q2; Q1 *steppe.* See STEPPE.

steep-down *adj.* Precipitous OTH 5.2.280 *Wash me in steep-down gulfs of liquid fire!*

steep-up *adj.* Precipitous, perpendicular SON 7.5 *the steep-up heavenly hill*, LLL 4.1.2, PP 9.5.

steepy *adj.* Difficult to ascend TIM 1.1.75 *the steepy mount*; (fig.) SON 63.5 *age's steepy night*.

steerage *n.* Direction (of one's life, affairs), steering ROM 1.4.112 *He that hath the steerage of my course* (F1 *stirrage*), PER 4.4.19.

stell *vb.*
1 Fix, place LUC 1444 *a face where all distress is stell'd.*
2 Portray, delineate SON 24.1 *Mine eyes have play'd the painter and hath stell'd Thy beauty's form in table of my heart* (or perh. sense 1).
▷ Capell's emendation. Q1 *steel'd*. See STEEL *vb.* sense 2.

stelled *ppl. adj.* Fixed LR 3.7.61 *The sea...would have buoy'd up And quench'd the stelled fires* (i.e. the fixed stars).

stem *n.* Prow (of a ship) PER 4.1.63 *they skip From stem to stern*, COR 2.2.107.
~ *vb.* Make headway against, breast 3H6 2.6.36 *Command an argosy to stem the waves*, JC 1.2.109.

step-dame *n.* Stepmother MND 1.1.5 *Like to a step-dame, or a dowager*, TRO 3.2.194, CYM 1.6.1.

steppe *n.* (?) (1) Steppe, vast, treeless plain; or (2) step (in travel or exploration) MND 2.1.69 *the far-thest steppe of India* (i.e. in sense 2 the utmost limit in travel, the furthest one has been).
▷ Q1; Ff, Q2 *steepe*. See STEEP.

sterling *adj.*
1 Lawful, genuine English money or coin; (hence) of full value 2H4 2.1.120 *with sterling money*, HAM 1.3.107; *be sterling* pass current, have its full value R2 4.1.264 *if my word be sterling.*

stern *n.* Rudder; (fig.) that which guides or controls affairs 1H6 1.1.177 *sit at chiefest stern of public weal* (i.e. in a position of supreme control).

sternage *n.* The sterns of a fleet collectively H5 3.Ch.18 *Grapple your minds to sternage of this navy* (i.e. so as to follow the vessels in your mind's eye).

stew *n.*
1 House of prostitution, brothel CYM 1.6.152 *to mart As in a Romish stew*; (pl.) R2 5.3.16 *he would unto the stews*, 2H4 1.2.54.
2 Vessel in which things are boiled or stewed, stewpan, cauldron MM 5.1.319 *Where I have seen corruption boil and bubble Till it o'errun the stew* (perh. with play on sense 1).

stick *vb.*
1 (lit. and fig.) Stab TRO 3.2.195 *to stick the heart of falsehood*, TGV 1.1.102, AYL 1.2.242.
2 Be fixed *on* (a person) like an ornament COR 1.1.271 *Opinion that so sticks on Marcius*; (with *off*) stand out in relief, be prominent HAM 5.2.257 *Your skill shall like a star...Stick fiery off indeed.*
3 Hesitate (to do something) 2H4 1.2.22 *he will not stick to say his face is a face royal*, COR 2.3.16, SON 10.6.

sticking-place *n.* Place in which a thing stops and holds fast MAC 1.7.60 *screw your courage to the sticking-place.*

stickler-like *adj.* Like an umpire or arbitrator at a tournament, etc. TRO 5.8.18 *night...stickler-like the armies separates.*

stiff *adj.*
1 Stout COR 1.1.161 *stiff bats and clubs*; formidable, grave ANT 1.2.100 *This is stiff news.*
2 Unbending, obstinate LR 4.6.279 *how stiff is my vile sense*, COR 1.1.241.

stiff-borne *adj.* Obstinately carried out 2H4 1.1.177 *The stiff-borne action.*

stiffly *adv.* Strongly HAM 1.5.95 *bear me stiffly up.*

stigmatic *n.* Person marked or branded (by nature) with some physical deformity or blemish 3H6 2.2.136 *a foul misshapen stigmatic*, 2H6 5.1.215.

stigmatical *adj.* Marked or branded by nature with a deformity, deformed ERR 4.2.22 *Stigmatical in making, worse in mind.*

still *adj.*
1 Silent; (with *be*) OTH 5.2.46 *Peace, and be still!*, LLL 1.2.181, 1H4 3.1.239; (with *hold oneself*) ERR 4.2.17 *I cannot, nor I will not, hold me still*, ERR 3.2.69, SON 85.1.
2 *be still* Rest in peace JC 5.5.50 *Caesar, now be still.*
3 (of music) Soft AYL 5.4.SD *Still music.*
4 Constant, continual R3 4.4.230 *still use of grief*, TIT 3.2.45.
~ *adv.* Always, ever, continually ROM 5.3.270 *We still have known thee for a holy man*, TGV 2.1.11, HAM 2.2.42; *still and anon* constantly from time to time JN 4.1.47 *I...Still and anon cheer'd up the heavy time*; (corr. to) *still an end* TGV 4.4.62 *A slave, that still an end turns me to shame.*
▷ When qualifying an adj. or pple. used attrib., *still* in this adv. sense is sometimes hyphened e.g. R2 5.5.8 *still-breeding*, LUC 84 *still-gazing*, TMP 1.2.229 *still-vex'd* (i.e. constantly troubled).

stillitory *n.* Alembic, still VEN 443 *from the stillitory of thy face* (Q7 *stillatorie*).

stillness *n.* Silence MV 1.1.90 *a wilful stillness*; quietness of behaviour H5 3.1.4 *modest stillness and humility.*

still-peering *adj.* (?) (1) Always peering; or (2) look-ing on unmoved AWW 3.2.110 *the still-peering air.*
▷ F1; Ff 2-4 *still(-)piercing*; many conjectures; most popular is *still-piecing* (i.e. 'constantly clos-ing itself up again').

still-stand *n.* Stand of a tide, the period at high or low water when no movement is visible 2H4 2.3.64 *That makes a still-stand, running neither way.*

stilly *adv.* Softly H5 4.Ch.5 *The hum of either army stilly sounds.*

sting *n.* Sharp stimulus, incitement LC 265 *O most potential love! vow, bond, nor space In thee hath neither sting, knot, nor confine*; carnal impulse, sexual desire MM 1.4.59 *The wanton stings and motions of the sense*, AYL 2.7.66, OTH 1.3.331.

stint *n.* (?) Check, stay PER 1.2.25 *with the stint of war.*
▷ Ff 3-4, Qq; Tyrwhitt *th'ostent* (i.e. display).
~ *vb.*
1 Cause to cease, stop H8 1.2.76 *We must not stint Our necessary actions*, TIM 5.4.83, TIT 4.4.86.
2 (intr.) Cease PER 4.4.42 *swears she'll never stint*, ROM 1.3.48.

stir *n.*
1 Stirring, movement JC 1.3.127 *no stir or walking in the streets*, MAC 1.3.144.
2 Event, happening ANT 1.4.82 *stirs abroad.*
3 Mental agitation CYM 1.3.12 *the fits and stirs of 's mind*, VEN 283.
~ *vb.* Move, be active MAC 5.5.12 *my fell of hair Would...rouse and stir.*

stirring *ppl. adj.* Moving, active TRO 2.3.137 *A stir-ring dwarf.*

stith, stithy *n.* Anvil or forge HAM 3.2.84 *as foul As Vulcan's stithy* (Qq; Ff *Styth(e)*).
~ *vb.* Forge TRO 4.5.255 *the forge that stithied Mars his helm.*

stoccado *n.* Thrust in fencing WIV 2.1.226 *your pas-ses, stoccadoes.*

stock *n.*[1] STOCCADO WIV 2.3.26 *to see thee pass thy puncto, thy stock.*

stock *n.*[2]
1 Senseless person, blockhead SHR 1.1.31 *Let's be no stoics nor no stocks.*
2 Stocking TN 1.3.135 *in a dun-colour'd stock,* TGV 3.1.309, SHR 3.2.66.
3 Dowry TGV 3.1.309 *What need a man care for a stock with a wench.*
~ *vb.* Put in the stocks as a punishment LR 2.2.139 *Stocking his messenger* (Ff; Qq *stopping*), LR 2.4.188, LR 3.4.135 (Ff *stockt, punish'd*; Qq 1–2 *stock-punisht*).

stockfish *n.* Dried codfish MM 3.2.109 *he was begot between two stockfishes; make a stockfish of* beat, as stockfish was beaten before it was cooked TMP 3.2.70; (applied as a term of contempt to a person) 1H4 2.4.245 *you bull's pizzle, you stockfish.*

stockish *adj.* Resembling a stock or block of wood, blockish, unfeeling MV 5.1.81 *nought so stockish, hard, and full of rage.*

stock-punished *pa. pple.* Punished by being set in the stocks LR 3.4.135 *who is whipt…and stock-punish'd* (Qq 1–2; Ff *stockt, punish'd*).

stoic *n.* One who practises repression of emotion, severe or rigorous person SHR 1.1.31 *Let's be no stoics nor no stocks.*

stole *n.* Long robe LC 297 *my white stole of chastity.*

stolen *ppl. adj.* Furtive, secret ROM 5.3.233 *their stol'n marriage-day,* OTH 3.3.338.

stomach *n.*
1 Appetite, relish for food ERR 1.2.50 *You have no stomach, having broke your fast,* 1H4 2.3.41, CYM 3.6.32; (with play on sense 3) TGV 1.2.68 *That you might kill your stomach on your meat,* SHR 4.1.158.
2 Inclination, disposition SHR 1.1.38 *as you find your stomach serves you,* JC 5.1.66, AYL 3.2.21; (with *to*) TRO 3.3.220 *my little stomach to the war,* H5 4.3.35.
3 Resentment, angry temper 1H6 4.1.141 *their grudging stomachs,* TIT 3.1.233, LR 5.3.74.
4 Pride, arrogant spirit H8 4.2.34 *a man Of an unbounded stomach,* SHR 5.2.176.
5 Courage, valour TMP 1.2.157 *An undergoing stomach,* HAM 1.1.100, 2H4 1.1.129.
~ *vb.* Resent, be offended at ANT 3.4.12 *if you must believe, Stomach not all.*

stomacher *n.* Ornamental covering for the breast worn by women under the lacing of the bodice WT 4.4.224 *Golden quoifs and stomachers;* (fig.) CYM 3.4.84 *you shall no more Be stomachers to my heart.*

stomaching *n.* Resentment, bitterness ANT 2.2.9 *'Tis not a time For private stomaching.*

stone *n.*
1 Mirror of polished stone or crystal LR 5.3.263 *Lend me a looking-glass, If that her breath will mist or stain the stone.*
2 Symbol of hardness or insensibility TN 3.4.201 *I have said too much unto a heart of stone,* TGV 2.3.10, SON 94.3; (occas. pl.) LR 5.3.258 *you are men of stones,* R3 3.7.224.
3 Symbol of dumbness ANT 2.2.110 *your considerate stone.*
4 Thunderbolt OTH 5.2.234 *Are there no stones in heaven But what serves for the thunder,* CYM 5.5.240.
5 Testicle MND 5.1.181 *Curs'd be thy stones for thus deceiving me,* WIV 1.4.112, ROM 1.3.53.
~ *vb.* Make as hard as stone OTH 5.2.63 *thou dost stone my heart.*

stone-bow *n.* Cross-bow for shooting stones TN 2.5.46 *O, for a stone-bow, to hit him in the eye.*

stonish *vb.* Shock, dismay, bewilder HAM 3.2.328 *O wonderful son, that can so stonish a mother!* (Ff *astonish*), VEN 825.

stool *n.* Commode, privy; (applied to a person contemptuously) TRO 2.1.42 *thou stool for a witch.*

stoop See STOUP.

stoop *vb.*
1 (of a hawk or other bird of prey) Descend (from the pitch) swiftly on its prey, swoop CYM 5.4.116 *the holy eagle Stoop'd, as to foot us,* CYM 5.3.42, SHR 4.1.191; (fig.) H5 4.1.107 *when they stoop, they stoop with the like wing.*
2 Bow (the head or neck) R2 3.1.19 *stoop'd my neck under your injuries,* 2H4 Ind.32; (fig.) humiliate, submit 2H4 5.2.120 *stoop and humble my intents To your…directions,* MM 2.4.182.
~ *adj.* Stooping, bent LLL 4.3.87 *As upright as the cedar.—Stoop, I say, Her shoulder is with child.*

stop *n.*
1 (in horsemanship) Sudden check in a horse's 'career'; (fig.) MND 5.1.120 *He hath rid his prologue like a rough colt; he knows not the stop* (quibble with sense 3), CYM 5.3.40.
2 Pause in speaking OTH 3.3.120 *these stops of thine fright me,* R2 5.2.4.
3 Mark of punctuation MV 3.1.15 *Come, the full stop,* MND 5.1.120 (see sense 1).
4 (in music) Closing of a finger-hole or ventage in a wind instrument so as to alter the pitch 2H4 Ind.17 *a pipe…of so easy and so plain a stop* (i.e. easy to play on), HAM 3.2.71; (fig.) LUC 1124 *My restless discord loves no stops nor rests;* frets on the fingerboard of a stringed instrument used to regulate the pitch ADO 3.2.60 *his jesting spirit, which is now crept into a lute-string, and now govern'd by stops.*
5 Filling or closing up a hole or aperture 2H6 3.1.288 *A breach that craves a quick expedient stop!*
~ *vb.*
1 Fill up, close by filling, 'stop up' JN 3.4.32 *stop this gap of breath with fulsome dust,* AYL 4.1.163, H8 5.2.58.
2 Check the bleeding of (a wound); (hence) heal MV 4.1.258 *stop his wounds, lest he do bleed to death,* COR 4.5.86, R3 5.5.40.
3 Fill (the ears) *with* (sound) R2 2.1.17 *it is stopp'd with other flattering sounds,* 2H4 1.1.79.
~ in combination
stop in Shut in, keep in ERR 1.2.53 *Stop in your wind,* WIV 3.5.112, R3 1.4.38 (Ff; Qq *kept in*). **stop up** Put a stop to AWW 4.5.75 *stop up the displeasure he hath conceiv'd.*

stopple *vb.* Stop up, close as with a stopple, plug LR 5.3.156 *Shut your mouth, dame, Or with this paper shall I stopple it* (Q1; F1 *stop*).

store *n.*
1 *in store* Laid up as in a storehouse TIT 1.1.94 *O sacred receptacle of my joys…How many sons of mine hast thou in store!*
2 Fertility, increase SON 11.9 *those whom nature hath not made for store,* SON 14.12.
~ *vb.* 'Stock with people, populate' (Schmidt) H5 3.5.31 *To new store France with bastard warriors,* OTH 4.3.85.

stored *ppl. adj.*
1 Laid up in store, accumulated, hoarded LR 2.4.162 *All the stor'd vengeances of heaven.*
2 Stocked, furnished, provided with a store, full (of) JN 5.4.1 *so stor'd with friends,* COR 2.1.18, PER 1.1.77.

storehouse *n.* Burial place MAC 2.4.34 *The sacred storehouse of his predecessors And guardian of their bones.*

storm *vb.* Make a storm or commotion in; (fig.) trouble, vex, disturb LC 7 *Storming her world with sorrow's wind and rain.*

story *n.* Theme for mirth MM 1.4.30 *make me not your story.*
~ *vb.* Tell the story of, give an account of CYM

1.4.33 *story him in his own hearing*, Ven 1013, Luc 106.

stoup *n.* Measure for liquor, two quarts (approx. two litres) TN 2.3.14 *a stoup of wine* (F *stoope*), Ham 5.2.267, Oth 2.3.30 (F1 *stope*).

stout *adj.*
1 Valiant, brave, resolute 1H6 1.1.106 *the stout Lord Talbot*, 1H4 5.4.93, R3 1.3.339.
2 Strong Tmp 5.1.45 *Jove's stout oak*, Tim 4.3.33, Son 65.7.
3 Proud, haughty TN 2.5.170 *I will be strange, stout*, 2H6 1.1.187, Cor 3.2.78.

stoutly *adv.*
1 With a 'stout' heart, valiantly, resolutely, boldly 3H6 2.5.79 *Thou that so stoutly hath resisted me*, Oth 3.1.44, Luc 1209.
2 Strongly Oth 2.1.48 *His bark is stoutly timber'd.*

stoutness *n.* Obstinate pride Cor 3.2.127 *Thy dangerous stoutness*, Cor 5.6.26.

stover *n.* Fodder for cattle Tmp 4.1.63 *flat meads thatch'd with stover.*

straggler *n.* Rover, vagabond R3 5.3.327 *Let's whip these stragglers o'er the seas again.*

straight *adv.* Immediately, without delay Ant 4.12.3 *I'll bring thee word Straight how 'tis like to go*, Oth 4.1.57, MM 1.2.162.

straight-pight *adj.* Erect Cym 5.5.164 *straight-pight Minerva.*

strain *n.*[1]
1 Race, stock, lineage JC 5.1.59 *the noblest of thy strain*, H5 2.4.51, Tim 1.1.250.
2 Natural character, quality, or disposition Lr 5.3.40 *you have show'd today your valiant strain*, Cym 4.2.24.
3 Kind, class, sort (of person) as determined by community of character, conduct, etc. Wiv 3.3.186 *I would all of the same strain were in the same distress.*

strain *n.*[2]
1 Strong impulse or motion of the mind, high-pitched feeling or emotion LLL 5.2.760 *love is full of unbefitting strains*, 2H4 4.5.170, Son 90.13.
2 Particular tendency or disposition Wiv 2.1.87 *unless he know some strain in me*, Tim 4.3.213.
3 *make no strain but that* Have no difficulty in believing that Tro 1.3.326.
4 Musical note or phrase, melody, tune JC 4.3.257 *touch thy instrument a strain or two*, AYL 4.3.68, Luc 1131.
~ *vb.*
1 Embrace H8 4.1.46 *when he strains that lady.*
2 Exert to the utmost Tim 5.1.227 *strain what other means is left unto us*, Ado 4.1.252, 1H6 1.5.10; (intr.) exert oneself Tim 1.1.143 *To build his fortune I will strain a little.*
3 Press, urge Oth 3.3.250 *if your lady strain his entertainment.*
4 Force, constrain Rom 2.3.19 *Nor aught so good but, strain'd from that fair use, Revolts from true birth*, Rom 4.1.47, Jn 3.3.46.
5 Exceed bounds WT 3.2.50 *With what encounter so uncurrent I Have strain'd, to appear thus; strain too far* put an exaggerated construction on matters 1H4 4.1.75.
6 Extract (liquor or juice) by pressure, squeeze out; (fig.) MV 4.1.184 *The quality of mercy is not strain'd.*
7 *strain courtesy* (1) Be punctiliously polite, stand upon ceremony, refuse to go first Ven 888 *They all strain courtesy who shall cope him first*; (2) act with less than due courtesy Rom 2.4.50 *in such a case as mine a man may strain courtesy.*
8 *strain at* Find difficulty in Tro 3.3.112 *I do not strain at the position.*

strained *ppl. adj.*
1 Excessive 2H4 1.1.161 *This strained passion doth you wrong*, Lr 1.1.169.
2 Purified as by filtering Tro 4.4.24 *so strain'd a purity* (Ff *strange*).
3 Forced, constrained Son 82.10 *What strained touches rhetoric can lend.*

strait *n.* Narrow way or path Tro 3.3.154 *honour travels in a strait so narrow.*
~ *vb.* (pass.) Be put in 'straits' or difficulties, be hard put to it, be at a loss WT 4.4.354 *you were straited For a reply.*
~ *adj.*
1 Narrow Cym 5.3.7 *a strait lane*, Cym 5.3.11.
2 Tight-fitting H5 3.7.54 *strait strossers.*
3 Strict MM 2.1.9 *most strait in virtue*, 1H4 4.3.79, 2H6 3.2.258; exacting Tim 1.1.96 *his creditors most strait.*
4 Niggardly, close Jn 5.7.42 *you are so strait And so ingrateful.*
~ *adv.* Severely oppressively 2H6 3.2.20 *Proceed no straiter 'gainst our uncle.*

straitly *adv.* Strictly R3 1.1.85 *hath straitly given in charge*, R3 4.1.17 (Ff *strictly*).

straitness *n.* Strictness MM 3.2.255 *the straitness of his proceeding.*

strange *adj.*
1 Belonging to another country, foreign LLL 4.2.130 *one of the strange queen's lords*, AYL 4.1.34, H8 3.1.45.
2 Belonging to another person or place, not one's own Son 53.2 *millions of strange shadows on you tend*, Ado 5.4.49, Cym 1.4.89.
3 Not known, used or experienced before, new, fresh LLL 5.1.6 *learned without opinion, and strange without heresy*, R2 5.5.66, Mac 1.3.145.
4 Not knowing, ignorant, unacquainted Tim 4.3.57 *in thy fortunes am unlearn'd and strange*, Tro 3.3.12; *strange to, unto* ignorant of Err 2.2.149 *As strange unto your town as to your talk*, Mac 3.4.111; *look strange (on)*, *put a strange face on* pretend unfamiliarity (with) Err 5.1.296 *Why look you strange on me?* (perh. also sense 5), Ado 2.3.47 *put a strange face on his own perfection*, Son 89.8; *make it strange* seem to be surprised or shocked Tit 2.1.81, TGV 1.2.99.
5 Estranged, not familiar, distant, (passing into the sense) shy, reserved, reluctant TN 5.1.212 *You throw a strange regard upon me*, Rom 3.2.15, JC 1.2.35.
6 Out of the common, remarkable, rare Ham 1.5.28 *most foul, strange, and unnatural*, Tmp 3.3.87, Cym 1.5.34.
~ *adv.* In a way that is unusual, remarkably, surprisingly Ham 1.5.170 *How strange or odd some'er I bear myself.*
~ *in combination*
strange-achieved Gained (?) (1) in foreign lands; or (2) by exceptional and hence wrong means; or (3) for the enjoyment of others 2H4 4.5.71 *The cank'red heaps of strange-achieved gold.* **strange-disposed** Of extraordinary character JC 1.3.33 *it is a strange-disposed time.*

strangely *adv.*
1 As a foreigner, as belonging to another country WT 2.3.182 *That thou commend it strangely to some place.*
2 As one who is or pretends to be a stranger, in a distant or reserved manner Son 49.5 *strangely pass, And scarcely greet me*, 2H4 5.2.63, H8 3.2.11.
3 In an uncommon or exceptional degree, extra-ordinarily, oddly, extremely Tmp 4.1.7 *thou Hast strangely stood the test*, Mac 4.3.150, Ado 3.2.132.

strangely-visited *adj.* Afflicted with disease Mac

4.3.150 *strangely-visited people All swoll'n and ulcerous.*

strangeness *n.* Absence of friendly feeling, distant behaviour, reserve TN 4.1.15 *ungird thy strangeness*, OTH 3.3.12, 2H6 3.1.5.

stranger *n.* One belonging to another country, foreigner ERR 4.2.9 *Then swore he that he was a stranger here*, H8 2.3.17, OTH 1.1.136.
~ *adj.*
1 Belonging to another country, foreign JN 5.1.11 *stranger blood*, LLL 4.2.139, R2 1.3.143.
2 Belonging to another person or place, not one's own MV 1.3.118 *And foot me as you spurn a stranger cur.*
3 Belonging to those not known, not familiar LUC 99 *she that never cop'd with stranger eyes.*

strangered *ppl. adj.* Made a stranger, estranged, alienated LR 1.1.204 *stranger'd with our oath.*

strangle *vb.* (fig.) Suppress, stifle, efface TN 5.1.147 *makes thee strangle thy propriety* (i.e. disown your identity), WT 4.4.47, SON 89.8.

strappado *n.* Form of punishment or of torture to extort confession in which the victim's hands were tied across his back and secured to a pulley; he was then hoisted from the ground and let down half way with a jerk 1H4 2.4.237 *and I were at the strappado, or all the racks in the world.*

stratagem *n.* Deed of great violence MV 5.1.85 *treasons, stratagems, and spoils*, 3H6 2.5.89, ROM 3.5.209.

straw *n.*
1 Symbol of something of small value, trifle WT 3.2.110 *I prize it not a straw*, JN 3.4.128, HAM 4.4.26.
2 *wisp of straw* Badge of disgrace for an immodest woman or scold 3H6 2.2.144 *A wisp of straw were worth a thousand crowns To make this shameless callet know herself.*

strawy *adj.* Like straw TRO 5.5.24 *the strawy Greeks* (Ff *straying*).

stray *n.*
1 Animal found wandering out of bounds H5 1.2.160 *impounded as a stray The King of Scots*; (fig.) vagabond 2H6 4.10.25 *Here's the lord of the soil come to seize me for a stray, for entering his fee-simple without leave*; (collect.) stragglers 2H4 4.2.120 *pursue the scatter'd stray.*
2 Act of straying LR 1.1.209 *I would not from your love make such a stray* (i.e. go so far away).
~ *vb.* Lead astray ERR 5.1.51 *his eye Stray'd his affection in unlawful love.*

strayed *ppl. adj.* That has gone astray, 'passing due bounds' (Johnson) LR 1.1.169 *strayed pride* (Qq; Ff *strain'd*).

straying *ppl. adj.* Wandering LLL 5.2.763 *like the eye, Full of straying shapes.*

streak *vb.* Rub or smear (a surface) *with* (some liquid substance) MND 2.1.257 *with the juice of this I'll streak her eyes.*

strength *n.*
1 *of strength* Strong TRO 5.2.113 *A proof of strength she could not publish more* (i.e. a stronger proof), 1H6 3.4.7.
2 Force, vehemence, intensity 1H4 1.3.25 *with such strength denied*, ANT 3.2.62, MV 5.1.198.
3 *in (the) strength of* With the full force or authority of COR 3.3.14 *I' th' right and strength a' th' commons*, LR 2.1.112, JC 3.1.174.
4 Armed force, army JN 2.1.388 *dissever your united strengths*, ANT 2.1.17, 1H6 4.1.73.

stretch *vb.*
1 Open wide H5 2.2.55 *stretch our eye*, H5 3.1.15, 2H6 3.2.171.
2 Strain to the utmost JC 4.1.44 *Our best friends*

made, our best means stretch'd, LR 2.2.104, PER 5.1.55.
3 Be protracted ANT 1.1.46 *There's not a minute of our lives should stretch Without some pleasure now.*

stretched *ppl. adj.* Strained, forced, affected TRO 1.3.156 *'Twixt his stretch'd footing and the scaffoldage*, SON 17.12.

stretch-mouthed *adj.* Wide-mouthed; (hence) of coarse speech, foul-mouthed WT 4.4.196 *where some stretch-mouth'd rascal would...mean mischief.*

strewing *n.* (pl.) Flowers (etc.) strewn on a grave CYM 4.2.285 *strewings fitt'st for graves.*

strewment *n.* (pl.) Flowers (etc.) strewn on a grave HAM 5.1.233 *Her maiden strewments.*

strict *adj.*
1 Close, tight VEN 874 *their strict embrace.*
2 Restricted in amount, narrow CYM 5.4.17 *take No stricter render of me than my all.*
3 Harsh, cruel PER 3.3.8 *the strict fates.*

stricture *n.* Strictness MM 1.3.12 *a man of stricture and firm abstinence.*

stride *vb.*
1 Step over (with a stride) CYM 3.3.35 *a debtor that not dares To stride a limit* (i.e. 'overpass his bound' Johnson).
2 Bestride COR 1.9.71 *I mean to stride your horse*, MAC 1.7.22.

strife *n.*
1 Striving, endeavour MM 3.2.232 *One, that above all other strifes, contended especially to know himself*, AWW Epil.4, ROM 2.2.152 (Q5 *suit*).
2 Emulation TIM 1.1.37 *Artificial strife Lives in these touches, livelier than life*, LUC 1377.

strike *vb.*
1 Blast, destroy by malign influence WT 1.2.201 *It is a bawdy planet, that will strike Where 'tis predominant*, COR 2.2.113, HAM 1.1.162.
2 Lower or take in sail R2 2.1.266 *We see the wind sit sore upon our sails And yet we strike not*; (as sign of surrender or deference) ANT 4.2.8 *I'll strike, and cry, 'Take all!'*, 3H6 5.1.52; (trans., fig.) 2H4 5.2.18 *strike sail to spirits of vile sort*, 3H6 3.3.5.
3 Strike up WT 5.3.98 *Music! awake her! strike!*, TIM 5.4.85, LR 5.3.81; (trans.) R3 4.4.149 *Strike alarum, drums!*, TRO 5.10.30, COR 2.2.76.
4 Fight (a battle) H5 2.4.54 *When Cressy battle fatally was struck.*
5 Tap (a cask) ANT 2.7.97 *Strike the vessels.*
~ *in combination*
strike away, off Cross out (a score); (fig.) blot out, efface, cancel (an obligation) TRO 3.3.29 *her presence Shall quite strike off all service I have done*, OTH 3.4.179, AWW 5.3.56.

striker *n.* Footpad, robber, pickpocket 1H4 2.1.74 *no long-staff sixpenny strikers* (i.e. robbers who will knock a man down for sixpence).

string *n.* Tendon, nerve, etc. JN 5.7.55 *My heart hath one poor string to stay it by*, ANT 3.11.57, HAM 3.3.70; *strings of life* heart-strings LR 5.3.217.

stroke *n.*
1 Striking of a clock R3 3.2.5 *Upon the stroke of four*, R3 4.2.122; *keep the stroke* keep on striking R3 4.2.114.
2 Fighting (of a battle) CYM 5.5.468 *the stroke Of this scarce-cold battle.*

strond *n.* Strand, sea-shore 1H4 1.1.4 *broils To be commenc'd in stronds afar remote*, MV 1.1.171, SHR 1.1.170.

strong *adj.*
1 Resolute, determined R2 5.3.59 *heinous, strong, and bold conspiracy*, TIM 4.3.46, LR 2.1.77 (F1 *strange*).

2 Certain, powerful to demonstrate, hard to confute PER 2.4.34 *Whose death indeed the strongest in our censure* (i.e. of whose death we are most strongly convinced), AWW 4.3.55.
3 *hold strong* Hold firmly by JC 5.1.76 *You know that I held Epicurus strong, And his opinion.*
strong-besieged *adj.* Hard pressed by siege LUC 1429 *strong-besieged Troy.*
strong-bonded *adj.* Conveying a strong obligation LC 279 *strong-bonded oath.*
strossers *n.* Breeches H5 3.7.54 *your French hose off, and in your strait strossers.*
strow (var. of) STREW.
stroy, 'stroy *vb.* (aphetic form of) Destroy ANT 3.11.54 *what I have left behind 'Stroy'd in dishonour.*
struck *ppl. adj.*
1 Wounded 1H4 4.2.19 *a struck fowl.*
2 Stricken R3 1.1.92 *Well struck in years* (i.e. of advanced age), SHR 2.1.360.
strumpet *n.* Unchaste woman, harlot, prostitute OTH 5.1.122 *I am no strumpet, but of life as honest...,* ERR 4.4.124, WT 3.2.102; (attrib.) MV 2.6.16 *the strumpet wind,* JN 3.1.61, HAM 2.2.493.
~ *vb.* Bring to the condition of a strumpet SON 66.6 *maiden virtue rudely strumpeted,* ERR 2.2.144.
strung *pa. pple.* Furnished or fitted with strings TGV 3.2.77 *Orpheus' lute was strung with poets' sinews,* LLL 4.3.340.
stubborn *adj.*
1 (of physical objects) Stiff, inflexible HAM 3.3.70 *stubborn knees,* TRO 3.1.150, H8 5.2.58.
2 Harsh, rude, rough TN 5.1.361 *some stubborn and uncourteous parts,* LR 2.2.126, 2H6 3.1.360; (of verse) rugged LLL 4.3.53 *these stubborn lines lack power to move.*
3 Ruthless, implacable, insensitive MV 4.1.32 *pluck commiseration...from stubborn Turks and Tartars,* TRO 5.2.131, MM 5.1.480.
stubbornness *n.* Roughness, harshness AYL 2.1.19 *That can translate the stubbornness of fortune Into so quiet and so sweet a style,* OTH 4.3.20.
stuck *n.* STOCCADO, thrust in fencing HAM 4.7.161 *your venom'd stuck,* TN 3.4.275.
studied *ppl. adj.*
1 Versed, practised (as in a part to be played) MV 2.2.196 *well studied in a sad ostent To please his grandam,* MAC 1.4.9.
2 Diligent H8 3.2.168 *My studied purposes.*
3 Inclined 2H4 2.2.8 *so loosely studied as to remember so weak a composition,* ANT 2.6.47.
studious *adj.* Diligent 1H6 2.5.97 *be wary in thy studious care.*
studiously *adv.* Carefully 1H6 3.1.2 *written pamphlets studiously devis'd.*
study *n.*
1 Solicitous endeavour, diligence LR 1.1.276 *Let your study Be to content your lord,* H8 5.2.69, AYL 5.2.79.
2 Getting up a part MND 1.2.67 *slow of study.*
~ *vb.*
1 (intr.) Think carefully, dwell in thought, be intent (*upon* something), take thought (*for* something) MM 2.4.7 *The state, whereon I studied,* ANT 5.2.10, 2H6 1.1.90.
2 (trans.) Think carefully about, meditate upon, devise R3 1.2.257 *To study fashions to adorn my body,* TGV 3.1.244; (with infin. or clause) LLL 1.1.61 *to study where I well may dine,* 1H6 3.1.110, 2H6 3.1.111; wonder *how* R2 5.5.1 *I have been studying how I may compare This.*
3 Learn by heart, con, get up HAM 2.2.541 *study a speech of some dozen lines,* AYL 3.2.274, TN 1.5.178.
4 Arrive at, work out by studious application LLL

1.2.53 *how easy it is to put 'years' to the word 'three', and study three years in two words.*
stuff *n.* Matter (of thought) HAM 2.2.311 *there was no such stuff in my thoughts.*
~ *vb.*
1 (fig.) Distend, expand (as if by padding) JN 3.4.97 *Grief...Stuffs out his vacant garments with his form.*
2 Fill out, complete LR 3.5.21 *it will stuff his suspicion more fully;* (with *up*) LUC 297 *his servile powers, Who...Stuff up his lust.*
stuffed *ppl. adj.*
1 Full ADO 1.1.58 *a stuff'd man* (viz., with eating); (fig.) WT 2.1.185 *stuff'd sufficiency;* (with *with*) full of ADO 1.1.56 *stuff'd with all honourable virtues,* ROM 3.5.181.
2 Stopped up, obstructed; (hence) having a heavy cold ADO 3.4.64 *I am stuff'd, cousin, I cannot smell;* (fig.) MAC 5.3.44 *with some sweet oblivious antidote Cleanse the stuff'd bosom.*
stumbling *ppl. adj.* Causing stumbling JN 5.5.18 *The stumbling night.*
stuprum [L.] Violation, rape TIT 4.1.78.
sturdy *adj.* Intractable, disobedient 3H6 1.1.50 *the sturdy rebel.*
sty *n.* (fig.) Place of bestial lust or of moral pollution HAM 3.4.94 *making love Over the nasty sty,* PER 4.6.97.
~ *vb.* Coop up as in a sty TMP 1.2.342 *here you sty me In this hard rock.*
style *n.* Title 1H6 4.7.72 *Here's a silly stately style indeed!,* AWW 2.3.195, 2H6 1.1.111.
sub-contracted *adj.* Bethrothed for the second time LR 5.3.86 *'Tis she is sub-contracted to this lord.*
subdue *vb.*
1 Make subject to punishment COR 1.1.175 *him ...whose offence subdues him.*
2 Bring to a low state, reduce LR 3.4.70 *nothing could have subdu'd nature To such a lowness but his unkind daughters.*
3 Make subject, subservient *to* ANT 4.14.74 *his face subdu'd To penetrative shame,* TMP 1.2.490, OTH 1.3.250.
subdued *ppl. adj.* Overcome OTH 5.2.348 *one whose subdu'd eyes...Drops tears* (i.e. overcome by grief).
subduement *n.* Conquest TRO 4.5.187 *Despising many forfeits and subduements.*
subject *n.*
1 People or subjects of a state (collectively) MM 3.2.136 *the greater file of the subject,* WT 1.1.39, HAM 1.2.33; (fig.) PER 2.1.48 *the finny subject of the sea.*
2 Creature, object COR 2.1.85 *such ridiculous subjects as you are,* ROM 3.5.210.
3 Something having an independent existence MM 5.1.453 *Thoughts are no subjects.*
subjected *ppl. adj.* Belonging to a subject, owed by a subject, submissive JN 1.1.264 *Needs must you lay your heart at his dispose, Subjected tribute to commanding love.*
subjection *n.* Submission, obedience, homage, obligation of a subject CYM 4.3.19 *he's true and shall perform All parts of his subjection loyally,* JN 5.7.105, H5 4.1.146.
submission *n.* Acknowledgement or admission of fault 1H4 3.2.28 *Find pardon on my true submission,* WIV 4.4.11, ROM 3.1.73.
submit *vb.* Expose (oneself to risk, etc.) JC 1.3.47 *I have walk'd...Submitting me unto the perilous night.*
suborn *vb.* Procure (a person) to do an evil action, bribe ERR 4.4.82 *Thou hast suborn'd the goldsmith to arrest me,* R3 4.3.4, MAC 2.4.24.
subornation *n.* Act of procuring or inducing a person to do an evil action by bribery, corruption,

etc. 1H4 1.3.163 *murderous subornation* (i.e. secret prompting to murder), 2H6 3.1.45, Luc 919.

suborned *ppl. adj.* Bribed or unlawfully procured to make false accusations Son 125.13 *Hence, thou suborn'd informer!*

subscribe *vb.*
1 Sign (one's name) LLL 1.1.19 *subscribe your names*; put (one) down for R2 1.4.50 *They shall subscribe them for large sums of gold*; (intr.) sign one's name Ant 4.5.14 *Write to him (I will subscribe)*.
2 Admit, acknowledge, assent to MM 2.4.89 *As I subscribe not that*, Ado 5.2.58, Tro 2.3.147; (intr.) admit one's inferiority or error 1H6 2.4.44 *If I have fewest, I will subscribe in silence*, 2H6 3.1.38.
3 Surrender, yield Lr 1.2.24 *subscrib'd his power* (Q; F *prescrib'd*); (intr.) yield, give in (to feelings of pity) Lr 3.7.65 *All cruels else subscribe* (F; Q *subscrib'd*).
~ in combination
subscribe for 1 Make an undertaking on behalf of Ado 1.1.41 *my uncle's fool...subscrib'd for Cupid.*
2 Answer for, vouch for (a person) AWW 3.6.83 *I know th' art valiant, and to the possibility of thy soldiership will subscribe for thee*, AWW 4.5.32.
subscribe to 1 Sign one's name to an undertaking, give full assent to LLL 1.1.23 *Subscribe to your deep oaths*, Per 2.5.69. 2 Acknowledge, admit AWW 5.3.96 *when I had subscrib'd To mine own fortune*, TGV 5.4.145. 3 Yield to, submit to Tro 4.5.105 *Hector in his blaze of wrath subscribes To tender objects*, Shr 1.1.81, Tit 4.2.130.

subscription *n.* Submission Lr 3.2.18 *You owe me no subscription.*

substance *n.*
1 Form, shape Mac 1.5.49 *sightless substances* (i.e. invisible forms); (hence) creature, being Per 2.1.3 *Wind, rain,...remember earthly man Is but a substance that must yield to you*, Lr 1.1.198.
2 Great wealth Tro 1.3.324 *the purpose is perspicuous as substance.*
3 *in the substance* In the mass or gross weight MV 4.1.328.

substitute *n.* Deputy, representative Oth 1.3.223 *we have there a substitute of most allow'd sufficiency*, MM 5.1.140, MV 5.1.94; *by substitute* by proxy R3 3.7.181.
~ *vb.* Delegate (to the position of leader) 2H4 1.3.84 *who is substituted against the French, I have no certain notice.*

substitution *n. out o' th' substitution* In consequence of being my deputy Tmp 1.2.103 *he did believe He was indeed the Duke, out o' th' substitution.*

substractor *n.* (perversion of) Detractor TN 1.3.34 *they are scoundrels and substractors that say so of him.*

subtle, subtil(e) *adj.*
1 Treacherously cunning, insidiously sly 1H4 1.3.169 *this subtle king*, TGV 4.2.95, TN 1.5.297; having a treacherous influence Tim 4.3.429 *the subtle blood o' th' grape.*
2 Fine, delicate; (fig.) Tmp 2.1.42 *of subtle, tender, and delicate temperance*, Tro 3.2.24 (some mod. edd. *subtle-potent*), Tro 5.2.151.
3 (of ground) Deceptively smooth, tricky Cor 5.2.20 *a bowl upon a subtle ground.*

subtlety *n.* Illusion Tmp 5.1.124 *You do yet taste Some subtleties o' th' isle.*
◇ Perh. with ref. to the use of *subtlety* in cookery for a fantastically decorated piece of pastry or confectionery.

subtle-witted *adj.* Crafty, treacherously cunning

1H6 1.1.25 *the subtle-witted French Conjurers and sorcerers.*

subtly, subtilly *adv.* Treacherously, deceitfully H5 4.1.258 *thou proud dream, That play'st so subtly with a king's repose*, Rom 4.3.25, Tro 3.3.232.

suburbs *n.* (pl.) Outskirts of a city; (esp.) area of inferior, debased, and licentious habits of life JC 2.1.285 *Dwell I but in the suburbs Of your good pleasure?*
◇ In S.'s time the area where brothels were to be found.

subvert *vb.* Destroy, raze to the ground 1H6 2.3.65 *Razeth your cities, and subverts your towns.*

succeed *vb.*
1 Follow 2H6 2.4.2 *after summer evermore succeeds Barren winter*, H8 5.4.23, Oth 2.1.193; (trans.) Per 1.4.104 *The curse of heaven and men succeed their evils!*; come to pass Lr 1.2.143 *the effects he writes of succeed unhappily.*
2 'Succeed to', inherit MM 2.4.123 *Owe and succeed thy weakness.*
3 Come down by inheritance, devolve *on* Oth 5.2.367 *seize upon the fortunes of the Moor, For they succeed on you* (Qq *to you*), AWW 3.7.23; (fig.) Per 1.1.114 *hope, succeeding from so fair a tree As your fair self.*

succeeding *n.* Consequence AWW 2.3.191 *bloody succeeding.*

success *n.*
1 Succession, descent as from father to son WT 1.2.394 *our parents' noble names, In whose success we are gentle*, 2H4 4.2.47.
2 What follows as the result of action or in the course of events, issue, result, fortune (good or bad) Ant 3.5.6 *what is the success?*, Oth 3.3.222, TGV 1.1.58.
3 *of success* Successful AWW 4.3.86 *an abstract of success.*

successantly *adv.* Following after another, in succession Tit 4.4.113 *Then go successantly, and plead to him.*
◇ Capell *incessantly.*

successfully *adv. look successfully* Seem likely to succeed AYL 1.2.153 *yet he looks successfully.*

succession *n.*
1 Following in another's steps AWW 3.5.23 *example...cannot for all that dissuade succession.*
2 Futurity, the future Err 3.1.105 *slander lives upon succession*, Ham 2.2.351.
3 Successors or heirs collectively Cym 3.1.8 *for him And his succession granted Rome a tribute*, Cym 3.3.102.
4 *to the succession of new days* From one day to the next Tim 2.2.20 *he hath put me off To the succession of new days this month.*

successive *adj.*
1 *successive heir* Heir by succession 2H6 3.1.49, Son 127.3.
2 *successive title* Title to the succession Tit 1.1.4.

successively *adv.* By right of succession R3 3.7.135 *as successively, from blood to blood*, 2H4 4.5.201.

successor *n.* Descendant Wiv 1.1.14 *All his successors (gone before him)*, H8 1.1.60.

succour *n.* Reinforcements H5 3.3.45 *The Dauphin, whom of succours we entreated.*

such *adj.*
1 *no such* No very great Ant 3.3.41 *by him, This creature's no such thing.*
2 *such another* (used pleonastically for) (1) Such (a), such a one, one of that kind TGV 3.1.133 *I'll get me one of such another length*, Ado 3.4.87; (2) (often with contempt) 'a real one', so-and-so Tro 1.2.271 *You are such another!* (F; Q *such a*), Oth

4.1.146; (3) another, a second OTH 5.2.344 *such an other world*, WIV 1.4.150.

sudden *n.* **on the, a sudden** Suddenly ROM 2.3.50 *Where on a sudden one hath wounded me*, COR 2.1.221, ANT 1.2.82; (with *upon*) COR 1.4.50 *who upon the sudden Clapp'd to their gates*; (with *of*) TIT 1.1.393 *the…Queen…Is of a sudden thus advanc'd*, SHR 1.1.147.

~ *adj.*

1 Not prepared, not provided for JN 5.6.26 *that you might The better arm you to the sudden time.*

2 (of speech) Extempore 1H6 3.1.6 *sudden, and extemporal speech*, H8 5.2.157.

3 Swift, speedy in a 'ion, hasty AYL 5.2.6 *my sudden wooing*, JN 4.1.27, JC 3.1.19.

4 Happening or performed immediately, immediate, very early OTH 4.2.189 *expectations…of sudden respect*, MM 2.2.83, HAM 5.2.46.

5 Impetuous, violent AYL 2.7.151 *sudden, and quick in quarrel*, MAC 4.3.59, OTH 2.1.272; (of storms) R2 2.1.35 *sudden storms are short*, 2H4 4.4.34.

6 Rash COR 2.3.251 *revoke Your sudden approbation.*

~ *adv.* Rashly LLL 2.1.107 *too sudden bold.*

suddenly *adv.*

1 Without preparation or premeditation, extempore H8 3.1.70 *to make ye suddenly an answer*, 1H6 3.1.5, 2H6 2.1.127.

2 Immediately, at once, without delay WIV 4.1.6 *desires you to come suddenly*, AYL 2.4.100, 1H4 1.3.294.

sue *vb.*

1 Beg, entreat, petition ANT 1.3.33 *When you sued staying* (i.e. begged to stay), TIM 3.5.94, WIV 2.2.164; (intr.) R3 4.4.94 *Who sues, and kneels, and says, 'God save the Queen'?*, 3H6 3.2.61, LR 1.1.30.

2 Make legal claim to SON 134.11 *that put'st forth all to use, And sue a friend came debtor for my sake*; (intr.) LLL 5.2.427 *how can this be true, That you stand forfeit, being those that sue?* (with play on the general sense), 2H6 1.3.39.

▷ **sue one's livery** R2 2.1.203, 1H4 4.3.62: see LIVERY.

3 Move for (a writ); (hence) enforce H8 3.2.341 *That therefore such a writ be sued against you.*

4 Woo, court LLL 3.1.189 *I love, I sue, I seek a wife*; be a suitor to TGV 2.1.137 *My master sues to her.*

suffer *vb.*

1 Allow, permit MND 3.2.327 *Why will you suffer her to flout me thus?*, TIT 4.4.83, PER 5.1.78.

2 'Acquiesce, put up with anything' (Schmidt) OTH 5.2.256 *Thou hast no weapon, and perforce must suffer*; (trans.) endure LR 3.4.148 *my duty cannot suffer T'obey…your daughters'…commands*, MV 4.1.12, TMP 3.2.37.

3 (pass.) Be allowed full liberty or scope, not be checked LR 1.2.51 *not as it hath power, but as it is suffer'd*, 2H6 3.2.262, 2H4 2.3.57; (of a fire) 3H6 4.8.8 *A little fire is quickly trodden out, Which being suffer'd, rivers cannot quench*, VEN 388.

4 Sustain loss, injury or damage, be abused TIM 1.1.165 *your jewel Hath suffer'd under praise*, SON 124.6, PER 4.4.23; (trans.) HAM 5.2.112 *his definement suffers no perdition in you.*

5 Inflict pain on 2H6 5.1.153 *being suffer'd, with the bear's fell paw.*

6 'Suffer death'; (hence gen.) perish MAC 3.2.16 *But let…both the worlds suffer*, TMP 2.2.36, MM 2.2.107.

sufferance *n.*

1 Permission, esp. allowing things to take their course without check or opposition H5 2.2.46 *by his sufferance* (i.e. by neglecting to punish him), AYL 2.2.3, 3H6 1.1.234.

2 Forbearance, endurance COR 3.1.24 *Against all noble sufferance* (i.e. so that none of the nobility can endure it), ADO 1.3.9, MV 1.3.110.

3 Suffering, distress, pain MM 2.4.167 *ling'ring sufferance*, ADO 5.1.38, JC 2.1.115.

4 Damage, injury, OTH 2.1.23 *a grievous…sufferance On most part of their fleet.*

5 Suffering of the penalty of death H5 2.2.159 *prevention, Which in sufferance…will rejoice.*

suffering *ppl. adj.* Acquiescing JC 2.1.130 *such suffering souls.*

suffice *vb.* Satisfy, content AYL 2.7.131 *till he be first suffic'd,…I will not touch a bit*, JN 1.1.191, SON 37.11; (refl.) AWW 3.5.10 *let's…suffice ourselves with the report of it.*

sufficient *adj.*

1 Able, fit for an office or position OTH 3.4.91 *You'll never meet a more sufficient man*, MM 2.1.273, 2H4 3.2.93.

2 Able to meet liabilities, solvent MV 1.3.17 *my meaning in saying he is a good man is…that he is sufficient*, MV 1.3.26.

suffigance *adj.* (Dogberry's blunder for) Sufficient ADO 3.5.52 *It shall be suffigance.*

suffocate *pa. pple.* Suffocated 2H6 1.1.124 *For Suffolk's duke, may he be suffocate*, TRO 1.3.125.

suggest *vb.*

1 Incite, prompt (a person) R2 1.1.101 *That he did …Suggest his soon-believing adversaries*, H8 1.1.164, VEN 651; insinuate (a false idea into a person's mind) COR 2.1.245 *We must suggest the people in what hatred He still hath held them*, COR 2.1.253, WIV 3.3.215.

2 Tempt, lead astray, seduce TGV 3.1.34 *tender youth is soon suggested*, AWW 4.5.45, H5 2.2.114.

suggestion *n.*

1 Prompting or urging to evil, temptation LR 2.1.73 *thy suggestion, plot, and damned practice*, JN 3.1.292, MAC 1.3.134; instigation R3 3.2.101 *Then was I going prisoner to the Tower, By the suggestion of the Queen's allies*, JN 4.2.166.

2 'Crafty dealing' (Wright), 'underhand practice' (Holinshed) H8 4.2.35 *one that by suggestion Tied all the kingdom.*

suit *n.*

1 Attendance at the court of a liege lord MM 4.4.17 *men of sort and suit* (i.e. such as owed attendance), LC 234; *out of suits with* not in the attendance of AYL 1.2.246; *out of all suit* beyond the limits of proper behaviour LLL 5.2.275 (with quibble).

2 Dress, apparel; (fig.) MV 2.2.202 *put on Your boldest suit of mirth*, HAM 1.2.86; (hence) *in all suits* in all points, in every detail SHR Ind.1.106 *dress'd in all suits like a lady.*

3 (fig., from legal sense) Entreaty, petition LR 2.2.63 *at suit of his grey beard*, COR 5.3.135, OTH 3.1.34; *suit of pounds* petition for money H8 2.3.85.

~ *vb.*

1 Clothe, dress CYM 5.1.23 *suit myself As does a Britain peasant*, AYL 1.3.116; (fig.) H5 4.2.53 *Description cannot suit itself in words*, SON 132.12, AYL 1.3.116 (with quibble on sense 2).

2 Agree *with*, accord *with* TN 1.2.50 *a mind that suits With this thy fair…character*, H5 1.2.17, MAC 2.1.60.

suited *ppl. adj.* Clothed, apparelled MV 1.2.74 *How oddly he is suited!*, LR 4.7.6, TN 5.1.234; (fig.) SON 127.10 *Her eyes so suited* (i.e. dressed in the same colour).

sullen *n.* (pl.) Dumps, melancholy, depression R2 2.1.139 *let them die that age and sullens have.*

~ *adj.*

1 Melancholy, mournful, dismal R2 5.6.48 *sullen black*, 2H4 1.1.102, ROM 4.5.88; depressing OTH 3.4.51 *a salt and sullen rheum* (Q1; Ff *sorry*).

2 Dark, dull 1H4 1.2.212 *like bright metal on a sullen ground*, 2H6 1.2.5, SON 29.12.

sully *n.* Blemish HAM 2.1.39 *You laying these slight sullies on my son* (Qq 3–4; F1 *sulleyes*; Q2 *sallies*).

sulphur *n.* Lightning COR 5.3.152 *to charge thy sulphur with a bolt; stones of sulphur* thunderbolts CYM 5.5.240.
◊ Lightning was supposed to be burning sulphur.

sulphurous *adj.* Having the qualities associated with burning sulphur; (applied to lightning) MM 2.2.115 *thy...sulphurous bolt*, PER 3.1.6.
◊ Cf. SULPHUR.

sum *n.*
1 Summary, epitome ANT 1.1.18 *News, my good lord from Rome.—...the. sum.* (i.e. tell me all briefly, give me the essence of it), PER 3.Gower.33, 2H4 1.1.131.
2 *grand sum* Grand total H8 3.2.293 *the grand sum of his sins.*

sumless *adj.* Incalculable H5 1.2.165 *sumless treasuries.*

summer *n.* (used attrib. or in genitive) Pleasant CYM 3.4.12 *summer news*, WT 4.3.11, R3 4.3.13; SON 98.7 *any summer's story*, 1H4 3.1.207.
~ *vb.* Nurture, keep during the summer H5 5.2.308 *maids, well summer'd and warm kept.*

summer(-)house *n.* Country house to spend the summer in 1H4 3.1.162 *In any summer house in Christendom.*

summer-seeming *adj.* Summer-like, transitory, short-lived MAC 4.3.86 *This avarice Sticks deeper, grows with more pernicious root Than summer-seeming lust.*

summon *vb.* Call to surrender COR 1.4.7 *Summon the town.*

summoner *n.* Officer who haled offenders before the ecclesiastical courts; (fig.) LR 3.2.59 *cry These dreadful summoners grace.*

sumpter *n.* Pack-horse; (fig.) drudge LR 2.4.216 *slave and sumpter.*

sun *n.*
1 *from sun to sun* From day to day R2 4.1.55 (Capell; Qq1-5 *sinne to sinne*); *'twixt sun and sun* in one day CYM 3.2.68.
2 *in the sun* In the manner of a carefree, idle life AYL 2.5.39 *Who doth ambition shun, And loves to live i' th' sun*, ROM 3.1.26, HAM 1.2.67 (with quibble on 'son').
3 *get the sun of* Get on the sunward side of (the enemies, so that the light shines in their eyes); (hence) get the advantage of LLL 4.3.366.

sunburnt *adj.* (euphemistically) Unattractive TRO 1.3.282 *The Grecian dames are sunburnt, and not worth The splinter of a lance*, ADO 2.1.319.
◊ A sunburnt skin was not a mark of beauty to the Elizabethans.

Sunday *n.* *Sunday citizens* Citizens in their Sunday clothes 1H4 3.1.256.

sup *vb.* Feed LLL 5.2.692 *no more man's blood...than will sup a flea*, SHR Ind.1.28.

super- *prefix* Excessively, over- SHR 2.1.188 *super-dainty*, MND 3.2.153 *superpraise*, OTH 1.3.356 *super-subtle* (see SUBTLE sense 2).

superfinical See FINICAL.

superfluous *adj.*
1 Excessive H8 1.1.99 *purchas'd At a superfluous rate!*, HAM 4.5.96.
2 Having more than enough LR 4.1.67 *superfluous and lust-dieted man*, LR 2.4.265, AWW 1.1.105; *superfluous riots* riotous revelling in luxuries PER 1.4.54.

superflux *n.* Superfluity, overflow, wealth above one's needs LR 3.4.35 *That thou mayst shake the superflux to them.*

supernal *adj.* That is above or on high, heavenly JN 2.1.112 *that supernal judge.*

superscript *n.* Address (of a letter) LLL 4.2.131 *I will overglance the superscript.*

superscription *n.* SUPERSCRIPT TIM 2.2.78 *read me the superscription of these letters*, 1H6 4.1.53.

superserviceable *adj.* Doing or offering service beyond what is desired, officious LR 2.2.18 *A knave, a...superserviceable, finical rogue.*

superstitious *adj.* Extravagantly or idolatrously devoted H8 3.1.131 *Been, out of fondness, superstitious to him?*

supervise *n.* Perusal HAM 5.2.23 *an exact command...That, on the supervise, no leisure bated, ...My head should be struck off.*
~ *vb.* Look over, peruse LLL 4.2.120 *Let me supervise the canzonet.*

supervisor *n.* Onlooker, spectator OTH 3.3.395 *Would you, the supervisor, grossly gape on?* (Q1; Q2, F *super(-)vision*).

supple *adj.*
1 *supple knee* Ref. to insincere or obsequious obeisance R2 1.4.33 *had the tribute of his supple knee*, TRO 3.3.48.
2 Complaint COR 2.2.26 *having been supple and courteous to the people*, COR 5.1.55.

suppliance *n.* *suppliance of a minute* Diversion, pastime to fill up a minute HAM 1.3.9.

suppliant, supplyant *adj.* Auxiliary, supplementary CYM 3.7.14 *whereunto your levy Must be supplyant.*

supply *n.*
1 Aid, relief HAM 2.2.24 *the supply and profit of our hope*, TIM 2.1.27, H5 Prol.31.
2 (sing. and pl.) Auxiliary forces, reinforcements JN 5.3.9 *the great supply...Are wrack'd*, 2H4 4.2.45 *We have supplies to second our attempt*, 1H6 1.1.159.
~ *vb.*
1 Reinforce MAC 1.2.13 *Macdonwald...from the Western Isles Of kerns and gallowglasses is supplied.*
2 Satisfy the desires of, gratify MM 5.1.212 *did supply thee...in her imagin'd person*, OTH 4.1.28.

supplyant See SUPPLIANT.

supplyment *n.* Continuance of support CYM 3.4.179 *I will never fail Beginning nor supplyment.*

support *vb.* Endure LR 5.3.198 *too weak the conflict to support*, OTH 1.3.258.

supportable *adj.* Endurable, bearable TMP 5.1.145 *supportable To make the dear loss, have I means much weaker Than you may call to comfort you.*

supportance *n.*
1 Support R2 3.4.32 *Give some supportance to the bending twigs.*
2 Maintenance, upholding TN 3.4.300 *for the supportance of his vow.*

supposal *n.* Estimate, opinion HAM 1.2.18 *Holding a weak supposal of our worth.*

suppose *n.* Supposition, conjecture TRO 1.3.11 *we come short of our suppose*, TIT 1.1.440, SHR 5.1.117.
~ *vb.*
1 Form an idea of, conceive 1H6 4.1.186 *more furious...broils Than yet can be imagin'd or suppos'd*, SON 57.10.
2 Picture to oneself, imagine H5 Prol.19 *Suppose within the girdle of these walls*, H5 3.Ch.3, PER 5.2.5.
3 Presume the truth of, conjecture ERR 3.1.101 *supposed by the common rout.*

supposed *ppl. adj.*
1 Imaginary LUC 455 *makes supposed terror true.*
2 Pretended, counterfeit WIV 4.4.62 *the supposed fairies*, TIM 5.1.12, LR 5.3.112.

supposing *n.* Imagination PER 5.Gower.21 *In your supposing...put your sight Of heavy Pericles.*

supposition n.

1 *in supposition* In uncertainty, of doubtful existence MV 1.3.17 *his means are in supposition.*

2 Notion, imagination, fancy ERR 3.2.50 *in that glorious supposition think He gains by death hath such means to die.*

supreme n. Chief VEN 996 *Imperious supreme of all mortal things.*

sur mes genoux [Fr.] On my knees H5 4.4.54.

sur-addition n. Additional title or name CYM 1.1.33 *gain'd the sur-addition Leonatus.*

surance n. Assurance, pledge, guarantee TIT 5.2.46 *give some surance that thou art Revenge.*

surcease n. Cessation MAC 1.7.4 *catch With his surcease, success.*

~ *vb.* Cease, stop COR 3.2.121 *Lest I surcease to honour mine own truth,* ROM 4.1.97, LUC 1766.

sure adj.

1 In safety, safe WIV 4.2.6 *sure of your husband* (i.e. safe from), TGV 5.1.12, TIM 3.3.39; *the surer side* the safer side TIT 4.2.126 *he is your brother by the surer side* (i.e. the mother's side).

2 Unable to do harm, harmless; (with *make*) put beyond the power of doing harm, secure; (hence) disable, kill 1H4 5.3.47 *I have made him sure* (i.e. I have killed him), TIT 2.3.133, PER 1.1.167; (with *bind*) TIT 5.2.160 *bind them sure,* TIT 5.2.165; (with *hold*) 2H4 2.1.25 *hold him sure,* TIT 5.2.76; (with *guard*) 2H6 3.1.188 *guard him sure,* 2H4 4.3.75.

3 Reliable, trustworthy ADO 1.3.69 *You are both sure, and will assist me?,* 1H4 3.1.1, COR 1.1.172.

4 Indissolubly joined, firmly united, joined in wedlock, married WIV 5.5.224 *she and I...Are now so sure that nothing can dissolve us,* AYL 5.4.135, LLL 5.2.285.

5 *sure-card* Expedient or person certain to bring success, winning card TIT 5.1.100 *That codding spirit...As sure a card as ever won the set;* (used as name) 2H6 3.2.86 *Master Surecard* (F1; Q *Soccard*).

~ *adv.*

1 Securely, safely JC 4.1.47 *How...open perils* [may be] *surest answered;* firmly 1H6 5.1.16 *And surer bind this knot of amity.*

2 Certainly, assuredly 1H6 5.3.85 *sure the man is mad,* TMP 2.1.325, LR 1.1.218.

3 Infallibly HAM 2.2.47 *this brain...Hunts not the trail of policy so sure...*

surety n.

1 Feeling of security, confidence TRO 2.2.14 *The wound of peace is surety, Surety secure.*

2 Certainty OTH 1.3.390 *as if for surety* (i.e. as if the thing were certain).

3 Stability JN 5.7.68 *What surety of the world, what hope, what stay.*

4 Reliable support TRO 1.3.220 *With surety stronger than Achilles' arm.*

5 Guarantee, warrant, ratification AWW 5.3.108 *She call'd the saints to surety,* H5 5.2.372, LLL 2.1.134.

6 One who makes himself liable for the default of another, bail MV 1.2.82 *the Frenchman became his surety,* TMP 1.2.476; *surety-like* as a guarantor SON 134.7 *He learn'd but surety-like to write for me Under that bond that him as fast doth bind;* hostage 2H6 5.1.116 *the bastard boys of York Shall be the surety for their traitor father.*

~ *vb.* Be surety or bail for AWW 5.3.297 *he shall surety me,* COR 3.1.177.

surgeon n. (sometimes in wide sense) Medical man, doctor MV 4.1.257 *Have by some surgeon, Shylock,* PER 4.6.26, OTH 2.3.254.

surly adj. Masterful, imperious, haughty, arrogant TN 2.5.150 *Be opposite with a kinsman, surly with servants,* JC 1.3.21, H5 1.2.202.

surmise n.

1 Formation of an idea in the mind, thought, reflection, conception LUC 1579 *Being from the feeling of her own grief brought By deep surmise of others' detriment,* LUC 83.

2 Conjecture, speculation MAC 1.3.141 *function Is smother'd in surmise,* 2H4 1.3.23.

~ *vb.* Imagine, conjecture HAM 2.2.108 *Now, gather, and surmise;* (trans.) 2H6 3.2.347 *my grief, 'Tis but surmis'd whiles thou art standing by.*

surmised ppl. adj. Imagined, fancied TRO 1.3.17 *the thought That gave't surmised shape.*

surmount vb. Rise above, surpass, excel LLL 5.2.670 *This Hector far surmounted Hannibal,* R2 2.3.64, SON 62.8; (intr.) be superior, excel, 1H6 5.3.191 *Bethink thee on her virtues that surmount.*

surprise n. Perplexity, alarm, bewilderment caused by a sudden calamity, attack, etc. PER 3.2.17 *Our lodgings...shook...Pure surprise and fear Made me to quit the house,* WIV 5.5.123.

~ *vb.*

1 Perplex, bewilder, astonish, overpower WT 3.1.10 *the ear-deafening voice...so surpris'd my sense,* TIT 2.3.211, TIM 5.1.156.

2 Capture, seize, take prisoner TIT 1.1.284 *Treason, my lord! Lavinia is surpris'd,* 2H6 4.9.8, 1H4 1.1.93.

sur-reined ppl. adj. Over-ridden H5 3.5.19 *sur-rein'd jades.*

survey vb. Perceive, notice MAC 1.2.31 *the Norweyan lord, surveying vantage.*

surveyor n. Overseer of a household, estate, etc. 2H6 3.1.253 *To make the fox the surveyor of the fold,* H8 1.1.115.

suspect n. Suspicion SON 70.13 *some suspect of ill,* ERR 3.1.87, 3H6 4.1.142.

suspense, suspense n. Doubt as to a person's character or conduct 2H6 3.1.140 *That you will clear yourself from all suspense.*

⟡ F1 *suspence;* some mod. edd. *suspect.*

suspicion n.

1 *of suspicion* Under suspicion, suspected ROM 5.3.222 *Bring forth the parties of suspicion;* *in strong suspicion* much to be suspected WT 5.2.29 *the verity of it is in strong suspicion; out of all suspicion* beyond a doubt ADO 2.3.160 *(out of all suspicion) she is virtuous.*

2 Suspicious circumstance ROM 5.3.187 *A great suspicion.*

suspiration n. Breathing HAM 1.2.79 *windy suspiration of forc'd breath.*

suspire vb. Breathe, draw breath JN 3.4.80 *since the birth of Cain...To him that did but yesterday suspire,* 2H4 4.5.33.

sustain vb. (refl.) Have its place OTH 5.2.260 *I have a weapon; A better never did itself sustain Upon a soldier's thigh.*

sustaining ppl. adj.

1 Nourishing LR 4.4.6 *our sustaining corn.*

2 That which bears up, supporting TMP 1.2.218 *On their sustaining garments not a blemish* (i.e. garments which bore them up in the sea).

sutler n. One who sells provisions to soldiers in a camp or garrison H5 2.1.111 *I shall sutler be Unto the camp.*

suum cuique [L.] To each man his due TIT 1.1.280.

swabber n. A member of the crew whose job it was to swab or clean the decks, etc. TMP 2.2.46 *The master, the swabber, the boatswain,* TN 1.5.203.

swaddling-clouts n. Bandages in which new-born children were wrapped HAM 2.2.383 *that great baby...is not yet out of his swaddling-clouts.*

swag-bellied adj. Having a pendulous paunch OTH 2.3.78 *your swag-bellied Hollander.*

swagger vb. Play the boaster, bully, bluster OTH

2.3.280 *squabble, swagger, swear*, TN 5.1.399, 2H4 2.4.99; (trans.) TRO 5.2.136 *Will 'a swagger himself out on 's own eyes?*, LR 4.6.238 *(zwaggered)*.

swaggerer *n.* Blusterer, bully AYL 4.3.14 *play the swaggerer*, 2H4 2.4.75.

swaggering *ppl. adj.* Blustering, bullying, boasting TN 3.4.180 *a swaggering accent*, 2H4 2.4.71.

swain *n.*
1 Peasant, shepherd AYL 2.4.89 *That young swain that you saw here*, WT 4.4.9, LUC 1504.
2 Person of low rank 2H6 4.1.50 *Obscure and lousy swain*, LLL 1.1.179, MND 4.1.65.
3 Young man in love, lover, sweetheart TGV 4.2.40 *what is she, That all our swains commend her*, TRO 3.2.173.

swallow *vb.* (fig.) Retract, disavow (a promise) MM 3.1.226 *swallow'd his vows whole*, R2 1.1.132.

swan *n.* Bird of the genus Cygnus; (with allusion to the legendary belief that the swan sings immediately or shortly before its death) OTH 5.2.247 *I will play the swan, And die in music*, JN 5.7.21, PHT 15.

swan-like *adj.* Like a swan (i.e. singing in death) MV 3.2.44 *he makes a swan-like end, Fading in music*.

swart *adj.* Of dark complexion, black, swarthy ERR 3.2.102 *Swart, like my shoe*, 1H6 1.2.84, JN 3.1.46.

swart-complexioned *adj.* Dark, black SON 28.11 *the swart-complexion'd night*.

swarth *n.* (var. of) SWATH *n.*¹; (fig.) heap TN 2.3.150 *an affection'd ass, that cons state without book, and utters it by great swarths*.

swarth *adj.* (var. of) SWART TIT 2.3.72 *your swarth Cimmerian* (Ff).

swarty *adj.* Of dark complexion, black TIT 2.3.72 *your swarty Cimmerian* (Qq).

swasher *n.* Blustering braggart, bully H5 3.2.29 *I have observ'd these three swashers*.

swashing *ppl. adj.*
1 Blustering AYL 1.3.120 *We'll have a swashing and a martial outside*.
2 (in sword fighting) Slashing with great force ROM 1.1.63 *remember thy swashing blow* (Q1; Ff, Qq 2–3 *washing*).

swath *n.*¹ Quantity cut by the mower with one sweep of the scythe TRO 5.5.25 *the strawy Greeks...Fall down before him like a mower's swath*.

swath *n.*² Swaddling-clothes TIM 4.3.252 *our first swath* (i.e. earliest infancy).

swathing-clothes, swathing-clouts *n.* Swaddling-clothes 1H4 3.2.112 *Mars in swathing clothes* (Qq *swathling*), HAM 2.2.383 (Qq *swadling*), CYM 1.1.59.

sway *n.*
1 Management, direction, control COR 2.3.182 *sway o' th' state*, JN 2.1.578, SON 66.8.
2 Power of rule, sovereignty TMP 1.2.112 *so dry he was for sway*, MV 4.1.193, MAC 1.5.70.
3 Realm JC 1.3.3 *when all the sway of earth Shakes like a thing unfirm* (perh. sense 1 'settled order').
~ vb.
1 Have under control, manage, direct, rule as a sovereign ADO 4.1.201 *let my counsel sway you*, JN 1.1.13, ANT 2.2.148.
2 (intr.) Rule, hold sway TN 4.1.52 *Let thy fair wisdom, not thy passion, sway*, COR 2.1.204, 1H6 3.2.135.
3 Have a certain direction in movement, move TN 2.4.31 *So sways she level in her husband's heart*, MAC 5.3.9, 2H4 4.1.24.
⟡ In TN and MAC perh. a play on sense 2.

swayed *ppl. adj.* (of a horse) Having a depression in the spinal column, caused by strain SHR 3.2.55 *sway'd in the back*.
⟡ Hanmer's conjecture; F1 *Waid*.

swear *vb.*
1 Take oath of allegiance MAC 4.2.47 *What is a traitor?—Why, one that swears and lies*.
2 Swear by LR 1.1.161 *Thou swear'st thy gods in vain*, JN 3.1.281.
3 Administer an oath to, make one swear MM 4.2.182 *Were you sworn to the Duke, or to the deputy?*, H8 1.2.165, JC 5.3.38.
~ in combination
swear out Forswear, renounce solemnly LLL 2.1.104 *your Grace hath sworn out house-keeping*.
swear over Outswear WT 1.2.424 *Swear his thought over By each particular star in heaven*.

swearing *n.* Oath, vow TN 5.1.270 *all those swearings keep as true*.

sweat *n.* Sweating sickness, a form of the plague MM 1.2.83 *what with the war, what with the sweat ...I am custom-shrunk*.
~ vb. Take the sweating cure (a treatment for venereal disease) TRO 5.10.55 *then I'll sweat and seek about for eases*.

sweep *n.* Moving along with a magnificent or impressive air TIM 1.2.132 *What a sweep of vanity comes this way*.
~ vb.
1 Move in a stately fashion or majestically 3H6 5.1.76 *And lo, where George of Clarence sweeps along*, AYL 2.1.55; (with *it*) 2H6 1.3.77 *She sweeps it through the court with troops of ladies*.
2 Carry, trail along in a stately manner 1H6 3.3.6 *like a peacock sweep along his tail*.

sweepstake See SWOOPSTAKE.

sweet *n.* Perfume (of a flower) SON 99.2 *whence didst thou steal thy sweet that smells*, SON 99.15; (pl.) substances having a sweet smell, fragrant flowers HAM 5.1.243 *Sweets to the sweet*, R3 4.4.10.
~ adj.
1 Perfumed, scented WT 4.4.250 *a pair of sweet gloves*, TIT 2.4.6, SHR Ind.1.35; fragrant MND 2.1.252 *sweet musk-roses*, VEN 1079, TN 1.1.39.
2 (of the heavens or heavenly powers) Gracious, 'dear' HAM 3.3.45 *the sweet heavens*, LLL 3.1.67, OTH 2.1.195.
3 Sweet-tongued, eloquent 2H6 4.1.136 *sweet Tully*.
4 Dear, precious to 1H6 4.6.55 *Thy life to me is sweet*, SON 136.12.

sweet-and-twenty *n. phr.* (term of endearment) Very precious one TN 2.3.51 *Then come kiss me sweet-and-twenty*.
⟡ See TWENTY.

sweeting *n.*
1 Sweet kind of apple ROM 2.4.79 *Thy wit is a very bitter sweeting*.
2 (term of endearment) Dear one, sweetheart SHR 4.3.36 *How fares my Kate? What, sweeting, all amort?*, OTH 2.3.252, TN 2.3.42.

sweetmeat *n.* Preserved or candied fruits ROM 1.4.76 *their breath with sweetmeats tainted are*, MND 1.1.34.

sweetness *n. saucy sweetness* Wanton pleasure, self-indulgence MM 2.4.45 *to remit Their saucy sweetness that do coin heaven's image In stamps that are forbid*.

sweet-seasoned *adj.* (of rain) Soft SON 75.2 *sweet-season'd showers*.

sweet-suggesting *adj.* Sweetly seductive TGV 2.6.7 *sweet-suggesting Love*.

swelled *ppl. adj.* Inflated CYM 5.5.162 *the swell'd boast*.

swelling *ppl. adj.*
1 Full to bursting or overflowing 1H4 3.1.199 *these swelling heavens* (i.e. eyes filled with tears), TIT 5.3.13.
2 Inflated with pride OTH 2.3.55 *Noble swelling*

spirits; inflated with anger R3 2.1.52 *swelling wrong-incensed peers*, R2 1.1.201, TIT 5.3.13.
3 Pompous, ostentatious MV 1.1.124 *something showing a more swelling port.*
4 Increasing in interest and grandeur H5 Prol.4 *the swelling scene*, MAC 1.3.128.
sweltered *ppl. adj.* Exuded like sweat (as if) by heat MAC 4.1.8 *Swelt'red venom.*
swerve *vb.* Go astray, err TRO 3.2.184 *If I be false, or swerve a hair from truth*, CYM 5.4.129, WT 4.4.374.
swerving *n.* Error, transgression ANT 3.11.50 *A most unnoble swerving.*
swift *adj.*
1 Done or finished in a short time, passing quickly, brief, of short duration PER 3.1.13 *make swift the pangs Of my queen's travails*, LUC 991, MND 1.1.144.
2 Ready-witted, quick-witted AYL 5.4.62 *he is very swift and sententious*, SHR 5.2.54.
swill *vb.*
1 Swallow greedily, gulp down R3 5.2.9 *The...boar, That...Swills your warm blood like wash.*
2 (of the sea) Wash, flow forcibly over H5 3.1.14 *a galled rock...his confounded base, Swill'd with the wild and wasteful ocean.*
swim *vb.* Float, be supported on water, not to sink AYL 4.1.38 *you have swam in a gondola*, JC 5.1.67.
swing *n.* Forcible motion TRO 1.3.207 *the great swing and rudeness of his poise.*
swinge *vb.* Thrash, beat, flog, whip TGV 2.1.82 *you swing'd me for my love*, JN 2.1.288, 2H4 5.4.21.
swinge-buckler *n.* Riotous person, swashbuckler 2H4 3.2.22 *You had not four such swinge-bucklers in all the Inns a' Court.*
swinish *adj.* Gross HAM 1.4.19 *with swinish phrase Soil our addition*, MAC 1.7.67.
Swissers See SWITZERS.
switch *n. switch and spurs* At full gallop, as hard as one can go ROM 2.4.69 *switch and spurs, or I'll cry a match* (F1 *swits*).
Switzer *n.* (pl.) Swiss guards HAM 4.5.98 *Where is my Switzers* (Qq *Swissers*).
swoond (var. of) Swoon ANT 4.9.26 *But he sleeps.— Swoonds rather*, JC 1.2.248.
swoopstake *adv.* By sweeping or winning all the stakes at once; (hence) indiscriminately HAM 4.5.143 *is't writ in your revenge That, swoopstake, you will draw both friend and foe.*
sword *n.* Symbol of regal power or authority OTH 5.2.17 *that dost almost persuade Justice to break her sword*, JN 1.1.12, MM 3.2.261.
sword and buckler *n. phr.* Fencing weapons in common use until the end of the 16C, but in S.'s time supplanted in gentlemen's use by rapier and dagger; (attrib.) 1H4 1.3.230 *that same sword-and-buckler Prince of Wales* (i.e. blustering, ruffianly).
sworder *n.* Gladiator 2H6 4.1.135 *A Roman sworder*, ANT 3.13.31.
swordman *n.* Man 'of the sword', fighter AWW

2.1.60 *Worthy fellows, and like to prove most sinewy swordmen.*
sworn *ppl. adj.*
1 *sworn counsel* Pledged secrecy AWW 3.7.9 *what to your sworn counsel I have spoken.*
2 Bound by a tie or obligation (of a friend), close, intimate WT 1.2.167 *my sworn friend*, H8 1.2.191, CYM 2.4.125; *sworn brother* one of two companions in arms pledged to share each other's good and bad fortunes H5 2.1.12 *sworn brothers to France*; (hence, in more general use) one pledged to another in comradeship, close friend ADO 1.1.7 *every month a new sworn brother*, COR 2.3.96, R2 5.1.20.
3 Inveterate, out-and-out TIM 3.5.67 *a sworn rioter*, 3H6 3.3.257, TN 3.4.169.
swoun *vb.* (var. of) Swoon MND 2.2.154 *I swoun almost with fear* (F1).
swound *vb.* (var. of) Swoon AYL 3.5.17 *counterfeit to swound* (F1), JN 5.6.22, TIM 4.3.368.
swounds *interj.* God's wounds, ZOUNDS HAM 2.2.576 *Hah, 'swounds, I should take it*, HAM 5.1.274.
swown *vb.* (var. of) Swoon 3H6 5.5.45 *Doth she swown?* (F1).
syllable *n.*
1 *to the last, utmost syllable of* To the utmost limit or extent of MAC 5.5.21 *To the last syllable of recorded time*, AWW 3.6.71 *to the utmost syllable of your worthiness.*
2 *by, the syllable* To the letter PER 5.1.167 *I will believe you by the syllable Of what you shall deliver*, TMP 1.2.501.
sympathize *vb.*
1 Be of the same mind TRO 4.1.26 *We sympathize.*
2 Have an affinity, agree in nature, disposition, etc., be in conformity (*with*) H5 3.7.147 *the men do sympathize with the mastiffs*, 1H4 5.1.7, TRO 1.3.82.
3 Agree with, answer or correspond to, match R2 5.1.46 *the senseless brands will sympathize The heavy accent of thy moving tongue, And in compassion weep the fire out*, LUC 1113; represent or express by something corresponding or fitting SON 82.11 *Thou, truly fair, wert truly sympathiz'd In true plain words.*
sympathized *ppl. adj.* Shared in (by all) ERR 5.1.398 *all...That by this sympathized one day's error Have suffer'd wrong.*
sympathy *n.* Agreement, conformity, correspondence OTH 2.1.229 *sympathy in years, manners, and beauties*, WIV 2.1.7, 2H6 1.1.23; equality of blood or rank MND 1.1.141 *a sympathy in choice*, R2 4.1.33; sympathy of likeness to LUC 1229 *Her circled eyne, enforc'd by sympathy Of those fair suns set in her mistress' sky.*
synod *n.* Legislative assembly ERR 1.1.13 *It hath in solemn synods been decreed*; (esp.) assembly of the gods ANT 3.10.5 *Gods and goddesses, All the whole synod of them!*, COR 5.2.69, HAM 2.2.494.
syrup *n.* Medicinal decoction ERR 5.1.104 *wholesome syrups, drugs*, OTH 3.3.331.

T

ta *pron.* (dial. form, after a dental, in interr. sentences) Thou 2H4 2.1.58 *thou wo't, wo't ta?* (Q; Ff *Thou wilt not?*).
table *n.*
1 One or both of the stone tablets containing the ten commandments R3 1.4.196 *the table of his law*, MM 1.2.9.
2 Writing tablet, memorandum book TGV 2.7.3

thee, Who art the table wherein all my thoughts Are visibly character'd, HAM 1.5.98; (esp. pl.) CYM 3.2.39 *young Cupid's tables* (i.e. love-letters), 2H4 2.4.266, SON 122.1.
3 Board or flat surface on which a picture is painted AWW 1.1.95 *to...draw His arched brows...In our heart's table*, JN 2.1.503, SON 24.2.
4 (in palmistry) Quadrangle formed by four main

lines in the palm of the hand MV 2.2.158 *a fairer table.*

5 Board on which backgammon, or any similar game is played; (pl.) backgammon LLL 5.2.326 *when he plays at tables.*

⇨ For H5 2.3.17 *a table of green fields* see FIELD.

~ *vb.* Set down in a table or list CYM 1.4.6 *though the catalogue of his endowments had been tabled.*

table-book *n.* Notebook WT 4.4.598 *brooch, table-book, ballad,* HAM 2.2.136.

table-sport *n.* Laughing-stock at table, butt of the company WIV 4.2.162 *let me for ever be your table-sport.*

tabor *n.* Small drum used on festive occasions LLL 5.1.154 *I will play On the tabor,* TMP 4.1.175, COR 5.4.50; used by professional clowns and jesters TN 3.1.2 *Dost thou live by thy tabor?—No, sir, I live by the church*; (coupled with 'pipe' as symbol of peaceful rejoicing) ADO 2.3.14 *now had he rather hear the tabor and the pipe,* WT 4.4.182.

taborer *n.* Drummer TMP 3.2.151 *I would I could see this taborer.*

taborin(e), tabourine *n.* Kind of drum, less wide and longer than the tabor ANT 4.8.37 *our rattling taborines,* TRO 4.5.275.

tackled *ppl. adj. tackled stair* Rope ladder ROM 2.4.189.

tackling *n.* Rigging of a ship, tackle R3 4.4.234 *a poor bark of sails and tackling reft,* 3H6 5.4.18.

taffeta *n.* Lustrous kind of silk 1H4 1.2.10 *in flame-colour'd taffeta,* 1H4 1.2.10.

~ *adj.* Dressed in taffeta AWW 2.2.22 *your taffeta punk* (F1 *taffety*); (fig.) LLL 5.2.406 *Taffeta phrases, silken terms precise* (i.e. fine speech).

tag *n.* Rabble COR 3.1.247 *Before the tag return.*

tag-rag *adj. tag-rag people* Rabble JC 1.2.258.

tailor *n.* (?) Posterior; (hence, as impolite interj.) MND 2.1.54 *down topples she, And 'tailor' cries.*

taint *n.*

1 Decay, corruption LR 1.1.221 *affection Fall into taint,* H8 5.2.63.

2 Stain, blemish ANT 5.1.30 *His taints and honours,* HAM 2.1.32, MAC 4.3.124; disgrace TRO 1.3.373 *taint of our best man.*

~ *vb.*

1 Affect in a slight degree, tinge, imbue slightly (with an undesirable quality) 1H6 5.3.183 *Never yet taint with love,* 3H6 3.1.40.

2 (intr.) Lose vigour or courage, become weak or faint MAC 5.3.3 *I cannot taint with fear.*

3 Infect with corruption, corrupt, deprave 1H6 5.4.45 *tainted with a thousand vices,* HAM 1.5.85, LUC 38; (intr.) become corrupted or stale TN 3.4.132 *lest the device take air, and taint.*

4 Injure, impair OTH 1.3.271 *That my disports corrupt and taint my business,* TN 3.4.13, OTH 4.2.161.

5 Sully, stain, bring into discredit H8 3.1.55 *To taint that honour,* TN 5.1.138, 1H6 4.5.46; disparage OTH 2.1.268 *tainting his discipline.*

6 Convey infection TRO 3.3.232 *danger like an ague subtly taints.*

taintingly *adv.* (app. misprint for) Tauntingly COR 1.1.110 *it taintingly replied* (Ff 1–3; F4 *tauntingly*).

tainture *n.* Defilement 2H6 2.1.184 *the tainture of thy nest* (F1 *Taincture*).

take *vb.*

1 Strike R3 1.4.154 *Take him on the costard*; (with double object) give (a person a blow) H5 4.1.215 *I will take thee a box on the ear,* MM 2.1.180, TN 2.5.67.

2 Strike with disease WIV 4.4.32 *he blasts the tree, and takes the cattle,* ANT 4.2.37; (absol.) HAM 1.1.163 *no planets strike, No fairy takes.*

3 Bewitch, captivate, charm WT 4.4.118 *daffodils,*

That...take the winds of March with beauty, TMP 5.1.314, PER 4.4.3.

4 Catch, meet, find ERR 3.2.167 *I thought to have ta'en you at the Porpentine,* H5 4.1.219.

5 Assume, pretend HAM 2.1.13 *Take you...some distant knowledge of him.*

6 Repair to (a place) for refuge ERR 5.1.36 *Run, ...take a house!,* ERR 5.1.94, TRO 5.4.19.

7 (intr.) Have recourse TGV 4.1.40 *have you anything to take to?*; (refl.) betake oneself H5 3.2.114 *ere these eyes of mine take themselves to slumber,* PER 3.4.10.

8 Hear, learn COR 3.1.140 *No, take more!,* JN 1.1.21; (chiefly in) *take it, this of me* let me tell you TIT 2.1.108, SHR 2.1.190, H8 5.1.30; (pregnantly) accept as true LR 4.6.141 *I would not take this from report.*

9 Receive without resistance, acquiesce in, put up with HAM 2.2.576 *Who does me this?...I should take it,* LR 2.2.100.

10 Accept (a person) as being, or suppose him to be so-and-so TIT 5.2.153 *The Empress' sons I take them,* AWW 3.5.52.

11 Arrange, conclude (truce, peace) VEN 82 *Till he take truce with her contending tears,* JN 3.1.17, ROM 3.1.157.

12 (intrans.) Catch fire H5 2.1.52 *I can take.*

13 'Take effect' COR 2.2.108 *His sword, death's stamp, Where it did mark, it took.*

~ *in phrases*

take on, upon oneself 1 Profess, pretend 2H4 4.1.60 *I take not on me here as a physician,* ERR 5.1.243, CYM 5.4.180; pretend to know LR 5.3.16 *take upon's the mystery of things*; make believe TRO 1.2.139 *she takes upon her to spy a white hair on his chin.* **2** Assume lofty airs 1H6 1.2.71 *She takes upon her bravely at first dash,* SHR 3.2.214. **take (it) on (one's) death, honour, salvation** Give a strong assurance, affirm vehemently WIV 2.2.13 *I took't upon mine honour thou hadst it not,* R2 5.3.11, JN 1.1.110. **take one's death 1** Die 3H6 1.3.35 *let me pray before I take my death.* **2** Take one's dying oath 2H6 2.3.88 *I will take my death I never meant him any ill.* **take one's haste** Make haste TIM 5.1.210 *To stop affliction, let him take his haste.* **take head** Run, rush JN 2.1.579 *this vile-drawing bias...Makes it take head from all indifferency.* **take the heat** Get the start 2H4 2.4.298 *he will...turn all to a merriment, if you take not the heat.* **take me with you** Speak so that I can understand you, be explicit ROM 3.5.141, 1H4 2.4.460. **take note of 1** Notice COR 4.2.10 *They have ta'en note of us.* **2** Know about TN 3.2.36 *my niece shall take note of it.* **take the wall of** Take the advantage of, get the better of ROM 1.1.12 *I will take the wall of any man or maid of Montague's.*

~ *in combination*

take away Clear the table TIT 3.2.81. **take in** Conquer, subdue COR 1.2.24 *To take in many towns,* WT 4.4.577, ANT 1.1.23. **take off 1** Dissuade, disincline MAC 2.3.33 *it sets him on, and it takes him off.* **2** Relieve one of (an office) OTH 5.2.331 *Your power and your command is taken off,* COR 3.3.61. **3** Make away with, destroy (a person or his life, etc.) MAC 5.9.37 *Took off her life,* CYM 5.5.47, PER 4.6.127. **4** *there's laying on, take it off who will* Proverbial phr. applicable to anything excessive TRO 1.2.207. **take on** Be furious, rage WIV 3.5.39 *she does so take on with her men,* MND 3.2.258, 3H6 2.5.104. **take out 1** Lead out from the company for a dance H8 1.4.95 *I were unmannerly to take you out And not to kiss you.* **2** Take a copy of OTH 3.4.180 *Take me this work out...I'd have it copied.* **take right** Have the right effect, have the intended result, succeed H8 3.2.219 *I know a way, if it take right...Will bring me off again.* **take up 1** Raise, levy 2H4 2.1.187 *You are to take soldiers up*, 2H4 4.2.26; enlist AWW 2.3.207 *yet art thou good for nothing but taking up*. **2** Arrest (with quibble on sense of TAKING-UP) ADO 3.3.178 *being taken up of these men's bills*, 2H6 4.7.127. **3** 'Oppose, encounter, cope with' (Schmidt) 2H4 1.3.73 *a third Must take up us*, COR 3.1.243. **4** Take to task, rebuke, reprimand CYM 2.1.4 *take me up for swearing*, TGV 1.2.131. **5** Retort to (a speech) H5 3.7.116 *I will take up that*. **6** Make up, settle, arrange amicably AYL 5.4.99 *seven justices could not take up a quarrel*, TIT 4.3.93, TN 3.4.292. **7** Occupy entirely, fill up; (hence) obstruct COR 3.2.116 *tears take up The glasses of my sight*, H8 1.1.56. **8** Trip up MAC 2.3.40 *he took up my legs*. **take up short** Give short shrift to H5 2.4.72 *Take up the English short*.

taking *n.*
1 Malignant influence LR 3.4.60 *Bless thee from …star-blasting, and taking!* **2** State of agitation or alarm WIV 3.3.180 *What a taking was he in…!*, LUC 453. **3** Handling TIM 1.2.154 *the worst is filthy, and would not hold taking* (i.e. would not bear handling).
~ *ppl. adj.* Blasting, blighting, pernicious LR 2.4.164 *Strike her…bones, You taking airs, with lameness!*

taking(-)off *n.* Murder LR 5.1.65 *devise His speedy taking off*, MAC 1.7.20.

taking(-)up *n.* Obtaining on credit 2H4 1.2.40 *if a man is through with them in honest taking-up, then they must stand upon security*.

tale *n.*
1 Talk ROM 2.4.95 *to stop in my tale*, VEN 74. **2** *in a tale* In agreement ADO 4.2.31 *they are both in a tale* (i.e. say the same).

talent *n.*[1] Sum of money, value of a talent weight in gold or silver TIM 1.1.95 *Five talents is his debt*; (hence) riches, treasure CYM 1.6.80 *In himself, 'tis much; In you,…beyond all talents* (perh. with play on the sense 'evil inclination'), LC 204.

talent *n.*[2] (common 16–17C form of) Talon LLL 4.2.63 *If a talent be a claw*.

talk *vb.*
1 (emphatically) Talk idly, talk nonsense OTH 4.3.25 *Come, come; you talk*, MAC 4.2.64, WT 3.2.41. **2** Speak (a word) R3 4.4.199 *I must talk a word with you*, LR 3.4.157; say *that* TMP 2.1.97 *we were talking that our garments seem now as fresh…*; tell (a person *of* something) OTH 3.4.92 *talk me of Cassio*.

tall *adj.*
1 Comely, fair, fine, handsome MND 5.1.144 *sweet youth and tall*, SHR 4.4.17. **2** (conventional epithet of ships of large build) Gallant, fine, large and strong LR 4.6.18 *yond tall anchoring bark*, R2 2.1.286, MV 3.1.6. **3** (freq. ironical) Good at arms, strong in fight, valiant ANT 2.6.7 *much tall youth*, ROM 2.4.30, WIV 2.2.11; brave H5 2.1.68 *Thy spirits are most tall*. **4** Long H8 1.3.30 *tall stockings*.

tallow *n.* Fat of an animal WIV 5.5.15 *who can blame me to piss my tallow?* (i.e. grow thin as a stag in rutting time), ERR 3.2.98, 2H4 1.2.158.

tallow-catch *n.* (?) Dripping-pan under roasted meat; (applied as a term of contempt to a very fat person) 1H4 2.4.228 *thou…greasy tallow-catch*.
▷ Ff, Qq; Hanmer *tallow ketch* 'tub of tallow'; Johnson *tallow-keech*. See KEECH.

tallow-face *n.* Pale-faced wretch ROM 3.5.157 *you green-sickness carrion!…You tallow-face!*

tally *n.* Stick or rod of wood, marked with transverse notches or scores representing the amount of a debt; the rod being cleft lengthwise across the notches, the debtor and creditor each retained one

of the halves, the agreement or tallying of which constituted legal proof of the debt SON 122.10 *Nor need I tallies thy dear love to score*, 2H6 4.7.35.

'tame *vb.* (apheptic form of 'attame') Broach, pierce, break into H5 1.2.173 *To 'tame and havoc more than she can eat*.

tame *adj.*
1 Subdued, subjected, subjugated, submissive *to* JN 4.2.262 *make them tame to their obedience*, LR 4.6.221, SON 58.7. **2** Tractable, pliant TRO 3.3.10 *all That time…and condition Made tame and most familiar to my nature*.

tamed *ppl. adj.* Broached, opened TRO 4.1.63 *He…would drink up The lees and dregs of a flat tamed piece* (with quibble on sense of 'spiritless, stale').

tang *n.* (?) (1) Sting, 'something that leaves a sting or pain behind it' (Johnson); or (2) sharp ringing sound, twang TMP 2.2.50 *she had a tongue with a tang*.
▷ S. may have associated the two uses of *tang* here.

tang *vb.* Utter with a tang, sound loud with, clang with TN 2.5.150 *let thy tongue tang arguments of state*; (intr.) TN 3.4.70 *let thy tongue tang with arguments of state* (Ff 2–4; F1 *langer*).

tangle *vb.* Entrap, snare TGV 3.2.68 *lay lime to tangle her desires*, 1H6 4.2.22, VEN 67.

tanling *n.* One tanned by the sun's rays CYM 4.4.29 *hot summer's tanlings*.

Tanta est erga te mentis integritas, regina serenissima [L.] Such whole-heartedness is there towards you, most serene highness H8 3.1.40.

Tantaene animis caelistibus irae? [L. Virgil, Aeneid i.15] Is such resentment in the mind of the gods? 2H6 2.1.24.

tap *vb.*
1 Draw liquor, act as a tapster WIV 1.3.11 *he shall draw, he shall tap*. **2** Draw *out* as liquor from a cask R2 2.1.127 *That blood…Hast thou tapp'd out and drunkenly carous'd*.

taper *n.* Candle OTH 1.1.141 *Give me a taper!*, JC 2.1.7, CYM 2.2.5.

tap-house *n.* House where beer drawn from the tap is sold in small quantities, ale-house MM 2.1.209 *any room in a tap-house*.

tapster *n.* One who draws beer, etc., for the customers in a public house or inn WIV 1.3.16 *A tapster is a good trade*, AYL 3.4.31, 2H4 1.2.170.

tardy *vb.* Delay WT 3.2.162 *the…mind of Camillo tardied My …command*.
~ *adj.* **1** *ta'en tardy* Taken unawares, surprised R3 4.1.51 *Be not ta'en tardy by unwise delay*. **2** *come tardy off* Fallen short, inadequately done HAM 3.2.25 *this overdone, or come tardy off*.

tardy-gaited *adj.* Slow-paced H5 4.Ch.20 *the cripple tardy-gaited night*.

targe *n.* Light shield LLL 5.2.553 *with targe and shield*, ANT 2.6.39, CYM 5.5.5.

target *n.* TARGE 1H4 2.4.202 *seven points in my target*, HAM 2.2.321, ANT 1.3.82.

tarre *vb.* Provoke, incite, hound *on* HAM 2.2.353 *to tarre them to controversy*, JN 4.1.116, TRO 1.3.390.

tarriance *n.*
1 Delay TGV 2.7.90 *I am impatient of my tarriance*. **2** Waiting in expectation PP 6.4 *A longing tarriance for Adonis*.

tarry *vb.*
1 Lodge (in a place) stay MV 4.2.18 *where I will tarry*. **2** Wait for, await WIV 4.5.20 *tarries the coming-*

down of thy fat woman, Tro 1.1.15; stay for (a meal) 2H4 3.2.192 *I cannot tarry dinner.*

tart *adj.* (fig.) Painful, grievous Lr 4.2.87 *The news is not so tart*; (of aspect) sour Ant 2.5.38 *so tart a favour.*

Tartar *n.* Tartarus, the infernal regions, hell TN 2.5.205 *the gates of Tartar*, H5 2.2.123, Err 4.2.32.

tartly *adv.* (of aspect) Sourly Ado 2.1.3 *How tartly that gentleman looks!*

tartness *n.* (fig.) Sourness Cor 5.4.17 *The tartness of his face sours ripe grapes*, AWW 4.3.83.

task *n.* **at task** Taken to task, blamed Lr 1.4.343 *at task for want of wisdom.*
    ◇ F1; Q1 *attask't*, Q2 *attask'd.* See ATTASK.
    ~ *vb.*
    1 Lay a tax upon, tax 1H4 4.3.92 *task'd the whole state.*
    2 Impose a task upon LLL 2.1.20 *to task the tasker*, Cor 1.3.36.
    3 Make demands upon, summon, challenge (a person *to* perform something) Tmp 1.2.192 *To thy strong bidding, task Ariel*, 1H4 4.1.9, Son 72.1.
    4 Occupy fully, put a strain upon, put to the proof H5 1.2.6 *things of weight That task our thoughts*, Wiv 4.6.30, Oth 2.3.42.
    5 Reproach Lr 3.2.16 *I task not you...with unkindness* (Q; Ff *tax*).

tasking *n.* Challenge 1H4 5.2.50 *How show'd his tasking?* (Q1; F1, Qq2–6 *talking*).

tassel-gentle *n.* TERCEL Rom 2.2.159 *a falc'ner's voice, To lure this tassel-gentle.*

taste *n.*
    1 Trial, test Lr 1.2.45 *an essay or taste of my virtue*, 2H4 2.3.52.
    2 Act of tasting Rom 2.6.13 *The sweetest honey...in the taste confounds the appetite*, R2 2.1.13; (fig.) experience (whether of joy or suffering) H5 2.2.51 *the taste of much correction*, 1H4 3.1.173, Son 40.8.
    3 Small quantity of a thing tasted as a sample; (fig.) AYL 3.2.233 *take a taste of my finding him, and relish it*, Tro 1.3.387; (hence) specimen, sample AYL 3.2.100 *For a taste*, Cor 3.1.316, Ham 2.2.431; *in some taste* in some degree, in some sense JC 4.1.34 *and in some taste is Lepidus but so.*
    4 Judgement, discrimination LLL 4.2.29 *we of taste and feeling are.*
    ~ *vb.*
    1 Put to the proof, try, test TN 3.4.244 *taste their valour*, 1H4 4.1.119, Tro 3.2.91; (used affectedly) TN 3.1.78 *Taste your legs*; (intr., with *of*) 2H4 4.1.190 *every idle...reason Shall to the King taste of this action.*
    2 Experience, feel Tmp 5.1.123 *You do yet taste Some subtleties o' th' isle*, MND 5.1.275 (Qq *take*), H5 4.7.65; have experience of the qualities of Tim 3.2.77 *I never tasted Timon*; (intr., with *of*) WT 3.2.179 *To taste of thy most worst*, Cym 5.5.308, Rom 2.3.72.
    3 Act as taster *to* Jn 5.6.28 *How did he take it? Who did taste to him?*

tattering *ppl. adj.* In rags, tattered Jn 5.5.7 *our tatt'ring colours* (F1 *tott'ring*).

tawdry-lace *n.* Silk 'lace' or necktie much worn by women in 16C and early 17C, cheap and showy ones being app. worn by country girls WT 4.4.250 *promis'd me a tawdry-lace.*
    ◇ 'So called from St. Audrey (Ethelreda) who thought herself punished [by a tumour in the throat] for wearing rich necklaces' (Blount's Glossographia, 1674).

tawny-coat *n.* Ecclesiastical apparitor or attendant, so-called from the colour of his livery 1H6 1.3.56 *Out, tawny-coats!*

tax *n.* Charge, accusation, censure AWW 2.1.170 *Tax of impudence.*

tax *n.* Charge, accusation, censure AWW 2.1.170 *Tax of impudence.*
    ◇ Hibbard (New Penguin) proposes *tax* in this sense as an emendation for Tim 1.1.47 *My free drift...itself In a wider sea of tax* (F1 *wax*). Cf. AYL 2.7.70–87.
    ~ *vb.*
    1 Censure, blame, accuse Ado 1.1.46 *you tax Signior Benedick too much*, Ham 1.4.18, AYL 2.7.71; (with *of*) AWW 5.3.122 *My...proofs...Shall tax my fears of little vanity*; (with *with*) MM 5.1.310 *to tax him with injustice*, Lr 3.2.16, AYL 3.2.349.
    2 TASK *vb.* sense 3 Ado 2.3.44 *tax not so bad a voice To slander music.*

taxation *n.*
    1 Demand, claim TN 1.5.209 *I bring...no taxation of homage.*
    2 Censure, slander AYL 1.2.85 *you'll be whipt for taxation one of these days.*

taxing *n.* Censure AYL 2.7.86 *If he be free, Why then my taxing like a wild goose flies, Unclaim'd.*

teach *vb.* Show how LLL 4.1.108 *Who is the shooter?—Shall I teach you to know?* (i.e. tell you), Rom 1.5.44, Ven 398.

teachy See TETCHY.

tear *vb.*
    1 Tear up; (hence) erase Rom 2.2.57 *Had I it written, I would tear the word.*
    2 *tear a cat* Play the part of a roistering hero, rant and bluster MND 1.2.29 *a part to tear a cat in.*

tear-distained *adj.* Stained with tears Luc 1586 *her tear-distained eye.*

tear-falling *adj.* Shedding tears R3 4.2.65 *Tear-falling pity dwells not in this eye.*

Te Deum [L.] Title of the canticle beginning 'Te Deum laudamus', We praise thee, O God H5 4.8.123.

tedious *adj.* Irksome, annoying, painful AYL 3.2.324 *heavy tedious penury*, R2 2.1.75, Mac 3.4.137; laborious 1H4 3.1.47 *the tedious ways of art* (i.e. magic); laboriously executed Tit 2.4.39 *a tedious sampler*; (humorously) long AWW 2.3.29 *that is the brief and the tedious of it.*

tediously *adv.* Slowly, tardily H5 4.Ch.22 *limp So tediously away.*

teem *vb.*
    1 Bring forth Mac 4.3.176 *Each minute teems a new one*, H5 5.2.51, Tim 4.3.179.
    2 Bear children, bring forth (young), be fruitful Lr 1.4.281 *If she must teem, Create her child of spleen*; (with *with*) Tim 4.3.190 *Teem with new monsters.*
    3 *teem with* Conceive *by* Oth 4.1.245 *If that the earth could teem with woman's tears.*

teeming *ppl. adj.* Fruitful, abundantly productive, fertile R2 2.1.51 *this teeming womb*, Son 97.6, MM 1.4.43; *teeming date* time of childbearing R2 5.2.91.

teen *n.* Affliction, grief, woe R3 4.1.96 *each hour's joy wrack'd with a week of teen*, Tmp 1.2.64, LLL 4.3.162.

tell *vb.*
    1 Count, reckon the number of Ven 277 *trots, as if he told the steps*, R3 1.4.119, Ham 1.2.237.
    2 Count (money) Tim 3.5.106 *they have told their money*, WT 4.4.184, Lr 3.2.91; (fig.) Tim 3.4.94 *Tell out my blood.*
    3 *tell the clock* Count the strokes of the clock, tell the time R3 5.3.276 *Tell the clock there*; (also simply *tell*) Tmp 2.1.15 *One. Tell*; (fig.) keep time *to*, be willing slaves *to* Tmp 2.1.289 *They'll tell the clock to any business that We say befits the hour.*
    4 (of a clock) Strike (the hour) MND 5.1.363 *The*

iron tongue of midnight hath told twelve, OTH 2.2.10.

5 Say (prayers) as on a string of beads 3H6 2.1.164 *Numb'ring our Ave-Maries with our beads? Or shall we on the helmets of our foes Tell our devotion ...?*

6 *tell over* Recount, go over R3 4.4.39 *Tell over your woes again*, SON 30.10, OTH 3.3.169.

7 *can tell* Know, understand H5 4.1.223 *if you could tell how to reckon* (i.e. knew), TIT 1.1.202; (esp. in negative) *I cannot tell* I do not know what to say or do R3 1.3.69 *I cannot tell, the world is grown so bad*, SHR 4.3.22, COR 5.6.14; (in expressions of derision, defiance, or evasion) ERR 3.1.52 *When? can you tell?* (i.e. Never!), 1H4 2.1.39.

8 *never tell me, tell not me* (expression of impatience) Nonsense, rubbish! 2H4 2.4.83 *Tilly-fally, Sir John, ne'er tell me*, TMP 3.2.1 *Tell not me. When the butt is out, we will drink water*, OTH 1.1.1.

temnest *adj.* (?) Most deserving of condemnation LR 2.2.143 *basest and temnest wretches*.

▷ Qq; Capell's conjecture *contemned'st*.

temper *n.*

1 Disposition, temperament, constitution MV 1.2.19 *a hot temper leaps o'er a cold decree*, 2H4 4.4.36, 2H4 5.2.15.

2 Good condition (of mind) LR 1.5.47 *Keep me in temper, I would not be mad!*

3 Self-restraint, moderation in or command over the emotions ANT 1.1.8 *his captain's heart...reneges all temper*, MM 2.2.184.

4 Degree of hardness and elasticity imparted to steel 2H6 5.2.70 *Sword, hold thy temper*, 1H6 2.4.13, R2 4.1.29.

~ *vb.*

1 Compound (a poison) CYM 5.5.250 *To temper poisons*, ADO 2.2.21, ROM 3.5.97.

2 Moisten (*with* a fluid) 2H6 3.1.311 *temper clay with blood*, TIT 5.2.199, LR 1.4.304.

3 Modify, qualify ROM 2.Ch.14 *Temp'ring extremities with extreme sweet*, LLL 4.3.344.

4 Work upon, mould (*to* a particular purpose or frame of mind) TGV 3.2.64 *you may temper her by your persuasion To hate young Valentine*, H5 2.2.118, TIT 4.4.109.

5 Blend *with*, accord *with* 3H6 4.6.29 *few men rightly temper with the stars*.

6 (of wax) Soften (by heating), melt; (fig.) 2H4 4.3.130 *I have him already temp'ring between my finger and my thumb, and shortly will I seal with him.*

temperality *n.* (Mistress Quickly's blunder for) Temper 2H4 2.4.23 *you are in an excellent good temperality.*

temperance *n.*

1 Climate, temperature TMP 2.1.43 *this island...must needs be of subtle...temperance.*

2 Moderation H8 1.1.122 *are you chaf'd? Ask God for temp'rance*, MM 3.2.237, HAM 3.2.7.

3 Chastity ANT 3.13.121 *Though you can guess what temperance should be, You know not what it is*, LUC 884.

temperate *adj.*

1 (of weather) Mild, equable H5 3.3.30 *the cool and temperate wind of grace*, SON 18.2.

2 Moderate TRO 1.2.146 *a more temperate fire*, JN 2.1.195, MAC 2.3.108.

3 Chaste TMP 4.1.132 *temperate nymphs*, SHR 2.1.294.

temperately *adv.* Moderately, calmly HAM 3.4.140 *My pulse, as yours, doth temperately keep time*, COR 2.1.224, COR 3.3.67.

tempering *n.* The action of the verb TEMPER sense 6,

softening VEN 565 *What wax so frozen but dissolves with tempering?*

temporal *adj.* Secular, civil, not ecclesiastical H5 1.1.9 *temporal lands*, MV 4.1.190, MM 2.2.155.

temporary *adj.* Belonging to the present life or this world, temporal, devoted to secular affairs MM 5.1.145 *a man divine and holy, Not...a temporary meddler.*

temporize *vb.* Compromise, come to terms, make terms JN 5.2.125 *will not temporize with my entreaties*, TRO 4.4.6, ADO 1.1.274.

tempt *vb.*

1 Put to the test, try TRO 4.4.96 *we will tempt the frailty of our powers*, TN 3.4.349, H8 1.2.55.

2 Venture upon, risk TRO 5.3.34 *tempt not yet the brushes of the war*, JN 4.3.84, JC 2.1.266.

ten *adj.* *ten groats* See GROAT.

tenable *adj.* Capable of being held, that may be kept back or kept secret HAM 1.2.247 *Let it be tenable in your silence still* (Ff *treb(b)le*).

tenant *n.* One who holds land of a lord, vassal R3 4.4.480 *Where be thy tenants and thy followers?*, H8 1.2.173, SON 46.10.

tench *n.* Freshwater fish, with red spots (like fleabites) on its body 1H4 2.1.15 *I am stung like a tench.*

tend *vb.*[1]

1 (intr.) Be in waiting or attendance HAM 1.3.83 *your servants tend*, HAM 4.3.45.

2 (trans.) Wait or attend upon TMP 1.2.47 *women ...that tended me*, LR 2.4.263, ANT 2.2.207.

3 Take care of, look after JN 5.6.32 *to tend his Majesty*, 2H6 1.1.204.

4 Guard R3 4.1.92 *good angels tend thee* (Qq 1-6 *garde* 'guard').

5 Accompany R2 4.1.199 *cares...tend the crown.*

~ in combination

tend on, upon 1 Wait upon, serve, follow 2H6 3.2.304 *threefold vengeance tend upon your steps!*, HAM 3.2.206, LR 2.1.95. **2** Attend to ADO 1.3.16 *tend on no man's business.* **tend to** Attend to, give attention to, listen to TMP 1.1.6 *Tend to th' master's whistle.*

tend *vb.*[2] Relate, refer, concern JC 3.2.58 *grace his speech Tending to Caesar's glories.*

tendance *n.*

1 Attention, care TIM 1.1.57 *His...fortune ...Subdues...to his love and tendance All sorts of hearts*, H8 3.2.149, CYM 5.5.53.

2 Attendants collectively, people in attendance, retinue TIM 1.1.80 *his lobbies fill with tendance.*

tender *n.*[1]

1 Offer (of anything) for acceptance HAM 1.3.99 *He hath...made many tenders Of his affection to me*, ROM 3.4.12, LLL 2.1.170.

2 Thing offered (esp. in payment) SON 83.4 *The barren tender of a poet's debt*, MND 3.2.87, LC 219.

▷ In HAM 1.3.106 *you have ta'en these tenders for true pay* perh. play on both senses.

~ *vb.*[1]

1 Exhibit, show forth LLL 2.1.244 *jewels... tend'ring their own worth from where they were glass'd*, HAM 1.3.109.

2 *tender down* (lit.) Pay down (money); (fig.) MM 2.4.180 *had he twenty heads to tender down On twenty bloody blocks*, TIM 1.1.54.

tender *n.*[2] Tender consideration, regard, care, solicitude 1H4 5.4.49 *thou mak'st some tender of my life*, LR 1.4.211.

~ *vb.*[2]

1 Have a tender regard for, be concerned for, care for H8 2.4.116 *You tender more your person's honour than Your high profession spiritual*, TGV 4.4.140, ROM 3.1.71.

2 Regard favourably LUC 534 *Tender my suit.*

3 Feel compassion for 1H6 4.7.10 *Tend'ring my ruin.*

~ *adj.*

1 Young, youthful, immature R2 2.3.42 *tender, raw, and young*, 3H6 2.2.28, VEN 1091.

2 (of climate, air) Mild, soft CYM 5.4.140 *tender air*, TMP 2.1.42.

3 Dear, beloved, precious TGV 5.4.37 *Whose life's as tender to me as my soul*, MAC 1.7.55.

4 Sensitively felt, that touches sensitive feelings or emotions TRO 4.5.106 *subscribes To tender objects.*

5 Finely sensitive in respect of physical perception or feeling LUC 695 *the full-fed hound ...Unapt for tender smell*, MND 4.1.25, SON 141.6.

6 *tender of* Sensitive to CYM 3.5.40 *tender of rebukes.*

7 *tender over, o'er* Having great consideration or compassion for WT 2.3.128 *tender o'er his follies*, WT 2.3.133, CYM 5.5.87.

tender-dying *adj.* Dying when young 1H6 3.3.48 *his tender-dying eyes.*

tender-feeling *adj.* Sensitive 2H6 2.4.9 *her tender-feeling feet.*

tender-hefted *adj.* 'Set in a delicate "haft" or bodily frame' (Wright); (hence) womanly, gentle LR 2.4.171 *Thy tender-hefted nature shall not give Thee o'er to harshness.*

tenderness *n. tenderness of years* Youth of tender years LLL 3.1.4 *Go, tenderness of years, take this key.*

tender-smelling *adj.* Having a finely sensitive perception of smell LLL 5.2.566 *Your nose smells 'no' in this, most tender-smelling knight.*

tending *n.* Attendance MAC 1.5.37 *Give him tending.*

tennis *n.* Game in which a ball is struck with a racket and driven to and fro by two players in an enclosed oblong court, specially constructed for the purpose H8 1.3.30 *The faith they have in tennis*, HAM 2.1.57.

➪ Lawn tennis, played on a court without walls, is a 19C modification.

tennis-ball *n.* Ball used in TENNIS ADO 3.2.47 *the old ornament of his cheek hath already stuff'd tennis-balls.*

➪ In S.'s day tennis-balls were made of white leather and stuffed with hair, generally dog's hair.

tennis-court *n.* Enclosed quadrangular area, or building, in which the game of TENNIS is played PER 2.1.60 *that vast tennis-court*; (attrib.) 2H4 2.2.18 *the tennis-court keeper.*

➪ See TENNIS note.

tenor *n.* (in law) Copy of an instrument not fully set out but containing only the substance or purport of it; (fig.) LUC 1310 *Here folds she up the tenor of her woe, Her certain sorrow writ uncertainly* (Q *tenure*).

tent *n.*[1] (pl.) Bed hangings SHR 2.1.352 *Costly apparel, tents, and canopies.*

➪ A 'tent-bed' was a bed with an arched canopy and covered sides.

~ *vb.* (fig.) Lodge (as in a tent) COR 3.2.116 *The smiles of knaves Tent in my cheeks.*

tent *n.*[2] Roll of lint used to search and cleanse a wound TRO 2.2.16 *the tent that searches To th' bottom of the worst.*

~ *vb.* Apply a tent to (a wound); (only fig.) probe HAM 2.2.597 *I'll tent him to the quick*, CYM 3.4.115; cure COR 1.9.31 *tent themselves with death*, COR 3.1.235.

tenth *n.*

1 One out of ten TRO 2.2.21 *If we have lost so many tenths of ours*, TIM 5.4.33.

2 Royal subsidy or aid, orig. being a levy of a tenth

part of a town-dweller's movables 1H6 5.5.93 *For your expenses...Among the people gather up a tenth.*

tenure See TENOR.

tercel *n.* Male of the falcon-gentle or peregrine falcon TRO 3.2.52 *you shall fight your hearts out...the falcon as the tercel.*

term *n.*

1 (Long) period of time SON 146.11 *Buy terms divine in selling hours of dross.*

2 Period of session of courts of law AYL 3.2.332 *lawyers...sleep between term and term*, 2H4 5.1.80.

3 (pl.) State, condition, position, circumstances H5 3.6.74 *what terms the enemy stood on* (i.e. the enemy's position), HAM 1.1.103, LC 176; (hence, vaguely or redundantly) respect, manner, relation MV 2.1.13 *In terms of choice* (i.e. in respect of my choice), AWW 2.3.166 *Without all terms of pity* (i.e. without pity in any form), H5 2.1.57 *in fair terms* (i.e. fairly), LUC 1706 *any terms* (i.e. anything); (once in sing.) OTH 1.1.39 *in any just term* (i.e. in any way justly).

Termagant *n.* Imaginary deity supposed in medieval Christendom to be worshipped by Mohammedans, represented in mystery plays as a violent overbearing personage HAM 3.2.13 *for o'erdoing Termagant.*

~ *adj.* Violent 1H4 5.4.113 *that hot termagant Scot.*

termination *n.* Term, expression ADO 2.1.249 *If her breath were as terrible as her terminations.*

termless *adj.* Indescribable, inexpressible LC 94 *that termless skin.*

terra [L.] Earth LLL 4.2.7 *the face of terra, the soil, the land, the earth.*

Terras Astraea reliquit [L.; Ovid, Metamorphoses 1.150] Astraea left the earth TIT 4.3.4.

terrene *adj.* Terrestrial ANT 3.13.153 *our terrene moon.*

terrestrial *n.* Human being, mortal; (hence) one concerned with secular or physical matters (applied jocularly to a doctor) WIV 3.1.106 *Give me thy hand, terrestrial; so. Give me thy hand, celestial; so* (i.e. 'healer of the body' as opposed to 'healer of the soul').

terrible *adj.* Terrified, frightened LR 1.2.32 *that terrible dispatch of it into your pocket.*

terribly *adv.* In a manner to excite terror or dread TMP 2.1.313 *It struck mine ear most terribly*, MND 1.2.74, TIM 4.3.137.

territory *n.* (pl.) Dependencies JN 1.1.10 *lays most lawful claim To this fair island and the territories, To Ireland, Poictiers...*

tertian *n.* (short for) Tertian fever, fever of which the paroxysm occurs every third (i.e. every other) day H5 2.1.122 *so shak'd of a burning...tertian.*

➪ See QUOTIDIAN.

test *n.* Witness, testimony OTH 1.3.107 *Without more wider and more overt test*, TRO 5.2.122 (Ff14; Q1 *th'attest*).

testament *n.* Will disposing of one's property after death AYL 1.1.74 *the poor allottery my father left me by testament*, AWW 5.3.197, JC 3.2.130; (fig.) R2 3.3.94 *to open The purple testament of bleeding war*, H5 4.6.27.

tested *ppl. adj.* Refined MM 2.2.149 *tested gold.*

tester *n.* Sixpence WIV 1.3.87 *Tester I'll have in pouch when thou shalt lack*, 2H4 3.2.277.

➪ A corr. of 'teston', through the form 'testern' (cf. next), the shilling of Henry VII, Henry VIII, and Edward VI, which was gradually debased in value.

testern *vb.* Give a TESTER to, tip TGV 1.1.145 *you have testern'd me.*

testimony *vb.* Test, prove MM 3.2.144 *Let him be*

but testimonied in his own bringings-forth, and he shall appear to the envious a scholar...

testril *n.* (fanciful form of) TESTER TN 2.3.33 *there is sixpence for you...- There's a testril of me too.*

tetchy *adj.* Fretful, peevish R3 4.4.169 *Tetchy and wayward was thy infancy,* TRO 1.1.96 (F1, Q *teachy*), ROM 1.3.32 (Qq *teachie*).

tetter *n.* Skin eruption TRO 5.1.23 *the rivell'd fee-simple of the tetter,* HAM 1.5.71.
~ *vb.* Affect with tetter COR 3.1.79 *those measles Which we disdain should tetter us.*

text *n.*
1 Quotation, quoted saying ROM 4.1.21 *What must be shall be.—That's a certain text,* TN 1.5.223, LR 4.2.37.
2 Capital (letter) LLL 5.2.42 *Fair as a text Be in a copy-book.*
~ *vb.* Inscribe, write in a text-hand or in capital or large letters ADO 5.1.183 *and text underneath, 'Here dwells Benedick...'.*

than *adv.* (old form of) Then LUC 1440 *their ranks began To break upon the galled shore, and than Retire.*
▷ Retained here in mod. edd. for the sake of the rhyme.

than *conj.*
1 As LLL 3.1.178 *A...pedant...Than whom no mortal so magnificent.*
2 Than that MM 2.4.133 *we are made to be no stronger Than faults may shake our frames,* AWW 2.1.85, WT 2.1.149.
▷ Commonly spelt *then* in Ff and Qq.

thane *n.* Former Scottish title nearly equivalent to 'earl' MAC 1.2.45 *The worthy Thane of Ross.*

thankful *adj.* Worthy of thanks PER 5.2.20 *your fancies' thankful doom.*

thankings *n.* (pl.) Thanks MM 5.1.4 *Many and hearty thankings,* CYM 5.5.407.

thanksgiving *n.* Thanking LLL 2.1.193 *I cannot stay thanksgiving.*

tharborough *n.* (var. of) THIRDBOROUGH, constable LLL 1.1.184 *I am his Grace's tharborough* (Q1 *farborough*).

that *adj.* (pl. *those*) Such AWW 5.3.86 *Had you that craft to reave her Of what should stead her most?,* R3 1.4.250, MAC 4.3.74.
~ *pron.*
1 (demonstrative) Such WIV 5.5.53 *those as sleep,* H8 3.1.167.
2 (used elliptically) That is so, precisely ADO 2.3.139 *she found 'Benedick' and 'Beatrice' between the sheet?—That,* JC 2.1.15.
3 (with ellipsis, uniting the functions of a demonstrative and a relative) He or she who(m) JC 2.1.309 *who's that knocks?,* TN 5.1.150, LR 1.4.257; that that, that which, what WIV 3.3.200 *May be the knave bragg'd of that he could not compass,* 1H6 2.4.60, TIM 4.3.292.
4 (relative, correlated with *so* and *such*) As TMP 5.1.270 *a witch...so strong That could control the moon,* JC 1.3.117, CYM 3.4.78.
~ *conj.*
1 In that, for the reason that, because TGV 4.4.64 *I have entertained thee Partly that I have need of such a youth,* ROM 1.1.216, LR 1.1.72; (esp. after a compar.) ADO 1.3.72 *their cheer is the greater that I am subdu'd,* 3H6 3.3.118.
2 In order that, so that (expressing purpose) WIV 4.2.52 *watch the door...that none shall issue out,* AYL 5.2.54, OTH 1.1.157.
3 (in a second clause supplying the place of a conj. introducing the preceding clause) LLL 5.2.803 *If ...But that...,* TN 5.1.122 *Since...And that...,* COR 5.6.42 *When...and that...,* HAM 1.2.2 *Though...and*

that..., OTH 2.1.300 *Till...Or, failing so, yet that...,* CYM 3.5.71 *for...And that*; (similarly after a conditional clause with inversion) MM 2.1.12 *Had time coher'd...Or that...,* SON 39.13.

thatched *ppl. adj.* Covered TMP 4.1.63 *meads thatch'd with stover.*

theft *n.*
1 Thing stolen HAM 3.2.89 *I will pay the theft.*
2 (quibbling) Stealing away AWW 2.1.34 *I 'll steal away.—There's honour in the theft,* MAC 2.3.145.

theme *n.*
1 What is said, discourse ERR 5.1.65 *the subject of my theme,* WT 5.1.100.
2 Business, undertaking 2H4 1.3.22 *in a theme so bloody-fac'd as this.*

then *conj.* (old form of) Than JN 4.2.42 *more [reasons], more strong then lesser is my fear* (F1).

thence *adv.* Away, absent 3H6 2.5.18 *They prosper best...when I am thence,* WT 5.2.109, TRO 1.1.31; (with *from*) away (from home) MAC 3.4.35 *To feed were best at home; From thence, the sauce to meat is ceremony.*

theoric *n.* Theory AWW 4.3.142 *the whole theoric of war,* H5 1.1.52, OTH 1.1.24.

there *adv.*
1 (as demonstrative) That AWW 2.3.22 *you shall read it in what-do-ye-call there*; (esp. in *there's*) AYL 1.3.58 *there's enough,* CYM 1.5.87, TIT 4.2.116; (*there was*) H8 3.2.407 *There was the weight that pulled me down.*
2 With that ADO 5.2.93 *There will I leave you* (i.e. with those words); by that ANT 2.5.92 *dost thou hold there still?*; in that ROM 3.3.138 *thou slewest Tybalt: there art thou happy,* HAM 3.1.64, LR 4.6.145.
3 At that, at that juncture, then MV 2.8.46 *And even there...he put his hand behind him,* HAM 2.1.19, LR 4.3.29.

thereabout *adv.* That part *of* HAM 2.2.447 *One speech in't I chiefly lov'd,...and thereabout of it especially when he speaks of...*

thereabouts *adv.* (fig.) Near to that state or action, about that, of that mind, pointing at that WT 1.2.378 *Do you know, and dare not? Be intelligent to me, 'tis thereabouts,* ANT 3.10.28.

thereafter *adv.* According as 2H4 3.2.50 *Thereafter as they be, a score of good ewes may be worth ten pounds.*

therefore *adv.* For that, for that purpose or reason, in respect of that MND 3.2.78 *what should I get therefore?,* TMP 3.3.100, 1H4 1.1.30.

thereto *adv.* In addition, besides WT 1.2.391 *a gentleman, thereto Clerk-like experienc'd,* OTH 2.1.132, CYM 4.4.33.

thereunto *adv.* THERETO OTH 2.1.141 *none so foul and foolish thereunto.*

therewithal *adv.*
1 By means of that TGV 4.4.170 *my poor mistress, moved therewithal, Wept,* LLL 5.2.848.
2 In addition to that, at the same time, moreover TGV 4.4.85 *give her that ring and therewithal This letter,* CYM 1.1.33, CYM 2.4.33.

these See THIS.

Thetis *n.* One of the Nereids or sea-nymphs; (confused with Tethys, wife of Oceanus and used for) the sea, the ocean PER 4.4.39 *Thetis...swallowed some part a' th' earth,* TRO 1.3.39.

thews *n.* (pl.) Bodily lineaments or parts, bodily strength 2H4 3.2.258 *the limb, the thews...of a man,* JC 1.3.81, HAM 1.3.12.

thick *adj.*
1 Rapid, frequent, uttered in quick succession CYM 1.6.67 *thick sighs,* LUC 1784.
2 (of sleep) Heavy PER 5.1.234 *thick slumber Hangs upon mine eyes.*

3 (of sight) Dim 2H4 3.2.313 *any thick sight*, JC 5.3.21.

~ *adv.* Fast, quickly 2H4 2.3.24 *speaking thick*, Tro 3.2.36, Ant 1.5.63.

thicken *vb.* Become dim Mac 3.2.50 *Light thickens,...Good things of day begin to...drowse*, Ant 2.3.28.

thick-eyed *adj.* Dim-sighted 1H4 2.3.46 *thick-ey'd musing*.

thick-pleached *adj.* Made with dense hedges of intertwined shrubs Ado 1.2.9 *a thick-pleach'd alley*.

thick-sighted *adj.* Dim-sighted Ven 136 *Were I ...wrinkled old,...Thick-sighted...*

thick-skin *n.* Blockhead MND 3.2.13 *The shallowest thick-skin...Forsook his scene*, Wiv 4.5.2.

thief *n.*

1 (term of reproach) Wretch, scoundrel MM 5.1.40 *an adulterous thief*, Ado 3.3.131, Cym 5.5.220.

2 (used affectionately) 2H4 5.3.57 *my little tiny thief*, 1H4 3.1.234.

thievery *n.* Result or produce of stealing, stolen property Tro 4.4.43 *his rich thiev'ry*.

thievish *adj.*

1 Infested with robbers Rom 4.1.79 *walk in thievish ways*.

2 Stealthy Son 77.8 *Time's thievish progress*, AWW 2.1.166.

thill *n.* (pl.) Shafts of a cart Tro 3.2.46 *we'll put you i' th' thills* (F *fils*).

thin *adj.* (of clothes) Scanty, light, wanting in fullness LLL 5.2.801 *thin weeds*, Err 3.1.70; lightly covered R3 2.1.118 *did give himself (All thin and naked) to the numb cold night.*

thin-belly *adj. thin-belly doublet* doublet with an unpadded 'belly' or lower part LLL 3.1.19.

thing *n.*

1 (applied to human beings) Being, creature TGV 4.2.51 *each mortal thing*, H8 1.1.91, Mac 5.4.13.

2 *a thing* Something LLL 4.3.179 *write a thing in rhyme*, Rom 4.1.74, Oth 3.3.301.

3 (pl.) All things, everything, creation Mac 3.2.16 *let the frame of things disjoint*, LR 3.1.7.

think *vb.*[1]

1 Meditate on, turn over in the mind, ponder over Mac 2.2.31 *These deeds must not be thought After these ways.*

2 Have despondent or melancholy thoughts Ant 3.13.1 *Think, and die.*

3 Bear in mind Mac 3.1.131 *always thought That I require a clearness.*

~ in combination

think on, upon 1 Remember, bear in mind, call to mind AWW 3.2.48 *Think upon patience*, Ham 3.2.134. **2** Have regard or thought for, provide for, think of WT 4.4.536 *Have you thought on A place whereto you'll go?*, 1H6 1.2.116, LR 5.3.251. **3** Hit upon (a way of doing something) by mental effort, contrive, devise Wiv 4.4.47 *What is your plot?—That likewise have we thought upon.* **4** Cherish kind thoughts of, have a good opinion of, esteem WT 4.4.520 *To have them recompens'd as thought on*, Cor 2.3.56.

think *vb.*[2] (impersonal)

1 *it thinks* It seems R3 3.1.63 *Where it thinks best unto your royal self* (Ff, Q3; Qq 1-2 *seems*), Ham 5.2.63.

2 *thinks* (app.) Methinks LC 91 *For on his visage was in little drawn What largeness thinks in Paradise was sawn.*

⇨ See METHINKS.

thinking *n.* Thought, cogitation H8 3.2.134 *His thinkings are below the moon*, AWW 5.3.128, Oth 3.3.131.

third *n.* (?) (var. of) Thread; (fig.) ultimate constitu-

ent, vital part Tmp 4.1.3 *a third of mine own life* (F1).

⇨ Some interpret in sense of 'third part'.

thirdborough *n.* Constable Shr Ind.1.12 *I must go fetch the thirdborough.*

⇨ Theobald's conjecture; F1 *Headborough*.

thirst *vb.* Desire to drink (*to* a person) Mac 3.4.90 *to all, and him, we thirst.*

thirsty *adj.* Causing thirst (for itself) MM 1.2.130 *A thirsty evil, and when we drink we die.*

this *adj.* (pl. *these*)

1 *this other day* The other day, just lately AWW 4.3.199, 1H4 3.3.133, LR 1.2.141.

2 *within this mile* Within a mile of this Cor 1.4.8, Mac 5.5.36.

3 (followed by *as*) Such TN 3.4.254 *do me this courteous office, as to know...*, JC 1.2.174.

4 *these and these* Such and such JC 2.1.31 *Would run to these and these extremities.*

5 *these many* So many JC 4.1.1 *These many then shall die.*

⇨ *This* is reduced to *'s* in Ham 3.2.127 *within's two hours.*

~ *pron.*

1 This person LLL 5.2.636 *Hector was but a Troyan in respect of this*, Ado 5.3.33, LR 1.1.20.

2 *this it is* (1) This is what it is, so it is TGV 5.2.49 *this it is to be a peevish girl*, R3 1.1.62, Ant 2.7.11; (2) it is as I shall tell you TGV 1.3.90 *this it is: my heart accords thereto, And yet...*, JC 4.3.198, Ant 4.10.4.

3 *by this* By this time JC 1.3.125 *by this they stay for me.*

4 *from this* Henceforward LR 1.1.116 *I...as a stranger to my heart...Hold thee from this for ever.*

5 *to this* To such an extent Ant 5.1.48 *let me lament...that our stars...should divide Our equalness to this.*

6 (elliptical) (It is) as follows Tro 1.2.12 *The noise goes, this: there is among the Greeks...*, Per 3.Gower.24.

⇨ *This* is occas. contracted to *this* MM 5.1.131 *This a good friar*, Shr 1.2.46, LR 4.6.183.

~ *adv.*

1 In this way, thus Ven 205 *that thou shouldst contemn me this?*, Jn 2.1.518.

2 So, thus Per 2.Gower.40 *this long's the text.*

⇨ Ff 3–4 *thus long's*; some read *this longs* i.e. belongs to.

thisne *adv.* [Northern and Midland dial.] In this way or manner, so MND 1.2.52 *I'll speak in a monstrous little voice, 'Thisne! Thisne! Ah, Pyramus, my lover dear! thy Thisby dear'.*

⇨ Perh. error on Bottom's part for 'Thisby'.

thitherward *adv.* On the way there AWW 3.2.53 *We met him thitherward, for thence we came* (i.e. on his way there).

thorough *adv.* Through Per 4.3.35 *It pierc'd me thorough*, 2H4 1.3.59 (Ff *through*).

~ *prep.* Through JC 5.1.109 *to be led...Thorough the streets of Rome*, 2H6 4.1.87, Luc 1851.

those See THAT.

thou *pron.* Pronoun of the second person, singular number, denoting the person spoken to; used in contrast with *you* to show variations in social or emotional status: (1) in addressing relatives or friends affectionately TGV 1.1.9 *since thou lov'st, love still*, LR 1.1.66, AYL 1.3.90; (2) by masters or superiors when speaking good-humouredly or confidentially to servants or inferiors TGV 2.1.42 *dost thou know my lady Silvia?*, Err 1.2.10, TN 1.5.1; (3) in contemptuous or angry speech TN 3.2.45 *If thou thou'st him some thrice, it shall not be amiss*, LR 1.1.262, Tmp 5.1.72; (4) in solemn style generally

TN 1.1.9 *O spirit of love, how quick and fresh art thou*, CYM 5.5.443, ERR 5.1.191.

though *adv. what though*
1 (with clause) Even though ADO 5.1.132 *What though care kill'd a cat, thou hast mettle enough in thee to kill care*, R3 1.1.154, VEN 574.
2 (with ellipsis of clause) What does it matter? What then? WIV 1.1.275 *But what though? yet I live like a poor gentleman born*, AYL 3.3.51, JN 1.1.169.

thought *n.*
1 Care, anxiety, sorrow, melancholy HAM 4.5.188 *Thought and afflictions*, AYL 4.1.212, TRO 4.2.6.
2 *with a thought* In an instant, in no time TMP 4.1.164 *Come with a thought*, 1H4 2.4.217, JC 5.3.19; (similarly) *upon a thought* MAC 3.4.54 *upon a thought He will be well again.*
3 *in thought* In silence, without (it) being spoken of R3 3.6.14 *When such ill dealing must be seen in thought.*

thoughten *adj.* Having thoughts, thinking PER 4.6.108 *For me be you thoughten That I came with no ill intent.*

thought-executing *adj.* Doing execution with the rapidity of thought LR 3.2.4 *thought-executing fires.*

thoughtful *adj.* Careful 2H4 4.5.72 *they have been thoughtful to invest Their sons with arts.*

thought-sick *adj.* Sick with anxiety HAM 3.4.51 *Heaven's face...Is thought-sick at the act.*

thrall *n.*
1 One who is in bondage to a lord or master, slave 1H6 1.2.117 *look gracious on thy prostrate thrall*, R3 4.1.45, SON 154.12.
2 Bondage, slavery PP 17.14 *Love hath forlorn me, living in thrall.*
~ *adj.* Enslaved VEN 837 *love makes young men thrall.*

thrasonical *adj.* Boastful AYL 5.2.31 *Caesar's thrasonical brag*, LLL 5.1.12.
▷ Thraso is a boastful character in Terence's *Eunuchus.*

thread *n.* Continued course of life; (in allusion to the thread of life spun and cut by the Fates) H5 3.6.47 *let not Bardolph's vital thread be cut*, MND 5.1.286, OTH 5.2.206.
~ *vb.* Pass through as a thread through the eye of a needle COR 3.1.124 *They would not thread the gates*, R2 5.5.17, LR 2.1.119.

threaden *adj.* Made of woven threads H5 3.Ch.10 *threaden sails*, LC 33.

threat *vb.* Threaten R3 1.3.112 *Threat you me with telling of the king?*, 2H6 1.4.48, VEN 620.

three-farthings *n.* Three-farthing silver piece coined under Elizabeth I, which was very thin and bore the queen's profile with a rose behind the ear JN 1.1.142 *my face so thin That in mine ear I durst not stick a rose Lest men should say, 'Look where three-farthings goes!'* (i.e. insignificant, paltry fellow).

three-hooped See HOOP *n.²*.

three-man See BEETLE *n.*

three-man-song-men *n.* (pl.) Singers of 'threemen(s) songs' (later called 'freemen(s) songs'), a lively kind of catch or round popular in Eliz. times WT 4.3.42 *the shearers* (*three-man song-men all...*).

three-nooked *adj.* Three-cornered ANT 4.6.5 *the three-nook'd world.*
▷ An allusion to either (1) the division of the world among the triumvirs, cf. JC 4.1.14 *The threefold world divided;* or (2) a common division of the world into Europe, Asia, and Africa, cf. JN 5.7.116 *the three corners of the world* (see CORNER).

three-pile *n.* Three-pile velvet, the most valuable

type WT 4.3.14 *in my time wore three-pile*, MM 4.3.10.

three-piled *adj.* Having a very thick pile; name of the richest kind of velvet MM 1.2.32 *thou art good velvet; thou'rt a three-pil'd piece*; (fig.) of highest quality; (hence) excessive, extreme LLL 5.2.407 *Three-pil'd hyperboles.*

three-suited *adj.* (app.) Having three suits of clothes a year, prob. a servant's allowance LR 2.2.16 *beggarly, three-suited, hundred-pound... knave.*

threne *n.* Funeral song or dirge PHT 49 *it made this threne.*
▷ Anglicized form of Gk. *threnos*; see title before PHT 52.

thrice-crowned *adj. thrice-crowned queen* Allusion to the goddess' threefold character as ruling in heaven (as Luna or Cynthia), on earth (as Diana), and in the lower world (as Hecate or Prosperpina) AYL 3.2.2 *thrice-crowned queen of night.*

thrice-driven *adj.* Thrice-winnowed, i.e. with the lighter down separated from the heavier by currents of air driven three times through it OTH 1.3.231 *My thrice-driven bed of down.*

thrift *n.*
1 Gain, profit MV 1.3.50 *my well-won thrift*, WIV 1.3.43, WT 1.2.311.
2 Thriving, success, advantage CYM 5.1.15 *to the doers' thrift*, MV 1.1.175.

thriftless *adj.* Unprofitable TN 2.2.39 *thriftless sighs*, SON 2.8.

thrifty *adj.*
1 Intent on gain MV 2.5.55 *Fast bind, fast find—A proverb never stale in thrifty mind*, TRO 5.1.55.
2 Obtained by economy, well-husbanded AYL 2.3.39 *The thrifty hire I sav'd under your father.*

thrilling *ppl. adj.* Causing one to shiver with cold MM 3.1.122 *thrilling region of thick-ribbed ice.*

thrive *vb. to thrive* Help (me) to succeed R2 1.3.84 *Mine innocence and Saint George to thrive!*

thriving *ppl. adj.* Successful WT 2.2.43 *A thriving issue* (i.e. a successful result).

throat *n.* Voice COR 3.2.112 *My throat of war to turn'd...into a pipe...*, AYL 2.5.4, OTH 3.3.355.

throe *vb.*
1 Cause to suffer throes, agonize as in childbirth TMP 2.1.231 *a birth...Which throes thee much to yield.*
2 Bring *forth*, give birth to ANT 3.7.79 *With news the time's with labour, and throes forth Each minute some.*
▷ Both citations F1 *throwes* (common Eliz. spelling for *throes*).

throne *vb.* Be enthroned COR 5.4.24 *He wants...a heaven to throne in.*

throng *vb.*
1 Crowd, cram; (hence) overwhelm PER 1.1.101 *to tell the earth is throng'd By man's oppression*, PER 2.1.73.
2 Push one's way as through a crowd or against obstacles, press LUC 1041 *Her breath...thronging through her lips.*

through *adv.* Thoroughly CYM 4.2.160 *seek us through* (i.e. follow us up with determination), TRO 2.3.221.

throughly *adv.* Thoroughly HAM 4.5.137 *I'll be reveng'd Most throughly for my father*, TMP 3.3.14, H8 5.1.110.

throw *n.*
1 Cast of the dice MV 2.1.33 *the greater throw May turn...from the weaker hand*, TN 5.2.544; (fig.) venture TN 5.1.42 *You can fool no more money out of me at this throw* (with quibble on sense of 'occasion, time').

2 Distance to which anything is to be thrown Cor 5.2.21 *Like to a bowl upon a subtle ground, I have tumbled past the throw* (i.e. gone beyond the mark).

~ *vb.*

1 Cast (dice) AWW 2.3.78 *throw ames-ace for my life*, LR 1.4.123; (fig.) stake or venture all one has R2 4.1.57 *Who sets me else? By heaven, I 'll throw at all.*

2 Cast (a look), direct (the eye) AYL 4.3.102 *He threw his eye aside*, TN 5.1.212, 3H6 2.5.85.

3 Shed MND 2.1.255 *there the snake throws her enamell'd skin.*

~ in combination

throw away Divert, deflect Son 145.13 *'I hate' from hate away she threw.* **throw by** Lay aside, cast off Luc 1814 *now he throws that shallow habit by*, PP 6.9. **throw down** Overthrow, bring low AYL 1.2.250 *My better parts Are all thrown down*, R2 3.4.66, Tro 3.3.208. **throw...on** 1 Bestow or confer upon Jn 4.2.12 *To throw a perfume on the violet*, Tit 4.3.19, Oth 1.1.52. **2** Put upon: (in favourable sense) bestow on Jn 4.2.12 *To throw a perfume on the violet*, Cym 3.5.75, Ant 1.2.187; (in unfavourable sense) inflict upon Err 5.1.202 *the wrong That she...hath...thrown on me*, R2 3.2.22, Oth 4.2.116.

thrum *n.* Tufted end of a weaver's warp; *thread and thrum* each length of the warp-yarn, and the tuft where it is fastened to the loom; (hence) the whole of anything, good and bad together MND 5.1.286 *O Fates, come, come, Cut thread and thrum.*
 ▷ See THREAD.

thrummed *ppl. adj.* Covered with thrums, having a nap or shaggy surface, fringed with thrums Wiv 4.2.78 *and there's her thrumm'd hat and her muffler too.*

thrusting on *n.* Impulse, compulsion LR 1.2.126 *a divine thrusting on.*

thunder-bearer *n.* The bearer of thunder or thunderbolts; (applied to a deity) LR 2.4.227 *I do not bid the thunder-bearer shoot.*

thunder-darter *n.* One who darts or casts thunder or thunderbolts; (applied to Jove) Tro 2.3.10 *O thou great thunder-darter of Olympus.*

thunderer *n.* He who thunders; (applied to Jove) Cym 5.4.95 *How dare you ghosts Accuse the thunderer.*

thunder-master *n.* Master of thunder; (applied to Jove) Cym 5.4.30 *No more, thou Thunder-master.*

thunder(-)stone *n.* Thunderbolt JC 1.3.49 *bar'd my bosom to the thunder-stone*, Cym 4.2.271.

thwart *vb.* Cross Per 4.4.10 *thwarting the wayward seas.*

~ *adj.* Perverse LR 1.4.283 *a thwart disnatur'd torment.*

~ *adv.* Crosswise, athwart, the wrong way Tro 1.3.15 *Sith every action...trial did draw Bias and thwart.*

Tib *n.* Typical name for a woman of the lower classes AWW 2.2.22 *As fit as...Tib's rush for Tom's forefinger*; common woman Per 4.6.166 *every Custrel that comes inquiring for his Tib.*

tice, 'tice *vb.* (aphetic form of) Entice Tit 2.3.92 *These two have 'ticed me hither.*

tickle *vb.*

1 Disturb by tickling Cym 4.2.210 *as some fly had tickled slumber.*

2 Touch pleasurably Cym 1.1.85 *How fine this tyrant Can tickle where she wounds!*, Son 128.9.

3 Flatter, gratify Cor 1.1.260 *Tickled with good success*, Jn 2.1.573.

4 Vex, irritate, nettle 2H6 1.3.150 *She's tickled now.*

5 Touch (one) up, pay (one) out, serve one well 1H4 2.4.444 *I 'll tickle ye for a young prince* (i.e.

I 'll show you what a young prince ought to be); (ironically) beat TN 5.1.193 *if he had not been in drink, he would have tickled you othergates than he did.*

~ *adj.* Easily shifted, unstable, insecure MM 1.2.172 *thy head stands so tickle on thy shoulders*, 2H6 1.1.216, Ham 2.2.324 (Ff *tickled*).

tickle-brain *n.* Strong liquor 1H4 2.4.397 *Peace, good pint-pot, peace, good ticklebrain.*

tickled *ppl. adj.* (app. error for) TICKLE *adj.* Ham 2.2.324 *whose lungs are tickled a' th' sere* (F1).

tickling *adj.* TICKLISH Tro 4.5.61 *every tickling reader* (Ff; Q *ticklish*).

ticklish *adj.* Easily tickled; (hence) wanton, prurient Tro 4.5.61 *every ticklish reader* (Q; Ff *tickling*).

tick-tack *n.* Form of backgammon in which pegs were driven into holes; (used with indelicate application) MM 1.2.190 *lost at a game of tick-tack.*

tide *n.*

1 Time, season Jn 3.1.86 *the high tides in the calendar* (i.e. the great festivals), Tim 1.2.56 (with pun), Rom 3.5.176 (Qq2–4).

2 Course (of time) JC 3.1.257 *the noblest man That ever lived in the tide of times.*

3 (short for) Flood-tide Tro 5.1.83 *I have important business, The tide whereof is now*, R2 2.2.98, Tim 3.4.116.

4 Flow (of tears) Ven 957 *her eyelids, who...stopp'd The crystal tide*, TGV 2.2.14, Luc 1789.

tide, 'tide *vb.* (aphetic form of) Betide, befall, happen MND 5.1.203 *'Tide life, 'tide death* (i.e. come life, come death).

tidy *adj.* In prime condition, fit for killing, fat, plump 2H4 2.4.231 *Thou whoreson little tidy Bartholomew boar-pig.*

tie *vb.*

1 Bring into bondage, restrict the liberties of H8 4.2.36 *one that by suggestion Tied all the kingdom.*

2 (fig.) Bind, confine Ant 2.1.23 *Tie up the libertine in a field of feasts*, Per 2.5.8.

3 Bind, oblige Shr 1.1.212 *I am tied to be obedient*, R2 1.1.63, Cor 2.2.65.

4 (fig.; of the eyes) Fix LC 24 *their poor balls are tied to th' orbed earth.*

tiger-footed *adj.* Fierce and swift Cor 3.1.310 *tiger-footed rage.*

tight *adj.*

1 (of ships) Not leaking, sound Tmp 5.1.224 *tight and yare*, Shr 2.1.379.

2 Able, deft Ant 4.4.15 *a squire More tight at this than thou.*

tightly *adv.*

1 Like a 'tight' ship, safely Wiv 1.3.79 *bear you these letters tightly; Sail like my pinnace to these golden shores.*

2 Soundly Wiv 2.3.65 *He will clapper-claw thee tightly.*

tike, tyke *n.* Small dog, cur LR 3.6.70 *bobtail tike or trundle-tail* (Q *tyke*; Ff 1–3 *tight*).
 ▷ See also TYKE.

tilly-fally, tilly-vally *interj.* (expression of contempt at something said) Nonsense! 2H4 2.4.83 *Tilly-fally, Sir John, ne'er tell me*, TN 2.3.78 *Tilly-vally! Lady!*

tilt *vb.* Thrust at Oth 2.3.183 *tilting one at other's breast*, Rom 3.1.158; fight, contend, engage in a contest Err 4.2.6 *his heart's meteors tilting in his face*, 1H4 2.3.92, LLL 5.2.483.

tilter *n.* (properly) One who runs a 'tilt' in a tournament AYL 3.4.43 *a puisne tilter, that spurs his horse but on one side*; (transf.) fighter, fencer MM 4.3.16 *Master Forthlight the tilter.*

tilth *n.* Tillage, cultivation MM 1.4.44 *tilth and husbandry*, Tmp 2.1.153.

timbered *ppl. adj.*
1 *Too slightly timbered* Of too light a wood HAM 4.7.22 *my arrows, Too slightly timber'd.*
2 *stoutly timbered* Strongly built OTH 2.1.48 *His bark is stoutly timber'd.*

time *n.*
1 Age, duration of life TGV 2.7.48 *a youth Of greater time,* LLL 1.2.17, CYM 1.1.43.
2 (one's) Life or lifetime LR 1.1.295 *The best and soundest of his time* (i.e. his best and sanest years), AYL 2.4.95, ROM 4.1.60; (without possessive) R2 1.1.177 *mortal times* (i.e. human existence), ANT 3.2.60 *the time* (i.e. the remainder of my life).
3 (chiefly *the time*) The present state of affairs, the present moment, present circumstances HAM 1.5.188 *The time is out of joint,* JC 2.1.115; *in time* in the present AWW 4.2.62.
4 The age in which one lives; (hence) the world, society, mankind, one's contemporaries R3 5.3.92 *deceive the time,* MAC 1.5.63, HAM 3.1.69.
5 (pl.) Times to come, the future JN 4.3.54 *the yet unbegotten sin of times.*
~ in phrases
at a time At some time or other OTH 2.3.314 *any men living, may be drunk at a time* (Ff; Qq *at some time*). **fair, good time of day** Good-day LLL 5.2.339 *All hail, sweet madam, and fair time of day,* R3 1.1.122, TIM 3.6.1; *give the time of day* greet 2H6 3.1.14; *not worth the time of day* not worth speaking to, worthless PER 4.3.35. **for this time** For the time being TGV 2.4.30 *Ay, sir and done too—for this time,* ERR 3.1.43. **good time** Happy issue, good fortune WT 2.1.20 *Good time encounter her,* CYM 4.2.108. **in good time** On a seasonable occasion, at the right moment ERR 2.2.64 *to jest in good time,* COR 4.6.10, LR 2.4.250; at a happy juncture, propitiously R3 2.1.45 *And in good time, Here comes Sir Richard Ratcliffe and the Duke,* MM 5.1.285; (hence, by ellipsis) well met ROM 1.2.44 *I must to the learned. In good time!,* TGV 1.3.44; (expressing ironical acquiescence, incredulity, amazement, scorn or the like) To be sure! indeed, very well OTH 1.1.32 *He, in good time, must his lieutenant be,* MM 3.1.179, SHR 2.1.195. (See also HAPPY sense 1.) **take (one's) time** Seize (one's) opportunity 3H6 5.1.48 *Come, Warwick, take the time,* ANT 2.6.23, TMP 2.1.302. **time and the hour** The mere passage of time MAC 1.3.147 *Time and the hour runs through the roughest day.* **(the) time was that, when** Once upon a time AWW 4.4.5 *Time was, I did him a desired office,* ERR 2.2.113, AYL 3.5.92; (also) *the time has been, the times have been* MAC 3.4.77, MAC 5.5.10; (similarly) *when time was* TMP 2.2.139. **to time** To the end of time, forever COR 5.3.127 *to keep your name Living to time,* SON 18.12.

timeless *adj.*
1 Untimely, premature 1H6 5.4.5 *thy timeless cruel death,* TGV 3.1.21, ROM 5.3.162.
2 Unseasonable LUC 44 *all too timeless speed.*

timely *adj.*
1 Early, speedy ERR 1.1.138 *my timely death.*
2 Opportune; (hence) welcome MAC 3.3.7 *To gain the timely inn.*
~ *adv.* Early MAC 2.3.46 *to call timely on him,* CYM 1.6.97, ANT 2.6.51.

timely-parted *adj.* Having died in the natural course of time 2H6 3.2.161 *a timely-parted ghost.*

time-pleaser *n.* One who adapts his conduct to the time or season, time-server, temporizer COR 3.1.45 *Time-pleasers, flatterers, foes to nobleness,* TN 2.3.148.

timorous *adj.* Full of fear, frightened, terrified OTH 1.1.75 *timorous accent.*

tinct *n.*
1 Colour CYM 2.2.23 *blue of heaven's own tinct,* HAM 3.4.91, ANT 1.5.37 (with allusion to sense 2).
2 The grand elixir of the alchemists AWW 5.3.102 *the tinct and multiplying med'cine.*

tincture *n.* Colour WT 3.2.205 *bring Tincture or lustre in her lip, her eye,* SON 54.6.
▷ In JC 2.2.89 *great men shall press For tinctures, stains, relics, and cognizance* also with allusion to the heraldic use of the word, and to the practice of dipping handkerchiefs in the blood of martyrs.

tinder-like *adj.* Flaring up quickly COR 2.1.50 *hasty and tinder-like.*

tine *n.* Wild tare, vetch OTH 1.3.322 *set hyssop and weed up tine.*
▷ F1, Q1 *time;* A.Walker *tine.*

tine, tyne *adj.* Very small, tiny TN 5.1.389 *a little tine boy,* TN 3.2.74, 2H4 5.1.28 (Ff; Q *tinie*).

tinker *n.* Proverbial type of tipplers and talkers TN 2.3.88 *gabble like tinkers,* 1H4 2.4.19.

tinsel *n.* Rich material of silk or wool interwoven with gold or silver thread ADO 3.4.22 *underborne with a bluish tinsel.*

tipstaff *n.* (pl. *tipstaves*) Official carrying a tipped staff, spec. one appointed to wait on a court in session and to take custody of committed persons H8 2.1.SD *Enter Buckingham…,Tipstaves before him.*

tire *n.*
1 Head-dress TGV 4.4.185 *If I had such a tire, this face of mine Were full as lovely as is this of hers,* ANT 2.5.22, SON 53.8.
2 Bed ornamentation or furniture PER 3.2.22 *having Rich tire about you.*

tire *vb.*
1 Prey or feed ravenously *upon* 3H6 1.1.269 *like an…eagle Tire on the flesh of me,* VEN 56; (fig.) TIM 3.6.4 *Upon that were my thoughts tiring* (i.e. busily engaged), CYM 3.4.94.
2 Cause to tire or feed ravenously, glut (the eyes) LUC 417 *in his will his wilful eye he tired.*

tired *ppl. adj.* (aphetic form of) Attired, clothed, dressed; (fig.) VEN 177 *Titan, tired in the midday heat;* adorned with trappings LLL 4.2.127 *the tired horse.*

tire-valiant *n.* Fanciful head-dress WIV 3.3.57 *Thou hast the right arch'd beauty of the brow that becomes…the tire-valiant.*

tiring *n.* Dressing the hair ERR 2.2.98 *to save the money that he spends in tiring.*
▷ F1 *trying;* Pope conjecture *tyring,* Collier conjecture *'tiring.*

tiring-house *n.* Dressing-room MND 3.1.4 *this hawthorn brake [shall be] our tiring-house.*

tirrit *n.* (Mrs. Quickly's speech) (?) Terrors 2H4 2.4.205 *these tirrits and frights.*

'tis *phr.* There's TGV 4.4.66 *'tis no trusting to yond foolish lout.*

tisick *n.* (var. of) Phthisis, consumptive cough TRO 5.3.101 *a…tisick so troubles me.*
▷ Used as a proper name in 2H4 2.4.85.

tissue *n.* Cloth made of gold thread and silk woven together ANT 2.2.199 *cloth of gold, of tissue.*
▷ See CLOTH OF GOLD.

tithe *vb.* Levy a tenth JN 3.1.154 *No Italian priest Shall tithe or toll in our dominions.*
~ *adj.* Tenth AWW 1.3.85 *One good woman in ten…we'd find no fault with the tithe-woman if I were the parson* (with quibble on sense 'woman who pays tenth part of produce, which was the parson's due'), TRO 2.2.19.

tithed *ppl. adj.* Involving the slaughter of a tenth TIM 5.4.31 *a tithed death* (i.e. decimation).

tithe-pig Pig paid as tithe ROM 1.4.79 *with a tithe-pig's tail Tickling a parson's nose as 'a lies asleep.*

tithe-woman See TITHE adj.

tithing n. District, rural division, orig. the tenth part of a hundred LR 3.4.134 whipt from tithing to tithing (i.e. as a vagabond).

title n.
1 Inscription, motto MV 2.9.35 thou silver treasure house, Tell me at once what title thou dost bear.
2 Name, appellation WIV 5.5.227 unduteous title (i.e. name of undutifulness), R3 4.4.350, MAC 5.7.8.
3 Interest, share, part (in something) R3 2.2.48 so much interest have I in thy sorrow As I had title in thy noble husband!
4 That to which one has a title, possession(s) MAC 4.2.7 to leave...his babes, His mansion and his titles, AWW 2.4.26, JN 1.1.13.
5 make title Lay claim AWW 1.3.103 she...may lawfully make title to as much love as she finds, H5 1.2.68.

titled ppl. adj. Having a (certain) name AWW 4.2.2 Titled goddess (i.e. having the name of a goddess), TRO 2.3.193 (F; Q liked).

tittle n. Point or dot; spec. applied to the dots commonly printed at the end of the alphabet in hornbooks LLL 4.1.83 What shalt thou exchange...for tittles? titles.

to adv.
1 (used as interj.) Go on! TRO 2.1.109 To, Achilles! to, Ajax! to—.
2 to and back To and fro ANT 1.4.46.

~ prep.
1 In addition to, besides, to accompany R3 3.1.116 that's the sword to it, TRO 1.1.7, ROM 1.3.105.
2 In opposition to, against LR 4.2.75 bending his sword To his great master, R2 1.1.76, H8 3.2.92.
3 In connexion or relation with TMP 3.3.69 that's my business to you, MND 3.2.62, WT 4.4.794.
4 Appropriate or pertinent to MM 5.1.90 The phrase is to the matter, TRO 3.1.30.
5 In accordance with, according to, to correspond with MV 2.9.20 To my heart's hope, LLL 5.2.365, TRO 4.4.133; to the utmost of MND 5.1.105 to my capacity, COR 2.1.246.
6 (denoting inclination or preparedness for something) For H5 4.3.35 he which hath no stomach to this fight, HAM 3.3.24, MM 3.1.167.
7 In comparison with, as compared with, to be compared to TMP 2.1.171 thou dost talk nothing to me, TGV 2.4.138, 2H4 4.3.51.
8 In respect of, with regard to TIM 1.1.147 Pawn me to this your honour, TIM 3.5.1, LR 3.1.52; (with guilty) see GUILTY.
9 In the character of, as, for MAC 4.3.10 As I shall find the time to friend (i.e. friendly), TMP 2.1.76, R2 4.1.308.
10 As to AYL 2.3.7 would you be so fond to overcome..., H8 3.1.86, VEN 350.
11 As far as, to the point of OTH 2.3.197 I am turn'd to danger (i.e. dangerously), PHT 58 to eternity doth rest (i.e. eternally).

toad-spotted adj. Stained with infamy, as a toad LR 5.3.139 A most toad-spotted traitor.

toast n.
1 Piece of toast put into liquor WIV 3.5.3 fetch me a quart of sack, put a toast in't; (fig.) TRO 1.3.45 made a toast for Neptune (i.e. swallowed up by the sea).
2 toasts-and-butter Eaters of buttered toast; (hence) delicate, weak fellows 1H4 4.2.21 I press'd me none but such toasts-and-butter.

toasting-iron n. Toasting-fork; (applied contemptuously to a sword) JN 4.3.99 you and your toasting-iron.

toaze See TOZE.

to-bless vb. Bless entirely PER 4.6.21 the gods to-bless your honour! (Q to bless).

tod n. Weight used in the wool trade (usu. 28 pounds or approx. 13 kg) WT 4.3.33 every tod yields pound and odd shilling.
~ vb. Yield a tod WT 4.3.32 every 'leven wether tods (i.e. every eleven sheep produce a tod).

todpole n. (var. of) Tadpole LR 3.4.130 the...frog, the toad, the todpole.

tofore adv. Previously LLL 3.1.82 that hath tofore been sain; formerly TIT 3.1.293 would thou wert so thou tofore hast been!

toge n. Toga COR 2.3.115 in this woolvish toge.
◊ F1 tongue; Ff 2–4 gowne; Steevens's conjecture toge.

toged ppl. adj. Wearing a toga, gowned OTH 1.1.25 the toged consuls (Q1; Ff, Qq 2–3 tongued).

togue See TOGE.

toil n. Net, snare HAM 3.2.347 drive me into a toil, LLL 4.3.2.

toil vb. Put to exertion, tax the strength of MND 5.1.74 toiled their...memories, 2H6 1.1.83, HAM 1.1.72.

token n. Mark on the body of disease or infection, esp. of the plague LLL 5.2.423 the Lord's tokens on you do I see (i.e. plague-spots), LUC 1748.

tokened ppl. adj. Marked with spots indicating disease ANT 3.10.9 the token'd pestilence (i.e. the plague).

tolerable adj. Passable AWW 2.3.202 Thou didst make tolerable vent of thy travel.
◊ Misused by Dogberry for 'intolerable' ADO 3.3.36 for the watch to babble...is most tolerable.

toll vb.[1]
1 Take toll, levy a tax JN 3.1.154 shall...toll in our dominions.
2 Take as a toll, collect 2H4 4.5.74 tolling from every flower The virtuous sweets (Q toling; Ff culling).
3 toll for Take out a licence for selling; (fig.) get rid of AWW 5.3.148 I will...toll for this. I'll none of him.

toll vb.[2]
1 (of a clock) Strike H5 4.Ch.15 the clocks do toll.
2 Ring the passing-bell for 2H4 1.1.103 a sullen bell, Rememb'red tolling a departing friend (Ff knolling).

Tom n.
1 Typical name of a servant or man of the lower class LLL 5.2.914 Tom bears logs into the hall, AWW 2.2.23, 1H4 2.1.5 (an ostler's name).
2 Tom O'Bedlam, one of the discharged, but only partly-cured, patients of Bedlam (an asylum for the insane), licensed to beg LR 2.3.20 Poor Turlygod! Poor Tom!
◊ The beggars freq. referred to themselves as 'poor Tom'.

tomb vb. Bury, entomb SON 4.13 Thy unus'd beauty must be tomb'd with thee.

tombless adj. Without a sepulchral monument H5 1.2.229 lay these bones in an unworthy urn, Tombless, with no remembrance over them.

tomboy n. Wanton CYM 1.6.122 tomboys hir'd.

tongs n. (pl.) Rustic musical instrument, struck with a key (as a triangle) MND 4.1.29 Let's have the tongs and the bones.

tongue n.
1 Language; the tongue the English language (Johnson) 1H4 3.1.123; the tongues foreign languages TGV 4.1.33 Have you the tongues?, ADO 5.1.166.
2 the common, general tongue Common report, general opinion TIM 1.1.174 he speaks the common tongue Which all men speak with him (i.e. says what everybody else says), ANT 1.2.105 mince not the general tongue.

3 Vote COR 3.1.34 *disclaim their tongues,* COR 2.3.208.

4 Interior projection on a mask or vizard, held in the mouth to keep the mask in place LLL 5.2.242 *was your vizard made without a tongue?*

~ *vb.*

1 Speak, utter CYM 5.4.146 *such stuff as madmen Tongue.*

2 Speak against, scold, abuse MM 4.4.25 *How might she tongue me!*

tongued See TOGED.

tongueless *adj.* Not spoken of WT 1.2.92 *one good deed dying tongueless.*

tonight *adv.* Last night MV 2.5.18 *I did dream of money-bags tonight,* ADO 3.5.30, ROM 2.4.2.

too *adv. and too* And at the same time ERR 3.1.110 *wild, and yet, too, gentle,* VEN 1155, JC 2.1.244.

too *prep.* (var. in F. of) To HAM 4.5.60 *if they come too't,* ANT 5.1.56, COR 1.9.94; (before infin.) TGV 2.4.120 *we look too hear from you.*
⇨ Freq. before BLAME.

tool *n.*

1 Weapon ROM 1.1.31 *Draw thy tool,* CYM 5.3.9, LUC 1039.

2 Sexual organ H8 5.3.34 *some strange Indian with the great tool.*

too much *n. phr.* Excess AWW 3.2.90 *The fellow has a deal of that too much,* HAM 4.7.118.

tooth *n.*

1 *colt's tooth* Symbol of youthful inexperience H8 1.3.48 *Your colt's tooth is not cast yet?*

2 *in, into, to* (one's) *teeth* In or to one's face ERR 2.2.22 *flout me in the teeth,* HAM 4.7.56 *tell him to his teeth,* 1H4 5.2.42.

3 *in despite of the teeth of* In defiance of WIV 5.5.125.

4 *from his teeth* Not from the heart ANT 3.4.10 *he not...did it from his teeth.*

toothpicker *n.* Toothpick ADO 2.1.266 *I will fetch you a toothpicker.*

top *n.*

1 Head LR 2.4.163 *fall On her ungrateful top,* AWW 1.2.43, CYM 4.2.354.

2 (in fig. phr.) Forelock ADO 1.2.15 *to take the present time by the top,* AWW 5.3.39.

3 (short for) Topsail MV 1.1.28 *Vailing her high top lower than her ribs.*

4 (fig.) Summit, acme MM 2.2.76 *He, which is the top of judgement* (i.e. God); *In top of* at the height of ANT 5.1.43 *my competitor In top of all design* (i.e. in the supreme conception of enterprise), 3H6 5.7.4, LC 55.

5 *in the top of* Above HAM 2.2.439 *whose judgements in such matters cried in the top of mine.*

~ *vb.*

1 Surpass COR 2.1.20 *topping all others in boasting,* HAM 4.7.88.

2 Copulate with, have sexual intercourse with OTH 5.2.136 *Cassio did top her.*

topfull *adj.* Full to the top, brim-full JN 3.4.180 *their souls are topfull of offence,* MAC 1.5.42.

top-gallant *n.* Top at the head of the topmast, and hence the highest point; (fig.) summit, highest point ROM 2.4.190 *the high top-gallant of my joy.*

topless *adj.* Immeasurably high TRO 1.3.152 *Thy topless deputation.*

top-proud *adj.* Excessively proud H8 1.1.151 *this top-proud fellow.*

torcher One who gives light, as by carrying a torch, torch-bearer; (fig.) light-bearer AWW 2.1.162 *Ere twice the horses of the sun shall bring Their fiery torcher his diurnal ring* (i.e. the sun).

torch-staff *n.* Staff or rod upon which a torch is carried H5 4.2.46 *horsemen...With torch-staves in their hand.*

torn *ppl. adj.* (of faith) Broken LLL 4.3.281 *prove ...our faith not torn,* SON 152.3.

tortive *adj.* Twisted, distorted TRO 1.3.9 *diverts his grain Tortive and errant from his course of growth.*

toss *vb.*

1 Carry aloft on the point of a pike 1H4 4.2.65 *I never did see such pitiful rascals—Tut, tut, good enough to toss;* (transf.) 2H6 5.1.11 *A sceptre...On which I'll toss the flower-de-luce of France.*

2 Turn over and over, turn the pages of (a book) TIT 4.1.41 *what book is that she tosseth so?*

3 *toss* (*a person*) *in a blanket* Throw (a person) upward in a blanket repeatedly as a form of punishment 2H4 2.4.222 *I will toss the rogue in a blanket.*

toss(-)pot *n.* One accustomed to toss off his pot of drink, a heavy-drinker, drunkard TN 5.1.403 *toss-pots still had drunken heads.*

tother *pron.* The other (of two) COR 1.1.243 *I'll lean upon one crutch and fight with tother* (F1), TRO 5.4.18 (Q), LR 3.7.71 (Qq; Ff *Th'other*).

~ *adj.*

1 The other (of two) ROM 2.4.50 *My back a tother side* (F1), TRO 5.4.9 (F1).

2 *tother day* The other day, a few days ago 2H4 2.4.85 *I was before...the deputy, tother day,* HAM 2.1.54 (Ff; Qq *th'other*).
⇨ In most mod. edd. spelt *t'other.*

tottered *ppl. adj.* Tattered, ragged R2 3.3.52 *this castle's tottered battlements* (Ff *tatter'd*), 1H4 4.2.34, SON 26.11.

tottering *ppl. adj.* Tattered, in tatters or rags JN 5.5.7 *our tott'ring colours.*

totters *n.* (pl.) Tattered or ragged clothing, rags HAM 3.2.10 *tear a passion to totters* (Qq; Ff *tatters*).

touch

1 Act or manner of touching or handling a musical instrument so as to bring out its tones, fingering or playing a musical instrument TGV 3.2.78 *Orpheus' lute...Whose golden touch could soften steel;* (hence) note or brief strain of instrumental music MV 5.1.57 *the touches of sweet harmony; know no touch* have no skill in playing (music) R2 1.3.165 *put into his hands That knows no touch to tune the harmony,* HAM 3.2.356.

2 Stroke of the brush SON 17.8 *Such heavenly touches ne'er touch'd earthly faces,* TIM 1.1.36, TIM 1.1.38; (fig.) SON 82.10 *What strained touches rhetoric can lend.*

3 (fig.) Stroke LLL 5.1.59 *a sweet touch* (i.e. of wit), MND 3.2.70.

4 Trait, feature AYL 5.4.27 *Some lively touches of my daughter's favour,* AYL 3.2.152, TRO 3.3.175.

5 Slight amount, trace, dash H5 4.Ch.47 *A little touch of Harry,* R3 4.4.158.

6 Hint H8 5.1.13 *Some touch of your late business.*

7 Feeling, (esp.) delicate or refined feeling TGV 2.7.18 *the inly touch of love,* R3 1.2.71, MAC 4.2.9; feeling of sympathy TMP 5.1.21 *a touch, a feeling Of their afflictions;* (transf.) something that touches one ANT 1.2.180 *The death of Fulvia, with more urgent touches, Do strongly speak to us.*

8 (short for) Touchstone R3 4.2.8 *now do I play the touch, To try if thou be current gold indeed;* (fig.) that which tests TIM 4.3.389 *thou touch of hearts.*

9 Trial of gold; (fig.) COR 4.1.49 *My friends of noble touch* (i.e. that have been tested and proved noble), 1H4 4.4.10.

10 Taint, sullying H8 2.4.156 *to the...touch of her good person.*

11 (euphemistically) Sexual contact or intercourse MM 5.1.141 *free from touch or soil,* OTH 4.2.84, SON 141.6.

~ vb.

1 Strike the strings, keys etc. of (a musical instrument) so as to make it sound, play on JC 4.3.257 *Canst thou...touch thy instrument a strain or two*, SHR 3.1.64.

2 Imbue *with* (some quality) LR 2.4.276 *touch me with noble anger*, LR 5.3.233, MV 4.1.25.

3 Infect, taint, sully AYL 3.2.348 *to be touch'd with so many giddy offences*, JN 5.7.2, MM 5.1.51.

4 Affect with some feeling or emotion ANT 2.2.139 *Not till he hears how Antony is touch'd With what is spoke already*, ANT 5.1.33, CYM 1.1.10.

5 Test as with the touchstone, try JN 3.1.100 *a counterfeit...which, being touch'd and tried, Proves valueless*, TIM 3.3.6, OTH 3.3.81.

6 (intr., of a ship) Arrive, call in passing WT 3.3.1 *our ship hath touch'd upon The deserts of Bohemia*; (trans.) land at R2 2.1.288 *to touch our northern shore*, TRO 2.2.76, WT 5.1.139.

7 Attain, reach to ANT 5.2.330 *thy thoughts Touch their effects* (i.e. attain realization), TIM 1.1.14, H8 3.2.223.

8 Wound, hurt, injure CYM 4.3.4 *How deeply you at once do touch me*, 1H4 2.4.300, TIM 3.5.19.

9 Succeed in getting at, hit upon TRO 2.2.194 *there you touch'd the life of our design!*

10 Mention in passing, touch upon in speaking R3 3.7.4 *Touch'd you the bastardy of Edward's children*, R3 3.5.93, ANT 2.2.24.

11 Produce an impression on, strike, impress (the senses or organs of sense) MV 5.1.76 *If...any air of music touch their ears*, COR 2.1.56, COR 5.2.11.

12 *touch ground* Reach or touch the bottom or seafloor 1H4 1.3.204 *Where fathom-line could never touch the ground*; (fig.) run aground 2H4 4.1.17 *Thus do the hopes we have in him touch ground And dash themselves to pieces.*

touching *prep.* In reference to, regarding, concerning JN 1.1.101 *To treat of high affairs touching that time*, H5 1.1.79, OTH 2.1.32.

touchstone *n.* Stone used for testing the quality of gold PER 2.2.37 *gold that's by the touchstone tried*; (used as proper name) AYL 3.2.12 *how like you this shepherd's life, Master Touchstone?*

tourney *vb.* Take part, tilt in a tournament PER 2.1.110 *to just and tourney for her love*, PER 2.1.144.

touse *vb.* Tear, pull out of joint MV 5.1.311 *We'll touse you Joint by joint* (F1 *towze*).

toward *adj.*

1 Disposed to do what is asked or required, docile, tractable, willing SHR 5.2.182 *'Tis a good hearing when children are toward*, VEN 1157, PP 4.13.

2 Promising, bold 3H6 2.2.66 *that is spoken like a toward prince.*

~ adv. About to take place, in preparation, forthcoming AYL 5.4.35 *There is sure another flood toward*, MND 3.1.79, HAM 5.2.365.

~ prep.

1 In the direction of, with implication of reaching, to MAC 1.3.152 *Let us toward the king*, ADO 3.2.2, AWW 2.5.90.

2 With a view to, tending to, aiming at, as a help to TIM 2.2.192 *to use 'em toward a supply of money*, JC 1.2.85, MAC 1.4.27.

3 With regard to, for TN 3.2.12 *a great argument of love in her toward you*, AWW 2.5.75, TIM 5.1.144.

4 With, in dealing with WIV 2.3.95 *I will be thy adversary toward Anne Page*, COR 2.2.53.

towardly *adj.* TOWARD *adj.* sense 1, well-disposed, willing TIM 3.1.34 *a towardly prompt spirit.*

towards *adv.* In preparation, about to take place ROM 1.5.122 *We have a trifling foolish banquet towards.*

~ prep.

1 In the direction of, with implication of reaching,

to, TOWARD *prep.* sense 1 2H6 4.3.18 *let's march towards London*, ROM 3.2.2, R3 1.2.29.

2 With a view to, tending to, aiming at, as a help to, TOWARD *prep.* sense 2 R2 2.1.160 *Towards our assistance we do seize to us The plate, coin...*, MAC 5.4.21.

3 With regard to, for, TOWARD *prep.* sense 3 H8 1.1.103 *a heart that wishes towards you Honour*, MAC 1.6.30, MV 1.2.34.

4 With, in dealing with, TOWARD *prep.* sense 4 CYM 2.3.63 *I' employ you towards this Roman*, COR 5.1.41.

5 About R3 3.5.101 *towards three or four a' clock.*

tower *vb.* Mount up, as a hawk or falcon, so as to be able to swoop down on the quarry 2H6 2.1.10 *My Lord Protector's hawks do tower so well*, MAC 2.4.12, LUC 506; (hence) soar aloft JN 5.2.149 *like an eagle o'er his aery tow'rs*; (fig.) JN 2.1.350 *how high thy glory towers.*

town *n. town of war* Garrison-town, fortified place, stronghold H5 2.4.7 *new repair our towns of war*, OTH 2.3.213.

town clerk *n.* Parish clerk ADO 4.2.SD *Enter...the Town Clerk.*

⟡ He is called *sexton* throughout the scene.

touze See TOUSE.

toy *n.*

1 Trifle, trifling ornament, trinket TN 3.3.44 *Haply your eye shall light upon some toy*, WT 4.4.319.

2 Thing of no substance or value, trifling matter, piece of nonsense 1H6 4.1.145 *a toy, a thing of no regard*, LLL 4.3.197, OTH 1.3.268; (used contemptuously of a person) WIV 5.5.42 *silence, you aery toys!*

3 Foolish tale, idle fancy, fantastic thought, whim MND 5.1.3 *I never may believe These antic fables, nor these fairy toys*, OTH 3.4.156, R3 1.1.60; *toys of desperation* desperate fancies HAM 1.4.75.

~ vb. Trifle amorously, dally, flirt VEN 106 *To toy, to wanton, dally, smile, and jest*, VEN 106.

toze *vb.* Separate or unravel the fibres of, pull asunder; (hence, fig.) separate, search out, tease out WT 4.4.735 *toze from thee thy business* (F1 *toaze*).

trace *vb.*

1 Travel or range over, tread, traverse, pass through ADO 3.1.16 *As we do trace this alley up and down*, MND 2.1.25.

2 Follow the footprints or traces of MAC 4.1.153 *his babes, and all...souls That trace him in his line*, HAM 5.1.203, CYM 1.1.65; (hence) follow, pursue 1H4 3.1.47 *trace me in the tedious ways of art*, H8 3.2.45, HAM 5.2.119.

⟡ OTH 2.1.303 *If this poor trash of Venice, whom I trace For his quick hunting* (Ff, Qq 2-3): perh. 'follow, pursue' and hence Dorsch 'whom I am hounding on so that he may hunt quickly'. Hulme (1962) relates to the sense in falconry of keeping a hawk hungry to sharpen its keenness for hunting. Steevens's conjecture *trash* (q.v.).

track See TRACT.

tract *n.*

1 Trace, track (of a path) TIM 1.1.50 *But flies an eagle...on...Leaving no tract behind.*

2 (of the sun) Course, path, way R3 5.3.20 *by the bright tract of his fiery car* (F1; Qq *track*), R2 3.3.66 (Qq *track*), SON 7.12.

3 (fig., of events) Course, manner of proceeding H8 1.1.40 *the tract of ev'ry thing.*

⟡ *Trace*, *track*, and *tract* were largely interchangeable in the Eliz. period.

trade *n.*

1 Course, way, path; (fig.) beaten path H8 5.1.36 *Stands in the gap and trade of moe preferments* (i.e. where more preferments are to be found); (hence)

passing to and fro as over a path, resort R2 3.3.156 *Some way of common trade*, 2H4 1.1.174.
2 Regular course of action, settled habit or custom MM 3.1.148 *Thy sin's not accidental, but a trade.*
3 Business (of any kind) TN 3.1.75 *if your trade be to her*, HAM 3.2.334.
~ *vb.* Have dealings with MAC 3.5.4 *how did you dare To trade and traffic with Macbeth In riddles and affairs of death.*

traded *ppl. adj.* Practised, experienced TRO 2.2.64 *traded pilots*, JN 4.3.109.

trade-fallen *adj.* Fallen or broken in trade, bankrupt, out of employment 1H4 4.2.29 *revolted tapsters, and ostlers trade-fallen.*

trader *n.* (short for) 'Trader in the flesh', brothelkeeper TRO 5.10.37 *O traders and bawds.*

tradition *n.* Old, established custom R2 3.2.173 *Tradition, form, and ceremonious duty*, AYL 1.1.47.

traditional *adj.* Observant of, bound by tradition, old-fashioned R3 3.1.45 *Too ceremonious and traditional.*

traducement *n.* Calumny, defamation, slander COR 1.9.22 *'Twere a concealment..., no less than a traducement, To hide your doings.*

traffic *n.*
1 Trade, commerce ERR 1.1.15 *To admit no traffic to our adverse towns*, TN 3.3.34, SHR 1.1.12.
2 Business, dealings, occupation ROM Prol.12 *the two hours' traffic of our stage*, 1H6 5.3.164.

trail *n.* Track, scent WIV 4.2.197 *If I cry out thus upon no trail*; (fig.) HAM 2.2.47 *Hunts not the trail of policy*; traces (of an animal) ANT 5.2.351 *an aspic's trail.*

train *n.¹*
1 Tail or tail-feathers of a bird 1H6 3.3.7 *pull his plumes and take away his train*; (applied to a comet) HAM 1.1.117 *stars with trains of fire.*
2 Troop, body of soldiers 2H4 4.2.93 *let our trains March by us*, H5 3.3.SD.

train *n.²* Lure, false device, trap MAC 4.3.118 *By many of these trains have sought to win me.*
~ *vb.* Entice, allure, lure ERR 3.2.45 *train me not, sweet mermaid, with thy note, To drown me*, LLL 1.1.71, 1H4 5.2.21.

traitor *n.* Person of bad character, harlot AWW 2.1.96 *A traitor you do look like, but such traitors His Majesty seldom fears*, LUC 888; (attrib.) LUC 73 *his traitor eye.*

traject *n.* Ferry MV 3.4.53 *Bring them...Unto the traject, to the common ferry.*
▷ Rowe; Ff, Qq *tranect.* Perh. for It. 'traghetto' (ferry).

trammel *vb.* Fasten *up* as in a trammel MAC 1.7.3 *If th' assassination Could trammel up the consequence.*
▷ A trammel could be either a shroud in which corpses were wrapped or a fishing net.

trance *n.*
1 Ecstasy, transport SHR 1.1.177 *stir him from his trance*, LUC 1595.
2 State of mental dread LUC 974 *Disturb his hours of rest with restless trances.*

tranced *ppl. adj.* In a trance, insensible LR 5.3.219 *There I left him tranc'd.*

tranect *n.* (prob. corr. of) TRAJECT.

tranquillity *n.* (concrete) People who live at ease 1H4 2.1.76 *I am joined...with nobility and tranquillity.*

transfix *vb.* Remove SON 60.9 *Time doth transfix the flourish set on youth.*

transform *vb.* Change (a person) into (something) 2H4 2.2.72 *if the fat villain hath not transform'd him ape.*

transformation *n.* Shape into which one is

changed TRO 5.1.53 *the goodly transformation of Jupiter there*, WIV 4.5.96.

transformed *ppl. adj.* That which effects a transformation MND 4.1.64 *this transformed scalp.*

translate *vb.*
1 Transform, change, alter MND 3.1.119 *Bottom!...Thou art translated*, AYL 5.1.53, HAM 3.1.112; (with allusion to translation from one language to another) 2H4 4.1.47 *translate yourself Out of the speech of peace*, AYL 2.1.19, WIV 1.3.49.
2 Interpret, explain, express the significance of HAM 4.1.2 *these profound heaves— You must translate, 'tis fit we understand them*, JN 2.1.513, TRO 4.5.112.

transmigrate *vb.* Pass after death into another body ANT 2.7.45 *crocodile—...the elements once out of it, it transmigrates.*

transparent *adj.* That shines through, penetrating 2H6 3.1.353 *the glorious sun's transparent beams.*

transport *vb.*
1 Remove from this world to the next MM 4.3.68 *A creature...unmeet for death; And to transport him...Were damnable.*
2 (Starveling's speech) Transform, transfigure (Aldis Wright) MND 4.2.4 *He cannot be heard of. Out of doubt he is transported.*
3 Carry away: (1) by violent passion WT 3.2.158 *transported by my jealousies*, COR 1.1.75; (2) by ecstasy TMP 1.2.76 *transported And rapt in secret studies*, MAC 1.5.56, WT 5.3.69.

transportance *n.* Conveyance TRO 3.2.11 *give me swift transportance to these fields.*

transpose *vb.* Change, transform MAC 4.3.21 *That which you are, my thoughts cannot transpose*, MND 1.1.233.

trans-shape *vb.* Alter the shape or form of, distort ADO 5.1.170 *Thus did she...trans-shape thy particular virtues.*

trapped *ppl. adj.* Adorned with trappings TIM 1.2.183 *Four milk-white horses, trapp'd in silver* (i.e. with silver trappings), SHR Ind.2.41.

trash *n.* Worthless, disreputable person OTH 5.1.85 *I do suspect this trash To be a party in this*, OTH 2.1.303.

trash *vb.* (hunting term) Check (a dog) by a cord or leash SHR Ind.1.17 *Trash Merriman, the poor cur, is emboss'd* (F1 *Brach*); (fig.) hold back, restrain TMP 1.2.81 *who t' advance, and who To trash for overtopping.*
▷ Steevens's conjecture of *trash* for OTH 2.1.303 *whom I trash for his quick hunting* does not seem to fit the context. Ff *trace.* See TRACE.

travail, travel *n.*
1 Labour, toil 1H6 5.4.102 *Is all our travail turn'd to this effect* (F1 *trauell*), TRO 1.1.70, SON 27.2.
2 Labour of childbirth H8 5.1.71 *With gentle travail*, ERR 5.1.403, ADO 4.1.213; (pl.) PER 3.1.14 *the pangs Of my queen's travails.*
3 Painful or wearisome journeying, or the fatigue caused by it TMP 3.3.15 *oppress'd with travail*, AYL 2.4.74, LUC 1543.
4 Journeying, travelling, wandering TN 3.3.8 *what might befall your travel* (F2; F1 *rrauell*), H8 1.3.31; (fig.) TN 2.5.53 *a demure travel of regard* (i.e. looking about).
5 Journey R2 1.3.262 *Call it a travel that thou tak'st for pleasure* (F1 *trauaile*), TGV 1.1.13, HAM 4.7.71.
~ *vb.*
1 Labour, work AWW 2.3.158 *which travails in thy good*, TIM 5.1.15.
2 (of actors or players) 'Stroll', go on tour HAM 2.2.329 *How chances it they travel* (F1 *trauaile*).
▷ In Ff and Qq both spellings used indiscrimi-

nately in the above senses, but in mod. edd. usu. differentiated according to meaning.

travailer, traveller *n*. Labourer MM 4.2.67 *as guiltless labour When it lies starkly in the travailer's bones* (F1 *Trauellers*), LLL 4.3.304 (F1 *trauayler*).
◊ Both spellings used indiscriminately in Ff and Qq.

travel See TRAVAIL.

traveller See TRAVAILER.

travel-tainted *adj*. Travel-stained 2H4 4.3.36 *travel-tainted as I am*.

traverse *vb*.
1 (military term) March, esp. backwards and forwards 2H4 3.2.272 *Hold, Wart, traverse*; (transf.) OTH 1.3.371 *Traverse, go, provide thy money*.
2 Move from side to side, dodge WIV 2.3.25 *To see thee fight…to see thee traverse*.
~ *adv*. Across AYL 3.4.42 *swears brave oaths, and breaks them bravely, quite traverse* (with allusion to the disgrace of breaking one's lance across one's opponent's body, instead of lengthways).

traversed *ppl. adj*. Placed or laid across; (?) (1) (of weapons) held in a position for carrying not for combat; or (2) (of the arms) folded TIM 5.4.7 *wander'd with our travers'd arms*.

tray-trip *n*. (var. of) Trey-trip, a game at dice in which success depended on the casting of a trey or three TN 2.5.190 *Shall I play my freedom at tray-trip*.
◊ See TREY.

treacher, treacherer *n*. Traitor LR 1.2.123 *knaves, thieves, and treachers* (Ff; Qq *Trecherers*).

treasure *n*. Treasury, treasure-house SON 136.5 *Will will fulfil the treasure of thy love*.
~ *vb*. Supply with treasure, enrich SON 6.3 *treasure thou some place With beauty's treasure*.

treasury *n*. Treasure 2H6 1.3.131 *cost a mass of public treasury*, LR 4.6.43, WT 4.4.350.

treatise *n*. Discourse, talk MAC 5.5.12 *my fell of hair Would at a dismal treatise rouse and stir*, ADO 1.1.315, VEN 774.

treaty *n*. Proposal of agreement, discussion of terms, negotiation ANT 3.11.62 *send humble treaties*, COR 2.2.55, H8 1.1.165.

treble *vb*. *Trebles thee o'er* Makes thee three times as great TMP 2.1.221.

treble-dated *adj*. Living three times as long as man PHT 17 *thou treble-dated crow*.

treble-sinewed *adj*. Triply strong ANT 3.13.177 *I will be treble-sinew'd*.

trecherer See TREACHER.

tree *n*. *Jove's tree* Oak AYL 3.2.236 *It may well be call'd Jove's tree*, 3H6 5.2.14.

trembling *ppl. adj*. Accompanied by trembling H8 1.2.95 *a trembling contribution*.

tremor cordis [L.] Palpitation of the heart WT 1.2.110.

trench *n*. (pl.) Furrows, wrinkles TIT 5.2.23 *these trenches made by grief and care*, SON 2.2.
~ *vb*.
1 Cut TGV 3.2.7 *a figure Trenched in ice*, VEN 1052.
2 Divert (a river) by means of a trench or new channel 1H4 3.1.111 *a little charge will trench him here*.

trenched *ppl. adj*. Cut MAC 3.4.26 *twenty trenched gashes on his head*.

trenchant *adj*. Cutting, sharp TIM 4.3.116 *thy trenchant sword*.

trencher *n*. Flat piece of wood on which meat was served and cut up, plate, platter 2H6 4.1.57 *Fed from my trencher*, ROM 1.5.2, SHR 4.1.165.

trencher-friend *n*. Parasite TIM 3.6.96 *You fools of fortune, trencher-friends*.

trenchering *n*. Trenchers collectively TMP 2.2.183 *Nor scrape trenchering, nor wash dish*.

trencher-knight *n*. Serving man attending at table LLL 5.2.464 *Some mumble-news, some trencher-knight*.

trencherman *n*. Feeder, eater ADO 1.1.51 *He is a very valiant trencherman* (i.e. he has a hearty appetite).

trenching *ppl. adj*. Cutting (into a surface), making (trenches or gashes) 1H4 1.1.7 *No more shall trenching war channel her fields*.

trey *n*. Three at dice LLL 5.2.232 *two treys…well run, dice!*

tribe *n*. One of the traditional three political divisions in ancient Rome COR 3.3.11 *Have you collected them by tribes?*

tribulation *n*. One who causes disturbance, disorderly person, rowdy H8 5.3.62 *no audience but the tribulation of Tower-hill*.
◊ App. a cant name for a gang of disturbers.

tribunal *n*. Raised platform, dais ANT 3.6.3 *on a tribunal silver'd, Cleopatra and himself in chairs of gold*.

tribunal plebs *n*. (Clown's blunder for) 'tribunus plebis', tribune of the people TIT 4.3.93.

tribune *n*. In ancient Rome, title of the representatives of the plebs or common people, orig. granted to them as a protection against the patricians and consuls COR 1.1.254 *we were chosen tribunes for the people*, TIT 1.1.46, CYM 3.7.8.

trice *n*. Instant, moment, very brief period LR 1.1.216 *in this trice of time*; (with *in*) TN 4.2.123 *in a trice*, CYM 5.4.167; (with *on*) TMP 5.1.238 *On a trice*.

trick *n*.
1 Custom, habit, way MM 3.2.52 *Which is the way? Is it sad, and few words? or how? The trick of it?*, AWW 3.2.8, HAM 4.7.187.
2 Art, knack, skill HAM 5.1.91 *and we had the trick to see't*, LLL 5.2.465, H8 1.3.40.
3 Characteristic expression (of the face or voice), peculiar feature, distinguishing mark AWW 1.1.96 *every line and trick of his sweet favour*, LR 4.6.106, 1H4 2.4.404.
4 Touch (of a disease) LLL 5.2.416 *I have a trick Of the old rage…I am sick*.
5 Trifling ornament or toy, trinket, bauble SHR 4.3.67 *A knack, a toy, a trick*, WT 2.1.51, COR 4.4.21.
~ *vb*.
1 (with *up*) Deck out, adorn H5 3.6.76 *the phrase of war, which they trick up with new-tun'd oaths*.
2 (in heraldry) Delineate arms, indicating colours by means of certain arrangements of dots or lines; (used allusively) 'blazon' (Dyce) HAM 2.2.457 *Now is he total gules, horridly trick'd With blood of fathers*.

tricking *n*. Ornamentation WIV 4.4.79 *tricking for our fairies*.

tricksy *adj*. Full of tricks or pranks, sportive, mischievous TMP 5.1.226 *My tricksy spirit*, MV 3.5.69.

tried *ppl. adj*. Refined MV 2.7.53 *tried gold*.

trifle *n*. *enchanted trifle* Trick of magic TMP 5.1.112 *some enchanted trifle to abuse me*.
~ *vb*.
1 (of time) Spend to no purpose, pass frivolously MV 4.1.298 *We trifle time*, H8 5.2.212.
2 Make trivial or insignificant MAC 2.4.4 *this sore night Hath trifled former knowings*.

trigon *n*. Triangle; in astrology, conjunction of three planets of the zodiac, distant 120 degrees from each other, as if at the angles of an equilateral triangle 2H4 2.4.265 *the fiery Trigon* (i.e. the three superior planets meeting in Aries, Leo, or Sagittarius).

trill *vb.* Trickle LR 4.3.12 *an ample tear trill'd down Her delicate cheek.*

trim *n.*
1 Fine attire, apparel, adornment, trappings COR 1.9.62 *My noble steed...With all his trim belonging*, 1H4 4.1.113, ANT 4.4.22; (fig.) H5 4.3.115 *our hearts are in the trim.*
2 (nautical sense) Condition of being fully rigged and ready to sail ERR 4.1.90 *The ship is in her trim*, TMP 5.1.236.
~ *vb.* Furnish, equip 2H4 1.3.94 *trimm'd in thine own desires* (i.e. furnished with what you desire).
~ *adj.* (ironically) Fine, nice, pretty MND 3.2.157 *a trim exploit*, 1H4 5.1.135, TRO 4.5.33. .
~ *adv.* Trimly, neatly ROM 2.1.13 *he that shot so trim.*

trinket *n.* (pl.) Tools, implements; (applied contemptuously to followers) trash, rubbish 2H6 1.4.53 *We'll see your trinkets here all forthcoming.*

trip *n.* Catch in wrestling by which one causes one's antagonist to lose his balance and fall; (fig.) TN 5.1.167 *That thine own trip shall be thine overthrow.*

tripe-visaged *adj.* With a face like tripe 2H4 5.4.8 *thou damn'd tripe-visag'd rascal* (i.e., perh., sallow, pitted).

triple *adj.* One of three, third AWW 2.1.108 *a triple eye*, ANT 1.1.12.
⟡ MND 5.1.384 *triple Hecate's*: see THRICE-CROWNED.

triple-turned *adj.* Thrice faithless ANT 4.12.13 *Triple-turn'd whore!*

triplex *n.* (in music) Triple time TN 5.1.37 *the triplex, sir, is a good tripping measure.*

tristful *adj.* Sad HAM 3.4.50 *With tristful visage* (F1; Qq *heated*).
⟡ In 1H4 2.4.393 *my trustful queen* (F1, Qq): Dering's emendation *tristful.* See TRUSTFUL.

triumph *n.*
1 Public festivity or rejoicing, festive show, entertainment MND 1.1.19 *with triumph, and with revelling*, TGV 5.4.161, 1H4 3.3.41; (spec.) tournament R2 5.2.52 *justs and triumphs*, 1H6 5.5.31, PER 2.2.1; (attrib.) R2 5.2.66 *the triumph day.*
2 Trump-card; (allusively) ANT 4.14.20 *she...has Pack'd cards with Caesar's, and false play'd my glory Unto an enemy's triumph.*
~ *vb.* Celebrate a Roman triumph COR 2.1.177 *weep'st to see me triumph.*

triumphant *adj.*
1 Triumphal, celebrating a triumph 1H6 1.1.22 *a triumphant car*, COR 5.5.3, R3 4.4.333.
⟡ SON 151.10 *his triumphant prize*: (?) (1) transf. use of sense 1, or (2) gained by conquest.
2 Splendid, glorious, magnificent ANT 2.2.184 *a most triumphant lady*, ROM 5.3.83, SON 33.10.

triumphantly *adv.* Festively MND 4.1.89 *Dance in Duke Theseus' house triumphantly.*

triumpher *n.* One who celebrated a Roman triumph TIT 1.1.170 *Gracious triumpher in the eyes of Rome* (hence, victorious general), TIM 5.1.196.

triumpherate *n.* (error in F1 for) Triumvirate ANT 3.6.28.

triumphery *n.* (error in F, Q for) Triumviry LLL 4.3.51.

Trojan *n.* (cant term) Boon companion, dissolute fellow H5 5.1.19 *Dost thou thirst, base Trojan* (F1 *Troyan*), LLL 5.2.636, 1H4 2.1.69.

troll *vb.* Run over (a song), sing TMP 3.2.117 *Will you troll the catch...?*

troll-my-dames *n.* Game played by ladies, resembling bagatelle, in which the object was to 'troll' or roll balls through arches set on a board WT 4.3.87 *A fellow, sir, that I have known to go about with troll-my-dames.*

troop *n.* (pl.) Retinue 2H6 1.3.77 *with troops of ladies*, ANT 4.14.53, R3 4.4.96.
~ *vb.* Associate *with*, go in company *with* LR 1.1.132 *all the large effects That troop with majesty*, ROM 1.5.48.

trophy *n.*
1 In ancient Greece and Rome, structure erected as a memorial of a victory in war, monument TIM 5.4.25 *these great towers, trophies, and schools*; (transf.) painted or carved figure of such a memorial COR 1.3.40 *it more becomes a man Than gilt his trophy.*
2 (fig.) Anything serving as a token or evidence of victory, valour, etc., token, sign H5 5.Ch.21 *Giving full trophy, signal, and ostent Quite from himself to God*, H5 5.1.72, LC 218; (applied to a crown or garland) JC 1.1.69 *let no images Be hung with Caesar's trophies*, HAM 4.7.174.
3 Emblem or memorial placed over a grave or on a tomb TIT 1.1.388 *with trophies do adorn thy tomb*, AWW 2.3.139, HAM 4.5.215.

tropically *adv.* Figuratively HAM 3.2.237 *'The Mouse Trap'. Marry, how? tropically: this play is the image of a murder done in Vienna.*

trossers See STROSSERS.

trot *n.* (usu. disparaging) Old woman SHR 1.2.79 *an old trot with ne'er a tooth in her head*; (applied to a man) MM 3.2.50 *What sayst thou, Trot?*

troth *n.*
1 Truth CYM 5.5.274 *I'll speak troth*, MND 2.2.36, COR 4.5.186.
2 Faithfulness, good faith, loyalty LLL 4.3.141 *break faith and troth*, LR 3.4.123, LUC 885; (used as an asseveration: simply) WIV 1.4.144 *Troth, sir, all is in His hands above*, MM 2.1.217; (duplicated) H8 2.3.34 *Nay, good troth.—Yes, troth and troth*; (with *good*) CYM 3.6.47 *Good troth*, OTH 4.3.70, H8 2.3.33; (with *by*) ERR 3.1.62 *By my troth*, ADO 1.1.224, R3 2.4.23; (with *in*) COR 1.3.106 *In troth, I think she would*; (with *o'*) TMP 2.2.34 *o' my troth!*, LLL 4.1.142.

trothed *ppl. adj.* Betrothed ADO 3.1.38 *my new trothed lord.*

troth-plight *n.* Act of plighting troth, solemn promise or engagement, esp. of marriage, betrothal WT 1.2.278 *As rank as any flax-wench that puts to Before her troth-plight.*
~ *ppl. adj.* Engaged by a 'troth', betrothed, affianced H5 2.1.19 *you were troth-plight to her*, WT 5.3.151.

trouble *vb.*
1 Agitate, disturb (water, the sky) SHR 5.2.142 *like a fountain troubled*, 2H6 4.1.72.
2 Interfere with, interrupt COR 5.6.127 *Trouble not the peace*, TMP 3.2.48, WT 5.3.129.

troubled *ppl. adj.* Agitated, disturbed 1H4 1.1.10 *the meteors of a troubled heaven*, JC 1.2.101, LUC 589.

troublous *adj.* Characterized by trouble, disordered, disturbed R3 2.3.9 *a troublous world*, 2H6 1.2.22, 3H6 2.1.159.

trow *vb.*
1 Believe LR 1.4.122 *Learn more than thou trowest.*
2 Think, suppose 2H6 2.4.38 *Trowest thou that e'er I'll look upon the world*, 3H6 5.1.85.
3 Know H8 1.1.184 *as I trow—Which I do well*, LR 1.4.214 (Ff *know*).
4 *I trow*: (1) I am pretty sure, I daresay SHR 1.2.4 *I trow this is his house*, R2 2.1.218, ROM 1.3.33. (2) I wonder WIV 1.4.132 *Who's there, I trow?*, WIV 2.1.64; (sometimes simply) *trow* CYM 1.6.47 *What is the matter, trow?*, ADO 3.4.59.
5 *trow you* Do you know?, can you tell? LLL 5.2.279 *And trow you what he call'd me?*, SHR 1.2.164, AYL 3.2.179.

Troyan See TROJAN.

truant *n.* One who begs without justification, idle rogue or knave Ado 3.2.18 *Hang him, truant, there's no true drop of blood in him…If he be sad, he wants money.*

~ *vb. truant with* Be unfaithful to Err 3.2.17 *'Tis double wrong, to truant with your bed.*

truce *n.* Peace 1H6 5.4.117 *peaceful truce shall be proclaim'd,* Err 2.2.145; *take (a) truce* make peace Jn 3.1.17, Rom 3.1.157, Ven 82.

truckle-bed *n.* Low bed running on truckles or castors usu. pushed beneath a high or 'standing bed' when not in use Wiv 4.5.7 *his standing-bed and truckle-bed* (F1; Q1 *trundle-bed*), Rom 2.1.39 (F1; Q1 *trundle-bed*).

true *adj.*
1 Honest Wiv 2.1.145 *the priest…commended him for a true man,* Tmp 5.1.268, 1H4 2.4.501; *true man* freq. opposed to 'thief' Cym 2.3.72 *sometime hangs both thief and true man* (F1 *True-man*) Ado, 3.3.51, Ven 724.
2 Trustworthy, reliable Tro 1.3.238 *strong joints, true swords,* Tit 5.1.102, Son 48.2.
3 Well-proportioned Lr 1.2.8 *my shape as true As honest madam's issue,* Son 62.6.

~ *adv.*
1 'Truly', truthfully AWW 4.2.22 *the plain single vow that is vow'd true,* Cor 5.2.32.
2 'Truly', genuinely, really 1H4 1.1.62 *a dear, a true industrious friend.*

true-confirmed *adj.* Faithful and steadfast, unwavering in faithfulness TGV 4.4.103 *I am my master's true-confirmed love* (F1 *true confirmed*).

true-man See TRUE *adj.* sense 1.

true-penny *n.* Honest fellow Ham 1.5.150 *Art thou there, true-penny?*

truest-mannered *adj.* Most honestly disposed Cym 1.6.166 *he is one The truest-manner'd* (F1 *truest manner'd*).

trump *n.* Trumpet 1H6 1.4.80 *Whilst any trump did sound, or drum struck up,* Oth 3.3.351, Tit 1.1.275.

trumpet *n.* One who blows on a trumpet, trumpeter H5 4.2.61 *I will the banner from a trumpet take,* 3H6 5.1.16, Tro 4.5.6.

truncheon *n.* Staff carried as a symbol of office, command or authority MM 2.2.61 *The marshall's truncheon,* Ham 1.2.204, Tro 5.3.53.

~ *vb.* Beat with a truncheon 2H4 2.4.142 *captains …would truncheon you out for taking their names upon you.*

truncheoner *n.* One armed with a 'truncheon' or cudgel H8 5.3.52 *some forty truncheoners draw to her succour.*

trundle-bed See TRUCKLE-BED.

trundle-tail *n.* Dog with a curly tail, low-bred dog Lr 3.6.70 *bobtail tike or trundle-tail.*

trunk sleeve *n.* Full, puffed sleeve Shr 4.3.141 *With a trunk sleeve.*

trunk-work *n.* Secret or clandestine action, as by means of a trunk WT 3.3.74 *This has been some stair-work, some trunk-work, some behind-door-work.*

truss *vb.* Pack 2H4 3.2.325 *you might have truss'd him…into an eel-skin* (Q *thrust*).

trust *n.*
1 Belief, conviction TN 4.3.15 *persuades me To any other trust but I am mad.*
2 Credit MV 1.1.185 *of my trust* (i.e. on my credit).
3 Trusted person 1H6 4.4.20 *the trust of England's honour,* Tit 1.1.181.

~ *in phrases*
for fear of trust Fearing to trust myself Son 23.5 *So I, for fear of trust, forget to say The perfect ceremony of love's rite.* **in trust** Enjoying one's confidence, confidential H8 1.2.125 *This was his*

gentleman in trust. **of trust** Trustworthy, reliable Cor 1.6.52 *their men of trust,* Lr 2.1.115, Ant 5.2.154. **on my trust** As I am to be trusted, on my word MM 5.1.147 *And on my trust, a man that never yet Did…misreport your Grace.* **put in trust** Entrust important matters to Lr 1.4.14 *to serve him truly that will put me in trust,* Oth 2.3.126. **What is the trust of…** What reliance can be placed upon…? 1H6 3.2.112 *What is the trust or strength of foolish man?*

~ *vb.* Believe, be sure of Shr 4.2.67 *If he be credulous, and trust my tale,* WT 2.3.49, Mac 1.3.120.

~ *in phrases*
trust me Believe me, truly TGV 1.2.44 *trust me, 'tis an office of great worth,* Wiv 2.1.33, Tit 1.1.261. **never trust me** (usu. the apodosis of a conditional sentence) TN 2.3.188 *If I do not, never trust me,* Tro 5.2.59. **never trust me then** Have no fear TN 3.2.58 *you'll not deliver't?—Never trust me then,* 1H6 2.2.48.

truster *n.* Creditor Tim 4.1.10 *Bankrupts…out with your knives And cut your trusters' throats!*

trustful *adj.* Faithful 1H4 2.4.393 *my trustful queen.*
⋄ F1, Qq. See TRISTFUL.

trustless *adj.* Faithless Luc 2 *the trustless wings of false desire.*

trusty *adj.* Requiring faithfulness or reliability AWW 3.6.15 *he might at some great and trusty business in a main danger fail you.*

truth *n.*
1 Honesty, righteousness Ado 4.1.35 *what authority and show of truth Can cunning sin cover itself withal,* Jn 4.3.144, Luc 1532.
2 Loyalty, faithfulness 3H6 4.8.26 *In sign of truth I kiss your Highness' hand,* R2 5.2.44, Son 41.12.

try *n.* Trial, test Tim 5.1.9 *a try for his friends.*

~ *vb.*
1 Separate the good part of a thing from the rest, sift, strain Tim 2.2.178 *try the argument of hearts.*
2 (fig.) Refine MV 2.9.63 *The fire seven times tried this,* MV 2.9.64.
3 Prove, demonstrate Rom 4.3.29 *he hath still been tried a holy man,* Ham 1.3.62, Ven 280; (intr.) Ado 1.1.260 *as time shall try.*
4 Sail close to the wind, lie to Tmp 1.1.35 *bring her to try with main course.*

tub *n.* Sweating-tub used in the treatment of venereal disease MM 3.2.57 *she is herself in the tub,* H5 2.1.75, Tim 4.3.87.

tub-fast *n.* Abstinence during treatment in the sweating-tub for venereal disease Tim 4.3.88 *the tub-fast and the diet.*

tuck *n.* Rapier TN 3.4.224 *Dismount thy tuck*; (applied contemptuously to a person) 1H4 2.4.248 *you vile standing tuck.*

tucket *n.* Flourish or preliminary signal given on a trumpet MV 5.1.SD. *A tucket sounds,* Lr 2.1.SD; (attrib.) H5 4.2.35 *The tucket sonance and the note to mount.*

tuffe *n.* (var. of) Tuft, bunch Wiv 5.5.70 *In em'rald tuffes.*
⋄ F1; mod. edd. freq. *tufts.*

tuft *n.* Small group of trees, clump AYL 3.5.75 *the tuft of olives here,* WT 2.1.34, R2 2.3.53.

tug *vb.*
1 Pull about roughly, buffet Mac 3.1.111 *tugg'd with fortune.*
2 Contend, strive in opposition WT 4.4.497 *let myself and fortune Tug for the time to come,* 2H6 3.2.173, 3H6 2.5.11.

tuition *n.* Protection Ado 1.1.281 *and so I commit you—To the tuition of God.*

tumble *vb.* Roll about on the ground, or in the water or air Tmp 2.2.11 *hedgehogs which Lie tumbling* *in my barefoot way*, JN 3.4.176, PER 2.1.30; (with lascivious connotations) WT 4.3.12 *While we lie tumbling in the hay*, ANT 1.4.17, HAM 4.5.62; (in a nautical sense) roll about the trough of the sea, wallow PER 5.Gower.13 *at sea, tumbled and tost* (Q4).

tun *n.*

1 Large cask or barrel, usu. for liquids; (fig.) 1H4 2.4.448 *an old fat man, a tun of man*; large vessel in general, chest H5 1.2.255 *This tun of treasure.*

2 Measure of capacity for liquids, usu. equivalent to 4 hogsheads WIV 2.1.65 *this whale (with so many tuns of oil in his belly)*, COR 4.5.99 (or sense 1).

tun-dish *n.* Funnel MM 3.2.172 *filling a bottle with a tun-dish.*

tune *n.*

1 Tone, accent (of the voice) COR 2.3.85 *the tune of your voices*, CYM 5.5.238, SON 141.5.

2 Temper, humour, mood HAM 5.2.190 *the tune of the time*, LR 4.3.39, MM 3.2.48.

~ *vb.* Utter or express musically, sing LUC 1107 *The little birds that tune their morning's joy*, LUC 1465, VEN 74.

tuneable *adj.* Tuneful, musical MND 1.1.184 *your tongue's sweet air More tuneable than lark to shepherd's ear*, MND 4.1.124.

tup *vb.* (of a ram) Copulate with (a ewe) OTH 1.1.89 *an old black ram Is tupping your white ewe.*

turf *n.* (Holofernes' speech) Clod LLL 4.2.88 *a turf of earth.*

Turk *n.*

1 (used generically) Infidel AYL 4.3.33 *she defies me, Like Turk to Christian*, WIV 1.3.88, R3 3.5.41; *turn Turk* change completely (as from a Christian to an infidel) HAM 3.2.276 *if the rest of my fortunes turn Turk with me*, ADO 3.4.57; (attrib.) 1H4 5.3.45 *Turk Gregory never did such deeds in arms.*

▷ To Christian nations the Turks were the typical Moslem power from 13C.

2 *The Turk* The Sultan of Turkey H5 5.2.209 *go to Constantinople and take the Turk by the beard*, AWW 2.3.88, OTH 1.3.20.

turlygod *n.* (app. a name for) Bedlam-beggar, person discharged from an asylum for the insane, freq. only part cured, and licensed to beg LR 2.3.20 *Poor Turlygod! Poor Tom!*

turmoiled *ppl. adj.* Harassed (with tumult and commotion) 2H6 4.10.16 *who would live turmoiled in the court.*

turn *vb.*

1 Shape on a lathe 1H4 3.1.129 *I had rather hear a brazen canstick turn'd.*

2 Compose (a poem or tune) LLL 1.2.184 *I shall turn sonnet*, AYL 2.5.3.

3 Fling back, return R2 4.1.39 *I will turn thy falsehood to thy heart*, 1H6 2.4.79, TIM 2.1.26.

4 Come back, return R3 4.4.185 *Ere from this war thou turn a conqueror*, TIT 5.2.141, OTH 4.1.254.

5 Go back on one's word; (hence) be inconstant or fickle TGV 2.2.4 *If you turn not*, MND 3.2.91, 1H6 3.3.85.

6 Change (one's countenance or colour) COR 4.6.60 *some news...That turns their countenances*, HAM 2.2.519, OTH 4.2.62.

~ *in phrases*

turn the balance, beam, scale Cause one scale of a balance to descend, said of an additional, usu. slight or just sufficient, weight, preponderate MM 4.2.31 *a feather will turn the scale*, MND 5.1.318, HAM 4.5.158. **turn head** (hunting term) Turn and face the enemy, show a bold opposing front H5 2.4.69 *Turn head, and stop pursuit.*

Turnbull Street *n.* (Eliz. corr. of) Turnmill Street, resort of dissolute and disorderly persons 2H4

3.2.306 *the feats he hath done about Turnbull Street.*

turning *ppl. adj.* Fickle H5 3.6.34 *she is turning, and inconstant.*

turtle *n.*

1 Turtle-dove, symbol of constancy in love WT 4.4.154 *Your hand, my Perdita. So turtles pair That never mean to part*, WIV 2.1.81, PHT 57.

2 (fig.) Applied to a person as a term of endearment, esp. to lovers in allusion to the turtle-dove's affection for its mate LLL 4.3.208 *Will these turtles be gone?*

tush *n.* Tusk VEN 624 *whom he strikes his crooked tushes slay*, VEN 617.

tutor *vb.* Teach (a thing) 2H4 4.1.44 *Whose learning and good letters peace hath tutor'd.*

twain *n.* Pair, couple TMP 4.1.104 *To bless this twain*, ANT 1.1.38.

~ *vb.* Part or divide in twain; (hence) weaken R2 5.3.134 *Twice saying 'pardon' doth not pardon twain, But makes one pardon strong.*

~ *adj.*

1 Two WT 4.4.660 *What have we twain forgot*, SHR 2.1.304, MAC 3.1.27; *in twain* into two parts or pieces, in two 1H6 4.5.49 *Than can yourself yourself in twain divide*, 2H6 1.2.26, TRO 1.1.35.

2 *both twain* (redundant use) Both LLL 5.2.459 *I remit both twain*, SON 42.11.

3 Separate, parted asunder ROM 3.5.240 *Thou and my bosom henceforth shall be twain*, TRO 3.1.102, SON 36.1.

tway *adj.* [Northern dial.] Two H5 3.2.119 *heard some question 'tween you tway.*

twelfe *adj.* (var. of) Twelfth TN 2.3.84 *the twelfe day of December* (F1).

▷ Spelt in the same way in the title of the play.

twelve score *n. phr.* (short for) Twelve score yards WIV 3.2.34 *as easy as a cannon will shoot pointblank twelve score*, 1H4 2.4.547, 2H4 3.2.46.

twenty *adj.*

1 Used indefinitely or hyperbolically to express a large number WIV 1.1.2 *if he were twenty Sir John Falstaffs*, LR 2.4.70, VEN 522.

2 *and twenty* Used as an intensive WIV 2.1.196 *Good even and twenty* (i.e. twenty times good), TN 2.3.51.

▷ In SHR 4.2.57 *That teacheth tricks eleven and twenty long* there is an allusion to the game of one and thirty.

twiggen *adj.* Having a wickerwork covering OTH 2.3.148 *I 'll beat the knave into a twiggen bottle* (Qq *wicker*).

twilled *adj.* (?) Ridged, raised up in ridges (perh. for layering hedges or plants) TMP 4.1.64 *Thy banks with pioned and twilled brims.*

twin *vb.*

1 Be born at the same birth *with*, be the twin of OTH 2.3.212 *Though he had twinn'd with me, both at a birth.*

2 Be like twins in resemblance or companionship COR 4.4.15 *who twin, as 'twere, in love Unseparable*, PER 5.Gower.8.

twink *n.* Winking of the eye, twinkling, instant (with *with*) TMP 4.1.43 *with a twink*; (with *in*) SHR 2.1.310 *in a twink.*

twinned *ppl. adj.*

1 Born at one birth, twin TIM 4.3.3 *Twinn'd brothers*, WT 1.2.67; (hence) exactly alike, resembling each other like twins CYM 1.6.35 *the twinn'd stones Upon the number'd beach.*

twire *vb.* Peep, twinkle SON 28.12 *When sparkling stars twire not.*

twist *n.* Cord COR 5.6.95 *twist of rotten silk.*

~ *vb.* Form, draw out (a thread) by spinning JN 4.3.128 *the smallest thread That ever spider twisted from her womb;* (fig.) ADO 1.1.311 *thou began'st to twist so fine a story.*

two-and-thirty See PEEP.

Tyburn *n.* Usual place of execution in London; (used allusively) LLL 4.3.52 *the triumviry, the corner-cap of society, The shape of love's Tyburn* (with ref. to the triangular form of the gallows).

tyke *n.* (var. of) (1) tick, a parasite; (2) TIKE; (applied as a term of contempt to a person) H5 2.1.29 *Base tyke* (F1).
▷ Either sense could be appropriate.

type *n.* Distinguishing mark, sign, stamp 3H6 1.4.121 *Thy father bears the type of King of Naples* (i.e. the crown), H8 1.3.31, LUC 1050.

tyrannically *adv.* Vehemently, violently HAM 2.2.341 *most tyrannically clapp'd for't.*

tyrannize *vb.* Play the tyrant; (hence) inflict pain or torment TIT 3.2.8 *This poor right hand of mine*

Is left to tyrannize upon my breast, JN 5.7.47, LUC 676.

tyrannous *adj.* (transf.) Of the nature of tyranny, oppressive, cruel, pitiless R3 4.3.1 *The tyrannous and bloody act is done,* HAM 2.2.460, LR 3.4.151.

tyranny *n.* Violence, outrage, cruelty AWW 1.1.50 *the tyranny of her sorrows,* COR 5.3.43, LR 3.4.2.

tyrant *n.*
1 One who seizes the sovereign power in a state without legal right, usurper 3H6 3.3.71 *To prove him tyrant this reason may suffice, That Henry liveth still.*
2 One who acts in a cruel manner, violent, pitiless one ADO 1.1.169 *a profess'd tyrant to their sex,* CYM 1.1.84, 2H4 Ind.14.
~ *adj.* Cruel, pitiless, violent JN 5.3.14 *this tyrant fever,* LUC 851, PHT 10.

U

umber *n.* Brown pigment, used to disguise the face AYL 1.3.112 *with a kind of umber smirch my face.*

umbered *adj.* Darkened as if with umber H5 4.Ch.9 *Each battle sees the other's umber'd face* (i.e. shadowed by firelight).

umbrage *n.* Shadow HAM 5.2.119 *his semblable is his mirror, and who else would trace him, his umbrage, nothing more.*

umpire *n.* (transf.) One who settles a matter and brings peace, 'friendly compounder of differences' (Cotgrave); (applied to Death) 1H6 2.5.29 *Just Death, kind umpire of men's miseries,...doth dismiss me,* ROM 4.1.63.

un boitier vert [Fr.] See UNE BOITRE VERTE.

un garçon, un paysan [Fr.] A boy, a peasant WIV 5.5.205.

unable *adj.* Weak, impotent, inadequate SHR 5.2.169 *froward and unable worms,* LR 1.1.60, 1H6 4.5.4.

unaccommodated *ppl. adj.* Unfurnished with necessaries (e.g. dress) LR 3.4.106 *unaccommodated man is no more but such a...bare...animal as thou art.*

unaccustomed *ppl. adj.* Strange, unusual, not customary 1H6 3.1.93 *set this unaccustom'd fight aside,* ROM 3.5.67, JC 2.1.199.

unacquainted *ppl. adj.*
1 Having no intimate knowledge of things TRO 3.3.12 *am become As new into the world, strange, unacquainted.*
2 Unfamiliar, strange JN 3.4.166 *unacquainted change,* JN 5.2.32.

unadvised *adj.*
1 By inadvertence TGV 4.4.122 *I have unadvis'd Deliver'd you a paper that I should not;* done in ignorance LUC 1488 *friend to friend gives unadvised wounds.*
2 Indiscreet, thoughtless, rash JN 2.1.191 *unadvised scold,* JN 5.2.132, TIT 2.1.38; imprudent, done without consideration ROM 2.2.118 *It is too...unadvis'd, too sudden.*
~ *adv.* Unwisely, rashly, thoughtlessly JN 2.1.45 *Lest unadvis'd you stain your swords with blood.*

unadvisedly *adv.* Unwisely, rashly, thoughtlessly R3 4.4.292 *Men shall deal unadvisedly sometimes.*

unagreeable *adj.* Unsuitable TIM 2.2.40 *The time is unagreeable to this business.*

unaneled *ppl. adj.* Unanointed; (hence) not having received the sacrament of extreme unction HAM 1.5.77 *Thus was I...Cut off even in the blossoms of my sin,...unanel'd.*

unapproved *ppl. adj.* Unconfirmed by trial, unproved LC 53 *unapproved witness.*

unapt *adj.*
1 Unfit SHR 5.2.166 *Unapt to toil,* LUC 695.
2 Not prepared or inclined COR 5.1.52 *We...are unapt To give or to forgive,* 1H4 1.3.2, 1H6 5.3.133.

unaptness *n.* Disclination TIM 2.2.131 *you...that unaptness made your minister.*

unarm *vb.* Take off, remove one's armour or arms (trans.) TRO 3.1.150 *To help unarm our Hector;* (refl.) TRO 5.3.35 *Unarm thee,* TRO 1.2.274; (intr.) TRO 5.3.25 *Unarm, sweet Hector* (i.e. remove your armour), TRO 5.3.3, ANT 4.14.35 *Unarm, Eros* (i.e. remove my armour).

unattainted *ppl. adj.* Unbiased ROM 1.2.85 *unattainted eye.*

unattempted *adj.* Not tempted, unassailed JN 2.1.591 *my hand, as unattempted yet,...raileth on the rich.*

unavoided *adj.*
1 Not avoided R3 4.1.55 *A cockatrice...Whose unavoided eye is murderous.*
2 Unavoidable, inevitable 1H6 4.5.8 *A terrible and unavoided danger,* R2 2.1.268, R3 4.4.218.

unawares *adv.* at unawares Suddenly, unexpectedly 3H6 4.2.23 *we...At unawares may beat down Edward's guard,* 3H6 4.8.63, TRO 3.2.38.

unbacked *adj.* Unridden TMP 4.1.176 *unback'd colts,* VEN 320.

unbanded *adj.* Having no hatband AYL 3.2.379 *your hose should be ungarter'd, your bonnet unbanded.*

unbarbed *adj.* Unarmed, not caparisoned; (hence) bare, not protected COR 3.2.99 *my unbarb'd sconce.*

unbated *adj.*
1 Unabated MV 2.6.11 *unbated fire.*
2 Not bated or blunted HAM 4.7.138 *A sword unbated* (i.e. without a button on the tip), HAM 5.2.317.

unbend *vb.* Make slack, relax, weaken MAC 2.2.42 *You do unbend your noble strength, to think So brain-sickly of things.*

unbent *ppl. adj.*
1 (of a bow) Not bent, released from tension; (hence) unprepared CYM 3.4.108 *To be unbent when thou hast ta'en thy stand.*
2 (of a brow) Not wrinkled or knit LUC 1509 *A brow unbent* (i.e. not frowning).

unbid *ppl. adj.* Uninvited; (hence) unwelcome 3H6 5.1.18 *O unbid spite.*

unbitted *ppl. adj.* Unbridled OTH 1.3.331 *unbitted lusts.*

unbless *vb.* Not make happy SON 3.4 *if now thou not renewest, Thou dost...unbless some mother.*

unblessed, unblest *ppl. adj.* Cursed, wretched OTH 2.3.307 *every inordinate cup is unbless'd, and the ingredient is a devil,* OTH 5.1.34.

unbodied *ppl. adj.* Incorporeal TRO 1.3.16 *that unbodied figure of the thought That gave't surmised shape.*

unbolt *vb.* (intr.) Disclose, explain TIM 1.1.51 *I will unbolt to you.*

unbolted *ppl. adj.* Unsifted; (hence) coarse LR 2.2.66 *I will tread this unbolted villain into mortar.*

unbonneted *ppl. adj.* Not wearing a bonnet, having the head uncovered LR 3.1.14 *unbonneted he runs;* (spec. as a mark of respect) OTH 1.2.23 *my demerits May speak, unbonneted, to as proud a fortune As this that I have reached.*

◇ In OTH the sense may be 'without taking the hat off', i.e. on equal terms. Cf. BONNET.

unbookish *adj.* Ignorant, unskilled OTH 4.1.101 *his unbookish jealousy must construe Poor Cassio's...behaviours Quite in the wrong.*

unborn *ppl. adj.* Non-existent COR 3.1.129 *All cause unborn* (i.e. without cause).

unbraced *pa. pple.* Unbuttoned, unfastened JC 1.3.48 *thus unbrac'd...Have bar'd my bosom to the thunder-stone* (i.e. with doublet unfastened), JC 2.1.262, HAM 2.1.75.

unbraided *ppl. adj.* Untarnished, not faded or shopsoiled WT 4.4.203 *unbraided wares.*

unbreathed *ppl. adj.* Unexercised MND 5.1.74 *their unbreathed memories.*

unbred *ppl. adj.* Unborn SON 104.13 *thou age unbred.*

unbruised *ppl. adj.* Unhurt ROM 2.3.37 *unbruised youth,* ADO 5.4.111, TRO Pr.14; undamaged JN 2.1.254 *helmets all unbruis'd.*

unbuckle *vb.* Tear off (a helmet) in a close fight COR 4.5.125 *Unbuckling helms, fisting each other's throat,* ANT 4.4.12.

uncape *vb.* Divest (one) of a cape or covering; (hence) uncover, drive out of hiding WIV 3.3.165 *we'll unkennel the fox...So, now uncape.*

uncase *vb.* (refl.) Undress SHR 1.1.207 *Uncase thee;* (intr.) LLL 5.2.701 *Pompey is uncasing for the combat.*

uncharge *vb.* Acquit of guilt HAM 4.7.67 *even his mother shall uncharge the practice, And call it accident* (i.e. fail to suspect the plot).

uncharged *ppl. adj.* Unattacked TIM 5.4.55 *your uncharged ports.*

uncharmed *ppl. adj.* *uncharmed from* Not subject to the spell of ROM 1.1.211 *From Love's...bow she lives uncharm'd.*

unchary *adv.* Carelessly TN 3.4.202 *I have said too much unto a heart of stone, And laid mine honour too unchary on't.*

unchecked *ppl. adj.* Not contradicted MV 3.1.2 *it lives there uncheck'd that...*

unclasp *vb.* Open, unfasten; (fig.) TRO 4.5.60 *wide unclasp the tables of their thoughts,* 1H4 1.3.188, TN 1.4.13; disclose WT 3.2.167 *He...to my kingly guest Unclasp'd my practice,* ADO 1.1.323.

uncleanly *adj.* Improper, indelicate, unbecoming JN 4.1.7 *Uncleanly scruples,* AYL 3.2.50, OTH 3.3.139.

unclew *vb.* (lit.) Unwind; (hence, fig.) ruin TIM 1.1.168 *If I should pay you for't as 'tis extoll'd, It would unclew me quite.*

uncoined *ppl. adj.* Not coined; (fig.) not fabricated, not invented or made up H5 5.2.153 *a fellow of plain and uncoin'd constancy.*

uncolted *adj.* Deprived of one's horse 1H4 2.2.39 *thou art not colted, thou art uncolted* (with quibble; see colt *vb.* sense 1).

uncomfortable *adj.* Comfortless, cheerless ROM 4.5.60 *Uncomfortable time.*

uncomprehensive *adj.* Illimitable, incomprehensible TRO 3.3.198 *The providence that's in a watchful state...Finds bottom in th' uncomprehensive depth.*

unconfirmed *adj.* Inexperienced LLL 4.2.18 *untrained...unlettered...unconfirmed fashion,* ADO 3.3.117.

unconstant *adj.* Sudden, abrupt, irregular, erratic LR 1.1.300 *unconstant starts.*

unconstrained *adj.* Not imposed against one's will; (hence) imposing no restraint LC 242 *unconstrained gyves.*

uncouple *vb.* Set (hounds) free for the chase VEN 674 *Uncouple at the...hare,* MND 4.1.107, TIT 2.2.3.

uncouth *adj.* Strange, wild, uncanny AYL 2.6.6. *this uncouth forest,* TIT 2.3.211, LUC 1598.

uncovered *ppl. adj.*
1 Not wearing a hat, etc., bareheaded 2H6 4.1.128 *let my head Stoop to the block...Than stand uncovered to the vulgar groom.*
2 Open, unconcealed ADO 4.1.305 *uncover'd slander.*

uncropped *adj.* Unplucked AWW 5.3.327 *a fresh uncropped flower.*

uncrossed *ppl. adj.* Not cancelled CYM 3.3.26 *keeps his book uncross'd* (i.e. remains unpaid).

unction *n.* Salve, ointment HAM 4.7.141 *I bought an unction;* (fig.) HAM 3.4.145 *Lay not that flattering unction to your soul* (i.e. soothing ointment).

unctious *adj.* Oily, fat TIM 4.3.195 *man, with...morsels unctious, greases his...mind.*

uncurbable *adj.* Unrestrainable ANT 2.2.67 *So much uncurbable, her garboils...Did you too much disquiet.*

uncurrent *adj.* Not commonly accepted or recognized WT 3.2.49 *With what encounter so uncurrent.*

uncurse *vb.* Remove a curse from R2 3.2.137 *uncurse their souls.*

undeeded *adj.* Having accomplished nothing MAC 5.7.20 *my sword...I sheathe...undeeded.*

under *adj.*
1 Infernal COR 4.5.92 *all the under fiends.*
◇ See UNDERGROUND.
2 Belonging to 'this world below', sublunary LR 2.2.163 *this under globe,* MM 4.3.89 (Hanmer; F1 *yond*); *each under eye* every mortal eye SON 7.2.
~ *prep.*
1 Under the pretence of TIM 3.3.32 *under hot ardent zeal,* MV 2.4.36.
2 Under the auspices of, authorized by, protected by SON 78.4 *under thee their poesy disperse;* (esp. with abstract nouns) LR 2.2.106 *Under th' allowance of your great aspect,* SHR 5.1.39 *under my countenance* (i.e. in my person), H8 1.2.56.
3 Next to COR 1.1.187 *under the gods.*
4 *go under* (1) Profess to be AWW 3.5.20 *their promises...are not the things they go under;* (2) adhere to (an opinion) TRO 1.3.382 *Yet go we under our opinion still.*

underbear *vb.*
1 Endure JN 3.1.65 *those woes...which I alone Am bound to underbear.*
2 Trim round the lower part ADO 3.4.21 *skirts, round underborne with a bluish tinsel.*

underbearing *n.* Endurance R2 1.4.29 *patient underbearing of his fortune.*

undercrest *vb.* Wear as if a crest COR 1.9.72 *To undercrest your good addition To th' fairness of my power.*

undergo vb.
1 Be liable or subject to, run the risk of ADO 5.2.57 *Claudio undergoes my challenge*, JN 4.1.133, 1H4 1.3.164.
2 Take upon oneself, undertake to perform JC 1.3.123 *To undergo...an enterprise*, WT 2.3.164, CYM 1.4.141.
3 (fig.) Bear the weight of, sustain MM 1.1.23 *of worth To undergo such ample grace and honour*, HAM 1.4.34.

undergoing ppl. adj. Enduring TMP 1.2.157 *which raised in me An undergoing stomach* (i.e. enduring spirit).

underground n. Region beneath the surface of the earth, underworld 2H6 1.2.79 *A spirit rais'd from depth of underground* (F1 *under ground*), 2H6 2.1.170.

underhand adj. Not open or obvious, unobtrusive AYL 1.1.140 *I had...notice of my brother's purpose..., and have by underhand means labour'd to dissuade him from it.*

under-honest adj. Wanting in straightforwardness TRO 2.3.124 *over-proud And under-honest.*

underpraise n. Dispraise TIM 1.1.166 *your jewel Hath suffered underpraise.—What, my lord, dispraise?*
◇ Reinterpretation by jeweller of the poet's *underpraise*.

under-skinker n. Assistant tapster, barman 1H4 2.4.24 *clapp'd...into my hand by an under-skinker.*

understand vb. (used quibblingly) Stand under TN 3.1.79 *my legs do better understand me*, ERR 2.1.54, TGV 2.5.32.

undertake vb.
1 Take charge of, conduct H8 2.1.97 *Sir Nicholas Vaux, Who undertakes you to your end.*
2 Assume SHR 4.2.107 *His name and credit shall you undertake.*
3 Engage with, have to do with WIV 3.5.125 *you'll undertake her no more?*, TN 1.3.58, CYM 2.1.26.
4 (intr.) Make an attempt or venture LR 4.2.13 *It is the cowish terror of his spirit That dares not undertake.*
5 Take up a matter *for* OTH 2.3.330 *I will beseech ...Desdemona to undertake for me.*

undertaker n. One who takes upon himself a task or business OTH 4.1.211 *let me be his undertaker* (i.e. I will settle him, I will dispatch him); one who takes up a challenge for another TN 3.4.318 *if you be an undertaker, I am for you.*

undervalued ppl. adj. Inferior in value *to* MV 1.1.165 *nothing undervalu'd To Cato's daughter*, MV 2.7.53.

underwork vb. Undermine JN 2.1.95 *thou hast underwrought his lawful king.*

underwrite vb. Subscribe to; (he 'ice) submit to TRO 2.3.128 *underwrite...His humorous predominance.*

underwrought See UNDERWORK.

undeserving n. 'Want of merit, unworthiness' (Schmidt) LLL 5.2.366 *My lady...In courtesy gives undeserving praise.*

undetermined ppl. adj. Not decided, not settled JN 2.1.355 *In undetermin'd differences* (perh. with quibble on the sense 'uncertain, not definitely identified').

undisposed ppl. adj. Not in a merry mood ERR 1.2.80 *that merry sconce of yours That stands on tricks when I am undispos'd.*

undistinguishable adj. Not discernible, incapable of being made out MND 2.1.100 *the...mazes in the...green, For lack of tread, are undistinguishable*, MND 4.1.187.

undistinguished ppl. adj.
1 Indefinable LR 4.6.271 *O undistinguish'd space of woman's will!* (Q2 *vndistinguisht*; Q1 *indistinguish'd*).
2 Not made distinct to perception, confused, not discernible in its nature LC 20 *undistinguish'd woe.*

undividable adj. Indivisible ERR 2.2.122 *undividable incorporate.*

undo vb.
1 Hinder, be a bar to, prevent from coming into existence LR 4.1.70 *distribution should undo excess*, PER 4.6.4, TIM 3.2.48.
2 Ruin, destroy ANT 2.5.106 *Lie they upon thy hand, And be undone by 'em!*, H8 2.1.159, COR 1.1.63.
3 Beggar (description) WT 5.2.58 *I never heard of such another encounter, which...undoes description to do it.*
4 (fig.) Unravel PER 1.1.117 *If...our secret be undone.*

undone ppl. adj. Ruined TIM 4.3.481 *his undone lord*, AWW 5.3.146, TRO 3.3.258.

undoubted ppl. adj.
1 Beyond a doubt, unquestioned JN 2.1.369 *A greater pow'r than we denies all this, And till it be undoubted...*
2 Fearless 3H6 5.7.6 *undoubted champions*; unmixed or not impaired with fear 1H6 3.3.41 *Burgundy, undoubted hope of France.*

undressed ppl. adj. Unformed LLL 4.2.16 *his undressed, unpolished...fashion.*

unduteous adj. Undutiful WIV 5.5.227 *unduteous title* (i.e. designation of undutifulness).

uneared ppl. adj. Untilled SON 3.5 *whose unear'd womb.*

unearned ppl. adj. Unmerited MND 5.1.432 *unearned luck Now to scape the serpent's tongue.*

uneath adv. With difficulty, scarcely 2H6 2.4.8 *Uneath may she endure the flinty streets.*

uneffectual adj. Losing its effect HAM 1.5.90 *The glow-worm...gins to pale his uneffectual fire.*

unequal adj. Unfair, unjust 2H4 4.1.100 *a heavy and unequal hand*, ANT 2.5.101.

uneven adj. Not smooth or level, irregular, broken; (fig.) ROM 4.1.5 *Uneven is the course*; disordered, confused MM 4.4.3 *In most uneven and distracted manner*, R2 2.2.121; embarrassing, disconcerting 1H4 1.1.50 *uneven and unwelcome news.*

unexecuted ppl. adj. Not put into practice, not used ANT 3.7.44 *leave unexecuted Your own renowned knowledge.*

unexperient adj. Inexperienced; (absol.) LC 318 *th' unexperient gave the tempter place.*

unexpressive adj. Inexpressible AYL 3.2.10 *The fair, the chaste, and unexpressive she.*

unfair vb. Rob of beauty SON 5.4 *Those hours ...Will...that unfair which fairly doth excel.*

unfamed adj. Not famous, not much spoken of, inglorious TRO 2.2.159 *none so noble Whose life were ill bestow'd, or death unfam'd, Where Helen is the subject.*

unfashionable adj. Badly fashioned, uncomely R3 1.1.22 *scarce half made up, And that so...unfashionable That dogs bark at me.*

unfathered adj. Fatherless; (hence) not produced in the ordinary natural course, unnatural 2H4 4.4.122 *Unfather'd heirs and loathly births of nature*, SON 97.10, SON 124.2.

unfeeling ppl. adj. Without sensation 2H6 3.2.145 *his hand unfeeling.*

unfellowed adj. Without an equal HAM 5.2.142 *in his meed he's unfellow'd.*

unfelt ppl. adj.
1 Not felt inwardly, not experienced MAC 2.3.136 *To show an unfelt sorrow is an office Which the false man does easy*, R3 1.4.80.

2 Not perceived by others R2 2.3.61 *unfelt thanks* (i.e. 'thanks not accompanied by any palpable proofs, expressed only in words', Wright), Luc 828.

unfenced *adj.* Defenceless Jn 2.1.386 *till unfenced desolation Leave them as naked as the vulgar air.*

unfirm *adj.*
1 Unstable JC 1.3.4 *all the sway of earth Shakes like a thing unfirm;* (hence, fig.) fickle TN 2.4.33 *Our fancies are more giddy and unfirm.*
2 Weak 2H4 1.3.73 *the unfirm king.*

unfix *vb.* Loosen, move from a fixed position Mac 1.3.135 *Whose horrid image doth unfix my hair,* Mac 4.1.96, 2H4 4.1.206.

unfledged *ppl. adj.* (fig.) Inexperienced, immature WT 1.2.78 *those unfledg'd days,* Ham 1.3.65, Cym 3.3.27.

unfold *vb.*
1 Disclose or reveal by statement, explain, make clear Lr 1.1.280 *Time shall unfold what plighted cunning hides,* Oth 3.3.243, Ham 1.1.2 (or sense 2); (hence) utter, communicate Cym 5.5.313 *I must...unfold a dangerous speech.*
2 Disclose or lay open to the view, display MND 1.1.146 *the lightning...That, in a spleen, unfolds both heaven and earth,* Cym 2.3.96, Luc 1146.
3 Expose, betray (a person) Oth 5.1.21 *the Moor May unfold me to him,* Oth 4.2.141, Ant 5.2.170.
4 Open (a letter) Ham 5.2.17 *to unfold Their grand commission* (Qq2–4; F1 *unseal*); (fig.) expand Cym 1.1.26 *I do...Crush him together rather than unfold His measure duly.*
5 (intr.) Open up, become plain TN 1.2.19 *Mine own escape unfoldeth to my hope.*

unfolding *n.* Disclosure, explanation Oth 1.3.244 *To my unfolding lend your prosperous ear.*

unfolding *ppl. adj. unfolding star* Star that by its rising tells the shepherd the time to release the sheep from the fold MM 4.2.203 *th' unfolding star calls up the shepherd.*

unfool *vb.* Take from (a person) the reproach of folly Wiv 4.2.115 *have you any way then to unfool me again?*

unfurnished *ppl. adj.*
1 Unmatched with its fellow MV 3.2.126 *leave itself unfurnish'd.*
2 Unprepared Rom 4.2.10 *We shall be much unfurnish'd for this time.*
3 Undefended H5 1.2.148 *his unfurnish'd kingdom.*
4 Not hung with tapestry R2 1.2.68 *unfurnish'd walls.*

ungalled *ppl. adj.* Uninjured Ham 3.2.272 *the hart ungalled,* Err 3.1.102.

ungenitured *adj.* Impotent MM 3.2.174 *This ungenitur'd agent.*

ungird *vb.* Take off; (hence) relax TN 4.1.15 *ungird thy strangeness.*

ungored *adj.* Uninjured Ham 5.2.250 *To keep my name ungor'd.*

ungot *ppl. adj.* Unbegotten, unborn MM 5.1.142 *as free...As she from one ungot.*

ungotten *ppl. adj.* Unbegotten H5 1.2.287 *some are yet ungotten and unborn.*

ungracious *adj.* Devoid of spiritual grace, graceless, profane, wicked Ham 1.3.47 *ungracious pastors,* R2 2.3.89, 1H4 2.4.445.

unguem [L.] *ad...unguem* To a nicety, perfectly LLL 5.1.79.

unguided *ppl. adj.* Ungoverned 2H4 4.4.59 *th' unguided days And rotten times that you shall look upon.*

unhair *vb.* Denude of hair Ant 2.5.64 *I 'll unhair thy head.*

unhaired *ppl. adj.* Beardless; (hence) youthful Jn 5.2.133 *This unhair'd sauciness and boyish troops.*

⇨ Theobald's conjecture; F1 *un-heard.*

unhandled *ppl. adj.*
1 Unresolved, not dealt with H8 3.2.58 *Has left the cause o' th' King unhandled.*
2 Not broken in, untamed MV 5.1.72 *unhandled colts.*

unhandsome *adj.*
1 Improper, unbecoming, indecent 1H4 1.3.44 *a slovenly unhandsome corse.*
2 Inexpert, unskilful, inept Oth 3.4.151 *unhandsome warrior as I am.*

unhap'ly *adv.* (contracted form of) Unhappily Luc 8 *Happ'ly that name of 'chaste' unhap'ly set This ...edge on his...appetite* (Q1).

unhappily *adv.*
1 Unfortunately, unluckily, regrettably MM 1.2.156 *With child perhaps?—Unhappily, even so.*
2 With evil fortune or mischance, wretchedly, miserably Lr 1.2.144 *the effects he writes of succeed unhappily.*
3 Mischievously, maliciously Son 66.4 *purest faith unhappily forsworn;* unfavourably H8 1.4.89 *I should judge now unhappily.*
4 Unpleasantly near the truth, shrewdly Ham 4.5.13 *there might be thought, Though nothing sure, yet much unhappily.*

unhappiness *n.* Evil nature R3 1.2.25 *heir to his unhappiness.*

unhappy *vb.* Make unhappy R2 3.1.10 *A happy gentleman...By you unhappied and disfigured clean.*
~ *adj.*
1 Fatal, pernicious, bringing misfortune Cym 5.5.153 *unhappy was the clock That struck the hour,* LLL 5.2.12, Luc 1565; (hence, used as a term of depreciation) miserable, wretched Oth 2.3.34 *I have very poor and unhappy brains for drinking,* Err 4.4.124, MV 5.1.238.
2 'Mischievously waggish' (Johnson) AWW 4.5.63 *A shrewd knave and an unhappy.*

unhatched *ppl. adj.*[1] (fig.) Not brought to maturity, 'not yet brought to light' (Schmidt) Oth 3.4.141 *some unhatch'd practice Made demonstrable,* Ham 1.3.65 (F1 *unhatch't*; Q1 *new hatcht*).

unhatched *ppl. adj.*[2] Not hacked or blunted; (hence) never used in combat TN 3.4.235 *dubb'd with unhatch'd rapier.*

unheard *ppl. adj.* Unheard-of, unexampled Jn 5.2.133 *This unheard sauciness.*
⇨ See UNHAIRED.

unheart *vb.* Dishearten Cor 5.1.49 *to bite his lip And hum at good Cominius much unhearts me.*

unheedful *adj.* Rash TGV 2.6.11 *unheedful vows,* 1H6 4.4.7.

unhoused *ppl. adj.*
1 Having no household ties or cares, unrestricted Oth 1.2.26 *my unhoused free condition.*
2 Houseless Tim 4.3.229 *the creatures...whose bare unhoused trunks...Answer mere nature.*

unhouseled *adj.* Not having received the holy sacrament Ham 1.5.77 *Thus was I...Of life...at once dispatch'd,...Unhous'led,...unanel'd.*

unimproved *ppl. adj.* (?) (1) Not turned to use or account; or (2) unreproved, uncensored, undisciplined, untried Ham 1.1.96 *Fortinbras, Of unimproved mettle hot and full.*

unintelligent *adj.* Unaware WT 1.1.14 *your senses* (*unintelligent of our insufficience*).

union *n.* Pearl Ham 5.2.272 *in the cup an union shall he throw* (Ff; Qq 2–4 *Onixe*), Ham 5.2.326 (Qq 3–4 *the Onixe*).

united *ppl. adj.* Conferring union; *united ceremony* ceremony of union, marriage Wiv 4.6.52 *in the law-*

ful name of marrying To give our hearts united ceremony.

unity *n.* Oneness, singleness TRO 5.2.141 *If there be rule in unity itself* (i.e. 'if there be a rule that one is one', Johnson).

universal *adj. universal earth, world* The whole world ROM 3.2.94 *sole monarch of the universal earth*, H5 4.1.66, H5 4.8.10.

unjust *adj.*
1 Unfaithful, false TGV 4.4.168 *Theseus' perjury and unjust flight*, 3H6 5.1.106, TRO 5.1.89.
2 Dishonest 1H4 4.2.28 *discarded unjust serving-men*, WT 4.4.674, 1H4 3.3.129.
3 Untrue ADO 5.1.218 *they have verified unjust things*.

unjustly *adv.*
1 Perfidiously LUC 1836 *this chaste blood so unjustly stained*.
2 Dishonestly, dishonourably AWW 4.2.76 *him that would unjustly win*.

unkennel *vb.*
1 Dislodge, drive (a fox) from its hole WIV 3.3.165 *I'll warrant we'll unkennel the fox*.
2 (fig.) Drive out from a place, bring to light, reveal HAM 3.2.81 *If his occulted guilt Do not itself unkennel in one speech*.

unkind *adj.* Unnatural, lacking in natural feeling TIT 1.1.86 *unkind and careless of thine own*, LR 3.4.71, JC 3.2.183.
▷ In VEN 204 *had my mother borne so hard a mind, She had not brought forth thee, but died unkind* perh. with play on 'without family, childless'.

unkindly *adv.* With resentment TIM 3.6.36 *I hope it remains not unkindly with your lordship that...*

unkindness *n.*
1 Ill-feeling, want of kindly feeling, enmity AWW 2.5.32 *Is there any unkindness between my lord and you...?*, JC 4.3.159, SHR 4.3.167.
2 Ingratitude, unthankfulness LR 3.2.16 *I tax not you, you elements, with unkindness; I never gave you kingdom*.

unkiss *vb.* Undo, unmake by a kiss R2 5.1.74 *Let me unkiss the oath 'twixt thee and me*.

unknown *ppl. adj.*
1 That may not be expressed or mentioned R3 1.2.217 *divers unknown reasons*, SON 117.5.
2 *an unknown fear* Fear of what is unknown AWW 2.3.6 *we make trifles of terrors, esconcing ourselves into seeming knowledge, when we should submit ourselves to an unknown fear*.

unlace *vb.* (fig.) Undo; (hence) destroy OTH 2.3.194 *That you unlace your reputation thus* (with quibble on 'strip of lace or ornament').

unlaid *ppl. adj. unlaid ope* Not laid open, undisclosed PER 1.2.89 *To keep his bed of blackness unlaid ope*.

unlearned *ppl. adj.*
1 Uninstructed, untaught, unacquired CYM 4.2.178 *That an invisible instinct should frame them To royalty unlearn'd, honour untaught*.
2 Not skilled or versed *in* TIM 4.3.57 *I know thee well; But in thy fortunes am unlearn'd and strange*, SON 138.4.

unless *conj.* If it be not, if there be not COR 5.1.71 *all hope is vain, Unless his noble mother and his wife* (i.e. there is no hope except in them), R2 5.3.32.
~ *prep.* Except, but TIT 2.3.97 *here nothing breeds, Unless the nightly owl or fatal raven*, OTH 1.1.24, AWW 4.1.5.

unlicensed *ppl. adj.* Not furnished with permission, without permission or consent PER 1.3.16 *Why, as it were unlicens'd of your loves, He would depart*.

unlike *adj.* Unlikely, improbable MM 5.1.52 *Make*

not impossible *That which but seems unlike*, COR 3.1.48, CYM 5.5.354.

unlimited *ppl. adj.* Not restricted to the 'unities of time and place' HAM 2.2.400 *poem unlimited*.

unlineal *adj.* Not related into the direct line of descent, not hereditary MAC 3.1.62 *an unlineal hand*.

unlive *vb.* Deprive of life LUC 1754 *Where shall I live now Lucrece is unlived?*

unlooked *ppl. adj.* (with *for*)
1 Not looked *for*, unexpected, unanticipated JN 2.1.79 *How much unlook'd for is this expedition!*, ROM 1.5.29, 3H6 5.1.14; (without *for*) R3 1.3.213 *some unlook'd accident*.
2 Disregarded, unheeded 1H4 5.3.60 *honour comes unlook'd for*, SON 25.4.

unloved *ppl. adj.* Not felt or pursued as love ANT 3.6.53 *The ostentation of our love, which, left unshown, Is often left unlov'd*.

unluckily *adv.* With ill omen JC 3.3.2 *things unluckily charge my fantasy*.

unmake *vb.* (fig.) Undo, ruin, bring to nothing MAC 1.7.54 *They have made themselves, and that their fitness now Does unmake you*.

unmanned *ppl. adj.* (in falconry) Not accustomed to the presence of man; (fig.) ROM 3.2.14 *Hood my unmann'd blood...With thy black mantle* (with quibble).

unmastered *ppl. adj.* Unrestrained HAM 1.3.32 *his unmaster'd importunity*.

unmeritable *adj.* Undeserving, without merit R3 3.7.154 *Your love deserves my thanks, but my desert Unmeritable shuns your high request*, JC 4.1.12.

unminded *ppl. adj.* Unregarded, unheeded 1H4 4.3.58 *A poor unminded outlaw sneaking home*.

unmoaned *ppl. adj.* Unlamented R3 2.2.64 *Our fatherless distress was left unmoan'd*.

unmoving *ppl. adj.* Devoid of motion; (hence) steady OTH 4.2.55 *The fixed figure for the time of scorn To point his slow unmoving finger at*.
▷ Qq; prob. error for F *slow, and mouing*.

unmuzzle *vb.* (fig.) Set free AYL 1.2.70 *Unmuzzle your wisdom*.

unmuzzled *ppl. adj.* Unrestrained TN 3.1.119 *unmuzzled thoughts*.

unnerved *ppl. adj.* Weak, drained of strength HAM 2.2.474 *Th' unnerved father falls*.

unnoted *ppl. adj.*
1 Unnoticed, unregarded AWW 1.2.34 *they may jest Till their own scorn return to them unnoted*, LUC 1014.
2 Having no outward signs, imperceptible TIM 3.5.21 *with such sober and unnoted passion*.

unnumbered *ppl. adj.* Innumerable JC 3.1.63 *The skies are painted with unnumb'red sparks*, LR 4.6.21.
▷ CYM 1.6.36 *the number'd beach*: F1; Theobald's conjecture *unnumber'd*. See NUMBERED.

unordinate *adj.* Inordinate, excessive OTH 2.3.307 *Every unordinate cup is unbless'd* (Q1; F, Q2 *inordinate*).

unowed *ppl. adj.* Having no owner, unowned JN 4.3.147 *and England now is left To tug...and to part by th' teeth The unow'd interest of proud swelling state*.

unparagoned *ppl. adj.* Matchless CYM 2.2.17 *Rubies unparagon'd*, CYM 1.4.80.

unpartial *adj.* Impartial H8 2.2.106 *the unpartial judging of this business*.

unpathed *adj.* Without paths, trackless, untrodden WT 4.4.567 *unpath'd waters, undream'd shores*.

unpaved *ppl. adj.* (jocular) Without 'stones' (i.e. testicles), castrated CYM 2.3.30 *unpav'd eunuch*.

unpay *vb.* Undo, make good 2H4 2.1.119 *Pay her the*

debt you owe her, and unpay the villainy you have done with her.

unpeaceable *adj.* Not disposed to peace, contentious TIM 1.1.270 *unpeaceable dog.*

unpeeled *ppl. adj.* Stripped LLL 2.1.88 *his unpeeled house* (Q1; F1, Q2 *unpeopled*).

unperfect *adj.* Not knowing one's part SON 23.1 *an unperfect actor.*

unperfectness *n.* Imperfection OTH 2.3.297 *one unperfectness shows me another.*

unpinked *ppl. adj.* Not ornamented by having patterns or eyelet-holes punched out, not scalloped SHR 4.1.133 *Gabr'el's pumps were all unpink'd i' th' heel.*

unpitied *ppl. adj.* Unmerciful MM 4.2.13 *an unpitied whipping.*

unplausive *adj.* Disapproving TRO 3.3.43 *unplausive eyes.*

unpleased *ppl. adj.* Not pleased, displeased R2 3.3.193 *my unpleased eye.*

unpolicied *ppl. adj.* Unskilled in the conduct of public affairs ANT 5.2.308 *That I might hear thee call great Caesar ass Unpolicied!* (perh. with play on sense of 'outwitted').

unpossessing *ppl. adj.* Having no rights to the inheritance of the estate of one's father LR 2.1.67 *Thou unpossessing bastard.*

unpregnant *adj.*
1 Unapt MM 4.4.20 *unpregnant And dull to all proceedings.*
2 *unpregnant of* Unquickened by, unmoved by HAM 2.2.568 *unpregnant of my cause.*

unprevailing *ppl. adj.* Unavailing, useless HAM 1.2.107 *throw to earth This unprevailing woe.*

unprevented *ppl. adj.* Not frustrated TGV 3.1.21 *A pack of sorrows which would press you down, Being unprevented, to your timeless grave.*

unprizable *adj.*
1 Not to be prized, worthless TN 5.1.55 *For shallow draught and bulk unprizable.*
2 Beyond all price, inestimable, invaluable CYM 1.4.90 *your brace of unprizable estimations.*

unprized *ppl. adj.* Not valued or appreciated LR 1.1.259 *this unpriz'd precious maid.*

unprofited *ppl. adj.* Profitless TN 1.4.22 *unprofited return.*

unproper *adj.* Not belonging exclusively to an individual, common OTH 4.1.68 *lie in those unproper beds Which they dare swear peculiar.*

unproperly *adv.* Unsuitably, unfittingly COR 5.3.54 *I…unproperly Show duty as mistaken all this while Between the child and parent.*

unproportioned *ppl. adj.* Inordinate HAM 1.3.60 *any unproportion'd thought.*

unprovide *vb.* Make unprepared, weaken the resolution *of* OTH 4.1.206 *lest her body and her beauty unprovide my mind again.*

unprovided *ppl. adj.*
1 Unprepared H5 4.1.173 *if they die unprovided,* 3H6 5.4.63.
2 Unarmed LR 2.1.52 *With his prepared sword he charges home My unprovided body,* R3 3.2.73.
3 Poorly dressed SHR 3.2.99 *you come so unprovided.*

unqualited, unqualitied *adj.* Divested of his (manly) qualities ANT 3.11.44 *He's unqualited with very shame.*

unquestionable *adj.* Unwilling to talk, taciturn AYL 3.2.374 *an unquestionable spirit.*

unraised *ppl. adj.* Unaspiring H5 Prol.9 *flat unraised spirits.*

unraked *ppl. adj.* (of a fire) Not raked together and covered with fuel so as to keep it in WIV 5.5.44 *Where fires thou find'st unrak'd.*

unready *adj.* Not fully clothed 1H6 2.1.39 *what, all unready so?*

unreasonable *adj.* Not endowed with reason 3H6 2.2.26 *Unreasonable creatures feed their young,* ROM 3.3.111.

unrecalling *ppl. adj.* Not to be recalled, unrecaliable, past recall LUC 993 *his unrecalling crime.*

unreclaimed *ppl. adj.* Untamed HAM 2.1.34 *unreclaimed blood.*

unreconciliable *adj.* Unreconcilable, not able to be brought into friendly relations ANT 5.1.47 *that our stars, Unreconciliable, should divide Our equalness to this.*

unrecuring *ppl. adj.* Incurable TIT 3.1.90 *some unrecuring wound.*

unreprievable *adj.* Without possibility of a reprieve JN 5.7.48 *unreprievable condemned blood.*

unresisted *ppl. adj.* Irresistible LUC 282 *fear Is almost chok'd by unresisted lust.*

unrespected *ppl. adj.* Unnoticed, not regarded SON 54.10 *They live unwoo'd, and unrespected fade,* SON 43.2.

unrespective *adj.*
1 Unobservant, heedless, inattentive R3 4.2.29 *iron-witted fools And unrespective boys.*
2 Making no distinction, undiscriminating TRO 2.2.71 *the remainder viands We do not throw in unrespective sieve.*

unreverend, unreverent *adj.* Irreverent, disrespectful JN 1.1.227 *thou unreverend boy,* SHR 3.2.112, R2 2.1.123.

unrightful *ppl. adj.* Having no rightful claim R2 5.1.63 *unrightful kings.*

unroll *vb.* Strike off the roll (of thieves) WT 4.3.122 *If I make not this cheat bring out another…let me be unroll'd.*

unroosted *ppl. adj.* Forced from a roost or perch; (hence) ousted from one's place WT 2.3.75 *thou art woman-tir'd; unroosted By thy Dame Partlet.*

unrough *ppl. adj.* Not rough-chinned, beardless MAC 5.2.10 *unrough youths.*

unsallied *ppl. adj.* Unsullied LLL 5.2.352 *as pure As the unsallied lily* (F1).

unsalted See VINEWED.

unsanctified *ppl. adj.*
1 Unconsecrated HAM 5.1.229 *in ground unsanctified.*
2 Wicked, damnable LR 4.6.274 *the post unsanctified Of murderous lechers,* MAC 4.2.81.

unscanned *ppl. adj.* Inconsiderate COR 3.1.311 *The harm of unscann'd swiftness.*

unsealed *ppl. adj.* Having no seal, not ratified (as by a seal) AWW 4.2.30 *your oaths Are words and poor conditions, but unseal'd.*

unseam *vb.* Rip up MAC 1.2.22 *he unseam'd him from the nave to th' chops.*

unseasonable *adj.* Not in season for hunting LUC 581 *a poor unseasonable doe.*

unseasoned *ppl. adj.*
1 Unseasonable, ill-timed WIV 2.2.168 *this unseason'd intrusion,* 2H4 3.1.105.
2 Immature, unripe AWW 1.1.71 *an unseason'd courtier.*

unsecret *adj.* Given to revealing secrets, indiscreet TRO 3.2.125 *Why have I blabb'd? Who shall be true to us, When we are so unsecret to ourselves* (i.e. not keeping our own counsel).

unseem *vb.* Not seem (to be willing *to*) LLL 2.1.155 *In so unseeming to confess receipt Of that which hath so faithfully been paid.*

unseminared *ppl. adj.* Deprived of virility ANT 1.5.11 *'Tis well for thee, That being unseminar'd, thy freer thoughts May not fly forth of Egypt.*

unset *ppl. adj.* Not planted or sown Son 16.6 *maiden gardens, yet unset.*

unsettled *ppl. adj.* Undecided H8 2.4.64 *to rectify What is unsettled in the King,* AWW 2.5.63.

unsevered *ppl. adj.* Inseparable Cor 3.2.42 *unsever'd friends.*

unshape *vb.* Deform; (hence) disturb, upset MM 4.4.20 *This deed unshapes me quite.*

unshaped *ppl. adj.* Not moulded into shape, imperfectly formed Ham 4.5.8 *Her speech is nothing, Yet the unshaped use of it doth move The hearers to collection.*

unshapen *ppl. adj.* Mis-shapen, deformed R3 1.2.250 *On me, that halt and am unshapen thus* (Qq1-6; Ff *halts...mishapen*).

unsheathe *vb.* Dislodge Luc 1724 *A harmful knife, that thence her soul unsheathed.*

unshorn *ppl. adj.* Having the nap unclipped LC 94 *unshorn velvet.*

unshout *vb.* Reverse by shouting the effect of (former shouting), annul with shouts Cor 5.5.4 *Unshout the noise that banish'd Marcius!* (Rowe; F1 *Vnshoot*).

unshrinking *ppl. adj.* Not shrinking, unyielding, firm Mac 5.9.8 *the unshrinking station where he fought.*

unshunnable *adj.* Inevitable Oth 3.3.275 *destiny unshunnable, like death.*

unshunned *ppl. adj.* Inevitable MM 3.2.60 *an unshunn'd consequence.*

unsifted *ppl. adj.* Untried Ham 1.3.102 *a green girl, Unsifted in such perilous circumstance.*

unsinewed, unsinowed *ppl. adj.* Weak, enfeebled Ham 4.7.10 *reasons Which may to you seem much unsinew'd, But yet to me th' are strong.*

unsisting *ppl. adj.* (?) Misprint in Ff 1-3 for F4 *insisting,* i.e persistent MM 4.2.89 *That spirit's possess'd with haste That wounds th' unsisting postern with these strokes.*

▷ Many conjectures.

unskilful *adj.* Undiscerning, unwise, foolish Ham 3.2.25 *though it makes the unskilful laugh,* Oth 1.3.27.

unskilfully *adv.* Without discernment, foolishly, ignorantly MM 3.2.147 *you speak unskilfully.*

unsorted *ppl. adj.* Ill-chosen 1H4 2.3.12 *the time itself unsorted.*

unsought *ppl. adj.* Unexamined, unexplored Err 1.1.135 *loath to leave unsought Or that, or any place that harbours men.*

unspeaking *ppl. adj.* Unable to speak Cym 5.5.178 *his description Prov'd us unspeaking sots.*

unsphere *vb.* Remove (a star) from its sphere WT 1.2.48 *t' unsphere the stars.*

unsquare, unsquared *ppl. adj.* Not adapted to the purpose, inapt, inappropriate Tro 1.3.159 *with terms unsquar'd* (F1; Q *vnsquare*).

unstaid *adj.*
1 Not staid in conduct; (transf.) unbecoming TGV 2.7.60 *how will the world repute me For undertaking so unstaid a journey?*
2 (of the mind) Not subjected to restraint, unregulated, giddy TN 2.4.18 *Unstaid and skittish in all motions else,* R2 2.1.2 (Q1 *unstayed*).

unstanched, unstaunched *ppl. adj.*
1 Not able to contain water, leaky Tmp 1.1.48 *though the ship were...as leaky as an unstanch'd wench.*
2 Insatiable 3H6 2.6.83 *unstanched thirst.*

unstate *vb.* Strip of state and dignity Lr 1.2.99 *I would unstate myself to be in a due resolution,* Ant 3.13.30.

unstayed See UNSTAID.

unsure *adj.*
1 Unsafe 2H4 1.3.89 *An habitation giddy and unsure.*
2 Uncertain Mac 5.4.19 *their unsure hopes,* TN 2.3.49, Oth 3.3.151.

unsured *ppl. adj.* Insecure, uncertain Jn 2.1.471 *tie Thy now unsur'd assurance to the crown.*

unswayed *ppl. adj.* Not wielded, uncontrolled R3 4.4.469 *Is the chair empty? is the sword unsway'd?*; ungoverned Son 141.11 *one foolish heart...Who leaves unsway'd the likeness of a man.*

untainted *ppl. adj.*
1 Unsullied, uncorrupted, without blemish R3 3.1.7 *the untainted virtue of your years,* 2H6 3.2.232, Son 19.11.
2 Unaccused R3 3.6.9 *Hastings liv'd, Untainted, unexamin'd, free.*

untaught *ppl. adj.* Uncultured, unmannerly, ill-bred MM 2.4.29 *their untaught love Must needs appear offence,* 1H4 1.3.43, Rom 5.3.214.

untempering *ppl. adj.* Not having a softening influence H5 5.2.224 *the...untempering effect of my visage.*

untented *ppl. adj.* (of a wound) Not tented or cleaned out, and so liable to fester Lr 1.4.300 *Th' untented woundings of a father's curse.*

unthread *vb.* Remove the thread from; (fig.) Jn 5.4.11 *unthread the rude eye of rebellion* (i.e. abandon rebellion).

unthrift *n.* Prodigal, spendthrift Son 9.9 *Look what an unthrift in the world doth spend,* Son 13.13; (hence) good-for-nothing R2 2.3.122 *my rights and royalties...given away To upstart unthrifts.*

~ *adj.* Prodigal, spendthrift, unthrifty MV 5.1.16 *Jessica...with an unthrift love did run from Venice,* Tim 4.3.311.

unthrifty *adj.*
1 Not eager for increase or profit, unprofitable WT 5.2.111 *Our absence makes us unthrifty to our knowledge* (i.e. not increasing in knowledge), Son 4.1.
2 Good-for-nothing MV 1.3.176 *an unthrifty knave,* R2 5.3.1.
3 Not bringing success, unlucky Rom 5.3.136 *some ill unthrifty thing.*

untie *vb.* (fig.) Solve (a difficulty) Cym 5.4.148 *Or senseless speaking, or a speaking such As sense cannot untie.*

untimbered *ppl. adj.* Not provided with timbers, frail Tro 1.3.43 *boat Whose weak untimber'd sides...*

unto *prep.*
1 In addition to AYL 1.2.238 *I should have given him tears unto entreaties,* R2 5.3.97, Jn 4.3.46.
2 In regard or relation to Ant 2.2.143 *His power unto Octavia.*
3 In accordance with, according to Per 2.1.157 *Unto thy value I will mount myself Upon a courser,* Ham 1.3.23.
4 Of JC 1.3.71 *To make them instruments of fear and warning Unto some monstrous state.*
5 Against 1H6 4.1.73 *Then gather strength and march unto him straight.*

untold *ppl. adj.* Unreckoned, uncounted Son 136.9 *in the number let me pass untold.*

untoward *ppl. adj.* Unmannerly Jn 1.1.243 *untoward knave,* Shr 4.5.79 (F1).

untowardly *adv.* Perversely Ado 3.2.131 *O day untowardly turn'd!* (i.e. perversely altered).

untraded *ppl. adj.* Unhackneyed, not customary Tro 4.5.178 *Mock not that I affect th' untraded oath.*

untread *vb.* Retrace (a path, steps) Jn 5.4.52 *We will untread the steps of damned flight,* MV 2.6.10, Ven 908.

untreasured *ppl. adj.* Robbed or emptied as of a

treasure, stripped (of something precious) AYL 2.2.7 *They found the bed untreasur'd of their mistress.*

untried *ppl. adj.* Unexamined WT 4.1.6 *I slide O'er sixteen years and leave the growth untried Of that wide gap.*

untrimmed *ppl. adj.* Stripped of ornament, unadorned JN 3.1.209 *the devil tempts thee here In likeness of a new untrimmed bride* (i.e. unclothed), SON 18.8.

untrue *adv.* Untruly, in defiance of the truth SON 72.10 *That you...speak well of me untrue.*

untrussing *n.* Untying points (see POINT *n.* sense 5); (hence) undressing MM 3.2.179 *Claudio is condemn'd for untrussing.*

untruth *n.* Unfaithfulness, disloyalty R2 2.2.101 *So my untruth had not provok'd him to it.*

untucked *ppl. adj.* Dishevelled LC 31 *Her hair...; For some untuck'd descended her sheav'd hat.*

untun(e)able *adj.* Discordant, unmelodious, harsh-sounding AYL 5.3.36 *the note was very untuneable,* TGV 3.1.209.

untuned *ppl. adj.*
1 Untuneful, discordant R2 1.3.134 *untun'd drums*; out of tune LR 4.7.15 *Th' untun'd and jarring senses.*
2 Put out of a state of harmony, changed from the customary tone ERR 5.1.311 *my feeble key of untun'd cares* (i.e. the weak tone of my voice, which is altered by sorrow), LUC 1214.

untutored *ppl. adj.*
1 untaught, uncultured 2H6 3.2.213 *Some stern untutor'd churl,* 3H6 5.5.32, SON 138.3.
2 Not produced or formed as the result of education, not improved by instruction LUC Ded.4 *my untutord Lines.*

untwind *vb.* Untwine; (hence) destroy, undo 2H4 2.4.199 *let...gaping wounds Untwind the Sisters Three!* (F3; F1 *vntwin'd,* Q *vntwinde*).

unum cita See MANU CITA.

unvalued *ppl. adj.*
1 Of no value HAM 1.3.19 *unvalued persons.*
2 Beyond price R3 1.4.27 *Inestimable stones, unvalued jewels.*

unvexed *ppl. adj.* Unmolested JN 2.1.253 *a blessed and unvex'd retire.*

unwares *n.* at *unwares* Unawares, unexpectedly, without warning TRO 3.2.38 *Like vassalage at unwares encount'ring The eye of majesty* (Q; F1 *at unawares*).
~ *adv.* Unawares, unintentionally, unknowingly 3H6 2.5.62 *Whom...I, unwares, have kill'd.*

unwarily *adv.* Unexpectedly JN 5.7.63 *the best part of my pow'r...Were...all unwarily Devoured by the unexpected flood.*

unwashed *ppl. adj.* do it *with unwash'd hands* Do it without waiting to wash your hands (i.e. at once) 1H4 3.3.184 *Rob me the exchequer the first thing thou doest, and do it with unwash'd hands.*

unwedgeable *adj.* Incapable of being split by wedges, uncleavable MM 2.2.116 *Thou...Splits the unwedgeable...oak.*

unweighed *ppl. adj.* Thoughtless, rash, hasty, inconsiderate WIV 2.1.23 *an unweigh'd behaviour.*

unweighing *ppl. adj.* Thoughtless, inconsiderate MM 3.2.139 *A very superficial, ignorant, unweighing fellow.*

unwholesome *adj.*
1 Foul, dirty TRO 2.3.120 *in an unwholesome dish.*
2 Impaired, defective OTH 4.1.121 *bear some charity to my wit, do not think it so unwholesome.*

unwish *vb.* Wish (persons) out of existence H5 4.3.76 *thou hast unwish'd five thousand men.*

unwit *vb.* Deprive of understanding OTH 2.3.182 *As if some planet had unwitted men.*

unworthy *adj.* Undeserved, unjustified, unwarranted, unfitting R3 1.2.88 *thyself, That didst unworthy slaughter upon others.*

unwrung *ppl. adj.* Not wrenched or galled, as by a bad saddle; (fig.) HAM 3.2.243 *Let the gall'd jade winch, our withers are unwrung.*

unyoke *vb.*
1 Free cattle from the yoke; (hence, fig.) finish one's work, cease from labour HAM 5.1.52 *tell me that, and unyoke.*
2 Disjoin JN 3.1.241 *shall these hands...Unyoke this seizure...?*

unyoked *ppl. adj.* Uncurbed, undisciplined 1H4 1.2.196 *The unyok'd humour of your idleness.*

up *adv.*
1 On foot, in motion, going on JC 5.1.68 *The storm is up,* TIT 2.2.1, CYM 3.3.107.
2 In a state of hostile activity, 'up in arms' 2H6 4.2.177 *Proclaim them traitors that are up with Cade,* 1H4 3.2.120, 2H4 1.1.189 (F1).
3 In confinement ANT 3.5.12 *the poor third is up.*
4 In a position or state of power, in force COR 3.1.109 *when two authorities are up, Neither supreme.*
5 *kill up* See KILL sense 3.
6 *up and down* Altogether, exactly TGV 2.3.29 *here's my mother's breath up and down,* ADO 2.1.118, TIT 5.2.107.

upbraid *vb.* Find fault with (a person's action) MAC 5.2.18 *upbraid his faith-breach,* TMP 2.1.287, TRO 3.2.191.

upcast *n.* Final shot or throw at the game of bowls CYM 2.1.2 *when I kiss'd the jack upon an upcast, to be hit away!* (perh. with quibble on the sense 'chance, accident').

upmost *adj.* Topmost JC 2.1.24 *when he once attains the upmost round, He then unto the ladder turns his back.*

upon *adv.*
1 In the direction towards something indicated; *look upon* look on, be a spectator WT 5.3.100 *Strike all that look upon with marvel,* TRO 5.6.10, 3H6 2.3.27.
2 On the surface MV 2.7.57 *A coin...that's insculp'd upon.*
3 (with advs. *near, hard, fast*) Almost immediately after the event in question, thereupon MM 4.6.14 *very near upon The Duke is ent'ring,* HAM 1.2.179, TRO 4.3.3.
~ *prep.*
1 On (the side, cause, party of) JN 2.1.237 *this ...hand, whose protection Is...vow'd upon the right Of him it holds,* MAC 3.6.30, 1H6 2.4.123.
2 In consequence of, in dependence on, on account of, because of, in pursuance of COR 2.1.228 *Upon their ancient malice,* ADO 4.1.223, JN 2.1.597; *upon the hand* by the hand MND 2.1.244 *To die upon the hand I love so well.*
3 On the strength of JC 3.1.221 *Upon this hope,* TIM 3.1.42, TGV 3.2.60.
4 With respect to, concerning COR 2.3.144 *upon your approbation,* COR 2.2.55.
5 Bent upon OTH 1.1.100 *Upon malicious bravery* (Qq; F *knauerie*).
6 At or just about (a certain time) HAM 1.1.6 *You come most carefully upon your hour,* MM 4.1.17, R3 3.2.5; (similarly) JN 2.1.50 *Lo upon thy wish Our messenger...is arriv'd!,* JC 3.2.266; *upon the moment* at once LC 248.
7 Against LR 3.6.89 *a plot of death upon him,* MAC 4.3.131, COR 3.3.47.
8 (with words denoting command or authority,

usu.) Over ANT 1.3.23 *I have no power upon you*, TGV 3.1.240, MAC 3.1.16.

9 For MV 1.1.74 *You have too much respect upon the world.*

10 At the risk of, on peril of PER 1.1.87 *upon thy life*, JN 5.6.7.

uprighteously *adv.* Righteously, in an upright manner MM 3.1.200 *you may most uprighteously do a poor wrong'd lady a...benefit.*

uproar *vb.* Disturb, throw into confusion MAC 4.3.99 *had I pow'r, I should...Uproar the universal peace.*

upshoot *n.* Best shot LLL 4.1.136 *get the upshoot by cleaving the pin.*

upshot *n.* Final shot in a match at archery; (hence) end, conclusion TN 4.2.71 *I cannot pursue...this sport t' the upshot*, HAM 5.2.384.

up-spring *adj.* Upstart, newly introduced HAM 1.4.9 *Keeps wassail and the swagg'ring upspring reels.*
◇ Some interpret as n. in the sense of 'a kind of wild dance'.

up-staring *pres. pple.* Standing on end TMP 1.2.213 *With hair up-staring.*

upstart *n.* One who has newly arrived, newcomer 1H6 4.7.87 *I think this upstart is old Talbot's ghost.*

upswarm *vb.* Raise in swarms 2H4 4.2.30 *You have ta'en up...The subjects of...my father, And both against the peace of heaven and him Have here upswarm'd them.*

up-till *prep.* Against, on PP 20.10 *She, poor bird, ...Lean'd her breast up-till a thorn.*

upward *n.* Top LR 5.3.137 *from th' extremest upward of thy head To the...dust below thy foot.*
~ *adj.* Upturned TIM 4.3.190 *thy upward face* (i.e. surface), JC 5.3.93.

urchin *n.*
1 Hedgehog TIT 2.3.101 *Ten thousand...toads, as many urchins, Would make such...confused cries, As...*
2 Goblin, elf WIV 4.4.50 *we'll dress Like urchins, ouphes, and fairies*, TMP 1.2.326; (attrib.) TMP 2.2.5 *Fright me with urchin-shows.*
◇ Sense 2 from the supposition that goblins occasionally assumed the form of a hedgehog; see TMP 2.2.10.

urchin-show See URCHIN n. sense 2.

urchin-snouted *adj.* Having a snout like a hedgehog VEN 1105 *this foul, grim, and urchin-snouted boar.*

urge *vb.*
1 (intr.) Put forward a strong plea or argument H8 2.1.16 *The King's attorney...Urg'd on the examinations...Of divers witnesses* (i.e. pleaded on the evidence of...); (with *against*) H8 5.2.83 *That...my accusers...may..freely urge against me*; (with *for*) TIM 3.2.12 *urged extremely for't.*
2 Bring forward, press (as a plea or argument) MV 1.1.144 *I urge this childhood*, R2 3.1.4, COR 5.1.10; put forward (a person's name) as a reason for action ANT 2.2.46 *my brother never Did urge me in his act* (i.e. make capital of my name in his war).

urinal *n.* Glass vessel to receive urine TGV 2.1.39 *these follies...shine through you like the water in an urinal*, WIV 3.1.14, WIV 3.1.88.

urn *n.*
1 (properly) Vessel to hold the ashes of the dead 1H6 1.6.24 *Her ashes, in an urn*, PHT 65; (transf.) grave H5 1.2.228 *lay these bones in an unworthy urn*, COR 5.6.144.
2 Water-jug; (fig. of the eyes) TIT 3.1.17 *rain, That shall distil from these two ancient urns* (F1, Qq1-3 *ruines*).

Ursa Major [L.] The constellation the Great Bear LR 1.2.130 *my nativity was under Ursa Major.*

usage *n.* Habit, mode of conduct or behaviour OTH

4.3.104 *God me such usage send, Not to pick bad from bad, but by bad mend* (Q1; F, Q2 *uses*).

usance *n.* Interest on money, usury MV 1.3.45 *The rate of usance*, MV 1.3.108, MV 1.3.141.

use *n.*
1 Habitual practice, custom MM 1.4.62 *use and liberty* (i.e. licentious practice), MV 4.1.268, OTH 4.1.274; (pl.) usages, ways HAM 1.2.134 *all the uses of this world*, OTH 4.3.104 (F, Q2; Q1 *usage*).
2 Common experience JC 3.1.265 *Blood and destruction shall be so in use* (i.e. of such common occurrence), JC 2.2.25, MAC 1.3.137.
3 Profit, advantage H8 3.2.420 *make use now, and provide For thine own future safety* (i.e. take advantage of the opportunity), JN 5.4.27.
4 Interest (on something lent) ADO 2.1.279 *he lent it me awhile, and I gave him use for it*, MM 1.1.40, SON 6.5; (with *put*) TN 3.1.50 *put to use*, VEN 768, SON 134.10.
5 Need TIM 2.1.20 *My uses cry to me*, TIM 3.2.45, CYM 4.4.7.
6 Present enjoyment or possession of the advantages of property, etc. belonging to another ANT 1.3.44 *my full heart Remains in use with you*, MV 4.1.383.
~ *vb.*
1 Be in the habit of doing (a thing), make a practice of LR 1.4.172 *I have us'd it, nuncle, e'er since thou mad'st thy daughters thy mothers*, MV 1.3.70; (with infin.) TRO 2.1.47 *If thou use to beat me.*
2 Be accustomed (with infin.) ANT 2.5.32 *we use To say the dead are well*, TMP 2.1.174, ANT 3.7.65.
3 Treat, deal with, behave towards (another) in a particular way JC 5.5.76 *According to his virtue let us use him*, H8 4.2.168, TGV 4.4.203.
4 (refl.) Behave oneself H8 3.1.176 *If I have us'd myself unmannerly.*
5 *use of* Deal with TIT 5.1.39 *brought him hither To use as you think needful of the man.*
6 Be familiar with, associate with, entertain MAC 3.2.10 *Using those thoughts which should indeed have died With them they think on.*

used *ppl. adj.* Familiar, accustomed PER 1.2.3 *so us'd a guest.*

usurer *n.* *usurer's chain* Chain such as was worn by wealthy citizens of the merchant or banker class ADO 2.1.189 *about your neck, like a usurer's chain.*

usuring *ppl. adj.* Usurious, grasping, stingy TIM 4.3.509 *a usuring kindness*, TIM 3.5.109.

usurp *vb.*
1 (intr.) Encroach or exercise unlawful influence upon TIT 3.1.268 *this sorrow...would usurp upon my wat'ry eyes*, HAM 3.2.260, PER 3.2.82.
2 (trans.) Encroach upon VEN 591 *a sudden pale ...Usurps her cheek.*

usurped *ppl. adj.* Possessed unjustly; (hence) false, counterfeit OTH 1.3.341 *defeat thy favour with an usurp'd beard.*

usurping *ppl. adj.* False LLL 4.3.255 *that painting and usurping hair Should ravish doters with a false aspect.*

usury *n.* Lending money at interest; (hence, fig.) prostitution (which produces increase) MM 3.2.6 *of two usuries the merriest was put down.*

ut *n.* Lowest note of the musical scale (now usually 'do') LLL 4.2.100 *Ut, re, sol, la, mi, fa*, SHR 3.1.76.

utensil *n.* Part of the human frame serving a special purpose TN 1.5.246 *my beauty...shall be inventoried, and every particle and utensil labell'd.*

utis *n.* (var. of) Utas, octave of a festival, i.e. the eighth day after the feast-day, or the period of eight days beginning with it; (hence, transf.)

merrymaking 2H4 2.4.19 *here will be old utis* (i.e. rare fun).

utmost *n.* Furthest point MM 2.1.36 *that's the utmost of his pilgrimage.*
~ *adj.* Furthest JN 2.1.29 *that utmost corner of the west,* OTH 5.2.268, 1H4 4.1.51.

utter *vb.*
1 Emit, exhale MND 4.2.43 *eat no onions nor garlic, for we are to utter sweet breath,* JC 1.2.246, WT 4.4.184.
2 Put forth, put in circulation, offer for sale, put on the market LLL 2.1.16 *Not utt'red by base sale of chapmen's tongues,* WT 4.4.323, ROM 5.1.67.

utterance *n. to the utterance, at utterance* To the uttermost, to the last extremity MAC 3.1.71 *champion me to th' utterance,* CYM 3.1.72 *keep at utterance.*
▷ 'A challenge or a combat a l'outrance, to extremity, was a fixed term of the law of arms' (Johnson, 1765).

uttermost *n.*
1 Utmost MV 1.1.156 *making question of my uttermost* (i.e. of my doing my utmost), SHR 4.3.80, TRO 4.5.91.
2 *the uttermost* The latest JC 2.1.213 *By the eighth hour; is that the uttermost?*
~ *adj.* Utmost, greatest in extent H5 3.6.9 *my uttermost power.*

V

vacancy *n.*
1 Empty space, vacuity ANT 2.2.216 *but for vacancy* (i.e. except that it would have created a vacuum), HAM 3.4.117.
2 Unoccupied time ANT 1.4.26 *If he fill'd His vacancy with his voluptuousness*; vacant interval TN 5.1.95 *a minute's vacancy.*

vacant *adj.* Devoid *of* H8 5.1.125 *of those virtues vacant.*

vade *vb.* Fade SON 54.14 *When that shall vade,* PP 13.2, R2 1.2.20 (Qq *faded*).

vaded *ppl. adj.* Faded PP 13.8 *vaded gloss,* PP 13.6.

vagabond *adj.* Moving to and fro ANT 1.4.45 *Like to a vagabond flag upon the stream.*

vagram *adj.* (Evans's speech) Fragrant WIV 3.1.25 *a thousand vagram posies.*

vagrom *adj.* (Dogberry's speech) Vagrant ADO 3.3.25 *you shall comprehend all vagrom men.*

vail *n.*[1] (pl.) Occasional emolument in addition to a regular salary, gratuity, perquisite PER 2.1.151 *There are certain condolements, certain vails.*

vail *n.*[2] Going down, setting TRO 5.8.7 *the vail and dark'ning of the sun.*
~ *vb.*
1 Let fall, lower 1H6 5.3.25 *France must vail her...crest,* LLL 5.2.297, PER 2.3.42; (fig.) COR 3.1.98 *vail your ignorance,* SHR 5.2.176, 2H4 1.1.129.
2 Do homage *to* PER 4.Gower.29 *when She would with rich and constant pen Vail to her mistress Dian.*

vailed *ppl. adj.* Lowered HAM 1.2.70 *thy vailed lids.*

vailful *adj.* Advantageous MM 4.6.4 *I am advis'd to do it, He says, to vailful purpose.*
▷ F *vaile full*; Malone's conjecture *veil full.*

vain *adj.*
1 Empty-headed, foolish, silly LR 4.2.61 *O vain fool!,* ERR 3.2.180, 1H4 3.2.67.
2 False ERR 3.2.27 *'Tis holy sport to be a little vain When the sweet breath of flattery conquers strife.*
3 *for vain* In vain, ineffectually, to no purpose MM 2.4.12 *an idle plume, Which the air beats for vain.*

vainly *adv.* Falsely, wrongly 2H4 4.5.238 *Jerusalem, Which vainly I suppos'd the Holy Land.*

vainness *n.* Boastfulness, vanity H5 5.Ch.20 *free from vainness and self-glorious pride,* TN 3.4.355.

valance *n.* Border of drapery hanging round the canopy of a bed, fringe SHR 2.1.354 *Valance of Venice gold in needle-work* (F1 *Vallens*).

valanced *adj.* Provided with a valance, fringed HAM 2.2.423 *thy face is valanc'd since I saw thee last* (i.e. fringed with a beard).

vale *n.* Dale, valley; (fig.) the world regarded as a place of sorrow or as the scene of life 2H6 2.1.68 *Great is his comfort in this earthly vale*; the declining years of a person's life, old age OTH 3.3.266 *I am declin'd Into the vale of years.*

valens, vallens See VALANCE.

validity *n.*
1 Strength HAM 3.2.189 *Of violent birth, but poor validity.*
2 Value AWW 5.3.192 *this ring Whose...rich validity,* TN 1.1.12, LR 1.1.81.

valuation *n.* Estimation 2H4 4.1.187 *our valuation shall be such That every...wanton reason Shall to the King taste of this action,* CYM 4.4.49.

value *n.*
1 Estimation, esteem, judgement of worth H8 5.2.143 *How much more is his life in value with him!* (i.e. valued by him).
2 Estimate COR 2.2.59 *A kinder value of the people.*
~ *vb.*
1 Rate, estimate 1H4 3.2.177 *Our business valued* (i.e. taking into consideration how long our business will take us), LLL 5.2.445, ADO 4.1.139; *valu'd with you* compared with you in respect of worth 1H4 5.2.59.
2 Be worth (so much) H8 2.3.52 *it values not your asking,* H8 1.1.88.

valued *ppl. adj.* Containing the value of each item set down, in which value is indicated MAC 3.1.94 *the valued file.*

vambrace *n.* Vantbrace, armour for the front part of the arm TRO 1.3.297 *in my vambrace put my withered brawns* (Q; F1 *Vantbrace*).

vanish *vb.* Escape *from* ROM 3.3.10 *A gentler judgement vanish'd from his lips.*

vanity *n.*
1 Character in old morality plays LR 2.2.36 *take Vanity the puppet's part,* 1H4 2.4.454 (with quibble).
2 Illusion TMP 4.1.41 *Some vanity of mine art.*

vant *n.* (old form of) Van, vanguard, front of an army or fleet ANT 4.6.8 *Plant those that have revolted in the vant.*

vantage *n.*
1 Superior position, superiority H5 3.6.144 *an enemy of craft and vantage,* MND 1.1.102, LUC 249.
2 ADVANTAGE sense 1 1H6 4.5.28 *for vantage* (i.e. to get a good opportunity), SHR 3.2.144, COR 5.6.53.
▷ For MAC 1.6.7 *coign of vantage* see COIGN.
3 Benefit, profit, gain CYM 5.5.198 *for my vantage, excellent,* JN 2.1.550, COR 1.1.160.
4 *of vantage, to the vantage* In addition, besides HAM 3.3.33 *some more audience...should o'erhear the speech, of vantage,* OTH 4.3.84.

vantbrace See VAMBRACE.

vaporous *adj.* *vap'rous drop* 'A foam which the moon was supposed to shed on particular herbs, or other objects, when strongly solicited by enchantment' (Steevens) MAC 3.5.24.

vapour *n.* (pl.) (Eliz. medical use) Exhalations supposed to be developed within the organs of the body and to have an injurious effect 2H4 4.3.98 *A good sherris-sack...ascends me into the brain, dries me there all the...vapours which environ it.*

vara *adv.* [dial. form] very LLL 5.2.487 *it is vara fine.*

variable *adj.* Various, diverse COR 2.1.212 *variable complexions* (i.e. all sorts of people), HAM 3.1.172, MV 2.8.13; *variable service* different courses (at a meal) HAM 4.3.23.

variation *n.* Variety 1H4 1.1.64 *Stain'd with the variation of each soil Betwixt that Holmedon and this seat*, SON 76.2.

varlet *n.*
1 Man or boy acting as an attendant or servant 2H4 5.3.12 *A good varlet*; (spec.) gentleman's son in the service of a knight or prince TRO 1.1.1 *Call here my varlet, I 'll unarm again*, H5 4.2.2.
2 Knave, rogue, rascal MM 2.1.190 *thou wicked varlet*, 1H4 2.4.432, WIV 4.2.102.

varletry *n.* Rabble ANT 5.2.56 *the shouting varletry Of...Rome.*

varletto *n.* (Host's Ital. form of) Varlet WIV 4.5.65 *Where be my horses? Speak well of them varletto.*

varlot *n.* (?) Blend of 'varlet' and 'harlot' TRO 5.1.15 *Thou art said to be Achilles' male varlot—Male varlot, you rogue! What's that?—Why, his masculine whore.*

vary *n.* Change, variation LR 2.2.79 *turn their halcyon beaks With every gale and vary of their masters* (i.e. changing wind).
~ *vb.* Express in different terms H5 3.7.32 *that cannot...vary deserv'd praise on my palfrey*, LLL 1.1.294.

vassal *n.*
1 Humble servant or subordinate LUC 666 *thy thoughts, low vassals to thy state.*
2 Base wretch, slavish fellow LR 1.1.161 *O vassal! miscreant!*, 2H6 4.1.111, LLL 1.1.253.
~ *adj.* Slavish, base 1H4 3.2.124 *vassal fear*, H5 3.5.51, SON 141.12.

vassalage *n.*
1 State or condition of a vassal, service, servitude SON 26.1 *Lord of my love, to whom in vassalage...*
2 Vassals collectively, subjects TRO 3.2.38 *Like vassalage...encount'ring The eye of majesty.*

vast *n.* (of the sea) Desolate, boundless expanse WT 1.1.30 *shook hands, as over a vast*, PER 3.1.1; (of night) desolate period HAM 1.2.198 *the dead vast and middle of the night* (Q1; F1 *waste*), TMP 1.2.327.
~ *adj.*
1 Waste, desolate R3 1.4.39 *the empty, vast, and wand'ring air*, TIT 4.1.53, TIT 5.2.36.
▷ The sense 'immense' is also present.
2 Extending far and wide JN 4.3.152 *vast confusion waits...The imminent decay of wrested pomp.*

vastidity *n.* Immensity MM 3.1.68 *though all the world's vastidity you had.*

vastly *adv.* Far and wide LUC 1740 *Who like a latesack'd island vastly stood Bare and unpeopled in this fearful flood.*

vasty *adj.* Vast, immense, boundless H5 Prol.12 *The vasty fields of France*, H5 2.4.105, 1H4 3.1.52.

vaultage *n.* Vaulted place or area H5 2.4.124 *caves and womby vaultages.*

vaulty *adj.* Arched, hollow, cavernous JN 3.4.30 *O...death!...I will...put my eyeballs in thy vaulty brows* (perh. with a ref. to burial vaults), ROM 3.5.22, LUC 119.

vaunt *n.* Beginning, rise TRO Prol.27 *our play Leaps o'er the vaunt and firstlings of those broils.*

vaunt *vb.* Exult R3 5.3.288 *the foe vaunts in the field*, SON 15.7.

vaunt-courier *n.* Herald, harbinger LR 3.2.5 *You sulph'rous...fires, Vaunt-couriers of...thunderbolts.*

vaward *n.* Vanguard H5 4.3.131 *I beg The leading of the vaward*, 1H6 1.1.132, COR 1.6.53; (fig.) beginning MND 4.1.105 *the vaward of the day*, 2H4 1.2.176.

vegetive *n.* (pl.) Vegetables, herbs, plants PER 3.2.36 *the blest infusions That dwells in vegetives, in metals, stones.*

vein *n.*
1 Disposition, humour ERR 2.2.20 *in this merry vein*, TRO 2.3.200, R3 4.2.116.
2 Particular style or manner of life or action MM 2.2.70 *Ay, touch him; there's the vein* (i.e. 'that's the right style'), MND 1.2.40, 1H4 2.4.387.

velure *n.* Velvet SHR 3.2.61 *a woman's crupper of velure.*

velvet *adj.* 'Sleek and prosperous' (Aldis Wright) AYL 2.1.50 *his velvet friends.*

velvet-guard *n.* (pl.) Wearers of velvet trimmings 1H4 3.1.256 *velvet-guards and Sunday-citizens.*
▷ See GUARD n. sense 3.

vendible *adj.* Saleable, in demand MV 1.1.112 *a maid not vendible* (i.e. marriageable), AWW 1.1.155.

Venetia, Venetia, Chi non ti vede non ti pretia [It.] Venice, Venice, who sees you not esteems you not LLL 4.2.97.
▷ It. proverb. F1, Q1 *Vemchi vencha, que non le unde, que non te perreche.*

venew See VENUE.

veney See VENUE.

vengeance *n.*
1 Mischief, harm AYL 4.3.48 *That could do no vengeance to me*, TIT 2.3.113.
2 Act or instance of retributive punishment; (imprecations) 2H6 3.2.304 *threefold vengeance tend upon your steps!*, TRO 2.3.18, LR 2.4.95; *What the vengeance* (oath used to strengthen interrogations) COR 3.1.261 *What the vengeance, Could he not speak 'em fair?*
~ *adv.* Exceedingly, intensely COR 2.2.5 *he's vengeance proud.*

vengeful *adj.* Revengeful, vindictive 2H6 3.2.198 *a vengeful sword*, TIT 5.2.51, SON 99.13.

veni, vidi, vici [L.] I came, I saw, I conquered LLL 4.1.67.

Venice gold *n.* Gold thread of Venetian manufacture SHR 2.1.354 *Valance of Venice gold in needlework.*

venison *n.* Beast of chase, wild animal hunted for food AYL 2.1.21 *shall we go and kill us venison?*, WIV 1.1.82, CYM 3.3.75.

venom *adj.* Poisonous 3H6 2.2.138 *venom toads*, R3 1.3.290 LUC 850; (fig.) ERR 5.1.69 *The venom clamours of a jealous woman*, R2 2.1.19.

venomed *ppl. adj.*
1 Poisoned R2 1.1.171 *slander's venom'd spear*, HAM 4.7.161, VEN 916.
2 Venomous R3 1.2.20 *any creeping venom'd thing*, TIM 4.3.182; (fig.) TRO 5.3.47 *venom'd vengeance.*
3 *venomed-mouthed* Having a venomous bite H8 1.1.120 *This butcher's cur is venom'd-mouth'd.*

venomous *adj.* (fig.) Injurious, pernicious TIT 5.3.13 *venomous malice*, COR 4.1.23; rancorous, spiteful, malignant TRO 4.2.12 *venomous wights.*

venomously *adv.* Spitefully, malignantly PER 3.1.7 *storm, venomously Wilt thou spit all thyself?*

vent *n.*[1]
1 Opening, aperture 2H4 Ind.2 *The vent of hearing* (i.e. the ear), TRO 5.3.82, LUC 310.
2 Emission, effusion ANT 5.2.349 *a vent of blood*; utterance (of words) VEN 334 *Free vent of words*; *make vent of* talk freely or copiously about AWW 2.3.202 *Thou didst make tolerable vent of thy travel.*

~ *vb.* Emit, void, get rid of COR 1.1.225 *to vent Our musty superfluity*, TMP 2.2.107, CYM 1.2.4; utter TMP 1.2.280 *thou didst vent thy groans*, TN 4.1.16, H8 1.2.23.

vent *n.²* Scent given off by a hunted animal; *full of vent* (of a hunting dog) full of the scent of a hunted animal; (hence) full of excitement and activity COR 4.5.223 *war...is...audible, and full of vent.*

ventage *n.* Opening, vent-hole; (pl.) stops of a flute HAM 3.2.357 *Govern these ventages with your fingers.*

venter See VENTURE.

ventricle *n. ventricle of memory* That one of the three divisions of the brain which was held to be the seat of memory LLL 4.2.68.

venture *n.* (aphetic form of ME. 'aventure', ADVENTURE).
1 Hazard, risk MAC 1.3.91 *Thy personal venture in the rebels' fight*, 2H4 Epil.7; *at a venture* at random 2H4 1.1.59 *Spoke at a venture* (F *adventure*).
2 One who puts his person at risk CYM 1.6.123 *to be partner'd with diseas'd ventures That play with all infirmities for gold That rottenness can lend nature.*
~ *vb. venture on* Dare, be so bold as to attack VEN 628 *on the lion he will venture.*
⟡ Both n. and vb. often spelt *venter* in Ff and Qq.

venue, veney *n.*
1 Thrust in fencing LLL 5.1.59 *a sweet touch, a quick venue of wit* (F1, Q1 *vene we*; F2 *venewe*), HAM 5.2.166 (Q1 *venies*; F1 *passes*).
2 Fencing-bout WIV 1.1.284 *three veneys.*

ver [L]. Spring LLL 5.2.891.

verbal *adj.* Verbose, talkative CYM 2.3.106 *You put me to forget a lady's manners By being so verbal.*

verbatim *adv.* By word of mouth, orally 1H6 3.1.13 *am not able Verbatim to rehearse the method of my pen.*

verdure *n.*
1 Fragrance, freshness VEN 507 *as they last, their verdure still endure, To drive infection from the dangerous year!*
2 Fresh or flourishing condition TMP 1.2.87 *The ivy which had hid my princely trunk And suck'd my verdure out*, TGV 1.1.49.

verge *n.*
1 Circle, circlet R3 4.1.58 *the inclusive verge Of golden metal that must round my brow*; (magic) circle 2H6 1.4.22 *Whom we raise We will make fast within a hallow'd verge.*
2 Limit R2 2.1.102 *incaged in so small a verge* (with allusion to 'the compass of the King's Court, an area of twelve miles extent around the king's court, wherever he happened to be, which was under the jurisdiction of the Lord High Steward of the Household'.

verify *vb.*
1 Affirm, maintain H5 3.2.71 *I will verify as much in his beard*, 1H6 1.2.32, ADO 5.1.218 (Dogberry's speech).
2 Support by testimony, vouch for COR 5.2.17 *I have ever verified my friends...with all the size that verity Would without lapsing suffer.*
⟡ F *verified*; Hanmer *magnified*, Edwards *varnished.*

verily *adv.* In truth, in fact, really TMP 2.1.321 *There was a noise, That's verily*, AYL 4.3.25, WT 1.2.49.

verity *n.* Truthfulness AYL 3.4.23 *his verity in love*, MAC 4.3.92.

versal *adj.* (aphetic form of) UNIVERSAL ROM 2.4.206 *the versal world.*

verse *vb.* Tell in verse, express in verse MND 2.1.67 *sat all day...versing love.*

very *adj.*
1 Veritable, real, true, that is indeed so TGV 3.2.41 *his very friend*, ADO 4.1.186, HAM 2.2.49; himself, itself CYM 4.2.107 *very Cloten*, TMP 2.2.105, WT 3.3.23.
2 Complete, thorough, perfect TN 1.3.24 *a very fool*, TRO 1.2.15, SHR 5.2.64.
3 Mere SHR 4.3.32 *thou...That feed'st me with the very name of meat*, HAM 3.4.137, VEN 441.
~ *adv.* Quite, exactly, just OTH 1.1.88 *very now*, LR 5.3.295, MM 4.3.38.

vesper *n.* Evening ANT 4.14.8 *black vesper's pageants.*

vessel *n.* Receptacle for holding liquids; (fig., applied to the human body as having the containing capacity or function of a vessel) OTH 4.2.83 *to preserve this vessel for my lord*; (hence) person WT 3.3.21 *I never saw a vessel of like sorrow So fill'd*, JC 5.5.13; *weaker vessel* woman ROM 1.1.16 *women, being the weaker vessels*, LLL 1.1.273, AYL 2.4.6.

vestal *n.* Priestess of Vesta, vowed to chastity, and having the charge of keeping alight the vestal fire ANT 3.12.31 *want will perjure The ne'er-touch'd vestal*, PER 4.5.7, VEN 752; (transf.) virgin MND 2.1.158 *a fair vestal throned by the west* (ref. to Queen Elizabeth I); (jocular) kitchen maid, 'her charge being, like the vestal virgins, to keep the fire burning' (Johnson) ERR 4.4.75 *the kitchen vestal.*
~ *adj.* Of Vesta or of the vestal virgins PER 3.4.10 *A vestal livery will I take me to* (i.e. I will embrace the life of a vestal); chaste ROM 3.3.38 *pure and vestal modesty*, ROM 2.2.8.

vesture *n.* (fig.) The human body as that in which the soul is clothed MV 5.1.64 *this muddy vesture of decay*, OTH 2.1.64.

vex *vb.* Disturb, agitate (mentally); (hence) afflict, harass, torment TN 3.4.209 *it hath no tongue to vex you*, LR 3.4.61, JC 4.3.115.

vexation *n.* Agitation, affliction, torment, uneasiness, anguish MND 4.1.69 *the fierce vexation of a dream*, R3 4.4.305, OTH 1.1.72.

vexed *ppl. adj.* Disturbed, agitated (physically) LR 4.4.2 *the vex'd sea*; (mentally) JN 3.1.17 *my vex'd spirits*, ROM 3.5.95.
⟡ TMP 1.2.229 *the still-vexed Bemoothes see* STILLVEXED.

via [It.] On, go on, say on, forward! 3H6 2.1.182 *Why, via! to London will we march*, LLL 5.1.149, WIV 2.2.153.
⟡ MV 2.2.11 *Fia* may be mispronunciation by Launcelot or may represent a southern dial. form. See also in VIA.

viage *n.* Voyage HAM 3.3.24 *Arm you...to this speedy viage* (Q; F1 *voyage*).

vial *n.* Bottle, flask ROM 4.1.93 *Take thou this vial...And this...liquor drink thou off*, R2 1.2.12, HAM 1.5.62; (spec.) bottle such as those found in ancient Roman tombs, commonly supposed to have been made to receive tears ANT 1.3.63 *the sacred vials thou shouldst fill With sorrowful water.*

vice *n.¹*
1 Sinful act, offence, transgression MM 2.4.116 *You...rather prov'd the sliding of your brother A merriment than a vice*, OTH 4.1.171, OTH 4.3.70.
2 (with capital V) Comic character in the old morality plays, also called INIQUITY TN 4.2.124 *Like to the old Vice...Who with dagger of lath...*, 2H4 3.2.319 (see DAGGER sense 2), R3 3.1.82; (allusion) 1H4 2.4.453 *that reverent Vice, that grey Iniquity*; (transf.) HAM 3.4.98 *a Vice of kings* (i.e. buffoon of a king).

vice *n.²* Screw ADO 5.2.21 *you must put in the pikes with a vice*; instrument for gripping things (fig.)

2H4 2.1.22 *and 'a come but within my vice* (F; Q *view*).

~ *vb.* Screw WT 1.2.416 *an instrument To vice you to't.*

vicegerent *n.* Deputy LLL 1.1.220 *the welkin's vicegerent.*

vicious *adj.*
1 Faulty, wrong, mistaken OTH 3.3.145 *Though I perchance am vicious in my guess,* CYM 5.5.65.
2 Constituting a defect HAM 1.4.24 *some vicious mole of nature.*

victor(-)sword *n.* Victorious sword LR 5.3.133 *Despite thy victor-sword and fire-new fortune* (F; Q *victor, sword*).

videlicet [L.] Namely WIV 1.1.138 (*fidelicet*; Evans's speech), LLL 4.1.69, AYL 4.1.97.

Videsne quis venit? Video et gaudeo [L.] Do you see who comes? I see and am glad LLL 5.1.30, 31.

vie *vb.* (orig. a term at cards)
1 Stake, wager; (fig.) SHR 2.1.309 *kiss on kiss She vied so fast* (i.e. as if to outdo me).
2 Compete *with* (another) in respect of (something) ANT 5.2.98 *Nature wants stuff To vie strange forms with fancy,* PER 3.1.26 (Steevens; Q *Vse*), PER 4.Gower.33.

view *n.*
1 Look, glance TRO 4.5.282 *gives all gaze and bent of amorous view,* WIV 1.3.61, LC 26.
2 Inspection, examination TN 2.2.19 *made good view of me* (i.e. examined me closely), TRO 3.3.241, TRO 4.5.232.
3 Outward appearance MV 3.2.131 *You that choose not by the view,* ROM 1.1.169.
~ in phrases
at ample view So as to be fully seen TN 1.1.26 *Shall not behold her face at ample view.* **from view of** Out of sight of CYM 3.3.28 *never wing'd from view o' th' nest.* **full cf view** Providing many opportunities of observation CYM 3.4.147 *a course Pretty and full of view.* **in (the) view** In (the) sight MM 4.2.167 *to deliver his head in the view of Angelo,* WT 5.2.70, TRO 1.3.273. **in common view** In the sight of all R2 4.1.155 *that in common view He may surrender.* **on more view** On closer inspection ROM 1.2.32 (Q4; F1, Qq 2–3 *Which one more view*; Q1 Such amongst view). **to the view** So as to be seen by all, to the public view ANT 5.2.211 *Uplift us to the view,* HAM 5.2.378, SON 110.2. **gave each thing view** Showed everything to full advantage H8 1.1.44. **to my sister's view** To see my sister ANT 2.2.167.

viewless *adj.* Invisible MM 3.1.123 *the viewless winds.*

vigil *n.* Eve of a festival H5 4.3.45 *yearly on the vigil.*

vigitant *adj.* (Dogberry's blunder for) Vigilant ADO 3.3.94 *Be vigitant.*

vigour *n.* Power or efficacy (of a poison) CYM 1.5.21 *To try the vigour of them, and apply Allayments to their act,* HAM 1.5.68; (fig.) MM 2.2.183 *her double vigour, art and nature.*
◇ In TIT 4.2.108 *The vigour and picture of my youth, vigour* is perh. a persistence of an earlier spelling of *figure* (S. Wells).

vild (var. of) VILE.

vildly (VAR. OF) VILELY.

vile, vild *adj.*
1 Low or mean in rank or condition 2H4 1.2.18 *neither in gold nor silver, but in vile apparel,* MV 2.4.6, H5 4.3.62.
2 Having a bad effect or influence, evil JC 2.1.265 *the vile contagion of the night,* R3 3.2.62, MAC 3.1.108.

vilely, vildly *adv.* Meanly, basely, of little worth

2H4 2.2.6 *Doth it not show vilely in me to desire small beer,* COR 3.1.10, CYM 5.5.198.

vile-drawing *adj.* Influencing or moving to evil JN 2.1.577 *this vile-drawing bias.*
◇ Pope; F1 *vile drawing.*

Vilia miretur vulgus; mihi flavus Apollo Pocula Castalia plena ministret aqua [L.; Ovid, *Amores* 1.15.35] Let the base vulgar admire trash; to me golden-haired Apollo shall serve goblets filled from the Castalian spring VEN Motto.

viliaco See VILLIAGO.

villagery *n.* Villages collectively MND 2.1.35 *Are you not he That frights the maidens of the villagery...?*

villain *n.*
1 Serf, bondman, servant AYL 1.1.56 *I am no villain* (with play on the sense 'rascal'), TIT 4.3.74, LR 3.7.78.
2 Used without serious implication of bad qualities, esp. as a term of address WIV 4.5.71 *They are gone but to meet the Duke, villain*; (hence) good-humouredly or as a term of endearment WT 1.2.136 *Sweet villain!,* ERR 1.2.19, 2H4 2.1.51; (applied to a woman) TRO 3.2.33 *the prettiest villain,* TN 2.5.13.

villainous *adj.* (informal) Abominably bad, wretched 1H4 2.4.333 *There's villainous news abroad,* WIV 3.5.92, 1H4 2.1.14.
~ *adv.* Wretchedly, horribly TMP 4.1.249 *apes With foreheads villainous low.*

villiago *n.* (var. of) Viliaco, villain, scoundrel, contemptible person 2H6 4.8.46 *I see them lording it in London streets, Crying 'villiago!' unto all they meet.*

vindicative *adj.* Vindictive, vengeful TRO 4.5.107 *he in heat of action Is more vindicative than jealous love.*

vinewed *adj.* (var. of) Finew, mouldy TRO 2.1.14 *thou vinewed'st leaven* (i.e. most mouldy).
◇ Ff *whinid'st* superlative degree form of 'vinnied', a by-form of 'vinewed'. Q *unsalted.*

viol *n.* Six-stringed instrument played with a bow R2 1.3.162 *an unstringed viol,* PER 1.1.81, PER 3.2.90 (Q1; Q4 *viall*).

viol-de-gamboys *n.* (var. of 'viola da gamba', i.e. 'leg viol') BASE-VIOL TN 1.3.26 *He plays o' th' viol-de-gamboys.*

violence *n.*
1 Vehemence of action, 'bold action' (Rolfe) OTH 1.3.249 *My downright violence.*
2 Vehemence of personal feeling, extreme ardour OTH 2.1.222 *with what violence she first lov'd the Moor,* HAM 3.2.196, ANT 1.5.60.

violent *vb.* Be violent, act or rage with violence TRO 4.4.4 *The grief...that I taste...violenteth in a sense as strong As that which causeth it.*

viperous *adj.* Venomous COR 3.1.285 *This viperous traitor,* CYM 3.4.39, 1H6 3.1.72.

Vir sapit qui pauca loquitur [L.] *The man is wise who says little* LLL 4.2.80.

virgin *vb. virgin it* Play the virgin, be chaste COR 5.3.48 *my true lip Hath virgin'd it e'er since.*
~ *adj.* Of a virgin MV 3.2.56 *The virgin tribute paid by howling Troy To the sea-monster*; of virginity MND 1.1.80 *my virgin patent* (i.e. my privilege of virginity), HAM 5.1.232, PER 2.5.12.

virginal *vb.* Play on the virginal, a keyed musical instrument resembling a spinet; (hence, fig.) finger WT 1.2.125 *Still virginalling Upon his palm?*
~ *adj.* Virgin, maidenly 2H6 5.2.52 *Tears virginal,* COR 5.2.43, 2H4 4.6.57.

virgin-knot *n.* 'Zone' or girdle anciently worn by maidens TMP 4.1.15 *If thou dost break her virgin-knot.*

virtue *n.*
1 (concrete use of the moral sense) One who displays or embodies virtue TIM 3.5.7 *an humble suitor to your virtues* (i.e. the senate; with quibble), 2H4 2.4.46, H8 3.1.103.
2 Valour, bravery LR 5.3.103 *Trust to thy single virtue*, 1H4 2.4.119, COR 1.1.40; (concrete) ANT 4.8.17 *O infinite virtue.*
3 Good quality or property, merit AYL 3.2.120 *that's the right virtue of the medlar*, ADO 2.1.122, 1H4 3.1.124.
4 Good accomplishment TGV 3.1.278 *'...She can milk'. Look you, a sweet virtue in a maid*, TGV 3.1.312, PER 4.6.184.
5 Power, efficacy (of a thing) JN 5.7.44 *some virtue in my tears*, MV 5.1.199, AYL 5.4.103; (hence, concrete) efficacious herb or plant LR 4.4.16 *you unpublish'd virtues of the earth.*
6 (a person's) Power, authority OTH 1.3.318 *it is not in my virtue to amend it*, 2H4 4.1.161, MAC 4.3.156 (i.e. power of healing).
7 Essence, essential part TMP 1.2.27 *touch'd The very virtue of compassion in thee*, MND 4.1.169, TIM 3.5.8.

virtuous *adj.*
1 Of efficacious or powerful properties MND 3.2.367 *Whose liquor hath this virtuous property*, OTH 3.4.111, MM 2.2.167.
2 Essential 2H4 4.5.75 *like the bee culling from every flower The virtuous sweets* (F1 *tolling*).

virtuously *adv.* Powerfully; (hence, affectedly) preciously, dearly TIM 1.2.226 *We are so virtuously bound.*

visage *n.* Appearance OTH 1.1.50 *visages of duty* (i.e. assumed appearance).

visit *vb.*
1 Afflict with disease LLL 5.2.422 *These lords are visited* (viz. by plague), 1H4 4.1.26.
2 Punish (sins) MV 3.5.14 *the sins of my mother should be visited upon me*, JN 2.1.179, H5 4.1.176.

visitation *n.*
1 Affliction, esp. attack of plague TMP 3.1.32 *thou art infected! This visitation shows it.*
2 Violent onset 2H4 3.1.21 *the visitation of the winds.*
3 Visiting, visit TIM 1.2.218 *your several visitations*, WT 1.1.6, R3 3.7.107.

visitor *n.* One who takes spiritual consolation (*comfort*) to others TMP 2.1.11 *He receives comfort like cold porridge.—The visitor will not give him o'er so.*

visor, vizor *n.* Mask to conceal the face, often kept in place by a tongue, or interior projection, held in the mouth (W. J. Lawrence, TLS 1923) ROM 1.5.22 *I have worn a visor and could tell A whispering tale in a fair lady's ear*, ADO 2.1.241, PER 4.4.44.
◇ See VIZARD.

viva voce [L.] So that their voices can be heard H8 2.1.18 *confessions Of divers witnesses, which the Duke desir'd To him brought viva voce to his face.*

vive le roi [Fr.] Long live the king JN 5.2.104.

vives See FIVES.

vizament *n.* (pl.) (Evans' speech; var. of) Avisement, consideration WIV 1.1.39 *Take your vizaments in that.*

vizard *n.* (altered form of 'vyzar') VISOR LLL 5.2.242 *was your vizard made without a tongue*, MAC 3.2.34, R3 2.2.28 (F1 *visor*).

vizarded *ppl. adj.* Wearing a vizard, masked WIV 4.6.40 *they must all be mask'd and vizarded*, TRO 1.3.83.

vizard-like *adj.* Like a VIZARD or mask 3H6 1.4.116 *thy face is vizard-like, unchanging.*

vizor See VISOR.

vlouting-stock *n.* (Evans's speech) FLOUTING-STOCK WIV 4.5.80 *full of gibes and vlouting-stocks.*

vlouting-stog *n.* (Evans's speech) FLOUTING-STOCK WIV 3.1.117 *he has made us his vlouting-stog.*

vocativo [L.] In the vocative case WIV 4.1.52.

vocatur [L.] Is called LLL 5.1.23.

voice *n.*
1 What one says, speech, words HAM 1.2.45 *lose your voice* (i.e. speak in vain), WIV 1.4.156, H5 5.2.93.
2 Utterance, expression of opinion TIM 2.2.204 *in a joint and corporate voice*, 2H4 4.1.134, TRO 2.3.140; (semi-concrete) TIT 5.3.140 *The common voice do cry it shall be so.*
3 General talk, rumour, report H8 3.2.405 *the voice is now full about her coronation*, TN 1.5.260, JC 2.1.146.
4 Judgement, opinion H8 2.2.87 *the voice of Christendom*, HAM 5.2.249, TRO 1.3.187; public opinion, (hence) reputation OTH 1.3.226 *opinion ...throws a more safer voice on you*, H5 2.2.113.
5 Vote, expression of opinion, choice or preference COR 2.2.140 *the people Must have their voices*, JC 3.1.177, TIT 1.1.218; (hence) support, authority, approval HAM 5.2.356 *he has my dying voice*, MND 1.1.54, R3 3.4.19.
6 *in my voice* (1) In my name MM 1.2.180; (2) far as my opinion is concerned AYL 2.4.87.
~ *vb.*
1 Acclaim TIM 4.3.82 *Is this th' Athenian minion, whom the world Voic'd so regardfully?*
2 Nominate COR 2.3.234 *To voice him consul.*

void *vb.* (aphetic form of AVOID)
1 Emit MV 1.3.117 *did void your rheum*, H5 3.5.52; *void up* vomit TIM 1.2.138 *spend our flatteries to drink those men Upon whose age we void it up again.*
2 Quit, abandon H5 4.7.59 *void the field.*
~ *adj.* Empty, deserted JC 2.4.37 *a place more void* (i.e. less occupied or crowded).

voiding(-)lobby *n.* Antechamber, anteroom, waiting-room 2H6 4.1.61 *How in our voiding lobby hast thou stood And duly waited for my coming forth?*

voke *n.* [dial. form] Folk LR 4.6.238 *let poor voke pass.*

volable *adj.* (Armado's speech) Fluent, quick-witted LLL 3.1.66 *A most acute juvenal, volable and free of grace!* (Q1; Ff, Q2 *voluble*).

volume *n. by th' volume* By the bookfull COR 3.3.33 *as an hostler, that for th' poorest piece Will bear the knave by th' volume* (i.e. will endure whole volumes of contemptuous epithets).

voluntary *n.* Volunteer JN 2.1.67 *Rash, inconsiderate, fiery voluntaries*, TRO 2.1.97.

vor' *vb.* [dial.] Warrant LR 4.6.240 *che vor' ye.*

votaress *n.* Woman that is under a vow MND 2.1.123 *His mother was a vot'ress of my order*, MND 2.1.163, PER 4.Gower.4.

votarist *n.*
1 VOTARY TIM 4.3.27 *I am no idle votarist.*
2 One devoted to the religious life MM 1.4.5 *the votarists of Saint Clare*, OTH 4.2.187.

votary *n.* One who has taken a vow LLL 2.1.37 *Who are the votaries...That are vow-fellows with this...Duke?*, TGV 1.1.52, SON 154.5.

vouch *n.* Testimony, witness MM 2.4.156 *My vouch against you*, H8 1.1.157, OTH 2.1.146.
~ *vb.*
1 Bear witness OTH 1.3.261 *Vouch with me, heaven.*
2 Affirm, assert, declare MM 5.1.323 *What can you vouch Against him?*, OTH 1.3.103, CYM 1.4.58.

vouched *ppl. adj.* Affirmed, declared TMP 2.1.61 *many vouch'd rarities.*

voucher *n.* Person who is called upon to warrant a

tenant's title HAM 5.1.105 *his double vouchers*, HAM 5.1.108; (transf.) CYM 2.2.39 *Here's a voucher, Stronger than ever law could make.*
vouchsafe, voutsafe *vb.*
1 Allow (a person to do something) ERR 5.1.283 *vouchsafe me speak a word*, ADO 3.2.4.
2 Deign to accept TIM 1.1.152 *Vouchsafe my labour*, JC 2.1.313, JN 3.1.294.
vow-fellow *n.* One under the same vow LLL 2.1.38 *vow-fellows with this...Duke.*
vox [L.] (lit.) Voice; (hence) appropriate tone, dramatic reading TN 5.1.296 *art thou mad?—No, madam, I do but read madness...you must allow vox* (i.e. loud, frantic tone).
vulgar *n.*
1 Common people JC 1.1.70 *drive away the vulgar from the streets*, LLL 1.2.48; (pl.) WT 2.1.94 *those That vulgars give bold'st titles*; common soldiers H5 4.7.77 *So do our vulgar drench their peasant limbs In blood of princes.*

2 'Vulgar tongue', vernacular, indigenous language LLL 4.1.68 *in the vulgar*, LLL 4.1.69, AYL 5.1.48.
~ *adj.*
1 Of the common people, plebeian COR 2.1.215 *a vulgar station* (i.e. a place among the crowd), COR 1.1.215, 2H4 1.3.90 (Q).
2 Public ERR 3.1.100 *A vulgar comment*, ANT 3.13.119, SON 112.2.
3 Commonly known or experienced, ordinary TN 3.1.124 *a vulgar proof* (i.e. common experience), HAM 1.2.99.
4 Common to all JN 2.1.387 *the vulgar air*; (in an unfavourable sense) HAM 1.3.61 *Be thou familiar, but by no means vulgar.*
◇ Erroneously used by Costard in LLL 4.1.142 *a most incony vulgar wit.*
vulgarly *adv.* Publicly MM 5.1.160 *So vulgarly and personally accus'd.*
vurther *adj.* [dial. form] Further LR 4.6.235 *without vurther cagion.*

W

wadge *vb.* (var. of) Wedge COR 2.3.28 *your wit...'tis strongly wadg'd up in a blockhead* (F1; F2 *wedged*).
wafer-cake *n.* Very light thin crisp cake; (hence used as a symbol of fragility) H5 2.3.51 *oaths are straws, men's faiths are wafer-cakes.*
waft *vb.*[1] Convey by water, carry across or over the sea etc. 2H6 4.1.115 *I charge thee waft me safely cross the Channel*, JN 2.1.73, 3H6 3.3.253.
waft *vb.*[2]
1 Beckon, signal to MV 5.1.11 *In such a night Stood Dido with a willow in her hand...and waft her love To come again*, HAM 1.4.78 (F1; Q1 *waves*), TIM 1.1.70.
2 Turn away, avert (the eyes) WT 1.2.372 *he, Wafting his eyes to th' contrary.*
waftage *n.* Conveyance across water by boat ERR 4.1.95 *to hire waftage*, TRO 3.2.10.
wafter See WAFTURE.
wafture *n.* WAVE JC 2.1.246 *with an angry wafture of your hand.*
◇ Rowe's emendation; F1 *wafter.*
wag *vb.*
1 Go forward, go one's way AYL 2.7.23 *how the world wags* (i.e. how affairs are going), WIV 1.3.7, ADO 5.1.16.
2 Go about, move about TIT 5.2.87 *the Empress never wags But in her company there is a Moor.*
wage *vb.*
1 Lay as a wager, stake CYM 1.4.132 *I will wage against your gold, gold to it*, LR 1.1.156, HAM 5.2.147 (F1).
2 Venture, hazard 1H4 4.4.20 *too weak To wage an instant trial with the King*, OTH 1.3.30, JN 1.1.266.
3 (intr.) Contend, struggle *against* LR 2.4.209 *To wage against the enmity o' th' air.*
4 Contend equally, be equal ANT 5.1.31 *His taints and honours Wag'd equal with him* (F; F2 *way*; Rowe *weigh'd*), PER 4.2.31.
5 Remunerate (as with wages) COR 5.6.39 *He wag'd me with his countenance.*
waggish *adj.* Frolicsome, roguish MND 1.1.240 *waggish boys*, CYM 3.4.157.
waggon *n.* Chariot, carriage WT 4.4.118 *Dis's waggon*, AWW 4.4.34, TIT 5.2.51.
waggoner *n.* Charioteer ROM 3.2.2 *such a waggoner As Phaeton*, ROM 1.4.67, TIT 5.2.48.
wagtail *n.* (used as term of contempt) Obsequious person LR 2.2.67 *you wagtail.*

waid See SWAYED.
wail *vb.*
1 (of the eyes) Weep LUC 1508 *eyes wailing still.*
2 (trans.) Bewail, lament, deplore LLL 5.2.749 *to wail friends lost*, R3 4.4.99, MAC 3.1.121.
wailing *ppl. adj.* *wailing robes* Mourning clothes 1H6 1.1.86 *Give me my steeled coat...Away with these disgraceful wailing robes!*
wain *n.* See CHARLES' WAIN.
wain *vb.* See WEAN.
wain-rope *n.* Waggon-rope TN 3.2.59 *oxen and wain-ropes cannot hale them together.*
waist *n.*
1 Girdle JN 2.1.217 *those sleeping stones That as a waist doth girdle you about*, 1H6 4.3.20, MM 3.2.40.
2 Part of a ship between the mainmast and foremast TMP 1.2.197 *Now in the waist, the deck, in every cabin.*
wait *vb.*
1 Remain expecting (something), await JN 4.3.152 *vast confusion waits...The imminent decay of wrested pomp*, LLL 5.2.63, PER 1.1.55.
2 Be in attendance ROM 1.3.103 *I must hence to wait* 1H4 1.2.70, 2H6 4.1.56.
3 *wait attendance* Remain in attendance TIM 1.1.161 *Wait attendance Till you hear further from me.*
waiting-woman *n.* *Diana's waiting-women* The stars TRO 5.2.91 *By all Diana's waiting-women yond.*
◇ Diana was the moon-goddess.
wake *n.*
1 Sleeplessness LR 3.2.34 *turn his sleep to wake.*
2 Feast of the dedication (or title) of a church and the merrymaking connected with it LR 3.6.74 *wakes and fairs*, LLL 5.2.318, WT 4.3.102.
~ *vb.*
1 (fig.) Arouse, excite R2 1.3.132 *To wake our peace*, MAC 3.6.31, ADO 5.1.102.
2 Be or remain awake, keep (oneself) awake TGV 1.1.80 *whether I wake or sleep*, 2H6 1.1.249, PP 20.52; (spec. of the eyes) CYM 3.4.101 *I'll wake mine eyeballs out first.*
◇ Johnson's conjecture; F *first*; Hanmer's conjecture *blind first.*
3 Sit up late for pleasure or revelry, turn night into day (with revelling) HAM 1.4.8 *The King doth wake to-night and takes his rouse*, SON 61.13.
~ *adj.* Awake LR 1.2.15 *Got 'tween asleep and wake.*

walk *n.*
1 (pl.) (a person's) Way or course MND 3.1.165 *Hop in his walks and gambol in his eyes,* TIT 2.4.8, SON 89.9.
2 Tract of garden, park, or forest 2H6 2.2.3 *In this close walk* (viz., the Duke of York's garden), 3H6 5.2.24, TIT 2.1.114.
3 Part of a masquerade or dance ADO 2.1.89 *I am yours for the walk.*
~ *vb.*
1 Go outside, withdraw WT 1.2.172 *We two will walk...And leave you to your graver steps,* LR 4.7.82, CYM 1.1.176.
2 *walk about* Promenade with a partner at a masquerade ADO 2.1.86 *Lady, will you walk about with your friend?,* ROM 1.5.17 (F1, Qq 2–4); (transf.) take part in a fencing bout ROM 3.1.75 *Tybalt...will you walk?*

walled See LADY *n.* sense 4.

wallet *n.*
1 Bag for holding provisions, etc., knapsack TRO 3.3.145 *Time hath...a wallet at his back.*
2 (transf.) Something (in a creature's body) protuberant and swagging TMP 3.3.46 *mountaineers...whose throats had hanging at 'em Wallets of flesh.*

wall-eyed *adj.* Having the iris of the eye discoloured, which gives a look of fierceness; (hence) glaring, fierce-looking JN 4.3.49 *wall-ey'd wrath,* TIT 5.1.44.

wall-newt *n.* Lizard LR 3.4.130 *Tom, that eats...the wall-newt, and the water.*

wan *vb.* Turn pale HAM 2.2.554 *Could force his soul so to his own conceit That from her working all the visage wann'd.*
▷ F1 *warm'd*; Qq 2–4 *wand*; Warburton's conjecture *wann'd.*

wandering *ppl. adj.*
1 *wandering knight* Knight errant MND 1.2.45 *What is Thisby? a wand'ring knight?*
2 (of the moon or stars) Not fixed, having a separate individual motion HAM 5.1.256 *whose phrase of sorrow Conjures the wand'ring stars* (i.e. the planets), MND 4.1.98, 2H6 4.4.16.

waned *ppl. adj.* Withered ANT 2.1.21 *all the charms of love...soften thy wan'd lip.*
▷ F *wand,* which might be for *wanned* 'paled'.

wan(n)ion *n.* *with a wanion* (exclamation of anger) With a vengeance PER 2.1.17 *Come away, or I'll fetch th' with a wanion.*

wanny *adj.* Pale, pallid ROM 4.1.100 *The roses in thy lips and cheeks shall fade To wanny ashes.*
▷ Kellner's conjecture; F1, Qq 2–3 *many*; Qq 4–5 *paly.*

want *vb.*
1 Be without, lack TMP 3.3.38 *they want the use of tongue,* JN 4.1.98, R3 5.3.13; (intr. with *of*) ROM 2.2.78 *wanting of thy love.*
2 Miss OTH 3.3.342 *nor wanting what is stol'n.*
3 Be lacking LR 4.6.264 *if your will want not,* TGV 1.2.92, LLL 4.3.233.
4 *Who cannot want the thought?* Who can help thinking...Mac 3.6.8.

wanton *n.*
1 Person of unrestrained, sportive, or roguish behaviour, trifler WIV 2.2.56 *your worship's a wanton,* MND 2.1.63, ROM 1.4.35; *play the wantons* dally, trifle, frolic R2 3.3.164 *shall we play the wantons with our woes...?*
2 Spoilt or pampered child, effeminate person HAM 5.2.299 *I am sure you make a wanton of me,* JN 5.1.70, CYM 4.2.8.
~ *vb.*
1 Sport amorously, play lasciviously TIT 2.1.21 *I will be bright...to wanton with this Queen.*

2 Play sportively or idly, frolic unrestrainedly, dally VEN 106 *To toy, to wanton, dally, smile, and jest,* WT 2.1.18, SHR Ind.2.52.
~ *adj.*
1 Unrestrained, sportive, frolicsome LLL 5.2.761 *All wanton as a child,* MV 5.1.71, H8 3.2.359.
2 Capricious, frivolous 2H4 4.1.189 *every idle, nice, and wanton reason,* 1H4 5.1.50.
3 Luxuriant, lush MND 2.1.99 *the wanton green,* R2 1.3.214, ROM 2.5.70.
4 Luxurious, effeminate 2H4 1.1.148 *a guard too wanton for the head Which princes...aim to hit,* 1H4 3.1.211, 2H4 4.1.55.

wantonly *adv.* Sportively SON 54.7 *The canker-blooms...play as wantonly.*

wantonness *n.*
1 Playful or frolicsome behaviour, sportiveness, caprice JN 4.1.16 *Young gentlemen would be as sad as night, Only for wantonness,* 1H4 5.2.68, HAM 3.1.145.
2 Capriciousness, perversity TRO 3.3.137 *While pride is fasting in his wantonness.*

wappened *ppl. adj.* Stale TIM 4.3.39 *the wappen'd widow.*
▷ Malone's conjecture *wapper'd* (i.e. fatigued).

ward *n.*
1 Guard, protection LLL 3.1.132 *the best ward of mine honour.*
2 Guard in fencing, posture of defence TMP 1.2.472 *Come, from thy ward,* 1H4 1.2.189, 1H4 2.4.195; (fig.) WIV 2.2.248 *I could drive her then from the ward of her purity,* TRO 1.2.259.
3 Bar, bolt TIM 3.3.37 *Doors, that were ne'er acquainted with their wards,* LUC 303.
4 Cell in a prison HAM 2.2.246 *a prison...in which there are many confines, wards, and dungeons,* MM 4.3.63; (fig.) MM 5.1.10 *lock it in the wards of covert bosom,* SON 48.4, SON 133.9.
5 *in ward* In the position of a ward, under (a person's) guardianship AWW 1.1.5 *his Majesty's command, to whom I am now in ward.*
6 *go to ward* Be placed in custody 2H6 5.1.112 *I know, ere they will have me go to ward, They'll pawn their swords for my enfranchisement.*
~ *vb.* Guard, protect TIT 3.1.194 *a hand that warded him From thousand dangers,* R3 5.3.254, TRO 1.2.267.

warden *n.* Variety of baking pear; (attrib.) made of Warden pears WT 4.3.45 *I must have saffron to colour the warden pies.*

warder *n.* Staff or mace held by one presiding over a combat R2 1.3.118 *the King hath thrown his warder down* (i.e. to stop the fight), 2H4 4.1.123.

ware *vb.* Beware of LLL 5.2.43 *Ware pencils ho!,* TRO 5.7.12.
~ *adj.* Aware (of) AYL 2.4.57 *Thou speak'st wiser than thou art ware of,* ROM 1.1.124, TRO 4.2.55.
▷ AYL 2.4.58 *I shall ne'er be ware of mine own wit till I break my shins against it:* with play also on the sense of 'cautious, wary'.

warm *adj.* Well-off, comfortable 1H4 4.2.17 *warm slaves, as had as lieve hear the devil as a drum.*

warn *vb.*
1 Summon JN 2.1.201 *hath warn'd us to the walls,* R3 1.3.39, JC 5.1.5.
2 *God warn us!* God keep us! AYL 4.1.77 *for lovers lacking (God warn us!) matter.*
▷ MND 1.1.320 *he for a man, God warn us* (F1 *warnd*): some mod. edd. emend to *warrant* or *warr'nt.*

warp *vb.*
1 Change the aspect of, distort AWW 5.3.49 *his scornful perspective...Which warp'd the line of*

every other favour, AYL 2.7.187; (intr.) WT 1.2.365 *My favour here begins to warp.*

2 Deviate MM 1.1.14 *our commission, From which we would not have you warp.*

warped *ppl. adj.* Perverse, malignant LR 3.6.53 *whose warp'd looks proclaim What store her heart is made on*, MM 3.1.141.

war-proof *n.* Valour proved in war H5 3.1.18 *Whose blood is fet from fathers of war-proof.*

▷ See PROOF sense 4.

warrant *n.*

1 Deed or document by which a person authorizes another to do something in his name WIV 1.1.10 *any bill, warrant, quittance.*

2 Pledge, assurance given CYM 1.4.59 *upon warrant of bloody affirmation*, R2 4.1.235, OTH 3.3.20.

3 Allowance, justification MAC 2.3.145 *There's warrant in that theft*, WIV 4.2.207, PER 4.2.128; *of warrant* warranted, allowed HAM 2.1.38 *a fetch of warrant* (F1; Q2 *wit*); *out of warrant* not allowed OTH 1.2.79 *a practiser Of arts inhibited and out of warrant.*

∼ *vb.*

1 Furnish (a person) with a guarantee or assurance ERR 1.1.139 *Could all my travels warrant me they live*, 1H4 2.4.405, PER 5.1.134.

2 Give (a person) security MM 4.2.169 *By the vow of mine order I warrant you*, ERR 4.4.3, TMP 1.1.46.

3 Keep, protect AYL 3.3.5 *Lord warrant us!*, MND 5.1.320.

▷ See WARN.

4 Justify, defend TRO 2.2.96 *that disgrace We fear to warrant.*

warranted *ppl. adj.*

1 Justified MAC 4.3.137 *our warranted quarrel.*

2 Requiring a warrant or guarantee MM 3.2.143 *a warranted need.*

warrantise, warrantize *n.*

1 Surety, guarantee 1H6 1.3.13 *I'll be your warrantize*, SON 150.7.

2 WARRANTY HAM 5.1.227 *As we have warrantise* (F1 *warrantis*).

warranty *n.* Authorization, permission OTH 5.2.60 *such general warranty of heaven*, MV 1.1.132, HAM 5.1.227 (F1 *warrantis*).

warren *n.* 'A Franchise or privileged Place by Prescription or Grant to keep Beasts and Fowl of Warren, as Conies, Hares, Partridges, and Pheasants' (Bailey), piece of land enclosed and preserved for breeding game ADO 2.1.215 *as melancholy as a lodge in a warren.*

warrener *n.* Keeper of a warren, gamekeeper WIV 1.4.27 *He hath fought with a warrener.*

wash *n.* Neptune's salt wash The sea HAM 3.2.156.

∼ *vb.*

1 *wash oneself of* Get rid of WIV 3.3.157 *I would I could wash myself of the buck* (pun on BUCK-WASHING).

2 *wash one's brain* Drink copiously ANT 2.7.99 *It's monstrous labour when I wash my brain And it grows fouler.*

washed *ppl. adj.* Bathed in tears LR 1.1.268 *wash'd eyes.*

washing *ppl. adj.* SWASHING sense 2 ROM 1.1.63 *remember thy washing blow* (Ff, Qq 2–3; Q1 *swashing*).

waspish-headed *adj.* Hot-headed, fiery TMP 4.1.99 *Her waspish-headed son has broke his arrows.*

wasp-stung *adj.* Irritable (as if stung by a wasp) 1H4 1.3.236 *what a wasp-stung and impatient fool* (Q1; F1 *Waspe-tongu'd*, Qq 2–6 *waspe-tongue*).

wassail *n.*

1 Spiced ale MAC 1.7.64 *with wine and wassail.*

2 Carousal, revelry LLL 5.2.318 *retails his wares At wakes and wassails*, HAM 1.4.9, ANT 1.4.56 (F1 *Vassailes*); (attrib.) 2H4 1.2.158 *A wassail candle* (i.e. large candle used at a feast).

waste *n.*

1 Wasting, squandering, devastation LR 2.1.100 *th' expense and waste of his revenues*, MV 1.1.157, H5 1.2.28.

2 Spoliation WIV 4.2.212 *he will never, I think, in the way of waste, attempt us again.*

3 (concrete) That which is laid waste or destroyed R2 2.1.103 *The waste is no whit lesser than thy land* (with quibble on the legal sense 'destruction of houses, woods, lands, etc., done by the tenant to the prejudice of the heir'), SON 12.10 *the wastes of time* (i.e. things devastated by Time).

▷ For HAM 1.2.198 *the dead waste and middle of the night* (F2; F1, Qq 2–4 *wast*; Q1 *vast*) see VAST sense 1.

∼ *vb.*

1 Spend (time, money, etc.), consume (food) AYL 2.7.134 *we will nothing waste* (i.e. eat), R2 2.1.252, 2H4 4.1.213.

2 Make as if non-existent PER 4.4.1 *Thus time we waste.*

∼ *adj.* Empty SON 77.10 *Look what thy memory cannot contain Commit to these waste blanks* (i.e. empty, blank sheets of paper).

wasted *ppl. adj.*

1 Consumed (by fire) MND 5.1.375 *the wasted brands do glow.*

2 (of time) Gone by, elapsed, past OTH 1.3.84 *some nine moons wasted*, SON 106.1.

wasteful *adj.* Devastating, consuming, destructive AYL 3.2.323 *wasteful learning*, H5 3.1.14, SON 55.5.

Wat *n.* (pet-form of) Walter; traditional name for the hare VEN 697 *poor Wat...stands on his hinderlegs.*

watch *n.*

1 Condition of being awake CYM 3.4.41 *in watch* (i.e. awake); *keep watch* be awake H5 4.1.283 *What watch the King keeps to maintain the peace*; state of sleeplessness HAM 2.2.148 *Fell into a sadness, then into a fast, Thence to a watch.*

2 Timepiece, clock LLL 3.1.192 *like a German clock...being a watch*, TMP 2.1.12, TN 5.1.162; (prob.) clock-face R2 5.5.52 *the outward watch.*

3 (?) (1) Watch-light, or candle divided into sections which burn through in a definite time; or (2) sentinel R3 5.3.63 *Give me a watch.*

4 One of three or four parts into which the night was formerly divided OTH 1.1.123 *this odd-even and dull watch o' th' night*, 2H4 4.5.28.

5 Intervals of time R2 5.5.52 *My thoughts are minutes, and with sighs they jar Their watches on unto mine eyes.*

6 Man or body of men charged with patrolling the streets at night, guard ADO 3.3.6 *the Prince's watch*, ROM 5.3.71, 1H4 2.4.483.

7 Sentinel's and watchman's cry MAC 2.1.54 *the wolf, Whose howl's his watch.*

∼ *vb.*

1 Be awake, lie awake, have no sleep, sit up at night LLL 3.1.200 *to sigh for her, to watch for her...!*, SHR 4.1.205, LR 2.2.155; remain awake for a specified purpose MAC 5.1.1 *I have two nights watch'd with you*, JN 4.1.30.

2 Keep (a hawk) awake in order to tame her; (fig.) OTH 3.3.23 *I'll watch him tame*, SHR 4.1.195, TRO 3.2.43.

3 Wait expectantly for, look out for JC 4.3.249 *we will stand and watch your pleasure*, 2H6 2.4.7, MND 1.1.177; (intr. with *for*) MV 2.6.24 *I'll watch as long for you then.*

4 Catch in the act Wiv 5.5.103 *do not fly, I think we have watch'd you now*, 2H6 1.4.42, 2H6 1.4.55.

watch-case *n*. Sentry-box 2H4 3.1.17 *O sleep... why...leavest the kingly couch A watch-case...?*

watcher *n*. One who remains awake Mac 2.2.68 *Get on your night-gown, lest occasion...show us to be watchers*, TGV 2.4.135.

watchful *adj*.

1 Marked by or causing loss of sleep JC 2.1.98 *watchful cares*, TGV 1.1.31, 2H4 4.5.25.

2 Used in keeping watch H5 4.Ch.23 *watchful fires*.

watchman *n*.

1 Sentry Ant 4.3.17 *let's see if other watchmen Do hear what we do*; one of a group charged with patrolling the streets at night Ado 3.3.40 *an ancient...watchman*; (fig.) Ham 1.3.46 *I shall the effect of this good lesson keep As watchman to my heart*, 1H6 3.1.66.

2 One who stays awake Son 61.12 *To play the watchman* (with quibble).

water *n*.

1 Tears 3H6 5.4.75 *the water of my eye*, 1H4 3.1.93, LC 291; (pl.) MM 4.3.146 *Command these fretting waters from your eyes With a light heart*, Jn 4.3.107, Lr 1.4.303; *raise the waters* call forth tears MV 2.2.49.

2 Lustre of a diamond Per 3.2.101 *diamonds Of a most praised water*, Tim 1.1.18.

3 *for all waters* Ready for anything TN 4.2.63.

water-fly *n*. Fly that hovers over water Ant 5.2.59 *let the water-flies Blow me into abhorring!*; (fig.) vain or busily idle person Ham 5.2.82 *Dost know this water-fly?*, Tro 5.1.34.

water-gall *n*. Secondary or imperfectly formed rainbow Luc 1588 *like rainbows in the sky. These water-galls in her dim element...*

watering *n*. Act of drinking 1H4 2.4.16 *when you breathe in your watering*.

waterish *adj*. Well-watered, abounding in rivers Lr 1.1.258 *wat'rish Burgundy* (with play on the sense 'poor, thin').

water-rat *n*. Pirate MV 1.3.23 *there be land-rats and water-rats, water-thieves and land-thieves, I mean pirates*.

water-rug *n*. Shaggy breed of water-dog Mac 3.1.93 *spaniels, curs, Shoughs, water-rugs...are clipt All by the name of dogs*.

water-standing *adj*. Flooded with tears 3H6 5.6.40 *many an orphan's water-standing eye*.

waterwork *n*. Imitation tapestry in size or distemper 2H4 2.1.145 *the German hunting in waterwork*.

watery *adj*.

1 (of the moon) Connected with water, either as controlling the tides or bringing rain MND 2.1.162 *the wat'ry moon*, R3 2.2.69; (hence) *wat'ry star* the moon WT 1.2.1.

2 'Watering', desirous Tro 3.2.21 *wat'ry palates*.

wave *vb*.

1 Waver, vacillate Cor 2.2.17 *he wav'd indifferently 'twixt doing them neither good nor harm*.

2 Make motions (with something held in the hand) by way of signal Cym 1.3.12 *he...with glove or hat or handkerchief Still waving*; (hence) signal to (a person), beckon Ham 1.4.61 *It waves you to a more removed ground* (F *wafts*), Ham 1.4.68, Ham 1.4.78.

3 Move (the head up and down) Cor 3.2.77 *waving thy head*, Ham 2.1.90.

wawl *vb*. Wail Lr 4.6.180 *We wawl and cry* (Ff; Qq *wayle, waile*).

wax *n*.

1 *man of wax* (term of emphatic commendation) Man perfect in beauty, faultless as if modelled in wax Rom 1.3.76 *such a man As all the world—why, he's a man of wax.*

2 *sea of wax* (?) Tablet of wax on which one could write Tim 1.1.47 *My free drift...moves itself In a wide sea of wax.*
▷ Hibbard's emendation seems more reasonable. See TAX.

wax *vb*.

1 Grow, increase Ham 1.3.12 *as this temple waxes*, Cor 2.2.99, LLL 5.2.10 (with quibble on 'wax' *n*. in the sense 'substance secreted by bees').

2 Become (so-and-so) Ham 1.4.87 *He waxes desperate with imagination*, H5 5.1.84, 2H6 3.2.76.

waxen *vb*. Increase MND 2.1.56 *waxen in their mirth*.

waxen *adj*. (fig.)

1 Easily impressed TN 2.2.30 *women's waxen hearts*, Luc 1240.

2 Easily effaced H5 1.2.233 *a waxen epitaph*.

3 Easily penetrable R2 1.3.75 *Mowbray's waxen coat.*

way *n*.

1 Passage, course Err 4.3.91 *Belike his wife...shut the doors against his way*, H8 2.4.129, Ant 3.6.85.

2 Freedom of action, scope, opportunity; (with *have*) MM 5.1.238 *Let me have way...To find this practice out*, AWW 3.6.2; (with *give*) Lr 2.4.298 *'Tis best to give him way, he leads himself*, 2H4 5.2.82, Cor 5.6.31; (hence) *give way* (*to*) humour, favour H8 3.2.16 *though now the time Gives way to us*, Per 4.6.19, Per 5.1.230.

3 'Way of thinking', belief H8 5.1.28 *a gentleman Of mine own way*, H8 1.3.61.

4 Best or most advisable course R3 1.1.78 *I think it is our way...To be her men*, Err 4.3.92.

~ in phrases

any way In any degree or respect Err 3.2.148 *if the wind blow any way from shore*, H8 3.1.56, 1H4 4.3.46. **by the way** Indirectly, by a side channel of information Mac 3.4.129 *I hear it by the way.* **in (the) way of** 1 As regards H8 3.2.272 *in the way of loyalty and truth Toward the King*, Tro 2.2.189, Lr 2.2.20. **2** As an instance or manifestation of, by way of Tro 3.3.13 *I do beseech you, as in way of taste, To give me now a little benefit*, Ham 1.3.95, H5 3.2.97. **out of the way** 1 Beside the mark, out of place, inappropriate Oth 1.3.359 *A pox of drowning thyself, it is clean out of the way*, LLL 4.3.74. **2** Gone astray, lost Oth 3.4.80 *Is't lost? Is't gone? Speak, is't out o' th' way?* **that way** 1 In that respect Wiv 1.4.14 *he is something peevish that way*, Tmp 2.1.240, Wiv 1.4.14. **2** By reason of that Cym 1.1.137 *Past hope, and in despair, that way past grace.* **this way** 1 In respect of this H8 2.2.68 *Our breach of duty this way Is business of estate.* **2** By acting thus Cym 4.4.4 *This way, the Romans Must or for Britains slay us or receive us For... revolts.*

ways (old genitive of 'way' *n*. used in adverbial expressions)

1 *come* (*your*) *ways* Come along MM 3.2.80 *Come your ways, sir, come*, AYL 1.2.209, AWW 2.1.93; *go* (*your*) *ways* move away, depart, get along, be off AYL 4.1.182 *Ay, go your ways, go your ways*, Shr 4.5.23, Wiv 2.2.138.

2 *this ways* This way Wiv 2.2.45 *come a little nearer this ways.*

wayward *adj*.

1 Untoward, perverse Per 4.4.10 *Pericles Is now again thwarting the wayward seas*, R2 2.1.142, TGV 1.2.57.

2 Perverted Mac 1.3.32 *The wayward sisters* (F1 *weyward*).
▷ With the connotation also of 'perverting'; cf. Matt 6.23 *If thine eye be weyward* (Wiclif). Theobald's conjecture *weird* (i.e. 'having the power to

control the fate or destiny of men') is popularly accepted.

weak *adj.*
1 Foolish, stupid TMP 2.2.145 *A very weak monster!*, ADO 3.1.54, ROM 2.4.170.
2 (of a thing) Of little account or worth, inconsiderable MND 5.1.427 *this weak and idle theme*, OTH 3.3.443, H5 3.6.133.

weak-hinged *adj.* Ill-balanced WT 2.3.119 *Not able to produce more accusation Than your own weak-hing'd fancy.*

weal *n.*
1 Welfare TIM 4.3.160 *the general weal*, JN 4.2.65, HAM 3.3.14.
2 Commonwealth COR 2.3.181 *th' body of the weal*, MAC 3.4.75 LR 1.4.211.

weal-balanced *adj.* Adjusted with due regard to the public welfare MM 4.3.100 *By cold gradation and weal-balanc'd form We shall proceed with Angelo.*

wealsman *n.* Statesman COR 2.1.54 *two such wealsmen.*

wealth *n.* Welfare, prosperity HAM 4.4.27 *th' imposthume of much wealth and peace*, MV 5.1.249.

wean, wain *vb.* (fig.) Turn away, alienate TIT 1.1.211 *I will restore to thee The people's hearts, and wean them from themselves*, 3H6 4.4.17.

wear *n.* Fashion MM 3.2.75 *I hope...your...worship will be my bail.—No...it is not the wear*, AYL 2.7.34, AWW 1.1.205.
~ *vb.*
1 Bear, carry MV 2.2.192 *Wear prayer-books in my pocket*; (fig.) bear, have, possess TIM 4.3.480 *Never did poor steward wear a truer grief For his undone lord*, CYM 4.2.202, 2H6 3.2.197; (proverbial) own ADO 5.1.82 *Win me and wear me*, H5 5.2.233.
2 Be worn, be fashionable AWW 1.1.158 *the brooch and the toothpick, which wear not now* (F1 *were*).
3 Fatigue, weary AWW 5.1.4 *To wear your gentle limbs in my affairs*, AYL 2.4.38 (F1; Ff 2–4 *wearying*).
4 Outlast LR 5.3.17 *we'll wear out...packs and sects of great ones*, ANT 4.14.133.
5 Spend, pass (a period of time) H8 2.4.229 *To wear our mortal state to come with her.*
6 (of time) Pass on, pass away WIV 5.1.7 *time wears*, SHR 3.2.111.
▷ See also WORN.
7 Gain more and more (of a person's) liking or admiration TN 2.4.30 *so wears she to him.*

wearer *n.* Bearer, owner MV 2.9.43 *O that...clear honour Were purchas'd by the merit of the wearer!*

wearing *n.* Clothes OTH 4.3.16 *my nightly wearing*, WT 4.4.9.

weary *adj.* Tiresome, irksome MM 1.4.25 *Not to be weary with you*, HAM 1.2.133 (F1; Qq2–4 *wary*), OTH 3.4.176.

weather *n.*
1 Storm, tempest TMP 1.1.37 *louder than the weather*, MV 2.9.29, JN 4.2.109.
2 (nautical) The direction in which the wind is blowing; (hence) *keeps the weather of* is to windward of; (fig.) *has the advantage of* TRO 5.3.26 *Mine honour keeps the weather of my fate.*

weather-bitten *adj.* Weather-worn, weathered WT 5.2.55 *a weather-bitten conduit of many kings' reigns.*

weather-fend *vb.* Protect from the weather TMP 5.1.10 *the line-grove which weather-fends your cell.*

web See PIN *n.* sense 3.

wedded *ppl. adj.* Nuptial ROM 1.5.135 *My grave is like to be my wedded bed* (F1; Qq *wedding*).

wedge *vb.* Cleave or split by driving in a wedge;

(fig.) TRO 1.1.35 *when my heart, As wedged with a sigh, would rive in twain.*

weed *n.*[1] Dress, garment LUC 196 *love's modest snow-white weed*, COR 2.3.221, SON 2.4; (pl.) HAM 4.7.80 *his sables and his weeds*, TN 5.1.273, TGV 2.7.42.

weed *n.*[2] Poor, leggy or ill-conditioned horse; (fig.) MM 1.3.20 *The needful bits and curbs to headstrong weeds.*
▷ F *weedes* (here perh. in simple sense of 'horse'); Theobald's conjecture *steeds*; Walker *wills.*

weed *vb.* (lit. and fig.) Clear from weeds, uproot, eradicate R2 2.3.167 *The caterpillars of the commonwealth, Which I have sworn to weed and pluck away*, OTH 1.3.322, COR 4.5.102.

weeding *n.* What is weeded out, weeds LLL 1.1.96 *He weeds the corn and still lets grow the weeding.*

weedy *adj.* Made or consisting of weeds HAM 4.7.174 *her weedy trophies.*

week *n.*
1 The six working days as opposed to Sunday HAM 1.1.76 *whose sore task Does not divide the Sunday from the week.*
2 *in by the week* Trapped, caught LLL 5.2.61 *O that I knew he were but in by th' week!*
3 *too late a week* 'Too late in the day' AYL 2.3.74 *At seventeen years many their fortunes seek, But at fourscore it is too late a week.*
4 *a whole week by days* See DAY *n.* sense 1.

ween *vb.* Imagine, expect, hope 1H6 2.5.88 *weening to redeem And have install'd me in the diadem*, H8 5.1.135.

weeping-ripe *adj.* Ready to weep LLL 5.2.274 *The King was weeping-ripe for a good word*, 3H6 1.4.172.

weet *vb.* Know ANT 1.1.39 *I bind...the world to weet We stand up peerless.*

weigh *vb.*
1 Consider, take into consideration JC 2.1.108 *Weighing the youthful season of the year*, WT 1.2.258, SON 120.8.
2 Estimate at a certain rate AWW 3.4.32 *her worth That he does weigh too light*, H5 2.4.43.
3 Esteem, value; (with neg.) esteem lightly, attach no value to, have no regard for LLL 5.2.27 *You weigh me not? O, that's you care not for me*, H8 5.1.124, SON 108.10.
4 Be equivalent to, balance LLL 5.2.26 *Indeed I weigh not you, and therefore light*, MAC 4.3.90, H8 1.1.11; (with *out*) counterbalance, countervail, outweigh H8 3.1.88 *my friends...that must weigh out my afflictions*; (intr., with *against*) 2H4 1.3.55 *To weigh against his opposite*; (with *with*) TIM 1.1.146 *in him I'll counterpoise, And make him weigh with her*, 2H4 2.2.176.
5 Hang or balance evenly TMP 2.1.131 *the fair soul...Weigh'd between loathness and obedience.*
6 Have weight, be heavy (with sadness) AWW 3.5.67 *Her heart weighs sadly*, MAC 5.3.45.
7 Have a certain value COR 2.2.74 *I love them as they weigh* (i.e. according to their worth).

weight *n.* (with *by*) With full measure, fully MM 1.2.121 *Make us pay down for our offence by weight The words of heaven*, TRO 5.2.168; (similarly with *in*) H5 3.6.128 *which in weight to re-answer, his pettiness would bow under*; (with *with*) HAM 4.5.157 *thy madness shall be paid with weight* (Qq; F1 *by*).

weighty *adj.* Grievous TIM 3.5.101 *our weightier judgement*, H8 3.1.58.

weird See WAYWARD.

welfare *n.* Health MV 5.1.114 *our husbands' welfare* (Q1 *health*), SON 118.7, LUC 263.

welked See WHELKED.

welkin *n.* Sky LLL 4.2.5 *the sky, the welkin, the heaven*, TMP 1.2.4, JN 5.5.2; (attrib.) heavenly WT 1.2.136 *your welkin eye* (or perh. 'blue').

◇ Used ludicrously in TN 3.1.58 *out of my welkin.*

well *n.* Spring of water PP 17.25 *Clear wells spring not,* TRO 5.10.19, LC 255.

well *adj.*

1 (of the dead) Happy, at rest ANT 2.5.33 *we use To say the dead are well,* ROM 5.1.17, WT 5.1.30.

2 *well to live* Well to do, prosperous MV 2.2.53 *an honest exceeding poor man and...well to live* (Old Gobbo's speech), WT 3.3.121.

well-a-day *n.* Woe, grief PER 4.4.49 *His daughter's woe and heavy well-a-day.*

~ *interj.* Alas ROM 3.2.37 *Ah, well-a-day, he's dead,* TN 4.2.108, WIV 3.3.99.

well-advised *adj.*

1 (of persons) Prudent, wary, circumspect R3 4.4.515 *any well-advised friend,* JN 3.1.5, TIT 4.2.10.

2 In one's right mind, sane ERR 2.2.213 *mad or well-advis'd.*

well-a-near *interj.* [Dial.] WELL-A-DAY PER 3. Gower. 51 *The lady shrieks, and well-a-near Does fall in travail.*

well-appointed *adj.* Well-equipped 2H4 1.1.190 *well-appointed pow'rs.*

well-balanced See WEAL-BALANCED.

well-beseeming *adj.* Very fitting TIT 2.3.56 *her well-beseeming troop,* 1H4 1.1.14.

well-breathed *adj.* (1) Sound or strong of wind; or (2) exercised so as to be in good wind VEN 678 *thy well-breath'd horse.*

well-derived *adj.* Inherited from good ancestors AWW 3.2.88 *My son corrupts a well-derived nature*; well-born TGV 5.2.23 *What says she to my birth?—That you are well-derived.*

well-desired *adj.* Much sought after OTH 2.1.204 *you shall be well-desir'd in Cyprus.*

well-entered *adj.* Well-instructed, highly trained AWW 2.1.6 *well-ent'red soldiers.*

well-favoured *adj.* Good looking, handsome, comely ADO 3.3.14 *To be a well-favour'd man is the gift of fortune,* WIV 2.2.273, LR 2.4.256.

well-foughten *adj.* Bravely contested H5 4.6.18 *in this glorious and well-foughten field.*

well-found *adj.*

1 Of tried goodness or merit AWW 2.1.102 *In what he did profess, well-found.*

2 Happily met with COR 2.2.44 *last general In our well-found successes* (perh. with play on sense 1).

well-given *adj.* Well-disposed JC 1.2.197 *He is a noble Roman, and well-given,* 2H6 3.1.72.

well-governed *adj.* Of good behaviour ROM 1.5.68 *a virtuous and well-govern'd youth.*

well-graced *adj.* Favourite, popular R2 5.2.24 *a well-graced actor.*

well-liking *adj.* In good condition, plump LLL 5.2.268 *Well-liking wits they have—gross gross, fat fat.*

well-painted *adj.* Skilfully feigned OTH 4.1.257 *well-painted passion.*

well-respected *adj.* Carefully weighed, well considered 1H4 4.3.10 *If well-respected honour bid me on.*

well said! *interj.* Well done! that's right! TIT 4.3.64 *Now masters, draw.* [They shoot.] *O, well said, Lucius!,* AYL 2.6.13, ANT 4.4.28.

well-wished *adj.* 'Attended by good wishes, beloved' (Schmidt) MM 2.4.27 *a well-wish'd king.*

Welsh hook *n.* Weapon with a curved or hooked blade 1H4 2.4.338 *and swore the devil his true liegeman upon the cross of a Welsh hook.*

wen *n.* Tumour, swelling; (fig., applied contemptuously to a person) 2H4 2.2.106 *I do allow this wen to be as familiar with me as my dog.*

wench *n.* Term of affectionate or familiar address

TMP 1.2.139 *Well demanded, wench,* H8 3.1.1, LUC 1273.

wenching *ppl. adj.* Womanizing, lecherous TRO 5.4.33 *the wenching rogues.*

wench-like *adj.* Womanish CYM 4.2.230 *do not play in wench-like words.*

weyward See WAYWARD.

wezand *n.* Windpipe TMP 3.2.91 *cut his wezand with thy knife.*

whale's bone *n.* Ivory, from walrus or similar animal LLL 5.2.332 *To show his teeth as white as whale's bone.*

◇ Ivory was supposed by some to come from the whale.

wharf *n.* Bank (of a river) HAM 1.5.33 *on Lethe wharf,* ANT 2.2.213.

what *pron.* and *adj.* A. Interrogative uses

1 (of a person in predicative use) Of what name?, who? OTH 1.1.94 *what are you?—My name is Roderigo,* MAC 5.7.2, MM 5.1.467.

2 For what reason?, why? TIT 1.1.189 *What should I don this robe and trouble you?,* ANT 5.2.313, 2H4 1.2.114.

3 How? ROM 1.5.55 *What dares the slave Come hither...?*

4 *What is the night?* What time of night is it? MAC 3.4.125.

5 *What though?* What does it matter?, No matter! AYL 3.3.51 *But what though? Courage!,* H5 2.1.8, JN 1.1.169.

6 *What to?* What about, what of? SHR 3.2.42 *what to thine old news?*

B. Exclamatory uses

7 (as an exclamation of surprise, impatience, exultation or encouragement) Why!, Come! SHR 4.1.108 *How now Grumio? What, Grumio!,* R3 4.4.320, ANT 4.8.19.

8 Used to summon or call the attention of a person TMP 4.1.33 *What, Ariel!,* WIV 3.3.1, ANT 2.7.131; (with *ho*) TMP 1.2.313 *What ho! slave! Caliban!,* MM 3.1.44, ROM 1.1.83.

9 What a...! JC 1.3.42 *Cassius, what night is this?,* WT 1.2.352, VEN 445.

10 What a thing MV 1.3.160 *what these Christians are...!,* CYM 4.1.15.

C. Relative uses

11 Whatever, any(thing) whatever TMP 1.2.158 *to bear up Against what should ensue,* WT 1.2.44, 3H6 3.1.51.

12 Whoever H8 2.1.65 *Be what they will, I heartily forgive 'em,* 1H6 5.3.45, LR 5.3.97.

13 *what time* At the time when TN 4.3.30 *What time we will our celebration keep According to my birth,* 3H6 2.5.3.

D. Idiomatic uses

14 *I'll tell you what* Let me tell you ADO 5.4.100 *I'll tell thee what, Prince,* TRO 5.2.21, JN 3.3.60; (similarly) *wot you what* R3 3.2.90 *Wot you what, my lord?*; *I know what* ROM 1.5.84 *This trick may chance to scathe you, I know what.*

15 *what with...what with* Partly by...and partly by 1H4 4.4.14 *What with the sickness of Northumberland...And what with Owen Glendower's absence thence,...I fear the power of Percy is too weak,* MM 1.2.82, 1H4 5.1.49; (without *with*) TRO 5.3.103 *what one thing, what another.*

whatever *pron.* (elliptical for) Whatever it be TRO 4.5.77 *Therefore Achilles, but whate'er, know this.*

whatsoever *pron.*

1 (elliptical for) Whatsoever it be, in any case SHR 1.2.215 *bear his charge of wooing, whatso'er.*

2 Whoever TN 1.3.117 *as any man in Illyria, whatsoever he be,* TN 3.4.147, CYM 2.1.40.

whatsomever *pron.*
1 Whatever ANT 2.6.97 *All men's faces are true, whatsome'er their hands are.*
2 Whoever AWW 3.5.51 *whatsome'er he is, He's bravely taken here.*

wheel *n.*
1 Spinning wheel AYL 1.2.32 *mock the good housewife Fortune from her wheel* (with ref. to sense 2), HAM 4.5.172.
2 Used as emblem of Fortune LR 5.3.175 *The wheel is come full circle.*
3 *wheel of fire* Form of torture in hell; (transf.) LR 4.7.46 *I am bound Upon a wheel of fire.*
4 *go on wheels* Pursue a course of ease and self-indulgence ANT 2.7.93 *the world...might go on wheels;* (similarly) TGV 3.1.315 *set the world on wheels.*
5 *turn in the wheel* Do the office of a turn-spit, as certain dogs were made to do by treading wheel ERR 3.2.146 *She had transform'd me to a curtal dog, and made me turn i' th' wheel.*
~ *vb.*
1 Turn round R3 4.4.105 *Thus hath the course of justice wheel'd about* (Qq; Ff *whirl'd*).
2 Make a circuit COR 1.6.19 *I was forc'd to wheel Three or four miles about.*
3 Range about, rove TRO 5.7.2 *Attend me where I wheel.*

wheeling *ppl. adj.* Wandering about, roving OTH 1.1.136 *an extravagant and wheeling stranger Of here and everywhere.*

wheeson *n.* [dial.] Whitsun 2H4 2.1.89 *upon Wednesday in Wheeson week* (Q; F1 *Whitson*).

whelk *n.* Pustule, pimple H5 3.6.103 *His face is all bubukles, and whelks, and knobs.*

whelked *adj.* Twisted, convoluted, or ridged like the shell of a whelk LR 4.6.72 *he had a thousand noses, Horns whelk'd and waved* (Qq *welkt, welk't;* Ff 1-2 *wealk'd*).

whelm *vb.* Submerge, drown WIV 2.2.137 *She is my prize, or ocean whelm them all.*

when *conj.*
1 As an exclamation of impatience JC 2.1.5 *when, Lucius, when?,* TMP 1.2.316, R2 1.1.162.
2 (after *seldom*) That 2H4 4.4.79 *'Tis seldom when the bee doth leave her comb,* MM 4.2.86.

whenas, when as *conj.* When ERR 4.4.139 *When as your husband all in rage today Came to my house,* 3H6 1.2.74, CYM 5.4.138.

whence *conj.* From the place where AWW 3.2.121 *come thou home...Whence honour but of danger wins a scar,* MAC 1.2.25; (with *from*) TIT 1.1.68 *Andronicus is returned From whence he...* (F1), TIM 1.1.22.

whe'r *conj.* (contracted form of) Whether ERR 4.1.60 *say whe'r you'll answer me or no,* TMP 5.1.111, SON 59.11.
▷ In Ff and Qq sometimes also spelt *where*.

where *n.* Place LR 1.1.261 *Thou losest here, a better where to find.*
~ *adv.*
1 (relative use) In which condition or action TN 5.1.86 *I...Drew to defend him...Where being apprehended,* WT 5.1.213; in a case in which, in circumstances in which TGV 1.1.29 *To be in love—where scorn is bought with groans,* TRO 4.4.33, VEN 1153; (hence) when JC 1.2.59 *I have heard Where many...Have wish'd,* TMP 5.1.236, MV 5.1.264.
2 (interr.) Whence H5 3.5.15 *where have they this mettle?,* JN 5.1.40, SON 76.8; from whom ANT 2.1.18 *Where have you this?*
~ *conj.*
1 Whereas LLL 2.1.103 *his ignorance were wise, Where now his knowledge must prove ignorance,* 1H6 5.5.47, LUC 792.

2 *where you are* What you are driving at AYL 5.2.29 *I know where you are.*
3 Wherever LR 4.5.10 *where he arrives he moves All hearts against us,* MND 5.1.93, 2H6 4.7.59.

whereabout *n.* What one is about, intention MAC 2.1.58 *Hear not my steps...for fear The very stones prate of my whereabout.*
~ *adv.* On what errand or purpose 1H4 2.3.104 *question me Whither I go, nor reason whereabout.*

whereagainst *rel. adv.* Against which COR 4.5.107 *that body, whereagainst My grained ash an hundred times hath broke.*

whereas *conj.* Where 2H6 1.2.58 *unto Saint Alban's, Whereas the king and queen do mean to hawk,* PER 1.4.70, PP 6.13.

whereby *adv.* Whereupon 2H4 2.1.96 *telling us they had a good dish of prawns, whereby thou didst desire to eat some,* 2H4 2.1.97.

wherefore *adv.*
1 (interr.) To what end?, For what purpose? R2 2.3.122 *Wherefore was I born?*
2 (interr.) For what cause?, On what account? 1H6 2.1.54 *Wherefore is Charles impatient with his friend?,* TMP 3.1.76, ROM 3.2.100.
3 (rel.) For which H5 5.2.1 *Peace to this meeting, wherefore we are met.*

wherein *adv.*
1 (interr.) In what AYL 3.2.221 *Wherein went he?* (i.e. in what clothes), 1H4 2.4.457, R2 2.3.107.
2 (rel.) In that in which, in whatever; (hence) though WT 1.1.8 *Wherein our entertainment shall shame us: we will be justified,* MND 3.2.179.

whereof *rel. adv.* By means of which, with which, wherewith AWW 1.3.229 *the desperate languishings whereof The King is render'd lost,* TIM 4.3.194.

whereout *rel. adv.* Out of which TRO 4.5.245 *make distinct the very breach whereout Hector's great spirit flew.*

whereuntil *rel. adv.* To what LLL 5.2.493 *we know whereuntil it doth amount,* LLL 5.2.500.

whereupon *rel. adv.*
1 On what, on what grounds, for what reason 1H4 4.3.42 *to know The nature of your griefs, and whereupon You conjure...,* JN 4.2.65.
2 Concerning which, about which H8 2.4.202 *Toward this remedy, whereupon we Are now present here together.*

whet *vb.* Incite, instigate JC 2.1.61 *Cassius first did whet me against Caesar,* JN 3.4.181, R3 1.3.331.

whether *pron.* Which of the two AWW 4.5.22 *Whether dost thou profess thyself—a knave or a fool?,* VEN 304, PP 14.8.
~ *conj.* (introducing a disjunctive direct question) Expressing doubt between alternatives JN 1.1.134 *Whether hadst thou rather be a Faulconbridge ...Or the reputed son of Coeur-de-Lion?,* MV 3.2.117; (with or introducing the first question) SON 114.1 *Or whether doth my mind...Or whether shall I say...?*

whey-face *n.* Pale-face MAC 5.3.17 *What soldiers, whey-face?*

which *pron.*
1 (used of persons) Who, whom MAC 5.1.60 *I have known those which have walked...,* TMP 1.2.32, 1H4 3.1.45.
▷ Freq. occurs as *the which.*
2 That which WT 3.2.60 *More than mistress of Which comes to me in name of fault.*
3 (correlative to such) As WT 1.1.24 *there rooted...such an affection, which cannot choose but branch now,* TN 5.1.350, COR 3.2.105.

whiffler *n.* Officer who clears the way for a procession H5 5.Ch.12 *the deep-mouth'd sea, Which* *like a mighty whiffler 'fore the king Seems to prepare his way.*

while *n. the while* (in exclamations) (At) the present time MV 2.1.31 *alas the while!*, JN 4.2.100, R3 3.6.10.
~ *conj.* Till, until R2 1.3.122 *let the trumpets sound While we return these dukes what we decree.*
~ *prep.* Till, until MAC 3.1.43 *while then, God be with you.*

while-ere *adv.* A little while ago, erewhile TMP 3.2.118 *will you troll the catch You taught me but while-ere?*

whiles *n. the whiles* During that time SHR 3.1.22 *play you the whiles.*
~ *conj.* Till, until TN 4.3.29 *He shall conceal it Whiles you are willing it shall come to note.*

whinid'st See VINEWED.

whip *vb.*
1 Move quickly (intr.) LLL 5.2.309 *Whip to our tents;* (refl.) ADO 1.3.60 *I whipt me behind the arras* (Q).
2 (esp. imperative as a mild execration) Confound PER 4.2.86 *Marry, whip the gosling*, 3H6 3.2.28, OTH 1.1.49.

whipping-cheer *n.* 'Banquet' of lashes with the whip, flogging 2H4 5.4.5 *she shall have whipping-cheer, I warrant her.*

whipster *n.* Insignificant or contemptible person OTH 5.2.244 *every puny whipster.*

whipstock *n.* Handle of a whip PER 2.2.51 *he appears To have practis'd more the whipstock than the lance*, TN 2.3.27.

whirligig *n.* Toy that spins and whirls, whipping-top; (fig.) circling course, revolution TN 5.1.376 *thus the whirligig of time brings in his revenges.*

whirling *ppl. adj.* Impetuous, violent HAM 1.5.133 *wild and whirling words* (Q1 *wherling*, Q2 *whurling;* Ff *hurling*).

whissing *ppl. adj.* (var. of) Wheezing TRO 5.1.20 *whissing lungs.*

whist *adj.* Silent, quiet, hushed TMP 1.2.378 *kiss'd, The wild waves whist.*

whistle *n. worth the whistle* Worthy of some notice LR 4.2.29 *I have been worth the whistle* (F1; Q1 *whistling*).
~ *vb.*
1 (in falconry) *whistle off* Send off by whistling, cast off, dismiss OTH 3.3.262 *if I do prove her haggard...I'ld whistle her off.*
2 Speak, tell, utter secretly, whisper WT 4.4.245 *to whistle of these secrets.*
◊ F1; Hanmer's conjecture *whistle off* (i.e. fig. use of sense 1).
3 *go whistle* (expression of contempt) Go hang, go and do what one will WT 4.4.698 *let the law go whistle.*

white *n.*
1 White spot in the centre of a target SHR 5.2.186 *'Twas I won the wager, though you hit the white.*
2 *spit white* Eject frothy-white sputum from the mouth 2H4 1.2.212 *I would I might never spit white again.*
~ *adj.*
1 Pale, esp. from fear; (hence) emblem of cowardice MV 3.2.86 *livers white as milk*, 2H4 4.3.104, MAC 2.2.62.
2 *white herring* Fresh or pickled (as opposed to red) herring LR 3.6.31.

white-limed *adj.* Whitewashed TIT 4.2.98 *Ye white-lim'd walls.*
◊ Ff 3-4. Ff 1-2 *-limb'd*, Qq *-limbde*, which are common 16-17C forms of 'limn'; hence Malone's conjecture *white-lim'nd* (i.e. painted white).

white-limned See WHITE-LIMED.

white-livered *adj.* Feeble-spirited, cowardly, lily-livered R3 4.4.464 *White-liver'd runagate*, H5 3.2.32.

whitely *adj.* Pale, whitish LLL 3.1.196 *A whitely wanton with a velvet brow.*
◊ Ff 1-2, Qq; see WIGHTLY.

whither *rel. adv.* Whithersoever, to whatever place 1H4 1.3.2 *a fool go with thy soul, whither it goes*, COR 1.2.16.

whiting-time *n.* Bleaching-time WIV 3.3.132 *it is whiting-time.*

whitster *n.* Bleacher of linen WIV 3.3.14 *carry it among the whitsters in Datchet-mead.*

whittle *n.* Small clasp-knife TIM 5.1.180 *There's not a whittle in th' unruly camp But I do prize it...*

who *pron.*
1 Which TMP 1.2.7 *a brave vessel, Who had, no doubt, some noble creature in her*, JC 4.3.112, ERR 1.2.37.
2 Whom LLL 4.1.74 *Who overcame he?*, 1H6 3.3.62, 2H6 3.2.127.
3 The person(s) that, he (etc.) who MAC 1.3.109 *Who was the thane lives yet*, ANT 1.2.98, TGV 5.4.79.
4 Whoever JC 1.3.80 *Let it be who it is*, WT 5.1.109.
5 *as who should say* As if to say R2 5.4.8 *he wishtly look'd on me As who should say, 'I would...'*, SHR 4.3.13, MV 1.2.46.

whoa ho ho(a) *interj.* (used to call attention from a distance) Hallo WIV 5.5.177 *Whoa ho, ho! father Page!*, WT 3.3.78.

whoe'er, whoever *pron.* Whomsoever TN 1.4.42 *Whoe'er I woo*, ROM 5.3.173, H8 2.1.47.

whole *adj.*
1 Well, in a healthy state, restored to health JC 2.1.327 *make sick men whole*, ANT 4.8.11, 2H6 4.7.10; (fig.) AWW 5.3.37 *My high-repented blames...pardon to me.—All is whole*, JN 1.1.35, 1H4 2.1.73.
2 Solid MND 3.2.53 *I 'll believe as soon This whole earth may be bor'd*, MAC 3.4.21.

wholesome *adj.*
1 Sound, healthy HAM 1.5.70 *The thin and wholesome blood*, HAM 3.2.260, HAM 3.4.65; (transf.) MAC 4.3.105 *thy wholesome days* (i.e. days of health), LR 1.4.211, WIV 5.5.59.
2 Reasonable, sensible HAM 3.2.316 *to make me a wholesome answer*, HAM 2.2.444, OTH 3.1.46.
3 Having the property of restoring health, curative, remedial ERR 5.1.104 *wholesome syrups, drugs, and holy prayers.*
4 Profitable, salutary, beneficial COR 2.1.69 *a good wholesome forenoon*, COR 2.3.60, LR 2.4.144; (with *to*) profitable, suitable *to* H8 3.2.99 *not wholesome to Our cause*, OTH 1.1.145.

whom *pron.*
1 Which 2H6 3.2.345 *the seal, Through whom a thousand sighs are breath'd for thee*, TRO 3.3.201.
2 Who TMP 5.1.76 *whom, with Sebastian...Would here have kill'd your king*, MM 2.1.72, JN 4.2.165.
3 The person that, him whom ERR 1.1.84 *Fixing our eyes on whom our care was fix'd*, 2H6 1.4.21, VEN 624.
4 Any(one) whom, whomever, whomsoever HAM 4.5.205 *Make choice of whom your wisest friends you will.*

whoobub *n.* Clamour WT 4.4.616 *with a whoobub against his daughter.*

whoop *interj.* Coarse exclamation expressing surprise, excitement, etc. WT 4.4.198 *he makes the maid to answer, 'Whoop, do me no harm, good man'*, LR 1.4.225.

whoop *vb.* See HOOP *vb.²*

whoremaster *n.* One who has dealings with whores, one who practises whoredom, fornicator, lecher 1H4 2.4.469 *that he is...a whoremaster, that I utterly deny*, MM 3.2.35, TIM 2.2.105.

whoremasterly adj. Lecherous TRO 5.4.7 that Greekish whoremasterly villain.

whoremonger n. One who has dealings with whores, one who practises whoredom, fornicator, lecher MM 3.2.36 If he be a whoremonger.

whoreson n.

1 Son of a whore, bastard son LR 1.1.24 and the whoreson must be acknowledg'd.

2 (freq. used in coarse playfulness) Fellow, 'dog' H8 1.3.39 the sly whoresons Have got a speeding trick to lay down ladies, ROM 4.4.20.

~ adj. (chiefly as a coarsely abusive epithet) Vile, abominable, detestable, 'wretched' TMP 1.1.43 you whoreson, insolent noisemaker, 2H4 2.2.85, TRO 2.1.41; (sometimes a mere intensive with little meaning) 2H4 3.2.181 What disease hast thou?—A whoreson cold, sir, HAM 5.1.172, HAM 5.1.176; (sometimes a coarse term of endearment or humorous familiarity) 2H4 2.4.209 you whoreson little valiant villain, you!

whorish adj. Lewd, unchaste TRO 4.1.64 whorish loins.

whosoever pron. (elliptical) No matter who it be TRO 1.2.192 He's one o' th' soundest judgements in Troy, whosoever.

why adv.

1 (used as an interj.) An emphasised call or summons, expressing some degree of impatience MV 2.5.6 What, Jessica!...Why, Jessica, I say!, 2H4 5.1.6.

2 why so (as an expression of content, acquiescence, or relief) Well, so let it be R3 2.1.1, COR 5.1.15, MAC 3.4.106.

3 for why (as conj.) Because SHR 3.2.167 Trembled and shook; for why, he stamp'd and swore, TGV 3.1.99, R2 5.1.46; (as rel.) for which OTH 1.3.257 The rites for why I love him (Qq for which).

wicked adj.

1 Harmful, baleful TMP 1.2.321 wicked dew, LR 2.1.39.

2 Unlucky, ill-starred MND 2.2.98 What wicked and dissembling glass of mine, TIM 3.2.44.

wide adj. Astray in opinion, mistaken, 'wide of the mark' TRO 3.1.88 No, no! no such matter, you are wide, LR 4.7.49; (with of) WIV 3.1.58 so wide of his own respect.

~ adv. Aside from the aim, astray HAM 2.2.472 Pyrrhus at Priam drives, in rage strikes wide, SON 140.14; (fig.) mistakenly ADO 4.1.62 Is my lord well, that he doth speak so wide?

wide-chapped adj. Opening the mouth wide (to eat or drink gluttonously), wide-mouthed TMP 1.1.57 this wide-chapped rascal (F1 wide-chopt).

widen vb. Open wide COR 1.4.44 the gates...fortune widens them.

widow vb.

1 Survive as a widow, become a widow of ANT 1.2.27 Let me be married to three kings in a forenoon, and widow them all.

2 Endow with a widow's right, settle a jointure upon MM 5.1.424 We do enstate and widow you with all.

widowhood n. Estate settled on a widow SHR 2.1.124 I'll assure her of Her widowhood.

wield vb. (fig.) Express LR 1.1.55 I love you more than words can wield the matter.

wife n. Woman H5 5.Ch.10 with men, wives, and boys, TN 5.1.136, WIV 2.2.98.

wight n. Human being, man or woman, person OTH 2.1.158 She was a wight (if ever such wights were), LLL 1.1.177, H5 2.1.60.

wightly adj. Active, nimble LLL 3.1.196 A wightly wanton.

◇ Aldis Wright's conjecture; Ff 1-2, Qq whitely. See WHITELY.

wild n.

1 Weald, name of the formerly wooded tract of country including Kent 1H4 2.1.55 a franklin in the wild of Kent.

2 Wild or waste region, wilderness MV 2.7.41 the vasty wilds Of wide Arabia; (fig.) MV 3.2.182 a wild of nothing, save of joy.

~ adj. Rash, inconsiderately venturesome COR 4.1.36 a wild exposture to each chance, WT 2.1.182, 1H6 4.4.7.

wilderness n. Wildness, barrenness MM 3.1.141 such a warped slip of wilderness (i.e. worthless slip).

wildfire n. Highly inflammable composition of gunpowder LUC 1523 Whose words like wildfire burnt the shining glory Of rich-built Ilion (i.e. with immense rapidity and effect), 1H4 3.3.40.

wild-goose chase n. Kind of horse-race in which the second or succeeding horse had to follow accurately the course of the leader like a flight of wild geese; (fig.) erratic course led by one and followed by another ROM 2.4.71 if our wits run the wild-goose chase.

wildly adj.

1 Without order, irregularly, in disorder or confusion JN 4.2.128 How wildly then walks my estate in France, WT 4.4.539.

2 Without cultivation, like a wild plant CYM 4.2.180 valour That wildly grows in them but yields a crop.

wild-mare See MARE n.[1]

wildness n. Madness HAM 3.1.39 Hamlet's wildness, CYM 3.4.9.

wilful adj.

1 Willing, eager MND 5.1.209 when walls are so wilful to hear without warning, ROM 1.5.89, WIV 3.2.43.

2 Obstinate, stubborn MV 1.1.90 a wilful stillness, R3 3.7.28.

~ adv. Obstinately, stubbornly JN 5.2.124 The Dauphin is too wilful-opposite (i.e. stubbornly hostile; F1 wilfull opposite), WT 1.2.255.

wilful-blame adj. Wilfully blameable, wittingly to blame 1H4 3.1.175 you are too wilful-blame.

will n.

1 good will (1) Acquiescence, consent ERR 3.2.70 I'll fetch my sister to get her good will, SHR 1.1.6, LR 5.3.79; (2) willingness, readiness MND 3.2.164 here, with all good will...I yield you up my part, TMP 3.1.30, ANT 2.5.8; (3) favourable regard, favour ADO 2.1.17 if 'a could get her good will, TGV 4.3.14, WIV 1.1.231.

2 by (my) will (1) Of (my) own accord, voluntarily ADO 3.3.63 I would not hang a dog by my will, TN 3.3.1; (2) with (my) consent 2H4 4.1.157 by my will we shall admit no parley, TRO 2.3.192, VEN 639; by, of one's (own) good will of one's own accord R2 4.1.177 To do that office of thine own good will, VEN 479; on my free will on my own accord ANT 3.6.57 I not constrain'd, but did it On my free will.

3 (transf.) That which one desires 3H6 1.4.144 Wouldst have me weep? why, now thou hast thy will, LUC 128; desire or wish as expressed in a request, request TGV 4.2.92 What's your will?, ANT 1.2.7.

4 Carnal appetite or desire, lust MM 2.4.164 yielding up thy body to my will, ANT 3.13.3, LR 4.6.271.

5 (euphemistically, usu. with quibble on other senses) Male or female sexual organ SON 135.5 Wilt thou, whose will is large and spacious, ANT 2.5.8, LUC 247.

~ vb.

1 Wish to have, desire, want AWW 1.1.163 Will you anything with it? (i.e. Is there anything else you'd like to know), AWW 2.1.70; (with neg.) have no

desire for, refuse to have, have nothing to do with 2H4 2.4.75 *I'll no swaggerers*, HAM 5.2.247, TRO 5.5.47.

2 Desire (a person) to do something; (hence contextually) bid, command H8 3.1.18 *They will'd me say so*, AWW 1.3.224, TIT 5.1.160.

3 (in ironical phrases) Will have it, pretend, claim (to) 1H6 2.3.58 *This is a riddling merchant for the nonce; He will be here, and yet he is not here*, 2H4 4.1.155, HAM 4.5.3.

4 *it will not be* It is no use, it is all in vain, it cannot be done 1H6 1.5.33 *It will not be, retire into your trenches*, VEN 607; *will it not be?* exclamation of impatience ROM 4.5.11, JN 3.1.298.

willing *adv*. Willingly R2 3.3.206 *I'll give you, and willing too*, TIM 3.6.30, H8 4.2.130.

willingly *adv*. Intentionally MND 3.2.346 *commit'st thy knaveries willingly* (F1; Qq *wilfully*).

willow *n*. Symbol of grief for unrequited love or the loss of a mate OTH 4.3.51 *Sing all a green willow must be my garland*, TN 1.5.268; (esp. in the phr.) *wear a willow garland* 3H6 3.3.228 *I wear the willow garland for his sake*, ADO 2.1.187.

wimpled *ppl. adj.* Blindfolded LLL 3.1.179 *This wimpled, whining, purblind, wayward boy.*

win *vb.* (with *of*) Gain the advantage of, get the better of JN 2.1.569 *he that wins of all*, H8 5.1.58, CYM 1.1.121; (similarly with *upon*) COR 1.1.220 *it will in time Win upon power* (i.e. get the better of authority), ANT 2.4.9.

wince See WINCH.

winch *vb.*

1 Start back, recoil, flinch, wince JN 4.1.80 *I will not stir, nor winch, nor speak a word.*

2 (of a horse) Kick restlessly from pain or impatience, wince HAM 3.2.243 *Let the gall'd jade winch* (F1, Q2; Q1 *wince*).

Winchester goose See GOOSE.

wind *n*. Breath as used in speaking; (hence) speech, talk ERR 1.2.53 *Stop in your wind*, HAM 4.7.66; (usu. coupled with *rain* i.e. tears) sighs AYL 3.5.50 *puffing with wind and rain*, MAC 1.7.25, LUC 1790.
~ in phrases
down the wind (in falconry) In the direction of the wind, as a hawk was made to do when dismissed OTH 3.3.262 *let her down the wind To prey at fortune.* **have in the wind** Get scent of AWW 3.6.114 *this same coxcomb that we have i' th' wind.* **have the wind of** Keep watch upon (as upon the game when following it down the wind) TIT 4.2.133 *My son and I will have the wind of you.* **keep the wind** Keep to the windward of the game so as to scent it or so that it does not scent me 3H6 3.2.14 *He knows the game; how true he keeps the wind!* **on the wind** Speedily and without impediment, as if on the 'wings of the wind' ANT 3.6.63 *his affairs come to me on the wind.* **recover the wind of** Get to windward of, regain the scent of in order to trap HAM 3.2.346 *why do you go about to recover the wind of me, as if you would drive me into a toil.* **sit in the wind against** Be in opposition to ANT 3.10.36 *though my reason Sits in the wind against me.*
~ *vb.*[1]
1 Blow (a blast on a horn) ADO 1.1.241 *I will have a recheat winded in my forehead*, MND 4.1.SD, SHR Ind.1.SD.
2 Scent TIT 4.1.97 *The dam will wake and if she wind ye once.*

wind *vb.*[2]
1 Turn or wheel (a horse) round 1H4 4.1.109 *To turn and wind a fiery Pegasus*; (intr.) JC 4.1.32 *a creature that I teach to fight, To wind, to stop.*
2 Pursue a devious course in argument; (with

about) use circumlocution or subtle terms of argument, approach indirectly MV 1.1.154 *herein spend but time To wind about my love with circumstance.*
3 (with *into*) Insinuate oneself COR 3.3.64 *to wind Yourself into a power tyrannical*, LR 1.2.98.
~ in combination
wind away Go away AYL 3.3.103 *Wind away, Be gone, I say.* **wind up 1** Furl JN 5.2.73 *thy threat'ning colours now wind up.* **2** Tune up (as the strings of a musical instrument) LR 4.7.15 *Th' untun'd and jarring senses O, wind up Of this child-changed father!* **3** Pass (time) H5 4.1.279 *Winding up days with toil.*

wind-changing *adj*. Inconstant as the wind 3H6 5.1.57 *Wind-changing Warwick.*

windgall *n*. Soft tumour on either side of a horse's leg just above the fetlock SHR 3.2.52 *full of windgalls.*

winding-sheet *n*. Sheet in which a corpse is wrapped for burial; (fig.) 3H6 2.5.114 *These arms of mine shall be thy winding-sheet*, 3H6 1.1.129.

windlass *n*. Roundabout proceeding, circuitous course of action HAM 2.1.62 *With windlasses and with assays of bias.*

window *n*.
1 (transf.) Eyelid R3 5.3.116 *let fall the windows of mine eyes*, ANT 5.2.316, ROM 4.1.100.
2 *in at the window* Born illegitimately JN 1.1.171 *a little from the right, In at the window.*

window-bar *n*. Latticed open-work of the bodice in a dress TIM 4.3.117 *for those milkpaps That through the window-bars bore at men's eyes* (F1 *window Barne*).

windowed *ppl. adj.*
1 Placed in a window ANT 4.14.72 *Wouldst thou be window'd in great Rome.*
2 Full of window-like holes LR 3.4.31 *Your loop'd and window'd raggedness.*

windring *adj*. (?) (no satisfactory explanation) TMP 4.1.128 *the windring brooks.*
▷ Most freq. emendations: *winding, wand'ring.*

windy *adj*.
1 Windward; *on the windy side of* (fig.) so as not to be scented and attacked by, out of the reach of, away from TN 3.4.164 *keep o' th' windy side of the law*, ADO 2.1.315.
2 (of speech, sighing, with various shades of meaning) Vehement, violent, verbose VEN 51 *her windy sighs*, JN 2.1.477, SON 90.7 (with quibble); (of a speaker) full of talk or verbiage, long-winded, empty and high-sounding R3 4.4.127 *Windy attorneys to their client's woes.*

wing *n*. Flight MAC 3.2.51 *the crow Makes wing to th' rooky wood*, TN 2.5.113, 1H4 3.2.30.

winged *pa. pple.* Flying 1H6 4.7.21 *Two Talbots, winged through the lither sky*, CYM 4.2.348.
~ *ppl. adj.* (military term) Protected by additional forces on the wing or flanks of an army R3 5.3.300 *whose puissance on either side Shall be well winged with our chiefest horse.*

wing-led *adj*. Led in the wings CYM 2.4.24 *wing-led with their courages* (F1; Ff2-4 *mingled*).

wink *n*.
1 Closing of the eyes TMP 2.1.285 *To the perpetual wink* (i.e. to death), WT 1.2.317.
2 Very small distance (i.e. that can be seen in a wink) TMP 2.1.242 *Ambition cannot pierce a wink beyond.*
~ *vb.*
1 Shut one's eyes, have the eyes closed H5 2.1.7 *I dare not fight, but I will wink and hold out mine iron*, TMP 2.1.216, CYM 5.4.186; (said of the eyes) close LUC 375 *his eyes begun To wink*, LUC 1139.
2 *wink at, upon* 'Shut one's eyes to', seem not to

see TGV 2.4.98 *Upon a homely object Love can wink*,
TIM 3.1.44, MAC 1.4.52; (hence) connive at ROM
5.3.294 *winking at your discords*, H5 2.2.55, 2H6
2.2.70.
3 Give a significant glance or look (as of command,
direction or invitation) H5 5.2.306 *I will wink on
her to consent*, TIT 3.2.43.
winking *n.*
1 Closing of the eyes HAM 2.2.137 *given my heart a
winking* (F1; Qq 2–4 *working*).
2 Significant glance or movement of the eyes JN
4.2.211 *on the winking of authority* (i.e. at the merest look or nod).
~ *ppl. adj.*
1 Closed CYM 2.3.24 *winking Mary-buds*, JN 2.1.215.
2 Blind CYM 2.4.89 *two winking Cupids*.
winnowed *ppl. adj.* Separated from or rid of worthless elements HAM 5.2.192 *the most profound and
winnow'd opinions* (i.e. select, sensible), TRO
3.2.167.
winter *adj.* Old, aged 2H6 5.3.2 *That winter lion*.
wintered *adj.* Adapted for or worn in winter AYL
3.2.105 *Wint'red garments must be lin'd*.
winter-ground *vb.* Cover up in the ground for protection against harsh weather (like a plant covered with straw etc.) CYM 4.2.229 *furr'd moss…To
winter-ground thy corse*.
winterly *adj.* Cheerless, cold CYM 3.4.13 *If 't be summer news…; if winterly…*
wipe *n.* Mark, brand LUC 537 *Worse than a slavish
wipe or birth-hour's blot*.
wiry *adj.*
1 *wiry friends* Hairs JN 3.4.64 *her hairs…ten thousand wiry friends*.
2 Played on stringed instruments SON 128.4 *The
wiry concord* (i.e. the harmony of the strings).
wis See I-WIS.
wisdom *n.*
1 Sanity, reason MM 4.4.5 *pray heaven his wisdom
be not tainted*.
2 *wisdom of nature* Natural science LR 1.2.104
Though the wisdom of nature can reason it thus.
wise *n.* Manner PER 5.2.11 *in no wise* (i.e. not at all),
PP 17.22.
~ *adj.* Sane OTH 4.1.234 *the love I bear to Cassio.—
Are you wise?*, LR 1.5.45.
~ *adv.* Wisely AYL 2.4.57 *Thou speak'st wiser than
thou art ware of*.
wise man *n.* One who is not a fool or a madman;
(usu. opposed to 'fool') AYL 5.1.32 *The fool doth
think he is wise, but the wise man knows himself to
be a fool*, LR 3.2.13, TN 3.1.68; (opposed to 'madman') R2 5.5.63 *For though it would have holp madmen to their wits, In me it seems it will make wise
men mad*.
wise woman *n.* Woman skilled in magic or occult
arts, witch WIV 4.5.26 *the wise woman of Brainford*,
TN 3.4.102.
wish *vb.* Recommend (a person) *to* (another), commend *to* SHR 1.1.112 *I will wish him to her father*,
SHR 1.2.60, SHR 1.2.64.
wishful *adj.* Full of desire, longing 3H6 3.1.14 *To
greet mine own land with my wishful sight*.
wishtly *adv.* Longingly, intently R2 5.4.7 *he wishtly
look'd on me As who should say, 'I would thou wert
the man…'* (Qq 1–2; F1, Qq 3–5 *wistly*).
wist See WIT.
wistly *adv.* (of looking) Steadfastly, attentively LUC
1355 *And blushing with him, wistly on him gazed*,
VEN 343, PP 6.12.
wit *n.*
1 Faculty of thinking and reasoning, mental capacity or powers, intellect TGV 1.1.47 *the young
and tender wit*, 1H6 1.2.73; (usu. pl.) COR 3.3.20 *our*

wits are so diversely colour'd, TGV 1.1.44, ADO
3.5.10; *five wits* common sense, imagination, fancy,
estimation, memory LR 3.4.58 *Bless thy five wits*,
ROM 1.4.47, SON 141.9.
2 Power of imagination or invention LLL 1.2.184
Devise, wit, write, pen, MND 4.1.205, H5 3.7.31;
(hence) ingenious plan, 'contrivance, stratagem,
power of expedients' (Johnson) LR 1.2.183 *Let me,
if not by birth, have lands by wit*, WIV 4.5.118.
3 Sound sense, good judgement, understanding,
intelligence HAM 2.2.90 *since brevity is the soul of
wit*, WT 2.2.50, JC 3.2.221.
⟡ In MV 2.1.18 *hedg'd me by his wit*, there may
also be a play on the sense of 'will, bequest'.
4 Wisdom, wise or prudent knowledge 3H6 4.7.61
Away with scrupulous wit! now arms must rule,
WIV 4.5.60, SON 140.5.
5 (used of persons) One of a certain mental capacity or turn of mind (expressed by a qualifying
word or phrase) H5 3.6.78 *ale-wash'd wits*, 2H4
2.2.35, VEN 850; one of understanding and intelligence SON 59.13 *I am the wits of former days* (incorporating senses 1 and 2), LLL 5.2.266.
6 *Wit, whither wilt thou?* Phrase addressed to a
person who is letting his tongue run away with
him or is talking foolishly AYL 4.1.165 *A man that
had a wife with such a wit, he might say, 'Wit,
whither wilt?'*; (alluded to) AYL 1.2.56 *How now,
wit, whither wander you?*
~ *vb.*
1 Know PER 4.4.31 *Now please you wit The epitaph
is for Marina writ*, 1H6 2.5.16.
2 *to wit* That is, namely H5 1.2.50 *this law: to wit, no
female Should be inheritrix*, MV 2.9.90, 3H6 5.6.51.
⟡ *Wist*, pa. t. form: Steevens, capell conjecture for
1H6 4.1.180 *if I wist he did*; F1 *wish*.
witch *vb.* Bewitch, enchant 1H4 4.1.110 *witch the
world with noble horsemanship*, 3H6 3.2.150 (Ff
'witch), TIM 5.1.155.
witching *ppl. adj.* Belonging or appropriate to the
deeds of witches or witchcraft, and hence to supposed supernatural occurrences HAM 3.2.388 *the
very witching time of night*.
with *prep.*
1 (expressing agency) By ANT 5.2.171 *must I be
unfolded With one that I have bred?*, MM 2.2.142,
JN 2.1.567.
2 (expressing means of nourishment) On LLL
1.1.301 *fast a week with bran and water*, R2 3.2.175,
MAC 5.5.13.
3 (with *possess*) Of JN 4.2.9 *possess'd with double
pomp*.
4 (with superlatives used absol.) At OTH 2.3.7 *with
your earliest*, ANT 5.1.67.
5 From, from association with CYM 4.2.60 *let the
stinking elder, grief, untwine His perishing root
with the increasing vine*, R2 1.4.10, JN 2.1.563.
6 In the opinion or estimation of COR 3.3.30 *that is
there which looks With us to break his neck*.
~ in phrases
be with 1 (used as menace, threat) Be avenged
on, chastise, be even with SHR 4.1.167 *What, do you
grumble? I'll be with you straight*, MND 3.2.403,
H8 5.3.29. **2** Understand 2H6 2.1.48 *Cardinal, I am
with you*. **not with himself** Beside himself TIT
1.1.368 *He is not with himself*. **What news or tidings with…?** What news has…? TGV 3.1.280
what news with your mastership?, 2H6 2.1.161.
with all my heart 1 Used as a salutation TIM
3.6.25 *With all my heart, gentleman both*. **2** Used
as a reply to a salutation LR 4.6.32 *Now fare ye
well, good sir.—With all my heart*, OTH 4.1.216.
withal *adv.*
1 With this, with it ERR 3.1.113 *Hath oftentimes*

upbraided me withal, MAC 2.2.53, H5 1.2.216; *I could not do withal* I could not help it MV 3.4.72.

2 In addition, besides, at the same time AYL 2.7.48 *I must have liberty Withal...To blow on whom I please,* HAM 1.3.14, SHR 3.2.25.

~ *prep.* (esp. at the end of a clause) With TGV 5.4.152 *These banish'd men, that I have kept withal,* ROM 1.5.115, 3H6 1.4.83.

withdraw *vb.*

1 Retract, revoke, take back ROM 2.2.130 *thy love's faithful vow...Wouldst thou withdraw it?*

2 Draw away TRO 5.4.22 *advantageous care Withdrew me from the odds of multitude.*

3 Take aside ADO 2.1.156 *my brother...hath withdrawn her father to break with him about it.*

4 (refl.) Remove oneself (from a place) R2 5.3.28 *Withdraw yourselves, and leave us here alone,* WT 2.2.15, 1H4 5.4.2.

5 Retire to a private place; (hence, ellipt.) *To withdraw with you* let me speak privately with you HAM 3.2.345.

wither *vb. wither out* Cause to dwindle, waste MND 1.1.6 *a dowager, Long withering out a young man's revenue.*

withers *n.* (pl.) In a horse, the highest part of the back, lying between the shoulder blades 1H4 2.1.6 *Poor jade is wrung in the withers,* HAM 3.2.243.

withhold *vb.* Detain, keep in custody MND 2.1.26 *she...withholds the loved boy,* VEN 612.

within *prep.*

1 *within oneself* In self-command or self-control ANT 2.5.75 *Good madam, keep yourself within yourself.*

2 At some time during H5 1.2.60 *King Pharamond...died within the year of our redemption.*

3 Inside the guard or defence of ERR 5.1.34 *Some get within him, take his sword away.*

without *conj.* Unless TGV 2.1.36 *without you...were so simple,* ERR 3.2.91, ADO 3.3.80.

~ *prep.*

1 Beyond the reach of TMP 5.1.271 *without her power,* MND 4.1.153, MAC 3.2.11.

2 *without book* Without the aid of a book, from memory, by rote ROM 1.2.59 *Perhaps you have learn'd it without book,* TN 1.3.27.

without-book *adj.* Recited by heart ROM 1.4.7 *no without-book prologue.*

without-door *adj.* Outward, external WT 2.1.69 *her without-door form.*

witness *n.*

1 Evidence (given in a court) H8 5.1.136 *in perjur'd witness.*

2 *with a witness* With a vengeance SHR 5.1.118 *Here's packing, with a witness.*

~ *vb.*

1 Give or show evidence of MM 4.3.95 *letters ...whose contents Shall witness to him I am near at home,* R2 2.4.22, SON 26.4.

2 Give formal or sworn evidence of (a fact, etc.) AWW 5.3.200 *Methought you said You saw one here in court could witness it.*

wit-old *adj.* Mentally feeble LLL 5.1.63 *which is wit-old* (with quibble on WITTOL).

wit-snapper *n.* One who seizes every opportunity of indulging in witticism MV 3.5.49 *what a wit-snapper are you!*

wittily *adj.*

1 Intelligently, cleverly VEN 471 *Which cunning love did wittily prevent.*

2 Wisely TN 4.2.13 *as the old hermit of Prague... very wittily said...*

wittol *n.* Contented cuckold, one who is complaisant about the infidelity of his wife WIV 2.2.299 *Cuckold! Wittol!*

wittolly *adj.* Cuckoldly WIV 2.2.272 *They say the jealous wittolly knave hath masses of money.*

witty *adj.*

1 Wise, prudent TN 1.5.36 *Better a witty fool than a foolish wit,* 3H6 1.2.43, OTH 2.1.131.

2 Clever, cunning, ingenious R3 4.2.42 *The deep-revolving witty Buckingham,* ADO 4.2.25.

wo ha ho *interj.* Falconer's cry to a hawk; (hence, transf.) call to attract attention MV 5.1.39 *Sola, sola! wo ha, ho!*

wod(d)e See WOOD.

woe *n.*

1 (pl., concrete) Objects of grief and misfortune ROM 5.3.179 *We see the ground whereon these woes do lie.*

2 Cry of 'woe', lament ADO 5.3.33 *this for whom we rend'red up this woe,* JN 5.7.110; plaint, complaint H5 1.2.26 *whose guiltless drops Are every one a woe...'Gainst him whose wrongs...*

3 (in exclamations) Alas for H5 4.7.75 *woe the while!* (i.e. alas for the times we live in), JC 1.3.82, TMP 1.2.15.

~ *adj.* Sorry, distressed TMP 5.1.139 *I am woe for't,* ANT 4.14.133, SON 71.8.

woman *n.*

1 Wife WIV 2.2.292 *the hell of having a false woman,* 1H4 2.3.39.

2 *woman's* Womanish, feminine 1H4 1.3.237 *to break into this woman's mood,* TGV 1.2.23, TRO 1.1.106.

3 *play the woman* Weep H8 3.2.430 *I did not think to shed a tear...but thou hast forc'd me...to play the woman.*

~ *vb.* Make like a woman in weakness or subservience, bend or subdue (like a woman) AWW 3.2.51 *I have felt so many quirks of joy and grief That the first face of neither...Can woman me unto't.*

womaned *ppl. adj.* Accompanied by a woman OTH 3.4.195 *nor my wish, To have him see me woman'd.*

woman-post *n.* Female messenger JN 1.1.218 *What woman-post is this?*

woman-queller *n.* Woman-killer 2H4 2.1.53 *a man-queller, and a woman-queller.*

woman-tired *adj.* Henpecked WT 2.3.75 *Thou dotard, thou art woman-tir'd.*

womb *n.*

1 Belly 2H4 4.3.22 *And I had but a belly of any indifferency...my womb undoes me.*

2 (transf.) Hollow space or cavity, something conceived as such (e.g. the earth, night) R2 2.1.83 *A grave, Whose hollow womb...,* ROM 5.1.65, LC 1.

~ *vb.* Enclose as in a womb WT 4.4.490 *for all the sun sees, or The close earth wombs.*

womby *adj.* Having a womb-like cavity, hollow H5 2.4.124 *caves and womby vaultages.*

wonder *n.*

1 Admiration TN 2.1.27 *such estimable wonder,* WT 5.1.133, LUC 84.

2 Miracle, miraculous quality, miraculous means ERR 3.2.30 *by what wonder you do hit of mine,* SHR 2.1.409, OTH 3.4.101.

~ *vb.* Admire SON 106.14 *we...Have eyes to wonder, but lack tongues to praise*; (with *at*) LLL 5.2.266 *Are these the breed of wits so wondered at?,* SON 98.9, 1H4 1.2.201.

wondering *n.* Admiration WT 4.1.25 *now grown in grace Equal with wond'ring,* 2H6 1.1.34.

wondered *ppl. adj.* Performing wonders or miracles TMP 4.1.123 *So rare a wond'red father.*

wont *n.* Custom, habit 2H6 3.1.2 *'Tis not his wont to be the hindmost man,* HAM 1.4.6.

~ *vb.* Be wont or accustomed, be in the habit of

1H6 1.2.14 *Talbot is taken, whom we wont to fear*, ERR 4.4.38, PP 17.19.

~ *pa. pple.* (with *be*) Accustomed, used TGV 2.4.126 *My tales of love were wont to weary you*, HAM 2.2.327, R3 1.4.118.

wood *adj*. Mad, frenzied MND 2.1.192 *here am I, and wood within this wood* (Q1 *wodde*), 1H6 4.7.35, TGV 2.3.27 (F1 *would-woman*).

woodbine *n*. One of various plants of a climbing habit; (spec.) honeysuckle ADO 3.1.30 *couched in the woodbine coverture*, MND 2.1.251.

▷ MND 4.1.42 *So doth the woodbine, the sweet honeysuckle, Gently entwist*: F1, in which *honeysuckle* acts as a synonym for *woodbine*. Some mod. edd. omit the commas thus making *woodbine* refer to a different plant.

woodcock *n*. Symbol of gullibility or folly; (hence, applied to a person) fool, simpleton, dupe HAM 5.2.306 *as a woodcock to mine own springe*, ADO 5.1.157, SHR 1.2.160.

wooden *adj*. Unintelligent, blockish 1H6 5.3.89 *I'll win this Lady Margaret. For whom? Why, for my king. Tush, that's a wooden thing*.

woodman *n*. One who hunts game in a wood or forest, hunter CYM 3.6.28 *You, Polydore, have prov'd my best woodman*, WIV 5.5.27, LUC 580; (fig.) woman-hunter MM 4.3.162 *He's a better woodman than thou tak'st him for*.

woollen *n*. Cloth or other fabric made of wool ADO 2.1.31 *I had rather lie in the woollen* (i.e. sleep between the blankets with no sheets).

~ *adj*.
1 Covered with woollen cloth MV 4.1.56 *a woollen bagpipe*.

▷ Qq, Ff 1–3; the allusion is uncertain. Capell's conjecture *wauling*.

2 Wearing woollen clothing as a mark of poor or lowly status, coarsely clad COR 3.2.9 *woollen vassals*.

woolward *adj*. Wearing wool next to the skin, esp. as a penance LLL 5.2.711 *I go woolward for penance*.

woosel See OUZEL.

woot, woo't *vb*. (2nd pers. sing. pres. of 'will') Wilt (thou) ANT 4.15.59 *Noblest of men, woo't die?*, HAM 5.1.275.

word *n*.
1 Watchword, password MV 3.5.52 *'cover' is the word*, HAM 1.5.110, LR 4.6.92.
2 Command, order, bidding JC 4.2.33 *Stand ho! Speak the word along*, JC 1.2.104, H5 4.6.38.
3 Promise, assurance, undertaking AWW 2.1.210 *If thou proceed As high as word* (i.e. if your deeds are as good as your undertaking), TGV 2.4.44, 2H4 2.3.10.
4 Utterance or declaration in the form of a phrase or sentence R2 1.3.152 *The hopeless word of 'never to return' Breathe I against thee*, R3 3.1.83.
5 Motto PER 2.2.21 *The word: 'Lux tua vita mihi'*, HAM 1.5.110.
6 *the word* The inspired word, Holy Writ, the Bible WIV 3.1.44 *the sword and the word?*, R2 5.5.13, 2H4 4.2.10; (similarly) MM 1.2.122 *The words of heaven*.
~ in phrases
at a word 1 (in phr. expressing prompt decision or action) Upon the utterance of a single word, as soon as a word is spoken, without more ado JC 1.2.267 *if I would not have taken him at a word*, WIV 1.3.14, 2H4 3.2.297. **2** In short, briefly, in a word WIV 1.1.106 *He hath wrong'd me, indeed he hath, at a word he hath*, ADO 2.1.114, COR 1.3.109. **break, change a word** Hold conversation, exchange words ERR 3.1.75 *A man may break a word with you*, LLL 5.2.238. **come to, give, have, maintain**

words Hold conversation ANT 2.6.3 *first we come to words*, HAM 1.3.134, JC 5.1.25, TN 4.2.99. **of my word** (as an asseveration) Assuredly, certainly, on my word TIT 4.3.60 *Of my word, I have written to effect*. **spend word for word** Hold conversation TGV 2.4.41 *if you spend word for word with me*. **with a word** In short, briefly, in a word 1H4 2.4.256 *and with a word, outfac'd you from your prize*.
~ *vb*.
1 Utter in words, speak ANT 4.13.9 *Say that the last I spoke was 'Antony', And word it, prithee, piteously*; (as distinct from singing) CYM 4.2.240 *I cannot sing. I'll weep, and word it with thee*.
2 Ply or urge with words ANT 5.2.191 *He words me, that I should not Be noble to myself*.
3 Represent as in words, speak of, pad out with words CYM 1.4.16 *words him...a great deal from the matter* (i.e. describes him in terms remote from the fact).

work *n*.
1 Fortification OTH 3.2.3 *I will be walking on the works*, H8 5.3.58.
2 **make work** Work havoc or confusion, cause trouble COR 1.4.20 *There is Aufidius. List what work he makes Amongst your cloven army*, JN 2.1.407.
~ *vb*. (pa. t. and pa. pple. *wrought*)
1 Act upon, affect, move powerfully TMP 4.1.144 *your father's in some passion That works him strongly*, MAC 1.3.149, OTH 5.2.345.
2 Strive to effect (something) H8 3.2.311 *You wrought to be a legate*, COR 2.3.246; bring about, effect ROM 3.5.144 *that we have wrought So worthy a gentleman to be her bridegroom*.
3 *work out* (1) Scent out like a dog TN 2.5.127 *Did not I say he would work it out?*; (2) bring through safely, procure by effort 2H4 1.1.182 *if we wrought out life*.
4 *let...work* Allow (a person or thing) to follow his or its course JC 2.1.209 *Let me work*, HAM 3.4.205.
5 Be agitated PER 3.1.48 *The sea works high*.
6 (with object and predicative adj.) Render by continuous action 2H4 4.4.119 *Th' incessant care and labour of his mind Hath wrought the mure...So thin*.

working *n*.
1 (pl.) Actions 2H4 5.2.90 *mock your workings*.
2 Effort, endeavour AYL 1.2.203 *his will hath in it a more modest working*, 2H4 4.2.22.
3 Mental or emotional activity, operation of the mind or heart LLL 4.1.33 *the working of the heart*, MM 2.1.10, HAM 2.2.554.
~ *ppl. adj*. Operative, effective, exciting the emotions H8 Prol.3 *things...Sad, high, and working, full of state and woe*.

working-day *adj*. Ordinary, trivial, workaday AYL 1.3.12 *this working-day world*.

working-house *n*. Workhouse, factory; (fig.) H5 5.Ch.23 *the quick forge and working-house of thought*.

workman *n*. Skilled or expert craftsman AWW 2.5.19 *a good workman, a very good tailor*, ANT 4.4.18, TIM 4.3.435.

worky-day *adj*. Ordinary, trivial, workaday ANT 1.2.54 *tell her but a worky-day fortune*.

world *n*.
1 Life, condition of existence ROM 3.1.99 *I am pepper'd...for this world*, TIM 4.3.253, MM 5.1.49; *both the worlds* this life and the next HAM 4.5.135; *the world to come* posterity, future generations TRO 3.2.173.
2 The microcosm of man LR 3.1.10 *his little world of man*, LC 7.

3 *matter of the world* Anything at all TRO 2.3.186 *never suffers matter of the world*; (with neg.) at all WT 5.3.72 *No settled senses of the world can match The pleasure of that madness.*

4 *it is a world to see* It is wonderful to see ADO 3.5.35, SHR 2.1.311.

5 *how goes the world?* How is the state of affairs?, how are matters with you? MAC 2.4.21, TIM 1.1.2, R3 3.2.96; *let the world slide, slip* allow things to take their course SHR Ind.1.5, SHR Ind.2.143.

6 *go to the world* Get married ADO 2.1.319 *Thus goes everyone to the world,* AWW 1.3.18; *woman of the world* married woman AYL 5.3.5 *desire to be a woman of the world.*

▷ From 13 to 16C 'word' was a spelling for *world.* There may be confusion between the two at AYL 2.7.13 *A miserable world,* so that *word,* in the sense of 'appellation, title', may have been intended (Hulme).

worldling *n.* Inhabitant of the world, human being, mortal AYL 2.1.48 *thou mak'st a testament As worldlings do,* 2H4 5.3.99.

worldly *adj.*

1 Belonging to this world or this life 2H4 4.5.230 *My worldly business* (i.e. my life), 2H6 1.2.45, CYM 4.2.260.

2 Mortal, earthly R2 3.2.56 *The breath of worldly men,* MM 3.1.128, TIT 1.1.152; *no worldly (good)* no (good) in the world TGV 3.1.9 *no worldly good should draw from me,* R3 3.7.63.

3 Pertaining to one's relations with the world (as opposed to private interests) TMP 1.2.89 *neglecting worldly ends, all dedicated To closeness,* R2 3.2.94, OTH 1.3.299 (Q1; F1 *wordly*).

world-without-end *adj. phr.* Eternal LLL 5.2.789 *a world-without-end bargain,* SON 57.5.

worm *n.*

1 Serpent, snake ANT 5.2.243 *the pretty worm of Nilus,* MND 3.2.71, 2H6 3.2.263; (fig.) VEN 933 *Death...earth's worm.*

2 Tick or mite breeding in the hand ROM 1.4.68 *a round little worm Prick'd from the lazy finger of a maid.*

3 (fig.) Human being likened to a worm as an object of pity, abject or miserable creature WIV 5.5.83 *Vile worm, thou wast o'erlook'd even in thy birth,* LLL 4.3.152, LR 4.1.33.

4 (fig.) Grief or passion that preys stealthily on a man's heart or torments his conscience R3 1.3.221 *The worm of conscience still begnaw thy soul.*

worn *ppl. adj.*

1 (of time) Spent, past WT 5.1.142 *infirmity (Which waits upon worn times)* (i.e. attends old age), MND 4.1.182.

2 (of persons) Exhausted, enfeebled COR 3.1.6 *the Volsces...are worn.*

3 Obliterated, effaced from the memory 2H6 2.4.69 *These few days' wonder will be quickly worn.*

worn-out *adj.* Past, departed LUC 1350 *worn-out age.*

worry *vb.* Strangle, choke; (transf.) kiss or hug vehemently WT 5.2.53 *then again worries he his daughter with clipping her.*

worship *n.*

1 Honour, distinction, good name WT 1.2.314 *bench'd and rear'd to worship,* JN 4.3.72, 3H6 4.3.16.

2 High rank, prominent place H8 1.1.39 *I belong to worship*; (pl.) position of honour or high place LR 1.4.266 *Men...That...in the most exact regard support The worships of their name.*

~ *vb.* Honour, dignify H5 1.2.233 *our grave...Not worshipp'd with a waxen epitaph.*

wort *n.*[1] Plant, herb, vegetable WIV 1.1.121 *Good worts? good cabbage.*

wort *n.*[2] Infusion of malt before it is fermented,

sweet unfermented beer LLL 5.2.233 *Metheglin, wort, and malmsey.*

worth *n.*

1 Wealth, riches, possessions ROM 2.6.32 *They are but beggars that can count their worth,* LR 4.4.10, TN 3.3.17.

2 Merit, deservingness, desert MM 1.1.22 *If any...be of worth To undergo such ample grace,* CYM 5.5.307.

~ *adj.* Of value, valuable 1H4 4.1.27 *His health was never better worth than now,* TRO 2.2.22.

worthiness *n.* Deservedness TRO 1.3.241 *The worthiness of praise.*

worthless *adj.* Unworthy 1H6 4.4.21 *worthless emulation*; not deserving of JC 5.1.61 *A peevish schoolboy, worthless of such honour.*

worthy *n.* Thing of worth or value, excellence LLL 4.3.232 *in her fair cheek, Where several worthies make one dignity,* TGV 2.4.166.

~ *vb.* Raise to honour or distinction, give (a person) a reputation for excellence LR 2.2.121 *he...put upon him such a deal of man That worthied him.*

~ *adj.*

1 Valuable TMP 1.2.247 *I have done thee worthy service,* AYL 3.3.59, JC 3.1.116.

2 Well-deserved, due R2 5.1.68 *worthy danger and deserved death,* 1H6 5.5.11, R3 1.2.87.

3 Legitimate, justifiable COR 3.1.240 *your worthy rage,* 1H4 3.2.98, OTH 3.3.254.

4 Befitting, fitted (for) TGV 1.3.33 *every exercise Worthy his youth,* MAC 1.2.10, JC 5.5.24.

wot *vb.*[1] (var. of) WIT, know WIV 2.2.87 *the picture...that you wot of,* R3 2.3.18, ROM 3.2.139; *wot you what let me tell you* R3 3.2.90, H8 3.2.122.

wot *vb.*[2] (var. of) Wilt 2H4 2.1.65 *thou wot, wot ta* (Q; F1 *thou wilt not*).

would *vb.*

1 Wish, desire TGV 2.4.116 *my lord your father would speak with you,* MAC 1.5.18, JC 2.1.12; (with *n.* or *pron.* as object) MV 2.2.121 *wouldst thou aught with me,* H5 4.1.32, H5 5.2.68; (with clause) HAM 1.2.234 *I would I had been there*; (with accus. and infin.) H5 2.Ch.18 *What mightst thou do, that honour would thee do.*

2 Require to HAM 3.3.75 *That would be scann'd,* MAC 1.7.34.

wound *ppl.adj.* Entwined TMP 2.2.13 *sometime am I All wound with adders.*

woundless *adj.* Invulnerable HAM 4.1.44 *hit the woundless air.*

wrack *n.*

1 Destruction, ruin AWW 3.5.22 *the wrack of maidenhood,* 2H6 1.2.105, MAC 1.3.114.

2 Wreck, shipwreck TMP 1.2.26 *The direful spectacle of the wrack,* OTH 2.1.23, ERR 5.1.49.

3 Wrecked ship or person TN 5.1.79 *a wrack past hope he was,* R3 1.4.24.

4 Wreckage H5 1.2.165 *sunken wrack.*

~ *vb.*

1 Destroy, ruin HAM 2.1.110 *meant to wrack thee,* R3 4.1.96.

2 Wreck (a ship), ruin by shipwreck TMP 1.2.236 *they saw the king's ship wrack'd,* MM 3.1.216, MV 3.1.3.

▷ COR 5.1.16 *A pair of tribunes that have wrack'd for Rome*: see RACK.

wrackful *adj.* Destructive SON 65.6 *the wrackful siege of batt'ring days.*

wrangle *vb.* Cheat, use subtlety, or deceive TMP 5.1.174 *for a score of kingdoms you should wrangle, And I would call it fair play.*

wrangler *n.* Adversary TRO 2.2.75 *The seas and winds, old wranglers, took a truce,* H5 1.2.264.

wrath *n.*
1 Impetuous ardour, rage or fury 2H4 1.1.109 *Harry Monmouth, whose swift wrath beat down The never-daunted Percy*, TN 3.4.232, HAM 2.2.461.
2 Ardour of passion AYL 5.2.40 *the very wrath of love.*
~ *adj.* Wrathful MND 2.1.20 *fell and wrath.*
wrathful *adj.* 'Impetuous, furious' (Schmidt) R2 1.3.136 *wrathful iron arms*, 2H4 3.2.160, 2H6 2.4.3.
wreak *n.* Vengeance, revenge TIT 4.4.11 *in his wreaks* (i.e. vindictive acts), TIT 4.3.34, COR 4.5.85.
~ *vb.*[1] Revenge TIT 4.3.52 *to wreak our wrongs*, ROM 3.5.101, VEN 1004.
wreak *vb.*[2] (var. of) RECK.
wreakful *adj.* Revengeful TIM 4.3.229 *in all the spite Of wreakful heaven*, TIT 5.2.32.
wreakless (var. of) RECKLESS.
wreathed *ppl. adj.* (of the arms) Folded LLL 4.3.133 *his wreathed arms.*
wrenching *n.* (var. of) Rinsing H8 1.1.167 *and like a glass Did break i' th' wrenching* (F1).
wrest *n.* Tuning-key; (fig.) TRO 3.3.23 *Antenor...is such a wrest in their affairs That their negotiations all must slack, Wanting his manage.*
~ *vb.*
1 Get as if by force TIT 3.2.44 *I, of these, will wrest an alphabet.*
2 Strain the meaning of (words) wilfully in the wrong direction, misinterpret ADO 3.4.33 *And bad thinking do not wrest true speaking*, H5 1.2.14, 2H6 3.1.186.
wretch *n.* (used as a term of endearment or pity) Person or little creature ROM 1.3.44 *The pretty wretch left crying*, OTH 3.3.90, ANT 5.2.303.
wretched *adj.* Hateful, loathsome R3 5.2.7 *The wretched, bloody, and usurping boar*, LUC 999.
wring *vb.*
1 Wrench, wrest (lit. and fig.) MM 5.1.32 *wring redress from you*, HAM 1.2.58, OTH 5.2.288 (Ff *Wrench*).
2 Writhe, suffer torture ADO 5.1.28 *wring under the load of sorrow*, CYM 3.6.78.
3 Subject (something) to a turning movement, drive or impel in this way TMP 1.2.135 *It is a hint That wrings mine eyes to't.*
4 Press tightly, pinch, squeeze VEN 421 *You hurt my hand with wringing*, VEN 475.
◇ See also WRUNG.
wringing *n.* Griping pain, suffering, writhing H8 2.2.27 *Dangers, doubts, wringing of the conscience* (i.e. pangs of remorse), H5 4.1.236.
wrinkle *vb.* Give wrinkles to, make appear old TRO 2.2.79 *whose youth and freshness Wrinkles Apollo's.*
writ *n.*
1 That which is written, writing, document TIT 2.3.264 *this fatal writ*, 2H6 1.4.57, HAM 5.2.51.

2 (esp. *holy writ*) Scripture AWW 2.1.138 *holy writ in babes hath judgement shown*, OTH 3.3.324, R3 1.3.336; (hence) 'gospel' truth PER 2.Gower.12 *each man Thinks all is writ he speken can.*
◇ HAM 2.2.401 *the law of writ and the liberty*: quibbling on two senses: (1) those districts in London under the jurisdiction of the Sheriff or city authorities (*the law of writ*) as opposed to the ones which were exempt from the Sheriff's writ (*the liberty*) and thus more suitable for the location of theatres; and (2) those plays written strictly according to orthodox rules of drama as opposed to those displaying freedom from such rules.
write *vb.* (pa. t. usu. *writ*, rarely *wrote*; pa. pple. *writ*, written, rarely *wrote*)
1 Sign or subscribe (*for*) 2H6 4.1.63 *This hand of mine hath writ in thy behalf*, SON 134.7, WIV 1.1.9.
2 Set oneself down as, call oneself AWW 2.3.198 *I write man* (see MAN *n.*), 2H4 1.2.26, LR 5.3.35; (hence) lay claim to AWW 2.3.61 *My mouth no more were broken than these boys', And writ as little beard.*
3 *write against* Denounce ADO 4.1.56 *I will write against it*, CYM 2.5.32.
4 Record in written form, specify, stipulate HAM 1.2.222 *we did think it writ down in our duty*, HAM 4.5.142.
5 *write over* (1) Re-write LLL 1.2.115 *I will have that subject newly writ o'er*; (2) copy out, transcribe R3 3.6.5 *Eleven hours I have spent to write it over.*
writer *n.* Law-clerk, notary ADO 3.5.63 *get the learned writer to set down our excommunication*, 1H4 3.1.141.
writhled *adj.* Wrinkled 1H6 2.3.23 *this weak and writhled shrimp.*
writing *n.* Words of a song LLL 1.2.114 *it would neither serve for the writing nor the tune.*
wroath *n.* (var. of) 'Ruth', calamity, ruin MV 2.9.78 *Patiently to bear my wroath* (Ff, Qq 1–2; Qq 2–3 *wroth*).
wrong *n.*
1 *have wrong* Suffer injury, injustice, or loss 2H4 5.1.52 *he shall have no wrong*, 3H6 4.1.102, JC 3.2.110.
2 *do oneself wrong* Put oneself in the wrong, be mistaken TMP 1.2.444 *I fear you have done yourself some wrong*, MM 1.2.40, WIV 3.3.207.
3 Wrong-doing, evil act, offence JN 2.1.116 *Under whose warrant I impeach thy wrong*, MM 2.2.103, R3 5.1.19.
wroth See WROATH.
wrung *ppl. adj.* Wrenched, galled 1H4 2.1.6 *Poor jade is wrung in the withers.*
wry *vb.* Swerve from the right course, go wrong CYM 5.1.5 *wives...wrying but a little.*
wry-necked *adj.* Having a wry or crooked neck MV 2.5.30 *the vile squealing of the wry-neck'd fife.*

Y

yallowness (var. of) YELLOWNESS.
yard *n.* Yard measure, yardstick SHR 4.3.112 *I shall so bemete thee with thy yard*, 1H4 2.4.247, ROM 1.2.40; *clothier's yard* 'cloth-yard shaft', arrow a cloth-yard long used with the long bow LR 4.6.88 *draw me a clothier's yard.*
◇ In LLL 5.2.669 *Loves her by the foot.—He may not by the yard* with quibble on sense of 'penis'.
yare *adj.*
1 Ready, prepared MM 4.2.58 *if you have occasion to use me...you shall find me yare.*
2 Alert, nimble, brisk TN 3.4.224 *be yare in thy*

preparation, ANT 3.13.131; (of a ship) moving lightly and easily, easily manageable ANT 3.7.38 *Their ships are yare, yours heavy*, TMP 5.1.224.
~ *adv.* Briskly, nimbly, quickly TMP 1.1.6 *cheerly, my hearts! yare, yare!*, ANT 5.2.283.
yarely *adv.* Nimbly, briskly, diligently ANT 2.2.211 *those...hands, That yarely frame the office*, TMP 1.1.4.
yaw *vb.* (of a ship) Deviate temporarily from the straight course, turn from side to side; (hence, fig.) deviate, go out of course, go or move unsteadily HAM 5.2.115 *to divide him inventorially would dozy*

th' arithmetic of memory, and yet but yaw neither in respect of his quick sail.

yawn vb.

1 Open wide, be wide open H5 4.6.14 gashes That bloodily did yawn upon his face, Ado 5.3.19, JC 2.2.18.

2 Gape in surprise or wonder Oth 5.2.101 that th' affrighted globe Did yawn at alteration, Cor 3.2.11, Ham 4.5.9 (Qq 2–4; Ff ayme, aim).

yawning ppl. adj. Lulling to sleep Mac 3.2.43 The...beetle with his drowsy hums Hath rung night's yawning peal.

yclad ppl. adj. Clad, clothed; (fig.) 2H6 1.1.33 Her words yclad with wisdom's majesty.

ycleped, ycliped pa. pple. Called LLL 1.1.240 it is ycleped thy park (Q, F ycliped), LLL 5.2.598.
▷ Pa. pple. of CLEPE.

yea adv.

1 (used, like NAY, before a clause, phrase, or word to correct or amplify) Indeed, and more Tmp 1.2.206 make his bold waves tremble, Yea, his dread trident shake, Ado 2.1.254, MV 4.1.210.

2 (prefixed to a question of reproof or surprise) Well, well then, indeed MND 3.2.411 Yea, art thou there?, Per 2.5.73, R3 1.4.88 (Qq 1-6; Ff What).

Yead n. (short for) YEDWARD Wiv 1.1.157 that cost me two shilling and two pence a-piece of Yead Miller.

yea-forsooth adj. Addicted to saying 'yea, forsooth' like a person of low station 2H4 1.2.36 a...yea-forsooth knave (i.e. one who readily gives superficial assent).

year n. (pl.) Mature age 2H6 2.3.28 I see no reason why a king of years Should be to be protected like a child, R2 2.3.66, Oth 1.2.60; in years old 1H4 2.4.454 that vanity in years, Rom 3.5.46, R2 1.3.171.
▷ LLL 5.2.465 smiles his cheek in years: see SMILE.

yearn vb. Vex, grieve Wiv 3.5.44 it would yearn your heart; (impersonal) H5 4.3.26 It yearns me not, R2 5.5.76 (Qq 1-4; Ff 1-3 yern'd).

yeast n. (transf.) Foam WT 3.3.93 the ship... swallow'd with yeast and froth (F1 yest).

yeasty adj. Foamy, frothy Mac 4.1.53 the yeasty waves (F1 yesty); (fig.) Ham 5.2.191 a kind of yeasty collection (i.e. superficial knowledge; F1 yesty; Q2 histy; Qq 3–4 misty).

Yedward n. Familiar form of Edward 1H4 1.2.134 Hear ye, Yedward.

yellowing ppl. adj. Yelping Tit 2.3.20 the hounds ...their yellowing noise (Q1; F1 yelping).

yellowness n. (fig.) Jealousy Wiv 1.3.102 I will possess him with yellowness (F1 yallowness).

yellows n. Jaundice in horses Shr 3.2.53 ray'd with the yellows.

yeoman n.

1 Attendant or assistant to an official, sheriff's officer 2H4 2.1.3 Where's your yeoman?; yeoman's service good and faithful service Ham 5.2.36 (Qq 2–3 yemans).

2 yeoman of the wardrobe Keeper of the wardrobe, an official in a noble household TN 2.5.40.

3 Member of the class holding small landed estates (who formed a large part of the infantry of English armies), freeholder under the rank of gentleman R3 5.3.338 Fight, gentlemen of England! fight, bold yeomen!, 1H4 4.2.15, H5 3.1.25; (contrasted with 'gentleman') Lr 3.6.10 whether a madman be a gentleman or a yeoman, 1H6 2.4.81.

yer prep. (var. of) Ere, before PP 18.26 yer night, PP 18.29.

yerk vb.

1 Strike smartly Oth 1.2.5 yerk'd him...under the ribs.

2 Move (some part of the body) with a jerk; (esp.) lash out with (the legs), as a horse H5 4.7.80

wounded steeds...Yerk out their armed heels at their dead masters.

yerwhile adv. (var. of) Erewhile, just now AYL 3.5.105 the youth that spoke to me yerwhile.

yes adv.

1 (in contradiction of or opposition to a neg. statement) On the contrary, but it is or was Cor 4.6.62 Yes, worthy sir, The slave's report is seconded, 2H4 1.3.36 (F1), Cym 1.4.49.

2 YEA sense 1 H8 1.2.176 take heed; Yes, heartily beseech you, Ham 1.5.135, Cym 1.4.49.

yest (var. of) YEAST.

yesty (var. of) YEASTY.

yet adv. Still, now as before, now as always Ham 1.3.54 Yet here, Laertes?, Wiv 2.2.140, R3 1.4.122; (similarly) as yet LC 75 I might as yet have been a spreading flower...if I had...

yield vb.

1 Bring forth, bear Per 5.3.48 she was yielded there, Tmp 2.1.231, AYL 2.3.64.

2 Reward Ant 4.2.33 the gods yield you for't!
▷ See GOD 'ILD.

3 Give, state, declare, communicate (something expressible in speech) AWW 3.1.10 The reasons of our state I cannot yield, TN 3.2.3; report (as being so-and-so) Ant 2.5.28 but well and free, If thou so yield him, there is gold.

yielded ppl. adj. Given up, surrendered Jn 5.2.107 the yielded set.

yielding n. Compliance LLL 1.1.118 How well this yielding rescues thee from shame!, Jn 2.1.474, Rom 2.2.105.

yoke n. Pair of oxen 2H4 3.2.38 a good yoke of bullocks; pair of servants Wiv 2.1.175 these that accuse him...are a yoke of his discarded men.

~ vb. Be joined or coupled 3H6 4.6.49 We'll yoke together, Cor 3.1.57; (with ref. to marriage) 3H6 4.1.23 To sunder them that yoke so well together.

yoked ppl. adj. Married Oth 4.1.66 Think every bearded fellow that's but yok'd May draw with you (with quibble).

yoke-devils n. (pl.) Devils linked together, companion devils H5 2.2.106 two yoke-devils sworn to either's purpose.

yoking ppl. adj. Linking, coupling; (hence) embracing Ven 592 on his neck her yoking arms she throws.

yon adj. That (those)...over there JC 2.1.103 yon grey lines, Ant 3.10.10, R3 1.2.260.

~ adv. Over there, yonder R2 3.3.91 for yon methinks he stands.

yond adj. That (those)...over there TGV 4.4.66 yond foolish lout, Ham 1.1.36, WT 2.1.31.

~ adv. Over there, yonder Tmp 1.2.410 say what thou seest yond, Tro 5.2.91, Oth 1.2.28.

~ pron. That one over there Tro 4.5.13 Is not yond Diomed...?, AWW 3.5.82 (perh. adv.).

yore n. of yore Once upon a time Son 68.14 what beauty was of yore.

young adj.

1 Raw, inexperienced AYL 1.1.54 you are too young in this, Mac 3.4.143, Cym 1.4.43.

2 Recent H8 3.2.47 this is yet but young.

younger n. Younger son MV 2.6.14 like a younger or a prodigal.
▷ Cf. Luke 15:12.

younger adv. Ago Per 1.4.39 Those palates who, not yet two summers younger.

young-eyed adj. Having the lively eyes of a young person, having a youthful vision MV 5.1.62 young-ey'd cherubins.

youngling n. Stripling, novice Shr 2.1.337 Youngling, thou canst not love so dear as I, Tit 2.1.73, PP 11.3.

youngly *adv.* Early in life COR 2.3.236 *How youngly he began*, SON 11.3.

younker *n.* Prodigal (see YOUNGER), greenhorn 1H4 3.3.80 *will you make a younker of me?*, 3H6 2.1.24.

youth *n.* Recentness, freshness MV 3.2.221 *the youth of my new int'rest here*.

youthful *adj.* Belonging to the period of youth, of or in youth TGV 4.1.34 *My youthful travel*, AYL 2.3.67, R2 1.3.70.

yravish *vb.* Ravish, entrance PER 3.Gower.35 *The sum of this...Yravished the regions round*.

yslacked *pa. pple.* Reduced to inactivity PER 3.Gower.1 *Now sleep yslacked hath the rout*.

Z

zany *n.* Buffoon who imitated the tricks of a professional clown or fool LLL 5.2.463 *some slight zany*, TN 1.5.89.

zeal *n.* Ardent or earnest desire 2H4 5.5.14 *this doth infer the zeal I had to see him*.

zenith *n.* (fig.) Highest point of one's fortune TMP 1.2.181 *I find my zenith doth depend upon A most auspicious star*.

zir *n.* [southern dial.] Sir LR 4.6.235 *Chill not let go*, *zir*, LR 4.6.244.

zo *adv.* [southern dial.] So LR 4.6.239 *zo long as 'tis*.

zodiac *n.*
1 Belt of the celestial sphere extending about 8 or 9 degrees on each side of the ecliptic, within which the apparent motions of the sun, moon, and principal planets take place TIT 2.1.7 *the...sun...Gallops the zodiac* (i.e. through the zodiac).
2 (transf.) Year MM 1.2.168 *nineteen zodiacs have gone round*.
▷ At the end of any nineteen-year period the new moon returns to the same day of the year.

zone *n.* *burning zone* Path or sphere of the sun, the region or belt in the celestial sphere between the tropics of Cancer and Capricorn HAM 5.1.282 *till our ground, Singeing his pate against the burning zone, Make Ossa like a wart!*

'zounds *interj.* God's wounds 1H4 2.1.79 *and yet*, *'zounds, I lie*, JN 2.1.466, ROM 3.1.100.
▷ Cf. SWOUNDS.

zwagger [southern dial] SWAGGER.